MAINTAINING AND REPAIRING PCs

MAINTAINING
AND REPAIRING
PCs

Vice President and Publisher: Natalie E. Anderson
Associate VP/ Executive Acquisitions Editor, Print: Stephanie Wall
Executive Editor, Media: Richard Keaveny
Executive Editor: Chris Katsaropoulos
Editorial Assistant: Lora Cimiluca
Product Development Manager: Eileen Bien Calabro
Senior Media Project Manager: Steve Gagliostro
Media Project Manager: Alana Meyers
Director of Marketing: Margaret Waples
Senior Marketing Manager: Jason Sakos
Career Channel Marketing Manager: John Wannemacher
Marketing Assistant: Ann Baranov
Customer Service Representative: Rebecca Scott
Managing Editor: Lynda Castillo
Production Project Manager: Lynne Breitfeller
Manufacturing Buyer: Natacha Moore
Cover art: Michael R. Hall

This book was set in Futura MD BT, Times New Roman, and Arial by Cathy J. Boulay, Educational Technologies Group. It was printed and bound by Quebecor World/Versailles. The cover was printed by Phoenix Color Corp.

Written by Charles J. Brooks

Pearson Education Ltd.
Pearson Education Singapore Pte. Ltd.
Pearson Education Canada, Ltd.
Pearson Education—Japan

Pearson Education Australia Pty. Limited
Pearson Education North Asia Ltd.
Pearson Educación de Mexico, S.A. de C.V.
Pearson Education Malaysia Pte. Ltd.

10 9 8 7 6 5 4 3 2 1

ISBN 0-13-240981-X

Trademark Acknowledgments

RECRUITS WANTED

TO ELIMINATE ALL EVIL COMPUTER BEHAVIOR

FAINT OF HEART NEED NOT APPLY

BECOME AN AGENT
APPLY ONLINE AT GEEKSQUAD.COM

PREFACE

FEATURING CASE STUDIES FROM THE GEEK SQUAD

Welcome to the 5th edition of the ETG/Marcraft *MAINTAINING & REPAIRING PCs* course. This edition of our course brings you the Geek Squad® from Best Buy®. We've included real scenarios, tips and situations provided to us by real Geek Squad Agents who are on the front lines of the PC service industry. In addition, they have made being referred to as a "Geek" a good thing.

The Geek Squad has created a polished standardized image for their computer service people that makes them instantly recognizable to computer users throughout the United States and beyond. This image is carefully maintained and honed to set the standard for computer repair personnel.

The changes in the structure of CompTIA's 2006 A+ exams reflect the type of structure businesses like Best Buy have in their computer service organizations. The Geek Squad begins with Counter Intelligence Agents (CIAs) that are posted at Geek Squad Precincts inside Best Buy stores. The next Geek Squad level is the Special Agent who is tasked with patrolling the streets protecting any computer used by any civilian, corporate or government individual that may be in harm's way and are denoted by their badges. Then you have the Double Agents that work in the Best Buy store but also climb into now famous Black and White Volkswagens with Geek Squad emblems on the doors and go to remote businesses and homes to install and repair PC equipment.

You may have noticed the title change from the previous *A+ Certification: Concepts and Practices* editions. While this edition covers all the objectives and sub-objectives for all four of CompTIA's new 2006 A+ exams, it also includes vital non-A+ materials designed to help students entering the PC repair and maintenance field understand the PC components better.

TWENTY YEARS OF PC MAINTENANCE AND REPAIR

This is not the first time the name of this book, lab guide and related course has changed. The original version appeared in 1987 as the *Marcraft Microcomputer Service Course*. This course taught IC level troubleshooting on PC-XT clones (that had a monochrome HGCA video display, 256K of RAM and a 360KB floppy disk drive. The operating system was MS-DOS 3.2).

The popularity of the courseware outside of the training course led to a better marketing name for that point in time— Microcomputer Systems Theory and Service. This name stuck until CompTIA introduced their A+ certification exams for computer technicians.

We saw the potential for these certifications to stabilize the computer repair training market, so we joined CompTIA and changed the name of the next edition to *A+ Certification - Concepts and Practice*. This title remained through four editions and has now been replaced by the current title.

The changes this book has covered in both hardware and operating systems have been tremendous. Our current troubleshooting trainer can handle a gigabyte of RAM, supports hundreds of GB HDDs and CD-ROM/DVD drives and employs the latest Windows operating system versions. However, if you knew where to look, you could find updated graphics and some reworked explanations from that original 1987 text. It will be very interesting to see what the next 20 years will produce in PC technology.

2006 Revisions

This version of the ETG/Marcraft *MAINTAINING & REPAIRING PCs* textbook is designed provide a solid theory basis for PC repair personnel. New information has been added to this book to cover the newest hardware and operating system technologies available. The most noticeable changes occur in the following areas:

1. The inclusion of a Professionalism and Communications domain. This is an area of technician development that the personal computer industry has been pushing forward since before the original A+ exam launched more than 12 years ago. Just having technical skills is not enough.

2. Coverage of new Processors and Chipset designs that have evolved since the last A+ exams were launched. This edition includes coverage of Pentium dual core processors as well as AMD's newest dual and single core processors. The chipset material has also been expanded to include the different variations associated with newer PCI and AGP bus standards.

3. Wireless networking coverage has been expanded to offer more complete coverage of wireless router installation and advanced WiFi communications.

4. One of the fastest areas of change in PC maintenance involves physical and data security systems. Coverage that centered on Virus infections three years ago has been expanded to cover anti virus protection, pop-up blockers, spam blockers, and social engineering efforts. The security material has also been enlarged to include hardware access protection devices such as Smart Cards and Biometric identification devices.

5. The operating system technologies material has changed significantly in that the only references to Windows 9X/Me or Windows NT involve upgrading from one of these operating systems to a Windows 2000 or Windows XP operating system. However, the Windows XP material has been widened to include information specific to Windows XP Home Edition and Windows XP Media Center Edition.

Pedagogical Features

The pedagogical features of this book were carefully developed to provide readers with key content information, as well as review and testing opportunities.

- Over 50 diagrams and screen dumps are included in each chapter to provide constant visual reinforcement of the concepts being discussed.

- Each chapter begins with a list of learning objectives that establishes a foundation and systematic preview of the chapter.

- Each chapter contains exam tips that correlate the material to specific A+ certification exam information.

- Key terms are presented in bold type throughout the text.

- Geek Squad Case File scenario challenges are scattered throughout each chapter to provide the reader with real, open-ended challenges that reinforce the material they have just studied. These scenarios challenge students to apply what they are learning to scenario-based situations that require more than a single word or sentence to evaluate.

- Each chapter concludes with a key-points review of its material.

A comprehensive glossary of terms appears at the end of the text to provide quick, easy access to key term definitions that appear in each chapter. The key terms work in conjunction with the extensive Glossary at the end of the book. Key thoughts in the chapter are presented in special boxes to call special attention to them.

An abundance of assessment materials are available with this course. At the end of each chapter there is a 10-question multiple-choice section and a 15-question section of open-ended review questions. The 10 multiple-choice questions test knowledge of the basic concepts presented in the chapter, while the 15 open-ended review questions are designed to test critical thinking.

Appendix A contains maps of CompTIA's new A+ exams that direct the reader to areas of the text and Lab Guide where each objective and sub-objective are covered.

In general, it is not necessary to move through this text in the same order that it is presented. Also, it is not necessary to teach any specific portion of the material to its extreme. Instead, the material can be adjusted to fit the length of your course.

ORGANIZATION

Chapter 1 – *Communications and Professionalism* introduces students to the fundamentals of good Customer Service and Customer Satisfaction. This facet of preparation is so much in demand by the PC service industry (as well as virtually every other entry level industry) that we have decided to start with this information before the first technical information is introduced. These topics have become this important in our industry.

Chapter 2 – *Basic PC Terms and Concepts* introduces microcomputer architecture and shows how those basic microcomputer structures come together to form a PC-compatible personal computer system. The chapter quickly charts the evolution of the PC from the days when small keyboard units were connected to a television set up to the powerful PCs available today. This chapter introduces the student to the components for every major subsection of the PC along with all the major variations of those sections. The main purpose here is to be able to compartmentalize the PC system, identify its components by name and sight, understand the function each is supposed to perform and be able to identify major variations of each component.

Chapter 3 – *Advanced System Boards* deals with the system boards that form the heart of every PC system. Microprocessors, microprocessor-support systems, and expansion buses are all covered in this chapter. The focus of the system board information in this chapter is based on older ATX and newer BTX and NLX standards being used throughout the industry. In addition, the chapter covers microprocessors from the Pentium through the Pentium 4 and Dual Core Pentium processors. The operating characteristics of all the Intel Pentium line of microprocessors are presented in this chapter.

The chapter also includes advanced system board-related technologies such as advanced cooling systems, current expansion bus technologies, and CMOS setup options (i.e., Microprocessor Health and Security).

Chapter 4 – *Standard I/O Systems* begins by examining basic input/output structures used in PCs. The computer's fundamental I/O devices are covered, including the most common ports found on the typical PC compatible system. This is one of the biggest changes in the industry since the last edition of this book appeared. I/O port types that had been staples of the PC industry for decades have almost disappeared from new PCs. The USB port has become the defacto port of choice on new PCs. Built in wireless networking has also become a major I/O system in new PCs. Older parallel and serial ports are becoming hard to find.

This chapter also provides information about typical I/O devices used with PCs. These include digital television and LCD displays, touch pads, digital cameras, and PDAs, as well as traditional keyboards, CRT monitors, mice, trackballs, joysticks, touch-sensitive screens, and scanners are covered.

Chapter 5 – *Mass Storage Systems* commonly used in PC systems are presented. These include floppy drives, hard drives, RAID systems, tape drives, CD-ROM drives and rewritable CD and DVD drives. The chapter has been expanded to include SATA interface specification, installation techniques and information, and advanced configuration information.

Chapter 6 – *Data Communications* focuses on Data Communications systems associated with PCs. This chapter covers both local and wide area networks, along with the equipment and software required to operate them. The LAN material has been modified and expanded to include newer Ethernet specifications, cabling information, and newer networking technologies. Dial-up networking and modems are discussed here along with expanded DSL, cable modem, wireless, and satellite networking information.

Chapter 7 – *Printers* covers printers from the workhorse dot-matrix printer to color ink-jet and high-speed laser printers. Theory, operation, and maintenance information is presented for all three types of printers. Specific troubleshooting information is also provided for each printer type in this chapter. The printers chapter includes up-to-date information on the newest interfaces commonly used with printers.

Chapter 8 – *Portable Systems* focuses on the unique structures associated with this type of computer and how they are installed, configured, and maintained. It also describes the types of problems that are inherent with smaller computer systems. The portable chapter has been expanded to include more information about installing, configuring, and repairing additional components associated with notebook computers.

Chapter 9 – *Operating System Fundamentals* provides a detailed examination of basic operating systems. In particular, it investigates the role of the system's BIOS and the Disk Operating System (DOS) in the operation of the system. The first half of the chapter covers topics associated with the ROM BIOS, including system bootup information, CMOS Setup routines, and Power On Self Test (POST) information.

The second half of the chapter is dedicated to command-line operations For the PC consumer working from the command line has passed away in favor of Graphical User Interfaces. However, the technician must be able to use command-line utilities and commands to access and restore defective systems. Topics covered here include Microsoft disk structures, and drive-level, directory-level, and file-level command-line operations.

Chapter 10 – *Windows Operating Systems* is an in-depth study of the Windows 2000 Professional and Windows XP Professional/Home Edition/Media Center Edition operating systems. This chapter addresses operating systems from a technician's point of view - Installation, Configuration, and Upgrading; Diagnosing and Troubleshooting; and Networking. Information that applies to all these versions is referred to as Windows 2000/XP, whereas items specific to one version or the other are referred to as Windows XP Home Edition or Windows XP Media Center Edition. This chapter also includes extensive information about handling application programs, printing, and wide and local area networking with Windows 2000/XP.

Chapter 11 – *Basic System Troubleshooting* addresses the fundamentals of troubleshooting microprocessor-based equipment. The chapter covers the use of diagnostic software to isolate system hardware problems. It also describes the Field-Replaceable Unit (FRU) method of hardware troubleshooting required for most field and bench repair work. The second half of the chapter deals with symptoms and troubleshooting procedures associated with the various hardware components typically associated with PCs. It also provides the first half of a comprehensive computer diagnosing and troubleshooting methodology.

Chapter 12 – *Operating System Troubleshooting* shifts the focus of troubleshooting to the software side of the system. It focuses on the three major categories of operating system-related problems: setup problems, startup problems, and operational problems. The chapter includes troubleshooting tools available with the different operating system versions and methods of using them. Important HDD support utilities, such as CHKDSK, backup, defragmentation, and anti-virus protection are highlighted here. This chapter also furnishes the second half of the complete computer troubleshooting methodology. Troubleshooting of application, printer, and networking problems related to operating systems is also covered here.

Chapter 13 – *Security and Preventive Maintenance* discusses important Security, Preventive Maintenance and Safety procedures and considerations. The first half of the chapter covers system and data security products and techniques. The initial sections of the chapter investigate topics including physical security devices such as smart cards and biometric identification devices. Successive sections cover information destruction/disposal procedures and data/network security tools and procedures.

The second half of the chapter covers Preventive Maintenance and safety issues, such as cleaning, electrostatic discharges, power line problems, and Universal Power Supplies (UPS) along with other power line conditioning devices. The chapter features preventive maintenance procedures for various system components. Suggested PM schedules are also presented. It also covers safety issues commonly associated with computer systems. Although not an intrinsically unsafe environment, some areas of a computer system can be harmful if approached unawares.

SUPPORT MATERIALS

In addition to the wealth of material in the theory manual, the ETA/Marcraft *MAINTAINING & REPAIRING PCs* course provides a significant amount of student and instructor support materials to make the course easier to implement. These include the following:

The Hands-On Lab Guide

Applying the concepts of the chapter to hands-on exercises is crucial to preparing for a successful career as a computer technician. The Lab Guide provides an excellent hands-on component to emphasize the theoretical materials. There are four types of Procedures included in the labs.

First, introductory labs act as introductions to hardware and different types of software.

A number of troubleshooting labs allow students to be tested under real problem situations. The instructor can insert software faults, simple hardware faults, or complex hardware faults into the system for the student to track down, isolate, and repair.

A pair of Research and Design labs present students with a realistic PC design and build situation that requires them to perform research on components and software that fit a certain customer's computer needs. Then they use the research to design the computer the customer wants. Finally, they do market analysis to determine whether their product competes well with products already in the market.

A number of hardware/software installation labs are included as well. This enables students to install and set up hard drives, CD-ROM drives, modems, network cards, and more.

The Lab Procedures in the ETG/Marcraft Lab Guide do require certain hardware and software components to perform—it is after all a hands-on lab guide. However, these procedures are written around industry standard, commercially available hardware and software components. Therefore, they can be performed on standard PC compatible systems, using standard Microsoft operating systems and commercially available diagnostic and anti-virus software.

ETG/Marcraft does provide lab kits and trainers that make it convenient to deliver these labs. However, none of these products are required to be purchased from ETG/Marcraft to perform the procedures.

Instructor Support

An instructor's guide accompanies the course.

- Answers for all of the end-of-chapter quiz questions are included along with a reference point in the chapter where a particular item is covered.

- Sample schedules are included as guidelines for possible course implementations.

- Answers to all lab review questions and fill-in-the-blank steps are provided so that there is an indication of what the expected outcomes should be.

- Full Power Point Slide Presentations including every graphic, table, question, objective and key text segment in the book. These slide sets can be edited to fit the class length and your delivery preference.

- Descriptions of the numerous ETG/Marcraft software faults, hardware faults, and extended hardware faults are presented, along with suggested faults for particular labs as appropriate.

Optional System Support

- Student Practice Test CD—ETG/Marcraft offers a Practice Test CD to prepare students to challenge the new A+ Certification exams. This CD contains over 1000 A+ preparation questions to prepare with.

- Classroom Management System—The TEAMs LAN-based, client/server classroom management system contains test banks that can be edited, added onto and rearranged for easy testing, quizzing and assessment. This engine can also be used with other ETG/Marcraft test banks or with test banks made up from your own question pool.

- Online LMS Delivery and Management System—ETG/Marcraft also provides interactive, online classrooms and self study seats for all of its products. The LMS tracks student progress, automatically grades exams and quizzes and places the scores in the electronic grade book.

- To order these products, or for more information, call 800-441-6006.

Reference Shelf CD

The **Reference Shelf** CD contains additional chapters of fundamental "How Things Work" information. You will find a table of contents for the individual subjects on the Reference Shelf CD.

This information is offered as support material for students so that they can gain a full knowledge of how the elements of the computer do what they do. It provides a base they can draw on as technology changes throughout their careers. We suggest that you incorporate information from these topics into your presentations as time allows.

The Reference Shelf contains additional information concerning:

1. How Microprocessors Work
2. How DMA Works
3. How Interrupts Work
4. Initiating I/O Transfers
5. Bits, Bytes, and Computer Words
6. Computer Buses
7. How a Parallel Printer Port Works
8. How a Serial Port Works
9. How Keyboards Work
10. How Magnetic Disks Work
11. How Video Displays Work
12. How Printers Work
13. How Modems Work
14. How Multimedia Works
15. How MACs Work
16. The Chips
17. Buses and Support Devices
18. The 8088 Microprocessor
19. Coprocessors
20. Soldering Techniques
21. The Standard Parallel Port
22. Operating System Fundamentals
23. Windows 9x
24. Extended Glossary

As you can see from the Reference Shelf topics, we have included sections on the Apple Macintosh and multimedia that may be of particular interest.

COVERING COMPTIA'S A+ EXAMS

While we have moved away from using the A+ exam in the title, we still cover all of the A+ exams in detail. We include different pedagogical features that relate the theory material to the 2006 A+ objectives. These features include Objective icons in the margin to mark passages of text the directly relate to the objectives in the four 2006 exams. The icons also identify the particular exam the material is related to.

We also place **Exam Tip** notices in the text at points where the material match up with known A+ test material.

An **Exam Map** in Appendix A tracks each objective and sub-objective in the 2006 exams to the area of the text and lab guides where they are covered.

Our Practice Test CD has over 1000 questions that map to all four 2006 A+ exams.

These questions have been updated to closely reflect the Domain and Objective structure published by CompTIA for the 220-601, 602, 603 and 220-6042 certification exams posted on their website (www.comptia.org) in October of 2006.

Test Taking Tips

The A+ exams are objective-based timed tests. They cover the objectives listed in Appendix A of this book in a multiple-choice format. There are two general methods of preparing for these tests. If you are an experienced technician using this material to obtain certification, use the testing features at the end of each chapter and on the Practice Test CD to test each area of knowledge. Track your weak areas and spend the most time concentrating on them.

If you are a newcomer to the subject of serious computer repair, plan a systematic study of the materials, reserving the testing functions until each chapter has been completed. In either case, after you complete the study materials, use the various testing functions available on the Test CD to practice taking the test. Use the Study and Exam modes to test yourself by chapter, or on a mixture of questions from all areas of the text. Practice until you are very certain that you are ready. The CD will provide you with explanations of questions and answers for your review.

- Answer the questions you know first. You can always go back later and work on questions you don't know.

- Don't leave any questions unanswered. They will be counted as incorrect.

- There are no trick questions. The correct answer is in there somewhere.

- Be aware of A+ questions that have more than one correct answer. Questions that have multiple correct answers can be identified by the special formatting applied to the letters of their possible answers. They are enclosed in a square box. When you encounter these questions, make sure to mark every answer that applies.

- Get plenty of hands-on practice before the test, using the time limit set for the test.

- Make certain to prepare for each test category listed above. The key is not to memorize, but to understand the topics.

- Take your watch. The A+ exam is a timed test. You will need to keep an eye on the time to make sure that you are getting to the items that you are most sure of.

- Get plenty of rest before taking the test.

ACKNOWLEDGMENTS

I would like to mention some of the people and groups who have been responsible for the success of this book. First I would like to thank Greg Michael, formerly of Howard W. Sams, for getting me involved in writing about microcomputer systems back in the early days of the IBM PC.

As always, I want to thank the staff here at ETG/Marcraft for making it easy to turn out a good product. Thanks to Gregory Ter-Oganov and Dan Smith from the Technical Services area for trying things out for me in the lab. Also, thanks to Mike Hall, Cathy Boulay, and Tony Tonda from the Product Development department for their excellent work in getting the text and lab books ready to go and looking good. Without these folks, there would be no timely delivery of the A+ product.

I also want to thank our new associates at Prentice Hall for all they bring to our projects and their excellent work in getting this book to you.

In addition, I would like to say thanks to Brian Alley of Boston University for his excellent guidance in bringing yet another version of this book up to speed.

As always, I want to thank my wife Robbie for all of her understanding, support, and help with these projects, as well as Robert, Jamaica, Michael, and Joshua.

TABLE OF CONTENTS

CHAPTER 1 - COMMUNICATIONS AND PROFESSIONALISM

OBJECTIVES 2
INTRODUCTION 3
CUSTOMER SERVICE SKILLS 4
    Prepare 5
    Establish Rapport 6
    Establish Your Presence 6
    Be Proactive 7
    Listen and Communicate 8
    Follow Up 11
    Be Responsive 11
    Be Accountable 12
    Be Flexible 12
    Be Professional 13
    Establish Integrity 13
    Handle Conflicts Appropriately 14
    Telephone Techniques 15
    Handle Paperwork and Finish Up 16
    Maintain an Orderly Work Area 16
KEY POINTS REVIEW 17
REVIEW QUESTIONS 18
EXAM QUESTIONS 19

CHAPTER 2 - BASIC PC TERMS AND CONCEPTS

OBJECTIVES 22
INTRODUCTION 23
PERSONAL COMPUTER EVOLUTION 23
    PC Compatibles 25
THE PC SYSTEM 25
    System Unit Cases 26
        Desktop Cases 26
        Tower Cases 28
        System Cooling 29
        Front Panels 30
        Back Panels 31
        Portable PCs 32
    Inside the System Unit 33
    Power Supplies 35
    System Boards 38
        Major System Board Components 40
        Microprocessors 42
            Pentium Processor Package Types 43
        Memory Units 45

ROM 45

RAM 46

Chipsets 46

System Configuration Settings 47

Front Panel Connections 48

Expansion Slots 49

Adapter Cards 51

Video Adapter Cards 53

Other Adapter Cards 54

The System Speaker 55

STORAGE DEVICES 56

Disk Drives 56

Hard Drives 57

CD-ROM Drives 58

Digital Versatile Discs 60

Tape Drives 60

Floppy Drives 61

Peripherals 63

External Devices and Connections 64

Keyboards 65

Video Displays 66

Other Peripherals 67

SOFTWARE 70

System Software 70

Basic Input/Output Systems 71

Plug-and-Play 74

CMOS Setup 75

Operating Systems 76

Graphical User Interfaces 77

Major Operating Systems 78

Application Software 78

Commercial Application Packages 79

Programming Packages 81

Games and Educational Packages 83

Version Numbers, Service Packs, and Patches 83

KEY POINTS REVIEW 84

REVIEW QUESTIONS 85

EXAM QUESTIONS 85

CHAPTER 3 - ADVANCED SYSTEM BOARDS

OBJECTIVES 88

INTRODUCTION 89

ATX SYSTEM BOARDS 90

BTX System Boards 91

Low-Profile Form Factors 95

System Board Compatibility Issues 96

Pentium Chipsets 97

System Bus Speeds 98

Configuring Microprocessors and Buses 99

Expansion Slots 101

PCI Local Bus 101

PCI Configuration 103

PCI-X 105

PCI Express 105
    PCIe Configuration 107
AGP Slots 107
Audio Modem Risers 108
On-Board Disk Drive Connections 110
PATA Connections 110
Serial ATA Connections 112
SCSI Connections 113
MICROPROCESSORS 114
Intel Processors 115
Processor Power Supply Levels 117
Advanced Pentium Architectures 118
Pentium MMX 118
Pentium Pro 119
Pentium II 121
Pentium III 122
Xeon 123
Pentium 4 124
Itanium Processors 124
Intel Dual-Core Processors 125
    Advanced Intel Microprocessor Technologies 128
    Dual-Core Intel Chipset 129
Hyperthreading Software Support 131
AMD PROCESSORS 132
Athlon Processors 132
Athlon 64 Processors 133
Duron Processors 134
Athlon Dual-Core Processors 134
Opteron Processors 137
PROCESSOR SOCKET SPECIFICATIONS 139
FANS, HEAT SINKS, AND COOLING SYSTEMS 142
BTX Thermal Module 143
Advanced Cooling Systems 144
MEMORY SYSTEMS 146
Random Access Memory 146
Advanced DRAM 147
Advanced SDRAM 147
SRAM 151
Memory Overhead 152
    DRAM Refresh 152
    Error Checking and Correcting 152
Advanced Memory Structures 154
    Cache Memory 154
    Memory Paging and Interleaving 156
RAM Speed Ratings 157
CMOS RAM 158
Typical CMOS Features Screens 160
The Advanced BIOS Features Setup Screen 162
The Chipset Features Screen 163
The PnP/PCI Configuration Screen 164
The Integrated Peripherals Setup Functions 165
Power Management Functions 166
PC Health Status 167
Security Subsystem 167
ADDING AND REMOVING FRU MODULES 168

Removing System Boards 168
    Removing External I/O Systems 169
    Removing the System Unit's Outer Cover 169
    Removing Adapter Cards 170
        Removing Cables from the System Board 170
        Removing the System Board 170
Replacing System Board FRU Devices 171
    Installing Microprocessors 172
    Installing Memory Modules 174
SYSTEM UPGRADING AND OPTIMIZING 174
    System Board Upgrading 175
        Microprocessor Upgrades 175
        Bus System Issues 176
        Installing Additional Processors 177
        Firmware Upgrades 178
        Cooling System Upgrades 179
        Memory Upgrades 180
        Cache Upgrades 180
KEY POINTS REVIEW 181
REVIEW QUESTIONS 182
EXAM QUESTIONS 183

CHAPTER 4 - STANDARD I/O SYSTEMS

OBJECTIVES 186
INTRODUCTION 187
SYSTEM INPUT/OUTPUT 188
    Moving Data 189
        PC Address Allocations 189
        System Board I/O Address Allocations 191
        Peripheral I/O Address Allocations 192
        Hexadecimal Addressing 192
        Initiating I/O Transfers 193
        Polling and Programmed I/O 193
        Interrupts 194
        Direct Memory Access 196
    System Resource Allocations 197
        Resources for Legacy Ports and Devices 198
PORTS, CABLES, AND CONNECTORS 199
    PS/2 Connectors 200
    Universal Serial Bus 200
        USB Cabling and Connectors 201
        USB Architecture 202
        USB Data Transfers 203
    IEEE-1394 Firewire Bus 205
        Infrared Ports 206
    Multimedia Connections 207
        MIDI Connections 209
    Legacy Ports 210
    Parallel Printer Ports 212
        The Centronics Standard 212
        EPP and ECP Parallel Port Operations 213
    RS-232 Serial Ports 213
        Serial Interface ICs 214

RS-232 Interfaces and Cables 215
  Game Ports 216
TYPICAL PERIPHERAL SYSTEMS 217
  Input Devices 218
    Keyboards 218
      Pointing Devices 220
      Installing Standard PC Input Devices 222
    Touch-Sensitive Screens 223
    Scanners 225
    Bar Code Scanners 227
      Installing Scanners 228
    Video Capture Cards 228
  Output Devices 230
    Video Displays 231
      Basic CRT Display Operations 231
      Color CRT Monitors 232
    Video Adapters 233
      Specialized Video Cards 234
    Screen Resolution 235
      Dot Pitch 236
      Digital Television Resolutions 237
      Digital Display Definitions 238
  Installing Video/Monitor Systems 238
    Sound Cards 239
      Installing Sound Cards 240
  Installing Other Peripherals 242
    Installing Digital Cameras 242
    Adapter Card-Based Peripherals 243
      Upgrading Adapters 243
    Installing Devices Using Advanced Buses and Ports 244
    Infrared Monitor 246
  Upgrading Peripheral Devices 246
KEY POINTS REVIEW 247
REVIEW QUESTIONS 248
EXAM QUESTIONS 249

CHAPTER 5 - MASS STORAGE SYSTEMS

OBJECTIVES 252
INTRODUCTION 253
MAGNETIC STORAGE 254
  Magnetic Disk Drives 254
    Reading and Writing on Magnetic Surfaces 256
  Contact versus Noncontact Recording 257
    Disk Drive Operations 258
      Initialization 259
      Track-Seek Operations 259
      Write Operations 260
      Read Operations 261
    Hard-Disk Drives 261
      Personal Video Recorders 263
      RAID Systems 265
    Floppy-Disk Drives 268
  Magnetic Tape Drives 269

QIC Tape Drives 270
DAT Drives 271
DLT Drives 271
OPTICAL STORAGE 273
CD-ROM Drives 273
CD-ROM Discs 274
CD Writers 274
Digital Versatile Discs 275
REMOVABLE STORAGE 276
Flash Memory 276
USB Flash Drives 277
Compact Flash Cards 278
Memory Sticks 279
Secure Digital Cards 280
DISK DRIVE INTERFACES 280
Internal Disk Drive Interfaces 281
IDE/ATA Interface 282
Advanced EIDE Specifications 283
Serial ATA Interface 284
Floppy Drive Interface 285
Small Computer System Interface 286
SCSI Specifications 286
SCSI Cables and Connectors 288
SCSI Signaling 289
INSTALLING INTERNAL STORAGE DEVICES 291
HDD Installation 292
Configuring PATA Drives 294
Installing SATA Drives 295
Installing SCSI Adapter Cards 297
Configuring SCSI Addresses 298
SCSI Termination 299
Hard Drive Preparation 300
Logical and Physical Drives 300
Installing CD-ROM/DVD Drives 303
Configuring CD-ROM Drives 304
Installing CDRW and DVDRW Drives 304
FDD Installation 304
Installing External Storage Devices 306
DISK DRIVE UPGRADING AND OPTIMIZING 306
HDD Upgrading 307
Disk Drive Subsystem Enhancements 308
RAID Adapter Enhancements 309
KEY POINTS REVIEW 310
REVIEW QUESTIONS 311
EXAM QUESTIONS 311

CHAPTER 6 - DATA COMMUNICATIONS

OBJECTIVES 314
INTRODUCTION 315
LOCAL AREA NETWORKS 315
LAN Topologies 316
Logical Topologies 317
Network Connectivity Devices 318

NETWORK TRANSMISSION MEDIA...320
    Twisted-Pair Cabling...321
        IDC Connections...323
    Coaxial Cable..324
        Coaxial Cable Specifications..325
    Fiber-Optic Cable...326
        Fiber-Optic Cable Types..327
    Plenum Cable...327
    Wireless Infrared Links 328
    Wireless RF Links 329
    Bluetooth Wireless...331
NETWORK CONTROL STRATEGIES 331
    Networking Protocols 333
    Network Architectures 334
        Ethernet..335
        The Ethernet Frame...336
        Ethernet Implementations..337
            Coaxial Ethernet Specifications 338
            Twisted-Pair Ethernet Specifications 338
        Fiber Ethernet Standards..339
            The FDDI Ring Standard...340
            Wireless Ethernet Standards 341
INSTALLING AND CONFIGURING LANS 341
    LAN Adapter Cards..341
    Installing LAN Cards...343
        Optimizing Network Adapters 344
        Installing Network Connectivity Devices 344
    Installing Wireless LANs...347
        Installing the Access Point 348
        Configuring the Access Point..349
            Installing Wireless Clients...350
            Establishing Wireless Security 350
WIDE AREA NETWORKS..351
    The Internet 352
        Internet Service Providers..353
            IP Addresses..355
        Subnets...356
        Private IP Classes 356
        Internet Domains..357
            DNS Name Resolution 358
INTERNET ACCESS METHODS 359
    LAN Access to the Internet..360
    Dial-Up Networking...361
        Modems 361
            Installing Modems...363
            Modem Configuration 364
    ISDN Connections...365
    Digital Subscriber Lines 366
        DSL Modems and Splitters 366
        DSL Versions 368
            Asymmetric DSL Versions 369
            Symmetric DSL Versions 369
    Cable Modems 370
    Installing Digital Modems 371
    Satellite Internet Access...373

Wireless Internet Access 375
TCP/IP 375
   The TCP/IP Suite 377
      Domain Name Service 378
      Windows Internet Naming Service 378
      Dynamic Host Configuration Protocol 379
   Voice Over IP 380
      VoIP Operations 380
   Internet Resources 382
   The World Wide Web 382
      File Transfer Protocol 384
         FTP Authentication 384
   E-mail 384
   Secure Socket Layer Protocol 385
   Telnet 385
   Web Browsers 386
KEY POINTS REVIEW 388
REVIEW QUESTIONS 390
EXAM QUESTIONS 391

CHAPTER 7 - PRINTERS

OBJECTIVES 394
INTRODUCTION 395
PRINTER FUNDAMENTALS 395
   Printing Methods 396
   Impact Printers 396
      Nonimpact Printers 397
   Character Types 397
      Fonts 399
   Print Quality 400
   Printer Mechanics 400
   Paper Handling 401
   Printer Controls 402
      Printer Interface 402
      Printer Controllers 403
   Dot-Matrix Printers 404
      Printhead Mechanisms 406
      Paper Handling 407
      Thermal Printers 407
   Ink-Jet Printers 409
      Ink-Jet Printer Components 411
         The Printhead Assembly 411
      Paper Handling 412
   Laser Printers 412
      Laser Printer Components 413
      Laser Printing Operations 415
      Component Variations 416
      Paper Handling 417
         Paper Specifications 419
   Dye Sublimation Printers 419
PRINTER CONNECTIONS AND CONFIGURATIONS 420
   Printer Interfaces 420
      USB Printers 420

Networked Printers 421
Infrared Printer Port Connections 422
Wireless Printer Interfaces 422
Parallel Printer Connections 423
Serial Printer Considerations 425
Serial Cabling Problems 425
Serial Printer Configuration 426
Printer Drivers 427
Special Print Drivers 428
Printer Control Panel Configuration 429
Printer Calibration 430
Printer Options and Upgrades 431
SERVICING PRINTERS 432
Troubleshooting Dot-Matrix Printers 433
Dot-Matrix Printer Configuration Checks 435
Dot-Matrix Printer Hardware Checks 436
Dot-Matrix Printer Power Supply Problems 436
Ribbon Cartridges 437
Printhead Not Printing 438
Printhead Not Moving 439
Paper Not Advancing 441
Troubleshooting Ink-Jet Printers 441
Ink-Jet Printer Configuration Checks 442
Ink-Jet Printer Hardware Checks 443
Power Supply Problems 443
Ink Cartridges 444
Printhead Not Printing 445
Printhead Not Moving 445
Paper Not Advancing 446
Troubleshooting Laser Printers 447
Laser Printer Configuration Checks 448
Laser Printer Hardware Checks 448
Printer Is Dead or Partially Disabled 449
Print on Page Is Missing or Bad 450
Paper Will Not Feed or Is Jammed 452
KEY POINTS REVIEW 454
REVIEW QUESTIONS 456
EXAM QUESTIONS 457

CHAPTER 8 - PORTABLE SYSTEMS

OBJECTIVES 460
INTRODUCTION 461
PORTABLE COMPUTER TYPES 461
Personal Digital Assistants 462
Portable Drawbacks 463
INSIDE PORTABLES 464
Portable System Boards 465
Microprocessors in Portables 466
Pentium IIIM and 4M Processors 467
Pentium M Processors 468
Centrino 469
Pentium M Celerons 470
Core Duo Processors 471

Memory for Portables 472
    Upgrading Portable Memory 473
Portable Drives 475
BASIC I/O 475
Portable Display Types 476
    Liquid Crystal Displays 476
Keyboards 478
Trackballs 480
Touch Pads 480
Pointing Sticks 482
EXTENDED I/O 482
PC Cards (PCMCIA) 483
    PC Card Types 484
    CardBus 485
    Installing PC Cards 485
    Installing PC Card Support 486
Mini PCI Express Cards 487
Networking Portables 488
    Built in WiFi 490
EXTERNAL DEVICES 491
Power Supplies 491
    Batteries 492
    Fuel Cells 492
Power Management 493
    ACPI 494
External Drive Units 494
    External CD-ROM and DVD Drives 494
    External FDDs 495
    Removable Storage 496
    Docking Stations 496
    Port Replicators 497
TROUBLESHOOTING PORTABLE SYSTEMS 498
Common LCD Display Problems 499
    Replacing the LCD Panel 500
Troubleshooting Touch Pads 501
    Troubleshooting Portable Keyboards 502
Troubleshooting Portable Unique Storage 502
    Troubleshooting PCMCIA 503
Troubleshooting Portable Power 504
Troubleshooting Docking Stations/Port Replicators 505
KEY POINTS REVIEW 507
REVIEW QUESTIONS 508
EXAM QUESTIONS 509

CHAPTER 9 - OPERATING SYSTEM FUNDAMENTALS

OBJECTIVES 512
INTRODUCTION 513
OPERATING SYSTEM BASICS 513
BOOTING THE SYSTEM 515
The Hardware Startup Process 515
The Operating System Bootup Process 517
    The Windows 2000/XP Boot Process 519
WINDOWS 2000/XP STRUCTURES 522

System Memory Management 524
    Virtual Memory.. 525
  Windows 2000/XP Registries 526
WINDOWS 2000/XP FILE SYSTEMS 528
  Managing Partitions.. 529
  High-Level Formatting 530
    FAT Disk Organization... 531
      File Allocation Tables 531
    The FAT32 File System 533
      The Root Directory... 533
    NTFS Disk Organization 534
      Master File Tables 535
      NTFS Clusters 536
    NTFS Advantages 537
WORKING FROM THE COMMAND LINE.. 538
  Command-Line Functions 540
  Drives and Disks 542
    Drive-Level Command-Line Operations 543
    Directories 543
CREATING AND MANAGING FILES 544
  Files and Filenames 545
  Command-Line Shortcuts 547
  Command-Line Utilities 548
KEY POINTS REVIEW 549
REVIEW QUESTIONS 551
EXAM QUESTIONS 551

CHAPTER 10 - WINDOWS OPERATING SYSTEMS

OBJECTIVES 554
INTRODUCTION 555
THE WINDOWS NT PRODUCT LINE 556
  Windows 2000... 558
    Windows 2000 Professional.. 559
    Windows 2000 Server 559
    Windows XP 560
    Windows XP Media Center Edition 561
    Windows 2003 Server 561
NAVIGATING WINDOWS 2000/XP 562
  Windows 2000/XP Desktops 563
    Locating, Accessing, and Retrieving Information in Windows 2000 and XP 564
    My Computer 564
    The Recycle Bin 565
    My Network Places 566
  Drop-Down Menus.. 567
    File Menus 568
    View Menu 569
    Tools Menu 570
  The Taskbar 570
  Start Menu 571
  Windows 2000 Control Panel 574
    Installation Wizards 575
    Administrative Tools... 576
      Windows 2000/XP Device Manager 579

Managing Symmetric Multiprocessing 580
The System Icon 581
The Display Icon 582
Windows Explorer 582
Windows XP Interface Variations 585
Windows XP Control Panel 588
Windows XP Media Center Interfaces 589
My TV 590
My Music 592
My Pictures 594
Other Features 595
WINDOWS 2000/XP FILES 595
File Encryption and Compression 596
Managing Windows 2000/XP NTFS 597
Formatting Volumes in Windows 2000/XP 598
INSTALLING WINDOWS 2000/XP 599
Installation Methods 600
Unattended Installations and Disk Images 601
Using Answer Files 601
Disk Cloning 601
Remote Installation Services Images 602
Creating Disk Images 602
Hard-Disk Drive Preparation 604
Patches and Service Packs 604
Installing Windows 2000 Professional 605
Upgrading to Windows 2000 608
Installing Windows XP Professional 611
Windows XP Professional Hardware Requirements 611
Windows XP MCE Hardware Requirements 612
Upgrading to Windows XP 613
Performing Local Upgrades 614
Dual Booting with NT Operating Systems 615
WINDOWS 2000/XP DEVICE DRIVERS 617
SATA Drivers 618
Finding Drivers 618
Driver Signing 619
PRINTING IN WINDOWS 2000/XP 620
Establishing Printers in Windows 2000/XP 622
Printer Properties 624
WINDOWS 2000/XP APPLICATIONS 625
Windows 2000/XP Application Installer 626
Launching Applications in Windows 2000/XP 626
WINDOWS 2000/XP NETWORK STRUCTURE 627
Configuring Windows 2000/XP Networking 629
Administering Windows 2000/XP Networks 629
Windows 2000/XP Policies 630
User Profiles 630
Group Policies 631
Network Shares 632
NTFS Permissions 634
Mapping a Drive 635
Installing Network Components in Windows 2000/XP Control Panels 636
Configuring Clients in Windows 2000/XP 639
Configuring Protocols in Windows 2000/XP 639
Configuring TCP/IP in Windows 2000/XP LANs 639

Manual TCP/IP Configuration 640
Networking with Novell NetWare 642
Installing NetWare Clients and Protocols.. 642
Installing Other Network Protocols... 643
NETWORK PRINTING WITH WINDOWS 2000/XP 643
Sharing Printers in Windows 2000/XP 644
WIDE AREA NETWORKING WITH WINDOWS 2000/XP 646
The Windows 2000/XP Internet Infrastructure 646
Establishing the Windows 2000/XP Dial-Up Configuration 647
Establishing Dialing Rules 647
Establishing Dial-Up Internet Connections.. 647
Establishing Internet Connection Sharing.. 649
WINDOWS SECURITY.. 650
Windows Portable Design 651
KEY POINTS REVIEW 652
REVIEW QUESTIONS 654
EXAM QUESTIONS 655

CHAPTER 11 - BASIC SYSTEM TROUBLESHOOTING

OBJECTIVES 658
INTRODUCTION.. 659
BASIC PC TROUBLESHOOTING... 660
Diagnostic and Repair Tools 660
Using a Multimeter 662
Using Software Diagnostic Packages... 664
Using POST Cards 666
Workspace 666
Gathering Information 667
Assessing the Situation 667
Assessing the Environment 668
Perform an Initial Inspection.. 668
Document the Process 669
Observe the Bootup Procedure... 669
Note Symptoms and Error Codes 670
Determining Hardware/Software/Configuration Problems.. 672
Field-Replaceable Unit Troubleshooting 675
COMMON SYMPTOMS AND TROUBLESHOOTING PROCEDURES 676
Isolating Power-Supply Problems... 676
Checking a Dead System.. 677
Other Power-Supply Problems... 678
Adding and Removing Power Supplies... 679
Power-Supply Upgrade Considerations 680
TROUBLESHOOTING THE SYSTEM BOARD 681
System Board Symptoms.. 681
Configuration Checks.. 683
Hardware Checks... 683
RAM 684
Microprocessor 685
ROM 685
Cooling Systems.. 686
CMOS Batteries 687
Exchanging the System Board 687
Troubleshooting Keyboard Problems 688

Keyboard Symptoms... 689
    Keyboard Configuration Checks 689
    Basic Keyboard Checks 689
    Keyboard Hardware Checks 690
Troubleshooting Mouse Problems 690
    Mouse Hardware Checks 691
    Mouse Configuration Checks 692
Troubleshooting Video 692
    Video Hardware Checks 694
    Windows Video Checks 694
Working with Monitors 696
    Diagnosing Display Problems 697
Troubleshooting HDDs 698
    Basic HDD Checks 700
    HDD Configuration Checks 701
    HDD Hardware Checks 702
Troubleshooting CD-ROM and DVD Drives 703
    Basic Checks 703
        Windows Checks 704
    CD-ROM/DVD Hardware Checks 704
    Writable Drive Problems 705
Troubleshooting FDDs 706
    Basic FDD Checks 707
Troubleshooting Port Problems 708
    Basic Port Checks 709
    USB Port Checks 709
    Legacy Port Problem Symptoms 711
    Basic Parallel Ports Check 711
    Basic Serial Ports 712
    Windows Parallel Ports 712
Troubleshooting Tape Drives 713
Troubleshooting Modems 714
    Modem Problem Symptoms 715
    COM Port Conflicts 716
    Windows Modem Checks 716
Communication Software 718
    The AT Command Set 718
    Using the AT Command Set 720
    Modem Hardware Checks 721
Troubleshooting Sound Cards 723
    Sound Card Configuration Checks 723
    Sound Card Hardware Checks 724
NETWORK TROUBLESHOOTING 725
Network Troubleshooting Basics 725
LAN Configuration Checks 726
Security Access Problems 726
LAN Hardware Checks 726
Troubleshooting Wireless Networks 728
    Testing Cable 729
KEY POINTS REVIEW 730
REVIEW QUESTIONS 732
EXAM QUESTIONS 733

CHAPTER 12 - OPERATING SYSTEM TROUBLESHOOTING

OBJECTIVES 736
INTRODUCTION 737
OPERATING SYSTEM UTILITIES 737
Windows Disk Management Tools 738
CHKDSK 738
HDD Defragmentation 739
Backups 741
Backup Types 742
Windows Data Backup 744
Advanced Backup Settings 745
Restoring Data 746
Advanced Restore Settings 747
System State Data Backups 747
Backup Scheduling 748
Backup Media Rotation 749
Removable Storage Utility 750
Windows 2000/XP System Management Tools 751
Event Viewer 751
Windows 2000/XP System Information 752
Task Manager 754
Device Manager 754
Using MSCONFIG.EXE 757
Windows XP Driver Rollback Feature 758
File Management Tools 758
System Editors 759
Dr. Watson 760
System File Checker 761
Windows Troubleshooting Help Files 761
Other Information and Troubleshooting Resources 764
Windows Resource Kits 764
Internet Help 764
Microsoft TechNet 765
TROUBLESHOOTING WINDOWS 766
TROUBLESHOOTING SETUP PROBLEMS 767
Windows 2000 Setup Problems 768
Windows XP Setup Problems 769
Upgrade Problems 770
TROUBLESHOOTING START-UP PROBLEMS 770
Windows 2000 Start-Up and Emergency Repair Disks 772
Creating the Windows 2000 ERD 772
Windows XP Boot Disk 773
Troubleshooting Windows 2000/XP Start-Up Problems 773
Windows 2000/XP Start-Up Tools 776
Altering BOOT.INI 776
Windows 2000/XP Start-Up Modes 776
Safe Modes 777
Other Windows Start-Up Options 778
Windows 2000/XP Recovery Console 779
Windows XP System Restore 782
Using System Restore 783
Performing an Emergency Repair 784
Windows XP Automated System Recovery 785
Conducting ASR Backups 786

ASR Restore Operations 787
Network Start-Up Problems 787
Authentication Problems 788
Common OS Operational Problems 788
Optional Devices Will Not Operate 788
Troubleshooting Stop Errors 789
Windows 2000/XP Application Problems 790
Applications Will Not Install 790
Application Will Not Start 790
Starting Applications from the Command Prompt 792
Locating Hidden Files 793
Applying Task Manager to Application Problems 793
Applying Event Viewer to Application Problems 794
Monitoring Application Performance with System Monitor 794
Other Operational Problems 795
REMOTE DESKTOP AND REMOTE ASSISTANCE 796
Using Remote Desktop 797
Configuring the Remote Desktop Function 797
Conducting Remote Desktop Sessions 798
Using Remote Assistance 800
Establishing Remote Assistance Sessions 800
The Remote Assistance Consoles 801
OPTIMIZING WINDOWS 2000/XP PERFORMANCE 803
Monitoring System Performance 805
Monitoring Performance with Task Manager 805
Monitoring Performance with System Monitor 806
Using Performance Logs and Alerts 807
Correcting Memory Performance Issues 809
Correcting Processor Performance Issues 809
Correcting Disk System Performance Issues 810
Troubleshooting Windows Printing Problems 810
Troubleshooting Local Area Networks 811
Windows 2000/XP Networking Problems 812
Troubleshooting Network Printing Problems 814
Troubleshooting WAN Problems 815
Network Troubleshooting Tools 818
Verifying TCP/IP Configurations 820
Troubleshooting Software Firewall Issues 821
KEY POINTS REVIEW 821
REVIEW QUESTIONS 822
EXAM QUESTIONS 823

CHAPTER 13 - SECURITY AND PREVENTIVE MAINTENANCE

OBJECTIVES 826
INTRODUCTION 827
PC SECURITY 828
Hardware Security 828
Smart Cards 829
Biometric Authentication Devices 831
Information Disposal/Destruction Policies 833
Software Security 833
Disposal and Destruction Policies 834
Network Security 835

    Administrative Security Settings...835
        Establishing User and Group Accounts 836
        Implementing Authentication Options 838
        Enabling System Auditing and Event Logging 840
        Establishing Firewall Settings 842
    Using the Encrypting File System..844
    Establishing Internet Browser Security Options 844
        Configuring Script Support 845
        Configuring Proxy Settings 845
        Locking the Computer..847
    Establishing and Implementing Malicious Software Protection...........848
MALICIOUS PROGRAM SECURITY 848
  Viruses 848
    Virus Symptoms..850
    Antivirus Software 851
  Grayware 852
    Spyware 852
        Spyware Prevention 853
    Adware...854
    Spam 854
  Social Engineering...854
PREVENTIVE MAINTENANCE 855
  Cleaning..855
  Preventive Maintenance Procedures 857
    Dust...857
    Heat Buildup Problems 857
    Handling Techniques 858
    Protecting Display Systems..858
    Protecting Hard-Disk Drives..859
    Protecting Removable Media Drives 861
        Protecting Removable Media 861
        Maintaining Removable Media Drives..861
    Protecting Input Devices 862
    Software PM 863
PRINTER PM AND SAFETY ISSUES 864
  Dot-Matrix Printers..864
  Ink-Jet Printers..865
  Laser Printers 866
  Preventive Maintenance Scheduling..867
    Daily Activities 868
    Weekly Activities 868
    Monthly Activities 868
    Six Months' Activities...869
    Annual Activities 869
SYSTEM PROTECTION 869
  Power Line Protection 869
    Surge Suppressers 870
    Uninterruptible Power Supplies 870
    Checking UPS Operation 873
  Protection During Storage 875
HAZARDS AND SAFETY PROCEDURES..875
  Avoiding Laser and Burn Hazards 876
ELECTROSTATIC DISCHARGE 877
  MOS Handling Techniques 878
  Understanding Grounds..880

HARDWARE DISPOSAL PROCEDURES...882
KEY POINTS REVIEW 883
REVIEW QUESTIONS 885
EXAM QUESTIONS 885

APPENDIX A

A+ OBJECTIVE MAP 887

GLOSSARY
....925

INDEX
....945

CHAPTER

1

PROFESSIONALISM AND COMMUNICATION

OBJECTIVES

Upon completion of this chapter and its related lab procedures, you should be able to perform these tasks:

1. Differentiate between general support and technical support.

2. State the purpose of providing customer education as part of customer service efforts.

3. Give reasons for customer service personnel to solicit feedback.

4. List steps involved in preparing for customer communications.

5. Address techniques for establishing rapport with customers.

6. Describe Active Listening.

7. Identify common body language signs.

8. Identify key words and phrases that turn off customers.

9. Describe steps and techniques that build customers' perceptions of your professionalism.

10. Describe proper telephone techniques for customer service.

11. Describe actions you can take to de-escalate problems.

12. Identify how and when to escalate problems to higher levels of administration.

13. Identify actions that create contention points with customers.

CHAPTER 1

PROFESSIONALISM AND COMMUNICATION

FROM THE GEEK SQUAD

A gent 97 is positioned at his station ready for his next action. His black pants, white shirt, and thin black tie identify him as one of the most well-known computer repair people in the world—a member of the Best Buy Geek Squad. Agent 97 is a double agent—he may be called on to work at the in-store counter, work in the back of the Geek Squad area installing or repairing computers brought into the store, or jump into one of their famous black and white Volkswagen Beetles and go to a customer's location to work on equipment there.

The Geek Squad has carefully honed its image so that people in need of computer information or repair think Geek Squad first. However, there is much more to the Geek Squad than their uniform appearance and famous black and white VWs. To maintain this image, Best Buy puts considerable efforts into two areas—technical capabilities and customer service. They control how their employees look and how they address and work with customers.

INTRODUCTION

One thing that is very apparent from the new A+ certification objectives is that Best Buy is not the only company that wants its people to have good interpersonal skills. Mostly, employers want employees to be aware of those behaviors that contribute to satisfying customers. These behaviors include such things as

- The quality of technician—customer personal interaction

- The way a technician conducts him- or herself professionally within the customer's business setting

- The credibility and confidence projected by the technician which, in turn, engenders customer confidence

- The resilience, friendliness, and efficiency that can unexpectedly delight the customer above and beyond the solving of a technical problem

customer service

customer satisfaction skills

CUSTOMER SERVICE SKILLS

The object of this chapter is to discuss **customer service** and **customer satisfaction skills** that employers find desirable in their employees. Many companies have formal Customer Service Guidelines that they make all employees aware of. However, these guidelines are not universal throughout the industry. Therefore, we offer a set of generic guidelines for your consideration.

> For the most part, a high level of technical proficiency alone is not enough to sustain a career in the world of computer service. For most of the service jobs available, good customer skills are just as important as good technical skills. In most cases, they are equal partners for a successful career. Good customer service skills are a must for those of us who work directly with the public.

Everything discussed so far in this text has concerned the development of good technical skills.

Marketing

Customer service is part of any company's sales and marketing effort and should be considered as such. As a part of the customer service team, you should think of yourself as part of that team as well. **Marketing** makes potential customers aware of the company's products and services. The salespeople follow up on the marketing efforts to ensure that the marketing materials are received and understood, and to convert the potential customer into an actual customer. Once the customer has chosen your company, the customer service effort comes into play to keep the customer. In every type of business, it costs far less to hang on to an existing customer than to find and convince new ones.

- Good customer service typically involves

- Educating the customer by providing useful and practical information, problem resolution, and support

- Informing the customer of goods and services

- Relating to the customer by learning their needs and concerns

- Delivering goods and services to the customer in a timely manner, and in a form desired by the customer

- Supporting the customer to the degree that they feel supported but not overwhelmed

general support

technical support

Customer service may take the form of **general support** or **technical support**. General support provides nontechnical care of the customer, while technical support deals with product installation, application, repair, and maintenance. In general, customer service supports the customer through education, personal service, and customer satisfaction monitoring.

Customer education

Personal service

feedback

Customer education refers to providing direction on the proper use of the product and advising customers of new services or product developments. **Personal service** involves answering questions and addressing specific concerns about products and services. This aspect also concerns assisting in the resolution of service or product problems. The customer service person solicits **feedback** from the customer concerning products and services.

The feedback aspect of customer service is one of the most important functions and one of the most under used. This phase is used to provide logs of customer problems and complaints, maintain positive feedback and suggestions, produce policy decisions to improve products and services, and promote goodwill in customers. Ideally, feedback should be solicited from the customer during every contact. You should routinely inquire about how the customer, and the product, are doing.

All of these customer service functions typically involve person-to-person activity. Therefore, the customer service person must be able to communicate effectively with users, and potential users, of technical equipment. As indicated earlier, they must be able to educate and support the user in the safe and proper use of such equipment.

| customer satisfaction |
| product |
| service |
| supplier |
| soft skills |

Both field and bench technicians must possess good interpersonal skills in order to properly handle customers. It has been said by some service managers that "We don't fix computers, we fix customers." In many ways, how service people are perceived is as important as how well we perform. In the end, it is **customer satisfaction** (with the **product**, the **service**, and the **supplier**) that creates a successful business, and continued employment.

Customer service skills are generally referred to as **soft skills**, because they cannot be tested easily with written or hands-on tests. However, they are skills that can be learned and practiced. The following paragraphs contain key points to consider in the area of providing customer service.

Prepare

Review customer history before contacting the customer, or going to the customer's site to perform work. In particular, see if the problem you are going to work on is a repetitive problem or a new occurrence. Check the urgency of the call and the customer's priority level.

| Research |

Research the type of equipment the call is concerning. Determine if there are any special tools that will be needed or any parts that may be involved in the repair. Make sure your documentation is in order. It may be necessary to check the customer's status with your company. Make certain that you have all the manuals, replacement parts, and tools you will likely need. Do you have the ESD equipment, meters, hand tools, and so forth needed? Make sure the tools and parts are in good working order.

Prioritize commitments and set realistic schedules. Resist the urge to overbook appointments. If it takes 30 minutes to get across town, never schedule an appointment there for a half-hour after you should be finished at the first site. Maintain time allotments established for completion of different tasks.

The best laid plans often go astray. There will be occasions where you just won't be able to keep an appointment. A previous service call runs long, the car breaks down, traffic on the freeway is stopped, and so on. When these occasions come up, make contact with the affected customers as soon as possible to let them know about your situation.

Always notify customers, as soon as possible, about any appointment changes, service delays, complications, or setbacks that may occur. Make contact with all of the customers affected by your schedule changes. Apologize for the inconvenience and ask them how they would like to proceed. These things happen to everyone, and your best defenses against customer dissatisfaction are **promptness** and **good communications**.

Establish Rapport

A good practice is to learn your customers by name and greet them by name. Collect business cards and include copies in customer folders—have them in your pocket during the call. Always deal with them as individuals, not by stereotypes such as order entry person, receptionist, manager, and so forth.

Be as open, friendly, and approachable as your personality will allow. This is an area that most of us can always work on. **Politeness** is a valuable quality to possess. However, it should never be forced, contrived, or overdone. Your greatest weapon in this area is your expertise. Avoid politically or racially sensitive topics. These have no place in business settings.

Establish Your Presence

Make eye contact when you speak to customers. Maintain alert body posture and calm facial expressions. Keep a calm voice level when perplexing situations arise. Your presence can be used to set the excitement level of the customer. If you appear calm, collected, and confident, the customer probably won't get too excited either. Avoid moodiness in the workplace. This can undermine your credibility with the customer. You begin each new customer contact with a 100% rating. At the end, you will be left with whatever points you have not given away.

Doing an **efficient**, **professional**, and **complete** job does more to ingratiate you to customers than almost anything else you can do.

If customers get to the place where they are sure that you will always be able to solve their problems, you have the best rapport that could be achieved in a business setting.

Be Proactive

Provide customers with appropriate preventive maintenance plans, and explain how they contribute to the continued productivity of their equipment. Take time to illustrate proper methods of handling consumables, and items to be on the watch for. Show them how to properly install and change printer ribbons, ink cartridges, toner cartridges, and so forth. Demonstrate the use of virus protection products and backup utilities, and advise the customer of potential environmental hazards, such as improperly disposing of toner cartridges.

GEEK SQUAD CASE FILE #12143

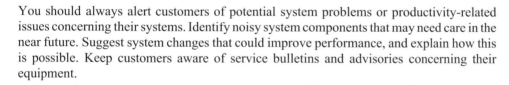

A customer calls with a RAM problem that has been common in a particular model of computer being sold. What should you tell the customer about the product?

    a. "Oh yeah, we have that happening all over. We're getting everyone fixed up ASAP."

    b. "We've had a whole batch of bad RAM in those machines."

    c. Troubleshoot the problem as you would any other phone support problem.

    d. Offer to send the customer replacement RAM.

You should always alert customers of potential system problems or productivity-related issues concerning their systems. Identify noisy system components that may need care in the near future. Suggest system changes that could improve performance, and explain how this is possible. Keep customers aware of service bulletins and advisories concerning their equipment.

Research customer requests for recommendations and advise them about future directions and equipment. However, this option should normally only be taken if requested by the customer. Also, be sensitive to the level of the person you are making recommendations to. There are people who have never met a new piece of hardware or software they didn't like. However, their superiors may be quite happy without the production/downtime/cost trade-offs that changing could bring. Don't incite the customer's employees with the latest and greatest product if their management hasn't signaled the way.

Listen and Communicate

One of the attributes that makes a good customer service or repair person is the ability to **actively listen** to the customer. Real listening means not just hearing what the customer has to say, but trying to pin down what they mean.

actively listen

Mentally (and maybe physically) identify key points as the customer describes the nature of the problem. Don't interrupt customer descriptions before you have all the details. Even if you are sure that you know what is going on after the first sentence, have patience to listen to the complete description. This is not only **common courtesy** but also serves to uncover extra data about the problem.

common courtesy

GEEK SQUAD CASE FILE #37170

You are sent to set up a desktop publishing computer for a publisher, and you discover that the company is using a publishing program that you know does not have all the features of a competing program. You're sure that the company could be much more productive using the other program. How do you convey this to the customer?

    a.   You don't because the company is installing a new program and does not need to be told this isn't the best.

    b.   Get the supervisor alone, and recommend the other program in private.

    c.   Mail an advertisement of the better product to the manager.

    d.   Tell the operators about the features of the other product in confidence so that they will know what to look for the next time.

body language

Pay attention to the customer's **body language** and other nonverbal clues. Pay attention to body posture, hand gestures, facial cues, and voice inflection to gauge anger, franticness, and so forth.

You should also be aware of your body language and what it is saying. Folding your arms while someone is speaking to you signals that you are not interested in what they are saying and that you are simply waiting for them to finish. Failure to make eye contact when you are talking conveys lack of commitment and may be taken as a sign you are being less than truthful. Closing books, returning pens to your pocket, or gathering tools while the customer is talking to you also sends a sign that you are finished and not paying real attention to them. Make sure to always pay *serious attention* to the customer.

Listening is also a good way to eliminate the user as a possible cause of the problems occurring. Many cartoons have been created in service newsletters about the strangest user-related calls ever received. Part of your job is to determine whether the user could be the source of the problem—either trying to do things with the system that it cannot do, or not understanding how some part of it is supposed to work. If you find this to be the case, work with the user to clarify the realistic uses of the system. This is a point where it may be appropriate to suggest advanced training options available. However, such suggestions should be made discreetly.

GEEK SQUAD CASE FILE #41217

You arrive on a service call, and the office supervisor turns on the malfunctioning machine. She begins to explain what she thinks the problem is, but you can tell from the operation of the machine that it is something else. What course of action should you pursue?

- a. Listen to the explanation until she is finished, and then fix the machine.

- b. Sit down and fix the machine while she is describing the rest of the problem to you.

- c. Begin troubleshooting the problem she is describing until she leaves, and then fix the problem.

- d. Stop the explanation, and tell her that you are pretty sure that you already know what the problem is.

The ability to **communicate clearly** is the other trait most looked for in service people. Allow customers to talk through their problems. Use probing questions for clarification purposes and to make sure you understand what the user is describing at each step. In doing so, they may come up with clues they haven't thought of before.

communicate
clearly

Help the customer think through the problem by asking them organized questions. With equipment down, the customer may be under some stress and might not be thinking as rationally as possible. Choose words and questions that do not put the customer, or their employees, in a bad light (i.e., What have you done now? is not likely to set the proper tone with a customer who has more problems than they need for the moment). Adjust the pace and flow of your conversation to accommodate the customer.

Avoid quick analysis statements. Repeatedly changing your position kills customer confidence. Also, avoid or minimize surprises that pop up (such as unexpected charges or time requirements). Try to manage the customer's expectations by being as up front as possible about what you can accomplish and the scope of services you can provide. If the customer has a networking problem, and you are the computer repair person, they shouldn't be allowed to believe that you are going to get everything working before you leave (unless the network falls within the scope of your normal work).

If the person you are working with in a company is the MIS person, network administrator, or engineer, take his or her lead and follow his or her instructions. Avoid situations of who knows more. Try to quickly recognize the technical abilities of the people you are working with. Adjust your conversation to accommodate them. For technically challenged customers, avoid jargon. It will be confusing to them and can be a cause of customer dissatisfaction with you, even if you do a great job.

Clarify your terminology with such people and be careful to avoid **patronizing** (talking down to) them. On the other hand, if the customer is technically literate, be careful not to insult their intelligence by overexplaining things to them. In this case, use technical terms as appropriate, and use them correctly. Watch for signs of misunderstanding, and explain things in greater detail as necessary.

GEEK SQUAD CASE FILE #02140

While working with a relatively inexperienced customer over the telephone, you become aware that the customer is having great difficulty following your directions. How can you help the customer even though he cannot see you?

    a.   Send the customer fax drawings of steps to perform.

    b.   Ask the customer if you can talk to someone else to get a fresh perspective on the problem.

    c.   Check your conversation, and try to communicate more clearly.

    d.   Ask the customer to fax you drawings of what he is experiencing.

There are some words and phrases that should automatically be avoided when talking to customers. Customers may be lost if certain key phrases, including the following, are used:

- *I don't know*—While this statement may be true, using it with a customer really means you don't care enough to go find out. Instead, substitute "I will have to find out and get back to you about that" instead. Write down the question, do the research, and make certain to follow up with the customer when you do know.

- *What was your name/problem?*—These questions show that you have not paid close enough attention to what the customer has already said, possibly causing a doubt that you are paying attention to anything. People usually call because they need a problem solved. This phrase will not go far in convincing them that you have the answers they need. Keep a writing instrument by the telephone and write down names and related information as soon as it is given.

- *I can't help you*—Once again, this may be a true statement; however, using this statement by itself indicates that you are not interested in helping. Add something, such as, "but, you might try ...," in an attempt to be helpful to the customer.

- *I'm/he's/she's busy*—So is everyone else. Saying this indicates that the recipient is less important than something else. Therefore, it almost automatically wounds the customer's ego and creates a bad atmosphere. If you/he/she is involved in something that cannot be interrupted right away, try to phrase the rejection so that it is delivered with a promise to get back to the caller as soon as possible and that the call is of value. Also, ask if the customer would like to leave a message for the other individual.

Follow Up

Follow up on unresolved issues. For incomplete calls, such as those requiring additional parts, assess the customer's need, and restore as much functionality to the system as possible or needed. Clean up and organize parts removed from the system, so that they will not be in the way or be removed before your return to the site. Keep the customer informed about progress of unresolved issues, such as when parts are expected. If problems are intermittent, set up a schedule and procedure to work with the customer to pin down circumstances that cause the problem to reoccur.

Be Responsive

Essentials 8.2

Concentrate on the customer's problem or request. Give preeminence to the customer's **sense of urgency**. Relegate paperwork and administrative duties to a secondary level, until the customer's problems have been fully aired. Don't undermine the customer's sense of urgency. Work with the customer's priorities. Schedule steps to fulfill any unresolved problems to show commitment to getting the customer's problems solved. In this way, the customer will be assured that he or she is not being left adrift.

sense of urgency

Don't multitask while working directly with a customer. Focus on the task at hand, and keep it in the forefront. Avoid distractions and interruptions in the customer's presence. Act on the customer's complaints.

GEEK SQUAD CASE FILE #21137

A customer who has picked up a repaired computer from your store brings it back within a few hours, complaining that it doesn't work. What should you say?

    a.   "What happened to it?"

    b.   "Sometimes I can't believe our technicians can find their way home at night. I'll get this thing fixed up for you."

    c.   "It was working when it left here. I don't know what could have happened to it. Let's take a look at it."

    d.   "Did it ever work when you got it home?"

Be Accountable

Document your promises and dates so that you may demonstrate accountability to your customers. Follow up on return dates for yourself and equipment. Take personal responsibility for being the single point for the service call—contacting specialists, dealing with parts vendors, and so on. It's your show, run it (unless your organization has someone in the structure that is supposed to take over this responsibility).

flexible

adaptable

GEEK SQUAD CASE FILE #51403

An irate customer calls, complaining that a technician from your company has recently performed a software upgrade on his system and now the modem will not connect with other modems. How should you handle the customer?

    a.   "I'm sure none of our technicians would have left a condition like that. Let's see what the problem is.

    b.   "Give me the technician's name, and I'll have him get back to you as soon as he returns to the office."

    c.   "Please describe the symptoms to me, so I can see what might be causing the problem."

    d.   "This is really easy. Take the top off of the computer, and check to see that the card is installed securely."

Be Flexible

Effective customer service must be **flexible** and readily **adaptable** to meet the needs of the customer. This does not mean that the *customer is always right*. But it does mean that you should be looking for the best way to help the customer meet his or her needs. This may involve looking for new and innovative methods of servicing the customer.

If a problem runs beyond the scope of your position, or your capabilities, take the initiative to move it to the next level of authority. Never leave a customer hanging without a path to follow to get the customer's problems addressed. Provide alternatives to the customer when possible (i.e., downtime scheduling, loaner equipment availability, etc.).

Be Professional

Essentials 8.2

Technical Support 6.2

IT Technician 8.2

While you may not work for the Geek Squad and have a uniform, you should always make certain that your attire is clean, neat, and appropriate. It should also be *businesslike*. Dress slacks (not jeans), a dress shirt with a collar, and a tie is the common standard. It may be different at your place of employment. Avoid excessive jewelry, or jewelry that might be offensive to your range of customers. Also, hold down the cologne or perfume—be moderate. Practice good hygiene by keeping hair washed and groomed, fingernails trimmed and clean, and breath fresh (use mouthwash or breath mints as needed, but not chewing gum).

You should establish a **good rapport** with your customers, but you should always maintain a professional distance from them. You cannot afford to be their support, or confidant, in dealings with the company you work for. The apparent opportunity to gain the inside track with the customer, at your company's expense, cannot work out in your favor. Remember, the customer sees you as an extension of that company. So, you can only be as good as your company is to the customer. If my computer is broken, I don't need a friend, I need the best technician I can find.

good rapport

Establish Integrity

The news media periodically produces undercover exposé's about service rip-offs in different industries. **Integrity** is the greatest asset a service person has. This is the main factor in creating continuous customer relationships and repeat business. Once it has been breached, it is nearly impossible to restore.

Integrity

It is much more beneficial to establish the relationship with the customer based on your abilities and integrity. Have something good to say about the customer's facilities, if possible. If not, don't comment on them at all. The same goes for equipment that they have chosen. They aren't paying you for consulting services, and disparaging comments about their choices won't win you any points.

From time to time, you may be exposed to customer information that is of a sensitive nature. Respect the confidentiality of this information. Never reveal financial information that you have obtained from a customer's system. This includes friends and, especially, employees of the customer.

GEEK SQUAD CASE FILE #62156

The technician received a telephone call from a customer who buys thousands of dollars of computer equipment from his company each year. The purchaser cannot get the company's computer to work with a printer that was purchased through another supplier. She wants the technician to get the system running. How should the technician react?

    a.   "I'm really sorry, but we can't work on equipment purchased from another vendor."

    b.   "Sure, how can I help you?"

    c.   "Let me clear this with my supervisor."

    d.   "You'll have to tell my supervisor that you want me to do this. I'm sure that it will be all right because you do so much business with us."

Avoid distracting employees while you are working at a customer's site. Work as unobtrusively as possible. **Ask permission** to use the customer's facilities, such as the telephone, copier, or other equipment. An example would be if paper is required to test a printer you are repairing—ask an appropriate person for it and don't just get it for yourself. Also ask permission from a supervisor if you must borrow equipment, enter areas of a facility that you have not expressly been authorized to be in, or move equipment around. Remember to straighten up the work area before leaving it (i.e., don't leave the paper from the print tests laying around).

Never break copyright regulations by loading, or giving away, illegal software. One of the leading causes of computer virus infection is pirated software. Not only do you run this risk in giving away copies, it's illegal, and it can get you introduced to various people you never really wanted to meet, such as lawyers and judges. On top of that, it could cost you your job.

Essentials 8.2

Handle Conflicts Appropriately

Successfully servicing a customer often means providing a positive solution to the customer's problem under negative circumstances. Inevitably, you will run into a customer who is having a bad day. No matter what you do, you will not be able to keep them from getting angry over their situation. What you can do is realize that this is the case, and attempt to **de-escalate** the situation.

de-escalate

This usually involves letting customers get pent-up frustrations off their chests by simply listening to them. The best thing to do is let the customer vent verbal frustrations without becoming defensive. It can be very frustrating to let customers vent without interrupting them, but that is an important part of successfully handling irate customers. Take notes during the emotional explosion and note the key issues. Taking notes and trying to figure out the real issues should keep you preoccupied so that the emotional part does not affect you as much.

Avoid arguing with the customer. When you do reply, remain calm, talk in a steady voice, and avoid making inflammatory comments. Also, try to avoid taking a defensive stance, as this signals a conflict point. Realize that criticism given out by customers is generally not personal—so don't take it that way. Information delivered with an aggressive attitude will normally lead to an aggressive, or retaliatory response from the customer.

After the customer has poured out the full story, try to redirect the conversation to creating solutions to the problems. However, do not minimize the customer's problems. Go over the important details one-at-a-time and explain how you will handle each concern, or who you must turn to for a final answer. Here again, be exact. Give the customer a time when you will be getting back to them with answers. Be specific if possible—next Tuesday morning is a better answer than some time next week.

If the customer is too angry to work through the details with you, conclude the encounter by trying to do or offer something to lessen the frustration level and make certain to follow up as you've indicated. As soon as possible, withdraw from the confrontation and let the situation cool off. Inform your superiors of the situation as quickly as possible, so that you have inside support, and so that a plan of relief can be implemented.

Telephone Techniques

All of the listening and communications skills are equally valuable when performing **phone support** work. Because you cannot see the customer, or interpret the customer's body language, it is even more important to assess the state of the customer quickly. It is also important to determine the technical abilities of the user as quickly as possible. Asking a receptionist to remove the cover of a computer is not normally an accepted practice.

phone support

When giving instructions over the phone, **be precise**. Provide detailed instructions for work to be done, and ask lots of questions about what is happening on the other end. Cellular or cordless phones are extremely valuable tools for customers using phone support. At your end of the phone, take good notes of what the user has been instructed to do, so that you can review them as needed.

be precise

Try to **answer the phone** on the second or third ring. First-ring answers can be startling for the customer, catching them unprepared. Customers will often assume that you are not available soon after the third ring. Voice mail answering systems are normally set up to assume the same thing, so your call may automatically get routed there after only a few rings. There are a number of people who do not care to be switched to a machine.

answer the phone

placing a call

When **placing a call**, let it ring up to six times if you are calling a business and ten times if calling a residence. Longer time may be required to get to the phone from some parts of a residence, such as the garage or basement.

Avoid rounds of **phone tag** by leaving a good time to call in your message. Don't forget to leave the telephone number where you can be reached at that time. Also provide a reason for the call along with any other pertinent information. Doing so will enable the other party to have any relevant documents or notes for the conversation. Do not leave the time or date of your call as part of your message unless the greeting tells you to do so. Most automated answering systems do this automatically.

phone tag

Always identify your company and provide your name when making or receiving telephone calls. Attempt to use the caller's name at least once, if not twice, in the conversation. This action personalizes the call and lets the customer know you are paying attention. (It also reminds you to pay attention.)

Avoid putting customers on hold if possible. If you must put them on hold, make certain to get their name and phone number in case anything happens. If you expect that the customer may be on hold for more than 30 seconds, ask them if you can call them back. Their time is as valuable as yours, and, unless they are calling on a toll-free or local line, they are paying for the call.

Take notes during the conversation, and recap the important points before hanging up. Reaffirm all commitments made, and include times and dates of any appointments or services scheduled. Always include date, time, and reasons for calls, as well as the customer's name and company information. These items can be very beneficial when preserved in note form. Good notes prevent missed, lost, or forgotten communications from ruining a good customer relationship.

Handle Paperwork and Finish Up

There are a number of nontroubleshooting, nonrepair activities that must be handled in order to have an efficient organization. As a service person, you are not alone. As indicated at the beginning of this chapter, you are part of a team that must communicate effectively in order for the system to operate smoothly. Other members of the team won't be able to do their jobs effectively if you don't follow through on yours. When the last nut has been tightened and the last cord plugged in on a service call, process the paperwork as soon as possible, so that it can be moving through your system.

Note any abnormalities, unusual situations, or memory-based activities in writing. As an example, say that you loan a customer an extension cord at their location and do not write a memo or work ticket entry about it. Would you reasonably expect to remember the place and situation after a couple of weeks, and dozens of service calls, have gone by? At some point, you, or one of your coworkers, will need that equipment, and there will be no record of where it is.

Follow up with people you have delegated tasks to, in order to make sure that those tasks are being taken care of. Use an organizational aid to coordinate jobs, appointments, and activities with coworkers.

Maintain an Orderly Work Area

Keep an inventory

Tag parts

Handle jobs one at a time, so that components from one job do not get mixed up with components from another job. Store equipment not being used, so that there is ample room to work, and so that these items do not become a safety hazard.

Keep an inventory of parts and equipment in your area of responsibility. Order parts needed for a job promptly, and keep a log of when they should arrive. If the parts do not arrive as scheduled, you should have a reminder that they are still missing. This reminder will allow you to track repair parts, so that when a customer calls to check on the equipment, or problem, you will have the information at hand.

Tag parts brought into the work area, so that they do not get lost or mishandled. Store them so that they will not be damaged by environmental factors, such as ESD. Include all pertinent information about the part, including the problem description, repair notes, and customer name and location.

KEY POINTS REVIEW

- Customer education refers to providing direction on the proper use of the product and advising customers of new services or product developments.

- Personal service involves answering questions and addressing specific concerns about products and services.

- The customer service person solicits feedback from the customer concerning products and services.

- Politeness is a valuable quality to possess. However, it should never be forced, contrived, or overdone.

- Make eye contact when you speak to customers.

- Be aware of your body language and what it is saying.

- Part of your job is to determine whether the user could be the source of the problem—either trying to do things with the system that it cannot do or not understanding how some part of it is supposed to work.

- Give preeminence to the customer's sense of urgency.

- Document your promises, and dates, so that you may demonstrate accountability to your customers.

- Always make certain that your attire is clean, neat, and appropriate.

- Integrity is the greatest asset a service person has—it is the main factor in creating continuous customer relationships and repeat business.

- Ask permission to use the customer's facilities, such as the telephone, copier, or other equipment.

- If the customer is too angry to work through the details with you, conclude the encounter as soon as possible, withdraw from the confrontation, and let the situation cool off. Inform your superiors of the situation as quickly as possible, so that you have inside support, and so that a plan of relief can be implemented.

- Avoid rounds of phone tag by leaving a good time to call in your message.

- Store equipment not being used, so that there is ample room to work, and so that these items do not become a safety hazard.

- Tag parts brought into the work area, so that they do not get lost or mishandled. Store them so that they will not be damaged by environmental factors, such as ESD. Include all pertinent information about the part, including the problem description, repair notes, and customer name and location.

The following questions test your knowledge of the material presented in this chapter.

1. What actions should be taken as soon as a situation goes beyond the scope of your position?

2. If you suspect that a customer may not be trained properly to perform operations associated with the items you are being asked to fix, what actions should you take and at what level?

3. List two tools that provide your best defense against customer dissatisfaction.

4. Describe the purpose of soliciting feedback from customers.

5. What is the main reason for including customer education as a major component of customer service?

6. List two items you should address in preparing to contact a customer or going to their location to work.

7. Under what conditions would it be bad business to discuss new equipment or software with employees of companies you are working with?

8. In terms of body language, what message is being sent if you keep your arms folded while a customer is explaining their problem to you?

9. In terms of body language, what message is being sent if you fail to make eye contact with customers when they are talking to you?

10. What is the most effective way to help customers think through the problems they are experiencing?

11. List the four negative phrases that should be avoided when talking to a customer.

12. What is the best way to protect your accountability level with a customer?

13. When dealing with an upset customer, what action can you take to prevent yourself from getting caught up in the emotions of the situation?

14. How can you avoid playing phone tag with customers?

15. What items should always be included in the notes you keep from customer contacts?

1. Identify the customer satisfaction elements that create a successful business. (Select all that apply.)
   a. Satisfaction with the organization (supplier)
   b. Satisfaction with the product
   c. Satisfaction with your personality
   d. Satisfaction with the service received

2. Choose the items that negatively impact your perception as a professional. (Choose all that apply.)
   a. Use of breath mints
   b. Wearing jeans
   c. Chewing gum
   d. Wearing Polo shirts

3. You have just finished repairing a remote printer connection at a customer's office and need some paper to test it. The paper tray is empty, and there is no one nearby. What should you do?
   a. Look for the supply closet.
   b. Find someone who works in the office and ask that person to get it for you.
   c. Find a manager from the office and ask permission to get and use their material.
   d. Leave a note for the operator to test the printer connection and get back to you if there are any problems.

4. What are the definite downsides of sharing copies of copyrighted software with customers or their employees? (Select all that apply.)
   a. The customer may acquire a virus from your copy.
   b. This action is illegal and could get you fired, or your customer sued.
   c. The customer will be disappointed in your ethics.
   d. The customer will likely call the software supplier for support.

5. When dealing with an irate customer, what action on your part should be avoided to ensure that a conflict point isn't established?
   a. Contacting your boss to escalate the problem resolution to a higher level.
   b. Aggressively defending your personal techniques and abilities.
   c. Attempting to divert the conversation to a solutions-oriented discussion.
   d. Going over details one at a time with the customer, as this will appear as a waste of time to them.

6. If you must put a customer on hold, at what point should you consider asking them if you can call them back?
   a. 10 minutes
   b. 5 minutes
   c. 1 minute
   d. 30 seconds

7. You receive a call from an office where Jim, another member of your team, has just repaired a computer system for them. Jim has left their offices, and they are telling you that the machine is down again. Which of the following is a proper customer service response?
   a. "The machine was working when Jim left your office. I can't imagine what could have happened to it. I'm busy right now, and I know Jim is on another appointment already. I'll have someone get back to you as soon as possible."
   b. "I'm not familiar with what Jim was working on at your place, but I will try to help you or have Jim get back to you as soon as possible."
   c. "I can't help you, but I will have Jim get back to you as soon as he can get free."
   d. "Give me your name, and I will have Jim get back to you as soon as he can."

8. You are on a job site with one of your company's best customers when one of the managers asks you to repair a printer that you know your company does not sell or service. How should you handle this request?
   a. Simply perform the work as requested.
   b. Offer to perform the work on your own time.
   c. Refer the request to your management.
   d. Decline the work, because it is not your responsibility.

9. When answering customer phone calls, what pieces of information should you always remember to include in your conversation? (Choose all that apply.)
   a. Your phone or extension number
   b. Your name
   c. The date and time
   d. The company's name

10. When you are performing troubleshooting or other customer support functions over the telephone, which of the following are key parts of a successful customer satisfaction effort? (Select all that apply.)
   a. Use precise directions and terminology.
   b. Include plenty of anecdotes to keep the customer calm.
   c. Ask questions before and after each instruction has been performed.
   d. Make sure the customer uses a corded phone so that they can clearly hear your instructions.

CHAPTER

2

BASIC PC TERMS AND CONCEPTS

OBJECTIVES

Upon completion of this chapter and its related lab procedures, you should be able to perform these tasks:

1. Locate the power supply unit, system board, system speaker, disk drive unit, adapter cards, and expansion slots.

2. Differentiate between typical PC case styles and explain the strengths and weaknesses associated with each.

3. Describe the function of the PC power supply unit.

4. Locate the system's RAM banks, and use documentation to determine the amount of RAM installed.

5. Identify system memory modules.

6. Identify common microprocessor IC package types.

7. Identify a Video Graphics Array (VGA) adapter card.

8. Recognize different disk drive types associated with PCs.

9. Describe typical external connections associated with purchase.

10. Define the functions of the computer's input/output (I/O) devices.

11. Explain the three classes of software used with computer systems.

12. Explain the function of the system ROM BIOS.

13. Describe the function and purpose of a disk operating system.

14. Describe the value of a graphical user interface.

15. Describe popular software application programs.

CHAPTER 2

BASIC PC TERMS AND CONCEPTS

FROM THE GEEK SQUAD

Jennifer is a salesperson at Best Buy store 224 where she wants to get into the Geek Squad. To do so, she knows that she must take an online assessment to show that she has the basic knowledge of computer systems to qualify for entry into the Geek Squad as a Counter Intelligence Agent. This assessment measures the applicant's knowledge of basic PC systems and operation. She needs to make sure that she has an accurate knowledge of basic PC terminology and that she is able to identify typical PC components, as well as describe their functions and characteristics.

INTRODUCTION

The first objective in the first domain of CompTIA's A+ Essentials exam states that the technician should be able to identify the names, purposes, and characteristics of various personal computer system modules. As with any group or industry, the PC world has produced a peculiar vocabulary to describe its products and their functions. As this A+ Essentials objective indicates, the computer technician must be able to use that vocabulary to identify personal computer products and to understand how they work and what they do.

Every computer system consists of two parts: *hardware devices* that perform physical operations and *software* (programs) that oversees and guides the actions of the hardware. Hardware consists of those parts of the computer that you can touch. Software is the logical, intangible parts of the computer. Like all other classes of computers, personal computers (PCs) involve hardware and software components. To this end, this chapter is designed to introduce you to personal computer fundamentals, including both hardware and software components. In particular, it provides an introduction to common PC components, including a brief discussion of their theories of operation and the basic functions that each component supplies. These discussions include the standards that the industry has developed for these components. This information serves as a foundation for presenting more advanced theory and troubleshooting materials in the following chapters.

Essentials 1.0

PERSONAL COMPUTER EVOLUTION

In the early years of microcomputer history, the market was dominated by small companies that produced computers intended mainly for playing video games. Serious computer applications were a secondary concern. Companies such as Commodore, Timex/Sinclair, Atari, and Tandy produced 8-bit machines for the emerging industry based on microprocessors from Intel, Motorola, Zilog, and Commodore.

In 1977, Apple Computers produced the Apple I. This was followed by a series of 8-bit microcomputers: the Apple II, Apple IIc, and Apple IIe. These units were single-board computers with built-in keyboards and a discrete monitor. With the IIe unit, Apple installed seven expansion connectors on its main board. They were included to allow the addition of adapter cards. Apple also produced a set of adapter cards that could be used with the IIe to provide additional capabilities. These units were very advanced for their time. In 1981, however, Apple introduced their relatively powerful 16-bit **Macintosh (Mac)** system to the market. The features offered by the Mac represented a major shift in computing power. Departing from command-line operations, it offered a graphical operating environment. Using a small input device called a mouse, visual objects were selected from the display monitor to guide the operation of the system. This operating method found an eager audience of nontechnical and public school system users.

Late in 1981, IBM entered the microcomputer market with the unveiling of their now famous IBM **personal computer (PC)**. At the time of its introduction, the IBM PC was a drastic departure from the status quo of the microcomputer world. The original Apple Mac and IBM PC are depicted in Figure 2-1.

The IBM PC employed an Intel 8088 16/8-bit microprocessor. (It processes data 16 bits at a time internally, but moves it around in 8-bit packages.) Relatively speaking, the IBM PC was fast, powerful, flexible, and priced within the range of most individuals. The general public soon became aware of the tremendous possibilities of the personal computer, and the microcomputer quickly advanced from a simple game machine to an office tool with a seemingly endless range of advanced personal and business applications.

| **Macintosh (Mac)** |
| **personal computer (PC)** |

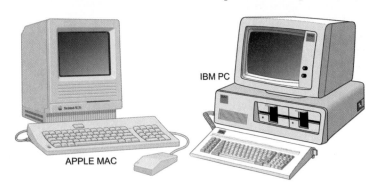

IBM PC

APPLE MAC

Figure 2-1: Apple Mac and IBM PC

| **extended technology (XT)** |
| **advanced technology PC (PC-AT)** |
| **pseudo-standards** |
| **Industry Standard Architecture (ISA)** |

In 1983, IBM added a small hard-disk drive to the PC and introduced its **extended technology (XT)** version. The success continued when, in 1984, IBM introduced the **advanced technology PC (PC-AT)**. The tremendous popularity of the original IBM PC-XT and AT systems created a set of **pseudo-standards** for hardware and software compatibility. The AT architecture was so popular that it became known as the **Industry Standard Architecture (ISA)**. Even today, the majority of microcomputers are both hardware and software compatible with the original AT design. The IBM PC-AT is depicted in Figure 2-2.

Figure 2-2: IBM PC-AT

PC Compatibles

The openness of the IBM PC architecture, coupled with an abundance of PC-compatible hardware and software components, enticed several companies to develop PC-like computers of their own. These computers were referred to as *PC look-alikes*, *PC clones*, or more commonly as **PC-compatibles**. The cloning process was made possible by two events. First, the government-backed *Electronic Research and Service Organization* (*ERSO*) in Taiwan produced a non-copyright-infringing version of the IBM-XT **firmware** (software stored in a hardware device that controlled the operation of the system). Second, IBM did not secure exclusive rights to the **Microsoft Disk Operating System**, which controlled the interaction between the PC system's hardware and application software.

The presence of several PC-compatibles in the marketplace fueled a race to introduce increasingly powerful hardware devices, operating system control software, and user applications. While most PCs are still based in some part on the PC-AT design, they incorporate improved microprocessors, memory management structures, and data storage units, as well as faster, more powerful expansion buses and **input/output (I/O)** connectors for adding peripheral devices to the basic system. The rapid advance of the PC market has also been aided by advances in input/output technologies, digital communication technologies, lowered cost of components, and the widespread acceptance of the Internet.

> **PC-compatibles**
>
> **firmware**
>
> **Microsoft Disk Operating System**
>
> **input/output (I/O)**

THE PC SYSTEM

The terms *Personal Computer* and *PC* have come to be used as references to a class of small, relatively inexpensive computers designed for individual users. A typical PC system, shown in Figure 2-3, is modular by design. It is called a *system*, because it includes all of the components required to have a functional computer:

> **Input devices**
>
> **Computer**
>
> **system unit**
>
> **Output devices**

- **Input devices**—keyboard and mouse

- **Processing system**—system unit

- **Output devices**—CRT monitor and a character printer

> The system unit is the main portion of the microcomputer system and is the basis of any PC system arrangement.

The components surrounding it vary from system to system, depending on the particular functions the system is designed to serve.

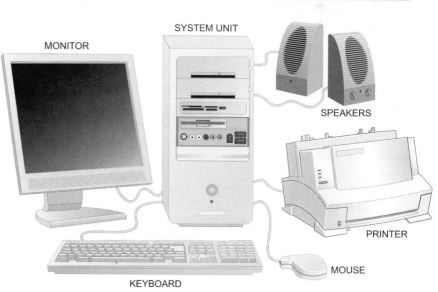

Figure 2-3: A Typical Personal Computer System

System Unit Cases

The system unit case is typically a metal chassis and removable cover that includes a plastic front panel for aesthetic purposes. This box typically contains the basic components that make up the computer system. PCs have been packaged in a number of different case designs. These designs fall into three basic styles: desktops, towers, and portables. Each case design type offers characteristics, as follows, that adapt the system for different environments:

- Mounting methods for the printed circuit boards

- Ventilation characteristics

- Total drive capacity

- Footprint (the amount of desk space they take up)

- Portability

Desktop Cases

desktop cases

As illustrated in Figure 2-4, **desktop cases** are typically wider than they are tall. This case style was used with the original IBM PCs and continues to be produced until the present. They are referred to as desktops, because they are designed to set on a standard desktop behind a keyboard and mouse, usually with the display monitor sitting on top of the case. Theoretically, this arrangement places the input devices in a good position for the user and sets the display device at normal eye level when the user is seated at a desk. These case types remained popular for many years but have largely given way to more space-conscience tower designs.

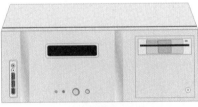

ATX CASE STYLE

BTX CASE STYLE

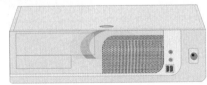

LOW-PROFILE CASE STYLE

Figure 2-4:
Desktop Case Designs

A special variety of desktop cases, referred to as **low-profile desktops**, reduce the vertical height of the unit. A short bus-extender card, called a **back plane**, mounts in an expansion slot on the system board and allows adapter cards to be mounted in the unit horizontally. The case is thus enabled to be shorter. The horizontal mounting of the adapter cards in a low-profile case tends to create heat buildup problems. The heat rising from the system board flows around the adapter cards, adding to the heat they are generating. A standard back plane card is depicted in Figure 2-5. Low-profile power supplies and disk drives are also required to achieve the reduced height.

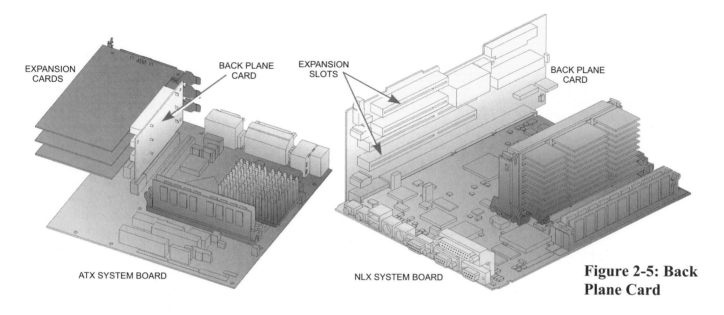

Figure 2-5: Back Plane Card

PC technicians frequently need to gain access to the insides of the system unit for installing or repairing components located inside. There are several common variations in how desktop cases are assembled and disassembled. In some designs, the cover of the system unit slides (or lifts) off the base, as shown in Figure 2-6. The top of some designs slides forward after screws securing it to the back panel have been removed. In this style of case, the plastic front panel usually slides off with the metal top. In other designs, the top swings up from the rear and slides backwards to clear the case. The tops of these units are secured to the base by screws in the rear of the unit and screws or clips along the sides of the case. The plastic front panel is attached directly to the case.

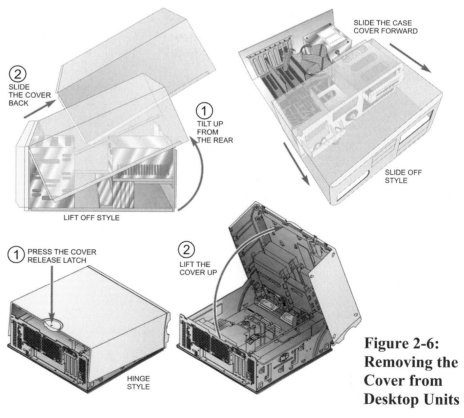

Figure 2-6: Removing the Cover from Desktop Units

The fit between the case top and the chassis is very important in achieving Federal Communications Commission (FCC) certification. A tight fit and electrical conductivity between the two pieces is necessary to prevent unwanted radio interference from escaping the interior of the case. The inside face or the plastic front panel is coated with a conductive paint to limit the radiomagnetic interference escaping from the case.

Tower Cases

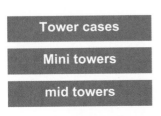

Tower cases are designed to set vertically on the floor beneath a desk. In the past, PC users often resorted to standing their desktop computers on their sides under the desk to provide more usable workspace on the desktop. This prompted computer manufacturers to develop cases that would naturally fit under the desk. IBM validated the tower design when they introduced their *Personal System 2* (*PS/2*) line of personal computers. Different tower case styles are depicted in Figure 2-7.

MINI TOWER

MID TOWER

FULL TOWER

Figure 2-7: Tower Case Designs

Mini towers and **mid towers** (tower cases somewhere between the full and mini towers in height) are short towers designed to take up less vertical space. Internally, their design resembles a vertical desktop unit. They are considerably less expensive than the larger towers due to the reduced materials needed to produce them. Unlike their taller relatives, mini towers do not provide abundant space for internal add-ons or disk drives. However, they do possess the shortcomings of the full towers. Mini towers exist more as a function of marketing than as an application solution.

Many easy-access schemes have been developed to enable quick or convenient access to the inside of the system unit. Some towers use removable trays that the system board and adapter cards can be attached to before being slid into the unit. This enables all of the boards to be assembled outside the system unit. Other tower cases use hinged doors on the side of the case, allowing the system and boards to swing away from the chassis. Figure 2-8 depicts different methods of removing the outer covers from tower cases.

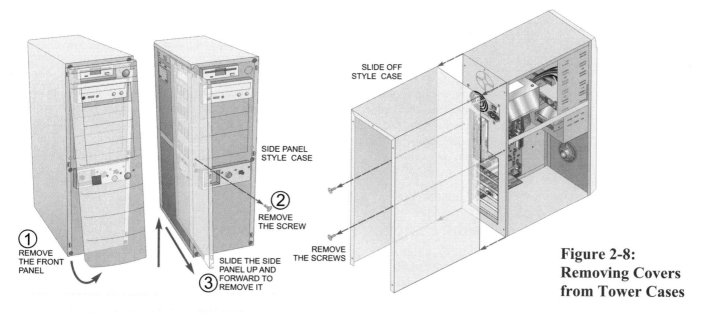

**Figure 2-8:
Removing Covers
from Tower Cases**

1. REMOVE THE FRONT PANEL
2. REMOVE THE SCREW
3. SLIDE THE SIDE PANEL UP AND FORWARD TO REMOVE IT

SIDE PANEL STYLE CASE

REMOVE THE SCREWS

SLIDE OFF STYLE CASE

NOTE

Although the term *desktop* has historically been used to refer to PCs with the case styles described above, current usage of the term has been expanded to refer to mini and mid towers as well. It is not uncommon for users to place the mini tower on the desktop surface to one side of, or behind, the input devices and display unit.

System Cooling

Excessive heat buildup is always a cause for concern with electronic equipment, because it can cause integrated circuit components to fail. The heat inside the system unit case increases as the internal components run faster and as more internal options are added to the system. Various fan arrangements are used to pull cooler outside air into the system unit to minimize heat buildup inside the case. Depending on the type of system, internal fans may be used to either pull fresh air in through slots in the front of the case, or through vents in the power supply unit located in the rear of the case.

In most systems, the power supply fan is the main source of airflow within the case. However, special **IC cooler fans** and **heat sink devices** are always added to advanced microprocessors and routinely installed on faster support devices for direct cooling of those devices. These fan units are designed so they can be attached directly to the IC and plug into one of the power supply's connectors or special connectors on the system board, as depicted in Figure 2-9.

IC cooler fans

heat sink devices

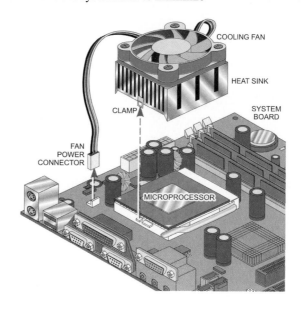

COOLING FAN
HEAT SINK
SYSTEM BOARD
CLAMP
FAN POWER CONNECTOR
MICROPROCESSOR

**Figure 2-9:
Microprocessor,
Heat Sink, and
Fan**

In some systems, it may become necessary to add additional fans to the case to compensate for additional heat buildup beyond the cooling capabilities of the power supply and IC fans. These fans may be attached to the front or rear panels of the system unit and used to channel airflow in directions determined by the system designer.

The ventilation characteristics of most tower units tend to be poor, because the plug-in adapter cards are mounted horizontally. This permits the heat produced by lower boards to rise past the upper boards, adding to the cooling problem. To compensate for this deficiency, most tower units include a secondary case fan to help increase the airflow and dissipate the heat buildup.

Essentials 1.1

Front Panels

indicator lights

control buttons

Case manufacturers place the system **indicator lights** and **control buttons** on the front panel for easy viewing and user access. Typical indicator lights include a power indicator light and a hard drive activity light. Control buttons normally include a power switch and a RESET button. Most desktop and tower units place the on/off switch on the machine's front panel and use an internal power cable between the switch and the power supply unit. Figure 2-10 shows typical front panel controls and indicators.

The system unit provides access to removable storage media and their drives through openings in the front panel. These openings exist in standard sizes to accommodate the two most common drive unit size —5.25" and 3.5" drives. In most desktop units, these openings are typically located at the right side of the case. On the other hand, tower units generally place the drives at the top of the case.

Inside the case, there are matching support structures for the drives called the drive cage. These cages provide standard-size mounting structures, called bays, for individual drives to be installed in. These structures also allow the drives to be secured to the chassis and to align correctly with the openings in the front panel.

Hard-disk drives do not require external access, so they may be hidden behind a blank insert. Likewise, blank inserts are used to cover empty drive bays in the system. This is done to prevent dust from being pulled into the system unit through the opening. The covers also preserve the case's designed airflow channels to insure proper cooling of the system unit's components.

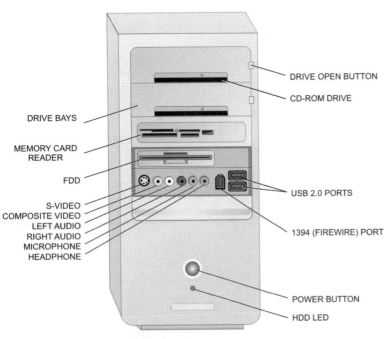

DRIVE OPEN BUTTON

CD-ROM DRIVE

DRIVE BAYS

MEMORY CARD READER

FDD

S-VIDEO
COMPOSITE VIDEO
LEFT AUDIO
RIGHT AUDIO
MICROPHONE
HEADPHONE

USB 2.0 PORTS

1394 (FIREWIRE) PORT

POWER BUTTON

HDD LED

Figure 2-10: Typical Front Panel Controls, Indicators, and Openings

Most current case designs include special front panel **memory card reader/writer** units that handle different types of memory modules used with other digital electronic devices, such as *Personal Digital Assistants* and *digital cameras*. This enables digital information, such as audio and video data stored on those memory modules, to be shared between the computer and the device for processing. Figure 2-11 depicts a *9-in-1* front panel memory card unit that accepts eight different types of memory modules, as well as supplying a single, front-mounted USB connection port. As the figure illustrates, these units provide multiple openings that are compatible with different standard memory module types. These modules and connection ports are covered in greater detail in Chapter 4, *Standard I/O Systems*.

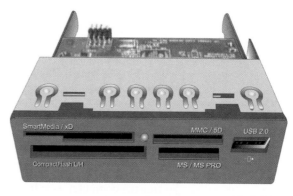

Many front panel designs also provide convenient standardized connection points (*hardware ports*) for input and output devices. Historically, I/O connections were all made at the rear of the system unit, out of sight of the

Figure 2-11: Front Panel Memory Card Reader

user and the public. This also served to keep connecting cables out of the way. However, as PC technology has advanced so that peripheral devices may be connected and disconnected while the system is in operation, many manufacturers have provided additional connections on the front panel. With this move, users do not have to gain access to the back of the unit to connect such a device to the system.

Back Panels

The PC's back panel has typically provided three points of interest for the technician—power supply connection and ventilation openings, standard input/output connection points, and openings (referred to as *expansion slots*) for add-on adapter cards. External connections to the system's power supply unit are made at the rear of the case, as illustrated in Figure 2-12.

There is also an opening for the power supply fan to move air in or out of the case. You may also find an on/off override switch for the power supply located here.

Traditionally, standard input devices have been connected to the rear of the system unit. This usually involves standard connections for a keyboard and a mouse, as well as an assortment of different industry standard connection ports that permit other devices to connect directly to the system. These connections are defined and discussed in detail in Chapter 4, *Standard I/O Systems*.

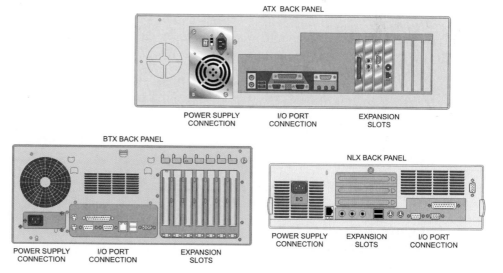

Figure 2-12: Typical Back Panel Layouts

PC systems have always provided special slot-type connectors to allow additional circuitry to be added to the system. The additional circuitry is provided in the form of plug-in **adapter cards** that snap into the slot connectors, which gives them direct access to the system board circuitry. These slots make the system very flexible and provide a method for attaching new inventions to the system. The system's installed adapter cards are also accessed through openings in the system's back panel.

Vacant slots and adapter cards that do not provide and external connections are covered with blank slot covers. The blank slot covers prevent dust from entering the system and act to maintain the integrity of the system unit's internal airflow patterns.

Portable PCs

To free the computer user from the desk, an array of **portable PCs** have been developed. These units package the system unit, input units, and output unit into a single, lightweight package that can be carried by the user.

Although early attempts at developing a portable PC produced smaller computers that could be carried by the user, they tended to be heavy and inconvenient to carry and had short operating times between battery recharges. However, continued advancements in IC and peripheral component designs have provided truly portable, PC-compatible computers.

A typical **notebook computer**, such as the one depicted in Figure 2-13, features an integrated video display, reduced-size keyboard, specialized pointing devices, hard drives that range into the tens of gigabytes, and CD-ROM/DVD drives. The capabilities of modern portable computers make them the equivalent of desktop or tower units in most respects.

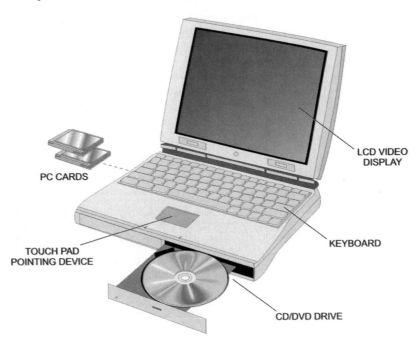

**Figure 2-13:
A Typical Portable
Computer**

Although portable systems operate in the same manner as desktop and tower PCs, they have characteristics that are considerably different than the other PC designs. Therefore, they are covered in detail in Chapter 8, *Portable Systems*.

Inside the System Unit

The components inside the system unit can be divided into four distinct subunits: a switching power supply, the disk drives, the system board, and the adapter cards, as illustrated in Figure 2-14.

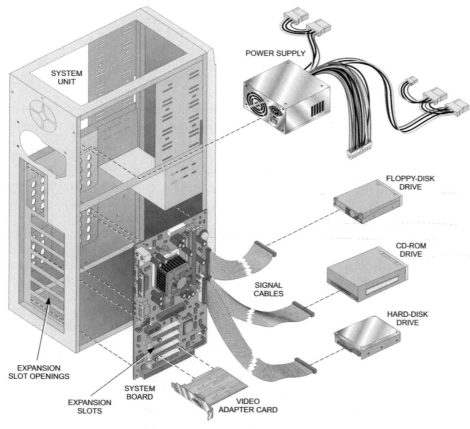

Figure 2-14: Components Inside the System Unit

TEST TIP

Know the names of all the components of a typical PC system and be able to identify them by sight.

> disk drives

A typical desktop/tower system unit contains a single power supply unit that converts commercial power into the various levels required by the different devices in the system. In desktop cases, the power supply is generally located in the right-rear corner of the system unit.

The number and types of **disk drives** in the system vary according to the application the system is designed for. The disk drive bays in most desktop cases are located in the front-right corner of the system unit.

The basic arrangement for disk drives in a PC system includes a single hard-disk drive unit and a single CD-ROM/DVD drive to handle the system's mass storage requirements. However, desktop/tower cases typically provide additional drive bays to accommodate several more disk drive units. Some systems may still include a floppy-disk drive as part of the system's mass storage devices.

The **system board,** also referred to as the **motherboard,** is the center of the PC system. It contains the portions of the system that define its computing power and speed. It also hosts a number of connection ports. Some protrude through the rear of the system unit, while others are provided through the system board's **expansion slot connectors**.

> system board
>
> motherboard
>
> expansion slot connectors

Expansion slots are located in the left-rear quadrant of the system board so that the external devices they serve can access them through the rear case openings.

The system board is located on the floor of the unit, toward the left-rear corner. Any number of plug-in adapter cards may be installed in the system board's expansion slots to handle a wide array of PC peripheral equipment. Older PCs normally had several adapter cards installed in their expansion slots. However, the only card typically installed in newer systems is the **video adapter card**. Most of the other basic functions historically served by adapter cards have been integrated directly into the system board.

video adapter card

In tower units, the system board is typically mounted to the right side-panel of the case. The power supply unit is attached to the back panel. Indicator lights and control buttons are located toward the upper part of the front panel. The drive units are mounted in the disk drive bays located in the upper half of the front panel. They also offer extended drive bay capabilities that make them especially useful in file server applications where many disk drives, CD-ROM/DVD drives, and tape drives are desired.

In both tower-style and desktop-style cases, the system board is attached to the case through brass standoffs that screw into the chassis. The standoffs are threaded into holes in the floor (or side panel) of the desktop (tower) system unit to anchor the system board to the chassis. The brass standoffs are inserted into the threaded holes before installing the system board. After the system board has been set in place on top of the standoffs, small machine screws are inserted through the system board openings and into the brass standoffs. This arrangement provides electrical grounding between the system board and the case and helps to reduce **electromagnetic field interference (EFI)** emitted from the board.

electromagnetic field interference (EFI)

Every electrical conductor radiates a field of electromagnetic energy when an electrical current passes through it. The intensity of these fields increases as the current is turned on and off. Computers are made of hundreds of conductors. Personal computers turn millions of digital switches in their ICs on and off each second. This results in a substantial amount of energy radiating from the computer. The levels generated by the components of a typical system can easily surpass maximum-allowable radiation levels set by the **Federal Communications Commission (FCC)**. The EFI fields generated can potentially interfere with reception of radio, television, and other communications signals under the FCC's jurisdiction. Therefore, computer manufacturers design grounding systems and case structures to limit the amount of EFI that can escape from the case. Basically, the FCC has established two certification levels for microcomputer systems:

Federal Communications Commission (FCC)

- Class A, for computers in business environments

- Class B, a stricter level directed at general consumers for the home environment

To be legal, FCC compliance stickers are required on computer units, along with certain information in their documentation.

Portable computers look very different inside than do tower/desktop units. Portable computer manufacturers are typically concerned with two main objectives: minimize power consumption and minimize the size of the unit as far as practical. To accomplish the latter objective, the designers create proprietary designs that squeeze internal components into the smallest space possible. The result of these designs is that no two models are alike. Each one has a different, nonstandard case and system board design. These factors are explored in Chapter 8, *Portable Systems*.

Power Supplies

The systems **power supply** unit provides electrical power for every component inside the system unit. It converts commercial electrical power received from a 120 Vac, 60 Hz (or 220 Vac, 50 Hz outside the United States) outlet into other levels required by the components of the system. In desktop and tower PCs, the power supply is the shiny metal box located at the rear of the system unit.

Several bundles of cable emerge from the power supply to provide power to the components of the system unit and to its peripherals. Typical desktop/tower power supplies produce four (or five) different levels of efficiently regulated DC voltage. These are +3.3, +5 V, –5 V, +12 V, and –12 V. The power supply unit also provides the system's ground. The +3.3 V and +5 V levels are used by the microprocessor. Other IC devices on the system board and adapter cards use the +5 V level. Figure 2-15 illustrates the typical power supply connections found in a desktop or tower PC.

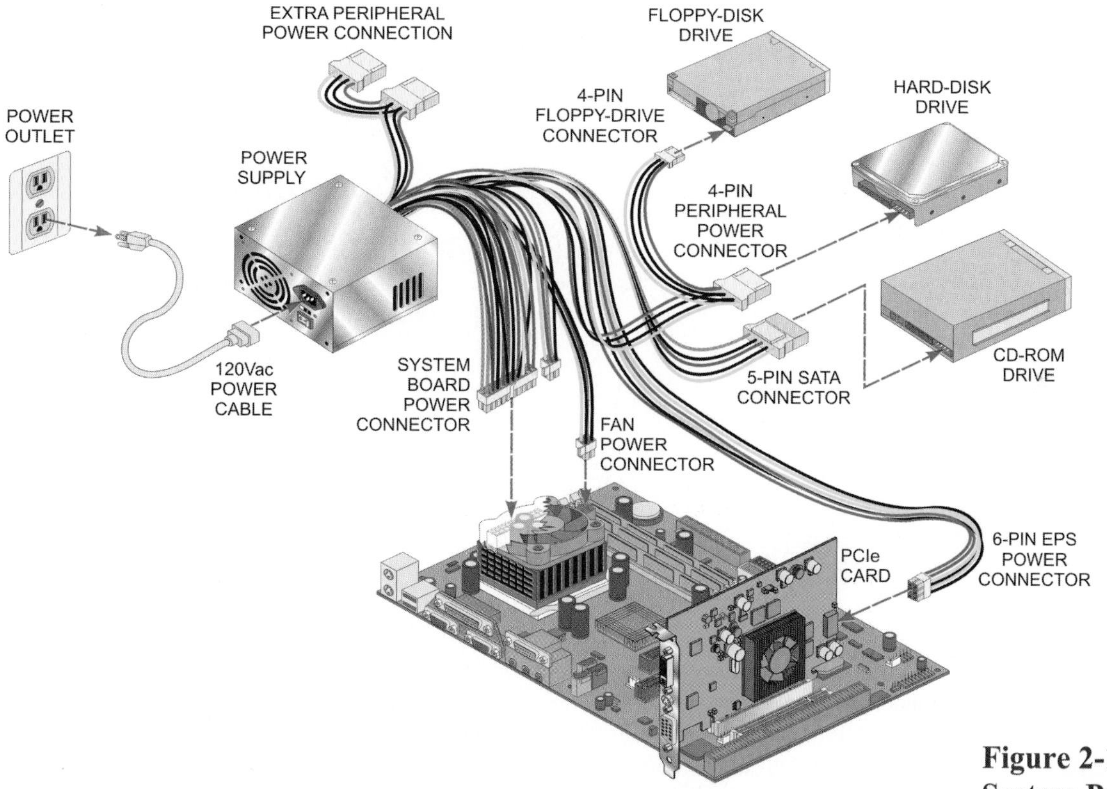

Figure 2-15: System Power Supply Connections

In the United States, a grounded, three-prong power cord provides the AC input voltage to the power supply. The smaller vertical blade in the connector is considered the hot or phase side of the connector. A small slide switch on the back of the unit permits the power supply to be switched over to operate on 220 Vac input voltages found outside the United States. When the switch is set to the 220 position, the voltage supplied to the power supply's monitor outlet will also be 220. In this position, it is usually necessary to exchange the power cord for one that has a plug suited to the country in which the computer is being used.

The power supply delivers power to the system board and its expansion slots through the system board power connector, as depicted in Figure 2-16. The ATX system board connector is a 20-pin connector that is keyed so that it cannot be installed incorrectly. It provides the system board components and the individual expansion slots with up to 1 ampere of current each. All of the voltage levels provided by the power supply are available to adapter cards through the system board's expansion slot connectors.

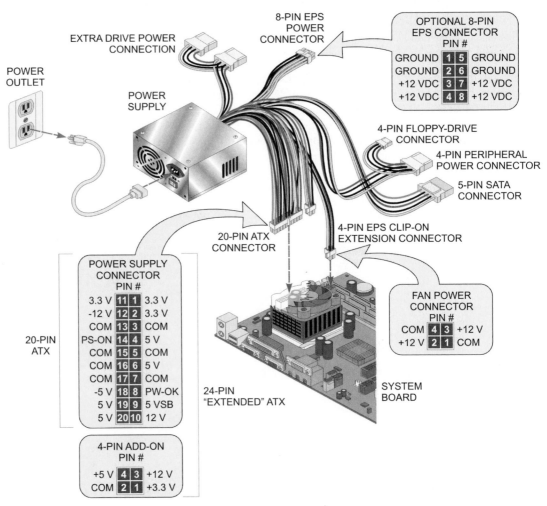

Figure 2-16: The System Board Power Connector

Newer power supplies offer a 4-pin clip-on extension to the standard 20-pin ATX power connector that converts it to meet the minimum requirements of the **entry-level power supply (EPS)** specification. This enhanced specification calls for additional conductors to provide additional 12-volt supply sources to the system board so it can deliver higher current capabilities required by high-end peripherals.

In addition to the lines that deliver different voltage levels to the system board, this connection contains a signal line that the system board can use to turn off the power supply. This is a power saving feature referred to as a *soft switch* and enables the system to shut itself off under control of the system software. This enables power management components of the operating system software to manage the hardware's power usage. This concept is discussed further in Chapter 3 (*Advanced System Boards*) and in Chapter 10 (*Windows Operating Systems*).

The other power supply bundles are used to supply power to optional systems, such as the disk drives, CD-ROM/DVD drives, and tape drives. These bundles provide a +5 and a +12 Vdc supply, as described in Figure 2-17. The larger 4-pin connector, referred to as the **peripheral power connector**, is carried over from older PC designs, while the smaller 4-pin **floppy connector** has gained widespread usage with smaller form factor disk drives. The +5 V supply provides power for electronic components on the optional devices, while the +12 V level is used for disk drive motors and other devices that require a higher voltage. As Figure 2-17 illustrates, these connectors are keyed, so they must be plugged in correctly.

peripheral power connector

floppy connector

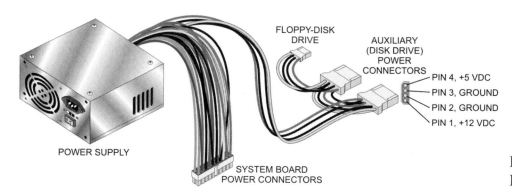

Figure 2-17: Auxiliary Power Connectors

More advanced power supplies offer additional power connection options, as illustrated in Figure 2-18. The wide-flat 5- and 15-pin **SATA connectors** are used to supply power to the newer **serial ATA**-style disk drive units.

SATA connectors

serial ATA

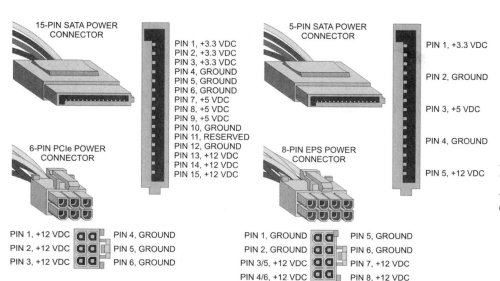

Figure 2-18: Advanced Auxiliary Power Connectors

The 6-pin **PCI express (PCIe)** power connectors are used to supply additional power to adapter cards mounted in the system board's PCIe expansion slots. Some of these cards may require more current from the power supply than the system board can deliver through its expansion slots.

PCI express (PCIe)

The 8-pin **EPS** connector provides the full implementation of the EPS specification for those system boards that require, or accommodate, this connector. The full EPS implementation delivers even more 12 Vdc power sources to the system board than standard ATX 20, 20+4 and 24-pin connections.

EPS

Like the standard options connectors, these advanced connectors are keyed, so they cannot be plugged in incorrectly.

Some power supply manufacturers offer modular connectivity units. With these power supplies, the number and types of cables and connectors is variable. This is possible because the power supply comes with a number of connection sockets mounted in its side, as illustrated in Figure 2-19. Different cable types can be plugged into any of the sockets to provide the levels of voltages and types of connectors needed for a given arrangement of components.

Power supply units come in a variety of form factors and power ratings. The form factor is important, because this specification indicates what case types the unit can be used with. The second important consideration when dealing with power supplies is their power rating (expressed as wattage rating). This is an indicator of the power supply's ability to deliver enough power to effectively drive all the devices in the system. Typical power ratings for PC power supplies range from 350-watt versions to over 1000 watts.

Selecting the correct power supply for a given computer system involves checking the power requirements of the various components and then adding them together. The value derived from this calculation represents the lowest power supply rating that can be used to power the system. The components that typically consume the most power in the PC are the microprocessor, the disk drives, and high-end video cards. These issues are discussed in greater detail in Chapter 11, *Basic System Troubleshooting*.

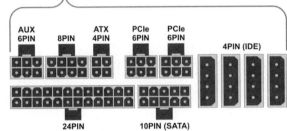

Figure 2-19: A Modular Power Supply

AUX 6PIN 8PIN ATX 4PIN PCIe 6PIN PCIe 6PIN 4PIN (IDE)

24PIN 10PIN (SATA)

TEST TIP

Be aware that a power supply's form factor and wattage ratings must be taken into account when ordering a replacement power supply for a given PC system.

Essentials 1.1

System Boards

The *system board* is the center of the PC-compatible microcomputer system. It contains the circuitry that determines the computing power and speed of the entire system. In particular, it contains the microprocessor and support devices that form the brains of the system.

form factor

There are several standard **form factor** specifications for system board layouts. Form factor is a description of the physical layout and interconnection ability of devices. A device's form factor involves its physical size and geometry, the positioning of key components, such as mounting holes, and the positioning and arrangement of interconnection points. These factors determine whether *component A* (such as a system board) will fit properly with *component B* (such as a system unit case) and connect to *component C* (such as a power supply). This concept is illustrated in Figure 2-20.

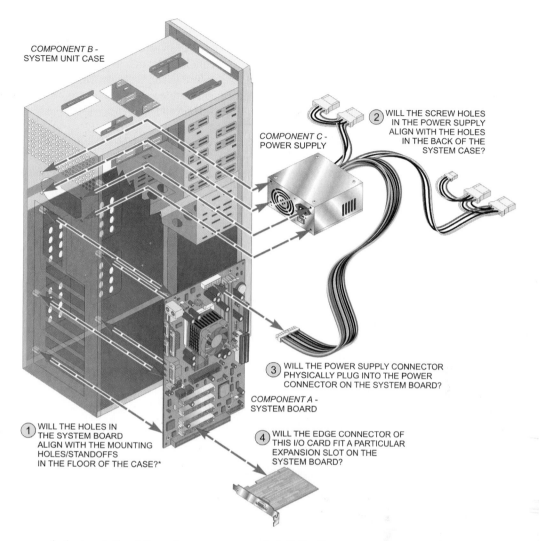

COMPONENT B - SYSTEM UNIT CASE

COMPONENT C - POWER SUPPLY

② WILL THE SCREW HOLES IN THE POWER SUPPLY ALIGN WITH THE HOLES IN THE BACK OF THE SYSTEM CASE?

③ WILL THE POWER SUPPLY CONNECTOR PHYSICALLY PLUG INTO THE POWER CONNECTOR ON THE SYSTEM BOARD?

COMPONENT A - SYSTEM BOARD

① WILL THE HOLES IN THE SYSTEM BOARD ALIGN WITH THE MOUNTING HOLES/STANDOFFS IN THE FLOOR OF THE CASE?*

④ WILL THE EDGE CONNECTOR OF THIS I/O CARD FIT A PARTICULAR EXPANSION SLOT ON THE SYSTEM BOARD?

Most manufacturers use industry-defined form factors to create their PCs. However, other manufacturers use their own versions of PC components so that they are not compatible with the same components produced by their competitors.

Figure 2-20: Key Form Factor Considerations

Although there are several active form factors for PC components, there are three standard form factors that CompTIA has listed for the A+ technician to be aware of. These are the *ATX*, *BTX*, and *NLX* form factors.

The **advanced technology extended (ATX)** form factor was introduced in the mid-1990s as an upgrade to the IBM PC-AT standard that had become the pseudo-standard form factor for PCs. It continues to be the most widely used form factor currently in use with PC components.

> **advanced technology extended (ATX)**

The **balanced technology extended (BTX)** form factor is a newer scalable form factor specification that provides for a wide range of system sizes and profiles. Its main goal is to establish component positions that optimize cooling inside the case to support higher component operating speeds. The BTX form factor design is incompatible with the ATX standard, except that you can use ATX power supplies with BTX system boards and cases.

> **balanced technology extended (BTX)**

The *new low-profile extended* (**NLX**) form factor is the replacement form factor specification from Intel for the older **LPX** low-profile specification. The NLX specification is designed to support newer PC technologies, such as larger memory modules, advanced microprocessors, and their cooling systems. The NLX system incorporates a backplane that mounts in a slot on the main board and enables adapter cards to be plugged in horizontally. This is one of the major keys to its low profile.

The three specified form factors are described in more detail in Chapter 3, *Advanced System Boards*. The differences between these form factors are relatively insignificant to the technician in most cases. Therefore, we will point out the differences in the following discussions when appropriate.

Major System Board Components

The major components of interest on a PC system board are the **microprocessor**, the system's primary **read only memory (ROM)**, **random access memory (RAM)**, and **cache memory** sections; expansion slot connectors; disk drive interface connectors; and the microprocessor support ICs that coordinate the operation of the system. A typical ATX system board layout is depicted in Figure 2-21.

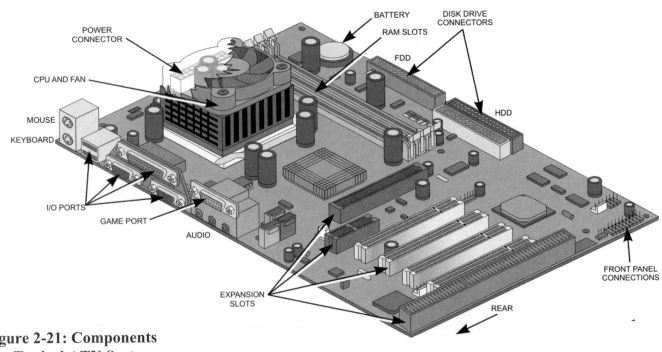

Figure 2-21: Components of a Typical ATX System Board

┌─ **TEST TIP** ──────────────────────────────┐
Know the parts of a typical system board and make sure that you can identify these components (and variations of them) from a pictorial or photographic representation.
└──┘

┌─ **NOTE** ──┐
For orientation purposes, the end of the board where the keyboard connector, expansion slots, and power connectors are located is generally referred to as the rear of the board.
└──┘

In Figure 2-21, the microprocessor is at the bottom of the cubic structure to the left (looking from the back of the board) of the system board. The cube-like structure actually includes the *socket* that the microprocessor is mounted in, a large block of metal called a *heat sink*, and finally, a *fan* unit that moves air across the heat sink unit to remove heat from the microprocessor.

Some systems use processors that come in a different type of packaging called *cartridge processors*. The microprocessors come in plastic packages that snap into a special slot connector on the system board. The processor cartridge is tall and thin in comparison to the socket-mounted processor assembly shown in Figure 2-21. However, the cartridge is normally held in place by a plastic support mechanism that includes a fan/heat sink module. These units are easy to locate, because they look very different from any of the other components attached to the system board.

The system's ROM BIOS may be difficult to locate on the system board, because it is an integrated circuit device and is similar in appearance to the other IC devices on the board. On some units the ROM IC is the only stand-alone socket-mounted IC device present; however, on most newer system boards, the ROM chip is soldered to the board.

On the other hand, the system's RAM modules are very distinctive. In a PC, they are mounted vertically in special snap-in memory slots on the system board. These slots are typically arranged side by side and may involve between three and four slots. The modules slide into the slots and are secured in place by locking tabs at each end of the slot. Any on-board cache memory can also be hard to identify simply by sight. Like the ROM IC, onboard cache memory is simply an IC device that looks like the other ICs on the board. To identify these devices you should refer to the system board manufacturer's user/installer's information guide.

For several generations, PC system boards have directly supported a standard set of disk drives. The disk drive control circuitry is an integral part of the microprocessor's supporting chipset. This enables the disk drives to communicate directly with the system through signal cables that plug into the system board without using an adapter card. On older Pentium boards, this involved three berg strip connectors—one 34-pin strip for the floppy-disk drive and two 40-pin strips for **parallel ATA (PATA)** hard disk and CD-ROM/DVD drives. These connectors can be mounted anywhere on the system board, but they tend to be placed toward the front right side so that they are close to the disk drive cage. Newer system boards provide two, 7-pin connectors to accommodate newer **serial ATA (SATA)** disk drives. These drives can operate at much higher speeds than the older PATA drives. Both types of drives are covered in detail in Chapter 5, *Mass Storage Systems*.

parallel ATA (PATA)

serial ATA (SATA)

I/O

As mentioned earlier, the system board can communicate with various optional **I/O** and memory systems through adapter cards that plug into its *expansion slots*. Figure 2-21 depicts a number of different types of expansion slots. In ATX systems, these slots are normally located along the left-rear portion of the system board in positions that permit connections from the back plates of the adapter cards to protrude through the back panel of the system unit case. The different types of slots depicted in Figure 2-21 are covered in detail in Chapter 3, *Advanced System Boards*.

Many I/O connection types have become standards in the PC environment. When I/O connections become standards they are typically integrated directly into the system board's chipset and BIOS/CMOS structures. To provide physical connectivity for these circuits, system board designers have developed standard blocks of I/O connections that they place along the back edge of the system board. The figure shows the typical blocks associated with the ATX system board form factor. These ports are covered in detail in Chapter 4, *Standard I/O Systems*.

Figure 2-21 shows typical appearances and locations of system board devices on an ATX form factor board, but the BTX and NLX specifications move these components around within the system unit in efforts to provide better system performance and optimized space considerations, respectively. The specifics of these form factor specifications are described fully in Chapter 3, *Advanced System Boards*.

Essentials 1.1

Microprocessors

The microprocessor is the major component of any system board. It can be thought of as the "brains" of the computer system, because it reads, interprets, and executes software instructions, and also carries out arithmetic and logical operations for the system.

Intel

The original PC and PC-XT computers were based on the 8/16-bit 8088 microprocessor from the **Intel** Corporation. The IBM PC-AT system employed a 16-bit 80286 microprocessor. The popularity of the 80286-based IBM PC-AT introduced many standards that are still being addressed by PCs today.

Since the days of the IBM PC-AT, Intel has introduced a series of ever more powerful microprocessors for the PC market. These include devices such as the 80386DX and SX, the 80486DX and SX, the Pentium (80586), the Pentium Pro (80686), and Pentium II/III/4 processors. All these microprocessors are backward compatible with the 8088—that is, programs written specifically for the 8088 can be executed by any of the other processors. These processors are depicted in Figure 2-22.

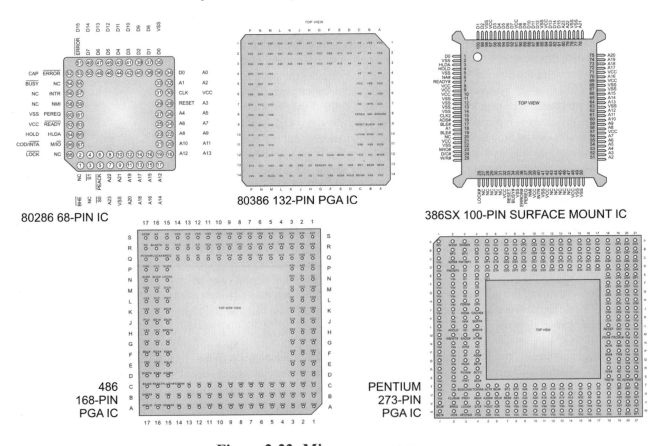

Figure 2-22: Microprocessors

Intel used the SX notation to define reduced function versions of existing microprocessors (e.g., the 80486SX was a version of the 80486DX that had some functionality removed). SX devices were normally created to produce price variations that kept the Intel product competitive with those of other manufacturers.

Other microprocessor manufacturers, including **American Micro Devices (AMD)** produce work-alike versions of the Intel processors that became known as **clone processors**. In response to clone microprocessor manufacturers using the 80 × 86 nomenclature, Intel dropped their 80 × 86 numbering system after the 80486 processor and adopted the **Pentium** name so that they could copyright it.

> ─ **NOTE** ──────────────────────
>
> Intel resorted to using the Pentium name when clone microprocessor manufacturers used the 80 × 86 nomenclature. Intel dropped the numbering system and adopted the name strategy so that they could copyright it.

The Pentium architecture has appeared in many different implementations and improvements. It has also appeared in a number of package styles and connection configurations. For A+ certification purposes, the only microprocessors specified are the Pentium class of processor. Therefore, all the Pentium processors and their clones are covered in detail in Chapter 3, *Advance System Boards*.

> For more in-depth information about how microprocessor systems actually work, refer to the Electronic Reference Shelf located on the CD that accompanies this book.

REFERENCE
SHELF

Pentium Processor Package Types

PC manufacturers mount microprocessors in **sockets** so that they can be replaced easily. This permits a failed microprocessor to simply be exchanged for a working unit. It also enables the system board to be upgraded with improved processors when they become available. With a socket, the existing microprocessor can be replaced with an improved compatible version to upgrade the speed or performance of the system.

Beginning with the 80386DX processor, microprocessor manufacturers began using a type of IC package called a **pin grid array (PGA)** for microprocessors. This arrangement, depicted in Figure 2-23, placed the actual integrated circuitry **chip** in a thin, square or rectangular package with connecting pins sticking straight down from the bottom of the package. Variations of this package type are still used with different microprocessors. The size of the package, the number of pins attached to it, and the scale of the IC chip circuitry inside the package change as processing power increases.

American Micro Devices (AMD)

clone processors

Pentium

sockets

pin grid array (PGA)

chip

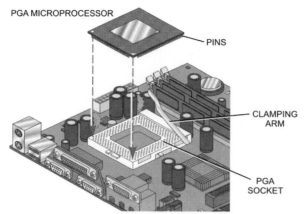

PGA MICROPROCESSOR

PINS

CLAMPING
ARM

PGA
SOCKET

**Figure 2-23:
Microprocessors
and Sockets**

In older systems, the microprocessors were forcibly inserted and removed from their sockets using an IC extractor tool. As the typical microprocessor's pin count increased, so did the amount of force required to install or remove them. To overcome this, special **zero insertion force (ZIF)** sockets were implemented that allowed the microprocessor to be set in the socket without force and then clamped in place. An arm-activated clamping mechanism in the socket shifts to the side, locking the pins in place.

The notches and dots on the various ICs are important keys when replacing a microprocessor. They specify the location of the IC's number 1 pin. This pin must be lined up with the *pin-1 notch* of the socket for proper insertion. The writing on the IC package is also significant. It contains the number that identifies the type of device in the package and normally includes a speed rating for the device.

TEST TIP

Know how to locate pin-1 of a microprocessor and be aware that this is one of the most important aspects of replacing or updating a microprocessor.

In a move to decrease the impact of clone processors, Intel changed the Pentium packaging to a proprietary cartridge and plug-in slot and microprocessor cartridge arrangement with the Pentium II processor. The original argument for this change centered on claims that the socket and pin arrangement had reached its speed limit, and the slot technology was supposed to provide the development pathway to higher speed processors.

Intel's main competitor **American Micro Devices (AMD)** responded by producing its own cartridge processor that used a mirror image connection configuration of the Intel cartridge and slot arrangement. Soon after the advent of the slot processor, both companies returned to producing processors using pin and socket versions of their new processors. A slot and cartridge microprocessor arrangement is depicted in Figure 2-24

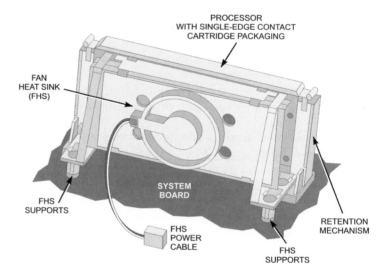

PROCESSOR
WITH SINGLE-EDGE CONTACT
CARTRIDGE PACKAGING

FAN
HEAT SINK
(FHS)

FHS
SUPPORTS

SYSTEM
BOARD

FHS
POWER
CABLE

RETENTION
MECHANISM

FHS
SUPPORTS

**Figure 2-24: Slot and
Cartridge Processors**

The full range of Pentium and clone socket and slot configurations are covered in detail in Chapter 3, *Advanced System Boards*, along with their significant variations.

Memory Units

All computers need a place to temporarily store information while other pieces of information are being processed. In digital computers, information storage is normally conducted at two different levels: **primary memory** (made up of semiconductor RAM and ROM chips) and **mass storage** (usually involving floppy- and hard-disk drives).

Most of the system's primary memory is located on the system board and typically exists in three forms:

- **Read Only Memory (ROM)**—memory that contains the computer's permanent start-up programs

- **Random Access Memory (RAM)**—memory that is quick enough to operate directly with the microprocessor and can be read from and written to as often as desired

- **Cache Memory**—a fast RAM system used to hold information that the microprocessor is likely to use

ROM devices store information permanently and are used to hold programs and data that do not change. RAM devices only retain the information stored in them as long as electrical power is applied to the IC. Any interruption of power will cause the contents of the memory to vanish. This is referred to as **volatile memory**. ROM, on the other hand, is **nonvolatile**. It retains the information even if power is removed from the device.

| primary memory |
| mass storage |
| Read Only Memory (ROM) |
| Random Access Memory (RAM) |
| Cache Memory |

┌─ **TEST TIP** ─────────┐
Be aware of which memory types are volatile and what this means.
└───────────────────────┘

| volatile memory |
| nonvolatile |

ROM

Every system board contains one or more ROM ICs that hold the system's **basic input/output system (BIOS)** program. The BIOS program contains the basic instructions for communications between the microprocessor and the various input and output devices in the system. Until recently, this information was stored permanently inside the ROM chips and could only be changed by replacing the chips.

Advancements in EEPROM technology have produced **flash ROM** devices that enable new BIOS information to be written (**downloaded**) into the ROM device to update it. This can be done from an update disk, or it can be downloaded from another computer. Unlike RAM ICs, the contents of the flash ROM remain after the power has been removed from the chip. In either case, the upgraded BIOS must be compatible with the system board it is being used with and should be the latest version available.

The information in the BIOS represents all of the intelligence the computer has until it can load more information from another source, such as a hard or floppy disk. Taken together, the BIOS software (programming) and hardware (the ROM chip) are referred to as **firmware**.

| basic input/output system (BIOS) |
| flash ROM |
| downloaded |
| firmware |

RAM

dual in-line memory modules (DIMMs)

RAM modules on Pentium-class system boards are supplied in the form of snap-in **dual in-line memory modules (DIMMs)**. These modules use special snap-in sockets that support the module firmly. DIMMs are keyed so they cannot be plugged in backwards. DIMMs come on 168-pin or 184-pin boards designed to work efficiently with Pentium-class microprocessors.

DIMM sockets are quite distinctive in that they are normally arranged side by side. However, they can be located anywhere on the system board. DIMMs come in 32- and 64-bit bus widths. They must be arranged properly to fit the size of the system data bus. DIMMs also come in 36- and 72-bit versions that include parity checking bits for each byte of storage.

PCs are usually sold with less than their full RAM capacity. This enables users to purchase less expensive computers to fit their individual needs and yet retain the option to install more RAM if future applications call for it. DIMM storage capacities are typically specified in an *a*-by-*b* format. Under this format, the capacity of the device (in bytes) is derived by multiplying the two numbers and then dividing by eight (or nine for parity chips). A typical DIMM module is depicted in Figure 2-25.

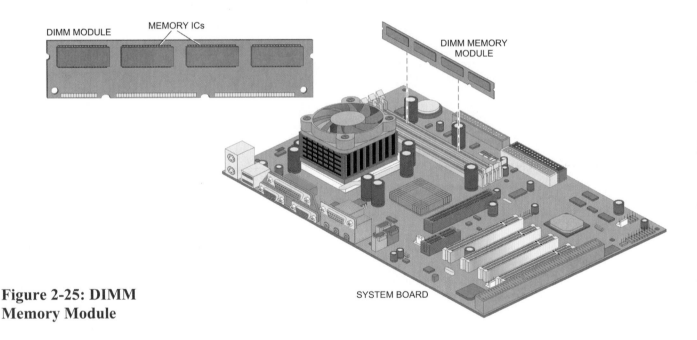

Figure 2-25: DIMM Memory Module

Essentials 1.1

Chipsets

integrated circuit (IC)

The first digital computers were giants that took up entire rooms and required several technicians and engineers to operate. They were constructed with vacuum tubes, and their computing power was very limited by comparison to modern computers. However, the advent of **integrated circuit (IC)** technology in 1964 launched a new era in compact electronic packaging. The much smaller, low-power transistor replaced the vacuum tube, and the size of the computer began to shrink.

Current IC technology permits millions of circuit elements to be constructed on a single small piece of silicon. Some **very large-scale integration (VLSI)** devices (devices that exceed 100,000 integrated electronic elements) contain complete computer modules. These devices are commonly referred to as **application-specific integrated circuits (ASICs)**. By connecting a few ASIC devices together on a printed circuit board, computers that once inhabited an entire room have been shrunk to fit on the top of an ordinary work desk and, now, into the palm of the hand.

> Microprocessor manufacturers and third-party IC makers produce microprocessor-support **chipsets** (collections of integrated circuits that provide a standard set of auxiliary services) for each type of microprocessor.

For the IC manufacturer, PC compatibility means designing chipsets that use the same basic memory map that was employed in the original IBM PC-AT (that is, the chipset's programmable registers, RAM, ROM, and other addresses have to be identical to those of the PC-AT). This insures that instructions and data in software programs will be interpreted, processed, and distributed the same way in both systems. In doing so, the supporting chipsets have decreased from as many as eight major ICs and dozens of **small scale integration (SSI)** devices to two or three VLSI chips and a handful of SSI devices. In some highly integrated system boards, the only ICs that remain on the board are the microprocessor, the ROM BIOS chip, a single chipset IC, and the system's memory modules.

All Pentium-based system boards rely on some variation of the Pentium/PCI chipset. Figure 2-26 illustrates the relatively compact structure provided by a basic Pentium/PCI chipset. As the figure illustrates, the *chip count* on a typical Pentium-class system board involves only seven major ICs, including the microprocessor.

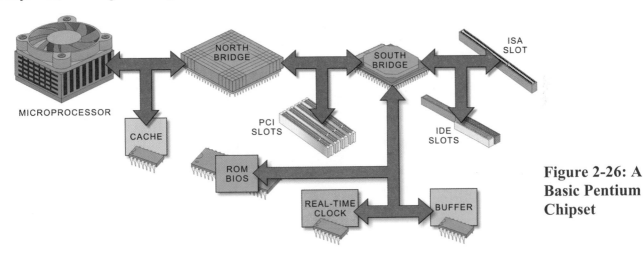

Figure 2-26: A Basic Pentium Chipset

Essentials 1.1

System Configuration Settings

> Each time the system is turned on, or reset, the BIOS program checks the system's **configuration settings** to determine what types of optional devices may be included in the system.

very large-scale integration (VLSI)

application-specific integrated circuits (ASICs)

chipsets

small scale integration (SSI)

configuration settings

The original PC-AT featured a battery-powered RAM area that held some of the system's advanced configuration information. This configuration storage area became known as **CMOS RAM**.

IC manufacturers quickly integrated the advanced software configuration function to their chipsets along with the system's **real time clock (RTC)** function. The RTC function keeps track of time and date information for the system. System board designers added a rechargeable nickel-cadmium (Ni-Cad) battery to their system boards to maintain the information when the system was turned off.

In newer systems, there are no rechargeable Ni-Cad batteries for the CMOS storage. Instead, the CMOS storage area and RTC functions have been integrated with a 10-year, nonreplaceable lithium cell in an independent RTC module.

Because the configuration settings are the system's primary method of getting information about what options are installed, they must be set to accurately reflect the actual options being used with the system. If not, an error will occur. You should always suspect a configuration problem if a machine fails to operate immediately after a new component is installed. The CMOS configuration values can be accessed for change by pressing the CTRL and DEL keys (or some other key combination) simultaneously during the bootup procedure.

In 1994, Microsoft and Intel teamed up to produce a set of system specifications that would enable options added to the system to automatically be configured for operation. To accomplish this, the system's BIOS, expansion slots, and adapter cards are designed so that the system software can reconfigure them automatically. This concept became known as **Plug and Play (PnP)** capability.

During the start-up process, the PnP BIOS examines the system for installed devices. Devices designed for Plug-and-Play compatibility can tell the BIOS what types of devices they are and how to communicate with them. This information is stored in an area of the CMOS memory so that the system can work with the device. Plug-and-Play information will be scattered throughout the remainder of the text as it applies to the topic being covered.

Front Panel Connections

System boards may possess *jumper blocks* (called **BERG connectors** after the BERG connector company that developed them) that can be used to select operating options such as processor speed, installed RAM type, and so forth. You may be required to alter these settings if you change a component or install a new module in the system.

The system board also uses a set of BERG connectors as a connection point for the system's front panel indicators and controls. Over time, the number and types of these connections have become fairly standard. The normal connections are the *power LED*, *hard drive activity indicator light*, system *reset switch*, and *system speaker*.

Placement of these connectors and color-coding of wiring varies between case and system board manufacturers. It is usually necessary to consult the PC board's installation guide to locate and properly set configuration jumpers and switches. The installation guide typically provides the locations of all the board's configuration jumpers and switches. It also defines the possible configuration settings, along with corresponding switch or jumper positions.

Figure 1-27 illustrates the use of BERG configuration jumpers. A metal clip in the cap of the jumper creates an electrical short between the pins it is installed across. When the cap is removed, the electrical connection is also removed, and an electrically open condition is created.

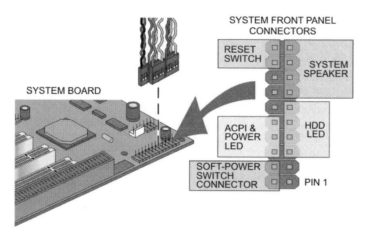

Figure 2-27: Front Panel and System Configuration Jumpers

Expansion Slots

Essentials 1.1

It would be very expensive to design and build a computer that fits every conceivable user application. With this in mind, computer designers include standardized connectors that enable users to configure the system to their particular computing needs.

Most PCs use standardized **expansion slot** connectors that enable various types of peripheral devices to be attached to the system. Optional **I/O devices**, or their **interface adapter cards**, are plugged into these slots to connect the devices to the system's address, data, and control buses.

The system board communicates with the various optional I/O and memory systems through adapter cards that plug into its expansion slots. These connectors have traditionally been located along the left-rear portion of the system board so that the external devices they serve can access them through openings at the rear of the case.

> expansion slot

> I/O devices

> interface adapter cards

Every expansion slot type contains three basic channels of information used to carry out data transfers between the system and the peripheral device associated with the adapter card. These channels are data, address, and control information. In addition, the expansion slot supplies all or some of the power required to operate the adapter card circuitry. However, different expansion slot types employ different connection layouts, timing and speed requirements, and operating signal levels. Therefore, you should be aware that given adapter cards can only be used in slots they are designed for. Therefore, it is important to know which type of slot is available when dealing with adapter cards.

Several different types of expansion slots may be found on current system boards. A particular system board design may contain only one type of slot, or it may have a mixture of expansion slot types. The following expansion slot types are commonly found on Pentium-class system boards:

Peripheral component interconnect (PCI)

Accelerated graphics port (AGP)

Audio modem riser (AMR)

Communications and networking riser (CNR)

PCI extended (PCI-X)

PCI express (PCIe)

Industry Standard Architecture (ISA)

advanced technology (AT) bus

- **Peripheral component interconnect (PCI)** slots—These 32/64-bit slots have been the most widely used expansion slots in the Pentium PC environment. They replaced the earlier 16-bit *Industry Standard Architecture* (*ISA*) slot as the main expansion slot in the PC. These slots can conduct data transfers at rates between 132 and 528 MBps.

- **Accelerated graphics port (AGP)** slots—The AGP slot is a 32-bit derivative of the PCI bus that was developed to provide a specialized interface for advanced video graphics adapters. Data pass back and forth between the system board and the AGP adapter card at rates of up to 2.1 GBps.

- **Audio modem riser (AMR)** slot—This is a special expansion slot specification developed to handle specialized modems and sound cards that interact directly with the system.

- **Communications and networking riser (CNR)** slot—The CNR slot is a revised expansion slot specification that replaces the AMR slot. Like the AMR specification, the CNR slot is designed to handle special communication and audio cards.

- **PCI extended (PCI-X)** slots—A high-performance version of the original PCI bus specification. These buses maintained the same connectors and form factor as the original PCI bus. They employed advanced signaling techniques to provide performance levels of 266 and 533 MHz and data transfer rates up to 2.1 and 4.3 GBps.

- **PCI express (PCIe)** slots—A collection of high-speed serial versions of the PCI bus standard. These PCI versions employ proprietary slot specifications that are not compatible with other PCI devices. They push performance levels to 2.5 GHz and data transfer rates to between 250 MBps and 4 GBps.

- **Industry Standard Architecture (ISA)** slots—You may still expect to encounter these 16-bit, non-Plug and Play, Legacy slots on older Pentium system boards. The ISA bus, also known as the **advanced technology (AT) bus** served as the standard expansion slot specification for many years and through several generations of processors. The reason this slot has continued well into PnP systems is that so many ISA-compatible adapter cards and devices were manufactured. Users have steadfastly hung onto these adapters and devices until the industry basically stopped including the slot in new designs. The ISA slot ran at 8.33 MHz and could transfer data at a whopping 8 MBps.

Common expansion slots associated with ATX system boards are depicted in Figure 2-28. All of the expansion slot types introduced here are discussed in greater detail in Chapter 3, *Advanced System Boards*.

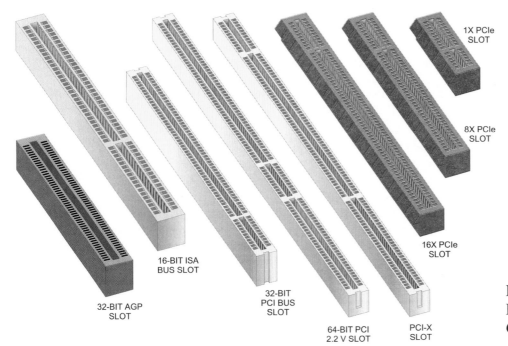

Figure 2-28: Typical
Expansion Slot
Connectors

1X PCIe
SLOT

8X PCIe
SLOT

16X PCIe
SLOT

PCI-X
SLOT

64-BIT PCI
2.2 V SLOT

32-BIT
PCI BUS
SLOT

16-BIT ISA
BUS SLOT

32-BIT AGP
SLOT

Adapter Cards

Essentials 1.1

The openness of the PC architecture has led many companies to develop a wide assortment of expansion devices for them. Several of these devices communicate with the basic system through **adapter cards** that plug into the expansion slots of the computer's system board, as illustrated in Figure 2-29. They typically contain the interfacing and controller circuitry for the peripheral device. However, in some cases, the entire peripheral may be contained on the adapter card.

adapter cards

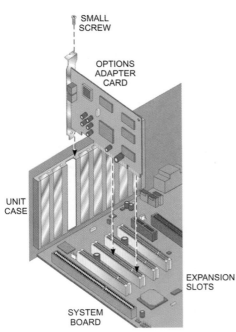

SMALL
SCREW

OPTIONS
ADAPTER
CARD

UNIT
CASE

EXPANSION
SLOTS

SYSTEM
BOARD

Figure 2-29:
Plugging in a Typical
Adapter Card

This expansion approach enables a wide variety of peripheral devices to be added to the basic system to modify it for particular applications. For example, adapter cards allow less expensive devices to be used with an introductory system and yet still permit high-end, high-performance peripherals to be used with the same system for advanced applications.

There are three important characteristics associated with any adapter card:

- Function
- Expansion slot connector style
- Physical size

Adapter cards have thin electrical contact pads arranged along either side of an extended section of their printed circuit boards. This extended edge is called the edge connector. These contact pads are electrical conductors that deliver power to the adapter card circuitry and carry signals back and forth between the system and the adapter. When the edge connector is pressed into the slot in the center of the expansion slot connector, its contacts align with corresponding spring-loaded contacts in the sides of the slots, forming a complete electrical connection.

The main factors that differentiate one type of expansion slot connector from another are the number, order, and functions specified for the contacts, and the physical dimensions and layout of the slot and **edge connector**. These items are determined by the organization that designs and sponsors the slot specification. Most slot specifications place a physical notch somewhere in the slot so that only adapter cards with matching notches can physically be installed in the slot, and so that they cannot be installed backwards.

The only real requirements for adapter cards now are that they fit securely in a compatible expansion slot, cover the slot opening in the rear of the system unit, provide standard connectors for the types of devices they serve, and be able to communicate with the system's PnP process. Various adapter card designs are depicted in Figure 2-30.

edge connector

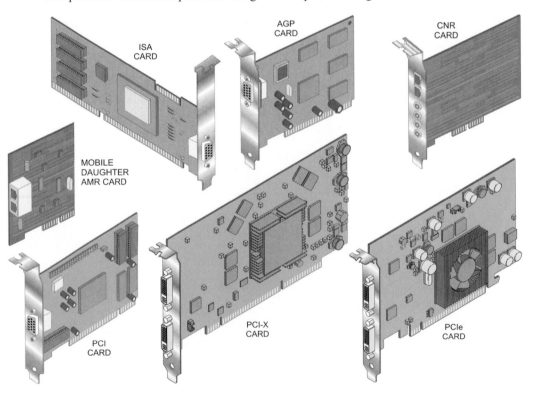

**Figure 2-30:
Adapter Card
Designs**

Early adapter card designs required technicians to set hardware jumpers or configuration switches to configure them for the specific application in which they were being used. The technician had to set up the card for operation and solve system resource or memory addressing conflicts that occurred. Such cards are referred to as **legacy cards**. Newer PnP adapter cards have the ability to identify themselves to the system during the start-up process, supply information about what type of device they are and how they are configured, as well as what system resources they need access to. The PnP system will automatically attempt to reconfigure these cards if a conflict is detected between it and another system device.

legacy cards

Video Adapter Cards

The **video adapter card** provides the interface between the system board and the display monitor.

video adapter card

The most common type of video adapter card currently in use is the **video graphics array** (**VGA**) card, like the one depicted in Figure 2-31. The system uses it to control video output operations.

video graphics array (VGA)

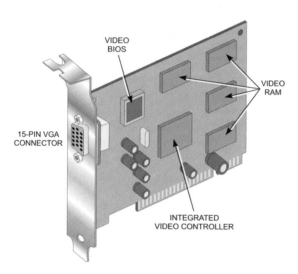

VIDEO BIOS

VIDEO RAM

15-PIN VGA CONNECTOR

INTEGRATED VIDEO CONTROLLER

Figure 2-31: A Typical VGA Card

Unlike most other computer components, the VGA standard uses analog signals and circuitry rather than digital signals. The main component of most video adapter cards is an ASIC device called the **integrated video controller**. It is a microprocessor-like chip that oversees the operation of the entire adapter. It is capable of accessing RAM and ROM memory units on the card. The video RAM holds the information that is to be displayed on the screen. Its size determines the card's maximum video **resolution** and color capacities.

integrated video controller

resolution

Most current video adapter cards are designed to use the system's AGP slot. High-end video adapter cards like those used by artists and serious game players are designed to plug into more advanced *PCI-X* or *PCIe* slots.

In some cases, the VGA adapter circuitry is built directly into the system board circuitry. With these on-board video system boards, the display monitor plugs directly into the VGA or other video connector on the back of the board. Video adapter cards with more advanced capabilities can still be added to the systems. However, it may be necessary to disable the on-board video before doing so.

Other Adapter Cards

Although the video display adapter card is typically the only adapter card required in the system, many other I/O functions can be added to the system through adapter cards. Some of the most popular cards in Pentium systems include

- **Internal Modem cards**—These devices are used to carry on data communications through traditional telephone lines.

- **Local Area Network cards**—LAN cards are used to connect the local system to a group of other computers so they can share data and resources.

- **Sound cards**—Sound cards are used to provide high-quality audio output for the computer system.

Still other adapter cards can be added to the system to provide additional connectivity and functionality. Some of the newer adapters finding their way into PC systems include:

- **SCSI adapters**—Most PCs include a built-in *Integrated Drive Electronic* (IDE) interface for disk drives. Many disk drive arrangements and peripherals are designed to use a small computer system interface (SCSI). For these devices to be used with the PC, a SCSI host adapter must be installed in one of the expansion slots to facilitate communications between the system and the device.

- **USB adapters**—Most new PCs include high-speed **universal serial bus (USB)** connections. However, you can install additional USB connection points in the system by installing a USB adapter card in one of the expansion slots.

- **IEEE-1394 Firewire adapters**—Although most newer PCs include a USB connection, they do not directly support **IEEE-1384 Firewire** connections commonly used with audio/video equipment. However, this bus specification can be supported by adding a firewire adapter card to the system.

- **Wireless network adapters**—PCs don't directly support wireless networks or printers. However, these functions can be supported by adding a **wireless networking adapter** card to the system.

Figure 2-32 shows examples of these cards and their connections. Although they represent most options added to computer systems, there are many other devices that can be plugged into expansion slots to enhance the operation of the system.

Internal Modem cards

Local Area Network cards

Sound cards

SCSI adapters

USB adapters

universal serial bus (USB)

IEEE-1394 Firewire adapters

IEEE-1384 Firewire

Wireless network adapters

wireless networking adapter

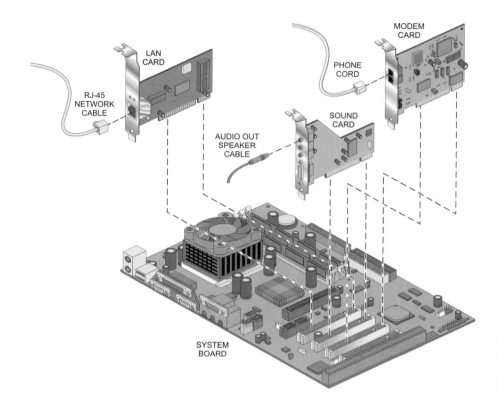

Figure 2-32:
Typical Adapter
Cards

The System Speaker

The system's primary audio output device is a 2.25-inch, 8-ohm, ½-watt speaker, similar to the one depicted in Figure 2-33. This unit can be located behind the vertical vents in the front panel or under the power supply unit in a small plastic retainer. The system uses the speaker to prompt the user during certain events and to indicate certain errors in the system, such as video display failures, which can't be displayed on the screen. The user can also control the operation of the speaker through software. Its output frequency range extends through the complete audio range and, with proper programming, can be used to create arcade sounds and music.

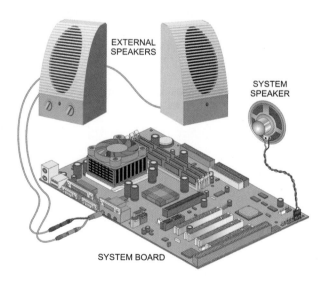

Figure 2-33:
System Speakers

As Figure 2-33 illustrates, most consumer-oriented PCs now include a set of additional external speakers to provide a much higher quality audio output than the traditional system speaker is capable of. However, the system speaker remains because of its ability to produce beep-coded error messages and audible event indications even when major portions of the system may not be functioning.

Essentials 1.1

STORAGE DEVICES

Programs and data disappear from the system's RAM when the computer is turned off. In addition, IC RAM devices tend to be too expensive to construct large memories that can hold multiple programs and large amounts of data. Therefore, storage systems that can be used for long-term data storage are desirable as a second level of memory.

With this in mind, a number of secondary memory technologies have been developed to extend the computer's memory capabilities and store data on a more permanent basis. These systems tend to be too slow to be used directly with the computer's microprocessor. The secondary memory unit holds the information and transfers it in batches to the computer's faster internal memory when requested.

> From the beginning, most secondary memory systems have involved storing binary information in the form of magnetic charges on moving magnetic surfaces. The major magnetic storage media are floppy disks, hard disks, and tape. However, optical storage technologies such as *compact discs* (*CD*s) and *digital video discs* (*DVD*s) have quickly moved to rival magnetic storage for popularity.

Disk Drives

| hard-disk drive (HDD) |
| CD-ROM/DVD drive |

| volumes |
| logical drives |

PC systems normally come from the manufacturer with at least one **hard-disk drive (HDD)** and one **CD-ROM/DVD drive** installed, as illustrated in Figure 2-34. However, the system's disk-drive capacity is usually not limited to the standard units installed. In most cases, the system's drive bay is designed to hold additional disk drive units. These units can consist of an additional FDD, HDD, or CD-ROM/DVD unit, or some combination of these devices. It is also possible for individual physical hard-disk drives to be *partitioned* into multiple **volumes** that the system recognizes as independent **logical drives**. In addition, external disk drives can be added to the system through standard I/O port connections.

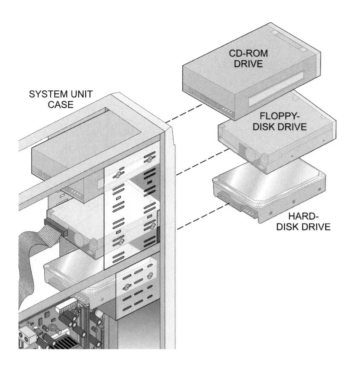

Figure 2-34:
The Disk Drives of
a Typical PC System

Hard Drives

The system's data storage potential is extended considerably by high-speed, high-capacity **hard-disk drive** units like the one shown in Figure 2-35. Hard drives contain rigid disks that are permanently sealed in the drive unit (nonremovable). The disks are aluminum platters coated with a nickel-cobalt or ferromagnetic material. Two or more platters are usually mounted on a common spindle, with spacers between them, to allow data to be recorded on both sides of each disk.

hard-disk drive

read/write (R/W)

Hard-disk drives used with personal computers typically contain between one and five disks that are permanently mounted inside a sealed, dust-free enclosure, along with the **read/write (R/W)** head mechanisms. There is one R/W head for each disk surface. The disks are typically turned at a speed between 5400 and 7200 RPM. This high rotational speed creates a thin cushion of air around the disk surface that causes the R/W heads to fly just above the disk.

Figure 2-35: Inside a Hard-Disk Drive

Hard-disk drives store information on the disks in the form of magnetized spot written on the disks as they spin. The spots are arranged in evenly sized blocks arranged in concentric circles around the disk. These circles are referred to as **tracks**, and the equal-sized storage blocks are called **sectors**. This arrangement is depicted in Figure 2-36.

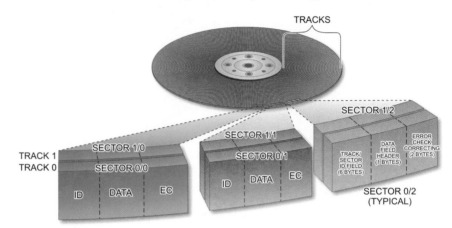

Figure 2-36: The Organizational Structure of a Magnetic Disk

Modern hard-disk drives come in 3.5 and 2.5-inch diameters. Of these sizes, the 3.5-inch version is by far the most popular due to their association with personal and business desktop computers. However, the popularity of the 2.5-inch drives is growing with the rising popularity of laptop and notebook-size computers.

Modern hard drives typically have storage capacities ranging up to hundreds of gigabytes. The capacity of a given drive is determined by the number of bytes of information stored in each sector, multiplied by the number of sectors, times the number of tracks, times the number of disk sides used, times the number of disks in the drive. These factors are referred to as the disk's geometry, which is determined initially by the system's BIOS configuration. Effective use of the disk's geometry is the responsibility of the operating system. Disk operation, geometry and usage are covered in more detail in Chapter 3, *Advanced System Boards*; Chapter 5, *Mass Storage Systems*; and Chapter 10, *Windows 2000 and XP Operating Systems*.

REFERENCE SHELF

For more in-depth information about how magnetic disk systems work, refer to the Electronic Reference Shelf located on the CD that accompanies this book.

CD-ROM Drives

Soon after the **compact disc (CD)**—the term "*disc*" is used in place of disk to denote the fact that it is an optical disc instead of a magnetic disk—became popular for storing audio signals on optical material, the benefits of storing computer information in this manner became apparent. The typical CD can hold upwards of 600 MB of programs and data on a single, inexpensive, removable media.

CD-ROM technology employs a laser to write data on optical material by burning small spots (pits) on the disc substrate. Data are read back from the disc by reflecting a laser light off the substrate. Differences between the pits and unburned areas on the disc reflect the light differently to create digital information that can be read by the drive.

Originally, information had to be placed on the CD by a disc manufacturer. Therefore, early discs used to hold digital data for computers were referred to as **CD-ROMs**. The ROM designation refers to the fact that most of the original discs and drives were *read-only* in nature. Newer optical technologies have produced low-cost drives and discs that can be written and erased multiple times. These drives and discs are referred to as **CD-R/W** devices. Figure 2-37 shows the components generally associated with a CD-ROM drive system.

CD-ROMs

CD-R/W

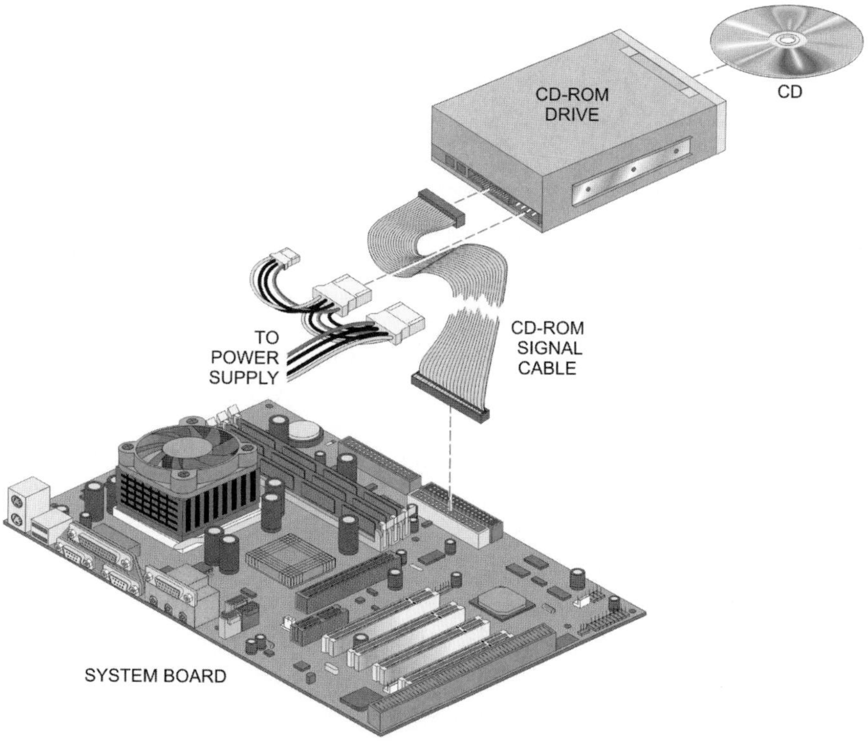

Figure 2-37: Components of a CD-ROM System

Typical CD-ROM drives are constructed to fit in standard 5-1/4" half-height disk drive openings. They require a signal cable to communicate with the system and a single options power connector. CDs are inserted into the drive using an automatic sliding tray mechanism that positions the disc for use.

Drives that operate at the speed of a conventional audio CD player are called **single-speed (1X) drives**. Single-speed drives transferred data at a rate of 150 kBps, double-speed drive transferred data at 300 kBps, and so on. Most manufacturers are now focusing on 50X and 52X drives.

single-speed (1X) drives

Computer CD-ROM drives are capable of playing audio CDs. However, standard CD players are not designed to produce output from the CD-ROM disc. CDs are classified by a color-coding system that corresponds to their intended use. CDs that contain digital data intended for use in a computer are referred to as **Yellow Book** CDs. **Red Book** CDs refer to those formatted to contain digital music. **Orange Book** refers to the standard for CDs that are used in WORM drives. **Green Book** CDs are used with interactive CD systems, and **Blue Book** CDs are those associated with laser disc systems.

Yellow Book

Red Book

Orange Book

Green Book

Blue Book

Digital Versatile Discs

REFERENCE
SHELF

Newer compact disc technologies have produced a high-capacity disc, called a **digital versatile disc**, **digital video disc**, or **DVD** for short. These discs have capacities that range between 4.7 GB and 17 GB of data. Transfer rates associated with DVD drives range between 600 kBps and 1.3 MBps.

Like CDs, DVDs are available in **DVD-ROM** (write-once) and **DVD-RAM** (rewritable) formats. There are also DVD-Audio and DVD-Video specifications that can store up to 75 songs or a complete full-length movie. The DVD-Video standard employs the MPEG-2 compression standard to compress and decompress video data on the disc.

> For more information about MPEG, video data compression, and multimedia, refer to the *How Multimedia Works* section of the Electronic Reference Shelf on the CD that accompanies this book.

Physically, the DVD drive looks and operates in the same manner as the traditional CD-ROM drive described earlier in this chapter. Newer manufacturing methods for the discs permit the minimum length of the pits and lands to be smaller. Therefore, they can be squeezed closer together on the disc. DVD drives also employ higher resolution lasers to decrease the track pitch (distance between adjacent tracks). Together, these two factors create the high data densities offered by DVD.

Tape Drives

Tape drive units are another popular type of information storage system. These systems can store large amounts of data on small **tape cartridges**, similar to the one depicted in Figure 2-38.

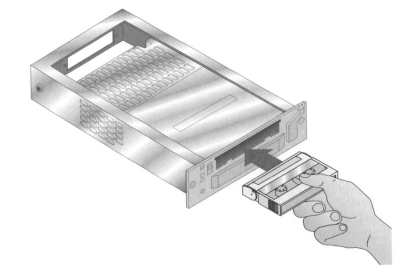

Figure 2-38: A Tape Drive and Cartridge

Tapes tend to be more economic than other magnetic media when storing large amounts of data. However, access to information stored on tape tends to be very slow. This is caused by the fact that, unlike disks, tape operates in a linear fashion. The tape transport must run all of the tape past the drive's R/W heads to access data that are physically stored at the end of the tape.

Therefore, tape drives are generally used to store large amounts of information that will not need to be accessed often, or quickly. Such information includes **backup copies** of programs and data. This type of data security is a necessity with records such as business transactions, payroll, artwork, and so forth.

Data backup has easily become the most widely used tape application. With the large amounts of information that can be stored on a hard-disk drive, a disk crash is a very serious problem. If the drive crashes, all of the information stored on the disk can be destroyed. This can easily add up to billions of pieces of information. Therefore, an inexpensive method of storing data away from the hard drive is desirable.

Floppy Drives

In older PCs, the floppy-disk drive was the most widely used data storage device. Floppy-disk drives store information in the form of tiny, magnetized spots on small flexible disks that can be removed from the drive unit. The disks are relatively inexpensive and are easy to transport and store. Once the information has been written on the disk, it will remain there until the disk is magnetically erased or written over. It will remain on the disk even if it is removed from the drive or if power is removed from the system. Whenever the information is required by the system, you can obtain it by inserting the disk back into the drive and reading the data from the disk. In addition, they can easily be removed and replaced if they become full. Figure 2-39 depicts the major components of a typical floppy-disk drive unit.

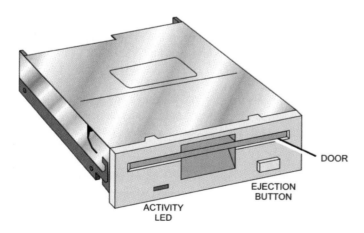

DOOR

EJECTION
BUTTON

ACTIVITY
LED

**Figure 2-39: The
Floppy-Disk Drive Unit**

In Pentium-class PCs, high-density, 3.5-inch floppy drives capable of holding 1.44 MB (1,474,560 bytes) are the norm. The typical floppy disk, depicted in Figure 2-40, is a flexible, 3.5-inch diameter mylar disk that has been coated with a ferromagnetic material. It is encased in a protective, hard plastic envelope that contains a low-friction liner that removes dust and contaminants from the disk as it turns within the envelope. These floppy disk referred to as *Double-Sided, High-Density* (DS-HD), because they can be recorded on both sides.

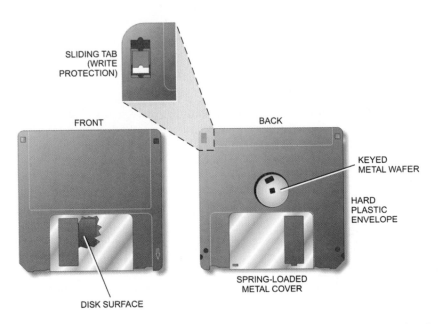

**Figure 2-40:
Floppy Disks**

Typical floppy drives turn the disk at 300 or 360 RPM, and the drive's R/W heads ride directly on the disk surface. Information is written to or read from the disk as it spins inside the envelope. The small LED on the front of the disk drive unit lights up whenever either of these operations is in progress.

The drive's read/write heads access the disk surface through a spring-loaded metal cover, which the drive unit moves out of the way. The drive spindle turns the disk by engaging a keyed metal wafer attached to the lower side of the disk. A small, sliding tab in the left-front corner of the envelope performs a write-protect function for the disk. If the tab covers the opening, the disk may be written to. If, however, the opening is clear, the disk is said to be "Write Protected," and the drive will not write information on the disk.

The major differences between floppy- and hard-disk drives are storage capacity, data transfer rates, and cost. Another difference to note is the fact that hard-disk drives tend to be more delicate than floppy drives. Therefore, they require some special handling considerations to prevent damage to the unit as well as loss of data. The disks in the HDD are not removable as floppy disks are. It is possible to fill up a hard-disk drive. When this occurs, it will be necessary to delete information from the drive to make room for new information to be stored. Conversely, floppy disks are prone to damage due to mishandling, static, temperature, and so on. In addition, they are easy to misplace, and they provide limited storage of application software.

Peripherals

> **Peripherals** are devices and systems that are added to the basic system to extend or improve its capabilities. These devices and systems can be divided into three general categories: **input systems**, **output systems**, and **memory systems**.

The standard peripherals associated with PCs are the alphanumeric **keyboard** and the **video monitor**. With the rapid growth of GUI-oriented software, the **mouse** has become a common input peripheral as well. The next most common peripheral is the **character printer,** which is used to produce hard-copy output on paper. Figure 2-41 depicts a sample system with these devices. Many other types of peripheral equipment are routinely added to the basic system.

| Peripherals |
| input systems |
| output systems |
| memory systems |

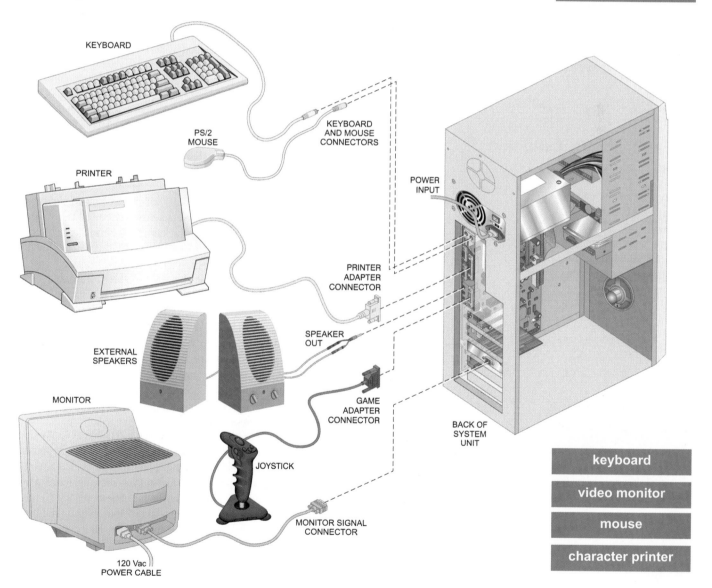

| keyboard |
| video monitor |
| mouse |
| character printer |

Figure 2-41: Typical PC Peripherals

External Devices and Connections

On the ATX back panel, many of the systemboard-related I/O functions have been integrated into a standardized block of system board-supported connections as illustrated. Figure 2-42 illustrates typical connectors found on the back panel of ATX systems. The back panels of specific PCs may have all the connections depicted in the figure, or they may have some subset of these connections.

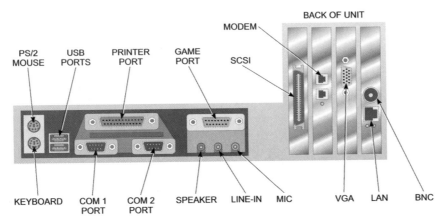

Figure 2-42: ATX Back Panel Connections

universal serial bus (USB)

video graphics array (VGA)

small computer system interface (SCSI)

local area network (LAN)

network interface card (NIC)

unshielded twisted pair (UTP)

The panel features two 6-pin PS/2 mini-DIN connectors. The (0.25"), 6-pin mini-DIN connector was adopted from the IBM PS/2 line of computers. This connector type is specified in the ATX form factor for both the mouse and the keyboard. The lower connector is designated for keyboards equipped with PS/2 connectors, while the upper connector is intended for use with a PS/2 mouse. Because these connectors are physically identical, it is relatively easy to confuse them. To compensate for this possibility, manufacturers have color-coded these connectors—pink indicates the connection is for the keyboard while green is used for the mouse. Just to the right of the keyboard and mouse ports are two **universal serial bus (USB)** connectors for attaching devices to the system using this high-speed serial interface.

Most PCs use detachable keyboards that are connected to the system by a coiled cable. This cable may plug into the PS/2 keyboard connector or one of the USB connectors. These connectors are keyed so they cannot be misaligned. The most widely used display device for current PCs is the color **video graphics array (VGA)** display. The display monitor's signal cable normally connects to a 15-pin D-shell connector at the back of the system unit. The mouse can be connected to the PC through the 6-pin mini-DIN or one of the USB connectors.

The complete ATX master I/O block contains two DB-9M COM port connectors for use with serial devices and a DB-25F parallel-port connector for SPP, EPP, and ECP parallel devices. This board also features a game port and built-in audio connections. The two-row DB-15F connector is the standard for the PC game port and is used to attach joysticks and other game-playing devices. The audio block features standard RCA jacks for the microphone, audio-in, and speaker connections.

In the expansion slots to the right of the ATX I/O block, you will see a DB-15F VGA video connector, a 50-pin Centronics **small computer system interface (SCSI)** bus connector, two RJ-11 jacks for an internal modem (one is for the phone line while the other is used to attach a traditional telephone handset), and an RJ-45 combination for making **local area network (LAN)** connections with the system's **network interface card (NIC)**. The DB-15F connector used with VGA video devices uses a three-row pin arrangement to differentiate it from the two-row DB-15F connector specified for the game port. This prevents them from being confused with each other. The RJ-45 jack on the NIC card is used with **unshielded twisted pair (UTP)** LAN cabling. Network cabling is discussed in detail in Chapter 6, *Data Communications*.

Keyboards

The keyboard type most widely used with desktop and tower units is a detachable, low profile 101/102-key model depicted in Figure 2-43. These units are designed to provide the user with a high degree of mobility and functionality. The key tops are slightly concave to provide a comfortable feel to the typist. In addition, the key makes a noticeable tap when it bottoms out during a keystroke.

Figure 2-43: An Alphanumeric Keyboard

As indicted earlier, there are currently two popular methods of connecting the keyboard to the system board—through one of its USB connectors or through the specified mini-DIN keyboard connector. Figure 2-44 shows the various connection schemes used with detachable keyboards. One advantage of using the USB option for connecting keyboards (and other devices) to the system is that these devices can be removed from the system and replaced while it is operational. This is known as **hot swapping** devices. The design of the PS/2 connector does not provide for hot swapping, so removing or installing a keyboard at this port can result in damage to the keyboard, the system's interface circuitry, or both.

hot swapping

> ┌─ **TEST TIP** ─────────────────────────┐
> Be aware that plugging non-hot-swappable devices such as the keyboard into the system while it is turned on can damage parts of the system.

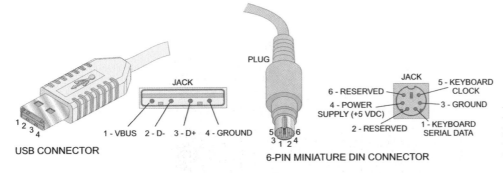

Figure 2-44: Connection Schemes for Detachable Keyboards

Video Displays

cathode-ray tube
(CRT)

liquid crystal
display (LCD)

plasma flat panel
displays

color CRT monitor

RGB monitor

There are two technologies commonly used to display video output from a personal computer—the color **cathode-ray tube (CRT)** display monitor and **liquid crystal display (LCD)** or **plasma flat panel displays**. In the past, the video display function was dominated by the CRT display similar to the one shown in Figure 2-45, as standard video output equipment. The **color CRT monitor** is sometimes referred to as an **RGB monitor**, because the three primary colors that make a color CRT are red, green, and blue.

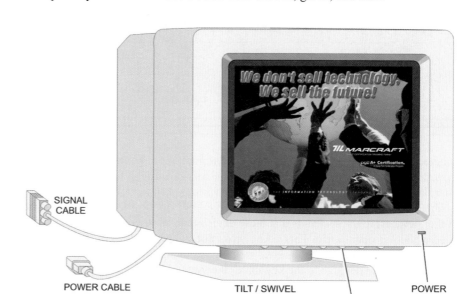

Figure 2-45: The CRT Display Monitor

However, LCD and plasma flat panel displays, like those depicted in Figure 2-46, are rapidly replacing the CRT in this role. These monitors are not as bulky as CRT-based monitors, so they take up less space than the same size CRT monitor. They are also lighter and use less energy than CRT monitors.

Figure 2-46: Flat Panel Displays

As mentioned previously, the monitor is attached to the video adapter card in the system unit via a **signal cable** or cables. The signal cable permits the monitor to be positioned away from the system unit if desired. With CRT monitors and with flat panel monitors designed strictly for use with PC systems, the signal cable is permanently attached to the monitor and plugs into the video adapter card using a 3-row, 15-pin **D-shell connector**.

Some flat panel displays intended for dual use as PC displays and as televisions offer several connection schemes, including standard **composite video** connections, **S-video** connections and three-wire **component video** connections associated with audio/video equipment. Some TV/monitor units also include advanced **digital visual interface (DVI)** and **high-definition multimedia interface (HDMI)** connections associated with high-definition television. These connection options are covered in more depth in Chapter 4, *Standard I/O Systems*.

The video display's normal external controls include

- Brightness and contrast

- Horizontal and vertical sizing

- Horizontal and vertical position

- Skew (sides and top/bottom of picture drawn in)

The controls for these functions are located in different positions on the monitor depending on its manufacturer. In addition, each function may be directly addressable or may be accessed through a menu system. There is also a power on/off switch on the monitor. Its location varies from model to model as well. If the monitor receives power through the system unit's power supply, the monitor's power switch can be set to on, and the monitor will turn on and off along with the system.

Other Peripherals

Mice, joysticks, trackballs, and touch pads belong to a category of input devices called **pointing devices**. They are all small, handheld input devices that enable the user to interact with the system by moving a cursor or some other screen image around the display screen, and to choose options from an onscreen menu, instead of typing commands from a keyboard. Because pointing devices make it easier to interact with the computer than other types of input devices, they are, therefore, friendlier to the user.

The most widely used pointing device is the **mouse**. Mice, like the one depicted in Figure 2-47, are handheld devices that produce input data by being moved across a surface, such as a desktop. The mouse has become a standard input device for most systems because of the popularity of graphics-based software.

signal cable

D-shell connector

composite video

S-video

digital visual interface (DVI)

high-definition multimedia interface (HDMI)

pointing devices

mouse

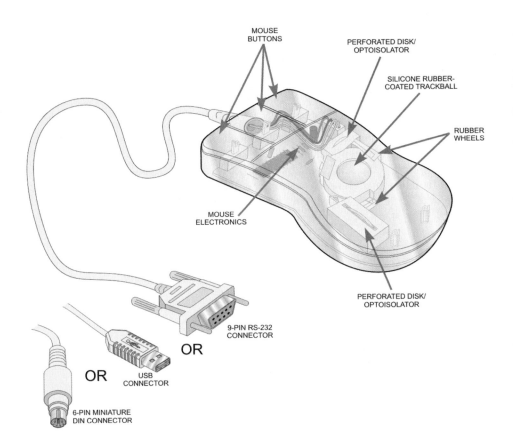

MOUSE BUTTONS

PERFORATED DISK/ OPTOISOLATOR

SILICONE RUBBER- COATED TRACKBALL

RUBBER WHEELS

MOUSE ELECTRONICS

PERFORATED DISK/ OPTOISOLATOR

9-PIN RS-232 CONNECTOR

OR

USB CONNECTOR

OR

6-PIN MINIATURE DIN CONNECTOR

Figure 2-47: A Typical Mouse

trackball mouse

The **trackball mouse** detects positional changes through the movement of a rolling trackball that it rides on. As the mouse moves across a surface, the mouse circuitry detects the movement of the trackball and creates pulses that the system converts into positional information.

Mice may have one, two, or three buttons that can be pressed in different combinations to interact with software running in the system. When the cursor has been positioned on screen, one or more of the mouse buttons can be "clicked" to execute an operation or select a variable from the screen. Specialized graphics software enables the user to operate the mouse as a drawing instrument.

wheel mouse

A newer mouse design, referred to as a **wheel mouse**, includes a small thumb wheel built into the top of the mouse between the buttons. This wheel enables the user to efficiently scroll up and down the video screen without using scroll bars or arrows. Some scrolling functions, such as click-and-drag text highlighting in a word processor, can be awkward when the text extends off the bottom of the screen. In faster computers, the automatic scroll functions in some software packages will take off at the bottom of the screen and scroll several pages before stopping. The wheel in the mouse is designed to control this type of action.

wireless mice

infrared (IR)

As the figure illustrates, there are currently two methods used to connect mice to the system—through the 6-pin PS/2 mouse connector or through one of the system's USB ports. Some **wireless mice** employ an **infrared (IR)** link between the mouse and an IR receiver which then communicates with the computer through a USB port.

Joysticks are very popular input devices used primarily with computer video games. However, they can also provide a convenient computer/human interface for a number of other applications. These peripherals are X−Y positioning devices with a *gimbal* (handle) that can be moved forward, backward, left, right, or at any angular combination of these basic directions to move a cursor or other screen element across a video display. Buttons on the joystick can be used in the same manner as buttons on a mouse. A typical joystick for use with PCs is shown in Figure 2-48.

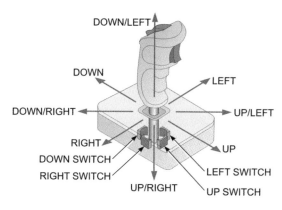

Figure 2-48: A Typical Joystick

Joysticks have traditionally used a special 2-row, 15-pin female D-shell **game-port** connector on the back panel of the computer. However, as with so many I/O devices, newer joystick designs employ the USB interface for connectivity to the system.

game-port

Touch pads (or *touch panels*) are pointing devices that supply X−Y positioning for cursors and other screen elements. The touch pad typically replaces the mouse in the system. The user controls the screen element by moving a finger across the pad surface. Clicking and double-clicking functions associated with mice can be accomplished by tapping a finger on the pad. Touch pads come as an integral part of many portable computers. However, they can be obtained as add-on devices that plug into standard USB or PS/2 mouse ports.

Touch pads

Character printers are widely used peripheral devices that provide hard copy output. The most common method of connecting newer printers to PCs is through high-speed *USB*, *Firewire*, or *direct network* connections. However, there is still a large installed base of printers that communicate with the host system through a standard parallel interface. Older **parallel printers** are connected to the 25-pin female D-shell connector at the rear of the system.

Character printers

parallel printers

There are also many older printers that use serial interfacing so that they can be located further from the computer. **Serial printers** normally plug into a 9-pin or 25-pin male D-shell connector on the computer. Most often, the serial printer is connected to the 25-pin connector that has been set up as the system's second serial port. The first serial port is typically implemented through the 9-pin connector and handles the mouse connection. These legacy interfaces are covered in greater detail in Chapter 7, *Printers*.

Serial printers

SOFTWARE

software

Once the system's components are connected together and their power connectors have been plugged into a receptacle, the system is ready for operation. However, there is one thing still missing—the **software**. Without good software to oversee its operation, the most sophisticated computer hardware is worthless.

There are actually three general classes of software that can be discussed:

- *System software*

- *Application software*

- *Games* and *learning software*

The bulk of the software discussed in this book falls into the system software category. This is because this type of software requires more technical skill to manipulate and, therefore, most often involves the service person.

Essentials 3.1

system software

basic input/output system (BIOS)

disk operating system (DOS)

ROM BIOS

System Software

The **system software** category consists of special programs used by the system to control the computer's operation. Two classic examples of this type of software are the system's **basic input/output system (BIOS)** program and the **disk operating system (DOS)**. These programs, described in Figure 2-49, control the operation of the other classes of software. The BIOS is located in a ROM IC device on the system board. Therefore, it is commonly referred to as **ROM BIOS**. The DOS software is normally located on a magnetic disk.

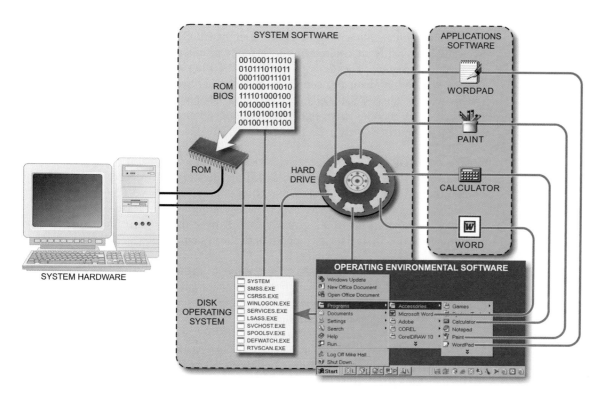

001000111010
010111011011
000110011101
001000110010
111101000100
001000011101
110101001001
001001110100

Figure 2-49:
System Software

Basic Input/Output Systems

When a PC is turned on, the entire system is reset to a predetermined starting condition. From this state, it begins carrying out software instructions from its BIOS program. This small program is permanently stored in the ROM memory ICs located on the system board. The information stored in these chips represents all the inherent intelligence that the system has to begin with.

A system's BIOS program is one of the keys to its **compatibility**. For example, to be IBM PC-compatible, the computer's BIOS must perform the same basic functions that the IBM PC's BIOS does. However, because the IBM BIOS software is copyrighted, the compatible's software must accomplish the same results that the original did in some different way.

compatibility

During the execution of the BIOS firmware routines, three major types of operations are performed. First, the BIOS performs a series of diagnostic tests on the system, called **POST** or **power-on self-tests**, to verify that it is operating correctly. If any of the system's basic components are malfunctioning, the tests will cause an error message or code to be displayed on the monitor screen, and/or an audio code to be output through the system's speaker.

POST (power-on self-tests)

The BIOS program also places starting values in the system's various programmable devices. These intelligent devices regulate the operation of different portions of the computer's hardware. This process is called **initialization**. When the system is first started, the BIOS moves starting address and mode information into the microprocessor's intelligent support devices so that they have the information they need to begin operation.

initialization

Plug and Play (PnP)

As part of the initialization process, a portion of the BIOS program examines the system to determine what hardware components are actually installed and pass that information to the initialization program. This activity is part of the **Plug and Play (PnP)** system used in modern PCs to automatically configure installed hardware devices. The complete PnP system involves the BIOS, the adapter cards, and the operating system that takes control of the system. Plug and Play is covered in more detail later in this chapter as well as in Chapter 3, *Advanced System Boards*.

master boot record (MBR)

Finally, the BIOS searches the system for a special program that it can use to load other programs into RAM. This program is called the **master boot record** (**MBR**). The boot record program contains information that allows the system to load a much more powerful disk operating system into RAM. After the operating system has been loaded into the computer's memory, the BIOS gives it control over the system. From this point, the operating system will oversee the operation of the system.

booting up

cold boot

reset

warm boot

This operation of transferring control of the system from the BIOS to the operating system is referred to as **booting up** the system. If the computer is started from the OFF condition, the process is referred to as a **cold boot**. If the system is restarted from the ON condition, the process is called a **reset**, or a **warm boot**.

The bootup process may take several seconds to perform depending on the configuration of the system. If a warm boot is performed, or if the POST has been disabled, the amount of time required for the system to get into operation is decreased. The four components of the bootup process are illustrated in Figures 2-50, 2-51, and 2-52.

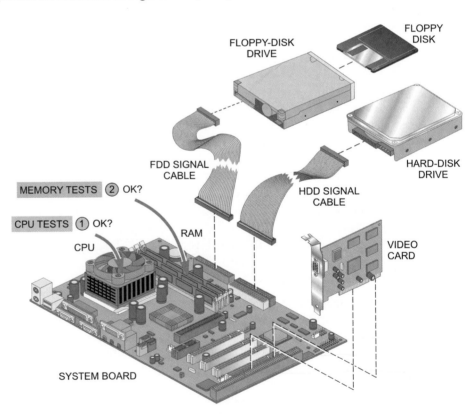

Figure 2-50:
The Steps of a Bootup:
Phase One—POST

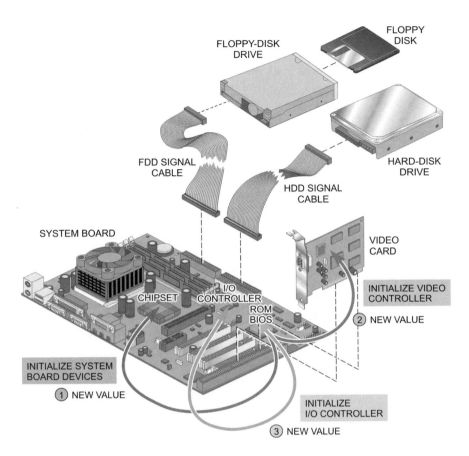

FLOPPY DISK

FLOPPY-DISK DRIVE

HARD-DISK DRIVE

FDD SIGNAL CABLE

HDD SIGNAL CABLE

SYSTEM BOARD

CHIPSET

I/O CONTROLLER

ROM BIOS

VIDEO CARD

INITIALIZE VIDEO CONTROLLER

② NEW VALUE

INITIALIZE SYSTEM BOARD DEVICES

① NEW VALUE

INITIALIZE I/O CONTROLLER

③ NEW VALUE

Figure 2-51:
The Steps of a Bootup:
Phase Two—Initialization

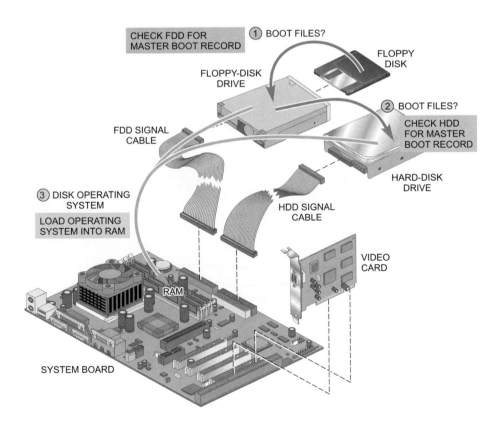

CHECK FDD FOR MASTER BOOT RECORD

① BOOT FILES?

FLOPPY DISK

FLOPPY-DISK DRIVE

② BOOT FILES?

CHECK HDD FOR MASTER BOOT RECORD

FDD SIGNAL CABLE

HARD-DISK DRIVE

③ DISK OPERATING SYSTEM

LOAD OPERATING SYSTEM INTO RAM

HDD SIGNAL CABLE

VIDEO CARD

RAM

SYSTEM BOARD

Figure 2-52:
The Steps of a Bootup:
Phase Three—Bootup

In the first phase of the operation, the BIOS tests the microprocessor (1) and the system's RAM memory (2). In the second phase, the system interrogates the system's hardware to determine what types of devices are installed and what system resources they need to operate. In this phase, the BIOS also furnishes starting information to the system's microprocessor support devices (1), video adapter card (2), and disk drive adapter card (3). Finally, the BIOS searches through the system in a predetermined sequence for a master boot record to turn over control of the computer to. In this case, it checks the floppy-disk drive first (1) and the hard-disk drive second (2). If a boot record is found in either location, the BIOS will move it onto the computer's RAM memory and turn over control to it (3).

Plug-and-Play

In the PC, the BIOS, peripheral devices, and operating system work together to provide *Plug-and-Play* features that enable the system to automatically determine what hardware devices are actually installed in the system and to allocate system resources to the devices to configure and manage them. This removes some of the responsibility for system configuration from the user or the technician. All three of the system components just mentioned must be PnP-compliant before automatic configuration can be carried out.

Basically, the PnP device communicates with the BIOS during the initialization phase of the start-up to tell the system what type of device it is, where it is located in the system, and what its resource needs are. This information is stored on the device in the form of firmware. The BIOS stores the PnP information it collects from the devices in a special section of the CMOS RAM known as the **extended system configuration data (ESCD)** area. This information is stored in the same manner as standard BIOS settings are stored. The BIOS and operating system both access the ESCD area each time the system is restarted to see if any information has changed. This enables the BIOS and operating system to work together in sorting out the needs of the installed devices and assigning them needed system resources. Figure 2-53 illustrates the basic PnP process.

extended system configuration data (ESCD)

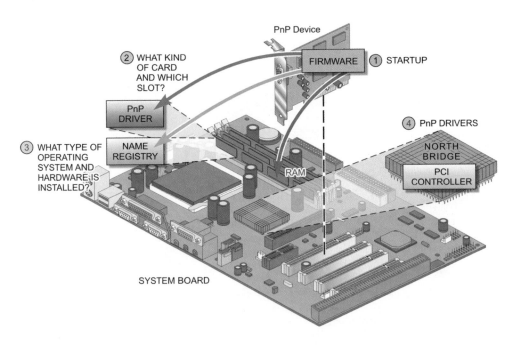

Figure 2-53: Plug-and-Play Operations

If no changes have occurred in the contents of the ESCD since the last bootup occurred, the BIOS will detect this and skip that portion of the boot process. When a PnP operating system checks the ESCD to see if any hardware changes have occurred, it will react accordingly and record any changes it finds in the hardware portion of its registry. On some occasions, the system's PnP logic may not be able to resolve all of its resource needs, and a configuration error will occur. In these cases, the technician, or the user, will have to manually resolve the configuration problem. The BIOS and operating system typically provide interfaces to the hardware configuration information so that users can manually override the system's Plug-and-Play resource assignments.

CMOS Setup

During the initialization process, PCs check a battery-powered storage area on the system board called the **CMOS RAM** to determine what types of options were installed in the system. During bootup, the BIOS permits users to have access to this configuration information through its **CMOS Setup utility**.

CMOS RAM

CMOS Setup utility

When the computer is set up for the first time, or when new options are added to the system, it is necessary to run the CMOS Configuration Setup utility. The values input through the utility are stored in the system's CMOS Configuration registers. These registers are examined each time the system is booted up to tell the computer what types of devices are installed. Early in the start-up process, the BIOS places a prompt on the display to tell the user that the CMOS Setup utility can be accessed by pressing a special key, or a given key combination. Typical keys and key combinations include the DEL key, the ESC key, the F2 function key, the CTRL and ESC keys, and the CTRL-ALT-ESC key combination.

The key combinations used to access the setup menus vary from one BIOS manufacturer to another. If the proper keys are not pressed within a predetermined amount of time, the BIOS program will continue with the bootup process. However, if the keys are pressed during this time interval, the bootup routine will be put on hold, and the program will display a "CMOS Setup Selection" screen.

Each chipset variation has a specific BIOS designed for it. Therefore, there are functions specific to the design of system boards using that chipset. The example screen shown in Figure 2-54 serves as the main menu for entering and exiting the CMOS Setup utility and for moving between its configuration pages.

A typical Configuration Setup screen is shown in Figure 2-54. Through this screen, the user enters the desired configuration values into the CMOS registers. The cursor on the screen can be moved from item to item using the keyboard's cursor control keys.

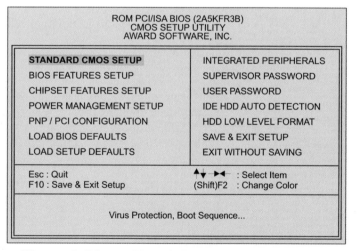

Figure 2-54: A CMOS Setup Selection Screen

Operating Systems

Every portion of the system must be controlled and coordinated so that the millions of operations that occur every second are carried out correctly and on time.

Operating systems are programs designed to control and coordinate the operation of the computer system. As a group, they are easily some of the most complex programs devised. Likewise, the operating system acts as an intermediary between nearly as complex software applications, and the hardware they run on.

In the personal computer environment, the operating system accepts commands from the computer user and carries them out to perform some desired operation. It is the job of the operating system to make the complexity of the personal computer as invisible as possible to the user.

The most widely used operating systems in the world have nothing to do with personal computers. These operating systems are found in automobiles and consumer electronics products. They receive input from sensing devices such as airflow sensors (instead of keyboards and mice), process a control program according to a set of instructions and input data, and provide output to electro/mechanical devices such as fuel injector pumps (not video displays and printers). They also don't have much to do with disk drives.

A **disk operating system** (**DOS**) is a collection of programs used to control overall computer operation in a disk-based system. These programs work in the background to allow the user of the computer to input characters from the keyboard, to define a file structure for storing records, or to output data to a monitor or printer. The disk operating system is responsible for finding and organizing your data and applications on the disk.

The disk operating system can be divided into three distinct sections:

- *Boot files* − take over control of the system from the ROM BIOS during start-up

- *File management files* − enable the system to manage information within itself

- *Utility files* − permit the user to manage system resources, troubleshoot the system, and configure the system

The operating system acts as a bridge between application programs and the computer, as described in Figure 2-55. These application programs allow the user to create files of data pertaining to certain applications such as word processing, remote data communications, business processing, and user programming languages.

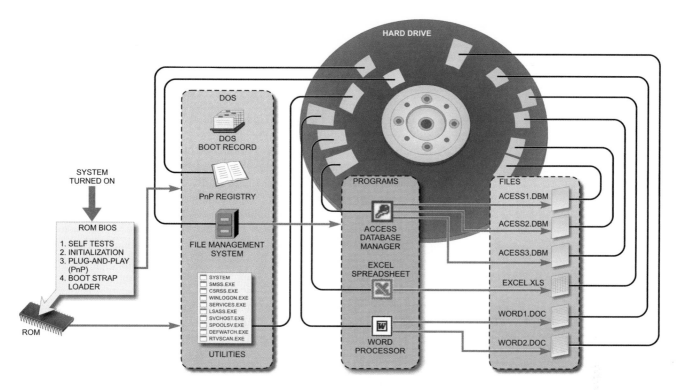

Notable disk operating systems include Windows 9X versions, Windows 2000 Professional, Windows XP Professional, Windows XP Home, Apple MAC OS x.x, and Apple OS X.

Network operating systems (NOS) are designed to extend the control of disk operating systems to provide for communications and data exchanges between computers connected by a communication media. Notable network operating systems include Windows NT Server, Windows 2000 Server, Windows 2003 Server, Linux, Unix, and Novell NetWare.

Figure 2-55: The Position of the DOS in the Computer System

Network operating system (NOS)

Graphical User Interfaces

Another form of operating environment, referred to as a **graphical user interface (GUI)**, has gained widespread popularity in recent years. GUIs, like the Microsoft Windows desktop depicted in Figure 2-56, employ a graphics display to represent procedures and programs that can be executed by the computer. These programs routinely use small pictures, called **icons**, to represent different programs. The advantage of using a GUI is that the user doesn't have to remember complicated commands to execute a program.

graphical user interface (GUI)

icons

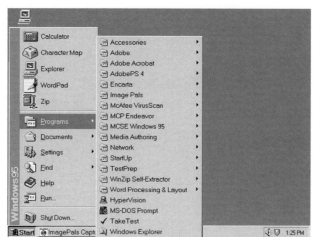

Figure 2-56: A Graphical User Interface Screen

Major Operating Systems

The most widely used disk operating systems with personal computers are the Windows line of operating systems from Microsoft. Windows is a GUI-based operating system that enables users to navigate through the system using a series of pop-up windows and menus.

Many personal computer users run versions of a freely distributed, open-source operating system called **Linux**. Linux is a very powerful, command-line operating system that can be used on a wide variety of hardware platforms including PC and **Apple Macintosh** systems. A community of programmers works with the Linux oversight committee to continually upgrade and enhance the basic Linux structure to keep it current and competitive. In addition, several companies have developed proprietary additions to the basic Linux structure to produce their own *distributions* (Linux speak for versions) of the operating system. Major Linux distributions include Redhat, SuSE, Slackware, Mandrake, Fedora, FreeBSD, Debian, and others.

While Linux is primarily thought of as a command-line-based operating system, multiple GUI-based desktop overlays have been developed to enable users to control the system in a manner similar to the Windows and Apple operating systems.

The other major line of the personal computers comes from Apple Computers. These personal computers are not compatible with the IBM line of PCs. They have distinctly different hardware designs and do not directly run software packages developed for the PC environment. All Apple computers originally ran proprietary versions of the Apple operating system. However, newer Apple Macintosh computers run on a proprietary version of Linux named **Apple OS X**. While the structure of OS X is Linux based, the user interaction portions of the system employ Apple's trademark GUI-based desktop. This gives the MAC a very powerful and stable engine with very user-friendly interfaces to work with.

For many years the vast majority of business PCs ran on a network operating system called Novell NetWare. However, Microsoft has taken over a large share of this market with Enterprise versions of its Windows operating systems. Originally, Novell developed and upgraded the complete structure of the NetWare operating system, including proprietary network management system, file management system, user and group control management and directory services.

Novell maintains a reasonable share of networked business users. Therefore, the computer technician must be aware of NetWare and how to work with it in a network environment. In an attempt to regain some of the desktop market, Novell has embraced its own version of the Linux operating system.

Application Software

The second major software category is application software. This category consists of programs that perform specialized tasks, such as word processing, accounting, and so forth. This category of software exists in two formats:

- Commercially available, user-oriented packages that may be purchased and used directly

- Programming language packages that developers can use to create user-oriented programs

Application software packages operate as extensions of the operating system. Depending on the type of operating system being used, an application program may directly control some system resources, such as printers and modems, while the operating system lends fundamental support in the background. In more advanced systems, the operating system supplies common input, output, and disk management functions for all applications in the system.

Commercial Application Packages

The openness of the personal computer market has generated a wide variety of different applications programs designed for use with them. Even a short discussion of all the software types available for the PC would take up more space than we can afford. However, a small group of these programs make up the vast majority of the software sold in this category. These programs are

- Word processors
- Spreadsheets
- Graphic design packages
- Personal productivity tools
- Database management systems (DBMS)

Word processors are specialized software packages that can be used to create and edit alphanumeric texts, such as letters, memos, contracts, and other documents. These packages convert the computer into a super typewriter. Unlike typewriters, word processors enable the user to edit, check, and correct any errors before the document is committed to paper. Many word processors offer extended functions such as spelling checkers, as well as online dictionary and thesaurus functions that aid the writer in preparing the document. A typical word processor working page is depicted in Figure 2-57.

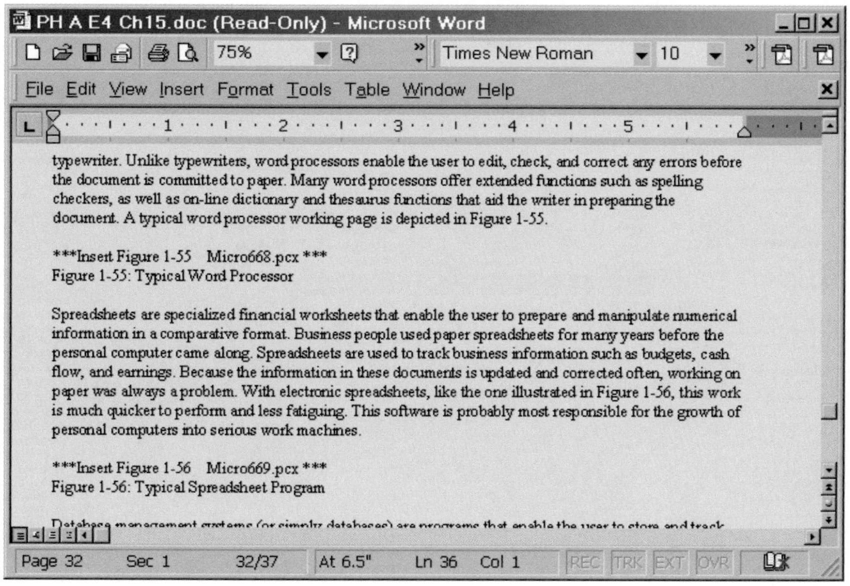

Word processors

Figure 2-57: Typical Word Processor

Spreadsheets

Spreadsheets are specialized financial worksheets that enable the user to prepare and manipulate numerical information in a comparative format. Business people used paper spreadsheets for many years before the personal computer came along. Spreadsheets are used to track business information such as budgets, cash flow, and earnings. Because the information in these documents is updated and corrected often, working on paper was always a problem. With electronic spreadsheets, like the one illustrated in Figure 2-58, this work is much quicker to perform and less fatiguing. This software is probably most responsible for the growth of personal computers into serious work machines.

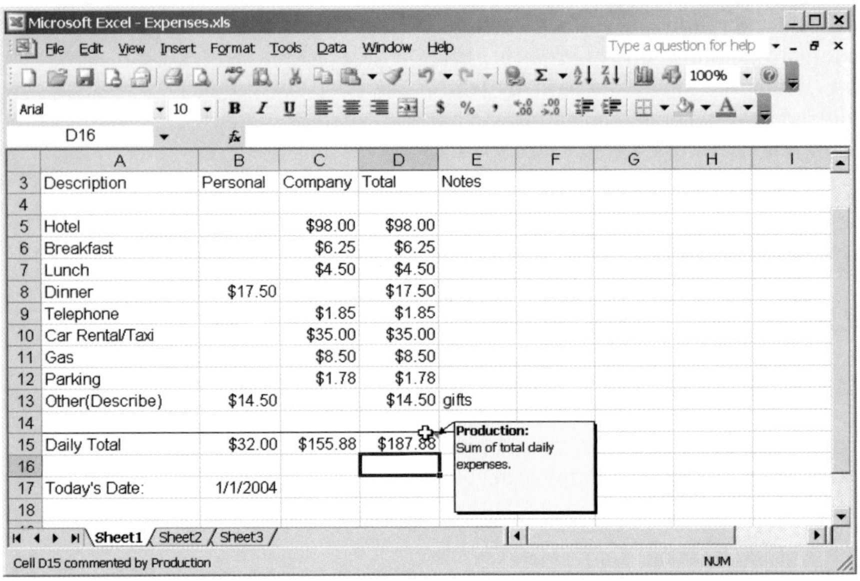

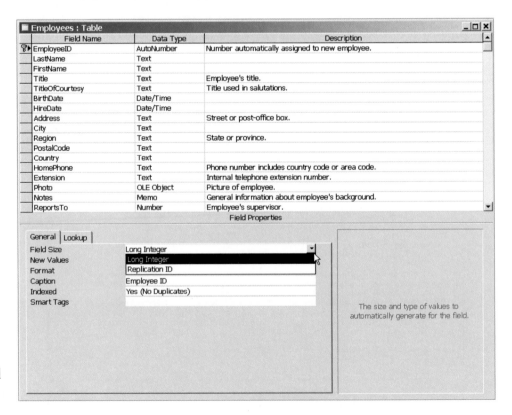

Figure 2-58: Typical Spreadsheet Program

Database management systems

databases

Database management systems (or simply **databases**) are programs that enable the user to store and track vast amounts of related information about different subjects. Databases can be thought of as electronic boxes of note cards. You can keep several pieces of information related to a given subject on these electronic note cards.

For example, you might keep information on note cards for each of your relatives. The cards might contain their phone numbers, addresses, and birthdays. The database enables you to search and sort through the information in different ways. With a database program, it would be no problem to sort out all of the relatives that have a birthday in a given month, or how many customers had purchased a given product from you in the last year. A typical database information page is depicted in Figure 2-59.

Figure 2-59: Typical Database Program

Graphics programs enable the user to create nonalphanumeric output from the computer. Simple graphics programs are used to create charts and graphs that represent data. More complex programs can be used to create artistic output in the form of lines, shapes, and images. Typically, graphic design programs produce graphics in two formats: as **bit-mapped images** and as **vector images**.

With bit-mapped graphics, every dot (**pixel**) in the image is defined in memory. Vector images are defined as a starting point and a set of mathematical formulas in memory. Because vector images exist only as a set of mathematical models, their size can be scaled up or down easily without major distortions. Vector images can also be rotated easily, allowing three-dimensional work to take place on these images. On the other hand, bit-mapped graphics are tightly specified collections of spots across and down the screen. These types of images would be difficult to scale or rotate without distortion. A typical graphics design package is depicted in Figure 2-60.

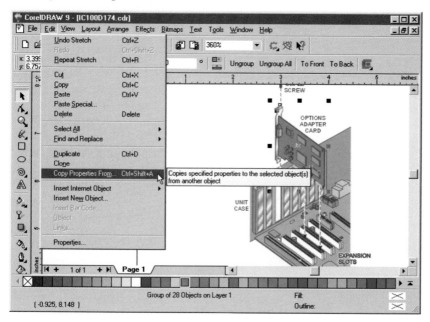

Figure 2-60: Typical Graphics Design Program

Personal productivity programs, also referred to as **desktop organizers**, encompass a variety of programs that simulate organizational tools found on typical business desks. They normally include items such as telephone directories, calculators, note pads, and calendar programs. Of course, many other types of application software are available for use with the PC. A meaningful discussion of all these software types is well beyond the scope of this book and certainly goes well beyond the scope of preparing for A+ testing.

Programming Packages

Because the only language that computers understand is their own machine language, and most humans don't relate well to machine languages, you'll need a piece of system software to convert whatever language you're programming into the machine's language. These conversion packages exist in two forms: **interpreters** and **compilers**. The distinction between the two is in how and when they convert the user language into machine language.

run

Interpreters convert the program as it is being **run** (executed). Compilers convert the entire user-language program into machine code before it is executed. Typically, compiled-language programs execute much faster than those written in interpretive languages. In addition, compiled languages typically provide the user with a much higher level of direct control over the computer's operation. In contrast, interpreted languages are usually slower, and less powerful, but their programs tend to be easier to write and use than those of compiled languages.

Visual Basic

BASIC

One of the most widely known programming environments is Microsoft's **Visual Basic** package. Unlike the previous command-line-driven **BASIC** language versions, Visual Basic is a graphical programming tool that allows programmers to develop Windows applications on an artistic rather than a command-line basis. The programmer draws graphic elements and places them on the screen as desired. This tool is so powerful that it is used to produce large blocks of major applications, as well as finished Windows products. The finished product can be converted into an executable file using a Visual Basic utility. The only major drawback of Visual Basic is that major applications written in Visual Basic tend to run slowly, because it is an interpreted language.

Assembly language

assembler

mnemonics

DEBUG

Another alternative in programming exists for your computer—that is, to write programs in **Assembly language** (one step away from machine language) and run them through an **assembler** program. Assembly language is a human-readable form of machine language that uses short, symbolic instruction words, called **mnemonics**, to tell the computer what to do. Each line of an Assembly language program corresponds directly to one line of machine code. Writing programs in Assembly language enables the programmer to precisely control every aspect of the computer's operation during the execution of the program. This makes Assembly language the most powerful programming language you can use. To its detriment, Assembly language is complex and requires the programmer to be extremely familiar with the internal operation of the system using the program.

For short and simple Assembly language programs, an MS-DOS utility called **DEBUG** can be used to enter and run machine language and limited Assembly-language programs, without going through the various assembly steps. A sample DEBUG program is shown in Figure 2-61.

```
c:\>debug
-r
AX=0000 BX=0000 CX=0000 DX=0000 SP=FFEE BP=0000 SI=0000 DI=0000
DS=20AB ES=20AB SS=20AB IP=0100 NU UP EI PL NZ NA PO NC
20AB:100 0F      DB    0F

-d
20AB:0100 0F 00 B9 A8  FFF3 AE 47-61 03 IF 8B C3 48 12 B1    .......Ga.........H..
20AB:0110 04 8B C6 F7 0A 0A D0 D3-48 DA 2B D0 34 00 9A 20    ..........H.+.4.......
20AB:0120 00 DB D2 D3 E0 03 F0 8E-DA 8B C7 16 C2 B6 01 16    ...........................
20AB:0130 C0 16 F8 8E C2 AC 8A D0-00 00 4E AD 8B C8 46 8A    ................N...F.
20AB:0140 C2 24 FE 3C B0 75 05 AC-F3 AA A0 0A EB 06 3C B2    ..$.<.U.............>.
20AB:0150 75 6D 6D 13 A8 01 50 14-74 B1 BE 32 01 8D 8B 1E    umm....P.+.2.......
20AB:0160 8E FC 12 A8 33 D2 29 E3-13 8B C2 03 C3 69 02 00    ......3.)......i.......
20AB:0170 0B F8 83 FF FF 74 11 26-01 1D E2 F3 81 00 94 FA    .......+.&..............
```

**Figure 2-61:
DEBUG Program**

Games and Educational Packages

Games and learning programs are among the leading titles in retail software sales. The games market has exploded as PC speeds have increased, and as output graphics have improved. However, on the technical side, there is generally not much call for repair associated with games software. Most games work with well-developed pointing devices, such as trackballs and joysticks, as the primary input devices. Although the housing designs of these products can be quite amazing, they tend to be simple and well-proven devices, requiring relatively little maintenance. Likewise, the software tends to be pretty straightforward from a user's point of view. It simply gets installed and runs.

Computer-aided instruction (CAI) and **computer-based instruction (CBI)** have become accepted means of delivering instructional materials. In CAI operations, the computer assists a human instructor in delivering information and tracking student responses. In CBI operations, the computer becomes the primary delivery vehicle for instructional materials.

As these teaching systems proliferate, more complex input, output, and processing devices are added to the system. A basic teaching system requires a minimum of a sound card, a fast hard drive, a CD-ROM drive, and a high-resolution video card. Beyond this, CAI and CBI systems may employ such wide-ranging peripherals as large LCD display panels, VGA-compatible overhead projectors, intelligent white boards, wireless mice, and touch-sensitive screens as input devices, full-motion video capture cards, and a host of other multimedia-related equipment.

> **Computer-aided instruction (CAI)**
>
> **computer-based instruction (CBI)**

Version Numbers, Service Packs, and Patches

Software products never seem to get completely finished. They tend to be supplied in the form of a starting component and then undergo minor periodic changes until a major change in the product occurs. So that the user and the industry can keep track of where software products are within that cycle, the manufacturers assign software products **version numbers**.

> **version numbers**

Traditionally, when a programmer releases a software program for sale, a version number is assigned to it, such as Windows 3.11 or MS-DOS 6.22. The version number distinguishes the new release from prior releases of that same software. The larger the version number, the more recent the program and, theoretically, the more functions and features it has (and hopefully, the fewer problems and bugs it has).

When new features or capabilities are added to a program, it is given a new version number. Therefore, referring to a software package by its version number indicates its capabilities and operation. The number to the left of the decimal point is the major revision number, which usually changes when new features are added. The number(s) to the right of the decimal are minor revision numbers, which usually change when corrections are made to the program.

In 1995, Microsoft began a new method of referring to its software products. The initial product offering is given a name with the year of its origin appended to it (e.g., Windows 2000, or Office 2003). Major upgrades are delivered in a form known as Service Packs (collections of fixes and upgrades). Minor revisions are referred to as Updates. When software vintage needs to be discussed, such as when you are asking for technical assistance, the service pack installation is used (e.g., Windows 2000 Server—Service Pack 3 is running). Upgrades are typically assigned a number that no one remembers or speaks of after it has been installed on the machine. In both cases, Microsoft's preferred delivery method is through the Internet—no telephone/personnel cost, no media costs, and no mailing costs are incurred.

KEY POINTS REVIEW

This chapter has covered the fundamental hardware structures and components associated with PC-compatible personal computer systems. Review the following key points before moving into the Review and Exam Questions sections to make sure you are comfortable with each point. Afterward, answer the Review Questions that follow to verify your knowledge of the information.

- The system unit is the main portion of the microcomputer system and is the basis of any PC system arrangement.

- The system board is the center of the system. It contains the portions of the system that define its computing power and speed.

- The system's power supply unit provides electrical power for every component inside the system unit.

- The system board communicates with various optional Input/Output (I/O) and memory systems through adapter boards that plug into its expansion slots. These connectors are normally located along the left-rear portion of the system board so that the external devices they serve can access them through openings at the rear of the case.

- The microprocessor is the major component of any system board. It executes software instructions and carries out arithmetic operations for the system.

- Microprocessor manufacturers always produce microprocessor-support chipsets that provide auxiliary services for the microprocessor.

- Each time the system is turned on, or reset, the BIOS program checks the system's Configuration Settings to determine what types of optional devices are included in the system.

- Newer microcomputers possess the capability to automatically reconfigure themselves for new options that are installed. This feature is referred to as Plug-and-Play (PnP) capability.

- The video adapter card provides the interface between the system board and the display monitor.

- The system unit normally comes from the manufacturer with at least one hard-disk drive (HDD) and a CD-ROM drive installed.

The following questions test your knowledge of the material presented in this chapter.

1. What advantage does the EPS power supply specification offer the system over the ATX specification?

2. List the four subunits typically found inside the system unit.

3. How can you avoid confusion between the DB-15F connectors for VGA and game-port connections?

4. List three types of memory typically found on modern system boards.

5. Describe how data are stored on a magnetic disk.

6. List the devices normally found outside the system unit.

7. How are legacy cards different from PnP cards, and how do they affect the system?

8. You are upgrading your system with a more powerful microprocessor. You have been advised that you will need a new ROM BIOS program to support the upgrade. How can you accomplish this part of the upgrade?

9. What do the terms SIMM and DIMM stand for, and what kinds of devices are they?

10. What functions do microprocessors perform for the system?

11. Name a major drawback of tower cases.

12. How are data placed on a DVD disc, and how does the system read this information back from the disc when called for?

13. What is ESCD, and how does it affect the operation of the system?

14. What is the data storage capacity of a typical CD-ROM?

15. List the three major sets of operations performed by the BIOS during start-up.

EXAM QUESTIONS

1. What type of IC is the brain of the PC system?
   a. The ROM BIOS
   b. The ASIC device
   c. The memory controller
   d. The microprocessor

2. Name one weak feature of tower cases.
   a. Weak framework due to its vertical height
   b. Airflow through tower cases is generally not good
   c. High EFI radiation
   d. Requires excessive desk space in an office environment

3. Where is the system's BIOS program located?
   a. In ROM ICs located on the system board
   b. In the CMOS chip
   c. In the keyboard encoder
   d. In the microprocessor's L2 cache

4. What function does Plug and Play perform in the computer system?
   a. Enables system to automatically reconfigure itself
   b. Enables system to test itself
   c. Enables system to automatically load operating system files
   d. Enables system to automatically repair legacy configuration

5. You are building a new computer for a friend. They want a starter system that they can use to surf the Internet, balance their checkbook, and handle their e-mail. They have purchased a low-end VGA card for the video display. Which expansion slot type are you most likely to use for this video adapter card?
   a. An ISA slot
   b. An AGP slot
   c. A PCI slot
   d. A PCIe slot

6. In a PC-compatible system, _____.
   a. the BIOS must perform the same functions as the BIOS in an IBM PC
   b. the operating system must perform the same functions as the OS in an IBM PC
   c. the system must use the same ICs that the IBM PC used
   d. the system must use an IBM BIOS

7. Starting the computer from the power off condition is known as _____.
   a. warm boot
   b. cold boot
   c. initialization
   d. reset

8. Which of the following is not part of the bootup process?
   a. POST tests
   b. Initialization
   c. Loading MBR
   d. Executing utility files

9. The process of placing the starting values in a system's programmable devices is known as _____.
   a. POSTing
   b. initializing
   c. booting
   d. resetting

9. The process of placing the starting values in a system's programmable devices is known as _____.
   a. POSTing
   b. initializing
   c. booting
   d. resetting

10. What is the main function of the MBR in a disk-based system?
   a. Test the basic system's hardware
   b. Load starting values into the system's intelligent devices
   c. Provide information to the system about loading the operating system
   d. Load the BIOS into RAM to start the system

CHAPTER 3

ADVANCED SYSTEM BOARDS

OBJECTIVES

Upon completion of this chapter and its related lab procedures, you should be able to perform these tasks:

1. Name popular Pentium-class microprocessors and describe their basic characteristics, such as speeds, voltages, form factors, and cache capabilities.

2. Differentiate between the characteristics of various types of RAM used in a PC system, including the different types of dynamic and static RAM.

3. Discuss typical memory organization schemes used with different system board types and, given a specific memory arrangement, identify the types of devices employed.

4. Identify the most popular types of motherboards, their components, and their architecture, including ATX, BTX, and NLX.

5. Identify typical system board components, including I/O ports, memory modules, and processor sockets.

6. Describe the characteristics of different expansion bus architectures, including PCI, PCI-X, PCIe, and AGP specifications.

7. Discuss basic compatibility guidelines for different types of disk drive interfaces found on Pentium system boards, including the various types of IDE and SCSI devices.

8. State the purpose of CMOS RAM, what items it typically contains, and how to change its basic parameters.

ADVANCED SYSTEM BOARDS

FROM THE GEEK SQUAD

A gent 54 is a Geek Squad Special Agent who has been asked by one of his salespeople to help a customer put together a system to serve as a high-end gaming computer. The main items that the customer has concerns about revolve around the system board—which processor will provide the performance desired, how much RAM is necessary to play the games the customer wants to participate in, what type of cooling system should be used?

Agent 54 must know which system board components can be used to optimize the application the customer wants to fill. In addition, he must be able to explain to the customer how the components he suggests affect the ability of the system to play games more effectively.

INTRODUCTION

Even though the system board's physical structure has changed over time, its logical structure has remained relatively constant. Since the original PC, the system board has been the component that contained the main components of the PC system—the microprocessor, its support devices, the system's primary memory units, and the expansion-slot connectors. Figure 3-1 depicts a typical system board layout.

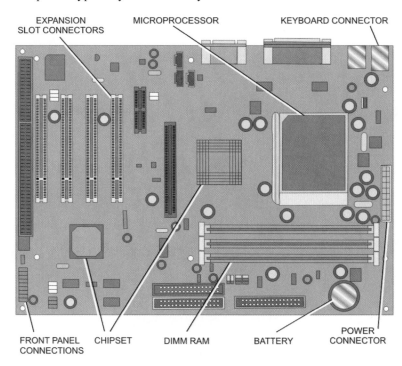

Figure 3-1: A Typical System Board Layout

In the PC industry, system board designs fundamentally change for four reasons: new industry form factors, new microprocessor designs, new expansion-slot types, and reduced chip counts. Reduced chip counts are typically the result of improved microprocessor support chipset designs. The progression of system board form factors include the PC and PC-XT form factor, followed by the Industry Standard Architecture PC-AT, which, in turn, gave way to the ATX architecture currently in widespread use.

Another line of form factors have existed for low-profile PC versions. The *low-profile extended* (*LPX*) form factor has been the standard for low-profile PCs since the late 1980s. The latest entry in the low-profile form factor line is the NLX architecture introduced in Chapter 2.

The A+ Essentials Objective 1.1 lists the ATX, BTX, and NLX architectures as those that all technicians should be familiar with at this point in time.

Essentials 1.1

ATX SYSTEM BOARDS

The mainstay of PC form factors has been the **ATX form factor** since the late 1990s. Intel developed this form factor for Pentium-based systems by evolving the older *Baby AT* form factor and moving the standard I/O functions to the system board. The **ATX specification** basically rotates the *Baby AT* form factor by 90 degrees, relocates the power supply connection, and moves the microprocessor and memory modules away from the expansion slots.

ATX form factor

ATX specification

NOTE

The Changing Face of System Boards—Chipset-based system boards and I/O cards tend to change often as IC manufacturers continue to integrate higher levels of circuitry into their devices.

Figure 3-2 depicts a Pentium-based, ATX system board that directly supports the FDD, HDD, serial, and parallel ports. The board is 12" (305 mm) wide and 9.6" (244 mm) long. A revised, mini-ATX specification allows for 11.2"-by-8.2" system boards. The hole patterns for the ATX and mini-ATX system boards require an ATX-compatible case that can accommodate the form factors of these boards. Although ATX shares most of its mounting-hole pattern with the older baby-AT specification, it does not match exactly.

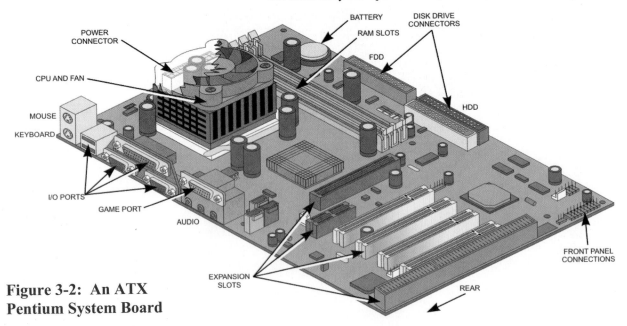

Figure 3-2: An ATX Pentium System Board

The power supply orientation enables a single fan to be used to cool the system. This provides reduced cost, reduced system noise, and improved reliability. The relocated microprocessor and memory modules allow full-length cards to be used in the expansion slots while providing easy upgrading of the microprocessor, RAM, and I/O cards.

BTX System Boards

PC designers continue to build faster, more powerful systems based on faster microprocessors, support chipsets, and adapter cards. Increased speed and power result in additional power usage, which translates directly to additional heat. To handle the additional heat buildup inside the system unit, manufacturers have had to install additional cooling elements and fans. The presence of the fans and the volume of air that must be pulled through the system unit to adequately cool the system can increase noise levels associated with PC systems.

The BTX form factor specification is designed to provide better thermal handling capabilities, better acoustic characteristics, and provisions for newer PC technologies. The BTX form factor is not compatible with the older ATX specification. It moves key components, such as the microprocessor, chipset, and video controller, to new general locations on the system board to achieve better airflow (and cooling) characteristics inside the system unit. Figure 3-3 depicts the recommended full-size version of a BTX system board.

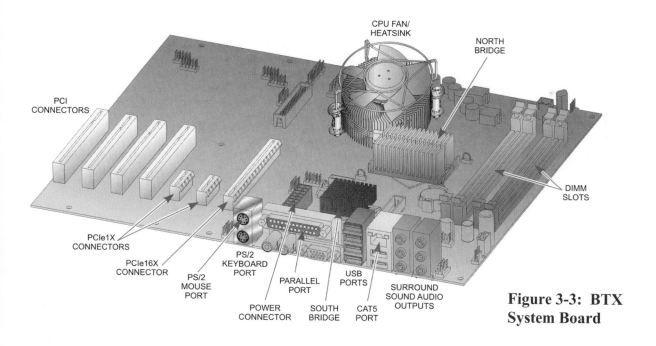

Figure 3-3: BTX System Board

thermal module

Notice that the microprocessor has been moved toward the front center section of the board, as have the chipset devices. The major source of cooling in the BTX system is the **thermal module** depicted in Figure 3-4. The thermal module mounts to the front of the system unit and sits directly over the microprocessor and chipset components to provide in-line airflow across the components. This reduces the need for additional cooling fans and heat sinks, which, in turn, lowers the cost of the unit. BTX thermal modules come in two varieties—a standard height Type I version, which is designed for full-height cases and a low-profile Type II version designed for small form factor cases.

Figure 3-4: BTX Thermal Module

media servers

This configuration also improves the *acoustics* of the unit, which is becoming an area of greater concern as PCs are increasingly being used as **media servers**. Media servers are specialized PCs designed specifically for delivering audio and video services in the home setting. In these applications, the sound levels generated by cooling and case fans can reach unacceptable levels.

Under the BTX specification, there are options for four different board widths that share common core design characteristics. The length of all the board types is 266.7 mm. One of the core design characteristics is that in each version the expansion slots have been moved to the right side of the BTX boards. This factor alone makes the BTX designs incompatible with cases with other PC form factors. The standard BTX board versions are described in Figure 3-5 and include

PicoBTX

NanoBTX

- **PicoBTX**—This is the smallest BTX variation at a width of 203.2 mm. It includes only a single expansion slot.

- **NanoBTX**—This BTX version increases the board width to 223.53 mm and provides for two expansion slots.

- **Micro BTX**—This medium-size BTX version includes four expansion slots on a board that is increased to a width of 264.16 mm.

Micro BTX

- **BTX**—The full-size BTX specification extends the number of expansion slots from the four in the smaller variations to a total of seven. The board width for the full version is 325.12 mm.

BTX

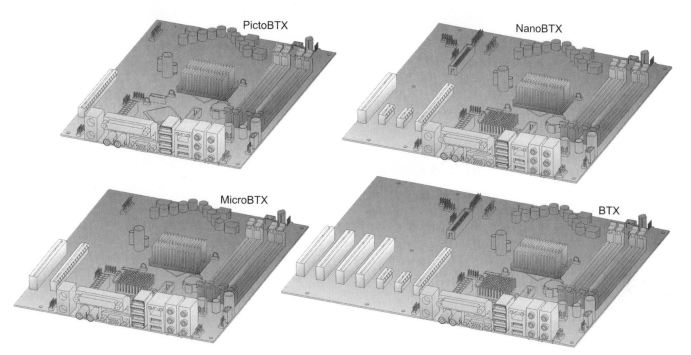

Figure 3-5: Standard BTX Size Variations

BTX system boards treat newer PC technologies as standard components. These system boards routinely include Serial ATA interface connections, USB 2.0 ports, and PCIe expansion slots. Notice that the BTX adapter slots are located at the right rear corner of the unit. The larger the board, the more adapter slots and slot types are included. Typical expansion slots used in BTX systems include PCI-5V, PCI-3.3V, AGP-3.3V, AGP-1.5V, and PCI express slots.

On the left side of the system, the DRAM slots are located just to the left of the microprocessor and its chipset. The power supply unit is located at the left rear of the unit with the system's disk drives occupying the front-left corner of the unit. The BTX specification makes provisions for using ATX power supplies as well as small form factor **low-profile form factor (LFX)** and **compact form factor (CFX)** power supplies.

low-profile form factor (LFX)

compact form factor (CFX)

The various BTX system board sizes are intended to allow the same technologies to be used in tower, desktop, and low-profile small form factor configurations. Figure 3-6 illustrates how these variations are implemented in the different case styles.

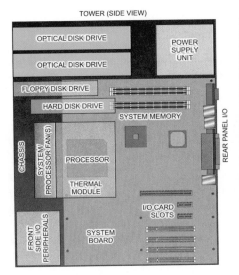

TOWER (SIDE VIEW)

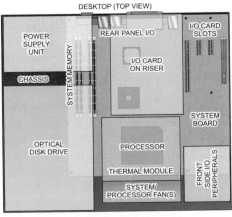

DESKTOP (TOP VIEW)

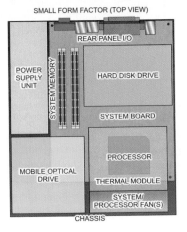

SMALL FORM FACTOR (TOP VIEW)

Figure 3-6: BTX Implementations

The BTX back panel moves the rear panel I/O connectors, depicted in Figure 3-7, to the center of the back panel. This layout is the result of better placement of the I/O controller on the system board. The system manufacturer determines the exact makeup of the BTX I/O back panel. Most back panels include traditional PS/2 mouse and keyboard connectors, VGA video connections, as well as legacy parallel printer and serial ports. In addition, the BTX back panel may offer a wide variety of consumer audio and video connection combinations.

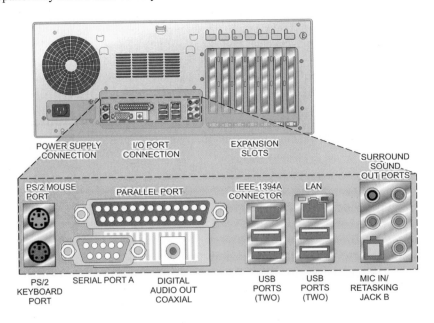

Figure 3-7: Typical BTX Back Panel Layout

Low-Profile Form Factors

Low-profile cases employ short back-planes to provide a lower profile than traditional desktop units. In low-profile cases, the adapter cards are mounted horizontally on the back-plane card that extends from an expansion slot on the motherboard. The expansion slot openings in the back panel of the case are horizontal as well. To accommodate the lower profiles, special lowered power supply versions have also been developed.

The **low-profile extended (LPX)** form factor, also referred to as the *slim line* form factor, was designed to reduce the height of the system unit. As such, the specification applied to system unit cases, power supply units, and expansion cards. The LPX form factor never became an official standard, but it gained enough industry support that millions of cases and power supply units were produced. LPX system boards typically incorporated built-in video so that no adapter card was needed for this function. Finally, LPX units typically had poor ventilation characteristics—the low case height and horizontally mounted adapter cards tended to trap heat near the system board surface.

Unlike the LPX specification, the **new low-profile extended (NLX)** form factor, depicted in Figure 3-8, did become a legitimate standard for cases, power supplies, and system boards. However, it has never really become a force in the industry. Manufacturers have chosen to produce low-profile units based on **microATX** and **miniATX** designs. These form factors followed the ATX design specification but reduced the size of the unit (and its associated costs) by limiting the number of expansion slots.

> Low-profile
>
> low-profile extended (LPX)
>
> new low-profile extended (NLX)
>
> microATX
>
> miniATX

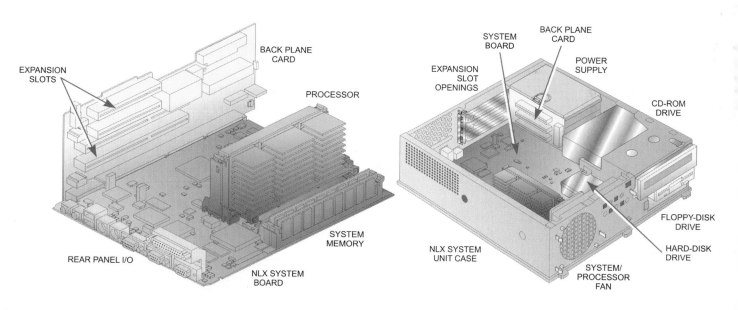

Figure 3-8:
NLX Components

System Board Compatibility Issues

The term *form factor* is used to refer to the physical size and shape of a device. However, in the case of system boards, it also refers to their case style and power supply compatibility, as well as their I/O connection placement schemes. These factors come into play when assembling a new system from components, as well as in repair and upgrade situations where the system board is being replaced. With this in mind, the first consideration when installing or replacing a system board is whether it will physically fit the environment and work with the other system components. In both of these situations, the following basic compatibility issues must be dealt with:

- The system board's form factor

- The case form factor

- The power supply connection type

System boards of different types have different mounting-hole patterns. Obviously the hole patterns of the replacement system board must match that of the case. If not, the replacement board cannot be installed or grounded properly. Some clone system boards do not observe standard sizes (only compatible standoff spacing). If the case has a power supply that mounts in the floor of the unit, there may not be enough open width in the case to accommodate an extra-wide system board. The same can be said for a full-height disk drive bay. If the disk drive bay reaches from the floor of the case to its top, there will be no room for a wide system board to fit under it.

In addition to the mounting hole alignment issue, the case openings for expansion slots and port connections must be compatible with those of the system board. Likewise, expansion-slot placement is likely to vary between different form factors. The bad alignment created by this situation can make it difficult to install I/O cards in some systems. Similarly, I/O connectors mounted directly on the backs of system boards may not line up with openings in other form factor case styles. The types of adapter cards in the system are another point of consideration when installing or replacing a system board. Make sure the new board has enough of the correct types of expansion slots to handle all the different adapter cards in the system.

Power supply size, orientation, and connectors present another compatibility consideration. The ATX specification calls for this device to be placed toward the right rear of the board so that its fan can push air directly across the microprocessor. Under the BTX specification, the processor placement is moved toward the front center of the board so that a front mounted thermal (cooling) unit can direct fresh air across it.

GEEK SQUAD CASE FILE #13345

You have been called in as a computer consultant for the world's third largest banking organization. It wants to upgrade its existing computer systems to Pentium-class systems. When you arrive, you discover that old Windows 3.11 operating systems are still running on 80386 computers. These systems use baby AT system boards, 2/3-size multi-I/O cards, 9-pin serial mice, and 500 MB IDE hard drives. What should you advise the customer to do in order to upgrade the machines with the least cost and the most advantage?

Pentium Chipsets

Several IC manufacturers have developed chipsets to support different Pentium processors and their clones. Most of these designs feature a two- or three-chip **chipset** that supports a combination PCI/ISA bus architecture. Figure 3-9 depicts a generic chipset arrangement for this type of system board.

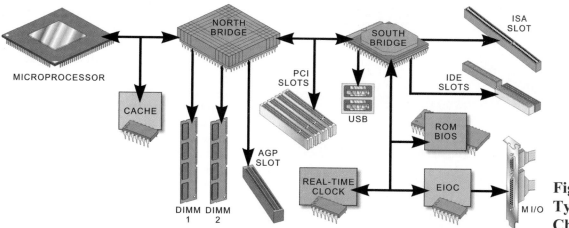

Figure 3-9: Typical Pentium Chipset

The typical Pentium chipset consists of a memory controller (called the **north bridge**), a PCI-to-ISA host bridge (referred to as the **south bridge**), and an enhanced I/O controller. The memory controller provides the interface between the system's microprocessor, its various memory sections, and the PCI bus. In turn, the host bridge provides the interface between the PCI bus, the IDE bus, and the ISA bus. The enhanced I/O controller chip interfaces the standard PC peripherals (LPT, COM, and FDD interfaces) to the ISA bus.

north bridge

south bridge

This typical chipset arrangement may vary for a couple of reasons. The first reason is to include a specialized function, such as an AGP or USB interface. The second reason is to accommodate changes in bus specifications such as PCI-X or PCIe slots. Figure 3-10 shows an advanced Pentium/PCI chipset design that includes an AGP slot. Notice that the AGP slot is local to the north bridge—meaning that it has very fast access to the microprocessor.

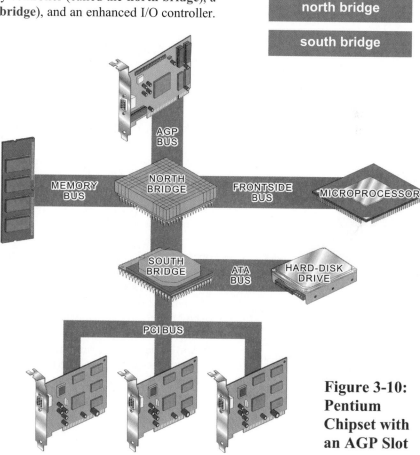

Figure 3-10: Pentium Chipset with an AGP Slot

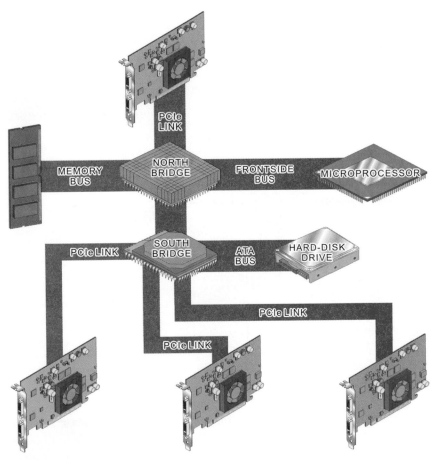

Likewise, Figure 3-11 depicts an advanced Pentium/PCI chipset that provides advanced PCIe expansion buses for multiple "links". Notice that each PCIe link is attached directly to the South Bridge (with the exception of a special PCIe link for the high-end video display adapter.

It is normal to consider the ROM BIOS as an integral part of any chipset model, because it is designed to support the register structure of a particular chipset. One of the major functions provided by the BIOS is the Chipset Features configuration screen in the CMOS Setup routine described later in this chapter. Technicians can use this tool to optimize the system settings to provide maximum internal performance. However, these settings tend to be very technical and require an extensive understanding of the specific system's component structure to configure. Therefore, replacing a ROM BIOS chip on a system board is not as simple as placing another ROM BIOS IC in the socket. The replacement BIOS must have correct information for the specific chipset it is being used with.

Figure 3-11: Advanced Pentium/PCIe Chipset

System Bus Speeds

core speed

bus speed

clock multiplier

front side bus (FSB)

back side bus (BSB)

Microprocessor and chipset manufacturers are continually developing products to speed up the operation of the system. The first method used to speed up the system is to separate the speed at which the internal core of the processor runs from that of all the buses and devices external to it. In the Pentium processor, two speed settings can be established for the microprocessor—one is the **core speed** at which the internal microprocessor operations take place, and the second is a derivative **bus speed** for its external bus transfers. These two operational speeds are tied together through an internal **clock multiplier** system.

The second method of speeding up the system is to speed up the movement of data across its data buses. Looking at the arrangement shown in Figure 3-9, you should note that the buses operating directly with the microprocessor and north bridge, referred to as the **front side bus** (**FSB**), are running at one speed, while the PCI bus is running at a different speed, and the ISA/MIO devices are running at still another speed. In Pentium processors, a parallel bus called the **back side bus** (**BSB**) connects the microprocessor with its internal L2 cache.

Historically, Pentium processors have operated at many speeds between 50 MHz and 3.4 GHz. At the same time, the front side buses have been operating at clock rates between 66 MHz and 1066 MHz. Likewise, the **PCI bus** has operated at standard speeds of 33 MHz, 44 MHz, and 66 MHz. The devices in the supporting chipset are responsible for coordinating data and control signal flow between the different buses. You can think of these buses as highways and streets where traffic travels at different speeds. The devices in the chipset act as on/off ramps and stoplights to effectively coordinate information movement across the buses. Using an example of a current Pentium system board, the processor may run at 3.0 GHz internally, while the front side bus runs at 800 MHz (200 MHz × 4), the PCI bus runs at 33 MHz, and the IDE bus runs at 100 MHz.

TEST TIP

Know which processors can be used with which system board bus speeds.

Configuring Microprocessors and Buses

Older Pentium system boards were designed so that they can support a variety of different microprocessor types and operating speeds. It was not uncommon for a particular system board to support a given type of Intel Pentium processor, its American Micro Devices clone processor, and a number of different speed ratings for each type. On newer system boards you are pretty much limited to a single type of processor from one or the other manufacturers. However, you can still generally upgrade that device with an upgraded version from the same manufacturer.

In older Pentium systems, the microprocessor's configuration settings were established largely through a series of jumpers on the system board. Some settings on system boards are still enabled and configured through on-board jumpers. Incorrectly setting processor-related system board jumpers causes a high number of failures for both new installations and upgrades. You should always refer to the system board's Installation Guide or User's Manual for definitions of these settings.

TEST TIP

Be aware of how PC systems determine what type of microprocessor is installed and what its capabilities are.

However, most system boards feature autodetection functions as part of the PnP process that automatically detect different FRU components on the board (i.e., processors, fans, RAM modules, and adapter cards) and synchronize the different bus speed configurations. For example, the autodetect feature will examine the installed microprocessor and the installed RAM modules to configure the front side bus for maximum microprocessor-memory operations. Similarly, the chipset may detect an advanced video adapter card in one of the expansion slots and adjust the expansion bus speed to maximize the performance of the video display. Likewise, the system will autodetect the installed hard drives and CD-ROM drives and adjust the IDE bus speed to provide the best drive system performance based on what it finds.

Finally, the system evaluates the information it has acquired about its components and buses and configures the north and south bridges to provide synchronization between their other buses and the PCI bus that connects them together. The PCI bus speed (and by default its AGP video slot derivative) does not change to accommodate different installed components. Its speed is established as a derivative of the microprocessor clock (not to be confused with the advertised speed rating of the microprocessor).

Key microprocessor and bus configuration settings typically included such items as

- *Microprocessor Type*—This setting tells the system what type of processor is installed. If this setting is incorrect, the system will assume that the installed processor is the one specified by the setting and try to interact with it on that basis. Depending on which microprocessor is indicated, the system POST might identify the processor incorrectly and still run, but not properly. In other cases, the processor might lock up during the POST or not run at all. In either case, the processor could be damaged.

- *Core-to-Bus Speed Ratio*—Again, depending on the exact mismatch, the system might overclock the processor and run, but erratically. If the overclocking is less than 20%, the system might run without problems. However, the processor's life expectancy will be decreased. If the deviation is greater than 20%, the system might not come up at all, and the processor might be damaged.

- *Bus Frequency Setting*—Configuring this setting incorrectly will cause the processor to run faster or slower. This is a common method employed by users to increase the operating speed of their older systems. If the variation is less than 20%, the system will probably work with a shortened processor life. Greater levels of overclocking the bus might cause the system to have random lockups.

- *Core Voltage Level*—This setting establishes the voltage level that the microprocessor core will operate at. The setting is linked to the processor's speed and power dissipation. Normally, the microprocessor will not operate at all if the voltage level is more than 20% too low. Conversely, if you operate a processor at a voltage level that is higher than its specified value, this can cause physical damage to it.

It should be obvious that all of these settings must be configured correctly for the type of microprocessor actually installed in the system. If the *core voltage* level is set too high, then the microprocessor will probably overheat slowly, or burn out, depending on the amount of voltage applied. Conversely, if the voltage level is configured too low for the installed processor, then the system will most likely refuse to start. Likewise, setting the speed selection jumpers incorrectly can cause the system to think that a different processor is installed in the system.

In newer systems, the BIOS version must support the parameters of the microprocessor so that the PnP process can correctly configure the device and the chipset. If a microprocessor upgrade is performed and the BIOS code does not fully support the new processor, all the problems described earlier can occur.

For example, if an 850 MHz Pentium III processor were installed in a system whose BIOS only supported processor speeds up to 600 MHz, the BIOS will only report a processor speed of 600 MHz during the POST portion of the startup. The system will actually be limited to running at 600 MHz. For this reason, the capabilities of the system BIOS should always be examined when performing microprocessor upgrades.

overclocking

Different groups of PC enthusiasts, such as *gamers*, make a practice of configuring the microprocessor clock to run at a higher speed than the IC manufacturer suggests. This is referred to as **overclocking** the processor and is done to squeeze additional performance out of the system.

Because the basic microprocessor is running faster than designed, both the front side bus and the PCI bus run faster than their stated values by a factor directly proportional to the amount that the microprocessor is overclocked. The additional speed also generates additional heat from both the processor and its supporting devices. This requires the installation of additional fans and cooling systems to prevent damage from the additional heat generated.

Expansion Slots

The system's expansion slots provide the connecting point for most of its I/O devices. Interface cards communicate with the system through the extended microprocessor buses made available through these slots. In the original PC, PC-XT, and PC-AT designs, the expansion slots were located in the slower portions of the system board's chipset.

In order to speed up the operation of their systems, system board manufacturers began to add proprietary bus designs to their boards to increase the speed and bandwidth for transfers between the microprocessor and a few selected peripherals. This was accomplished by creating special **local buses** between the devices that would enable the peripherals to operate at speeds close to that of the microprocessor. This technique assured faster operations for these selected components by giving them more direct access to the microprocessor (the equivalent of driving on a freeway versus city streets with lots of stop signs).

local buses

Although there were several local bus designs introduced, the PCI expansion bus specification eventually became the dominant expansion bus and slot configuration for PCs. Continued advancement of the PCI architecture has prevented it from being replaced by another type of bus/slot architecture.

Newer Pentium system boards include a combination of different PCI slots and an AGP slot. However, it is not uncommon to find systems boards with other types of expansion slots onboard. Some boards still include an ISA slot for use with older AT-compatible legacy cards. Other boards include AMR and CDR risers for special modem and audio cards.

With the exception of the ISA slot, all of the other expansion bus specifications include slot addressing capabilities and reserve memory space to allow for plug-and-play reconfiguration of each device installed in the system. However, because no identification or reconfiguration capabilities were designed into the ISA bus specification, the presence of ISA-compatible slots on the system board can seriously disrupt plug-and-play operations.

TEST TIP

Remember which expansion slot types are most prevalent on a modern system board.

PCI Local Bus

The **peripheral component interconnect (PCI)** local bus was jointly developed by IBM, Intel, DEC, NCR, and Compaq. Its design incorporates three elements: a low-cost, high-performance local bus, the automatic configuration of installed expansion cards (plug-and-play), and the ability to expand with the introduction of new microprocessors and peripherals. The data transfer performance of the PCI local bus is 132 MBps using a 32-bit bus and 264 MBps using a 64-bit bus. This is accomplished even though the bus has a maximum clock frequency of 33 MHz.

peripheral component interconnect (PCI)

The PCI peripheral device has 256 bytes of on-board memory to hold information as to what type of device it is. The peripheral device can be classified as a controller for a mass-storage device, a network interface, a display, or other hardware. The configuration space also contains control, status, and latency timer values. The latency timer register on the device determines the length of time that the device can control the bus for bus mastering operations.

Figure 3-12 illustrates the structure of a system based on PCI local bus chipset components.

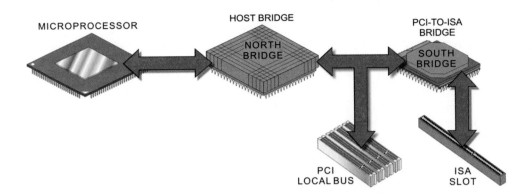

**Figure 3-12:
PCI Bus
Structure**

host bridge

The main component in the PCI-based system is the PCI bus controller, called the **host bridge**. This device monitors the microprocessor's address bus to determine whether addresses are intended for devices on the system board, in a PCI slot, or in one of the system board's other expansion slots.

mezzanine bus

PCI-to-ISA bridge

In older PC-compatible systems, the PCI bus normally coexisted with an ISA bus. The PCI portion of the bus structure functions as a **mezzanine bus** between the ISA bus and the microprocessor's main bus system. The figure also depicts a **PCI-to-ISA bridge** that allows ISA adapters to be used in the PCI system. Other bridge devices can also accommodate advanced PCI-X or PCIe adapters.

The host bridge routes PCI data directly to the PCI expansion slots through the local bus. These transfers occur at speeds compatible with the microprocessor. However, it must route non-PCI data to the PCI-to-ISA bridge that converts it into a format compatible with the ISA expansion slot. In the case of ISA slots, the data are converted from the 64/32-bit to the 16-bit ISA format. These transfers occur at typical ISA bus speeds.

The original PCI bus employed 32-bit address and data buses. Its specification also defined a 64-bit multiplexed address and data bus variation for use with 64-bit processors, such as the Pentium. Its clock line was originally defined for a maximum frequency of 33 MHz and a 132 Mbps transfer rate. However, it can be used with microprocessors operating at higher clock frequencies (e.g., 66 MHz under the PCI 2.1 specification).

The PCI 2.2 and PCI 2.3 versions of the bus implemented two new slot structures to provide a true 64-bit data bus, as illustrated in Figure 3-13. The new PCI specification runs at 66 MHz to provide a 264 Mbps data throughput. The slot also features a reduced 3.3 Vdc power supply voltage to decrease signal interference levels generated by the 33 MHz operations. Adapters placed in the 32-bit section of the PCI 2.2 slot can operate with the 5 Vdc or 3.3 V supply levels. The back portion of the slot remains pin and signal compatible with the older 32-bit PCI slots. It retained its +5 Vdc operating voltage to remain compatible with older PCI 1.1 and 2.0 adapters.

An additional PCI bus improvement has been developed using a new slot layout for PCI 2.3. This slot is similar to the PCI 66-32/64 intermediate slot in size and appearance. However, it is keyed in such a manner that only adapter cards designed for this slot (or universal PCI cards) can be inserted. The slot also features a reduced 3.3 Vdc power supply voltage to decrease signal interference levels generated by the 66 MHz operations.

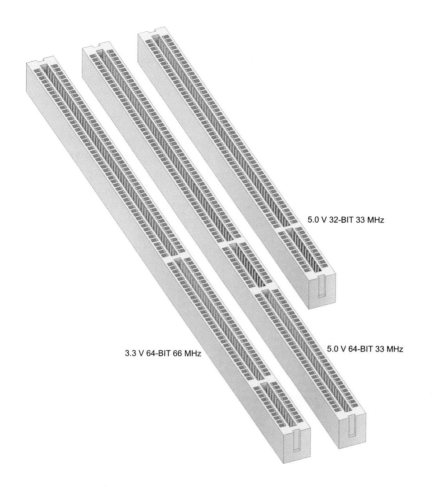

5.0 V 32-BIT 33 MHz

3.3 V 64-BIT 66 MHz   5.0 V 64-BIT 33 MHz

**Figure 3-13:
32-bit and 64-bit
PCI Slots**

PCI Configuration

The PCI standard is part of the plug-and-play hardware standard. As such, the system's BIOS and system software must support the PCI standard. Although the PCI function is self-configuring, many of its settings can be viewed and altered through the CMOS Setup utility. Figure 3-14 depicts the PCI PnP configuration information from a typical BIOS.

```
                    ROM PCI/ISA BIOS (P155TVP4)
                         PNP AND PCI SETUP
                       AWARD SOFTWARE, INC.

Slot  1  (Right) IRQ    : Auto          DMA  1  Used By ISA      : No/ICU
Slot  2  IRQ            : Auto          DMA  3  Used By ISA      : No/ICU
Slot  3  IRQ            : Auto          DMA  5  Used By ISA      : No/ICU
Slot  4  IRQ            : Auto
PCI  Latency Timer      : 32 PCI Clock  ISA MEM Block BASE       : No/ICU

                                        NCR SCSI BIOS            : Auto
IRQ  3   Used By ISA  : No/ICU          USB Function             : Disabled
IRQ  4   Used By ISA  : No/ICU
IRQ  5   Used By ISA  : No/ICU
IRQ  6   Used By ISA  : No/ICU
IRQ  7   Used By ISA  : No/ICU
IRQ  8   Used By ISA  : No/ICU
IRQ  9   Used By ISA  : No/ICU
IRQ 10 Used By ISA  : No/ICU
IRQ 11 Used By ISA  : No/ICU
IRQ 12 Used By ISA  : No/ICU
IRQ 13 Used By ISA  : No/ICU          ESC  : Quit         ↑↓←→        : Select Item
IRQ 14 Used By ISA  : No/ICU          F1   : Help         PU/PD/+/-   : Modify
IRQ 15 Used By ISA  : No/ICU          F5   : Old Values   (Shift) F2  : Color
                                      F6   : Load BIOS Defaults
                                      F7   : Load Setup Defaults
```

**Figure 3-14:
PCI Configuration
Settings**

detection phase

handle

PnP registry

resource conflicts

During a portion of the bootup known as the **detection phase**, the PnP-compatible BIOS checks the system for devices installed in the expansion slots to see what types they are, how they are configured, and which slots they are in. For PnP-compatible I/O cards, this information is held in a ROM device on the adapter card.

The BIOS reads the information from all of the cards and then assigns each adapter a **handle** (logical name) in the **PnP registry**. It then stores the configuration information for the various adapters in the registry as well. This process is shown in Figure 3-15. Next, the BIOS examines the adapter information against the system's basic configuration for **resource conflicts**. After evaluating the requirements of the cards and the system's resources, the PnP routine assigns system resources to the cards as required.

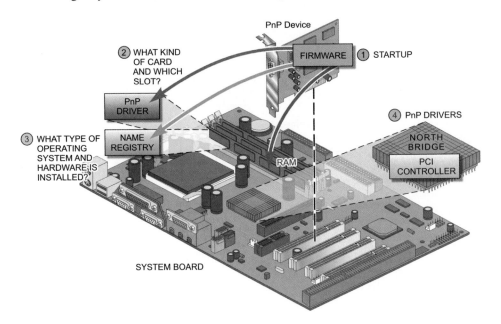

Figure 3-15: PCI Information Acquisition

Because the PnP process has no method for reconfiguring legacy devices during the resource assignment phase, it begins by assigning resources, such as IRQ assignments, to legacy devices before servicing the system's PnP devices.

┌─ **TEST TIP** ─────────────┐
Know which system resources the PnP system must assign first and why.
└──────────────────────────┘

Likewise, if the BIOS detects the presence of a new device during the detection phase, it disables the resource settings for its existing cards, checks to see what resources are required and available, and then reallocates the system's resources as necessary.

┌─ **TEST TIP** ─────────────┐
Know the process the PnP system employs to allocate resources to a new device in an existing system.
└──────────────────────────┘

Depending on the CMOS settings available with a particular PCI chipset, the startup procedure may be set up to configure and activate all of the PnP devices at startup. With other chipsets, it may also be possible to check all cards, but only enable those actually needed for startup. Some CMOS routines may contain several user-definable PCI configuration settings. Typically, these settings should be left in default positions. The rare occasion for changing a PCI setting occurs when directed to do so by a product's installation guide.

PC systems may theoretically contain an unlimited number of PCI slots. However, a maximum of four PCI slots are normally included on a system board due to signal loading considerations. The PCI bus includes four internal interrupt lines (INTa through INTd, or INT1 through INT4) that allow each PCI slot to activate up to four different interrupts. PCI interrupts should not be confused with the system's IRQ channels, although they can be associated with them if required by a particular device. In these cases, IRQ9 and IRQ10 are typically used.

PCI-X

PCI bus versions after PCI 2.3 were given a designation of PCI-X (along with a description of their operating speeds, e.g., PCI-X 66). These PCI-X specifications are enhanced versions of the 64-bit 66 MHz PCI 2.3 bus specification.

- PCI-X 1.0 was based on the previous PCI 2.3 architecture and offers support for 3.3 V and universal PCI cards. Therefore, conventional 33/66 MHz PCI cards can be used in PCI-X 1.0 slots. Conversely, PCI-X 1.0 cards could be used in standard PCI slots. PCI-X 1.0 provides 66 and 133 MHz bus speed options.

- PCI-X 2.0 was derived from PCI-X 1.0 and introduced an error correction code (ECC) feature to improve data transfer reliability. It also introduced two new speed options—PCI-X 266 MHz (that provides 2.13 GB/sec transfer rates) and PCI-X 533 MHz (with 4.26 GB/sec transfer rates).

All the PCI-X versions are backward compatible with the original PCI specifications (e.g., they employ the same form factors, pin-outs, connector, 32/64-bit bus widths, and protocols as the original PCI specification. However, the slowest board installed in one of the PCI-X slots determines the operating speed for all the PCI devices. While these versions offered some improvements over previous PCI versions, they have never been widely used in desktop PCs or network workstations. Instead, boards with these slots have typically been used in more powerful network server computers.

PCI Express

Originally, there was a PCI-X 1066 expansion slot version envisioned. However, as signal speed increases in parallel bus connections, it becomes much more difficult to reliably transmit and receive data. The electrical quantities associated with insulated, parallel conductors eventually outweigh the advantages of sending multiple bits of data at the same time. When this point is reached in any type of communications setting, the answer is always to implement some type of serial (one bit at a time using one communication path) method of moving the information from point A to point B. In the following chapters of this book, you will see that most of the functions that have historically been performed using parallel communications paths are now conducted using serial communications techniques. These techniques are discussed in much greater depth in Chapter 4, *Standard I/O Systems*.

In a forward looking move to prepare their expansion slot specification for future viability, the PCI-CIG organization that oversees the PCI specification shifted to a serial PCI expansion scheme that they titled **PCI express (PCIe)**. The Pentium/PCIe chipset employs the same software driver support as traditional PCI interfaces. However, under PCIe, the data moving back and forth across the bus are formed into serialized packets before being sent and then converted back to parallel format after the data have been received.

PCI express (PCIe)

The basic PCIe architecture employs two *low-voltage differential signal* (*LVDS*) pairs of data lines that carry data back and forth at rates up to 5.5 GBps in each direction. Each two-pair communication path is referred to as a **lane** and is capable of transmitting one byte at a time in both directions at once. This full-duplex communication is possible, because each lane is made up of one send and one receive path.

lane

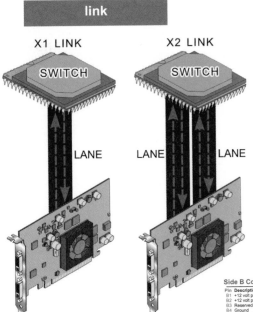

link

X1 LINK   X2 LINK

SWITCH   SWITCH

LANE   LANE   LANE

Figure 3-16: PCIe Lanes and Links

Under the PCIe specification, multiple lanes can be added together to provide additional bandwidth between the PCIe host and the PCIe device. Each complete connection between a host and a device (or slot) is referred to as a **link**. Figure 3-16 illustrates the relationship between PCIe lanes and Links.

Currently, PCIe supports x1, x2, x4, x8, x12, x16, and x32 lane links. However, available PCIe chipsets provide only for 20 lanes—16 are typically used for the x16 PCIe graphics slot, as illustrated in Figure 3-11. To date, this slot is the most successful implementation of the PCIe standard. The other four lanes can be distributed between any combination of x1, x2, or x4 slots.

PCIe employs four different slot connector sizes. The 1x slot contains 36 contact positions. The x4 slot is physically larger and has 64 pins, the x8 version uses 98 pins, and the x16 has 164 pins. Figure 3-17 shows the different PCIe expansion slots and their pin assignments.

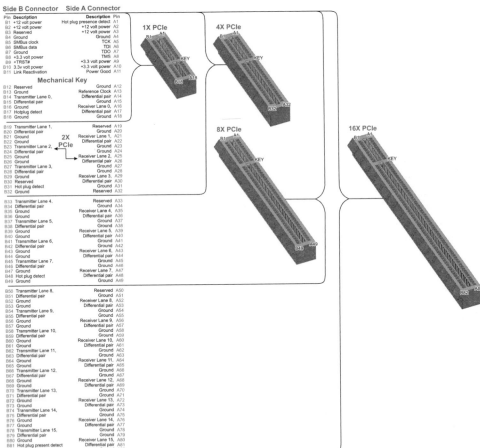

Figure 3-17: PCIe Slots

The number and arrangement of PCIe slots on system boards are largely up to the discretion of the system board manufacturer. The BTX form factor specification calls for one x16 slot and two x1 slots for its system boards. The x16 slot replaces the traditional AGP slot (covered in the next section of this chapter) for the graphic display adapter. Some system boards include two x16 slots, while others offer a mixture of x8, x4, and x1 slots. These system boards may also include some number of traditional PCI slots.

It is permissible to plug PCIe adapter cards with fewer lanes into larger slots (i.e., a x8 card into a x16 slot). The card's edge connector will not fill the slot, but the electrical contact connections should line up properly, and the card should function correctly. The PCIe host adapter (known as a **PCIe switch**) portion of the chipset will automatically assess the card in the slot during startup and assign the required number of lanes to the slot. The unused lanes are then available for use in other PCIe slots.

System boards designs may include both traditional PCI and PCIe slots. A **PCI-to-PCIe bridge** translates PCIe information into standard PCI signals. This bridging enables standard PCI devices to be included in the PCIe system. The bridging circuitry is starting to be included in PCIe chipsets. On these boards, the PCI bridge is part of the south bridge device. In other cases, the bridge is included in the adapter card.

PCIe Configuration

During the PnP process, the PCIe switch portion of the chipset negotiates with any PCIe devices to establish the maximum number of lanes available for the link. The outcome of the negotiation depends on three factors:

- The number of physical lanes the link can support

- The number of lanes the device requires

- The number of lanes the PCIe switch can support

If the device, such as an advanced PCIe video card, contains 16 lanes, it will need to be inserted into an x16 slot. However, if the device only has 8 lanes, the PCIe switch will detect this and only allocate the 8 lanes required. If the link supports more than 16 lanes, the extra lanes will be ignored. On the other hand, if the device has more lanes than the link can furnish, then the device and the switch throttle back to the number of lanes available. The one situation where this would not be the case is where the physical edge connector does not match the physical connector.

AGP Slots

Newer Pentium systems include an advanced **accelerated graphics port** (AGP) interface for video graphics. The AGP interface is a variation of the PCI bus design that has been modified to handle the intense data throughput associated with three-dimensional graphics.

The AGP specification was introduced by Intel to provide a 32-bit video channel that runs at 66 MHz in basic 1X video mode. The standard also supports three high-speed modes that include a 2X (5.33 MBps), a 4X (1.07 GBps), and an 8X (2.1 GBps) mode.

┌─ **TEST TIP** ─────────────┐
Know what type of device is plugged into an AGP slot.
└──────────────────────────┘

The AGP standard provides for a direct channel between the AGP graphic controller and the system's main memory, instead of using the expansion buses for video data. This removes the video data traffic from the PCI buses. The speed provided by this direct link permits video data to be stored in system RAM instead of in special video memory. System boards designed for portable systems and single-board systems may incorporate the AGP function directly into the board without using a slot connector.

As illustrated in Figure 3-18, there have been three different types of slot connectors used to deliver the AGP function for system boards used in desktop and tower units. The system board typically features a single slot that is supported by a Pentium/AGP-compliant chipset. The original slot configuration had a key located toward the rear of the board. These slots were used with 3.3 V (2X) adapters. The second AGP slot version moved the key toward the front of the board so that it was not physically compatible with the older AGP adapters. These slots were used with 1.5 V (4X) adapters. The final revision of the AGP slot is the universal AGP slot that removes all keys so that it can accept any type of AGP card (including universal adapters). These slots can be used with 3.3 V, 1.5 V, and 0.8 V (2X/4X/8X) adapters.

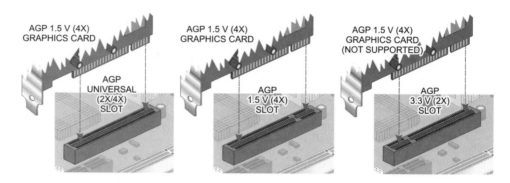

Figure 3-18: AGP Slots

The 8X specification employs a lower supply voltage (0.8) than the 2X and 4 X specifications. When upgrading an AGP card or system board containing an AGP slot, you should always consult the system board and AGP adapter card's documentation to verify their compatibility with each other. Usually the Chipset Features page of the CMOS Setup utility provides user-configurable AGP slot parameters that can be used to manually configure the adapter's parameters.

The default setting for this option is *Autodetect*. In this mode, the PnP process will detect the card and assign the correct voltages and maximum speed settings for that type of card.

Audio Modem Risers

audio modem riser (AMR)

mobile daughter card (MDC)

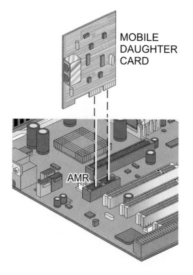

Figure 3-19: Audio Modem Riser Components

Intel has developed a new audio/modem standard for system board designs. This standard includes an expansion slot connection, called the **audio modem riser** (**AMR**), and a companion expansion card format, known as the **mobile daughter card** (**MDC**). These components are depicted in Figure 3-19.

The design specification separates the analog and digital functions of audio (sound card) and modem devices. The analog portion of the function is placed on the MDC riser card, while the digital functions are maintained on the system board. This permits the system board to be certified without passing through the extended FCC and international telecom certification process attached with modem certifications. Only the MDC needs to pass the FCC certification process.

The contents of the MDC basically consist of an analog audio **coder/decoder** (**codec**) or a modem circuit. The digital functions performed by the system board are a function of software instead of a hardware device such as a **universal asynchronous receiver transmitter** (**UART**). The system microprocessor basically performs the UART functions under the control of the audio or modem software. This relationship makes the AMR device much less expensive but places additional overhead on the operation of the microprocessor.

AMR slots are already being replaced in Pentium systems by a new design called the **communications and networking riser** (**CNR**) card, depicted in Figure 3-20. This specification improves on the AMR specification by including support for advanced V.90 analog modems, multichannel audio, telephone-based dial-up networking, and USB devices, as well as 10/100 Ethernet-based LAN adapters.

| coder/decoder (codec) |
| universal asynchronous receiver/transmitter (UART) |
| communications and networking riser (CNR) |

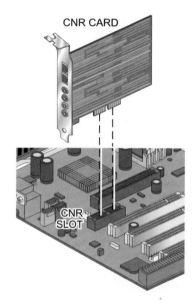

Figure 3-20: Communications and Networking Riser Card

Table 3-1 compares the capabilities of the various bus types commonly found in personal computers. It is quite apparent that the data transfer rates possible with each new version increase dramatically. The reason this is significant is that the expansion bus is a speed-limiting factor for many of the system's operations. Every peripheral access made through the expansion slots requires the entire computer to slow down to the operating speed of the bus.

Table 3-1: Expansion Bus Specifications

BUS TYPE	TRANSFER RATE	DATA BITS	ADDRESS BITS	DMA CHANNELS	INT CHANNELS
ISA	8 MBps	16	24	8	11
PCI 2	132/264 MBps	32/64	32	None	3
PCI 2.1	264/528 MBps	32/64	32	None	3
PCI-X 1.0	1.06 GBps	64	64	None	3
PCI-X 2.0	2.13/4.26 GBps	64	64	None	3
PCIe	250 MBps per lane	Serial	None	None	None
AGP	266/533/1,070 MBps	32	32	None	3

On-Board Disk Drive Connections

Pentium system boards provide the system's hard-disk/CD-ROM/DVD drive and floppy-disk drive controller functions and interface connections. There are currently three common disk drive connection interfaces provided on system boards—**parallel advanced technology attachment (PATA)** and **serial AT attachment (SATA)** connectors for **integrated drive electronics (IDE)** drives, and (possibly) a **floppy-disk drive controller (FDC)** interface connection.

PATA and SATA interfaces are designed to serve a particular type of drive that places the bulk of the drive controller circuitry on the disk unit instead of on an adapter card. These drives are referred to as IDE drives. The IDE designation was originally used to refer to all ATA devices until the advent of the serial ATA interface. At this point, discussions of IDE drives and their interfaces had to be segmented into terms of parallel and serial ATA drives. Figure 3-21 provides an example of a system board that supplies the system's PATA and SATA host adapter connections, along with the FDC interface connection.

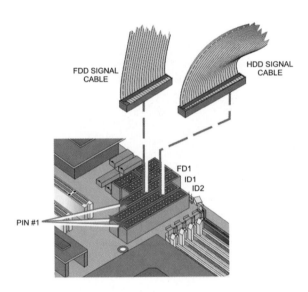

Figure 3-21: System Board Disk Drive Connections

The FDC portion of the chipset can control two floppy-disk drives with signal cable that connects to the system board at the 34-pin BERG connector (labeled FD1 in Figure 3-21). As with any disk drive connection, caution must be taken when connecting the floppy-disk drive signal cable to the system board; pin 1 of the connector must line up with the signal cable's indicator stripe.

PATA Connections

The parallel IDE host adapter portion of the chipset furnishes two complete IDE channels—IDE1 and IDE2—that can handle one master and one slave device each. The IDE hard drives and CD-ROM drives are attached to the system board via ribbon cables that connect to two 40-pin BERG connectors labeled ID1 and ID2. There are several versions of the PATA/IDE interface. Fortunately most of these versions are only concerned with the software and drivers that control the flow of information through the interface.

System boards that used the original PATA/IDE specification provided one 40-pin connector on the board and offered a single IDE channel that could control two IDE devices (one master and one slave). Eventually, system boards that support the **enhanced IDE (EIDE)** standards for communications and feature two physical IDE connectors were introduced to the market. Each EIDE channel is capable of handling its own master and slave devices. Over time, the EIDE interface has been redefined to provide faster transfer rates, as well as to handle larger storage capacities. EIDE interfaces can also be used to control drive units such as a tape or CD-ROM. The EIDE interface is often described as an **ATAPI (AT attachment packet interface)**, or a **fast ATA (fast AT attachment)** interface.

The original PATA/IDE interface employed 40-wire cables between the system board interfaces and the drive units. Of these 40 wires, only 7 were ground wires. As transfer speeds across the PATA cabling increased, the large separation between each signal line and its respective return ground line resulted in decreased reliability over this cable. For transfer rates greater than 33 MHz, the original 40-wire cable was replaced by an 80-wire version that alternates ground and signal lines. This arrangement reduces interference between signal lines, which greatly increased the reliability of each line at higher frequencies. These cables have a maximum length specification of 18 inches.

You should be aware that the 80-pin cables still use the 40-pin IDE connector at each end to remain compatible with standard PATA connections. They are color coded to prevent them from being confused with older 40-wire cables, which are typically gray in color. However, when newer EIDE devices are connected to the system using an older 40-conductor cable, they will default to operating speeds compatible with the older IDE standards.

When attaching either type of PATA signal cable to the system board or an IDE device, you must properly align pin #1 of the cable with pin #1 of the connector on the board and device. In many cases, the connector is keyed so that it cannot be plugged in backward. However, like the floppy-disk drive cable mentioned earlier, the colored alignment stripe along one side of the cable indicates the position on pin #1 in the cable. This pin should be aligned with pin #1 on the device and the system board connector. Figure 3-22 provides an example of the proper alignment of the PATA and FDD cables with their system board interface connectors.

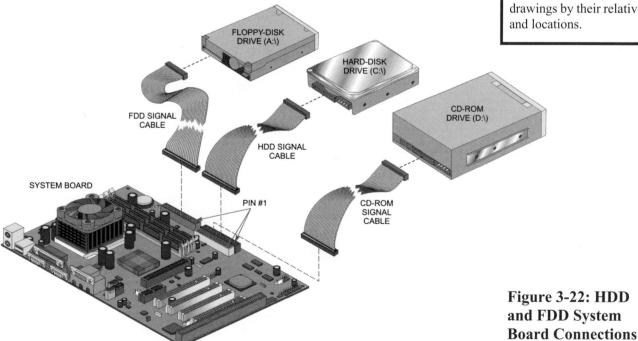

Figure 3-22: HDD and FDD System Board Connections

After the EIDE hardware has been installed, its operating mode must be configured correctly through the system's CMOS Setup utility. Newer system boards possess an autodetect feature in the BIOS that communicates with the hard drives and automatically configures them for optimum use with the system. The CMOS Setup utility can be used to manually configure IDE channel parameters. Both IDE channels can be Enabled, Disabled, or placed in Autodetect mode through CMOS settings. These settings are discussed under the "*Chipset Features Screen*" heading later in this chapter.

Serial ATA Connections

As with all other parallel I/O schemes, the ATA specification eventually ran into performance limitations associated with parallel transmissions. The negative electrical properties associated with having multiple conductors running side by side eventually overcomes the advantage of sending multiple bits of information at the same time. The two factors that adversely affect parallel cabling are signal speed and distance. As either of these quantities increase, the performance of the connection decreases.

The SATA interface specification was designed to replace the PATA interface and overcome its electrical restraints. Although it replaces the physical interface connection and cabling structures, the SATA specification remains compatible with the supporting ATA software embedded in existing operating systems.

Figure 3-23 depicts the flat 7-pin SATA signal cable connector and its configuration. Four of the wires are used to form two differential signal pairs (A+/A- and B+/B-), while the other three wires are used for shielded grounds. The cable is only 0.5 inches wide. This feature makes cable routing inside the system unit simpler and provides less resistance to airflow through the case. The maximum length for an internal SATA cable is specified as 36 inches (1 meter).

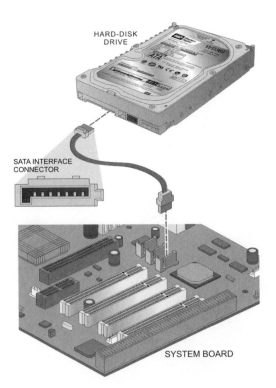

**Figure 3-23:
The Serial ATA
Interface Connector**

Unlike its PATA counterpart, the SATA interface has made provisions for connections outside the system unit case. This type of connection is referred to as the **external SATA** or **eSATA** interface. Figure 3-24 illustrates the implementation of a single-lane external SATA interface. An interface consists of a SATA cable that links the SATA interface on the system board to a eSATA connector on an expansion slot cover mounted in the rear of the system unit. A shielded eSATA cable is used to connect the drive unit to the slot-mounted interface. The maximum cable length for the external eSATA cable is 6 feet (2 meters).

external SATA

eSATA

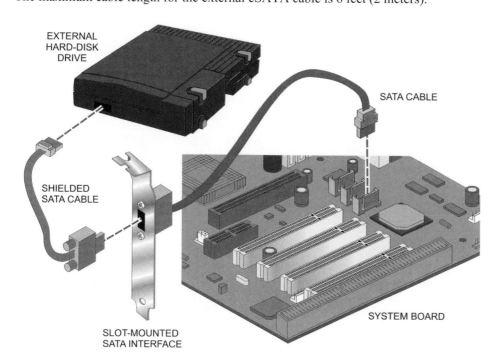

Figure 3-24: eSATA Interface Connections

EXTERNAL HARD-DISK DRIVE

SATA CABLE

SHIELDED SATA CABLE

SLOT-MOUNTED SATA INTERFACE

SYSTEM BOARD

SCSI Connections

There are no industry-accepted equivalents for on-board SCSI adapters. Although a few such system board designs are available, they are not standard boards and have probably been created to fill the specific needs of a particular application. Therefore, SCSI devices require that a SCSI host adapter card be installed in most systems.

The built-in SCSI connector on the system board will normally be made through a 50-pin BERG header. Like the IDE drives, support for the on-board SCSI controller must be established through the CMOS Setup utility. The system BIOS provides support for the built-in SCSI controller through its CMOS Setup utility, whereas add-on adapter cards feature a BIOS extension on the card.

Your colleague has faxed you a drawing of an old, stripped system board he is planning to repopulate for use as a Linux mail server. He is not sure about which components he must obtain to make it work again. From the drawing, what can you tell him about what he will need to get the board up and running again?

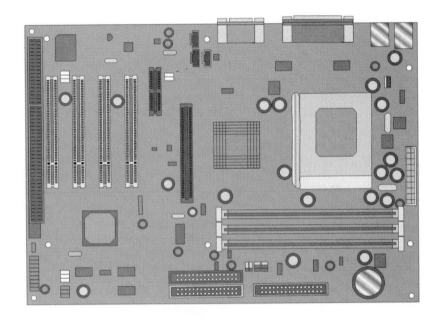

Essentials 1.1

MICROPROCESSORS

A portion of A+ Essentials objective 1.1 states that the test taker should be able to distinguish between popular CPU chips and technologies in terms of their basic characteristics. As mentioned in Chapter 2, there were originally several competitors in the PC-compatible microprocessor market. However, over time the market has really come down to two major players competing for market domination—Intel and American Micro Devices (AMD). Intel has set the standard for processor performance throughout most of the personal computer era. However, AMD has shown itself a worthy opponent, frequently taking the market lead with speed increases and new innovations.

Pentium

For the most part, the previous generations of microprocessors have disappeared from the marketplace, leaving the **Pentium** and its clones as the only processor types that need to be discussed in detail. The following sections will look at the advancements Intel has produced and then focus on the AMD processors that compete with them.

Intel Processors

When Intel introduced the Pentium processor, it discontinued the 80X86 naming convention it had previously used for its microprocessors. This allowed Intel to copyright the name (numbers cannot be copyrighted) and prevent clone microprocessor manufacturers from using the same convention. Therefore, the 80586 became the *Pentium*.

The Pentium is a 32/64-bit microprocessor contained in a ceramic pin grid array package. The internal architecture of the Pentium is shown in Figure 3-25. The registers for the microprocessor and floating-point sections of the Pentium are identical to those of the 80486. It has a 64-bit data bus that allows it to handle **Quad Word** (or **Qword**) data transfers. The Pentium also contains two separate 8 kB caches, compared to only one in the 80486. One of the caches is used for instructions or code, and the other is used for data. The internal architecture of the Pentium resembles an 80486 in expanded form. The floating-point section operates up to five times faster than that of the FPU in the 80486.

Quad Word

Qword

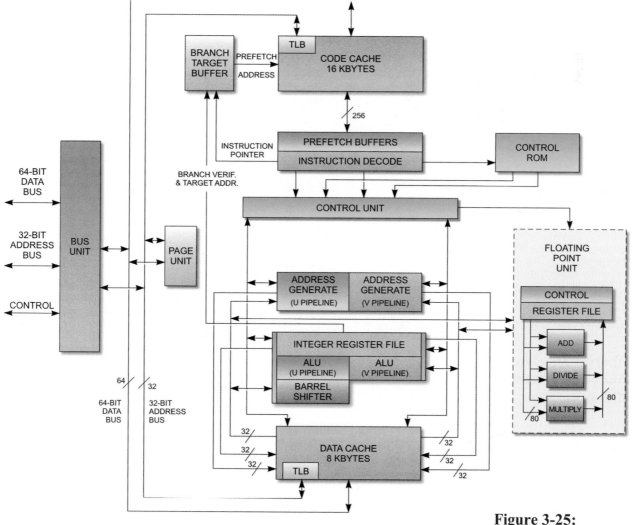

**Figure 3-25:
Inside the Pentium
Microprocessor**

The Pentium is referred to as a **superscalar** microprocessor because its architecture allows multiple instructions to be executed simultaneously. This is achieved through a **pipelining** process. Pipelining is a technique that uses multiple **stages** to speed up instruction execution. Each stage in the pipeline performs a part of the overall instruction execution, with all operations being completed at one stage before moving on to another stage. This technique allows streamlined circuitry to perform a specific function at each stage of the pipeline, thereby improving execution time. When an instruction moves from one stage to the next, a new instruction moves into the vacated stage. The Pentium contains two separate pipelines that can operate simultaneously. The first is called the **U-pipe** and the second the **V-pipe**.

The original Pentium processor architecture has appeared in three generations. The first-generation design, code-named the P5, came in a 273-pin PGA package and operated at 60 or 66 MHz speeds. It used a single +5 Vdc operating voltage, which caused it to consume a large amount of power and generate a large amount of heat. The Pentium processor generated so much heat during normal operation that an additional **CPU cooling fan** was usually required. A pin-out for the first-generation Pentium is shown in Figure 3-26.

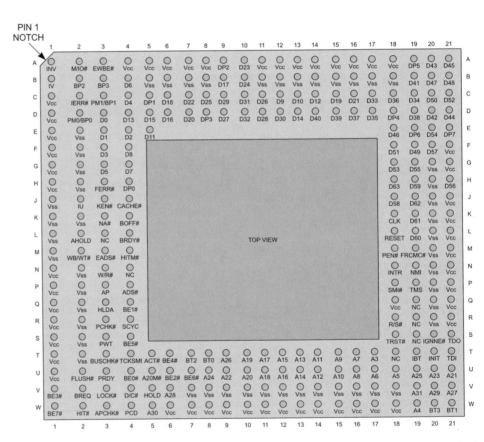

Figure 3-26: The Pins of the Pentium Microprocessor

The second-generation Pentiums, referred to as **P54Cs**, came in a 296-pin **staggered pin grid array (SPGA)** package and operated at 75, 90, 100, 120, 133, 150, and 166 MHz in different versions. For these devices, Intel reduced the power supply voltage level for the core of the processor to +3.3 Vdc to consume less power and provide faster operating speeds. The SPGA packaging made the second generation of Pentium devices incompatible with the first-generation system boards. The external interfaces of the processor continue to operate at +5 Vdc to be compatible with other system board components.

The second-generation devices also employed internal clock multipliers that could be used to increase performance. In this scenario, the system's buses run at the same speed as the clock signal introduced to the microprocessor. However, the internal clock multiplier causes the microprocessor to operate internally at some multiple of the external clock speed (i.e., a Pentium operating from a 50 MHz external clock and a 2x internal multiplier is actually running at 100 MHz inside).

Processor Power Supply Levels

Beginning with the second-generation Pentium, Intel adopted dual-voltage supply levels for the overall IC and for its processor core. This was done for two reasons—to make the processor's switching time faster so that it can be clocked faster and to reduce the processor's power consumption/dissipation (in the form of heat).

The transistors that make up the microprocessor (and every other digital device) have maximum turn on and turn off rates. When the system clock nears this point, there can be no further performance increase without a change that allows the transistor to be clocked faster. The answer was to move the core's high and low logic voltage levels (that represent 1 and 0) closer to each other (0 and 1.7 vs. 0 and 5) so that it requires less time to switch back and forth between them. At the maximum change rate of the transistors, it doesn't take as long to get from 0 to 1.7 V as it does to get from 0 to 5.0 V. Therefore, you can turn the devices on and off more often with a smaller voltage separation.

The second reason for using the lower voltage level in the processor core is also electrical—transistors dissipate power in the form of *heat*. In electronic devices, power dissipation is directly proportional to both voltage and current. Therefore, if the current or the voltage associated with an electronic component like a transistor is lowered, so is the level of power that will be generated. Although the power associated with a single microprocessor is very small, when you multiply that value by millions of transistors, you get a very large number.

Common Intel voltage supplies are +5/+5 for older units and +3.3/+3.3, +3.3/+2.8, +3.3/+1.8, and +3.3/1.45 for newer units. Clone processors may use compatible voltages (especially if they are pin compatible), or they may use completely different voltage levels. Common voltages for clone microprocessors include +5, +3.3, +2.5, and +2.2. The additional voltage levels are typically generated through special regulator circuits on the system board. In each case, the system board's user guide should be consulted any time the microprocessor is being replaced or upgraded.

From the second-generation Pentiums forward, system boards have employed **voltage regulator modules (VRMs)** to supply special voltage levels associated with different types of microprocessors that might be installed. The VRM module may be designed as a plug-in module so that it can be replaced easily in case of component failure. This is a somewhat common occurrence with voltage regulator devices. It also enables the system board to be upgraded when a new Pentium device is developed that requires a different voltage level, or a different voltage pairing.

voltage regulator
modules (VRMs)

Some multiprocessor system boards have spaces for two or more VRM modules to be installed. The additional modules must be installed in VRM sockets, as illustrated in Figure 3-27, to support additional processors. VRMs can also be a source of server board failures. You should always check the processor voltages on a malfunctioning system board to verify that they are being supplied correctly. While VRMs rarely fail, you must be aware of them and know how they can affect the system's operation.

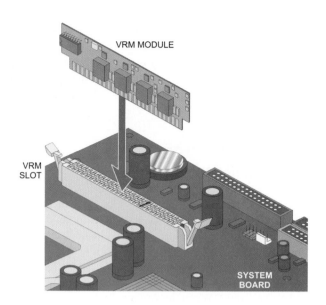

**Figure 3-27:
VRM Sockets**

Advanced Pentium Architectures

Intel has continued to advance its Pentium line of microprocessors by introducing additional specifications including the Pentium MMX, Pentium Pro, Pentium II, Pentium III, XEON, Pentium 4, Pentium D, Pentium EE, and Itanium processors. At the same time, Intel's competitors have developed clone designs that equal or surpass the capabilities of the Intel versions.

Pentium MMX

P55Cs

The third-generation Pentiums, referred to as the **P55Cs**, employed a 296-pin SPGA arrangement that adhered to the 321-pin Socket-7 specification designed by Intel. The P55C has been produced in versions that operate at 150, 166, 180, 200, and 233 MHz. This generation of Pentium devices operates at voltages below the +3.3 level established in the second generation of devices.

**Pentium MMX
(Multimedia
Extension)**

The P55C is known as the **Pentium MMX (Multimedia Extension)** processor. In this processor, the multimedia and communications processing capabilities of the original Pentium device were extended by the addition of 57 multimedia-specific instructions to the instruction set.

Intel also increased the on-board L1 cache size to 32 kB in the MMX processor. The cache was divided into two separate 16 kB caches: one was the instruction cache, while the other was designated as the data cache. L2 cache sizes used with the MMX were 256 kB and 512 kB.

The MMX added an additional multimedia-specific stage to the integer pipeline. This integrated stage handled MMX and integer instructions quickly. Improved branching prediction circuitry was also implemented to offer higher prediction accuracy and, thereby, provide higher processing speeds. The four Prefetch buffers in the MMX could hold up to four successive streams of code. The four write buffers were shared between the two pipelines to improve the memory write performance of the MMX.

The Pentium MMX processor was produced in 166, 200, and 233 MHz versions and required two separate operating voltages. One source was used to drive the Pentium processor core, while the other was used to power the processor's I/O pins. The pin-out of the Pentium MMX is shown in Figure 3-28.

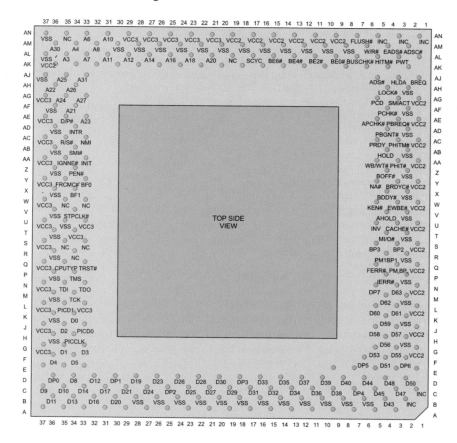

**Figure 3-28:
The Pins of the
Pentium MMX
Microprocessor**

Compare Figures 3-26 and 3-28. Notice the staggered pin arrangement of the MMX device compared to the uniform row and column arrangement of the original Pentium devices. Also, notice the new signals added to the Pentium architecture for later versions. Some of these additional signals were used to implement the VRM and internal clock multiplier functions for the advanced Pentiums.

Pentium Pro

Intel departed from simply increasing the speed of its Pentium processor line by introducing the **Pentium Pro** processor. While compatible with all of the previous software written for the Intel processor line, the Pentium Pro is optimized to run 32-bit software.

Pentium Pro

However, it did not remain pin-compatible with the previous Pentium processors. Instead, Intel adopted a 2.46" × 2.66", 387-pin PGA configuration to house a Pentium Pro **processor core**, and an on-board 256 kB (or 512 kB) L2 cache. The L2 cache complements the 16 kB L1 cache in the Pentium core. This arrangement is illustrated in Figure 3-29. Notice that while they are on the same PGA device, the two components are not integrated into the same IC. The unit is covered by a gold-plated, copper/tungsten heat spreader.

processor core

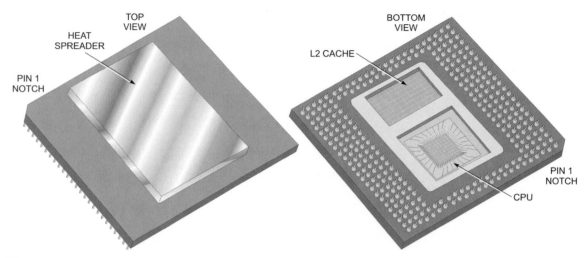

**Figure 3-29:
The Pentium Pro
Microprocessor**

The L2 on-board cache stores the most frequently used data not found in the processor's internal L1 cache, as close to the processor core as it can be without being integrated directly into the IC. A high-bandwidth cache bus (referred to as the backside bus) connects the processor and cache unit together. The bus (0.5 inches in length) allows the processor and external cache to communicate at a rate of 1.2 GB/second.

The Pentium Pro is designed in a manner so that it can be used in typical, single-microprocessor applications or in multiple-processor environments, such as high-speed, high-volume file servers and workstations. Several dual-processor system boards have been designed for twin Pentium Pro processors. These boards, like the one shown in Figure 3-30, are created with two Pentium Pro sockets so that they can operate with either a single processor or with dual processors. When dual processors are installed, logic circuitry in the Pentium Pro's core manages the requests for access to the system's memory and 64-bit buses.

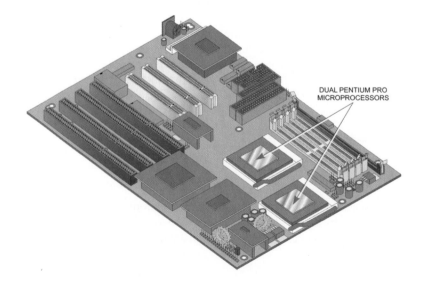

**Figure 3-30:
A Dual-Processor
System Board**

Pentium II

Intel radically changed the form factor of the Pentium processors by housing the **Pentium II** processor in a new, **single edge contact (SEC) cartridge**, depicted in Figure 3-31. This cartridge uses a special **retention mechanism** built into the system board to hold the device in place. The new proprietary socket design is referred to as the **Slot 1** specification and is designed to allow the microprocessor to eventually operate at bus speeds in excess of 300 MHz. This is the upper operating frequency limit for pin grid sockets.

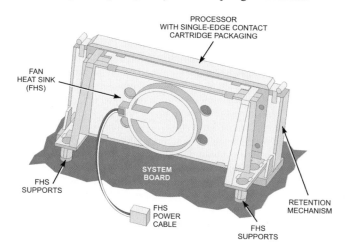

**Figure 3-31:
The Pentium II
Cartridge**

The cartridge also requires a special **fan heat sink (FHS)** module and fan. Like the SEC cartridge, the FHS module requires special support mechanisms to hold it in place. The fan draws power from a special power connector on the system board, or from one of the system's optional power connectors.

Inside the cartridge, there is a substrate material on which the processor and related components are mounted. The components consist of the Pentium II processor core, a **Tag RAM**, and an **L2 Burst SRAM**. Tag RAM is used to track the attributes (read, modified, etc.) of data stored in the cache memory.

The Pentium II includes all of the multimedia enhancements from the MMX processor, as well as retain the power of the Pentium Pro's dynamic execution and 512 kB L2 cache features. The L1 cache is increased to 32 kB, while the L2 cache operates with a half-speed bus.

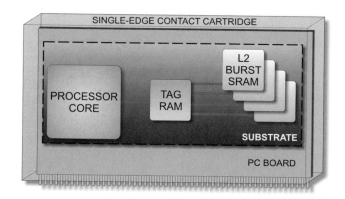

**Figure 3-32:
Inside the Pentium
II Cartridge**

Figure 3-32 depicts the contents of the Pentium II cartridge.

A second cartridge type, called the single edged processor package (SEPP), has been developed for use with the Slot 1 design. In this design, the boxed processor is not completely covered by the plastic housing as it is in the SEC design. Instead, the SEPP circuit board is accessible from the back side.

You can upload processor update information into the BIOS that has **application programming interface (API)** capabilities built into it to modify the operation of Pentium Pro and Pentium II/III/4 processors. The microprocessor manufacturer places updated information on its Web site that can be downloaded by customers. The user transfers the update information from the update media to the system's BIOS via the API routine. If the updated data are relevant (as indicated by checking its processor stepping code), the API writes the updated microcode into the BIOS. This information will, in turn, be loaded into the processor each time the system is booted.

Pentium III

Intel followed the Pentium II processor with a new Slot 1-compatible design it called the **Pentium III**. The original Pentium III processor (code-named Katmai) was designed around the Pentium II core but increased the L2 cache size to 512 kB. It also increased the speed of the processor to 600 MHz including a 100 MHz front side bus speed.

> **— NOTE ————————————————**
>
> In addition to the 80×86 numbering system, Intel used a Px identification up to the Pentium II. The Pentium II is identified as the Klamath processor. Subsequent microprocessor versions have been dubbed Deschutes, Covington, Mendocino, Katmai, Willamette, Northwood, Flagstaff (P7), Merced, and Tahoe.

Intel followed the Pentium III design with a less expensive version that it named the Pentium **Celeron**. Unlike the original Pentium III, the Celeron version featured a 66 MHz bus speed and only 128 kB of L2 cache. Initially, the **Celeron Mendocino** was packaged in the SEC cartridge.

> **— TEST TIP ————————**
>
> Be able to state the difference between Pentium II and Pentium III processors.

Later versions of the Pentium III and Celeron processors were developed for the Intel **Socket 370** specification. This design returned to a 370-pin, ZIF socket/SPGA package arrangement, depicted in Figure 3-33.

The first pin grid array versions of the Pentium III and Celeron processors conformed to a standard called the **plastic pin grid array (PPGA)** 370 specification. Intel repackaged its processors into a PGA package to fit this specification. The PPGA design was introduced to produce inexpensive, moderate-performance Pentium systems. The design topped out at 533 MHz with a 66 MHz bus speed.

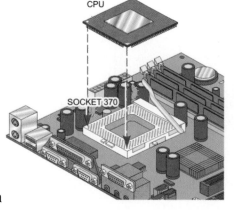

**Figure 3-33:
Socket 370/Celeron**

Intel upgraded the Socket 370 specification by introducing a variation called the **flip chip pin grid array (FC-PGA)** 370 design. Intel made small modifications to the wiring of the socket to accommodate the Pentium III processor design. In addition, they employed a new 0.18 micron IC manufacturing technology to produce faster processor speeds (up to 1.12 GHz) and front-side bus speeds (100 MHz and 133 MHz). However, the new design provides only 256 kB of L2 cache.

flip chip pin grid
array (FC-PGA)

Pentium III and Celeron processors designed with the 0.18 micron technology are referred to as **Coppermine** and **Coppermine 128** processors, respectively (the L2 cache in the Coppermine 128 is only 128 kB). Further developments of the Coppermine versions, referred to as *Tualatin*, employed 0.13 micron IC technology to achieve 1.4 GHz operating speeds with increased cache sizes (256 kB or 512 kB).

Coppermine

Coppermine 128

Xeon

Intel has produced three special versions of the Pentium III that they have collectively named the **Pentium Xeon**, as shown in Figure 3-34. These processors are designed to work with an edge-connector-based **Slot 2** specification that Intel has produced to extend their Slot 1/boxed-processor scheme to a 330-contact design. Each version features a different level of L2 cache (512 kB, 1 MB, 2 MB). The Xeon designs were produced to fill different, high-end server needs.

Pentium Xeon

Slot 2

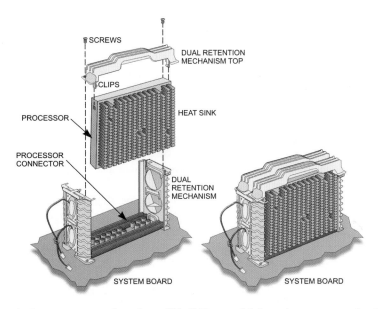

Figure 3-34: The Xeon Processor

The Xeon designs were produced to fill different, high-end server needs. The Xeon processor functions at speeds up to 866 MHz and is built upon the 0.18-micron process technology. The processor allows for highly scalable server solutions that support up to 32 processors. Benefits of the Xeon processor include

- Scalability—Start small and add more processors later

- Faster I/O—Incorporates a I2O architecture and faster PCI

- Better Manageability—IPMI management allows cluster to be managed as one

- Flexibility—Designed to industry-open physical and mechanical specifications

Pentium 4

Pentium 4

Late in 2000, Intel released a Pentium version called the Williamette 423, or **Pentium 4** microprocessor. However, the Pentium 4 was not a simple continuation of the Pentium design. It was actually a new design (IA-32 NetBurst architecture) based on 0.18-micron IC construction technology. It employed a modified Socket 370 PGA design that uses 423 pins and boasts operating speeds up to 2.0 GHz. The system's FSB bus was increased from 64 to 128 bits and operates at up to 400 MHz. The bus is actually clocked at 100 MHz, but data were transferred four times in a single clock cycle (referred to as a **quad-pumped bus**). Therefore, the bandwidth of the bus is considered to be 400 MHz.

quad-pumped bus

In addition to the new FSB size, the Pentium 4 features new WPNI (Williamette Processor New Instructions) in its instruction set. The L1 cache size has been reduced from 16 kB in the Pentium III to 8 kB for the Pentium 4. The L2 cache is 256 kB and can handle transfers on every clock cycle.

The operating voltage level for the Pentium 4 core is 1.7 Vdc. To dissipate the 55 watts of power (heat) that the microprocessor generates at 1.5 GHz, the case incorporates a metal cap that acts as a built-in heat sink. Firm contact must be maintained between the microprocessor's case and its built-in heat sink feature.

Newer .13-micron versions code-named *Northwood* operate at speeds up to 3.06 GHz. This newer Pentium 4 design employs an improved 478-pin version of the chip that increased the L2 cache size to 512 KB. This type of P4 processor has been produced in versions that run at 2.0, 2.2, 2.4, 2.8, and 3.06 GHz. The 2.4 GHz version increased the speed of the quad-pumped bus to 533 MHz (133 × 4). Some variations of the 2.4 to 3.06 processors were produced with support for 800 MHz FSB operations.

hyperthreading technology (HTT)

The evolution of the Pentium 4 processor topped out with the delivery of a 3.2 and 3.4 GHz version in 2004. The 3.06 MHz version of the P4 brought **hyperthreading technology** (**HTT**) to the Intel line of processors. Hyperthreading is an architecture that enables multiple program threads to be run in different sections of the processor simultaneously. Basically, the structure fools the operating system into thinking there are two processors available.

Pentium 4 Extreme Editions

The most advanced versions of the P4 processor are the **Pentium 4 Extreme Editions** (**P4EE**). In its ongoing battle with AMD for microprocessor supremacy, Intel added 2 MB of Level 3 (L3) cache to the Xeon core and called them P4EE. Later versions of these processors have been clocked at 3.73 GHz and are equipped with 1066 MHz front side buses. They are available in either Socket 603 or LGA 775 versions.

Itanium Processors

Itanium

explicitly parallel instruction computing (EPIC)

The Intel **Itanium** processor, depicted in Figure 3-35, provides a new architecture specifically for servers. It maximizes server performance through special processing techniques Intel refers to as **explicitly parallel instruction computing** (**EPIC**). The Itanium architecture provides the following performance enhancements using the EPIC technology:

- *Predication*—the ability to identify a certain condition inline, rather than rely on inefficient test and branch algorithms. It uses branch prediction to work more efficiently with "if-then-else" statements. This eliminates or minimizes the number of memory accesses required to execute an instruction.

- *Speculation*—a function that improves the performance of the Itanium processor by allowing the compiler to schedule and store load instructions ahead of branches to reduce memory latency.

- *Parallelism*—delivers higher performance and scalability by enabling the compiler to provide more information to the processor, allowing it to execute multiple operations simultaneously on a sustained basis.

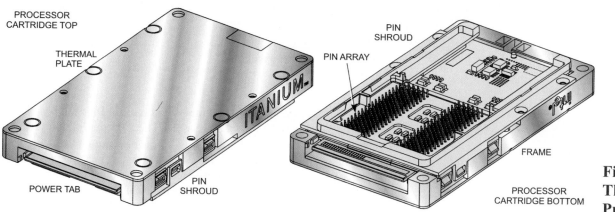

Figure 3-35: The Itanium Processor

The Itanium processor design features a new three-level, on-board cache system. The L1 cache size is 32 kB operating fully pipelined, while the L2 cache size is 96 kB, and the new **L3 cache** is available in two size—2 MB or 4 MB. The cartridge's edge connector specification provides separate voltage levels for the processor and cache devices to improve signal integrity.

L3 cache

Because Itanium processors are designed to be available 100 percent of the time, they tend to be very expensive—often more expensive than the complete network operating system that it is running. However, the cost of the processor is nothing compared to the cost of most online businesses going down for just 1 hour.

Intel Dual-Core Processors

Dual-core processors provide two execution cores in one physical processor package. The two cores are actually produced on the same piece of silicon (on the same *die*). This enables the system to divide processing tasks up between the two cores. Therefore, it can do twice as many things, such as editing video while downloading audio streams, in a given amount of time and appear to be running much faster. Figure 3-36 depicts a dual-core processor arrangement.

Dual-core processors

As is the case with the other major components we've discussed in this chapter, it becomes increasingly difficult to make digital devices run faster after a certain point. In the case of the microprocessor, creating serial communications paths has not been an option. However, fitting two processors into a single package theoretically doubles the computing power of the device without having to clock it twice as fast. Both major microprocessor manufacturers have launched dual processor products.

Figure 3-36: Dual-Core Processors

Pentium D

Pentium Extreme Edition (EE)

hyperthreading

Intel has launched two dual processor versions—the mainline **Pentium D** line of processors and the **Pentium Extreme Edition (EE)** line of processors. The Extreme Edition versions employ Intel's **hyperthreading** technology that enables a single processor core to simulate dual logical processors that can be used to work on different program segments simultaneously. Including the hyperthreading technology in a dual-core processor package enables it to process four different threads simultaneously (e.g., it functions like four different single-core processors). Table 3-2 lists the key characteristics of the Intel dual-core processors.

Table 3-2: Intel Dual-Core Processors

PROCESSOR	CLOCK FREQUENCY	L2-CACHE	FRONT SIDE BUS SPEED	CLOCK MULTIPLIER	CORE VOLTAGE	POWER DISSIPATION
Pentium D 805	2.667 GHz	2 × 1 MB	533 MT/s	20x	1.25/1.4 V	95 W
Pentium D 820	2.800 GHz	2 × 1 MB	800 MT/s	14x	1.2/1.4	95 W
Pentium D 830	3 GHz	2 × 1 MB	800 MT/s	15x	1.2/1.4	130 W
Pentium D 840	3.2 GHz	2 × 1 MB	800 MT/s	16x	1.2/1.4	130 W
Pentium D 920	2.8 GHz	2 × 2 MB	800 MT/s	14x	1.2/1.337 V	130 W
Pentium D 930	3 GHz	2 × 2 MB	800 MT/s	15x	1.2/1.337 V	130 W
Pentium D 940	3.2 GHz	2 × 2 MB	800 MT/s	16x	1.2/1.337 V	130 W
Pentium D 950	3.4 GHz	2 × 2 MB	800 MT/s	17x	1.2/1.337 V	130 W
Pentium D 960	3.6 GHz	2 × 2 MB	800 MT/s	18x	1.2/1.337 V	130 W
Pentium Extreme Edition 840	3.2 GHz	2 × 1 MB	800 MT/s	16x	1.2/1.4 V	130 W
Pentium Extreme Edition 955	3.466 GHz	2 × 2 MB	1066 MT/s	13x	1.2/1.337 V	130 W
Pentium Extreme Edition 965	3.733 GHz	2 × 2 MB	1066 MT/s	14x	1.2/1.337 V	130 W

As shown in Table 3-2, most of the dual-core Intel designs employ an 800 MHz FSB to communicate with the rest of the system. So far, the exceptions to this are the Pentium EE 955 and EE 965 processors that use a 1066 MHz FSB. The table specifies the front side bus speed in terms of *mega transfers per second* (MT/s). This is a realistic measurement of the bus' channel speed instead of its clock speed. For instance, if the bus transfers data on both the rising and falling edges of its clock signal, then a 400 MHz clock would effectively yield a 800 MT/s throughput rate.

In both designs, the two cores communicate with each other through a special bus interface block, or through the FSB. They can also access each others L2 caches through this interface. However, each core can use only half of the FSB bandwidth frequency when working under heavy load. The 8XX models include 1 MB of L2 cache for each core, while the 9XX models have enlarged the L2 cache to 2 MB for each core

The *Smithfield* core used in the first Pentium D models is basically made up of two *Prescott* Pentium 4 processor cores and includes 1 MB of Level 2 cache for each processor. This is all placed on a 206 mm chip, which makes the Pentium D core roughly twice the physical size of the Prescott processor. Newer Pentium D 920, 930, 940, and 950 processors are based on the *Presler* core, which is a derivation of pairing two *Cedar Mill* cores. This core is produced using 65 nm technology and can work with the same chipsets as the Smithfield core.

All of the current and planned dual-core processors from Intel are designed to use a new type of socket called the **land grid array (LGA) 775**. Unlike previous socket types, the LGA775, also referred to as *Socket-T*, places contact pins on the system board and contact pads on the bottom of the microprocessor. A hinged metal rim folds down over the microprocessor package and holds its contact pads securely against the signal pins on the system board. A locking arm is used to clamp the processor package in place. The heat sink and fan unit are connected directly and securely to the system board on four points. Figure 3-37 shows the LGA775 socket arrangement.

land grid array (LGA) 775

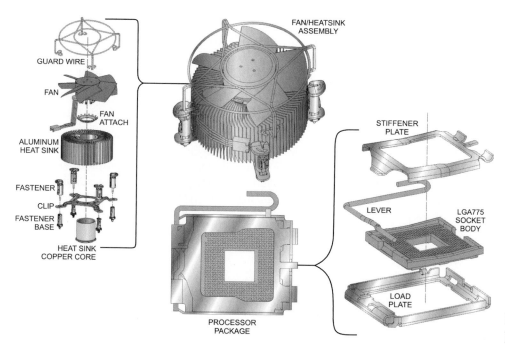

Figure 3-37: The LGA775 Socket

Advanced Intel Microprocessor Technologies

Both dual-core processor types incorporate advanced technologies into their feature sets. All Smithfield-based processors support the Intel *Execute Disable Bit virus protection* (*XD bit*), *EM64T* 64-bit extension, and enhanced *SpeedStep* technologies. The Presler designs also include **virtualization technology** (**VT**), which enables a single machine to run multiple operating systems at once.

virtualization technology (VT)

XD-bit technology is used to separate areas of memory into regions for distinct uses. For example, a section of memory can be set aside exclusively for storing processor instructions (*code*), while another section can be marked only for storage of data.

In the case of Intel processors, any section of memory marked with the XD attribute means it's only for storing data. Therefore, processor instructions cannot be stored there. This is a popular technique for preventing malicious software from taking over computers by inserting their code into another program's data storage area and then running that code from within this section. This is known as a *buffer overflow attack* and is discussed in more detail in Chapter 13, *Preventive Maintenance and Security*.

EM64T

EM64T is a 64-bit microprocessor architecture and corresponding instruction set that is an extension of the x86 instruction set used with all Intel processors. Intel has included this technology and instruction set in its Pentium 4, Pentium D, Pentium Extreme Edition, Celeron D, and Xeon processors.

Enhanced Intel SpeedStep Technology (*EIST*) enables the operating system software to dynamically control the clock speed of a processor. Running the processor at higher clock speeds provides better performance. However, running the processor at a lower speed provides for reduced power consumption and heat dissipation. This technique is used to conserve battery power in notebooks, extend processor life, and reduce noise from cooling devices.

Each processor type has a range of core operating speeds that it can work at. For example, a Pentium M processor designated as a 1.5 GHz processor can actually operate safely at any speed between 600 MHz and 1.5 GHz. The Intel dual-core designs leave some margin for processor overclocking to satisfy the PC performance enthusiast. *Overclocking* is covered later in this chapter.

The SpeedStep technology enables the user or the operating system to change the speed setting in 200 MHz increments. Windows operating systems prior to Windows XP require a special driver and a dashboard application to provide speed control for the processor. However, Windows XP has speed step support built into the Control Panel's Power Management Console. This technology is discussed in greater detail in Chapter 8, *Portable Systems*.

Dual-Core Intel Chipsets

Intel has also introduced a new series of system board chipsets to support the Pentium D line of processors. These include the Intel 975X, 955X, 945G, 945GZ, 945P, 945PL Express chipsets. Figure 3-38 depicts the block diagram of a typical Pentium D processor chipset. The chipset described in the figure is the 955X chipset. This chipset is primarily intended to support Pentium D and Pentium Extreme Edition processors. However, Intel also lists it as supporting all other Intel microprocessors using the LGA775 socket.

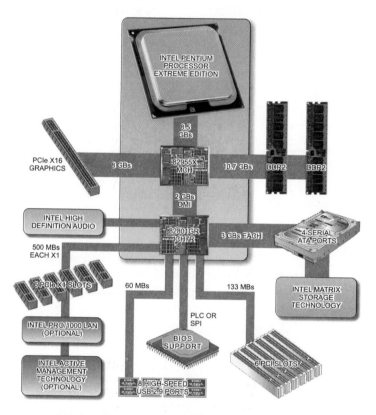

Figure 3-38: An Intel Dual-Core Processor Chipset

Chipsets designed to support the Pentium Extreme Edition processors with hyperthreading technology include the Intel 975X, 955X, 945G, 925XE, 925X, and 915G Express chipsets. Figure 3-39 depicts the block diagram of a typical Pentium Extreme Edition processor chipset. This particular chipset is the 975X chipset designed for high-performance gaming, multimedia, and business applications. Notice the extremely fast front side bus capabilities, the number of PCIe options available, and the number of different I/O options supported.

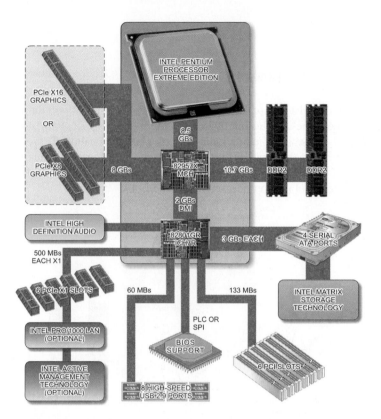

Figure 3-39: An Intel Pentium Extreme Edition Chipset

The 910GL Express chipset is used with the Intel Celeron D processor. Likewise, a low-power chipset has been developed to support the Core Duo processors in mobile computing environments. This chipset is the Intel 945GTExpress chipset. Figure 3-40 depicts the block diagram of the Pentium Celeron D processor chipset. Notice the reduced set of features compared to the previous chipset architectures. Also notice the reduced speeds associated with the major buses and I/O connections.

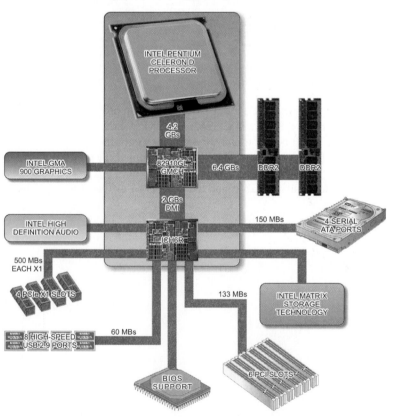

Figure 3-40: An Intel Pentium Celeron D Chipset

Table 3-3 compares the attributes of the different dual-core Pentium chipsets.

**Table 3-3: Dual-Core
Pentium Chipsets**

PRODUCT	FSB SPEEDS	MEMORY TYPES	EXPANSION BUSES	DISK DRIVE SUPPORT
Pentium D				
975X Express	800/1066	DDR2-533/667 (8GB)	PCIe x16/x1	SATA—3 Gbps
945G Express	533/800/1066	DDR2-400/533/667	PCIe x16/x1 (4/6)	SATA—3 Gbps/4
945GZ Express	533/800	DDR2-400/533	PCIe x1 (4/6)	SATA—3 Gbps/4
945P Express	533/800/1066	DDR2-400/533/667	PCIe x16/x1 (4/6)	SATA—3 Gbps/4
945PL Express	533/800	DDR2-400/533	PCIe x16/x1 (4/6)	SATA – 3 Gbps/4
Pentium EE				
975X Express	800/1066	DDR2-533/667 (8 GB)	PCIe x16/x1	SATA—3 Gbps
955X Express	800/1066	DDR2-533/667 (8 GB)	PCIe x16/x1	SATA—3 Gbps
945G Express	533/800/1066	DDR2-400/533/667	PCIe x16/x1 (4/6)	SATA—3 Gbps
925XE Express	800/1066	DDR2-400/533	PCIe x16/x1	SATA—1.5 Gbps
925X Express	800	DDR2-400/533	PCIe x16/x1	SATA—1.5 Gbps
915G Express	533/800	DDR/DDR2-533	PCIe x16/x1	SATA—150 Mb
Celeron D				
910GL Express	533	DDR-333/400	PCIe x1 (4/6)	SATA—150 Mb

Hyperthreading Software Support

The presence of two microprocessors does not automatically double system performance. The controlling operating system software must distribute tasks to all available processor resources. This requires the OS to handle multiple program execution threads that can run independently. The problem is that software has not traditionally been written with multiple threading capabilities—most existing software applications are single threaded, meaning they are written so only one task is worked on at a time. In these cases, the dual-core processor performs just like its single-core version.

On the other hand, modern operating systems can deliver multitasking operations—operations where the system works on more than one application at a time. The operating system actually switches from one task to another in a predetermined order. This is done so quickly that the system appears to be working on multiple tasks at the same time. Operating systems can use processors with **hyperthreading** technology to provide smooth and responsive operations during intensive multitasking operations. Multitasking and other multiple process computing techniques are described in greater detail in Chapter 9, *Operating System Fundamentals*.

hyperthreading

AMD PROCESSORS

Advanced Micro
Devices (AMD)

Advanced Micro Devices (AMD) offers several clone microprocessors: the 5x86 (X5), the 5x86 (K5), the K6, the K6PLUS-3D, and K7 microprocessors. The X5 offers operational and pin compatibility with the DX4. Its performance is equal to that of the Pentium and MMX processors. The K5 processor is compatible with the Pentium, and the K6 is compatible with the MMX. Both the K5 and K6 models are Socket-7 compatible, enabling them to be used in conventional Pentium and Pentium MMX system-board designs (with some small modifications). The K6 employs an extended 64 kB L1 cache that doubles the internal cache size of the Pentium II.

The K6PLUS-3D is operationally and performance compatible with the Pentium Pro, and the K7 is operationally and performance compatible with the Pentium II. However, neither of these units has a pin-out compatibility with another processor.

AMD continues to produce clone versions of Pentium processors. In some cases, the functions and performance of the AMD devices go beyond the Intel design they are cloning. Two notable AMD clone processors are the Athlon and the Duron.

Athlon Processors

Athlon

Slot A

The **Athlon** is a Pentium III clone processor. It is available in a Slot 1 cartridge clone, called the Slot A specification. Figure 3-41 depicts the cartridge version of the Athlon processor with a **Slot A** connector.

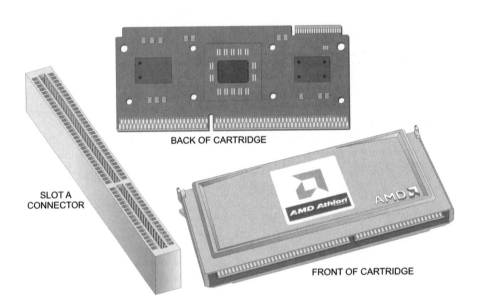

BACK OF CARTRIDGE

SLOT A
CONNECTOR

FRONT OF CARTRIDGE

**Figure 3-41: Slot
A/Athlon Version**

The Athlon is also available in a proprietary SPGA Socket A design that mimics the Intel Socket 370 specification. The **Socket A** (also known as *Socket 462*) specification employs a 462-pin ZIF socket and is supported by only two available chipsets.

Socket A

Three versions of the Athlon processor have been introduced so far. The first version was the K7 version that ran between 500 MHz and 700 MHz, provided a 128 kB L1 cache and a 512 kB L2 cache, and employed a 100 MHz system bus.

Subsequent Athlon versions have included the K75, Thunderbird, Thoroughbred, and Barton versions. Both versions are constructed using the 0.18-micron manufacturing technology. The K75 processor ran between 750 MHz and 1 GHz. Like the K7 version, it provided a 128 kB L1 cache and a 512 kB L2 cache, and employed a 100 MHz system bus. The Thunderbird version ran between 750 MHz and 1.2 GHz, provided a 128 kB L1 cache and a 256 kB L2 cache, and employed a 133 MHz system bus. The Thoroughbred featured 256 kB of L2 cache and the standard 64+64 kB L1 cache. It operated at speeds up to 2.8 GHz.

A later evolution of the Athlon processor was given the title of **Athlon XP**. These versions were based on the *Thoroughbred* and the newer *Barton* core versions. The Barton versions feature a 512 kB L2 cache, a slower clock speed, and a maximum processor speed of 3.0 GHz.

Athlon XP

Athlon 64 Processors

AMD made several technology changes to the Athlon processor when they unveiled their **Athlon 64** line of processor. These processors are built on a new K8 core that includes AMD's **AMD64** 64-bit architecture. This architecture is an extension of the **x86 Instruction Set** that was originally create by Intel for its 80 × 86 line of processors. In addition, the Athlon 64 implemented additional internal registers to handle **SSE** (*streaming single-instruction/multiple data extensions*) instructions designed to support independent floating point math operations.

Athlon 64

AMD64

Instruction Set

SSE

no-execute (NE)

A new **no-execute (NE)** bit technology was also introduced with the Athlon. NE technology marks different areas of memory as being for use with data or as reserved for instructions. Any attempt to execute code from a memory page that has been tagged as a no-execute page will result in a memory access violation error. This feature makes it more difficult for certain types of *malware* to take control of the system and execute its payload.

The Athlon 64 processor brought another considerable change to Pentium class PC architecture by moving the memory controller from the supporting system board chipset into the microprocessor package. This effectively removes the front side bus from the system architecture and improves memory access operations by avoiding external bus access overhead.

Instead of continuing the traditional FSB structure, AMD adopted a special bidirectional, serial/parallel I/O bus and controller technology from the *HyperTransport Technology Consortium* for their Athlon 64 processors. The **hypertransport (HT)** technology handles the I/O functions previously performed across the FSB at speeds much higher than existing FSB clocking.

hypertransport (HT)

As we shall see shortly, AMD was also looking forward to multiple-core processors when they adopted the hypertransport technology. AMD also employs this bus to interconnect multiple processor cores to provide efficient cooperation between the cores.

The **Athlon 64 FX** is a special designation given to some Athlon 64 versions. These processors are typically clocked faster than the traditional Athlon versions to make them more interesting to gamers and other enthusiasts.

Athlon 64 FX

There are two common socket sizes used with Athlon 64 processors—a 754-pin socket for a value/budget version of the Athlon 64 that only provides a 64-bit, single-channel memory interface, and a 939-pin version that is the standard for all other Athlon 64 versions.

Duron Processors

Duron

The **Duron** processor is a Celeron clone processor that conforms to the AMD Socket-A specification. The Duron features processor speeds between 600 MHz and 800 MHz. It includes a 128 kB L1 cache and a 64 kB L2 cache. Like the newer Celerons, the Duron is constructed using 0.18-micron IC manufacturing technology.

Athlon Dual-Core Processors

AMD took the lead in the processor development races by pushing dual-core processors to the forefront. Unlike the Intel dual-core processors discussed earlier in the chapter, AMD designed their dual-core devices to fit in the same 939-pin socket interface they were already using for their single-core **Athlon 64** processor. In addition, the existing Athlon 64 chipset had been designed with this possibility in mind. These features make upgrading to dual-core processors relatively easy and attractive. All that is required is to physically exchange the microprocessor packages and perform a logical upgrade by flashing the system's ROM BIOS with programming to support the new processor.

Athlon 64

Athlon 64 X2 Dual-Core

direct connect architecture

Figure 3-42 provides a block diagram of the AMD **Athlon 64 X2 Dual-Core** processor design. Like the Intel processors, the two processor cores in the 64 X2 can communicate with each other through the System Request Interface. This interface enables the communications to take place at the core clock speed of the processors. The AMD multicore technology also changed the front side bus arrangement found in existing Pentium/PCI systems. This portion of the system has been redesigned in a **direct connect architecture** that directly connects the processor, the memory controller, and the I/O controller to the CPU. Therefore, there is no loss due to I/O manipulation and bottlenecks associated with the operation of the front side bus.

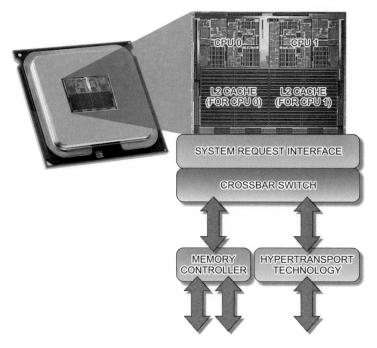

Figure 3-42: AMD Dual-Core Processors Design

Notice in the figure that in the AMD 64 processors, a 128-bit ECC memory controller has been integrated into the microprocessor die. This gives the processors direct access to the memory controller (as opposed to having to access an external bus to get to the north bridge).

The complete line of AMD64 devices (single and dual core) offers AMD's advanced *hypertransport* bus interface technology for high speed I/O communication. In the AMD processors, this interface consists of an integrated *hypertransport controller* and a 16-bit, 1 GHz bus that interconnects the cores of the multicore AMD processor through their *direct connect architecture* and provides 8 GBps transfer rates. The HyperTransport interface also connects the processor package to the system board's chipset. This connection scheme is illustrated in Figure 3-43.

The AMD 64 X2 has been built on two different microprocessor core types—the *Toledo* core and the *Manchester* core. Both versions include dual AMD64 microprocessor cores. These cores are rated to operate at core voltages between 1.35 V and 1.4 V. Likewise, they both contain dual 64+64 (Data/Instructions) L1 cache memory units. They also run identical microprocessor instruction sets and extensions. Finally, they both work with Socket-939 structure and provide 1 GHz hypertransport high-speed I/O interfaces.

In the Toledo core, each processor core is supported by a 1 MB full-speed L2 cache. On the Manchester core, the L2 cache is limited to 512 KB for each core. Power consumption for the Toledo core is 89 or 110 Watts, depending on the version, while the power consumption in the Manchester core is 110 W max.

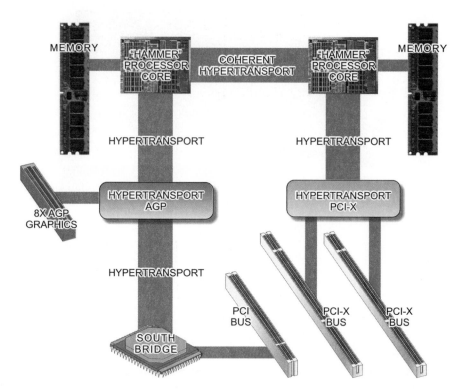

Figure 3-43: HyperTransport Links

Models built on the Toledo core include the 4400+ and 4800+ processors, while Manchester models include the 3800+, 4200+, and 4600+ processors. The 4400+ runs on a 2.2 GHz clock, and the 4800+ uses a 2.4 GHz clock. On the Manchester side, the 3800+ is designed for a 2.0 GHz clock, the 4200+ uses a 2.2 GHz clock, and the 4600+ model employs a 2.4 GHz clock.

The Athlon 64 X2 is supported by a number of different chipsets from many different manufacturers. These include

- NVIDIA—Nforce4 Series chipsets

- ATI—Radeon Xpress 200 Series chipsets

- VIA—K8 Series chipsets

- SiS—75x Series chipsets or greater

In the case of the *NVIDIA nFORCE Professional* chipset designed to support the AMD dual-core processor, this is a single chip, as illustrated in Figure 3-44. The AMD processors provide direct connection to the system's DDR memory through its direct connect architecture, while the nFORCE chipset handles the PCIe graphics, Ethernet networking, and SATA disk drive interfaces.

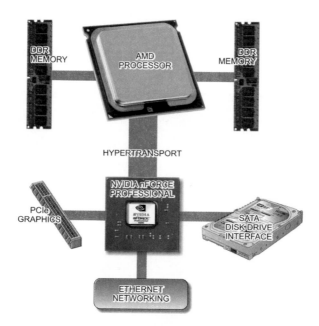

**Figure 3-44:
Single-Chip AMD
Chipset**

Like the dual-core Intel processors, the Athlon 64 X2 supports a 64-bit extension to the x86 Instruction set, enhanced virus protection with supported operating systems, and speed throttling features. In the AMD environment, these features are known as AMD64, NX (no execute bit), and CoolnQuiet. The functions associated with these features are roughly the same as those of the Intel EM64T, XD bit, and SpeedStep features described earlier in this chapter.

Opteron Processors

AMD has also produced a line of dual-core, high-end **Opteron** processors for network server and workstation units. These units are built on AMD's K8 core and are intended to compete with Intel's Xeon line of processors in the network server market. The original 1XX Opteron versions were built to fit in a 939-pin socket. However, newer 2XX and 8XX 940-pin versions have been introduced. Table 3-4 lists the prominent features of the dual-core Opteron processors from AMD.

Opteron

Table 3-4: AMD Dual-Core Opteron Processors

MODEL	CLOCK FREQUENCY	L2-CACHE	MEMORY	MULTIPLIER	VOLTAGE	TDP	SOCKET
165	1.8 GHz	2 × 1 MB	up to PC-3200	9x	1.35/1.3 V	110 W	Socket 939
170	2.0 GHz	2 × 1 MB	up to PC-3200	10x	1.35/1.3 V	110 W	Socket 939
175	2.2 GHz	2 × 1 MB	up to PC-3200	11x	1.35/1.3 V	110 W	Socket 939
180	2.4 GHz	2 × 1 MB	up to PC-3200	12x	1.35/1.3 V	110 W	Socket 939
185	2.6 GHz	2 × 1 MB	up to PC-3200	13x	1.35/1.3 V	110 W	Socket 939
265/865	1.8 GHz	2 × 1 MB	up to PC-3200R	9x	1.35/1.3 V	95 W	Socket 940
270/870	2.0 GHz	2 × 1 MB	up to PC-3200R	10x	1.35/1.3 V	95 W	Socket 940
275/875	2.2 GHz	2 × 1 MB	up to PC-3200R	11x	1.35/1.3 V	95 W	Socket 940
280/880	2.4 GHz	2 × 1 MB	up to PC-3200R	12x	1.35/1.3 V	95 W	Socket 940
285/885	2.6 GHz	2 × 1 MB	up to PC-3200R	13x	1.35/1.3 V	95 W	Socket 940

Table 3-5: Microprocessor Characteristics

Table 3-5 summarizes the characteristics of common Intel and AMD microprocessors.

MICROPROCESSOR	DIAMETER SIZE (mm)	VRM (VOLTS)	SPEED (MHz)	CACHE ON DIE (kB)	CACHE ON CARTRIDGE	CACHE ON BOARD (kB)	SOCKETS OR SLOT TYPES
Pentium	23.1 x 23.1	2.5–3.6	75–166	L1—8+8	-	L2—256/512	Socket 7
Pentium MMX	25.4 x 25.4	2.0–3.5	166–233	L1—16+16	-	L2—256/512	Socket 7
AMD - K6-2:K6-3	33.5 x 33.5	2.2–3.3	300–550	L1—32+32	-	L2—256/512	Super Socket 7
Pentium Pro	24.2 x 19.6	3.1–3.3	150, 166, 180, 200	L1—8+8	L2—256/512/1000	-	Socket 8
Pentium II/III Celeron (.25 micron)	25.4 x 25.4 18 x 62 x 140 Box	1.5–2.6	233–1000	L1—16+16	L2—256/512 128 kB	-	Slot 1
Xeon II/III (330) (.25 micron)	27.4 x 27.4 18 x 87 x 125 Box	1.5–2.6	500/550 700/900	L1—16+16	L2—512 kB 1 MB 2 M	-	Slot 2
Pentium III Celeron (.25 micron)	25.4 x 25.4 Slug 27.4 x 27.4 Opening	1.1–2.5	300–566	L1—16+16 L2—128/256	- -	- -	Socket 370 PPGA
Pentium III (Coppermine) Celeron (.18 micron)	9.3 x 11.3	1.1–2.5	667–1000	L1—16+16 L2—128/256	- -	- -	Socket 370 FC-PGA
Pentium III (Tualatin) Celeron (.13 micron)	31 x 31	1.1–2.5	800–1500	L1—16+16 L2—128/256/512	- -	- -	FC-PGA2
Pentium 4 (.18 micron)	31 x 31	1.75	1300–2000	L1—12+8 L2—256	- -	- -	Socket 423 FC-PGA
Pentium 4 (.18 micron) (.13 micron)	31 x 31 33 x 33	1.75 1.50	1400–2000 1800–3400	L1—12+8 L2—512	- -	- -	FC-PGA2
Pentium Xeon (.18 micron)	31 x 31	1.4–1.8 1.7	1400–2000	L1—12+8 L2—256	- -	- -	Socket 603 FC-BGA
Pentium Xeon (.13 micron)	35 x 35	1.4–1.8 1.475	1800–3400	L1—12+8 L2—512	- -	- -	Socket 603 FC-BGA2
Itanium (.18 micron) (266 MHz)	71.6 x 127.7	1.7	733/800	1—16+16 L2—512	L3—2 MB 4 MB	- -	PAC-418
Celeron D	125.0 x 90nm x 81mm	1.25–1.4	2133–3333	L1-12+16KB/L2-256KiB	-	-	Socket 478/LGA775
Pentium 4 Extreme Edition	169.0 x 130nm x 237mm	1.2/1.25–1.337/1.4	3200–3733	L1-12+8/L2-2x1024KiB or 2x2048KiB	L3-2MB	-	FC-LGA775
Pentium D	230.0/376.0 x 90/65nm x 206/280mm	1.2/1.25–1.337/1.4	2667–3600	L1-24+32KB/L2-2x1024KiB or 2x2048KiB	-	-	FC-LGA775
Athlon/Duron	9.1 x 13.1	1.75	800–1400	L1—64+64	L2—256 kB	-	Slot A 242 CPGA
Athlon/Duron	11.1 x 11.6	1.75	733–1800 1400–3200	L1—64+64	L2—256 kB	-	Socket A 462 ORGA
Athlon XP-M	68.5 x 130nm x 144mm	1.5–1.75	1333–2333	L1—64+64	L2—128KiB/ 256KiB/512KiB	-	Socket A/462
Athlon 64	105.9/68.5/76 x 130/130/90nm x 193/144/84mm	1.25–1.40, 1.35, 1.4, 1.5	2133–3333	L1—64+64	L2—1024KiB/ 512KiB	-	Socket 754/939
Athlon 64 FX	233.0 x 90nm x 199mm	1.50–1.55, 1.50, 1.35/1.4	1.3–1.35V, 2200–2800	L1—64+64	L2—1024KiB	-	Socket 754/939/ 940/AM2
Opteron	114.0/105.9 x 90/130nm x 115/193mm	1.50–1.55/ 1.35–1.4	1400–2400/ 1600–3000	L1—64+64	L2—1024KiB	-	Socket 939/940

GEEK SQUAD CASE FILE #50144

Agent 1355 is a Geek Squad Double Agent who has been called out to the ACME Widget corporate office to do some consulting work for them. ACME does not want to replace all of its computers at this time. As a matter of fact, what they really want to do is spend a little money to upgrade all their computers as much as they can for now and wait as long as possible to replace them. Their board of directors has asked Agent 1355 for a plan to upgrade their systems. He knows that nearly all the systems in the company are Pentium II 350 MHz machines. What is the most current, fastest upgrade Agent 1355 can recommend to this company's board of directors?

PROCESSOR SOCKET SPECIFICATIONS

In addition to the clone processors, Intel has always developed lines of upgrade microprocessors for their original offerings. These are referred to as **OverDrive** processors. An OverDrive unit may simply be the same type of microprocessor running at a higher clock speed, or it may be an advanced architecture microprocessor designed to operate from the same socket/pin configuration as the original. To accommodate this option, Intel created specifications for eight socket designs, designated Socket 1 through Socket 8.

The specifications for **Socket 1** through **Socket 3** were developed for 80486SX, 80486DX, and 80486 OverDrive versions that use different pin numbers and power supply requirements. Likewise, the **Socket-4** through **Socket 6** specifications deal with various Pentium and OverDrive units that have different speeds and power supply requirements.

The **Socket-7** specification enabled system boards to be configured for different types and versions of microprocessors using different internal core and FSB operating speeds. Its design includes provision for a **voltage regulator module (VRM)** to allow various power settings to be implemented through the socket. The Socket-7 specification corresponds to the second generation of Pentium devices that employ SPGA packaging. It is compatible with the **Socket 5**, straight-row PGA specification that the first-generation Pentium processors employed. Finally, the **Socket 8** specification is specific to the Pentium Pro processor.

Although the Intel **Slot 1** design was originally developed for the Pentium II, it also serves its Celeron and Pentium III processor designs. Like Socket 7, the Slot 1 specification provides for variable processor core voltages (2.8 to 3.3) that permit faster operation and reduced power consumption. In addition, some suppliers have created daughter boards containing the Pentium Pro processor that can be plugged into the Slot 1 connector. This combination Socket 8/Slot 1 device is referred to as a slotket processor.

The **Slot 2** specification from Intel expands the Slot 1 SECC technology to a 330-contact cartridge (**SECC-2**) used with the Intel Xeon processor.

AMD produced a reversed version of the Slot 1 specification for its Athlon processor by turning the contacts of the Slot 1 design around. They titled the new design **Slot A**. Although serving the same ends as the Slot 1 design, the Slot A and Slot 1 microprocessor cartridges are not compatible.

OverDrive

Socket 1
Socket 3
Socket 4
Socket 6
Socket 7
voltage regulator module (VRM)
Socket 5
Socket 8
Slot 1

Slot 2
SECC-2
Slot A

ADVANCED SYSTEM BOARDS   139

Socket 370

plastic pin grid array (PPGA)

flip chip pin grid array (FC-PGA)

In a departure from its proprietary slot connector development, Intel introduced a new ZIF socket standard, called **Socket 370**, for use with its Celeron processor. There are actually two versions of the Socket 370 specification. The first is the PPGA 370 variation intended for use with the **plastic pin grid array (PPGA)** version of the Celeron CPUs. The other is the **flip chip pin grid array (FC-PGA)** version.

The term *flip chip* is used to describe a group of microprocessors that have provisions for attaching a heat sink directly to the microprocessor die. The processors in this category include the Cyrix III, Celeron, and Pentium III. Although the PPGA and FC-PGA processors will both plug into the 370 socket, this does not mean they will work in system boards designed for the other specification.

As the Pentium 4 processor continued to be upgraded, Intel rolled out a couple of different socket types to keep up with the improvements. The original P4 was delivered in a Socket 423 configuration. Subsequent versions have been produced using **Socket 478** or **flip chip LGA775** sockets. Intel has continued to employ the LGA775 socket arrangement for a number of its newer processor designs, including

Socket 478

flip chip LGA775

- Pentium 4 (2.66–3.800 GHz)
- Celeron D (2.527–3.333 GHz)
- Pentium 4 Extreme Edition (3.2 GHz, 3.400–3.73 GHz)
- Pentium D (2.80–3.40 GHz)

They have also offered a variety of front side bus speed options through this socket type, including 133 MHz/533 FSB, 200 MHz/800 FSB, 266 MHz/1066 FSB, and 333 MHz/1333 FSB speeds. The LGA775 package features 250 power and 273 ground pins to accommodate the processor's 130 W of power dissipation.

In the AMD camp, a 462-pin ZIF socket specification was adopted for the PGA versions of its Athlon and Duron processors. This has been followed by a line of advanced sockets to keep pace with the updated features of the AMD processors:

- Socket 563—Athlon XP-M (low power mobile)
- Socket 754—Athlon 64
- Socket 939—Athlon 64/ Athlon 64 FX
- Socket 940—Opteron/Athlon 64 FX
- Socket 462/Socket A—Athlon, Duron, Athlon XP, Athlon XP-M, Athlon MP, and Sepron

AMD is also preparing the next generation of sockets to support their anticipated processor upgrades. These include a Socket 1207 (also known as Socket F) to replace the Socket 940 for dual processor applications, a Socket AM2 to replace the current Socket 754 and 939 offerings, and the Socket S1 which will replace the Socket 754 in the portable computing market.

Table 3-6 summarizes the attributes of the various industry socket and slot specifications.

Table 3-6:
Industry Socket
Specifications

NUMBER	PINS	VOLTAGES	MICROPROCESSORS
Socket 1	169 PGA	5 V	80486 SX/DXx, DX4 Overdrive
Socket 2	238 PGA	5 V	80486 SX/DXx, Pentium Overdrive
Socket 3	237 PGA	5/3.3 V	80486 SX/DXx, Pentium Overdrive
Socket 4	237 PGA	5 V	Pentium 60/66, 60/66 Overdrive
Socket 5	320 SPGA	3.3 V	Pentium 75-133, Pentium Overdrive
Socket 6	235 PGA	3.3 V	Never Implemented
Socket 7	321 SPGA	VRM (2.5 V-3.6 V)	Pentium 75-200, Pentium Overdrive
Socket 8	387 SPGA	VRM (2.2 V-3.5 V)	Pentium Pro
Slot 1	242 SECC/SEPP	VRM (1.5 V-2.5 V)	Celeron, Pentium II, Pentium III
Slot 2	330 SECC-2	VRM (1.5 V-2.5 V)	Xeon
Super Socket 7	321 SPGA	VRM (2.0 V-3.5 V)	AMD K6-2, K6-2+, K6-III, K6-III+, Pentium MMX
Socket 370	370 SPGA	VRM (1.1 V-2.5 V)	Cyrix III, Celeron, Pentium III
Slot A	242 Slot A	VRM (1.2 V-2.2 V)	AMD Athlon
Socket A	462 SPGA	VRM (1.2 V-2.2 V)	AMD Athlon, Duron
Socket 423	423 FC-PGA	VRM (1.7 V)	Pentium IV (1.3 GHz – 2.0 GHz)
Socket 478	478 FC-PGA	VRM (1.5 V-1.7 V)	Pentium IV Xeon (1.4 GHz – 2.2 GHz)
Socket 603	603 INT-PGA	VRM (1.5 V-1.7 V)	Pentium IV (1.4 GHz – 2.2 GHz)
Socket 418	418 INT-PGA	VRM (1.7 V)	Itanium/Intel (733 MHz – 800 MHz)
FC-LGA775 (Socket T)	775 LGA	1.2V-1.4 V,	Pentium 4/Extreme Edition/D; Celeron D
Socket 563	563 microPGA	1.5-1.75 V	Athlon XP-M
Socket 754	754 PGA	0.8-1.55 V	Athlon 64
Socket 939	939 PGA	0.8-1.55 V	Athlon 64, Athlon 64 FX
Socket 940	940 PGA	0.8-1.55 V	Opteron, Athlon 64 FX

TEST TIP

Know which processors can be used with Slot 1 and Socket 370 connections. Also know which processors can be used in Slot A.

GEEK SQUAD CASE FILE #87888

ACME's board of directors approves your recommendation for upgrading their existing systems as outlined in Case File #50144 (the previous case file). When Agent 1355 upgrades the first system, he finds that it is only running at 450 MHz. What should Agent 1355 do to get the system up to the speed you recommended to ACME's board?

FANS, HEAT SINKS, AND COOLING SYSTEMS

The Pentium processor requires the presence of a heat-sinking device and a microprocessor fan unit for cooling purposes. As Figure 3-45 illustrates, these devices come in many forms, including simple **passive heat sinks** and fan-cooled, **active heat sinks**.

Passive heat sinks are finned metal slabs that can be clipped or glued with a heat-transmitting adhesive onto the top of the microprocessor. The fins increase the surface area of the heat sink, enabling it to dissipate heat more rapidly. Active heat sinks add a fan unit to move air across the heat sink. The fan moves the heat away from the heat sink and the microprocessor more rapidly.

ATX-style systems employ power supplies that use a reverse-flow fan that brings in cool air from the back of the unit and blows it directly onto the microprocessor. For this to work properly, the system board must adhere to the *ATX form factor* guidelines and place the microprocessor in the correct position on the system board.

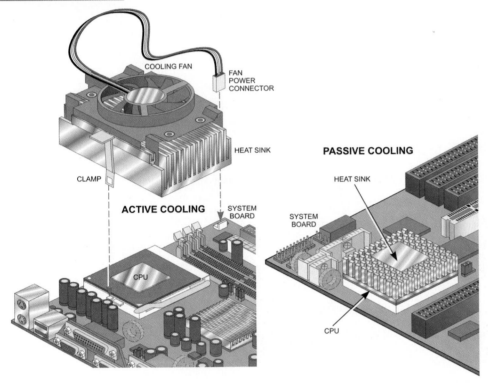

Figure 3-45: Typical Microprocessor Cooling Systems

In newer Pentium systems, the BIOS interrogates the processor during start-up and configures it appropriately. This prevents the user from subjecting the processor to potentially destructive conditions, such as overclocking. In addition, these systems can monitor the **health** of the processor while it is in operation and take steps to compensate for problems such as overheating. This normally involves speeding up or slowing down the processor fan to maintain a given operating temperature.

Be aware that not all heat sinks and fans are created equal. The fan module must be one that is supported by the installed BIOS. If a fan unit is installed that does not have proper stepping in the BIOS routines, the system will not be able to correctly control the fan speed. Therefore, it may not be able to keep the processor cool enough for proper operation. Also, some fans are built better than others. For instance, fans that use ball bearings instead of slip ring bearings tend to run smoother and make less noise. However, they are usually more expensive than the slip ring versions.

BTX Thermal Module

The BTX form factor design is based on creating specific airflow zones within the case. The component responsible for generating the airflow is the **BTX thermal module**. The thermal module combines a heat sink and fan into a special duct that channels the air across the system board's main components. Figure 3-46 shows the components of the BTX thermal module.

The duct fits tightly against large air vents in the front center portion of the case. The fan draws air in from the front and pushes it directly over the microprocessor mounted under the assembly in a linear flow pattern. The air continues toward the back of the case passing over the graphics card and major chipset components. A fan in the power supply unit draws some of the air across the memory devices before exhausting it out through the rear of the unit. Figure 3-46 depicts the flow of air through the BTX case.

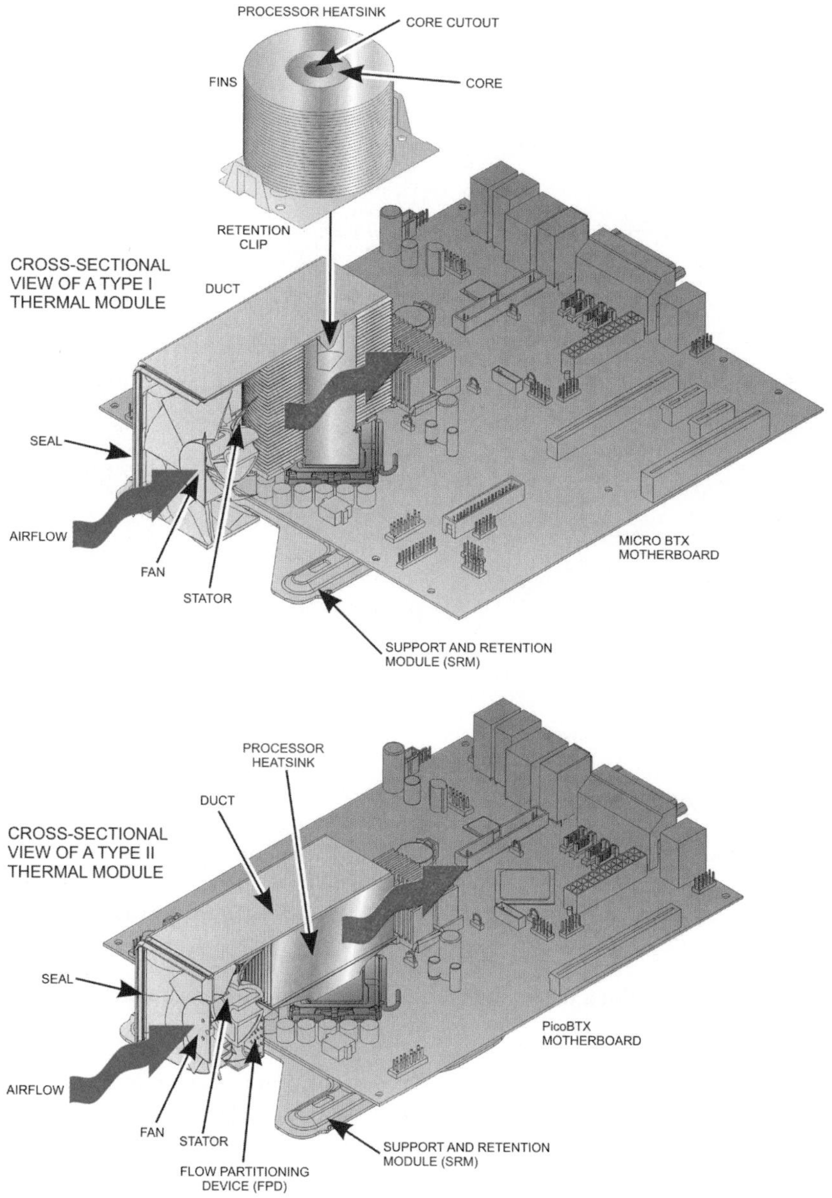

Figure 3-46: BTX Thermal Module Components

Advanced Cooling Systems

As system designers continue to push microprocessors for more speed, they also increase the amount of power that they dissipate. The latest microprocessor design techniques have created processors that generate over 80 W of power that must be dissipated as heat. This is comparable to the heat generated by a heat lamp. It is beyond the capabilities of normal processor fans and heat sinks to effectively dissipate this much heat.

Simple air-cooling systems cannot create a large enough temperature differential to cool the processor. Therefore, system designers have begun to equip very high-speed systems with refrigerated cooling systems. Originally, the designers adopted water-based cooling systems that cooled and circulated water to carry heat away from the processor. Figure 3-47 depicts the components of a water-based cooling system typically used to cool processors that have been configured to run in overclocking conditions.

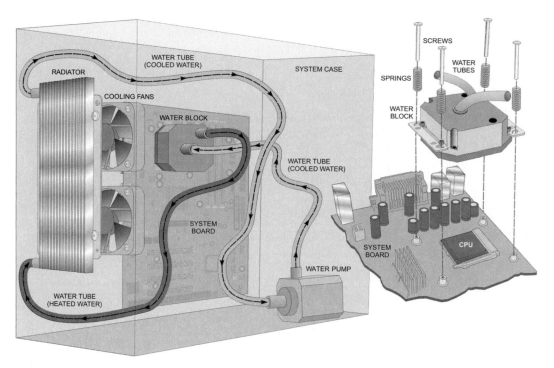

**Figure 3-47:
Water-Based
Microprocessor**

The water cooler system consists of

- A water reservoir tank

- A water pump that circulates water throughout the cooling system

- A condenser coil radiator with fans that cool the water and exhaust heat into the outside atmosphere

- A **CPU cooling block** that connects directly to the microprocessor and extracts heat from it

The water pump operates from inside the reservoir tank and is used to force cooling water through the system. Most of the pumps for these systems are adaptations of home aquarium pumps and are designed for 120 Vac operation; therefore, they must have an external power cord.

CPU cooling block

The CPU cooling block consists of a copper-finned heat sink that mounts to a bracket installed around the microprocessor. Pentium 4 system boards have standard hole patterns already supplied to permit such devices to be attached to them. The heat sink is enclosed in a water jacket that permits cooling water to circulate around the fins. This enables heat to be removed from the processor faster than an air-cooled heat sink.

Heated water from the CPU cooler is pumped through the radiator. The radiator is composed of several coils of tubing to maximize the surface area that is used to dissipate heat. The additional fans push air across the coils and speed up the radiation process in the same manner as conventional CPU fans do for air-cooled heat sinks. The cooled water returns to the reservoir for recirculation.

More advanced liquid-based cooling systems have migrated to nonwater coolants like those used in residential refrigerators or automobile air conditioners. Figure 3-48 shows the components associated with a refrigerated cooling system used with a PC system.

- An **evaporator** that mounts on top of the microprocessor

- A **condenser** with cooling fan that mounts to the case so that air can be exhausted to the outside of the case

- A **compressor** that places the cooling liquid under pressure so that it can perform refrigeration

- A **flow control/expansion device** that acts as a restriction in the lines of the system that causes the refrigerant to lose pressure and partially vaporize

- Insulated tubing that connects the four major components in a closed-loop cooling circuit

As the figure illustrates, the components of the PC cooling system do not fit inside a typical desktop or tower unit. Instead, they must be used in cases that have been modified for them, or in cases that have been designed specifically for them.

The four major components of the system are interconnected by a sealed piping system that holds a refrigerant liquid. The compressor is used to compress the refrigerant and pump it through the system. The high-pressure, high-temperature refrigerant first passes through the condenser unit where it exchanges heat with the surrounding air and cools somewhat.

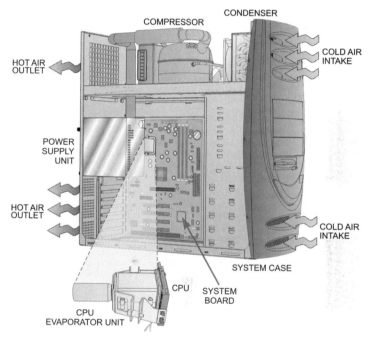

evaporator

condenser

compressor

flow control/
expansion device

**Figure 3-48: PC
Refrigerant Coolers**

Next, the refrigerant is forced through the flow control/expansion device, which restricts its flow and causes it to lose pressure as it passes through the device. The loss in pressure causes some of the refrigerant to change into a gas. In the process, the gaseous portion of the refrigerant extracts heat from the remaining liquid and thereby cools it.

The refrigerant is then passed through the evaporator on the microprocessor in the form of a warm liquid. As air passes over the evaporator, heat is extracted from the processor body and passed to the cooler refrigerant. The remainder of the liquid refrigerant becomes a cool gas as it gathers heat from the evaporator and is drawn back to the compressor where the process begins again.

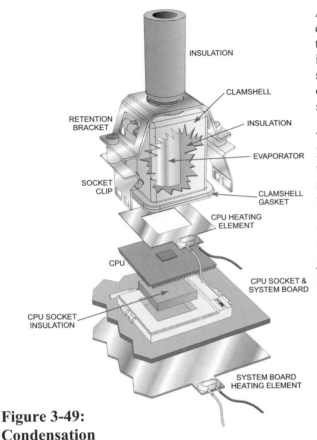

INSULATION

CLAMSHELL

RETENTION
BRACKET

INSULATION

EVAPORATOR

SOCKET
CLIP

CLAMSHELL
GASKET

CPU HEATING
ELEMENT

CPU

CPU SOCKET &
SYSTEM BOARD

CPU SOCKET
INSULATION

SYSTEM BOARD
HEATING ELEMENT

**Figure 3-49:
Condensation
Prevention**

As the air passes over the evaporator and cools, moisture can condense around the processor in the form of condensate. In order to protect the processor and printed circuit board around it, special insulating foam pads must be mounted around the microprocessor socket. In addition, special heating elements are typically mounted on the backside of the system board under the microprocessor socket position as illustrated in Figure 3-49.

The BIOS controls the refrigerant cooling system through its Health Management system. This includes monitoring the actual temperature of the microprocessor and manipulating the cooling system to maintain a designated temperature level. It also controls the temperature of the heating pad under the printed circuit board.

This technology is not widely used in PCs. While the military has been using this type of cooling system for more than five years, it is just beginning to be used with commercial PCs. Because the liquid refrigerants used in these systems are considered hazardous to the environment, you must be aware that only individuals licensed to handle refrigerants can legally work on these units.

Essentials 1.1

MEMORY SYSTEMS

As mentioned in Chapter 2, *Basic PC Terms and Concepts*, there are normally three types of semiconductor memory found on a typical system board. These include the system's ROM BIOS ICs, the system's RAM memory, and the second-level cache memory unit.

A typical PC system board uses ROM chips to hold the system's BIOS firmware. The system's memory map reserves memory locations from F0000h to FFFFFh for this purpose. These chips contain the firmware routines to handle start-up of the system, the changeover to disk-based operations, video and printer output functions, as well as the Power-On Self-Tests.

Random Access Memory

static RAM (SRAM)

dynamic RAM
(DRAM)

Two types of semiconductor RAM, **static RAM (SRAM)** and **dynamic RAM (DRAM)**, are used on system boards. Although they both perform the same types of functions, the methods they use are completely different. Static RAM stores bits in such a manner that they will remain as long as power to the chip is not interrupted. Dynamic RAM requires periodic refreshing to maintain data, even if electrical power is applied to the chip.

Dynamic RAM stores data bits on rows and columns of IC capacitors. Capacitors lose their charge over time. This is the reason that dynamic RAM devices require data refreshing operations. Static RAM uses IC transistors to store data and maintain it as long as power is supplied to the chip. Its transistor structure makes SRAM memory much faster than ordinary DRAM. However, it can only store about 25% as much data in a given size as a DRAM device. Therefore, it tends to be more expensive to create large memories with SRAM.

Whether the RAM is made up of static or dynamic RAM devices, all RAM systems have the disadvantage of being volatile. This means that any data stored in RAM will be lost if power to the computer is disrupted for any reason. On the other hand, both types of RAM have the advantage of being fast, with the ability to be written to and read from with equal ease.

Generally, static RAM is used in smaller memory systems, such as cache and video memories, where the added cost of refresh circuitry would increase the cost-per-bit of storage. Cache memory is a special memory structure that works directly with the microprocessor, whereas video memory is a specialized area that holds information to be displayed on the screen. On the other hand, DRAM is used in larger memory systems, such as the system's main memory, where the extra cost of refresh circuitry is distributed over a greater number of bits and is offset by the reduced operating cost associated with DRAM chips.

Advanced DRAM

Both types of RAM are brought together to create an improved DRAM, referred to as **enhanced DRAM (EDRAM)**. By integrating an SRAM component into a DRAM device, a performance improvement of 40% can be gained. An independent write path allows the system to input new data without affecting the operation of the rest of the chip. These devices are used primarily in L2 cache memories.

enhanced DRAM
(EDRAM)

Another modified DRAM type, referred to as **synchronous DRAM (SDRAM)**, employs special internal registers and clock signals to organize data requests from memory. Unlike asynchronous memory modules, SDRAM devices operate in synchronicity with the system clock. Once an initial Read or Write access has been performed on the memory device, additional accesses can be conducted in a high-speed burst mode that operates at one access per clock cycle. This enables the microprocessor to perform other tasks while the data are being organized.

synchronous DRAM
(SDRAM)

Special internal configurations also speed up the operation of the SDRAM memory. The SDRAM device employs internal interleaving that permits one side of the memory to be accessed while the other half is completing an operation. Because there are two versions of SDRAM (2-clock and 4-clock) you must make certain that the SDRAM type you are using is supported by the system board's chipset.

Advanced SDRAM

Advanced versions of SDRAM include

- **SDR-SDRAM**—Single Data Rate SDRAM. This version of SDRAM transfers data on one edge of the system clock signal.

SDR-SDRAM

SGRAM

- **SGRAM**—Synchronous Graphics RAM. This type of SDRAM is designed to handle high-performance graphics operations. It features dual-bank operations that permit two memory pages to be open at the same time.

ESDRAM

- **ESDRAM**—Enhanced SDRAM. This advanced form of SDRAM employs small cache buffers to provide high data access rates. This type of SDRAM is used in L2 cache applications.

VCM-SDRAM

- **VCM-SDRAM**—Virtual Channel Memory SDRAM. This memory design has on-board cache buffers to improve multiple access times and to provide I/O transfers on each clock cycle. VCM SDRAM requires a special chipset to support it.

DDR-SDRAM

- **DDR-SDRAM**—Double Data Rate SDRAM. DDR is a form of SDR-SDRAM that can transfer data on both the leading and falling edges of each clock cycle. This capability doubles the data transfer rate of traditional SDR-DRAM. It is available in a number of standard formats including SODIMMs for portables.

EDDR-SDRAM

- **EDDR-SDRAM**—Enhanced DDR SDRAM. EDDR is an advanced form of DDR SRAM that employs on-board cache registers to deliver improved performance.

DDR2

- **DDR2**—Double Data Rate SDRAM 2. DDR2 is an improved version of the DDR memory devices. These devices employ advanced electrical interface technologies to improve the effective clock frequency of the memory module over older DDR devices. These interface technologies include bigger pre-fetch buffers, off-chip driver devices, and on chip termination. Improved manufacturing processes enable the DDR2 operating voltage to be dropped to 1.8 V. DDR2 devices are not compatible with DDR slots. The notch in the edge connector of the DDR2 device is in a different location than that of a DDR module.

Table 3-7 summarizes the characteristics and usage of various types of SDRAM.

Table 3-7: SDRAM Types

	CONFIGURATION	VOLTAGE	DENSITY	FREQUENCY (MHz)	PACKAGE
RDRAM RIMM	32 x 16 32 x 18 64 x 16 64 x 18 128 x 16	2.5 V	64 MB 72 MB 96 MB 108 MB 128 MB 144 MB	300, 356, 400	184-pin RIMMs
DDR SRAM DIMMs (Unbuffered)	16 x 64 32 x 64	2.5 V	128 MB 256 MB	200, 266	184-pin DIMMs
DDR SRAM DIMMs (Registered)	32 x 72	2.5 V	256 MB	200, 266	184-pin DIMMs
SDRAM AIMM*	1 x 32	3.3 V	4 MB	166	66-pin AIMM
100-Pin DIMMs	1 x 32 2 x 32	3.3 V	4 MB 8 MB	100, 125	100-pin DIMMs
	2 x 32	3.3 V	8 MB	125	100-pin DIMM
	4 x 32 8 x 32	3.3 V	16 MB 32 MB	100, 125	100-pin DIMMs
	16 x 32	3.3 V	64 MB	100, 125	100-pin DIMM
	16 x 32 32 x 32	3.3 V	64 MB 128 MB	100, 125	100-pin DIMMs

* AIMM is a special memory card format used with AGP expansion slots.

Table 3-7: SDRAM Types (continued)

	CONFIGURATION	VOLTAGE	DENSITY	FREQUENCY (MHz)	PACKAGE
144-Pin SODIMMs	4 x 64	3.3 V	32 MB	100, 125, 133	144-pin SODIMM
	8 x 64	3.3 V	64 MB	66, 100	144-pin SODIMM
	8 x 64	3.3 V	64 MB	100, 133	144-pin SODIMM
	16 x 64	3.3 V	128 MB	66, 100	144-pin SODIMM
	32 x 64	3.3 V	256 MB	100, 133	144-pin SODIMM
168-Pin DIMMs	4 x 64 8 x 64 16 x 64	3.3 V	32 MB 64 MB 128 MB	66, 100, 133	168-pin SDRAM DIMMs
	8 x 64 16 x 64	3.3 V	64 MB 128 MB	66, 100, 133	168-pin DIMMs
	16 x 64 32 x 64	3.3 V	128 MB 256 MB	100, 133	168-pin DIMMs
	4 x 72 8 x 72 16 x 72	3.3 V	32 MB 64 MB 128 MB	66, 100, 133	168-pin DIMMs
	8 x 72 16 x 72	3.3 V	64 MB 128 MB	66, 100, 133	168-pin DIMMs
	8 x 72 16 x 72	3.3 V	64 MB 128 MB	100, 133	168-pin DIMMs
	16 x 72 32 x 72	3.3 V	128 MB 256 MB	100, 133	168-pin DIMM
	16 x 72 32 x 72 64 x 72	3.3 V	128 MB 256 MB 512 MB	100, 133	168-pin DIMM
	32 x 72 64 x 72	3.3 V	256 MB 512 MB	100, 133	168-pin DIMMs
	64 x 72	3.3 V	512 MB	100, 133	168-pin DIMMs
	64 x 72 128 x 72	3.3 V	512 MB 1 GB	100, 133	168-pin DIMMs

Table 3-7:
SDRAM
Types
(continued)

	CONFIGURATION	VOLTAGE	DENSITY	SPEED (ns)	PACKAGE
	1 x 32 2 x 32	3.3 V	4 MB 8 MB	50 (EDO only), 60	100-pin DIMM
	1 x 32 2 x 32 4 x 32	3.3 V	4 MB 8 MB 16 MB	50, 60	100-pin DIMMs
	4 x 32 8 x 32	3.3 V	16 MB 32 MB	50, 60	72-pin SODIMMs
	4 x 32 8 x 32	3.3 V	16 MB 32 MB	50, 60	144-pin SODIMMs
	4 x 64 8 x 64	3.3 V	32 MB 64 MB	50, 60	168-pin DIMMs
EDO/FPM DRAM **DIMMs/SODIMMs**	4 x 64 8 x 64	3.3 V	32 MB 64 MB	50, 60	168-pin DIMMs
	8 x 64 16 x 64 32 x 64	3.3 V	64 MB 128 MB 256 MB	50, 60	168-pin DIMMs
	4 x 72	3.3 V	32 MB	50, 60	168-pin DIMMs
	4 x 72	3.3 V	32 MB	50, 60	168-pin DIMMs
	8 x 72 16 x 72 32 x 72	3.3 V	64 MB 128 MB 256 MB	50, 60	168-pin DIMMs
	8 x 72 16 x 72 32 x 72	3.3 V	64 MB 128 MB 256 MB	50, 60	168-pin DIMMs

Extended data out (EDO)

Extended data out (EDO) memory increases the speed at which RAM operations are conducted by cutting out the 10-nanosecond wait time normally required between issuing memory addresses. This is accomplished by not disabling the data bus pins between bus cycles. EDO is an advanced type of fast page-mode DRAM, also referred to as hyper page-mode DRAM. The advantage of EDO DRAM is encountered when multiple sequential memory accesses are performed. By not turning off the data pin, each successive access after the first access is accomplished in two clock cycles rather than three.

┌─ **TEST TIP** ──────────────┐
│ Know the difference between EDO and fast │
│ page-mode DRAM. │
└────────────────────────────┘

Rambus

Rambus DRAM (RDRAM)

Direct Rambus DRAM (DRDRAM)

Rambus In-line Memory Module

heat spreader

A company named **Rambus** has designed a proprietary DRAM memory technology that promises very high data delivery speeds. The technology has been given a variety of different names that include **Rambus DRAM (RDRAM)**, **Direct Rambus DRAM (DRDRAM)**, and RIMM. The RIMM reference applies to a special 184-pin memory module that is designed to hold the Rambus devices. While these devices are often referred to as **Rambus Inline Memory Modules**, according to the Rambus company, this is not actually the source for the acronym RIMM. Figure 3-50 shows that RIMMs look similar to DIMMS. However, their high-speed transfer modes generate considerably more heat than normal DIMMs. Therefore, RIMM modules include an aluminum heat shield, referred to as a **heat spreader**, to protect the chips from overheating.

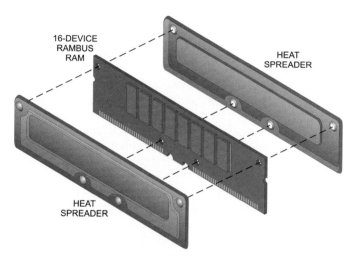

16-DEVICE
RAMBUS
RAM

HEAT
SPREADER

HEAT
SPREADER

Figure 3-50:
RIMM Modules

The Rambus technology employs a special, internal 16-bit data channel that operates in conjunction with a 400 MHz clock. The 16-bit channel permits the device to operate at much higher speeds than more conventional 64-bit buses.

RIMMs look similar to DIMMs, but they have a different pin count. While RIMMs transfer data in 16-bit chunks, the faster access and transfer speed generate more heat.

SRAM

Like DRAM, SRAM is available in a number of different types. Many of the memory organization techniques described for DRAM are also implemented in SRAM.

- **Asynchronous SRAM** is standard SRAM that delivers data from the memory to the microprocessor and returns it to the cache in one clock cycle.

- **Synchronous SRAM** uses special clock signals and buffer storage to deliver data to the CPU in one clock cycle after the first cycle. The first address is stored and used to retrieve the data, while the next address is on its way to the cache.

- **Pipeline SRAM** uses three clock cycles to fetch the first data and then accesses addresses within the selected page on each clock cycle.

- **Burst-mode SRAM** loads a number of consecutive data locations from the cache, over several clock cycles, based on a single address from the microprocessor.

Asynchronous SRAM
Synchronous SRAM
Pipeline SRAM
Burst-mode SRAM

In digital electronics terms, a buffer is a holding area for data shared by devices that operate at different speeds or have different priorities. These devices permit a memory module to operate without the delays that other devices impose. Some types of SDRAM memory modules contain buffer registers directly on the module. The buffer registers hold and retransmit the data signals through the memory chips.

The holding aspect permits the module to coordinate transfers with the outside system. The retransmission factor lowers the signal drain on the host system and enables the memory module to hold more memory chips. Registered and unbuffered memory modules cannot be mixed. The design of the chipset's memory controller dictates which types of memory the computer can use.

Memory Overhead

It has already been mentioned that DRAM devices, commonly used for the system's RAM, require periodic refreshing of their data. Some **refreshing** is performed simply by regular reading and writing of the memory by the system. However, additional circuitry must be used to ensure that every bit in the memory is refreshed within the allotted time frame. In addition to the circuitry, the reading and writing times used for refreshing must be taken into account when designing the system.

Another design factor associated with RAM is data **error detection**. A single incorrect bit can shut down the entire system instantly. With bits constantly moving in and out of RAM, it is crucial that all of the bits be transferred correctly. The most popular form of error detection in PC compatibles is **parity checking**. In this methodology, an extra bit is added to each word in RAM and checked each time it is used. Like refreshing, parity checking requires additional circuitry and memory overhead to operate.

DRAM Refresh

Dynamic RAM devices require that data stored in them be **refreshed**, or rewritten, periodically to keep the data from fading away. As a matter of fact, each bit in the DRAM must be refreshed at least once every 2 milliseconds or the data will dissipate. Because it can't be assumed that each bit in the memory will be accessed during the normal operation of the system (within the time frame allotted), the need to constantly refresh the data in the DRAM requires special circuitry to perform this function.

The extra circuitry and inconvenience associated with refreshing may initially make DRAM memory seem like a distant second choice behind static RAM. However, due to the simplicity of DRAM's internal structure, the bit-storage capacity of a DRAM chip is much greater than that of a similar static RAM chip, and it offers a much lower rate of power consumption. Both of these factors contribute to making DRAM memory the economical choice in certain RAM memory systems, even in light of the extra circuitry necessary for refreshing.

Error Checking and Correcting

Parity checking is a simple self-test used to detect RAM read-back errors. When a data byte is stored in memory, the occurrences of logic "1s" in the byte are added together by the parity generator/checker chip. This chip produces a parity bit that is added to, and stored along with, the data byte. Therefore, the data byte becomes a 9-bit word. Whenever the data word is read back from the memory, the parity bit is reapplied to the parity generator and recalculated.

> **TEST TIP**
> Know that parity is a method of checking stored data for errors by adding an additional bit to it when it is read from memory.

The recalculated parity value is then compared to the original parity value stored in memory. If the values do not match, a parity-error condition occurs, and an error message is generated. Traditionally, there are two approaches to generating parity bits; the parity bit may be generated so that the total number of 1-bits equals an even number (**even parity**) or an odd number (**odd parity**).

To enable parity checking, an additional ninth bit is added to each byte stored in DRAM. On older systems, an extra memory chip was included with each bank of DRAM. In newer units, the extra storage is built into the DIMM modules. Whether a particular system employs parity check or not depends on its chipset. Many newer chipsets have moved away from using parity checking altogether. In these cases, DIMMs with parity capability can be used, but the parity function will not function. In Pentium systems, the system board's user's guide or the BIOS' Extended CMOS Setup screen should be consulted to determine whether parity is supported. If so, the parity function can be enabled through this screen.

Figure 3-51 illustrates how the system's RAM and parity checking circuit work together.

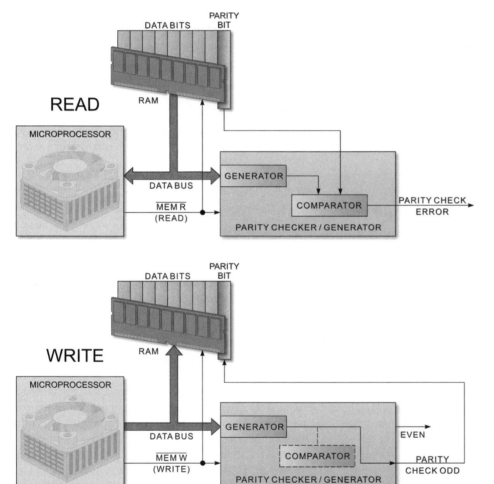

**Figure 3-51:
How Parity
Checking Works**

When a parity error occurs, a **nonmaskable interrupt (NMI)** signal is cogenerated in the system, causing the BIOS to execute its NMI handler routine. This routine will normally place a parity error message on the screen, along with an option to shut down the system, or continue.

nonmaskable
interrupt (NMI)

error checking and
correcting (ECC)

In some applications, stability is of the utmost concern for the system design. In these systems, advanced RAM types that include **error checking and correcting (ECC)** capabilities are used. ECC provides additional data integrity by detecting and often correcting errors in the information they process. However, the additional data manipulation that goes on inside the memory devices causes ECC RAM to provide lower performance than its non-ECC counterparts.

┌─ **TEST TIP** ─────────────┐
│ Be aware of the types of problems │
│ that can create NMI errors and what │
│ the consequences of these errors are. │
└──────────────────────────┘

GEEK SQUAD CASE FILE #56878

Special Agent 147 has been called on to check out a failing computer in the production department. When Agent 147 arrives, he finds that the system is continually locking up and rebooting when the operating system loads. What type of problem is the system likely to be having, and what should Agent 147 do about it?

Advanced Memory Structures

As the operating speeds of microcomputers have continued to increase, it has become increasingly necessary to develop new memory strategies to keep pace with the other parts of the system. Some of these methods, such as developing faster DRAM chips, or including wait states in the memory-access cycles, are fundamental in nature. However, these methods do not allow the entire system to operate at its full potential. Other, more elaborate memory management schemes have been employed on faster computers to maximize their overall performance.

Cache Memory

caching

One method of increasing the memory-access speed of a computer is called **caching**. This memory management method assumes that most memory accesses are made within a limited block of addresses. Therefore, if the contents of these addresses are relocated into a special section of high-speed SRAM, then the microprocessor can access these locations without requiring any wait states.

Cache memory is normally small to keep the cost of the system as low as possible. However, it is also very fast, even in comparison to fast DRAM devices.

Cache memory operations require a great deal of intelligent circuitry to operate and monitor the cache effectively. The cache controller circuitry must monitor the microprocessor's memory-access instructions to determine if the specified data is stored in the cache. If the information is in the cache, the control circuitry can present it to the microprocessor without incurring any wait states. This is referred to as a **hit**. If the information is not located in the cache, the access is passed on to the system's RAM, and it is declared a **miss**.

hit

miss

The primary objective of the cache memory's control system is to maximize the ratio of hits to total accesses (hit rate), so that the majority of memory accesses are performed without wait states. One way to do this is to make the cache memory area as large as possible (thus raising the possibility of the desired information being in the cache). However, the relative cost, energy consumption, and physical size of SRAM devices work against this technique. Practical sizes for cache memories working directly with the microprocessor run between 16 kB and 512 kB. As you will see in the following section, additional levels of on-board and remote cache can be much larger. However, these caches require more management circuitry.

The Intel 80486 and the original Pentium microprocessors (Pentium I and Pentium MMX) had a built-in first-level cache, referred to as **L1 cache**, that was used for both instructions and data. The internal cache in these units was divided into four 2 kB blocks containing 128 sets of 16-byte lines each. Control of the internal cache is handled directly by the microprocessor. However, many system boards that supported these processors extended their caching capabilities by adding an external, second-level 256 kB/512 kB memory cache, referred to as an **L2 cache**.

With the Pentium Pro, Intel moved the 256 kB or 512 kB L2 cache from the system board to the processor package. This design technique continued through the Pentium II and III slot processors, so that the 256 kB/512 kB L2 cache resided in the microprocessor cartridge. In their Celeron and Coppermine devices, Intel moved the L2 cache (128 kB /256 kB and 256 kB/512 kB, respectively) onto the actual microprocessor dye. Moving the L2 cache onto the dye made the microprocessor directly responsible for managing the cache and enabled it to run at full speed with the microprocessor. In all of these systems, no cache existed on the system board.

When Intel designed the Itanium processor, they built in capabilities for managing an additional external level of cache in the microprocessor cartridge. This additional cache level was dubbed **L3 cache**. The Xeon processor has continued this design concept and improved it by moving a 1 MB or 2 MB L3 cache onto the microprocessor dye. Once again the external cache is able to run at full speed with the microprocessor.

The computer industry has taken a more liberal definition of L3 cache, sometimes referring to L3 cache as cache memory mounted on system boards where the processors already possess on-board L1 and L2 cache. An external cache memory system is depicted in Figure 3-52.

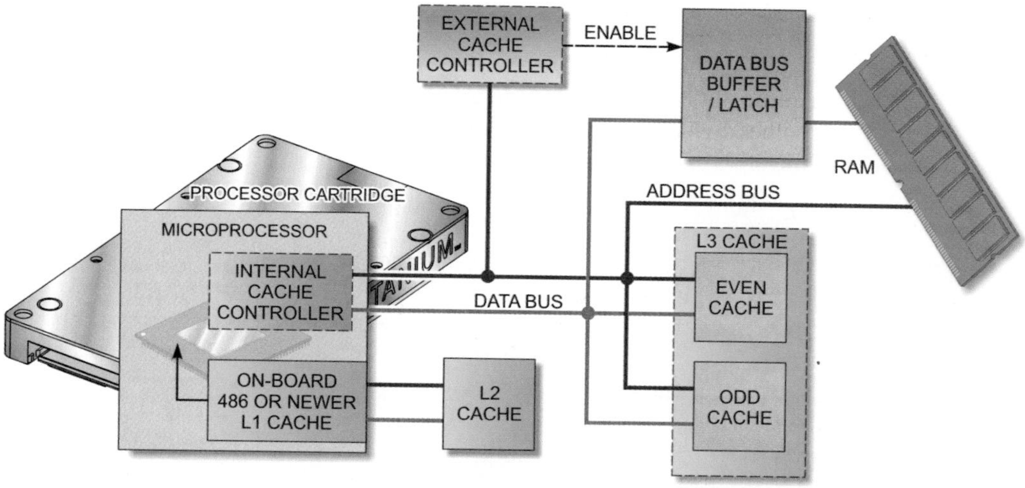

Figure 3-52: An External Cache

Paging

interleaving

page-mode RAM

static-column RAM

pages

row address strobe
(RAS)

Fast page-mode RAM

column address
strobe (CAS)

Memory Paging and Interleaving

There are also other commonly used methods of organizing RAM memory so that it can be accessed more efficiently. Typically, memory accesses occur in two fashions—instruction fetches (which are generally sequential) and operand accesses (which tend to be random). **Paging** and **interleaving** memory schemes are designed to take advantage of the sequential nature of instruction fetches from memory.

The basic idea of page-mode DRAM operations is illustrated in Figure 3-53. Special memory devices called **page-mode** (or **static-column**) **RAM** are required for memory paging structures. In these memory devices, data are organized into groups of rows and columns called **pages**. Once a ROW access is made in the device, it is possible to access other column addresses within the same row without precharging its **row address strobe (RAS)** line. This feature produces access times that are half that of normal DRAM memories. **Fast page-mode RAM** is a quicker version of page-mode RAM that has improved **column address strobe (CAS)** access speed.

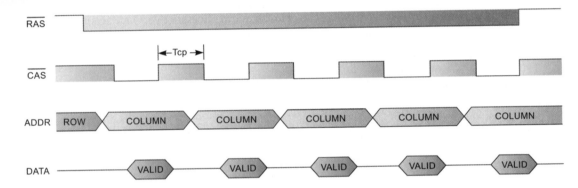

Figure 3-53: Page-Mode DRAM Operation

The operating principle behind memory interleaving is shown in Figure 3-54. Typical interleaving schemes divide the memory into two banks of RAM with one bank storing even addresses and the other storing odd addresses.

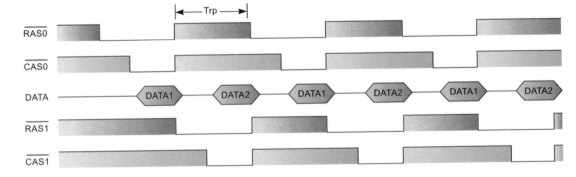

Figure 3-54: Memory Interleaving

precharge

The RAS signals of the two banks overlap so that the time required to **precharge** one bank's RAS line is used for the active RAS time of the other bank. Therefore, there should never be a precharge time for either bank, as long as the accesses continue to be sequential. If a nonsequential access occurs, a miss is encountered, and a wait state must be inserted in the timing. If the memory is organized into two banks, the operation is referred to as two-way interleaving. It is also common to organize the memory into four equal-sized banks. This organization effectively doubles the average 0-wait state hit space in the memory.

GEEK SQUAD CASE FILE #53339

Double Agent 957 has been assigned to upgrade the memory in a number of your office's computers. When the agent opens them, he discovers that they have a three-slot DIMM arrangement. Also, they cannot locate a system board user manual for these computers. Agent 957 installs a 128 MB DIMM in each slot. When he starts the computer, he sees from the POST that the system only recognizes 256 MB of RAM. What happened to the other 128 MB of RAM, and how can Agent 957 get the system to recognize it?

RAM Speed Ratings

Essentials 1.1

Depot Technician 1.1

IT Technician 1.1

Another important factor to consider when dealing with RAM is its speed. Manufacturers mark RAM devices with speed information. DRAM modules are marked with a numbering system that indicates the number of clock cycles required for the initial Read operation, followed by information about the number of reads and cycles required to move a burst of data. As an example, a fast page-mode DRAM marked as 6-3-3-3 requires six cycles for the initial read and three cycles for each of three successive reads. This will move an entire 4-byte block of data. EDO and FPM can operate with bus speeds up to 66 MHz.

SDRAM devices are marked differently. Because they are designed to run synchronously with the system clock and use no wait states, a marking of 3:3:3 at 100 MHz on an SDRAM module specifies that

- The CAS signal setup time is 3 bus cycles.

- The RAS to CAS changeover time is 3 cycles.

- The RAS signal setup time is 3 clock cycles.

The bus speed is specified in MHz. These memory modules have been produced in the following versions:

- PC66 (66 MHz or 15 nanoseconds)

- PC83 (83 MHz or 12 nanoseconds)

- PC100 (100 MHz or 10 nanoseconds)

- PC133 (133 MHz or 8 nanoseconds)

- PC150 (150 MHz or 4.5 nanoseconds)

- PC166 (166 MHz or 4 nanoseconds)

The PC66 and PC83 specifications were the first versions produced using this system. However, they never really gained widespread acceptance. On the other hand, the PC100 and PC133 versions did gain acceptance and are widely available today. The PC150 and PC166 versions are also common.

Continued advancements in memory module design have made the MHz and CAS setup time ratings obsolete. On-board buffering along with advanced clocking and access strategies have made these measurements inconsequential. Instead, memory performance is now measured by total data **throughput** (also referred to as **bandwidth**) and in terms of gigabytes per second (GBps). As an example, some of the new standard specifications include the following *double-pumped* **double data rate (DDR)** modules:

throughput

bandwidth

double data rate (DDR)

- PC1600 (1.6 GBps/200 MHz/2:2:2)

- PC2100 (2.1 GBps/266 MHz/2:3:3)

- PC2600 (2.6 GBps/333 MHz/3:3:3)

- PC3200 (3.2 GBps/400 MHz/3:3:3)

Likewise, there is a range of specifications for **dual-channel, double data rate 2 (DDR2)** modules. These include

dual-channel, double data rate 2 (DDR2)

- PC2-3200 (3.2 GBps/200 MHz/3:3:3)

- PC2-4200 (4.267 GBps/266 MHz/3:3:3)

- PC2-5300 (5.333 GBps/333 MHz/3:3:3)

- PC2-6400 (6.4 GBps/400 MHz/3:3:3)

TEST TIP

Be aware of the consequences of mixing RAM with different speed ratings within a system.

The system board's documentation will provide information about the types of devices it can use and their speed ratings. It is important to install RAM that is compatible with the bus speed the system is running. Normally, installing RAM that is rated faster than the bus speed will not cause problems. However, installing slower RAM or mixing RAM speed ratings in a system will cause the system to not start or to periodically lock up.

Essentials 1.1

Depot Technician 1.1

CMOS RAM

During the POST process, you can press the DEL key to access the CMOS Setup routines that modify the operation of some BIOS functions. In other BIOS types, the CTRL/ALT/ESC key combination can also be used to access the Setup utilities. The CMOS Setup utility's Main Menu screen, similar to the one depicted in Figure 3-55, appears whenever the CMOS Setup utility is engaged. This menu allows the user to select setup functions and exit choices. The most used entries include the **Standard CMOS Features, Advanced BIOS Features**, and **Advanced Chipset Features Setup** options. Selecting these, or any of the other Main Menu options, will lead into a corresponding submenu.

Standard CMOS Features

Advanced BIOS Features

Advanced Chipset Features Setup

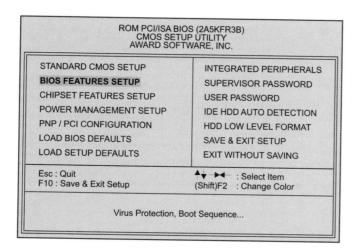

```
                ROM PCI/ISA BIOS (2A5KFR3B)
                    CMOS SETUP UTILITY
                    AWARD SOFTWARE, INC.

   STANDARD CMOS SETUP          INTEGRATED PERIPHERALS
   BIOS FEATURES SETUP          SUPERVISOR PASSWORD
   CHIPSET FEATURES SETUP       USER PASSWORD
   POWER MANAGEMENT SETUP       IDE HDD AUTO DETECTION
   PNP / PCI CONFIGURATION      HDD LOW LEVEL FORMAT
   LOAD BIOS DEFAULTS           SAVE & EXIT SETUP
   LOAD SETUP DEFAULTS          EXIT WITHOUT SAVING

   Esc : Quit                   ▲▼ ►◄   : Select Item
   F10 : Save & Exit Setup      (Shift)F2  : Change Color

              Virus Protection, Boot Sequence...
```

Figure 3-55: CMOS Main Menu Screen

Other typical menu items include **Power Management Setup, PnP/PCI Configuration, Integrated Peripherals, PC Health Status,** and **Password Maintenance Services.** A given CMOS Setup utility may contain the same options as those listed in the sample, options that perform the same functions under a different name, or it may not contain options at all. This example also offers two IDE HDD-related utilities, two options for starting with default system values, and two exit options.

BIOS designers have built two options (**Auto Configuration** and **Default Settings**) into newer versions to help users deal with the complexity of the advanced CMOS configuration. Newer system boards use an autoconfiguration mode that takes over most of the setup decisions. This option works well in most cases, producing settings for an efficient, basic level of operation for standard devices in the system. However, it doesn't optimize the performance of the system. To do that, it's necessary to turn off the autoconfiguration feature and insert the desired parameters into the configuration table. Two options typically exist for the autoconfiguration function: **Auto Configure with Power-On Defaults** and **Auto Configure with BIOS Defaults.**

The autoconfiguration power-on defaults provide the most conservative system options from the BIOS, and the most effective method of detecting BIOS-related system problems. These settings replace any user-entered configuration information in the CMOS Setup registers, disabling the turbo speed mode, turning off all memory caching, and setting all wait states to maximum, thus enabling the most basic part of the system for starting.

If these default values fail to boot the system, it indicates possible hardware problems such as incorrect jumper settings or bad components.

If you have entered an improper configuration setting and cannot determine which setting is causing the problem, using the autoconfiguration with the BIOS defaults provides more flexibility than the power-on option. This selection also replaces the entered configuration settings with a new set of parameters from the BIOS, and gets you back into the CMOS Setup screen so that you can track down the problem. This is also the recommended starting point for optimizing the system's operation.

Power Management Setup

PnP/PCI Configuration

Integrated Peripherals

PC Health Status

Password Maintenance Services

Auto Configuration

Default Settings

Auto Configure with Power-On Defaults

Auto Configure with BIOS Defaults

WARNING

Set values with caution—The settings in these menus enable the system to be configured and optimized for specific functions and devices. The **default values** are generally recommended for normal operation. Because incorrect Setup values can cause the system to fail, you should only change Setup values that really need to be changed. If changes are made that disable the system, pressing the Insert key on reset will override the settings and start the system with default values.

default values

Typical CMOS Features Screens

Standard CMOS Features

Standard CMOS Features screens from various manufacturers are depicted in Figure 3-56. They all provide the same basic information. They can be used to set the system clock/calendar, establish disk drive parameters and video display type, and specify which types of errors will halt the system during the POST.

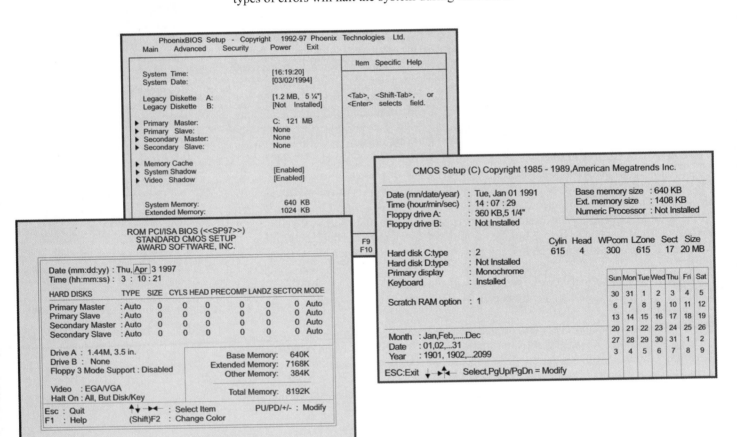

Figure 3-56: Standard CMOS Setup Screens

The BIOS uses military time settings (i.e., 13:00:00 = 1 PM). The PgUp and PgDn keys are used to change the setting after it has been selected using the arrow keys. Some BIOS versions support Daylight Savings time by adding an hour when Daylight Savings time begins and subtracting it when standard time returns.

Current BIOS typically support 360 kB, 720 kB, 1.2 MB, 1.44 MB, and 2.88 MB floppy drive formats. The other area in this screen that may require some effort to set up is the HDD parameters section. All BIOS come with a list of hard drive types that they can support directly. However, they also provide an entry for user-definable drive settings. Historically, this entry has been referred to as the "Type 47" but may be located at any number in the list.

Most BIOS possess **Auto Detect** options to detect the type of hard drives installed in the system and automatically load their parameters into CMOS. Systems with Enhanced IDE capabilities support up to four IDE drives. However, the CMOS does not typically display information about CD-ROM drives or SCSI devices.

Auto Detect

When the Auto Detect selection is chosen, the BIOS attempts to detect IDE devices in the system during the POST process and to determine the specifications and optimum operating modes for those devices. The drive specifications can also be selected from a built-in list of drive parameters, or they can be entered directly using the User option at the end of the list.

Four **translation modes** can be selected for each drive type: Auto, Normal, Large, and LBA. In Auto mode, the BIOS will establish the best operating mode for the drive. In Normal mode, the BIOS will support a maximum **Cyl/Hds/Sec (CHS)** setting of 1024/16/63. For larger drives (above 1024 cylinders), the Large and LBA modes are used. The Large option can be used with large drives that do not support **logical block addressing (LBA)** techniques. For those drives that do, the LBA mode should be selected. In this mode, the IDE controller converts the sector/head/cylinder address into a physical block address that improves data throughput. Care should be taken when changing this BIOS setting, because data loss may occur.

translation modes

Cyl/Hds/Sec (CHS)

logical block addressing (LBA)

Similarly, most BIOS still support standard EGA/VGA formats, as well as older 40- and 80-column CGA and monochrome formats. In the case of errors detected during the POST process, the BIOS can be set up to halt on different types of errors, or to ignore them and continue the bootup process. These settings include

> **TEST TIP**
>
> Know that the LBA mode for SCSI and IDE disk drives must be enabled in the CMOS to support hard drive sizes over 528 MB.

- *No Errors.* The POST does not stop for any errors.

- *All Errors.* The POST stops for all detected errors and prompts the user for corrective action.

- *A series of "All But" options.* The POST stops for all errors except those selected (i.e., all but disk or keyboard errors).

> **TEST TIP**
>
> Be aware that changing the translation mode setting for an existing drive may result in loss of all data.

Finally, the screen displays the system's memory usage. The values displayed are derived from the POST process and cannot be changed through the menu. The BIOS displays the system's total detected RAM, base memory, extended memory, and other memory (between the 640 kB and 1 MB marks). In most CMOS displays, the total memory does not equal the summation of the base and extended memory. This is because the BIOS reserves 384 kB for shadowing purposes. Newer BIOS versions may only show the total installed system memory.

The Advanced BIOS Features Setup Screen

Advanced BIOS Features

virus warning utility

> **TEST TIP**
>
> Be aware that you should turn off any BIOS anti-virus protection settings when changing operating systems.

The **Advanced BIOS Features** Setup screen, shown in Figure 3-57, provides access to options that extend the standard BIOS functions. This BIOS example includes a built-in **virus warning utility** that produces a warning message whenever a program tries to write to the boot sector of an HDD partition table. This function should be enabled for normal operations. However, it should be turned off when upgrading to the operating system. The built-in virus warning utility checks the drive's boot sector for changes. The changes that the new operating system will attempt to make to the boot sector will be interpreted as a virus, and the utility will act to prevent the upgrade from occurring. If a warning message is displayed under normal circumstances, a full-feature anti-virus utility should be run on the system.

```
                    ROM PCI/ISA BIOS (2A5KFR3B)
                       STANDARD CMOS SETUP
                       AWARD SOFTWARE, INC.

Virus Warning               : Disabled  | Video     BIOS Shadow : Enabled
CPU Internal Cache          : Enabled   | C8000-CBFFF Shadow    : Disabled
External Cache              : Enabled   | CC000-CFFF  Shadow    : Disabled
Quick Power On Self Test    : Disabled  | D0000-D3FFF Shadow    : Disabled
Boot Sequence               : A,C, SCSI | D4000-D7FFF Shadow    : Disabled
Swap Floppy Drive           : Disabled  | D8000-DBFFF Shadow    : Disabled
Boot Up Floppy Seek         : Enabled   | DC000-DFFFF Shadow    : Disabled
Boot Up Numlock Status      : On        |
Boot Up System Speed        : High      |
Gate A20 Option             : Fast      |
Memory Parity Check         : Disabled  |
Typematic Rate Setting      : Disabled  |
Typematic Rate (Chars/Sec)  : 6         |
Typematic Delay (Msec)      : 250       |
Security Option             : Setup     | ESC : Quit        ↑↓→←  : Select Item
PCI/VGA Palette Snoop       : Disabled  | F1  : Help        PU/PD/+/- : Modify
OS Select For DRAM > 64M    : Non-OS2   | F5  : Old Values  (Shift)F2  Color
                                        | F6  : Load BIOS  Defaults
                                        | F7  : Load Setup Defaults
```

Figure 3-57: BIOS Features Setup Screen

The Advanced BIOS Features Setup screen is used to configure different bootup options. These options include establishing the system's bootup sequence. Most BIOS versions typically provide user definable boot sequences for up to four devices. The most commonly used sequence simply checks the first hard drive as the first boot source. Newer BIOS versions can be configured to boot from a CD-ROM device. The sequence can be set so that the system checks the floppy drive for a boot sector first.

Swap Floppy Drive

Other common bootup options include Floppy Drive Seek, Numlock Status, and System Speed settings. The **Swap Floppy Drive** option can be enabled to route commands for logical drive A to physical drive B. This option can be used to isolate FDD problems in dual-drive units. Likewise, the Drive A option should be enabled if the system cannot boot to the hard-disk drive.

parity checking

Gate A20

The system board's cache memory organization is displayed in the screen's External Cache Memory field. The CMOS provides options for controlling the system's A20 line and **parity checking** functions. The operation of the A20 line is connected to the system's changeover from Real mode to Protected mode and back. When set to the Fast mode, the chipset controls the operation of the system's A20 line. If the Normal mode setting is selected, the keyboard controller circuitry controls the **Gate A20** function. The operating system uses this function to enable the Real mode changeover. The system's parity checking function is used to check for corruption in the contents of data read from DRAM memory.

The operation of the keyboard can be modified from this screen. **Typematic Action** refers to the keyboard's ability to reproduce characters when a key is held down for a period of time. This action is governed by two parameters set in the BIOS Features screen—Typematic Rate and Typematic Delay. **Typematic Rate** refers to the rate at which characters will be repeated when the key is held down, while **Typematic Delay** defines the amount of time between the initial pressing of the key and when the repeating action begins. Typematic action is normally enabled, and values of six characters/second and 250 milliseconds are typical for these settings.

GEEK SQUAD CASE FILE #68349

CIA 555 is working the Geek Squad counter when a customer brings in a system that will not bootup to the hard drive. So Agent 555 places a bootable CD-ROM in the drive and tries to restart the system. The agent watches the start-up sequence closely and discovers that the system does not appear to check the CD-ROM drive for a disc. What should Agent 555 do to get the system to look for a disc in the CD-ROM drive as part of the bootup activities?

The Chipset Features Screen

An Advanced Chipset Features screen, depicted in Figure 3-58, contains advanced setting information that system designers and service personnel use to optimize the chipset. The options and submenus associated with this page can vary greatly from chipset to chipset. Obviously, the options that you can configure here depend on the functions the chipset provides (e.g., FSB options, processor speed/voltage options, AGP configurations, thermal throttling, memory timing options, etc.).

```
              ROM PCI/ISA BIOS (2A5KFR3B)
                 CHIPSET FEATURES SETUP
                  AWARD SOFTWARE, INC.

Auto Configuration     : Enabled   Word Merge          : Enabled
AT Bus Clock           : CLK2/4    Byte Merge          : Disabled
Asysc. SRAM Write WS   : X-3-3-3   Fast Back-to-Back   : Disabled
Asysc. SRAM Read WS    : X-3-3-3   PCI Write Burst     : Enabled
EDO Read WS            : X-3-3-3   SDRAM Access Timing : Normal
Page Mode Read WS      : X-3-3-3   SDRAM CAS Latency   : 3
DRAM Write WS          : X-2-2-2   TAG [10-8] Config   : Default
CPU to DRAM Page Mode  : Disabled
DRAM Refresh Period    : 60 us
DRAM Data Integrity Mode : Parity
Pipelined Function     : Disabled
16 Bit ISA I/O Command WS : 2 Wait
16 Bit ISA Mem Command WS: 2 Wait
Local Memory 15-16M    : Enabled
Passive Release        : Enabled
ISA Line Buffer        : Enabled   ESC : Quit       ↑↓ →← : Select Item
Delay Transaction      : Enabled   F1  : Help       PU/PD/+/- : Modify
Primary Frame Buffer   : 2 MB      F5  : Old Values  (Shift)F2 : Color
VGA Frame Buffer       : Enabled   F6  : Load BIOS Defaults
Linear Merge           : Enabled   F7  : Load Setup Defaults
```

Figure 3-58: Chipset Features Screen

The **Auto Configuration** option selects predetermined optimal values for the chipset to start with. When this feature is enabled, many of the screen's fields are not available to the user. When this setting is disabled, the chipset's setup parameters are obtained from the system's CMOS RAM. Many of the system's memory configuration parameters are established in this screen.

Data Integrity

error checking and correcting (ECC)

These parameters can include wait state timing for asynchronous SDRAM read and writes, as well as EDO and page-mode RAM reads. Special DRAM paging operations can be enabled in the Chipset Features screen. When this option is disabled, the chipset's memory controller closes the DRAM page after each access. When enabled, it holds the page open until the next access occurs. DRAM refresh period and **Data Integrity** functions are also established here. This particular chipset features both parity error checking and **error checking and correcting (ECC)** error handling modes.

TEST TIP

Be aware that parity checking detects only data errors, whereas ECC can detect and correct data errors.

The PnP/PCI Configuration Screen

The BIOS holds information about the system's resource allocations and supplies it to the operating system as required. Figure 3-59 shows the PCI Configuration screen from the sample CMOS Setup utility. The operating system must be PnP-compatible in order to achieve the full benefits of the PnP BIOS. In most newer PCs, the standard operating system is some version of Windows, which is PnP compliant.

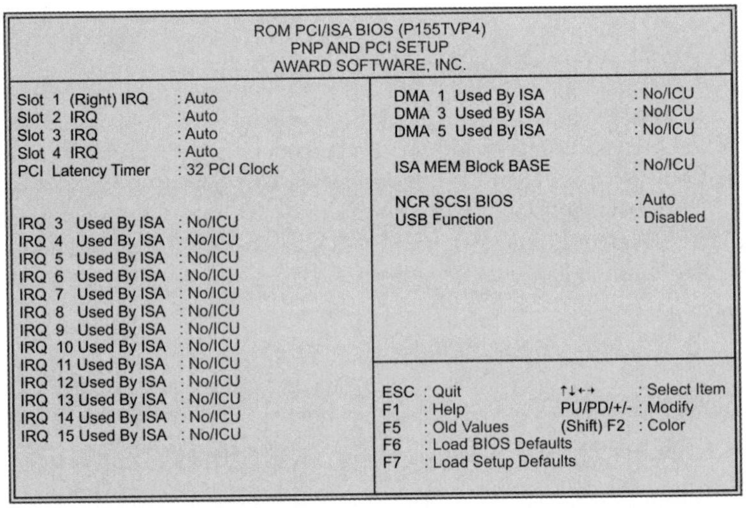

Figure 3-59: PnP/PCI Configuration Options Screen

Auto mode

This CMOS utility can automatically configure all PnP devices if the **Auto mode** is enabled. Under this condition, the system's IRQ and DMA assignment fields disappear as the BIOS assigns them to installed devices. When the configuration process is performed manually, each resource can be assigned as either a legacy device or a PnP/PCI device. The legacy device is one that is compatible with the original ISA slot and requires specific resource settings. The PnP/PCI device must be compliant with the Plug-and-Play specification.

TEST TIP

Know which portion of the BIOS is responsible for implementing the PnP process.

PCI IRQ Map-to

With this chipset, the system board's IDE channels are coordinated with the operation of the PCI bus. The **PCI IRQ Map-to** function lets the user establish the PCI IRQ mapping for the system. Because the PCI interface in the sample chipset has two channels, it requires two interrupt services. The primary and secondary IDE interrupt fields default to values appropriate for two PCI IDE channels. The primary channel has a lower interrupt number than the secondary channel. Normally, ISA interrupts reserved for IDE channels are IRQ14 for the primary channel and IRQ15 for the secondary channel.

The secondary IDE channel can be deactivated through the PCI IDE Second Channel option. This setting is usually disabled so that an add-on IDE host adapter card can be added to the system. Only the secondary on-board IDE channel is disabled through this setting. The type of action required to trigger the interrupt can also be established in this screen. The PCI IRQ activated by option is normally set to Level unless a device that requires an ISA-compatible, edge-triggered interrupt is added to the system.

The Integrated Peripherals Setup Functions

In most Pentium-based systems, the standard I/O functions are configured through the BIOS' **Integrated Peripherals** screen, depicted in Figure 3-60. This screen provides configuration and enabling settings for the system board's IDE drive connections, floppy-disk drive controller, on-board UARTs, and on-board parallel port.

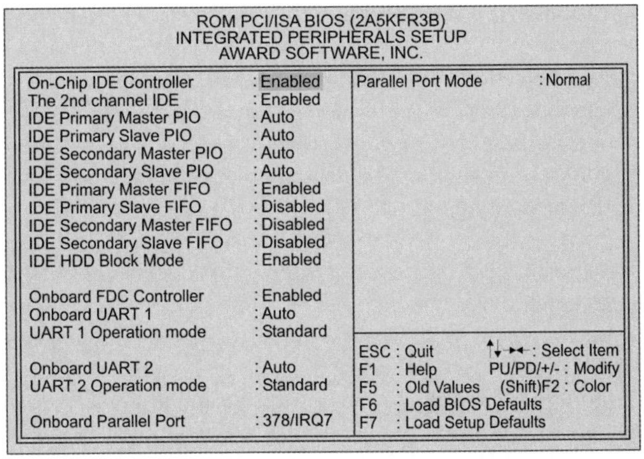

Integrated Peripherals

```
              ROM PCI/ISA BIOS (2A5KFR3B)
              INTEGRATED PERIPHERALS SETUP
                   AWARD SOFTWARE, INC.

 On-Chip IDE Controller      : Enabled    Parallel Port Mode      : Normal
 The 2nd channel IDE         : Enabled
 IDE Primary Master PIO      : Auto
 IDE Primary Slave PIO       : Auto
 IDE Secondary Master PIO    : Auto
 IDE Secondary Slave PIO     : Auto
 IDE Primary Master FIFO     : Enabled
 IDE Primary Slave FIFO      : Disabled
 IDE Secondary Master FIFO   : Disabled
 IDE Secondary Slave FIFO    : Disabled
 IDE HDD Block Mode          : Enabled

 Onboard FDC Controller      : Enabled
 Onboard UART 1              : Auto
 UART 1 Operation mode       : Standard
                                          ESC : Quit         ↑↓→← : Select Item
 Onboard UART 2              : Auto       F1  : Help      PU/PD/+/- : Modify
 UART 2 Operation mode       : Standard   F5  : Old Values   (Shift)F2 : Color
                                          F6  : Load BIOS Defaults
 Onboard Parallel Port       : 378/IRQ7   F7  : Load Setup Defaults
```

Figure 3-60: Integrated Peripherals Screen

The Integrated Peripherals screen is used to enable the on-board IDE controller. As mentioned earlier in this chapter, the second IDE channel can be enabled or disabled independently of the first channel, provided that the controller has been enabled. Any of the four possible devices attached to the interface can be configured for Master or Slave operation.

On older systems, each IDE device can also be enabled for **programmed input/output (PIO)** modes and **first in/first out (FIFO) buffering**. The PIO field permits the user to select any of four PIO modes (0−4) for each device. The PIO mode determines how fast data will be transferred between the drive and the system. The performance level of the device typically increases with each higher mode value.

programmed input/output (PIO)

first in/first out (FIFO) buffering

Most BIOS versions provided for a manual PIO configuration setting. In Mode-0, the transfer rate is set at 3.3 MB/second with a 600 nanosecond (ns) cycle time. Mode-1 steps up to 5.2 MB/s with a 3.3 ns cycle time. Mode-2 improves to 8.3 MB/s using a 240 ns cycle time.

However, the newer ATA standards provide for different *programmed I/O (PIO)* modes that offer higher performance capabilities. Most of the faster drives support PIO Modes-3 and -4 through the ATA-2 specification. These modes use 11.1 MB/s with a 180 ns cycle time and 16.6 MB/s using a 120 ns cycle time, respectively. These modes require that the IDE port be located on a local bus, such as a PCI bus. However, the IDE port must be attached to the PCI bus to use these modes. Newer BIOS versions also support PATA devices with ultra DMA options and PIO selections.

If the *Auto mode* option is selected, the system will determine which mode is best suited for each device. If FIFO operation is selected, the system establishes special FIFO buffers for each device to speed up data flow between the device and the system.

The IDE HDD Block mode selection should be set to *Enabled* for most new hard drives. This setting, also referred to as Large Block Transfer, Multiple Command, and Multiple-Sector Read/Write mode, supports LBA disk drive operations so that partitions larger than 528 MB can be used on the drive.

TEST TIP

Remember that ECP and EPP modes for the parallel port must be enabled through the CMOS Setup utility.

The other on-board I/O functions supported through the CMOS utility include enabling the FDD controller, selecting the logical COM port addressing and operating modes for the system's two built-in UARTs, and selecting logical addressing and operating modes for the parallel port.

The UARTs can be configured to support half-duplex or full-duplex transmission modes through an infrared port, provided the system board is equipped with one. This allows wireless communications with serial peripheral devices over short distances.

standard parallel port (SPP)

extended parallel port (EPP)

extended capabilities port (ECP)

Infrared data association (IrDA) ports

The parallel printer port can be configured for **standard parallel port** (SPP) operation, for extended bidirectional operation (**extended parallel port—EPP**), for fast, buffered bi-directional operation (**extended capabilities port—ECP**), or for combined ECP+EPP operation. The normal setting should be selected unless both the port hardware and driver software support EPP or ECP operation.

Infrared data association (IrDA) ports provide short-distance wireless connections for different IrDA-compliant devices, such as printers and personal digital assistants. Because the IrDA port communicates by sending and receiving a serial stream of light pulses, it is normally configured to work with the UART of the system's second serial port. This arrangement is established through the Integrated Peripherals page of the CMOS Setup utility. In this manner, the infrared port is assigned the same system resources normally reserved for the COM2/COM4 serial ports.

To enable the IrDA port, the mode for the COM2 UART must be set to automatic, and one of the infrared protocol settings (*HPSIR* or *ASKIR*) must be selected. In addition, the transmission duplex mode must be selected (normally half duplex). The operation of the infrared port and the second serial port are mutually exclusive. When the infrared option is enabled in CMOS, the second serial port will be disabled.

MIDI

Other functions configured through this screen include on-board audio and local area networking interfaces as well as on-board USB and IEEE-1394 Firewire ports. Some boards may also offer built in support for game ports and **MIDI** music ports.

Power Management Functions

Power Management

Doze

Standby

Suspend

The **Power Management** fields allow the user to select from three power-saving modes: **Doze**, **Standby**, and **Suspend**. These are green PC-compatible power saving modes that cause the system to incrementally step down from maximum power usage. The Doze setting causes the microprocessor clock to slow down after a defined period of inactivity. The Standby mode causes the hard drive and video to shut down after a period of inactivity. Finally, everything in the system except the microprocessor shuts down in Suspend mode. Certain system events, such as IRQ and DRQ activities, cause the system to wake up from these modes and resume normal operation.

PC Health Status

The PC Health menu, shown in Figure 3-61, displays status information for the critical elements of the system board, including the microprocessor temperature, fan speeds, and actual voltage levels. The page also enables you to establish set points for issuing notifications and alarms when these variables are outside of the desired ranges of operation.

Temperature monitoring can be as simple as tracking the microprocessor's package temperature or it can include monitoring the case temperature in multiple locations. Key voltage levels tracked by the BIOS include the microprocessor core voltage, the expansion slot voltages, and the various voltage levels being provided to the system board by the power supply.

Finally, this screen enables you to establish a warning and system shut down level that will either warn the user something is going bad or will go ahead and shut the system down to protect the microprocessor from harm.

```
                  Phoenix - AwardBIOS CMOS Setup Utility
                             PC Health Status

  Show PC Health in POST      [Enabled]                      Item Help
  Smart CPU Fan Temperature   [Disabled]
  Current System Temperature  29°C/84°F          Menu Level    ▶
  Current CPU Temperature     40°C/104°F
  Current System FAN Speed    0 RPM
  Current CPU FAN Speed       0 RPM
  Current Power FAN Speed     0 RPM
  CPU Voltage                 1.53 V
  AGP Voltage                 1.50 V
  Chipset Voltage             1.60 V
  + 5 V                       4.97 V
  DIMM Voltage                2.72 V
  Battery Voltage             3.20 V
  5V Standby                  5.05 V
  ACPI Shutdown Temperature   [75°C/167°F]


  ↑↓←→:Move  Enter:Select  +/-/PU/PD:Value  F10:Save  ESC:Exit  F1:General Help
       F5: Previous Values     F6: Fail-Safe Defaults   F7: Optimized Defaults
```

**Figure 3-61:
PC Health Menu**

Security Subsystem

Newer BIOS offer a variety of **security options** that can be set through the CMOS setup utility. Figure 3-62 displays a typical security configuration screen. Typically, these options include items such as setting **passwords** and **supervisory passwords** to control access. The password setting options permit the user to enter and modify password settings. Password protection can be established for the system, so that a password must be entered each time the system boots up or when the Setup utility is entered, or it can simply be set up so that it is only required to access the Setup utility.

security options

passwords

supervisory passwords

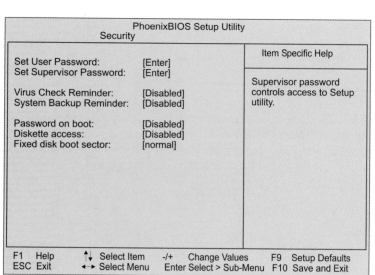

```
                      PhoenixBIOS Setup Utility
              Security

  Set User Password:         [Enter]          Item Specific Help
  Set Supervisor Password:   [Enter]
                                             Supervisor password
  Virus Check Reminder:      [Disabled]      controls access to Setup
  System Backup Reminder:    [Disabled]      utility.

  Password on boot:          [Disabled]
  Diskette access:           [Disabled]
  Fixed disk boot sector:    [normal]




  F1   Help      ↑↓ Select Item   -/+   Change Values    F9   Setup Defaults
  ESC  Exit      ←→ Select Menu   Enter Select > Sub-Menu  F10 Save and Exit
```

**Figure 3-62:
CMOS Security
Configuration**

The security configuration screen may also include options for setting virus check and backup reminders that will pop up periodically when the system is booted. In addition to enabling these settings, administrators can specify the time interval between notices.

One of the main sets of security options in the CMOS Setup utility consists of those that can be used to control access to the system. For the most part, these options cover such things as access permitted through the floppy drive and access to the boot sector of the drive. This section may also provide for a password on bootup.

ADDING AND REMOVING FRU MODULES

Portions of objective 1.1 for both the A+ Depot Technician and IT Technician exams state that the test taker should be able to identify basic procedures for adding and removing field replaceable modules. As these objectives point out, PC technicians should be aware of typical personal computer components that can be exchanged in the field. They should be able to install, connect, and configure these components to upgrade or repair an existing system. The following sections of this chapter present standard procedures for installing and removing typical field replaceable units in a microcomputer system.

Removing System Boards

System boards are generally removed for one of two possible reasons. Either the system board has failed and needs to be replaced, or the user wants to install a new system board with better features. In either case, it will be necessary to remove the current system board and replace it. The removal procedure can be defined in five steps, as described in the following process:

1. Remove all external I/O systems.

2. Remove the system unit's outer cover.

3. Remove the adapter cards.

4. Remove the cables from the system board.

5. Remove the system board.

To replace a system board, it is necessary to disconnect several cables from the old system board and reconnect them to the new system board. The easiest method of handling this is to use tape (preferably masking tape) to mark the wires and their connection points (on the new system board) before removing them from the old system board.

Removing External I/O Systems

Unplug all power cords from the commercial outlet. Remove all peripherals from the system unit. Disconnect the mouse, keyboard, and monitor signal cable from the rear of the unit. Finally, disconnect the monitor power cable from the system (or the outlet). Figure 3-63 illustrates the system unit's back panel connections.

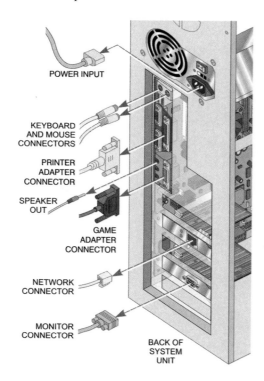

POWER INPUT

KEYBOARD AND MOUSE CONNECTORS

PRINTER ADAPTER CONNECTOR

SPEAKER OUT

GAME ADAPTER CONNECTOR

NETWORK CONNECTOR

MONITOR CONNECTOR

BACK OF SYSTEM UNIT

Figure 3-63: System Unit Back Panel Connections

Removing the System Unit's Outer Cover

Unplug the 120 Vac power cord from the system unit. Determine which type of case you are working on. If the case is a desktop model, does the cover slide off the chassis in a forward direction, bringing the front panel with it, or does it raise off the chassis from the rear? If the back lip of the outer cover folds over the edge of the back panel, then the lid raises up from the back after the retaining screws are removed. If the retaining screws go through the back panel without passing through the lip, then the outer cover will slide forward after the retaining screws have been removed.

Determine the number of screws that hold the outer cover to the chassis. Do not confuse the power supply retaining screws with those holding the back panel. The power supply unit requires four screws. Check for screws along the lower edges of the outer cover that hold it to the sides of the chassis. Remove the screws that hold the cover to the chassis. Store the screws properly. Remove the system unit's outer cover by lifting or sliding it away from the chassis.

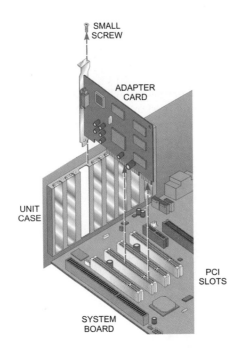

Removing Adapter Cards

Remove the retaining screws that secure the adapter cards to the system unit's back panel. Remove the adapter cards from the expansion slots. It is a good practice to place adapter cards back into the same slots they were removed from, if possible. Store the screws properly. Refer to Figure 3-64 to perform this procedure.

Disconnect any I/O port connections or auxiliary power connector from the card before removing it from the expansion slot.

Figure 3-64: Removing Adapter Cards

Removing Cables from the System Board

The system board provides an operator interface through a set of front panel indicator lights and switches. These indicators and switches connect to the system board by BERG connectors, as depicted in Figure 3-65.

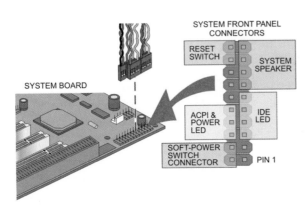

The front panel connectors must be removed in order to exchange the system board for a new one. Because it is quite easy to get these connections reversed, make sure that you mark them for identification purposes before removing them from their connection points. Record the color and function of each connection. Trace each wire back to its front panel connection to determine what its purpose is. This will ensure that all the wires are reinstalled correctly after the exchange is completed.

Remove the HDD and CD-ROM/DVD drive signal cables from the system board. Disconnect the power supply connections from the system board as well.

Figure 3-65: Front Panel Connections

Removing the System Board

Verify the positions of all jumper and switch settings on the old system board. Record these settings and verify their meanings before removing the board from the system. This may require the use of the board's user's manual, if available. Remove the grounding screws that secure the system board to the chassis. Store the screws properly.

In some cases you will be able to lift the system board straight out of the chassis, as illustrated in Figure 3-66. However, in other cases, you will need to guide some portion of the board around overhanging disk drive cages and power supply mounts. Normally, you simply need to tilt the board back and forth to clear these obstacles on the way out. Be careful not to snag any of the system board devices on these structures as you remove the board from the case. The same will be true when you install the replacement system board in the unit.

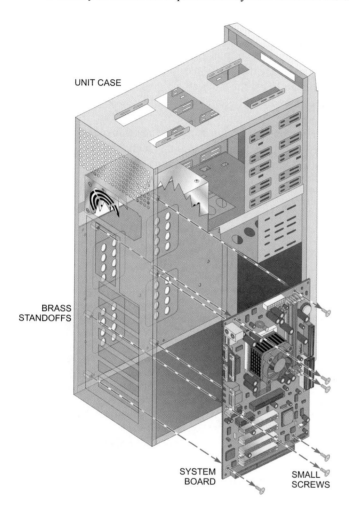

UNIT CASE

BRASS
STANDOFFS

SYSTEM
BOARD

SMALL
SCREWS

Figure 3-66: Removing the System Board

Replacing System Board FRU Devices

There are a few serviceable devices on the system board. These include

- The microprocessor

- The system RAM modules

- Specialized support ICs

As with the system board, there are really only two reasons for servicing any of these devices: to replace a failed unit or to upgrade the unit.

Installing Microprocessors

sockets

PC manufacturers mount microprocessors in **sockets** so that they can be replaced easily. This enables a failed microprocessor to simply be exchanged with a working unit. More often though, the microprocessor is replaced with an improved version to upgrade the speed or performance of the system.

pin-1 notch

The notches and dots on the various IC devices are important keys when replacing a microprocessor. They specify the location of the IC's number 1 pin. This pin must be lined up with the **pin-1 notch** of the socket for proper insertion. In older systems, the microprocessors had to be forcibly removed from the socket using an IC extractor tool. As the typical microprocessor's pin count increased, special Zero Insertion Force (ZIF) sockets were designed that allowed the microprocessor to be set in the socket without force and then be clamped in place. An arm-activated clamping mechanism in the socket shifts to the side, locking the pins in place. A microprocessor and ZIF socket arrangement are depicted in Figure 3-67.

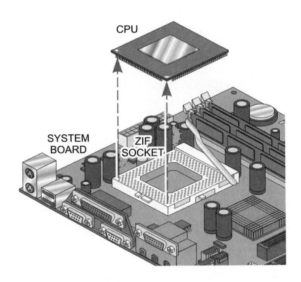

Figure 3-67: A Microprocessor and ZIF Socket

To release the microprocessor from the socket, the lever arm beside the socket must be pressed down and away from the socket. When it comes free from the socket, the arm raises up to release the pressure on the microprocessor's pins.

A notch and dot in one corner of the CPU mark the position of the processor's #1 pin. The dot and notch should be located at the free end of the socket's locking lever for proper installation. Both the CPU and the socket have one corner that does not have a pin (or pin hole) in it. This feature prevents the CPU from being inserted into the socket incorrectly.

Pentium processors generate a considerable amount of heat during normal operation. To prevent this heat from reaching a destructive level, all Pentiums require that a CPU cooling fan and heat sink unit be installed on the microprocessor. These units are available in glue-on and snap-on models. A special heat-conducting grease is typically used with snap-on heat sinks to provide good thermal transfer between the microprocessor and the heat sink. Power for the fans is normally obtained from one of the system's options power connectors, or from a special jumper block on the system board. These items must be installed before operating the microprocessor.

From the Pentium II processor forward, Intel has offered microprocessors in single edge cartridges (SEC). These processors mount vertically in an edge connector slot on the system board. The slot concept is similar to the expansion slot connectors used with adapter cards. Because the cartridge mounts vertically on the system board, special mechanical supports must be installed on the system board to help hold it in place. These supports are normally preinstalled on the system board by its manufacturer.

The processor cartridge slides into the upright supports as illustrated in Figure 3-68. It should be pressed firmly into the slot to ensure good contact.

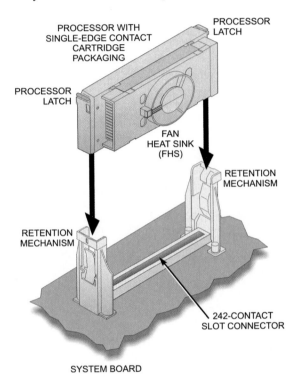

PROCESSOR WITH SINGLE-EDGE CONTACT CARTRIDGE PACKAGING

PROCESSOR LATCH

PROCESSOR LATCH

FAN HEAT SINK (FHS)

RETENTION MECHANISM

RETENTION MECHANISM

242-CONTACT SLOT CONNECTOR

SYSTEM BOARD

Figure 3-68: Installing a Cartridge Processor

As with other Pentium-class processors, the cartridge-mounted Pentium processors require heat sinks and cooling systems to dissipate the tremendous amount of heat they generate. These processors employ special snap-in fan units that attach to the system board through special holes designed into the board. The fan is encased in a support structure that holds it in place. The fan unit receives power and speed control information from the system board through a two- or three-wire cable and connector.

The microprocessor's internal core voltage supply is controlled through a VRM located on the system board. Older Pentium system boards employed jumpers to establish the proper +3 V and CPU core voltage settings for the particular type of microprocessor being installed. These boards also used jumpers to establish the external/internal clock ratio for the microprocessor, as well as its external front-side bus frequency. Newer systems autodetect the type of microprocessor installed through the PnP BIOS and configure these settings for their optimum values. However, they can usually be modified manually through the CMOS Setup utility.

Installing Memory Modules

Modern system boards provide rows of **dual in-line memory module (DIMM)** sockets. These sockets accept piggy-back memory modules that can contain various combinations of DRAM devices. DIMMs use edge connectors that snap into a retainer on the system board. The DIMM socket accepts 168-pin or 184-pin DIMM units. The DIMM modules simply slide vertically into the sockets and are locked in place by a tab at each end, as illustrated in Figure 3-69. DIMMs are also keyed, so that they cannot be plugged in backwards.

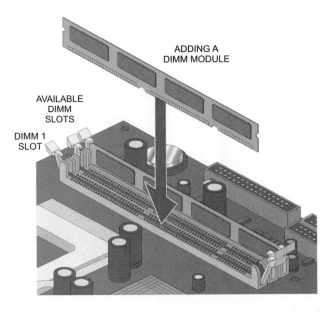

Figure 3-69: Installing a DIMM Module

On most Pentium system boards, the DIMM sockets are organized so that slots 1 and 2 make up **bank-0**, while slots 2 and 3 form **bank-1**. Each bank can be filled with single-sided (32-bit) DIMMs or double-sided (64-bit) DIMMs. The system can be operated with only bank-0 full. It will also operate with both banks full. However, it cannot be operated with a portion of any bank filled (a bank in use must be full).

SYSTEM UPGRADING AND OPTIMIZING

The modular design of the PC-compatible system enables portions of the system to be up-graded as new, or better, components become available, or as the system's application changes. As this A+ objective points out, computer technicians must be capable of upgrading the system's BIOS as part of a system upgrade. Technicians should also be able to optimize PC hardware to obtain the best performance possible for a given system configuration. The following sections cover upgradable components found in common PC systems, including information about when and how to upgrade them.

System Board Upgrading

There are typically five serviceable components on the system board. These include

- The microprocessor
- The RAM modules
- The CMOS backup battery
- The ROM BIOS
- The cache memory

Of the five items listed, three—the microprocessor, the RAM modules, and the cache memory—can be exchanged to increase the performance of the system. These devices are normally mounted in sockets to make replacing or upgrading them an easy task.

Great care should be taken when exchanging these parts to avoid damage to the ICs from **electrostatic discharge (ESD)**. ESD prevention is covered in detail in Chapter 13, *Preventive Maintenance*. In addition, care should be taken during the extraction and replacement of the ICs to avoid misalignment and bent pins. Make sure to correctly align the IC's pin #1 with the socket's pin #1 position. In the case of microprocessors that plug into standard sockets, the force required to insert them may overstress the system board if it is not properly supported.

electrostatic discharge (ESD)

Microprocessor Upgrades

Microprocessor manufacturers have devised upgrade versions for virtually every type of microprocessor in the market. It is also common for clone microprocessors to be pin-for-pin compatible with older Intel socket designs. This strategy enables the end user to realize a speed and performance increase by upgrading the microprocessor and its support systems.

Actually, upgrading the processor is a fairly easy operation after gaining access to the system board. In most cases, you simply remove the microprocessor from its socket and replace it with the upgrade processor. However, you should check the system board's documentation before selecting an upgrade microprocessor for it. You must make certain that the system board will support the new processor in terms of the following:

- *Physical compatibility*—Such as socket versus slot, or socket type-A versus socket type-B compatibility. When moving a microprocessor to a new board, it must be socket compatible, voltage compatible, and speed compatible with the new board.

- *Speed/clocking ratings*—There is no need to purchase a 2 GHz processor with a 200 MHz front-side bus capability if the system only supports 1.2 GHz operation using a 133 MHz front-side bus speed. If you do so, the new processor will be limited to operating at all of the system board's lower capabilities.

- *Technology*—A 0.13 micron processor will not work in a socket system designed to support processors built with 0.18 micron technology.

- *Logical upgradability*—Verify that the existing BIOS can be upgraded to support the new microprocessor specifications.

Table 3-8 shows the upgrade paths available to the major microprocessor types used in PCs.

Table 3-8: Microprocessor Upgrade Paths

SOCKET TYPE	MICROPROCESSOR
Socket 7	Pentium (75 MHz-200 MHz)
Socket 8	Pentium Pro
Slot 1	Celeron, Pentium II, Pentium III
Slot 2	Xeon
Super Socket 7	AMD K6-2, K6-2+, K6-III, K6-III+, Pentium MMX
Socket 370	Cyrix III, Celeron, Pentium III
Slot A	AMD Athlon
Socket A	AMD Athlon, Duron
Socket 423	Pentium 4 (1.3 GHz-2.0 GHz)
Socket 478	Pentium 4 (1.4 GHz-2.2 GHz)
Socket 603	Pentium 4 Xeon (1.4 GHz-2.2 GHz)
Socket 418	Itanium/Intel (733 MHz-800 MHz)

Several adapters are available to match different processors to otherwise incompatible sockets and slots. These adapters include products that adapt socket-mounted processors to slotted system boards, and to convert from one technology to another. Microprocessor conversion products can be found through the Internet by searching on the key words "computer upgrade" or "microprocessor upgrade."

After the new processor has been installed, you should verify the operation of the upgrade. The initial test will be to bootup the system and see if you receive an error code, and to verify that the system recognizes the newly installed processor.

Bus System Issues

Different portions of the system's buses run at different speeds. When an upgrade microprocessor is installed in a system, the coordination between it and the other devices requires that the timing relationships between all of the buses be recalculated. This process begins with the microprocessor and its front-side bus. However, the other buses in the system must run at predetermined speeds to maintain compatibility with the types of devices they serve. The chipset devices must be reset so they can act to synchronize the movement of information between the different buses.

Most current system boards feature autodetection functions as part of the PnP process that automatically detect the presence of the new processor on the board and synchronize the different bus speed configurations. These systems exchange information with the system's PnP BIOS during the configuration portion of the boot procedure to obtain the optimum chipset settings.

However, some microprocessor-related settings on system boards may still be enabled and configured through on-board jumpers. Incorrectly setting processor-related jumpers causes a high number of failures for both new installations and upgrades. You should always refer to the system board's installation guide or user's manual for definitions of these settings. In particular, the Core Voltage, Bus Frequency, and Bus Ratio settings must be properly configured for the new processor. If these items are not set correctly, you may have the following types of problems:

- Overheating and destruction of the new microprocessor
- Inability to start the system
- Encountering of random errors during normal operations
- Failure to start the operating system
- Receipt of incorrect processor type or Incorrect processor speed messages during the POST

On many system boards, it is possible to tweak the board to clock the microprocessor above its stated characteristics. In these systems, the microprocessor clock is set at a higher speed than the IC manufacturer suggests. This is referred to as overclocking the processor. This typically involves manually setting the processor configurations for higher microprocessor clock settings. Overclocking the processor normally includes updating the BIOS to support the upgraded processor and improving the processor's cooling system.

Installing Additional Processors

Some system boards provide multiple processor sockets or slots that permit additional processors to be added to distribute the processing load. You can use all, some, or just one of the available sockets by removing the terminator from the socket and installing the new processor. Adding additional processors represents the most effective means to upgrade the performance of the computer. However, there are several steps that should be taken before installing additional processors.

1. *Verify processor compatibility*—Ensure that the processor you are adding is compatible with the socket type on the board (preferably the same brand that is already on the board). You should also check the production run number of the processor to ensure that it is within one production run of its companion processors. In the case of Intel processors, this is referred to as a "stepping level." For example, if you have a Pentium III 750 MHz processor from stepping level four, you should install additional processors that are defined as stepping 3, 4, or 5.

   For optimum stability, you should install the same make, model, and clock speed for all processors. This would include using the same bus speed and multiplier settings and the same cache size to ensure there is no speed difference between cache feeds. Refer to the system board's manual or online documentation for detailed information about processor compatibility issues.

2. *Perform a BIOS upgrade*—Multiple processor system boards include a BIOS version with multiple processor support. This BIOS should be sufficient when installing directly compatible additional processors. However, for major upgrades, such as installing newer and faster processors, the BIOS may need to be upgraded. In many cases, newer BIOS versions are developed by the system board's manufacturer to permit the installation of faster processors as they enter the market. Therefore, check the manufacturer's Internet support site to determine whether your system board can support the processor type and speed you intend to use.

3. *Verify upgrade*—Verifying a processor upgrade is fairly simple. Bootup the system to see if an error code is generated and to verify that the system recognizes the newly installed processor.

NOTE

You should not interpret an automatic entry into the CMOS Setup utility as an error when the system is initially booted after adding an additional processor. This is the process that systems often use to recognize new processors. You can use the system's CMOS Setup utility (or their administrative tools package) to ensure that the system board is recognizing all the installed processors and that they are working properly.

Firmware Upgrades

The physical microprocessor upgrade should also be accompanied by a logical upgrade. For major upgrades, such as installing newer and faster processors, the BIOS may need to be upgraded as well. Later BIOS versions are often developed by the system board's manufacturer to permit installation of faster processors as they come on the market.

When the microprocessor is upgraded, the BIOS should be *flashed* with the latest compatibility firmware. If the BIOS does not possess the flash option and does not support the new microprocessor, a new BIOS chip that does support it must be obtained. If not, the entire system board will typically need to be upgraded.

flash

When you **flash** firmware, you direct the system board to send electrical charges into a ROM chip that will rewrite its programming. In order to flash the ROM device, you must have a program from its vendor that can be downloaded into the IC. This program will write the updated information into the chip so that the physical device now holds the latest version of information.

The same technique is used for flashing the system's ROM BIOS, as well as the various ROM BIOS extensions associated with video cards, network cards, modem, and RAID controllers. Each peripheral device will have its own utility program for flashing their ROM devices.

Even though there are many different types of devices whose BIOS you can flash, the general process to do so remains the same:

- Document the CMOS settings.

- Back up the original BIOS program. In case the process fails, you can use the original BIOS program to attempt to restore the settings back to the original form.

- Flash the BIOS with the new program according to the directions of the device manufacturer.

TEST TIP

Know what precautions to take before upgrading the system's BIOS.

A graphical representation of this process is shown in Figure 3-70.

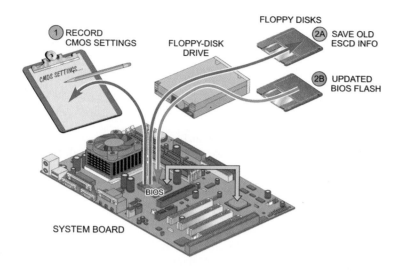

Figure 3-70:
Flashing BIOS

Cooling System Upgrades

In any modern PC, the cooling system will include a passive heat sink device and a processor cooling fan. These items work alongside the power supply fan to cool the system and the processor. A special **thermal compound** (thermal grease) is placed between the heat sink and the processor to increase the rate of heat transfer to the heat sink. In some situations, additional case fans are installed to increase or redirect the airflow through the chassis.

When microprocessors are upgraded (or overclocked), the processor cooling system may also need to be improved. In most cases, the new microprocessor comes with a properly sized heat sink and fan. These are referred to as boxed processors and provide longer warranties than stand-alone OEM (original equipment manufacturer) processors. However, OEM processors do not include a fan or heat sink, and you must research and locate a proper cooling system for them.

To accomplish this, you must find the microprocessor's operating temperature specification. For Pentium processors the recommended operating temperature was 30 degrees C. However, with the appearance of the Pentium III and Pentium 4 processors, Intel switched to 35 degree C. The AMD processors typically run much hotter than Intel versions (i.e., 45–50 degrees C). Then, you must find a fan that is rated to work with that processor's temperature/speed specification.

The Health configuration settings in the system's CMOS Setup utility can be set to automatically control the fan speed to provide optimum cooling. This setting can also be switched to permit manual configuration of the cooling system. These settings work in conjunction with fan speed control values obtained from the BIOS. If the cooling system fails to maintain the processor temperature, it can shut down the system and prevent it from starting back up. Optimizing the speed of the fan lowers the relative dust accumulation that can lead to thermal failure.

Some computer manufacturers include air baffles (guides) that channel air through the chassis in specific paths. Others include foam filters at chassis openings to filter the incoming air, removing dust particles that accumulate on electronic devices and cause overheating.

At present, high-end servers are available with liquid-cooled and refrigerated processor cooling systems. Only serious hardware users employ these options with their PCs. However, future processor development plans (i.e., Pentium 5+) are considering liquid versus refrigerated cooling systems as standard equipment.

Memory Upgrades

Upgrading system board memory is also a fairly simple process. Having more RAM on board allows the system to access more data from extended or expanded memory, without having to access the disk drive. This speeds up system operation considerably. Normally, upgrading memory simply amounts to installing new memory modules in vacant DIMM slots. If the slots are already populated, it will be necessary to remove them to install faster or higher-capacity modules.

Although a 168-pin or 184-pin DIMM from one board can physically be transferred to another system board, it must still have a sufficient speed rating to work in the new system. Consult the system board user's guide to determine what speed the memory devices must be rated for. You should be aware that RAM and other memory devices are rated in access time instead of clock speed. Therefore, a 70-nanosecond (ns) RAM device is faster than an 80-nanosecond device. The guide should also be checked for any memory configuration settings that must be made to accept the new memory capacity.

You must ensure that the memory type and size you want to install are supported by the system board and that the system board does not already have the maximum amount of memory installed. The system board's manual will include information on the type, configuration, and size of memory it will accept. In addition, verify that the memory you wish to install is compatible with the memory currently installed on the board. For example, if the memory currently installed in the machine is rated as PC2-6400, you would not want to install an additional PC2-3200-type memory module.

Normally you should use the same type, brand, and speed of memory devices for RAM upgrades. Because the information detailing the RAM module's type and speed is rarely annotated on the device, you may need to check the signal to clock rate (CAS) for comparison. For instance, if your current memory modules are described as CAS3 units, then you should get CAS3 type memory for a compatible replacement, or for adding additional memory.

To verify the memory upgrade, attempt to observe the memory test display during the POST process to ensure that the system sees the additional memory. Afterwards, boot into the operating system and verify that it also recognizes the installed memory.

Cache Upgrades

If the system has socketed cache memory, some additional performance can be gained by optimizing the cache. Upgrading the cache on these system boards normally requires only that additional cache ICs be installed in vacant sockets. If the sockets are full but the system's cache size is less than maximum, it will be necessary to remove the existing cache chips and replace them with faster, higher-capacity devices. Make sure to observe the pin #1 alignment as well as check the system board's user's guide for any configuration jumper changes.

Before upgrading the system board's FRU units, compare the cost of the proposed component upgrade against the cost of upgrading the system board itself. In many cases, the RAM from the original board can be used on a newer, faster model that should include a more advanced microprocessor. Before finalizing the choice to install a new system board, however, make sure that the current adapters, software, and peripherals will function properly with the updated board. If not, the cost of upgrading may be unexpectedly higher than simply replacing an FRU component.

KEY POINTS REVIEW

This chapter has examined the major components that make up typical PC-compatible system boards. These items include microprocessors, memory types, microprocessor support systems, and expansion buses. Review the following key points before moving into the Review and Exam Questions sections to make sure you are comfortable with each point. Afterward, answer the Review Questions that follow to verify your knowledge of the information.

- The system board contains the components that form the basis of the computer system.

- System boards fundamentally change for three reasons: new microprocessors, new expansion-slot types, and reduced chip counts. Reduced chip counts are typically the result of improved microprocessor support chipsets. Chipsets combine PC- and AT-compatible structures into larger integrated circuits.

- Because chipset-based system boards require much fewer IC devices to produce, printed-circuit-board manufacturers have been able to design much smaller boards.

- Chipset-based system boards and I/O cards tend to change often as IC manufacturers continue to integrate higher levels of circuitry into their devices.

- The system's expansion slots provide the connecting point for most of its I/O devices. Interface cards communicate with the system through the extended microprocessor buses in these slots.

- In order to speed up the operation of their systems, system board manufacturers began to add proprietary bus designs to their board to increase the speed and bandwidth for transfers between the microprocessor and a few selected peripherals. This was accomplished by creating special local buses between the devices that would enable the peripherals to operate at speeds close to that of the microprocessor.

- The main component in the PCI-based system is the PCI bus controller, called the host bridge. This device monitors the microprocessor's address bus to determine whether addresses are intended for devices on the system board, in a PCI slot, or in one of the system board's other expansion slots.

- The Pentium is a 32/64-bit microprocessor contained in a ceramic pin grid array package. The registers for the microprocessor and floating-point sections of the Pentium are identical to those of the 80486. It has a 64-bit data bus that allows it to handle Quad Word (or Qword) data transfers. The Pentium also contains two separate 8 kB caches. One of the caches is used for instructions or code, and the other is used for data.

- In the Pentium MMX processor, the multimedia and communications processing capabilities of the original Pentium device are extended by the addition of 57 multimedia-specific instructions to the instruction set.

- Intel departed from simply increasing the speed of its Pentium processor line by introducing the Pentium Pro processor. While compatible with all of the previous software written for the Intel processor line, the Pentium Pro is optimized to run 32-bit software.

- The Pentium II includes all of the multimedia enhancements from the MMX processor, as well as retaining the power of the Pentium Pro's dynamic execution and 512 kB L2 cache features. The L1 cache is increased to 32 kB, while the L2 cache operates with a half-speed bus.

- There are normally three types of semiconductor memory found on a typical system board. These include the system's ROM BIOS ICs, the system's RAM memory, and the second-level cache memory unit.

- The microprocessor, the RAM modules, and the cache memory can be exchanged to increase the performance of the system. These devices are normally mounted in sockets to make replacing or upgrading them an easy task.

- One method of increasing the memory access speed of a computer is called caching. This memory management method assumes that most memory accesses are made within a limited block of addresses.

- When the contents of a section of RAM addresses are relocated into the high-speed SRAM cache, the microprocessor can access these locations without requiring any wait states.

- Typically, memory accesses occur in two fashions: instruction fetches (which are generally sequential) and operand accesses (which tend to be random). Paging and interleaving memory schemes are designed to take advantage of the sequential nature of instruction fetches from memory.

REVIEW QUESTIONS

The following questions test your knowledge of the material presented in this chapter.

1. What part of the ATX Pentium system board is responsible for controlling the operating temperature of its microprocessor?

2. Identify two options that can be implemented to cool microprocessors that run outside their operating temperature range. Also, indicate what conditions might cause this to occur.

3. Where is the L1 cache located in the Pentium microprocessor?

4. You are upgrading a PC's memory capabilities. The system has one bank of PC-3200 DIMMs installed. You want to upgrade the system to have two banks of PC2-6400 DIMMs. What actions do you need to take to install these memory modules?

5. Compare the data transfer performance of the PCI local bus using a 32-bit bus versus a 64-bit bus running at the same speed.

6. Where is the microprocessor located in a BTX form factor system?

7. What function does parity checking provide for the system?

8. What type of data transfers occur across the PCIe expansion slot?

9. Describe the main function of the north bridge in a Pentium/PCI chipset.

10. What feature in AMD processors provides a level of malicious code protection?

11. Which type of memory device comes in a 168-pin module?

12. Describe the steps required to update a system board processor from an AMD Athlon 64 processor to a dual-core Athlon 64 X2 processor.

13. How are local buses different than other expansion buses?

14. Which memory device employs special clock signals and buffer storage to deliver data to the microprocessor in one clock cycle?

15. Name two advantages of using chipsets to design circuit boards.

EXAM QUESTIONS

1. What does the Suspend mode actually do?
   a. Suspend mode causes the microprocessor clock to slow down after a defined period of inactivity.
   b. Suspend mode causes everything in the system except the microprocessor to shut down.
   c. Suspend mode causes the microprocessor clock to slow down after a defined period of inactivity.
   d. Suspend mode causes the system to stop its system clock until F5 is pressed.

2. What is the maximum data throughput of a video card that is AGP 8x compliant used in a motherboard with an AGP slot that is AGP 8x?
   a. 1.07 GBPs
   b. 2.1 GBps
   c. 5.33 GBps
   d. 7.33 GBps

3. You install a Pentium processor rated to operate at 850 MHz in a system. When you start the system up, the speed is indicated as 600 MHz. Which part of the system should you most likely check?
   a. The microprocessor because it has obviously been mislabeled
   b. The chipset is obviously not rated to manage this processor speed
   c. The system's RAM must not be rated to run at this speed
   d. The BIOS because it does not support this level of microprocessor operating speeds

4. In a water-cooled system, what device is used to cool the water and exhaust heat into the outside atmosphere?
   a. Water reservoir tank
   b. Water pump
   c. Condenser coil radiator
   d. CPU cooling block

5. When you install an upgrade processor in an existing system, what actions do you have to take to make sure the system recognizes it?
  a. Update its device driver
  b. Configure its core voltage level and frequency multiplier settings
  c. Access the system's CMOS Setup utility to ensure that the system board is recognizing all the installed processors
  d. Upgrade the CMOS configuration

6. If the front side bus of a PC system is specified as running at 800 MHz quadpumped, what is the actual clock speed of the bus and its data throughput level?
  a. 800 MHz.
  b. 400 MHz.
  c. 200 MHz.
  d. 100 MHz.

7. How are the Dual-Core Athlon chipsets different than other Pentium class chipsets?
  a. They do not contain a front side bus
  b. They do not contain a back side bus
  c. They do not contain a north bridge
  d. They do not contain a south bridge

8. What typical section of the CMOS Setup utility would you use to establish time intervals between the appearances of Notices to Backup when the system is booted?
  a. The Chipset Features Screen
  b. The PnP/PCI Configuration Screen
  c. Security Subsystem
  d. Power Management Functions

9. In a Pentium system that uses two IDE controllers (ID1 and ID2), what will the primary partition of the drive attached to ID2 be?
  a. C:\
  b. D:\
  c. E:\
  d. F:\

10. What type of device is used with microprocessors to supply special voltage levels for different types of microprocessors that might be installed?
  a. RAM
  b. Voltage Module Regulator
  c. Voltmeter
  d. Voltage Regulator Module

CHAPTER 4

STANDARD I/O SYSTEMS

OBJECTIVES

U pon completion of this chapter and its related lab procedures, you should be able to perform these tasks:

1. Define the functions associated with the PC's input/output units.

2. Describe four common methods of initiating a data transfer in a PC.

3. Identify the various port connectors used in PC-compatible systems.

4. Describe connection techniques for attaching multimedia equipment to a PC.

5. Define digital television standards including LDTV, SDTV, EDTV, and HDTV and describe how they relate to personal computers.

6. Differentiate between resolution formats associated with PC display monitors and digital televisions.

7. Describe the operation of the Universal Serial Bus.

8. List the events that occur when a key is depressed on the keyboard.

9. Describe the operation of a video capture card.

10. Install different types of mice and describe their operation.

11. Identify game port connectors used with joysticks and game paddles.

12. Describe the operation of flat-bed and bar code scanners.

13. Describe the physical aspects of a cathode-ray tube.

14. Explain how a single dot can be positioned anywhere on the face of the CRT, using raster scanning.

15. Describe how color images are created on a CRT video display screen.

16. Identify connection types associated with typical and advanced sound cards.

17. Describe the function of a shadow mask in a CRT monitor.

18. State the characteristics of the VGA video standard, including the type of physical connector specified for this video standard.

19. Identify standard PC-compatible resource allocations.

20. Differentiate between the operating characteristics of IEEE-1394 and USB ports.

STANDARD I/O SYSTEMS

FROM THE GEEK SQUAD

A gent 235 is a Geek Squad Special Agent who has been asked to help a customer design a media center computer to handle video and audio input from his digital cameras, a personal video recorder, the television and the customer's whole-home audio system. In addition, the system must be able to output the digital media to advanced video displays as well as the whole-home audio system. The main items that the customer has concerns about revolve around the system's input output devices—what types of video and sound cards will provide the performance desired, which I/O expansion bus will enable the customer to connect his multimedia devices to the system?

Agent 253 must know which system components can be used to optimize the application the customer wants to fill. In addition, he must be able to explain to the customer how the components he suggests affect the ability of the system to handle audio and video media more effectively.

INTRODUCTION

Although the circuitry on the system board forms the nucleus of the personal computer system, it cannot stand alone. The computer must be able to acquire data from the outside world. In most applications, it must also be able to deliver results of operations it performs to the outside world in a useful format. Many different systems have been developed for both inputting and outputting data.

While the microcomputer is a completely digital electronic device that uses parallel words of given lengths and adheres to basic digital logic levels, its peripheral devices tend to be more mechanical and analog in nature. In many cases this is because the peripheral devices must accommodate humans, which are analog in nature. In other cases, the form that data take is not for the convenience of human beings, but the form most suitable to carry out the function of the I/O device.

This chapter examines peripheral I/O systems in detail. The first portion covers types of I/O operations and the standard I/O port assignments and configurations in PC systems. The second half of the chapter deals with typical I/O devices associated with PC systems.

SYSTEM INPUT/OUTPUT

The computer's input and output units enable it to communicate with the outside world. An *I/O unit* typically consists of **interface circuitry**, a **peripheral device**, and some type of standard connection point, or **port connector**. The interface circuitry may be located on a plug-in adapter card or in one of the system board's chipset components. Likewise, the I/O port connector may be mounted on the back of an adapter card, on the back of the system board so that it is accessible from the rear of the system, on the front panel of the system unit case, or somewhere on the system board. Finally, the peripheral device can plug directly into one of the port connectors, or it can be attached to the system through some type of standard signal cable.

interface circuitry

peripheral device

port connector

The system's input units contain all of the interface circuitry necessary to accept data and programs from peripheral input devices such as keyboards, scanners, mice, joysticks, and so on, and convert the information into a digital form that is usable by the microprocessor.

The output units contain all of the interface circuitry necessary to convert information from the computer's digital language into a form that is more convenient for the outside world. Most often this is in the form of alphanumeric characters or graphical images, which are convenient for humans to use. Common output devices include video display monitors, audio speakers, and character printers. Figure 4-1 depicts several common I/O devices associated with personal computers.

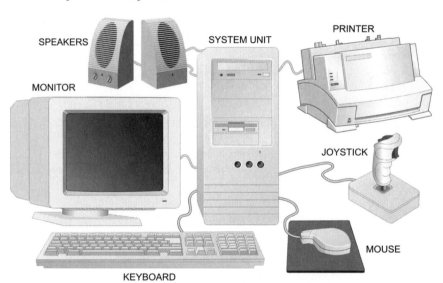

Figure 4-1: Common I/O Devices Used with PCs

Some computer peripherals do double duty as both input and output units. These devices are collectively referred to as I/O devices and include secondary storage devices such as hard-disk drives, floppy-disk drives, and magnetic tape drives, as well as modems and sound cards.

Moving Data

The most frequent operation performed in a computer is the movement of information from one location to another. This information is moved in the form of words. These transfers can occur in one of two modes—**parallel mode**, where an entire word is transferred from location A to location B by a set of parallel conductors at one instant, and **serial mode**, where the bits of the word are transmitted along a single conductor, one bit at a time.

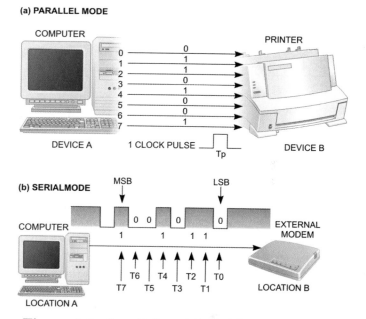

parallel mode

serial mode

Serial transfers require more time to accomplish than parallel transfers because a clock cycle must be used for each bit transferred. Parallel transfers require only one clock pulse to complete. Examples of both parallel and serial transfers are depicted in Figure 4-2. Because speed is normally of the utmost importance in computer operations, all data movements within the computer are conducted in parallel, as shown in (a). But when information is being transferred between the computer and its peripherals (or another computer), conditions may dictate that the transfer be carried out in serial mode, as shown in (b).

– Peripheral devices may use parallel or serial transmission modes between themselves and the system board. While parallel buses have historically been used for high-speed I/O devices, such as disk drives and some printers, newer serial technologies have replaced parallel interfaces for most nonsystem board applications. In addition, serial transmission techniques are used with remotely located devices or with devices whose operation is more compatible with serial data flow, such as monitors, modems, certain input devices, and some printers.

Figure 4-2: Parallel and Serial Data Transfers

PC Address Allocations

The most important part of moving data in the PC is to get the data to and from where it should be. Just like moving mail and e-mail, the PC employs **addresses** to access and move data. One of the three major buses in the PC is the address bus, which interconnects all of the system's intelligent devices and memory structures with the microprocessor. In the PC system, there are two types of addressing to contend with—addresses that refer to locations in the system's *memory map* (i.e., RAM and ROM addresses) and those that apply to I/O device locations. Table 4-1 provides an abbreviated listing of the standard PC memory map. Notice that these addresses are the same as those stated for the Interrupt Vectors in system memory. This method of dual addressing is referred to as *redundant addressing*.

addresses

In addition to the millions of possible memory locations in a PC, there are more than 65,000 input and output addresses allocated for use with peripheral systems. For an I/O device to work with the system's microprocessor, it must have an address (or group of addresses) where the system can communicate with it. In fact, most I/O devices and subsystems require at least a small block of addresses for their individual uses.

Table 4-1:
System Memory
Map

ADDRESS	FUNCTION
0–3FF	Interrupt Vectors
400–47F	ROM-BIOS RAM
480–5FF	BASIC and Special System Function RAM
600–9FFFF	Program Memory
A0000–BFFFF	VGA/EGA Display Memory
B0000–B7FFF	Monochrome Display Adapter Memory
B8000–BFFFF	Color Graphics Adapter Memory
C0000–C7FFF	VGA/SVGA BIOS
C8000-CBFFF	EIDE/SCSI ROM (also older HDD Types)
D0000–D7FFF	Spare ROM
D0000–DFFFF	LAN Adapter ROM
E0000–E7FFF	Spare ROM
E8000–EFFFF	Spare ROM
F0000–F3FFF	Spare ROM
F4000–F7FFF	Spare ROM
F8000–FBFFF	Spare ROM
FC000–FDFFF	ROM BIOS
FE000–FFFFF	ROM BIOS

There are two groups of I/O addresses in the PC system—the system board's on-board I/O systems (System), and peripheral devices that interact with the system through its expansion slots or port connectors (I/O). The various I/O port addresses listed in Table 4-2 are used in the PC-compatible system.

Table 4-2:
I/O Port
Addresses

HEX ADDRESS	DEVICE	USAGE
000–01F	DMA Controller (South Bridge)	System
020–03F	Interrupt Controller (South Bridge)	System
040–05F	Timer/Counter (South Bridge)	System
060–06F	Keyboard Controller	System
070–07F	Real-Time Clock, NMI Mask (South Bridge)	System
080–09F	DMA Page Register (South Bridge)	System
0A0–0BF	Interrupt Controller (South Bridge)	System
0F0	Clear Math Coprocessor Busy	System
0F1	Reset Math Coprocessor	System
0F8–0FF	Math Coprocessor	System
170–177	Second IDE Controller	I/O
1F0–1F7	First IDE Controller	I/O
200–207	Game Port	I/O
278–27F	Parallel Printer Port #2	I/O
2F8–2FF	Serial Port #2	I/O
378–37F	Parallel Printer Port #1	I/O
3B0–3BF	MGA/first Printer Port	I/O
3D0–3DF	CGA	I/O
3F0–3F7	FDD Controller	I/O
3F8–3FF	Serial Port #1	I/O
FF80-FF9F	USB Controller	I/O

System Board I/O Address Allocations

In a PC-compatible system, certain I/O addresses are assigned to intelligent devices (**controllers**) on the system board, such as the interrupt and DMA controllers, timer counter channel controller, and keyboard controller. The on-board address decoder, illustrated in Figure 4-3, has been a part of the south bridge for many chipset generations and converts addresses from the system's address bus into enabling bits for the different intelligent devices. These addresses are included in the overall I/O address map of the system.

controllers

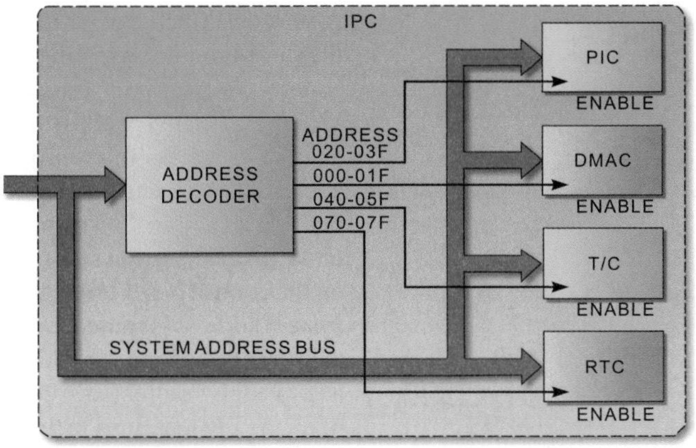

Figure 4-3:
System Board I/O
Address Decoding

Likewise, the integrated peripheral controller (IPC) portion of the south bridge is responsible for decoding addresses intended to activate the system board's built in I/O port controllers. These include the system's keyboard, controller, HDD/CD-ROM/DVD controller, floppy controller (if present), parallel printer ports, RS-232 serial ports, USB ports, and game port. Figure 4-4 depicts address decoding for the system board's various standard integrated peripheral controllers.

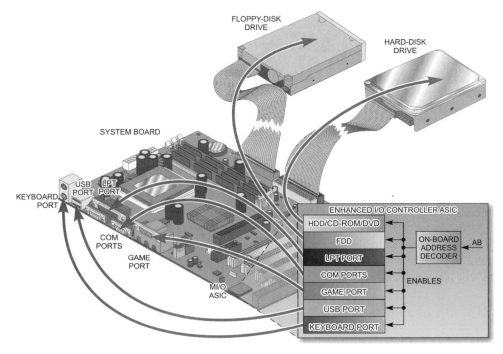

Figure 4-4:
Addressing System
Board I/O Port
Controllers

Peripheral I/O Address Allocations

Some I/O ports and their interfaces are located on adapter cards. In particular, it is common for PCs to use adapter card-based video adapters, sound cards, network interface cards, and modem. In each of these examples, a specialized intelligent controller device is the center of the peripheral. The system communicates with these controllers and their interface circuitry through the expansion slot's address, data, and control buses. Some of the adapters employ one of the data transfer initiation techniques described earlier in this chapter when they need to interact with the system.

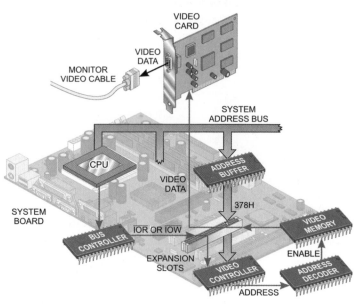

When the system needs to interact with the adapter card, its microprocessor places the address of the controller device on the address bus and an active read (input from the device) or write (information sent to the device) signal on the control bus. Figure 4-5 illustrates how a system address is routed through the system to an I/O port location. The address is decoded to activate the designated controller location out of all the I/O locations in the system. The R/W signals determine what type of operation is conducted with that location after it has been accessed by its address. Finally, the system moves data into the device in a write operation and retrieves data from the device in a Read operation.

Figure 4-5: Address Routing to an I/O Port

Hexadecimal Addressing

Addresses in PC systems are always referred to by their hexadecimal value. The reason for this is that digital computers are built on components that only work with two logic levels: On/Off, High/Low, 1/0. This corresponds directly to the base-2 or binary numbering system. In the binary system, each piece of information represents a binary digit, or bit.

The power of the digital computer lies in how it groups bits of information into words. The basic word length in PCs is the 8-bit word called a byte. Some computers can handle data as 16-, 32-, and 64-bit words. With the byte as the basic data unit, it is easier for humans to speak of computer numbers in the base-16 or **hexadecimal (hex)** numbering system. In this system, groups of 4 bits can be represented directly by a single hex character (i.e., 1001 base2 = 09 base16). For human representation, the values in the hexadecimal numbering system run from 0 to 9 and then from A through F, as illustrated in Table 4-3.

hexadecimal (hex)

DECIMAL (10)	BINARY (2)	HEXADECIMAL (16)
0	0000	0
1	0001	1
2	0010	2
3	0011	3
4	0100	4
5	0101	5
6	0110	6
7	0111	7
8	1000	8
9	1001	9
10	1010	A
11	1011	B
12	1100	C
13	1101	D
14	1110	E
15	1111	F
16	10000	10

**Table 4-3:
Decimal, Binary, and
Hexadecimal Numbers**

While this may seem a little inconvenient for those of you not familiar with binary and hexadecimal systems, it is much easier to convey the number 3F8 to someone than it is 001111111000. The real difficulty of reconciling a hexadecimal value comes when you try to convert binary or hexadecimal values to the decimal (base 10) number system you are familiar with.

Initiating I/O Transfers

While executing a program, the microprocessor constantly *Reads* from or *Writes* information to memory locations. The program is also likely to call on the microprocessor to Read from or Write to the system's I/O devices. Regardless of how the peripheral is connected to the system (serial or parallel), one of four methods is used to initiate data transfer between the system and the peripheral device. These methods are listed as follows:

- **Polling**—where the microprocessor examines the status of the peripheral under program control.

- **Programmed I/O**—where the microprocessor alerts the designated peripheral by applying its address to the system's address bus.

- **Interrupt-driven I/O**—where the peripheral alerts the microprocessor that it's ready to transfer data.

- **DMA**—where the intelligent peripheral assumes control of the system's buses to conduct direct transfers with primary memory.

Polling

Programmed I/O

Interrupt-driven I/O

DMA

Polling and Programmed I/O

Both polling and programmed I/O represent software approaches to data transfer, whereas interrupt-driven and DMA transfers are basically hardware approaches.

In a polling operation, the software periodically checks with the system's I/O devices to determine if any device is ready to conduct a data transfer. If so, it will begin reading or writing data to the device's corresponding I/O port. The polling method is advantageous in that it is easy to implement and reconfigure, because the program controls the entire sequence of events during the transfer. However, polling is often inconvenient, because the microprocessor must be totally involved in the polling routine and cannot perform other functions.

With the programmed I/O method, the software calls for the microprocessor to alert the desired peripheral of an I/O operation by issuing that device's unique port address. The peripheral can delay the transfer by asserting its Busy line. If the system receives a Busy signal from the peripheral, the program continues performing other tasks but periodically checks the device's location until the Busy signal is replaced by a Ready signal.

This back and forth communication between the system and the device to establish an orderly flow of data during the transfer is known as handshaking. A number of **handshakes** may occur between the peripheral and the system to control the flow of information. Handshaking may involve different hardware control lines as illustrated in this example, or it may involve special software codes that pass back and forth between the device and the system. In either case, handshaking prevents the microprocessor from sending or requesting data at a faster rate than the peripheral can handle. In both polling and PI/O methods, the main system resource that is used is the microprocessor's time.

Interrupts

In the course of normal operations, the PC's I/O devices, such as the keyboard, and disk drives require servicing from the system's microprocessor. These devices generally have the capability to interrupt the microprocessor while it is executing a program. The I/O device does this by issuing an **interrupt request** (**IRQ**) input signal to the microprocessor. Each device in a PC-compatible system that is capable of interrupting the microprocessor must be assigned its own unique IRQ number. The system uses this number to identify which device is in need of service. If two interrupt signals occur at the same instant, the interrupt that has the highest priority will be serviced first.

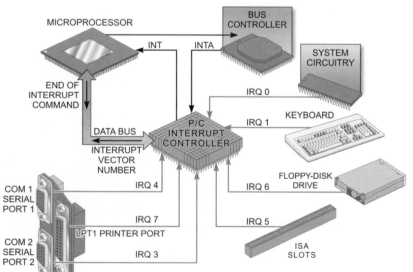

A typical IRQ operation is illustrated in Figure 4-6. The *interrupt controller* portion of the chipset accepts prioritized IRQ signals from the system's peripheral devices when they desire to communicate with the microprocessor. The controller responds by passing an INT signal to the microprocessor and then prompting the microprocessor to jump into the **interrupt service routine** associated with the IRQ number it receives. The service routine is written specifically to service the interrupting device. In the PC environment, this routine is part of the **device driver** program produced by the manufacturer of the peripheral device that has been assigned to the IRQ channel. After the processor finishes servicing the interrupting device, it returns to the original program at the point where the interrupt occurred.

Figure 4-6: Programmable Interrupt Controller Channels

Two varieties of interrupts are used in PCs:

- *Maskable interrupts* (*IRQs*)—which the computer can ignore under certain conditions

- *Non-maskable interrupts* (*NMI*)—which the microprocessor must always respond to

Of the 16 IRQ channels available in a PC (IRQ0 through IRQ15), one is used inside the IRQ controller and several are reserved for use inside the PC. Therefore, they are not available as external IRQ lines. IRQ channel 2 is used inside the controller to maintain compatibility with older IRQ operations. The other IRQ inputs are available to the system for user-definable interrupt functions. Each IRQ input is assigned a priority level. The priority orders for IRQs in a PC-compatible machine begin with IRQ0 as the highest, followed by IRQ1, IRQ8 through IRQ15, and finally IRQ3 through IRQ7.

Table 4-4 lists the designations for the traditional interrupt allocations in the PC system. The PnP process attempts to implement these resources as described in the table, however, it will ultimately assign the system's resources as necessary. The widespread use of USB ports, which require a single IRQ channel, for connecting all types of peripheral devices to the system has decreased the use of traditional PC I/O ports and adapter card-based peripheral systems. In turn, this has decreased the usage of the PC's available IRQ channels for I/O operations.

INTERRUPT	DESCRIPTION	INTERRUPT	DESCRIPTION
NMI	I/O CHANNEL CHECK OR PARITY CHECK ERROR		
INTC1		INTC2	
IRQ0	TIMER/COUNTER ALARM	IRQ8	REAL-TIME CLOCK
IRQ1	KEYBOARD BUFFER FULL	IRQ9	SPARE
IRQ2	CASCADE FROM INTC2	IR110	SPARE
IRQ3	SERIAL PORT 2	IRQ11	SPARE
IRQ4	SERIAL PORT 1	IRQ12	SPARE PS/2 MOUSE
IRQ5	PARALLEL PORT 2	IRQ13	COPROCESSOR
IRQ6	FDD CONTROLLER	IRQ14	PRIMARY IDE CTRL
IRQ7	PARALLEL PORT 1	IRQ15	SECONDARY IDE CTRL

Table 4-4:
Traditional System
Interrupt Levels

TEST TIP

Memorize the system resources available in an ISA-compatible system and what their typical assignments are.

There are two system board-based conditions that will cause a **nonmaskable interrupt (NMI)** signal to be sent to the microprocessor. The first condition occurs when an active **IO channel check (IOCHCK)** input is received from an adapter card located in one of the board's expansion slots. The other event that will cause an NMI signal to be generated is the occurrence of a **parity check (PCK) error** in the DRAM memory.

PCI system boards bring four flexible PCI interrupt lines (INTa through INTd, or INT1 through INT4) to the system. Adapter cards in the PCI slots can use these lines to activate up to four different interrupts that are mapped to the system's standard IRQ channels (typically IRQ9 through IRQ12) as part of the PnP operation. You may see these interrupts described in the PnP and PCI Configuration screen of the CMOS Setup utility. The operating system can manipulate the use of the PCI interrupts and steer them to different IRQ lines so that there is never a conflict between devices sharing them.

nonmaskable
interrupt (NMI)

IO channel check
(IOCHCK)

parity check (PCK)
error

TEST TIP
Know what types of problems can cause an NMI to occur.

Don S., Special Agent 67 is adding a wide carriage dot matrix printer to his workstation so that he can print multipart forms. He already has a color ink-jet printer attached to the computer using IRQ7. He has no idea of which resources to assign to the new printer. What will you tell him when he asks for help?

Direct Memory Access

direct memory access (DMA)

The final data movement technique used in personal computers is **direct memory access (DMA)**. DMA operations involve a high-speed *DMA Controller* taking over the system's buses to perform data transfer operations between the I/O device and primary memory, without the intervention of the system microprocessor. The mechanics of the DMA transfers are similar to that of an IRQ operation. However, the microprocessor is not only interrupted, it is removed from the activity of the system while the transfer is carried out. Figure 4-7 illustrates the DMA process.

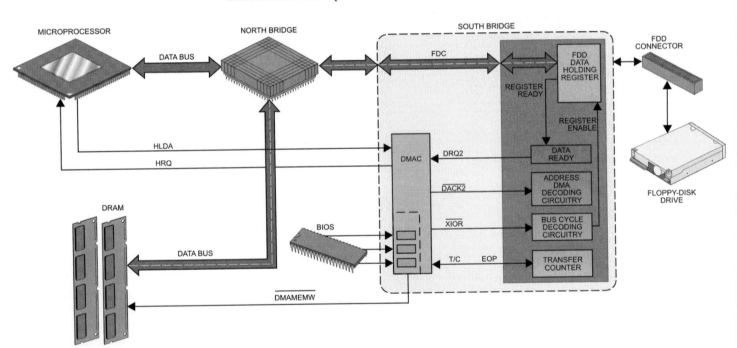

**Figure 4-7:
DMA Operations**

DMA request (DRQ)

DMA controller

When the peripheral device has data ready to be transferred, it sends a **DMA request (DRQ)** signal to the system's **DMA controller**, which in turn sends a *HOLD* input signal to the microprocessor. The microprocessor finishes executing the instruction it is currently working on and places its address and data pins in a floating state, effectively disconnecting the microprocessor from the buses. At this time, the microprocessor issues a *Buses Available* (*BA*) or *Hold Acknowledge* (*HLDA*) signal to the DMA controller. The DMA controller, in turn, issues a *DMA Acknowledge* (*DACK*) to the peripheral and all the necessary R/W and enable signals for the data transfer to begin.

The key to DMA operations is that the DMA controller has been designed specifically to transfer data bytes faster than the microprocessor can. In modern PCs, the controller is part of the chipset's south bridge circuitry. The controller provides eight DMA channels as described in Table 4-5.

CHANNEL	FUNCTION	CONTROLLER	PAGE REGISTER ADDRESS
CH0	SPARE	1	0087
CH1	SDLC (NETWORK)	1	0083
CH2	FDD CONTROLLER	1	0082
CH3	SPARE	1	0081
CH4	CASCADE TO CNTR 1	2	
CH5	SPARE	2	008B
CH6	SPARE	2	0089
CH7	SPARE	2	008A

Table 4-5: Traditional DMA Channel Allocations

System Resource Allocations

Each I/O controller or interface in the system requires certain system resources to support its operation and interaction with the system. Most intelligent devices in the PC system will require at least two of the following system resources:

- IRQ interrupt channels
- DMA channels
- I/O port address allocations
- Buffer memory address allocation (in system RAM)

Most current system boards include multiple **universal serial bus (USB)** connectors as a standard part of their I/O port offering. The on-board **USB controller** portion of the south bridge resides between the I/O addresses of FF80 and FF9F. It is also assigned an open IRQ channel (such as IRQ10) by the PnP process.

A similar high-speed peripheral bus called the **IEEE-1394** or **Firewire bus** is not considered a standard part of the PC port package. However, these ports are often added to the system in the form of an adapter card. When these ports are installed in a system they require the same types of resources used by the USB bus. Because most Firewire ports are installed in the PC on a PCI adapter card, the resources allocated to the port are actually PCI resources. Therefore, the IRQ assignment for a Firewire host adapter is typically assigned by the operating system through the PnP process. From Windows 98 forward, Microsoft operating systems have included drivers for Firewire ports. However, many times the drivers supplied with the Firewire adapter card work much better than those provided by Microsoft.

Infrared data association (IrDA) ports are very popular with notebook computers. These infrared light ports provide short-distance wireless connections for different IrDA-compliant devices, such as printers and personal digital assistants. Because the IrDA port communicates by sending and receiving a serial stream of light pulses, it is normally configured to work with the UART of the system's second serial port. In this manner, the infrared port is assigned the system resources normally reserved for the COM2/COM4 serial ports (that is, IRQ3, 2F8-2FF, or 2E8-2EF).

universal serial bus (USB)

USB controller

IEEE-1394

Firewire bus

Pentium-based system boards with support for PATA drives include two enhanced IDE controllers to handle their HDD/CD-ROM/DVD drive hosting function. Each controller can handle up to two IDE drives. The first, or primary IDE, controller is assigned IRQ14, whereas the secondary controller uses IRQ15 to interrupt the system. Likewise, the first IDE drive controller responds to I/O addresses between 1F0 and 1F7, whereas the second answers to addresses between 170 and 177.

Many new system board designs do not support floppy-disk drives. However, for those that still do, the FDC portion of the system board's chipset provides a programmable, logical interface for up to two FDD units. This controller resides in the I/O address range between locations 370 and 37F. The FDC receives and decodes instructions from the system to the floppy-disk drive at these addresses.

In a PC system, the FDC operates in conjunction with the system's DMA controller and is assigned to the DRQ-2 and DACK-2 lines. In operation, the FDC presents an active DRQ-2 signal to the DMA controller for every byte of data to be transferred. After the last byte has been transferred, the FDC interrupt is generated. The floppy-disk drive controller is assigned the IRQ6 channel in PC-compatible systems.

When the system starts up, the operating system searches for traditional parallel ports installed at hex addresses 3BC, 378, and 278 consecutively. The operating system links the addresses of any printer ports it finds to logical names, LPT1, LPT2, or LPT3, that software uses to identify the ports. If a printer port is found at location 3BC, the operating system assigns it the title of LPT1. If no printer port is found at 3BC, but there is one at 378, the system will assign LPT1 to the latter address.

Likewise, a system that has printer ports at physical addresses 378 and 278 would have LPT1 assigned to the port at 378, and LPT2 will be established at location 278. Normal IRQ settings for printer ports in a PC are IRQ5 or IRQ7. IRQ7 is normally assigned to the LPT1 printer port, whereas IRQ5 typically serves the LPT2 port, if installed.

An RS-232 port in a PC can be designated as logical port COM1, COM2, COM3, or COM4, as long as two ports are not assigned the same COM port number. In most PCs, COM1 is assigned to port address 3F8 and uses IRQ channel 4. A second COM2 port is typically assigned port address 2F8 and IRQ3. Likewise, COM3 uses IRQ4 and is assigned an I/O address of 3E8, while COM4 usually resides at 2E8 and uses IRQ3.

Resources for Legacy Ports and Devices

legacy devices

In Pentium-based systems the PnP BIOS normally detects all the ports and devices in the system and allocates the appropriate resources to each. The exception to this is the presence of non-PnP devices, also referred to as a **legacy devices**. Older ISA adapter cards typically had no PnP function and had to be configured manually. In these situations, the system had no way to reconfigure the card, so you had to tell it which resources are required for it. This function is performed through the *PnP and PCI Setup* screens in the CMOS Setup routine and reserves certain resources so that they are available for the legacy device.

When you manually configure such a device, you must be aware of which system resources it needs and what settings it can work with. This information can typically be found in the device's installation guide. If the guide is not available, you should check the Internet for the manufacturer's Web site to determine whether any configuration information is available there. In addition, there may be third-party sites on the Internet that can supply the configuration information that you need for the device.

GEEK SQUAD CASE FILE #13345

One of the CIA agents has called you because he is working on a system that has several legacy devices installed and he does not remember what resources are assigned to typical devices in a PC-compatible system. He needs you to fax him a list of these devices. Because you have become a very successful Geek Squad technician, you are on a cruise and do not have access to your resource materials. What information can you send the agent from your memory?

Essentials 1.1

PORTS, CABLES, AND CONNECTORS

A variety of different peripheral devices can be added to a PC-compatible system. Most of these devices are designed to employ some type of standard PC-compatible I/O connection method. As this A+ objective indicates, the computer technician must be able to recognize what type of port the device requires, locate standard I/O port connections, and determine what type of cabling is required to successfully connect the port and the device in order to successfully add peripheral devices to a PC system.

One of the most noticeable changes in the PC industry since the previous edition of this book was produced three years ago is the change in I/O port usage. A single port type has mostly replaced three port types that had been standards of the industry for over 25 years. The USB port that was touted as one of the new entries in the I/O connectivity race in the previous edition has emerged as the go-to port for nearly everything in the PC. This has led to the steady disappearance of the older ports from newer PC models. In addition, new devices are not being designed with these ports as an option. However, these legacy ports are still found and used in millions of existing computers and peripherals in the world. Therefore, they are covered later in the chapter.

The standard I/O port types commonly found on new computers include

- PS/2 keyboard and mouse ports

- USB ports

- Firewire ports

- Infrared ports

PS/2 Connectors

6-pin mini-DIN

PS/2 connector

PC-compatible systems still offer a pair of round (quarter-inch) **6-pin mini-DIN** connectors (also referred to as a **PS/2 connector**) for connecting the keyboard and mouse to the system. These connectors are built into the system board, and their controllers are an integral part of the chipset.

When the ATX form factor specification adopted identical connectors for both the keyboard and mouse, it introduced an opportunity to plug these devices into the wrong connector. Although they are physically the same, the pin assignments and signal levels are completely different, as Figure 4-8 illustrates. Later PC system boards and peripherals have adopted an informal color coding system to avoid this confusion—the keyboard connector and port are color coded purple, whereas the mouse connection is green.

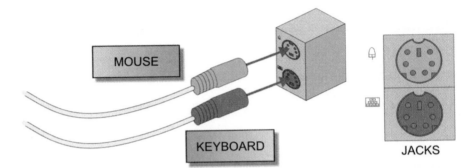

Figure 4-8: Mouse and Keyboard Connectors

TEST TIP

Be aware that it is quite possible to confuse the PS/2 mouse and keyboard connections on most PC systems.

Although many newer peripheral devices can safely be unplugged and reattached to the system while power is applied, this is not so with the standard keyboard or mouse. Plugging these devices into the system while power is applied can cause the system board or the device to fail due to the power surge and **electrostatic discharge (ESD)** that might occur between the keyboard and the system board.

TEST TIP

Be aware that plugging non-hot-swappable devices such as the keyboard into the system while it is turned on can damage parts of the system.

Universal Serial Bus

universal serial bus (USB)

The most widely used I/O interface scheme in current PCs is the **universal serial bus (USB)**. This high-speed serial interface has been developed to provide a fast, flexible method of attaching up to 127 peripheral devices to the computer. USB peripherals can be daisy-chained or networked together using connection hubs that enable the bus to branch out through additional port connections. This connection format has been designed to replace the system's traditional serial- and parallel-port connections. A practical USB desktop connection scheme is presented in Figure 4-9.

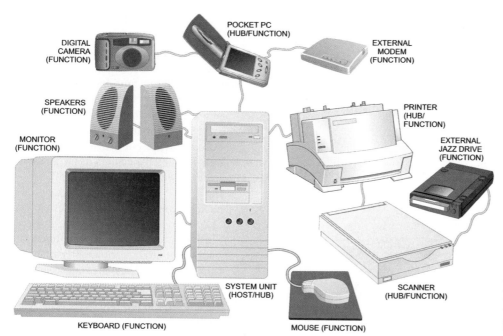

Figure 4-9: USB Desktop Connection Scheme

Figure 4-9: USB Desktop Connection Scheme

In this example, some of the peripheral devices are simply devices, whereas others serve as both devices and connection hubs. The system provides a USB host connection that serves as the main USB connection.

USB devices can be added to or removed from the system while it is powered up and fully operational. This is referred to as hot-swapping or hot-plugging the device. The Plug-and-Play capabilities of the system will detect the presence (or absence) of the device and configure it for operation.

USB Cabling and Connectors

USB transfers are conducted over a four-wire cable, as illustrated in Figure 4-10. The signal travels over a pair of twisted wires (D+ and D–) in a 90-ohm cable. The differential signal and twisted-pair wiring provide minimum signal deterioration over distances and high **noise immunity**.

noise immunity

A Vbus and Ground (GND) wire are also present. The Vbus is the +5 Vdc power cord. The interface provides power to the peripheral attached to it. The root hub provides power directly from the host system to those devices directly connected to it. Hubs also supply power to the devices connected to them. Even though the interface supplies power to the USB devices, they are permitted to have their own power sources if necessary.

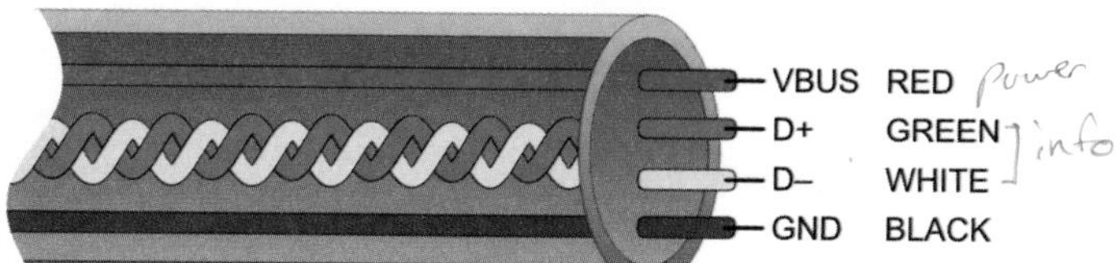

VBUS RED — power
D+ GREEN ⎤ info
D– WHITE ⎦
GND BLACK

Figure 4-10: The USB Cable

In these instances, the device must be designed specifically to avoid interference with the bus' power distribution scheme. The USB host's power-management software can apply power to devices when needed and suspend power to them when not required.

The USB specification defines two types of plugs: series-A and series-B. Series-A connectors are used for devices where the USB cable connection is permanently attached to devices at one end. Examples of these devices include keyboards, mice, and hubs. Conversely, the series-B plugs and jacks are designed for devices that require detachable cabling (printers, scanners, and modems, for example). Both are four-contact plugs and sockets embedded in plastic connectors, as shown in Figure 4-11. The sockets can be implemented in vertical, right-angle, and panel-mount variations. The icon used to represent a USB connector is depicted by the centers of the A and B "plug connectors."

The connectors for both series are keyed so that they cannot be plugged in backward. All hubs and functions possess a single, permanently attached cable with a series-B connector at its end. The connectors are designed so that the A- and B-series connections cannot be interchanged.

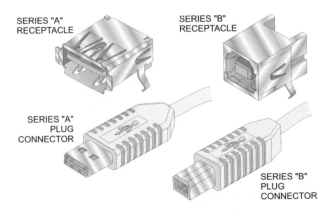

Figure 4-11: USB Connectors

USB Architecture

When USB devices are daisy-chained together, the resulting connection architecture forms a tiered-star configuration, like the one depicted in Figure 4-12.

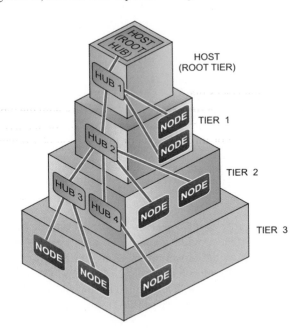

Figure 4-12: Universal Serial Bus Architecture

TEST TIP

Memorize the number of devices that can be attached to a USB port.

The USB system is composed of a USB host and USB devices. The devices category consists of hubs and nodes. In any system, there is one USB host. This unit contains the interface that provides the USB host controller. The controller is actually a combination of USB hardware, firmware, and software.

Hubs are devices that provide additional connection points for other USB devices. A special hub, called the **root hub**, is an integral part of the host system and provides one or more attachment points for USB devices.

ATX and BTX system boards feature built-in USB host ports. ATX boards feature a pair of USB port connectors as part of their master I/O connection block. BTX boards routinely provide five or more built-in USB ports. You can also install PCI card-mounted USB ports to attach even more USB devices to the system. These host ports function as the system's root hub.

In the case of built-in USB ports, the operation of the port connections is controlled by settings in the system board's CMOS Setup utility. In most cases, it will be necessary to access the CMOS Setup utility's PCI Configuration Screen and enable the USB function and assign the ports IRQ channels to use. If no USB device is being used with the system, the IRQ allocation should be set to "NA" to free up the IRQ line for use by other devices.

It is evident that some of the components of the system serve as both a function and as a hub (that is, the keyboard and monitor). In these devices, the package holds the components of the function, as well as provides an embedded hub that other functions can be connected to. These devices are referred to as compound devices.

Although the tiered architecture described in Figure 4-12 approaches the complexity and capabilities of the LAN architectures covered in Chapter 5, *Data Communications*, the overhead for managing the port is much easier to implement. As mentioned earlier, USB devices can be added to or removed from the system while it is fully operational. In reality, this means that the USB organizational structure is modified any time a device is added to or removed from the system.

USB Data Transfers

Unlike traditional serial interfaces that transmit framed characters one at a time, data move across the USB in the form of **data packets**. Packet sizes vary with the type of transmission being carried out. However, they are typically 8, 16, 32, or 64 bytes in length. All transmissions require that two or three packets of information be exchanged between the host, the source location, and the destination location. Figure 4-13 demonstrates the USB's four packet formats: **token packet**, the **start-of-frame (SOF)** packet, the **data packet**, and the **handshake packet**.

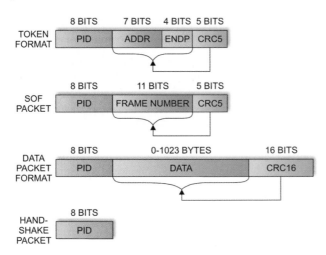

Figure 4-13: USB Packet Formats

packet ID (PID)

cyclic redundancy check (CRC)

Each type of packet begins with an 8-bit **packet ID (PID)** section. The SOF packet adds an 11-bit frame-number section and a 5-bit **cyclic redundancy check (CRC)** error-checking code section. In the data packet, a variable-length data section replaces the frame-number section, and the CRC frame is enlarged to 16 bits. The data section can range up to 1023 bytes in length. The handshake packet just consists of a PID byte.

bus enumerating

hot-swap

The USB management software dynamically tracks what devices are attached to the bus and where they are. This process of identifying and numbering bus devices is known as **bus enumerating**. The USB specification promotes **hot-swap** peripheral connections that do not require the system to be shut down. The system automatically detects peripherals and configures the proper driver. Instead of just detecting and charting devices at startup in a PnP style, the USB continuously monitors the bus and updates the list whenever a device is added to or removed from it.

The USB specification provides for the following four types of transfers to be conducted:

Control transfers

Bulk data transfers

Interrupt transfers

Isochronous transfers

- **Control transfers** are used by the system to configure devices at startup or time of connection. Other software can use control transfers to perform other device-specific operations.

- **Bulk data transfers** are used to service devices that can handle large batches of data (scanners and printers, for example). Bulk transfers are typically made up of large bursts of sequential data. The system arranges for bulk transfers to be conducted when the bus has plenty of capacity to carry out the transfer.

- **Interrupt transfers** are small, spontaneous transfers from a device that are used to announce events, provide input coordinate information, or transfer characters.

- **Isochronous transfers** involve large streams of data. This format is used to move continuous, real-time data streams such as voice or video. Data delivery rates are predetermined and correspond to the sampling rate of the device.

┌─ **TEST TIP** ─────────┐
Be aware of the USB high-speed data streaming mode.
└────────────────────────┘

low-speed USB

full-speed USB

USB 2.0

[handwritten: signal degregation will lose signal]

USB devices are rated as full-speed and low-speed devices based on their communication specification. Under the USB 1.1 specification, **low-speed USB** devices run at 12 Mbps. The length limit for cables serving low-speed devices is 9 feet 10 inches (3 meters). On the other hand, **full-speed USB** devices operate under the **USB 2.0** specification (also referred to as *high-speed USB*) and support data rates up to 480 Mbps. The maximum cable length for full-speed USB communication is 16 feet 5 inches (5 meters).

┌─ **TEST TIP** ───┐
Know the length limits for full- and low-speed USB devices. It should help you to remember that the low-speed distance is actually shorter than the high-speed length.
└──┘

The low-speed USB data rate is sufficient for many PC peripherals such as telephones, keyboards, mice, digital joysticks, floppy drives, digital speakers, and low-end printers. The higher bandwidth of high-speed USB enables peripherals such as higher-resolution full motion video cameras, high-resolution scanners and printers, fast data storage devices, and broadband Internet connections to operate smoothly.

High-speed USB ports are available on PCI adapter cards for upgrading older PC systems. Likewise, USB drivers for Windows 2000 and Windows XP can be downloaded from the Microsoft Windows update Web site.

IEEE-1394 Firewire Bus   *Camera + video captures*

While the USB specification was being refined for the computer industry, a similar serial interface bus was being developed for the consumer products market. Apple Computers and Texas Instruments worked together with the **IEEE (Institute of Electrical and Electronic Engineers)** to produce the **Firewire (or IEEE-1394)** specification. The new bus offers a very fast option for connecting consumer electronics devices, such as camcorders and DVDs, to the computer system.

The Firewire bus is similar to USB in that devices can be daisy-chained to the computer using a single connector and host adapter. It requires a single IRQ channel, an I/O address range, and a single DMA channel to operate. Firewire is also capable of using the high-speed isochronous transfer mode described for USB to support data transfer rates up to 400 Mbps. This actually makes the Firewire bus superior to the USB 1.1 bus but slower than USB 2.0. Its high-speed capabilities make Firewire well suited for handling components, such as video and audio devices, which require real-time, high-speed data transfer rates.

A single IEEE-1394 connection can be used to connect up to 63 devices to a single port. However, up to 1023 Firewire buses can be interconnected. PCs most commonly employ a PCI expansion card to provide the Firewire interface. While AV equipment typically employs 4-pin 1394 connectors, computers normally use a 6-pin connector, with a 4-pin to 6-pin converter. The maximum segment length for an IEEE-1394 connection is 4.5 m (14 ft). Figure 4-14 depicts the Firewire connector and plug most commonly used with PCs.

The IEEE-1394 cable is composed of two twisted-pair conductors similar to those used in the local area networks described later in the chapter. Like USB, it supports both PnP and hot-swapping of components. It also provides power to the peripheral devices through one pair of the twisted conductors in its interface cable.

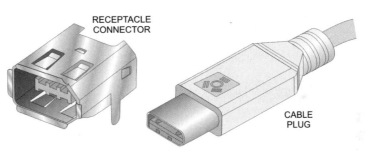

RECEPTACLE CONNECTOR

CABLE PLUG

Figure 4-14: Firewire Plug and Connector

A proposed version of the IEEE-1394 standard (titled *P1394b*) provides an additional electrical signaling method that permits data transmission speeds of 800 Mbps and greater. The new version of the standard also supports new transport media including glass and plastic optical fiber, as well as Category 5 copper cable. With the new media comes extended distances, for example, 100 meters over CAT5 cabling.

> ### IEEE (Institute of Electrical and Electronic Engineers)
> ### Firewire
> ### IEEE-1394

> ┌─ **TEST TIP** ─────────┐
> Be aware that the Firewire bus is faster than the USB bus.

> ┌─ **TEST TIP** ─┐
> Remember how many devices can be attached to a single IEEE-1394 port.

GEEK SQUAD CASE FILE #27846

The ACME company is moving strongly into multimedia systems that include professional electronic music and video devices. Their boss has asked the local Geek Squad which type of interface the company should standardize on. What should you tell their boss about this?

Infrared Ports

Infrared Data
Association (IrDA)

The **Infrared Data Association (IrDA)** has produced a wireless peripheral connection standard based on infrared light technology, similar to that used in consumer remote control devices. Many system board designs include an IrDA-compliant port standard to provide wireless communications with devices such as character printers, Personal Digital Assistants, and notebook computers. Figure 4-15 illustrates an IrDA-connected printer. The same technology has been employed to carry out transfers between computer communications devices such as modems and Local Area Network cards.

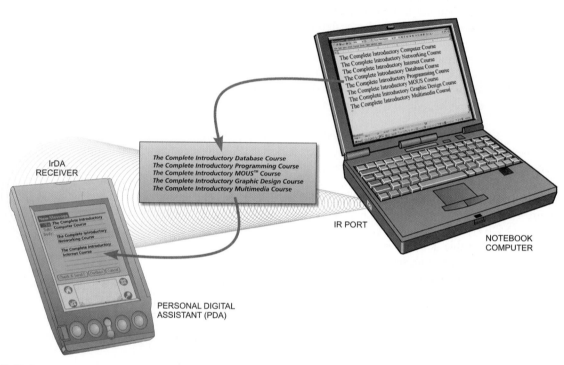

Figure 4-15: An IrDA Device Connection

The IrDA standard specifies four protocols that are used with different types of devices:

- *IrLPT*—This is used with character printers to provide a wireless interface between the computer and the printer.

- *IrDA-SIR*—The standard infrared protocol used to provide a standard serial port interface with transfer rates ranging up to 115 kbps.

- *IrDA-FIR*—The fast infrared protocol used to provide a high-speed serial port interface with transfer rates ranging up to 4 Mbps.

- *IrTran-P*—This is used to provide a digital image transfer standard for communications with digital image capture devices.

TEST TIP

Remember that the IrLPT port is a new, high-speed printer interface that can be used to print from a wide array of computing devices.

These protocols specify communication ranges up to 2 meters (6 feet), but most specifications usually state 1 meter as the maximum range. All IrDA transfers are carried out in half-duplex mode and must have a clear line of sight between the transmitter and receiver. The receiver must be situated within 15 degrees of center with the line of transmission.

The Windows operating system supports the use of infrared devices. The properties of installed IrDA devices can be viewed through its Device Manager. Likewise, connections to another IrDA computer can be established through the Windows Network Dialup Connections applet. By installing a **point-to-point protocol** (**PPP**) or an **IrDA LAN protocol** through this applet, you can conduct wireless communications with other computers without a modem or network card.

GEEK SQUAD CASE FILE #27846

Special Agent 632 is setting up an IrDA printer in a remote location. He has called you because he cannot get the system to see the infrared printer connection. To check the printer, the agent connected it to the host computer using a normal parallel interface and it ran successfully. Which items should you suggest that Agent 632 check to verify the operation of the infrared port?

Multimedia Connections

Essentials 1.12

Another noticeable change in PC systems since the last edition of this book is the rapid integration of the PC with consumer audio and video (A/V) systems. Special hardware and operating system versions have been produced under the banner of **media centers** in an effort to integrate mainstream PC systems for home entertainment applications. Figure 4-16 depicts a typical PC media center and its I/O components.

This integration has led to the inclusion of many connector types commonly found in consumer audio and video systems. These connections range from the standard RCA mini-jacks and plugs associated with traditional PC sound cards to advanced video cables and connectors used with **high-definition television (HDTV)** systems. They enable A/V source components such as AM/FM stereo receivers, MPEG players, and DVD/CD players to be connected to the PC system. They also enable the PC system to operate with advanced A/V output devices, such as large-screen HD televisions and high-end stereo amplifiers and speaker systems.

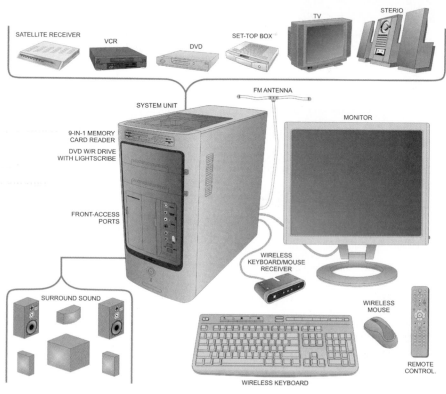

Figure 4-16: Media Center Components

Figure 4-17 depicts common audio connector schemes. To the right of the figure are the typical *Microphone*, *Speaker*, and *Line-In* connectors found on PC sound cards. On the left side of the figure are plugs and connectors used for stereo audio connections. These connectors typically use a red connector and jack for the right stereo channel and a white connector for the left channel.

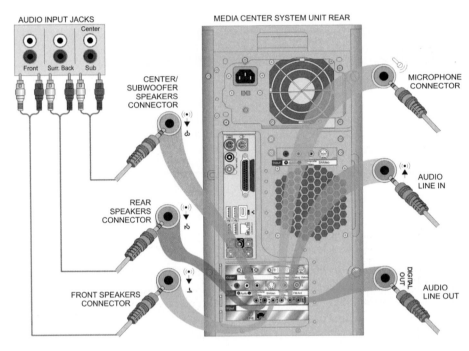

Figure 4-17: Audio Connection Methods

Composite Video

Component Video

Luminance

synchronization

For many years, the standard video connection for PCs has been the 15-pin VGA D-shell connector used to connect video adapter cards to video monitors. However, as the PC is increasingly integrated into home entertainment systems, standard consumer electronics connectors have been adopted to accommodate these applications. Just as the PC industry has developed standardized connections for most components, consumer electronics connections are standardized by function. Figure 4-18 shows different video connection options adopted from the consumer A/V market.

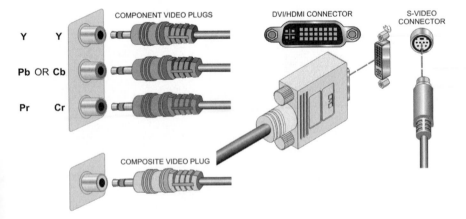

Figure 4-18: Advanced Video Connection Options

- **Composite Video**—a video connection scheme where all video color and synchronization information is transmitted as one combined signal. These cables and connectors are typically color coded yellow. This is typically the cheapest and lowest quality method of transporting audio signals. *Yellow, 3ft, 6ft₂₁ /3A*

- **Component Video**—an analog video connection method where three color video signals (red, green, blue—RGB) are transmitted on separate lines and combined inside the video equipment. **Luminance** and **synchronization** signals are added to one or more of the color signal line. This method delivers signal quality levels between the composite video and the S-video method described next. Component video connections are typically color coded as red, blue, and green.

Digital component video is also referred to as 4:2:2. These numbers represent an encoded luminance factor followed by a *Blue Difference* (Pb) and a *Red Difference* (Pr) value that make up the color signal. Digital component video can be used with 480p, 720p, 1080i, and 1080p video display systems.

- **S-video**—a high-performance multi-pin video cable and connector specification that splits the video signal into separate color components, **chrominance**, and luminance channels to provide high-quality video output.

- **Digital Video Interface (DVI)**—a relatively new video signal connection scheme adopted from high-definition (HD) television systems. DVI is a video-only connection scheme. DVI can deliver quality video in video systems running resolutions up to 1080p.

- **High-definition multimedia interface (HDMI)**—an advanced version of the DVI interface that offers high definition video and multichannel (up to 8) audio transfers in a single cable. Like the DVI interface, HDMI is capable of handling signals for video systems running resolutions up to 1080p.

| S-video |
| chrominance |
| Digital Video Interface (DVI) |
| High-definition multimedia interface (HDMI) |

MIDI Connections

Most sound cards possess only the ability to capture audio signals, digitize them, and play them back as they were recorded. Some sound cards have the ability to generate synthetic sounds that are not a function of a digitizing process. Musical instrument makers created the **musical instrument digital interface (MIDI)** standard to enable music synthesizers, and other electronic music devices, to communicate with computers and with each other.

| musical instrument digital interface (MIDI) |

The MIDI specification began as a hardware connectivity format that included a protocol for exchanging data and a cabling scheme for hooking devices together. The agreement was so widely accepted by the music industry that virtually every electronic instrument manufactured today conforms to the MIDI standard.

Figure 4-19 shows a typical MIDI system. The system contains a MIDI-equipped computer, a keyboard controller/synthesizer, and an audio mixer/recorder, along with related sound modules. The computer contains a MIDI interface card. While a mixer has been shown in this figure, advances in MIDI software have led to systems where the mixer has been eliminated in favor of software mixing. Sophisticated MIDI systems, with a large number of instruments, still opt for hardware mixing consoles. MIDI software contains programming called *MIDI Machine Control* (MMC) that actually controls intelligent MIDI devices, such as mixers, stage lights, etc. A sound module is actually a hardware component containing ROM devices that hold the sampled sounds of the real instruments being produced.

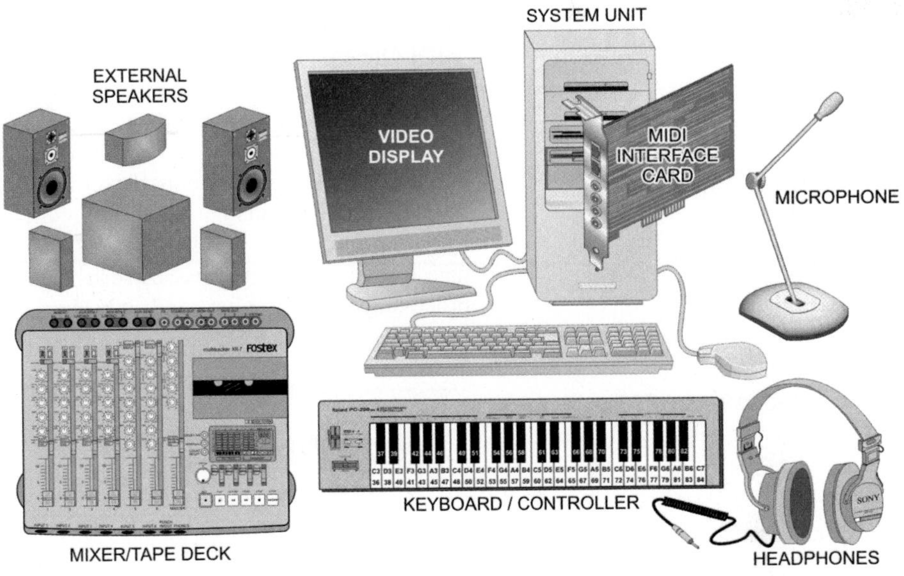

Figure 4-19: A Typical MIDI System

All MIDI devices communicate serially through round, 5-pin DIN connectors, as described in Figure 4-20. Three types of connections are possible in a MIDI system. These are the *MIDI-In*, *MIDI-Out*, and *MIDI-Thru* connections. A single connection cable can be used for all three connection types. The synthesizer/controller requires two connections to the MIDI interface in the computer. The first deals with the controller portion of the keyboard. A MIDI cable runs from MIDI-Out of the controller, to MIDI-In of the interface. On the synthesizer side of the keyboard, a MIDI-In from the keyboard must be connected to MIDI-Out of the interface card.

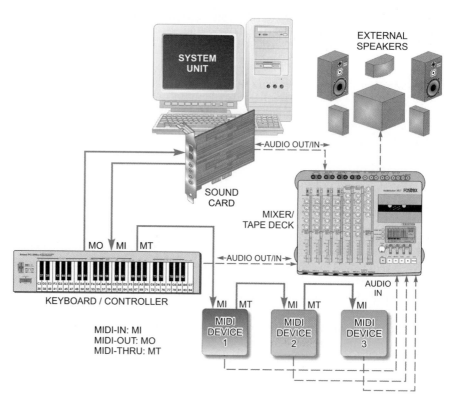

**Figure 4-20:
MIDI Cable
Connections**

To continue the MIDI connection scheme, the interface would require an additional MIDI-Out connection. Alternately, MIDI-Thru connections can be used to serially connect all of the other MIDI devices to the system. The various devices are connected to the mixer/recorder through audio out/in *Patch Cords*.

MIDI data transfers are conducted serially. Each MIDI device contains a MIDI controller, as does the MIDI adapter card in the computer system. In the MIDI device, the data produced by the equipment are applied to the MIDI controller, which converts the data into the MIDI data format. The signal passes serially to the MIDI adapter card in the computer. After processing, the computer sends it back to the MIDI device.

Essentials 1.1

Legacy Ports

As indicated earlier in this chapter, there are three port types that have been I/O standards since the original IBM PCs were introduced:

- Centronic parallel ports
- RS-232C serial ports
- Game ports

To their credit, these older ports are still included on many PCs. However, with the advent of several newer, faster, and more flexible connectivity schemes, these ports are becoming **legacy ports** and will probably disappear from PCs in the near future.

legacy ports

Table 4-6 summarizes the types of connectors typically found on the back panel of system units, along with their connector and pin count information. These connector types are described in Figure 4-21.

PORT	CONNECTOR
Keyboard	PS/2 6-pin mini-DIN
Mouse	PS/2 6-pin mini-DIN
COM1	DB-9M
COM2	DB-9M
LPT	DB-25F
VGA	DB-15F (3 row)
Game	DB-15F (2 row)
Modem	RJ-11
LAN	BNC/RJ-45
Sound	RCA 1/8" mini or 3/32" sub mini-jacks
SCSI	Centronics 50-pin
USB	4-pin USB Socket

Table 4-6: Typical I/O Ports

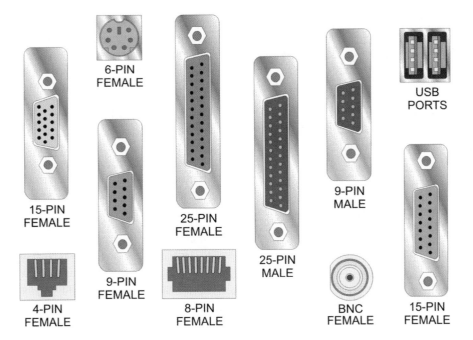

15-PIN FEMALE
6-PIN FEMALE
25-PIN FEMALE
9-PIN FEMALE
25-PIN MALE
9-PIN MALE
USB PORTS
4-PIN FEMALE
8-PIN FEMALE
BNC FEMALE
15-PIN FEMALE

Figure 4-21: Typical I/O Port Connectors

┌─ **TEST TIP** ─────────┐
Memorize the appearance, type, and pin configuration of the standard PC port connectors (i.e., parallel ports use 25-pin female D-shell connectors).
└────────────────────────┘

Parallel Printer Ports

Parallel printer ports

Parallel printer ports have been a staple of the PC system since the original PCs were introduced. In their day, the parallel port's ability to quickly transfer bytes of data in parallel mode caused it to be adopted to interface a number of different peripheral devices to the PC. These devices include CNC mills and lathes; X−Y plotters; fast computer-to-computer transfer systems; high-speed, high volume, removable disk backup systems; and optical scanners.

Centronics connector

standard parallel port (SPP)

mini Centronic

Centronics standard

The Centronics Standard

The original Centronics interface that existed prior to the original IBM PC employed a 36-pin D-shell connector on the printer adapter and a 36-pin **Centronics connector** on the printer end. The Centronics connector on the printer features a female slotted connector with contacts embedded on the top and bottom of the slot.

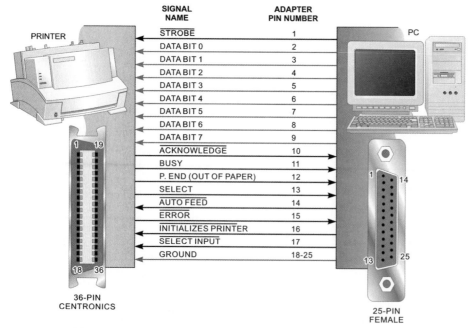

Figure 4-22: Parallel-Port Connector and Signals

The IBM version of the interface, which became known as the **standard parallel port (SPP)** specification for printers, reduced the pin count to 25 using a 25-pin, female D-shell connector at the computer's back panel. However, at the printer end of the cable, IBM continued with the standard 36-pin Centronics connector. Some printer connections employ a 36-pin **mini Centronic** connector at the printer end of the cable.

Figure 4-22 shows a typical parallel printer connection, using the IBM version of the **Centronics standard**. This interface enables the computer to pass information to the printer, 8 bits at a time, across the 8 data lines. The other lines in the connection carry control signals (handshaking signals) back and forth between the computer and the printer.

Because parallel signals can deteriorate quickly with long lengths of cable, the length of a parallel printer cable should be less than 10 feet. If longer lengths are needed, the cable should have a low-capacitance value. The cable should also be shielded to minimize **electromagnetic field interference (EFI)** peripherals.

electromagnetic field interference (EFI)

EPP and ECP Parallel Port Operations

Enhanced parallel port (EPP) and **Extended capabilities port (ECP)** can be converted between unidirectional and bidirectional operation through the CMOS setup screen. If a bidirectional port is being used to support an I/O device, such as a local area network adapter or a high-capacity storage device, this feature would need to be checked at both the hardware and software levels.

Enhanced parallel port (EPP)

Extended capabilities port (ECP)

The parallel cable should also be checked to see that it complies with the **IEEE-1284** standard for use with bidirectional parallel ports. Using a traditional SPP cable could cause the device to operate erratically or fail completely.

When EPP mode is selected in the port's configuration register, the standard and bidirectional modes are enabled. The functions of the port's pins are redefined under the EPP specification. When the EPP mode is enabled, the port can operate either as a standard bidirectional parallel port or as a bidirectional EPP port.

The ECP mode provides a number of advantages over the SPP and EPP modes. The ECP mode employs DMA operations to offer higher performance than either of the other two modes.

RS-232 Serial Ports

As the distance between the computer and a peripheral reaches a certain point (10 feet), it becomes less practical to send data as parallel words. An alternative method of sending data is to break the parallel words into their individual bits, and transmit them, one at a time, in a serial bit stream over a single conductor.

This reduces the number of conductors between the computer and the peripheral from 25 or more to as little as a single line. Therefore, when a peripheral device must be located at some distance from the computer, using serial communication techniques reduces the cost of connecting the equipment. Before the widespread acceptance of newer USB and FireWire serial ports, serial communications were conducted using one of the PC's standard **RS-232 communication (COM) ports**.

RS-232 communication (COM) ports

When data are transferred asynchronously, the receiving system is not synchronized with the sending system. The standard serial ports in a PC employ this transmission method. The transmitted material is sent character by character (usually ASCII), with the beginning and end of each character framed by character Start and Stop bits. Between these bits, the bits of the character are sent at a constant rate, but the time interval between characters may be irregular, as illustrated in Figure 4-23.

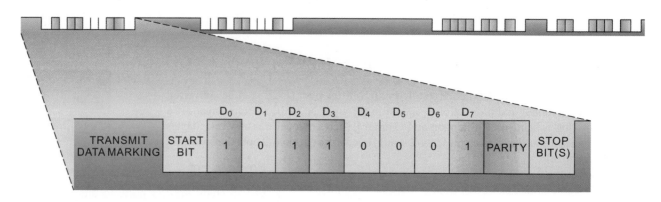

Figure 4-23: Asynchronous Transmission

Over a given period of time, synchronous communications are much faster than asynchronous methods. This is due to the extra number of bits required to send each character asynchronously. PC serial ports and analog modems use asynchronous communications methods, whereas digital modems and local area network adapters use synchronous methods.

Serial Interface ICs

universal asynchronous receiver/transmitter (UART)

USARTs (universal synchronous/ asynchronous receiver/transmitters)

The PC's RS-232 serial port circuitry has always been based on a specialized device called a **universal asynchronous receiver/transmitter** or **UART**. Synchronous devices are usually called **USARTs (universal synchronous/asynchronous receiver/transmitters)**. Not only do these devices provide the parallel-to-serial and serial-to-parallel conversions required for serial data communications, but they also handle the parallel interface requirements for the computer's internal buses and all the control functions associated with the transmission.

The original UARTs used in PC systems featured programmable baud rates from 50 to 9600 baud, a fully programmable interrupt system, and variable character lengths (5-, 6-, 7-, or 8-bit characters). In addition, the adapter added and removed start, stop, and parity bits; had false start-bit detection, line-break detection, and generation; and possessed built-in diagnostics capabilities. However, advanced UARTs have enabled serial ports to reach data transmission rates of up to 115 kbps. UARTs were originally mounted on serial port adapter cards and inside dial-up modems. They eventually became part of the ATX chipset. Currently, UARTs are primarily found in analog modems used for dial-up connections to the Internet.

RS-232 Interfaces and Cables

Historically, the most popular serial interface standard for PCs has been the **Electronic Industry Association (EIA)** RS-232C interface standard. The IBM version of the **RS-232C** standard calls for a 25-pin, male D-type connector, as depicted in Figure 4-24. It also designates certain pins for data transmission and receiving, along with a number of control lines. The standard was developed to cover a wide variety of peripheral devices, and therefore, not all the lines are used in any given application. Normally, only nine of the pins are active for a given application. The other lines are used for secondary, or backup, lines and grounds. Different device manufacturers may use various combinations of the RS-232C lines, even for peripherals of the same type.

In addition to defining the type of connector to be used, and the use of its individual pins, the RS-232 standard also establishes acceptable voltage levels for the signals on its pins. These levels are generally converted to and from standard digital logic levels. These levels can produce a maximum baud rate of 20,000 baud over distances less than 50 feet.

Since the advent of the PC AT, the system's first serial port has typically been implemented in a 9-pin D-shell male connector on the computer. Figure 4-25 depicts a typical 9-pin to 25-pin connection scheme. Notice the crossover wiring technique employed for the TXD/RXD lines displayed in this example.

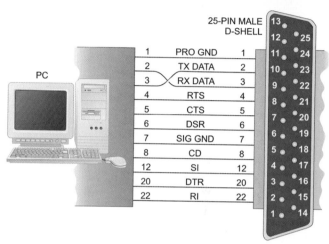

Electronic Industry Association (EIA)

RS-232C

Figure 4-24: RS-232C Connector

TEST TIP

Know the maximum recommended length of an RS-232 cable.

Figure 4-25: A 9-Pin to 25-Pin RS-232 Cable

PC		MODEM
3	TX DATA	2
2	RX DATA	3
7	RTS	4
8	CTS	5
6	DSR	6
5	SIG GND	7
1	CXR	8
4	DTR	20
9	RI	22

null modem

In cases where the serial ports are located close enough to each other, a null modem connection can be implemented. A **null modem** connection allows the two serial ports to communicate directly without using modems. A typical null modem connection scheme is illustrated in Figure 4-26.

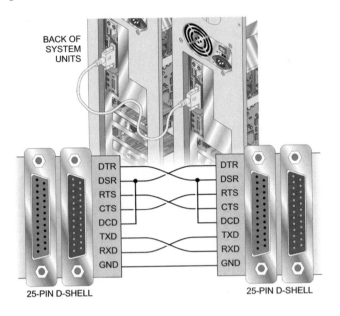

**Figure 4-26:
A Null Modem
Cable**

Game Ports

game control port

fire buttons

The IBM version of the **game control port** enables two joysticks to be used with the system. The adapter converts resistive input values into relative joystick positions, in much the same manner as described in the previous section. This adapter can also function as a general-purpose I/O converter, featuring four analog and four digital input points. As with the parallel printer and RS-232 serial ports, the game port has mostly been replaced on newer PC models by USB ports and devices.

The input to the game port is generally a pair of resistive joysticks. Joysticks are defined as having two variable resistances, each of which should be variable between 0 and 100 kilohms. Joysticks may have one or two normally open **fire buttons**. The order of fire buttons should correspond with that of the resistive elements (A and B or A, B, C, and D). The wiring structure for the two-row, 15-pin D-shell female connector is shown in Figure 4-27.

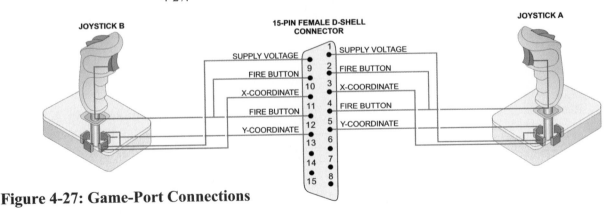

Figure 4-27: Game-Port Connections

TYPICAL PERIPHERAL SYSTEMS

Peripherals are devices and systems that are added to the basic system to extend its capabilities. These devices and systems can be divided into three general categories: **input systems**, **output systems**, and **memory systems**. The standard peripherals associated with personal computers typically include two input devices and two output devices. The typical input devices are the *keyboard* and the *mouse*. Likewise, most systems employ two output devices: the *VGA display monitor* and the *character printer*.

input systems

output systems

memory systems

On the other hand, there are many other types of peripheral equipment that have routinely been added to the basic PC system. As long as there are open expansion slots, or available I/O connectors, it is possible to add compatible devices to the system. Figure 4-28 illustrates external connections for a basic PC system configuration.

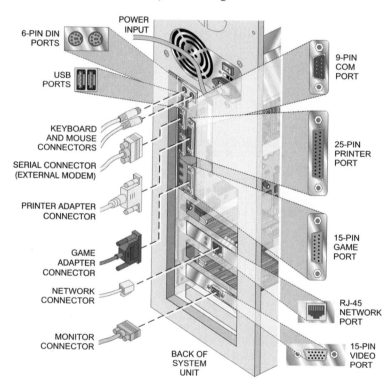

Figure 4-28: External Connections

The procedures for installing external storage devices are presented in Chapter 5, *Mass Storage Systems*. Likewise, modems, transceivers and wireless access points are covered in Chapter 6, *Data Communications*. UPS and power line suppressors are considered to be system protection devices and are covered in Chapter 13, *Preventive Maintenance*. Finally, there is an entire domain concerning printers, and all of this information is covered in Chapter 6, *Printers*. Therefore, the installation processes involved with these devices are covered in those chapters.

Input Devices

Input devices convert physical quantities into electronic signals that can be manipulated by interface units. The input devices typically used with microcomputers convert human physical activity into electronic impulses that can be processed by the computer. The chief devices of this type are keyboards, joysticks, mice, trackballs, and touch pads. Some of these devices are illustrated in Figure 4-29. Other types of input devices convert physical quantities (such as temperature, pressure, and motion) into signals that can be processed. These devices are normally found in industrial control applications.

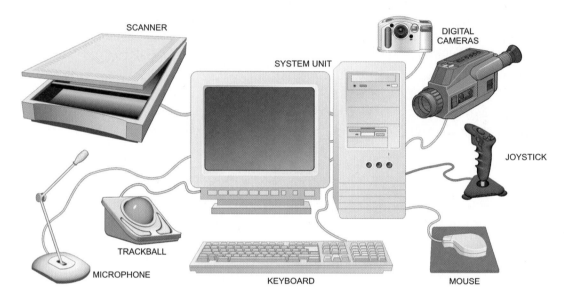

**Figure 4-29:
Typical Input
Devices**

Keyboards

The alphanumeric keyboard is the most widely used input device for microcomputers. It provides a simple, finger-operated method of entering numbers, letters, symbols, and special control characters into the computer. Modern computer keyboards are adaptations of earlier typewriter-like keyboards used with teletypewriters. In addition to the alphabetic and numeric keys found on conventional typewriters, the computer keyboard may also contain any number of special function and command keys to extend its basic operation and provide special-purpose entry functions.

Inside, a keyboard is basically an $X-Y$ matrix arrangement of switch elements, as shown in Figure 4-30. To produce meaningful data from a key depression, the keyboard must be capable of detecting and identifying the depressed key and then encoding the key closure into a data form the computer can use.

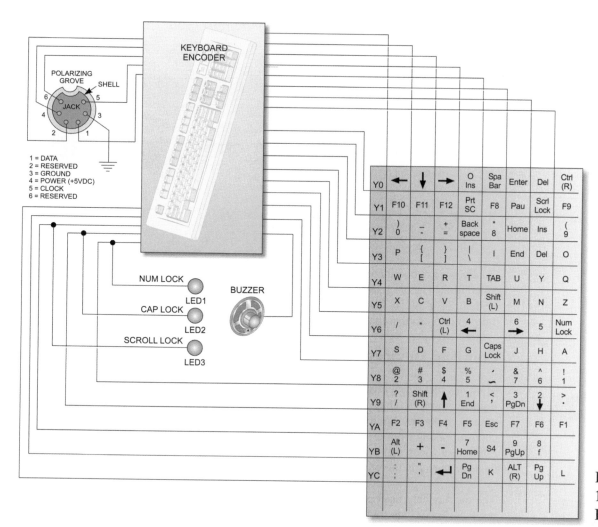

Figure 4-30: 101-Key Keyboard

PC keyboards employ a dedicated microprocessor, called a **keyboard encoder**, to scan the lines of the matrix sequentially at a rate much faster than it is humanly possible to close one of the key switches and release it. Pressing a key shorts a particular Strobe line to a Sense line which the encoder interprets as the key corresponding to that location in the matrix. When it detects a key closure, the encoder pauses for a few milliseconds to enable the switch closure to settle out and sends an interrupt request signal to the system. Afterward, the keyboard encoder stores the closure in its buffer and continues scanning until all the rows have been scanned. A typical encoder scans the entire keyboard within 3 to 5 milliseconds.

Each time the keyboard encoder receives a valid key closure from the matrix, it generates two serially coded characters: a scan code that corresponds to the key closure, and a break code that is generated when the key closure is broken. The encoder notifies the system unit that it is ready to transmit a scan code by sending it a start bit, followed by a serial string of coded bits.

On the PC system board, an intelligent **keyboard controller** built into the system's chipset handles the keyboard-interfacing function. When the keyboard controller receives the serial data from the keyboard, it checks the parity of the data, converts it into a scan code, and generates a keyboard interrupt request (IRQ1) to the system. The keyboard encoder transmits the codes to the keyboard controller through the cable, as illustrated in Figure 4-31. The keyboard controller releases the code to the system's keyboard interrupt handler routine.

keyboard encoder

keyboard controller

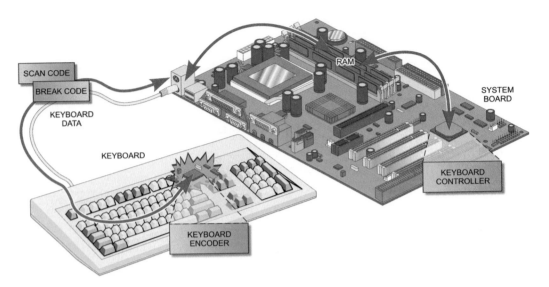

**Figure 4-31:
Moving Keyboard
Data**

Finally, the keyboard handling routine sends the ASCII character code to the program that called for it. The program, in turn, delivers the code to the activated output device (monitor, modem, or printer). This is referred to as an *echo* operation and may be suppressed by programming so that the character is not displayed.

Pointing Devices

pointing devices

Mice, joysticks, trackballs, and touch pads belong to a category of input devices called **pointing devices**. They are all small, handheld input devices that allow the user to interact with the system by moving a cursor, or some other screen image, around the display screen to choose options from an on-screen menu, instead of typing commands from a keyboard. Pointing devices make it easier to interact with the computer than other types of input devices; they are, therefore, friendlier to the user.

mouse

The most widely used pointing device is the **mouse**. A mouse is a handheld device that produces input data by being moved across a surface, such as a desktop. The mouse has become a standard input device for most systems due to the popularity of GUI-based software.

The most common mouse type is the trackball mouse, depicted in Figure 4-32. The trackball mouse detects positional changes through the movement of a rolling trackball that it rides on. As the mouse is moved across a surface, its circuitry detects the movement of the trackball, and creates pulses that the system converts into positional information.

The movement of the mouse causes the trackball to roll. Inside the mouse, the trackball drives two small wheels that are attached to the shafts of two potentiometers (one X and one Y). As the trackball rolls, the wheels turn and the resistance of the potentiometers varies proportionally. The varying resistance is converted to an analog signal that undergoes an analog-to-digital conversion process, by which it is changed into a digital input that represents the movement of the mouse.

The trackball mice use opto-coupling techniques to generate a string of digital pulses when the ball is moved. These devices are referred to as opto-mechanical mice. The trackball turns two perforated wheels by friction. Light from light-emitting diodes shines through holes in the wheels (which are not attached to potentiometers) as the mouse moves. The light pulses are detected by a photoconductive device that converts them into digital voltage pulses. The pulses are applied to counters that tabulate the distance (both X and Y) that the mouse moves.

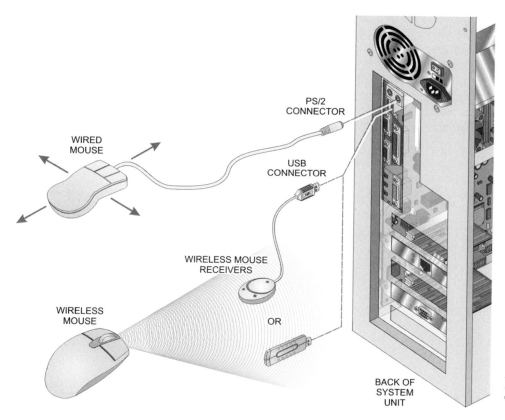

PS/2
CONNECTOR

WIRED
MOUSE

USB
CONNECTOR

WIRELESS MOUSE
RECEIVERS

WIRELESS
MOUSE

OR

BACK OF
SYSTEM
UNIT

Figure 4-32: Typical Trackball Mouse

Another popular type of mouse is the **optical mouse**. In these mice, a light-emitting diode and light sensor arrangement replaced the **trackball**. The mouse detects motion by emitting an infrared light stream, which is reflected off the surface when the mouse moves. The sensor detects the movement and direction by subtle changes in the angle of the received light and converts it into $X-Y$ position changes. Both trackball and optical mice have similar appearances, except for the trackball underneath the mouse.

As indicated by Figure 4-32, there are currently two methods used to connect mice to the system—through the 6-pin PS/2 mouse connector or through one of the system's USB ports. Some **wireless mice** employ an **infrared (IR)** link between the mouse and an IR receiver which then communicates with the computer through a USB port.

There are two major types of joysticks that can be used with PC-compatible systems: analog and digital joysticks. The analog version employs two resistive potentiometer elements, one for the X-direction and one for the Y-direction. Both potentiometers are mechanically connected to the movable **gimbal** that causes the resistance elements to produce variable levels of output signal when the gimbal is moved along the X-axis, Y-axis, or at some angle between them (this varies both the X and Y voltages).

The computer's game port interface uses these analog signals to produce digital $X-Y$ coordinate information for the system. When this type of joystick is used to position a screen image, the position of the image on the screen corresponds to the $X-Y$ position of the gimbal.

optical mouse

trackball

wireless mice

infrared (IR)

gimbal

A somewhat simpler design is used in the construction of digital joysticks. The gimbal is used to mechanically open and close different combinations of an internal, four-switch arrangement, as depicted in Figure 4-33. The joystick produces a single-byte output, which encodes the gimbal's movement in any of eight possible directions. Unlike analog joysticks, the position of the controlled image on the screen does not correspond to the $X-Y$ position of the gimbal. Instead, the gimbal position only produces the direction of movement for the screen image. When the gimbal is returned to its neutral position, the screen image simply stops where it is.

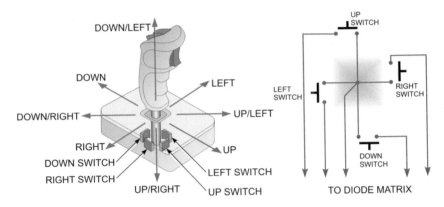

Figure 4-33: A Digital Joystick

Installing Standard PC Input Devices

Essentials 1.2

Technical Support 1.1

In a Windows-based system, the steps for installing a keyboard or a mouse are simple—plug the device's cable into the appropriate connector at the back of the unit. Then, turn the system on and let the operating system detect and automatically configure them.

While the traditional method of connecting keyboards and pointing devices to the system has involved plugging the device's PS/2 connector into the proper socket on the back of the system unit, other options have appeared. Newer keyboards, mice, and pointing devices often use a USB port instead of the more traditional PS/2 port. This connection may also involve wireless links (*infrared* [IR] or *radio frequency* [RF]) between the device and a small receiver that plugs into the USB port.

When I am conducting training sessions, I like to move around through my students instead of standing at a podium. I typically use a wireless handheld mouse to control my computer, which in turn employs a projector to display my presentations on a large screen. On the back of the computer, a small wireless RF receiver plugs into the USB port and communicates between the handheld and the system—therefore, there are no wires to restrict my movement.

The only additional steps that might be required to get a different type of pointing device operational is to ensure that its port hardware is properly selected and enabled, and that its driver software has been loaded into the operating system.

device driver

If the driver for the device is proprietary and cannot be identified by the system during the PnP phase of the start-up process, you will need to select a **device driver** program for the device, or use one obtained from the device manufacturer. These *drivers* might be located on a CD (or a floppy if it's really old) that comes with the device, on the manufacturer's Web site, or on one of the third-party driver Web sites on the Internet. If you cannot find the driver in any of these locations, you will need to contact the device manufacturer through other means to obtain it.

Touch-Sensitive Screens

Touch-sensitive screens, or simply *touch screens*, employ different sensing mechanisms to divide the display screen into rows and columns that correspond to X and Y coordinates and to detect the location of any contact made with the screen. When a user touches an area of the screen, the screen coordinates for the point are captured and passed to the system as input information. The supporting software application matches that coordinate with items displayed on the screen and determines what type of action is appropriate for the definition of the corresponding screen item.

These input devices are widely used in business settings for **point of sale (POS)** operations, such as computerized cashier stations. They are also popular as input devices for customer information and service **kiosks** (self-service computer stations). The lack of easily detachable items and mechanical mechanisms makes the touch screen very attractive for these applications.

point of sale (POS)

kiosks

Two techniques are commonly used to construct touch screens. The first technique employs see-through membranes arranged in rows and columns over the screen, as illustrated in Figure 4-34.

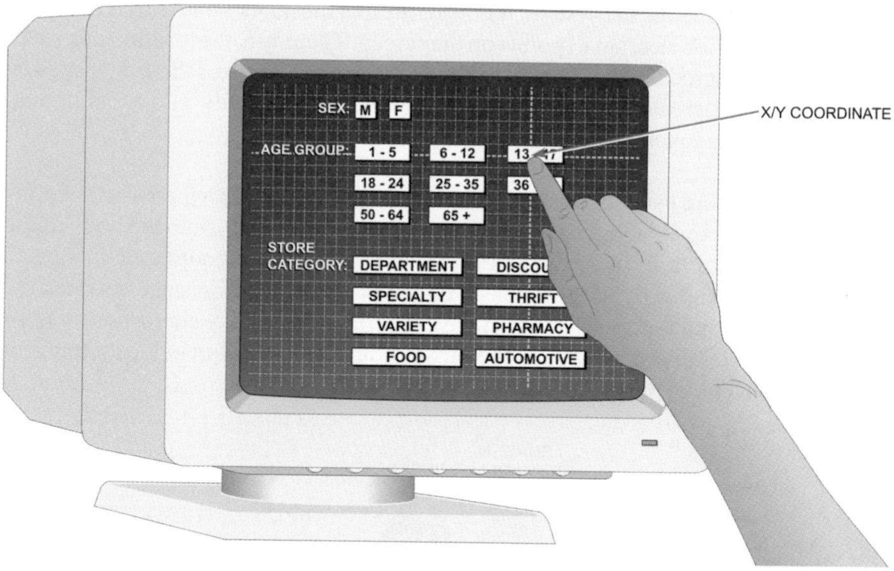

Figure 4-34: Membrane Strip Touch Screen

When the user presses the touch-sensitive panel, the transparent strips are pressed together. When strips from a row and a column make contact with each other, their electrical qualities change. The signal generated between the two strips is decoded to an approximate X/Y position on the screen by the panel's decoding circuitry.

The second type of touch-sensitive screen technology employs infrared techniques to section the screen. Banks of LEDs and sensors arranged around the face of the monitor, as illustrated in Figure 4-35, divide the screen into a grid pattern. When an object interrupts the signal paths between a pair of horizontal and vertical LEDs and sensors, a decodable signal is produced that can be related to an X/Y coordinate on the screen.

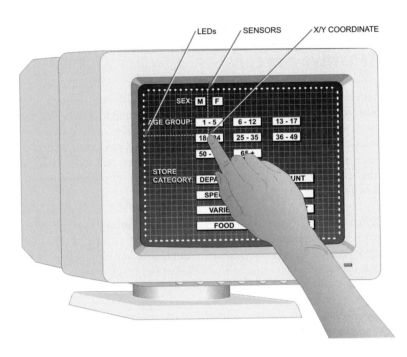

**Figure 4-35:
LED Sensor Touch
Screen**

The main drawback associated with using touch screens involves the excessive arm movements required to operate the system. It is also true that the human fingertip is not a fine enough pointing device to select small points on the screen. Therefore, the location of a small item pointed to on the screen may not be exact due to the relative size of the fingertip. The software designer must create screen displays that take this possibility into account, and compensate for it where touch screens are used.

parallax errors

Touch-sensitive panels are available as built-in units on some monitors, whereas other units are designed as add-ons to existing monitors. These units clip, or strap, onto the body of the monitor, and hang down in front of the screen. In add-on units, the coordinate mismatch problem can be compounded by the addition of **parallax errors**. The distance between the screen and the sensors and the angle at which the user views the display are responsible for these types of errors. Parallax error causes the image to appear at a different location than it actually is. This concept is illustrated in Figure 4-36.

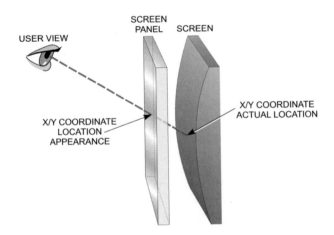

**Figure 4-36:
Parallax Error**

Scanners

Scanners convert pictures, line art, photographs, and text into electronic signals that can be processed by software packages such as desktop publishers and graphic design programs. These programs, in turn, can display the image on the video display or can print it out on a graphics printer.

Scanners

Scanners are typically classified by the types of images they can reproduce. Some scanners can differentiate only between different levels of light and dark. These scanners are called **grayscale scanners**. **Color scanners**, on the other hand, include additional hardware that helps them distinguish among different colors. The software included with most scanners provides the user with at least a limited capability to manipulate the image after it has been scanned.

grayscale scanners

Color scanners

In a typical **flatbed scanner**, the scanner body remains stationary as a scan head moves past the paper. Figure 4-37 describes this process. The paper is placed face down on the scanner's glass window. The light source from the scanning mechanism is projected up through the glass and onto the paper. The lighter areas of the page reflect more light than do the darker areas.

flatbed scanner

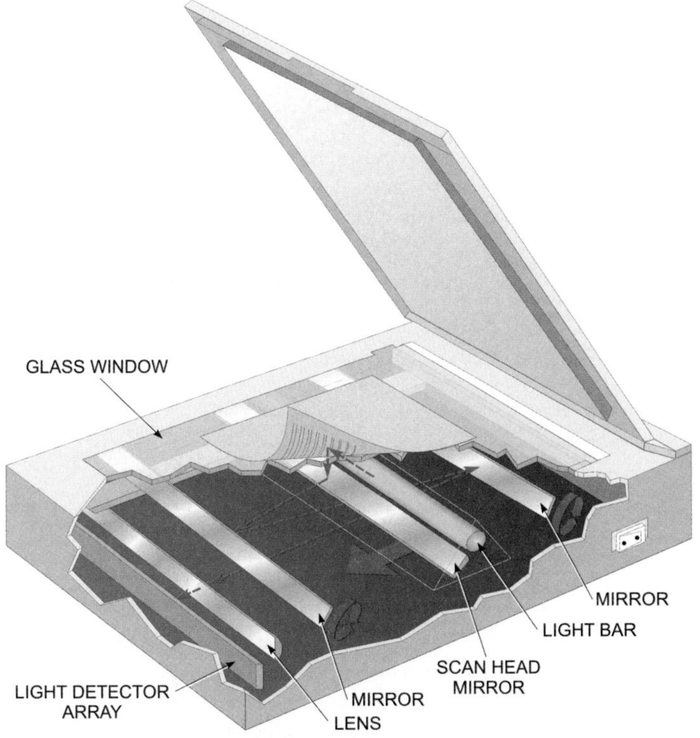

GLASS WINDOW

MIRROR

LIGHT BAR

SCAN HEAD
MIRROR

LIGHT DETECTOR
ARRAY

MIRROR

LENS

**Figure 4-37:
A Flatbed Scanner**

A precision positioning motor moves the scan head below the paper. As the head moves, light reflected from the paper is captured and channeled through a series of mirrors. The mirrors pivot to continually focus the reflected light on a light-sensitive diode. The diode converts the reflected light intensity into a corresponding digital value.

A normal scanner resolution is 300 dots (or pixels) per inch. Newer flatbed scanners can achieve resolutions up to 4800 dpi. At these resolutions, each dot corresponds to about 1/90,000 of an inch. The higher the selected scanning resolution, the slower the computer and printer operate, because of the increased amount of data that must be processed.

The digitized information is routed to the scanner adapter card in one of the PC's expansion slots. In main memory, the graphic information is stored in a format that can be manipulated by graphic design software.

Grayscale scanners can differentiate between varying levels of gray on the page. This capability is stated in shades. A good-quality grayscale scanner can differentiate between 256 levels of gray. Color scanners, on the other hand, use three passes to scan an image. Each scan passes the light through a different color filter to separate the colors from each other. The red, blue, and green filters create three different electronic images that can be integrated to form a complete picture. For intermediate colors, varying levels of the three colors are blended to create the desired shade. Figure 4-38 illustrates this concept.

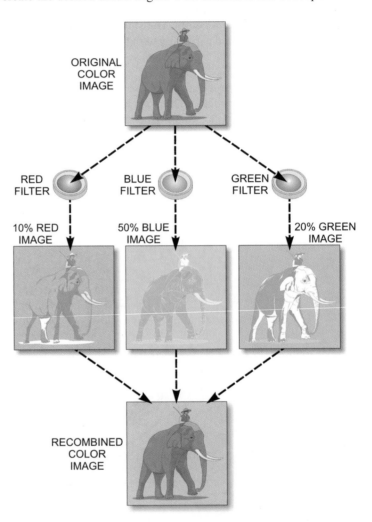

**Figure 4-38:
Color Filters**

Most scanners are currently produced as part of a multifunction office printer. These units combine several technologies together to offer multiple standard office machine functions from a single machine. The functions normally provided by these units include scanner, printer, fax, and photocopier. The heart of these machines is the photo-drum technology shared between the scanner, the copier, and the printer. This drum is described in some detail in Chapter 7, *Printers*.

Bar Code Scanners

A special type of optical scanner called **bar code scanners** or *bar code readers* are designed to optically read information that has been encoded in a standard striping arrangement. Figure 4-39 shows a handheld bar code scanner. The stripes in the code are created in different widths of dark and light stripes to represent numbers and letters. Some scanners have trigger mechanisms that must be engaged to read bar codes, while other models are triggerless and automatically recognize bar code patterns when they are exposed to them.

Like the flatbed scanner, a light source in the bar code reader is scanned across the coded stripes, and the light/dark image is reflected to the photo sensor in the reader. Decoder circuitry in the reader converts the light level changes into digital code. The decoded information can be transmitted directly to a host computer, or it may be stored in the reader and downloaded into a host computer in a batch transfer operation. Some scanner models must be pressed directly on the code to get a reading, while other models have a "field of depth" range that describes how far away from the code they can be and still get a reading.

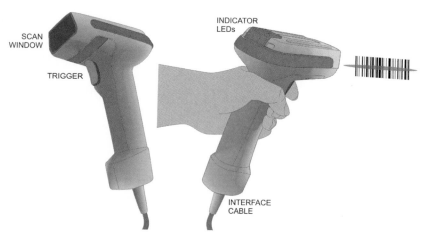

Bar code scanners are typically connected to the computer system using a PS/2 or USB cable. However, there are also versions that employ wireless **Bluetooth** connections to the computer. Some models are connected into the keyboard input using a Y-cable arrangement. In this scenario, the keyboard remains a usable input device. The hard-wired devices receive power through their interface cables, while the wireless scanners are battery operated. These connections are depicted in Figure 4-40.

Figure 4-39: A Handheld Bar Code Scanner

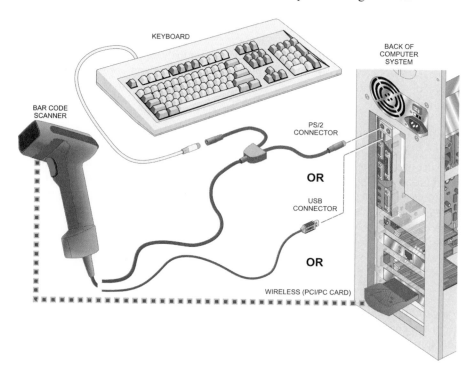

Figure 4-40: Connecting a Bar Code Scanner

Essentials 4.2

IT Technician 4.2

Depot Technician 3.2

Technical Support 3.2

Installing Scanners

Although some older scanners employed proprietary adapter cards, most scanners connect to one of the system's standard I/O ports, such as the system's EPP or ECP-enabled parallel port, as illustrated in Figure 4-41. When using one of these ports to support a scanner, it is important to use an approved IEEE-1284 compliant cabling. Older parallel printer cables were designed for *unidirectional* low-speed communications and may prevent a bidirectional high-speed device like a scanner from working correctly.

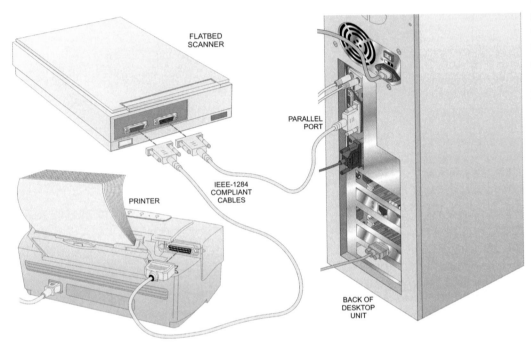

**Figure 4-41:
Connecting an
IEEE-1284–
Compliant Scanner**

On the other hand, newer scanners may employ a SCSI bus extension or USB port connection. These scanners must be installed in accordance with the appropriate SCSI or USB installation procedures. They will usually require that a supporting software application be installed in the system to take advantage of their feature sets.

As with installing printers and other peripheral devices, there is more to installing a scanner than simply hooking it up to the computer and turning it on. First you should verify that the scanner is compatible with the system's I/O port options and its current operating system and applications. Make sure there are device drivers available to support the scanner in question.

You should also take time to educate yourself or the user in the operation of the scanner being installed. Scanners can be configured to provide various levels of copy quality from basic draft level to near perfect picture level. The trade off for quality scanning is always file size and memory usage.

The challenge is to balance these trade offs to achieve the desired output results (i.e., draft quality wedding photos will probably not make the customer happy even though the files are smaller and they do not take up valuable storage space). These variables can be manipulated by configuring the scan for appropriate size/resolution and file format (some formats are more compact than others). Run test pages and experiment with how changing these variables affects the output.

Video Capture Cards

Video capture cards

Video capture cards are responsible for converting video signals from different sources into digital signals that can be manipulated by the computer. The video capture card samples the incoming video signal by feeding it through an analog-to-digital converter, as depicted in Figure 4-42.

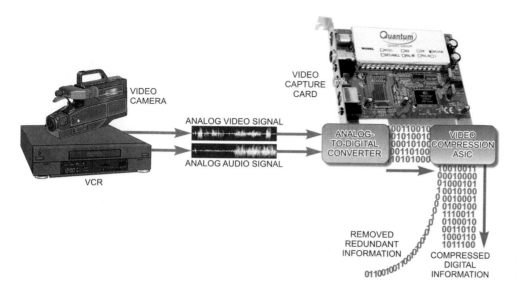

Figure 4-42: Video Capture Operations

The digitized output from the A-to-D converter is applied to a *video compression ASIC*. The compression chip reduces the size of the file by removing *redundant information* from consecutive frames. This reduction is necessary due to the extreme size of typical digitized video files. Video-compression schemes can reduce the size of a video file by a ratio of up to 200:1. The audio signal is not compressed, but it is synchronized to the video signal so that it will play in the right places when the video is rerun.

Sources for video capture normally include CD and DVD players, VCRs, and camcorders. Some capture cards include an RF demodulator and a TV tuner so that video can be captured from a television broadcast signal or a cable TV input. The signals received from analog video-producing devices can be **composite TV** or analog **S-video** signals. However newer digital video capture cards feature DVI or HDMI connections to support digital HDTV signals.

composite TV

S-video

The connection points for a typical video capture card are displayed in Figure 4-43. Low-end analog video capture cards simply supply an input connector for the video source. Other analog capture cards may supply both an input and output connection scheme. More advanced digital capture cards provide connection types that can act as both inputs and outputs.

A video decoder circuit is used to convert analog video signals into a stream of digital signals. However, these are not the RGB digital signals useful to the video adapter card. The characteristics of the decoded TV signal are defined in television industry terms as **YUV**. The Y portion of the term refers to the **luminance** of the signal color, and the UV portion describes the **color component** of the signal.

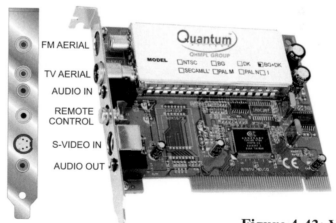

Figure 4-43: Video Capture Connections

YUV

luminance

color component

color space conversion

One of the jobs of the video capture card is to convert the YUV format into an RGB VGA-compatible signal. An encoding circuit samples the incoming analog signal and then performs an operation known as **color space conversion** on it. Color space conversion is the process of converting the YUV signal into the RGB format acceptable to the video adapter's screen memory.

When the digitized video is recalled for output purposes, the file is reapplied to the compression chip, which restores the redundant information to the frames. The output from the compression chip is applied to the digital-to-analog portion of the video-processing circuitry. In the case of analog capture cards, the video signals are converted back into the proper video format and are applied to the video-out connector at the back plate of the card.

video editing cards

More expensive video capture cards, referred to as **video editing cards**, contain special hardware to provide video editing and processing functions, such as rendering figures and performing MPEG encoding. They may also feature dual monitor capabilities that enable you to attach two monitors to the card and spread the display across the two screens, which enables you to work in one screen and view the results in the other without opening and closing windows to do so.

Output Devices

video graphics array (VGA)

Common output devices are depicted in Figure 4-44. The most widely used display device for current PCs is the **video graphics array (VGA)** color display monitor. On most PCs, the monitor's signal cable connects to a 15-pin D-shell VGA connector at the back of the system unit. After the video display monitor, the next most often added output device is the character printer. These peripherals are used to produce hard copy output on paper. They convert text and graphical data from the computer into print on a page.

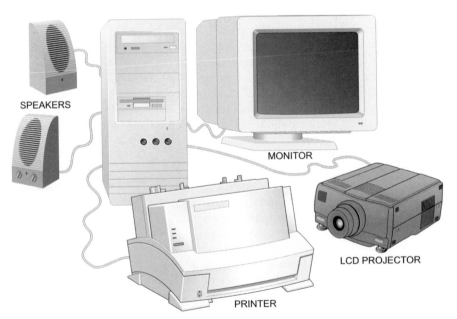

Figure 4-44: Typical Output Devices

Video Displays

The video display monitor has long been one of the most popular methods of displaying computer data. For many years the most widely used version of this output device in PCs was the **cathode-ray tube (CRT)** video display monitor. At the heart of the monitor is the cathode-ray tube familiar to many of us from the television receivers we have in our homes. In fact, the early personal computers used televisions as video units. The basic difference between the television and a monitor is that no radio-frequency demodulation electronics are used in the video monitor.

cathode-ray tube (CRT)

However, newer, lightweight, reduced power consumption display technologies have begun to replace the CRT display in home and office PCs. Originally, the popularity of portable computers created a large market for lightweight, low power display devices. The main devices used in this market are the **liquid crystal display (LCD)** displays. These devices do not use a CRT tube or its supporting circuitry, so the weight associated with the CRT and its high-voltage components is not present. The flat-panel nature of these devices also works well in the portable computer due to its reduced size. LCD displays are covered in detail in Chapter 8, *Portable Systems*.

liquid crystal display (LCD)

In addition to their use in portable PCs, LCD displays have gained widespread acceptance in the large-screen, high-definition television market. Coupled with the explosion of digital A/V systems, this has helped the PC become a pivotal component in home entertainment systems, using the LCD television as a video display and a television/video viewing system.

Basic CRT Display Operations

A CRT is an evacuated glass tube with an **electron gun** in its neck, and a fluorescent coated surface opposite the electron gun. A typical CRT is depicted in Figure 4-45. When activated, the electron gun emits a stream of electrons that strike the fluorescent coating on the inside of the screen, causing an illuminated dot to be produced.

electron gun

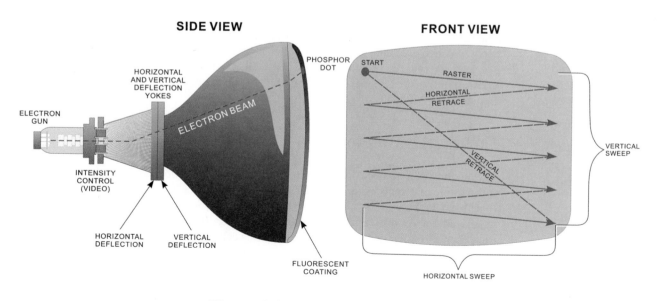

Figure 4-45: A Cathode-Ray Tube

The sweeping electron beam begins at the upper left-hand corner of the screen and moves across its face to the upper right-hand corner, leaving a line across the screen. This is called a **raster line**. Upon reaching the right side of the screen, the trace is blanked out, and the electron beam is repositioned to the left side of the screen, one line below the first trace in an operation called the **horizontal retrace**. At this point, the horizontal sweep begins producing the second display line on the screen. The scanning continues until the horizontal sweep reaches the bottom of the screen, as shown in Figure 4-46. At that point, the electron beam is blanked again and returned to the upper-left corner of the screen in a move referred to as the **vertical retrace**, completing one **field**.

As the beam moves across the screen, it leaves an illuminated trace, which requires a given amount of time to dissipate. The amount of time depends on the characteristics of the fluorescent coating and is referred to as **persistence**. Video information is introduced to the picture by varying the voltage applied to the electron gun as it scans the screen. The human eye perceives only the picture due to the blanking of the retrace lines, and the frequency at which the entire process is performed.

Typically, a horizontal sweep across the screen requires about 63 microseconds to complete, while a complete field requires approximately 1/60 of a second, or 1/30 of a second per frame. The **National Television Standards Committee** (**NTSC**) specifies 525 lines per frame, composed of two fields of 262.5 lines, for television pictures. The two fields, one containing the even-numbered lines, and the other containing the odd-numbered lines, are interlaced to produce smooth, flickerless images. This method of creating display images is referred to as **interlaced scanning** and is primarily used with television. Most computer monitors use **noninterlaced scanning** methods.

In text mode operations, the most common monitor arrangement calls for 25 lines of text to be created on the 525 scan lines. Each text line has a maximum of 80 characters per line. This requires that the top row of 80 character blocks be serialized during the first horizontal trace of the CRT. Afterwards, the second line of 80 character blocks is serialized for the second horizontal trace. This serialization is repeated until all the horizontal traces have been made.

Standard VGA monitors employ a 31.5 kHz horizontal scanning rate, while Super VGA monitors use frequencies between 35 and 48 kHz for their horizontal sync, depending on the **vertical refresh rate** of the adapter card. Standard VGA monitors repaint the screen (vertical refresh) at a frequency of 60 or 70 Hz, while Super VGA vertical scanning occurs at frequencies of 56, 60, and 72 Hz.

Color CRT Monitors

The monitor we have been discussing so far is referred to as a *monochrome* monitor, because it is capable of displaying only shades of a single phosphor color. A color monitor, on the other hand, employs a combination of three color phosphors, red, blue, and green, arranged in adjacent trios of dots or bars, called **pixels** or **PELs**. By using a different electron gun for each element of the trio, the individual elements can be made to glow at different levels to produce almost any color desired. The electron guns scan the front of a screen in unison, in the same fashion as described earlier for a monochrome CRT. Color CRTs add a metal grid in front of the phosphor coating called a **shadow mask**. It ensures that an electron gun assigned to one color doesn't strike a dot of another color. The basic construction of a color CRT is shown in Figure 4-47.

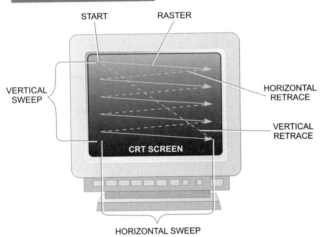

Figure 4-46 Raster Scan Video

raster line
horizontal retrace
vertical retrace
field

persistence
National Television Standards Committee (NTSC)
interlaced scanning
noninterlaced scanning
vertical refresh rate

pixels
PELs
shadow mask

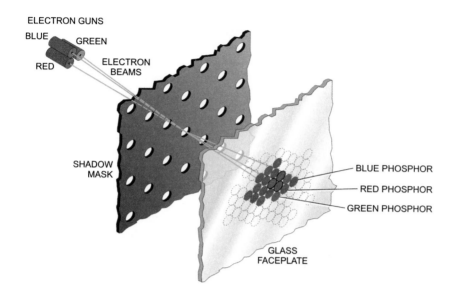

ELECTRON GUNS
BLUE
GREEN
RED
ELECTRON
BEAMS

SHADOW
MASK

BLUE PHOSPHOR
RED PHOSPHOR
GREEN PHOSPHOR

GLASS
FACEPLATE

**Figure 4-47: A Color
CRT Construction**

Video Adapters

At the heart of any video adapter is the video controller. This device is a specialized microprocessor-like device that develops the video signals for the display. It employs a video **DAC (digital-to-analog converter)** to convert digital data from the PC into the analog signal used to drive the video display.

The video controller also generates horizontal (*HSYNC*) and vertical (*VSYNC*) synchronization signals to control the placement of dots on the display screen. As described earlier, these signals are used to sweep the electron beam across and down the screen to paint the image on the display screen.

The adapter card's extended BIOS and device drivers set the rates for these signals which are required to support the vertical refresh rate of the monitor (i.e., if the video adapter card has lower vertical resolution capabilities than the monitor, the screen image will be created at the vertical resolution of the adapter card). If this is a problem, there are three options—update the Video BIOS, update the adapter card's device drivers, or get a better video adapter card.

The **vertical hold** control setting located on the monitor is used to fine-tune the response of the monitor to the vertical refresh signal received from the video adapter and the operation of the monitor's VSYNC generating circuitry. These variations can cause the display to roll, jump or flash.

After a line, or a page, of text has been displayed on the screen, it must be rewritten periodically to prevent it from fading away. In order for the rewrite to be performed fast enough to avoid display **flicker**, the contents of the display are stored in a special memory, called the **screen memory**. This memory is typically located on the video adapter card in the form of discrete memory devices or as an integral part of the video controller IC. On the other hand, some newer systems use sections of the system's on-board memory for the video screen memory function. In our example of 25 lines of text at 80 characters per line, the memory must be able to hold at least 2000 bytes of screen data for a single display.

DAC (digital-to-
analog converter)

vertical hold

flicker

screen memory

The 80 × 25 format described for alphanumeric text mode will typically require at least two bytes of screen memory for each character position on the screen. The first byte is for the ASCII code of the character itself, and the second byte is used to specify the screen attributes of the character and its cell. Under this scenario, the screen memory must be capable of holding at least 4000 bytes. The attribute byte specifies how the character is to be displayed. Common attributes include underlining, blinking, and the color of a text character for the color displays.

video BIOS ROM

Video adapters also have a **video BIOS ROM** that is similar to the ROM BIOS on the system board. The video BIOS acts as an extension of the system BIOS and is used to store firmware routines that are specific only to video functions.

You should also be aware that the video adapter circuitry can be integrated directly into the system board. In these cases, there is no video adapter card present in the system—only a 15-pin D-shell VGA connector on the back panel of the system unit. Even though the system board may come with integrated video capabilities, you are not necessarily stuck with them. You can deactivate the on-board video interface circuitry and install a higher performance video card in the system at any time.

Specialized Video Cards

High-end computers, such as media center computers or specialized gaming computers, typically employ a high-end video adapter card to display streaming video and other multimedia presentations. This type of video adapter card, depicted in Figure 4-48, normally includes at least a heat sink and possibly a snap-on fan unit to cool its video controller IC. The operating speeds and complexity of these devices have increased to the point where *active cooling* methods are required. Cooling units that include fans require a power connection to drive the fan. This connection can be made on a special connector on the video card or to the system board.

Digital visual interface (DVI)

high-definition multimedia interface (HDMI)

ultra extended VGA (UXGA)

high-definition TV (HDTV)

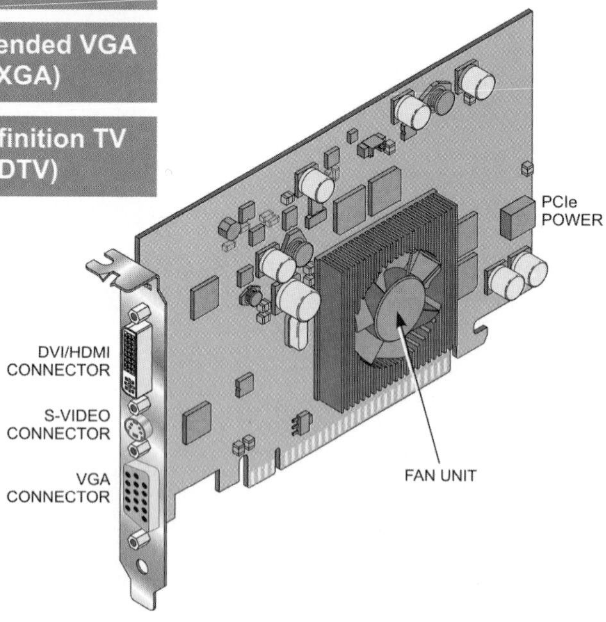

Figure 4-48: An Advanced Video Card

Digital visual interface (DVI) and **high-definition multimedia interface (HDMI)** cards are specialized video adapters that provide both analog and digital video signals to accommodate both analog and digital monitors. The DVI standard specifies a single plug and connector arrangement that can accommodate traditional legacy VGA connections as well as newer digital interfaces. The DVI interface operates with signal bandwidths that support new **ultra extended VGA (UXGA)** video display specifications, as well as **high-definition TV (HDTV)** signals.

High-end video adapter cards normally include a heat sink and possibly a snap-on fan unit to cool the video controller IC, as illustrated in Figure 4-48. The operating speeds and complexity of these devices have increased to the point where active cooling methods are required. Cooling units that include fans require an additional power connection to drive the unit. This connection can be made on a special connector on the video card or to the system board.

Some very high-end video adapters provide internal VGA−to−TV converters that enable them to deliver output directly to a typical television display. This output signal is provided through standard RCA mini-jacks mounted on the back of the card. In addition to standard VGA and SVGA compatible outputs, these cards generate NTSC-compatible (or European PAL compatible) raster scan video signals compatible with television sets. These signals can be delivered in the form of composite TV or analog S-video formats.

Screen Resolution

The quality of the image produced on the screen is a function of two factors: the speed at which the image is retraced on the screen, and the number of **pixels** (picture elements) on the screen. The more pixels on a given screen size, the higher the image quality. This quantity is called *resolution*, and is often expressed in an X-by-Y format. Using this format, the quality of the image is still determined by how big the viewing area is (e.g., an 800×600 resolution on a 14-inch wide display will produce much better quality than the same number of pixels spread across a 27-inch display).

pixels

Standard VGA resolution is defined as 720×400 pixels using 16 colors in text mode, and 640×480 pixels using 16 on-screen colors in graphics mode. However, improved-resolution VGA systems, referred to as **super VGA (SVGA)**, are now commonly available in formats of 1024×768 with 256 colors, 1024×768 with 16 colors, and 800×600 with 256 colors. The SVGA definition continues to expand, with video controller capabilities ranging up to 1280×1024 (with reduced color capabilities).

super VGA (SVGA)

IBM produced its own **extended graphics array** standard, called the **XGA**. This standard was capable of both 800×600 and 1024×768 resolutions, but added a 132-column, 400-scan line resolution. Unfortunately, IBM based the original XGA on interlaced monitors, and therefore never received a large following. However, several newer XGA standards have made it to the market. These include

extended graphics array

XGA

- **Super XGA (SXGA)** specification capable of displaying 1280×1024 resolution

- **Ultra XGA (UXGA)** specification capable of displaying 1600×1200 resolution

- **Wide UXGA (WUXGA)** specification that is capable of displaying 1920×1200 resolution.

super XGA (SXGA)

Ultra XGA (UXGA)

Wide UXGA (WUXGA)

As previously mentioned, the maximum resolution/color capabilities of a particular VGA adapter are ultimately dependent on the amount of on-board memory the adapter possesses. The standard 640×480 display format, using 16 colors, requires nearly 256 kB of video memory to operate ($640 \times 480 \times 4/8 = 153,600$ bytes). With 512 kB of video memory installed, the resolution can be improved to 1024×768, but only 16 colors are possible ($1024 \times 768 \times 4/8 = 393,216$ bytes). To achieve full 1024×768 resolution with 256 colors, the video memory has to be expanded to a full 1 MB ($1024 \times 768 \times 8/8 = 786,432$ bytes).

A summary of the different video standards is presented in Table 4-7.

Table 4-7: Video Standards

STANDARD	RESOLUTION (HXV PIXELS)	A/N DISPLAY	A/N CHARACTER	REFRESH RATE	HORIZONTAL SWEEP RATE	BUFFER ADDRESS
MDA (Monochrome Display Adapter)	720 x 348 720 x 348	80 x 25	7 x 9 in 9 x 14	50/60	Non-interlaced	B0000–B7FFF B0000–B7FFF B0000–BFFFF
CGA (Color Graphics Adapter)	640 x 200 160 x 100 320 x 200 640 x 200	80 x 25	7 x 7 in 8 x 8	60	15 kHz	B8000–BBFFF
HGA (Hercules Graphics Adapter)	720 x 348	80 x 25	7 x 9 in 9 x 14	50	18.1 kHz	B0000–BFFFF
EGA (Extended Graphics Adapter)	640 x 350 640 x 350	80 x 25 80 x 43	7 x 9 in 8 x 14	60 Hz	22.1 kHz	0A0000
VGA (Video Graphics Array Adapter)	720 x 400 640 x 480	80 x 25 80 x 43	9 x 16	60 or 70 Hz	31.5 kHz	0A0000–0BFFFF
Super VGA (SVGA)	1280 x 1024 1024 x 768 800 x 600	80 x 25 80 x 43	9 x 16	50, 60, or 72	35-48 kHz	0A0000–0BFFFF
XGA	1024 x 768 800 x 600	132 x 25	9 x 16 8 x 16	44/70	35.5 kHz	0A0000–0BFFFF
Super XGA (SXGA)	1280 x 1024	-	-	60/70/72/75/80/100 Hz	24.8–82 kHz (analog) 65 kHz (digital)	0A0000–0BFFFF
Ultra XGA (UXGA)	1600 x 1200	-	-	60/70/72/75/80/100 Hz	21–100 kHz (analog) 31–100 kHz (digital)	0A0000–0BFFFF
Wide UXGA (WUXGA)	1920 x 1200	-	-	60/70/72/75/80/100 Hz	24–100 kHz (analog) 31–100 kHz (digital)	0A0000–0BFFFF

Dot Pitch

While X-by-Y resolution specifications are largely a function of the video controller card, from the monitor's point of view, resolution can be expressed as a function of how close pixels can be grouped together on the screen. This form of resolution is expressed in terms of **dot pitch**. A monitor with a .28 dot pitch has pixels that are located .28 mm apart. In monochrome monitors, dot pitch is measured from center to center of each pixel. In a color monitor, the pitch is measured from the center of one dot trio to the center of the next trio.

dot pitch

```
┌─ TEST TIP ──────────┐
│  Be able to explain the definition │
│  of dot pitch.       │
└─────────────────────┘
```

Digital Television Resolutions

The convergence of computer video and digital television has introduced a whole new set of video resolution definitions and terms to the computer industry. The television industry has established a new **Advanced Television Systems Committee (ASTC)** and has produced new high-definition digital television specifications that offer much better viewing than the old NTSC standard.

Digital televisions can produce displays in two general formats—**interlaced displays** like those used in NTSC television that use two different frames to create a complete picture and **progressive displays** (or noninterlaced displays) that paint the entire picture in one sequential set of horizontal lines. Under the new specifications, interlaced display resolutions are denoted by a lowercase "i" following the *vertical resolution* description, while progressive resolutions are designated by a lowercase "p". The vertical resolution value is fixed by the specification, while the horizontal resolution is allowed to vary to permit different standard video sources to be displayed on a digital display device.

Different content sources employ different width-to-height ratios when displaying images (i.e., standard television, high-definition television, DVDs, camera phones, etc.). The mathematical relationship between the width and height of images is called the **aspect ratio**. For example, displaying NTSC programming on a digital television set produces a display screen of 640 pixels by 480 pixels. The ratio of these two values is expressed as a 4:3 aspect

ratio. On the other hand, theater quality video is presented in an aspect ratio of 16:9. The goal of the HDTV specification is to bring home entertainment displays up to the level of these displays.

16:9 Ratio

Where aspect ratio most often becomes apparent is when viewing a movie from a DVD. You are often given two viewing options—*full screen* and *wide screen*. These options refer to the aspect ratio you want to display the film in. If you select full screen and you are watching on a traditional NTSC display, the version of the film altered to provide a 4:3 aspect ratio will fill up the screen. To accomplish this, the film has been edited and picture elements that do not fit in the 4 × 3 box have been cut off, which is referred to as *letter boxing*. Figure 4-49 illustrates the difference between displaying images in 4:3 versus 16:9 resolutions.

On the other hand, if you select the wide-screen option and you are watching an NTSC display, you will see the complete width of the movie including all the screen elements, but you will have black bars at the top and bottom of the display. If you were watching the movie on a digital display with a 16:9 aspect ratio, the movie will fill the screen without losing any picture. As you might expect, if you watch an NTSC program on a wide-screen digital display you will see black bars at both sides of the display.

4:3 Ratio

Figure 4-49: Aspect Ratio Affects

Digital Display Definitions

The new digital television display standards have also caused a reevaluation of display-related terms.

Low-Definition TV (LDTV)

- **Low-Definition TV (LDTV)**—Display systems that produce lower resolutions than the NTSC standard. These systems are digital and provide video for Internet distribution, where higher bandwidth video streams associated with higher-resolution video streams would slow down or crash the system. Typical resolutions associated with LDTV are 240p and 288p. Screen refresh rates used with LDTV include 24, 30, and 25 Hz. LDTV is used with *Apple iPods*, *Sony Playstations*, and video CDs.

Standard-Definition TV (SDTV)

- **Standard-Definition TV (SDTV)**—Digital display systems that have lower resolutions than the high-definition TV specification calls for. These include the standard digital television displaying NTSC broadcasts. SDTV resolutions include 480i for displaying NTSC programming and 480p for European PAL-M programming. SDTV screen refresh rates are 60, 24, and 30 Hz. For PAL and SECAM formats, the resolutions are 576i and 576p using 50 and 25 Hz refresh rates.

Enhanced-Definition TV (EDTV)

- **Enhanced-Definition TV (EDTV)**—A gray area of picture quality that falls between traditional NTSC/PAL picture quality and the definitions set for HDTV images. DVD players with progressive scan output are a good example of EDTV. The EDTV image has a horizontal resolution of 704 pixels regardless of the aspect ratio—the picture is stretched to fit 4:3 or 16:9 aspect ratios.

High-Definition TV (HDTV)

- **High-Definition TV (HDTV)**—Under the ATSC standard, HDTV is any image being displayed at a resolution of 720 or more using a 16:9 aspect ratio. Cinematic video is produced in 720p or 1080p formats using a 24 frame per second refresh rate. Noncinematic HDTV images are produced in 720p or 1080i formats with refresh rates of 24, 25, 30, 50 or 60 Hz, depending on the producer of the content. In computer terms, these are screen resolutions of 1280 × 1024 and 1920 × 1080, respectively.

Installing Video/Monitor Systems

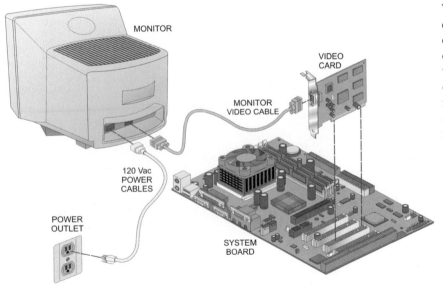

The video display system is one of the easiest systems to add to the computer. The components associated with the video display are depicted in Figure 4-50. The video adapter card typically plugs into one of the system's expansion slots. The monitor's signal cable plugs into the video adapter card. The monitor's power cable may be plugged into a commercial wall outlet.

Figure 4-50: Video System Components

After the video card has been installed and the monitor has been connected to the video card and plugged into the power outlet, the correct drivers for the video card must be loaded or installed. The Windows operating systems should automatically detect the video card, start the system with basic VGA video drivers and ask whether you want to install the manufacturer's video drivers. The Windows 2000 operating system is even more proactive. It will detect the new video card, tell you that it has found the new card, and then automatically load its video drivers. The only time that you should need to be directly involved with the system's video drivers is when the PnP process fails or the video card is not recognized by the operating system.

Sound Cards

The sound-producing capabilities of early PCs were practically nonexistent. They included a single, small speaker that was used to produce beep-coded error messages. Even though programs could be written to produce a wide array of sounds from this speaker, the quality of the sound was never any better than the limitations imposed by its small size. This led various companies to design audio digitizer cards for the PC that could both convert sound into digital quantities that the computer could manipulate and play back digitized sound produced by the computer. These cards are referred to as **sound cards**.

sound cards

A typical audio digitizer system is depicted in Figure 4-51. A microphone converts sound waves from the air into an encoded analog electrical signal. The analog signal is applied to the audio input of the sound card. On the card, the signal is applied to an A/D converter circuit, which changes the signal into corresponding digital values, as described in Figure 4-52.

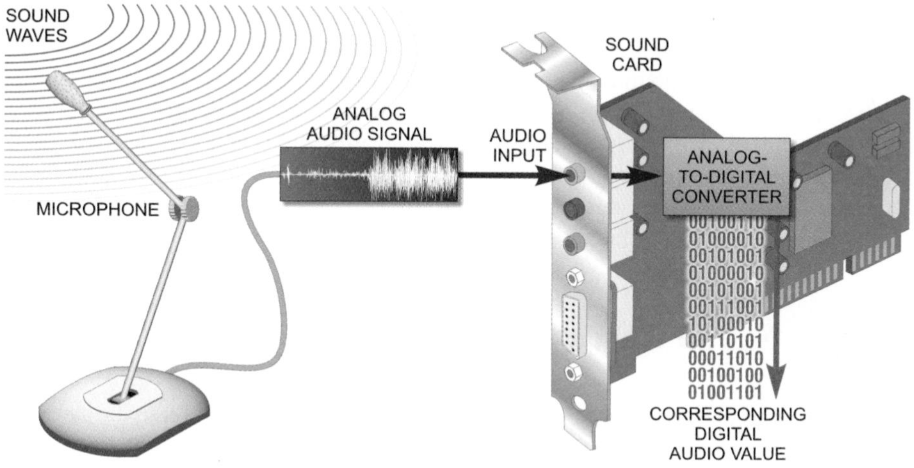

**Figure 4-51:
A Typical Audio
Digitizer System**

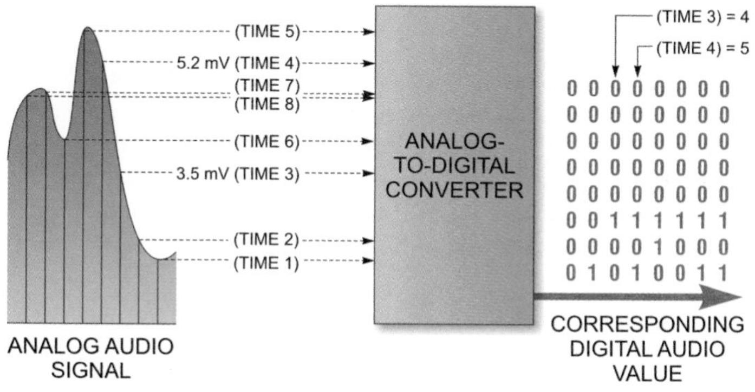

**Figure 4-52:
Converting Analog
Signals to Digital Values**

The sound card takes samples of the analog waveform at predetermined intervals and converts them into corresponding digital values. Therefore, the digital values approximate the instantaneous values of the sound wave.

The **fidelity** (the measure of how closely the original sound can be reproduced) of the digital samples is dependent on two factors: the accuracy of the samples taken and the rate at which the samples are taken. The accuracy of the sample is determined by the *resolution* capabilities of the A/D converter. Resolution is the capability to differentiate between values. If the value of the analog waveform is 15.55 microvolts at a given point, how closely can that value be approximated with a digital value?

The number of digital output bits an A/D converter can produce determines its resolution capabilities. For example, an 8-bit A/D converter can represent up to 256 (2 raised to the 8) different values. On the other hand, a 16-bit A/D converter can represent up to 65,536 (2 raised to the 16) different amplitudes. The more often the samples are taken, the more accurately the original waveform can be reproduced.

Playback of the digitized audio signal is accomplished by applying the digital signals to a D/A converter at the same rate the samples were taken. When the audio files are called for, the sound card's software driver sends commands to the audio output controller on the sound card. The digitized samples are applied to the audio output IC and converted back into the analog signal.

The analog signal is applied to an audio preamplifier that boosts the power of the signal and sends it to an RCA, or mini jack. This signal is still too weak to drive conventional speakers. However, it can be applied to an additional amplifier, or to a set of speakers that have an additional amplifier built into them.

A CD-quality audio signal requires a minimum of 16-bit samples, taken at approximately 44 kHz. If you calculate the disk space required to store all of the 16-bit samples collected in 1 minute of audio at this rate, the major consideration factor associated with using digitized audio becomes clear ($16 \times 44,000 \times 60 \times 8 = 5.28$ MB). If you want stereo sound, this will double to a whopping 10.56 MB. Therefore, CD-quality audio is not commonly used in multimedia productions. The audio sampling rate used in multimedia titles is generally determined by the producer. An alternative to lowering the sampling rate is to limit the digitized audio used in a product to short clips.

Installing Sound Cards

Installing a sound card is similar to installing any other adapter card. Refer to the card's user guide to determine what hardware configuration settings might need to be made before inserting the card into the system. It might also be beneficial to run a diagnostic software package to check the system's available resources before configuring the card.

After the hardware configuration has been completed, simply install the card in one of the system's vacant expansion slots and secure it to the back panel of the system unit. Plug the microphone and speakers into the proper 1/4" **RCA mini jacks** (you may also encounter 1/8" or 3/32" sub mini RCA jacks) on the card's back plate. With the card installed, the system loads its software drivers according to the directions in the user guide. Figure 4-53 depicts the connectors located on the back of a typical sound card.

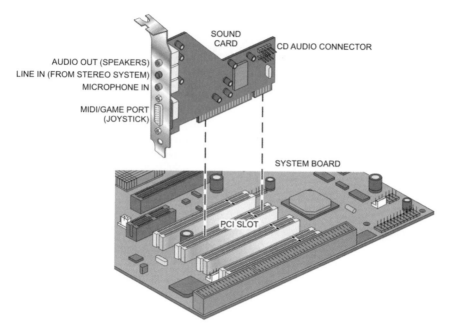

Figure 4-53: Sound Card Connections

Most sound cards support *microphones* through a mono RCA 1/4" mini jack. Microphone jacks are typically color coded pink. A similar green *speaker* jack is also normally present on the back of the card. Depending on the card, the jack might be designed for mono or stereo output. When stereo connections are provided, the jack is wired so that it can deliver separate sound channels through the same connection. The RCA mini-plug used with this connection must also have a stereo configuration.

A separate **Line In** connector is provided for making connections with audio equipment that have audio industry standard Line Out connections. These are nonamplified signals meant to be transported from device to device. Because the signal has not been amplified, it is considered to be cleaner from a sound quality point of view.

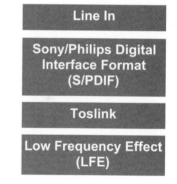

Advanced sound cards may include a number of multimedia connectors. Figure 4-54 shows an advanced sound card that offers connectors for full 7.1 Surround Sound outputs. It also features **Sony/Philips Digital Interface Format (S/PDIF)** digital/optical **Toslink** connectors to transfer multi-channel DVD sound to external Audio/Video equipment associated with home theater systems. The RCA mini jacks for the Front Out and Rear Out functions are stereo connectors that provide for separate Left and Right sound channels. The Center/LFE jack provides the Center sound speaker and the **Low Frequency Effect (LFE)** Sub Woofer channels. This sound card example also provides two onboard connectors along the top of the card that allow it to directly interface with CD players and other auxiliary audio sources.

Other sound cards feature IEEE-1394 Firewire ports and 15-pin D-shell MIDI/joystick connectors, as well as telephone answering ports.

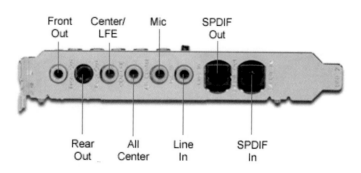

Figure 4-54: Advanced Sound Card Connections

Installing Other Peripherals

The typical PC features built-in logic and physical connection support for the standard PC peripherals. The system board provides the controllers and connectors for the system's hard- and floppy-disk drives. It also furnishes the standard keyboard (and possibly the mouse) connection. As we have seen, newer systems provide industry standard parallel- and serial-port connections, and may supply a game port connector.

Installing Digital Cameras

Digital cameras are mobile devices that are mostly plugged into the computer simply to download pictures. Therefore, most digital cameras feature the capability of being connected to parallel ports, serial ports, and USB ports. Some cameras can also communicate through IEEE-1394 Firewire ports. USB and Firewire ports feature hot-swap capabilities that permit the camera to be plugged into the system and removed while power is still applied. Figure 4-55 shows a typical digital camera connection scheme.

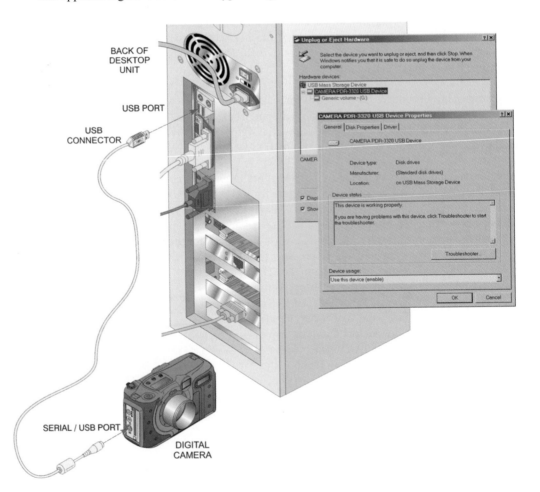

**Figure 4-55:
Digital Camera
Connection**

Software applications for downloading the pictures from the camera must be loaded on the PC before any transfers can be conducted. Likewise, the software supplied with the camera can be used to display the images and typically offers a limited number of graphic manipulation features (e.g., rotate, color balance, crop, and resize). Most digital cameras deliver the images to the PC in a JPEG format. This format is compact, but it can be manipulated with virtually any commercial graphic design software.

Adapter Card-Based Peripherals

In addition to installing hard drives and peripheral devices that connect to standard I/O ports, technicians must be able to successfully install and configure peripheral devices (or systems) that connect to the system in other ways, such as through the system's expansion slots. The steps for installing these types of peripherals and systems are generally similar from device to device:

1. Remove the system unit's cover and take out an expansion slot cover.

2. Check the adapter card's user's manual for any manual configuration information and set up the card as required.

3. Insert the card into the empty expansion slot.

4. Connect any necessary cabling to the adapter card.

5. Connect any external power supply connections to the peripheral device.

6. Start the machine. The Windows operating system should detect the new device if it is PnP-compatible. If it does not, you will need to load drivers for the device from its installation media (disk or CD).

7. Shut down the system, turn it off, and reinstall the system unit's outer cover.

This process can be used to install diverse I/O devices such as modems and LAN adapters, as well as scanners and other devices that use adapter cards in expansion slots. However, for many devices, the advent of newer hot-swap I/O buses, such as USB and Firewire, has reduced this process to more or less just connecting the device to the bus.

Upgrading Adapters

Essentials 1.12

Depot Technician 1.1

Normally, updating adapters in a PC involves installing additional NIC cards, modems, or other proprietary adapter cards. You should always use the following guidelines for upgrading adapter card-based peripherals in a system:

1. *Verify compatibility*—When you are installing adapter cards, you should verify their compatibility with the system board, its adapter slot, and the other cards installed in the system. For example, if you are upgrading a PCI card, you should make sure that the voltage is compatible with the available PCI slot. If your PCI slots only support 3.3 V adapters, then the card you are upgrading to also needs to be 3.3 V.

PCI cards that operate on 3.3 V and those that use 5 V are configured differently. Therefore, a 3.3 V card will only fit in a 3.3 V slot, whereas 5 V cards will only fit in 5 V slots. The 3.3 V and 5 V PCI slot configurations were discussed in detail in Chapter 3, *Advanced System Boards*. On the other hand, there are some PCI cards that support both 5 V and 3.3 V operation. There is less to worry about with such dual-voltage cards.

2. *Perform BIOS upgrade*—A system BIOS upgrade is not required when upgrading adapter cards, but some adapter cards contain their own specific BIOS. These BIOS may need to be upgraded to permit the adapter to work with the other components in the system. If in doubt, refer to the installation documentation and the manufacturer's Web site for specific information pertaining to the adapters you are using.

3. *Obtain the latest drivers*—In most cases, the drivers that came with an adapter card include the necessary drivers for the operating system you are using. However, the latest driver on the CD-ROM or floppy disk supplied with the component is often not the latest driver available for the noted operating system. Check the manufacturer's Web site for newer versions.

4. *Implement ESD best practices*—To prevent the adapter from being damaged, make sure that it is enclosed in an antishock bag when not in use. Make sure that you wear an antistatic device when handling the adapter. Most adapters include static-sensitive components that can be damaged by very small electromagnetic shocks, so take extra care when handling or installing your adapter cards.

5. *Verify upgrade*—There are specific attributes that are common when verifying proper installation of a wide variety of adapter cards. For instance, all adapters use resources, such as IRQ, I/O memory, or base memory address. You must make sure that none of these settings conflict with those of other hardware devices in the system.

You can check this in Windows by checking the system properties in the Control Panel and looking at the *Hardware* tab for hardware errors. Some adapter cards require jumper settings to be preset for these attributes, whereas others do not require jumpers, or include jumperless BIOS. The newer PnP operating systems in use today will usually automatically set up your adapter to preclude conflicts.

Installing Devices Using Advanced Buses and Ports

Most new I/O ports and buses (e.g., USB, IEEE-1394, PCMCIA, and IrDA) feature hot insertion and removal capabilities for their devices. These are in addition to the traditional PnP operation. The devices that connect to these ports and buses are designed to be plugged in and removed as needed. Installing these devices is practically a hands-off operation.

Installing a USB or Firewire device usually involves the following steps:

1. Enable the USB resources in the CMOS Setup screen, as illustrated in Figure 4-56. In some cases, this involves enabling the port and reserving an IRQ resource for the device.

2. Plug the device into an open USB connector.

3. Wait for the operating system to recognize the device and configure it through the PnP process.

Microsoft's Windows 2000 or Windows XP operating systems will detect the presence of the USB or Firewire device and start their Found New Hardware Wizard program, depicted in Figure 4-57, to guide the installation process. Simply follow the instructions provided by the wizard to set up the new device—there is no need to shut down or turn off the computer.

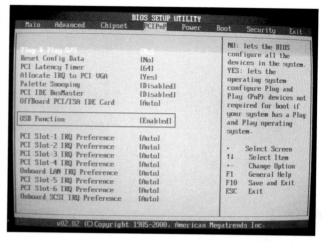

Figure 4-56: Enabling the USB Resources

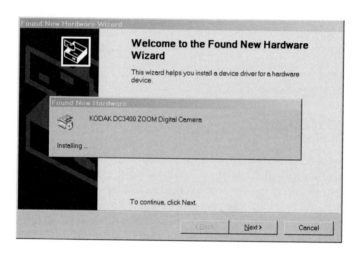

Figure 4-57: The Windows Found New Hardware Wizard

Installing an IrDA device in an infrared-enabled system is a fairly simple process. When an IrDA device is installed in the system, a *Wireless Link* icon appears in the Windows Control Panel as depicted in Figure 4-58. (Remember, infrared port operations must first be enabled through the CMOS Setup utility.) When another IrDA device comes within range of the host port, the *Infrared* icon will appear on the Windows desktop and in the taskbar. In the case of an IrDA printer, a printer icon will appear in the Printer folder.

Installing

┌─ **TEST TIP** ─────┐
Be aware that IrDA operations must be enabled in CMOS before any infrared activities can occur.
└────────────────┘

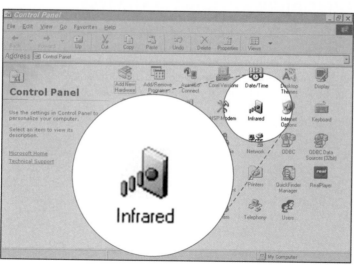

Figure 4-58: The Windows Wireless Link Icon

Right-click the *Infrared* icon on the taskbar to turn on the infrared communication function. Make sure that the *Enable Infrared* communication check box is checked. To turn off infrared communications, make sure that this item is not checked. When infrared communication has been turned off, the *Search for Devices Within Range* and *Enable Plug and Play* functions are also turned off. To engage support for infrared Plug-and-Play devices, right-click the *Infrared* icon on the taskbar.

Make sure that the *Enable Plug and Play* option is checked. Conversely, to turn off support for Plug-and-Play device installation, make sure that this item is not checked. It will only be available if the infrared and searching functions are enabled. If the taskbar icon is not visible, click on the *Related Topics* option.

TEST TIP

Be aware of how to know that an IrDA-capable device is within range of a host system.

Simply right-click the *Infrared* icon on the taskbar to install software for an infrared device. Make sure that the *Enable Plug and Play* check box is checked, and verify that the new device is within range. If you are not sure whether the device you are installing is Plug-and-Play capable, check its user's guide. If it is not a Plug-and-Play device, install its drivers by accessing the *Add New Hardware* icon in the Control Panel.

Infrared Monitor

Infrared Monitor

Windows provides an **Infrared Monitor** utility that can be used to track the computer's activity. When this utility is running, it will alert you when infrared devices are within range of your computer by placing the *Infrared* icon on the taskbar. The Infrared Monitor not only notifies you when the computer is communicating with an infrared device, but it also indicates how well it is communicating. Other functions that can be performed through the Infrared Monitor include controlling how the system reports the status of the infrared activity it detects and what types of infrared activity it can conduct.

Upgrading Peripheral Devices

Devices that come under this category include printers, external modems, external CD devices, and input devices, such as the keyboard and mouse. The steps involved in this process are similar to those listed for upgrading adapter cards presented earlier in this chapter. You should use the general procedure that follows when you are upgrading a system's peripheral devices:

1. *Verify compatibility*—Because peripheral devices can vary greatly in their configuration and use, you should always refer to the device's documentation to ensure that it will work properly with your system. Because external devices must connect to the computer through its interface ports (i.e., serial and parallel ports, USB, Firewire, and in some cases external SCSI connectors), you must ensure that the proper port is available for the device to be installed.

2. *Perform firmware upgrade*—Prior to installing a peripheral, consult the manufacturer's Web site for any updates that may exist for its firmware, or any updated device drivers that may be available. To apply firmware updates, you must first obtain the firmware update tool from the manufacturer.

3. *Obtain the latest drivers*—In most cases, the installation software that came with the peripheral will have the necessary drivers for the operating system you are using. The latest driver on the installation CD or floppy disk is usually only the latest driver available at the time the peripheral shipped.

4. *Implement ESD best practices*—Peripherals tend to be less sensitive to electrostatic damage than PC board devices and are often directly grounded through their power cords. However, because peripheral devices tend to be expensive, you may still want to properly ground yourself before working with them. It is always better to be safe than sorry.

5. *Verify the upgrade*—Because peripheral devices can vary greatly in their configuration and use, there are a variety of ways that you can test your upgrade. For instance, with a printer you can print a test page, print a page from a client, or print multiple print jobs to test the queue. For a zip disk, this may include moving data onto the disk and then trying to examine the data on another computer later.

6. *Check system resources*—Normally, peripherals use the resources associated with the port they are attached to. If the peripheral tests OK, you will normally not have to verify system resources.

KEY POINTS REVIEW

The first half of this chapter examined standard I/O port assignments in a PC-compatible system. The second half of the chapter dealt with common input/output devices used with PCs. Review the following key points before moving into the Review and Exam Questions sections to make sure you are comfortable with each point. Afterward, answer the Review Questions that follow to verify your knowledge of the information.

- In addition to the millions of possible memory locations in a PC, there are typically thousands of addresses set aside for input and output devices in a system. In order for any device to operate with the system's microprocessor, it must have an address (or group of addresses) at which the system can find it.

- Interface circuits are necessary because the characteristics of most peripherals differ greatly from those of the basic computer. Most interface circuits in the PC-compatible world have been integrated into application-specific ICs.

- When dealing with a PC-compatible, there are two forms of I/O to contend with. These include the system board's on-board I/O, and peripheral devices that interact with the system through its expansion slots.

- Parallel ports have been a staple of the PC system since the original PCs were introduced.

- Microsoft operating systems keep track of the system's installed printer ports by assigning them the logical device names (handles) LPT1, LPT2, and LPT3. Whenever the system is booted up, the operating system searches the hardware for parallel ports installed at hex addresses 3BC, 378, and 278 consecutively.

- As the distance between the computer and a peripheral reaches a certain point (10 feet), it becomes less practical to send data as parallel words. An alternative method of sending data is to break the parallel words into their individual bits, and transmit them, one at a time, in a serial bit stream over a single conductor.

- Two methods are used to provide the proper timing for serial transfers: The data bits may be sent synchronously (in conjunction with a synchronizing clock pulse) or asynchronously (without an accompanying clock pulse).

- The operating system assigns COM port designations to the system's serial ports during bootup.

- COM port designations are normally COM1 and COM2 in most systems, but they can be extended to COM3 and COM4 in advanced systems.

- Peripherals are devices and systems that are added to the basic system to extend its capabilities. These devices and systems can be divided into three general categories: input systems, output systems, and memory systems.

- The universal serial bus (USB) was developed to provide a fast, flexible method of attaching up to 127 peripheral devices to the computer. The USB provides a connection format designed to replace the system's traditional serial and parallel port connections.

REVIEW QUESTIONS

The following questions test your knowledge of the material presented in this chapter.

1. Explain the differences between SDTV and HDTV.

2. Where would you be likely to find an S/PDIF connector in a PC system?

3. Describe the different methods commonly used to interface bar code readers to a PC system.

4. Which type of data transfer technique involves a high-speed device taking over the system busses from the microprocessor to conduct I/O read and write operations?

5. An executive of a small company is concerned about purchasing digital cameras for her assessment team. Her main concern is that the digital camera connect to the workstation properly. List all the traditional connections that a digital camera can use to connect to a workstation.

6. What is the function of a shadow mask in a CRT display?

7. A user wishes to connect a Firewire-compatible video camera with his workstation. However, before he requests a purchase for all required devices, he wants to make sure that the cable segment will be long enough so he can place the video camera on a tripod in a specific place at his office and still be connected to the workstation. What is the maximum segment length for an IEEE-1394 connection in terms of feet?

8. You are establishing a component video connection between a media center PC and a flat panel television/video display, how many cables should this involve and what colors should they be?

9. How many USB devices can be attached to the USB port of a PC?

10. What is the maximum recommended distance for an IrDA link?

11. State the maximum segment lengths for low- and high-speed USB connections.

12. How many devices can be connected to a single IEEE-1394 port?

13. Which port types include high-speed data streaming modes that can transfer large streams of data such as audio or video information?

14. What type of device normally uses IRQ14?

15. When reviewing the specification for a particular video display, you read that it features a 0.28 mm dot pitch. What does this mean?

EXAM QUESTIONS

1. Which device or port uses IRQ8 in a PC-compatible system?
   a. Keyboard buffer
   b. Math coprocessor
   c. RAM refresh controller
   d. Real-time clock module

2. At what I/O port addresses does the system communicate with the primary hard disk (IDE) controller?
   a. 0F8-0FF
   b. 1F0-1f8
   c. 200-207
   d. 278-27F

3. What type of connector is normally found on PC-compatible keyboards? (Select all that apply.)
   a. A 6-pin mini-DIN connector
   b. A 5-pin DIN connector
   c. An RJ-11 connector
   d. An RJ-45 connector

4. Which type of I/O port employs a 2-row 15-pin, D-shell female connector?
   a. VGA port
   b. ATX mouse port
   c. LAN port
   d. Game port

5. Which video display standard is capable of providing a maximum output resolution of 1600 × 1220 pixels?
   a. WVXGA
   b. SXGA
   c. UXGA
   d. SVGA

6. Select the option that is not found on the back plate of a typical audio sound card.
   a. Line-in
   b. Line-out
   c. Speaker
   d. Microphone

7. If you establishing a component video connection between a media server PC and a television/video display unit, what connection standard offers the best performance?
   a. SVGA
   b. S-video
   c. DVI
   d. HDMI

8. A user complains that he is unable to find a cord or plug to connect his brand-new PDA to the workstation. Reading through the PDA manual, you note no mention of additional cords to interface with the PDA. All other functions of the PDA appear to be working. What is the most likely solution?
   a. A The PDA is defective.
   b. The PDA is missing cabling.
   c. The PDA uses wireless connections to transfer data.
   d. The PDA does not have batteries installed.

9. Which DMA channel has a dedicated function in a standard PC?
   a. Channel 6 for the FDD controller
   b. Channel 2 for the FDD controller
   c. Channel 3 for the EPP port controller
   d. Channel 1 for the keyboard controller

10. Choose the event that will cause an NMI error to occur.
    a. Adapter card error
    b. Hard drive failure
    c. Power failure port
    d. User error

CHAPTER 5

MASS STORAGE SYSTEMS

Upon completion of this chapter and its related lab procedures, you should be able to perform these tasks:

1. Identify and differentiate between different types of storage systems such as hard drives, tape drives, CD-ROM/DVD drives, and floppy-disk drives.

2. State reasons for the popularity of magnetic disks as computer data storage systems.

3. Describe the format or organization of a typical hard disk.

4. Identify different types of removable Flash Memory formats.

5. Explain how to determine whether an HDD in a given system should be upgraded.

6. Differentiate between common connecting cables and interfaces (e.g., SCSI, IDE, SATA, FDD).

7. Discuss the different RAID advisory levels and apply them to given applications.

8. Install PATA and SATA devices, including setting Master/Slave/Single designations.

9. Install and configure single and complex SCSI device chains.

10. Establish proper addressing and termination for SCSI devices to avoid conflicts and problems.

11. Describe the operation of a writable CD drive.

12. Differentiate between different types of CD formats.

13. Install and configure a CD-ROM/DVD drive for operation.

14. Describe actions that can be taken to optimize disk drive performance.

MASS STORAGE SYSTEMS

FROM THE GEEK SQUAD

Juan G, Geek Squad Agent 107, was working the morning shift at the workbench in store 445 when he received a work order informing him that he was to install a new serial ATA drive in a customer's ATX class computer. The customer purchased the drive over the weekend and could not get it installed at home, so he brought it in to have it installed.

Agent 107 must be familiar with the characteristics of this type of drive and what is required to install it in a given system. There may be good reasons why the customer could not get the drive to work in the system. Therefore, Juan must be able to explain to the customer how the component he has selected interacts with the system and why it did not work as the customer had expected it to.

INTRODUCTION

The problem with electronic memory devices is that programs and data disappear from them when the device is turned off or loses power. Also, the costs associated with IC RAM devices tend to make them too expensive to be used for constructing large memories that can hold multiple programs and large amounts of data. Therefore, storage systems that can be used for long-term data storage are necessary as a second level of memory for the computer. Like IC ROM devices, these systems must be able to hold information even when the computer is turned off. On the other hand, they need to be like RAM devices in that their information can be updated and changed often.

With this in mind, a number of secondary memory technologies have been developed to perform mass storage duties for the computer. Unlike primary memory devices, which are fast and have a relatively low storage capacity, secondary memory systems are typically slower and possess much larger storage potential. The mass storage unit holds information and transfers it in batches to the computer's faster internal memory when requested.

All personal computers include one or more mass storage systems. The most widely used mass storage systems have typically involved covering some medium with a magnetic coating. However, optical storage technologies such as *compact discs* (*CD*s) and *digital video discs* (*DVD*s) have made great inroads into the digital data storage market. In addition, many small form factor *flash storage* technologies have been introduced to the PC market.

MAGNETIC STORAGE

> From the early days of digital computers, most secondary memory systems have involved storing binary information in the form of magnetic charges on moving magnetic surfaces.

Magnetic storage has remained popular due to three factors:

- Low cost-per-bit of storage
- Intrinsically nonvolatile nature
- It has successfully evolved upward in capacity

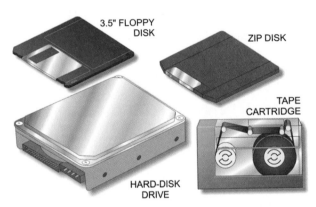

Typical magnetic storage media include flexible Mylar disks (called floppy disks), rigid aluminum hard disks, and various widths of flexible Mylar tape, as illustrated in Figure 5-1. The information to be stored on the medium is converted into electromagnetic pulses, which in turn are used to create tiny positive and negative magnetized spots on the magnetic surface. To retrieve, or read, the information back from the surface, the storage system needs only to detect the spots and decode them. The stored information can be changed at any time by remagnetizing the surface with the new information.

Figure 5-1:
Typical Magnetic
Storage Systems

Magnetic Disk Drives

Magnetic disks resemble grooveless phonograph records and fall into two general categories: high-speed hard disks and slower flexible disks. Data bits are stored as magnetic spots recorded serially in concentric circles around the disk. These circles are referred to as **tracks** and are numbered, beginning with 0, from the outside edge inward. The number of tracks may range from 40 up to 2048, depending on the type of disk and drive being used.

tracks

Because the tracks toward the outer edge of the disk are longer than the inner tracks, all tracks are divided into an equal number of equal-size data blocks called **sectors**. This arrangement is used so that the logic circuitry for processing data going to or coming from the disk can be as simple as possible. Therefore, each block of data has an address, which is the combination of its track number and its sector number. This means that each sector on the disk can be accessed for a read or write operation as fast as any other sector on the disk. The number of sectors on a track may range from eight to more than 60, depending on the disk and drive type, and the operating system software used to format it.

sectors

The tracks of the disk are numbered, beginning with 00, from the outer edge of the disk inward. Each side of the disk may hold 80 or more tracks, depending on the type of disk and the drive being used. When multiple disks are stacked together on a common spindle, as they are in a hard-disk drive, all of the tracks having the same number are referred to collectively as a **cylinder** (e.g., all of the track-0 tracks are taken together to form cylinder-0).

cylinder

In floppy- and hard-disk systems, track and sector address information is contained in a track/sector identification table recorded on the disk. This method of address specification is known as **soft sectoring**, because the sector information is written in software. PC-compatible systems use soft-sectored disks.

For more in-depth information about how magnetic disk systems work, refer to the Electronic Reference Shelf located on the CD that accompanies this book.

REFERENCE
SHELF

formatting

The typical PC floppy disk is a good simple example of magnetic disk organization. When hard disks and floppy disks (as well as magnetic tapes) are created, they are magnetically blank. The PC system must prepare them to hold data before they can be used. The system's disk-drive control circuitry accomplishes this by writing track/sector identification and gap locations on the disk surfaces in a process known as **formatting**.

In a PC, the typical floppy will be formatted to have 80 tracks on each side. Each track is divided into nine, or 18 sectors each. in the IBM-compatible/Microsoft world, each sector holds 512 bytes of data. Each sector is separated from the previous and following sectors by a small gap of unrecorded space.

Within these confines, the sector is segmented, beginning with an ID field header, which tells the controlling circuitry that an ID area containing the physical address information is approaching. A small data field header precedes the actual data field. The data field is followed by a postamble, containing error-checking and correcting (ECC) codes for the data recorded in the sector. The organizational structure of a typical magnetic disk is illustrated in Figure 5-2.

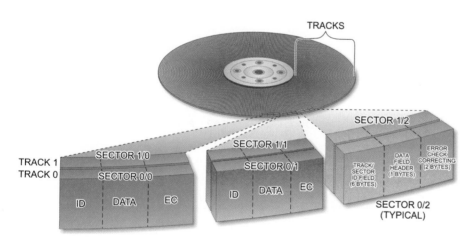

Figure 5-2: The Organizational Structure of a Magnetic Disk

Reading and Writing on Magnetic Surfaces

Read/Write (R/W)
head

Data is read from, or written to, the disk one sector at a time. In order to perform a read or write operation, the address of the particular track and sector to be accessed is applied to a stepper motor, which moves a **Read/Write (R/W) head** over the desired track. As the desired sector passes beneath the R/W head, the data transfer occurs. Information read from, or written to, the disk is usually held in a dedicated part of the computer's RAM memory. The system then accesses the data from this memory location at microprocessor-compatible speeds.

The R/W head consists of a coil of wire wrapped around a soft iron core, as depicted in Figure 5-3. A small air gap in the core rides above the magnetic coating on the disk's surface. Data are written on the disk by applying pulses to the coil, which produces magnetic lines of flux in the soft iron core. At the air gap, the lines of flux dip down into the disk's magnetic coating, due to its low reluctance (compared to the air). This, in turn, causes the magnetic domains in the recording surface to align in a direction dictated by the direction of current flow through the coil. The magnetic domains of the surface can assume one of three possible states depending on the direction of current flow through the R/W head:

- Unmagnetized (randomly arranged domains)

- Magnetized in a positive direction

- Magnetized in a negative direction

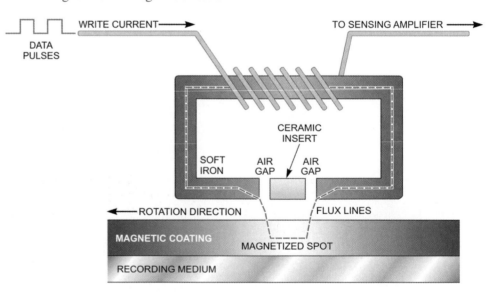

Figure 5-3: A Typical R/W Head

Data are read from the disk in a reversal of this process. As the magnetized spots on the surface pass by the R/W head, changes in magnetic polarity of the spots induce lines of flux into the R/W head's core. This, in turn, induces a small voltage in the R/W head that is sensed and amplified to the proper digital logic levels by the drive's Read circuitry.

Contact versus Noncontact Recording

Depending on the nature of the magnetic medium being read from or written to, the R/W head may ride directly on the medium's surface (contact recording), or it may "fly" slightly above it on a thin cushion of air created by the moving surface (noncontact recording). Hard disks, whether fixed or removable, must use flying heads, whereas flexible media (tapes and disks) generally use contact recording.

Hard disks use noncontact heads that fly over the medium. The extremely high speed of the medium, and the thin and fragile nature of its magnetic oxide coating, makes almost any contact between the R/W head and the disk surface a cause of considerable damage to both the head and the disk. Such contact is known as **head-to-disk interference (HDI)**, or simply as a **head crash**. Recent advances, such as smaller and lighter R/W heads, and ever-harder damage-resistant disk surfaces, have lowered the possibilities of damaging crashes somewhat. Because the medium is dimensionally stable, and spins at a high rate of speed, the data density associated with hard disks is relatively high.

> **head-to-disk interference (HDI)**
>
> **head crash**

The flying R/W head glides over the disk at a height of approximately 50 microinches. This may seem like an unimportant measurement until you consider the size of a common dust particle or a human hair.

This relationship is illustrated in Figure 5-4. If the R/W head should strike one of these contaminants as the disk spins at high speed, the head would be lifted into the air and then crash into the disk surface, damaging the R/W head or the disk surface. To avoid this, hard disks are encased in sealed protective housings. It is important to realize that at no time should the disk housing be opened to the atmosphere. Repairs to hard-disk drives are performed in special repair facilities having ultra-clean rooms. In these rooms, even particles the size of those described in the figure have been removed from the air.

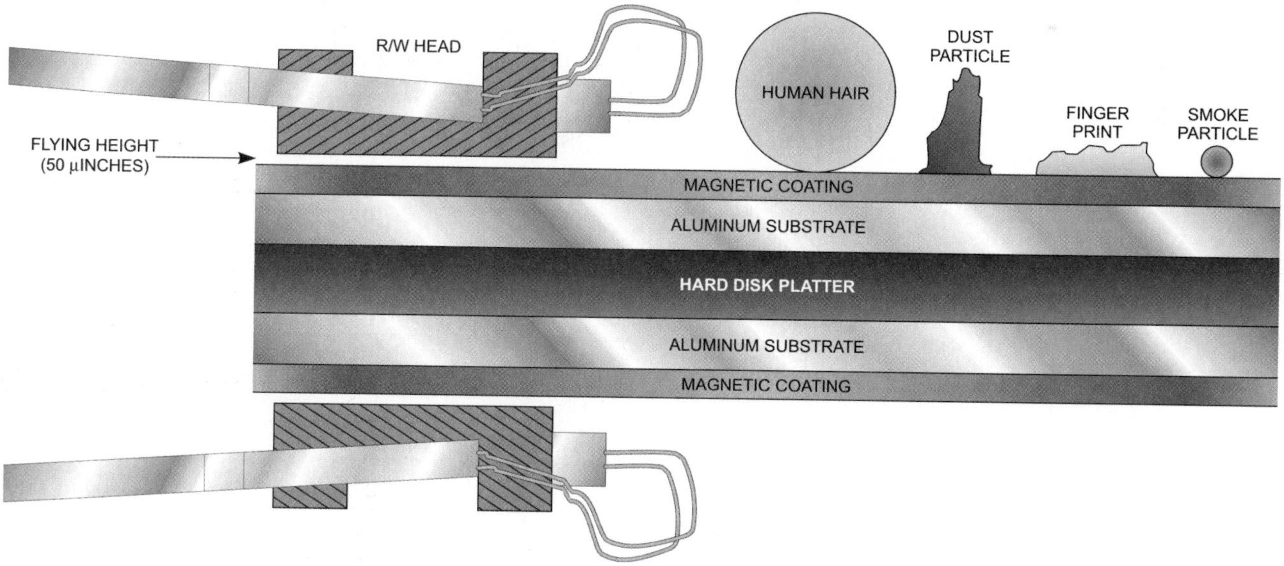

Flexible media such as floppy disks and tape expand and shrink with temperature and humidity variations. This causes the data tracks on the media to migrate in terms of track-location accuracy of the R/W head. To compensate for such shifting, the R/W heads ride directly on the media's surface, the track density is kept low, and the heads are made more complex to create special zones in the track construction, which compensate for some of the misalignment due to shifting.

Figure 5-4: Flying R/W Heads

Disk Drive Operations

The basic organization of both hard- and floppy-disk drives is similar in many respects. Both have drive spindles, which are actuated by precision synchronous motors, and a set of movable R/W heads that are positioned by a digital stepper motor, or voice coil. In addition, both systems have intelligent control circuitry to position the R/W head and to facilitate the transfer of information between the disk and the computer's memory. Figure 5-5 depicts the major components of a typical disk drive system.

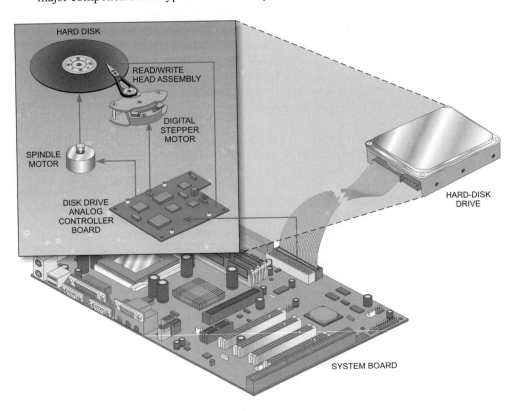

**Figure 5-5:
Disk Drive
Components**

disk-drive controller

The heart of the disk drive's circuitry is the **disk-drive controller**. The controller is responsible for providing the necessary interfacing between the disk drive and the computer's I/O channel. It does this by decoding the computer's instructions to the disk drive and generating the control signals that the disk drive must have to carry out the instruction. The controller must also convert back and forth between the parallel data format of the computer's bus and the serial format of the disk drive.

In addition, the controller must accurately position the R/W heads, direct the read and write operations, check and correct data received from the processor, generate error-correction codes for outbound data, and mark the location of defective sectors on the disk, closing them to use. After all of these responsibilities, the disk controller must also provide addressing for the tracks and sectors on the disk and control the transfer of information to and from the internal memory.

Initialization

To transfer a file from the system to the disk (a Write operation), the operating system sends the disk-drive controller a Write command, along with parameters required to carry out the operation. It also specifies the track and sector number where writing will begin. It obtains this information by referring to the disk's file system table (FAT) and locating the address of the next available sector. Figure 5-6 illustrates the type of information used to initialize a disk drive for operation.

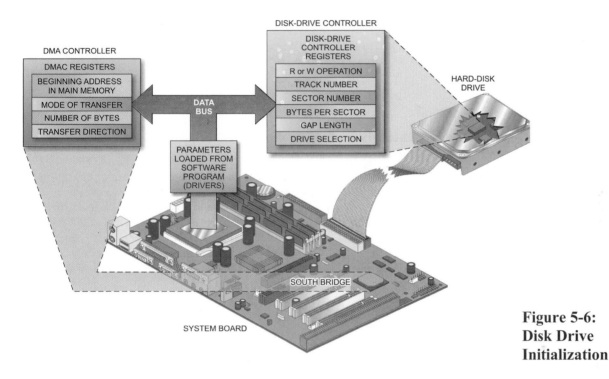

**Figure 5-6:
Disk Drive
Initialization**

Track-Seek Operations

To position the drive's R/W heads over the desired track, the controller must conduct a **track-seek** operation. In this operation, the controller enables the drive and produces a burst of step pulses to position the R/W head over the proper track. The controller accomplishes this by keeping a record of the current track location of the drive's R/W heads.

When the controller receives a Read or Write command from the system, it compares the current location information to the track number specified by the command. The controller decides which direction the head must be moved, issues a direction signal to the drive on its **direction** line, and begins producing step pulses on its **step** line. Each step pulse causes the drive unit to move the R/W heads over one track, in the direction specified by the direction signal. When the value of the present location matches the track number that was specified for the Read or Write operation, the step-pulses stop, and the R/W heads settle over the desired track. The positioning of the R/W heads is illustrated in Figure 5-7.

track-seek

direction

step

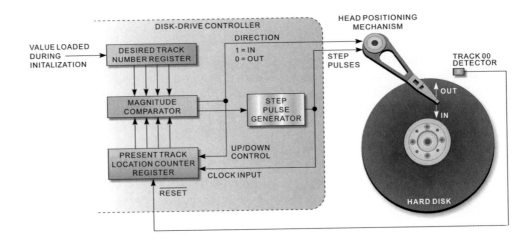

Figure 5-7:
A Track-Seek
Operation

Write Operations

When the system wants to send data to the disk drive for storage, it sends a **Write command** to the drive. But first, it performs a lookup operation on the drive's FAT to determine where to store the data. It then performs a track-seek operation to position the R/W heads over the designated track. When the head is over the track, the controller begins looking for the proper sector by reading the sector headers as they pass by. Once the sector is found, the controller changes from Read to Write operations, and data serialization/transfer begins. The disk controller obtains the byte from the data bus, encodes it into the proper form, and applies it to the R/W head, as illustrated in Figure 5-8.

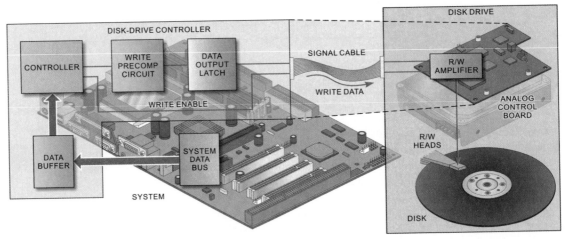

Figure 5-8:
Data Transfers

If the data from the computer require more than one sector to be written, as is usual, these logically related sectors typically are not located sequentially on the disk. When data are transferred a block at a time, some time will be required to process each sector of data. In order to give the drive time to process the information, logically sequential sectors are *interleaved* (separated) by a fixed number of other sectors. This way, the motion of the disk is moving the second sector into position to be written (or read), while the drive is processing the previous sector of information. A common interleaving factor is eight sectors between logically related sectors on a floppy drive, a factor of three on older hard disk systems, and a factor of one on newer systems.

Read Operations

When a **Read operation** is performed, the operating system examines the disk's directory to get the starting track/sector address of the data to be read. This address is loaded into the disk controller, and a track-seek operation is performed. The R/W heads are stepped to the desired track, and the designated head is enabled. After a few milliseconds delay to permit the R/W head to settle precisely over the track, the operating system gives the disk controller the command to Read the desired sector. The controller begins reading the sector ID headers, looking for the assigned sector.

When the sector is identified, the preamble is read, and the controller synchronizes its operation with the incoming bit stream from the disk drive. At the beginning of the sector's data field, a data start marker coordinates the first bit of the first data byte with the controller's operation. At this point, the controller begins dividing the incoming bit stream into bytes for transmission to the system. The transfer may continue over multiple sectors or tracks until an end-of-file marker is encountered, indicating that the entire file has been transferred. Figure 5-9 depicts the process of a typical disk drive Read operation.

Read operation

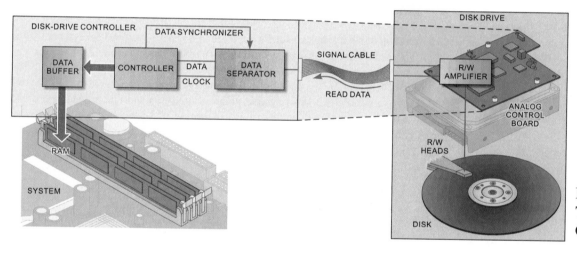

Figure 5-9: The Read Operation

Hard-Disk Drives

Essentials 1.1

Modern PC systems feature hard drives with storage capacities that typically range well into the gigabyte (GB) of storage as standard equipment. Physically, the hard drive is organized as a stack of rigid disks that turn in unison on a common spindle and are accessed by a bank of coordinated read/write heads. Each surface is divided into tracks, which are, in turn, divided into sectors. Each disk possesses a matching set of tracks on the top and bottom of the disk. The disks are stacked on top of each other, and the R/W heads move in and out between them. Because there are matching tracks on the top and bottom of each disk in the stack, the HDD controller organizes them into cylinders. For example, cylinder 1 of a four-platter HDD would consist of track 1 of each disk surface. The cylinder concept is described in Figure 5-10.

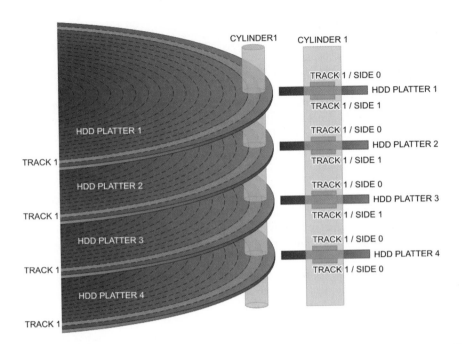

Figure 5-10:
HDD Cylinders

The physical makeup of a hard disk system is depicted in Figure 5-11. It involves a controller (either on an I/O card, or built into the system board), one or more signal cables, a power cable, and a disk drive unit. In some cases, floppy- and hard-disk drive signal cables may look similar. However, there are some slight differences in their construction that prevent them from being compatible. Therefore, great caution must be used when installing these cables. Many skilled technicians have encountered problems by not paying attention to which type of cable they were installing with a particular type of drive.

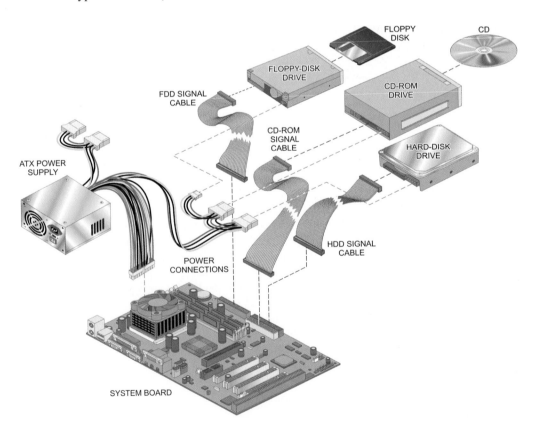

Figure 5-11:
Components of the
HDD System

The system's CMOS Setup holds the HDD configuration settings. As with other configuration settings, these must be set correctly for the installed drive. Typical HDD information required for the CMOS setup includes its capacity, number of cylinders, number of R/W heads, number of sectors per track, amount of signal *precompensation* applied, and the track number to be used as the landing zone for the R/W heads when the drive is shut down.

In Pentium-class systems, the PnP BIOS and operating system work with the newer system-level drives to **autodetect** the drive and supply its configuration information to the CMOS Setup utility. Otherwise, this information must be obtained from the drive manufacturer, or a third-party maintenance. Most BIOS also provide a user-definable HDD entry, where the drive's geometry values can be entered manually into the CMOS settings.

autodetect

The other important hard-disk drive specifications to consider are access time, seek time, data transfer rate, and storage capacity. These quantities designate how much data the drive can hold, how fast it can get to a specific part of the data, and how fast it can move it to the system.

Personal Video Recorders

Personal video recorders (**PVRs**), also known as **digital video recorders** (**DVRs**), are hard-disk drive based devices designed to record digitized audio and video for storage and replay. These devices have become very popular with television viewers, as they are able to perform recording and replay functions much simpler than existing *Video Cassette Recorders*. However, they have also been an important component in the development of media center PCs that allow users to integrate their PC functions with Audio/Video entertainment systems in their homes and offices.

Personal video recorders (PVRs)

digital video recorders (DVRs)

There are two types of PVRs—*PC-based PVRs* and *stand-alone PVRs*. **PC-based PVR** systems employ a video capture card to capture and digitize video images in MPEG-1 or MPEG-2 formats for storage on the hard drive. Stand-alone PVRs are designed specifically to be digital video recorders. These units contain a firmware-based operating system and application software. There are two popular stand-alone PVR systems in the marketplace—*TiVo* and *ReplayTV*. These systems involve subscription services to deliver television programming information and scheduling controls.

PC-based PVR

The PC-based PVR is a specialized multimedia version of the PC, which includes a video capture card, a fast hard-disk drive, lots of RAM, a TV tuner, and a high-end video card. A typical PC-based PVR is depicted in Figure 5-12. Mainstream PC manufacturers have attempted to create these PCs in case styles similar to those encountered in consumer A/V electronics products (stereo receivers, tape decks, and amplifiers). This has been done in an effort to make Media Center PCs blend in with the "family room" environment.

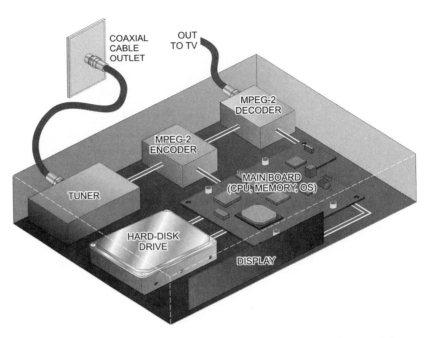

Figure 5-12:
A Personal Video
Recorder

The PC-based PVR also requires software to help the user select and control the recoding, organization and play back of audio and video media. The key to the popularity of PVRs is the ability to record multimedia materials at the same time you are watching or listening to another piece of material. There are several applications software packages available for this function , and some are even available as freeware.

Windows XP Media Center Edition

Microsoft has entered the PC-based PVR market by including PVR control software in its Windows XP operating system. This version is known as **Windows XP Media Center Edition**. Media Center Edition is a special superset of the Windows XP Professional operating system, as illustrated in Figure 5-13. It has been modified to limit its use in networked office environments and to provide additional multimedia features that enable the user to view different types of stored digital media (pictures, video, and music) on PC monitors, televisions, or home theater systems. It also gives the user the ability to record and pause live television on demand, or to automatically record an entire series of a program with only a couple of button presses of a remote controller.

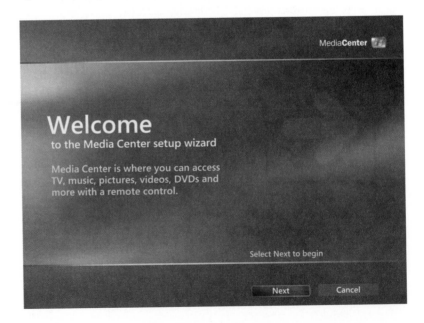

Figure 5-13:
Windows XP
Media Center

RAID Systems

As applications pushed storage capacity requirements past available drive sizes, it became logical to combine several drives together to hold all of the data produced. In a desktop unit, this can be as simple as adding an additional physical drive to the system. Wide area and local area networks connect computers together so that their resources (including disk drives) can be shared. If you extend this idea of sharing disk drives to include several different drive units operating under a single controller, you have a **drive array**. A drive array is depicted in Figure 5-14.

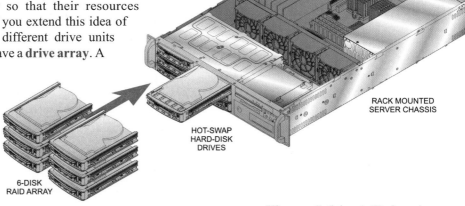

RACK MOUNTED SERVER CHASSIS

HOT-SWAP HARD-DISK DRIVES

6-DISK RAID ARRAY

Drive arrays have evolved in response to storage requirements for local area networks. They are particularly useful in client/server networks, in which the data for the network tend to be centrally located and shared by all of the users around the network.

Figure 5-14: A Drive Array

In the cases of multiple drives within a unit, and drives scattered around a network, each drive assumes a different letter designation. In a drive array, the stack of drives can be made to appear as a single large hard drive. The drives are operated in parallel so that they can deliver data to the controller in a parallel format. If the controller is simultaneously handling 8 bits of data from eight drives, the system will see the speed of the transfer as being eight times faster. This technique of using the drives in a parallel array is referred to as a striped drive array.

drive array

It is also possible to simply use a small drive array as a data backup system. This is referred to as a **mirrored drive array**, in which each drive is supplied with the same data. In the event that the data from one drive are corrupted, or one of the drives fails, the data are still safe. Both types of arrays are created through a blend of connection hardware and control software.

mirrored drive array

RAID

redundant arrays of inexpensive disks (RAID)

The most common drive arrays are **RAID** systems. RAID is an acronym for **redundant arrays of inexpensive disks**. Later usage of the term RAID exchanges the word independent to inexpensive. Five levels of RAID technology specifications are given by the **RAID Advisory Board**.

RAID Advisory Board

RAID 0

The RAID Advisory Board designated the classic striped array described above as RAID level-0 (**RAID 0**—*Striped Disk Array without Fault Tolerance*). Likewise, the mirrored drive array described above is labeled RAID 1. The operation of a striped disk array is shown in Figure 5-15.

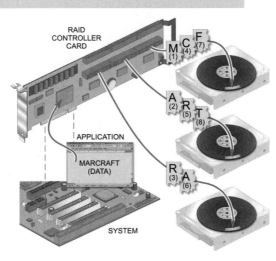

RAID CONTROLLER CARD

APPLICATION

MARCRAFT (DATA)

SYSTEM

Figure 5-15: Operation of a Striped Array

RAID 1 (*mirroring and duplexing*) is a redundancy scheme that uses two equal-sized drives, where both drives hold the same information. Each drive serves as a backup for the other. Figure 5-16 illustrates the operation of a mirrored array used in a RAID 1 application.

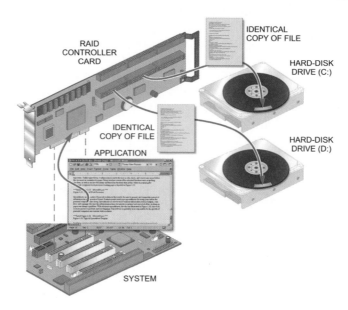

Figure 5-16: Operation of a Mirrored Array

Duplicate information is stored on both drives. When a file is retrieved from the array, the controller reads alternate sectors from each drive. This effectively reduces the data read time by half.

The **RAID 2** (*data striping with error recovery*) strategy interleaves data on parallel drives, as shown in Figure 5-17. Bits or blocks of data are interleaved across the disks in the array. The speed afforded by collecting data from the disks in a parallel format is the biggest feature of the system. In large arrays, complete bytes, words, or double words can be written to, and read from, the array simultaneously.

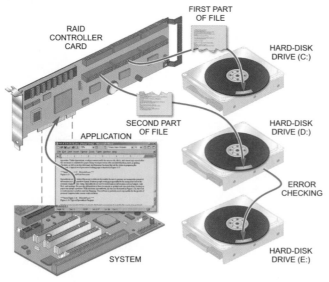

Figure 5-17: Interleaved Data on Parallel Drives

The RAID 2 specification uses multiple disks for **error-detection and correction functions**. Depending on the error-detection and correction algorithms used, large portions of the array are used for nondata storage overhead. Of course, the reliability of the data being delivered to the system is excellent, and there is no need for time-consuming corrective read operations when an error is detected. Arrays dealing with large systems may use between three and seven drives for error-correction purposes. Because of the high hardware overhead, RAID 2 systems are not normally used with microcomputer systems.

When the array is used in this manner, a complex **error-detection and correction algorithm** is normally employed. The controller contains circuitry based on the algorithm that detects, locates, and corrects the error without retransmitting any data. This is a very quick and efficient method of error detection and correction.

In Figure 4-37, the data block being sent to the array is broken apart and distributed to the drives in the array. The data word already has a parity bit added to it. The controller generates parity for the block and stores it on the error-detection drive. When the controller reads the data back from the array, it regenerates the error-check character and compares it to the one written on the error-check drive. By comparing the error-check character to the rewritten one, the controller can detect the error in the data field and determine which bit within the field is incorrect. With this information in hand, the controller can simply correct that bit as it is being processed.

In a **RAID 3** (*parallel transfer with parity striping*) arrangement, the drives of the array operate in parallel like a RAID 2 system. However, only parity checking is used for error detection and correction, requiring only one additional drive. If an error occurs, the controller reads the array again to verify the error. This is a time-consuming, low-efficiency method of error correction.

A **RAID 4** (*independent data disks with shared parity disk*) controller interleaves sectors across the drives in the array. This creates the appearance of one very large drive. The RAID 4 format is generally used for smaller drive arrays but can be used for larger arrays as well. Only one parity-checking drive is allotted for error control. The information on the parity drive is updated after reading the data drives. This creates an extra write activity for each data read operation performed.

The **RAID 5** scheme (*independent data disks with distributed parity blocks*) alters the RAID 4 specification by allowing the parity function to rotate through the different drives. Under this system, error checking and correction are the function of all the drives. If a single drive fails, the system is capable of regenerating its data from the parity information on the other drives. RAID 5 is usually the most popular RAID system, because it can be used on small arrays, and it has a high level of error recovery built in. The operation of a RAID 5 array is shown in Figure 5-18.

A variation of RAID 5 that implements two independent error-correcting schemes (independent data disks with two independent distributed parity schemes) has been devised and labeled **RAID 6**. This format is relatively expensive, but it provides an extremely high fault tolerance level for critical applications. This RAID level requires at least two additional drives to operate.

The **RAID 10** (*very high-reliability/high-performance RAID*) specification combines mirroring and striping to produce a high-performance, high-reliability backup system. This arrangement combines RAID 1 striped array segments with mirroring to provide increased performance to a RAID 1 installation.

A variation of RAID 3 referred to as **RAID 53** (*high I/O Rates and data transfer performance RAID*) combines RAID 0 striped arrays with RAID 3 parallel segments. The result is a high-performance RAID 3 system.

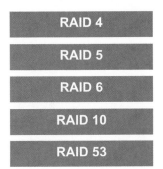

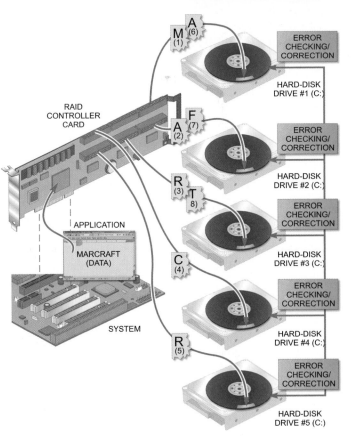

Figure 5-18: Operation of a RAID 5 Array

Floppy-Disk Drives

The discussion of general disk drive operations earlier in the chapter applies to both hard and floppy drives alike. However, the physical construction and operation of the drives are quite different. The floppy-disk drive (FDD) is an exposed unit, with an opening in the front to allow the floppy disk to be inserted and removed. In addition, the R/W heads are open to the atmosphere and ride directly on the surface of the disk. Modern 3-1/2" floppy-disk drives have ejection buttons that kick the disk out of the drive when they are pushed.

Data moves back and forth between the system's RAM memory and the floppy disk surface. Along the way, the data pass from the system RAM to the **floppy-disk controller (FDC)**, through the floppy drive signal cable, and into the floppy drive's analog control board. The analog control board converts the data into signals that can be applied to the drive's Read/Write heads, which in turn produce the magnetic spots on the disk surface.

Under direction of the operating system, the FDC divides the 3-1/2" floppy disk into 80 tracks per side, with nine or eighteen 512-byte sectors per track. This provides the system with 737,280 (720 kB) or 1,474,560 (1.44 MB) total bytes of storage on each disk. Table 5-1 lists the operating specifications for a typical 3-1/2" floppy-disk drive unit.

floppy-disk controller (FDC)

Table 5-1: FDD Drive Specifications

DRIVE UNIT PART	DSSD	DSHD
Track	80	80
Heads	2	2
Sectors per Track	9	18
Bytes per Sector	512	512
Formatted Capacity	720 kB	1.44 MB
Unformatted Capacity	1 MB	2 MB
Rotational Speed (RPM)	300	300
Recording Density (bits/inch)	8717	17,432
Tracks per Inch	135	135
Transfer Rate Unformatted (kbps)	250	500

The FDC also supplies interface signals that permit it to be connected to microprocessor systems with or without DMA capabilities. In most systems, however, the FDC operates in conjunction with the system's DMA controller and is assigned to the DRQ2 and DACK2 lines. In operation, the FDC presents a DRQ2 request for every byte of data to be transferred. In addition, the disk-drive controller is assigned to the IRQ6 line. The FDC generates an interrupt signal each time it receives a Read, Write, or Format command from the system unit. An interrupt will also be generated when the controller receives a Ready signal from one of the disk drive units.

Magnetic Tape Drives

Tape drives are available in a variety of types and configurations. Tape drives intended for desktop computers are available in both 5-1/4" and 3-1/2" drive form factors. These units are designed for mounting inside the system unit as part of the system's permanent drive capabilities.

Removable tape cartridges like the one depicted in Figure 5-19 are inserted into the front of the drive and locked into place by an internal mechanism. The drive's R/W heads access the tape through an opening in the front of the cartridge. Likewise, a *capstan* in the drive is used to turn a drive wheel inside the cartridge, which in turn moves both tape spools simultaneously.

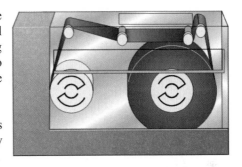

The drive also has a sensor that detects the position of the tape's Write-Protect switch. This switch disables the drive's write circuitry so that important data on the tape cannot be written over by mistake.

With the exception of their front panels, internally mounted tape drives share a great deal of their form with internal floppy and hard drive units. They feature a signal interface connection to connect them to their controller and standard options power supply connectors that deliver power to the drive.

Figure 5-19: Data Storage Cartridge

Internal tape drives are available for most of the standard drive interface types (i.e., floppy drive connection as well as IDE and internal SCSI buses). In many cases, tape drives are supplied with proprietary controller cards that plug into one of the system's expansion slots. Other older models are even capable of using the system's B: drive floppy connection as their interface connection.

For portable systems, tape drives are designed as external units that connect to one of the portable's external port or bus connections. These units typically employ one of the PC's standard I/O port or extension bus connections to communicate with the system (i.e., external SCSI, USB, or IEEE-1394 buses). These units usually include an external housing for aesthetic purposes. They also normally derive power independently from the host computer through their own detachable power pack unit.

Because tape drives are not considered standard PC peripherals, they are not directly supported by the available operating systems. These operating systems support the bus or port operation, but not the drive. However, the Backup utility in newer versions of Windows will treat tape drives as another storage device after their drivers have been installed.

Tape drive manufacturers normally supply device drivers for their own tape drives. In most cases, the manufacturer provides the entire application software package for the tape drive. These packages are installed under the operating system in the same manner as other application packages.

QIC Tape Drives

As more users employed tape as a backup media, standards for tape systems were formed. The most widely used tape standard is the **quarter inch cartridge** (**QIC**) standard. This standard calls for a tape cartridge like the one depicted in Figure 5-20. Its physical dimensions are 6" × 4" × 5/8". The cartridge has a head access door in the front that swings open when it is inserted into the drive unit.

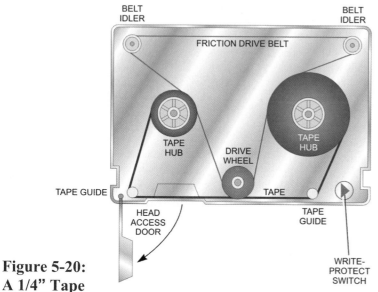

Figure 5-20: A 1/4" Tape Cartridge

The R/W heads magnetize the tape as it passes by, in much the same manner as described for other magnetic storage media. The data are placed on the tape serially as the data moves past the head. The tape is organized into sectors of data, separated by intergap blocks. The data can be applied in parallel tracks (using multiple R/W heads), in a continuous stream of data (streaming tape systems), or in a high-speed serpentine manner, where the data are applied to the tape in one direction for odd tracks, and in the other direction for even tracks.

Magnetic tape must be formatted before use, just like a magnetic disk. In the formatting process, the controller marks the tape off into sectors. In addition, it establishes a file allocation table in its header, similar to that of a floppy or hard disk. The header also contains a bad-sector table to prevent defective areas of the tape from being used. Some of the tape is devoted to the error-detection and correction information that must be used with tape systems. Table 5-2 provides a sample list of QIC standard numbers.

Table 5-2: QIC Standard Numbers

SPECIFICATION	TRACKS	CAPACITY	CARTRIDGE
QIC-02	9	60 MB	DC-3000
QIC-24	9	60 MB	DC-6000
QIC-40	20	40 MB	DC-2000
QIC-80	32	80 MB	DC-2000
QIC-100	12 / 24	100 MB	DC-2000
QIC-150	18	250 MB	DC-6000
QIC-1000	30	1.0 GB	DC-6000
QIC-1350	30	1.35 GB	DC-6000
QIC-2100	30	2.1 GB	DC-6000

DAT Drives

The **digital audiotape (DAT)** format has found little success in the public market for the storage of audio but has found great success in the computer storage industry. The unique design of the DAT drive allows it to back up large volumes of data onto small tape cartridges.

When performing a restore with DAT drives, the backup software first reads the entire directory of the tape. It then winds the tape to the appropriate spot and reads the contents into the controller's buffer. The controller uses CRC code to make sure the information is correct. If an error is detected, the ECC can be used to fix them. After the data have been verified as correct, the contents are written to the hard disk.

The most popular format for DAT today in terms of data storage is the **digital data storage (DDS)** standard. Table 5-3 shows the different DDS standards and technical information. All of these standards are backward compatible.

STANDARD	CAPACITY	MAX DTR
DDS	2 GB	55 kBps
DDS-1	2/4 GB	0.55/1.1 MBps
DDS-2	4/8 GB	0.55/1.1 MBps
DDS-3	12/24 GB	1.1/2.2 MBps
DDS-4	20/40 GB	2.4/4.8 MBps

**Table 5-3:
DDS Standards**

The increased data storage capacity provided by DAT drives comes at a price. A DAT drive can easily cost nearly twice as much as a QIC drive. Also, DAT drives only employ SCSI interfaces. However, the additional cost associated with DAT tape may be well worth it when comparing the usability of the tapes.

DLT Drives

Digital linear tape (DLT) drives use half-inch-wide metal particle tapes. The media is 60% wider than 8 mm tape. Data are recorded on these tapes in a serpentine pattern on parallel tracks that run the entire length of the tape. When data are recorded, the first set of tracks is recorded along the whole length of the tape. After reaching the end of the tape, the heads are repositioned to record a new set of tracks in the opposite direction. The process continues until the tape is full. A DLT drive is shown in Figure 5-21.

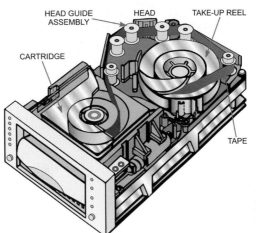

**Figure 5-21: A
DLT Drive**

On a DLT drive, data are recorded and read using multiple parallel channels simultaneously. DLT technology segments tape media into parallel, horizontal tracks and records data by running the tape past a stationary head. Current products record two channels simultaneously using two read/write elements in the head, effectively doubling the transfer rate possible at a given drive speed and recording density.

Another measure of tape performance is the time required to locate a file. This criterion is especially important in near-line applications, such as image manipulation, that frequently search for files and append or restore data. DLT technology minimizes search time through a file mark index located at the logical end of the tape. Using this index, the drive "steps" to the track containing the file and performs a high-speed streaming search to the file. This feature enables DLT products to find any file in a 20-gigabyte capacity tape in an average of 45 seconds.

Table 5-4 gives some examples of some of the more common DLT formats.

Table 5-4: Common DLT Formats

TYPE	DISK SPACE PER TAPE (NATIVE/COMPRESSED)	DATA TRANSFER BANDWIDTH
DLT 2000	15 GBs/30 GBs	2.5 MB/sec
DLT 4000	20 GBs/40 GBs	3 MB/sec
DLT 7000	35 GBs/70 GBs	10 MB/sec

super digital linear tape (SuperDLT)

The **super digital linear tape (SuperDLT)** specification is a natural progression of the DLT standard, increasing its capacity as well as its transfer rates. The general properties are comparable to DLT and are backward compatible with the DLT standard. Drives based on SuperDLT technology will far exceed the 35 GB native capacity of the DLT 7000 format and be backward compatible.

As Table 5-5 illustrates, the ultimate goal is to cram up to 1.2 TB of uncompressed data onto a single cartridge with uncompressed transfer rates rising to an eventual 100 MBps. Initial products, however, offer a more modest 110 GB with sustained data transfer rates of 11 MBps in native mode.

Table 5-5: SDLT Standards

	SDLT 220	SDLT 320	SDLT 640	SDLT 1280	SDLT 2400
Native Capacity	110 GB	160 GB	320 GB	640 GB	1.2 TB
Compressed Capacity (2:1 compression)	220 GB	320 GB	640 GB	1.28 TB	2.4 TB
Native DTR	11 MBps	16 MBps	32 MBps	50+ MBps	100+ MBps
Compressed DTR	22 MBps	32 MBps	64 MBps	100+ MBps	200+ MBps
Interfaces	Ultra2 SCSI LVD HVD	Ultra2 SCSI Ultra160 SCSI	Ultra 320 SCSI Fiber channel	TBD	TBD

OPTICAL STORAGE

Although magnetic disk drives have dominated the secondary memory function in PCs for decades, newer optical storage technologies have taken a large share of that category over the last 20 years. The main optical storage contenders in the PC market are the CD-ROM disc and the DVD or Digital Versatile Disc and their variants. Continued development and success of these two storage media has led to lower costs and greater demand. Practically every new PC sold comes with at least one CD/DVD drive installed. In many cases they include more than one drive.

CD-ROM Drives

Data are written on a CD digitally on a light-sensitive material by a powerful, highly focused laser beam. The writing laser is pulsed with the modulated data to be stored on the disc. When the laser is pulsed, a microscopic blister is burned into the optical material, causing it to reflect light differently from the material around it. The blistered areas are referred to as **pits**, while the areas between them are called **lands**. Figure 5-22 illustrates the writing of data on the optical disc.

The recorded data are read from the disc by scanning it with a lower-power, continuous laser beam. The laser diode emits the highly focused, narrow beam that is reflected back from the disc. The reflected beam passes through a prism and is bent 90 degrees, where it is picked up by the diode detector and converted into an electrical signal. Only light reflected from land areas on the disc is picked up by the detector. Light that strikes a pit is scattered and is not detected. The lower power level used for reading the disc ensures that the optical material is not affected during the read operation.

With an audio CD, the digital data retrieved from the disk are passed through a digital-to-analog converter (DAC) to reproduce the audio sound wave. However, this is not required for digital computer systems, because the information is already in a form acceptable to the computer. Therefore, CD players designed for use in computer systems are referred to as **CD-ROM drives**, to differentiate them from audio CD players. Otherwise, the mechanics of operation are similar between the two devices.

pits

lands

CD-ROM drives

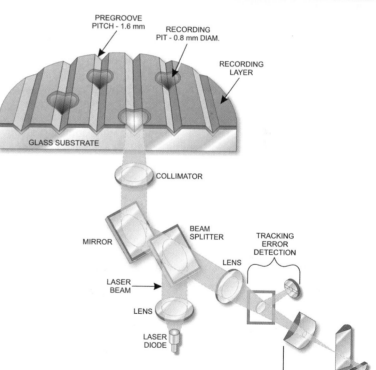

Figure 5-22: Writing on a CD-ROM Drive

CD-ROM Discs

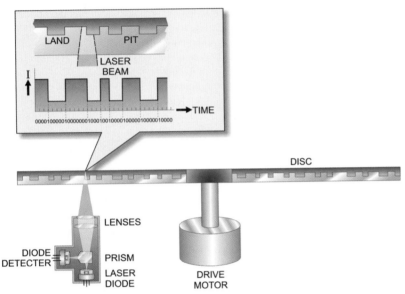

Figure 5-23: Encoding Data on a CD-ROM

spiral track

A typical CD-ROM disc is 4.7 inches in diameter, and consists of three major parts:

- Acrylic substrate

- Aluminized, mirror-finished data surface

- Lacquer coating

The scanning laser beam comes up through the disc, strikes the aluminized data surface, and is reflected back. Because there is no physical contact between the reading mechanism and the disc, the disc never wears out. This is one of the main advantages of the CD system. The blisters on the data surface are typically just under 1 micrometer in length, and the tracks are 1.6 micrometers apart. The data are encoded by the length and spacing of the blisters and the lands between them. This concept is illustrated in Figure 5-23.

The information on a compact disc is stored in one continuous **spiral track**, unlike floppy disks, where the data are stored in multiple, concentric tracks. The compact disc storage format still divides the data into separate sectors. However, the sectors of a CD-ROM disc are physically the same size. The disc spins counterclockwise, and it slows down as the laser diode emitter/detector unit approaches the outside of the disc.

The disc begins spinning at approximately 500 RPM at its inner edge and slows down to about 200 RPM at its outer edge. The spindle motor controls the speed of the disc, so that the track is always passing the laser at between 3.95 and 4.6 feet per second. Therefore, CD-ROM drives must have a variable-speed spindle motor, which cannot just be turned on and off like a floppy drive's spindle motor. The variable speed of the drive allows the disc to contain more sectors, thereby giving it a much larger storage capacity. In fact, the average storage capacity of a CD-ROM disc is about 680 MB.

CD Writers

write once, read many (WORM) drive

Another type of CD drive is a **write once, read many (WORM) drive**. As the acronym implies, these drives allow users to write information to the disc once and then retrieve this information as you would with a CD-ROM drive. Once information is stored on a WORM drive, the data cannot be changed or deleted.

CD-recordable (CD-R)

CD-RW disc

CD Writers record data on blank **CD-recordable (CD-R)** discs. A CD-R is a *write once, read many* media that is generally available in 120 mm and 80 mm sizes. The drives are constructed using a typical 5.25" half-height drive form factor. This form factor is convenient in that it fits into a typical PC drive bay. The CD-R technology has continued to evolve into a recordable, rewritable compact disc, called a **CD-RW disc**. These discs can be recorded, erased, and rewritten just like a floppy disk.

The physical construction of the CD-R disc is considerably different than that of the CD-ROM disc. The writable disc is constructed as described in Figure 5-24. The CD-R disc is created by coating a transparent polycarbonate substrate with an opaque polymer dye. The dye is covered with a thin layer of gold and topped with a protective lacquer layer and a label. The CD-R writing mechanism is not as strong as that of a commercial CD-ROM duplicator. Instead of burning pits into the substrate of the disc, the CD writer uses a lower-power laser to discolor the dye material.

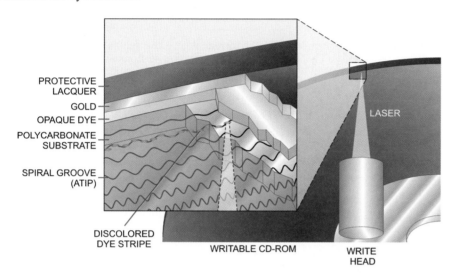

Figure 5-24:
Writable CD-R Disc

The CD-R disc format is identical to that of a CD-ROM, and information written on it can be read by a typical CD-ROM drive. The spiral track formation and sectoring are the same as those used with CD-ROM discs. In addition, the CD writer can produce recordings in the standard CD book formats (i.e., red, yellow, orange, and green).

During the write operation, the CD Writer uses a medium-intensity laser to write the data on the thermally sensitive media. The laser light is applied to the bottom side of the disc. It passes through the substrate to the reflective layer and is reflected back through the substrate. The light continues through the drive's optics system until it reaches the laser detector.

When the polymer is exposed to the light of the writing laser, it heats up and becomes transparent. This exposes the reflective gold layer beneath the polymer. During readback, the reflective layer reflects more light than does the polymer material. The transitions between lighter and darker areas of the disc are used to encode the data.

CD writers are typically able to write to the CD-R at either 4x or 8x CD speeds. These settings have nothing to do with playback speeds. CD-RW drives are specified in a record × write-once × rewrite speed format (e.g., a 32 × 8 × 4 CD-RW can read at 32x, write at 8x, and rewrite at 4x speeds).

Digital Versatile Discs

DVD drives and discs are identical in form factor and appearance to CD-ROM drives and discs. As a matter of fact, DVD drives are backward compatible with old CD-ROM discs, and newer DVD drives can be used to read CD-R and CD-RW discs. The discs are inserted into the front of the unit just like CD-ROM discs. The drive's circuitry senses the type of disc being used and automatically adjusts for it.

DVD drives

Within the DVD specification, there are several disc types that are associated with different DVD standards. These include

DVD Recordable (DVD-R) and (DVD+R)

DVD Rewritable (DVD-RW) and (DVD+RW)

DVD-RAM

- **DVD Recordable (DVD-R)** and **(DVD+R)**—Separate recordable DVD formats where the media can only be used to record data once, and then the data become permanent on the disc. The disc cannot be recorded onto a second time.

- **DVD Rewritable (DVD-RW)** and **(DVD+RW)**—Separate re-recordable DVD formats where data on the disc can be erased and recorded over numerous times.

- **DVD-RAM**—A specialized DVD format where the media can be recorded and erased repeatedly. The DVD-RAM specification is nonstandard, so DVD-RAM discs can only be used with drives manufactured by the companies that support the format.

There are two variations of the DVD-R disc—DVD-RG and DVD-RA. The DVD-RG designation is associated with general-use media, and the DVD-RA standard is provided for authoring and mastering DVD video and data. DVD-RA media is generally not available for general use. The DVD-RAM format supports 2.6 GB of storage per disc, and the DVD-RW standards supports 3.0 GB per disc.

Essentials 1.1

REMOVABLE STORAGE

removable storage

In a PC, **removable storage** includes all of the removable technologies we have already described (i.e., floppies, CD/CDRWs and DVD/DVDRWs, and tapes). However, there are several other types of emerging and lesser-known removable storage systems. These systems include cartridge-mounted high-capacity floppy disks (ZIP drives), solid-state USB drives (IC memory devices configured to operate like a mechanical disk drive), and PC Card drives. PC Card drives are removable storage devices that can hold miniature (1.8 inch) mechanical or solid-state disk drives.

Most external storage systems employ the PC's standard I/O ports (i.e., ECP Parallel, SCSI, USB, or Firewire). This permits the system's PnP operation to detect the new hardware attached to the system. However, most of the devices are nonstandard in nature and require that OEM applications package be installed to control them. On the other hand, newer *flash memory drives* automatically load USB drivers and function as another drive in the system (i.e., drive e:). These removable storage systems have the advantage of being **hot swappable**—they can be added to or removed from the system while it is in operation.

hot swappable

Flash Memory

Flash memory

Flash memory is an all-electronic storage technology that can be written to, erased, and rewritten in the same manner as a magnetic disk drive. When power is removed from the memory module, the data stored inside remain and do not dissipate. This technology has been used to create a number of digital memory devices for use in PDAs, digital cameras, video game units, and notebook computers.

There are many different types and form factors of flash memory devices currently in use. The original flash memory systems associated with personal computers involved making ROM-BIOS devices so they could be updated electronically, and PCMCIA cards developed as memory adapter cards for portable computer systems. PCMCIA devices are covered in detail in Chapter 8, *Portable Systems*.

Subsequently, many new form factor flash memory systems have been introduced into both the personal computer and consumer electronics markets. The most notable formats include USB flash memory drives, CompactFlash cards, Memory Sticks, and Secure Digital cards. They all provide small form factor, power free storage capacity.

The *Memory Card reader* described in Chapter 2 has become a common feature on new desktop PCs. These units are installed in one of the system's disk drive bays and provide a physical and logical interface for various flash memory device types. In addition to providing an interface to connect additional disk-drive-like storage to the PC, it also allows digital information from other non-PC digital devices, such as digital pictures and video clips from cameras and different types of files from PDAs, to be moved back and forth between the device and the PC.

USB Flash Drives

A **USB flash drive** is a flash memory unit equipped with a USB interface and connector and mounted in a high-impact plastic or metal case. This enables USB drives to plug into a standard USB port and function as an additional disk drive. They are removable and rewritable and can hold up to 64 GB of data. However, the most popular sizes for these devices range between 512 MB and 2 GB. Figure 5-25 depicts a USB drive being plugged into a computer's standard USB port.

USB flash drive

Figure 5-25: Connecting a USB Drive

Because the USB drive is based on flash memory technology, it does not require any power when it is not connected to the USB port. When it is installed, it draws power directly from the USB port. Most USB drive manufacturers supply a protective cap that snaps over the USB connector when the drive is not in use. The caps typically include an opening for attaching a chain or cord to the drive, which allows it to be attached to a key ring or other personal device for convenient carrying.

The appearance of "Boot from USB" options in the CMOS Setup utilities of newer system boards has made it possible to install operating systems and diagnostic utilities on USB drives so they can be used for emergency start-up purposes.

USB drives are also referred to as **pen drives**, **thumb drives**, **flash drives**, or **USB keys**. While they are sometimes referred to as Memory Sticks, this is an improper reference, because that name is a trademark of the Sony Corporation and describes a different memory card specification. USB drives are supported directly by modern versions of Linux, Apple, and Windows operating systems.

Compact Flash Cards

The **Compact Flash (CF)** card, depicted in Figure 5-26, is another flash memory form factor specification. Compact flash cards are very thin flash-memory-based devices that provide battery-free, removable data storage. These units are widely used in the professional camera market.

**Figure 5-26:
CompactFlash Cards**

There are multiple form factors within the CF specification. The Type I CF card is 1.7" × 1.4" × 0.13" (43 mm × 36 mm × 3.3 mm). Type II CF cards measure 1.7" × 1.4" × 0.19" (43 mm × 36 mm × 5.0 mm) in size. Otherwise the Type I and Type II cards are the same. CF cards are available in storage capacities up 137 GB and can offer data transfer rates up to 16 MBps for Type II CF cards and 66 MBps for newer CF 3.0 devices. These cards employ Ultra DMA 33 and Ultra DMA 66 techniques developed for traditional parallel disk drive interfaces (discussed later in this chapter) to achieve these transfer rates.

The connector and socket arrangement used with CF cards is similar to the older PCMCIA Card connector used in portable PC systems. However, the CF card and socket only has 50 pins instead of the 68 pins in the PCMCIA specification. The CF connection specification supports both 3.3 V and 5 V operation, allowing CF cards to be interchanged between 3.3 V and 5 V systems. Therefore, any CF card can operate at either voltage. Special 68-pin PCMCIA Type II to CF Type II *adapters* can be used to enable CF cards to be installed in a standard PCMCIA slot.

CF cards provide complete PCMCIA compatibility. In addition to flash memory applications, CF cards have been developed to fill a wide range of I/O functions for PCs. Common I/O devices available in a CF form factor include dial-up modems, Ethernet network adapters, 802.11b WiFi wireless network adapters, serial ports, and Bluetooth wireless ports, to mention a few. Type I CF cards can be used in both Type I and Type II CF slots. On the other hand, Type II CF cards will only fit in CF Type II slots.

There is a special 1-inch hard drive designed to fit in a Type II CF card slot. These drives, called **microdrive cards**, can store up to 10 GB of data. Like other electromechanical HDDs, microdrives must be formatted and have an operating system installed to be useful. Microdrive cards consume more power than other CF cards and devices, so they may not work properly in all systems with Compact Flash support

microdrive cards

Memory Sticks

Memory Stick is a proprietary 1.96" × 0.84" × 0.11" (50.0 × 21.5 × 2.8 mm) removable flash memory card format introduced by the Sony Corporation. These devices are available in transfer rates of 2.5 MBps and storage capacities ranging up to 128 MB. A newer version of the Memory Stick, known as **Memory Stick Pro**, offers higher storage capacities (theoretically ranging up to 32 GB) along with higher data transfer rates (20 MBps).

Small form factor versions of the Memory Stick, called the **Memory Stick Duo** and **Memory Stick Pro Duo** 1.22" × 0.78" × 0.06" (31.0 mm × 20.0 × 1.6 mm) have been developed to compete with the very successful *SD flash device* format. These devices feature 128 MB storage capacities and transfer rates up to 20 MBps.

Finally, an even smaller **Memory Stick Micro (M2)** device 0.59" × 0.49" × 0.05" (15 × 12.5 × 1.2 mm) is available and also provides data transfer rates up to 20 MBps and capacities that theoretically range up to 32 MB. Figure 5-27 shows different types of memory stick cards.

Memory Stick
Memory Stick Pro
Memory Stick Duo
Memory Stick Pro Duo
Memory Stick Micro (M2)

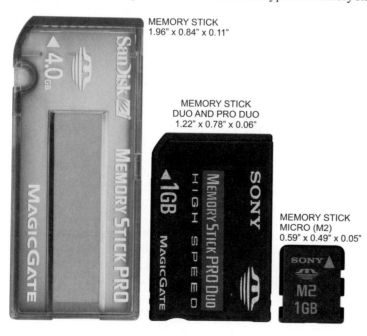

MEMORY STICK
1.96" x 0.84" x 0.11"

MEMORY STICK
DUO AND PRO DUO
1.22" x 0.78" x 0.06"

MEMORY STICK
MICRO (M2)
0.59" x 0.49" x 0.05"

**Figure 5-27:
Memory Stick Cards**

Secure Digital Cards

Secure Digital (SD) is a flash memory card format used in a variety of different portable devices, including digital cameras, notebook computers and PDAs. SD cards generally measure 1.26" × 0.94" × 0.08" (32 mm × 24 mm × 2.1 mm), but can be as thin as 0.055" (1.4 mm). These cards are based on an older **Multi Media Card (MMC)** form factor, but tend to be slightly thicker than MMC cards. New **miniSD** 0.79" × 0.86" × 0.055" (20 mm × 21.5 mm × 1.4 mm) and **microSD** 0.59" × 0.43" × 0.039" (15 mm × 11 mm × 1 mm) formats have also been introduced to provide even smaller form factor memory devices to the market. Figure 5-28 depicts typical SD cards.

SECURE DIGITAL (SD) CARD	MULTI MEDIA CARD (MMC)	miniSD	microSD
1.26" x 0.94" x 0.08"	1.26" x 0.94"	0.79" x 0.86" x 0.055"	0.59" x 0.43"

Figure 5-28: Secure Digital Cards

SD cards are sold according to their storage capacities as well as their data transfer rates. SD cards are available in 2 GB, 4 GB and 8 GB versions. Transfer rates for SD cards are specified in terms of 150 KBps multiples (e.g., an 1x version runs at 150 KBps and an 2x device transfers data at 300 KBps). Basic SD cards transfer data at 6x speeds—the speed of a standard CD-ROM drive. Higher-speed 1.01 SD cards operate at transfer rates up to 66x, and SD 1.1 cards operate at 133x speeds.

Mini and Micro SD cards can be used in standard SD slots by first inserting them in special adapters. Likewise, the standard SD devices can be used in Compact Flash or PC Card slots with an adapter. Some SD cards come with built-in USB connectors to provide dual-purpose usage of the device. Most SD cards also offer security feature such as a locking *write-protect switch* on the side of the device to prevent accidental overwriting of the contents, and on-board **digital rights management (DRM)** software to prevent unauthorized copying of the contents. (This feature is intended for use by the software, music, and movie industries to protect their materials from being copied).

DISK DRIVE INTERFACES

In the computer industry, there is a continuing race between interface specification groups to be the only interface in the PC environment. For now, the main participants in this race include the USB bus, the IEEE-1394 bus, the SATA interface, and the latest SCSI interface. These interfaces and buses, in turn, compete with the different types of local area networks. All of these interfaces are based on serial data transmission methods. Modern serial transmission modes are fast and provide high performance.

For installation purposes, storage devices fall into one of two categories: internal or external. Internal devices are typically mounted in the system unit's drive bays and connect to the system board or one of its adapter cards. External devices normally connect to one of the system's standard I/O port connectors. Whereas internal devices typically derive their power from the system unit's power supply, external storage devices tend to employ separate, external power supply units.

Modern PCs employ one of two standard *system-level interface* types to communicate with their internal disk drive systems—**integrated drive electronics (IDE)**, also known as the **AT attachment (ATA)** interface, or **small computer system interface (SCSI)** interfaces. Both interface types place most of the controller electronics directly on the drive unit. Therefore, data travel in parallel between the computer and the drive unit. The controller circuitry on the drive handles all of the parallel-to-serial and serial-to-parallel conversions. This permits the interface to be independent of the host computer design. The system sees the entire HDD system as an attachment to its bus systems.

Most newer external HDD and CD-ROM/DVD drives employ USB or IEEE-1394 Firewire interfaces. These interfaces were discussed in detail in Chapter 4, *Standard I/O Systems*. However, there are external disk drive systems that employ SCSI interfaces, or local area networks to communicate with the system.

Memory Stick Duo
integrated drive electronics (IDE)
AT attachment (ATA)
small computer system interface (SCSI)

Internal Disk Drive Interfaces

As we saw in Chapter 3, most *internal* hard drives and CD-ROM/DVD drives typically connect to one of the system board's parallel IDE/EIDE-ATA (**PATA**) interface connections, or one of its **serial ATA (SATA)** interface connections. On some system boards, you will find only PATA connectors, on others you will find only SATA connectors, and on some you will find a mixture of both. A mixed version system board layout is depicted in Figure 5-29.

PATA
serial ATA (SATA)

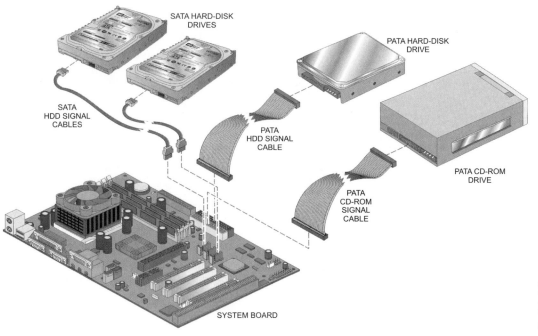

Figure 5-
Disk D
Con

he other internal drive option is the small computer system interface (SCSI). Most PC stem boards do not physically or logically (in the BIOS) support SCSI interface devices. erefore, an adapter-card-based controller is usually required to accommodate these ves. The host adapter card plugs into one of the system board's expansion slots and vides a BERG pin connector for the system's internal SCSI ribbon cable.

ever, there are many versions of the SCSI standard and several types of SCSI ecting cables. An internal SCSI CD-ROM drive must be capable of connecting to the of SCSI cable being used. The SCSI interface that employs a Centronics-type connector is the most widely used method for connecting external CD-ROM drives to systems.

IDE/ATA Interface

AT attachment
(ATA)

Master

Slave

The original IDE interface standard was also referred to as the **AT attachment (ATA)** interface. (*IDE and ATA were involved in the same standard.*) This interface originally appeared on adapter cards and supported two drive units that shared a single communications channel (one cable). If two drives were attached to the cable, one was designated as the **Master** drive and the other as the **Slave** drive. With the introduction of the ATX form factor specification, the IDE host adapter function and physical interface was integrated into the system board.

IDE drives store their low-level formatting information directly on the drive. This information is placed on the drive by its manufacturer, and is used by the controller for alignment and sector sizing of the drive. The IDE controller extracts the raw data (format and actual data information) coming from the R/W heads and converts the data into signal that can be applied to the computer's buses. Therefore, the system basically sees the drive as an extension of its buses. The IDE interface used a single 40-pin ribbon cable to connect the hard drive to the host adapter card or system board and supported a maximum throughput of 8.3 MBps. Its signal cable arrangement is depicted in Figure 5-30.

PIN DESCRIPTION

Pin	Description	Pin	Description
1	Reset	2	Ground
3	Data 7	4	Data 8
5	Data 6	6	Data 9
7	Data 5	8	Data 10
9	Data 4	10	Data 11
11	Data 3	12	Data 12
13	Data 2	14	Data 13
15	Data 1	16	Data 14
17	Data 0	18	Data 15
19	Ground	20	Unused
21	Unused	22	Ground
23	$\overline{\text{IOW}}$	24	Ground
25	$\overline{\text{IOR}}$	26	Ground
27	IOCHRDY	28	Bale
29	Unused	30	Ground
31	IRQ14	32	$\overline{\text{IOCS16}}$
33	A1	34	$\overline{\text{PDAIG}}$
35	A0	36	A2
37	$\overline{\text{HDCS0}}$	38	$\overline{\text{HDCS1}}$
39	$\overline{\text{SLV ACT}}$	40	Ground

CONNECTOR ENDS

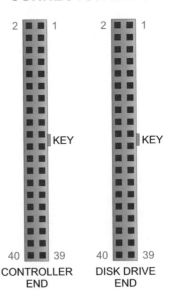

CONTROLLER END

DISK DRIVE END

Advanced EIDE Specifications

There are a variety of IDE-related specifications. Updated IDE specifications have been developed to enable more than two drives to exist on the interface. This was accomplished by creating two separate IDE channels, with two controllers and two 40-pin interface connections. The first channel is referred to as the primary channel, and the other is the secondary channel. Each channel is capable of handling its own master and slave drive independent of the other channel.

This new IDE specification is called **enhanced IDE (EIDE)**, or the **ATA-2** interface, and actually includes the ATA-2/EIDE/ATAPI specifications (the ATAPI standard is a derivative of the ATA-2 standard). The **AT attachment packet interface (ATAPI)** specification provides improved IDE drivers for use with CD-ROM drives and new data transfer methods. This specification provides maximum throughput of 16.7 MBps through the 40-pin IDE signal cable.

The ATA standards provide for different **programmed I/O (PIO)** modes that offer higher performance capabilities, as illustrated in Table 5-6. Most IDE devices are now capable of operating in modes 3 or 4. However, the IDE port must be attached to the PCI bus to use these modes. Some system boards only place the IDE1 connection on this bus, while the IDE2 connection is a function of the ISA bus. In these cases, devices installed on the IDE2 connector will only be capable of mode-2 operation.

enhanced IDE (EIDE)

ATA-2

AT attachment packet interface (ATAPI)

programmed I/O (PIO)

PIO MODE	TRANSFER	ATA VERSION
0	3.3 MB/sec	ATA-1
1	5.2 MB/sec	ATA-1
2	8.3 MB/sec	ATA-1
3	11.1 MB/sec	ATA-2
4	16.6 MB/sec	ATA-2
4	33.3 MB/sec	ATA-3/Ultra DMA 33
4	66.6 MB/sec	ATA-4/Ultra DMA 66
4	100 MB/sec	ATA 100

Table 5-6: ATA PIO Modes

An additional development of the ATA standard has provided the ATA-3/Ultra ATA 33 specification that boosts throughput between the IDE device and the system to 33.3 MBps. This standard still employs the 40-pin IDE signal cable. It relies on the system to support the 33.3 MBps burst mode transfer operation through the **Ultra DMA (UDMA)** protocol.

Ultra DMA (UDMA)

Newer IDE enhancements called ATA-4/Ultra ATA 66 and Ultra ATA 100 provide even higher data throughput by doubling the number of conductors in the IDE signal cable. The IDE connector has remained compatible with the 40-pin IDE connection, but each pin has been provided with its own ground conductor in the cable. The Ultra ATA 66 specification provides 66 MBps, and the Ultra ATA 100 connection provides 100 MBps.

Both Ultra ATA versions support 33.3 MBps data rates when used with a standard 40-pin/40-conductor IDE signal cable. Therefore, Ultra ATA 66 and 100 devices can still be used with systems that don't support the new IDE standards.

┌─ **TEST TIP** ────────┐
│ Remember how the Ultra ATA 66 │
│ interface cable can be identified. │
└──────────────────────┘

These operating modes must be configured correctly through the system's CMOS Setup Utility. These settings were discussed under the *Chipset Features Setup Functions* heading in Chapter 3, *Advanced System Boards*.

Serial ATA Interface

serial ATA

The newest ATA implementation from the IDE development community is the **serial ATA (SATA)** standard. This interface standard has been developed to compete with other interface types that employ serial data transmission types. The current SATA specification supports data transfer rates at up to 150 MBps using 250 mV differential signaling techniques. Serial ATA needs only two data channels—one for sending and one for receiving.

The seven-wire data cable used with the SATA connection is considerably different from the traditional ribbon cables used with parallel interfaces. They are thin and flexible and their connectors are just 8 mm wide. These cables can range up to a meter in length, meaning that there is no problem connecting a disk drive that is mounted in the top bay of a large tower case.

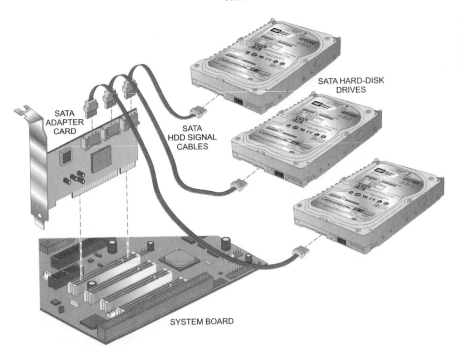

With SATA drives there is no master/slave relationship or configuration to perform. Each SATA drive has its own host connector and cable. Host connectors can be located on a host adapter card that plugs into one of the system board's PCI expansion slots, or it can be mounted directly on the system board. Figure 5-31 depicts a typical SATA adapter card. These cards may contain between one and four SATA connectors. There is no particular connection order that needs to be followed as there is in the master/slave–primary/secondary PATA interface.

You can mix PATA and SATA drives in a system as long as the system board or host adapter card supports both types of interfaces. This permits SATA drives to be added to older PATA systems by simply installing a host adapter card, without removing the existing PATA drives.

Figure 5-31: SATA Adapter Card

device drivers

Depending on the system board and drive types installed, you may need to load **device drivers** for the SATA controller after a Windows operating system detects the new drive in the system. These drivers should be located on the installation disc that comes with the drive or adapter card. You should also check the manufacturers' Internet Web page for the latest drivers available.

Floppy Drive Interface

A single ribbon cable is used to connect the floppy drive to the system board's FDD adapter connector when present. The signal cable has two 34-pin, two-row BERG headers along its length. The other end of the cable terminates in a 34-pin, two-row BERG header. A small colored stripe normally runs along one edge of the cable, as illustrated in Figure 5-32. This is the **Pin #1 indicator stripe** that marks the side of the cable, which should be aligned with the #1 pin of the FDD connector and the disk drive's signal connector. The location of this pin is normally marked on the drive's printed-circuit board.

The 34-pin interface connection enables the FDC to manage two floppy-disk drive units. Figure 5-33 depicts the connections between the disk drive adapter and the disk drives. The directions of signal flow between the drives and the adapter are indicated by the arrow tips.

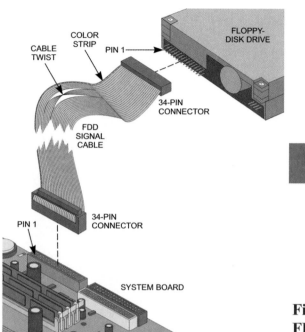

Pin #1 indicator stripe

Figure 5-32: The FDD Signal Cable

SIGNAL NAME	ADAPTER PIN NUMBER
GROUND (ODD NUMBERS)	1-33
DENSITY SELECT	2
UNUSED	4, 6
INDEX	8
MOTOR ENABLE A	10
DRIVE SELECT B	12
DRIVE SELECT A	14
MOTOR ENABLE B	16
DIRECTION	18
STEP	20
WRITE DATA	22
WRITE ENABLE	24
TRACK 0	26
WRITE PROTECT	28
READ DATA	30
SELECT HEAD 1	32
DISK CHANGE	34

DISK DRIVE — MULTI I/O

Figure 5-33: FDD Cable Signal Definitions

The floppy-disk drive connected to the 34-pin header at the end of the cable will be designated as drive A by the system. A floppy drive attached to the connector in the middle of the cable will be designated as the B drive. A small twist of wires between the A and B connectors reroutes key lines that determine which drive is which.

Small Computer System Interface

The **small computer system interface (SCSI)**, often referred to as the "**scuzzy**" standard, like the IDE concept, provides a true system-level interface for the drive. Nearly all of the drive's controller electronics are located on the peripheral device. As with the IDE host adapter, the duties of the **SCSI host adapter** are reduced to mostly physical connection functions, along with some signal compatibility handling.

With this arrangement, data arrive at the system interface in a form that is already usable by the host computer. This can be seen through the SCSI interface description in Figure 5-34. Note that the original SCSI interface described in the figure only makes provisions for 8-bit parallel data transfers.

The SCSI interface can be used to connect diverse types of peripherals to the system. As an example, a SCSI chain could connect a controller to a hard drive, a CD-ROM drive, a high-speed tape drive, a scanner, and a printer. Additional SCSI devices are added to the system by daisy-chaining them together: The input of the second device is attached to the SCSI output of the first device, and so forth.

PIN DESCRIPTION

Pin	Description	Pin	Description
1	Ground	2	Data 0
3	Ground	4	Data 1
5	Ground	6	Data 2
7	Ground	8	Data 3
9	Ground	10	Data 4
11	Ground	12	Data 5
13	Ground	14	Data 6
15	Ground	16	Data 7
17	Ground	18	Data Parity (Odd)
19	Ground	20	Ground
21	Ground	22	Ground
23	Ground	24	Ground
25	No Connection	26	No Connection
27	Ground	28	Ground
29	Ground	30	Ground
31	Ground	32	Attention
33	Ground	34	Ground
35	Ground	36	Busy
37	Ground	38	ACK
39	Ground	40	Reset
41	Ground	42	Message
43	Ground	44	Select
45	Ground	46	C/D
47	Ground	48	Request
49	Ground	50	I/O

CONNECTOR ENDS

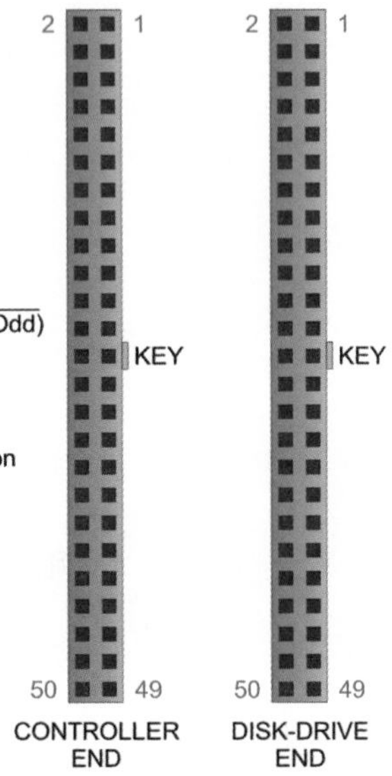

CONTROLLER END — DISK-DRIVE END

Figure 5-34: The SCSI Interface Connection

SCSI Specifications

The original **SCSI-1** specification established a data bus width of 8 bits and permitted up to eight devices to be connected to the bus (including the controller). The maximum speed of the SCSI-1 bus is 5 MBps (1 byte × 5 MHz = 5 MBps.) The maximum recommended length for a complete standard SCSI chain is 20 feet (6 m). However, unless the cables are heavily shielded, they become susceptible to data corruption caused by induced noise. Therefore, a maximum single SCSI segment of less than 3 feet (1 m) is recommended. Don't forget the length of the internal cabling when dealing with SCSI cable distances. You can realistically count on about 3 feet of internal cable, so reduce the maximum total length of the chain to about 15 feet (4.5 m). This specification became known as Narrow SCSI.

TEST TIP
Memorize the permissible lengths stated for SCSI cables and chains.

An updated SCSI specification was developed by the ANSI committee to double the number of data lines in the standard interface to 16 bits (2 bytes). It also adds balanced, dual-line drivers that allow much faster data transfer speeds to be used. This implementation is referred to as **Wide SCSI-2**. The specification expands the SCSI specification into a 16/32-bit bus standard and increases the cable and connector specification to 68 pins. This enhancement enabled the SCSI bus to transfer data twice as fast (2 bytes × 5 MHz = 10 MBps).

Wide SCSI-2

A different improvement to the original specification increased the synchronous data transfer option for the 8-bit interface from 5 Mbps to 10 Mbps. This implementation became known as **Fast SCSI-2**. Under this system, the system and the I/O device conduct nondata message, command, and status operations in 8-bit asynchronous mode. After agreeing on a larger or faster file-transfer format, they conduct transfers using an agreed-upon word size and transmission mode. As the speed of the bus was increased, it caused **cross talk** to occur earlier, which cut the maximum usable cable length in half (from 6 meters to 3 meters, or about 10 feet). Fast SCSI-2 connections use 50-pin connectors.

Fast SCSI-2

cross talk

A third version brought together both improvements and became known as **Wide Fast SCSI-2**. This version of the standard doubles the bus size to 16 bits and employs the faster transfer methods to provide a maximum bus speed of 20 MBps (2 bytes × 10 MHz = 20 MBps) supporting a chain of up to 15 additional devices. The maximum cable length is still specified at 3 meters, because the bus can run at 10 MHz.

Wide Fast SCSI-2

After increasing the bus width of the SCSI-2 specification to 16 bits, the next step in the evolution of the specification was to speed up the bus again. The newer version, referred to as **Ultra SCSI** (ultra meaning ultra-fast), pushed the bus speed from 10 MHz to 20 MHz, using the original SCSI-1 interface. Naturally, this move increased the maximum transfer rate from 5 MBps to 20 MBps (1 byte × 20 MHz), but it also reduced the maximum useful cable length of 1.5 meters. This distance tends to physically limit the number of devices that you can attach to the cable; however, it is still suitable for most installations. The Ultra SCSI specification also makes provisions for a special high-speed serial transfer mode and special communications media, such as fiber-optic cabling.

Ultra SCSI

This update has been combined with both wide and fast revisions to produce

- Ultra SCSI
- Ultra2 SCSI
- Wide Ultra SCSI
- Wide Ultra2 SCSI
- Wide Ultra3 SCSI

Of course, the next logical SCSI standard advancement was to once again increase the data bus width. This revision is called **Wide Ultra SCSI**. The addition of the Wide specification doubles the number of devices that can be serviced by the interface. Likewise, the Ultra designation indicates a speed increase due to improved technology. Combining the two technologies yielded a 4x increase in data throughput (i.e., Wide Ultra SCSI = 40 MBps compared to Ultra SCSI = 20 MBps and Wide and Fast SCSI = 10 MBps), while still keeping the cable length at 1.5 meters.

Wide Ultra SCSI

At this point, the SCSI development community could not increase the speed of the bus using the existing hardware interface. Increasing the speed again would limit the maximum cable length to the point where it would be unusable in the real world. To increase the bus speed to 40 MHz, the specification switched to low-voltage differential (LVD) signaling techniques described later in this section.

Ultra2 SCSI

By employing LVD technology, the **Ultra2 SCSI** specification doubled the data throughput of the 8-bit SCSI bus (1 byte × 40 MHz = 40 MBps). However, the presence of the LVD technology enabled the maximum cable length for this specification to be increased to 12 meters. Single LVD devices connected solely to a single controller may use up to 25 meters of cable.

Wide Ultra2 SCSI

Quickly, the SCSI community mixed the LVD technology with the increased bus width of the Wide SCSI specification to produce **Wide Ultra2 SCSI**. This specification increased the maximum data throughput to 80 MBps (2 bytes × 40 MHz = 80 MBps), while the cable length remained at 12 meters.

double transition
(DT) clocking

ULTRA160 SCSI

The next improvement to the SCSI technology was the introduction of **double transition (DT) clocking** techniques. DT clocking enabled an **ULTRA160 SCSI** controller to send data on both the rising and falling edges of its clock cycles. Although the bus width remained at 16 bits and the bus clock frequency stayed at 40 MHz, the new technique increased the maximum throughput to 160 MBps (2 bytes × 40 MHz × 2 =160 MBps). The maximum cable length also remained at 12 meters with the new specification, although the specifications for the cable type had to be made more stringent.

Ultra 320 SCSI

single connector
attachment (SCA)

The latest SCSI specification, referred to as **Ultra 320 SCSI**, increased the clock speed from 40 MHz to 80 MHz, while still employing the DT clocking scheme. Together, these steps boosted the maximum bus speed to 320 MBps (2 bytes × 80 MHz × 2 = 320 Mbps), using a 16-bit bus and supporting up to 15 external devices. The Ultra 320 SCSI connection employs a special 80-pin **single connector attachment (SCA)** connector.

ULTRA640 SCSI

There is currently a proposal in place for a new **ULTRA640 SCSI** specification. This specification proposes to increase the throughput of the interface to 640 MBps. While this proposal is currently in development, it may not be released for quite some time. In the development papers, it mentions that the cable length will need to be shortened to increase the standard's integrity, but does not mention by how much.

SCSI Cables and Connectors

The SCSI standard has been implemented using a number of different cable types. In PC-compatible systems, the SCSI interface uses a 50-pin signal cable arrangement. Internally, the cable is a 50-pin flat ribbon cable. However, 50-pin shielded cables, with Centronic connectors, are used for external SCSI connections. The 50-pin SCSI connections are referred to as **A-cables**.

A-cables

Advanced SCSI specifications have created additional cabling specifications. A 50-conductor alternative cable using 50-pin D-shell connectors has been added to the A-cable specification for SCSI-2 devices. A second cable type, referred to as **B-cable**, was added to the SCSI-2 specification to provide 16- and 32-bit parallel data transfers. However, this arrangement employed multiple connectors at each end of the cable and never received widespread acceptance in the market. A revised 68-pin **P-cable** format, using D-shell connectors, was introduced to support 16-bit transfers in the SCSI-3 specification. A 68-pin **Q-cable** version was also adopted in SCSI for 32-bit transfers. The P and Q cables must be used in parallel to conduct 32-bit transfers.

B-cable

P-cable

Q-cable

For some PS/2 models, IBM used a special 60-pin Centronics-like connector for their SCSI connections. The version of the SCSI interface used in the Apple Macintosh employs a variation of the standard that features a proprietary miniature 25-pin D-shell connector.

These cabling variations create a hardware incompatibility between different SCSI devices. Likewise, there are SCSI devices that just will not work with each other due to software incompatibilities.

In addition, SCSI devices may be classified as internal or as external devices. An internal SCSI device has no power supply of its own and, therefore, must be connected to one of the system's options power connectors. On the other hand, external SCSI devices come with built-in or plug-in power supplies that need to be connected to a commercial AC outlet. Therefore, when choosing a SCSI device, always inquire about compatibility between it and any other SCSI devices installed in the system.

Figure 5-35 depicts a 25-pin D-shell, a 50-pin Centronics, and a 68-pin Centronics-type and an 80-pin SCA SCSI connector used for external connections. Inside the computer, the SCSI specification employs 50-pin and 68-pin ribbon cables with BERG pin connectors, or the 80-pin SCA connector for Ultra 320 devices.

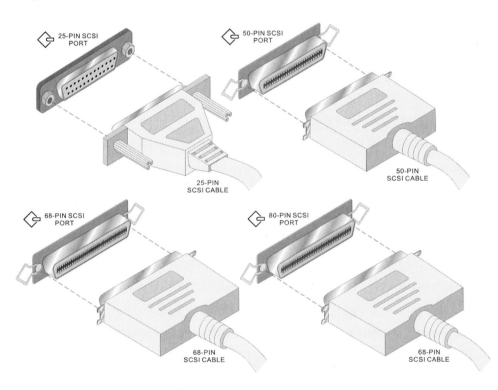

**Figure 5-35:
SCSI Connectors**

SCSI Signaling

You should also be aware that two types of signaling are used with SCSI interfaces—**single-ended (SE)** and **differential**. Single-ended signaling transmits signals in a straightforward manner where the information is applied to a signal line and referenced to ground. Differential signaling applies reciprocal versions of the same signal to two wires in the cable and compares them at the other end of the cable. This differential signal technique provides exceptional noise rejection properties and enables the signal to be transmitted much further (from 3/6 meters using SE up to 25 meters using differential) before it significantly deteriorates. For this reason, a single-ended interface uses half as many active conductors in the cable as do differential cables. The other conductors in the SE cable are used to provide grounds for the individual signal cables. In a differential cable, the ground conductors are used to carry the differential portion of the signal.

single-ended (SE)

differential

Single-ended and differential SCSI cables are available for A, P, and Q applications. Because they are electrically different, confusing them with each other would be problematic (i.e., using a differential cable to connect single-ended devices together could damage the devices because of the missing ground capabilities). For this reason, the industry has adopted different symbols, as illustrated in Figure 5-36, to identify SE and differential cables and devices. These symbols are placed on the connectors of the cables and ports so that they are not confused with each other. Fortunately, most PC applications use single-ended connections. Therefore, you are unlikely to run into differential cables or devices.

SINGLE-
ENDED
(SE)

LOW-VOLTAGE
DIFFERENTIAL
(LVD)

LOW-VOLTAGE
DIFFERENTIAL /
MULTIMODE
SINGLE-ENDED
(LVD / MSE)

HIGH-
VOLTAGE
DIFFERENTIAL
(HVD)

**Figure 5-36:
SCSI Symbols**

There have been two different differential signal specifications used in the SCSI environment. These are

High-Voltage
Differential (HVD)

- **High-Voltage Differential (HVD)**—The high differential refers to the +5 Vdc and 0 Vdc signal levels used to represent data bits. These voltage levels were implemented with the original SCSI-1 bus and have been included with all of the specifications up to the Wide Ultra SCSI version.

Low-Voltage
Differential (LVD)

- **Low-Voltage Differential (LVD)**—This is similar to the move in microprocessors to reduce the core voltage to 3.3 V to make them run faster and consume less power. LVD interfaces operate on 3-volt logic levels instead of the older TTL-compatible 5-volt levels.

multimode

Unlike the earlier HVD interfaces that were incompatible with SE devices, LVD SCSI devices actually operate in what is known as **multimode** (i.e., they can shift back and forth between traditional SE mode and LVD mode). The LVD is backward compatible with single-ended SCSI. However, connecting one single-ended peripheral to a multimode LVD bus will cause the entire bus to switch to the single-ended mode for protection. With the switch, the single-ended limitations on data throughput and cable length come into play. LVD mode was not defined in the original SCSI standards. If all devices on the bus support LVD, then operations at up to 12 meters are possible at full speed. However, if any device on the bus is singled-ended only, then the entire bus switches to single-ended mode, and the distance is reduced to the 3/6 meters.

To add a single-ended peripheral to an LVD bus and preserve the data throughput and cable length of the LVD, you can add a SCSI expander called an LVD-to-SE or LVD/MSE-to-LVD/MSE converter. This converter divides the SCSI domain into two bus segments. One segment can operate at the LVD data throughput rate and cable length, while the other segment uses the single-ended data throughput and cable length ratings. Most LVD controllers employ a single-ended connector for connecting to slower tape drives so that they can preserve the speed and cable length of the LVD segment.

TEST TIP

Know the number of devices that can be attached to IDE, EIDE, and standard SCSI interfaces.

The speed capabilities of the SCSI interfaces make them attractive for intensive applications such as large file servers for networks, and multimedia video stations. However, the PATA and SATA interfaces are generally more widely used due to lower cost and nearly equal performance. Table 5-7 contrasts the specifications of the PATA, SATA, and SCSI interfaces.

Table 5-7: PATA/SATA/SCSI Specifications

INTERFACE	BUS SIZE	# DEVICES	ASYNC. SPEED	SYNC. SPEED
IDE (ATA-1)	16 bits	2	4 MB/s	3.3/5.2/8.3 MB/s
EIDE (ATA-2)	16 bits	2	4 MB/s	11/16 MB/s
SATA	Serial	4	150 MB/s	-
SCSI (SCSI-1)	8 bits	7	2 MB/s	5 MB/s
Wide SCSI (SCSI-2)	8/16 bits	15	2 MB/s	5 MB/s
Fast SCSI (SCSI-2)	8/16 bits	7	2 MB/s	5/10 MB/s
Wide Fast SCSI (SCSI-2)	8/16 bits	15	2 MB/s	10/20 MB/s
Ultra SCSI	8 bits	7	2 MB/s	10/20 MB/s
Wide Ultra SCSI (SCSI-3)	16 bits	15	2 MB/s	10/20/40 MB/s
Ultra2 SCSI	8 bits	7	2 MB/s	10/20/40 MB/s
Wide Ultra2 SCSI	16 bits	15	2 MB/s	10/20/40/80 MB/s
Wide Ultra3 SCSI	16 bits	15	2 MB/s	10/20/40/160 MB/s
Ultra320 SCSI	16 bits	15	2 MB/s	10/20/40/320 MB/s

Essentials 1.2

INSTALLING INTERNAL STORAGE DEVICES

Most internal storage devices conform to traditional disk drive form factors. Therefore, the hardware installation procedures for most storage devices are the same. To install a storage device in a disk drive bay, disconnect the system's power cord from the back of the unit. Slide the device into one of the system unit's open drive bays, and install two screws on each side to secure the unit to the disk drive cage. If the unit is a 3-1/2" drive, and it is being installed into a 5-1/4" drive bay, you will need to fit the drive with a *universal mounting kit*. These kits attach to the drive and extend its form factor, so that it fits correctly in the 5-1/4" half-height space.

Connect the device's signal cable to the proper interface header on the system board (or on an I/O card). Then connect the signal cable to the storage device. Use caution when connecting the disk drives to the adapter. Make certain that the Pin #1 indicator stripe on the cable aligns with the Pin #1 position of the connectors on both the storage device and its controller. Proper connection of a signal cable is depicted in Figure 5-37. Finally, connect one of the power supply's optional power connectors to the storage device.

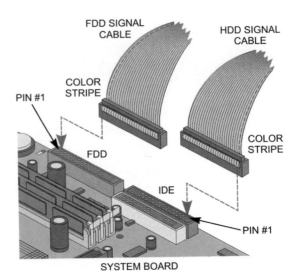

Figure 5-37:
Connecting a Drive's
Signal Cable

HDD Installation

The HDD hardware installation process is similar to that of other storage devices, as illustrated in Figure 5-38. Simply slide the hard-drive unit into one of the system unit's open drive bays, install two screws on each side to secure the drive to the system unit, and connect the signal and power cables to it.

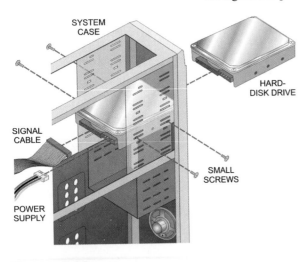

Figure 5-38:
Securing the
Drive Unit

It is a good idea to confirm the IDE drive's master/slave/single, or the SCSI drive's ID configuration setting before installing the unit in the drive bay. Likewise, in a SCSI system, make sure that the drive is correctly configured and terminated for its position in the system before performing the physical install. These settings are harder to configure after the drive has been placed in the drive bay. These settings were described later in this chapter.

When you are installing the HDD signal cable in an IDE-based system, you should recall that there are two similar types of cables used with IDE devices. The newer ATA-4/Ultra ATA 66, Ultra ATA 100, and Ultra ATA 133 IDE enhancements provide higher data throughput by doubling the number of conductors in the signal cable to 80. The IDE connector has remained compatible with the original 40-pin IDE connection, but each pin has been provided with its own ground conductor in the cable. All three Ultra ATA versions support 33.3 Mbps data rates when used with a standard 40-pin/40-conductor IDE signal cable. Therefore, Ultra ATA 66, 100, and 133 devices can still be used with systems that don't support the new IDE standards, but they will operate well below their potential.

┌─ **TEST TIP** ─────────────────────────────────┐
│ Remember how the Ultra ATA 66 interface cable can be identified │
│ and what the effects of using the older signal cable have on these │
│ faster interfaces. │
└───┘

When dealing with SCSI systems, verify that the SCSI host adapter and all the SCSI devices installed in the system are supported and will work together. For example, a standard SCSI-I host adapter will not support a Fast-Wide SCSI device. The physical cable and the communication speed differences between the two specifications will not match.

When handling hard drives, make sure to practice proper **electrostatic discharge (ESD)** precautions to prevent damage to the drive's electronic control circuitry. For instance, the hard drive should be kept inside its antistatic bag until installation. Also, make sure that during installation, your technicians are wearing an anti-static device, such as a grounded wrist or ankle strap. If a replacement hard drive is being installed for repair or upgrading purposes, the data on the original drive should be backed up to some other media before replacing it (if possible). These precautions and device are discussed in Chapter 13, *Preventive Maintenance*.

electrostatic discharge (ESD)

After completing the hardware installation process, the drive must be configured and formatted. Hard-disk drives are created in a wide variety of storage capacities and geometries. When the disk is created its surface is electronically blank. With system-level drive types, the manufacturer performs the low-level formatting process. To prepare the disk for use by the system, three levels of preparation must take place. The order of these steps is as follows:

1. Verify the CMOS configuration for the drive.

2. Partition the drive.

3. High-level format the drive.

The system's CMOS Setup holds the hard drive's configuration settings. As with other I/O devices, these settings must be established correctly for the type of drive being installed. Newer BIOS versions possess **autodetection** capabilities that enable them to find and identify the drives in the system. The physical geometry of the drive might be different than the logical arrangement that the controller displays to the CMOS. The IDE controller handles the translation between the drive parameters the system believes to exist and the actual layout of the drive.

autodetection

However, if the BIOS does not support autodetection, you must move into the CMOS Setup utility and identify the drive type being installed. The Hard Disk C: Type entry is typically located in the CMOS Setup utility's main screen. Simply move to the entry and scroll through the HDD selections until an entry is found that matches the type you are installing. In some cases, such as with SCSI drives, the CMOS configuration entry must be set to *None Installed* before the drive will operate correctly. Store this parameter in the CMOS configuration file by following the directions given on the menu screen. This utility can also be used to manually configure various IDE channel selections. Both IDE channels can be Enabled, Disabled, or placed in Autodetect mode through the CMOS.

Older BIOS versions provide for a manual PIO configuration setting. The ATA standards provide for different **programmed I/O (PIO)** modes that offer higher performance capabilities. Most EIDE devices are now capable of operating in modes 3 or 4. However, the IDE port must be attached to the PCI bus to use these modes. Some system boards only place the IDE1 connection on this 64-bit bus, whereas the IDE2 connection is a function of the ISA bus. In these cases, devices installed on the IDE2 connector will only be capable of mode 2 operations. Newer BIOS versions do not offer manual PIO configuration capabilities.

programmed I/O (PIO)

nfiguring PATA Drives

IDE/EIDE interface has been the standard PC disk drive interface for some time. The controller structure is an integrated portion of most PC system boards. This structure ades BIOS and chipset support for the IDE versions the board will support, as well as the sical PATA host connector.

se include providing the select signals to differentiate between a **single-drive** system, or **master** and **slave** drives. The relationships between the host adapter, the system buses, the IDE interfaces are described in Figure 5-39.

single-drive
master
slave

┌─ **TEST TIP** ─────────────────┐
│ Memorize the three configurations that can be set on an IDE drive. │
└────────────────────────────────┘

Most IDE drives come from the manufacturer configured for operation as a single drive, or as the master drive in a multidrive system. In order to install the drive as a second, or slave,

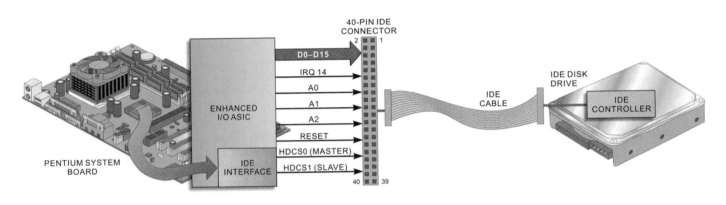

Figure 5-39: The Host Adapter, System Buses, and IDE Interface

drive, it is usually necessary to install, remove, or move a jumper block, as illustrated in Figure 5-40. Some hosts disable the interface's Cable Select pin for slave drives. With these types of hosts, it is necessary to install a jumper for the Cable Select option on the drive. Consult the system's user's manual to see if it supports this function.

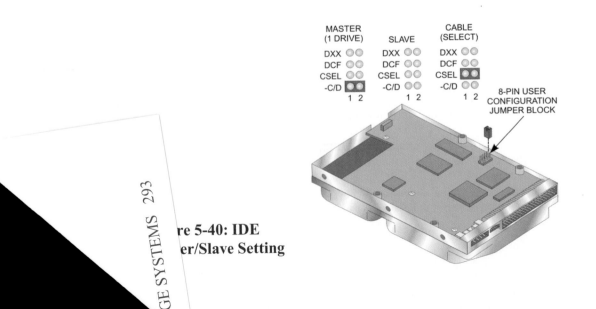

re 5-40: IDE
er/Slave Setting

In the FAT-based system, the primary partition of the drive attached to the ID1 connector will always be designated as a logical C: drive. On an IDE drive that is partitioned into two logical drives, the system will identify them as drives C: and D:. The hierarchy of assigning logical drive designations in the IDE interface calls for the primary partitions to be assigned sequentially from ID1 master, ID1 slave, ID2 master, to ID2 slave.

This is followed by assigning letters to the *extended partitions* on each drive in the same order (drive partitions are logical divisions of hard-disk drives and are covered in detail in the following section). For example, if a second drive is attached to ID1 as a slave, its primary partition will be designated as a logical D: drive. The system will reassign the partitions on the first drive to be logical drives C: and E:, and the partitions on the slave drive will assume the letters D: and F:.

GEEK SQUAD CASE FILE #15593

You are installing PATA drives in a new system. The buyers want to include a large HDD, a standard CD-ROM drive and a rewritable CD-ROM drive. Their company needs to have Windows 2000 and MS-DOS operating systems on the machine, so they want you to divide the hard drive into two equal-sized drives. You connect the hard drive to the system board's IDE1 connector and the two CD-ROM drives to the cable connected to its IDE2 connector. How will their drive-specific MS-DOS programs need to be configured if MS-DOS is placed on the drive's extended partition?

Installing SATA Drives

The physical installation of SATA drives is performed in the same manner as PATA drives, with the exception that there is no master/slave configuration that needs to be made. Before installing the drive in the drive bay, connect the signal cable to the drive. Figure 5-41 shows the connectors on a typical SATA drive unit. The larger connector is the power connector, and the smaller one is the signal cable connector. Both connectors are keyed at the drive so they will only connect in one way. Therefore, they cannot be connected backward. The jumpers beside the signal connector are not for user configurations and should not be moved.

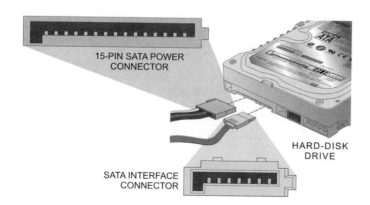

**Figure 5-41:
SATA Connections**

Next, install and secure the drive unit in an open disk drive bay. Then, attach the power supply cable to the drive and the signal cable to the host adapter (either on a SATA adapter card or on the system board). You are now ready to start the system.

When you start the system, it should automatically detect the presence of the new drive. If not, you should restart the system and enter the CMOS Setup routines when prompted to do so by the start-up procedure. Enable the SATA interface controller under the Integrated Peripherals' Onboard Devices submenu, as illustrated in Figure 5-42.

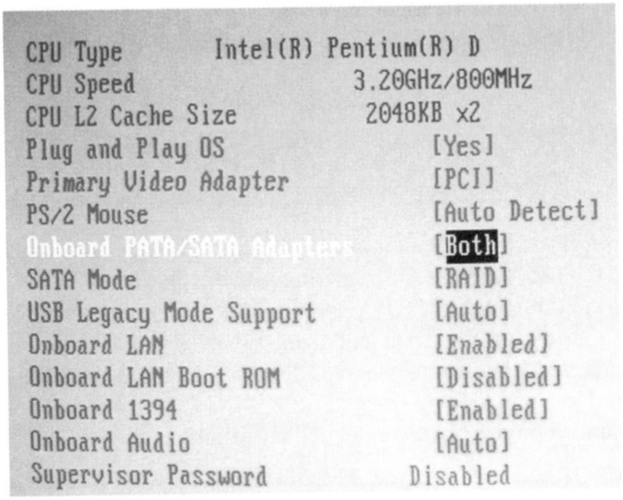

**Figure 5-42:
Enabling the SATA
Interface**

You may also need to *enable* the SATA DMA options and *disable* the IDE channel that is being used for the SATA drive. These options are typically established through the IDE Function Setup page of the Integrated Peripherals menu, as shown in Figure 5-43. Then, reboot the system and allow the PnP process to detect the additional drive. The presence of the drive should now show up in the Standard CMOS Setup page.

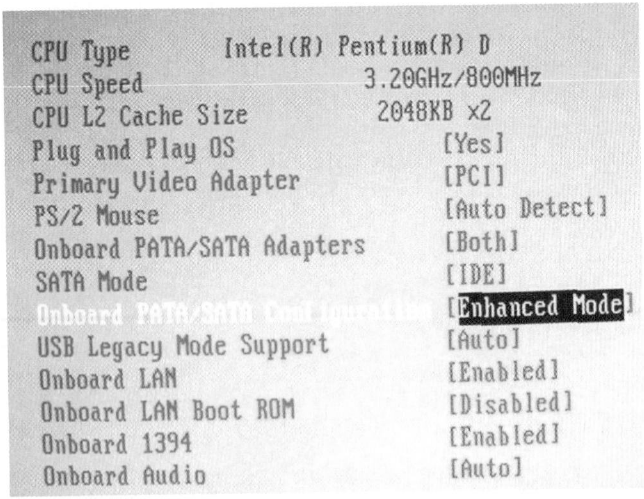

**Figure 5-43:
Configuring the
SATA Interface
in CMOS**

If the SATA drive you are installing is the system's boot drive, you may have to change the Boot Order sequence in the CMOS Setup to boot from a SATA drive. Because SATA is a new interface type, older systems may recognize the presence of a SATA host adapter card and mistakenly classify it as a SCSI device. It may also represent the drive simply as a model number in the listing. You should be aware of these possibilities and treat them as normal events even though the drive is not SCSI.

You may also need to load device drivers to enable the operating system to work with the SATA drive. SATA drives are not native to Windows operating systems, so you will need to install the manufacturer's drivers for Windows, so it can recognize the SATA device. Download the SATA drivers from the Web site of the company that manufactured the SATA adapter card (or system board) you are installing. If you are installing the SATA drive in a system with existing disk drives, you can load the drivers at any time. However, if you are performing a new Windows operating system install on the drive, the drivers must be added during the install process when requested by the installer routine. (Windows install procedures are covered in Chapter 10, *Windows Operating Systems*.)

Installing SCSI Adapter Cards

In the PC environment, SCSI devices are not standard. Even though newer system boards and operating systems do support SCSI operation, it has never been incorporated into the PC as a standard interface. Therefore, to use SCS devices with a PC, you will typically need to install a SCSI host adapter card.

Older ISA SCSI adapters required considerable manual configuration effort and careful consideration for installing cabling and terminators. (These activities are described in great detail in Chapter 6, *Data Communications*.)

With newer PCI SCSI host adapter cards, the installation and configuration process is much simpler. These cards possess PnP capabilities that enable the system to automatically configure them with the system resources they need to operate. PnP SCSI adapters are normally configured by default for ID = 7. However, you can change this setting by using the card's OEM software to update the BIOS extension on the card. This will cause the PnP process to configure the card with resources for the new ID setting when it is started again.

After the SCSI host adapter card has been installed in the system and secured, the cables must be attached to the card and the devices it supports. This could involve internal ribbon cables, external cables with D-shell connectors, or a combination of internal and external cables. One of the major tasks in getting SCSI systems installed and operating has been properly terminating the cables that run to the different SCSI devices in the system. Many newer SCSI adapters have autotermination capabilities built into them to reduce the effort required to achieve satisfactory termination. As with any type of device you are installing in a PC system, you should refer to the adapter's documentation to determine its termination and configuration needs.

The Windows 2000 and Windows XP operating systems offer support for most SCSI adapters. If the PnP process does not recognize a given SCSI adapter, it will ask for the OEM driver disk so that it can upload the drivers required to support the card. In some cases, these drivers may need to be loaded through the Windows Add/Remove Hardware applet in the Control Panel.

Configuring SCSI Addresses

SCSI-In

SCSI-Out

The original SCSI specification allows up to eight SCSI devices to be connected together. The standard SCSI1 port can be daisy-chained to permit up to six external peripherals to be connected to the system. To connect multiple SCSI devices to a SCSI host, all of the devices, except the last one, must have two SCSI connectors: one for **SCSI-In** and one for **SCSI-Out**. Which connector is which does not matter. However, if the device has only one SCSI connector, it must be connected to the end of the chain.

┌─ **TEST TIP** ────────────────┐
│ Remember how many devices can be │
│ daisy-chained on a standard SCSI interface, and │
│ which ID numbers are assumed automatically. │
└──────────────────────────────┘

It is possible to use multiple SCSI host adapters within a single system to increase the number of devices that can be used. The system's first SCSI controller can handle up to seven devices, whereas the additional SCSI controller can boost the system to support up to 14 SCSI devices.

SCSI ID numbers

SCSI-7

SCSI-0

Each SCSI device in a chain must have a unique ID number assigned to it. Even though there are a total of eight possible **SCSI ID numbers** for each controller, only six are available for use with external devices. The SCSI specification refers to the SCSI controller as **SCSI-7** (by default) and then classifies the first internal hard drive as **SCSI-0**. If two devices are set to the same ID number, one or both of them will appear invisible to the system. This type of identification is also used for Wide SCSI. The difference is that the bus can now support up to 16 devices with the bus being 16 bits wide. The addressing scheme changes to SCSI-0 to SCSI-15.

┌─ **TEST TIP** ────────────────┐
│ Be aware of how SCSI ID priorities are set. │
└──────────────────────────────┘

With older SCSI devices, address settings were established through jumpers on the host adapter card. Each device had a SCSI number selection switch, or a set of configuration jumpers for establishing its ID number. Figure 5-44 illustrates a three-jumper configuration block that can be used to establish the SCSI ID number. In the figure, an open jumper pair is counted as a binary 0, and a shorted pair represents a binary 1. With a three-pair jumper block, it is possible to represent the numbers 0 through 7. In PnP systems, the BIOS will configure the device addresses using information obtained directly from the SCSI host adapter during the bootup process.

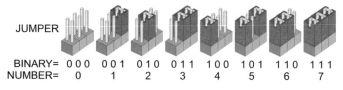

JUMPER								
BINARY=	000	001	010	011	100	101	110	111
NUMBER=	0	1	2	3	4	5	6	7

Figure 5-44: Configuring a SCSI ID Number

GEEK SQUAD CASE FILE #87220

Maria, a Double Agent at store 256 is installing an older SCSI device that must have its SCSI ID setting manually configured. The device has a 3-position, 2-pin BERG jumper for configuration and she needs to configure the device ID to 5. Maria has no documentation for the device, so she must guess at the setting. How should she arrange the three jumpers on the card? Explain your reasoning.

All newer BIOS versions are able to detect SCSI drives during the PnP process and can even be set to boot to a SCSI device. In addition, all current Windows versions offer native SCSI support. Because SCSI drives use a system-level interface, they require no low-level formatting. Therefore, the second step involved in installing a SCSI drive is to partition it.

SCSI Termination

The SCSI daisy chain must be **terminated** with a resistor network pack at both ends. Single-connector SCSI devices are normally terminated internally. If not, a SCSI terminator cable (containing a built-in resistor pack) must be installed at the end of the chain. SCSI termination is a major cause of SCSI-related problems. Poor terminations cause a variety of different system problems, including

- Failed system start-ups

- Hard drive crashes

- Random system failures

Several different types of termination are commonly used with SCSI buses. They differ in the circuitry that is used to terminate the bus. The better the termination method, the better the quality of signal moving along the bus, making it more reliable. In general, the slower bus specifications are less particular in the termination method required, while the faster buses require better termination techniques. The different types of termination commonly used with SCSI systems include

- **Passive Termination**—This is the simplest and least reliable method of termination. It employs nonactive resisters to terminate the bus. Passive termination is fine for short, low-speed SCSI-1 buses; however, it is not suitable for faster SCSI buses.

- **Active Termination**—Adding active elements such as voltage regulators to the resistors used in passive termination provides for more reliable and consistent termination of the bus. Active termination is the minimum requirement for any of the faster single-ended SCSI buses.

- **Forced Perfect Termination (FPT)**—FPT is a more advanced form of active termination, where the diode clamps are added to the circuitry to force the termination to the correct voltage. FPT virtually eliminates any signal reflections or other problems and is the best form of termination of a single-ended SCSI bus.

Newer SCSI buses that employ low-voltage differential signaling require special types of terminators. In addition, there are special LVD/SE terminators designed for use with **multimode LVD** devices that can function in either LVD or SE modes. When the bus is in single-ended mode, they behave like active terminators. LVDs are currently more popular than HVDs due to the fact that LVDs can support the Wide Ultra 2 SCSI, so the bandwidth is effectively doubled from 80 to 160 MB/sec.

Newer SCSI technologies often provide for automatic cable termination. Many of the latest internal SCSI cables provide the termination function on the cable itself. The terminator is permanently applied at the end of the cable. For this reason, you should always verify the type of SCSI cables and components you are using before installation. This will help to ensure that your SCSI installation process moves along as effortlessly as possible.

In these systems, after a SCSI component has been installed, the system queries the device to detect modifications to the SCSI configuration. It then provides termination as required to enable the system to operate properly. In addition, these intelligent systems can also assign SCSI IDs as required. Even in these systems you can still manually select ID numbers for the devices. In many cases, this is the best option because it enables you to document each SCSI component's ID for future reference.

Denita, CIA 327 is installing SCSI devices in a new system. Inside the case, there is a SCSI host adapter card, a hard-disk drive, and a CD-ROM drive. The SCSI cabling runs from the host adapter to the hard drive and ends at the CD-ROM drive. External to the case, Denita must make connections for a SCSI flatbed scanner and a SCSI printer. The external cabling runs from the host adapter to the scanner and ends at the printer. Where should the terminator packs be installed?

Essentials 1.2

Hard Drive Preparation

low-level format

partition

high-level format

Hard-disk drives are created in a wide variety of storage capacities. When the drive is created, its surface is electronically blank. To prepare the disk for use by the system, three levels of preparation must take place. These are, in order, the **low-level format,** the **partition**, and the **high-level format**.

A low-level format is similar to a land developer sectioning off a field for a new housing development. The process begins with surveying the property, and placing markers for key structures such as roads, water lines, and electrical service. The low-level format routine is similar in that it marks off the disk into cylinders and sectors and defines their placement on the disk. As mentioned earlier in this chapter, system-level drive types, such as PATA, SATA, and SCSI drives, come with the low-level format already performed. Therefore, they do not require any low-level formatting from the user.

Attempts to perform low-level formats on IDE and SCSI drives may result in damage to the drive. This is not physical damage, but the loss of prerecorded bad track and sector information that would occur during a low-level format. The drive also contains alignment information used to control the R/W heads for proper alignment over the tracks. This alignment information would also be lost during a low-level format. If this occurs, it will normally be necessary for the drive to be sent to the manufacturer to restore this information to the disk.

Logical and Physical Drives

Partitioning

logical drives

Before a disk drive can have a high-level format applied to it so that it can be used to perform useful functions for the system, the drive must be partitioned. **Partitioning** is the practice of dividing a physical drive into multiple logical storage areas and then treating each area as if it were a separate disk drive. This is normally done for purposes of organization and increased access speeds. However, drives may also be partitioned to enable multiple operating systems to exist on the same physical drive. Figure 5-45 illustrates the concept of creating multiple logical drives on a single physical hard drive.

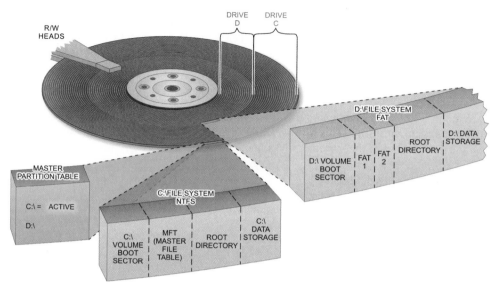

Figure 5-45: Partitions on an HDD

FAT-based systems provide for two partitions on a physical hard-disk drive. The first partition is referred to as the **primary partition** and must be created on the disk first. After the primary partition has been established and properly configured, an additional partition referred to as an **extended partition** can be created on any unused disk space that remains. In addition, the extended partition may be subdivided into 23 **logical drives** (the letters of the alphabet minus a, b, and c). These drives are dependent on the extended partition, so it cannot be deleted if logical drives have been defined within it.

<table>
<tr><td>primary partition</td></tr>
<tr><td>extended partition</td></tr>
<tr><td>logical drives</td></tr>
</table>

When the primary partition is created on a hard disk, a special table is created in its **master boot sector** called the **partition table**. This table is used to store information about the partitions and logical drives on the disk. It includes information about where each partition and logical drive begins and ends on the physical drive. This is expressed in terms of beginning and ending track numbers. Each time a logical drive is added to the system, a complete disk structure, including a boot sector and preliminary directory management structure, is created. Its beginning and ending locations are also recorded in the partition table when the new drive is created.

> **NOTE**
>
> When a drive is partitioned in the Microsoft operating system environment, each logical drive is assigned a different drive letter (such as C, D, E, and so on) to identify it to the system.

<table>
<tr><td>master boot sector</td></tr>
<tr><td>partition table</td></tr>
</table>

The table also includes a setting that identifies the partition or logical drive that is **active**. The active partition is the logical drive that the system will boot to. On a partitioned drive, only one logical drive can be active at a time. When the system checks the drive's master boot sector looking for a **master boot record** (**MBR**) during bootup, it encounters the partition table and checks it to determine which portion of the disk has been marked as active. With this information, the system jumps to the first track of the active partition and checks its boot sector for a **partition boot record** (an MBR for that partition). If an operating system has been installed in this partition, the boot sector will contain an MBR for it, and the system will use it to boot up with. This arrangement enables a single physical disk to hold different operating systems that the system can boot to.

<table>
<tr><td>active</td></tr>
<tr><td>master boot record (MBR)</td></tr>
<tr><td>partition boot record</td></tr>
</table>

Most PCs can have multiple physical hard-disk drive units installed in them. In a system using a Microsoft operating system, the primary partition is on the first disk drive designated as drive C. The system files must be located in this partition, and the partition must be set to Active for the system to boot up from the drive.

In local and wide area networks, the concept of logical drives is carried a step further. A particular hard-disk drive may be a logical drive in a large system of drives along a peer-to-peer network. On the other hand, a very large centralized drive may be used to create several logical drives for a server/client type of network. Local area networks are covered in detail in Chapter 6, *Data Communications*.

Disk Management

In Windows 2000 and Windows XP, the disk portioning function is performed using the **Disk Management** utility. This utility can be used to partition drives, and both will show you the basic layout of the system's disks, including

- The size of each disk

- The size and file system type used in each logical drive

- The size and location of any unformatted (free) space on the drive

volumes

However, these advanced disk utilities can also provide many advanced functions associated with enterprise (large-scale business-oriented) computing systems. The Disk Management utility can be used to create both traditional primary and extended partitions for Windows 2000 and Windows XP systems. They can also be used to create **volumes** (partitions that involve space on multiple physical drives) like those shown in Figure 5-46.

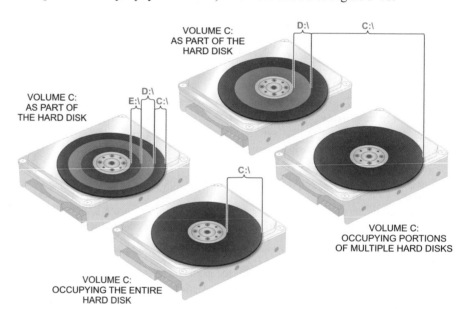

Figure 5-46: Volume Types

When newer operating system versions provided for partitions larger than 528 MB, another limiting factor for the size of disk partitions was encountered—the BIOS. The original AT-compatible BIOS featured a 504 MB capacity limit. To overcome this, newer BIOS include enhanced modes that employ special **logical block addressing (LBA)** techniques to utilize the larger partition sizes available through newer operating systems. This technique—known as **enhanced cylinder, heads, sectors (ECHS)**—effectively increases the number of R/W heads the system can recognize from 16 to 256. The maximum allowable disk drive parameters of 1024 cylinders, 63 sectors/track, and 512 bytes/sector remained unchanged.

logical block addressing (LBA)

enhanced cylinder, heads, sectors (ECHS)

The high-level format procedure is performed by the operating system and fills in or recreates the preliminary logical structures on the logical drive during the partitioning process. These structures tell the system what files are in the logical disk and where they can be found. Windows 2000 and Windows XP both support multiple types of file systems and partitions. In either of these systems, you may use the format process to create **file allocation table (FAT)** and **root directory** structures for the partition. These structures are compatible with older operating systems. However, their native files system structure relies on a more flexible **master file table (MFT)** structure used in the NTFS file management system. Chapter 9, *Operating System Fundamentals*, provides more detailed information about the organization of disks, including FATs, MFTs, and directory structures.

Hard-disk drives are the mainstays of mass data storage in PC-compatible systems. In modern PC systems, IDE and SCSI drives are most commonly used. Therefore, the computer technician must be able to successfully install and configure both IDE and SCSI drives, as well as other devices that employ IDE and SCSI interfaces. The following sections of the chapter cover the characteristics of these two interfaces, including standard variations and common connector types associated with each.

| file allocation table (FAT) |
| root directory |
| master file table (MFT) |

| low-level format |

NOTE

A **low-level format** routine marks off the disk into cylinders and sectors and defines their placement on the disk. System-level interface devices, such as IDE and SCSI drives, come with automatic low-level formatting routines already performed. Therefore, no low-level formatting needs to be performed on these drives before they can be partitioned and high-level formatted. Low-level formatting will not produce physical damage, but it may cause the loss of prerecorded bad track and sector information, as well as loss of information used to control the R/W heads for proper alignment over the tracks. If this occurs, it will normally be necessary to send the drive to the manufacturer to restore this information to the disk.

Installing CD-ROM/DVD Drives

Before installing an internal CD-ROM or DVD drive, confirm its master/slave/single, or SCSI ID configuration setting. Afterwards, install the drive unit in one of the drive bays, connect the power and signal cables, and load the drive's driver software if needed. (Due to their widespread use with portable systems, the procedure for installing external CD-ROM drives is presented in Chapter 7, *Portable Systems*.)

Figure 5-47 illustrates the installation of an internal CD-ROM drive. If the interface type is different than that of the HDD, it will be necessary to install a controller card in an expansion slot. Finally, refer to the drive's documentation regarding any necessary jumper or switch settings.

To connect the drive to the system, hook up the CD-ROM drive to the HDD signal cable, observing proper orientation. Connect the audio cable to the drive and to the sound card's **CD input** connection (if a sound card is installed).

| CD input |

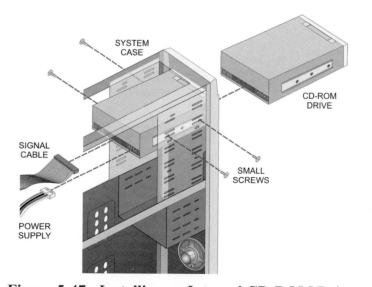

Figure 5-47: Installing an Internal CD-ROM Drive

Configuring CD-ROM Drives

As previously indicated, the CD-ROM drive must be properly configured for the system it is being installed in. In a PATA system, the master/slave setting must be confirmed. In a SCSI system, the ID setting must be correct. In a SCSI system, the only requirement is that a valid ID setting be configured. In a PATA system, however, some thought may be required as to how to configure the drive.

In a single-HDD system, the CD-ROM drive can be set up as the slave drive on the primary interface. However, the operation of the drives is much cleaner if the CD-ROM is set up as the master drive on the secondary PATA interface. In this manner, each drive has access to a full IDE channel instead of sharing one. Likewise, in a two-HDD system, the CD-ROM drive would most likely be configured as the master or single drive on the secondary interface. If the system also contains a sound card that has a built-in IDE interface, it should be disabled to prevent it from interfering with the primary or secondary interfaces. After the hardware has been installed, it will be necessary to install its software drivers.

Consult the drive's documentation for instructions on software installation. Typically, all that is required is to insert the OEM driver disk into the floppy drive, and follow the manufacturer's directions for installing the drivers. If the drive fails to operate at this point, reboot the system using single-step verification and check the information on the various boot screens for error messages associated with the CD-ROM drive.

Installing CDRW and DVDRW Drives

The hardware installation process involved with rewritable CD-ROM and DVD drives is identical to that used with standard CD-ROM and DVD drives. However, prior to the Windows XP operating system, rewritable CDRW and DVDRW drives required third-party application packages to perform write and rewrite functions. These applications had to be installed from the OEM CD that was packaged with the drive, or a CD obtained from an independent supplier.

In the Windows XP environment, rewritable drives are supported directly from the operating system and don't require any third-party applications. When you insert a blank disc in one of these drives, the operating system detects it and pops up a dialog box that asks you what you want to do with the disc. Most users still prefer to install a third-party program to manage all of the functions of these drives.

FDD Installation

The FDD installation procedure follows the sample procedure described earlier. Simply slide the FDD into one of the system unit's open drive bays, install two screws on each side to secure the drive to the system unit, and connect the signal and power cables to the drive. Figure 5-48 illustrates the steps required to install the floppy drive.

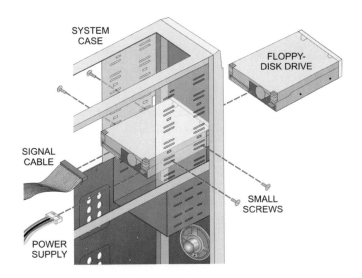

Figure 5-48: Installing a Floppy-Disk Drive

The PC-compatible FDD unit uses a 34-pin signal cable. The FDD signal cable is designed to accommodate two FDD units, as illustrated in Figure 5-49. If the drive is the only floppy in the system, or intended to operate as the A: drive, connect it to the connector at the end of the cable. If it is being installed as a B: drive, attach it to the connector toward the center of the cable. On older floppy drives, the cable connected to an edge connector on the drive's printed-circuit board. With newer units, the connection is made to a BERG connector.

┌─ **TEST TIP** ─────
Know what makes a floppy drive an A: or B: drive in a PC system.
└──────────────────

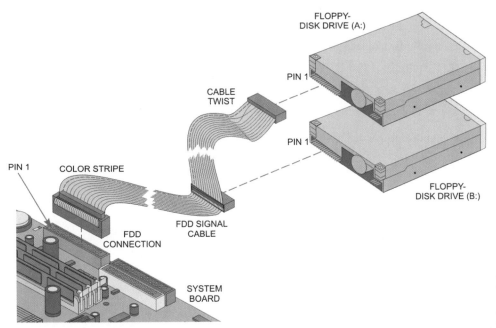

Figure 5-49: Connecting Floppy Drives

On some Pentium system boards and on all-in-one system boards, check the system board's documentation for an FDD enabling jumper and make certain that it is set correctly for the FDD installed. In newer systems, the FDD enabling function should be set in the Advanced CMOS Setup screen.

Reinstall the system unit's power cord and boot up the computer. As the system boots, move into the CMOS Setup utility and configure the CMOS for the type of FDD being installed.

Installing External Storage Devices

External storage devices normally connect to adapter cards installed in the system board's expansion slots. They also tend to employ separate, external power supply units. Several newer storage technologies, such as removable hard drive media, have been designed to take advantage of the enhanced parallel port specifications of modern systems. These devices can be connected directly to the system's parallel port, or can be connected to the system through another device that is connected to the port. The device's installation software is used to configure it for use in the system.

The general procedure for installing external storage devices is

1. Configure the device for operation.

   a. Refer to the device's user's manual regarding any IRQ and COM jumper or switch settings.
   b. Record the card's default IRQ and COM settings.
   c. Set the device's configuration jumpers to operate at the default setting.

2. Install the device's adapter card (if necessary).
   a. Turn the system off.
   b. Remove the cover from the system unit.
   c. Locate a compatible empty expansion slot.
   d. Remove the expansion slot cover from the rear of the system unit.
   e. Install the adapter card in the expansion slot.
   f. Reinstall the screw to secure the card to the back panel of the system unit.

3. Make the device's external connections.
   a. Connect the device's signal cable to the appropriate connector at the rear of the system.
   b. Connect the opposite end of the cable to the device.
   c. Verify that the power switch or power supply is turned off.
   d. Connect the power supply to the external storage unit.

4. Configure the device's software.
   a. Turn the system on.
   b. Check the CMOS Setup to ensure that the port setting is correct.
   c. Run the device's installation routine.

Essentials 1.2

IT Technician 1.1

DISK DRIVE UPGRADING AND OPTIMIZING

As with other modules in the PC, the hard disk and CD-ROM/DVD drives can be upgraded as new, or better, components become available, or as the system's application changes. PC technicians must be capable of upgrading the various components of the system—including its disk drives. The technician should also be able to optimize the operation of the drive to obtain the best performance possible for a given system configuration.

HDD Upgrading

One of the key components in keeping the system up to date is the hard-disk drive. Software manufacturers continue to produce larger and larger programs. In addition, the types of programs found on the typical PC are expanding. Many newer programs place high demands on the hard drive to feed information, such as large graphics files or digitized voice and video, to the system for processing.

Invariably, the system will begin to produce error messages that say that the hard drive is full. The first line of action is to use software disk utilities to optimize the organization of the drive. These utilities, such as **CHKDSK**, **SCANDISK**, and **DEFRAG**, are covered in detail in Chapter 12, *Operating System Troubleshooting*. The second step is to remove unnecessary programs and files from the hard drive. Programs and information that are rarely, or never, used should be moved to an archival media, such as removable disks or tape.

CHKDSK

SCANDISK

DEFRAG

In any event, there may come a time when it is necessary to determine whether the hard drive needs to be replaced in order to optimize the performance of the system. One guideline suggests that the drive should be replaced if the percentage of unused disk space drops below 20%.

Another reason to consider upgrading the HDD involves its ability to deliver information to the system. If the system is constantly waiting for information from the hard drive, replacing it should be considered as an option. Not all system slowdowns are connected to the HDD, but many are. Remember that the HDD is the mechanical part of the memory system, whereas everything else is electronic.

As with the storage space issue, HDD speed can be optimized through software configurations, such as a more efficient disk cache. However, once it has been optimized in this manner, any further speed increases must be accomplished by upgrading the hardware.

When considering an HDD upgrade, determine what the real needs are for the hard drive. Multimedia-intensive applications can place heavy performance demands on the hard-disk drive. Moving large image, audio, and video files into RAM on demand requires high performance from the drive. Critical HDD specifications associated with disk drive performance include:

- **Access Time**—The average time, expressed in milliseconds, required to position the drive's R/W heads over a specified track/cylinder and to reach a specified sector on the track.

Access Time

- **Track-Seek Time**—The amount of time required for the drive's R/W heads to move between cylinders and settle over a particular track following the seek command being issued by the system.

Track-Seek Time

- **Data Transfer Rate**—The speed, expressed in megabytes per second (MBps), at which data is transferred between the system and the drive.

Data Transfer Rate

These factors should be checked thoroughly when upgrading an HDD unit for speed-critical applications. In contemporary systems, the choice of hard drives for high-performance applications is between SATA drives and SCSI drives. The SATA drives are competitive and relatively easy to install, whereas the high-end SCSI specifications offer additional performance but require additional setup effort and an additional host adapter card.

Disk Drive Subsystem Enhancements

When upgrading a PATA hard drive, make sure that the system board supports the type of PATA drive you are installing. If your system board only supports ATA-100 drives, there is little reason to purchase an ATA-133 drive, unless you plan to upgrade the system board in the near future. Also verify that the correct cabling is being used to connect the new drive to the system. You should know that installing a new ATA-100 or ATA-133 drive in a system using the old 40-pin IDE cable will cause the drive's operation to be diminished to the level of the old drive. Without new cables, communications with the drives will be limited to the lesser standard determined by the 40-conductor signal cable. Check the master/slave jumper settings to see that they are correct for the new system before the drive is actually mounted in the system.

When upgrading SCSI systems, prepare a scheme for SCSI identification and termination ahead of time, and ensure that you have the necessary cabling and terminators. Take care to ensure that the new drive is correctly configured and terminated for its position in the system. Verify that the SCSI host adapter will support the new drive type. For example, a standard SCSI-I host adapter will not support a Fast-Wide SCSI drive. The physical cable and the communication speed differences between the two specifications will not match.

Likewise, when you upgrade a SCSI component, you should be aware that the SCSI host controller and the SCSI devices have the ability to adapt to lower functionality. If you upgrade one or more SCSI devices in a system, but do not upgrade the SCSI host adapter, then the devices will probably operate, but they will only operate at the maximum performance level of the adapter.

On the other hand, if you update the SCSI adapter and one or more SCSI devices, but you still have some older SCSI devices installed, devices that can operate at higher performance levels will attempt to do so. However, slower devices will work at their designated speed. The fact that the controller must slow down to work with the slower devices will effectively slow the operation of the entire SCSI system.

Before upgrading the HDD unit, make certain that the existing drive is providing all of the performance that it can. Check for VCACHE arrangements at the software configuration level and optimize them if possible. Also, determine how much performance increase can be gained through other upgrading efforts before changing out the hard drive.

If the drive is being upgraded substantially, such as from a 10 GB IDE drive to a 500 GB PATA drive, check the capabilities of the system's ROM BIOS. If the current BIOS does not support the drive type or size you intend to install, you must upgrade it to support the new hard drive installation. The best place to find out the type and size of hard drives your current BIOS supports is the system board's documentation. The best place to find out whether a new BIOS version is available to support the new hard drive is the system board manufacturer's Internet support site. This Web site typically makes provisions for downloading the new BIOS material and loader utility.

After the drive upgrade has been performed, you should verify the system's operation. When you start up the system, its POST routines will examine the drive's configuration and notify you if it has been detected. This is the most basic verification. An additional level of verification occurs at bootup. After the operating system starts up, you can open a file manager to see if the drive exists and how much space it presents to the system. You can also see the file system structure on the drive. In Figure 5-50, you can see the Windows 2000/XP Disk Management utility displaying information about a connected hard drive.

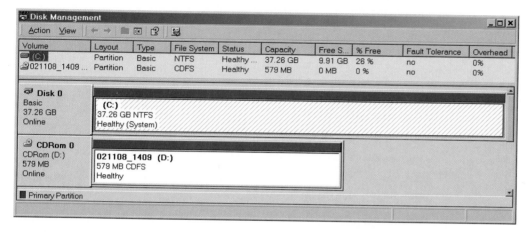

**Figure 5-50:
Windows 2000 Disk
Management Utility**

Finally, you should determine how much longer the unit in question is likely to be used before being replaced. If the decision to upgrade the HDD stands, ultimately, the best advice is to get the biggest, fastest hard drive possible. Don't forget that a different I/O bus architecture might add to the performance increase.

RAID Adapter Enhancements

RAID systems are available in two basic varieties—PATA and SCSI RAID systems. In each case, the components of the system include a RAID controller (usually an adapter card) and the RAID drives. At the center of each system is the RAID controller card. Therefore, the speed and efficiency of the RAID system cannot be upgraded with upgrading the adapter card.

If you are working with an ATA133 PATA RAID adapter and you install new PATA drives, the system will be limited to the operating speed and characteristics of the controller card. Likewise, if the RAID system is built on Wide SCSI 2 devices and you upgrade the drives to Wide-Fast SCSI 2 devices, the system would still function as a Wide SCSI 2 system.

GEEK SQUAD CASE FILE #15593

A customer's PATA hard drive is continually producing "Out of Hard Drive Space" error messages. These messages continue to be a problem even after you have optimized the drive through the Defrag utility and removed as much old information as possible. They are thinking of upgrading to a new high-speed, high-capacity 500 GB ATA-133 drive. What system considerations does the customer need to resolve before buying this drive?

KEY POINTS REVIEW

This chapter has explored the use of magnetic media to provide long-term, high-volume data storage for personal computer systems. Review the following key points before moving into the Review and Exam Questions sections to make sure you are comfortable with each point. Afterward, answer the Review Questions that follow to verify your knowledge of the information.

- From the beginning, most secondary memory systems have involved storing binary information in the form of magnetic charges on moving magnetic surfaces.

- The most common drive arrays are RAID systems. RAID is an acronym for redundant arrays of independent (inexpensive) disks. The RAID Advisory Board has established five major levels of RAID technology specifications.

- Soon after compact discs became popular for storing audio signals on optical material, the benefits of storing computer information in this manner became apparent. With a CD, data are written digitally on a light-sensitive material by a powerful, highly focused laser beam.

- The information on a compact disc is stored in one continuous spiral track, unlike floppy disks, where the data are stored in multiple, concentric tracks. The compact disc storage format still divides the data into separate sectors. However, the sectors of a CD-ROM disc are physically the same size. The disc spins counterclockwise, and it slows down as the laser diode emitter/detector unit approaches the outside of the disc.

- A Write Once, Read Many (WORM) drive allows users to write information to the disc once, and then retrieve this information as they would with a CD-ROM drive. With WORM drives, once data is stored on a disc, it cannot be changed or deleted.

- Tape drive units are another popular type of information storage system. These systems can store large amounts of data on small tape cartridges.

- Tape drives are generally used to store large amounts of information that will not need to be accessed often, or quickly. Such information includes backup copies of programs and data. This type of data security is a necessity with records such as business transactions, payroll, artwork, and so on.

- Operating systems can partition, or divide large physical drives into multiple logical drives. Each logical drive is identified by a different drive letter, such as C, D, E, etc.

- The high-level format procedure is performed by the operating system. This format routine creates a blank file allocation table (FAT) and root directory on the disk.

REVIEW QUESTIONS

The following questions test your knowledge of the material presented in this chapter.

1. What is the logical structure that replaces the function of the FAT on an NTFS drive?

2. Describe the process that the system used to determine where to boot from using a hard-disk drive with multiple partitions?

3. Name the tool that is used to perform partitioning in an NTFS system such as Windows 2000 and Windows XP.

4. In what order should SATA drives be connected to the host adapter or system board?

5. Name two types of HDD interfaces most commonly used with PC systems.

6. If you are installing a single PATA drive in a new computer, how would it be configured so that it appears to the system to be drives C:, D:, and E:?

7. What type of connector is used for the SATA signal connection to the system board?

8. What action should be taken if a SCSI drive option appears in the CMOS Setup Boot Sequence order after you've installed a new SATA drive?

9. Describe how data are stored on a magnetic disk.

10. List the steps you would use to install a hard-disk drive in a desktop system.

11. Describe the differences between the two types of drive array applications.

12. How and why is a cartridge tape different than a standard audiocassette tape?

13. Describe formatting as it applies to a magnetic disk.

14. What is the major procedural difference between installing a PATA drive and a SATA drive?

15. What is the main function of the high-level format?

EXAM QUESTIONS

1. RAID 0 is also known as ___.
   a. striped disk array
   b. mirroring
   c. duplexing
   d. parity

2. What action should always be taken before upgrading a hard-disk drive?
   a. Use the DOS VER command to determine what version of DOS is currently in use.
   b. Use the FDISK command to locate any lost cluster chains on the original drive.
   c. The contents of the installed drive should be backed up to some other media.
   d. Save the values of the installed drive's CMOS setup values for use with the new drive.

3. Head-to-disk interference (HDI) is also referred to as _____.
   a. a head crash
   b. R/W head bounce
   c. interleaving
   d. data compression

4. Identify the function that you would not employ on a SCSI drive when installing it.
   a. Low-level formatting
   b. Partitioning
   c. Formatting
   d. Installing the operating system on it

5. Where do the boot files in a Microsoft Windows system need to be located in order to boot the system?
   a. In the primary partition on the first disk drive
   b. In the extended partition on the first disk drive
   c. On the first disk drive
   d. In the master boot sector

6. The _____ partition is the partition that the system will boot to.
   a. active
   b. primary
   c. system
   d. extended

7. Which of the following is not a disk optimization utility?
   a. CHKDSK
   b. DEFRAG
   c. FDISK
   d. SCANDISK

8. What is the main purpose of a RAID 1 drive array?
   a. To act as an error-checking and correction method
   b. To create the appearance of one very large drive
   c. To act as a redundant data-backup method
   d. To act as a high-speed retrieval system

9. Which type of SCSI signal specification uses a core voltage of 3.3 V?
   a. LVD
   b. HVD
   c. Ultra Wide
   d. Single-Edged

10. Which IDE interface version employs an 80-wire, 40-pin cable?
    a. IDE
    b. ATA-2
    c. ATA-66
    d. EIDE

CHAPTER 6

DATA COMMUNICATIONS

OBJECTIVES

Upon completion of this chapter and its related lab procedures, you should be able to perform these tasks:

1.   Install internal and external modems.

2.   Define standard IP address classes.

3.   Install wireless networks.

4.   Describe the operation and hardware of an Ethernet LAN system.

5.   Differentiate among typical LAN topologies.

6.   Differentiate between different types of network media, including copper cabling, fiber cabling, and wireless connectivity.

7.   Define the term wide area network (WAN).

8.   Describe the function of routers, hubs, and bridges in network systems.

9.   Discuss basic concepts relating to Internet access (i.e., dial-up, ISP connections, browsers).

10.   Discuss ISDN, DSL, and cable modem connections.

11.   Describe FTP operations.

12.   Discuss common Internet concepts and terminology (such as e-mail).

13.   Discuss the purpose and use of Internet browsers.

DATA COMMUNICATIONS

FROM THE GEEK SQUAD

Mary A., Geek Squad Double Agent 245, is often called to perform installations and repairs at customer's homes. Today Agent 245 has been assigned to set up a small office network in a local residence. The network is supposed to interconnect five computers in the residence. The three computers in the home office handle e-mail and printing functions for the customer's home business. Printing, copying, and scanning functions are performed by a network-ready multifunction printer. The other computers are for personal use by the family. One functions as the home's media server and the other is a notebook computer that the family uses wirelessly from different rooms in the house.

Because the Geek Squad is called to perform tasks in both residential and small business settings, Agent 245 must be familiar with concepts and techniques associated with both residential and business network environments. In addition, she must be able to configure both peer-to-peer and client/server networks.

INTRODUCTION

The most explosive area of personal computer use is in the realm of data communications. Increasingly, personal computers are being connected to one another. Data communications can be as simple as connecting two units together so they can talk to each other. This can be accomplished by wiring their serial, or parallel, ports together when they are in close physical proximity to each other (up to a few feet). Communicating over longer distances requires additional hardware in the form of a modem, or a network card, and software, in the form of drivers and protocols.

When more than two computers are linked together so they can share information, a network is formed. Networks in a relatively confined geographical area are called local area networks (LANs), while networks distributed over wider geographical areas are referred to as wide area networks (WANs).

LOCAL AREA NETWORKS

Local area networks (LANs) are systems designed to connect computers together in relatively close proximity. These connections enable users attached to the network to share resources such as printers and modems. LAN connections also enable users to communicate with each other and share data among their computers.

Essentials 5.0

Technical Support 4.0

IT Technician 5.0

Local area networks (LANs)

Essentials 5.1

topology

protocol

When discussing LANs, there are two basic topics to consider: the LAN's **topology** (hardware connection method) and its **protocol** (communication control method). In concept, a minimum of three stations must be connected to have a true LAN. If only two units are connected, point-to-point communications software and a simple null modem could be employed.

LAN Topologies

Network topologies are physical connection/configuration strategies. LAN topologies fall into four types of configurations:

- **Bus**
- **Ring**
- **Star**
- **Mesh**

Bus

Ring

Star

Mesh

bus topology

nodes

stations

Figure 6-1 illustrates all four topologies. In the **bus topology**, the **nodes**, or **stations**, of the network connect to a central communication link. Each node has a unique address along the bus that differentiates it from the other users on the network. Information can be placed on the bus by any node. The information must contain the network address of the node, or nodes, that the information is intended for. Other nodes along the bus will ignore the information.

In a ring network configuration, the communication bus is formed into a closed loop. Each node inspects the information on the LAN as it passes by. A repeater, built into each ring LAN card, regenerates every message not directed to it and sends it to the next appointed node. The originating node eventually receives the message back and removes it from the ring.

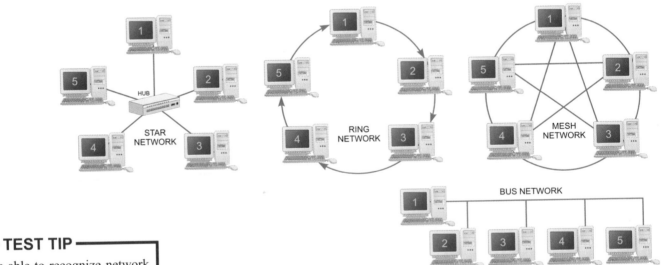

TEST TIP

Be able to recognize network topologies from this type of drawing.

Figure 6-1: Star, Bus, Ring, and Mesh Configurations

Ring topologies tend to offer very high data transfer rates but require additional management overhead. The additional management is required for dependability. If a node in a ring network fails, the entire network fails. To overcome this, ring designers have developed rings with primary and secondary data paths as depicted in Figure 6-2. If a break occurs in a primary link, the network controller can reroute the data onto the secondary link to avoid the break.

Ring topologies

star topology

In a **star topology**, the logical layout of the network resembles the branches of a tree. All the nodes are connected in branches that eventually lead back to a central unit. Nodes communicate with each other through the central unit. The central station coordinates the network's activity by polling the nodes, one by one, to determine whether they have any information to transfer. If so, the central station gives that node a predetermined slice of time to transmit. If the message is longer than the time allotted, the transmissions are chopped into small packets of information that are transmitted over several polling cycles.

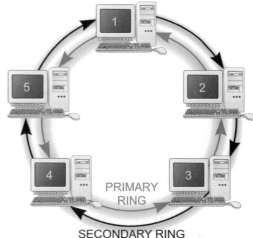

The **mesh design** offers the most basic network connection scheme. In this design, each node has a direct physical connection to all the other nodes in the network. While the overhead for connecting a mesh network topology together in a LAN environment is prohibitive, this topology is employed in two very large network environments—the public telephone system and the Internet.

Figure 6-2: Primary/ Secondary Ring Topologies

mesh design

Logical Topologies

It would be easy to visualize the connections of the **physical topologies** just described if the nodes simply connected to each other. However, this is typically not the case in newer LAN arrangements. This is due to the fact that most LAN installations employ connection devices, such as **hubs**, **switches**, and **routers**, which alter the appearance of the actual connection scheme. Therefore, the **logical topology** will not match the appearance of the physical topology. The particulars of the connection scheme are hidden inside the connecting device.

physical topologies

hubs

routers

logical topology

As an illustration, Figure 6-3 shows a typical network connection scheme using a router. The physical topology appears as a star. However, the internal wiring of the connecting router provides a logical bus topology. It is not uncommon for a logical ring or mesh topology to be implemented in a physical star topology.

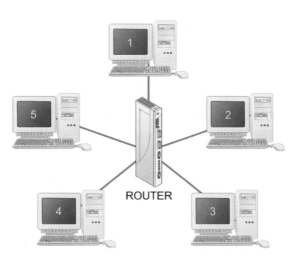

Figure 6-3: Logical Topologies

Network Connectivity Devices

While each computer or device attached to the network must have a **network interface adapter** capable of physically connecting to computer to the network transmission media, there are other connectivity devices that may be in the network to connect different portions of the network together and perform different network management functions. As described in the preceding section, these connectivity devices are usually *hubs*, *switches*, or *routers*. In large or complex networks, you may also find devices called *bridges* used to interconnect sections of the network. While each device provides physical connectivity, they also each have specific methods of operation that make them suitable for use in a specific network application. In some cases, a device with more features may be used to perform the functions of a lower-featured device.

A **hub** is a relatively simple connectivity device used to connect multiple network devices together so they work like a single segment. When it receives a packet of network information at one of its ports, it simply sends that information out to all its other ports, making it a repeater. Hubs are also referred to as concentrators, because their main function is to concentrate the network segment connections together in one place. However, hubs do possess some built-in intelligence that enables them to monitor its ports and detect excessive collisions (bad behavior) at a particular port and disconnect it from the other ports. This prevents a port from disabling the entire network segment. Hubs also provide port status lights that can be used to troubleshoot network connectivity problems. Hubs require a separate (usually DC) power supply to operate.

A **switch** connects network devices together to form a *local area network*. Instead of repeating a received messages at all its other ports, the switch can direct the information to its intended receiver if the address of the receiver is known. The switch keeps track of devices attached to it through a **media access control (MAC) address** table. All network devices have a MAC address assigned to them when they are manufactured. Because the information is sent only to the port where it is intended, the performance of the entire network is improved greatly. For this reason, switches have largely replaced hubs as the most basic connectivity device in local area networks. If the address is not known, the switch will broadcast the information to all of its ports in the same manner as a hub does. Like the hub, switches provide status lights for troubleshooting and require external power supplies to operate. Figure 6-4 shows a typical network switch connection scheme.

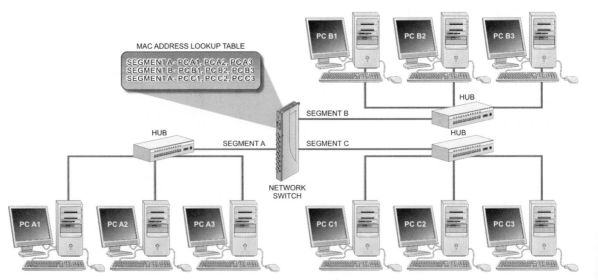

**Figure 6-4:
A Network
Switch
Connection**

Routers are network connectivity devices that forward network information in a manner similar to switches. However, unlike switches, routers can forward information across different network segments. This gives routers the ability to join different networks together through a process known as routing. For example, a router is commonly used to connect small residential networks to the biggest network in the world—the Internet.

Likewise, routers are used in commercial and governmental environments to break large networks up into more manageable subnetworks. This enables different sections of organizations to have their own network space while still being able to share information with other parts of the organization when needed. Such an *internetworked* arrangement increases the efficiency of all segments of the network by confining information moving *across* the network to only those things that need to be shared. Otherwise, local network traffic is confined within the local network by the presence of the router. Figure 6-5 illustrates using routers to break networks into individual segments.

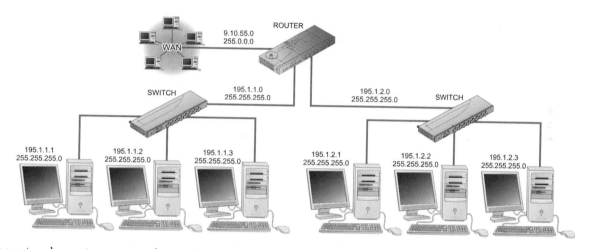

In large networks, routers communicate with other routers using a routing protocol to build and maintain routing tables. These tables are used to record the best route between different network locations. Unlike the MAC table used in switches, routing tables store address and *hop information* about the path between devices.

There is often confusion about connectivity devices because of the way they are marketed. For example, switch and router functions are sometimes built into the same piece of equipment and marketed as a multiport router. Routers may be labeled by the function they perform (e.g., a router connecting a network to the Internet may be referred to as an *edge router*, while a pair of routers simply connecting two network segments together are called *core routers*).

When the router is used to connect networks to always-on, broadband Internet connections they are referred to as **Internet gateways**. In addition to performing the routing functions, Internet Gateway routers typically supply a number of other Internet related services, such as automatic address assignments and firewall services. These services are described in detail later in this chapter. You may also encounter routing switches (called *LAN switches*) that have routing capabilities built into them.

A **network bridge**, sometimes referred to as a *network switch*, bridges network segments together and forwards traffic from one network to another. Like the switch, a bridge uses MAC addresses to guide information to the correct port; however, it also passes broadcast information to all of its ports. Therefore, the bridge gathers network connections into a single common segment while a router separates them into different segments. Figure 6-6 illustrates the operation of a network bridge.

Figure 6-5:
Segmenting a Network

Internet gateways

network bridge

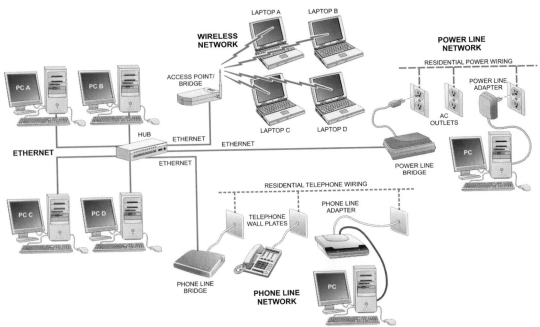

Figure 6-6:
Network Bridges

Essentials 5.1

NETWORK TRANSMISSION MEDIA

Basically, four media are used to transmit data between computers. These media include

- Copper cabling
- Fiber-optic cabling
- Infrared light
- Wireless radio frequency (RF) signals

noise immunity

Each media type offers advantages that make them useful for networking in certain conditions. The main media-related considerations include their cost to implement, maximum data transmission rates, and **noise immunity** characteristics.

In the implementation phase of a network, the cost to install the medium is a primary concern. This cost exists in two facets—the actual relative cost of the media and its adapter/connections and the cost associated with installing and configuring the network.

Bandwidth

Attenuation

Likewise, each media type has some limitations on its ability to transfer information. This factor is also wrapped up in two considerations—its bandwidth and its attenuation. **Bandwidth** is the media's total ability to carry data at a given instance. **Attenuation** is a measure of how much signal loss occurs as the information moves across the medium. As you will see in the following sections, some media types can literally carry a signal for miles and still deliver it as recognizable information.

To some degree the network transmission media determines the mode that can be used to transfer data back and forth. There are three basic transmission modes for transmitting data:

Simplex

- **Simplex** mode—Data is only transmitted in one direction.

- **Half Duplex** mode—Data can be transmitted in both direction, but only in one direction at a time. A walkie-talkie is the typical example used to describe this type of communications - users can only transmit information when they have access to the communication media.

- **Full Duplex** mode—Data can be transmitted in both directions at the same time. This effectively doubles the operating speed of a connection using this mode. The telephone system is the typical example of a full duplex communication system - users can talk and hear at any time a connection is present. Full duplex communications require either dual physical communication links or a multiplexer/demultiplexer system to separate transmitted and received data from each other on the same communication media.

Half Duplex

Full Duplex

The final media-related consideration is its noise immunity capabilities. Stray electrical energy (referred to as noise) moves through the atmosphere as a natural course. Electrical machines and devices can also generate electronic noise. These stray signals can interfere with organized data signals and make them unrecognizable. Therefore, cabling used to transmit data is expected to have some resistance to these stray signals.

Under the heading of copper cabling, there are basically two categories to consider—twisted-pair cabling and coaxial cabling. Twisted-pair cabling consists of two or more pairs of wires twisted together to provide noise reduction. The twist in the wires causes induced noise signals to cancel each other out. In this type of cabling, the number of twists in each foot of wire indicates its relative noise immunity level.

Twisted-Pair Cabling

When discussing twisted-pair cabling with data networks, there are two basic types to consider: **unshielded twisted pair (UTP)** and **shielded twisted pair (STP)**. UTP networking cable contains four pairs of individually insulated wires as illustrated in Figure 6-7. STP cable is similar with the exception that it contains an additional foil shield that surrounds the four-pair wire bundle. The shield provides extended protection from induced electrical noise and **cross talk** by supplying a grounded path to carry the induced electrical signals away from the conductors in the cable.

One of the specifications associated with the *physical* layer of the OSI model is the **EIA/TIA-568** specification for network wiring. Two groups have established this specification jointly—the Electronic Industry Association (EIA) and the Telecommunications Industry Association (TIA)—to standardize the use of UTP cable for different networking applications. These organizations have categorized different grades of cable along with connector, distance, and installation specifications to produce the EIA/TIA UTP wiring **category (CAT) ratings** for the industry (i.e., CAT 3, CAT 5, CAT 5e, and CAT 6 cabling).

The telephone cabling inside residence and office buildings is typically **CAT3** cabling. The CAT3 cabling is made up of three pairs of conductors. The wire pairs are made up of a tip and a ring wire. These terms are used for polarity purposes and are carried over from old RCA telephone plugs and jacks. These plugs had an electrical contact point at the tip of the plug and another through a ring around the shaft of the plug. The voltage applied to the tip wire is 0 Vdc, whereas the ring voltage is −48 Vdc (this voltage level is specific to the phone line at the company office [CO]—it is less at a residence or business location due to voltage drop of 5 Vdc to 12 Vdc along the transmission line).

unshielded twisted pair (UTP)

shielded twisted pair (STP)

cross talk

EIA/TIA-568

category (CAT) ratings

CAT

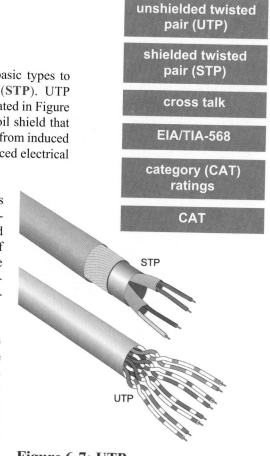

STP

UTP

Figure 6-7: UTP and STP Cabling

Table 6-1 lists tip and ring pairing for different types of cabling used to handle analog voice communications. The polarity of these wires is very important in DSL installations.

Table 6-1: Tip and Ring Wiring

	TIP	RING
Residential Cabling		
Pair 1	Green	Red
Pair 2	Black	Yellow
Pair 3	White	Blue
RJ-11 Plugs and Jacks		
Pair 1	3	4
Pair 2	5	2
Pair 3	1	6
Business Cabling		
Pair 1	White/Blue Band	Blue/White Band
Pair 2	White/Orange Band	Orange/White Band
Pair 3	White/.Green Band	Green/White Band
Pair 4	White/Brown Band	Brown/White Band
RJ-45 Plugs and Jacks		
Pair 1	5	4
Pair 2	3	6
Pair 3	1	2
Pair 4	7	8

CAT5

CAT5e

CAT6

CAT 5 cabling is still currently the most widely used specification for data communication wiring. However, an enhanced **CAT 5e** version adds far-end cross talk prevention to provide higher performance capabilities. It is often used for 1000Base-T networks. These cables are used in networks that operate at speeds of 10 Mbps, 100 Mbps, and 1 Gbps.

Table 6-2: UTP Cable Category Ratings

CATEGORY	MAXIMUM BANDWIDTH	WIRING TYPES	APPLICATIONS
3	16 MHz	100 Ω UTP; Rated Category 3	10 Mbps Ethernet; 4 Mbps Token Ring
4	20 MHz	100 Ω UTP; Rated Category 4	10 Mbps Ethernet; 16 Mbps Token Ring
5	100 MHz	100 Ω UTP; Rated Category 5	100 Mbps TPDDI; 155 Mbps ATM
5e	160 MHz	100 Ω UTP; Rated Category 5E	1.2 Gbps 1000Base-T High-Speed ATM
6	250 MHz	100 Ω UTP; Rated Category 6	1.2 Gbps 1000Base-T High-Speed ATM and beyond
7 Proposed	600–862 MHz	100 Ω UTP; Rated Category 7	1.2 Gbps 1000Base-T High-Speed ATM and beyond

The Category 6 (**CAT6**) specification provides even stricter regulation that gives it performance levels up to 250 MHz. CAT6 is backward compatible with CAT3 and CAT5/5e specifications. It can be used in 10Base-T, 100Base-TX, and 1000Base-T (Gigabit Ethernet) networks. Like CAT5, CAT6 has four wire pairs of 23 AWG copper wire (slightly larger than 24 AWG wire used in CAT5).

CAT 5/5e and CAT 6 cables have a maximum length of 100 meters. This measurement includes a 90-meter horizontal cable designation and 10 meters of drop (connection) cables on either end. Table 6-2 lists the industry's various CAT cable ratings that apply to UTP data communications cabling.

┌─ **TEST TIP** ─────────
│ Know what type of cabling is
│ involved in the CAT 5 cable
│ rating.
└──────────────────────

The connector and color-coded connection schemes specified for 4-pair, EIA/TIA 568-A and 568-B CAT 5 and CAT 6 UTP network cabling configurations are illustrated in Figure 6-8. In both cases, the UTP cabling is terminated in an 8-pin RJ-45 plug. The color codes for attaching the connector to the cable are also provided in the figure.

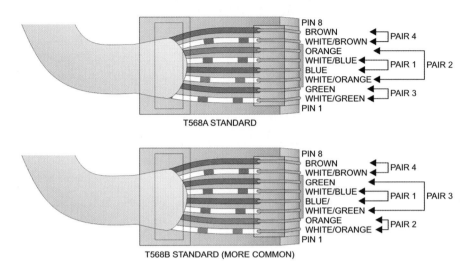

Figure 6-8: UTP Cable Connection Specifications

UTP LAN connections are made through modular RJ-45 registered jacks and plugs. RJ-45 connectors are similar in appearance to the RJ-11 connectors used with telephones and modems. However, the RJ-45 connectors are considerably larger than the RJ-11 connectors. Some Ethernet adapters include 15-pin sockets that enable special systems, such as fiber-optic cabling, to be interfaced to them. Other cards provide specialized ST connectors for fiber-optic connections.

IDC Connections

While UTP cabling is typically terminated in an RJ-45 connector at the computer end of the network, other types of connectors are used when the cables become part of the structured wiring of a facility. These connections are normally made in areas of the facility designated as the entrance facility or the telecommunications closet.

A standard method for terminating telecommunications wiring at these locations is to route all the data/telecommunications wiring to a connection block that employs an **insulation displacement connector (IDC)**. This connection method offers faster installation and more reliable connections.

IDCs do not require the conductors to be stripped of their insulation. Instead, the conductor is forced into a terminal strip, which not only holds it firmly in place, but also pierces the insulation to make an electrical connection.

The two most common styles of IDC are the **type-66** and **type-110 termination blocks**, depicted in Figure 6-9. Older type-66 blocks are insulation displacement system designed to wire up telephones and similar communications systems. They usually contain 200 metal slots (for interfacing 50 pairs from two sources), and come in various formats for those pins.

insulation displacement connector (IDC)

type-66 termination blocks

type-110 termination blocks

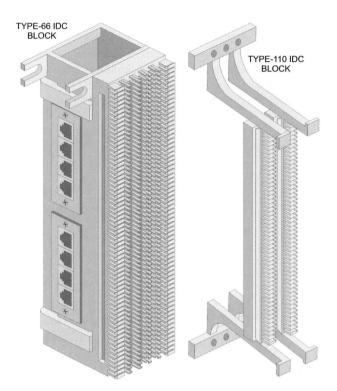

TYPE-66 IDC
BLOCK

TYPE-110 IDC
BLOCK

Figure 6-9:
IDC Connection

They are designed to work with solid wire (22- to 26-gauge), which is forced or "punched" into each slot, displacing the insulation and making the connection. Although they were not originally intended for use in data connections, some newer versions are used for this purpose.

Type-110 blocks are newer types of IDC blocks that occupy less space than type-66 blocks for an equal number of connections. These blocks are more likely to be rated for CAT 5 wire than type-66 blocks, and often have RJ-11 or RJ-45 connectors already attached to them.

Computer and network technicians are not typically involved with these connections, but be aware that they exist as part of the communications infrastructure that enables them to communicate outside their local facility.

Coaxial Cable

Coaxial cable (often referred to simply as "coax") is familiar to most people as the conductor that carries cable TV into their homes. Coaxial cable is constructed with an insulated solid or stranded wire core surrounded by a dielectric insulating layer and a solid or braided metallic shield. Both the wire and shield are wrapped in an outer protective insulating jacket, as illustrated in Figure 6-10.

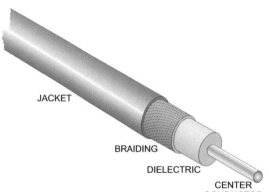

JACKET

BRAIDING

DIELECTRIC

CENTER
CONDUCTOR

Figure 6-10:
Coaxial Cable

In the past, coaxial cable was widely used for Ethernet LAN media. However, because the thickness and rigidity of coaxial cable make it difficult and time consuming to install, the networking industry and network standards development groups have abandoned coaxial cable in favor of unshielded twisted pair cabling.

Coax cable continues to be used for some applications, such as Internet service delivered to residential settings through the commercial cable television (CATV) system. In addition, several varieties of coaxial cable are available for transporting video and high-data rate digital information. This comes into play as computers, audio/video equipment, and intelligent home products with residential networks.

Coaxial Cable Specifications

Typically, coax cable is specified by an **RG rating** that is appropriate for a given application (such as RG-58 cable for use in Ethernet data network applications or RG-59 for CATV). The "RG" designation stands for radio grade, a term used in military specifications. Some grades of coaxial cable have similar outer appearances (i.e., RG-58 and RG-59). However, it is not advisable to mix different cable and terminator specifications as we once did when we switched from an older ArcNet LAN to an Ethernet LAN. Make sure that you have the correct grade of cable and the corresponding correct terminator for the intended coaxial application.

RG rating

Coaxial cables are typically categorized according to their size (diameter), shielding and core construction, type of dielectric, impedance, velocity factor, fire rating, and attenuation rating.

- *RG-6*—RG-6 coaxial cable is the preferred type of coaxial cable for residential structured wiring. It is widely used for video distribution and also for connecting satellite receiving antenna systems to standard, digital, and high-definition television (HDTV) receivers. RG-6 cable has an impedance of 75 ohms and uses 18-gauge wire. This type of coaxial cable connects to equipment through a threaded "F" connector.

- *RG-8*—Referred to as **Thicknet** coax cabling, RG-8 was widely used in 10Base-5 Ethernet networking. RG-8 cable has an impedance of 50 ohms and uses 19/10-gauge wire centers. The Thicknet cable does not actually connect to the network adapter in the computer. Instead, a device called a **medium attachment unit (MAU)** is inserted in line with the cable as illustrated in Figure 6-11. An interface cable referred to as an **attachment unit interface (AUI)** connects the MAU to the network adapter card through a 15-pin AUI cable.

Thicknet

medium attachment unit (MAU)

attachment unit interface (AUI)

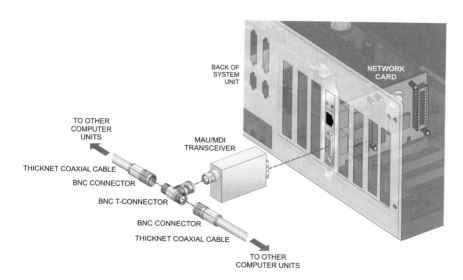

Figure 6-11: Thicknet Connections

- *RG-58*—**Thinnet** Ethernet cabling used for 10Base-2 networks. RG-58 cable has an impedance of 50 ohms and uses 24-gauge wire centers. These cables attach to equipment through BNCs (British Naval Connectors). In 10Base-2 LANs, the node's LAN adapter card is usually connected directly to the LAN cabling, using a T-connector for peer-to-peer networks, or a BNC connector in a client/server LANs.

- *RG-59*—RG-59 cable is widely used for CATV and video services. It is similar in appearance to RG-58 cabling.

Fiber-Optic Cable

Fiber-optic cable is plastic or glass cable designed to carry voice or digital data in the form of light pulses. The signals are introduced into the cable by a laser diode and bounce along its interior until they reach the end of the cable, as illustrated in Figure 6-12. At the end, a light-detecting circuit receives the light signals and converts them back into usable information. This type of cabling offers potential signaling rates in excess of 200,000 Mbps. However, current access protocols still limit fiber-optic LAN speeds to 100 Mbps.

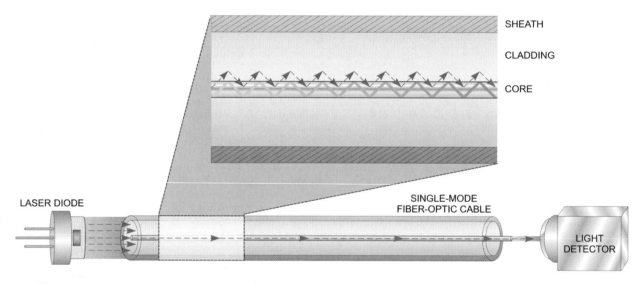

**Figure 6-12:
Transmitting Over
Fiber-Optic Cable**

Because light moving through a fiber-optic cable does not attenuate (lose energy) as quickly as electrical signals moving along a copper conductor, segment lengths between transmitters and receivers can be much longer with fiber-optic cabling. In some fiber-optic applications, the maximum cable length can range up to 2 kilometers.

Fiber-optic cable also provides a much more secure data transmission medium than copper cable, because it cannot be tapped without physically breaking the conductor. Basically, light introduced into the cable at one end does not leave the cable except through the other end. In addition, fiber-optic cable electrically isolates the transmitter and receiver so that no signal level matching normally needs to be performed between the two ends.

Getting the light out of the cable without significant attenuation is the key to making fiber-optic connections. The end of the cable must be perfectly aligned with the receiver and be free from scratches, film, or dust that would distort or filter the light.

Fiber-Optic Cable Types

As indicated earlier in this chapter, fiber-optic cabling offers the prospect of very high-performance links for LAN implementation. It can handle much higher data-transfer rates than copper conductors and can use longer distances between stations before signal deterioration becomes a problem. In addition, fiber-optic cable offers a high degree of security for data communications: Because it does not radiate EMI signal information that can be detected outside the conductor, it does not tap easily, and it shows a decided signal loss when it is tapped into

There are two basic types of fiber-optic cabling used in networking applications. These are

- *Multimode Fiber-Optic Cable*—**Multimode fiber-optic cable** is designed so that light travels in many paths from the transmitter to the receiver. Light rays that enter the cable reflect off the cladding at different angles as they move along the length of the cable. These rays disperse in the cladding and are useless as signals. Only those light rays introduced to the core of the cable within a range of critical angles will travel down the cable. Even with the excessive signal attenuation created by this method, it is still the most commonly used cable type, because it is cheaper and will transmit light over sufficient distances for use in local area networks.

- *Single-Mode Fiber-Optic Cable*—In a **single-mode fiber-optic cable**, the diameter of the core is reduced so that just one wavelength of the light source will travel down the wire. The light source for this type of cable is a laser. Laser diodes (LDs) produce the in-phase, single-frequency, unidirectional light rays required to travel down such a cable. These cables are normally reserved for use in high-speed, long-distance cable runs.

Figure 6-13 depicts two types of fiber-optic connectors. The connector on the top is a **SC connector**, and the one on the bottom is a **straight tip (ST) connector**. The SC connector is the dominant connector for fiber-optic Ethernet networks. In both cases, the connectors are designed so that they correctly align the end of the cable with the receiver.

Two newer connectors you may find when dealing with fiber optic network connectivity include the LC connector and the MT-RJ connector. The LC connector is a small form factor (half size) SC connector developed by Lucent Technologies for use in telephone environments. Likewise, The MTRJ connector is a small form factor fiber optic connector that resembles an RJ-45 connector. It was designed by AMP to provide an inexpensive, easy to implement fiber connection method. These smaller fiber connectors provide higher connection densities than the ST and SC connectors and are as easy to connect and disconnect as RJ-11 and RJ-45 connectors. In addition, they fit in conventional RJ-45 faceplates and patch panel openings. Figure 6-14 depicts the LC and MT-RJ connectors.

Multimode fiber-optic cable

single-mode fiber-optic cable

SC connector

> **TEST TIP**
>
> Know that single-mode and multimode are the two types of fiber-optic cable.

Straight Tip (ST) connector

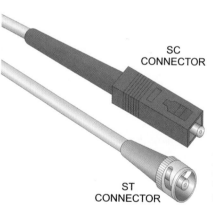

SC CONNECTOR

ST CONNECTOR

**Figure 6-13:
Fiber-Optic Cable
Connectors**

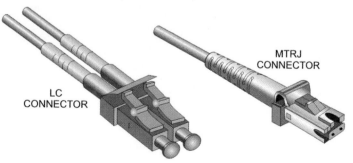

LC CONNECTOR

MTRJ CONNECTOR

**Figure 6-14:
Small Form
Factor Fiber
Connectors**

Plenum Cable

Another important rating for all cable types comes into play when you must install a cable in a space that is primarily involved in moving air throughout a facility. According to the *National Electrical Code* 2005 (NEC), a **plenum** is "a compartment or chamber to which one or more air ducts are connected and that forms part of the air distribution system." Likewise, the BICSI (*Building Industry Consulting Services International*) standards organization defines *plenum* as "a designated closed or open area that is used for transport of environmental air."

According to the *National Electrical Code*, when you install cables in plenums, you must use special plenum rated cables that are listed as "Type CMP" (Communications Plenum) cable. In certain cases, "Type MPP" (Multipurpose Plenum) Cables offer an acceptable substitute for Type CMP cables. **Plenum rated cables** are suitable for use in ducts, plenums, and other spaces used for environmental air because they have adequate fire-resistant and low smoke-producing characteristics. The reason for this requirement is that when the protective insulation placed around cabling burns, it gives off toxic gases. If these cables are located in a plenum area, the dangerous gases will be spread throughout the facility as part of the air circulation system.

Wireless Infrared Links

The **IrDA** infrared transmission specification makes provisions for multiple IrDA devices to be attached to a computer so that it can have multiple, simultaneous links to multiple IrDA devices. Figure 6-15 shows how IrDA links can be used to share computers and devices through a normal Ethernet hub. In these scenarios, the IrDA link provides the high-speed transmission media between the Ethernet devices.

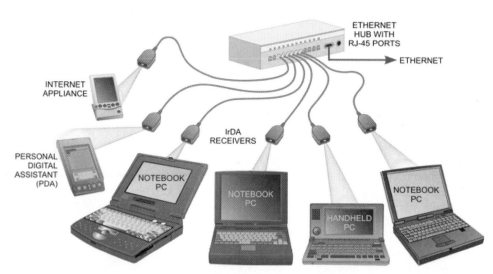

**Figure 6-15:
IrDA Networking**

One drawback of infrared transmissions in general is that they only provide line-of-sight communications over short distances and can be interfered with easily. In addition, they have very narrow lines of site (15 degrees of center with the line of transmission). IrDA devices cannot offer dependable communication paths if an object, such as a person, interrupts the path of the light from the transmitter to the receiver. And they also cannot penetrate walls or other solid objects and cannot communicate around corners.

Wireless RF Links

Recently, a variety of **wireless local area networking (WLAN** or **LAWN)** specifications have been introduced into the market. These networks connect computer nodes together using high-frequency radio waves. The IEEE organization has presented a specification titled IEEE-802.11 to describe its wireless networking standard. The IEEE-802.11b wireless standard originally gained wide acceptance as the preferred wireless networking technology for both business and home network applications. Most current wireless LANs are based on this specification and operate at transfer rates in the range of 1 Mbps.

The wireless networking community is working with two **spread spectrum** technologies as the basis of their transmission method. In spread spectrum transmissions, the frequency of the radio signal hops in a random, defined sequence that is known to the receiving device. These technologies are referred to as **frequency hopping spread spectrum (FHSS)** and **direct sequence spread spectrum (DSSS)**. The FHSS method spreads the signal across the time spectrum using **time division multiplexing (TDM)** techniques. The DSSS method combines the data with a faster carrier signal according to a predetermined frequency spreading ratio for transmission.

Time division multiple access (TDMA) technology employs TDM to divide a radio carrier signal into time-slices, called **cells**, and then funnel data from different sources into the cells. This technique enables a single-frequency signal to serve a number of different customers simultaneously. A similar technology known as **CDMA (code division multiple access)** does not assign users a specific frequency. Instead, it spreads the user's data across a range of frequencies in a random digital sequence.

A typical wireless LAN, depicted in Figure 6-16, consists of a device known as an **access point** and any number of wireless network-capable devices. The wireless access point acts as a bridging device that connects the wireless network computers with the wired network. The access point uses antennas and a radio receiver/transmitter to communicate with the other devices through radio frequency signals in the unlicensed 2.4 GHz radio band. Conversely, it communicates with the host computer through a physical interface known as an Ethernet hub or router, which provides connectivity between the access point and the wired Ethernet LAN.

wireless local area networking (WLAN or LAWN)
spread spectrum
frequency hopping spread spectrum (FHSS)
direct sequence spread spectrum (DSSS)
time division multiplexing (TDM)
Time division multiple access (TDMA)
cells
CDMA (code division multiple access)
access point

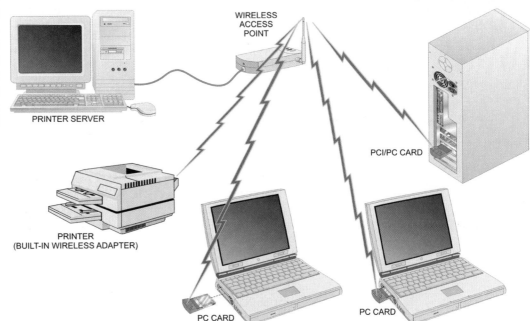

Figure 6-16: A Wireless LAN

Wireless network client computers also require a network interface consisting of a radio transmitter, receiver, and antenna. **Wireless LAN (WLAN) adapters** for PCs are typically available in the form of plug-in PCI and PCMCIA cards, or as attachable USB devices.

Each client computer that has a wireless network interface can communicate with other wireless equipped computers or with the access point. Wireless network computers are also able to communicate with wired network computers on an Ethernet LAN using the access point as the connection between the two networks.

Even though wireless networks are gaining popularity for their ease of installation, some security issues remain concerning using them to communicate personal or otherwise sensitive information. The following list describes the fundamental pros and cons associated with wireless networking:

┌─ **TEST TIP** ─────┐

Know what type of device is the main connection device used with 802.11b wireless networks.

- *Installation flexibility*—Wireless LANs provide the maximum amount of flexibility for connecting home and office networking components. Because no wires are required to connect devices to the wireless network, the users have considerable mobility. Laptop computers may be used throughout the home as long as they are within range of other wireless terminals or the access point. Installing the needed adapter cards and network software is all that is necessary to start sharing data and resources.

- *Services for mobile users*—Typical distances covered by wireless LANs are limited to specific indoor office locations or retail business locations called "hotspots." These are WiFi-enabled locations where customers with wireless-equipped portable computers can connect to the Internet while enjoying a coffee break or snack such as in an airport, hotel lobby, fast food restaurant, or coffee shop. WiFi is a trademark used by wireless LANs that operate on unlicensed radio spectrum and are therefore restricted to limited transmitter power covering an area of 200−300 feet from the antenna.

- *Security issues*—Transmissions from wireless network devices cannot simply be confined to the local environment of a home or business. Although the range is limited to a few hundred feet, radio signals can easily be intercepted even outside the vicinity of the stated security perimeter. Any other unauthorized mobile terminal can accomplish this using an 802.11 receiver. In order to minimize the risk of security compromise on a wireless LAN, the IEEE-802.11b standard provides a security feature called **wired equivalent privacy (WEP)**. WEP provides a method for encrypting data transmissions and authenticating each computer on the network. The 802.11b standard is discussed in detail later in this chapter.

- *Multipath problems and signal strength*—Signal strength at the received nodes on a wireless LAN can be impacted by signals bouncing off walls and objects in an indoor environment. The radio waves may arrive from multiple directions and in some cases can cancel or severely reduce the signal strength between portable users.

This effect is called multipath and is eliminated by analyzing the signals with test instruments or moving the nodes to a different location. Microwave radio emissions from other devices using the unlicensed 2.4 GHz radio spectrum are also a source of electromagnetic interference. The WLAN adapter cards and the access point should be installed in such a way that they provide the maximum exposure for the antenna to maximize signal strength.

Although there are still problems to overcome, the wireless network is becoming a popular option for connecting devices in the home and small office environments. It is also becoming an economical choice for locations where installing cable is not practical or is prohibited by historic building codes or other restrictions. Home networks where maximum flexibility and mobility for the network devices is desired also make wireless LAN technology an attractive technology.

Bluetooth Wireless

Although WiFi networks dominate the desktop and portable computer networking environment, a separate networking specification for **personal area networks** (**PANs**) has gained widespread acceptance. This specification is called **Bluetooth** (or **IEEE-802.15.1**) and was developed by a consortium made up of Ericsson, IBM, Intel, Nokia, and Toshiba as an avenue to connect and exchange information between personal devices such as PDAs, cell phones, and digital cameras, as well as PCs, notebooks, and printers. The meshing together of personal computers, cell phones, Web devices, LAN devices, and other intelligent devices in a common forum is referred to as **convergence**. The Bluetooth specification is intended to promote convergence of these systems.

Bluetooth devices use low power consumption, short-range radio frequency signals to provide a low-cost, secure communication link. The specification provides three power level/range options that include 100 mW/100 meters, 2.5 mW/10 meters, and 1 mW/1 meter.

Bluetooth employs **adaptive frequency hopping spread spectrum** (**AFHSS**) in the license-free 2.4 GHz range to provide security and avoid crowded frequency ranges. The Bluetooth protocol divides the 2.4 GHz frequency range into 79 1 MHz communication channels. The frequency hopping mechanism changes channels up to 1600 times per second. The data transfer rate for Bluetooth 1.1 and 1.2 devices is 723.1 Kbps, and it is 2.1 Mbps for Bluetooth 2.0 devices.

The most widely used application of Bluetooth is to provide point-to-point wireless communications between cell phone and hands-free headsets. It is also used to provide point-to-point communications between MP3 players, PDAs and digital cameras, and host computer systems. These devices can only be connected to one device at a time and connecting to them will prevent them from connecting to other devices and showing up in inquiries until they disconnect the other device. However, the standard also provides for constructing multi-point wireless networks using Bluetooth technologies.

Under the Bluetooth specification, up to eight devices can be grouped together to form a **piconet**. Any device can become the **master device** and assume control of the network by issuing a request broadcast. The other seven devices become **slave devices** until the master device releases its position. The master device uses time division multiplexing to rapidly switch from one slave device to another around the network. In this manner, the Bluetooth network operates like a wireless USB network. Any device in the network can assume the master device role when it is available.

> personal area networks (PANs)
>
> Bluetooth
>
> IEEE-802.15.1
>
> convergence
>
> adaptive frequency hopping spread spectrum (AFHSS)
>
> piconet
>
> master device
>
> slave devices

Essentials 5.1

NETWORK CONTROL STRATEGIES

When you begin to connect computers and devices together so that they can share resources and data, the issue of who will control the network (and how) comes up very quickly. In some applications, such as developing a book like this one, it is good for the author, artists, and pagination people to be able to share access to text and graphics files, as well as access to devices such as printers. However, in a business network, companies must have control over who can have access to sensitive information and company resources, as well as when and how much.

Control of a network can be implemented in two ways:

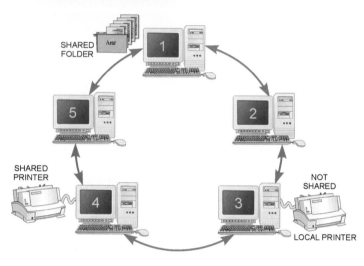

peer-to-peer network

client/server network

file server

1. As a **peer-to-peer network** where each computer is attached to the network in a ring or bus fashion and is equal to the other units on the network.

2. As a **client/server network** where dependent workstations, referred to as clients, operate in conjunction with a dedicated master computer (**file server**).

Figure 6-17 illustrates a typical peer-to-peer network arrangement. In this arrangement, the users connected to the network can share access to different network resources, such as hard drives and printers. However, control of the local unit is fairly autonomous. The nodes in this type of network configuration usually contain local hard drives and printers that the local computer has control of. These resources can be shared at the discretion of the individual user. A common definition of a peer-to-peer network is one in which all of the nodes can act as both clients and servers of the other nodes under different conditions.

Figure 6-18 depicts a typical client/server LAN configuration. In this type of LAN, control tends to be very centralized. The server typically holds the programs and data for its client computers. It also provides security and network policy enforcement.

Figure 6-17: A Peer-to-Peer Network

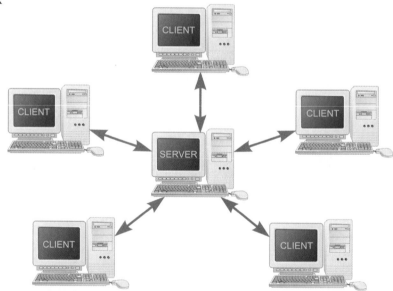

Figure 6-18: A Client/Server Network

workstation

In some cases, the client units do not even include a local hard drive or floppy drive unit. The bootup process is performed through an onboard BIOS, and no data are stored at the client machine. This type of client is referred to as a diskless **workstation**.

The major advantages of the client/server networking arrangement include

- Centralized administration
- Data and resource security

┌─ **TEST TIP** ─────────────────┐
│ Know the characteristic differences │
│ between peer-to-peer and client/server │
│ networks. │
└────────────────────────────────┘

GEEK SQUAD CASE FILE #33213

ACME Publishers has contacted your Geek Squad store about setting up a new production room for creating textbooks and multimedia presentations. They will employ writers, artists, document layout and paste up professionals, multimedia animators, and multimedia presentation designers. Their board of directors has asked you for input about how to set up the system. They anticipate tying everyone into the company's existing client/server network, but someone has suggested looking into peer-to-peer networks. What will you recommend to them and why?

GEEK SQUAD CASE FILE #63605

The ACME Publishing board of directors has asked you to give them a report on implementing a peer-to-peer network for the entire company. This would include the development room from challenge 1 and would also include the accounting office, the technical services department, and the warehouse/shipping department. They have been told that peer-to-peer networks are relatively inexpensive and very flexible. What would you tell them about implementing this idea?

Networking Protocols

Essentials 5.1

Technical Support 4.1

IT Technician 5.1

When more than two computers are involved in the communications pathway, a network is formed, and additional controls must be put into place to make certain that information is sent to the correct member of the network. This is in addition to controlling the flow of information on the network connection. A **network protocol** is a set of rules that governs how communications are conducted across a network. In order for devices to communicate with each other on the network, they must all use the same network protocol.

network protocol

While there are many different types of network protocols in use throughout the world, there are four that are widely accepted and must typically be dealt with in normal network environments:

- *NetBEUI*—**NetBIOS enhanced user interface (NetBEUI)** is a fast, efficient protocol, suitable for use on smaller Microsoft networks. It doesn't require any configuration to implement and is very simple to administer. NetBEUI is the fastest networking protocol because it has very low nondata overhead. However, NetBEUI is not a routable protocol, and therefore, it cannot be used in complex, multisegment networks that use routers. Therefore, the NetBEUI protocol is not used much anymore, because the TCP/IP protocol has become the protocol of choice for most networks.

NetBIOS extended user interface (NetBEUI)

- *NWLink*—NWLink is Microsoft's version of the **internetwork packet exchange/sequenced packet exchange (IPX/SPX)** network protocol used in Novell NetWare environments. While NetWare has used IPX/SPX for the majority of its networking functions, with the release of NetWare 5.0 Novell changed NetWare's primary protocol from IPX/SPX to TCP/IP. Even so, the majority of the installed NetWare networks continue to run IPX/SPX for at least some networking functions. IPX/SPX is a routable protocol, and therefore is suitable for use in larger multisegment network environments.

  NWLink is relatively easy to install and manage and is also a routable protocol. While IPX/SPX nearly became the most widely used network protocol, it has taken a second place behind TCP/IP because of the Internet. The IPX/SPX protocol is slower than NetBEUI, but it is faster than TCP/IP.

- *Appletalk*—**Appletalk** is used to communicate with Apple Macintosh computers. Historically, Apple has used Appletalk for the majority of the functions in their networking environment. However, Apple now supports TCP/IP as well. Appletalk is a routable protocol. In a PC environment, the Appletalk protocol is normally only implemented to communicate with Macintosh computers on your network.

- *TCP/IP*—**Transmission control protocol/Internet protocol (TCP/IP)** is the most popular network protocol currently in use due largely to the fact that the Internet is based on it. However, TCP/IP has rapidly become the protocol of choice for corporate networks, because most operating systems support this protocol. This fact becomes very useful when you are trying to network different types of systems (e.g., Windows, Apple Macs, Linux machines) to one another. Also, TCP/IP is a routable protocol, so its packets can be transferred across many different types of networks before they reach their final destination.

While TCP/IP is much slower than either IPX/SPX or NetBEUI, because it is a very reliable protocol, it has the ability to ensure that data will be delivered to the receiver correctly. These network protocols will be visited again later in this chapter as we apply them to the Internet, and then again in Chapters 9 and 10 when we set up LAN and WAN connections for different operating systems.

Network Architectures

Networks are complex, multifaceted structures that require a tremendous amount of interaction between computer designers, network equipment designers, operating system manufacturers, and networking application providers. Several initiatives have been put forward to provide models to serve as blueprints for these groups to follow in designing their products. While you should be aware that different hierarchical networking models exist, the most widely discussed initiative is the **open systems interconnection (OSI)** model put forward by the International Standards Organization.

The layers of the OSI model are shown in Figure 6-19. In the figure, each layer on the left is matched with a group of protocols that operate within it on the right. As you can see, there are many protocols at work in network architectures. Local area networking environments are primarily concerned with the first four layers of the model, while layers four through seven are more widely dealt with in wide area network environments. Basically, there are two de facto **network architectures** in use with local area networks: Ethernet and Token Ring.

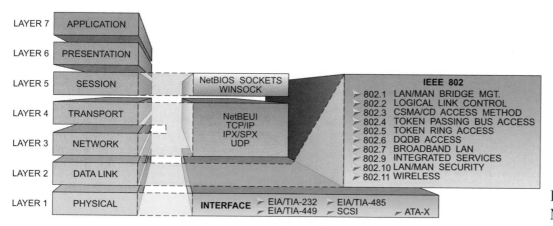

Figure 6-19: The OSI Networking Model

NOTE

Don't worry about memorizing the layers of the OSI model and their related protocols. The OSI model is not tested for on the A+ exam, but it puts the following discussions of different protocols in perspective. You should be aware as we describe different protocols in subsequent discussion that they are working together to get data where the data are supposed to go. However, you may want to start getting familiar with the OSI model if you intend to pursue the Network+ and i-Net+ exams after you complete the A+ exams.

Ethernet

Xerox developed **Ethernet** in 1976. The standard specification for Ethernet has been published by the **International Electrical and Electronic Association (IEEE)** as the **IEEE-802.3 Ethernet protocol** (Refer to the *Data Link* layer of the OSI model). Local area networks are designed so that the entire network runs synchronously at one frequency. Therefore, only one set of electronic signals may be placed on the network at one time. However, data can move in both directions between network locations. By definition, this makes local area network operations half-duplex in nature (i.e., information can travel in both directions, but not at the same time).

In a network, some method must be used to determine which node has use of the network's communications paths, and for how long it can have it. The network's access protocol handles these functions, and it is necessary to prevent more than one user from accessing the bus at any given time. If two sets of data are placed on the network at the same time, a data collision occurs, and data are lost.

The Ethernet methodology for access control is referred to as **carrier sense multiple-access with collision detection (CSMA/CD)**. Using this protocol, a node that wants to transfer data over the network first listens to the LAN to determine whether it is in use. If the LAN is not in use, the node begins transmitting its data. If the network is busy, the node waits for the LAN to clear for a predetermined time, and then takes control of the LAN.

If two nodes are waiting to use the LAN, they will periodically attempt to access the LAN at the same time. When this happens, a data collision occurs, and the data from both nodes are rendered useless. The receiver portion of the Ethernet controller monitors the transmission to detect collisions. When it senses the data bits overlapping, it halts the transmission, as does the other node. The transmitting controller generates an abort pattern code that is transmitted to all the nodes on the LAN, telling them that a collision has occurred. This alerts any nodes that might be waiting to access the LAN that there is a problem.

Ethernet

International Electrical and Electronic Association (IEEE)

IEEE-802.3 Ethernet protocol

carrier sense multiple-access with collision detection (CSMA/CD)

The receiving node (or nodes) dump any data that it might have received before the collision occurred. Other nodes waiting to send data generate a random timing number and go into a holding pattern. The timing number is a waiting time that the node sits out before it tries to transmit. Because the number is randomly generated, the odds against two of the nodes trying to transmit again at the same time are very low.

The first node to time out listens to the LAN to determine whether any activity is still occurring. Because it almost always finds a clear LAN, it begins transmitting. If two of the nodes do time out at the same time, another collision happens, and the abort pattern/number generation/time-out sequence begins again. Eventually, one of the nodes will gain clear access to the network and successfully transmit its data.

Limitations of Ethernet

Limitations of Ethernet—The Ethernet strategy provides for up to 1024 users to share the LAN. From the description of its collision-recovery technique, however, it should be apparent that with more users on an Ethernet LAN, more collisions are likely to occur, and the average time to complete an actual data transfer will be longer.

The Ethernet Frame

frame

Under the Ethernet standard, information is collected into a package called a **frame**. Figure 6-20 depicts a typical Ethernet frame. The frame carries the following six sections of information:

- A preamble

- A destination address

- An originating address

- A type field

- The data field

- The frame check error-detection and correction information

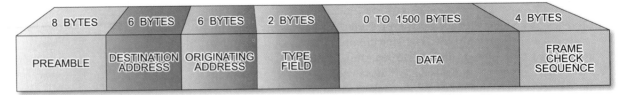

Figure 6-20: A Typical Ethernet Frame

This organizational structure is similar to that of a sector on a hard disk. The preamble synchronizes the receiver's operation to that of the transmitter. This action also tells the other nodes that a transmission is under way. The Ethernet preamble is a 64-bit string made up of alternating 1s and 0s, and ending in two consecutive 1s.

The destination address field is 6 bytes long and is used to define one of three address locations. This number can represent the individual node address of the intended receiver or the address of a grouping of nodes around the LAN, or it can be a broadcast code that allows the node to send a message to everyone on the LAN.

The originating address field contains the identification address for the transmitting node. The type field is a 2-byte field that identifies the user protocol of the frame.

The data field is a variable-length field that contains the actual information. Because it is sent in a synchronous mode, the data field can be as long as necessary. The Ethernet standard does not allow for data fields less than 46 bytes, however, or longer than 1500 bytes.

The frame-check block contains an error-detection and correction word. Like parity and other error-detection schemes, the receiver regenerates the error code from the received data (actually the data, the address bytes, and the type field) and compares it to the received code. If a mismatch occurs, an error signal is generated from the LAN card to the system.

Ethernet Implementations

In earlier discussions, the Ethernet and Token Ring architectures were described in terms of where they operated on the OSI model, but no mention was made of how those protocols were implemented at the *Physical* layer. Ethernet is classified as a bus topology that has been implemented across several different network media, including

- Coaxial cable
- Twisted-pair copper cable
- Fiber-optic cable
- Wireless RF

Figure 6-21 depicts typical coaxial and UTP connections.

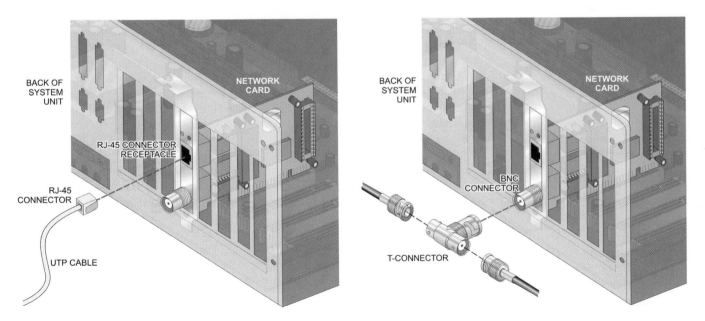

Figure 6-21: Typical Coax and UTP Connections

Coaxial Ethernet Specifications

The original Ethernet scheme was classified as a 10 Mbps transmission protocol. The maximum length specified for Ethernet is 1.55 miles (2.5 km), with a maximum segment length between nodes of 500 meters. This type of LAN is referred to as a 10Base-5 LAN by the IEEE organization.

The XXBaseYY IEEE nomenclature designates that the maximum data rate across the LAN is 10 Mbps, that it is a baseband LAN (versus broadband), and that its maximum segment length is 500 meters. One exception to this method is the 10Base-2 implementation. The maximum segment length for this specification is 185 meters (almost 200).

Coaxial Ethernet connections can be made through 50-ohm RG-8 *thicknet* coaxial cable (10Base-5) or *thinnet* coaxial cable (10Base-2). The original 10Base-5 connection scheme required that special transceiver units be clamped to the cable. A pin in the transceiver pierced the cable to establish electrical contact with its conductor. An additional length of cable, called the drop cable, was then connected between the LAN adapter card and the transceiver. The 10Base-2 Ethernet LAN uses thinner, industry-standard RG-58 coaxial cable and has a maximum segment length of 185 meters. Both coaxial connection methods require that a terminating resistor be installed at each end of the transmission line. Ethernet systems use 52-ohm terminators.

Twisted-Pair Ethernet Specifications

The **unshielded twisted pair (UTP)** Ethernet specifications are based on telephone cable and are normally used to connect a small number of PCs together. The twisted pairing of the cables uses magnetic-field principles to minimize induced noise in the lines. The original UTP LAN specification (10Base-T) had a transmission rate that was stated as 1 Mbps. Using UTP cable, a LAN containing up to 64 nodes can be constructed with the maximum distance between nodes set at 250 meters. Newer Ethernet implementations are producing LAN speeds of up to 100 Mbps using UTP copper cabling.

unshielded twisted pair (UTP)

For these networks, the IEEE adopted 10Base-T, 100Base-T, and 100Base-TX designations, indicating that they operate on twisted-pair cabling and depend on its specifications for the maximum segment length. The 100BASE designation is referred to as Fast Ethernet. The TX version of the Fast Ethernet specification employs two pairs of twisted cable to conduct high-speed, full-duplex transmissions. The cables used with the TX version can be CAT 5 UTP or STP. There is also a 100Base-FX Fast Ethernet designation that indicates the network in using fiber-optic cabling. This specification is described later in this chapter.

Network cards capable of supporting both transmission rates are classified as 10/100 Ethernet cards. The recommended maximum length of a 10/100Base-T segment is 100 meters (actually, the maximum segment length of any Ethernet connection designated with a T is 100 meters).

The latest Ethernet designations for copper cabling are the 1000Base-T Gigabit Ethernet specification that delivers 1 Gigabit (1000 Mbps) data transfers over Category 5 UTP cable and the 1000Base-CX specification that provides the same Gigabit transfer rate over two pairs of STP cable.

UTP systems normally employ *connection concentrators* built into routers, switches, or hubs for connection purposes, as shown in Figure 6-22.

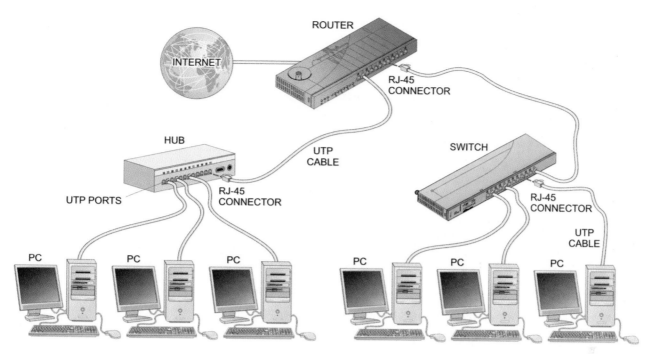

Hewlett Packard and AT&T jointly developed a completely different 100 Mbps standard referred to as the **100VG (Voice Grade) AnyLAN**. The 100VG AnyLAN runs on UTP cabling. It simultaneously employs four pairs of cable strands for transfers. Instead of using CSMA/CD for collision avoidance, the 100VG AnyLAN employs an access protocol called **demand priority**. This scenario requires that the network nodes request and be granted permission before they can send data across the LAN. The overwhelming popularity of the Fast Ethernet specification has caused 100VG AnyLAN to nearly disappear from the market.

Figure 6-22: UTP Network Connectivity Device

> 100VG (Voice Grade) AnyLAN

> demand priority

Fiber Ethernet Standards

The IEEE organization has created several fiber-optic variations of the Ethernet protocol. They classify these variations under the **IEEE-803** standard. These standards are referenced as the **10/100Base-F** specification. Variations of this standard include

- **10Base-FP**. This specification is used for passive star networks running at 10 Mbps. It employs a special hub that uses mirrors to channel the light signals to the desired node.

- **10Base-FL**. This specification is used between devices on the network. It operates in full-duplex mode and runs at 10 Mbps. Cable lengths under this specification can range up to 2 kilometers.

- **100Base-FX**. This protocol is identical to the 10Base-FL specification with the exception that it runs at 100 Mbps. This particular version of the specification is referred to as *Fast Ethernet*, because it can easily run at the 100 Mbps rate.

- **1000Base-LX**. *Gigabit Ethernet* delivered over two multimode or single-mode optical fiber cables using long-wave laser techniques.

- **1000Base-SX**. *Gigabit Ethernet* delivered over two multimode or single-mode optical fiber cables using short-wave laser techniques.

> IEEE-803

> 10/100Base-F

> 10Base-FP

> 10Base-FL

> 100Base-FX

> 1000Base-LX

> 1000Base-SX

Table 6-3: Ethernet
Specifications

Table 6-3 summarizes the different Ethernet specifications. Other CSMA/CD-based protocols exist in the market. Some are actually Ethernet compatible. However, these systems may, or may not, achieve the performance levels of a true Ethernet system. Some may actually perform better.

CLASSIFICATION	CONDUCTOR	MAX. SEGMENT LENGTH	NODES	MAX. LENGTH	TRANS. RATE
10Base2	RG-58	185 m	30/1024	250 m	10 Mbps
10Base5	RG-8	500 m	100/1024	2.5 km	10 Mbps
10Base-T	UTP/STP	100 m/200 m	2/1024	2.5 km	10 Mbps
100Base-T	UTP	100 m	2/1024	2.5 km	100 Mbps
100Base-FX	FO	412 m	1024	5 km	100 Mbps
1000Base-T	UTP	100 m	1024	-	1000 Mbps
1000Base-SX	FO (multimode)	275 m-550 m	1024	-	1000 Mbps
1000Base-LX	FO (single mode)	500 m-550 m-5 km	1024	-	1000 Mbps

┌─ **TEST TIP** ──
Know the types of connectors and physical cable used with each network type.
└──

The FDDI Ring Standard

fiber distributed data interface (FDDI)

There is a Token Ring-like network standard that has been developed around fiber-optic cabling. This standard is the **fiber distributed data interface (FDDI)** specification. The FDDI network was designed to work almost exactly like a Token Ring network, with the exception that it works on two counter-rotating rings of fiber-optic cable, as illustrated in Figure 6-23. All other differences in the two specifications are associated with their speed differences.

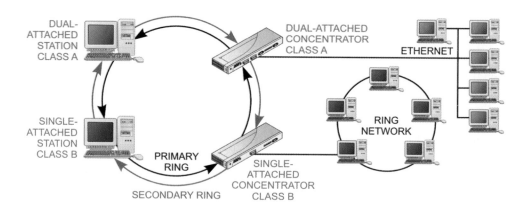

Figure 6-23: An FDDI Network

full-duplex communication

FDDI employs token-passing access control and provides data-transfer rates of 100 Mbps. Using the second ring, FDDI can easily handle multiple frames of data moving across the network at any given time. This provides the FDDI system a type of **full-duplex communication** capability (i.e., data can travel in both directions at the same time—in this case on two different conductors). Of course, the dual ring implementation provides additional network dependability, because it can shift over to a single ring operation if the network controller senses that a break has occurred in one of the rings.

Wireless Ethernet Standards

Wireless networking standards fall under the designation of *802.11x*. Current standard versions include 802.11a, b, g, and i. These are sometimes referred to as wireless Ethernet standards; however, true Ethernet protocols are classified under IEEE-802.3 standards.

The IEEE 802.11b (also known as *802.11 High Rate* or *Wi-Fi*) wireless standard has gained wide acceptance as the preferred wireless networking technology for both business and home network applications. Most current wireless LANs are based on this specification and operate at transfer rates in the range of 11 Mbps, with fallback operations at 5.5 Mbps, 2 Mbps, and 1 Mbps. This version of the 802.11 specification provides Ethernet-like functionality.

Typically, the effective range of the 802.11b signal is from 100 to 300 meters. However, these signals assume a direct line of site and can be affected by intervening objects, such as walls and trees. The practical range for 802.11b is 150 feet. Other 802.11 wireless specifications include

- **802.11**—The original wireless LAN specification that furnishes 1 or 2 Mbps data rates using FHSS or DSSS signaling techniques in the 2.4 GHz frequency range.

- **802.11a**—An upgraded 802.11 specification that provides up to 54 Mbps data rates in the 5.2 GHz frequency range. The practical range for 802.11a signals is less than the 802.11b specification (225 feet, with direct line of site).

- **802.11g**—A newly completed wireless specification that delivers data transfer rates in excess of up to 54 Mbps in the 2.4 GHz band. The practical distance for 802.11g signals is the same as the 802.11b specification.

- **802.11x**—A group of pending 802.11 WLAN update standards being developed to support the general 802.11 specification. These include Quality of Service (802.11e), Access Point Interoperability (802.11f), Interference (802.11h), and Security (802.11i).

| 802.11 |
| 802.11a |
| 802.11g |
| 802.11x |

INSTALLING AND CONFIGURING LANS

Essentials 5.2

Technical Support 4.2

Because PC technicians are typically responsible for maintaining the portion of the network that attaches to the computer, they must be able to install, configure, and service the network adapter card and cable. The following sections deal with installing and configuring LAN cards.

LAN Adapter Cards

In a LAN, each computer on the network requires a **network adapter card** (also referred to as a **network interface card** or **NIC**), and every unit has to be connected to the network by some type of cabling. These cables are typically either twisted-pair wires, thick or thin coaxial cable, or fiber-optic cable.

| network adapter card |
| network interface card (NIC) |

LAN adapter cards must have connectors that are compatible with the type of LAN cabling being used. Ethernet LAN cards come equipped with an RJ-45 connector.

Figure 6-24 depicts a typical LAN card. In addition to its LAN connectors, the LAN card may have a number of configuration jumpers that must be set up.

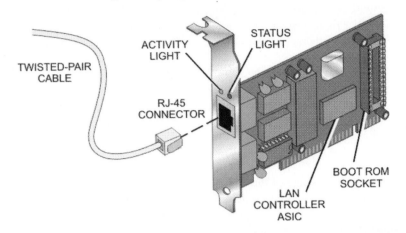

STATUS
LIGHT

ACTIVITY
LIGHT

TWISTED-PAIR
CABLE

RJ-45
CONNECTOR

BOOT ROM
SOCKET

LAN
CONTROLLER
ASIC

**Figure 6-24: A
Typical LAN Card**

WARNING

Use the user guide—Although some cards may have jumper instructions printed directly on them, the card's user manual is normally required to configure it for operation. Great care should be taken with the user manual, because its loss might render the card useless. At the very least, the manufacturer would have to be contacted to get a replacement.

---

bootup ROM

Another item that can be found on many LAN cards is a vacant ROM socket. This socket is included so that it can be used to install a **boot ROM** that will enable the unit to be used as a diskless workstation.

One or more activity or status lights may also be included on the card's back plate. These lights can play a very important part in diagnosing problems with the LAN connection. Check the card's user manual for definitions of its activity lights.

Each adapter must have an adapter driver program loaded in its host computer to handle communications between the system and the adapter. These are the Ethernet and Token Ring drivers loaded to control specific types of LAN adapter cards.

transport protocol

In addition to the adapter drivers, the network computer must have a network protocol driver loaded. This program may be referred to as the **transport protocol**, or just as the protocol. It operates between the adapter and the initial layer of network software to package and unpackage data for the LAN. In many cases, the computer may have several different protocol drivers loaded so that the unit can communicate with computers that use other types of protocols.

**internetworking
packet exchange/
sequenced packet
exchange (IPX/SPX)**

**transmission control
protocol/Internet
protocol (TCP/IP)**

Typical protocol drivers include the **internetworking packet exchange/sequenced packet exchange (IPX/SPX)** model produced by Novell, and the **standard transmission control protocol/Internet protocol (TCP/IP)** developed by the U.S. military for its **ARPA** network. Figure 6-25 illustrates the various LAN drivers necessary to transmit, or receive, data on a network.

ARPA

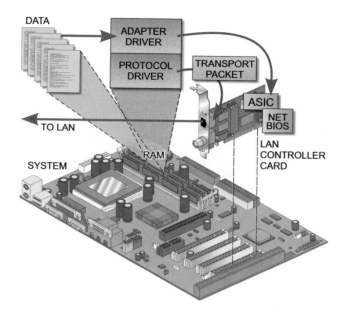

Figure 6-25:
Various LAN
Drivers

Installing LAN Cards

The process for installing a LAN card in a PC follows the basic steps as installing most peripheral cards in a PnP system. Consult the NIC's installation guide for any special settings that the card may require. If there are no special installation instructions for the card, simply place the adapter card in a vacant expansion slot, secure it to the system unit's back plate and turn the system on. The system's PnP function should detect the presence of the card and load the correct device drivers for it.

Connect the LAN card to the network media and check the activity lights on the back of the NIC card to insure that a connection to the network has been obtained. Figure 6-26 illustrates connecting the computer to the LAN using UTP cable. As the figure illustrates, the line drop to the computer comes from a network connectivity device. In some office environments the connection comes from a wall plate that has network cabling that runs back to the connectivity equipment.

After the card has been installed and physically connected to the network transmission media, you must install and configure the client options and network protocols described in the previous section. These items are operating system specific, so we will deal with them in the networking sections of the various operating systems described in Chapter 10, *Windows Operating Systems*.

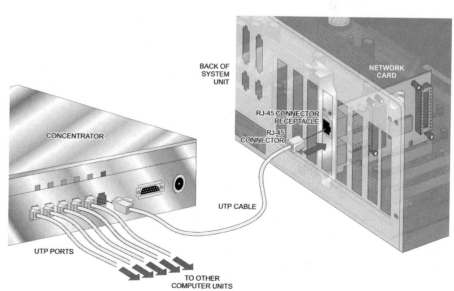

Figure 6-26: Connecting the Computer to the LAN

If a configuration conflict appears, reset the conflicting settings so that they do not share the same value. Which component's configuration gets changed is determined by examining the options for changing the cards involved in the conflict. A sound card may have many more IRQ options available than a given network card. In that case, it would be easier to change sound card settings than network card settings.

After the card has been installed and physically connected to the network transmission media, the driver and protocols described in the previous section must be installed. These items are operating system specific, so we will deal with them in the networking sections of the various operating systems chapters later in the book.

Optimizing Network Adapters

In a networked system, by design, all the nodes in the network run at the same speed. That means that the performance of the network is limited by its slowest component. If the system is using mostly adapter cards and devices rated for 100 MHz operation but one or more of the cards is rated only for 10 MHz operation, then the system will be limited to 10 MHz operation. Therefore, all of the adapters in the system should be updated to use the 100 MHz speed.

Installing Network Connectivity Devices

For the most part, installing a hub or switch in a network involves attaching the network media connections to the device, connecting the power unit to the device and turning on the power switch.

In the case of routers in the network, you may be required to install connecting cables that link the router to another router. Otherwise, the physical installation is the same as that described for hubs and switches.

The CAT5 wiring scenarios presented in the previous section are normally wired in a *straight-through cable* arrangement (that is, Pin 1 at both ends of the cable wired together, as are all the other connections). However, you must be aware that not all CAT5 cables are wired this way.

A CAT5 *crossover cable* is a good tool to have for troubleshooting NICs and hubs. These cables can also be used to connect two computers together without a hub or other network connectivity device. They might also be required to connect two hubs together.

Figure 6-27 depicts the wiring specification for such a crossover cable. Notice that the wire pairs remain constant with the earlier straight-through CAT5 wiring examples. The only difference with the crossover cable is that the Transmit pair of one end (TX+ and TX−) is crossed over to match the Receive pair (RX+ and RX−) at the other end.

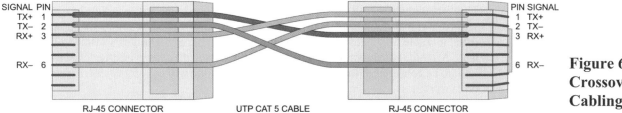

SIGNAL PIN
TX+ 1
TX− 2
RX+ 3

RX− 6

RJ-45 CONNECTOR   UTP CAT 5 CABLE   RJ-45 CONNECTOR

PIN SIGNAL
1 TX+
2 TX−
3 RX+

6 RX−

Figure 6-27: Crossover Cabling

Cabling from a NIC to a hub or router is normally performed with a straight-through cable. Crossover cables are typically used for connecting two hubs together. Hubs typically have markings on their ports to indicate whether a straight-through or crossover cable is required. The markings that are used to identify straight-through and crossover cables are

- **MDI (media dependent interface)**—This connection requires an external crossover (either the cable or the other hub must perform the crossover function).

- **MIDX (media independent interface crossover)**—This type of connection can be switched so that the port performs the crossover function. This allows a straight-through cable to be used to make the connection when engaged.

If there is no marking on the port, it is generally assumed that the hub performs the crossover. However, you should always check the hub documentation to verify this arrangement.

After the router has been connected, you must configure it for operation. Routers typically employ a browser-based wizard for this purpose. To begin the configuration process, start one of the computers in the network and open its browser. Next, enter the router's IP address in the browser's navigation window. The normal default value for most routers is the private network address 192.168.0.1. This should produce a configuration wizard screen similar to the one depicted in Figure 6-28.

> **MDI (media dependent interface)**

> **MIDX (media independent interface crossover)**

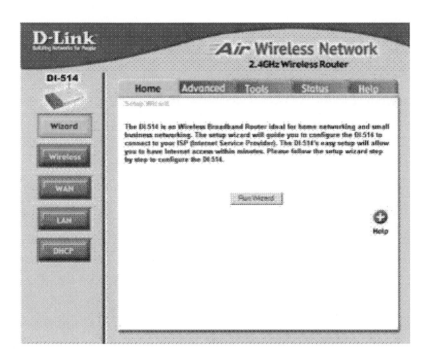

Figure 6-28: A Router Configuration Screen

The first thing you will be asked to do is enter a username and password to get into the wizard. Typical default usernames and passwords for different router manufacturers are listed in Table 6-4. These items are normally available in the router's installation guide as well. After the configuration wizard has been accessed there are a number of items that may need to be configured. In the following paragraphs, we will cover the generic feature found on most routers.

Table 6-4: Typical Default Router Login Information

ROUTER	USERNAME	PASSWORD
Linksys	no username	admin
Cisco	cisco	cisco
Netgear	admin	admin
SMC	no username	admin
Proxim	public	public

- *Administrative Password*—It is a good idea to change the password from the default value. This setting should be a strong setting since the router protects the entire network. If the password is forgotten you can always physically reset the router and re-establish the password setting. It's not a good idea to allow your browser to remember your username and password for this function if you are in an open environment where others can access the network through your computer.

- *Router IP Address*—some routers allow you to change their IP addresses from the factory default. Changing the address can add some additional level of security to the network.

- *DHCP Server*—Where you set this configuration depends on how your network is set up. To communicate in a modern network, every client must have a unique IP address that identifies its location to the rest of the network. Network clients can be configured with constant IP addresses—called static IPs—or they can be assigned one from a list of available IP addresses. There are two possible sources for IP addresses in a local area network—a computer providing the dynamic host configuration protocol (DHCP) function or the router performing this function. If both devices are active in the network, confusion occurs as the devise log on a receive conflicting information from two sources.

If you are setting up a relatively small network, such as a residential or small office network, consider using static IP addressing and assigning each computer a unique address. In this case, you would choose to *Disable* the DHCP server function on the router (as you would if you have a DHCP server computer operating in the network). If you do need to run the DHCP function on the router, you might want to consider limiting the number of IP addresses the router can issue to just a couple more than the number of computers you currently have connected to the network (for expansion purposes). DHCP is covered in detail later in this chapter.

Virtual servers

- *Access to Virtual Servers or Port Forwarding*—**Virtual servers** are the computers in the local network that interface directly with the Internet. Unless you are running a Web business where you have need to have servers connected to the Internet, *Disable* this option.

- *Exclusive Applications*—This setting allows applications to access and receive information directly from the Internet without controls from the router. This is a potential point of attack and should only be enabled if the system must use software that requires this feature.

- *Enable Access to Known MACs*—Also known as *Mac filtering*, this option enables you to configure the router to permit devices with known MAC addresses to access it. If you Enable this feature, you should only allow MAC addresses you recognize from your network to have access.

- *Wireless AP*—Many wireless access points also possess the ability to perform the routing functions. In network environments that have no wireless network devices, this function should be *Disabled*.

- *Remote Management*—This feature permits you to access your network from a remote location to perform management functions. Unless you have a specific need to do this, you should Disable this setting. It can always be reset to *Enable* if you find that you do need to perform remote management functions later.

- *Discard Ping from WAN side*—This is a troubleshooting setting that enables you to hide your network from unknown Internet users who may be trying to verify your location for malicious purposes. Enabling this setting prevents them from getting responses back from Ping operations and makes it look like your network is not present. If you are setting up the router as an internal connection, there is no need to enable this setting. The Ping utility is covered in Chapter 12, *Operating System Troubleshooting*.

- *UPnP*—This setting (**universal Plug and Play**) applies to allowing operating systems to manage stand-alone network devices such as the router. This option makes the router and the network more vulnerable to attacks. Therefore, this setting should be *Disabled*.

> **universal Plug and Play**

Installing Wireless LANs

> *Essentials 5.2*
>
> *Technical Support 4.2*

Wireless LANs provide the maximum amount of flexibility for connecting home and office networking components. Because no wires are required to connect devices to the wireless network, the users have considerable mobility. The wireless network is becoming a popular option for connecting devices in residential and small office environments. It is also becoming an economical choice for locations where installing cable is not practical or is prohibited by historic building codes or other restrictions.

The process for setting up a wireless network involves four steps:

1. Install the Access Point

2. Configure the AP

3. Install the Client Adapters

4. Configure Security

Installing the Access Point

access point

As Figure 6-29 illustrates, the **access point** is the mainstay of the wireless network. These devices serve as the central connection point for all the network devices within its range. The access point also provides the physical connection with wired networks. The access point can be connected to a host computer that is a node on an existing hard-wired network, or it can be connected directly into a connectivity device such as a network hub or router. Installing the access point is normally a matter of connecting it to the network host, installing its power adapter, and loading its network drivers and protocols on the host computer.

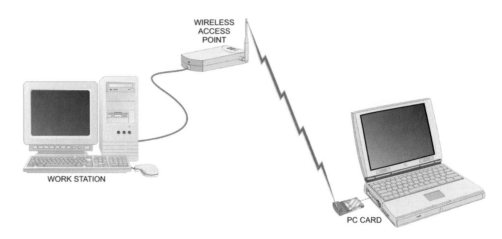

**Figure 6-29:
Wireless Network
Components**

hotspot

clients

The antennas on the access point establish a range of transmission around the access point called a **hotspot**. Other wireless computing devices (**clients**) may access the network throughout the hotspot as long as they are within range of other wireless terminals or the access point. Wireless clients can be any type of computer or peripheral designed to use the same wireless protocol that the access point is using. These devices include desktop computers with wireless PCI cards, laptop computers using PCMCIA cards, and wireless peripheral equipment using built-in wireless interfaces.

While the physical installation and configuration of wireless networks is typically simple when computers are close to each other and there are no physical barriers to their line-of-sight transmissions, installations can become more difficult when you have clients located at distances from the access point or when there are physical barriers of any type (e.g., walls). The RF signal strength at wireless LAN clients can be negatively impacted by signals bouncing off walls and objects in an indoor environment. The radio waves may arrive from multiple directions and in some cases can cancel or severely reduce the signal strength between portable users. This effect is called **multipath.** Microwave radio emissions from other devices using the unlicensed 2.4 GHz radio spectrum are also a source of electromagnetic interference.

multipath

site survey

The first step in overcoming these types of obstacles is to perform a **site survey** to analyze the network signal strength in each section of the network. Site checks can be performed using specialized test equipment or with software built into wireless devices. Most access points include software-based signal strength analysis tools as part of their support package. Likewise, the wireless support built into the Windows operating system provides a signal strength meter. These tools can be used to test for signal strength when the computers have been brought online.

The simplest site survey method involves setting up the AP in some initial position then walking around the site with a portable computer noting the power level at each section of the site. After the site has been mapped, you can locate network nodes to maximize connectivity between all the nodes and the access point. You may also find that you need to relocate the AP or add another AP to the network to gain better coverage. Generally, the best place to locate the AP is in the center of the area you need to cover. All the WLAN adapter cards and the access point should be installed in such a way that they provide the maximum exposure for the antenna to maximize signal strength. You should keep the AP's antenna as close to vertical as possible.

You may want to hang the AP on a wall or from the ceiling to get the best clear path for its wireless signals. Generally, the higher in the room the better, as this avoids typical obstacles found in most rooms. However, you should be aware that the weakest signal point for the AP is typically directly above and below the unit. Also be aware that hanging the AP on an exterior wall will limit its useful range (unless you want to work outside, in which case you should put the access point near a window).

Typical obstacles to the wireless network signals include large metal or water-filled objects, such as filing cabinets and fish tanks. Other items that tend to affect wireless network communications include other 2.4 GHz devices such as cordless telephones.

Configuring the Access Point

After the best location for the AP has been established and it has been connected to the network host you will need to configure it for operation. Most APs provide their own browser-based wizard for this purpose. Other APs come with CD-based configuration programs. In either event, you will need to start a browser on one of the network's computers and access the AP.

Using the browser method to access the AP's configuration wizard involves entering its IP address in the browser's navigation window. The factory default IP address for many APs is in the private address range of 192.168.x.x. When the wizard starts, you will be guided through the configuration process. Information you will need to enter includes password, **service set identifier (SSID)** name and AP channel. The SSID is a 32-character identifier that is attached to the front end of packets sent across wireless networks. You can select 11 different channels for the AP's operation. The factory default channel setting for most APs is 6. If problems occur with this channel setting, try channels 1 or 11. If you are adding an AP to a network that already has an AP set to channel 6, set the second AP to channel 1 operation—never set two APs in the same network to the same channel.

Next, you will be asked to enable encryption and security features. This option should be bypassed until the wireless client computers have been set up. To complete the AP configuration, you must apply the settings to the AP. The AP will reset itself, momentarily dropping connectivity with the network. You will need to come back to the wizard to configure the security setting after configuring the client computers.

service set identifier (SSID)

Installing Wireless Clients

For most client computers, all that is necessary to start sharing data and resources wirelessly is to install the proper wireless adapter and configure the network software. The adapter card can be a PCI-based wireless adapter in a desktop unit, or a PC Card-based adapter in a notebook computer. Computers built to meet Intel's **Centrino** mobile technology standard have built in wireless networking capabilities. No additional wireless adapter is needed. Simply configure the internal wireless adapter and push the button to activate the circuitry.

Centrino

For most computers, you simply need to install the wireless USB, PCI, or PC Card adapter card in the computer and turn it on. In Windows systems the operating system will display a *Found New Hardware* wizard page like the one depicted in Figure 6-30. Normally, you should select the *Install the Software Automatically* option. This will cause Windows to search for the appropriate driver. If the drivers are already installed, Windows will automatically use those drivers and attempt to establish a wireless network connection. If the drivers are not present, the operating system will produce a prompt asking for the location of the driver software. If there is more than one possible driver for the adapter, Windows will prompt the user to select the proper driver.

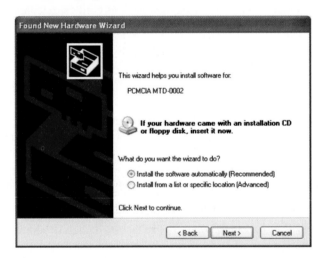

**Figure 6-30:
Windows Found
New Hardware
Wizard**

Many wireless network adapters come with additional software with their products to give them an advantage over their competitors. This software typically replaces Windows built-in wireless configuration software. However, other wireless adapters come with driver software that must be installed before you install the hardware. If you install the adapter first, the computer will not have the proper drivers installed and the adapter will not work.

Establishing Wireless Security

While wireless networks are gaining popularity for their ease of installation, there are a number of security issues concerning using them to communicate personal or otherwise sensitive information. Transmissions from wireless network devices cannot simply be confined to the local environment of a residence or business. Although the range is typically limited to a few hundred feet, RF signals can easily be intercepted even outside the vicinity of the stated security perimeter. Any unauthorized mobile terminal can accomplish this using an 802.11 receiver.

In order to minimize the risk of security compromise on a wireless LAN, the IEEE-802.11b standard provides a security feature called **wired equivalent privacy (WEP)**. WEP provides a 128-bit mathematical key encryption scheme for **encrypting** data transmissions and **authenticating** each computer on the network. Enabling the WEP function adds security for data being transmitted by the workstations. WEP is included on most APs and is relatively easy to install.

All of the computers in the network must be configured to use the same key to communicate. Therefore, if you enable WEP on the AP, you will need to enable the same WEP key on each computer in the network. WEP is enabled and configured by returning to the browser-based configuration wizard and accessing the WEP settings page (the same page as the SSID and channel settings). If the configuration wizard provides for multiple encryption levels, you should select the highest (strongest) level of encryption.

TEST TIP
Be aware of the security-related problems associated with wireless networking and know how to compensate for them.

You will also need to enter the WEP key value (password), either in the form of hexadecimal number string or as an ASCII character string. The ASCII option is easier for most people to work with. Record this string for use with the network's client computers. Each client computer will need to have the key installed the next time they attempt to connect to the network. When requested by the system, enter and confirm the WEP key.

While WEP is a strong encryption method, serious hackers can crack it. This has led the wireless industry to create a stronger **WiFi Protected Access (WPA)** standard. WPA adds improved data encryption, using **temporary key integrity protocol (TKIP)** and IEEE 802.1X **extensible authentication protocol (EAP)** user authentication protocol to provide increased security. This combination requires users to use usernames and passwords to access the network. After the user logs in, the AP generates a temporary key that is used to encrypt data transfers between the AP and the client computer.

If possible, you should set up the router to use **WPA-PSK** along with a encryption algorithm. The PSK option enables WPA to use **preshared keys** instead of a separate **certificate authority (CA)** computer to provide user authentication. The PSK allows a password to be set on the router and shared with the rest of the users. If the router does not offer WPA as an option, check the router manufacturer's Web site for a firmware upgrade. While you are there, you should also check for driver upgrades to enable WPA-PSK to work on the wireless network cards.

If WPA is simply not an option, you should enable WEP with 128-bit encryption. In addition, after you've installed and authenticated all the wireless clients, you should set the *SSID Broadcast* option to *Disable* so that outsiders do not use SSID to acquire your address and data. Also change the SSID name from the default value if you have not already done so.

WIDE AREA NETWORKS

Essentials 5.1

A **wide area network (WAN)** is similar in concept to a widely distributed client/server LAN. In a wide area network, some distances typically separate computers. A typical WAN is a local city- or countywide network, like the one in Figure 6-31. This network links network members together through a **bulletin board service (BBS)**. Users can access the bulletin board's server with a simple telephone call.

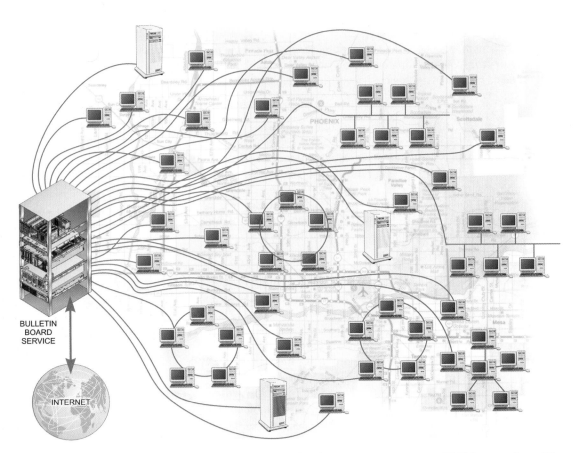

**Figure 6-31:
County-Wide
Network**

BULLETIN
BOARD
SERVICE

INTERNET

Several different types of communication systems connect WANs together. These communication paths are referred to as **links**. In some areas, high-speed intermediate-sized networks, referred to as **metropolitan area networks (MANs)**, are popping up. These networks typically cover areas up to 30 miles (50 kilometers) in diameter and are operated to provide access to regional resources. They are like LANs in speed and operation but use special high-speed connections and protocols to increase the geographic span of the network, like a WAN.

The Internet

The most famous WAN is the **Internet**. The Internet is actually a network of networks, working together. The main communication path for the Internet is a series of networks, established by the U.S. government, to link supercomputers together at key research sites.

This pathway is referred to as the **backbone**, and is affiliated with the **National Science Foundation (NSF)**. Since the original backbone was established, the Internet has expanded around the world and offers access to computer users in every part of the globe.

The TCP/IP protocol divides the transmission into packets of information, suitable for retransmission across the Internet. Along the way, the information passes through different networks that are organized at different levels. Depending on the routing scheme, the packets may move through the Internet using different routes to get to the intended address. At the destination, however, the packets are reassembled into the original transmission.

This concept is illustrated in Figure 6-32.

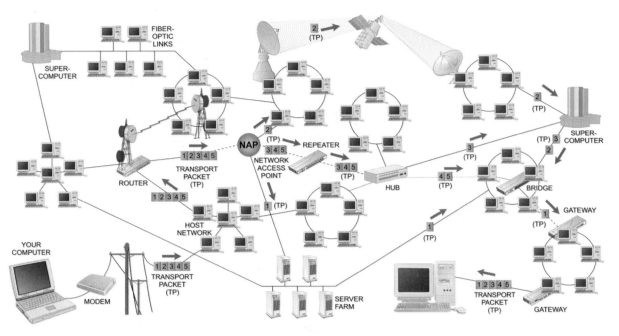

As a message moves from the originating address to its destination, it may pass through LANs, mid-level networks, routers, repeaters, hubs, bridges, and gateways. A mid-level network is simply another network that does not require an Internet connection to carry out communications.

Figure 6-32: Packets Moving Through the Internet

Internet Service Providers

Connecting all of the users and individual networks together are **Internet service providers (ISPs)**. ISPs are companies that provide the technical gateway to the Internet. These companies own blocks of access addresses that they assign to their customers to give them an identity on the network.

Some service providers, such as **America Online (AOL)** and **Earthlink**, have become very well known.

Technical Support 4.1

IT Technician 5.1

Internet service providers (ISPs)

America Online (AOL)

Earthlink

However, there are thousands of lesser-known, dedicated Internet access provider companies offering services around the world. Figure 6-33 illustrates the service provider's position in the Internet scheme, and shows the various connection methods used to access the Internet.

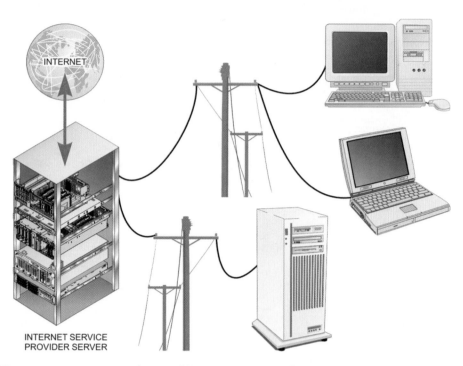

Figure 6-33: Service Provider's Position

INTERNET

INTERNET SERVICE
PROVIDER SERVER

When you connect to a service provider, you are connecting to its computer system, which, in turn, is connected to the Internet through devices called routers. A router is a device that intercepts network transmissions and determines for which part of the Internet they are intended. It then determines the best routing scheme for delivering the message to its intended address. The routing schedule is devised based on the known available links through the Internet and the amount of traffic detected on various segments. The router then transfers the message to a **network access point** (**NAP**).

network access point (NAP)

Service that most ISPs deliver to their customers include

- Internet identity through IP addresses
- E-mail services through POP3 and SMTP servers
- Internet News Service through USENET archive servers
- Internet routing through DNS servers

All of these services will be discussed in detail later in this chapter.

No matter which connection technology is employed for Internet access, most users are actually connecting to Internet service providers (ISPs) organizations at the other end of their connection. Only very large businesses and organizations can afford to act as their own ISPs and provide a technical gateway to the Internet. These companies own blocks of access addresses that they assign to their customers to give them an identity on the network.

In addition to e-mail and Usenet services, the ISP's main responsibility is to provide its customers with access to the Internet. At the root, this involves providing them with an IP address that gives them an Internet identity. IP addresses and the TCP/IP protocol that drive the Internet are described in the next section of this chapter.

The customer's Internet identity can be permanent if the ISP provides the user with a static IP address from its stockpile of IP addresses. Or it can be assigned dynamically to customers as they initiate contact with the ISP. The dynamic host configuration protocol (DHCP) is typically used to provide this function. The DHCP protocol issues and tracks IP addresses from the ISP's store of IP addresses. The DHCP protocol is covered in detail later in this chapter.

The other key function that ISPs perform is to act as the first stop in the Internet routing process. The structure of the Internet is built on a hierarchical system of servers that route transmissions according to a standard called the Domain Naming System (DNS). These DNS servers keep track of who is where and act as traffic cops on the Internet. The DNS system is also described later in this chapter.

IP Addresses

Essentials 5.1

The blocks of Internet access addresses that ISPs provide to their customers are called Internet protocol addresses, or **IP addresses**. The IP address makes each site a valid member of the Internet. This is how individual users are identified to receive file transfers, e-mail, and file requests.

IP addresses exist in the numeric format of XXX.YYY.ZZZ.AAA. Each address consists of four 8-bit fields separated by dots (.). This format of specifying addresses is referred to as **dotted decimal notation**. The decimal numbers are derived from the binary address that the hardware understands. For example, a binary network address of

      10000111.10001011.01001001.00110110 (binary)

corresponds to

      135.139.073.054 (decimal).

Each IP address consists of two parts: the network address and the host address. The network address identifies the entire network; the host address identifies an intelligent member within the network (a router, a server, or a workstation). Three classes of standard IP addresses are supported for LANs: Class A, Class B, and Class C. These addresses occur in four-octet fields like the example shown earlier.

- **Class A addresses** are reserved for large networks and use the last 24 bits (the last three octets or fields) of the address for the host address. The first octet always begins with a 0, followed by a 7-bit number. Therefore, valid Class A addresses range between 001.x.x.x and 126.x.x.x. This allows a Class A network to support 126 different networks with nearly 17 million hosts (nodes) per network.

> ┌─ **NOTE** ─────────────────────────────
> The 127.x.x.x address range is a special block of addresses reserved for testing network systems. The U.S. government owns some of these addresses for testing the Internet backbone. The 127.0.0.1 address is reserved for testing the bus on the local system.

Class B addresses

- **Class B addresses** are assigned to medium-sized networks. The first two octets can range between 128.x.x.x and 191.254.0.0. The last two octets contain the host addresses. This enables Class B networks to include up to 16,384 different networks with approximately 65,534 hosts per network.

Class C addresses

- **Class C addresses** are normally used with smaller LANs. In a Class C address, only the last octet is used for host addresses. The first three octets can range between 192.x.x.x and 223.254.254.0. Therefore, the Class C address can support approximately 2 million networks with 254 hosts each.

Subnets

intranets

Sections of the network can be grouped together into *subnets* that share a range of IP addresses. These groups are referred to as **intranets**. An intranet requires that each segment have a protective gateway to act as an entry and exit point for the segment. In most cases, the gateway is a device called a router. A router is an intelligent device that receives data and directs it toward a designated IP address.

firewall

Some networks employ a **firewall** as a gateway to the outside. A firewall is a combination of hardware and software components that provide a protective barrier between networks with different security levels. Administrators configure the firewall so that it will only pass data to and from designated IP addresses and TCP/IP ports.

Subnets

Subnets are created by masking off (hiding) the network address portion of the IP address on the units within the subnet. This, in effect, limits the mobility of the data to those nodes within the subnet because, they can reconcile only addresses from within their masked range. There are three common reasons to create a subnet:

- To isolate one segment of the network from all the others— Suppose, for example, that a large organization has 1000 computers, all of which are connected to the network. Without segmentation, data from all 1000 units would run through every other network node. The effect of this would be that everyone in the network would have access to all the data on the network, and the operation of the network would be slowed considerably by the uncontrolled traffic.

- To efficiently use IP addresses—Because the IP addressing scheme is defined as a 32-bit code, there are only a certain number of possible addresses. Although 126 networks with 17 million customers might seem like a lot, in the scheme of a worldwide network system, that's not a lot of addresses to go around.

- To utilize a single IP address across physically divided locations—For example, subnetting a Class C address between remotely located areas of a campus would permit half of the 253 possible addresses to be allocated to one campus location, and the other half to be allocated to hosts at the second location. In this manner, both locations can operate using a single Class C address.

Private IP Classes

Because the Internet is basically a huge TCP/IP network in which no two computers connected to it can have the same address, networks connected to the Internet must follow a specific IP addressing scheme assigned by an *Internet service provider* (*ISP*). However, any IP addressing scheme can be used as long as your network is not connected to the Internet. This is referred to as a *private network*.

When configuring a private network, you must design an IP addressing scheme to use across the network. Although, technically, you could use any IP addressing scheme you want in a private network without consulting an ISP, special ranges of network addresses in each IP class have been reserved for use with private networks. These are reserved addresses that are not registered to anyone on the Internet.

If you are configuring a private network, you should use one of these address options rather than create a random addressing scheme. The total number of clients on the network typically dictates which IP addressing class you should use. The following list of private network IP addresses can be used:

- An IP address of 10.0.0.0, with the subnet mask of 255.0.0.0

- An IP address of 169.254.0.0, with the subnet mask of 255.255.255.0 (the Microsoft AIPA default)

- An IP address of 172.(16−32).0.0, with the subnet mask of 255.240.0.0

- An IP address of 192.168.0.0, with the subnet mask of 255.255.0.0

In addition, remember that all *hosts* must have the same network ID and subnet mask and that no two computers on your network can have the same IP address when you are establishing a private IP addressing scheme.

Internet Domains

The IP addresses of all the computers attached to the Internet are tracked using a listing system called the **domain name system (DNS)**. This system evolved as a way to organize the members of the Internet into a hierarchical management structure.

domain name system (DNS)

domains

domain name

The DNS structure consists of various levels of computer groups called **domains**. Each computer on the Internet is assigned a **domain name**, such as *mic-inc.com*. The "mic-inc" is the user-friendly domain name assigned to the Marcraft site.

In the example, the .com notation at the end of the address is a top-level domain that defines the type of organization or country of origin associated with the address. In this case, the .com designation identifies the user as a commercial site. The following list identifies the Internet's top-level domain codes:

* .com = Commercial businesses
* .edu = Educational institutions
* .gov = Government agencies
* .int = International organizations
* .mil = Military establishments
* .net = Networking organizations
* .org = Nonprofit organizations

* .au = Australia
* .ca = Canada
* .fr = France
* .it = Italy
* .es = Spain
* .tw = Taiwan
* .uk = United Kingdom

| fully qualified |
| domain names |
| (FQDN) |

| host name |

On the Internet, domain names are specified in terms of their **fully qualified domain names (FQDN)**. An FQDN is a human-readable address that describes the location of the site on the Internet. It contains the host name, the domain name, and the top-level domain name. For example, the name "www.oneworld.owt.com" is an FQDN.

The letters "www" represent the **host name**. The host name specifies the name of the computer that provides services and handles requests for specific Internet addresses. In this case, the host is the World Wide Web. Other types of hosts include ftp and http sites.

The .owt extension indicates that the organization is a domain listed under the top-level domain heading. Likewise, the .oneworld entry is a subdomain of the .owt domain. It is very likely one of multiple networks supported by the .owt domain.

At each domain level, the members of the domain are responsible for tracking the addresses of the domains on the next-lower level. The lower domain is then responsible for tracking the addresses of domains, or end users, on the next level below it.

DNS Name Resolution

| DNS name server |

| DNS server |

| DNS database |

| DNS client |

Each domain must have a **DNS name server** that is responsible for registering its clients with the next higher level of the network. Any computer that provides domain name services is technically referred to as a **DNS server**. All DNS servers maintain a **DNS database** listing of name to IP address mappings that they are responsible for.

When a **DNS client** submits a *name resolution request* to a local DNS server, the server will search through its DNS database, and if necessary through the hierarchical DNS system, until it locates the host name or FQDN that was submitted to it. At this point, it resolves the IP address of the requested host name and returns it back to the client.

The simplified DNS process is as follows:

1. When you enter a Web page address in a Web browser, the client makes a *query* (a request for access) to a particular computer name, such as *www.west.mic-inc.com*.

2. The local DNS server (the DNS server that the client computer is assigned to) checks to determine whether it has that domain name in its memory cache.

3. If the local DNS server cannot answer a query, it will normally forward the query to a root DNS server looking for a match (all functional DNS servers, including the local DNS server, contain a static list of the IP addresses of all root DNS servers).

4. The root server will refer the local DNS server to a list of primary .com (domain) servers. In turn, the local DNS server will select one of the .com servers from the list and query it for the address of *west.mic-inc.com*.

5. In response, the .com domain DNS server will refer you to a list of *mic-inc.com* subdomain servers (if any exist).

6. The local DNS server will then query the mic-inc.com subdomain DNS server (or one of them) for the address of *west.mic-inc.com*.

7. Depending on the structure of the eitprep.com subdomain, the selected *mic-inc.com* server may refer you to a list of *mic-inc.com* subdomain DNS servers for the *west.mic-inc.com* address, or, if there are no additional subdomains, it will return the IP address for *west.mic-inc.com*.

INTERNET ACCESS METHODS

Over the past 3 years, a major shift has occurred in how users connect to the Internet. At that time, it was common for users to connect to the Internet via standard telephone lines, using dial-up modems. However, it is now as common for users to have high-speed broadband access to the Internet as dial-up.

Dial-up connections are generally the slowest way to connect to a network, but they are inexpensive to establish and use. Other users, who require quicker data transfers, contract with the telephone company to use special high-speed **digital subscriber line (DSL)**, **integrated service digital network (ISDN)**, or cable TV lines. These types of links require a **digital modem** to conduct data transfers. Because the modem is digital, no analog conversion is required.

Users who require very high volumes lease dedicated **T1 and T3 lines** from the telephone company. These applications generally serve businesses that put several of their computers or networks on-line. Once the information is transmitted, it may be carried over many types of communications links on its way to its destination. These interconnecting links can include fiber-optic cables, satellite up and down links, UHF, and microwave transmission systems. Figure 6-34 illustrates different ways to access WANs.

Dial-up connections
digital subscriber line (DSL)
integrated service digital network (ISDN)
digital modem
T1 and T3 lines

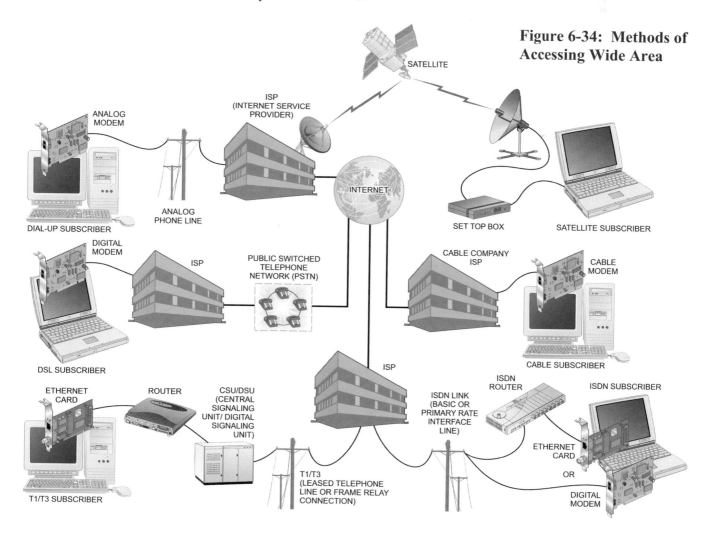

Figure 6-34: Methods of Accessing Wide Area

LAN Access to the Internet

As the figure illustrates, there are several methods of contacting an ISP to gain access to the Internet. You can dial them up directly using an analog modem and the **plain old telephone system (POTS)**. Or you can make special arrangements with service providers for special always-on services such as DSL, ISDN, **cable**, or **satellite services**. These services can be obtained through direct links to the phone company or an ISP that represents such services. Most residential users access the Internet in this manner.

However, in commerce and industrial settings, it is more common for users to work in a LAN environment. In these environments, Internet access is generally provided through the existing local area network structure. One or more of the LAN's network devices are used to provide some type of **gateway** to the Internet as illustrated in Figure 6-35. This arrangement may involve a third-party ISP, or in large organizations, the company may act as its own ISP.

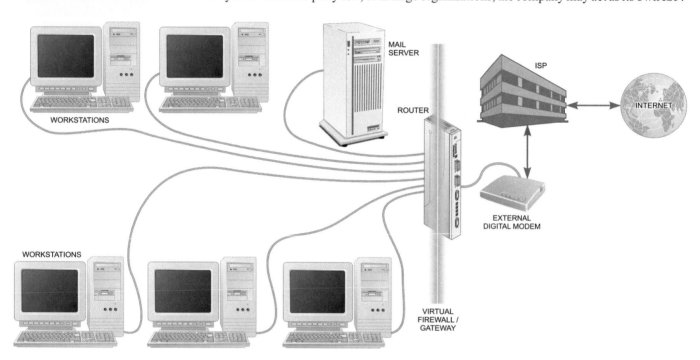

Figure 6-35: Internet Gateways

The network device that offers the gateway service may be a stand-alone router, or it could be one of the LAN's servers acting as a router for the LAN. The example of using a router as a gateway to the outside world has led to the terms *router* and *gateway* being used interchangeably. When the router is used as the gateway, the outside world only sees the router, not the individual computers attached to the LAN.

When a computer is used to serve as the gateway, it may actually be configured to perform several connection functions. Of course the server's first function is to perform all of the routing services for the LAN. This includes properly routing incoming messages to the proper node on the LAN and forwarding outgoing messages to the Internet. To accomplish this, the server must possess an **Internet connection sharing** utility that will enable it to represent the other computers on the LAN.

The server may also act as a **proxy server** for the LAN. A proxy server is a computer used to perform services locally and then forward requests for services that it cannot fulfill to an appropriate server. In this case, the proxy server function of the gateway computer could be used to cache (store) Web pages that have recently been accessed from the Internet, so that if they are needed again, they can be accessed locally instead of trying to reach them over the Internet. This improves network performance by reducing the load placed on the bandwidth capabilities of the link between the company and the Internet. If the requested page is not in the proxy cache, the server forwards the request to the Internet for resolution.

proxy server

The gateway computers may also act as a **firewall**. A firewall is a combination of hardware and software components that provides a protective barrier between networks with different security levels (e.g., the LAN and the Internet). Rules for transmitting and receiving information to and from the other network can be established for the firewall so that specific types of items or addresses will not be allowed to pass between the networks.

firewall

In some versions of this LAN connection scheme, a router is placed between the gateway computer and the Internet. In this case, the router is the only device seen by the outside world, but its function is single-ended in that the LAN server still represents the other computers on the LAN. However, the router can still be used to provide the firewall services referred to earlier.

The physical connection between the LAN and the Internet can be a dial-up connection using the telephone network, or it may involve one of the newer faster **always-on** access methods—ISDN, DSL, cable, or satellite. Corporate customers and large organizations may lease special multichannel T1 or T3 telephone lines for direct access to the Internet or ISP. The following sections of this chapter deal with these various Internet connectivity technologies.

always-on

Dial-Up Networking

Essentials 5.1

Technical Support 4.1

The world's largest communications network is the public telephone system. When computers use this network to communicate with each other it is referred to as **dial-up networking (DUP)**. Computers connect to the phone system through devices, called modems, and communicate with each other using audio tone signals. In order to use the telephone system, the modem must duplicate the dialing characteristics of a telephone and be able to communicate within the frequencies that occur within the audible hearing range of human beings (after all, this is the range that telephone lines are set up to accommodate).

dial-up networking (DUN)

Modems

If a peripheral is located at a distance greater than about 50 ft from the computer, you cannot simply use a longer cable for the communication. As the connecting cable gets longer, its natural resistance and distributive capacitance tend to distort digital signals until they are no longer digital. In order to overcome this signal deterioration, a device called a **modem** (short for modulator/demodulator) is used to convert the parallel, digital signals of the computer into serial, analog signals that are better suited for transmission over wire.

modem

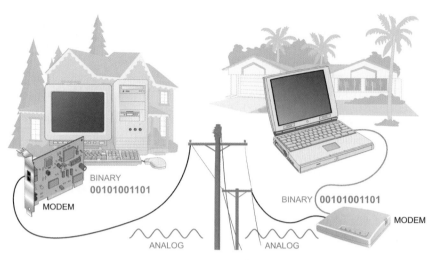

As the distance between terminals increases, it soon becomes impractical to use dedicated cabling to carry data. Fortunately, there is already a very extensive communications network in existence—the public telephone network. Unfortunately, the phone lines were designed to carry analog voice signals instead of digital data. The design of the public phone system limits the frequency at which data may be transmitted over these lines. Modems enable computers to communicate with other computers through the telephone lines, as depicted in Figure 6-36.

Figure 6-36: Modem Communications

┌─ TEST TIP ─────────

Be able to state the difference between simplex, half-duplex, and full-duplex transmissions and as you move through the text, be able to identify which communications systems use each type.

simplex mode

half-duplex mode

full-duplex mode

In its simplest form, a modem consists of two major blocks, a modulator and a demodulator. The modulator is a transmitter that converts the parallel/digital computer data into a serial/analog format for transmission. The demodulator is the receiver that accepts the serial/analog transmission format and converts it into a parallel/digital format usable by the computer, or peripheral.

When a modem is used to send signals in only one direction, it is operating in **simplex mode**. Modems capable of both transmitting and receiving data are divided into two groups, based on their mode of operation. In **half-duplex mode**, modems exchange data, but only in one direction at a time, as illustrated in Figure 6-37. Multiplexing the send and receive signal frequencies will allow both modems to send and receive data simultaneously. This mode of operation is known as **full-duplex mode**.

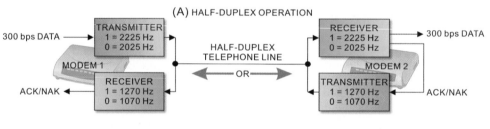

Figure 6-37: Half-Duplex and Full-Duplex Communications

REFERENCE SHELF

For more in-depth information about how modems actually work, refer to the Electronic Reference Shelf on the CD that accompanies this book.

Installing Modems

Modems can be either internal or external devices, as illustrated in Figure 6-38. An **internal modem** is installed in one of the computer's expansion slots and has its own interfacing circuitry. The **external modem** is usually a box that resides outside the system unit and is connected to one of the computer's serial ports by an RS-232 serial cable. These units depend on the interfacing circuitry of the computer's serial ports. External modems also require a separate power source.

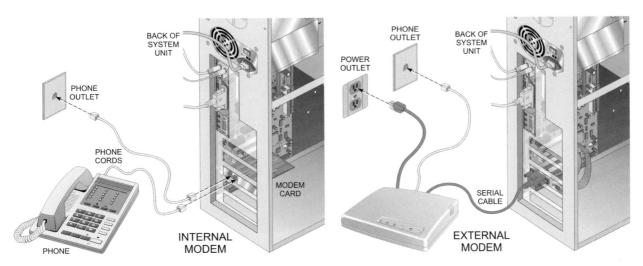

In both cases, the modem typically connects to the telephone line through a standard 4-pin RJ-11 telephone jack. The RJ designation stands for **registered jack**. A second RJ-11 jack in the modem allows an additional telephone to be connected to the line for voice usage. A still smaller 4-pin RJ-12 connector is used to connect the telephone handset to the telephone base. Be aware that an RJ-14 jack looks exactly like the RJ-11, but that it defines two lines to accommodate advanced telephone features such as caller ID and call waiting.

Figure 6-38: Internal and External Modems

The procedures for installing a modem vary somewhat depending on whether it is an internal or external device. To install an internal modem you must remove the cover from the system unit, locate a compatible empty expansion slot, remove the expansion slot cover from the rear of the system unit, and install the modem card in the system. Connect the phone line to the appropriate connector on the modem, as shown in Figure 6-39. Then, connect the other end of the phone line to the commercial phone jack. Finally, replace the system unit cover. All modern modems should automatically be configured through the Plug-and-Play procedure.

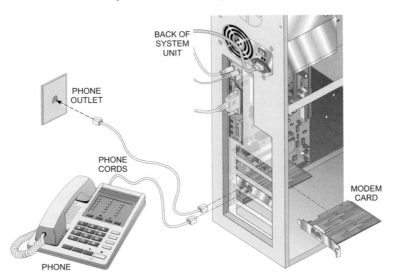

Figure 6-39: Installing an Internal Modem

It is somewhat simpler to install an external modem. There is no need to remove the system unit cover to install an external modem. Simply connect the serial signal cable to the serial COM port connector on the rear of the system, and connect the opposite end of the cable to the RS-232 connector of the external modem unit. Next, connect the phone line to the appropriate connector on the modem and the other end to the phone system jack. You can also connect a telephone to the appropriate connector on the modem. Finally, verify that the power switch or power supply is turned off, connect the power supply to the external modem unit, and verify this connection arrangement in Figure 6-40.

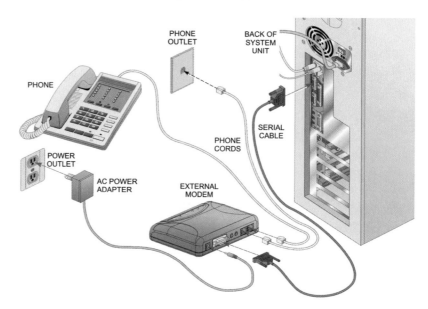

Figure 6-40: Installing an External Modem

Modem Configuration

With PCI-based internal modems, the configuration process is simple, because these cards possess PnP capabilities that enable the system to automatically configure them with the resources they need to operate.

If the PnP process does not recognize a given modem, the operating system will request that the OEM driver disk be inserted in the floppy or CD-ROM drive so that it can obtain the drivers required to support the modem. In some cases, these drivers may need to be loaded through the Windows Add/Remove Hardware applet in the Control Panel.

With external modems, the system interacts with the host port, and the port's UART interacts with the system. Even if there is no device connected to a COM port, the computer knows the port is there. Software supplied with the modem controls the communication process.

After the modem hardware has been installed, you will need applications to make use of the modem. These applications can be third-party calling programs (usually supplied with the modem) or programs built into the operating system (such as Browsers—*Internet Explorer* or *Firefox*—and e-mail programs—*Outlook* or *Outlook Express*). These programs must be configured to work with the modem hardware. Procedures for configurating these sections of the Windows operating systems are covered in detail in Chapter 10, *Windows Operating Systems*.

ISDN Connections

As discussed earlier in the chapter, ISDN service offers high-speed access to the public telephone system. However, ISDN service requires digital modems (also referred to as **terminal adapters**, or **TAs**). Not only does the end-user require a digital modem, the telephone company's switch gear equipment must be updated to handle digital switching. This fact has slowed implementation of ISDN services until recently.

Three levels of ISDN service are available: **basic rate interface (BRI)** services, **primary rate interface (PRI)** services, and **broadband ISDN (BISDN)** services.

BRI services are designed to provide residential users with basic digital service through the existing telephone system. The cost of this service is relatively low, although it is more expensive than regular analog service. BRI service is not available in all areas of the country, but it is expanding rapidly.

Typical residential telephone wiring consists of a four-wire cable. Up to seven devices can be connected to these wires. Under the BRI specification, the telephone company delivers three information channels to the residence over a two-wire cable. The two-wire system is expanded into the four-wire system at the residence through a **network terminator**. The ISDN organizational structure is depicted in Figure 6-41.

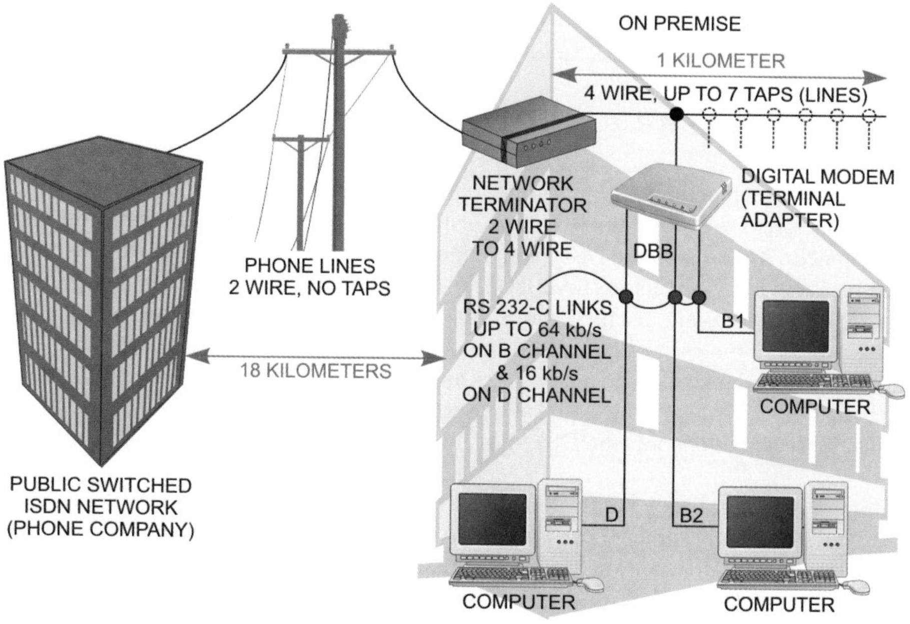

terminal adapters (TAs)

basic rate interface (BRI)

primary rate interface (PRI)

broadband ISDN (BISDN)

network terminator

**Figure 6-41:
ISDN Organizational
Structure**

The BRI information channels exist as a pair of 64 kbps channels and a 16 kbps control channel. The two 64 kbps channels, called **bearer** or **B channels**, can be used to transmit and receive voice and data information. The 16 kbps **D channel** is used to implement advanced control features such as call waiting, call forwarding, caller ID, and others. The D channel also can be used to conduct packet-transfer operations.

bearer

B channels

D channel

PRI services are more elaborate ISDN services that support the very high data rates needed for live video transmissions. This is accomplished using the telephone company's existing wiring and advanced ISDN devices. The operating cost of PRI service is considerably more expensive than BRI services. The higher costs of PRI tend to limit its usage to larger businesses.

The fastest, most expensive ISDN service is broadband ISDN. This level of service provides extremely high transfer rates (up to 622 Mbps) over coaxial or fiber-optic cabling. Advanced transmission protocols are also used to implement broadband ISDN.

ISDN modems are available in both internal and external formats. In the case of external devices, the analog link between the computer and the modem requires D-to-A and A-to-D conversion processes at the computer's serial port and then again at the modem. Of course, with an internal digital modem, these conversion processes are not required.

Digital Subscriber Lines

digital subscriber lines (DSL)

The telephone companies have begun to offer a new high-bandwidth connection service to home and business customers in the form of **digital subscriber lines** (**DSL**). This technology provides high-speed communication links by using the existing telephone lines to generate bandwidths ranging up to 9 Mbps or more. However, distance limitations and line quality conditions can reduce the actual throughput that can be achieved with these connections.

DSL Modems and Splitters

DSL modem

ADSL terminal unit (ATU)

As with ISDN connections, DSL communications requires a special **DSL modem** (also known as an **ADSL terminal unit** [**ATU**]) to provide the interface between the computer (or the computer network) and the DSL phone line. DSL modem connections are illustrated in Figure 6-42. DSL modems are available in both internal and external configurations. Internal DSL modems are installed in one of the host computer's expansion slots, similar to an analog dial-up modem. External DSL modems connect to the computer through a USB port, or network adapter card. In many cases, an Ethernet router is installed between the DSL modem and the LAN to provide equal access to the Internet connection. Normally, a CAT 5 UTP cable is used to connect the DSL modem to a port on the router.

POTS splitter

splitter-based DSL

splitter-less DSLs

Installing a device called a **POTS splitter** in the DSL connection separates the telephone voice band (0−4 kHz) and the DSL band used to transmit digital information. This enables the DSL phone line connection to be used for both telephone/voice and data communications. Depending on the DSL service provider, the splitter may be manually installed at the subscriber location (**splitter-based DSL**), or the signal splitting may be provided remotely from the telephone exchange carrier local office (**splitter-less DSL**). A splitter variation referred to as *Distributed Splitter DSL service* lowers the complexity at the subscriber location but is more complex to implement at the local office.

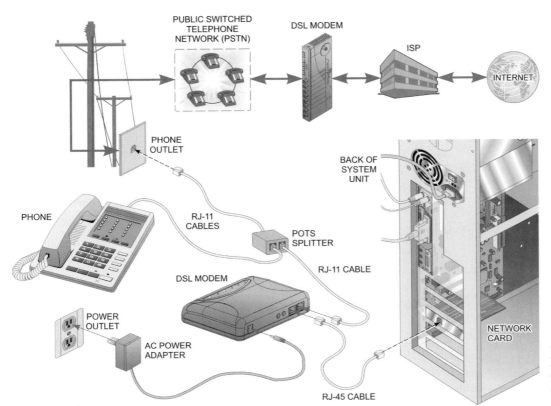

Figure 6-42: DSL Modem Connections

With most new DSL installations, line splitters are not required. Instead, telephone line filters are used to separate voice information from communications data. This is achieved by placing line filters on all the lines used by telephones. These filters are placed inline with the phones, as illustrated in Figure 6-43, so that users do not hear the sound of the digital communications going on. It is important to note that no line filter should be placed in line with the network and computer equipment, because it will prevent the digital data from reaching it.

┌─ **TEST TIP** ──────────
Be aware of the consequences of placing a line filter inline with the computer and network equipment in a DSL installation.
└───────────────────────

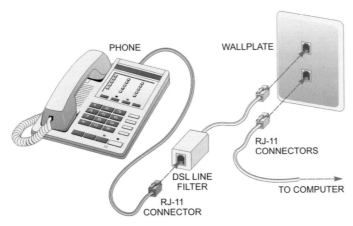

Figure 6-43: DSL Line Filters

There are several advantages to using a DSL connection over standard dial-up connections. Some of these advantages include

- The speed of DSL connections (1.5 Mbps) is much higher than that of dial-up connections using regular modems (56 kbps).

- The Internet connection can remain open while the phone line is used for voice calls.

- DSL service employs existing telephone wires between the home and the telephone-switching center (referred to as the local office).

- The local exchange carrier that offers DSL usually provides the DSL modem as part of the installation.

However, there are disadvantages associated with using DSL technology:

- A DSL connection works better when you are closer to the provider's central office.

- The connection is faster for receiving data than it is for sending data over the Internet.

- DSL service is not available in all locations.

DSL Versions

xDSL

asymmetric DSL
(ADSL)

symmetric DSL
(SDSL)

high-data-rate DSL
(HDSL)

symmetric DSL
(SDSL)

The term **xDSL** is used to refer to all types of DSL collectively. There are two main categories of DSL —**asymmetric DSL (ADSL)** and **symmetric DSL (SDSL)**. Two other types of xDSL technologies that have some promise are **high-data-rate DSL (HDSL)** and **symmetric DSL (SDSL)**.

SDSL is referred to as *symmetric* because it supports the same data rates for upstream and downstream traffic. Conversely, ADSL (also known as rate-adaptive DSL) supports different data transfer rates when receiving data (referred to as the *downstream* rate) and transmitting data (known as the *upstream* rate). SDSL supports data transfer rates up to 3 Mbps in both directions, and ADSL supports data transfer rates of from 1.5 to 9 Mbps downstream and from 16 to 640 kbps upstream. Both forms of DSL require special modems that employ sophisticated modulation schemes to pack data onto telephone wires. However, you should be aware that access speeds may also vary from provider to provider, even if they are using the same central office to provide service.

TEST TIP

Be aware that ADSL provides different upload and download speeds.

POTS (plain old
telephone system)

xDSL is similar to the ISDN arrangements just discussed in that they both operate over existing copper **POTS (plain old telephone system)** telephone lines. Also, they both require short geographical cable runs (less than 20,000 feet) to the nearest central telephone office. However, as we've just stated, xDSL services offer much higher transfer speeds. In doing so, the xDSL technologies use a much greater range of frequencies on the telephone lines than do the traditional voice services. In addition, DSL technologies use the telephone lines as a constant connection so that users can have access to the Internet and e-mail on a 24/7 basis. There is no need to connect with an ISP each time you want to go online.

TEST TIP

Know that the maximum distance that is specified between the subscriber location and the local office for ADSL is 18,000 feet.

Asymmetric DSL Versions

Asymmetric DSL (ADSL)

Asymmetric DSL (ADSL) works by splitting the phone line into two frequency ranges. The frequencies below 4 kHz are reserved for voice, and the range above that is used for data. This makes it possible to use the line for phone calls and data network access at the same time. This type of DSL is called "asymmetric" because more bandwidth is reserved for receiving data than for sending data. Asymmetric variations include ADSL, G.lite ADSL, RADSL, and VDSL. The collection of ADSL standards facilitates interoperability between all standard forms of ADSL.

- *Asymmetric DSL (ADSL)*—Full-rate ADSL offers differing upload and download speeds and can be configured to deliver up to 6 megabits of data per second (6000 K) from the network to the customer, that is, up to 120 times faster than dial-up service and 100 times faster than ISDN. ADSL enables voice and high-speed data to be sent simultaneously over the existing telephone line.

- *G.lite ADSL*—The *G.lite* standard was specifically developed to meet the plug-and-play requirements of the consumer market. It is a medium bandwidth version of ADSL that provides Internet access at up to 1.5 megabits downstream and up to 500 kilobits upstream.

- *Rate Adaptive DSL (RADSL)*—RADSL is a nonstandard version of ADSL, although standard ADSL also permits the ADSL modem to adapt speeds of data transfer.

- *Very High Bit Rate DSL (VDSL)*—VDSL offers transfer rates of up to 26 Mbps, over distances up to 50 meters on short loops such as from fiber to the curb. VDSL lines are normally served from neighborhood cabinets that link to a central office through fiber-optic cabling. This type of DSL is particularly useful for campus-type environments.

TEST TIP

Be aware that ADSL has the slowest upstream rate, and VDSL has the fastest upstream rate.

Table 6-5: ADSL Performance versus Local Loop Length

Table 6-5 illustrates the downstream performance of ADSL as a function of the distance from the subscriber to the local office.

One disadvantage of ADSL service is that when the ADSL local loop length increases, the available bandwidth decreases for both upstream (not shown) and downstream traffic. These numbers assume 24-gauge wire; performance decreases significantly if 26-gauge wire exists on the local loop.

CABLE LENGTH (FEET)	BANDWIDTH AVAILABILITY (kbps)
18,000	1,544
16,000	2,048
12,000	6,312
9,000	8,448

Symmetric DSL Versions

symmetric DSL

As with ASDSL, there are several varieties of **symmetric DSL**. These versions include SHDSL, HDSL, HDSL-2, and IDSL. The equal upstream and downstream speeds make symmetric DSL versions useful for LAN access, videoconferencing, and for locations that host their own Web sites.

- *Symmetric DSL (SDSL)*—SDSL is a vendor-proprietary version of symmetric DSL that may include bit-rates to and from the customer ranging of 128 kbps to 2.32 Mbps. SDSL is an umbrella term for a number of supplier-specific implementations over a single copper pair providing variable rates of symmetric service.

TEST TIP

Know that SDSL has the slowest downstream rate, and VDSL has the fastest downstream rate.

- *Symmetric HDSL (SHDSL)* (also known as G.shdsl)—SHDL is the newest, industry standard symmetric DSL version. This service can operate at bit-rates ranging from 192 kbps up to 2.3 Mbps, depending on the type of customer and installation parameters. Overall, it achieves 20% better useful distance than previous versions of symmetric DSL (i.e., 1.2 Mbps transmissions at distances over 20,000 feet using 26 AWG wire).

  SHDSL is designed for data-only applications that require high upstream bit-rates. Though SHDSL does not carry voice like ADSL, new **voice-over-DSL** techniques permit these services to be used for transmitting digitized voice and data.

- *High Data Rate DSL (HDSL)*—This DSL variety delivers symmetric service at speeds up to 2.3 Mbps in both directions. Available at 1.5 or 2.3 Mbps, this symmetric fixed-rate application does not provide standard telephone service over the same line.

- *High Data Rate DSL, 2nd-generation (HDSL2)*—This HDSL delivers 1.5 Mbps service each way, supporting voice, data, and video using either ATM (asynchronous transfer mode), private-line service, or frame relay over a single copper pair. This standard for this symmetric service gives a fixed 1.5 Mbps rate both upstream and downstream. HDSL2 does not provide standard voice telephone service on the same wire pair. The HDSL2 standard employs one pair of wires to transmit data at 1.5 Mbps, whereas HDSL requires two pairs.

- *Integrated Services Digital Network DSL (ISDL)*—This DSL type supports symmetric data rates of up to 144 kbps using existing phone lines. It is unique in that it has the ability to deliver services through a remote device, called a *digital loop carrier (DLC)*, that is positioned in planned neighborhoods to simplify the distribution of cable and wiring from the phone company.

Cable Modems

Another competitor in the high-speed Internet connection market involves the local cable television service companies. These companies act as ISPs and provide Internet access through their existing **broadband** cable television networks. To accomplish this, the cable companies offer special **cable modems** that attach the computer to an existing **cable TV (CATV)** network connection in the home.

The cable modem typically features two main connections—one to the host computer's USB port or 10/100 Ethernet network adapter and the other to the CATV coaxial cable outlet on the wall. A CAT 5 UTP cable normally provides the communication path between the cable modem and the NIC card. The cable modem has a BNC connector that is used to attach the coaxial cable from the cable system to the cable modem. Figure 6-44 illustrates this connection scheme.

When a cable modem subscriber configures multiple computers in a LAN environment, the connection between the cable modem and the network may be made through a gateway/router. This places the router between the modem and the other computers on the network. As with the LAN/Internet connection scheme described earlier, the router provides each computer on the LAN with equal access to the Internet through the modem.

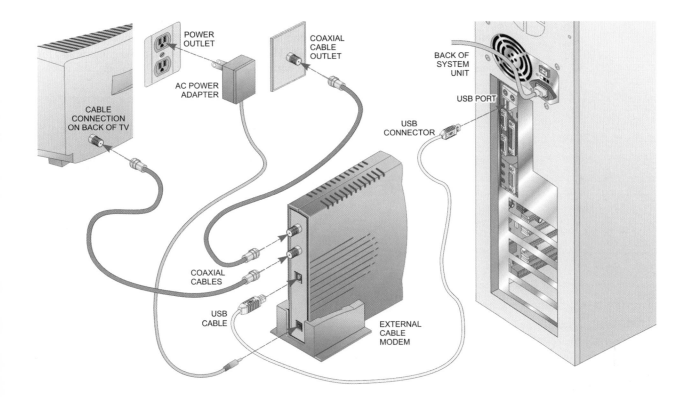

The cable modem is similar to an ASDL modem, because it establishes two different transmission rates. They provide for the uploading of data (information leaving the subscriber PC to the server) to have a slightly slower speed than the downloading of information (the server sending information to the subscriber). The typical cable modem transfers data at speeds up to 38 Mbps downstream and 10 Mbps upstream. For comparison, this is about 1000 times faster than the fastest analog modem connections using dial-up service. However, these rates vary depending upon the number of users on the cable (because cable Internet access is a shared service).

There is a standard for cable modems in North America called **DOCSIS (data over cable service interface specification)**. To deliver DOCSIS data services over a cable television network, one 6 MHz radio frequency (RF) channel is typically allocated for downstream traffic to residential subscribers. Another frequency channel is used to carry upstream signals.

Figure 6-44: A Cable Modem Configuration

DOCSIS (data over cable service interface specification)

Essentials 5.2

Installing Digital Modems

Although dial-up modems continue to play a large part in the WAN field, they tend to be limited in their capability to move data. However, several high-speed broadband communications technologies have become available to most users. These technologies include ISDN, DSL, cable modems, and satellite communication links.

Each of these technologies is provided through a service provider that supplies the service for a fee. These technologies also all involve some type of specialized digital modem to make the connection.

Figure 6-45 illustrates a typical digital modem connection scheme. Although each digital modem type employs different connection media, the structure of the physical installation is identical for all the different technologies. The modem sits between the computer and the outside service media (such as telephone wires, CATV cable, or satellite dish).

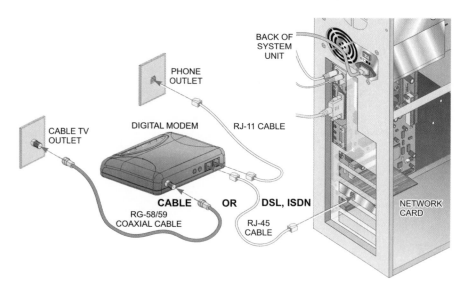

**Figure 6-45:
Installing Digital
Modems**

The host system sees the digital modems in ISDN, DSL, and cable modem connections through a network adapter card, so the system must be configured for network operation. No OEM drivers need to be loaded for these devices to function. In the case of the satellite connection, the host computer's USB port is used. Because satellite modems are not typical connectivity devices, you might need to load OEM drivers supplied by the manufacturer for the system to work with the PC.

In residential installations, this connection scheme is normally direct. However, in business environments, one computer is typically used as a gateway between the internal LAN and the external network (that is, the Internet). Some LAN connection schemes include a router between the gateway computer and the outside network to represent the complete LAN as a single unit. This makes unauthorized access to the internal LAN harder for outsiders to accomplish.

The basic steps for installing a broadband cable modem or DSL modem include the following:

1. Obtain the digital modem and support documentation from the service company. This should come as part of the cable or DSL service agreement.

2. Install a network adapter card in the host computer.

3. For broadband DSL connections, place filters on all phone and fax connections throughout the residence—except for the one the DSL modem will use. Note: this must include telephone connections to satellite receivers, answering machines, and computer fax modems.

4. Connect the digital modem to the commercial connection (i.e., the broadband interface for the cable or the telephone line) and power up the modem. For cable modems, connect the CATV cable to the modem. Connect DSL modem to the phone line.

5. Connect the digital modem to the network adapter or a router. In both cases, this involves connecting a CAT5 cable between the digital modem and NIC (or router). If a router is used, the host computer must be connected through the router.

6. Start the host computer and configure the network connection for DHCP operation. Verify that all of the status lights on the digital modem are active (typically, Power, Activity, and Link lights—Power and Link should be on and solid, Activity may flicker depending on the activity level of the network).

7. Configure authentication for the connection. Depending on the service provider's requirement, you may need to run their installation disk. Typical required information includes account number, username, and password (assigned by the service provider when the kit is delivered).

There are two different processes you may encounter for configuring authentication for the connection—**point-to-point protocol over Ethernet (PPoE)** and non-PPoE. If there is an installation CD, the authentication process will be performed automatically as part of the setup. However, if no installation CD is provided, you must manually configure the router to perform the authentication process.

point-to-point protocol over Ethernet (PPoE)

Under the PPoE method, the authentication requires that a username and password (supplied by the service provider) be entered in the router's configuration table. Under the non-PPoE method, the MAC address of the NIC or router connected directly to the digital modem must be supplied to the service provider (usually over the telephone).

8. Verify that you have received an IP address from the router (ipconfig /all). The IP address of the machine should be in the range supplied by the router (typically 192.168.1.X). You should also see a gateway address that should match the address of the router (typically 192.168.1.1).

9. Ping the default gateway (router) to confirm connectivity.

10. Open a browser and attempt to access a Web site (*www.mic-inc.com*).

If you cannot access the Internet, obtain a known IP address from the Web and attempt to Ping it. If this does not work, contact the technical support service of the service provider.

Satellite Internet Access

Two major companies (DirecTV and Dish Network) have successfully entered the market for television distribution using signals delivered to the customer via satellite. In these distribution systems, television signals are transmitted up to a satellite in orbit around the earth (**uplinked**) and then retransmitted to satellite receiver dishes installed in residences and offices (**downlinked**). These companies have not been content to simply compete for television distribution markets. They have also taken on the cable distribution companies by providing Internet access via satellite link.

uplinked

downlinked

These services have been provided using two methods—two-way satellite link and separate up- and downlink channels using satellite and dial-up telephone lines. In most systems, the satellite dish has no uplink capabilities, so users cannot send data to retrieve information from the Web. This function must be supplied through the telephone connection. Download speeds are very good (up to 1.5 Mbps), but upload speeds are limited to the 56 kbps speed of the dial-up modem. In other systems, the dish is equipped with multiple transceivers that provide both up- and downlinks through the satellite link.

Figure 6-46 depicts a typical satellite/Internet communications configuration.

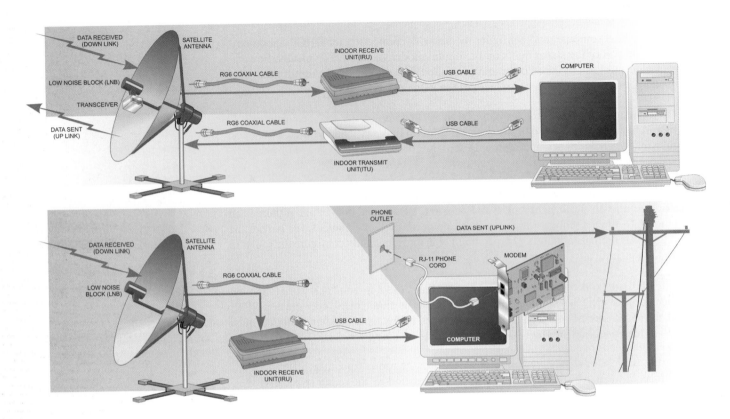

Figure 6-46:
Satellite Internet
Access

low noise block (LNB)

satellite receiver

As the figure illustrates, the satellite dish is the transmitter and the receiver for both the television and Internet signals. The dish holds a device known as a **low noise block (LNB)** converter that receives the satellite signal, removes the noise from it, and converts it into a digital signal that is compatible with the **satellite receiver**. RG-6 coaxial cable is used to connect the LNBs and the satellite receiver. The receiver unit separates the received demodulated signal into the individual television and Internet channels. It typically furnishes multiple methods for connecting to the television sets in the facility, including through RG-59 coaxial cabling and S-video/optical audio cabling options.

Most receiver models employ a dial-up connection for the uplink portion of the Internet operation but employ the satellite channel to provide very high-speed downloads and streaming media service. However, some more expensive models provide an *"always-on"* uplink through the satellite system as well. On the downlink side, the Internet access signal is considered to be just another channel coming from the satellite that gets filtered out and sent to the computer system, normally through a standard USB port. However, when satellite uplink method is included, two USB satellite units are required. These units include the receiver (also called the *indoor receive unit* or *IRU*) and an additional *indoor transmit unit* (*ITU*). The ITU unit is connected to a digital-to-Rf converter mounted on the dish that performs the uplink function. The IRU unit shares the USB connection to the computer with the ITU unit.

Wireless Internet Access

Many businesses have installed networks with wireless access points in their facilities to provide Internet services to their customers who carry Internet-ready wireless computing devices. In these settings, businesses such as restaurants, hotels, and airports become wireless service providers by installing access points that provide their customers with Internet access within the WiFi-enabled **hotspot** they establish. Customers with wireless-equipped portable computers can connect to the Internet while they patronize the business. **WiFi (wireless fidelity)** is a trademark used by wireless LANs that operate on unlicensed radio spectrum and are therefore restricted to limited transmitter power covering an area of 200–300 feet from the antenna. In most cases, this Internet connectivity is a for-pay service that the customer signs up for.

Broadband wireless Internet access has also begun to appear in some markets. This service employs a long-range wireless modem to transmit to and receive signals from **cellular** towers instead of using traditional dial-up phone line connections. The wireless broadband modem simply connects into the computer or network connectivity device. Then you install the software that comes with the modem, and it's up and working. You can connect the modem into a wireless router/AP and have both wired and wireless Internet access throughout the network. The modem is highly portable. It can also be taken along with the computer to other areas where the broadband wireless hosting service is available, and it will work there as well.

There are a number of computing devices that have moved into the wireless Internet access market. In particular, cellular telephones, personal digital devices, and **tablet PCs** have become major technologies involved in the wireless Internet market. Tablet PCs are small computer systems that offer a trade-off between PDAs and notebooks. They feature touch-screen operation like a PDA, but tend to include items such as multiple-gigabyte hard drives and USB ports. They typically work with docking stations just like a laptop to provide removable drives and usually have built-in wireless networking.

Cell phones are widely used to send and receive text messages, e-mail, graphics transmissions, and Internet downloads. In the same vein, many PDA manufacturers have included wireless Internet access capabilities with their devices. National ISPs or telephone providers typically supply the actual Internet access service.

hotspot
WiFi (wireless fidelity)
Broadband wireless Internet
cellular
tablet PCs

TCP/IP

The key to the Internet is the **transmission control protocol/Internet protocol (TCP/IP)**. The U.S. Department of Defense originally developed the TCP/IP protocol as a hacker-resistant, secure protocol for transmitting data across a network. It is considered to be one of the most secure of the network protocols. Because the U.S. government developed TCP/IP, no one actually owns the TCP/IP protocol, and so it was adopted as the transmission standard for the Internet. Due to its ability to connect to many different types of computers and servers, TCP/IP is used in the majority of all computer networks and is the preferred network protocol for Windows 2000.

transmission control protocol/Internet protocol (TCP/IP)

network packets

header fields

IP header

TCP header

However, the main reason that TCP/IP is the most widely used network protocol today is the Internet. No matter what type of computer platform or software is being used, information must move across the Internet in the form of TCP/IP packets. This protocol calls for data to be grouped together in bundles called **network packets**. The TCP/IP packet is designed primarily to allow for message fragmentation and reassembly. It exists through two **header fields**, the **IP header** and the **TCP header**, followed by the data field, as illustrated in Figure 6-47.

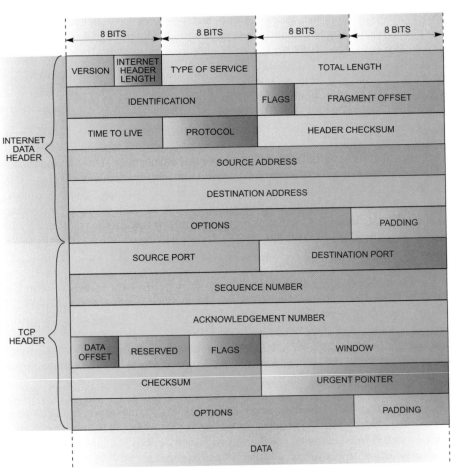

**Figure 6-47:
TCP/IP Packet**

┌─ **TEST TIP** ─┐
Know what TCP/IP
is and what it does.
└─────────────┘

The TCP/IP protocol was so widely accepted by the Internet community that virtually every network operating system supports it, including Apple, MS-DOS/Windows, UNIX, Linux, OS/2, and even networked printers. It can also be used on any topology (e.g., Ethernet, Token Ring, etc.). Therefore, all of these computer types can exchange data across a network using the TCP/IP protocol.

┌─ **TEST TIP** ─────────────┐
Know the advantages of using the
TCP/IP protocol.
└──────────────────────────┘

The TCP/IP Suite

Over time, the TCP/IP protocol has expanded to include many options that network technicians and administrators must understand to ensure proper configuration and operation of TCP/IP systems. First of all, the TCP/IP protocol is not a single protocol—it is actually a *suite of protocols* that were originally developed by the Department of Defense in 1969. TCP/IP consists of two main parts—transmission control protocol (TCP) and Internet protocol (IP). These protocols work together with a number of other protocols in a structure referred to as a protocol stack.

As was mentioned earlier, the most important function of the network protocol is to make sure that information gets to the network location it is intended for. Ultimately this is the real function of the TCP/IP protocol. It accomplishes this by routing packets of information to locations specified by IP addresses. In Figure 5-46 you should have noticed that the TCP/IP header contained two addresses—the source address that the message comes from and the destination address that it is being sent to.

Because humans don't relate to strings of numbers very well, computers are typically identified by name. For information to get to the address humans want it to go, there has to be some resolution between the numerical IP addresses understood by computers and the alphanumeric names we give them. To accomplish this, TCP/IP relies on a group of protocols and services that represent special advanced name and address resolution functions. These protocols and services include

- *DNS (Domain Name System) service*—a service that works with the hierarchical DNS naming system employed by the Internet

- *WINS (Windows Internet Name Service)*—a service that works with the Microsoft naming system used with earlier Microsoft networks

- *DHCP (Dynamic Host Configuration Protocol)*—a protocol that is used by ISPs and other networks to automatically assign users IP addresses from a rotating pool of available addresses

- *ARP (Address Resolution Protocol)*—this protocol/utility is used to modify tables that translate IP-to-Ethernet addresses

In addition to these supporting protocols associated with IP/computer name resolution, the TCP/IP protocol suite includes support for

- Electronic mail transportation

- File and print services

- Web browsing

- Network troubleshooting

The information in the remainder of this chapter deals primarily with IP address issues. However, the other TCP/IP components will be examined in the different operating system chapters, Chapters 9 and 10, while the troubleshooting tools are described in Chapter 12, *Operating System Troubleshooting*.

In addition to its domain name tracking function, the DNS system resolves (links) individual domain names of computers to their current IP address listings. Some IP addresses are permanently assigned to a particular domain name so that whenever the domain name is issued on the Internet, it always accesses the same IP address. This is referred to as **static IP addressing**. However, most ISPs use a **dynamic IP addressing** scheme for allocating IP addresses.

If an ISP wanted to service 10,000 customers within its service area using static IP addressing, it would need to purchase and maintain 10,000 IP addresses. However, because most Internet customers are not online all of the time, their IP addresses are not always in use. This allows the ISP to purchase a reasonable number of IP addresses that it can hold in a bank and dynamically assign to its users as they log on to their service. When the user logs out, the IP address returns to the bank for other users.

The Internet software communicates with the service provider by embedding the TCP/IP information in a **point-to-point protocol (PPP)** shell for transmission through the modem in analog format. The communications equipment, at the service provider's site, converts the signal back to the digital TCP/IP format. Older units running the **UNIX** operating system used a connection protocol called **Serial Line Internet Protocol (SLIP)** for dial-up services.

Domain Name Service

In order to communicate with another computer in a TCP/IP network, your computer must have the IP address of the destination host. As users, we generally specify the name of a computer when establishing connections, such as Marcraft1, not the IP address. These names need to be converted into the IP address of the destination computer. The process of matching a computer name to an IP address is called *name resolution*. The **domain name service (DNS)** can be used to perform name resolution for any TCP/IP client.

DNS is a service that runs on one or more servers in the network. These servers have databases that are used to perform the DNS name to IP address resolution function for the network. If your network employs DNS for name resolution, you must configure all the clients with the IP address of one or more DNS servers. Procedures for enabling and configuring DNS as part of the TCP/IP package are presented in later sections of this chapter. DNS is also the name resolution service used for the Internet.

Windows Internet Naming Service

While the DNS naming service is used exclusively by the Internet, it is not the only name-resolution service available to PCs. In the case of older Windows LANs, the **Windows Internet Naming Service (WINS)** service can be installed on one or more servers in the network to perform name resolution on TCP/IP networks. The WINS service can be used to translate IP addresses to *NetBIOS names* within a Windows LAN environment. As with a DNS system, there must be a Windows Name server running the WINS server software present in the network to maintain the WINS database used for resolving IP addresses/NetBIOS names for the LAN.

Pre-Windows 2000 clients can use WINS for name resolution of other Windows computers on the network. However, they will still employ DNS for the name resolution of hosts on the Internet. To use WINS for name resolution, you must configure the clients with the IP address of one or more WINS servers. Each client in the WINS network must contain the WINS client software and be WINS enabled.

┌─ TEST TIP ─────────────┐
│ Know what DNS and WINS are, what │
│ they do, and how they are different. │
└────────────────────────┘

Dynamic Host Configuration Protocol

The **dynamic host configuration protocol (DHCP)** is an Internet protocol that can be used to automatically assign IP addresses to devices on a network using TCP/IP. Using DHCP simplifies network administration, because software, rather than an administrator, assigns and keeps track of IP addresses. For this reason, many ISPs use the dynamic IP addressing function of DHCP to provide access to their dial-up users. The protocol automatically delivers IP addresses, subnet mask and default router configuration parameters, and other configuration information to the devices on the network.

> **dynamic host configuration protocol (DHCP)**

The dynamic addressing portion of the protocol also means that computers can be added to a network without manually assigning them unique IP addresses. As a matter of fact, the devices can be issued a different IP address each time they connect to the network. In some networks, the device's IP address can even change while it is still connected. DHCP also supports a mix of static and dynamic IP addresses.

DHCP is an open standard, developed by the **Internet Engineering Task Force (IETF)**. It is a client–server arrangement in which a DHCP client contacts a DHCP server to obtain its configuration parameters. The DHCP server dynamically configures the clients with parameters appropriate to the current network structure.

> **Internet Engineering Task Force (IETF)**

The most important configuration parameter carried by DHCP is the IP address. A computer must be initially assigned a specific IP address that is appropriate to the network to which the computer is attached, and that is not assigned to any other computer on that network. If a computer moves to a new network, it must be assigned a new IP address for that new network. DHCP can be used to manage these assignments automatically. The DHCP client support is built into Windows 9x, Windows NT 4.0 Workstation, and Windows 2000 Professional. Windows NT 4 and Windows 2000 Server versions include both client and server support for DHCP. These operating systems and DHCP are covered in greater detail in Chapters 9 and 10.

GEEK SQUAD CASE FILE #93144

You work as a Double Agent in store 1009. One day, you receive a call from a customer wondering why her IP address changes periodically. She doesn't have a problem with the operation of her computer, so what do you tell her?

Voice Over IP

Another technology that has advanced rapidly since the last version of this book came out is **voice over IP**, or **VoIP** technology. Sending and receiving data over the Internet has become an efficient, robust, and inexpensive process for billions of people. It was only a matter of time before someone considered replacing the data payload in the IP packet with digitized voice information. Instead of communicating over a fixed-connection circuit switched network (the telephone system), VoIP employs the packet switching technology used on the Internet to provide low-cost, worldwide voice communications.

The major advantage of VoIP communications for the user is cost savings. Most conventional telephone users pay a monthly flat fee for local telephone calls and a per-minute charge for long-distance calls. Because VoIP calls typically use the Internet, these calls are combined into the monthly flat fee structure of the Internet connection. In addition, VoIP users can drop their standard telephone service and use the Internet connection for both data and voice traffic.

The savings is also worldwide. International calls, which can be very costly through the telephone network, can be made with no additional cost through the Internet. Conversely, the VoIP user can place and receive fee-less calls from anywhere in the world as long as they have Internet access. All VoIP calls perform like local telephone calls regardless of where they are made to or from.

IP telephony can be integrated into other Internet services such as audio- and videoconferencing and instant messaging. Like other IP-based services, VoIP is susceptible to viruses, worms, and other malicious hacking. Although this is rare, it is possible, and the VoIP industry is developing encrypting tools to prevent these types of activities from occurring.

VoIP Operations

VoIP communications are sometimes referred to as **broadband phones** because they are most often used with DSL connections. While VoIP does not require DSL connections to operate, the quality of service is certainly better with a broadband connection. VoIP can also be carried out over cable modem connections to the Internet.

There are three commonly used connectivity schemes for placing VoIP calls:

- Using an **analog telephone adapter** (**ATA**) to interface conventional telephones to the computer so that it can use VoIP drivers to take advantage of its Internet connection. Commercial VoIP companies bundle ATA devices with their proprietary hosting services and application and driver software packages. The installation process is straightforward, install the ATA, connect the phone to it, load and configure the VoIP drivers and software, and make IP telephony calls.

- Through special **IP phones** that connect directly to the network (router or hub) using an RJ-45 connector instead of the standard RJ-11 telephone connector. These phones contain all the circuitry and firmware to perform VoIP operations without a host computer.

- **Computer-to-computer VoIP** using the computer's sound card, microphone, and speakers, along with third-party VoIP application software and an Internet connection. This removes all costs from the VoIP operation except the ISP's hosting fee.

Computer-to-computer VoIP

VoIP communications are not limited strictly to the Internet. IP telephony can be used on an IP-based network, such as a LAN. IP telephony calls can be placed to other VoIP devices as well as to normal telephones on the PSTN.

When you initiate a VoIP call, by picking up the handset or activating the application package, a connection is established with the **call processor** running at the VoIP service provider's location. The local VoIP equipment (ATA, IP phone, or VoIP software) returns a dial tone to your handset (or speakers) telling you that a connection to the Internet exists. When you dial a number, a special mapping database program running on the call processor, referred to as a **soft switch**, translates the number into an IP address and establishes a session with the remote number when the handset on the other end picks up.

call processor

soft switch

The Internet handles the VoIP conversation just as it would e-mail or Web page accesses. Packets pass back and forth between the two computers and are converted into analog voice signals by the ATA, IP phone, or VoIP software (depending on the type of connection being used). These elements also keep the session open between the two end users while the call is in progress. When you end the call by hanging up, the handset sends a signal to the ATA (or its equivalent), which, in turn, sends a signal to the soft switch terminating the session. Figure 6-48 illustrates the operation of a VoIP call.

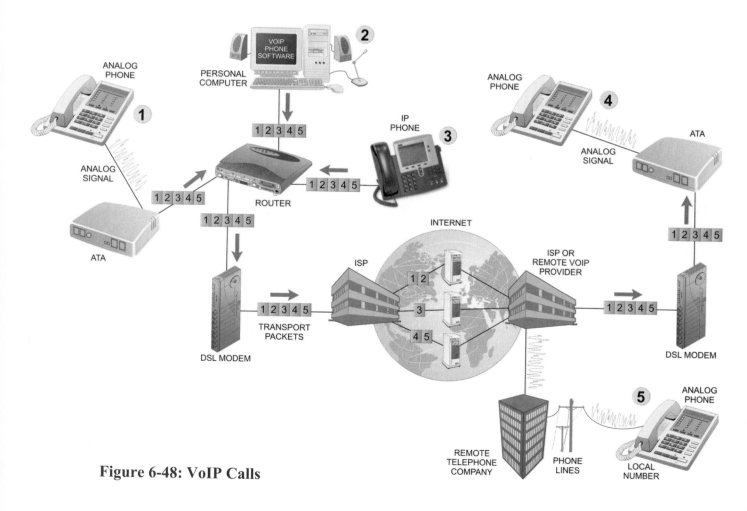

Figure 6-48: VoIP Calls

Internet Resources

The Internet is constructed of resources, or services, offered to users. The range of services available includes file transfers, database access, e-mail, or access to linked documents on the World Wide Web.

uniform resource locator (URL)

A **uniform resource locator** (**URL**) is used to access services on the Internet. A URL is composed of two parts. The first part specifies an Internet resource that's to be accessed. HTTP or FTP are examples of an Internet resource. Frequently, the resource is the name of a particular protocol. For example, both FTP and HTTP are well-established protocols used on the Internet. The second part of a URL lists the name of the server. The server name is followed by the directory path and filename of a particular document.

For example, consider the URL *HTTP:\\help.com/documents/security.txt*. The URL consists of the following parts:

HTTP

help.com

/documents/

security.txt

- **HTTP:** The protocol, or service, that will be accessed.

- **help.com:** The server name (also called the host name or domain name) that is accessed for files.

- **/documents/:** The directory path from which one, or many, specific files may be accessed.

- **security.txt:** The name of the file to be accessed.

┌ **TEST TIP** ─────────┐
Be able to identify the individual
parts of a URL.
└───────────────────────┘

Other common ways of referring to an Internet name are to call it a Web address, Internet address, or Web site. This is a reference to the static IP address assigned to the server name.

The World Wide Web

World Wide Web (WWW)

Web servers

> The **World Wide Web** (**WWW**) is a menu system that ties together Internet resources from around the world. These resources are scattered across computer systems everywhere. **Web servers** inventory the Web's resources and store address pointers, referred to as links, to them.

To access a Web site, the user must place the desired URL on the network. Each URL begins with http:// or https://. These letters stand for hypertext transfer protocol and identify the address as a Web site. The rest of the address is the name of the site being accessed (e.g., *http://www.mic-inc.com* is the home page of Marcraft, located on a server at One World Telecommunications). Each Web site begins with a home page. The home page is the menu to the available contents of the site.

There are numerous types of resources available on the Internet. Typical Internet resources include the following:

hypertext transfer protocol (HTTP)

- The **hypertext transfer protocol** (**HTTP**) is used to access linked documents on the World Wide Web. The documents are prepared with the hypertext markup language (HTML).

- The **hypertext transfer protocol secure (HTTPS)** is used to access linked documents on the World Wide Web that are located on a secure server. A secure server typically requires that a password be entered before access is granted. In some applications, https:// means that documents are encrypted (using the Secure Socket Layer protocol as described in detail later in this chapter) before sending them to a user that connects to the secure site.

- The **file transfer protocol (FTP)** is used to copy files to and from a remote server. When a URL has the ftp:// prefix, it means that the user is accessing a site from which files can be downloaded or uploaded.

- The **mailto:** prefix is used to access an e-mail server. Once the e-mail server is accessed (usually after entering a username and password), the e-mail application is started, and the user can read or write e-mail.

- The **news:** prefix starts the newsgroup application on the Internet. A newsgroup is a bulletin board arranged by specific discussion group titles such as the Internet, Networking, or Computers. There are thousands of newsgroups on the Internet.

- The **gopher://** prefix is used to access the database area of the Internet. Largely replaced by the World Wide Web, Gopher consists of a series of linked menu items.

- The **telnet://** prefix is used to connect a user to a remote server. Once the connection is established, the user has access to software or tools located on the server. When telnet is specified, a separate telnet application begins on the user's workstation. Like Gopher, telnet is being used less and less. Network operating systems like Windows NT and Novell NetWare contain remote access services that have largely replaced telnet.

- The **simple mail transfer protocol (SMTP)** is used to send e-mail across the Internet. E-mail uses conventions that are somewhat different than those used with other services.

- The **file://** prefix is used to access a file on a local server that supports Internet applications. For example, assume the URL *http://inet.com/document/help.txt* is accessed. Once the help.txt file is open, it may include references to other documents on the inet.com server. The file:// prefix can be used to directly connect to one of the other documents.

These utilities must be accessed through the *Tools* option of the Outlook Express applet. From the *Tools* option on the Outlook Express menu bar, select the *Accounts* entry, highlight an account name, and click the *Properties* tab. Finally, click the *Servers* tab to access the e-mail account configuration, as depicted in Figure 6-49.

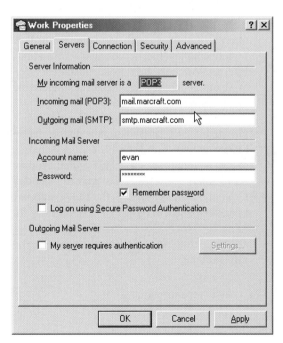

Figure 6-49: E-mail Account Configurations

File Transfer Protocol

A special application, called the **file transfer protocol (FTP)**, is used to upload and download information to, and from, the Net. FTP is a client/server type of software application. The server version runs on the host computer, and the client version runs on the user's station.

To access an FTP site, the user must move into an FTP application and enter the address of the site to be accessed. After the physical connection has been made, the user must log on to the FTP site by supplying an account number and password. When the host receives a valid password, a communication path opens between the host and the user site, and an FTP session begins.

Around the world, thousands of FTP host sites contain millions of pages of information that can be downloaded free of charge. However, most FTP sites are used for file transfers of things like driver updates and large file transfers that are too large for e-mail operations.

FTP Authentication

FTP sites exist on the Internet in two basic formats—private and public. To access most **private FTP sites**, you must connect to the site and input a username and password designated by the FTP host. Most **public FTP sites** employ **anonymous authentication** for access to the site. Anonymous authentication is an interaction that occurs between the local browser and the FTP host without involving the remote user. (That is, no username or passwords are required to gain access.)

E-mail

One of the most widely used functions of WANs is the **electronic mail (e-mail)** feature. This feature enables Internet users to send and receive electronic messages to each other over the Internet. As with the regular postal service, e-mail is sent to an address, from an address. With e-mail, however, you can send the same message to several addresses at the same time, using a mailing list.

On the Internet, the message is distributed in packets, as with any other TCP/IP file. At the receiving end, the e-mail message is reassembled and stored in the recipient's mailbox. When the recipient opens his e-mail program, the e-mail service delivers the message and notifies the user that it has arrived. The default e-mail reader supported by the Windows Outlook Express applet is the **POP3** standard. Likewise, it includes a standard **simple mail transfer protocol (SMTP)** e-mail utility for outgoing e-mail.

When setting up an e-mail account, you must supply the following configuration information:

- Account name
- Password
- POP3 server address
- SMTP server address

Secure Socket Layer Protocol

The **secure socket layer (SSL)** protocol is used to authenticate users or e-commerce servers on the Internet, and to encrypt/decrypt messages (particularly credit card purchases) by using a security process called public-key encryption. SSL encrypts data that moves between the browser and the server.

The SSL protocol consists of a digital certificate that the e-commerce site must possess before a Web browser can authenticate Web servers at the e-commerce site. The digital certificate is issued by a **certificate authority (CA)**. The role of the CA in the SSL session is to authenticate the holder of a certificate (such as an e-commerce server) and to provide a digital signature that will reveal whether the certificate has been compromised. CA certificates are pre-installed in all modern Web browsers.

> **TEST TIP**
> Be aware that SSL is used to protect credit card information during online transactions.

The reason sites need to be authenticated is that it's relatively easy to copy a complete Web site and then repost it using a domain name that's similar to the "real" site. For example, it is easy to mistake the site *micrsoft.com*, for *microsoft.com*. A purchaser may be lured to the first site, make a purchase, and never receive the purchased item.

A connection to a certificate server that uses SSL will use a URL that begins with https://. For example, a site called *https://buy.now.com* is a secure site in which messages between the browser and server are encrypted. The browser indicates that the connection is secure by displaying a locked padlock, or key, near the bottom corner of the browser.

> **TEST TIP**
> Know that when a Web site URL starts with https:// it is using SSL.

Telnet

Telnet is a service that enables you to "telephone-net" into another computer so that you can utilize the resources of the computer in a command-line interface environment. While most Web browsers do not include a client for telnet access, most operating systems include a utility that will enable you to launch telnet. In Windows, you can enter telnet from the command line. In other operating systems, a terminal emulator utility may be required in addition to a telnet client. A terminal emulator is a software package that allows a computer to mimic a dumb terminal.

Telnet enables users at remote computers to connect to a remote server. The client computer doesn't have to be running the same operating system as the remote server. This is an ideal situation for a PC-to-mainframe connection where the PC environment is radically different than that of the mainframe.

> **TEST TIP**
> Know how to connect to servers running different operating systems.

Table 6-6 summarizes common Internet service protocols and includes the **well-known port number** for each resource. In networking terms, port numbers are used to represent services running on computers. Network security systems open and close ports to control access to systems and services. Port numbers are discussed in greater detail in Chapter 10, *Windows Operating Systems*.

Table 6-6: Common Internet Protocols and Well-Known Port Numbers

URL PREFIX	DESCRIPTION	PORT NUMBER
http://	Specifies an address on the World Wide Web	80
https://	Specifies a secure address on the World Wide Web	443
ftp://	Specifies file transfers	20/21
mailto:	Initiates e-mail	24
news:	Initiates access to newsgroups	144
gopher://	Initiates access to database information	70
telnet://	Initiates direct access to a remote computer	23
SMTP:	Initiates e-mail over the Internet	25
file://	Initiates access to a file on a local server	59

Web Browsers

hypertext links

Web

As the Internet network has grown, service providers have continued to provide more user-friendly software for exploring the World Wide Web. These software packages are called browsers, and are based on **hypertext links**. Browsers use hypertext links to interconnect the various computing sites in a way that resembles a spider's Web, hence the name **Web**.

Browsers are to the Internet what Windows is to operating environments. Graphical browsers such as Netscape Navigator and Microsoft Internet Explorer enable users to move around the Internet and make selections from graphically designed pages and menus, instead of operating from a command line. The original Internet operating environment was a command-line program called UNIX. Fortunately, the UNIX structure and many of its commands were the basis used to create MS-DOS. Therefore, users who are DOS literate do not require extensive training to begin using UNIX. With the advent of a variety of browsers, however, it is unlikely that most users will become involved with UNIX.

National Center for Supercomputing Applications

hypertext markup language (HTML)

The **National Center for Supercomputing Applications** introduced the first graphical browser in 1993. This program was known as Mosaic. As its name implies, Mosaic allowed graphical pages to be created using a mixture of text, graphics, audio, and video files. It translated the **hypertext markup language (HTML)** files that were used to create the Web, and that ultimately link the various types of files together.

┌─ **TEST TIP** ─┐
Be aware of the different file types used with the Internet.
└────────────────┘

The Netscape Navigator and the Microsoft Internet Explorer browsers quickly followed Mosaic. Figure 6-50 depicts the home page (presentation screen) for the Netscape Navigator from Netscape Communications Corporation.

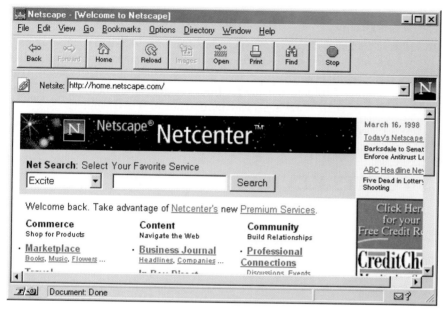

Figure 6-50:Netscape Navigator Home Page

Figure 6-51 illustrates the Microsoft Internet Explorer. Its features are similar to those of the Netscape Navigator. Both provide a graphical interface for viewing Web pages. Links to **search engines** are useful for finding information on the Internet. Both have links to built-in e-mail facilities, and to their respective creator's home pages.

Figure 6-51: Internet Explorer Home Page

search engines

┌─ TEST TIP ─────────┐
Memorize the Internet-related abbreviations and acronyms.
└────────────────────┘

In the Netscape navigator, searches look at Netscape-recommended sites, while the Explorer first checks out Microsoft sites. Operating either browser in Windows versions before Windows 95 requires an external **Windows socket** program to be loaded before running the browser. With Windows 95, the socket was integrated directly into the operating environment.

Several software packages allow users to generate their own Web pages. Programs such as word processors and desktop publishers have included provisions for creating and saving HTML files called **applets** that can be used as home pages. Internet browsers, such as Netscape and Internet Explorer, include facilities for generating home page documents. **Scripting languages**, such as **Java**, also are used to create HTML applets.

KEY POINTS REVIEW

This chapter has investigated the two major areas of data communications associated with personal computer systems: LANs and WANs. Review the following key points before moving onto the Review and Exam Questions sections to make sure you are comfortable with each point. Afterward, answer the Review Questions that follow to verify your knowledge of the information.

- Local area networks (LANs) are systems designed to connect computers together in a relatively close proximity. These connections allow users attached to the network to share resources, such as printers and modems. LAN connections also allow users to communicate with each other and share data between their computers.

- Control of the network can be implemented in two ways: as peer-to-peer networks, in which each computer is equal to the other units on the network, or as client/server networks, in which dependent workstations (referred to as clients) operate in conjunction with a dedicated master computer (server).

- In a network, some method must be used to determine which node has use of the network's communications paths, and for how long it can have it. The network's protocol handles these functions, and it is necessary to prevent more than one user from accessing the bus at any given time.

- The Ethernet strategy allows up to 1024 users to share the LAN. However, from the description of its collision-recovery technique, it should be clear that with more users on an Ethernet LAN, more collisions are likely to occur, and the average time to complete an actual data transfer will be longer.

- Ethernet is classified as a bus topology. The original Ethernet scheme was classified as a 10 Mbps transmission protocol. The maximum length specified for Ethernet is 1.55 miles (2.5 km), with a maximum segment length between nodes of 500 meters. This type of LAN is referred to as a 10Base-5 LAN by the IEEE organization.

- In a LAN, each computer on the net requires a network adapter card (also referred to as a NIC), and every unit is connected to the network by some type of cabling. These cables are typically either twisted-pair wires, thick or thin coaxial cable, or fiber-optic cable.

- In its simplest form, a modem consists of two major blocks, a modulator and a demodulator. The modulator is a transmitter that converts the parallel/digital computer data into a serial/analog format for transmission. The demodulator is the receiver that accepts the serial/analog transmission format and converts it into a parallel/digital format usable by the computer, or peripheral.

- The standard telephone system accommodates a range of frequencies between 300 and 3300 Hz, or a bandwidth of 3000 Hz. This is quite adequate to transmit voice, but severely distorts digital data. In order to use the audio characteristics of the phone lines to their best advantage, the modem encodes the digital 1s and 0s into analog signals within this bandwidth.

- In order to maintain an orderly flow of information between the computer and the modem, and between the modem and another modem, a protocol, or set of rules governing the transfer of information, must be in place. All of the participants in the "conversation" must use the same protocols to communicate.

- A wide area network is similar in concept to a widely distributed client/server LAN. In a wide area network, computers are typically separated by distances that must be serviced via modems instead of network cards.

- The most famous wide area network is the Internet. The Internet is actually a network of networks working together. The main communication path for the Internet is a series of networks, established by the U.S. government, to link supercomputers together at key research sites.

- Connecting all of the users and individual networks together are Internet service providers (ISPs). ISPs are companies that provide the technical gateway to the Internet. These companies own blocks of access addresses that they assign to their customers to give them an identity on the network.

- The IP addresses of all the computers attached to the Internet are tracked using a listing system called the Domain Name Service (DNS). This system evolved as a method of organizing the members of the Internet into a hierarchical management structure.

- The TCP/IP protocol divides the transmission into packets of information, suitable for retransmission across the Internet. Along the way, the information passes through different networks that are organized at different levels. Depending on the routing scheme, the packets may move through the Internet using different routes to get to the intended address. At the destination, however, the packets are reassembled into the original transmission.

- ISDN service offers high-speed access to the public telephone system. However, ISDN service requires digital modems, also referred to as terminal adapters. Not only does the end user require a digital modem, the telephone company's switch gear equipment must be updated to handle digital switching. This fact has slowed implementation of ISDN services until recently.

- A special application, called the file transfer protocol (FTP), is used to upload and download information to, and from, the Internet.

- One of the most widely used functions of wide area networks is the electronic mail (e-mail) feature. This feature allows Internet users to send, and receive, electronic messages to and from each other over the Internet.

- The World Wide Web (WWW) is a menu system that ties together Internet resources from around the world. These resources are scattered across computer systems everywhere. Web servers inventory the Web's resources and store address pointers, referred to as links, to them.

- As the Internet has grown, service providers have continued to provide more user-friendly software for exploring the World Wide Web. These software packages are called browsers and are based on hypertext links.

REVIEW QUESTIONS

The following questions test your knowledge of the material presented in this chapter.

1. What is the primary difference between a client/server network and a peer-to-peer network?

2. What is indicated if you encounter an IP Address of 127.0.0.1?

3. Describe three methods of implementing VoIP communications?

4. What is TCP/IP, and what does it mean?

5. The CIO of the company asks you for technical assistance about choosing an Internet service provider for your company. Due to cost cutting, she is interested in choosing a satellite Internet access solution but is unfamiliar with how uplinked versus downlinked satellites operate. Explain how uplinked versus downlinked satellites function.

6. You join a new division as part of the technical staff of a large company. This new division integrates Windows XP workstations with an older network that uses NetWare 4.0 and older software. Due to software incompatibility, TCP/IP is not a viable option. What sort of networking protocol should the network be using?

7. A fellow technician receives an order to purchase coaxial cable from a supplier. The supplier offers RG 6, RG 58, and RG 59 coaxial cable. The technician is unable to tell the difference between the three and enlists your help to explain the difference between the three cable types.

8. Describe the function of the World Wide Web.

9. What is the purpose of a router in a network?

10. Your network consists of PCs and a number of older Macintosh computers that are used for digital editing purposes. The users would like to be able to have the PCs and Macintosh computers networked together; however, the Macintosh computers are unable to use the TCP/IP protocol. What protocol should you attempt to try next?

11. Describe the function of the DNS.

12. Define the acronym URL and describe what it is used for.

13. Describe the functions of an Internet service provider.

14. What protocol is used to send large files on the Internet?

15. Describe plenum cabling, and explain why it's required for specific situations.

1. You install a new wireless network for a client. However, your client has been reading about network security and asks you to increase the security of the network while maintaining the wireless nature of the network. What do you suggest to accomplish this?
   a. Connect all workstations to the wireless access point using CAT5.
   b. Turn on wired equivalent privacy.
   c. Install more wireless access points throughout the network.
   d. Change encryption from 40-bit keys to 16-bit keys.

2. What type of topology is typically used by the Ethernet?
   a. A token-passing topology
   b. A star topology
   c. A ring topology
   d. A bus topology

3. State the maximum segment length of a 10Base-2 Ethernet network.
   a. 100 feet
   b. 185 meters
   c. 185 feet
   d. 100 meters

4. What does the designation 100Base-T tell you about a network?
   a. Its maximum cable segment length is 100 meters, and it uses BNC T connectors.
   b. Its maximum data rate is 100 Mbps, and it uses UTP cabling.
   c. Its maximum data rate is 100 MHz, and it uses BNC-type T connectors.
   d. Its maximum cable segment length is 100 feet, and it uses UTP cabling.

5. In a client/server network, _____.
   a. at least one unit is reserved just to serve the other units
   b. at least one unit depends on the other units for its information
   c. each unit has its own information and can serve as either client or server
   d. each unit handles some information for the network

6. What is the range of a 1 mW Bluetooth device?
   a. 100 meters
   b. 50 meters
   c. 10 meters
   d. 1 meter

7. What popular networking protocol is also the same protocol that the Internet uses?
   a. TCP/IP
   b. Appletalk
   c. IPX/SPX
   d. NetBEUI

8. The maximum segment length of a 10Base-5 network connection is _____.
   a. 15 meters
   b. 185 meters
   c. 500 meters
   d. 1000 meters

9. Which file type is associated with the Internet?
   a. HTML
   b. COM
   c. EPS
   d. DLL

10. In order to connect to the Internet, a computer must be able to use the protocol _____.
    a. MAU
    b. NIC
    c. PPP
    d. TCP/IP

CHAPTER
7

PRINTERS

OBJECTIVES

Upon completion of this chapter and its related lab procedures, you should be able to perform these tasks:

1. Describe the various methods currently used to place computer print on paper.

2. Discuss characteristics of dot-matrix characters.

3. Discuss the types of paper handling common to different printer technologies.

4. Install and configure a printer.

5. List special considerations that must be observed when installing or repairing serial printers.

6. Identify a given type of cable connection between the printer and the computer.

7. Discuss data flow-control methods as they apply to serial printers.

8. Identify the major components of a dot-matrix printer.

9. Describe troubleshooting techniques associated with dot-matrix printers.

10. Relate symptoms to associated components in a dot-matrix printer.

11. Describe general alignment procedures for printhead mechanisms.

12. Describe the operation of a typical ink-jet printer.

13. Identify the major components of an ink-jet printer.

14. Describe troubleshooting techniques associated with ink-jet printers.

15. Relate symptoms to associated components in an ink-jet printer.

16. Describe the process for applying print to a page in a laser printer.

17. Identify the major components of a laser printer.

18. Describe troubleshooting techniques associated with laser printers.

19. Relate symptoms to associated components in a laser printer.

CHAPTER 7

PRINTERS

FROM THE GEEK SQUAD

John H., Agent 991, has just advanced to become a Double Agent. This means that he will be expected to work inside Store #449, but he will also have to go to people's homes to install and service equipment. He is particularly worried about his knowledge of printers.

John is quite familiar with the newer printer models that Best Buy sells in its stores, but he feels that he is less familiar with the older types of printers that he knows still exist in great numbers. The printers from the store are largely USB and network ready units that require very little work beyond connecting them to the host, plugging them in, and turning them on. Agent 991 is very aware that he needs to be familiar with the older printer types that require a little more effort to install so that he will not be embarrassed when he encounters them on a job.

INTRODUCTION

There are many instances when a permanent copy of a computer's output may be desired. The leading hard-copy output device is the **character printer** (that is, letters, numbers, and graphic images). Character printers are the second most common output peripheral used with PCs (behind the video display). As computer systems and their applications have diversified, a wide variety of printer systems have developed to fill the particular printing needs created by the marketplace. These developments have yielded faster and higher-quality printing capabilities than ever before. In addition, these printers are now much less expensive than they have ever been before.

character printer

PRINTER FUNDAMENTALS

Currently, laser and ink dispersal printers are the most widely used printing technologies in the personal computer environment. In times past, dot matrix printers were the printer technology of choice because they were relatively inexpensive and fast. However, advanced functionality, such as color and graphical printing, has combined with decreasing costs of laser and ink-jet technology to relegate dot matrix printers to multipart continuous-form printing operations.

Essentials 4.0

Technical Support 3.0

IT Technician 4.0

Depot Technician 3.1

| impact |
| nonimpact |
| low speed |
| high speed |
| letter quality |
| near-letter quality |
| draft quality |
| fully formed |
| dot-matrix |

The other categories of printer technologies also represent different niche areas of the PC printing market. Thermal printing techniques are very old and at one point had nearly vanished. However, they continue to remain in use with specialized peripherals such as credit card receipt printers. Thermal wax printing is used to produce near photographic reproductions of images. Similarly, professional graphics companies have used dye sublimation printing to produce high-quality reproductions of photographic images. However, smaller versions designed for the consumer market have been introduced to provide personal printing capabilities for digital camera users.

Along with the diversity of printer systems have come various methods of classifying printers. Printers may be classified in a number of ways:

- Their method of placing characters on a page (**impact** or **nonimpact**)

- Their speed of printing (**low speed** and **high speed**)

- The quality of the characters they produce (**letter quality**, **near-letter quality**, or **draft quality**)

- Or, how they form the character on the page (**fully formed** or **dot-matrix**)

Printing Methods

The first method of differentiating printers is by how they deliver ink to the page. Impact printers produce the character by causing the print mechanism, or its ink ribbon, to impact the page. Conversely, nonimpact printers deliver ink to the page without the print mechanism making contact with the page.

Impact Printers

Impact printers place characters on the page by causing a hammer device to strike an inked ribbon. The ribbon, in turn, strikes the printing surface (paper).

The print mechanism may have the image of the character carved on its face, or it may be made up of a group of small print wires, arranged in a matrix pattern. In this case, the print mechanism is used to create the character on the page by printing a pattern of dots resembling it.

Generally, the quality and, therefore, the readability of a fully formed character is better than that of a dot-matrix character. However, dot-matrix printers tend to be less expensive than their fully formed character counterparts. In either case, most printers in use today are of the impact variety. Figure 7-1 depicts both fully formed and dot-matrix type characters.

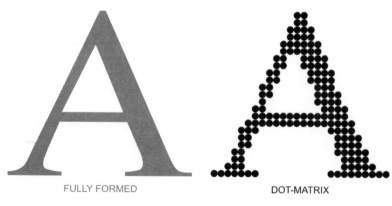
FULLY FORMED   DOT-MATRIX

Figure 7-1: Fully Formed and Dot-Matrix Characters

Nonimpact Printers

Several nonimpact methods of printing are used in computer printers. Older, nonimpact printers relied on special **heat-sensitive** or **chemically reactive paper** to form characters on the page. Newer nonimpact methods use ink droplets, squirted from a jet-nozzle device (**ink-jet printers**), or a combination of laser/xerographic print technologies (laser printers) to place characters on a page. Currently, the most popular nonimpact printers use ink-jet or laser technologies to deliver ink to the page.

heat-sensitive

chemically reactive paper

ink-jet printers

In general, nonimpact printers are less mechanical than impact counterparts. Therefore, they tend to be more dependable. Also, to their advantage, nonimpact printers tend to be very quiet and faster than comparable impact printers. The major disadvantage of nonimpact printers is their inability to produce **carbon copies**.

carbon copies

Character Types

Basically, there are two methods of creating characters on a page. One method places a character on the page that is fully shaped and fully filled-in. This type of character is called a fully formed character. The other method involves placing dots on the page in strategic patterns to fool the eye into seeing a character. This type of character is referred to as a dot-matrix character.

A fully formed impact print mechanism is depicted in Figure 7-2. The quality of **fully formed characters** is excellent. However, creative choices in print fonts and sizes tend to be somewhat limited. To change the size or shape of a character, the print mechanism would need to be replaced. Conversely, the flexibility of using dots to create characters allows them to be altered as the document is being created. The quality of dot matrix characters runs from extremely poor to extremely good, depending on the print mechanism.

fully formed characters

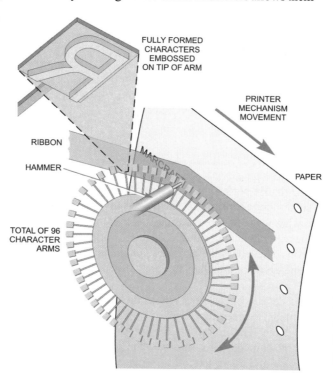

FULLY FORMED CHARACTERS EMBOSSED ON TIP OF ARM

PRINTER MECHANISM MOVEMENT

RIBBON

HAMMER

PAPER

TOTAL OF 96 CHARACTER ARMS

Figure 7-2: A Fully Formed Character Mechanism

Dot-matrix characters are not fully formed characters. Instead, they are a pattern of dots produced to represent the character, as illustrated in Figure 7-3. The reader's eye fills in the gaps between the dots. Today's dot-matrix printers offer good speed and high-quality characters that approach those created by good typewriters, and they offer nearly limitless printing flexibility.

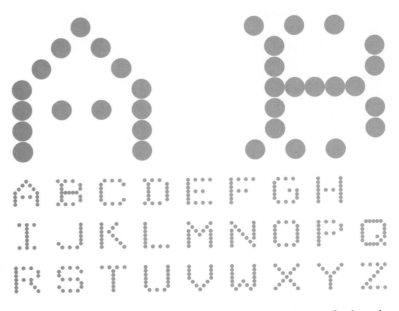

**Figure 7-3:
Dot-Matrix
Characters**

Basically, the printhead in a dot-matrix printer is a vertical column of print wires that are controlled by electromagnets, as depicted in Figure 7-4. Dots are created on the paper by energizing selected electromagnets, which extend the desired print wires from the printhead. The print wires impact an ink ribbon, which impacts the paper. It's important to note that the entire character is not printed in a single instant of time. A typical printhead may contain 9, 18, or 24 print wires. The number of print wires used in the printhead is a major determining factor when discussing a printer's character quality.

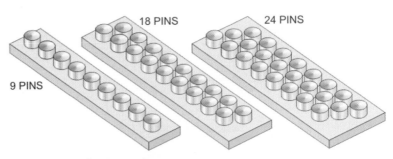

**Figure 7-4:
Dot-Matrix Printhead
Configurations**

character cells

pitch

The matrix portion of this printer's name is derived from the manner in which the page is subdivided for printing. The page is divided into a number of horizontal rows, or text lines. Each row is divided into groups of columns, called **character cells**. A character cell defines the area in which a single character is printed. The size of the character cell is expressed in terms of **pitch**, or the number of characters printed per inch. Within the print cell, the matrix dimensions of the character are defined.

The density of the dots within the character cell determines the quality of the character printed. Common matrix sizes are 5×7, 24×9, and 36×18, to mention only a few of those available. The more dots the printhead produces within the character cell the better the character looks. This is because the dots are closer together, making the character more fully formed and easier to read.

Fonts

The term **font** refers to variations in the size and style of characters. With true fully formed characters, there is typically only one font available without changing the physical printing element. With all other printing methods, however, it is possible to include a wide variety of font types and sizes.

There are three common methods of generating character fonts. These are as bit-mapped, or raster-scanned fonts, as vector-based fonts, and as TrueType outline fonts. **Bit-mapped fonts** store dot patterns for all of the possible size and style variations of the characters in the set. Because a complete set of dots must be stored for each character and size that may be needed, this type of font tends to take up large amounts of memory. For this reason, the number of character sizes offered by bit-mapped fonts is typically limited. Font styles refer to the characteristics of the font, such as **normal**, **bold**, and **italic** styles. Font size refers to the physical measurement of the character. Type is measured in increments of 1/72 of an inch. Each increment is referred to as a **point**. Common text sizes are 10-point and 12-point type.

Vector-based fonts store the outlines of character styles and sizes as sets of starting points and mathematical formulas. Each character is composed of a set of reference points and connecting lines between them. When a particular character is needed, the character generator sets the starting point for the character in the print cell and generates its outline from the formula. These types of fonts can be scaled up and down to achieve various sizes.

The vector-based approach requires much less storage space to store a character set, and all of its variations then would be necessary for an equivalent bit-mapped character set. In addition, vector-based fonts can be scaled and rotated, while bit-mapped fonts typically cannot. Conversely, bit-mapped characters can be printed out directly and quickly, while vector-based characters must be generated when called for.

TrueType fonts are a newer type of outline fonts that are commonly used with Microsoft Windows. These fonts are stored as a set of points and outlines that are used to generate a set of bit maps. Special algorithms adjust the bit maps so that they look best at the specified resolution. Once the bitmaps have been created, Windows stores them in a RAM cache that it creates. In this manner, the font is only generated once when it is first selected. Afterward, the fonts are simply called out of memory, thus speeding up the process of delivering them to the printer. Each TrueType character set requires an **.FOT** and a **.TTF** file to create all of its sizes and resolutions.

font

Bit-mapped fonts

normal

bold

italic

point

Vector-based fonts

TrueType fonts

.FOT

.TTF

TEST TIP
Be aware of the benefits and drawbacks of bit-mapped characters.

TEST TIP
Know which font types are generated by establishing starting points and then calculating mathematical formulas.

Print Quality

The last criterion for comparing printers is the quality of the characters they produce. This is largely a function of how the characters are produced on the page. Printers that produce fully formed characters are described as **letter quality (LQ)** printers. All elements of the character appear to be fully connected when printed. On the other hand, printers that produce characters by forming a dot pattern are simply referred to as matrix printers. Upon close inspection of a character, one can see the dot patterns. The characters produced on some matrix printers are difficult to distinguish from fully formed characters. These printers have been labeled **correspondence quality (CQ)**, or **near-letter quality (NLQ)** printers. Often, dot-matrix printers have two printing modes, one being standard dot matrix (sometimes called **utility** or **draft mode**), and the other a near-letter quality mode.

Printer Mechanics

By the very nature of their operation, printers tend to be extremely mechanical peripherals. During the printing operation, the print mechanism must be properly positioned over each character cell in sequence.

Loss of synchronization in impact printers can lead to paper jams, tearing, smudged characters, or printhead damage. Nonimpact printers may produce totally illegible characters if synchronization is lost. The positioning action may be produced by moving the paper under a stationary printhead assembly or by holding the paper stationary and stepping the printhead carriage across the page. In the latter operation, the **printhead carriage** rides on rods extending across the front of the page, as shown in Figure 7-5.

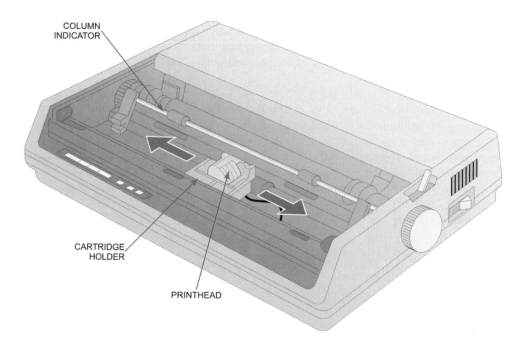

Figure 7-5: The Printhead Carriage

Depending upon the type of print mechanism used, the carriage may be stepped across the page at a rate of one character cell at a time (fully formed characters) or in sub-character-cell steps (dot-matrix characters). Printing may occur in only one direction (unidirectional) or in both directions (bidirectional). In bidirectional printers, the second line of characters is stored in the printer's buffer memory and printed in the opposite direction, saving the time that would normally be used to return the carriage to the start of the second line.

The printhead carriage assembly is stepped across the page by a **carriage motor/timing belt** arrangement. With many printer models, the number of character columns across the page is selectable, producing variable characters spacing (expressed in **characters per inch**, or **cpi**), which must be controlled by the carriage position motor. Dot-matrix printers may also incorporate variable dot-densities (expressed as **dot-pitches**). Dot-pitch is also a function of the carriage motor control circuitry. Obviously, this discussion excludes continuous-stream, ink-jet printers, in which printing is done by electromagnetic deflection of the ink drops, and laser printers, in which the beam is reflected from a revolving mirror.

carriage motor/timing belt
characters per inch (cpi)
dot-pitches

Paper Handling

In addition to positioning the print mechanism for printing, all printer types must feed paper through the print area. The type of **paper handling mechanism** in a printer is somewhat dependent on the type of form intended for use with the printer, and its speed.

paper handling mechanism
continuous forms
single-sheet forms
Friction-feed
platen
Pin-feed
tractor

Paper forms fall into two general categories, **continuous forms**, which come in folded stacks and have holes along their edges, and **single-sheet forms**, such as common typing paper. There are two common methods of moving paper through the printer:

- **Friction-feed** uses friction to hold the paper against the printer's **platen**. The paper advances through the printer as the platen turns.

- **Pin-feed** pulls the paper through the printer by a set of pins that fit into the holes along the edge of the form, as shown in Figure 7-6. The pins may be an integral part of the platen or may be mounted on a separate, motor-driven **tractor**.

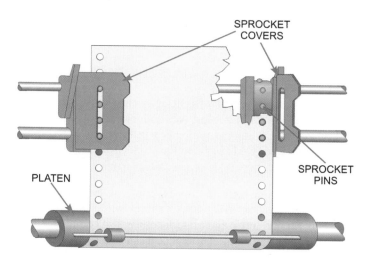

Figure 7-6: A Pin-Feed Tractor Mechanism

Friction-feed is normally associated with single-sheet printers. The sheet feeding system can be manual or automatic. Platen pin-feed and pin tractors are usually employed with continuous and multilayer forms. These mechanisms can control paper slippage and misalignment created by the extra weight imposed by continuous forms. Platen pin-feed units can handle only one width of paper, whereas tractors can be adjusted to handle various paper widths. **Tractor feeds** are used with very heavy forms, such as multiple-part continuous forms, and are most commonly found on dot-matrix printers. Most ink-jet and laser printers use single-sheet feeder systems.

The gear trains involved in the paper handling function can be treated as an FRU item in some printers. While it is possible to replace the gears, or gear packs, in dot-matrix and ink-jet printers (if they can be obtained from the manufacturer as separate items), it is usually not economical to do so. Laser printers, on the other hand, are normally expensive enough to warrant replacing the gear trains and clutch assemblies that handle the paper movement through the printer.

Printer Controls

Although printers vary considerably from type to type and model to model, there are some elements that are common to all printers. These elements are depicted in Figure 7-7.

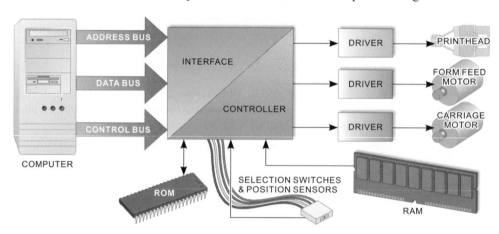

**Figure 7-7:
Common Printer
Components**

Printer Interface

interface/controller

Like most other peripherals, the heart of a character printer is its **interface/controller** circuitry. The interface circuitry accepts data and instructions from the computer's I/O port. This includes decoding the computer's instructions to the printer, converting signal logic levels, and passing data to the printer's controller.

The most widely used connection interface for new printers is the USB port. This is followed by the direct network connection using CAT5 cables with RJ-45 connectors. Wireless Wi-Fi, Bluetooth, and infrared link printer interfaces are also common. However, there are still so many older printers using parallel printer ports and serial interfaces that you must be able to identify them and work with them.

Historically, parallel-port connections were the primary choice when the printer was located in close proximity to the computer. If the printer had to be located remotely, the RS-232 serial interface became more appropriate. Many manufacturers offered both connections as standard equipment. Other models offered the serial connection as an option. More is said about these two interfaces later in this section.

A third less common method of connecting printers to computers uses the SCSI interface as the connection port. As with other SCSI devices, the printer must be set up as a unique SCSI device, and proper connection and termination procedures should be observed.

Printer Controllers

The controller section receives the data and control signals from the interface section and produces all of the signals necessary to select, or generate, the proper character to be printed. It also advances the print mechanism to the next print position, and feeds the paper at the proper times. In addition, the controller generates status and control signals that tell the computer what is happening in the printer.

Due to the complexity of most character printers, a dedicated **microcontroller** is typically employed to oversee the complete operation of the printer. The presence of the dedicated microprocessor provides greater flexibility, and additional options, for the printer. Along with the dedicated processor, the printer normally contains IC memory in the form of RAM, ROM, or both. A speed mismatch exists between the computer and the printer, since the computer is usually capable of generating characters at a much higher rate than the printer can print them. In order to minimize this speed differential, printers typically carry **onboard RAM** memory buffers to hold characters coming from the computer. In this way, the transfer of data between the computer and the printer occurs at a rate that is compatible with the computer's operating speed. The printer obtains its character information from the on-board buffer.

In addition to character print information, the host computer can also store printer instructions in the buffer for use by the dedicated processor. The printer may also contain **onboard ROM** in the form of **character generators**, or **printer initialization programs** for start-up. Some printers contain EPROM, instead of ROM, to provide a greater variety of options for the printer, such as **downloadable type fonts** and **variable print modes.**

Basically, the controller must produce signals to drive the print mechanism, the paper feed motor, the carriage motor, and possibly optional devices, such as single-sheet feeders and add-on tractors. Most of these functions are actually performed by precision stepper motors. There are usually hardware driver circuits between the motors and the controller to provide current levels high enough to activate the motors.

The controller also gathers information from the printer through a variety of sensing devices. These include position sensing switches and user-operated, front-panel-mounted, mode-control switches. Some of the more common sensing switches include the **home-position sensor**, the **end-of-paper sensor**, and the **carriage position sensor**. The controller also responds to manual input command switches, such as **on/off line**, **form feed (FF)**, and **line feed (LF).**

microcontroller

onboard RAM

onboard ROM

character generators

printer initialization programs

downloadable type fonts

variable print modes

home-position sensor

end-of-paper sensor

carriage position sensor

on/off line

form feed (FF)

line feed (LF)

operator control
panel

The sensors and switches can be treated as FRUs in many printers. This is particularly true with more expensive laser printers. In most printers, the entire **operator control panel** can be exchanged for another unit. This effectively changes all of the user-operated input switches at one time.

Essentials 4.1

Technical Support 3.1

IT Technician 4.1

Depot Technician 3.1

power supply board

main control board

printhead assembly

ribbon cartridge

paper feed motor

printhead positioning
motor

Dot-Matrix Printers

At one time, dot-matrix impact printers were the stalwarts of the microcomputer printing market. The components of a typical dot-matrix printer are depicted in Figure 7-8. They consist of a **power supply board,** a **main control board**, a **printhead assembly**, a **ribbon cartridge**, a **paper feed motor** (along with its mechanical drive gears), and a **printhead positioning motor** and mechanisms.

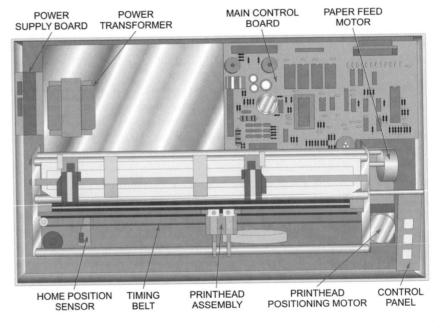

Figure 7-8: Parts of a Dot-Matrix Printer

The power supply board is called on to provide various voltages to power the electronics on the control board. It also drives both the printhead positioning and paper feed motors, and energizes the wires of the printhead so that they will strike the ribbon as directed by the control board. The control board is typically divided into four functional sections, as described in Figure 7-9. These functional blocks include

- Interface circuitry

- Character generation circuitry

- Printer controller circuitry

- Motor control circuitry

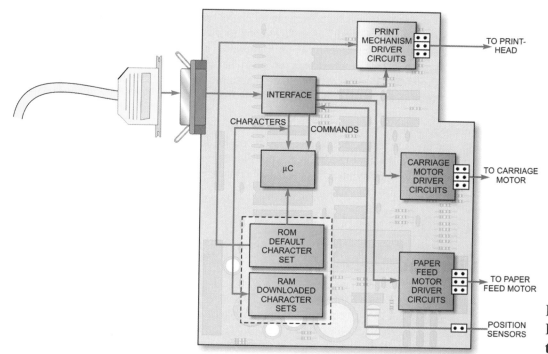

**Figure 7-9:
Logical Parts of
the Control Board**

The control board contains the logic circuitry required to convert the signals received from the computer's I/O port into character patterns, as well as to generate the proper control signals to position the printhead properly on the page, fire the correct combination of printhead wires to create the character, and advance the paper properly. The on-board microcontroller, character generators, RAM, and ROM are found on the control board.

The status of the printer's operation is monitored by the control board through a number of sensors. These sensors typically include

- Paper out

- Printhead position

- Home position (for the printhead carriage)

Input from the printer's control panel is also routed to the control board. Operator panel information includes

- On-line

- Form feed

- Line feed

- Power/paper out

The control panel may contain a number of other buttons and indicator lights, whose functions are specific to that particular printer. Always consult the printer's user's manual for information about the operation of the control panel buttons and indicators.

TEST TIP

Remember the types of connectors used at the computer and the printer ends of a parallel printer cable.

Dot-matrix printers process bit patterns in much the same way that CRT controllers do. The dot patterns are accessed from a character generator ROM. In addition to the standard ASCII character set, many printers feature preprogrammed sets of block-graphics characters that can be used to create nontext images on a page. Most manufacturers use EPROM (erasable-programmable ROM) character generators instead of the older ROM type. This allows their units to accept downloadable fonts from software.

Where used with a high-quality printhead, a variety of typefaces, such as **Roman Gothic**, italic, and foreign language characters, can be loaded into the programmable character generator from software. In addition, it is possible for users to create their own character sets, typefaces, and graphic symbols. Some manufacturers even offer standard bar-code graphics software sets for their machines.

Roman Gothic

Printhead Mechanisms

printhead

The **printhead** is a collection of print wires set in an electromagnetic head unit. The printhead assembly is made up of a permanent magnet, a group of electromagnets, and a housing. In the printhead, the permanent magnet keeps the wires pulled in until electromagnets are energized, causing them to move forward.

printhead carriage assembly

timing belt

printhead positioning motor

The printhead is mounted in the **printhead carriage assembly**. The carriage assembly rides on a bar that passes along the front of the platen. The printhead carriage assembly is attached to the printhead positioning motor by a **timing belt**.

The **printhead positioning motor** is responsible for moving the printhead mechanism across the page and stopping it in just the right places to print. The printhead rides back and forth across the printer on a pair of carriage rods. A timing belt runs between the printhead assembly and the printhead positioning motor, and converts the rotation of the motor into the linear movement of the printhead assembly. The printhead must stop each time the print wires strike the paper. If this timing is off, the characters will be smeared on the page, and the paper may be damaged. The motor steps a predetermined number of steps to create a character within a character cell. Figure 7-10 illustrates a dot-matrix printhead delivering print to a page.

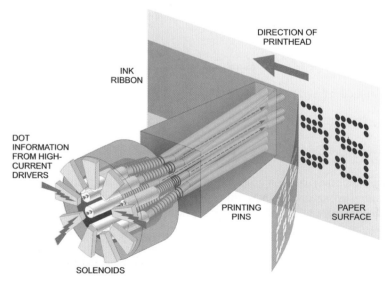

Figure 7-10: Dot-Matrix Printhead

Paper Handling

The **paper feed motor** and **gear train** move the paper through the printer. This can be accomplished by driving the **platen assembly**. The platen can be used in two different ways to move the paper through the printer. After the paper has been wrapped halfway around the platen, a set of rollers are used to pin the paper to the platen as it turns. This is **friction-feed paper handling**. As described earlier, the platen may have small pins that can drag the paper through the printer as the platen turns. In either case, the paper feed motor drives the platen to move the paper.

The feed motor's gear train can also be used to drive the extended gear train of a **tractor assembly** when it is installed. The gears of the feed motor mesh with those of the tractor, causing it to pull, or push, the paper through the printer. To use a tractor, the friction-feed feature of the platen must be released. Otherwise, the tractor and the platen may not turn at the same rate, and the paper will rip or jam. The installation of a tractor assembly is illustrated in Figure 7-11.

paper feed motor
gear train
platen assembly
friction-feed paper handling
tractor assembly

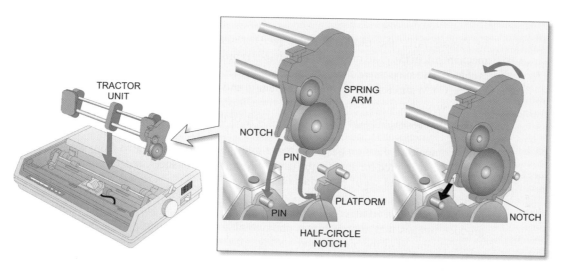

Figure 7-11: Installing a Tractor Assembly

Thermal Printers

As mentioned earlier in this section, thermal printing techniques were at one time widely used with PC printing. These printers use heated elements to burn or melt dot pattern characters on special paper. There are two types of thermal printers:

- **Direct thermal printers**

- **Thermal wax transfer printers**

Direct thermal printers
Thermal wax transfer printers

Direct thermal printers work in much the same manner as the ink cartridge dot-matrix printers described in the preceding section. The major difference between the two technologies is that the print wires are heated in the thermal printer so that they can burn dot patterns into special thermal paper. Early facsimile (fax) machine technology was based on this type of thermal printing. Even now, thermal printers are widely used for bar code printing, battery-powered handheld printing devices, and credit card receipt printers.

The other difference between direct thermal and dot-matrix printers is that in the thermal printer, the printhead does not move across the page. Instead, different pins in a row of heating elements are extended as the paper passes over the print bar. This makes thermal printing quiet and efficient. There is also no ink ribbon to change or run out of.

The drawback to direct thermal printing is the special thermal paper required for operation (using regular paper would present a fire hazard). In addition, the paper does not age well. Over time the entire page will darken and become difficult to read.

The other variation of thermal printers is the **thermal wax transfer printer**. In these units, a thermal printhead melts dots of wax-based ink from the transfer ribbon onto the paper. When the wax cools, it is permanently attached to the page. Unlike the direct thermal printer, thermal wax transfer printers do not require special paper to print on.

These printers are available in monochrome (one color) and multicolor versions. The multicolor versions can be three-color printers (cyan, magenta, and yellow—CMY color) or four-color printers (CMY + black = **CMYK color**). These thermal printers use a high volume of wax to print each page. Each page requires a complete covering of wax to print regardless of how many characters are placed on the page.

In Figure 7-12, the thermal printer feeds a sheet of paper into the thermal printing mechanism. In the print mechanism the paper is brought together with a roll of color film that is coated with successive sheets of inked wax. Each sheet on the roll contains one of the basic colors (CYM and K) and is equal to the length and width of the sheet of paper. As the paper moves through the print engine the first time, it is matched with one of the color sheets as it passes through a compression roller and a strip of thermal print heating elements (pins). The heating elements are turned on and off to melt selected dots of colored wax onto the paper. After completing the first pass, the paper and the film are separated from each other, the paper is repositioned for another run using the second color sheet, and the process is repeated to place the second set of color dots on the page. This cycle is repeated until all the colors have been applied to the page. This type of printer is used in professional color printing because it provides vivid reproductions of picture and artwork. However, they can't actually produce images that approach real photographic quality, because they use color dots to create the image of the picture, and photographs are made up of continuous tones.

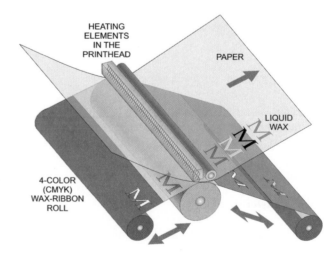

Figure 7-12: Color Thermal Printing

Ink-Jet Printers

Ink-jet printers produce characters by squirting a precisely controlled stream of ink drops onto the paper, as shown in Figure 7-13. The drops must be controlled precisely in terms of their aerodynamics, size, and shape, or the drop placement on the page becomes inexact and the print quality falters.

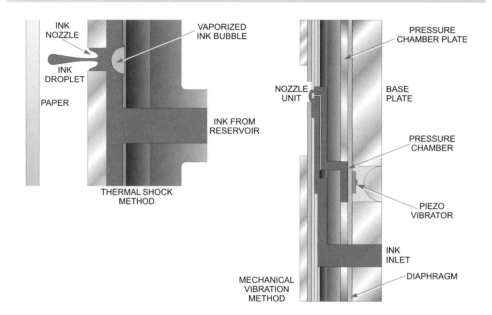

Figure 7-13: Ink-Jet Printers

The drops are formed by one of two methods:

- **thermal shock** heats the ink in a capillary tube, just behind the nozzle. This increases the pressure of the ink in the tube and causes it to explode through the opening.

- **mechanical vibration** uses vibrations from a piezoelectric crystal to force ink through a nozzle.

The ink-jet nozzle is designed to provide the proper shape and trajectory for the ink drops so that they can be directed precisely toward the page. The nozzle is also designed so that the surface tension of the ink keeps it from running out of the nozzle uncontrollably.

Two methods are used by ink-jet printers to deliver the drops to the page: the **interrupted-stream (drop-on-demand)** method and the **continuous-stream** method. The drop-on-demand system forms characters on the page in much the same manner does as a dot-matrix printer. As the printhead mechanism moves across the character cells of the page, the controller causes a drop to be sprayed, only where necessary, to form the dot pattern of a character. Drop-on-demand printing is illustrated in Figure 7-14.

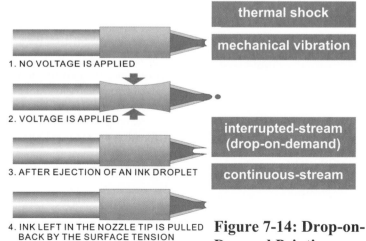

Figure 7-14: Drop-on-Demand Printing

Continuous-stream systems, like the one shown in Figure 7-15, produce characters that more closely resemble fully formed characters. In these systems, the printhead does not travel across the page. Instead, the drops are given a negative charge in an ion chamber and are passed through a set of deflection plates, similar to the electron beam in a CRT tube. The plates deflect the drops to their proper placement on the page, and unused drops are deflected off the page into an ink recirculation system.

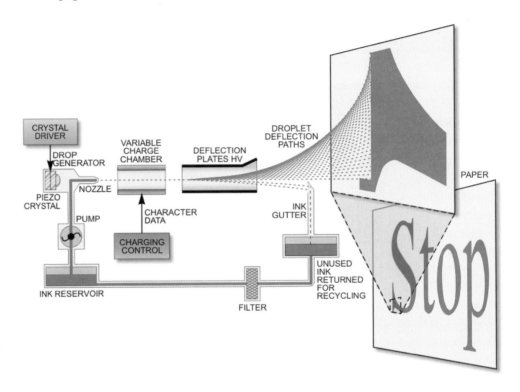

**Figure 7-15:
Continuous-Stream
Printing**

While capable of delivering very high-quality characters at high speeds, continuous-stream systems tend to be expensive, and therefore are not normally found in printers for the consumer market. Instead, they are reserved for high-volume commercial printing applications. The ink-jet printers in the general consumer market use drop-on-demand techniques to deliver ink to the page.

Some ink-jet printers incorporate multiple jets to permit color printing. Four basic colors may be mixed to create a palette of colors by firing the ink jets in different combinations.

solid ink-jet printers

A special variety of ink-jet printers referred to as **solid ink-jet printers** (also called *wax-jet printers*) combines thermal printer technology with ink-jet–type operations to produce brilliantly colored pictures and images. Instead of working with inks, these printers melt dyed waxes and then spray them on the page using ink-jet–like dispersal methods. The wax base used for the printing process produces exceptionally bright colors on all types of paper; however, because these printers are slow and relatively expensive, they are typically only found in professional reproduction and advertising settings.

Ink-Jet Printer Components

Aside from the printing mechanism, the components of a typical ink-jet printer are similar to those of a dot-matrix printer. Its primary components are

- The printhead assembly

- The power board

- The control board

- The printhead positioning motor and timing belt

- The paper feed motor and gear train

- The printer's sensors

These components are shown in Figure 7-16.

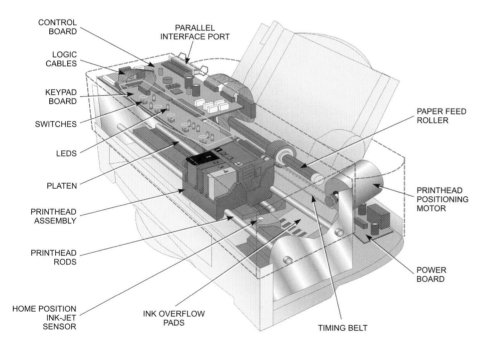

CONTROL BOARD

PARALLEL INTERFACE PORT

LOGIC CABLES

KEYPAD BOARD

SWITCHES

LEDS

PLATEN

PRINTHEAD ASSEMBLY

PRINTHEAD RODS

HOME POSITION INK-JET SENSOR

INK OVERFLOW PADS

TIMING BELT

PAPER FEED ROLLER

PRINTHEAD POSITIONING MOTOR

POWER BOARD

Figure 7-16: Ink-Jet Printer Components

The Printhead Assembly

The ink cartridge snaps into the printhead assembly that rides in front of the platen on a rail or rod. The printhead assembly is positioned by a timing belt that runs between it and the positioning motor. A flexible cable carries ink-jet firing information between the control board and the printhead. This cable folds out of the way as the printhead assembly moves across the printer.

Paper Handling

The paper feed motor turns a gear train that ultimately drives the platen, as depicted in Figure 7-17. The paper is friction-fed through the printer, between the platen and the pressure rollers. Almost all ink-jet printers used with microcomputer systems are single-sheet, friction-feed systems. The control board, power supply board, and sensors perform the same functions in an ink-jet printer that they did in the dot-matrix printer.

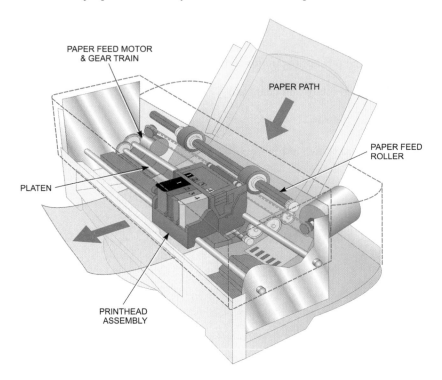

Figure 7-17: Ink-Jet Paper Handling

Laser Printers

laser printer

The **laser printer** modulates a highly focused laser beam to produce CRT-like raster-scan images on a rotating drum, as depicted in Figure 7-18.

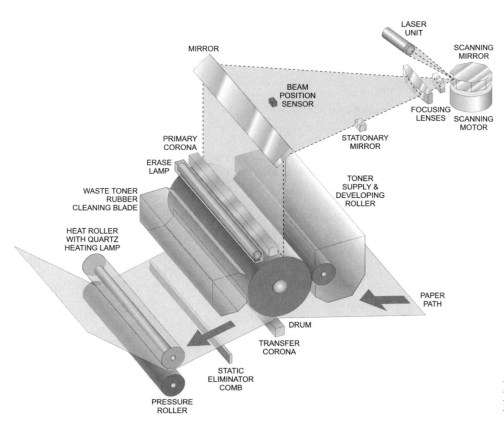

Figure 7-18: A Typical Laser Printer

The **drum** is coated with a photosensitive plastic, which is given a **negative electrical charge** over its surface. The modulated laser beam creates spots on the rotating drum. The spots written by the laser take on a **positive electrical charge**. A negatively charged **toner material** is attracted to the positively charged, written areas of the drum. The paper is fed past the rotating drum, and the toner is transferred to the paper. A pair of compression rollers is combined with a high-temperature lamp to fuse the toner to the paper. Thus, the image, written on the drum by the laser, is transferred to the paper.

The laser beam scans the drum so rapidly that it is not practical to do the scanning mechanically. Instead, the beam is bounced off a rotating, **polygonal** (many-sided) **mirror**. The faces of the mirror cause the reflected beam to scan across the face of the drum as the mirror revolves. Using the highest dot densities available, these printers produce characters that rival typeset text in quality. Larger laser printers produce characters at a rate of 20,000 lines per minute. Laser printers intended for the personal computer market generate 6 to 45 pages per minute.

drum
negative electrical charge
positive electrical charge
toner material
polygonal mirror

Laser Printer Components

From manufacturer to manufacturer, and model to model, the exact arrangement and combinations of components may vary in laser printers. However, the order of operations is always the same. The six stages of operation in a laser printer include

- Cleaning
- Conditioning
- Writing
- Developing
- Transferring
- Fusing

TEST TIP

Memorize the stages of a typical laser printer.

To accomplish these objectives, all laser printers possess the following logical blocks:

- Power supply
- Control board
- Laser writing unit
- Drum unit

- Fusing assembly
- Paper feed motor and gear train
- System's sensors
- Control panel board

The blocks of the typical laser printer are illustrated in Figure 7-19.

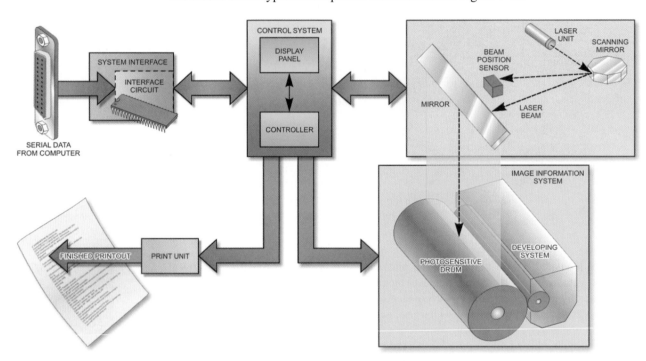

Figure 7-19: Block Diagram of a Laser Printer

AC power

high-voltage DC supply

static charges

DC operating voltages

registration

The laser printer power supply unit is the most complex found in any type of printer. It must deliver **AC power** to the fuser unit. This unit requires power for its fusing heaters and image erase lamps. The power supply also delivers a **high-voltage DC supply** (+1000 Vdc) to the toner transfer mechanisms in the drum area. The high voltages are used to create the **static charges** required to move toner from one component to another (i.e., from the drum to the paper). Finally, the power supply unit must deliver **DC operating voltages** to the scanning and paper handling motors, as well as the digital electronic circuitry on the control board.

The control board contains all of the circuitry required to operate the printer and control its many parts. It receives control signals from the computer and formats the data to be printed. The control board also monitors the conditions within the printer and responds to input from its various sensors.

When data are received from the host computer, the control board generates all of the enabling signals needed to place the information on the page as directed. The character information is converted into a serial bit stream, which can be applied to the scanning laser. The photosensitive drum rotates as the laser beam is scanned across it. The laser creates a copy of the image on the photosensitive drum in the form of a relatively positive-charged drawing. This operation is referred to as **registration**.

Laser Printing Operations

Before the laser writes on the drum, a set of erase lamps shine on the drum to remove any residual traces of the previous image. This leaves the drum with a neutral electrical charge. A high voltage, applied to the **primary corona wire**, creates a highly charged negative field that **conditions** the drum to be written on by applying a uniform negative charge (–1000 V) to it.

primary corona wire

conditions

> As the drum is written on by the laser it turns through the **toner powder**, which is attracted to the more positively charged image on the drum.

toner powder

Toner is a very fine powder, bonded to iron particles that are attracted to the charges written on the drum. The **developer roller** in the toner cartridge turns as the drum turns, and expels a measured amount of toner past a **restricting blade**, as illustrated in Figure 7-20. A regulating AC voltage assists the toner in leaving the cartridge, but also pulls back some excess toner from the drum. Excess toner is recycled within the toner cartridge so that it can be used again.

developer roller

restricting blade

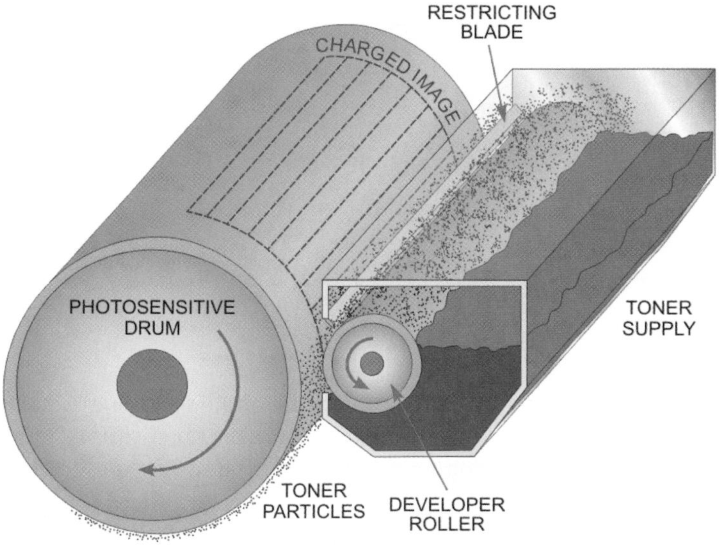

Figure 7-20: The Developer Roller

Great care should be taken when installing a new drum unit. Exposing the drum to light for more than a few minutes may damage it. The drum should never be touched, as this too can ruin its surface. Keep the unit away from dust and dirt, as well as away from humidity and high-temperature areas.

> **TEST TIP**
>
> Know that you should never expose the drum of a laser printer to sunlight or any other strong light source.

The **transfer corona wire (transfer roller)** is responsible for transferring the toner from the drum to the paper. The toner is transferred to the paper because of the highly positive charge that the transfer corona wire applies to the paper. The positive charge attracts the more negative toner particles away from the drum and onto the page. A special, static-eliminator comb acts to prevent the positively charged paper from sticking to the negatively charged drum.

transfer corona wire

transfer roller

> **TEST TIP**
>
> Know the functions of the two corona wires in a laser printer.

After the image has been transferred to the paper, a pair of **compression rollers** in the **fusing unit** act to press the toner particles into the paper, while they melt them to it. The top compression roller, known as the **fusing roller**, is heated by a quartz lamp. This roller melts the toner to the paper as it exits the fusing unit, while the lower roller applies pressure to the paper. A cleaning pad removes excess particles and applies a silicon lubricant to prevent toner from sticking to the Teflon-coated fusing roller. The complete transfer process is shown in Figure 7-21.

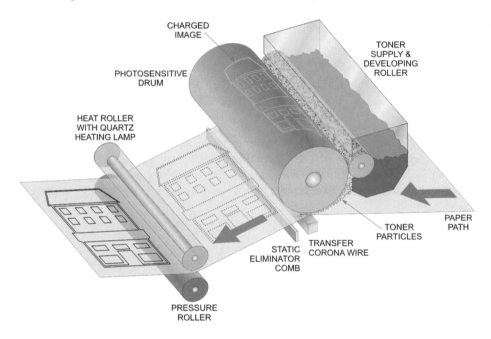

Figure 7-21: The Transfer Process

Component Variations

In Hewlett Packard printers, the main portion of the printing system is contained in the **electrophotographic cartridge**. This cartridge contains the **toner supply**, the **corona wire**, the **drum assembly**, and the **developing roller**. The HP cartridge configuration is depicted in Figure 7-22.

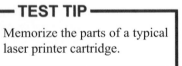

── **TEST TIP** ──

Memorize the parts of a typical laser printer cartridge.

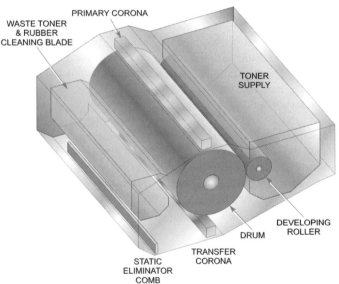

Figure 7-22: The HP Cartridge Configuration

In other laser printers, like the one depicted in Figure 7-23, the basic components are combined so that the printer consists of a **developer unit**, a **toner cartridge**, a **drum unit**, a **fuser unit**, and a **cleaning pad**. In this case, the developer unit and toner cartridge are separate units. With this configuration, changing the toner does not involve changing some of the other wear-prone components. While it is less expensive to change toner, attention must be paid to how much the other units are wearing. Notice that the photosensitive drum is also a separate component.

Color laser printers operate on the same principles as the monochrome version we have described as an example. However, color lasers use four different color toners. From earlier discussions of other color printers, you may be able to guess that the four toners are combined in different ratios on the page to form the different colors in the spectrum. Likewise, from the description of how images are written on the drum of a laser printer and transferred to the paper, you can probably imagine that the voltages used to control the attraction properties of the toner to the drum and paper are much more complex than they are for a single-color laser printer. However, for the technician, color laser printers still work like their single-color relatives.

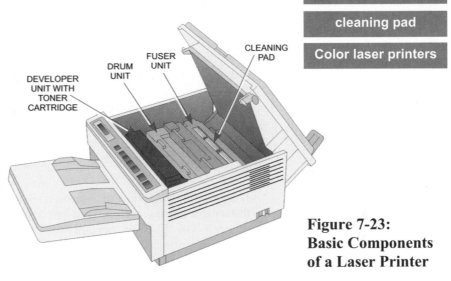

| developer unit |
| toner cartridge |
| drum unit |
| fuser unit |
| cleaning pad |
| Color laser printers |

Figure 7-23: Basic Components of a Laser Printer

Paper Handling

Laser printers are very mechanical in nature. The paper handling motor and the gear train assembly perform a tremendous number of operations to process a single sheet of paper. The **paper transport mechanics** must pick up a page from the paper tray and move it into the printer's registration area. After the drum has been written with the image, the paper handling mechanism moves the paper into registration. A roller system moves the page past the drum and into the fusing unit. When the page exits through the fusing rollers, the printer senses that the page has exited and resets itself to wait for another page to print.

| paper transport mechanics |

In addition to the motor and gear train, the printer uses a number of sensors and solenoid-accuated clutches to control the paper movement. It uses solenoids to engage and disengage different gear sets, and clutches, at appropriate times during the printing process.

Laser printer sensors—A typical laser printer has sensors to determine what paper trays are installed, what size paper is in them, and whether the tray is empty. It also uses sensors to track the movement of the paper through each stage of the printer. This allows the controller to know where the page is at all times and to sequence the activities of the solenoids and clutches properly.

| Laser printer sensors |

Figure 7-24 gives a summary of the sensors found in a typical laser printer.

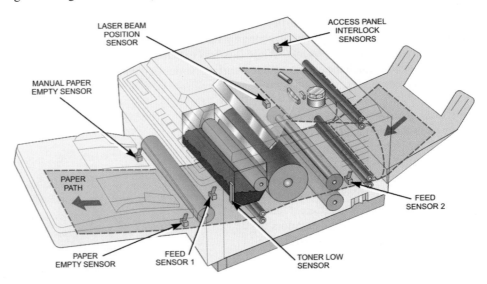

**Figure 7-24:
Sensor Summary**

If the page does not show up at the next sensor at the appropriate time, the printer will know that a paper jam has occurred and will create an error message that indicates the area of the printer it is in. When a paper jam occurs, it will be necessary to remove the paper from the inside of the printer and reset the print operation. Gaining access to the area where the jam is usually requires direction from the printer's user's manual. The printer should always be allowed to cool and should always be turned off before reaching inside the unit.

Another set of sensor switches monitor the printer's access doors to protect personnel from potentially dangerous conditions inside the printer. The **interlock switch** blocks the laser beam as a vision-protection measure. Likewise, the high-voltage supplies to various printer components are also shut down. To observe the operation of the printer, it will be necessary to locate, and bypass, these interlocks. However, you should always be aware that these interlocks are present for protection, and great care should be taken when working with them defeated.

Still other sensors are used to monitor the temperatures within different sections of the printer. A **thermal sensor** in the fusing unit monitors the temperature of the unit. This information is applied to the control circuitry so that it can keep the fuser temperature between 140°C and 230°C. If the temperature of the fuser is not controlled correctly, it may cause severe damage to the printer, as well as present a potential fire hazard.

A **thermal fuse** protects the fuser assembly from overheating and damaging the printer. The thermal fuse should normally snap back after the temperature condition is cleared. If the switch is open under cool conditions, it will need to be replaced. This is normally an indication that the thermal sensor has failed, or that the fuser assembly has been installed improperly.

When the laser beam is turned on, a **beam detector sensor** in the writing unit alerts the control circuitry that the writing process has begun. This signal synchronizes the beginning of the laser-modulating data with the beginning of the scan line.

interlock switch

thermal sensor

thermal fuse

┌─ **TEST TIP** ─┐
Remember the purpose of the thermal fuse in laser printers.

beam detector
sensor

Paper Specifications

One reason for faint printing is that the paper thickness lever is set to the wrong position for the weight of paper being used.

> **Paper weight**—Paper is specified in terms of its **weight** per 500 sheets at 22" × 17" (e.g., 500 sheets of 22" × 17", 21-pound bond paper weighs 21 pounds).

The thickness setting will also cause smudged characters when the paper is too thick for the actual setting. In this case, adjust the thickness lever one or two notches away from the paper.

> **TEST TIP**
> Know how paper weight is specified and how many sheets are involved.

Dye Sublimation Printers

Earlier in this chapter, we discussed thermal wax printers that could produce vivid high-quality graphics. However, the images they produce can never approach photographic quality because of their dot composition. A variation of that printer type, referred to as a **dye sublimation printer**, has been produced to provide photographic quality, continuous tone images.

Figure 7-25 illustrates the dye sublimation process. Although the printing mechanism appears similar to the thermal wax printer described earlier, there are some distinct differences. In a dye sublimation printer, sheets of special paper or transparencies are fastened securely to a print drum. Clamping the page to the drum ensures good **registration** between the different colors that will be printed on the paper in successive color passes.

The drum with the paper is rotated in conjunction with a continuous roll of plastic film containing successive CYMK color sheets that have the same dimensions as the page. At the point where the paper and film come together, a heating element strip is used to heat the color substance on the film so that it vaporizes (sublimates) and is absorbed into the paper. The heating element contains thousands of small heat points that can create extremely fine patterns of color dots. In addition, each element can be used to supply hundreds of different temperatures, which leads to hundreds of different amounts of ink transferred to the page and results in hundreds of different shades that can be produced.

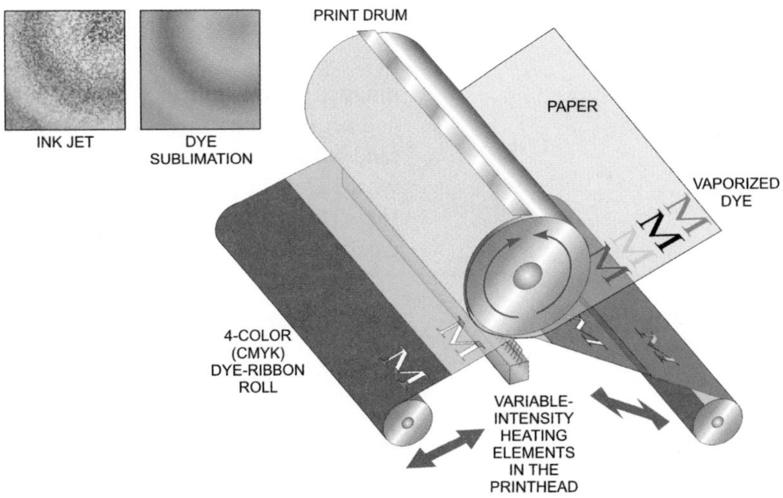

Figure 7-25: Dye Sublimation Printing

After the length of the page has been printed with one color, the drum cycles again, and the process is repeated until all the colors have been transferred to the page.

These printers tend to be very slow and expensive. However, due to their ability to produce continuous-tone quality images, these printers are widely used by professional graphics businesses to produce posters and large-scale reproductions.

With the popularity of digital cameras continuing to increase, users have many more options for how they handle, view, and display their photographs. Because digital photographs can be viewed without sending them to a print house, many users simply store their images on an electronic storage medium such as a disk drive or CD. However, there are always some photographs that people want to create hard copies of. For these occasions, some small consumer versions of the dye sublimation printer have been introduced to the market to enable users to reproduce electronic photographs without using a print service.

Essentials 4.1

PRINTER CONNECTIONS AND CONFIGURATIONS

The connection method between the printer and the computer will affect many of the troubleshooting steps necessary to isolate printing problems. Likewise, connecting a printer to a network will affect how the technician approaches its configuration and troubleshooting.

Printer Interfaces

As mentioned earlier in this chapter, the traditional parallel and serial ports that have been used with printers for decades are quickly fading from prominence as newer, faster, more powerful interfaces are gaining acceptance. As a matter of fact, there has been somewhat of an interface/bus war going on for supremacy of the personal computer world. These buses and interfaces were discussed in Chapter 4, *Standard I/O Systems* and include SCSI buses, USB ports, Firewire ports, and infrared ports along with direct-connect and wireless network adapter technologies. Therefore, it is not uncommon for printers to feature a variety of different connection options.

For many of the organizations that design and support given technologies, the idea is to develop a single dominant connection method that will permit any type of device to be plugged directly into the connection channel (buses and ports), be recognized by the system, and begin functioning without any further human intervention. For example, the USB port (and bus) can support up to 127 hot-swappable devices on a single-port hub. Try to imagine what 127 devices you would connect to your PC today. However, these groups are planning for a future where everything can be connected to the PC, including residential entertainment systems and automotive devices.

USB Printers

To install a USB printer, simply connect the USB signal cable to the computer and to the printer, plug in the printer's power cord, and then allow the system to detect the printer through the PnP process when it is started up. When the operating system detects the new printer, it may automatically install the printer's drivers without any additional efforts. If the operating system does not recognize the printer, a *Found New Hardware* wizard will appear, and you will need to select the proper driver from a Windows list, or supply an OEM driver from a disc. If the operating system does not detect the printer, you must install it using the Add Hardware wizard.

GEEK SQUAD CASE FILE #103452

You are working the evening shift in Store 54 when a local office manager comes to you complaining about the noise level in their accounting office caused by the dot-matrix printers they have to use. The wide-carriage dot-matrix printers are required because everyone in the department must print multipart invoices. After they have been printed, the invoices are separated from each other and taken to the warehouse for processing. The warehouse is well beyond the 10-feet range of the parallel printers you are using now. What option can you present to the office manager to lower the noise level in their accounting office?

Networked Printers

If a printer is installed in a computer system that is part of a network, it is possible for any other computer on the network to send work to the printer. Historically, the **local computer** has been attached to the printer through one of the normal printing interfaces (i.e., parallel, serial, or USB) and also connected to the other **remote computers** through its network connection. In addition to the signal cable, the local computer's operating system must be configured to permit the remote stations on the network to print through it to its printer. This relationship is known as **print sharing**.

Newer printers, referred to as **network-ready printers**, or simply as **network printers**, come with built-in network interfacing that enables them to be connected directly into the local area network. Most network printers contain an integrated network controller and Ethernet LAN adapter that enable them to work on the LAN without a supporting host computer.

Other printers may be connected directly to the local area network through a device called a **print server port**. This device resembles a network hub in appearance and can be used to connect up to three printers directly into the network. While some older network printers used coaxial cable connections, newer network printers feature RJ-45 jacks for connection to twisted-pair Ethernet networks.

It is relatively easy to determine whether a printer is networked by the presence of a coaxial or a twisted-pair network signal cable connected directly to the printer. The presence of the RJ-45 jacks on the back of the printer also indicates that the printer is network capable, even if it is not being used in that manner. These cables are covered in Chapter 6, *Data Communications*. In Windows, you can determine that a printer is networked by the appearance of its icon in the *Printers* folder. The icon will graphically illustrate the network connection. You can also check the *Details* tab of the printer in its Windows Properties page.

While parallel printers are easy to set up and check, and serial printers require a little more effort to set up, networked printers add another set of variables to the configuration and troubleshooting processes. To avoid dealing directly with the complexity of the network, it is normal to handle printer configuration and troubleshooting at the local level first. Once the operation of the local computer/printer interface has been established, or verified, the network portion of the system can be examined. The "Network Troubleshooting Basics" section of Chapter 11 deals with typical network troubleshooting procedures, while Windows-related network printing problems are covered extensively in the "Troubleshooting Local Area Networks" section of Chapter 12.

local computer

remote computers

print sharing

network-ready printers

network printers

print server port

TEST TIP

Know how to determine whether a printer is networked or not.

TEST TIP

Know how to identify the presence of a network-ready printer.

Infrared Printer Port Connections

The **IrLPT** IrDA standard provides specifications for implementing an infrared printer connection as illustrated in Figure 7-26. In this example, the printer connection is an IrDA printer connector and a receiver that is placed in line with the standard parallel printer port connection. The receiver has power supplied to it through its own power adapter.

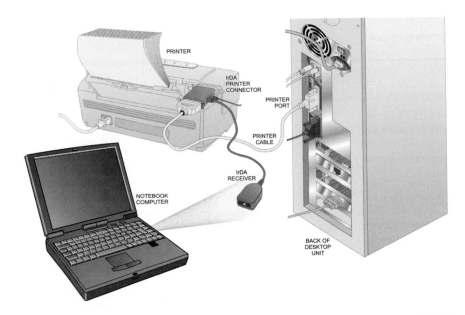

Figure 7-26: IrDA Printer Connections

The computer and printer communicate with each other over the infrared link that is established between their IrDA ports. The printer receives data and control signals from the computer and responds with status and error information. As with all IrDA connections, the distance and angle of transfer are limited. The recommended clear distance between the two devices is 1 meter, and the maximum angle between the transmitters and receivers is 15 degrees. The driver for the IrDA port of the printer must be loaded in the host machine for communications to occur.

Wireless Printer Interfaces

Just as it is common to find printers with built-in network adapters, it is almost as common to find printer models that feature wireless 802.11 and Bluetooth connectivity. These interfaces provide relatively easy, no-wires methods of attaching printers to existing networks. These units typically offer an embedded wireless network adapter as one of multiple interface options. In some cases, the printer may need to be physically connected to the network or a host computer to be configured. Afterward it can be used as a wireless device.

Small, inexpensive 802.11b/g **wireless print server** hub devices (or *Wi-Fi adapters*) have been developed to eliminate the need for a dedicated PC to handle print functions. These hubs typically connect to the USB port of network-capable, wired printers (or multifunction printer/scanner/copier/fax devices) and transform them into wireless printers. Some models also provide *Web server* functionality to enable remote configuration, printer management, and troubleshooting through a Web browser.

The Bluetooth option enables users to print directly from notebooks, PDAs, or cell phones. Bluetooth can be added to an existing USB or parallel port printer through a small Bluetooth receiver that plugs into the port. It also makes printer placement a simple and dynamic activity. You only need to position the printer within the specified range (e.g., 20 meters) of the Bluetooth device to achieve connectivity. Also, you can pick up the printer and relocate it in another room or office.

Bluetooth adapters feature *flashRAM* memory that can be flashed with the latest software updates to provide additional functionality. They also include traditional RAM memory to buffer pages of print data being sent to it across the network.

Parallel Printer Connections

Generally speaking, one of the least difficult I/O devices to add to a microcomputer system is a **parallel printer**. This is largely due to the fact that, from the beginning of the PC era, a printer has been one of the most standard pieces of equipment to add to the system. This standardization has led to fairly direct installation procedures for most printers: Obtain an IBM Centronics printer cable, plug it into the appropriate LPT port on the back of the computer, connect the Centronic-compatible end to the printer, plug the power cord into the printer, load a device driver to configure the software for the correct printer, and print.

parallel printer

At the printer end of a **Centronics parallel port**, a 36-pin connector, like the one depicted in Figure 7-27, is used. Of course, the computer end of the cable should have a DB-25M connector to plug into the system's DB-25F LPT port.

Centronics parallel port

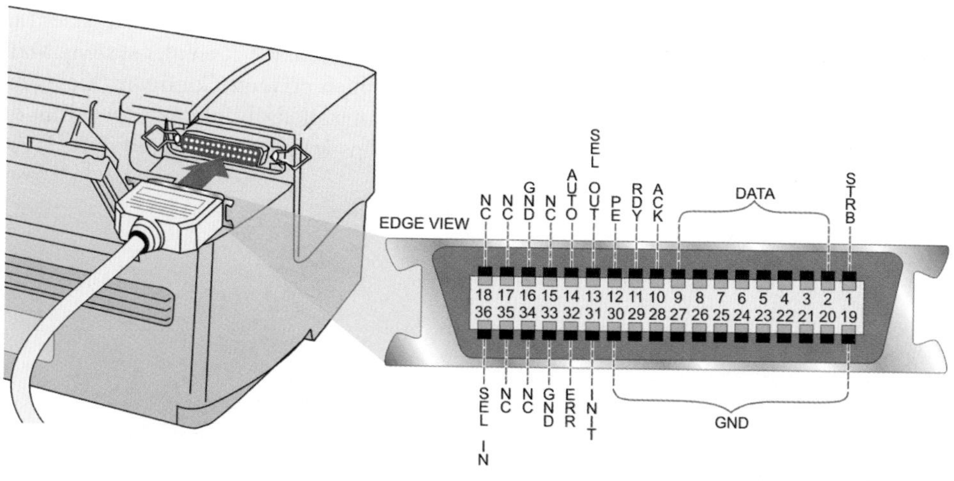

Figure 7-27: A Parallel Connection at the Printer

The major limiting factor for parallel printer connections is length. While cables purchased from reputable suppliers are typically correct in length and contain all of the shielding and connections required, cheaper cables and homemade cables often are lacking in some of these areas. The recommended signal cable lengths associated with standard parallel printers is: 0–10 ft (3 meters), although some equipment manufacturers specify 6 ft (1.8 meters) maximum for their cables. You should believe these recommendations when you see them.

One note of caution concerning parallel printer cables—the IEEE has established specifications for bidirectional parallel printer cables (**IEEE-1284**). These cables affect the operation of EPP and ECP parallel devices. Refer to the "Enhanced Parallel Port Operations" section of Chapter 4, *Standard I/O Systems*, for additional information about these ports. Using an older, noncompliant unidirectional cable with a bidirectional parallel device will prevent the device from communicating properly with the system and may prevent it from operating.

Some parallel printer cabling failures will produce error messages, such as "**Printer Not Ready**," while others will simply leave the data in the computer's **print spooler**. The symptom most often associated with this condition is that the parallel device simply refuses to operate. If an ECP or EPP device successfully runs a self-test, but will not communicate with the host system, check the *Advanced BIOS Setup* screens to make certain that bidirectional printing has been enabled for the parallel port. If so, check the printer cable by substituting a known 1284-compliant cable for it.

GEEK SQUAD CASE FILE #986543

You are Special Agent 554 working out of store 54. You have been called out to a customer's site to check his laser printer. The printer sits on the desk next to the host computer and is attached to the 25-pin D-shell connector on the back of the system. When you start the printer, it shows no startup errors and prints a page from a self-test. So, you check the system's CMOS settings to verify that the printer port is enabled and that it is set for ECP operation. Still, you cannot get the system to print a page from the printer. What should you check next?

Regardless of the type of printer being installed, the steps for adding a printer to a system are basically the same: Connect the printer to the correct I/O port at the computer system. Make sure the port is enabled. Set up the appropriate printer drivers. Configure the port's communication parameters, if a serial printer is being installed. Install the paper. Run the printer's self-test, and then print a document. These steps are summarized in Figure 7-28.

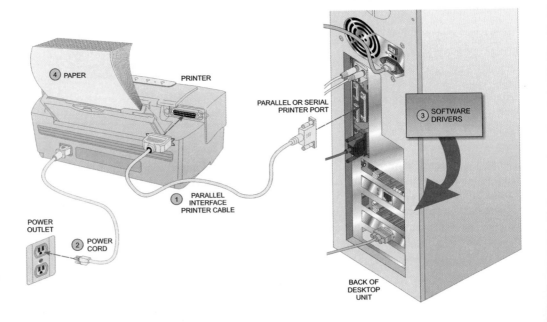

Figure 7-28: Printer Installation Steps

Serial Printer Considerations

In some applications, it is simply impossible to locate the printer close enough to the host computer to use the parallel connection. In these cases, serially interfaced printers come into play. Printers using an RS-232 serial interface connection add an extra level of complexity to the system. Unlike the parallel printer interface that basically plugs and plays on most systems, serial interface connections require additional hardware and software configuration steps. Serial printers are slightly more difficult to set up, because serial printers are not PnP compliant, and the communication definition must be manually configured between the computer and the printer. The serial port must be configured for speed, parity type, character frame, and protocol.

Serial printer problems basically fall into three categories:

- Cabling problems
- Configuration problems
- Printer problems

Serial Cabling Problems

Not all serial cables are created equal. In the PC world, RS-232 serial cables can take on several configurations. First, they may use either 9-pin or 25-pin D-shell connectors. The cable for a particular serial connection will need to have the correct type of connector at each end. Likewise, the connection scheme inside the cable can vary from printer to printer. Normally, the Transmit Data line (TXD—pin 2) from the computer is connected to the Receive Data line (RXD—pin 3) of the printer. Also, the Data Set Ready (DSR—pin 6) is typically connected to the printer's **Data Terminal Ready** (DTR—pin 20) pin. These connections are used as one method to control the flow of information between the system and the printer. If the printer's character buffer becomes full, it will signal the computer to hold up sending characters by deactivating this line.

Different or additional pin interconnections can be required for other printer models. The actual implementation of the RS-232 connection is solely up to the printer manufacturer. Figure 7-29 depicts typical connection schemes for both 9-pin and 25-pin connections to a typical printer. The connection scheme for a given serial printer model is usually provided in its user's manual.

> **TEST TIP**
> Remember the types of connectors used at both the computer and the printer ends of an RS-232 serial printer cable.

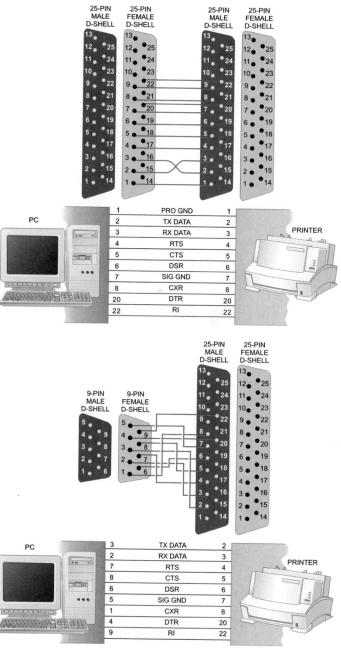

Figure 7-29: Serial Printer Connection Schemes

TEST TIP

Know the recommended maximum length of an RS-232 serial printer cable.

Like parallel printer cables, there is a practical length limit for serial cables. The recommended signal cable length associated with RS-232 serial printers is 10–50 ft (15.25 meters). However, some references use 100 ft as the acceptable length of an RS-232C serial cable. Serial connections are tricky enough without problems generated by the cable being too long. Make the cable as short as possible.

GEEK SQUAD CASE FILE #102938

Debra G., Special Agent 318 has been called to the ACME Warehouse. Their warehouse manager wants Debra to install a 20-foot printer cable so that he can move his wide-carriage dot-matrix printer out of his office and into the warehouse where the noise level caused by the dot-matrix printer will not be a problem. He must use the dot-matrix printer because he has to print multipart invoice forms. What can you suggest to the warehouse manager that would solve his problem?

Serial Printer Configuration

After the correct connector and cabling scheme has been implemented, the printer configuration must be established at both the computer and the printer. The information in both locations must match in order for communications to go on. On the system side of the serial-port connection, the software printer driver must be set up to match the settings of the printer's receiving section.

First, the driver must be directed toward the correct serial port. In a Windows-based system, this is typically COM2. Second, the selected serial port must be configured for the proper character framing. The number of start, stop, data, and parity bits must be set to match what the printer expects to receive. These values are often established through hardware configuration switches located on the printer.

Flow control

software handshaking

hardware handshaking

The printer driver must also be set up to correctly handle the flow of data between the system and the printer. Incorrect flow control settings can result in slow response, lost characters, or continuous errors and retries. **Flow control** can be established through **software** or **hardware handshaking**. In a hardware handshaking mode, the printer tells the port that it is not prepared to receive data by deactivating a control line, such as the DTR line. Conversely, in a software handshaking environment, control codes are sent back and forth between the printer and the computer to enable and disable data flow.

Software data flow control—Two popular methods of implementing software flow control are Xon/Xoff and ETX/ACK. In the Xon/Xoff method, special ASCII control characters are exchanged between the printer and the computer to turn the data flow on and off. In an ETX/ACK protocol, ASCII characters for End-of-Text (ETX) and ACKnowledge (ACK) are used to control the movement of data from the port to the printer.

Basically, the computer attaches the ETX character to the end of a data transmission. When the printer receives the ETX character, it checks the incoming data, and when ready, returns an ACK character to the port. This notifies the system that the printer is capable of receiving additional characters. This concept is illustrated in Figure 7-30. In any event, the devices at both ends of the interface connection must be set to use the same flow control method.

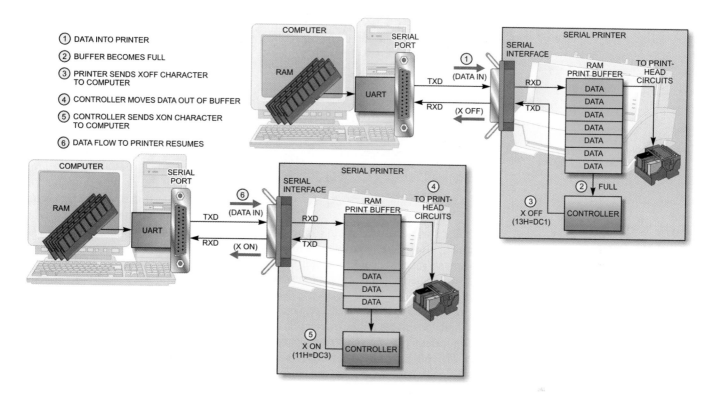

Figure 7-30: Software Flow Control

Printer Drivers

Essentials 4.2

Technical Support 3.2

All peripheral devices require device driver programs to coordinate their operation with the system. These programs are installed on the host computer and create a software interface between the operating system's printing subsystem, the port, and the printer's intelligent devices. For the most part, modern operating systems supply a wide variety of device drivers (including **printer drivers**) as an integral part of their packages.

printer drivers

When a new printer is installed, it should be detected by the system's PnP process the next time the system is started. In many cases, the operating system will be able to determine which type of printer is attached and automatically load a standard driver for it. In other cases, the PnP process will request that the user insert an OEM driver disk so that it can load a driver for the new drive.

When the new printer is not detected, the user must manually install the printer (and its driver program) through a configuration program (wizard) in the operating system. Figure 7-31 illustrates the functional position of a printer driver in the system.

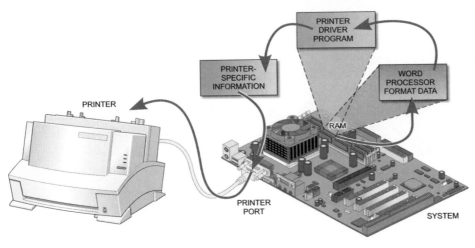

Printer drivers can also be a source of many printing problems and are generally one of the first things checked when a new printer installation does not function. These programs can also become corrupted in some operating systems when new devices are installed that write over .dll portions of their code. Therefore, it may be necessary to reload printer drivers in these situations.

Faulty or incorrect printer drivers will typically produce garbled print (because the driver is not giving the printer information that it can recognize) or no print at all. If you suspect that a printer driver problem is occurring, you must reinstall or replace the driver. In a PnP system, you can remove the existing driver through the installation wizard and restart the system so it can detect the printer and install a new copy of the driver. In a non-PnP system, you must manually reinstall the driver.

Figure 7-31: Printer Driver Position

If you are going to reinstall the driver, you should check the printer manufacturer's Web site for new updated drivers for the printer you are working with. Printer manufacturers typically supply proprietary driver programs that may be newer than the version in your operating system. Theoretically, these newer drivers should work better or offer improved features over the older versions.

Special Print Drivers

page description languages (PDLs)

graphics device interface (GDI)

Postscript

There are applications, such as desktop publishing, where you will need to install specialty drivers to extend the font capabilities of the printer. The two most widely used drivers for this function are Postscript and PCL. Postscript and PCL are actually **page description languages** (**PDL**s) that describe the arrangement of text and graphics on a printed page. In Windows, the default page descriptions for graphics output devices are supplied by its **graphics device interface** (**GDI**) library. To implement Postscript and PCL functions on the PC, it is necessary to install the driver software for that PDL.

Postscript was developed by *Adobe* is the defacto PDL standard for printing in commercial typesetting and print houses. The driver enables the system to scale characters to size using an interpreter. Thereby, removing the necessity of storing a variety of font types and sizes in disk or in memory. It is recommended for use with color documents and documents that have complex page layout formatting or that contain several graphical images. In addition, the Postscript driver offers more options and handles graphic processing more efficiently than other print drivers.

Printer control language (PCL) is a page description command language developed by Hewlett Packard for its Laser Jet to support scalable fonts. Its use has been so widely accepted that PCL has become the de facto standard in many printer models. It is best suited for use with text documents that are monochrome and have relatively simple formatting. With these types of pages, the PCL driver will offer quicker printing than a Postscript driver.

The printer has three options for accessing these types of fonts—internal fonts, soft fonts, and cartridge fonts. *Internal fonts* are those fonts stored in the printer's on-board ROM and always available. *Soft fonts* are downloadable fonts that reside on a disk somewhere and can be transferred to the printer's memory when needed. Cartridge fonts are provided in plug-in modules that are inserted directly into slots in the printer housing. The printer simply retrieves the fonts from the cartridge when called for.

When a page references one of these PDLs, the printer will check for the indicated font internally. If it does not find the font there, it will check with the host computer and download it into memory if available. If the font is not available in the printer or the computer, the printer will attempt to convert a bitmapped font into a simulated Postscript font. This often produces pages with mangled text and graphic positioning and characters of much lower quality than expected.

Postscript and PCl soft font drivers for different printers can be downloaded to the host computer and must then be installed. These fonts are installed in Windows through the printer's *Properties* dialog box. In the printer properties dialog box, select the *Device Settings* tab, click *External Fonts*, and then select *Properties*. Next, you must tell the installation wizard where the fonts are located by entering the path to the folder or drive where the fonts are located. You must have Manage Printers permissions in a network environment to add these fonts to the system.

Printer Control Panel Configuration

As indicated earlier in this chapter, most printer models have an operator **control panel** of some sort that can be used to configure printer options. Some control panels are a collection of a few buttons, while others have buttons and visual displays (usually small LCD screens). Some high-end printers feature touch screens that both display information about the printer and enable the user to configure printer settings through touch screen menus.

In any case, the use of the operator control panel to configure printer settings is often less than straightforward. Likewise, information that the printer supplies to the user through the control panel may be cryptic in nature. Therefore, you should always refer to the printer's user's manual to determine what options are available and how to go about changing default settings when an application calls for something different. For example, in the case of PCL and Postscript printers described in the previous section, you may need to configure internal font usage through the control panel on the front of the printer. For some configuration items, it is possible to establish their settings through the printer driver (using the *Properties* page) or through the operator control panel.

The operator's control panel is also the main source of information about the printer's operation and errors that occur. Like the computer, the printer or scanner may try to issue coded messages to you through beeps or flashing light sequences. The meaning of these coded messages and the recommended steps to correct them are located in the user's manual.

Printer Calibration

There are basically two common methods of adjusting printer output. The first is to adjust the output through the printer's driver settings. The other method involves using **color management** functions to match **International Color Consortium (ICC)** profiles. The key to using either method involves first correctly calibrating the display to which you can match a **test image** printout. This will enable you to effectively evaluate the quality of the image being produced.

There are several sources of good test images available on the Internet. These images are specially constructed to show the full capabilities of the printer (e.g., crispness, color, grayscale, brightness, contrast). One of the easiest methods of obtaining printer test pages is to use an Internet search engine to search for "printer test page." These pages can be downloaded to your system and displayed on a calibrated monitor as the standard to which to adjust the printer output.

Printer driver adjustments begin in the printer's Properties window, as illustrated by the sample Printer Properties window depicted in Figure 7-32. To achieve maximum control of the printing process, you must select a *Custom Mode* option and click on the *Advanced* button to access the **color management** functions.

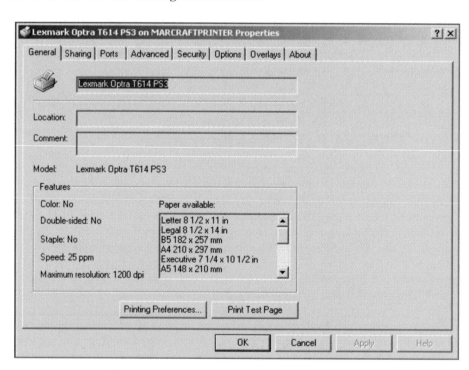

Figure 7-32: Printer Properties

This page will enable you to adjust brightness, contrast, saturation, and CMYK color settings as in Figure 7-33. You must adjust these settings and print test pages until you achieve the print output you want. It is best to make the first print using the default settings and then adjust one setting at a time until the desired qualities are achieved. You can change more than one adjustment at a time for expediency, but you should always record the previous settings so that you can come back to them if needed.

You should also be aware that the actual appearance of printed material can change based on the media type you are printing on. Many printer Properties pages allow you to select a media type to compensate for changes caused by the media.

Color management is a set of tools used to establish and maintain consistent image appearance between different devices, such as cameras, displays, scanners, and printers. Each of these devices has different color responses when displayed. Also, there is no direct correlation between RGB color in monitors and CYMK colors in printers and scanners. However, color management acts to coordinate the appearance of these color types between the devices.

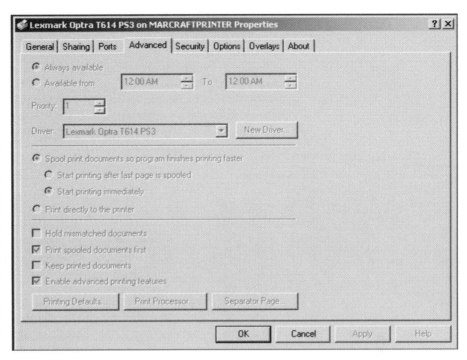

**Figure 7-33:
Advanced Printer
Properties**

Color management is based on *Image Color Management* (*ICM*) standards established by the ICC. **ICC profiles** are files that map color settings between devices. Depending on the type of profile, the color match may be linked between printers and monitors, printers and scanners, or monitors and scanners. These profiles are identified by a common filename extension of *.icm*. ICC profiles can be downloaded from Internet sources and should be placed in the Windows ICC profile folder. In Windows 2000, this is *WinNT\System32\Spool\Drivers\Color*, and in Windows XP it is *WINDOWS\system32\spool\drivers\color*.

After the profile has been installed, application programs that are ICM-aware, such as *Photoshop*, can use them. If the printer can use ICC profiles, they can be applied through the Printing Preferences dialog box. With the correct printer profile installed and a properly calibrated monitor, the match between the monitor and the printer output should be very good.

Printer Options and Upgrades

Printer FRU modules—In some printers, the microcontroller, RAM modules, and ROM/EPROM devices may be treated as FRU components. Many laser printers come with something less than their maximum amount of RAM installed. However, they also provide optional hardware to permit the memory to be upgraded if desired. Many high-speed laser printers require additional RAM to be installed to handle printing of complex documents, such as desktop-published documents containing large *Encapsulated Post Script* (*EPS*) graphics files.

Essentials 4.2

Technical Support 3.2

IT Technician 4.2

Similarly, ROM and EPROM devices that contain BIOS or character sets have often been placed in sockets so that they can be replaced or upgraded easily. However, newer printers have followed the ROM technologies used in computers and installed ROM devices that can be flashed. As with the gears and gear trains discussed earlier in the chapter, how replaceable these units are depends on the ability to source them from a supplier. In most cases, the question is not whether the device can be exchanged, but whether it makes economical sense to do so. For a given printer type and model, the manufacturer's service center can provide information about the availability of replacement parts.

In many cases, printers in business environments are becoming their own node of the company network. Increasingly, these printers are being equipped with their own built-in network adapters and computer-like peripherals so that they can function in a stand-alone manner. Figure 7-34 depicts a high-end laser printer intended for multiple-user or network printer applications.

Initially, these units were only equipped with an Ethernet network adapter and enough electronics to let them function as a network node and provide printing services for other network nodes. However, it has become common to integrate other computer peripherals such as hard drives into the printer unit to make them more efficient. For example, the hard-disk drive unit is used in a high-volume printer to store information coming to it from across the network. The HDD unit makes it possible for the printer to spool large amounts of data that it receives so that the network does not get congested waiting for the printer to print user's documents.

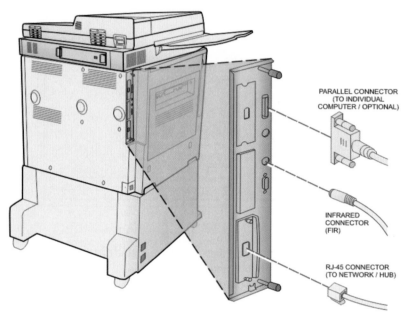

PARALLEL CONNECTOR
(TO INDIVIDUAL
COMPUTER / OPTIONAL)

INFRARED
CONNECTOR
(FIR)

RJ-45 CONNECTOR
(TO NETWORK / HUB)

Figure 7-34: Stand-Alone Multiple-User Printer

In all but the most basic printer installation, several time- and labor-saving peripherals and devices may be attached to printers. The technician must be aware of these devices and their functions, because they can fail in printer installations. It is not unusual for commercial office printers to offer several types of add-on components for their machines, such as the following:

- *An automatic sheet feeder*—a device that mounts on the printer to enable special paper types to be fed directly into the printer. This unit can be combined with a scanner unit so that hard-copy documents can be scanned directly into the printer for printing.

- *Multiple paper trays*—storage bins that can be used to supply different sizes and types of papers to the printer without having to manually load them, or change paper in a single tray. They can also be used to store large volumes of standard paper so that the printer does not need human attention as often.

- *A duplexer*—a device that reroutes paper through the printer so that copies can be made on both sides.

- *A collator*—a device that sorts multipage documents as they are printed so that they are in a prescribed order (i.e., page 1, page 2, etc.)

- *A stapler/stacker*—an add-on that is used to staple multipage documents after they have been sorted and collated and stack them for distribution.

As mentioned earlier in this chapter, laser printers share their basic technologies with other office machines, such as copiers, scanners, and plain paper faxes. Because of this, combination products have been developed to bring all of these functions together in a single unit, like the one depicted in Figure 7-35. These units offer considerable savings over buying separate machines for each function.

In combination units, the ELP drum provides the central function for each operation. In a scanner operation, the image is scanned from an inserted document and digitized. The digitized image can then be stored as an electronic file. Because the document is in a digital form, it can also be converted to a proper format for faxing to another fax machine. And yes, the unit can act as a laser printer that accepts information from a host computer, scans it on the drum, and prints it out.

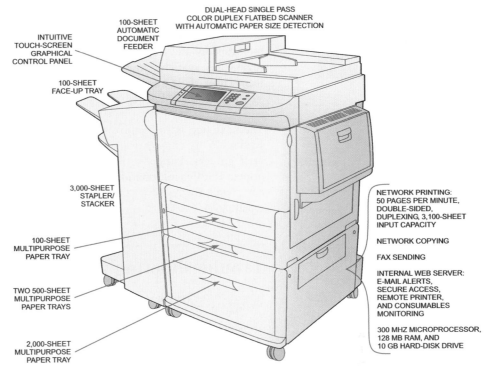

Figure 7-35: Office Automation Unit

SERVICING PRINTERS

Essentials 4.3

Technical Support 3.3

IT Technician 4.3

Depot Technician 3.3

Printers are connected to personal computers and they break down. Therefore, the computer technician should be familiar with common printer problems and be able to demonstrate current service techniques.

The preliminary steps for troubleshooting printer problems are similar to those used with other electronic devices. Begin with the simple and obvious possibilities. These include talking to the user or operator to gather information about the problem. Then check for simple causes such as the printer being plugged in to the power source and connected to the host computer. It is a good practice to cycle the power on the printer off and back on to see if problems clear up by resetting the printer system.

You should note any visual error indicators, codes or messages presented by the printer. These messages are often coded and will require that you refer to the user's manual for explanation. It makes much more sense to look up the meaning of a code than to try to go directly to troubleshooting activities. The device is trying to make your life easier—listen to it. You may simply need to add paper, clear a jammed page from the printer, clear the printer queue, or restart the print spooler.

However, if these simple things are not the cause of a problem you are trying to isolate, some organizations suggest that you divide the troubleshooting process into activities—*review and analyze the data you've collected* and then *identify solutions for the problem*. Use any printer diagnostic tools available. These include diagnostic utilities provided by the manufacturer as well as third party tools. The Internet is a good source of general (and sometimes specific) printer troubleshooting information, as well as a source of troubleshooting utilities.

Begin the review process by establishing probable causes for the problem you are observing—hardware, software, drivers, or connectivity. Then review the printer (or multifunction device) service documentation for information related to the problem. Also review any available **knowledge bases** for references to the problem being observed. In many cases, these knowledge bases have built-in search functions that let you go directly to information related to key words used to describe the problem.

The next step is to identify solutions for the problem you're observing. The following sections of this chapter deal with typical problems encountered with dot-matrix, ink-jet, and laser printers. They also include troubleshooting methods associated with each type of printer. Use this information to define a specific cause and apply a fix to the problem. When completed, always verify the printer's functionality and get the owner/user to sign off on the repair.

Troubleshooting Dot-Matrix Printers

The classical first step in determining the cause of any printer problem is to determine which part of the printer-related system is at fault—the **host computer**, the **signal cable**, or the **printer**.

host computer

signal cable

printer

built-in self-test

Nearly every printer is equipped with a **built-in self-test**. The easiest way to determine whether the printer is at fault is to run its self-test. Consult the printer's user's manual for instructions on running its self-test. Some printers are capable of producing audible tones to indicate the nature of an internal problem. Refer to the printer's user's manual for the definitions of the coded beep tones, if they are available.

If a printer runs the self-test, and prints clean pages, then most of the printer has been eliminated as a possible cause of problems. The problem could be in the computer, the cabling, or the interface portion of the printer. However, if the printer fails the self-test, it will be necessary to diagnose the printer's problem. The following section presents typical problems encountered in dot-matrix printers.

The following are symptoms for dot-matrix printer problems:

- No lights or noise from printer
- Printhead moving but not printing
- Dots missing from characters
- Light or uneven print being produced
- Printhead is printing but does not move
- Paper will not advance

┌─ **TEST TIP** ─────────────────┐
Know what it means if the printer produces a satisfactory self-test printout but does not print from the computer.
└────────────────────────────────┘

Dot-Matrix Printer Configuration Checks

The presence of on-board microcontrollers allows modern printers to be very flexible. Like other peripheral devices, printers can be configured to operate in different modes. Operating configuration information can be stored in CMOS RAM on the control board. Some configuration settings may be made through DIP switches mounted inside the printer. These switches are read by the printer's microcontroller at start-up.

In the case of dot-matrix printers, the configuration settings are normally entered into the printer through the buttons of its control panel. Typical dot-matrix configuration settings include

- Printer mode

- Perforation skip (for continuous forms)

- Automatic line feed at the bottom of the page

- Paper handling type

- ASCII character codes (7-bit or 8-bit)

- Basic character sets

Other quantities that can be set up include

- Print font

- Character pitch

- Form length

Most dot-matrix printers contain two or three on-board fonts (character styles) that can be selected through the printer's configuration routines. In many dot-matrix printer models, it is also possible to download other fonts from the computer. Typical fonts included in dot-matrix printers are

- Draft

- Courier

- Prestige

- Bold Prestige

The **character pitch** refers to the number of characters printed per inch. Common pitch settings include 10, 11, 12, and 14 characters per inch. Consult the printer's user's guide to find the definitions of such settings.

character pitch

Dot-Matrix Printer Hardware Checks

To perform work inside the printer, it will be necessary to disassemble its case. Begin by removing any add-on pieces, such as dust covers and paper feeders. Next, remove the paper advancement knob located on the right side of most dot-matrix printers. Turn the printer over, and remove the screws that hold the two halves of the case together. These screws are sometimes hidden beneath rubber feet and compliance stickers. Finally, it may be necessary to disconnect the printer's front panel connections from the main board to complete the separation of the two case halves. This procedure is shown in Figure 7-36.

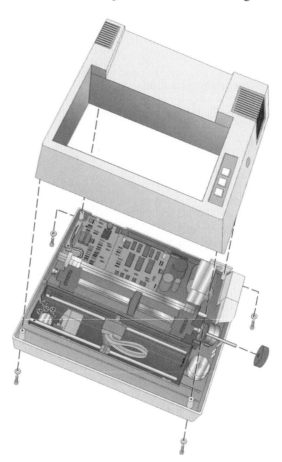

**Figure 7-36:
Disassembling
the Printer**

Dot-Matrix Printer Power Supply Problems

If the printer does not function, and displays no lights, no sounds, and no actions, the power supply is generally involved. Troubleshoot printer power supply problems in the same manner as you would a computer power supply problem. As a matter of fact, the power supply troubleshooting routine is the same.

Check the online light. If the printer is offline, no print action will occur. A missing, or improperly installed, ribbon cartridge will also prevent the unit from printing. Install the ribbon correctly. Check the power outlet to make certain that it is live. Plug a lamp, or other device, into the outlet to verify that it is operative. Check to see that the power cord is plugged securely into the printer and the socket. Make sure the power switch is on.

If everything is plugged in and in the on position but still not working, turn OFF the power, and unplug the printer from the outlet. Remove the top of the printer's case, and find the power supply board. Check the power supply's fuse to make sure that it is good. If the fuse is blown, replace it with a fuse of the same type and rating. Do not replace a blown fuse with a conductor or a slow-blow fuse. Doing so could lead to more extensive damage to the printer, and possibly unsafe conditions.

Also, check the power supply and control boards, as well as the paper feed and printhead positioning motors for burnt components, or signs of defect. Fuses usually do not blow, unless another component fails. Another possible cause of excessive current occurs when a motor (or its gear train) binds, and cannot move. Check the drive mechanisms and motors for signs of binding. If the gear train or positioning mechanisms will not move, they may need to be adjusted before replacing the fuse.

If none of the printer sections work when everything is connected and power is applied, it will be necessary to exchange the power supply board for a new unit. Unlike the computer's power supply, the typical printer power supply is not enclosed in a protective housing and, therefore, presents a shock hazard anytime it is exposed.

To exchange the power supply board, disconnect the power cable from the printer. Disconnect and mark the cabling from the control board, and any other components directly connected to the power supply. Remove any screws or clips that secure the power supply board to the case. Lift the board out of the cabinet. Install the new board, and reconnect the various wire bundles to it.

Ribbon Cartridges

The single item in a dot-matrix printer that requires the most attention is the **ribbon cartridge**. It is considered a consumable part of the printer and must be changed often. The ink ribbon is stored in a controlled wad inside the cartridge and moves across the face of the platen, as depicted in Figure 7-37. A take-up wheel draws new ribbon out of the wad as it is used. As the ribbon wears out, the printing will become faint and uneven. When the print becomes noticeably faint, the cartridge should be replaced. Most dot-matrix printers use a snap-in ribbon cartridge.

> **ribbon cartridge**

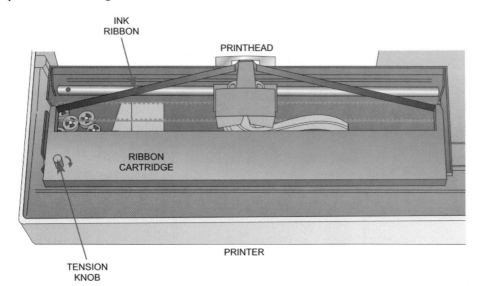

> **TEST TIP**
>
> Know what the most likely cause of uneven or faded print with a dot-matrix printer is and how to correct it.

**Figure 7-37:
The Printer
Cartridge**

To replace a typical ribbon cartridge, move the printhead carriage assembly to the center of the printer. Remove the old cartridge by freeing it from its clips or holders and then lifting it out of the printer.

Tighten the ribbon tension by advancing the tension knob on the cartridge, in a counterclockwise direction, until the ribbon is taut. Snap the cartridge into place, making certain that the ribbon slides between the printhead and the ribbon mask. Slide the printhead assembly back and forth on the rod to check for proper ribbon movement.

Printhead Not Printing

head gap lever

If the printhead is moving but not printing, begin by checking the printer's **head gap lever** to make sure that the printhead is not too far back from the paper. If the printhead does not operate, components involved include

- The printhead

- The flexible signal cable between the control board and the printhead

- The control board

- Possibly the power supply board

Run the printer's self-test to see if the printhead will print from the on-board test. Check the flexible signal cable to make sure that it is firmly plugged into the control board, and that it is not damaged or worn through. If none of the print wires are energized, then the first step should be to exchange the control board for a known good one of the same type. If the new control board does not correct the problem, replace the printhead. A power supply problem could also cause the printhead to not print.

A related problem occurs when one, or more, of the print wires does not fire. If this is the case, check the printhead for physical damage. Also check the flexible signal cable for a broken conductor. If the control board is delivering any of the other print wire signals, the problem is most likely associated with the printhead mechanism. Replace the printhead as a first step. If the problem continues after replacing the printhead, however, exchange the control board for a new one.

┌─ **TEST TIP** ─────────────────┐
Know what causes tops of characters to be missing from dot-matrix characters and how to correct the problem.
└────────────────────────────────┘

If the tops of characters are missing, the printhead is misaligned with the platen. It may need to be reseated in the printhead carriage, or the carriage assembly may need to be adjusted to the proper height and angle.

To exchange the printhead assembly, make sure that the printhead assembly is cool enough to be handled. These units can get hot enough to cause a serious burn. Unplug the printhead assembly from the control board. Slide the printhead assembly to the center of the printer, and rotate the **head-locking lever** to release the printhead from the assembly. Remove the printhead by lifting it straight up. Install the new printhead by following the disassembly

head-locking lever

┌─ **TEST TIP** ─────────────────┐
Remember that the printhead of a dot-matrix printer generates a great deal of heat and can be a burn hazard when working on these units.
└────────────────────────────────┘

procedure in reverse. Adjust the new printhead for proper printing. In some printers, the printheads are held in the printhead assembly with screws. To remove the printhead from these units, it will be necessary to remove the screws so that the printhead can be exchanged. Refer to the printer's documentation for directions concerning exchanging the printhead mechanism.

If the output of the printer gets lighter as it moves from left to right across the page, it may become necessary to adjust the spacing of the printhead mechanism to obtain proper printing. This procedure is illustrated in Figure 7-38. To print correctly, the printhead should be approximately 0.6 mm from the platen when the head position lever is in the center position. Move the printhead to the center of the printer. Adjusting this setting requires that the nut at the left end of the rear carriage shaft be loosened. Using a feeler-gauge, set the distance between the platen and printhead (not the **ribbon mask**). Tighten the nut, and check the spacing between the printhead and platen at both ends of the printhead travel.

ribbon mask

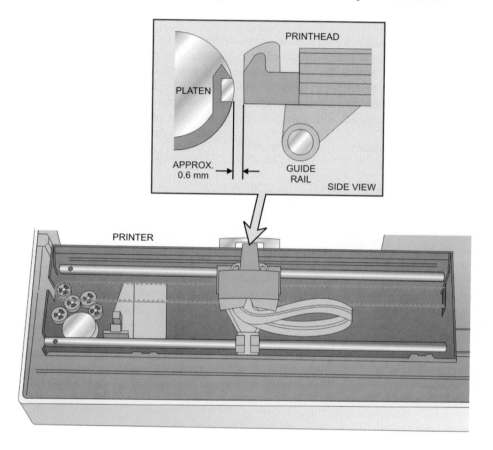

Figure 7-38: Adjusting the Printhead Spacing

Finally, check the distance between the platen and the ribbon mask. This space should be 0.3 mm. If not, loosen the screws that hold the ribbon mask to the printhead assembly, and adjust the gap with feeler gauges. There should also be a 0.1 mm space between the printhead and the ribbon mask. After setting the various gaps, run the printer's self-test to check for print quality.

┌─ **TEST TIP** ─────────┐
Know the most likely cause of print that fades from one side of the page to the other.
└────────────────────────┘

Printhead Not Moving

If the printhead is printing but not moving across the page, a single block of print will be generated on the page. When this type of problem occurs, the related components include the printhead positioning motor, the timing belt, the **home position** and **timing sensors**, the control board, and possibly the power supply board.

home position

timing sensors

With the power off, manually move the printhead to the center of the printer. Turn the printer on to see if the printhead seeks the home position at the far left side of the printer. If it moves to the left side of the printer and does not shut off or does not return to the center of the printer, then the home position sensor is malfunctioning and should be replaced. If the printhead moves on start-up and will not move during normal printing, the control board should be replaced. In the event that the printhead assembly will not move at any time, the printhead positioning motor should be replaced. If the print is skewed from left to right as it moves down the page, the printer's bidirectional mode settings may be faulty, or the home-position/end-of-line sensors may be defective.

Testing the timing sensor would require test equipment, in the form of a logic probe or an oscilloscope, to look for pulses produced as the printhead is manually moved across the printer. Figure 7-39 depicts the components associated with the printhead's timing belt. Replacing the timing belt requires that it be removed from the printhead assembly. In many cases, the belt is secured to the printhead assembly with adhesive cement. This will require that the adhesive seal be cut with a single-edged razor blade, or a hobby knife.

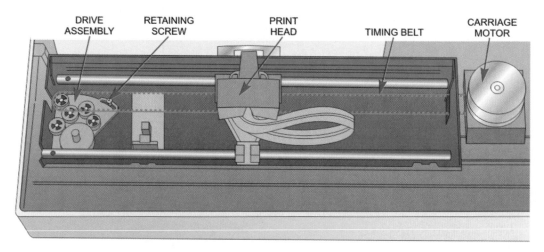

Figure 7-39: Printhead Timing Belt

After the seal has been broken, it should be possible to shove the belt out of the clips that secure it to the printhead assembly. Next, remove the belt from the drive pulley assembly at the positioning motor. It may be necessary to remove the positioning motor from the case to gain access to the pulley.

To reinstall the timing belt, apply a small drop of adhesive to the belt, and reattach it to the printhead assembly. Wrap the belt around the positioning motor's drive pulley, and reinstall the motor. Following this, it will be necessary to adjust the tension on the belt. To set the tension on the belt, loosen the adjustment screw on the belt-tension adjustment plate. Tighten the timing belt until it will not move more than 1/4" when the printhead is at either end of the carriage shaft and the belt is pressed inward. Tighten the retaining screw to lock the tension plate in place. Run the printer's self-test, and check the distance between the characters. If the character spacing is not uniform, replace the belt and perform the check again.

Paper Not Advancing

When the paper does not advance, the output will normally be one line of dark blocks across the page. Examine the printer's **paper feed selector lever** to make sure that it is set properly for the type of paper feed selected (i.e., friction feed, pin feed, or tractor feed). If the paper feed is set correctly, the printer is online, and the paper still does not move, it will be necessary to troubleshoot the paper handling motor and gear train. Check the motor and gear train by setting the printer to the offline mode and holding down the *Form Feed (FF)* button.

If the feed motor and gear train work from this point, the problem must exist in the **control board**, the **interface cable**, the **printer's configuration**, or the **computer system**. If the motor or gear train do not respond, unplug the paper feed motor cable, and check the resistance of the motor windings. If the windings are open, replace the paper feed motor.

To replace the paper feed motor or gear train, remove the screws that hold the paper feed motor to the frame of the printer. Create a wiring diagram that describes the routing of the feed motor's wiring harness. Disconnect the wiring harness from the control board.

Prepare a drawing that outlines the arrangement of the gear train (if multiple gears are used). Remove the gears from the shafts, taking care not to lose any washers, or springs, that may be located behind the gears. After reinstalling the gears and replacing the motor, adjust the motor and gear relationships to minimize the **gear lash** so that they do not bind or lock up. Use the printer's self-test to check the operation of the motor and gears.

> ### GEEK SQUAD CASE FILE #654910
>
> Special Agent 318 gets a call from the ACME warehouse manager complaining about the serial printer she installed in his warehouse earlier in the chapter. It seems that soon after she installed the new dot-matrix printer, the text on the multipart forms became uneven from side to side and printed with an uphill slant. When Debra checks out the printer, she determines that the paper is slipping from the weight of the multipart continuous forms. What can Agent 318 do to fix this printing problem on the new printer?

Troubleshooting Ink-Jet Printers

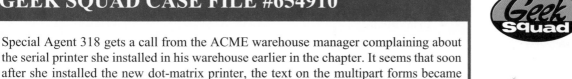

As with the dot-matrix printer, the first step in determining the cause of an ink-jet printer problem is to determine which part of the printer system is at fault—the **host computer**, the **signal cable**, or the **printer**.

Ink-jet printers are equipped with built-in self-tests. The easiest way to determine if the printer is at fault is to run its self-tests. Consult the printer's user's manual for instructions in running its self-tests. If the printer runs the self-tests, and prints clean pages, then most of the printer has been eliminated as a possible cause of problems. The problem could be in the **computer**, the **cabling**, or the **interface** portion of the printer.

However, if the printer fails the self-tests, it will be necessary to diagnose the printer problem. The following section presents typical problems encountered in ink-jet printers.

The following are symptoms of ink-jet printer problems:

- No lights or noise from the printer

- Light or uneven print being produced

- Printhead is moving but is not printing or is printing erratically

- Lines on the page

- Printhead is printing but does not move

- Paper will not advance

Ink-Jet Printer Configuration Checks

The presence of an on-board microcontroller allows modern printers to be very flexible. Like other peripheral devices, printers can be configured to operate in different modes. Operating configuration information can be stored in RAM, on the control board.

In the case of ink-jet printers, the configuration settings are normally entered into the printer through software. Typical configuration information includes

- **Paper size**
- **Print quality**
- **Page orientation** (landscape or portrait)
- **Collation**

Landscape printing is specified when the width of the page is greater than the length of the page. **Portrait printing** is specified when the length of the page is greater than the width. In an ink-jet printer, the quality of the printout is specified in the number of dots per inch (dpi) produced. Typical ink-jet resolutions run from 180 × 180 dpi to 720 × 720 dpi. Ink-jet printers have the capability to download additional fonts from the host computer.

┌─ **TEST TIP** ───┐
│ Be aware that print density can be adjusted through software in an ink-jet printer. │
└──┘

You can also configure the basic appearance of color and **grayscale** images produced by the ink-jet printer. A color ink-jet printer uses four ink colors to produce color images. These are **cyan**, **magenta**, **yellow**, and **black** (referred to as **CMYK color**). To create other colors, the printer prints a predetermined percentage of the basic colors in close proximity to each other.

The different percentages determine what the new color will be. The eye does not differentiate the space between them and perceives only the combined color. This is referred to as **halftone color**. Typical color configurations include setting up the **brightness**, the **contrast**, and the **saturation** settings of images.

Paper size

Page orientation

Print quality

Collation

Landscape printing

Portrait printing

grayscale

cyan

magenta

yellow

black

CMYK color

halftone color

brightness

contrast

saturation

Ink-Jet Printer Hardware Checks

To perform work on the printer's hardware, it will be necessary to disassemble the printer's case. Begin by removing all of the add-on pieces, such as dust covers and paper feeders. Remove the screws that hold the outer panels of the case to the printer frame. Removing the access panels of a typical ink-jet printer is shown in Figure 7-40. The retaining screws are sometimes hidden beneath rubber feet and compliance stickers. Finally, it may be necessary to disconnect the printer's front panel connections from the control board to complete the disassembly of the case.

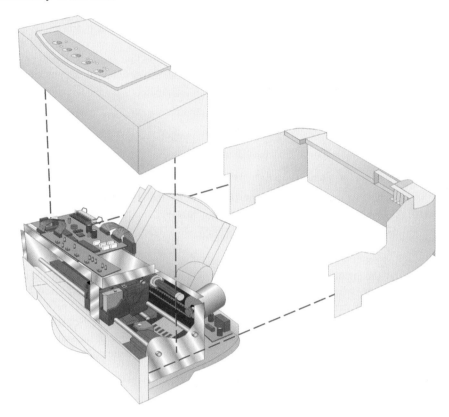

**Figure 7-40:
Printer Case**

Power Supply Problems

If the printer does not function, and displays no lights, no sounds, and no actions, the power supply is generally involved. Check the online light. If the printer is offline, no print action will occur. A missing, or improperly installed, ink cartridge will prevent the unit from printing. Install the ink cartridge correctly. Check the power outlet to make certain that it is live. Plug a lamp or some other device into the outlet to verify that it is operative. Check to see that the power cord is plugged securely into the printer and the socket. Make sure the power switch is ON.

If the unit is plugged in and turned ON, but still not working, turn it off and unplug it. Remove the top of the printer's case, and locate the power supply board. Check the power supply's fuse to make sure that it is good. If the fuse is blown, replace it with a fuse of the same type and rating. Do not replace a blown fuse with a conductor, or a slow-blow fuse. Doing so could lead to more extensive damage to the printer and possible unsafe conditions.

Also, check the power supply and control boards, as well as the paper feed and printhead positioning motors, for burnt components or signs of defect. Fuses usually do not blow unless another component fails. Another possible cause of overcurrent occurs when a motor (or its gear train) binds and cannot move. Check the drive mechanisms and motors for signs of binding. If the gear train, or positioning mechanisms, do not move, they may need to be adjusted, or replaced, before replacing the fuse.

If none of the printer sections work, everything is connected, and power is applied, it will be necessary to exchange the power supply board for a new unit. Unlike the computer's power supply, the typical power supply in a printer is not enclosed in a protective housing and therefore presents a shock hazard any time it is exposed.

To exchange the power supply board, disconnect the power cable from the printer. Disconnect and mark the cabling from the control board and any other components directly connected to the power supply. Remove any screws or clips that secure the power supply board to the case. Lift the board out of the cabinet. Install the new board, and reconnect the various wire bundles to it.

Ink Cartridges

ink cartridge

The single item in an ink-jet printer that requires the most attention is the **ink cartridge** (or cartridges). As the ink cartridge empties, the printing will eventually become faint and uneven, and the resolution of the print on the page will diminish.

The density of the printout from an ink-jet printer can be adjusted through its printing software. However, when the print becomes noticeably faint, or the resolution becomes unacceptable, the cartridge will need to be replaced. Most ink-jet printers use a self-contained, snap-in ink cartridge, like the one shown in Figure 7-41. Some models have combined ink cartridges that replace all three colors and the black ink at the same time. Other models use individual cartridges for each color. In this way, only the colors that are running low are replaced.

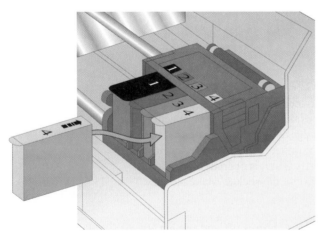

The ink cartridge can be popped out of the printhead assembly to inspect the ink jets. If any of the jets is clogged, it is normally possible to clear them by gently wiping the face of the cartridge with a swab. A gentle squeeze of the ink reservoir can also help to unblock a clogged jet. Using solvents to clear blockages in the jets can dilute the ink and allow it to flow uncontrollably through the jet.

To replace a typical ink cartridge, move the printhead carriage assembly to the center of the printer. Remove the old cartridge by freeing it from its clips or holders and lifting it out of the printer.

Figure 7-41:
Self-Contained, Snap-In
Ink Cartridge

After replacing the ink cartridge, you should cycle the printer on so that it will go through its normal warm-up procedures. During these procedures, the printer does a thorough cleaning of the ink-jet nozzles and gets the ink flowing correctly from the nozzles. Afterward, print a test page to verify the output of the new ink cartridge.

Printhead Not Printing

If the printhead is moving but not printing, begin by checking the ink supply in the print cartridge. The reservoir does not have to be completely empty to fail. Replace the cartridge(s) that appear(s) to be low. Some or all of the jets may be clogged. This is particularly common if the printer has not been used for a while. If there are cleaning instructions in the user's manual, clean the jets and attempt to print from the self-test.

If the printer will not print from the self-test, the components involved include

- The printhead

- The flexible signal cable (between the control board and the printhead)

- The control board

- Possibly the power supply board

Check the flexible signal cable to make sure it is firmly plugged into the control board and that it is not damaged or worn through. If none of the ink jets are firing, the first step should be to exchange the ink cartridges for new ones. If a single ink jet is not firing, replace the cartridge that is not working.

Next, use the ohmmeter function of a multimeter to check the continuity of the conductors in the flexible wiring harness that supplies the printhead assembly. If one of the conductors is broken, a single jet will normally be disabled. However, if the broken conductor is a ground, or common connection, all of the jets should be disabled. Exchange the control board for a known good one of the same type. If the new control board does not correct the problem, replace the printhead. A power supply problem could also cause the printhead to not print.

If a single jet is not functioning, the output will appear as a white line on the page. If one of the jets is activated all of the time, then black or colored lines will be produced on the page. Use the following steps to isolate the cause of these problems—replace the print cartridge; check the flexible cabling for continuity and for short circuits between adjacent conductors; exchange the control board for a known good one; and finally, check the power supply.

Printhead Not Moving

If the printhead is printing but not moving across the page, a single block of print will normally be generated on the page. When this problem occurs, the related components include the printhead positioning motor, the timing belt, the **home position sensor**, the control board, and possibly the power supply. These components are depicted in Figure 7-42.

home position sensor

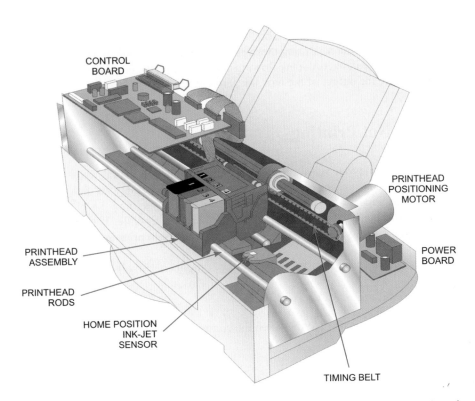

CONTROL
BOARD

PRINTHEAD
POSITIONING
MOTOR

PRINTHEAD
ASSEMBLY

POWER
BOARD

PRINTHEAD
RODS

HOME POSITION
INK-JET
SENSOR

TIMING BELT

**Figure 7-42: Printhead
Positioning Components**

With the power off, manually move the printhead to the center of the printer. Turn the printer on to see if the printhead seeks the home position at the far end of the printer. If the printhead moves to the end of the printer and does not shut off or does not return to the center of the printer, then the home position sensor is malfunctioning and should be replaced. If the printhead moves on start-up, and will not move during normal printing, the control board should be replaced. In the event that the printhead assembly will not move at any time, check to see if the printer is in **maintenance mode**. In this mode, the printer typically keeps the printhead assembly in the home position. If no mode problems are present, the printhead positioning motor should be replaced.

`maintenance mode`

If characters are unevenly spaced across the page, the timing sensor may be failing. To test the timing sensor would require test equipment, such as a logic probe or an oscilloscope, to look for pulses produced as the printhead is manually moved across the printer.

Replacing the timing belt requires that the belt be removed from the printhead assembly. In many cases, the belt will be secured to the printhead assembly with adhesive cement. This will require that the adhesive seal be cut with a single-edged razor blade, or a hobby knife. After the seal has been broken, it should be possible to shove the belt out of the clips that secure it to the printhead assembly. Next, remove the belt from the drive pulley assembly at the positioning motor. It may be necessary to remove the positioning motor from the case to gain access to the pulley.

Paper Not Advancing

When the paper does not advance, the output will normally be a thick, dark line across the page. Check the control panel to see that the printer is online. If the printer is online and the paper will not move, it will be necessary to troubleshoot the paper handling motor and gear train. Check the motor and gear train by setting the printer to the offline mode and holding down the *Form Feed* button.

If the feed motor and gear train work from this point on, the problem must exist in the control board, the **interface cable**, the printer configuration, or the computer system. If the motor or gear train does not respond, unplug the paper feed motor cable, and check the resistance of the motor windings. If the windings are open, replace the paper feed motor.

To replace the paper feed motor or gear train, remove the screws that hold the paper feed motor to the frame of the printer. Create a wiring diagram that describes the routing of the feed motor's wiring harness. Disconnect the wiring harness from the control board.

Draw an outline of the gear train arrangement (if multiple gears are used). Remove the gears from their shafts, taking care not to lose any washers or springs that may be located behind the gears. After reinstalling the gears and replacing the motor, adjust the motor and gear relationships to minimize the gear lash so that they do not bind or lock up. Use the printer's self-test to check the operation of the motor and gears.

If the printer's paper thickness selector is set improperly, or the rollers in its paper feed system become worn, the paper can slip as it moves through the printer and cause wavy graphics to be produced. Check the printer's paper thickness settings. If they are correct and the print output is disfigured, you will need to replace the paper feed rollers.

interface cable

┌─ **TEST TIP** ─
│ Know what types of problems
│ can cause disfigured print in an
│ ink-jet printer.

Troubleshooting Laser Printers

Many of the problems encountered in laser printers are similar to those found in other printer types. For example, notice that most of the symptoms listed in the following section relate to the printer **not printing**, or **not printing correctly**, and **not moving paper**.

not printing

not printing correctly

not moving paper

paper jams

pickup area

registration area

fusing area

Due to the extreme complexity of the laser printer's paper handling system, **paper jams** are a common problem. This problem tends to increase in frequency as the printer's components wear from use. Basically, paper jams occur in all three main sections of the printer. These sections are

- The **pickup area**
- The **registration area**
- The **fusing area**

If the rubber separation pad in the pickup area is excessively worn, more than one sheet of paper may be drawn into the printer, causing it to jam.

┌─ **TEST TIP** ─
│ Memorize places where paper jams are
│ likely to occur in a laser printer.

If additional paper handling features, such as **duplexers** (for double-sided copying) and **collators** (for sorting) are added to the printer, they will contribute to the possibility of jams as they wear. Paper problems can also cause jams to occur. Using paper that is too heavy or too thick can result in jams, as can overloading paper trays. Similarly, using the wrong type of paper can defeat the separation pad and allow multiple pages to be drawn into the printer. In this case, the multiple sheets may move through the printer together, or they may result in a jam. Using coated paper stock can be hazardous, because the coating may melt or catch fire.

duplexers

collators

┌─ **TEST TIP** ─
│ Remember that paper jams in a laser printer
│ can be caused by incorrect paper settings.

Be aware that laser printers can be a source of electrocution, eye damage (from the laser), and burns (from the fuser assembly).

WARNING

Laser printer dangers—Unlike other printer types, the laser printer tends to have several high-voltage and high-temperature hazards inside it. To get the laser printer into a position where you can observe its operation, it will be necessary to defeat some interlock sensors. This action will place you in potential contact with the high-voltage, high-temperature areas mentioned above. Take great care when working inside the laser printer.

The following are symptoms of laser printer problems:

- Printer dead: power on, but no printing
- The print on the page is light, or washed out
- A blank page is produced
- Stains, or black dust, on paper
- Vertical lines on paper
- The printer will not load paper
- Paper jams in printer
- A paper jam has been cleared, and the unit still indicates a jam is present

Laser Printer Configuration Checks

configure the
computer

configure the printer

configure the
software

Like other complex peripheral equipment, laser printers must be configured for the desired operational characteristics. The printer is an extension of the computer system and, therefore, must be part of the overall configuration. In order to make the system function as a unit, **configure the computer**, **configure the printer**, and **configure the software**. Review and record the computer's configuration information for use in setting up the printer and software. Configure the printer with the parameters that you want it to use, record these settings, and then set up the software to match. Consult the printer's user's manual for configuration information specific to setting up that particular printer.

Laser Printer Hardware Checks

Variations in the hardware organization of different laser printers make it impossible to write a general troubleshooting routine that can be applied to all of them without being specific to one model. The following troubleshooting discussions are general and will require that the user do some interpretation to apply them to a specific laser printer.

Fortunately, laser printer hardware has become highly modularized. This allows entire sections of hardware to be checked by changing a single module. Unfortunately, the mechanical gear train and sensor systems are not usually parts included in the modules. Therefore, their operation will need to be checked individually.

Printer Is Dead or Partially Disabled

As usual, when the printer appears to be dead, the power supply is suspected. Again, as usual, the power supply can affect the operation of basically every section of the printer. In the laser printer, this is particularly complicated, because there are three types of power being delivered to the various printer components.

If the printer does not start up, check all of the usual, power supply-related check points (e.g., **power cord, power outlet, internal fuses**, etc.). If the printer's fans and lights are working, other components that are associated with a defective power supply include

- Main motor and gear train
- High-voltage corona wires
- Drum assembly
- Fusing rollers

There are four basic reasons why the main motor does not run when the printer is supposed to print. These include

- The portion of the power supply that supplies the motor is defective
- The control circuitry is not sending the enabling signals to turn the motor on
- The motor is dead
- The gear train is bound and will not let the motor turn

In these instances, there should be sounds from the fan running, and lights on the control panel. Isolate the failure, and troubleshoot the components involved in that section.

If the high-voltage portion of the power supply that serves the corona wires and drum sections is defective, the image delivered to the page will be affected. If the high-voltage section of the power supply fails, then transfers of toner to the drum, and then to the paper, cannot occur. The contrast control will also not be operational.

In cases of partial failure, the image produced will have a washed-out appearance. Replace the high-voltage section of the power supply or the drum unit. If a separate corona wire is used, let the printer cool off sufficiently, and replace the wire. Never reach into the high-voltage, high-temperature corona area while power is applied to the printer. Also, avoid placing conductive instruments in this area.

If the DC portion of the power supply fails, the laser beam will not be produced, creating a **Missing Beam** error message. The components involved in this error are the **laser/scanning module**, the control board, and the DC portion of the power supply. Replace the laser/scanning module, the DC portion of the power supply, and the main control board.

When the heating element or lamp in the fusing area does not receive adequate AC power from the power supply, the toner will not affix to the page as it should. This condition will result in smudged output.

power cord

power outlet

internal fuses

Missing Beam

laser/scanning module

If the printer remains in a constant state of starting up, this is equivalent to the computer not passing the POST portion of the bootup process. If the printer starts up to an offline condition, there is likely a problem between the printer and the host computer's interface. Disconnect the interface cable, and check to see if the printer starts up to a ready state. If so, then the problem is in the host computer, its interface, its configuration, or its signal cable. Troubleshoot the system accordingly.

If the printer still does not start up, note the error message produced, and check the sections of the printer related to that message. Check to see if the printer is connected to the system through a print-sharing device. If so, connect the printer directly to the system and try it. It is not a good practice to use laser printers with this type of device.

A better arrangement is to install or simply use an LPT2 port to attach an additional printer to the system. If you need more than two printers, it would be better to network the printers to the system.

Print on Page Is Missing or Bad

Many of the problems encountered in laser printers are associated with missing or defective print on the page. Normal print delivery problems fall into eight categories. These include the following:

- Black pages
- White (blank) pages
- Faint print
- Random specks on the page
- Faulty print at regular intervals on the page
- White lines along the page
- Print missing from some portion of the page
- Smudged print

A **black page** indicates that toner has been attracted to the entire page. This condition could be caused by a failure of the **primary corona**, the laser scanning module, or the main control board. If the laser is in a continuous on condition, the entire drum will attract toner. Likewise, if the primary corona is defective, then the uniform negative charge will not be developed on the drum to repel toner. Replace the primary corona drum assembly. If the problem continues, replace the laser scanning module and the main control board.

On the other end of the spectrum, a **white page** indicates that no information is being written on the drum. This condition basically involves the laser scanning module, the control board, and the power supply. Another white page fault occurs when the corona wire becomes broken, contaminated, or corroded, so that the attracting charge between the drum and paper is severely reduced.

Specks and **stains** on the page may be caused by a worn-out cleaning pad or a defective corona wire. If the cleaning pad is worn, it will not remove excess toner from the page during the fusing process. If the corona wire's grid does not regulate the charge level on the drum, dark spots will appear in the print. To correct these situations, replace the corona assembly by exchanging the toner cartridge or drum unit. Also, replace the cleaning pad in the fusing unit. If the page still contains specks after changing the cartridge, run several pages through the printer to clear excess toner that may have collected in the printer.

black page

primary corona

white page

TEST TIP
Know what types if problems produce blank pages from a laser printer.

Specks

stains

White lines along the length of the page are generally caused by poorly distributed toner. Try removing the toner cartridge and gently shaking it to redistribute the toner in the cartridge. Other causes of white lines include damaged or weakened corona wires. Check and clean the corona wires, if accessible, or replace the module containing the corona wires.

White lines

Faint print in a laser printer can be caused by a number of different things. If the contrast control is set too low, or the toner level in the cartridge is low, empty, or poorly distributed, print quality can appear washed out. Correcting these symptoms is fairly easy; adjust the contrast control, remove the toner cartridge, inspect it, shake it gently (if it is a sealed unit), and retry it. If the print does not improve, try replacing the toner cartridge. Other causes of faint print include a weakened corona wire or a weakened high-voltage power supply that drives it. Replace the unit that contains the corona wire. Replace the high-voltage power supply. Make sure that latent voltages have been drained off the high-voltage power supply before working with it.

Faint print

Faults in the print that occur at regular intervals along the page are normally caused by mechanical problems. When roller and transport mechanisms begin to wear in the printer, bad registration and print appear in cyclic form. This can be attributed to the dimensions of cyclic components such as the drum, the developing roller in the toner cartridge, or the fusing rollers. Examine the various mechanical components for wear or defects.

Missing print is usually caused by a bad or misaligned laser scanning module. If this module is not correctly installed, then it will not be able to deliver lines of print to the correct areas of the page. Likewise, if the scanning mirror has a defect, or is dirty, portions of the print will not be scanned on the drum. Another cause of missing print involves the toner cartridge, and low or poorly distributed toner. If the toner does not come out of the cartridge uniformly, areas of missing print can be created. A damaged or worn drum can also be a cause of repeated missing print. If areas of the drum do not hold the charge properly, toner will not transfer to it, or the page, correctly.

Missing print

Smudged print is usually a sign of failure in the fusing section. If the fusing roller's temperature or pressure is not sufficient to bond the toner to the page, the print will smudge when touched. Examine the fuser unit, the power supply, and the fusing roller's heating unit.

Smudged print

GEEK SQUAD CASE FILE #297546

You are working the morning shift at Store 54 when one of your customers calls complaining that the pages coming out of his laser printer have spots where the print does not show up. He has changed the toner cartridge, but nothing improved. Now he wants your advice on what to do next. What should you tell him?

Paper Will Not Feed or Is Jammed

If the paper will not feed at all, then the place to begin checking is the paper tray area. The **paper trays** have a complex set of sensors and pickup mechanisms that must all be functioning properly to begin the paper handling. Due to the complexity of the paper pickup operation, jams are most likely to occur in this area. Check each paper tray to make sure that there is paper in it, and that it has the correct size of paper in it. Each tray in a laser printer has a set of tabs that contact sensor switches to tell the control circuitry that the tray is installed, and what size paper is in it. A mechanical arm and photodetector are used to sense the presence of paper in the tray. If these switches are set incorrectly, the printer could print a page that is sized incorrectly for the actual paper size. The various paper tray sensors are illustrated in Figure 7-43.

paper trays

TEST TIP

Be aware of the consequences of incorrectly setting the paper tray switches in a laser printer.

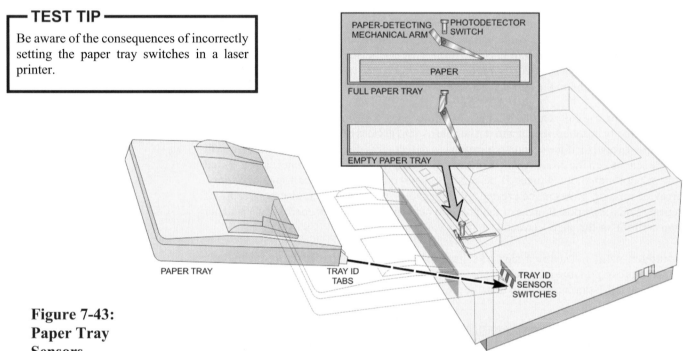

**Figure 7-43:
Paper Tray
Sensors**

Paper-Out error

If the printer's display panel indicates a **Paper-Out error** message, locate and actuate the paper detector by hand (lift it up). While holding the paper sensor, check the sensor switches by pressing each one individually. If the Paper Out message does not go out when any of the individual switches is pressed, replace that switch. If none of the switches show good, replace the paper sensor and arm. Also, check the spring-loaded plate in the bottom of the tray to make sure that it is forcing paper up to the **pickup roller** when the tray is installed in the printer.

pickup roller

The paper pickup roller must pull the top sheet of paper off the paper stack in the tray. The controller actuates a solenoid that engages the pickup roller's gear train. The pickup roller moves the paper into position against the registration rollers. If the printer's display panel shows a jam in the pickup area, check to make sure that the paper tray is functional, and then begin troubleshooting the pickup roller and main gear train. If the gear train is not moving, then the main motor and controller board need to be checked. The power supply board may also be a cause of the problem.

If the paper feeds into the printer but jams after the process has begun, troubleshoot the particular section of the printer where the jam is occurring—**pickup**, registration, fusing area, and **output devices** (collators and duplexers). This information is generally presented by the laser printer's display panel. Figure 7-44 shows the paper path through a typical laser printer.

pickup

output devices

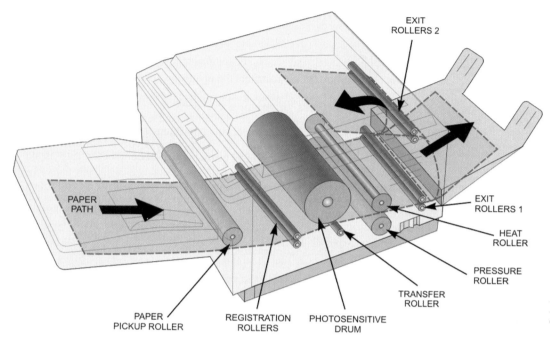

Figure 7-44:
The Paper Path

In each stage, you will need to check the action of the gear train in the area. Also, inspect the various rollers in that stage for wear or damage. If the motor and gear train operate but no action occurs in the pickup roller or registration rollers, check the solenoid and clutches for these units.

Another cause of jams is the presence of some obstruction in the paper path. Check for pieces of paper that have torn loose and lodged in the printer's paper path. In most laser printers, mechanical components are part of a replaceable module (i.e., the drum unit, the developing unit, or the fusing unit). If the motor and all the exposed gears are working, replace these units one at a time.

Many times, a paper-jam error will remain even after the paper has been removed from the laser printer. This is typically caused by an interlock error. Simply opening the printer's main access door should clear the error.

KEY POINTS REVIEW

The focus of this chapter has been printers. Review the following key points before moving into the Review and Exam Questions sections to make sure you are comfortable with each point. Afterward, answer the Review Questions that follow to verify your knowledge of the information.

- Impact printers place characters on the page by causing a hammer device to strike an inked ribbon. The ribbon, in turn, strikes the printing surface (paper).

- Several nonimpact methods of printing are used in computer printers. Older nonimpact printers relied on special heat-sensitive, or chemically reactive paper to form characters on the page. Newer methods of nonimpact printing use ink droplets squirted from a jet-nozzle device (ink-jet printers), or a combination of laser/xerographic print technologies (laser printers), to place characters on a page.

- Currently, the most popular nonimpact printers use ink-jet or laser technologies to deliver ink to the page. Basically, there are two methods of creating characters on a page. One method places a character that is fully shaped and fully filled-in. This type of character is called a fully formed character. The other method involves placing dots on the page in strategic patterns to fool the eye into seeing a character. This type of character is referred to as a dot-matrix character.

- The term font refers to variations in the size and style of characters. With true fully formed characters, there is typically only one font available without changing the physical printing element. However, with all other printing methods, it is possible to include a wide variety of font types and sizes.

- By the very nature of their operation, printers tend to be extremely mechanical peripherals. During the printing operation, the print mechanism must be properly positioned over each character cell in sequence.

- In addition to positioning the print mechanism for printing, all printer types must feed paper through the print area. The type of paper handling mechanism in a printer is somewhat dependent on the type of form intended for use with the printer and the printer's speed.

- Like most other peripherals, the heart of a character printer is its interface/controller circuitry. The interface circuitry accepts data and instructions from the computer's bus systems and provides the necessary interfacing (serial or parallel) between the computer and the printer's control circuitry.

- The printhead is a collection of print wires set in an electromagnetic head unit. The printhead assembly is made up of a permanent magnet, a group of electromagnets, and a housing. In the printhead, the permanent magnet keeps the wires pulled in until electromagnets are energized, causing them to move forward.

- Ink-jet printers produce characters by squirting a stream of ink drops onto the paper. The drops must be controlled precisely in terms of their aerodynamics, size, and shape, or their placement on the page becomes inexact, and the print quality falters.

- The laser printer modulates a highly focused laser beam to produce CRT-like raster-scan images on a rotating drum.

- As the drum is written on by the laser, it turns through the toner powder, which is attracted to the charged image on the drum.

- A typical laser printer has sensors to determine what paper trays are installed, what size paper is in them, and whether a tray is empty. It will also use sensors to track the movement of the paper through each stage of the printer. This allows the controller to know where a page is at all times and sequence the activities of the solenoids and clutches properly.

- Paper is specified in terms of its weight per 500 sheets at 22" × 17" (e.g., 500 sheets of 22" × 17", 21-pound bond paper weighs 21 pounds).

- Generally speaking, one of the least difficult I/O devices to add to a microcomputer system is a parallel printer. This is largely due to the fact that, from the beginning of the PC era, a parallel printer has been a standard piece of equipment to add to the system.

- Serial printers are slightly more difficult to set up, because the communication definition must be configured between the computer and the printer. The serial port will need to be configured for speed, parity type, character frame, and protocol.

- Like mice, printers require device driver programs to oversee their operation.

- The classical first step in determining the cause of any printer problem is to determine which part of the printer-related system is at fault—the host computer, the signal cable, or the printer.

- As with the dot-matrix printer, the first step in determining the cause of an ink-jet printer problem is to determine which part of the printer system is at fault—the host computer, the signal cable, or the printer.

- You can configure the basic appearance of color and grayscale images produced by the ink-jet printer. A color ink-jet printer uses four ink colors to produce color images. These are cyan, magenta, yellow, and black (referred to as CMYK color). To create other colors, the printer prints a predetermined percentage of the basic colors in close proximity to each other.

- The single item in an ink-jet printer that requires the most attention is the ink cartridge (or cartridges). As the ink cartridge empties, the printing will eventually become faint and uneven, and the resolution of the print on the page will diminish.

- Many of the problems encountered in laser printers are similar to those found in other printer types. For example, notice that most of the symptoms listed relate to the printer not printing, or not printing correctly, and not moving paper.

- Unlike other printer types, the laser printer has several high-voltage and high-temperature hazards inside it. To get the laser printer into a position where you can observe its operation, it will be necessary to defeat some interlock sensors. This action will place you in potential contact with the high-voltage, high-temperature areas mentioned above. Take great care when working inside the laser printer.

REVIEW QUESTIONS

The following questions test your knowledge of the material presented in this chapter.

1. Describe the function of the transfer corona wire in a laser printer.

2. What common transmission parameters must be established for a serial printer interface?

3. Describe the purpose for using platen pin-feed mechanisms to move paper through the printer.

4. Describe the reason for using tractor-feed paper handling.

5. If the resolution of an ink-jet printer becomes unacceptable, what action should be taken?

6. Describe the function of the fuser unit in a laser printer.

7. Compare how a direct thermal printer operates versus a thermal wax transfer printer.

8. If a laser printer continues to show a paper jam after the paper has been cleared, what type of problem is indicated, and what action should be taken?

9. List the three primary areas where paper jams occur in a laser printer, as well as any other areas where jams are likely to occur.

10. Describe two methods used by ink-jet printers to put ink on the page.

11. Does a successful self-test indicate that the printer is not the cause of the problem? List the parts of the system that can still be problem causes if the self-test runs successfully.

12. How does a dot-matrix printer actually deliver ink to a page?

13. Describe how a dye sublimation printer operates.

14. List four things that can be damaging to the photosensitive surface of the laser printer's drum.

15. List the basic components of an ink-jet printer.

1. List three common pin configurations for dot-matrix printers.
   a. 10, 20, and 30 pins
   b. 5, 10, and 15 pins
   c. 9, 18, and 24 pins
   d. 3, 6, and 9 pins

2. Name the four basic components of an HP electrophotographic cartridge.
   a. Laser, toner supply, drum, and fuser
   b. Toner supply, corona wire, drum assembly, and developing roller
   c. Laser, toner supply, corona wire, and drum
   d. Toner supply, corona wire, drum assembly, and fuser

3. What is the purpose of the primary corona wire in a laser printer?
   a. It cleans the paper as it enters the printer.
   b. It conditions the drum for printing.
   c. It transfers toner from the drum to the paper.
   d. It fuses the toner to the paper.

4. What is the first action that should be taken if the print generated by a dot-matrix printer becomes faded or uneven?
   a. Change the ribbon cartridge.
   b. Add ink.
   c. Adjust the print carriage.
   d. Add toner.

5. What is the purpose of a printer driver?
   a. Energizes the pins to strike the ribbon
   b. Translates between the application and the printer hardware
   c. Moves paper through the printer
   d. Moves the print mechanism across the page

6. What type of electrical charge must be placed on the corona wire to transfer toner from the drum to the paper?
   a. Negative
   b. None
   c. Neutral
   d. Positive

7. List the six stages of a typical laser printer.
   a. Pick up, registration, transfer, printing, fusing, and finishing
   b. Pick up, conditioning, transfer, developing, fusing, and finishing
   c. Cleaning, conditioning, writing, developing, transferring, and fusing
   d. Cleaning, registration, writing, transferring, fusing, and finishing

8. List the fundamental parts of a dot-matrix printer.
   a. Power supply, microprocessor, tractor feed motor, printhead mechanism, and printhead positioning motor
   b. Power supply, interface board, paper feed motor, printhead mechanism, and printhead positioning motor
   c. Interface board, ink cartridge, printhead mechanism, printhead positioning motor, and sensors
   d. Controller, paper feed motor, ribbon cartridge, and printhead positioning motor

9. What type of ink delivery system is normally found in ink-jet printers built for personal computers?
   a. Drop-on-demand ink delivery
   b. Continuous stream ink delivery
   c. Impact ink delivery
   d. Compact spray ink delivery

10. The specification for 60-pound bond paper means that _____.
    a. 100 22" × 17" sheets weigh 60 pounds
    b. 500 8.5" × 11" sheets weigh 60 pounds
    c. 100 11" × 17" sheets weigh 60 pounds
    d. 500 22" × 17" sheets weigh 60 pounds

CHAPTER 8

PORTABLE SYSTEMS

OBJECTIVES

Upon completion of this chapter and its related lab procedures, you should be able to perform these tasks:

1. Identify the unique components of portable systems and their unique problems.

2. Describe basic procedures for adding and removing FRU modules associated with portable systems.

3. Identify proper procedures for installing peripheral devices commonly used with portable systems.

4. Describe the applications that the three types of PCMCIA cards can be used to perform.

5. Discuss and recognize the different PCMCIA devices currently available.

6. Describe the purpose of a docking station.

7. Differentiate between typical power-saving modes as they apply to portable computers.

8. Describe portable display technologies and associated resolutions.

9. Identify input devices associated with portable computer systems.

10. Identify typical communication connections used with portable computers.

PORTABLE SYSTEMS

FROM THE GEEK SQUAD

Agent 37 is working the Geek Squad counter on the evening shift. He has experience working on the different desktop computers sold in the store. The day shift has left a notebook computer with wireless networking built in, a touch pad, and CD-ROM/DVD burner. Agent 37 is not familiar with the particulars of working with notebook computers. He must update his knowledge base to include the peculiarities of portable computers and adapt his desktop knowledge to work with notebook systems.

INTRODUCTION

Portable computers represent a large and growing portion of the personal computer market. Therefore, the computer technician must be aware of how they vary from traditional desktop units and how their service requirements are different.

PORTABLE COMPUTER TYPES

Essentials 2.0

IT Technician 2.0

Depot Technician 2.0

The original portables were called **luggables**. Although they were smaller than desktop computers they were not truly convenient to transport. The first portables included small built-in CRT displays and detachable keyboards. Their batteries and CRT equipment made them extremely bulky and heavy to carry. Therefore, they never really had a major impact on the PC market. However, they set the stage for the development of future portable computer systems. Examples of different portable computer designs are shown in Figure 8-1.

luggables

Figure 8-1: Portable Computers

With advancements in battery design and the advent of usable, large-screen, flat panel displays, the first truly portable PCs, referred to as **laptops**, were introduced. These units featured all-in-one, AT-compatible PC boards. The system board included the I/O and video controller functions. Laptops featured built-in keyboards and hinged LCD display panels that flipped up from the case for use. They also used an external power supply and a removable, rechargeable battery.

The battery life of typical laptops was minimal, and their size was still large enough to be inconvenient at times. However, the inclusion of LCD viewing screens and external power supply/battery arrangements made them useful enough to spawn a healthy portable computer market. Even though these units could weigh in excess of seven pounds, the user could easily take work from the office to the home, or to a hotel room while traveling. Users could also get work done at traditionally nonproductive times, such as on long automobile or airplane rides. An occasional game of computerized cards or golf was always at hand as well.

Continued advancements in integrated circuitry and peripheral technology allowed the PC's circuitry to be reduced. This allowed portable sizes to be reduced further so that they could achieve sizes of 8.75"d × 11"w × 2.25"h and smaller. Portables in this size range are referred to as **notebook computers**. The weight of a typical notebook dropped down to 5 or 6 pounds.

notebook computers

subnotebook PCs

palmtop PCs

Even smaller **subnotebook PCs** have been created by moving the disk drives outside the case and reducing the size of the display screen. These units tend to be slightly thinner than traditional notebooks and weigh in the neighborhood of 3 to 4 pounds. Very small subnotebooks, referred to as **palmtop PCs**, were produced for a short time in the pre-Windows days. These units limited everything as far as possible to reach sizes of 7"w × 4"d × 1"h and weights of 1 to 2 pounds. Subnotebooks have decreased in popularity as notebooks have continued to decrease in weight and cost.

Personal Digital Assistants

Palmtop computers

ergonomics

Palmtop computers are a class of very small computers designed to fit in most users' hands. The palmtop market was diminished for some time because of the difficulty of running Windows on such small displays. Human **ergonomics** also come into play when dealing with smaller notebooks. The smaller display screens become difficult to see, and keyboards become more difficult to use as the size of the keys decreases.

personal digital assistants (PDAs)

However, the market was revived by the introduction of palmtops known as **personal digital assistants (PDAs)**. Figure 8-2 depicts a typical PDA. These handheld devices use a special stylus, referred to as a pen, to input data and selections instead of a keyboard or mouse. Basically, the PDA is an electronic time management system that may also include computer applications such as word processors, spreadsheets, and databases.

Two items have made PDAs popular—their size and their ability to communicate with the user's desktop computer system. The PDA's display is a touch-screen LCD display that works in conjunction with a graphical user interface running on top of a specialized operating system. Some PDAs employ a highly modified, embedded (on a chip) version of Microsoft Windows, called **Windows CE**, as their operating system. These devices are particularly well suited for exchanging and synchronizing information with larger Windows-based systems.

Early PDAs exchanged information with full-sized computers through standard serial port connections. Newer models communicate with the user's desktop computer through USB port, an infrared communications link, or a docking cradle.

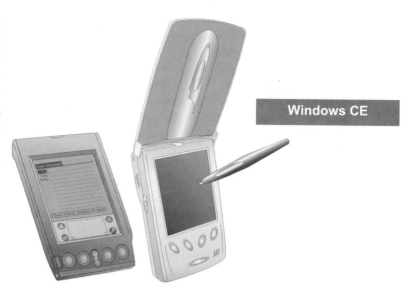

Windows CE

Figure 8-2: A Personal Digital Assistant

Portable Drawbacks

From a service point of view, the greatest drawback of portable computers is that conventions and compatibility disappear.

The continued minimization of the system comes at a cost. Most notably, the number of I/O ports, memory, and disk drive expansion capabilities are limited. In addition, there is no chance to use common full-sized adapter cards that are inexpensive and easy to find.

One of the biggest problems for portable computers is heat buildup inside the case. Because conventional power supplies (and their fans) are not included in portable units, separate fans must be designed into portables to carry heat out of the unit. The closeness of the portable's components and the small amount of free air space inside its case also adds to heat-related design problems.

The internal PC boards of the portable computer are designed to fit around the nuances of the portable case and its components, rather than to match a standard design with standard spacing and connections. Therefore, interchangeability of parts with other machines or makers goes by the wayside. The only source of most portable computer parts, with the exception of PC Cards and disk drive units, is the original manufacturer. Even the battery case may be proprietary. If the battery dies, you must hope that the original maker has a supply of that particular model.

Access to the notebook's internal components is usually challenging. Each case design has different methods for assembly and disassembly of the unit. Even the simplest upgrade task can be difficult with a notebook computer. Although adding RAM and options to desktop and tower units is a relatively easy and straightforward process, the same tasks in notebook computers can be difficult.

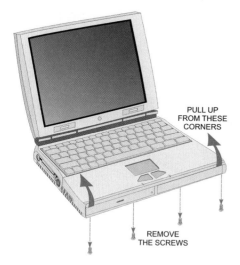

Figure 8-3: Disassembling a Notebook Computer

PULL UP FROM THESE CORNERS

REMOVE THE SCREWS

In some notebooks, it is necessary to disassemble the two halves of the case and remove the keyboard in order to add RAM modules to the system. In other portables, the hinged display unit must be removed to disassemble the unit. Once inside the notebook, you may find that several of the components are hidden behind other units. Figure 8-3 demonstrates a relatively simple disassembly process for a notebook unit.

In this example, a panel in front of the keyboard can be removed to gain access to the notebook's internal user-serviceable components. Four screws along the front edge of the unit's lower body must be removed. Afterward, the LCD panel is opened, and the front panel of the notebook's chassis is pulled up and away to expose a portion of the unit's interior.

To overcome the shortfalls of miniaturization, a wide variety of specialty items aimed at the portable computer market have emerged. Items such as small 2-1/2 inch hard-disk drives have been developed especially for use in portable computers. Other such items include small internal and external modems, special network adapters that plug into parallel printer ports, docking stations (or ports), special carrying cases and briefcases, detachable keypads, clip-on or built-in trackballs, and touch-sensitive mouse pads.

In addition, a sequence of special credit card—like adapter cards have been designed expressly for use with portable computers. These adapters are standardized through the Personal Computer Memory Card International Association (PCMCIA) and are commonly referred to as PC Cards. The different types of PCMCIA cards are covered in greater detail later in this chapter.

Essentials 2.1

INSIDE PORTABLES

Portable computers have two ideal characteristics: They are compact and lightweight. Portable computer designers work constantly to decrease the size and power consumption of all the computer's components. Special low-power chipsets and disk drives have been developed to extend battery life.

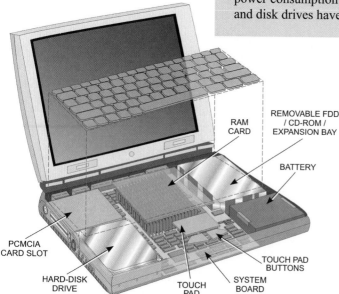

RAM CARD

REMOVABLE FDD / CD-ROM / EXPANSION BAY

BATTERY

PCMCIA CARD SLOT

HARD-DISK DRIVE

TOUCH PAD

SYSTEM BOARD

TOUCH PAD BUTTONS

Likewise, cases have been designed to be as small as possible while providing as many standard features as possible. Figure 8-4 shows the inside of a typical portable computer. Notice how the components are interconnected by the design. The system board is designed so that it wraps around other components whose form factors cannot be altered, such as the disk drive units. The components also tend to be layered in portable designs. Disk drives cover portions of the system board, whereas the keyboard unit covers nearly everything. The internal battery may slide into a cutout area of the system board, or more likely, it may be located beneath the system board.

Figure 8-4: Inside a Portable Computer

Portable System Boards

A typical notebook system board is depicted in Figure 8-5. The first thing you should notice about it is its unusual shape. As noted earlier, system boards for portable computers are not designed to fit a standardized form factor. Instead they are designed to fit around all of the components that must be installed in the system. Therefore, system boards used in portable computers tend to be proprietary to the model they are designed for. Mounting-hole positions are determined by where they will best suit the placement of the other system components.

The second item to notice is that none of the "desktop standard" expansion slots or adapter cards are present on the portable's system board. These system board designs typically include standard I/O and video circuitry as an integral part of the board. They also provide the physical connections for the unit's USB, serial, parallel and game ports, as well as on-board connectors for the disk drives, display unit, and keyboard units.

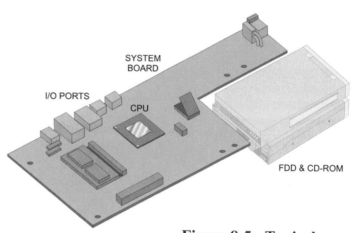

The computer's external I/O connections are arranged on the system board so that they align with the corresponding openings in the portable case. It is highly unlikely that a system board from another portable would match these openings. On the maintenance side, a blown USB-port circuit would require that the entire system board be replaced in order to correct the problem. In a desktop unit, a simple I/O card could be installed in an expansion slot to overcome such a situation.

Figure 8-5: Typical Notebook System Board

On newer notebook PCs, the most widely used I/O connections included in most notebook computers consist of two or more USB ports, an external VGA monitor connector, a built-in LAN connection, a built-in modem port, external microphone and speaker jack sound card connections, and a pair of PC Card slots. Older notebooks included legacy parallel printer ports, PS/2 external mouse/keyboard connectors, and proprietary docking port expansion buses. Figure 8-6 shows the port connections associated with most portable systems. This example places different port connectors on the back and sides of the unit. Other models may place most of their port connectors on the back of the unit. Some connectors may be hidden behind hinged doors for protection. These doors usually snap closed.

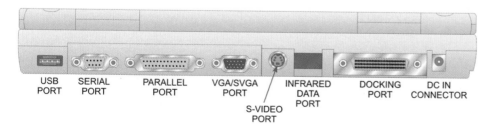

Figure 8-6: Notebook Back Panel Connections

Microprocessors in Portables

The portable computer market is so large that it even influences the microprocessor and chipset manufacturers. They produce special low-power-consumption microprocessors and chipsets specifically for portable computer systems. Standard Pentium processors produce large amounts of heat, even by desktop standards. Most of the portables currently in the market are based on Pentium devices.

To minimize the heat buildup condition, Intel has produced a complete line of **mobile Pentium processors** for use in portable systems. Mobile devices differ from standard microprocessor devices in terms of both their internal construction and their external packaging. In mobile microprocessors, both design aspects have been optimized to provide minimum size and power consumption, as well as maximum heat reduction.

Figure 8-7 depicts a mobile Pentium MMX processor. It is constructed using Intel's **Voltage Reduction Technology**, which enables the processor to run at lower core voltages (1.8−2.0 Vdc) and, thereby, consume less energy and generate less heat. The package style created for the mobile Pentium is referred to as a **Tape Carrier Package (TCP)**. The microprocessor chip is embedded in a polyimide film (tape) that is laminated with a copper foil. The leads of the IC are etched into the foil and attached to the processor.

mobile Pentium processors

Voltage Reduction Technology

Tape Carrier Package (TCP)

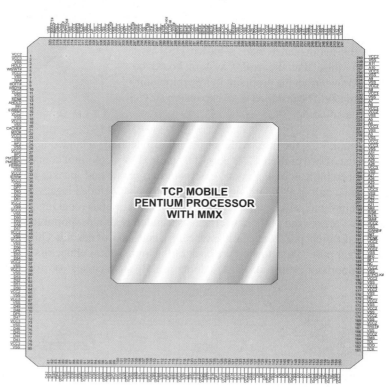

**Figure 8-7:
The Mobile Pentium**

The tape package arrangement makes the mobile package much smaller and lighter than the PGA and SPGA packages used with the standard Pentium devices. It also mounts directly to the PC board instead of plugging into a bulky heavy socket. A special insertion machine cuts the strip of microprocessors into individual 24 mm units as it is soldered to the system board. The system board furnishes a heat sink area beneath the processor that helps to dissipate heat. A layer of thermal conductive paste is applied to this connection prior to the soldering process to increase the heat transfer away from the processor. This design enables the full-featured Pentium processor to run at competitive speeds without additional heat sinks and fan modules. The cross section of the complete mobile Pentium attachment is depicted in Figure 8-8.

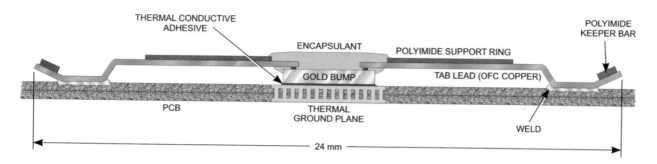

The attachment of the mobile microprocessor to a system board makes the arrangement permanent for all practical purposes. To allow for microprocessor upgrading, portable system boards often employ mobile processors mounted on plug-in daughter boards, or modules. Intel produced two Pentium plug-in variations. One is a mobile Pentium mounted on a 4" × 2.5" × 0.3" **mobile module**, referred to as an **MMO**. This module is attached to the system board via screws and plugs through a 280-pin connector. The other Intel module is a mini-cartridge for the Pentium II.

Figure 8-8: The Mobile Pentium Installation

mobile module (MMO)

Pentium IIIM and 4M Processors

With the Pentium IIIM and Pentium 4M processors, Intel began to design mobile processors with a real concentration on the needs of portable computers. Their previous mobile processor designs were all based on processors designed specifically for desktop computers. Even with Intel's efforts to design more mobile friendly, the core architecture of these processors were still based on desktop processor cores. This continued to limit the amount of power savings that they could engineer into the finished products.

The Pentium IIIM design included

- 1.2GHz Core

- 133MHz FSB

- 512KB L2 Cache

- Socket 478

- 830 Chipset

Likewise, the Pentium 4M design included

- 2.6GHz core

- 400MHz FSB

- 512KB L2 cache

- Socket 478

- i845MP chipset

Both processors were built on 0.13 micron technology and provide a number of power-saving features not found in the desktop versions of these processors. These features include the enhanced SpeedStep technology described in Chapter 3, *Advanced System Boards*, which enables the system to be throttled back based on software performance requirements, and a *Deeper Sleep Alert State* that enables the processor to run on very little power and still be capable of *waking up* rapidly.

Pentium M Processors

The **Pentium M** processor, depicted in Figure 8-9, was the first line of Intel mobile processors designed specifically to address the limitations of earlier mobile processors. The *Wall Street Journal* carried a very interesting column about the difficulties Intel had in changing the mindsets of their design engineers in producing new notebook systems for the market. The engineers had been so conditioned to produce the next fast processor, that when the company identified that what notebook users really wanted was greatly installed battery life and integrated networking, they had to become very stern with the engineers to get them to think in terms of slower processors and different chipset features to achieve the desired results.

TOP VIEW   BOTTOM VIEW

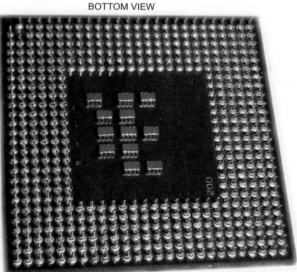

Figure 8-9: The Pentium M Processor

The Pentium M brought together a Pentium III core with a Pentium 4 bus interface (instead of using a modified desktop Pentium 4). The processor core has been optimized for greater power saving to provide extended battery life. The voltage level for standard Pentium M processors is a low 1.5 V. Low and Ultra-Low version cores run on 1.18 V and 1.1 V respectively. The Pentium M processor's power dissipation varies from 5 watts when idle to 27 watts when fully loaded.

The Pentium M processors also employ a more flexible SpeedStep (described in Chapter 3, *Advanced System Boards*) technology that provides better control of the system's clock frequency and **Mobile Voltage Positioning (MVP IV)** technology that dynamically lowers voltage based on processor activity to reduce power usage based on the tasks it is performing. For example, a 1.6 GHz Pentium M can throttle its clock speeds to 600 MHz, 800 MHz, 1000 MHz, 1200 MHz, 1400 MHz, and 1600 MHz. Older mobile processors such as the Pentium 4M had fewer possible steps to work with.

The Pentium M processors are combined with improved, power-efficient Intel 915 Express and 855 chipsets. Together, all of the power-saving features were adopted to provide notebook computers that can operate for five or more hours on a single battery.

Pentium M versions come in a variety of core clock speeds ranging from 1 GHz to 2.26 GHz that feature 400 and 533 FSB speeds. They also employ 478-pin **Micro FCPGA** and 479-pin **Micro FCBGA** packaging and ZIF socket technology that has been designed to provide a range of thinner processors. Execute disable bit technology to prevent certain classes of malicious "buffer overflow" attacks when combined with a supporting operating system. Intel also modified the 1 MB and 2 MB L2 cache structures so that they avoid turning on sections of the cache that are not being used. This technique significantly decreases power usage associated with the cache.

The first Pentium M processors (code-named *Banias*) were built using .13 micron technology and either carried no identifying number scheme or a 705 number. Advanced versions (code-named *Dothan*) began to show up using a 7XX numbering series that does not relate directly with the processor's clock speed. The Dothan versions are built on 90 nm technology that provides decreased power consumption.

All of these features combine to provide performance levels in the Pentium M processor that surpass those of faster Pentium 4M processors. This has caused some confusion in customers who had become used to relying on processor speed ratings for performance specifications. This led Intel to create a massive "Centrino" advertising campaign to focus customer attention away from sheer clock speed as the major factor in defining performance. Intel also decided to stop using clock speed as part of the processor's specification.

Centrino

In their battle to change the perception of performance associated with portable PCs, Intel introduced a product badge system, called **Centrino**, that identified the product as supporting those qualities that Intel had determined were essential for portable computers. To achieve this badge, the manufacturer must incorporate the following three items in their portable PC product:

- Intel Pentium M processor
- Intel 855PM or 855GM chipsets
- Intel PRO/Wireless 2100

The major emphasis of the Centrino specification is that the chipsets and the Pentium M processors deliver outstanding performance while providing very lower power usage. Users can use these systems to work for up to 5 hours without having to swap the battery or plug into an external power source. This relates to being able to work on a cross-country flight without having to give up halfway across the country. The second emphasis point in the Centrino specification is seamless, built-in wireless networking.

However, not all of Intel's vendors were happy with the requirement to include the PRO/Wireless 2100 chipset, because it only supported the 802.11b wireless communication protocol. There are many competing 802.11a and 802.11g products for notebook systems. In addition, many organizations are not comfortable with wireless communications due to security concerns. This has led many notebook manufacturers to advertise the Pentium M processor without the Centrino branding badge.

Pentium M Celerons

Intel produced its original *Banias 512* **Celeron M** processor by removing half of the L2 cache from a Pentium M processor. They followed up with a *Dothan 1024* Celeron M version that had half the cache of the 90 nm Pentium M versions. All of the Pentium M Celeron are designed to fit the Socket 479 specification and feature a 400 MHz FSB rating. Core speeds for the different Celeron M versions range from 900 MHz to 1.7 GHz. Figure 8-10 shows a typical Celeron M processor.

TOP VIEW

BOTTOM VIEW

Figure 8-10: The Celeron M Processor

Intel produced a more advanced *Yonah 1024* Pentium M based on its advanced Core Solo processor designed for desktop unit. This processor boosted the front side bus speed to 533 MHz and brought XD-bit protection to the Celeron M series. However, it still has only half the L2 cache of the Pentium M processors. The Yonah version of the Celeron M processor employs the FCPGA6 (478-pin) package and socket.

The other Celeron M version in production is the *Northwood 256* processor. The L2 cache in this version of the Celeron M is only 256 KB. This celeron version employs a Socket 478 design and 400 MHz FSB. Different Northwood versions have been produced with core frequencies between 1.4 GHz and 2.5 GHz.

None of these units support the variable clock speed SpeedStep functionality, and their battery life characteristics are much shorter than the standard Pentium M powered systems. By definition, any portable computers based on one of the Celeron M processors cannot be branded with the Centrino label.

Core Duo Processors

Intel has unveiled a series of special low power consumption dual-core processors for mobile computing environments. They have branded these products under the Intel **Core Duo** product name. They are mainly found in Intel's high-end *Centrino* mobile products and in some new **Viiv** applications.

| Core Duo |
| Viiv |

As with the Pentium D and Pentium EE products used in desktop PCs, the Core Duo processors are optimized for multithreaded applications and multitasking operations. They can simultaneously execute multiple applications such as graphics-intensive games or serious computing applications while downloading large audio/video files from the Internet or running antivirus security programs in the background. In addition, special energy-efficient power management technologies built into the Core Duo architecture transfer power only to those areas of the processor that need it, thereby enabling laptops to save power.

Structurally, the Core Duo processor consists of two Pentium cores, a 2 MB L2 cache that is shared by the two cores, and a bus arbiter that coordinates the activities of the L2 cache and FSB accesses. These processors communicate with the system board's chipset over a 166 MHz *quad-pumped* (667 MHz) front side bus. Figure 8-11 depicts the structure of a Core Duo processor.

Figure 8-11: The Core Duo Processor Structure

At the same time the Core Duo was rolled out, Intel also introduced the **Core Solo** processor, which is a single-core version of the Core Duo product. Like the Core Duo, the Core Solo processor communicates with the chipset using a 667 MHz FSB. Future versions of the Core Duo processor are scheduled to have a BIOS configurable option that will permit one of the cores to be turned off to reduce power consumption.

Intel has implemented a naming scheme for its Core processors that uses a "T" to mark "performance" processors and an "L" to mark "low-power" processors. The letters are followed by a four-digit code that, like the Pentium M, is not directly related to clock speed as performance. Examples of the Core line of processors include

- T1200 Core Solo: 1.5 GHz

- T1300 Core Solo: 1.66 GHz

- T2300 Core Duo: 1.66 GHz

- T2400 Core Duo: 1.83 GHz

- T2500 Core Duo: 2.0 GHz

- T2600 Core Duo: 2.16 GHz

- L2300 Core Duo: 1.5 GHz (low power, dual-core)

- L2400 Core Duo: 1.66 GHz (low power, dual-core)

Both Core processors employ the 478-pin FCPGA6 package and socket. However, the pinout of these processors and new chipset functions make the Core processors incompatible with previous Pentium M system boards. The Core Duo is matched up with the *945GTExpress* chipset that delivers a 533/667 FSB and supports up to 4GB of dual channel DDR 667 memory. The chipset also provides PCIe x16 expansion slots and 3GBps SATA interfaces for PCs. In addition, the Core Duo became the first Intel processor to be used in Apple Macintosh production systems.

Essentials 2.1

Memory for Portables

Notebook and other portable computer manufacturers do not use traditional DIMM modules in their designs. Special form factor DIMMs, called the **small outline DIMM (SODIMMs)**, were developed specifically for use in notebook computers. The basic difference between SODIMMs and regular DIMMs is that the SODIMM is significantly smaller than the standard DIMM so that it takes up less space in notebook computers. Figure 8-12 depicts a 72-pin and a 144-pin SODIMM. The 72-pin SODIMM has a 32-bit data bus, and the 144-pin version is 64 bits wide.

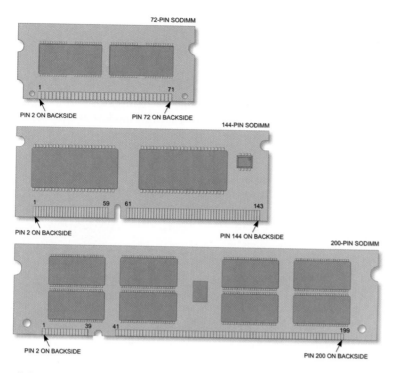

**Figure 8-12: Small
Outline DIMMs**

A new small form factor memory module referred to as **MicroDIMM** has been introduced for the micro devices market (subnotebook PCs) where size and performance are crucial. These units are nearly square 144-pin 32 Mb × 64 plug-in modules that are available with either SDRAM or DDR SDRAM components on board. Figure 8-13 shows a MicroDIMM module. They are 1.54" (38.0 mm) by approximately 1" (25.4 mm) high and unlike SODIMMs do not have any notches along their edge connector contacts. The height of MicroDIMM modules varies from manufacturer to manufacturer.

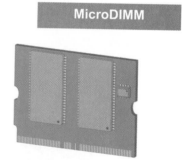

**Figure 8-13:
MicroDIMM**

MicroDIMM modules slide into a specialized spring-loaded socket. When the module is fully seated in the socket, two plastic clips snap into place to hold it securely. To release the module from the socket, simply spread the clips apart, and the spring will shove the module out of the socket.

Upgrading Portable Memory

The key to upgrading or replacing internal RAM in a portable computer can be found in its documentation. Only memory modules recommended by the portable manufacturer should be installed, and only in the configurations suggested.

The voltage level support for the memory devices in portable computers is critical. Using RAM devices that electrically overload this supply will cause memory errors to occur.

If the type of RAM device being installed is not one of the recommended types, the notebook might not be able to recognize the new memory. If the new RAM is being added to expand the existing banks of memory, the system might not recognize this additional RAM. The problem will show up in the form of a short memory count during the POST routines. However, if only the new RAM type is installed, the system could present a number of different symptoms, including

- Not working at all
- Giving beep coded error messages

- Producing soft memory errors
- Producing short memory counts in the POST
- Locking up while booting the operating system

As with disk drives, changing memory in a portable PC involves disassembling the computer case. Figure 8-14 shows the replacement of a SODIMM module in a particular notebook computer. The location of and process of accessing the memory in the unit vary from manufacturer to manufacturer and model to model.

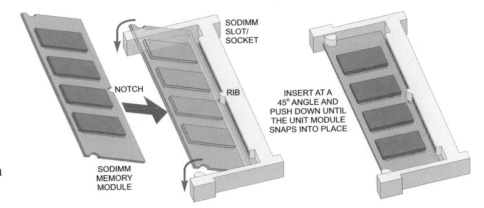

Figure 8-14: Replacing a SODIMM Module

In notebook computers, it is also possible to increase memory by installing PC-card—based memory cards described later in this chapter. These memory units can increase the portable computer's memory capabilities without the need to take it apart. In addition, they can be removed when additional memory space is not in high demand. A newer memory add-on technology that has found some favor in the notebook computer arena is the USB plug-in memory module.

GEEK SQUAD CASE FILE #986543

Your friend has brought you his notebook computer and wants you to upgrade the memory in it. He has also brought several different 184-pin 512 MB RIMM modules with him that he had in his office. What can you tell your friend about his upgrade?

shared video memory

IT Technician 2.2

Depot Technician 2.2

Portable PCs typically use a technique called **shared video memory**. Under shared memory, the system uses a portion of its main memory to hold screen information for the display. In desktop PCs, this memory is distributed to the video adapter card. The disadvantage of shared memory is that it takes up RAM that applications would normally use. In addition, DRAM devices used for system memory are typically not as fast as specialized video memory used on stand-alone display adapter cards. System performance also suffers due to bus contention issues created by the processor and video controller requiring access to the same memory devices. If you are upgrading memory in the portable system, you must take into account that the amount of RAM available for use by the system will not be the same as the installed RAM.

Portable Drives

Smaller 2.5" form factor hard drives, low-profile 3.5" floppy drives, and combination FDD/CD-ROM drives have been developed to address the portable computer market's need for compact devices. Older portables included one FDD and one HDD as standard equipment. Newer models tend to include a CD-RW/DVD drive and an HDD as their standard internal units.

While it is possible to install internal DVDRW drives in portable computers, these tend to only be installed in very high-end versions. On the other hand, external CDRW and DVDRW units are also widely used with portable computers. These drive units are described in greater detail later in this chapter. Figure 8-15 shows the placement of drives in a high-end notebook unit that includes one of each drive type.

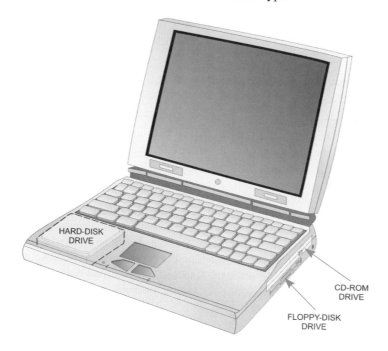

HARD-DISK
DRIVE

CD-ROM
DRIVE

FLOPPY-DISK
DRIVE

**Figure 8-15:
Portable Disk Drives**

Newer portable models include swappable drive bays that permit the combination of internal drives in the unit to be changed as dictated by the work being performed. In some units, a disk drive that is not needed for a particular task may be removed and replaced by an extra battery.

There are basically three considerations that should be observed when replacing disk drives in portable computers. These are its physical size and layout, its power consumption, and whether the existing BIOS will support it.

BASIC I/O

Personal computer users are creatures of habit as much as anyone else. Therefore, as they moved toward portable computers, they wanted the types of features they had come to expect from their larger desktops and towers. These features typically include an alphanumeric keyboard, a video display, and a pointing device.

Portable Display Types

Portable computers continue to gain popularity due to their ability to travel with the user. Most portable computing devices, including notebook and laptop computers, use non-CRT **liquid crystal display (LCD)** panels for their main video output device. These display systems are well suited to the portability needs of portable computers. They are much lighter and more compact than CRT monitors and require much less electrical energy to operate. These displays are powered by low-voltage DC power sources such as a battery or converter.

liquid crystal display (LCD)

TEST TIP

Know that notebook display panels are powered by low-voltage DC power sources such as a battery or converter.

Liquid Crystal Displays

Liquid crystal displays

Liquid crystal displays are the most common flat panel displays used with portable PCs. They are relatively thin, flat, and lightweight, and require very little power to operate. In addition to reduced weight and improved portability, these displays offer better reliability and longer life than CRT units.

thermotropic
picture element
pixel
polarizer

The LCD, illustrated in Figure 8-16, is constructed by placing **thermotropic** liquid crystal material between two sheets of glass. A set of electrodes is attached to each sheet of glass. Horizontal (row) electrodes are attached to one glass plate, and vertical (column) electrodes are fitted to the other plate. These electrodes are transparent and let light pass through. A **picture element**, or **pixel**, is created in the liquid crystal material at each spot where a row electrode and a column electrode intersect. A special plate called a **polarizer** is added to the outside of each glass plate. There is one polarizer on the front, and another on the back of the display.

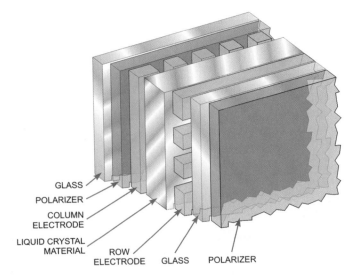

GLASS
POLARIZER
COLUMN ELECTRODE
LIQUID CRYSTAL MATERIAL
ROW ELECTRODE   GLASS   POLARIZER

Figure 8-16: LCD Construction

The display is designed so that when the pixel is off, the molecules of the liquid crystal twist from one edge of the material to the other, as depicted in Figure 8-17. The spiral effect created by the twist polarizes light and prevents it from passing through the display. When an electric field is created between a row and column electrode, the molecules move, lining up perpendicular to the front of the display. This allows light to pass through the display, producing a single dot on the screen.

Depending on the orientation of the polarizers, the energized pixels can be made to look like a dark spot on a light screen, or a light dot on a dark screen. In most notebook computers, the display is lit from behind the panel. This is referred to as **backlighting**. Some units are constructed so that the display can be removed from the body of the computer and used with an overhead projector to display computer output on a wall or large screen.

Because no current passes through the display to light the pixels, the power consumption of LCD displays is very low. The screen is scanned using IC multiplexers and drivers to activate the panel's row and column electrodes. The scanning circuitry addresses each row sequentially, column by column. Although the column electrode is activated for a short portion of each horizontal scan, the pixels appear to be continuously lit because the scanning rate is very high. The electrodes can be controlled (turned on and off) using standard TTL voltage levels. This translates into less control circuitry required to operate the panel. LCDs using this type of construction are referred to as **dual scan** or **passive matrix** displays. Advanced passive matrix technologies are referred to as **Color Super-Twist Nematic (CSTN)** and **Double-layer Super-Twist Nematic (DSTN)** displays.

An improved LCD approach is similar in design to the passive matrix designs, except that it adds a transistor at each of the matrix's row-column junctions to improve switching times. This technology produces an LCD display type referred to as an **active matrix display**. In these displays, a small current is sent to the transistor through the row−column lines. The energized transistor conducts a larger current, which, in turn, is used to activate the pixel seen on the screen. The active matrix is produced by using **thin film transistor (TFT)** arrays to create between one and four transistors for each pixel on a flexible, transparent film. TFT displays tend to be brighter and sharper than dual-scan displays. However, they also tend to require more power to operate and are more expensive.

Color LCD displays are created by adding a three-color filter to the panel. Each pixel in the display corresponds to a red, blue, or green dot on the filter. Activating a pixel behind a blue dot on the filter will produce a blue dot on the screen. Like color CRT displays, the dot color on the screen of the color LCD panel is established by controlling the **relative intensities** of a three-dot (RGB) pixel cluster.

The images produced by color LCD panels are heavily influenced by the **backlight** that shines through the panel and provides its brightness. The backlight also alters the actual color of the pixels produced on the screen and tends to wash them out. The measure of how distinguishable colors are on a video display is its **contrast ratio**. The higher this value, the better the colors should appear on the screen. However, with LCD and other flat panel displays, this specification can be misleading. The quality of the image is affected by the angle at which it is viewed.

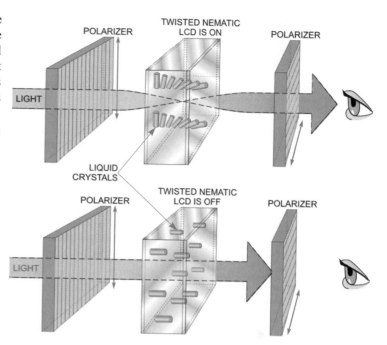

Figure 8-17: LCD Operation

backlighting

dual scan

passive matrix

Color Super-Twist Nematic (CSTN)

Double-layer Super-Twist Nematic (DSTN)

active matrix display

thin film transistor (TFT)

relative intensities

backlight

contrast ratio

The construction of LCD displays prevents them from providing multiple resolution options like an adapter-driven CRT display can. The resolution of the LCD display is dictated by the construction of the LCD panel and this value is known as its **native resolution**. To display image signals specified in higher or lower resolutions (DVD, HDTV, etc.) requires the video display system to convert the image to the native resolution to be displayed correctly.

If the display image has more pixels than the display's native resolution it will lose some of its picture information and sharpness when displayed. On the other hand, if the image has less pixels than the display, you will see all of the pixels displayed but there will be no increased quality due to the additional resolution capabilities of the display. The additional picture elements added to fill in the image may make the image look worse.

The life and usefulness of the portable's LCD panel can be extended through proper care and handling. The screen should be cleaned periodically with a glass cleaner and a soft, lint-free cloth. Spray the cleaner on the cloth and then wipe the screen. Never spray the cleaner directly on the screen. Also, avoid scratching the surface of the screen. It is relatively easy to damage the front polarizer of the display. Take care to remove any liquid droplets from the screen because they can cause permanent staining. After cleaning, allow 30 minutes for complete drying.

The screen should be shielded from bright sunlight and heat sources. Moving the computer from a warmer location to a cold location can cause damaging moisture to condense inside the housing (including the display). It should also be kept away from ultraviolet light sources and extremely cold temperatures. The liquid crystals can freeze in extremely cold weather. A freeze/thaw cycle may damage the display and cause it to be unusable.

Essentials 2.1

Keyboards

The most widely used notebook keyboard is the 84-key version. The keys are slightly smaller and shorter than those found in full-size keyboards. A number of keys or key functions may be combined or deleted from a notebook keyboard.

A typical notebook keyboard is illustrated in Figure 8-18.

Because a portable keyboard tends to be more compact than the detachable models used with desktop units, many of its keys are typically given dual or triple functions. The portable keyboard normally contains an **Fn** function key. This key activates special functions in the portable, such as display brightness and contrast. Other common Fn functions include Suspend mode activation and LCD/external-CRT device selection.

Figure 8-18: 84-Key Notebook Keyboard

Newer keyboard models may also include left and right Windows keys (**WIN keys**), and an **application key**, as identified in Figure 8-19. The WIN keys are located next to the ALT keys and provide specialized Windows functions, as described in Table 8-1. Similarly, the application key is located near the right WIN key, or the CTRL key, and provides context-sensitive help for most applications.

WIN KEY   APPLICATION KEY

Figure 8-19: WIN and Application Keys

KEY STROKE	ACTION
WIN/E	Start Windows Explorer
WIN/F	Start Find files or folders
Ctrl/WIN/F	Find the computer
WIN/M	Minimize All
Shift/WIN/M	Undo Minimize All
WIN/R	Display Run dialog box
WIN/F1	Start Help
WIN/Tab	Move through Taskbar objects
WIN/Break	Show System Properties dialog box

Table 8-1: WIN Key Definitions

Most portables offer standard connectors to enable full-size keyboards and VGA monitors to be plugged in, as shown in Figure 8-20. The VGA connector is usually the standard 15-pin D-shell type, while the external keyboard connector is generally the 6-pin mini-DIN (PS/2) type. When an external keyboard is plugged in, the built-in keyboard is disabled. The portable's software may allow both displays to remain active while the external monitor is connected.

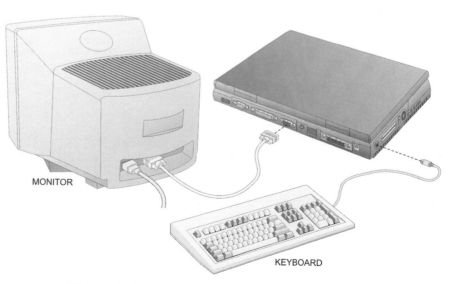

MONITOR

KEYBOARD

Figure 8-20: Attaching Standard I/O Devices

Trackballs

trackball

In some systems, such as notebook computers, it is desirable to have a pointing device that does not require a surface to be moved across. The **trackball** can be thought of as an inverted mouse that allows the user to directly manipulate it. Trackballs, like the one depicted in Figure 8-21, may be separate units that sit on a desk, or clip to the side of the computer, and connect to one of the system's serial ports. In many laptop and notebook computers, trackballs are frequently built directly into the system housing and connected directly to its I/O circuitry. Like mice, trackballs may come with one to three buttons.

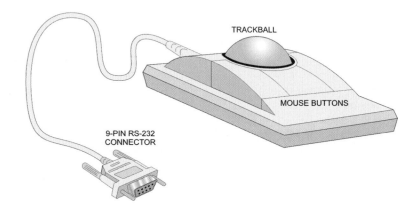

**Figure 8-21:
A Trackball Unit**

Touch Pads

touch screen
monitor

touch pad

Hewlett-Packard introduced the first **touch screen monitor** in 1983. These screens divide the display into rows and columns that correspond to X and Y coordinates on the screen. This technology has been adapted to notebook computers in the form of **touch pad** pointing devices, like the one illustrated in Figure 8-22.

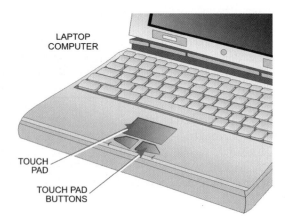

**Figure 8-22: A
Touch Pad**

This pointing device normally takes the place of the mouse as the pointing device in the system. The user controls the screen cursor by moving a finger across the pad surface. Small buttons are included near the pad to duplicate the action of the mouse buttons. With some touch pads, single- and double-clicking can be simulated by tapping a finger on the pad.

The touch pad contains a grid work of electric conductors that organize it in a row and column format, as described in Figure 8-23. When the user presses the touch pad, the protective layer over the grid flexes and causes the capacitance between the two grids within the pad to change. This produces a signal change that is detected by the touch pad controller at one X-grid line and one Y-grid line. The controller converts the signal generated between the two strips into an approximate X/Y position on the video display.

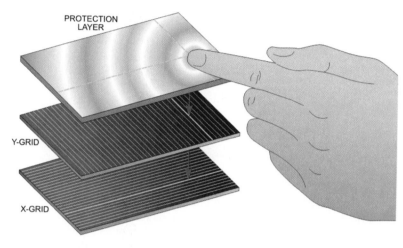

PROTECTION LAYER

Y-GRID

X-GRID

Figure 8-23: Inside a Touch Pad

The human fingertip is broad and does not normally provide a fine enough pointing device to select precise points on the screen. Therefore, accurately locating a small item on the screen may be difficult. Touch pad software designers have created drivers that take this possibility into account and compensate for it.

Touch pads are available as built-in units in some portables, while others are designed as add-ons to existing units. These units clip onto the body of the computer, or sit on a desktop, and plug into one of the system's I/O ports, just as a mouse or trackball does.

As with the portable's LCD panel, the life and usefulness of a touch pad can be extended through proper care and handling. The panel should be cleaned periodically with mild soap and water and a soft, lint-free cloth. Rinse the residue from the pad by wiping it with a cloth dampened in clear water. Never pour or spray liquids directly on the computer or the touch pad. After cleaning, allow 30 minutes for complete drying.

Like the other portable components, the touch pad should be shielded from bright sunlight and heat sources, as well as extremely cold temperatures. Never use sharp or pointed objects to tap the pad, as these items may damage the surface of the pad.

Pointing Sticks

pointing stick

TrackPoint

Some notebook computers feature a small fingertip operated pointing device called the **pointing stick,** or **TrackPoint** in IBM *ThinkPad* notebooks. These devices, depicted in Figure 8-24, are small joystick-like devices that enable users to position screen cursors by applying pressure to the top of the stick. The stick is positioned between the G, H, and B keys on the keyboard and have additional mouse click buttons located just below the Spacebar.

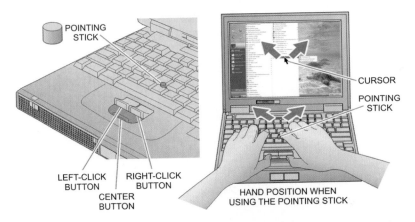

Figure 8-24: The Pointing Stick

Pointing sticks sense force applied to the top of the stick through changing resistance of a material. The velocity of the cursor movement on the screen is proportional to the amount of force applied to the stick. The pointing stick is preferred over other types of pointing devices by many touch-typists because it doesn't require the user to relocate their fingers away from the home row of keys.

Essentials 2.1

EXTENDED I/O

As more and more desktop users began to use laptop and notebook computers, they demanded that additional peripheral systems be included. With the limited space inside these units, it became clear that a new method for installing options would need to be developed.

At first, laptop and notebook manufacturers included proprietary expansion connections for adding such devices as fax/modems, additional memory, and additional storage devices. Of course, these devices tended to be expensive, because they were proprietary to a single vendor. In addition, they were not useful as the user upgraded to newer or more powerful units.

To meet the growing demand for flexible I/O capabilities for notebook computers and other portable systems, a variety of portable specific I/O ports and peripheral systems have been developed. In the following sections we will examine these systems.

PC Cards (PCMCIA)

In 1989, the **Personal Computer Memory Card International Association's (PCMCIA)** bus standard was introduced to provide a standard I/O adapter specification for the notebook and subnotebook computer markets. A small form factor expansion-card format, referred to as the **PC Card** standard was also adopted for use. This format, based on the 68-pin JEIDA connector, depicted in Figure 8-25, was derived from earlier proprietary laptop/notebook memory card designs.

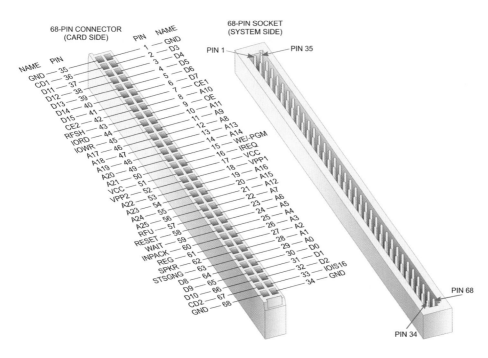

Figure 8-25: PCMCIA Connector Standard

The PCMCIA slot connector is typically recessed in the portable's case. The credit card–sized PC Cards slide into bays in the side of the case. They are normally pushed through a spring-loaded door on the side of the case and slide along guide rails molded into the sides of the bay. When fully inserted, the sockets built into the end of the cards engage the pins of the recessed connector.

Peripheral devices are attached to the exposed end of the card through a small PC-card connector, as illustrated in Figure 8-26.

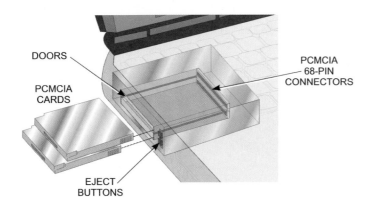

Figure 8-26: PCMCIA Connections

The interface is designed so that cards can be inserted into the unit while it is turned on (**hot insertion**). Although the PC Card connection scheme was never intended for use with a full-size unit, its design is compatible with all the other expansion bus types. As a matter of fact, PCMCIA adapters have been mounted on PCI cards so that they can be used in desktop and tower units. The PCI card is placed in one of the system board's expansion slots and the removable PC Cards can be inserted and removed through an opening in the PCI card's slot cover.

The PC Card standard defines a methodology for software programmers to write standard drivers for PC Card devices. The standard is referred to as **socket services** and provides for a software head to identify the type of card being used, its capabilities, and its requirements. Although the card's software driver can be executed directly on the card (instead of moving it into RAM for execution), the system's PC Card enablers must be loaded before the card can be activated. This is referred to as **execute-in-place mode**. In addition, PC Cards can use the same file allocation system used by floppy- and hard-disk drives. This also makes it easier for programmers to write code for PCMCIA devices.

PC Card Types

Three types of PCMCIA adapters currently exist. The **PCMCIA Type I** cards, introduced in 1990, are 3.3 mm thick and work as memory expansion units. In 1991, the **PCMCIA Type II** cards were introduced. They are 5 mm thick and support virtually any traditional expansion function, except removable hard drive units. Type II slots are backward compatible so that Type I cards will work in them. Currently, **PCMCIA Type III** cards are being produced. These cards are 10.5 mm thick and are intended primarily for use with removable hard drives. Both Type I and Type II cards can be used in a Type III slot.

All three card types adhere to a form factor of 2.12"w × 3.37"l and use a 68-pin, slide-in socket arrangement. They can be used with 8-bit or 16-bit data bus machines and operate on +5 V or +3.3 V supplies. The card's design allows it to be installed in the computer while it is turned on and running. Figure 8-27 shows the three types of PCMCIA cards.

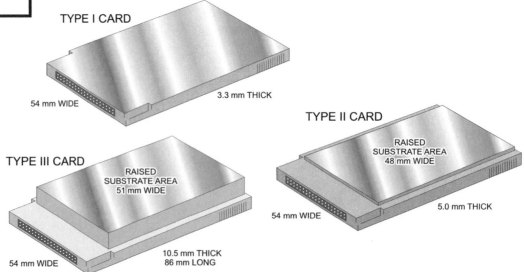

Figure 8-27: PCMCIA Cards

PC Card versions of most adapter types are available in the market place. Even PC Card hard drives (with disks the size of a quarter) can be found. Other common PC Card adapters include fax/modems, SCSI adapters, network adapters, and IDE host adapters. The PCMCIA standard allows up to 255 adapters, each capable of working with up to 16 cards. If a system implemented the standard to its extreme, it could, theoretically, work with over 4000 PC Cards installed. Most portable designs include only two PC Card slots.

CardBus

The latest variation of the PCMCIA standard is CardBus. CardBus is a redefined and enhanced 32-bit version of the PC Card standard. The main purpose of this new specification is to extend the PCMCIA bus to higher speeds with more powerful devices, and to provide support of 32 bit I/O and memory data paths.

The CardBus slot has intelligent software that interrogates cards when they are inserted into the slot. If the slot finds that the card is a PC Card, then it configures itself to function like a conventional PCMCIA slot. However, if an advanced CardBus card has been inserted, the slot reconfigures itself to use the 32-bit bus width, increases speed and low-voltage capabilities of the CardBus specification.

Although the CardBus slot is designed to work with older PCMCIA and PC Card devices, the same is not true concerning using CardBus cards in older slot types. The CardBus card is keyed with a physical sheath around its pins so that it will not plug into the traditional PC Card socket. On the software side, for a CardBus device to work in a given system, the its operating system must support 32-bit data paths.

You can use the following procedure to determine whether a particular system is a CardBus-enabled system:

1. Insert the CardBus card into your system's PC Card slot, if it doesn't insert completely, then the slot is not a CardBus slot.

2. Check the system BIOS setup and verify that the *PC Card* option is set to the *CardBus* option. If there is no option for CardBus, then the system does not support CardBus devices.

3. Check the version of Windows 95 installed on your system under Settings, Control Panel, System, General. If you do not have version 4.00.950B or later, you do not have the necessary software to use CardBus PC Cards.

Installing PC Cards

Although portable computers do not include standard desktop expansion slots for adding peripheral devices to the system, they typically include a couple of PC Card slots. Most notebooks provide two PCMCIA slots that can accept a wide variety of I/O device types. PC Cards are relatively easy to install in a PnP system that has the PCMCIA card services function running. Simply slide the card into an open PC Card slot and turn the machine on. The PnP function should detect the card in the slot and configure it with the proper drivers.

The operating system must support the PCMCIA slots at two levels—at the socket level (universal support for all PCMCIA devices) and at the card level (specific drivers to handle the function of the particular card installed). Because PCMCIA cards are hot-swappable, the operating system's socket service must update the system when a new card is installed or an existing card is removed. If not, the system would lose track of its actual resources. The card service portion delivers the correct device driver for the installed PC Card (that is, when a PC Card modem is removed and replaced with a LAN card, the operating system must automatically update its capability of controlling and using the new card).

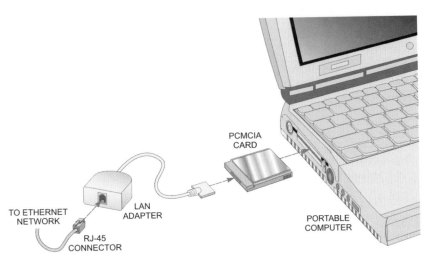

In many cases, the PC Card must furnish a standard I/O connector for connection to the full-sized world. Often, these connections are made through nonstandard connectors at the PC Card end but terminate in standard connectors at the I/O device end. For example, a PC Card LAN adapter, such as the one depicted in Figure 8-28, is not physically thick enough to accommodate a standard RJ-45 plug used with Ethernet networks. To overcome this, a thin connector is attached to the card, and a standard connector is used at the other end of the cable. Depending on their specific function, some PC Cards require an external power supply to acquire enough power to operate efficiently.

Figure 8-28: PC Card Connections

Installing PC Card Support

There are three ways in which the card services utility delivers the proper drivers to the card:

- The PnP operating system immediately recognizes the card and installs the driver without restarting.

- The operating system recognizes the card and has its driver but needs to reboot the operating system for the driver to be loaded.

- The operating system does not recognize the card and requires that an external driver be loaded. Under Windows 9x, a PC Card Wizard is started to guide the user through the driver installation process. Windows 2000 does not supply a PC Card installation wizard.

To install the PC Card (PCMCIA) Wizard on a Windows 9x system, you must navigate the *Start/Settings/Control Panel* path and access the *Add/Remove Programs* applet. Click the *Windows Setup* tab, select a category, and then click on the *Details* tab. If you don't see the component listed in the *Add/Remove Programs* dialog box, it might be one that is only present on the Windows 9x distribution CD. In this case, you can download the component from an online service, such as The Microsoft Network, or from the Microsoft Download Service at the main Microsoft Web site.

At different times, you might want to stop a PC Card driver from being loaded. To turn off support for a PC Card, access the *Device Manager* tab and expand the PC Card slot node. Then, double-click the PC Card controller and in the Device usage area, check the *Disable in This Hardware Profile* check box option.

The proper procedure for removing a PC Card from the computer begins with clicking on the PC Card status indicator on the taskbar. Then, select the command to stop the operation of the PC Card you want to remove. When the operating system prompts you, physically remove the PC Card from the system.

GEEK SQUAD CASE FILE #836666

You are traveling away from Geek Squad headquarters, and you want to get as much work done on the airplane as possible. You notice that the notebook takes several minutes during the PnP configuration portion of the boot process. Your notebook has a PCMCIA modem and network card, and you want to disable these devices while you are traveling so that their drivers are not loaded. How can you do this without permanently removing them? (You want to use them when you get back to HQ.)

Mini PCI Express Cards

The **Mini PCI** specification has been developed in an effort to extend the PCI bus into portable PCs. This specification extends the PCI version 2.2 standard to operate on a PC Card-like socket and slide in card. This arrangement is depicted in Figure 8-29. This version of the PCI bus only implements the 3.3 V, 32-bit variety of PCI. Therefore, no special keying is required for Mini PCI cards.

Mini PCI

There are three Mini PCI slot and card form factors, Type I, Type II, and Type III. Type I and II cards use a 100-pin connector like the PC Card slots do. However, the Type III cards employ a 124-pin edge connector interface similar to a traditional adapter card used in desktop PCs. For cards that provide an external interface, Type I and III cards provide support for a remote RJ-45 connector. The Type II cards include mounted RJ-11 and RJ-45 connectors.

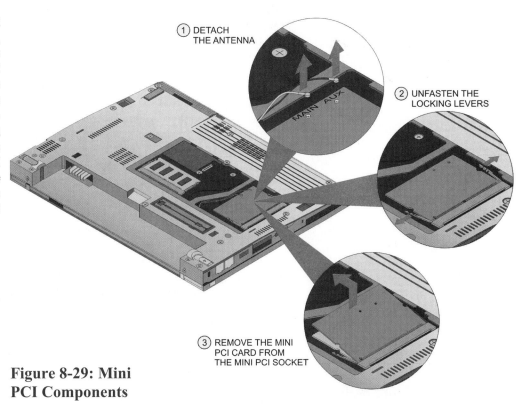

Figure 8-29: Mini PCI Components

The Mini PCI form factor also defines eight card sizes as described in Table 8-2

**Table 8-2: Mini
PCI Card
Specifications**

CONNECTOR	BOARD TYPE	DIMENSIONS
100-Pin Stacking	Type IA	7.5 × 70 × 45 mm
100-Pin Stacking	Type IB	5.5 × 70 × 45 mm
100-Pin Stacking	Type IIA	7.5 × 70 × 45 mm
100-Pin Stacking	Type IIB	17.44 × 78 × 45 mm
124-Pin Card Edge	Type IIIA	5.5 × 78 × 45 mm
124-Pin Card Edge	Type IIIB	5 × 64.7 × 55.8 mm
124-Pin Card Edge	Type IIIA	2.4 × 59.6 × 50.95 mm
124-Pin Card Edge	Type IIIB	2.4 × 59.6 × 44.6 mm

Typical applications associated with the Mini PCI card designs include PATA and SATA controller cards, wireless network cards, modems and sound cards.

Networking Portables

When the portable computer returns to the office, there is usually a gap between what is on the portable and what is on the desktop machine. One alternative is to use a docking station to allow the notebook to function as both a portable and as a desktop system. This concept is explored later in this chapter. The other alternative is to make the portable computer network-ready so that it can plug into the network in the office.

There are PC Card network adapters that can be used with a network socket device to enable the portable to be connected into the office network. The socket device has internal circuitry that prevents the open net connection from adversely affecting the network when the portable is removed. Some network adapters use the system's parallel port and a pocket LAN adapter to connect portables to the network. The LAN adapter actually works between the network, the computer, and its printer, as shown in Figure 8-30.

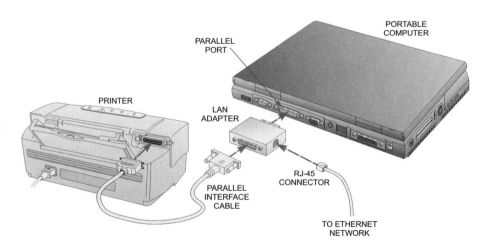

**Figure 8-30: A
LAN Adapter**

Notebook computers are natural selections for use as wireless networking clients. Because they are portable, they can be used anywhere within any wireless access point's hotspot. As mentioned in Chapter 6, many enterprises have created hotspots to enable traveling computer users to network through their access point—for a fee.

For the most part, the installation process involves inserting the wireless card in the PCMCIA slot and supplying the OEM drivers from the manufacturer's CD. Notebook computers typically use PC Card–based wireless network adapters like the one depicted in Figure 8-31. The wireless PC Card adapter slides into one of the notebook's PCMCIA slots and should be autodetected by the system. The card communicates with a remote access point through the embedded antenna that sticks out of the computer's PC Card slot.

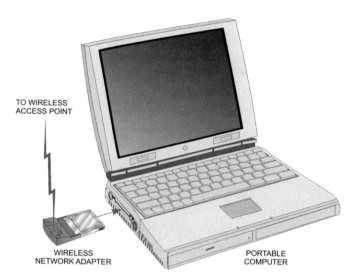

Figure 8-31: A Wireless Network Adapter PC Card

Part of configuring the drivers involves identifying the name of the access point that the card should use. Afterward, you simply need to configure networking support in the operating system. The device should be capable of functioning on the wireless LAN provided the card's driver and the operating system's networking components have been set up properly for communications.

Because wireless units can and do move, there are certain wireless connectivity issues that you must be aware of. Type 802.11b cards have a limited range of operation (i.e., about 500 ft). This estimation relies on a clear line of sight pathway existing between the card and the access point. The signals used under this wireless specification do not travel well through objects. In addition, if the card is used in a multiple access point environment, it will always try to communicate with the access point it has been configured to use. To switch to another access point, this setting must be reconfigured.

Many wireless configuration applications include a built-in *power meter* application that shows the relative signal strength being received from the access point. When you're positioning a computer that has a wireless network card, you should use this tool to maximize the location of the computer. Likewise, if you are operating in a multiple access point environment, you can use this tool to identify the best access point to use in a given location.

Notebook computers can also be used in dial-up networking environments by installing a PC Card modem as described in Figure 8-32. These modems slide into Type II PCMCIA slots and connect to the telephone jack through a special phone cable. The cable plugs into a small slot on the card and into the phone jack using a standard RJ-11 connector.

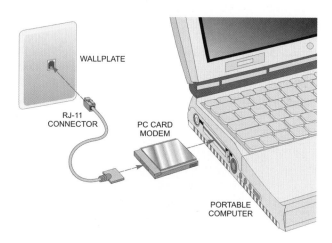

Figure 8-32: A PC Card Modem

Essentials 2.1

IT Technician 2.1

Depot Technician 2.1

Built in WiFi

As mentioned earlier in this chapter, embedded WLAN adapters have become a common feature of many notebook computer designs. Notebook computers with built-in WAN adapters often include a physical On/Off button to activate this feature. This button provides power savings by permitting the user to disable the circuitry while not online and to comply with regulations that require the transmit/receive portions of devices to be turned off while traveling by air.

There is one important consideration when purchasing or recommending wireless networking for portable computers. By definition, the wireless networking modules in *Centrino*-branded notebooks are limited to 802.11b wireless connectivity. On the other hand, *Pentium M*-portables are free to include the latest standards and features in wireless networking. In particular, these units include multimode WLAN adapters that support 802.11a/b/g WLAN capabilities. In general, non-Centrino notebooks offer longer battery life and greater networking performance than do the Centrino models.

802.11b products, like those in Centrino laptops, use the same 2.4 GHz frequency band used by cordless phones, microwave ovens, security cameras, and Bluetooth devices. These devices can interfere with the WLAN signal, slowing or disabling the connection. In addition, you should recall that the maximum data transmission rate for these devices is 11 Mbps under ideal conditions.

On the other hand, the 802.11a wireless products run up to 54 Mbps in the 5 GHz spectrum. This frequency band is much more restrictive and offers less interference than the 802.11b channel. The 5MHz band also offers more usable channels (13) to avoid conflicts with other WLAN access points. 802.11g devices also communicate at a 54 MHz rate but do so in the 2.4 GHz spectrum. This makes these devices subject to the same interference problems as the 802.11b products. However, it is still a good idea to have backward compatibility with 802.11b systems because of the large installed base of these products still in use.

EXTERNAL DEVICES

The basic portable should contain all of the devices that the user needs to do work while away from the office. However, there are always additional items that users have become accustomed to using with their computers. For this reason, portable computers typically offer a full range of I/O port types.

Power Supplies

Essentials 2.1

IT Technician 2.1

Depot Technician 2.1

Notebooks and other portables use a detachable, rechargeable battery and an external power supply, as illustrated in Figure 8-33 (battery sizes will vary from manufacturer to manufacturer). They also employ power-saving circuits and ICs designed to lengthen the battery's useful time. The battery unit contains a recharging regulator circuit that allows the battery to recharge while it is being used with the external power supply. As with other hardware aspects of notebook computers, there are no standards for their power supply units. They use different connector types and possess different voltage and current delivery capabilities. Therefore, a power supply from one notebook will not necessarily work with another portable model.

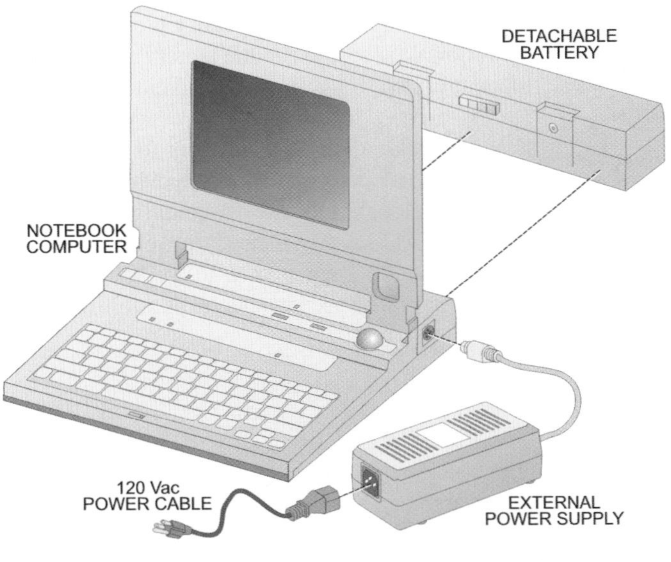

**Figure 8-33:
Laptop/Notebook
Power Supplies**

Because the premise of portable computers is mobility, it can be assumed that they should be able to run without being plugged into an AC outlet. The question for most

portables is how long it will run without being plugged in. This is the the aspect in which portable designs lead the industry. They continuously push forward in three design areas:

- Better battery design

- Better power-consumption devices

- Better power management

TEST TIP

Be aware that the external power supply used with portable systems basically converts AC voltage into a DC voltage that the system can use to power its internal components and recharge its batteries.

Batteries

nickel cadmium
(Ni-Cad)

nickel metal-hydride
(NiMH)

lithium-ion (Li-ion)

lithium-ion polymer

To be honest, the desktop world doesn't really pay much attention to power conservation issues. Conversely, portable computer designers must deal with the fact that portable computers are tied to a battery. Older portable designs included the battery as an external, detachable device, as depicted in the previous figure. These units normally contained rows of **nickel cadmium (Ni-Cad)** batteries wired together to provide the specified voltage and current capabilities for the portable. The housing was constructed both to hold the Ni-Cads and to attach to the portable case.

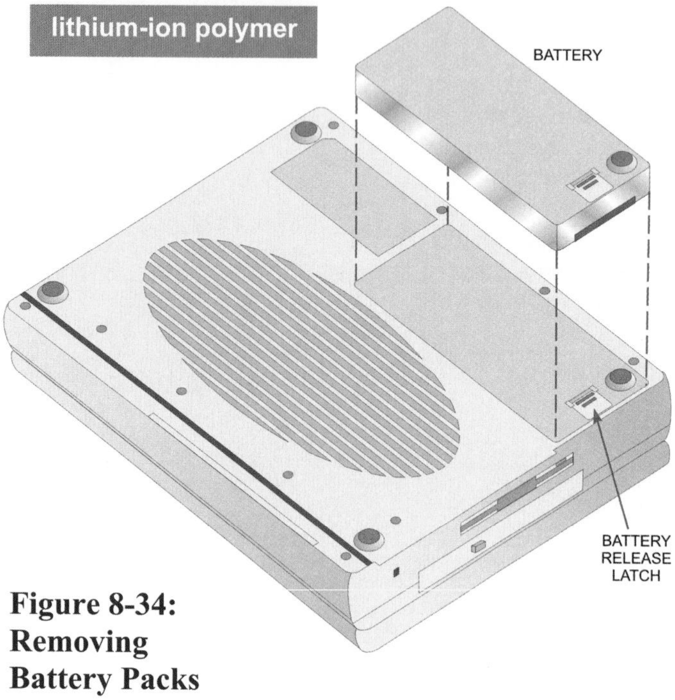

BATTERY

BATTERY
RELEASE
LATCH

**Figure 8-34:
Removing
Battery Packs**

Typical Ni-Cad batteries offer operating times approaching 2 hours in some models. As with other devices that rely on Ni-Cads, computer battery packs constructed with this type of battery suffer from the charge/discharge cycle "memory effect" problem associated with Ni-Cads. A full recharge for some Ni-Cad packs could take up to 24 hours to complete. For these reasons, Ni-Cad battery packs have all but disappeared from the portable computer market.

Newer portable designs have switched to **nickel metal-hydride (NiMH)**, **lithium-ion (Li-ion)**, or **lithium-ion polymer** batteries. These batteries are housed in a plastic case that can be installed inside the portable's case, as illustrated in Figure 8-34. These types of batteries typically provide up to 2 or 3 hours of operation. It is best to run the battery until the system produces a low battery warning message, indicator, or chime.

It should take about 2 to 3 hours to fully recharge the typical Ni-MH battery pack and about 4 to 5 hours for a Li-ion pack. The battery packs should always be fully recharged before using. When the AC adapter is used, a trickle charge is applied to the battery pack to keep it in a fully charged condition. The AC adapter should be used whenever possible to conserve the battery.

Fuel Cells

fuel cell

A relatively new power source for portable computers and handheld devices is the **fuel cell**. Fuel cells are power-generating technologies that use electrochemical reactions between hydrogen and oxygen to produce electrical power. One fuel cell technology does this using hydrogen extracted from methanol, whereas the other major fuel cell technology employs pure hydrogen. In both cases, the reaction between hydrogen and oxygen produces water vapor, heat, and electrical power.

Fuel cells small enough to be used with mobile computing systems are still primarily in the development stage, although some companies have already produced prototypes. Mobile computer manufacturers plan to routinely include fuel cells in their mobile products, including notebook PCs, digital still cameras, PDAs, and cell phones. These units will act as small wireless rechargers for the high-density lithium batteries already being used in notebook computers and PDAs. Current fuel cell designs in this category have about ten times the energy capacity of a similar-size typical portable computer battery.

Power Management

As mentioned earlier, power consumption consideration has been built into most devices intended for use with portable computers. Many of the PnP BIOS provide a **standby mode** that turns off selected components, such as the hard drive and display, until a system event, such as a keyboard entry or a mouse movement, occurs. The next level of power saving is called **suspend mode,** which places the system in a shutdown condition except for its memory unit. An additional power-saving mode, known as **hibernate mode**, writes the contents of RAM memory to a hard drive file and completely shuts the system down. When the system is restarted, the feature reads the hibernate file back into memory, and normal operation is restarted at the place it left off.

Each sector of the portable computer market has worked to reduce power consumption levels, including software suppliers. Advanced operating systems include power management features that monitor the system's operation and turn off some higher-power-consumption items when they are not in use (Standby mode), and will switch the system into a low-power-consumption **sleep mode** (Suspend mode) if inactivity continues.

These modes are defined by a Microsoft/IBM standard called the **Advanced Power Management (APM)** standard. The hardware producers refer to this condition as a **green mode**. The standard is actually implemented through the cooperation of the system's chipset devices and the operating system. Control of the APM system is provided through the BIOS' CMOS Setup utility, as described in Chapter 3, *Advanced System Boards*.

Most new portable PCs possess a number of automatic power-saving features to maximize battery life. Some can be controlled through the Power menu of the *Advanced CMOS Setup* utility. If the *Hard Disk Timeout* value is set to 3 minutes, the *Standby Timeout* to 5 minutes, and the *Auto Suspend* value to 10 minutes, the following activities will occur:

1. The hard disk will spin down after 3 minutes of inactivity.

2. After 2 additional minutes of inactivity, the system will enter the standby mode.

3. After 10 additional inactive minutes, the system will store the hibernation file on the hard drive and enter suspend mode.

The suspend mode can also be entered by pressing a key combination for those times when the user must step away from the computer for a few minutes but does not want to shut down. When the system suspends operation, the following events take place:

1. The video screen is turned off.

2. The CPU, DMA, clocks, and math coprocessor are powered down.

3. All controllable peripheral devices are shut down.

The amount of time the unit can remain in suspend mode is determined by the remaining amount of battery power. For this reason, data should be saved to the hard drive before voluntarily going to suspend mode. Pressing the computer's power button will return the system to its previous operational point.

standby mode

suspend mode

hibernate mode

sleep mode

Advanced Power Management (APM)

green mode

ACPI

advanced configuration and power interface (ACPI)

The **advanced configuration and power interface (ACPI)** is a power management specification supported in all modern versions of the Microsoft Windows operating systems. It was designed to improve APM activities described above by enabling the *operating system* to control the amount of power provided to each device or peripheral in the system. In addition, the specification permits power management functions to evolve independently in hardware devices, such as the BIOS, and the operating systems.

ACPI is particularly important in the portable computer market, because it provides greatly improved power management function that extends the battery life of those systems. It also enables the system to be reactivated by input from an external device, such as a mouse movement or a key closure.

BIOS ACPI error

Just as PnP requires a compatible BIOS for proper operation, ACPI must also be supported at the BIOS level to work. If these two items are not compatible, you can receive a **BIOS ACPI error**, telling you that they are not working together. This error has appeared with Windows XP installations and upgrades. In these cases, it is necessary to upgrade the BIOS so that it supports ACPI operation.

External Drive Units

The first laptops and notebooks incorporated the traditional single floppy drive and single hard drive concept that was typical in most desktop units. However, as CD-ROM drives and discs became the norm for new operating systems and software packages, a problem arose. There is simply not enough room in most notebook computers for three normal-size drive units. Even with reduced-size drives, the size limitations of most portables require that one of the three major drives be external.

External CD-ROM and DVD Drives

Prior to the CD-ROM drive becoming an accepted part of the notebook PC, some manufacturers produced external CD-ROM drives for use with these machines. Now, external DVD drives have become popular add-ons for notebook computers. External CD-ROM drives typically connect to a SCSI host adapter, or to an enhanced parallel port on the host computer. The latter connection requires a fully functional bidirectional parallel port and a special software device driver to operate properly.

Figure 8-35 illustrates the installation of an external SCSI CD-ROM drive. Because the drive is external, connecting the CD-ROM unit to the system usually involves simply connecting a couple of cables together. First, connect the CD-ROM's power supply to the external drive unit. Before making this connection, verify that the power switch, or power supply, is turned off. Connect the signal cable to the computer. Finally, connect the opposite end of the cable to the external CD-ROM unit. Complete the installation by installing the CD-ROM driver software on the system's hard-disk drive.

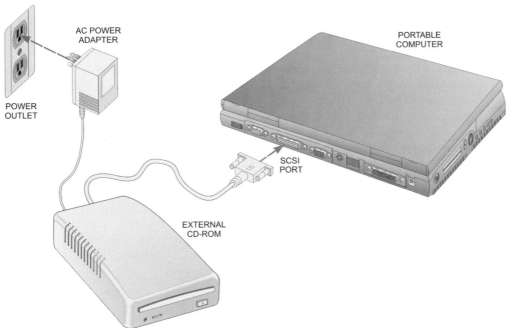

Figure 8-35: Installing an External CD-ROM Drive

External FDDs

Internal floppy drives have disappeared from portable computers for the most part. So much of the latest software is distributed on CD-ROM that CD-ROM drives now have preference in newer designs. Even so, there are still a few external FDD models available, but they are always an add-on option for a new notebook. There continue to be software components, such as OEM device drivers and utilities, that are distributed on floppy disks. Likewise, many users have volumes of cherished data stored on floppies. In these cases, having an external floppy drive for a portable computer makes sense.

The external floppy comes as a complete unit with an external housing and a signal cable. As with other external devices, it requires an independent power source, such as an AC adapter pack. The few remaining external floppy drive models available typically employ a USB interface for their signal cables, as illustrated in Figure 8-36.

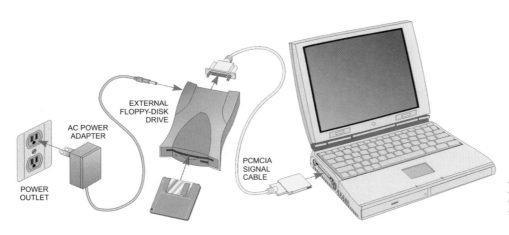

Figure 8-36: An External Floppy Drive

Removable Storage

For most portable PCs, the main removable storage system is the CD-RW/DVD drive. As long as you have a writable CD-R disk, you have additional storage. They also are likely to feature internal PC Card slots that can hold hot-swappable memory cards. These cards can be added to the system or removed while the system is in full operation.

Through modern I/O interface strategies, portable PCs can employ the same removable storage devices that desktop units do. It is not uncommon for a notebook computer to feature different flash memory card reader slots, as depicted in Figure 8-37. These slots are designed to handle CF cards, memory sticks, SD cards, and others. Like the PC Card devices, flash card devices are also hot-swappable and can be inserted or removed from the system at any time.

**Figure 8-37:
Portable PC Memory
Card Slots**

Virtually all new notebook computers employ USB ports as their main I/O interface. Some portable PC models provide additional USB ports to extend the number of USB devices that can be plugged into the system. These devices include USB flash drives and can increase the system's storage capacity significantly. As we've already discussed, USB devices, including memory devices using USB interfaces can be connected to the system and removed at any time.

All of the devices covered in this section are hot-swappable. They give portable systems a great deal of flexibility in meeting storage needs. While they are all hot-swappable, you must remember to *eject* them through the operating system software before you physically remove them from the system.

Essentials 2.1

Docking Stations

docking station

docking port

A **docking station**, or **docking port**, is a specialized structure that allows the notebook unit to be inserted into it. Once the notebook is inside, the docking port extends its expansion bus so that it can be used with a collection of desktop devices, such as an AC power source, a full-sized keyboard and display monitor, as well as modems, mice, and standard PC port connectors. A typical docking station is depicted in Figure 8-38.

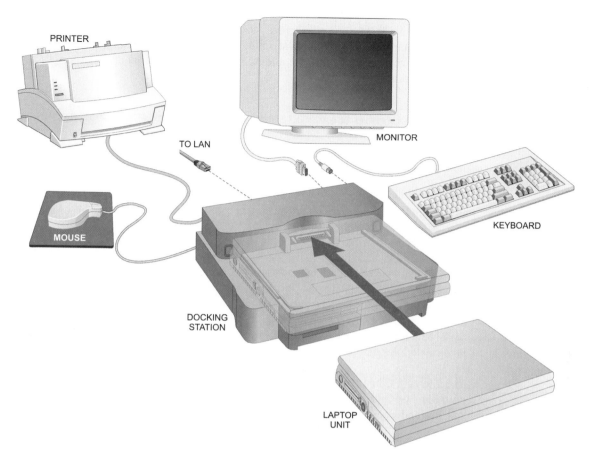

PRINTER

TO LAN

MONITOR

MOUSE

KEYBOARD

DOCKING
STATION

LAPTOP
UNIT

The notebook and the docking station communicate with each other through a special docking port connector in the rear of the notebook. When the notebook is inserted into the docking station, the extension bus in the docking station plugs into the expansion connector in the notebook. Most docking stations provide standard PC expansion slots so that non-notebook peripheral devices, such as network adapters and sound cards, can be used with the system.

When the notebook is in the docking station, its normal I/O devices (keyboard, display, and pointing device) are disabled, and the docking station's peripherals take over.

For the most part, docking stations are proprietary to the portable they were designed to work with. The docking port connection in the docking station must correctly align with the connector in the notebook. The notebook unit must also fit correctly within the docking station opening. Because there are no standards for these systems, the chances of two different manufacturers locating the connectors in the same places or designing the same case outline are remote.

Figure 8-38:
A Docking Station

Port Replicators

Many notebook computer manufacturers offer devices similar to docking stations that are called **port replicators**. These devices plug in to the notebook computer and contain common PC ports, such as serial and parallel ports. The purpose of these devices is to enable users to attach portable computers to standard, nonportable devices such as printers and monitors.

port replicators

Notebook manufacturers typically offer port replicators as additional proprietary options for their computers. Although these systems are similar to docking stations, they do not provide the additional expansion slots for adding options adapter cards and disk drives found in docking stations.

Essentials 2.3

IT Technician 2.3

TROUBLESHOOTING PORTABLE SYSTEMS

From a service point of view, the greatest drawback of portable computers is that conventions and compatibility disappear. The continued minimization of the system comes at a cost. Most notably, the number of I/O ports, memory, and disk drive expansion capabilities are limited. In addition, there is no chance to use common, full-sized options adapter cards that are inexpensive and easy to find.

One of the biggest problems for portable computers is heat buildup inside the case. Because conventional power supplies (and their fans) are not included in portable units, separate fans must be designed into portables to carry the heat out of the unit. The closeness of the portable's components and the small amount of free air space inside their cases also adds to heat-related design problems.

The internal PC boards of the portable computer are designed to fit around the nuances of the portable case and its components, rather than to match a standard design with standard spacing and connections. Therefore, interchangeability of parts with other machines or makers goes by the wayside. The only source of most portable computer parts, with the exception of PC Cards and disk drive units, is the original manufacturer. Even the battery case may be proprietary. If the battery dies, you must hope that the original maker has a supply of that particular model.

Access to the notebook's internal components is normally challenging. Each case design has different methods for assembly and disassembly of the unit. Even the simplest upgrade task can be difficult with a notebook computer. Although adding RAM and options to desktop and tower units is a relatively easy and straightforward process, the same tasks in notebook computers can be difficult.

In some notebooks, it is necessary to disassemble the two halves of the case and remove the keyboard in order to add RAM modules to the system. In other portables, the hinged display unit must be removed to disassemble the unit. Once inside the notebook you may find several of the components are hidden behind other units. Figure 8-39 demonstrates a relatively simple disassembly process for a notebook unit.

In this example, a panel in front of the keyboard can be removed to gain access to the notebook's internal user-serviceable components. Four screws along the front edge of the unit's lower body must be removed. Afterward, the LCD panel is opened and the front panel of the notebook's chassis is pulled up and away to expose a portion of the unit's interior.

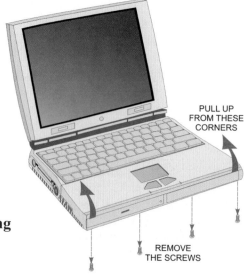

PULL UP
FROM THESE
CORNERS

REMOVE
THE SCREWS

**Figure 8-39:
Disassembling
a Notebook
Computer**

Common LCD Display Problems

The most common problems associated with LCD displays are

- A cracked screen

- A screen with lines (horizontal or vertical)

- A dim display

- No display

There are relatively few components to worry about in the LCD display of a portable computer. These are the **LCD panel**, the **inverter**, the **video cable**, the **case-closed switch**, the exterior bezel, an internal metal frame, and hinges. Of these items, only the *LCD panel*, the *inverter*, the *video cable*, and the *case-closed switch* are active components. The other item to consider is the video adapter, but this component is integrated into the notebook's system board and cannot be treated as an FRU component. Figure 8-40 shows the components of a notebook computer LCD display.

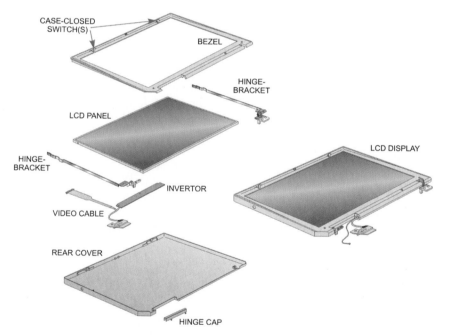

Figure 8-40:
LCD Display
Components

A cracked LCD screen normally occurs because the computer has been dropped or mishandled. The crack can appear as a visible crack or it can simply look like there is liquid floating on the screen. In either case, you will need to replace the LCD panel as described in the following section of this chapter.

If lines appear in the screen (either horizontal or vertical), you should plug an external display into the notebook's external VGA port to determine whether the problem is with the display or the display adapter. If the lines do not appear on the external display, there is either some problem with the LCD panel or the video signal ribbon cable that connects the LCD panel to the adapter. Inspect the pins of the cable to see if there is a problem with one of them. If the pins are OK and the external display is good, the problem is with the LCD panel and you will need to replace it.

If you have a dim screen on a portable system there are two likely candidates—the *LCD panel* and the *Inverter* card. The inverter provides power for the LCD panel's backlight. In most cases of a dim screen, the inverter is the source of the problem. This unit is normally a separate unit and is much less expensive to replace than an LCD panel. You can install a generic inverter to get the display running, but you must install the correct inverter for the display to receive optimal brightness and uniformity from the display. Refer to the following section for information related to replacing the inverter. If replacing the inverter does not restore the brightness to the display, you are looking at replacing the LCD panel.

If there is no display on the portable's display, there are a couple of portable PC-specific items to check before using the same troubleshooting procedures you would for a desktop PC. The Fn key of portable computers can be used to redirect the video output to the external VGA port. If you suspect this to be the case, you will need to check the user's guide for directions in redirecting the video back to the main display. The other item specific to portables is the case closed switch that suspends operation of the video display when the display is down. If this switch sticks in the closed position, the display will not activate. You must troubleshoot the switch action and may need to adjust or replace it.

Replacing the LCD Panel

To replace the LCD display on a portable PC, you must begin by locating all the screws that hold the panel between the front and back halves of the plastic bezel. Most displays are held together by between four and six small machine screws. These screws are typically hidden under small pieces of rubber and may be located on the front of the display or on its sides. Use a sharp tool such as an Exacta Knife to remove the covers from the screws. Finally, use a screwdriver to remove the all screws from the bezel and place them in a container.

Next, you will need to pull the two halves of the bezel shell apart. Use your fingers to separate the two halves at the seam that divides them. The front bezel typically snaps off fairly easily. If not, check for any missed screws in the frame. Work around the frame until the two halves are separated. You may need to work with the button that controls the latch, as it may need to be in a certain position to separate the two halves. With the front of the bezel removed, you should see the LCD panel and its metal frame as depicted in Figure 8-41.

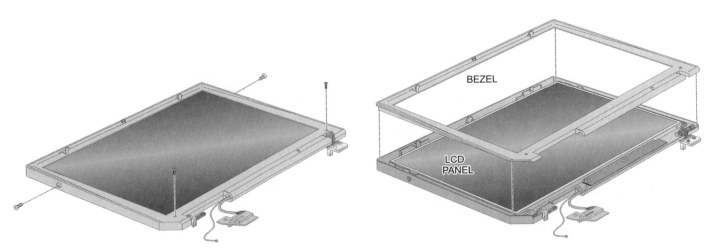

Figure 8-41: An Open LCD Display Panel

After removing the front half of the bezel from the display, cover the keyboard with a protective cloth. Pull the LCD panel and its metal bracket forward away from the rear half of the bezel to gain access to the screws that hold the LCD panel to the metal bracket. Remove the screws and store them securely.

After releasing the LCD panel from its frame, gently tilt the LCD panel forward onto the protective covering on the keyboard. Remove the video cable from the rear of the LCD panel. Remove any pieces of tape or clips that secure the video cable to the rear of the LCD panel. Take care to avoid damaging the video signal cable or is pins. Portable PCs that feature wireless networking may place the antenna behind the LCD panel. If present, this item must also be gently removed from the LCD panel before replacing it.

Unplug the LCD panel's inverter cable from the inverter module. In some units, you may need to release the inverter module from the system by removing its retaining screws to gain access to the connector. At this point, the LCD panel is completely free from the system. Remove the LC panel from the frame and check for its manufacturer's part number. Use this number to order the replacement LCD panel.

Reinstalling the replacement LCD panel is a matter of reversing the steps outlined above. Remember that the LCD panel is delicate and must be handled properly to avoid damage.

Troubleshooting Touch Pads

When troubleshooting touch pad problems, there are really only three components to consider. These are the touch-sensitive pad, the I/O port the pad is attached to, and its driver software. Review the user's manual for the pad to check its software setup for possible configuration problems. Examine the I/O port connection and configuration to make sure it is properly set up to support the pad. If the pad is an add-on unit, check the port specification to make sure that it is compatible with the touch pad unit. Reinstall the touch pad driver software, carefully reviewing each step. Check for the presence of diagnostic routines in the touch pad's software. Check the I/O port settings.

Smaller transparent touch pads or touch screens, such as those on PDAs, work with special pens called **stylus**. The stylus is required to interact with the touch pad because the screen icons and menus are too small to be manipulated by human fingers. The coordinates of the touch pad are calibrated with the screen elements displayed underneath. When the alignment between the screen elements and the touch pad coordinates gets out calibration, the system will not correctly interpret the input taps from the touch pad.

stylus

The alignment can get out of calibration due to temperature and humidity changes, differences in users perception, or a hard system reset. To correct this problem you must access the touch screen's recalibration utility and establish the starting point and length/width points. The touch screen can become so out of calibration that it is impossible to initiate the recalibration process. In this case you should check the Internet to download a third party calibration utility. You should also check the device manufacturer's web site to download an updated version of the device's driver—particularly if you are experiencing frequent recalibration problems.

Troubleshooting Portable Keyboards

If you have problems with the keyboard in a portable system it is not as easy (or as cheap) to replace as desktop keyboards. Therefore, if you have a problem that only affects selected keys, such as sticky or inoperable keys, you should to clean the keyboard out first. The keys may have built up dust or particles that keep the switches from making contact—use static-free compressed air to blow dust, dirt or liquids out of the keyboard.

Check for spyware on the system as these types of malware monitor the keystrokes you make and can affect the operation of the keyboard. Check the portable's Users Manual for an explanation of its function keys. In some units a function key (such as F11 or F13) can be used to disable the keyboard. Check the keyboard to system board connector as a single bad connection in this connector can produce errors that appear in groups of keys.

If the keyboard problem is associated with all its keys, you may have a loose connection. Moving can jar connectors loose—check the keyboard connection to the system board to make sure that it is securely plugged in.

In either case, you can run a diagnostic program (either the one supplied by the portable manufacturer or a third party diagnostic) to check for failures before you begin to disassemble the portable. You might also consider using a desktop keyboard with the portable if it has a PS/2 or USB port.

Troubleshooting Portable Unique Storage

Other than CD-ROM/DVD drives and floppy drives, all of the removable storage devices associated with portable computers are purely electronic devices—they have no movable parts. Therefore, causes for failures in these devices are limited to just a few possibilities—the part failed, the part has been physically damaged, the system does not recognize the device, or the system is not configured correctly to use the device. If the device has failed or been damaged to the point where it will not work, it is likely that you will need to simply replace it. On the other hand, if the system does not recognize the device, or it can see the device but cannot work with it, you typically need to straighten out its driver arrangements.

The general procedure for troubleshooting USB devices is covered in detail in Chapter 11, *Basic System Troubleshooting*. When you plug a USB memory device into the USB port, the system should recognize it and automatically load its drivers. At that point, you should be able to see the device listed as a drive in the *My Computer* window of any Windows operating system.

If the USB device does not appear, you should use the *Device Manager* utility to check for conflicting device drivers. You may also need to check the CMOS configuration pages to make certain that the USB ports are enabled there. If Windows simply will not work with the device you are trying to install, you need to obtain a Windows-compatible device driver for the device.

Likewise, all of the different flash memory card readers used with portable computers should automatically recognize the presence of the device when it is inserted. If not, you should use the *Device Manager* utility to check the status of the device and to determine whether there are any conflicts with its driver.

These types of devices can also generate error messages and failures when they are removed or turned off during an operation that involves them. For example, if you remove an SD card and then reinsert it into the system, the system may not use it. In the *Device Manager* utility, you will find a yellow triangle with an exclamation point beside the device. The operating system has not released the system resources dedicated to the device and believes that a new device has been installed. It cannot issue another set of resources to the device. This problem has been corrected in newer Windows Service Pack updates. These updates can be downloaded and installed from the Microsoft Web site.

You may also encounter problems with removable media devices when you reformat them under Windows. If you run the Windows Format utility to reformat a removable media device from the Windows Explorer, other devices, such as digital cameras, may not be able to recognize the device. This indicates that the PC and the camera are not using the same file system. You must make sure that the devices are set to the same file system type when using the formatting utility. This typically involves setting the operating system's formatting utility to use FAT or FAT16 formatting. *File systems* and *formatting* are discussed in detail in the next chapter.

Troubleshooting PCMCIA

The process for troubleshooting PC Cards is nearly identical to troubleshooting other I/O adapter cards. PCMCIA cards can be plugged into the system at any time, and the system should recognize them. In most cases, the Windows operating system will have a copy of the necessary driver software for the PCMCIA adapter being installed and will install it automatically when it detects the adapter. Most Windows operating system versions will display messages telling you that they are installing the drivers required. However, Windows 2000 and Windows XP simply install the drivers without a notice.

In cases where the operating system does not have the necessary driver software, it will display a prompt asking the user for a path to the location where the driver can be loaded, when it detects the adapter. PCMCIA manufacturers typically supply drivers for various operating systems on a floppy disk or a CD that comes with the adapter.

To verify that the PC Card device is working, access the *Device Manager* under the Windows Control Panel's System applet. If there is a problem with the PC Card device, it will be appear in the Device Manager. If the adapter's icon shows an exclamation mark on a yellow background, the card is not functioning properly. Turn the system off, and reinsert the device in a different PCMCIA slot. If the same problem appears, there are three possible sources of problems—the card may be faulty, the PC Card controller in the PC may be faulty, or the operating system may not support the device in question.

If the Windows Device Manager displays the PCMCIA socket but no name for the card, then the card insertion has been recognized but the socket could not read the device's configuration information from the card. This indicates that there is a problem with the PCMCIA socket installation. To correct this problem, remove the PCMCIA socket listing from the Device Manager, reboot the computer, and allow the Windows PnP process to detect the socket and install the appropriate driver for it. If the names of the PCMCIA cards do not appear after the restart, then the reinstallation process was not successful. Therefore, the PCMCIA socket you are using is not supported by the operating system version.

If the names of other PCMCIA cards appear in the Device Manager, but the card in questions does not, it is likely that the card has been damaged. To test the PC Card device, insert a different PC Card device of any type in the slot. If the other card works, it is very likely that the card in question has been damaged.

As with other PCMCIA devices, PC Card hard drives are self-contained. Plug them into the PCMCIA slot and the system should detect them (they are hot-swappable). If the system does not detect the card/hard drive, use the troubleshooting steps described for other PCMCIA devices.

Troubleshooting Portable Power

If you turn your portable computer on and nothing happens, the first things to check out include the AC power adapter and the battery. If the power adapter is plugged in, the computer should startup when the On/Off switch is engaged. Check for the presence of a power light on the AC adapter and verify that it is on. If not, either power is not reaching the adapter or it is defective.

However, if the computer is running on battery power and the system will not startup, the battery could be bad or need to be charged up. Verify that the battery doesn't need a recharge by trying to start the system with the AC power adapter plugged in. Remove all unnecessary peripherals from the system to reduce the load on the portable's battery and/or power adapter.

Check the power indicator in the computer. If it is on, then power is being supplied to the portable. If the indicator is not on, make sure that the power cord is securely connected to a live power source. Check all the power connections to make sure that the AC adapter jack is securely connected to the AC adapter port. If the portable still won't start up, you must troubleshoot the system board. If the system runs from the ac adapter, then the battery needs to be recharged or replaced.

Verify that the battery doesn't need a recharge by trying to start the system with the AC power adapter plugged in. Check the power indicator in the system display panel. If it is on, then power is being supplied to the portable. If the indicator is not on, make sure that the power cord is securely connected to a live power source. Check all the power connections to make sure that the AC adapter jack is securely connected to the AC adapter port. If the portable still won't start up, you must troubleshoot the system board. If the system runs from the AC adapter, then the battery needs to be recharged or replaced.

While a dead system is a classic battery/power supply problem, there are several other battery-related problems that you may encounter with portable computers. These include problems that present the following types of symptoms:

- Receiving warning messages about the battery not charging
- Intermittent system shut downs when operating only on the battery
- The computer does not recognize its network connection when operating with only the battery
- The computer and input devices are slow when operating with only the battery
- The computer loses the time and date information when operating on battery power

A loose or improperly installed battery can cause these problems. They can also appear when the battery is toward the end of its charge/recharge cycle. Check the installation and attempt to recharge the battery using the portable computer's AC adapter.

The actual life of a laptop computer battery varies from just under 1 hour to over 2 hours in each sitting. If you are experiencing battery life cycles that are significantly shorter than this (i.e., 10 to 15 minutes), you may have a problem referred to as battery memory. Battery memory is a condition that occurs with some types of batteries where the battery becomes internally conditioned to run for less time than its designed capacity (i.e., if you routinely operate the computer using the battery for an hour and then plug it back into an AC source, the battery can become conditioned to run only for that amount of time).

To correct battery memory problems, you must fully discharge the battery and then recharge it. To accomplish this, turn the portable's Power Management feature off by accessing the Power Management icon in the Windows Control Panel. Then restart the computer and access the CMOS setup utility during bootup. Disable the power management functions in the CMOS settings. Finally, start the portable computer using only the battery and allow it to run until it completely discharges the battery and quits. Then recharge the battery for at least 12 hours. Repeat this process several times, watching for consistently increasing operating times.

Adding peripheral devices to a portable system does not typically present the same load on its power system as it does in a desktop system. Most portable peripheral devices added to portable computers come with their own AC adapters. However, you should still be conscience of the power drain placed on the system by its peripherals. Refer to the "Power Supply Upgrade Considerations" section of Chapter 11, *Basic Troubleshooting*.

Troubleshooting Docking Stations/Port Replicators

Most docking stations offer an internal power supply that can operate the portable and its peripheral attachments—external parallel port for printers, a serial port for serial devices (mice and modems), USB ports, external VGA/DVI video and full-size keyboard connections, and audio connections for external speakers. In addition, the docking station can host several types of external storage devices, including full-sized FDD/HDD/CD-ROM/DVD drives.

Docking stations may also include one or two PCI slots that allow full-sized desktop adapter cards (SCSI or specialized video or LAN card) to be added to the system when it is docked. They may also provide multiple PCMCIA slots that add to the existing PC Card capabilities of the portable it is supporting.

For the most part, these connections are simply physical extensions of the ports provided by the portable. Therefore, if the port works on the portable and doesn't when connection is made through the docking station, then generally, somethings wrong with the docking station/port replicator. However, many portable computers employ special keystroke combinations (Fn + some other key) to activate external devices such as video display monitors or full-size keyboards.

For example, some portables will detect that the external video display has been attached. Others will use an Fn key combination to switch the display to the external monitor only, and then use another Fn key combination to send the display to both the LCD panel and the external display (i.e., internal, external, or both). If a peripheral device is not working, one of the first steps to take is to refer to the portable's documentation to insure that the external device has been activated.

For audio problems, make sure the speakers are connected to the correct RCA mini-jacks (not the line-in or microphone jacks). Check the documentation to make sure the sound output has not been muted using an Fn key combination

Under Windows operating systems, the hardware profile information for the portable computer can be configured differently for docked and undocked situations. When the computer is docked and turned on, its configuration is reset and the *Eject PC* option will appear on the Start menu. However, when the computer is not docked, the *Eject PC* option is automatically removed from the Start menu.

The *Windows XP Professional* operating system uses hardware profiles to determine which drivers to load when the system hardware changes (docked or undocked). It uses the Docked Profile to load drivers when the portable computer is docked and the Undocked Profile when the computer starts up without the docking station. These hardware profiles are created by the Windows XP operating system when the computer is docked and undocked if the system is PnP compliant. If a portable is not PnP compliant, you must manually configure the profile by enabling and disabling various devices present when docked and undocked.

The first check to make when you encounter docking station/port replicator problems is the same as with any other electronic device—check the power cord and docking power supply. Also, use the presence or activity levels of any indicator lights to determine if they are correct.

Next, verify that the portable has been properly inserted in the docking station or port replicator. If a single connection does not work, bypass the docking station/replicator and try to operate the peripheral directly with the portable unit. Check the power supply for both the docking station and the peripheral device and make sure that both are turned on. Reboot the portable while it is attached to the docking station. Then check any signal cables between the docking station and the peripheral.

If the PS/2 mouse connection does not work, verify that it has not been installed in the PS/2 keyboard connector by mistake. Make sure the mouse port is enabled in the CMOS Setup utility. Likewise, if you are using a serial mouse make sure the port is enabled in CMOS and that it is connected to the correct port. Check the serial port's configuration settings to verify that a proper device driver has been installed for the serial mouse. If the portable's touch pad works but the external mouse does not, check the documentation for an **Fn key** combination requirement for the mouse.

KEY POINTS REVIEW

The focus of this chapter has been portable computer systems. Review the following key points before moving into the Review and Exam Questions sections to make sure you are comfortable with each point. Afterward, answer the Review Questions that follow to verify your knowledge of the information.

- Continued advancements in chipset and peripheral technology allowed the PC's circuitry to be reduced. This allowed portable sizes to be reduced further so that they could achieve sizes of 8.75"d × 11"w × 2.25"h and smaller. Portables in this size range are referred to as notebook computers. The weight of a typical notebook dropped down to 5 or 6 pounds.

- Personal digital assistants (PDAs) are handheld devices that use a special stylus, referred to as a pen, to input data and selections instead of a keyboard or mouse. Basically, the PDA is an electronic time management system that may also include computer applications such as word processors, spreadsheets, and databases.

- The drawback of portable computers from a service point of view is that conventions and compatibility disappear. Therefore, interchangeability of parts with other machines or makers goes by the wayside.

- One of the biggest problems for portable computers is heat buildup inside the case. Because conventional power supplies (and their fans) are not included in portable units, separate fans must be designed into portables to carry the heat out of the unit. The closeness of the portable's components and the small amount of free air space inside its case also add to heat-related design problems.

- Portable computers have two ideal characteristics: they are compact and lightweight.

- The I/O ports included in most notebook computers consist of two or more USB ports, a built-in LAN adapter, sound card connections, and a dial-up modem connection.

- With the Pentium IIIM and Pentium 4M processors, Intel began to design mobile processors with a real concentration on the needs of portable computers.

- It is not a common practice for notebook and other portable computer manufacturers to use traditional DIMM modules in their designs. Instead, these types of computers routinely use the smaller SODIMMs and MicroDIMMs form factor memory modules.

- The key to upgrading or replacing internal RAM in a portable computer can be found in its documentation. Only memory modules recommended by the portable manufacturer should be installed, and only in the configurations suggested.

- The most common flat panel displays used with portable PCs are liquid crystal displays (LCDs). They are relatively thin, flat, and lightweight, and require very little power to operate. In addition to reduced weight and improved portability, these displays offer better reliability and longer life than CRT units.

- The most widely used notebook keyboard is the 84-key version. Its keys are slightly smaller and shorter than those found in full-size keyboards. A number of keys or key functions may be combined or deleted from a notebook keyboard.

- Three types of PCMCIA adapters currently exist. The PCMCIA Type I cards, introduced in 1990, are 3.3 mm thick and work as memory expansion units. In 1991, the PCMCIA Type II cards were introduced. They are 5 mm thick and support virtually any traditional expansion function, except removable hard drive units. Type II slots are backward compatible so that Type I cards will work in them. Currently, PCMCIA Type III cards are being produced. These cards are 10.5 mm thick and are intended primarily for use with removable hard drives. Both Type I and Type II cards can be used in a Type III slot.

- The PCMCIA bus was developed to accommodate the space-conscious notebook and subnotebook computer market.

- The Mini PCI specification has been developed in an effort to extend the PCI bus into portable PCs. This specification extends the PCI version 2.2 standard to operate on a PC Card-like socket and slide-in card.

- Portable computer designers work constantly to decrease the size and power consumption of all the computer's components. Special low-power consumption processors, chipsets, and disk drives have been developed to extend the battery life of portable computers.

- A docking station is a specialized structure that extends its expansion bus so that it can be used with a collection of desktop devices, such as an AC power source, a full-sized keyboard and display monitor, as well as modems, mice, and standard PC port connectors.

- Intel introduced a product badge system, called Centrino, that identified the product as supporting those qualities that Intel had determined were essential for portable computers.

- The pointing stick, or TrackPoint, devices are small joystick-like devices that enable users to position screen cursors by applying pressure to the top of the stick.

- Many of the PnP BIOS provide a standby mode that turns off selected components, such as the hard drive and display, until a system event, such as a keyboard entry or a mouse movement, occurs.

- The second level of power saving is called suspend mode, which places the system in a shutdown condition except for its memory unit.

- An additional power-saving mode, known as hibernate mode, writes the contents of RAM memory to a hard drive file and completely shuts the system down.

REVIEW QUESTIONS

The following questions test your knowledge of the material presented in this chapter.

1. How are mobile processors optimized for use in portable units?

2. List three considerations that must be taken into account when replacing disk drives in a portable.

3. What is the purpose of a docking station?

4. List three power management modes and describe how they are different.

5. What is the purpose of the Fn key on a portable computer keyboard?

6. How are notebook and laptop computers different?

7. Where is the network adapter normally located in a portable computer?

8. Describe some of the major maintenance problems that are associated with notebook computers.

9. How are active and passive matrix LCD displays different?

10. What type of device is a touch pad?

11. Describe two typical connection methods for adding an external CD-ROM drive to a portable system.

12. Which type of LCD panel uses less power than the others?

13. Describe two methods of connecting a portable computer to a network.

14. Describe what a port replicator does.

15. What functions do socket services provide for PC Cards in a notebook computer?

EXAM QUESTIONS

1. What form factor does a notebook computer's system board conform to?
   a. AT
   b. Baby AT
   c. ATX
   d. None

2. A Type I PCMCIA card is _____ thick.
   a. 3.3 mm
   b. 5.0 mm
   c. 7.5 mm
   d. 10.5 mm

3. A Type II PCMCIA card is _____ thick.
   a. 3.3 mm
   b. 5.0 mm
   c. 7.5 mm
   d. 10.5 mm

4. A Type III PCMCIA card is _____ thick.
   a. 3.3 mm
   b. 5.0 mm
   c. 7.5 mm
   d. 10.5 mm

5. Where would you usually expect to find a PCMCIA card?
   a. In an ISA expansion slot
   b. In a serial port
   c. In a notebook computer
   d. In an MCA expansion slot

6. Which of the following functions can be served by a Type I PCMCIA card?
   a. Memory expansion functions
   b. Serial port functions
   c. Parallel port functions
   d. Game port functions

7. Which of the following functions cannot be performed with a Type II PCMCIA card?
   a. Memory expansion functions
   b. Removable hard drive functions
   c. Serial port functions
   d. Parallel port functions

8. Select the battery technology that would not likely be used to provide power to a notebook computer.
   a. Nickel metal-hydride
   b. Lithium-ion
   c. Nickel cadmium
   d. Lithium-ion polymer

9. What sort of power source uses electrochemical reactions between hydrogen and oxygen to produce electrical power?
   a. Lithium batteries
   b. NiCad batteries
   c. Solar power batteries
   d. Fuel cells

10. Which of the following items cannot be used with portable computer systems?
    a. Full-size keyboards
    b. VGA monitors
    c. 3-button mice
    d. PCI modem

CHAPTER 9

OPERATING SYSTEM FUNDAMENTALS

OBJECTIVES

Upon completion of this chapter and its related lab procedures, you should be able to perform these tasks:

1. Describe the basic functions of an operating system.

2. Differentiate between single-process and multiple-process systems.

3. Differentiate between multiuser, multitasking, and multiprocessor operations.

4. Explain the structure of Windows 2000/XP operating systems.

5. Describe procedures for locating, accessing, and retrieving information in a command-line environment.

6. Identify basic concepts and procedures for creating and managing files and directories from the command-line environment.

7. List the events that occur during the bootup process.

8. Explain the basic organization of a FAT-based disk.

9. Describe the operation of the Microsoft command line.

10. Identify and use disk-level commands.

11. Create, delete, and navigate through various directories.

12. Discuss naming conventions as they apply to various types of files.

13. Find, copy, rename, delete, and move files in a command-line environment.

14. Manipulate file attributes from the command line.

15. List the core files in the Windows 2000 and XP structures.

16. Describe the bootup sequence employed by Windows 2000 and Windows XP.

17. Describe common command-line utilities associated with Windows 2000 and Windows XP.

OPERATING SYSTEM FUNDAMENTALS

FROM THE GEEK SQUAD

Jerry works as a sales associate at Best Buy store 254. He wants to join the Geek Squad and learn to work on computers. He has been talking to one of the store's Double Agents (DA) about what he needs to know to work in the Geek Squad.

Before talking to the DA, Jerry thought that he knew a lot about computer systems. However, he now finds that his computer knowledge set is much different than that of a technician. Jerry knows a lot of marketing and consumer-related information about computers but not a lot about their technical structure and repair side. Mainly, Jerry did not understand much of what the DA said when they were talking about operating systems and their structures. He must build a technician's view of operating systems, because this is half of the computer system and a much larger percentage of the problems users encounter with PCs.

INTRODUCTION

The general responsibilities of an operating system were presented in Chapter 2. This chapter will build on that description by presenting concepts that are fundamental to all operating systems. Every portion of the computer system must be controlled and coordinated so that the millions of operations that occur every second are carried out correctly and on time. In addition, it is the job of the operating system to make the complexity of the personal computer as invisible as possible to the user.

Operating systems are programs designed to control the operation of a computer system. As a group, they are easily some of the most complex programs devised. Likewise, the operating system acts as an intermediary between software applications nearly as complex, and the hardware they run on. Finally, the operating system accepts commands from the computer user and carries them out to perform some desired operation.

OPERATING SYSTEM BASICS

Essentials 3.0

IT Technician 3.0

Depot Technician 2.0

Literally thousands of different operating systems are in use with microcomputers. The complexity of each operating system typically depends on the complexity of the application the microcomputer is designed to fill.

Single-process systems

Multiple-process systems

batch mode

interactive mode

Multiuser

Multitasking

Multiprocessor

threads

tasks

command-line interpreter

graphical user interface (GUI)

parallel processing

There are two basic types of operating systems used with personal computers:

- **Single-process systems**—Systems that can work on only one task at one time
- **Multiple-process systems**—Systems that can work on several tasks at one time

In a single-process system, the operating system works with a single task only. These operating systems can operate in **batch mode** or **interactive mode**. In batch mode, the operating system runs one program until it is finished. In interactive mode, the operation of the program can be modified by input from external sources, such as sensors, or a user interface device.

Multiple-process operations can be organized in three different ways:

- **Multiuser**—Systems that accommodate more than one user at a time
- **Multitasking**—Systems that work on more than one task at a time
- **Multiprocessor**—Systems that divide the processing load into **threads** and distribute them between different processors

In multiuser and multitasking operations, the appearance of simultaneous operation is accomplished by switching between different **tasks** in a predetermined order.

The multiuser system switches between different users at multiple locations, whereas multitasking systems switch between different applications at a single location. In the large, multiple-user system, the operating system is likely to be stored on disk and have sections loaded into RAM when needed. This type of operating system must control several pieces of hardware, manage files created and used by various users, provide security for each user's information, and manage communications between different stations. The operating system is also responsible for presenting each station with a user interface that can accept commands and data from the user. This interface can be a **command-line interpreter** or a **graphical user interface (GUI)**.

In a multiprocessor operating system, tasks are divided among multiple microprocessors. This type of operation is referred to as **parallel processing**. All three types of multiple-process operating systems are described in Figure 9-1.

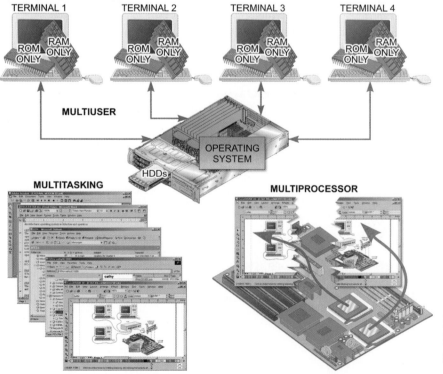

**Figure 9-1:
Multiple-Process
Operating Systems**

While simple microcomputers store the entire operating system in ROM, most microcomputers use a **bootstrapping** process to load the operating system into RAM. Bootstrapping describes an arrangement where the operating system is loaded into memory by a smaller program called the **bootstrap loader**.

The operating system can be loaded from a ROM chip, a floppy disk, a hard-disk drive, or another computer. The term **bootstrap** refers to the system pulling itself up by its own bootstraps, because in loading the more-powerful operating system files from the disk, it increases its on-board intelligence considerably. In personal computers, the bootstrap operation is one of the functions of the ROM BIOS.

bootstrapping

bootstrap loader

bootstrap

BOOTING THE SYSTEM

The *bootstrap* process is primarily used in disk drive−based systems to load an operating system to assume control of the system. All disk operating systems use the same basic process for booting up to the system hardware. In this section, we will describe a generic bootup process that covers the basic steps of booting up. This process exists in two distinct stages—*starting up the hardware* and *booting the operating system*. In the sections that follow, we will apply this general process to the bootup activities for Microsoft FAT−based and NTFS−based systems.

The Hardware Startup Process

The system startup sequence is basically a hardware-oriented operation until the bootstrap process begins. At this point, the hardware begins looking for an operating system to take over control of the hardware to increase its functionality. This process represents the starting point of everything related to operating systems. With the exception of some hardware configuration information that is collected during the initialization phase of the startup process and is eventually passed to the operating system, modern operating systems do not care what goes on prior to the bootup process. Until the bootstrap process occurs, the system runs the same no matter which operating system may eventually be started to take over control of the system.

At this point, we will review the basic hardware startup sequence. The key components and events of the PC-compatible hardware system are as follows:

- *System Startup or Reset*—When the system is started up or reset, the microprocessor is reset so that it begins taking instructions from a specified location in the ROM BIOS address range to test and initialize the system for operation.

- *POST*—The POST is a series of tests that are performed each time the system is turned on. The different tests check the operation of the microprocessor, the keyboard, the video display, the floppy- and hard-disk drive units, as well as both the RAM and ROM memory units.

checksum

DRAM tests

- *Initial POST Checks*—The first instruction that the microprocessor executes causes it to jump to the POST test, where it performs standard tests such as the ROM BIOS **checksum** test (that verifies that the BIOS program is accurate), the system's various **DRAM tests** (that verify the bits of the memory), as well as a test of the system's CMOS RAM (to make certain that its contents have not changed due to a battery failure). During the memory tests, the POST displays a running memory count to show that it is testing and verifying the individual memory locations.

During these tests, the BIOS determines whether the system is being started from an off condition or being reset from some other state. When the system is started from an off condition, a cold boot is performed. However, simultaneously pressing the CTRL, ALT, and DEL keys while the system is in operation will generate a reset signal in the system and cause it to perform a shortened bootup routine. This operation is referred to as a **warm boot**, and allows the system to be shut down and restarted without turning it off. This function also allows the computer's operation to be switched to another operating system.

warm boot

- *System Initialization*—During this part of the program, startup values stored in the ROM BIOS IC are moved into the system's programmable devices to make them functional. These include the IRQ and DMA channel configurations along with the standard I/O addresses that make the system PC-compatible.

Plug and Play (PnP)

software handle (name)

resource conflicts

- *Plug-and-Play Configuration*—During the initialization process, the **Plug and Play (PnP)** BIOS checks the devices installed in the expansion slots to see what types they are, how they are configured, and which slots they are in. It then assigns each adapter a **software handle (name)** and stores its name and configuration information in a RAM table. Next, the BIOS performs an enumeration process to verify the adapter information against the system's basic configuration for **resource conflicts**. If no conflicts are detected, all the devices required for bootup will be activated.

- *CMOS Setup Checks*—During the initialization process, the BIOS checks the battery-powered CMOS RAM configuration storage area to determine what types of options are installed in the system. In PnP systems, these settings are established by the PnP process's autodetect functions. However, the CMOS settings can be entered for manual configuration during this period.

BIOS extension

C8000

C8800

- *Additional POST Checks*—After the final memory test and basic system configuration steps have been performed, the remaining I/O devices and adapters are tested.

- *BIOS Extensions*—After the POST and initialization processes have been completed, the BIOS checks the area of memory between C0000 and DFFFF for **BIOS extension** programs. IBM system designers created this memory area so that new or nonstandard BIOS routines could be added to the basic BIOS structure. BIOS extensions are created in 512-byte blocks that must begin at a 2 kB marker (e.g., **C8000**, C8200, C8400, **C8800**, etc.), as illustrated in Figure 9-2. These extended firmware routines match software commands from the system to the hardware they support. Therefore, the software running on the system does not have to be directly compatible with the hardware.

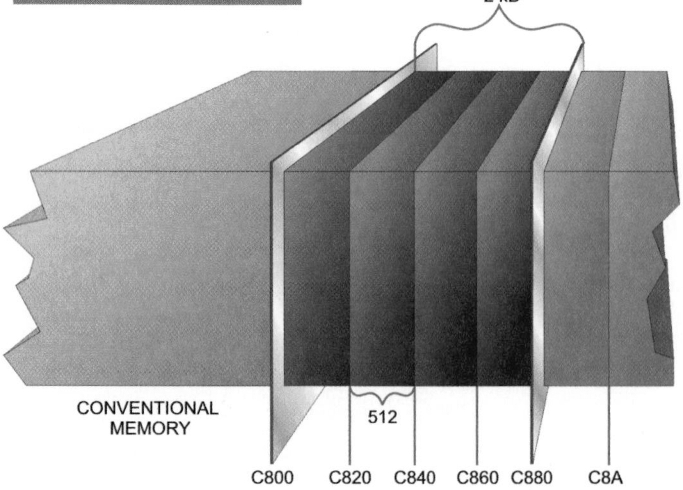

Figure 9-2: BIOS Extension Blocks

Advanced video cards contain **video BIOS** code, either in a ROM IC or built directly into the video controller ASIC. The IBM EGA and VGA standards allow for on-board ROM that uses addresses between C0000 and C7FFF. Likewise, different types of HDD controller cards contain a BIOS extension IC that uses the address space between C8000 and C9FFF. Some current HDD controllers, such as SCSI adapters, reserve memory blocks between C8000 and CBFFF.

video BIOS

Another type of device that commonly uses the C000-D000 blocks are network adapter cards. These cards enable the computer to be connected to other computers in the local area. The BIOS extension code on a network card may contain an **initial program load** (**IPL**) routine that will cause the local computer to load up and operate with an operating system from a remote computer. This is the principle behind diskless workstations that boot up to remote computers and have no local disk drives.

initial program load (IPL)

At the successful completion of these tests, most systems produce a single beep tone through the system speaker to announce the end of the hardware portion (POST/Initialization) phase of the start-up process and the beginning of the software portion (bootup) of the start-up sequence.

The Operating System Bootup Process

After the POST and initialization phases have been completed, the BIOS begins the process of booting up to an operating system. As we've already mentioned, this operation can occur on a local computer through its disk drives, or it can be performed from a remote computer across a network. A simple, single-operating system, single-disk bootup process is described in Figure 9-3. As you can see, it is a multiple-access operation that uses two different bootstrap routines to locate and load two different programs.

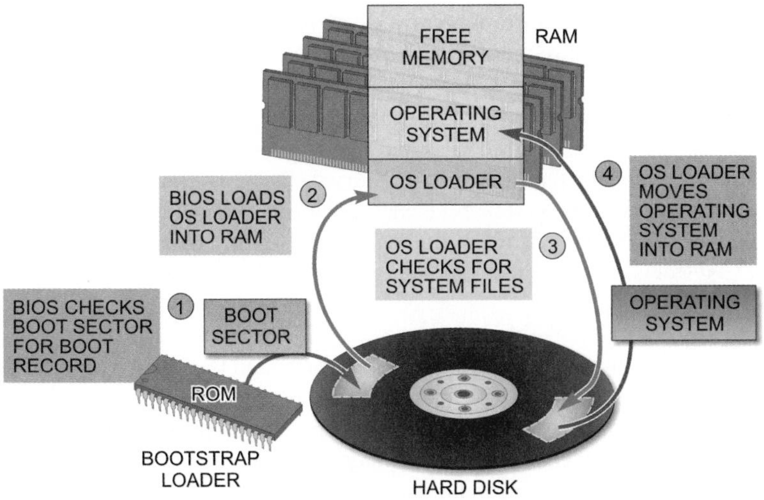

**Figure 9-3:
The Bootstrap
Operation**

The **bootup** process starts when the BIOS begins looking through the system for a **master boot record** (**MBR**). Older BIOS programs would automatically search for the master boot record in FDD drive A: first. However, in modern PC systems, the order in which the BIOS searches through the system drives for the boot record is governed by information stored in the system's CMOS. The order can be set to check the floppy drive first (if available) and then the hard drive, or to check the hard drive first, or to check the hard drive only. It can also be set to check the CD-ROM drive for a bootable disc.

bootup

master boot record (MBR)

boot sector

bootable disk

system disk

data disk

primary bootstrap loader

partition table

secondary bootstrap loader

partition loader

operating system loader

operating system boot record

command line

The very first section on any logical disk is called the **boot sector**. This sector may or may not contain an MBR. If the disk possesses a master boot record, it can boot up the hardware system to an operating system. The disk is then referred to as a **bootable disk**, or a **system disk**. If not, the disk is simply a **data disk** that can be used for storing information.

The MBR can reside on a local drive (A:, C:, D:, etc) or at any other location, such as a remote disk drive somewhere on another computer. In a networked system, a bootstrap loader routine can also be located in the ROM extension of a network card as described earlier. When the system checks the BIOS extensions, the bootstrap routine redirects the bootup process to look for a boot record on the disk drive of another computer. Any boot record on the local drives will be bypassed.

If the local boot sequence is not preempted by a network redirection, the BIOS routine executes a *Disk Drive Interrupt Service Routine* to activate the **primary bootstrap loader** program. This program checks for an MBR in the boot sector of each drive in the order it has been instructed to search. The first boot sector that the routine encounters that has an MBR is the one that will be used to boot the system. If the BIOS checks through the complete list of CMOS boot drive options and does not find an MBR, it will produce a message that might read "NO ROM BASIC—SYSTEM HALTED." This message is left over from the very first PCs that defaulted to a ROM-based BASIC programming tool when no bootable disk was found. While there is no more ROM BASIC to default to, the message provides a good troubleshooting tool in that you know the system could not find the boot files it needed to start up.

When a bootable disk is found, the primary bootstrap loader routine moves the MBR into RAM and then begins the process of loading the operating system. This step marks the end of the BIOS routine's active participation in the bootup process. However, the BIOS remains an integral part in the PC's operation as long as the system is in operation.

On hard-disk drives, the MBR contains two major sections—the **partition table** that contains information about how the disk is organized and the **secondary bootstrap loader** (also called the **partition loader** or **operating system loader**) code that contains directions for how and where the boot process should be conducted.

This routine looks for an **operating system boot record**, typically located on the disk. When it finds it, it loads the bigger boot record into RAM and begins executing it. This boot record brings special operating system files into memory so that they can control the operation of the system (i.e., the operating system). These files can belong to any operating system, such as Microsoft MS-DOS, Microsoft Windows, Linux, UNIX, Novell NetWare, or Apple OS-X. In PC systems, the dominant operating systems are different versions of Microsoft Windows.

In old MS-DOS systems, the command processor provided the basic user interface, called the **command line**. Users controlled the operation of the system by entering text-based commands and instructions at this prompt to run application programs from the other two software categories. However, in Windows systems, it launches the *graphical user interface* loader, which, in turn, loads the remainder of the operating system's structures and user interfaces. The total bootup process is shown in Figure 9-4.

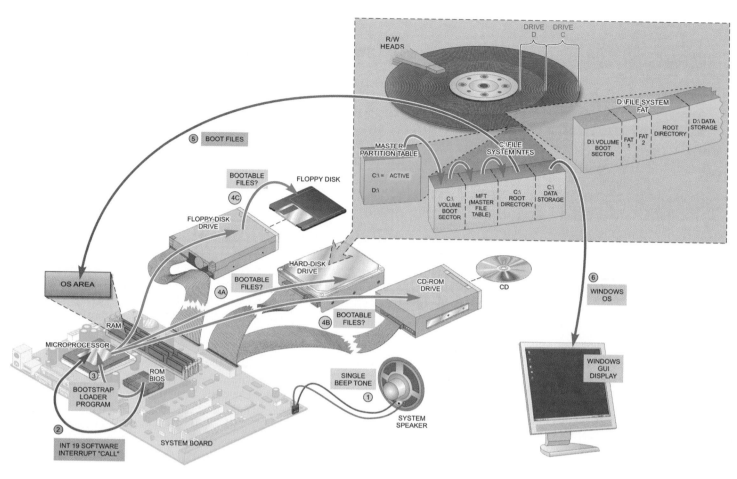

Now the operating system will control the movement of data and overall operation of the system. Up to this point, the user hasn't had anything to do with the operation of the system. This is why operating system software is referred to as system software.

Figure 9-4: The Bootup Process

The Windows 2000/XP Boot Process

All **Windows NT** (*New Technology*) operating system versions, which include Windows 2000 and all Windows XP variations, can work with two very different disk management structures. These Windows NT versions can work with the **file allocation table (FAT)**–based file management system used with older, consumer-oriented Microsoft operating systems (e.g., MS-DOS, Windows 3.x, and Windows 9x/Me). However, they also offer their own proprietary **Windows NT File System (NTFS)**. The NTFS structure is designed to provide better data security and to operate more efficiently with larger hard drives than do FAT systems.

Like any other PC system, the Windows PC starts up by running its POST, performing an initialization of its intelligent system devices, and performing a system boot process. It is in the boot process that the descriptions of the two operating systems diverge.

When the BIOS accesses the MBR on the hard drive, the MBR examines the disk's partition table to locate the active partition. The boot process then moves to the boot sector of that partition (referred to as the **partition boot sector**) located in the first sector of the active partition. Here the MBR finds the code to begin loading the secondary bootstrap loader from the root directory of the boot drive.

Essentials 3.1

Windows NT

file allocation table (FAT)

Windows NT File System (NTFS)

partition boot sector

NT Loader

NTLDR

kernel

minifile

BOOT.INI

Advanced Boot
Options Menu

NTDETECT.COM

registry

BOOTSECT.DOS

In the case of a Windows NTFS partition, the operating system loader is the **NT Loader** file named **NTLDR**. This file is responsible for loading the complete operating system into memory. Afterward, NTLDR passes control of the system over to the **kernel** and support files that make up the Windows operating system.

When the NTLDR file gains control of the system, its first action is to initialize the video hardware and switch the microprocessor into protected mode. NTLDR switches the processor to 32-bit flat memory mode.

Next, a temporary **minifile** system that can read both FAT and NTFS file structures is loaded to aid NTLDR in reading the rest of the system. Recall that Windows NT has the capability to work in either FAT or proprietary NTFS partitions. However, at this stage of the boot process, the operating system is still uncertain as to which system it will be using.

With the minifile system in place, the NTLDR can locate and read a special hidden boot loader menu file named **BOOT.INI**. If there is more than one operating system option defined in the BOOT.INI file, NTLDR uses this text file to generate the **Advanced Boot Options Menu** that is displayed on the screen. If no selection has been made after a given time delay, the default value is selected.

If Windows 2000 or Windows XP is designated as the operating system to be used, the NTLDR program executes a hardware detection file called **NTDETECT.COM**. This file is responsible for collecting information about the system's installed hardware devices and passing it to the NTLDR program. This information is later used to upgrade the Windows **registry** files that keep track of all the system's users, hardware devices, and settings.

If a different operating system is to be loaded, as directed by the *Advanced Boot Options Menu* entry, the NTLDR program loads a file called **BOOTSECT.DOS** and passes control to it. From this point, the BOOTSECT file is responsible for loading the desired operating system.

At this point, Windows 2000 places a progress bar on the screen along with the "*Starting Windows 2000*" message. No such message is displayed in Windows XP versions. Prior to this point, the user had the option to access the *Advanced Boot Menu* by pressing the F8 function key. This action is normally taken to enter a diagnostic start-up mode because something has gone wrong on a previous start-up attempt. Figure 9-5 shows a typical Advanced Boot Menu.

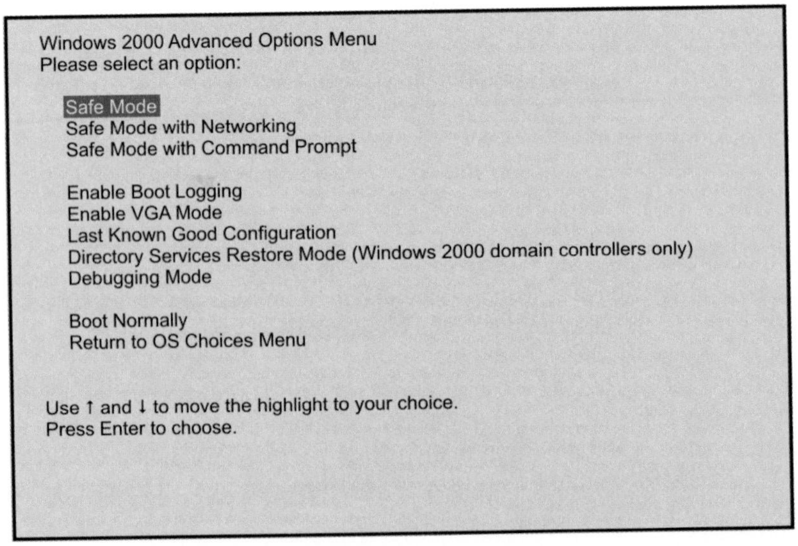

Figure 9-5: Windows 2000 Advanced Boot Menu

```
Windows 2000 Advanced Options Menu
Please select an option:

    Safe Mode
    Safe Mode with Networking
    Safe Mode with Command Prompt

    Enable Boot Logging
    Enable VGA Mode
    Last Known Good Configuration
    Directory Services Restore Mode (Windows 2000 domain controllers only)
    Debugging Mode

    Boot Normally
    Return to OS Choices Menu


Use ↑ and ↓ to move the highlight to your choice.
Press Enter to choose.
```

Next, NTLDR examines the partition for a pair of files named **NTOSKRNL.EXE** and **HAL.DLL**. NTOSKRNL.EXE is the Windows NT **kernel file** that contains the Windows NT core and loads its device drivers. HAL.DLL is the *Hardware Abstraction Layer* driver that holds the information specific to the microprocessor that the system is being used with.

NTOSKRNL.EXE

HAL.DLL

kernel file

Even though NTLDR reads the NTOSKRNL and HAL files at this time, it does not load or execute them. Instead, it uses a file named NTDETECT.COM to gather information about the hardware devices present and passes it to the NTLDR. The information gathered by NTDETECT is stored to be used later for updating the Hardware Registry hive. In particular, the NTDETECT checks for the following hardware items:

- Machine ID
- Bus types
- Video type
- Floppy drives
- Keyboard

- Pointing devices
- Parallel ports
- COMM ports
- SCSI adapters
- Math coprocessor

Once the information has been passed back to NTLDR, it opens the **System hive** portion of the registry to find the *Current Control Set*. This configuration information is moved into memory and is used to implement the system's **hardware profile**. The NTLDR file loads start-up device drivers into memory. At this point, the system displays the Starting Windows 2000 or Windows XP logo on the display along with a sliding progress bar that shows the degree of progress being made in loading the drivers.

System hive

hardware profile

After the drivers have been loaded, the NTLDR program passes control to the NTOSKRNL file to complete the bootup sequence. When NTOSKRNL gains control of the system, it initializes the HAL.DLL file along with the BOOTVID.DLL file and shifts the video display to graphics mode. It then initializes the drivers prepared by NTLDR and uses the NTDETECT information to create a temporary **Hardware hive** in memory.

Hardware hive

At this point, NTOSKRNL executes a *Session Manager* file titled SMSS.EXE to carry out prestart functions such as running a boot-time version of CHKDSK called AUTOCHK utilities to verify the readiness of the system. It also establishes parameters concerning the Windows 2000/XP virtual memory paging file (PAGEFILE.SYS) to hold RAM memory swap pages.

After these tasks have been performed, the Session Manager loads the console log-on service file (WINLOGON.EXE) to begin the authentication verification process. WINLOGON starts the local security authority subsystem (LSASS.EXE) and the print spooler (SPOOLS.EXE) along with their supporting files.

At this point in the start-up process, some Windows versions produce a CTRL+ALT+DEL window prompting the user to clear the system. When this key combination is pressed, the log-on screen is displayed, as shown in Figure 9-6. The Windows 2000/XP log-on process enables the operating system to configure itself specific for different users. Normal log-on involves entering a username and password. If no log-on information is entered, then default values will be loaded into the system. In Windows 2000, the log-in screen always appears even if the system is not being used with a network.

Figure 9-6: The Windows Logon Dialog Box

Finally, WINLOGON loads the Service Controller (SCREG.EXE) that completes the loading process by bringing in the remaining devices and services, including the Windows shell and desktop. The Windows 2000 and Windows XP shell program is the **Windows desktop**. Figure 9-7 depicts the Windows desktop. This interface is somewhat different for each Windows version, and each is covered in detail in Chapter 10.

Windows desktop

┌─ **TEST TIP** ─────────┐
Memorize the files involved
in the Windows 2000/XP boot
process and the order in which
they are executed.
└──────────────────────┘

Figure 9-7: The Windows Desktop

┌─ **TEST TIP** ─────────┐
Be aware of what the
NTBOOTDD.SYS file
does in a Windows
2000/XP system.
└──────────────────────┘

Using NTBOOTDD.SYS—If the Windows 2000/XP system employs a SCSI disk drive, and the system does not have a BIOS with SCSI support, a driver file named NTBOOTDD.SYS will need to be present in the root directory of the system partition. This condition must also be noted in the BOOT.INI file by placing a mark in its SCSI(x) or Multi(x) locations.

Essentials 3.1

WINDOWS 2000/XP STRUCTURES

When fully loaded into the system, the Windows 2000/XP logical structure exists as depicted in Figure 9-8. It is a modular operating system that allows for advances in computing technology to be integrated into the system. The operating system exists in two basic layers referred to as *modes*. These two levels are the **kernel mode** and the **user mode**.

kernel mode

user mode

Basically, the operating system runs in the *kernel mode*, whereas applications run in the *user mode*. The kernel mode is the operating mode in which the program has unlimited access to all memory, including those of system hardware, the user mode applications, and other processes (such as I/O operations). The user mode is a more restrictive operating mode in which no direct access of hardware is permitted.

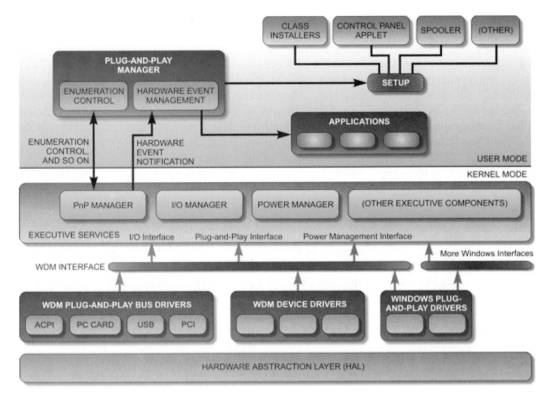

Figure 9-8:
Windows 2000/XP
Organizational
Structure

Application programming interfaces (APIs) are routines, protocols, and tools built into the operating system that provide application designers with consistent building blocks with which to design their applications. For the user, these building blocks lead to consistent interfaces being designed for all applications.

Application programming interfaces (APIs)

The Windows 2000/XP **Hardware Abstraction Layer (HAL)** is a library of hardware drivers that operate between the actual hardware and the rest of the system. These software routines act to make the architecture of every device look the same to the operating system. The **Microkernel** works closely with the HAL to keep the system's microprocessor as busy as possible. It does this by scheduling threads for introduction to the microprocessor on a priority basis.

Hardware Abstraction Layer (HAL)

Microkernel

The **PnP manager** employs the enumeration process to discover PnP devices installed in the system. Afterwards, it loads appropriate drivers and creates registry entries for those devices. These drivers and entries are based on *Information* (*INF*) scripts developed by Microsoft and the hardware vendors for the device being configured. The PnP manager then allocates the system's resources (IRQ settings, DMA channels, and I/O addresses) to the devices that require them.

PnP manager

The **power manager** interacts with key system components to conserve energy (especially useful for portable computers) and reduce wear on system devices. Both managers depend on PnP-compliant system components as well as the APM and ACPI power management standards described in Chapter 8, *Portable Systems*.

power manager

System Memory Management

Most modern operating systems, including Windows 2000, Windows XP, UNIX, and LINUX, do not employ the address segmentation features of the Intel microprocessors to divide up the computer's memory allocations. Because segments can overlap, memory usage errors can occur when an application attempts to write data into a space being used by the operating system or by another application.

Using the **flat memory model**, the memory manager sections map each application's memory space into contiguous pages of physical memory. Using this method, each application is mapped into a truly unique address space that cannot overlap any other address space. The lack of segment overlap reduces the chances of applications interfering with each other and helps to ensure data integrity by providing the operating system and other processes with their own memory spaces.

Figure 9-9 illustrates the flat memory model concept. In this example, the 32-bit address produced by the microprocessor contains three parts dictated by the operating system. The highest 10 bits of the address point to the page table directory. This table sets the address boundaries for each page of memory in the memory. This guarantees that there is only one method of entering the page space—through this table. Therefore, there is no chance for poorly written software to stray into a page on which it has not been assigned. The lower 22 bits of the address are used to access a particular page within the block of addresses specified in the Page Table Directory (bits $12-21$), and then to select a particular physical address within the page (bits $0-11$).

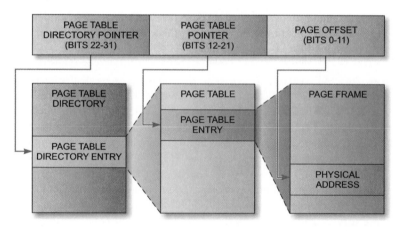

Figure 9-9: Flat Memory Model

In Windows 2000 and basic versions of Windows XP, the memory management scheme employs a full 32-bit architecture with a flat memory model that provides direct access to up to 4 GB of memory. In this model, the **virtual memory manager (VMM)** assigns unique memory spaces to every active 32-bit and 16-bit application. Under *Windows XP Professional x64 Edition*, this structure is expanded to provide a 64-bit memory model that provides the ability to access up to 128 GB of RAM.

The VMM module maps each application's memory space into contiguous 4 kB pages of physical memory. Using this method, each application is mapped into a truly unique address space that cannot overlap any other address space. The lack of segment overlap reduces the chances of applications interfering with each other and helps to ensure data integrity by providing the operating system and other processes with their own memory spaces.

Virtual Memory

The term **virtual memory** is used to describe memory that isn't what it appears to be. Virtual memory is actually disk drive space that is manipulated to seem like RAM. Software creates virtual memory by **swapping files** between RAM and the disk drive, as illustrated in Figure 9-10. This memory management technique effectively creates more total memory for the system's applications to use. However, because there is a major transfer of information that involves the hard-disk drive, an overall reduction in speed is encountered with virtual memory operations.

virtual memory

swapping files

Windows 2000/XP establishes virtual memory by creating a **PAGEFILE.SYS** file on the disk when the operating system is installed. Its default size is typically set at 1.5 times the amount of RAM installed in the system. It is possible to optimize the system's performance by distributing the swap file space between multiple drives. It can also be helpful to relocate the swap file away from slower or heavily used drives. The swap file should not be placed on mirrored or striped volumes. Also, don't create multiple swap files on logical disks that exist on the same physical drive.

PAGEFILE.SYS

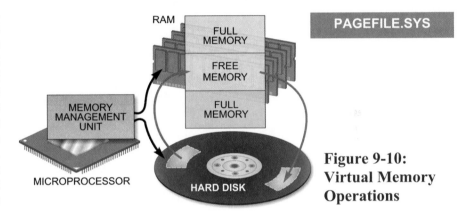

Figure 9-10:
Virtual Memory
Operations

When the Windows 2000/XP VMM has exhausted the physical RAM locations available, it maps memory pages into virtual memory addresses, as described in Figure 9-11. The VMM shifts data between RAM memory and the disk in 4 kB pages. This theoretically provides the operating system with a total memory space that equals the sum of the system's physical RAM and the capacity of the hard-disk drive.

TEST TIP

Memorize the filenames of the Windows 2000/XP virtual memory swap file.

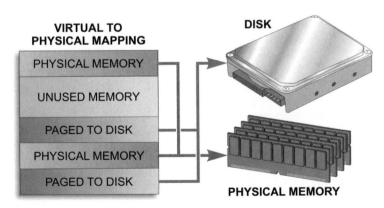

Figure 9-11:
Virtual Memory in
Windows 2000/XP

To take advantage of high RAM capacity, Windows automatically tunes itself to take advantage of any available RAM. The VMM dynamically balances RAM between paged memory and the virtual memory disk cache.

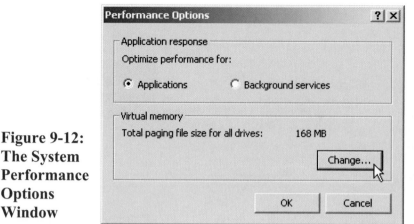

In Windows 2000 and XP, the virtual memory functions are located under the Control Panel's System icon. Simply click on its *Advanced* tab followed by the *Performance Options* button to view the dialog window depicted in Figure 9-12.

Figure 9-12: The System Performance Options Window

Clicking on the *Change* button in the dialog window will produce the *Virtual Memory* dialog window shown in Figure 9-13. Through this dialog window, you can establish and configure an individual swap file for each drive in the system. By highlighting a drive, you can check its virtual memory capabilities and settings. Entering new values in the dialog windows and clicking on the *Set* button will change the values for the highlighted drive.

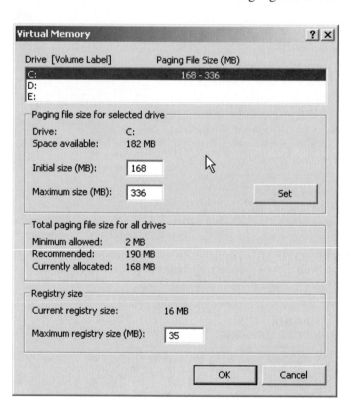

Figure 9-13: The Virtual Memory Dialog Window

Windows 2000/XP Registries

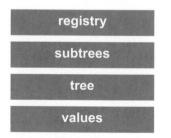

Windows 2000 and Windows XP use a multipart database, called the **registry**, to hold system and user configuration information. The Windows 2000/XP registry organization is depicted in Figure 9-14. The registry is segmented into Headkeys, Subkeys, and Values. The HKEYs are also referred to as **subtrees**, while the registry is referred to as the **tree**. Under each subtree are one or more subkeys, which, in turn, will have one or more **values** assigned to them.

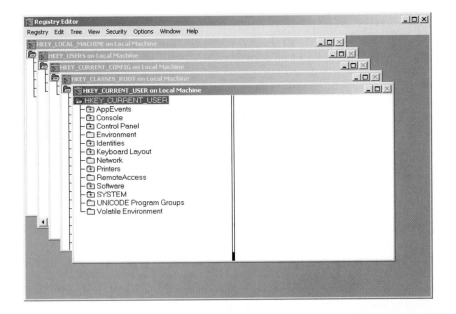

Figure 9-14: The Windows 2000/XP Registry

In Windows 2000 and Windows XP, the contents of the registries are physically stored in five files referred to as **hives**. Hives represent the major divisions of all the registry's keys, subkeys, subtrees, and values.

The hives of the Windows 2000/XP registry are:

- The **SAM hive**
- The **Security hive**
- The **Software hive**
- The **System hive**
- The **Default hive**

These files are stored in the *\Winnt\System32\Config* directory along with a backup copy and log file for each hive.

Configuration information about every user who has logged into the system is maintained in a named subfolder of the *\Winnt\Profiles* directory. The user settings portion of the registry is stored in the NTUSER.DAT file located in the *\Documents_and_Settings\userxxx* folder. The system portions of the registry are stored in the Software, System, Security, and SAM hives. These files are stored in the *\Winnt\System32\Config* folder. The major Windows hives and their files are described in Table 9-1.

SUBTREE/KEY	FILE	LOG FILE
HKEY_LOCAL_MACHINE\SOFTWARE	SOFTWARE	SOFTWARE.LOG
HKEY_LOCAL_MACHINE\SECURITY	SECURITY	SECURITY.LOG
HKEY_LOCAL_MACHINE\SYSTEM	SYSTEM	SYSTEM.LOG
HKEY_LOCAL_MACHINE\SAM	SAM	SAM.LOG
HKEY_CURRENT_USER	NTUSER.DAT	NTUSER.DAT.LOG
HKEY_USERS\DEFAULT	DEFAULT	DEFAULT.LOG

Table 9-1: Major Windows Hives and Their Files

hives

SAM hive

Security hive

Software hive

System hive

Default hive

The HKEY_LOCAL_MACHINE subtree is the registry's major branch. It contains five major keys. The SAM and SECURITY keys hold information such as user rights, user and group information for domain or workgroup organization, and password information. The HARDWARE key is a database built by device drivers and applications during bootup. The database is updated each time the system is rebooted. The SYSTEM key contains basic information about start-up including the device drivers loaded and which services are in use. The **Last Known Good configuration** settings are stored here. Finally, the SOFTWARE key holds information about locally loaded software, including file associations, OLE information, and configuration data.

The second most important subtree is HKEY_USERS. It contains a subkey for each local user that accesses the system. These subkeys hold desktop settings and user profiles.

The Windows 2000/XP **Control Panel wizards**, described in the following chapter, are designed to safely and correctly make changes to the registry in a manner in which the operating system can understand. Editing the registry directly opens the possibility of changing an entry in a manner that the operating system cannot accept, and thereby, of crashing the system. In either event, it is a good practice to back up the contents of the registry before installing new hardware or software or directly modifying the registry.

┌─ **TEST TIP** ─────────┐
Be aware of the utility used to directly edit registry entries of the various operating systems.
└────────────────────────┘

The contents of the registry can be edited directly using the Windows 2000/XP **RegEdit** utility (**Regedt32.exe**). Although there is a RegEdit tool in Windows 2000, this tool was designed to work with Windows 9x clients. The editor used to manage the Windows 2000/XP registry is Regedt32. However, in some instances, such as registry searches, the RegEdit utility offers superior operation, even in Windows 2000 and XP. This file is located in the *\Winnt\System32* folder. As with the Windows 9x packages, most changes to the registry should be performed through the wizards in the Windows 2000/XP Control Panels.

GEEK SQUAD CASE FILE #92189

Agent 42 has been dispatched to a customer site to upgrade one of their old Windows NT 4.0 workstations to Windows 2000 Professional. Because the equipment is getting a little old, he wants to protect the system in case he needs to reinstall it. Agent 42 is not too familiar with Windows NT, but he knows that there is a utility for creating a backup of the system's registry. What is this utility named and where can he access it?

WINDOWS 2000/XP FILE SYSTEMS

As mentioned earlier in this chapter, all Windows NT operating system versions can employ two very different disk management structures—*FAT systems* and *NTFS structures*. The Windows 2000/XP component responsible for implementing and managing these files systems (along with the CDFS file system used with CR-ROM drives and UDF file system used with DVDs and other digital media devices) is the **installable file system** (IFS) Manager section of the I/O manager. The following sections will cover the structures and operations associated with both major Windows file systems.

Managing Partitions

Physical hard-disk drives can be divided into multiple **logical drives**. This operation is referred to as **partitioning** the drive. When a physical drive is partitioned, it is divided into multiple logical drives that are handled by the file management system as separate, independent drives. This is because each logical drive has been given logical structures required to let it operate as an independent drive unit.

logical drives

partitioning

With earlier versions of MS-DOS, partitioning became necessary because the capacity of hard drives exceeded the ability of the existing FAT structure to track all of the possible sectors. Dividing the physical disk space into multiple logical drives where each new drive contains another *complete file tracking structure* solved this dilemma. The operating system sees each logical drive on the hard drive as a completely new disk to which it assigns a new, unique drive letter.

Figure 9-15 illustrates the concept of creating multiple logical drives on a single hard drive. This is usually done for purposes of organization and increased access speeds. The operating system's partitioning utility creates the disk's boot sector and establishes partition parameters (partition table) for the system's use.

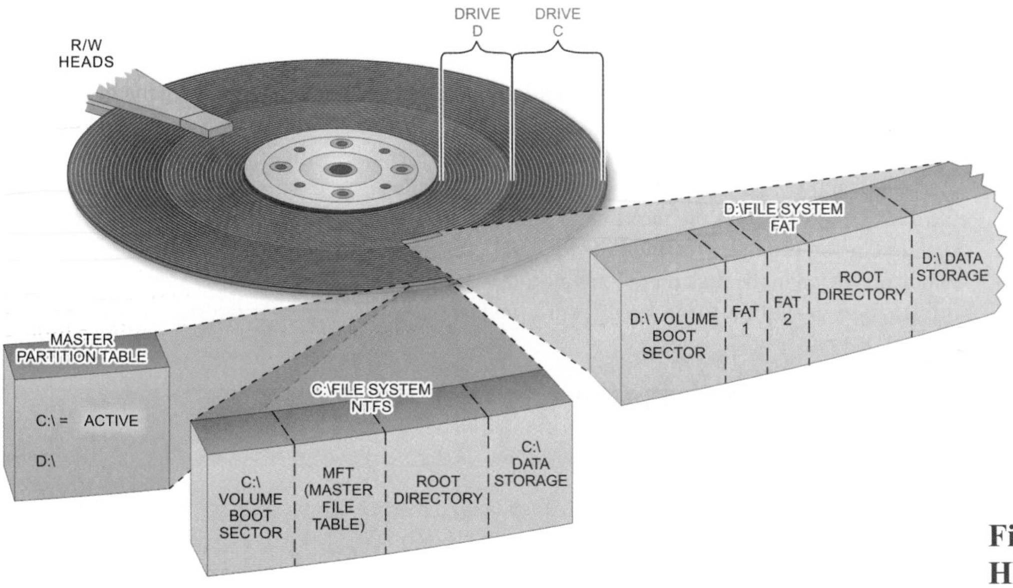

Figure 9-15: HDD Partitions

FAT systems provide for two partitions on an HDD unit. The first, or the **primary partition**, must exist as drive C. After the primary partition has been established and properly configured, an additional partition, referred to as an **extended partition**, is also permitted. However, the extended partition may be subdivided into 23 logical drives. The extended partition cannot be deleted if logical drives have been defined within it.

primary partition

extended partition

active partition

The **active partition** is the logical drive that the system will boot to. The system files must be located in this partition, and the partition must be set to "Active" for the system to boot up from the drive.

┌─ **TEST TIP** ─────────────────────
Be aware of how the primary partition, the extended partition, and the active partition are related.
└────────────────────────────────

An NTFS system can accommodate up to four primary partitions. It also supports extended partitions. If extended partitions are used, the system has a maximum of three primary partitions and a single extended partition. As with the FAT system, extended partitions cannot be marked as active in the NTFS system. NTFS extended partitions can also be divided into logical drives. However, only primary partitions and logical drives can be formatted and assigned a drive letter. The total number of primary partitions plus logical drives cannot exceed 32 for a single hard drive.

You may also hear or see partitions referred to as volumes when dealing with Windows 2000 and Windows XP. In instances involving a single physical drive, these terms will work interchangeably. However, the volume takes on a different meaning when applied to contiguous memory spaces that span multiple physical drives, such as RAID volumes.

In local and wide area networks (LANs and WANs), the concept of logical drives is carried a step further. A particular hard-disk drive may be a logical drive in a large system of drives along a peer-to-peer network. On the other hand, a very large, centralized drive may be used to create several logical drives for a client/server type of network. This is accomplished by creating a logical **mapping** between the operating system and the desired drive, so that the local system handles the mapped drive as one of its own drives.

mapping

In some applications, partitioning is used to permit multiple operating systems to exist on the same physical drive. Because each partition on the drive contains its own boot sector, FAT, and root directory, each partition can be set up to hold and boot up to a different operating system.

partition table

On a partitioned drive, a special table, called the **partition table**, is created in the boot sector at the very beginning of the disk. This table holds information about the location and starting point of each logical drive on the disk, along with information about which partition has been marked as active and a master boot record. The partition table is located at the beginning of the disk, because this is the point where the system looks for bootup information. When the system checks the MBR of the physical disk during the boot process, it also checks to see which partition on the disk has been marked as active. It then jumps to that location, reads the information in that partition boot record, and boots to the operating system in that logical drive.

GEEK SQUAD CASE FILE #88188

Trent K., Special Agent 26, has been approached by a customer who has a new computer with Windows 2000 Professional installed on it. However, she has several LINUX-based applications that she routinely uses and wants to move those applications onto the new computer. How can you help the special agent accomplish this?

High-Level Formatting

The high-level format procedure is used to load the operating system into a partition on the disk. In the case of disks with multiple partitions, it is possible to load different operating systems in each partition. Most operating systems are capable of operating with different file systems.

For example, Windows 2000 and Windows XP can work with either **FAT partitions** or **NTFS partitions**. This is referred to as creating a **dual boot** system. However, under some configurations, the system will not be able to use space in both partitions at the same time. Some thought must go into setting up and operating disks that contain multiple partition formats. Likewise, other operating systems, such as Linux and NetWare, can be loaded into partitions on disks that also contain Windows versions.

Root Directory

NTFS partitions

dual boot

FAT Disk Organization

In a FAT-based system, this operation re-creates the two **file allocation tables (FATs)** along with a **root directory** on the disk. These elements tell the system what files are on the disk and where they can be found. Modifying the Format command with a /S after the drive letter designation moves the operating system files to the drive.

file allocation tables (FATs)

root directory

Figure 9-16 describes the organization of a FAT disk and illustrates the position of the boot sector, the file allocation tables, and the root directory. The remainder of the disk is dedicated to data storage. As mentioned previously, the first area on each logical disk or partition is the boot sector. Although all formatted partitions have this sector, they do not all have the optional master boot record located in the sector. Only disks created to be bootable disks have this record.

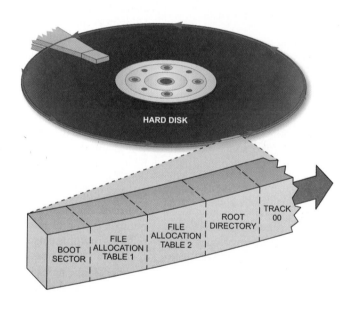

Figure 9-16: FAT Disk Organization

File Allocation Tables

The second logical section of a FAT disk is occupied by the file allocation tables (FATs). This area consists of information about how the disk is organized. Basically, the system logs two copies of disk space usage and availability in these tables.

In older versions of MS-DOS, the amount of space dedicated to tracking the sectors on the disk was 16 bits. Therefore, only 65,536 sectors could be accounted for. This parameter limited the size of an MS-DOS partition to 32 MB (33,554,432 bytes). To more effectively manage the space on larger disks, modern disk operating systems versions divide the disk into groups of logically related sectors called **allocation units**, or **clusters**. In a FAT-based system, the cluster is the smallest piece of manageable information.

The sectors on a FAT disk hold 512 bytes each. Files, on the other hand, can be any length. Therefore, a single file may occupy several sectors on the disk. The operating system's disk handling routine breaks a file into sector-sized chunks and stores it in a cluster of sectors. In this manner, DOS uses the cluster to track files instead of sectors. Because the file allocation table only has to handle information for a cluster, instead of for each sector, the number of files that can be tracked in a given length table is greatly increased.

The organization of a typical FAT is described in Table 9-2. The first two entries are reserved for DOS information. Each cluster after that holds a value. Each value may represent one of three conditions. A value of 0 indicates that the cluster is available and can be used for storage. Any number besides 0 or FFF indicates that the cluster contains data, and the number provides the location of the next cluster in a chain of clusters. Finally, a value of FFF (or FFFF in a 16-bit entry) indicates the end of a cluster chain.

allocation units

clusters

TEST TIP

Know what the smallest unit of storage in a disk-based system is.

TEST TIP

Know the size of sectors in an IBM/PC-compatible disk.

Table 9-2: File Allocation Table Structure

CLUSTER NUMBER	CONTENTS
Cluster 0	Reserved for DOS
Cluster 1	Reserved for DOS
Cluster 2	3 (contains data; go to cluster 3)
Cluster 3	4 (contains data; go to cluster 4)
Cluster 4	7 (contains data; go to cluster 7)
Cluster 5	0 (free space)
Cluster 6	0 (free space)
Cluster 7	8 (contains data; go to cluster 8)
Cluster 8	FFF (end cluster chain)
Cluster 9	0 (free space)
●	●
Cluster X	0 (free space)
Cluster Y	0 (free space)
Cluster Z	0 (free space)

On floppy disks, common cluster sizes are one or two sectors long. With hard disks, the cluster size may vary from 1 to 16 sectors in length. The FAT keeps track of which clusters are used and which ones are free. It contains a 12- or 16-bit entry for each cluster on the disk. The 12-bit entries are used with floppy disks and hard disks that are smaller than 17 MB. The 16-bit entries are employed with hard-disk drives larger than 17 MB. Obviously, the larger entries allow the FAT to manage more clusters.

In free clusters, a value of zero is recorded. In used clusters, the cluster number is stored. In cases where a file requires multiple clusters, the FAT entry for the first cluster holds the cluster number for the next cluster used to store the file. Each subsequent cluster entry has the number of the next cluster used by the file. The final cluster entry contains an end-of-file marker code that tells the system that the end of the file has been reached.

cluster links

cross-linked

These **cluster links** enable the operating system to store and retrieve virtually any size file that will fit on the disk. However, the loss of any link will make it impossible to retrieve the file and use it. If the FAT becomes corrupted, chained files can become **cross-linked** with each other, making them useless. For this reason, two complete copies of the FAT are stored consecutively on the disk under the FAT-based disk structure. The first copy is the normal working copy, and the second FAT is used as a backup measure in case the contents of the first FAT become corrupted.

The FAT32 File System

The OSR2 version of Windows 95 introduced an enhanced FAT32 file management system as an upgrade for the existing FAT16 file system. FAT32 was designed to optimize storage space and is based on the fact that the size of the registers in the operating system's FAT determines the size of the clusters for a given size disk partition.

Smaller cluster sizes are better because even a single byte stored in a cluster will remove the entire cluster from the available storage space on the drive. This can add up to a lot of wasted storage space on larger drives. The default cluster size set by Microsoft for FAT32 is 4 kB. Table 9-3 describes the relationships between clusters and maximum partition sizes for various FAT entry sizes.

The structure of the FAT32 system makes it incompatible with other versions of Windows file systems including FAT16 and NTFS. Therefore, it is also not compatible with disk utilities and troubleshooting packages designed for those file systems.

Table 9-3:
FAT Relationships

FAT TYPE	PARTITION SIZE	CLUSTER SIZE (IN BYTES)
FAT12	16 MB	4096
FAT16	32 MB	2048
FAT16	128 MB	2048
FAT16	256 MB	4096
FAT16	512 MB	8192
FAT16	1 GB	16384
FAT16	2 GB	32768
FAT32	<260 MB	512
FAT32	8 GB	4096
FAT32	16 GB	8192
FAT32	32 GB	16384
FAT32	>32 GB	32768

The Root Directory

The next section following the FAT tables is the disk's root directory. This is a special directory that is present on every FAT-based disk. It is the main directory of every logical disk and serves as the starting point for organizing information on the disk.

The location of every directory, subdirectory, and file on the disk is recorded in this table.

Each directory and subdirectory (including the root directory) can hold up to 512 32-byte entries that describe each of the files in them. The first eight bytes contain the file's name, followed by three bytes for its filename extension.

The next 11 bytes define the file's **attributes**. Attributes for DOS files include

- Read only
- System file
- Volume label
- Subdirectory entry
- Archive (backup) status

TEST TIP

Remember the number of entries that directories in a FAT-based system can hold.

---

attributes

Two bytes are used to record the time the file was created or last modified. This is followed by two additional bytes that record the date the file was created or last modified. The final four bytes are divided equally between the value of the *starting cluster number* and a *byte count number* for the file. Unlike the previous information in the directory, the information associated with the last four bytes is not displayed when a directory listing is displayed on the screen.

Because each root directory entry is 32 bytes long, each disk sector can hold 16 entries. Consequently, the number of files or directories that can be listed in the root directory is dependent on how many disk sectors are allocated to it. On a hard-disk drive, there are usually 32 sectors set aside for the root directory. Therefore, the root directory for such a disk can accommodate up to 512 entries. A typical 3-1/2" 1.44 MB floppy has 16 sectors reserved for the root directory and can hold up to 224 entries.

On a floppy disk, the logical structure usually has a group of files located under the root directory. Directory structures can be created on floppies, but due to their relatively small capacity, this is not normally done. A hard drive, however, is another matter. With hard drives, it is normal to organize the disk into directories and subdirectories as described earlier in the previous chapter.

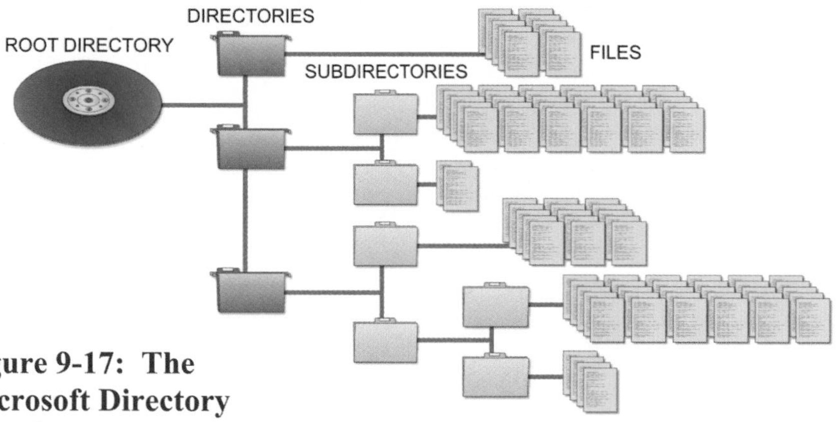

Technically, every directory on a disk is a subdirectory of the root directory. All additional directories branch out from the root directory in a tree-like fashion. Therefore, a graphical representation of the disk drive's directory organization is called a **directory tree**. Figure 9-17 depicts the directory organization of a typical hard drive.

directory tree

Figure 9-17: The Microsoft Directory Tree Structure

NTFS Disk Organization

The Windows NTFS structure uses 64-bit entries to keep track of storage on the disk (as opposed to the 16- and 32-bit entries used in FAT and FAT32 systems). When a partition is formatted in an NTFS system, several system files and the MFT are created on the disk. These files contain the information required to implement the file system structure on the disk. The system files produced during the NTFS formatting process include th following:

1. A pair of MFT files (the real one and a shorter backup version).

2. A log file to maintain transaction steps for recovery purposes.

3. A volume file that includes the volume name, NTFS version, and other key volume information.

4. An attribute definition table file.

5. A root filename file that serves as the drive's root folder.

6. A cluster bitmap that represents the volume and shows which clusters are in use.

7. The partition boot sector file.

8. A bad cluster file containing the locations of all bad sectors identified on the disk.

9. A quota table for tracking allowable storage space on the disk for each user.

10. An upper case table for converting lowercase characters to Unicode uppercase characters.

Unicode is a 16-bit character code standard, similar to 8-bit ASCII, used to represent characters as integer numbers. The 16-bit format allows it to represent over 65,000 different characters. This is particularly useful for languages that have very large character sets.

Figure 9-18 illustrates the organization of an NTFS disk volume. The first information in the NTFS volume is the 16-sector **partition boot sector**. The sector starts at physical sector-0 and is made up of two segments—the **BIOS parameter block** and the **code section**. The BIOS parameter block holds information about the structures of the volume and disk file system. The code section describes the method to be used to locate and load the start-up files for the specified operating system. This code loads the Windows NT bootstrap loader file **NTLDR** in Intel-based computers running Windows NT.

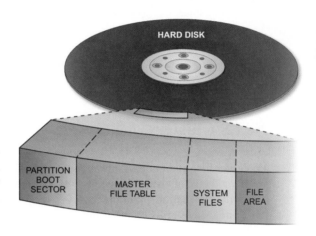

**Figure 9-18:
The Organization of an
NTFS Disk Volume**

Master File Tables

The core component of the NTFS system is the **master file table (MFT)**. This table replaces the file allocation tables in FAT-based systems and contains information about each file stored on the disk. In order of occurrence, this information includes

- Header information

- Standard information

- Filename

- Security information

- Data

The MFT contains information about each folder and file on the volume. The NTFS system relates to folders and files as a collection of attributes. All the folder's, or file's, elements (i.e., filename, security information, and data) are considered to be attributes. The system allocates space in the MFT for each file or folder based on the cluster size being used on the disk.

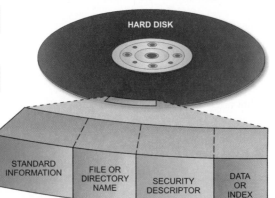

standard information

security descriptor

resident attributes

**Figure 9-19: Basic
NTFS Master File
Table Record**

Figure 9-19 shows a typical MFT record. The first section of the record contains **standard information** about the file or folder, such as its date and time stamp and number of links. The second section contains the file's or folder's name. The next section contains the file's or folder's **security descriptor** (which holds information about who can access the file, who owns it, and what they may do with it).

The next section of the MFT record is the data (or index) area. The information for smaller files and folders is stored in the MFT. The data area is 2 kB long on smaller drives but can be bigger on larger drives. When the data fit within the MFT record, the various portions of the file are referred to as **resident attributes**.

NTFS Clusters

data runs

**virtual cluster
numbers (VCNs)**

**nonresident
attributes**

attribute list

For larger files and folders that cannot be stored in a single MFT, the NTFS may resort to two other methods of using the MFT. For medium-size folders and files, the system stores standard information about the folder or file, such as its name and time information, in the MFT and then establishes index links to external cluster locations to store the rest of the data. The external clusters are referred to as **data runs** and are identified by 64-bit **virtual cluster numbers (VCNs)** assigned to them. The attributes stored outside the MFT are referred to as **nonresident attributes**. An **attribute list** that contains the locations of all the file's or folder's nonresident attributes is created in the data area of the MFT record. This arrangement is depicted in Figure 9-20.

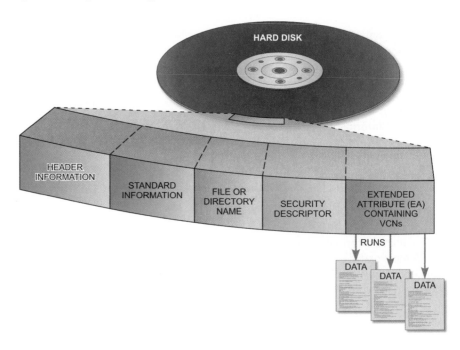

**Figure 9-20:
Extended MFT
Record Organization**

For extremely large files that cannot be identified by a single MFT record, multiple MFT records are employed. The first record contains a pointer to the additional MFT records. The original MFT record contains the file's or folder's standard information, followed by index links to other MFT records that, in turn, have index links to the actual data runs. In these cases, the data are stored outside the table and can theoretically range up to 16 EB (exabytes, 2^{60}).

All entries in the MFT are stored in alphabetical order by filename. Like FAT systems, NTFS systems use the cluster as the basic unit of disk storage. In Windows 2000 and XP, NTFS clusters could range between 512 bytes and 64 kB, depending on the size of the drive and how the disk was prepared. Clusters can range up to 64 kB when established using the FORMAT command from the command prompt. Clusters are numbered sequentially on the disk from start to end. These numbers are referred to as **logical cluster numbers (LCNs)**. The default cluster size is determined by the volume size and can be specified in the Disk Administrator utility. Table 9-4 lists the default cluster sizes for NTFS systems in Windows 2000/XP environments.

logical cluster
numbers (LCNs)

PARTITION SIZE	SECTORS/CLUSTER	CLUSTER SIZE
<512 MB	1	512 bytes
512 MB-1 GB	2	1 kB
GB-2 GB	4	2 kB
2 GB-4 GB	8	4 kB
4 GB-8 GB	16	8 kB
8 GB-16 GB	32	16 kB
16 GB-32 GB	64	32 kB
>32 GB	128	64 kB

**Table 9-4:
NTFS Cluster Sizes**

The smaller cluster size of the NTFS format makes it more efficient than FAT formats for storing smaller files. It also supports larger drives (over 1 GB) much more efficiently than FAT16 or FAT32 structures. The NTFS system is more complex than the FAT systems and, therefore, is not as efficient for smaller drives.

NTFS Advantages

The Windows 2000 operating system supports several file management system formats including FAT, FAT16, FAT32, **CDFS** (the **compact disk file system** is used on CD-ROM disks), and NTFS4, along with its own **NTFS5** format. The latter version enables administrators to establish **disk quotas** limiting the amount of hard drive space users can have access to. The new NTFS system also offers enhanced system security. NTFS5 provides an **encrypted file system** and secure network protocol and authentication standards.

In most situations, the NTFS system offers better performance and features than a FAT16 or FAT32 system. The exceptions to this occur when smaller drives are being used, other file systems are being used on the same drive, or the operating system crashes.

compact disk file
system (CDFS)

NTFS5

disk quotas

encrypted file system

┌─ **TEST TIP** ─────
Be aware of the different file system types supported by Windows 2000 and Windows XP.

In most other situations, the NTFS system offers

- More efficient drive management due to its smaller cluster size capabilities

- Support for very large drives made possible by its 64-bit clustering arrangement

- Increased folder and file security capabilities

- Disk quotas governing how much disk space individual users can take up

- Disk compression that enables the system to create more available disk space by compressing folders and files

- File encryption that encodes data stored on the hard drive, making it much more difficult for data to be stolen

- Recoverable file system capabilities

- Built-in RAID support

share permissions

NTFS permissions

In Windows 2000 and Windows XP, the administrator has the tools to limit what the user can do to any given file or directory. This is accomplished through two types of security permissions—**share permissions** and **NTFS permissions**. Both of these permission types are discussed in the Administrating Windows section of Chapter 10, *Windows Operating Systems*.

The NTFS structure provides recoverable file system capabilities including a hot-fix function and a full recovery system to quickly restore file integrity. The NTFS system maintains a copy of the critical file system information. If the file system fails, the NTFS system will automatically recover the system from the backup information as soon as the disk is accessed again. In addition, NTFS maintains a transaction log to ensure the integrity of the disk structure even if the system fails unexpectedly.

Security is a critical issue in large business networks. The NTFS file system provides security for each file in the system, as well as complete file access auditing information to the system administrator. NTFS files and folders can have permissions assigned to them whether they are shared or not. Data security is also improved by the ability of Windows to support mirrored drives.

You should recall from the RAID discussions in Chapter 5, *Mass Storage Systems*, that mirroring is a technique of storing separate copies of data on two different drives. This protects the data from loss due to hard drive failures. This is a very important consideration when dealing with server applications. Additional fault tolerance capabilities such as disk mirroring, drive duplexing, striping, RAID, and support for UPS are provided with the Windows 2000 and Windows XP operating systems.

WORKING FROM THE COMMAND LINE

Even though MS-DOS is a thing of the past, you should not take this to mean that command-line operations have gone away—quite the contrary. Computer technicians are regularly required to perform tests at the command-line level because the system is broken and cannot be taxed to support convenient graphical displays. Therefore, you must understand how Microsoft organizes disks so that you can navigate through their systems to find needed information and tools during the troubleshooting process.

The organizational structure of a computer's logical disks or partitions is typically described as being like a common office file cabinet, similar to the one depicted in Figure 9-21. Think of the drives in a computer as the file cabinet structure. Our example has three drawers that can be opened. Think of these drawers as **disk drives** labeled A, B, and C/D. Inside each drawer are hanging folders that can hold different types of items. Think of these as **directories** (although Microsoft refers to them as folders in their Windows products).

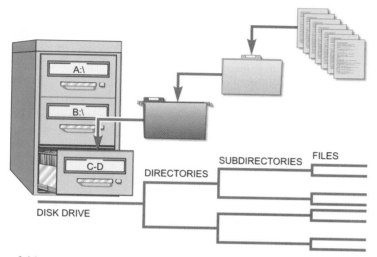

Figure 9-21: Microsoft Disk Organizational Structure

The hanging folders may contain different types of items or other individual folders. Think of these individual folders as **subdirectories**. For organizational purposes, each hanging folder and each individual folder must have a unique label on it.

Inside each hanging folder, or individual folder, are the items being stored. In a real file cabinet, these items in the folders are usually documents of different types. However, pictures and tapes and other items related to the folders can also be stored in them.

Think of the items inside the folders as **files**. Disk-based systems manage data blocks by giving them file names. Recall that a file is simply a block of logically related data, given a single name, and treated as a single unit. Like the contents of the folders, files can be programs, documents, drawings or other illustrations, sound files, and so on.

In order to find an item in the cabinet, you simply need to know which drawer, hanging folder, and folder it is located in. This concept can be translated directly to the computer system. To locate a particular file, you simply need to know which drive, directory, and subdirectory it is located in. In FAT systems, the **path** to any file in the system can be written as a direction to the computer so that it will know where the file is located. This format for specifying a path is as follows:

C:\directory name\subdirectory_name\filename

where the C: specifies the C disk drive. The directory name, subdirectory name, and filename would naturally be replaced by real names. The **backslashes** (\) after each item indicate the presence of a directory or subdirectory. The first slash indicates a special directory, called the root directory, which is present on all logical disks.

filename

extension

If the direction is to a file, the **filename** is always placed at the end of the path. MS-DOS allowed for basic filenames of up to eight characters. It also provided for an **extension** of up to three characters. The extension is separated from the main portion of the filename by a period and is used to identify what type of file it is (e.g., the filename *file1.ltr* could be used to identify a letter created by a word processor). This arrangement has become known as the 8.3 format.

.COM

.SYS

NOTE

Filename extensions are not actually required for most files. However, they become helpful in sorting between files in a congested system. You should be aware that the operating system reserves some three-letter combinations, such as **.COM** and **.SYS**, for its own use. More information about filenames and extensions is presented in the subsequent section concerning file-level commands.

Command-Line Functions

user interface

graphical user interfaces (GUIs)

Command Prompt

CMD (or COMMAND)

The operating system is responsible for providing the system's **user interface**. All operating systems for PCs provide some type of command-line user interface. The command line was the user interface for MS-DOS systems and remains the interface of choice for many LINUX and UNIX users. In the PC environment, different **graphical user interfaces (GUIs)** are the interfaces of choice for consumers. However, technicians often use the command-line environment for troubleshooting and repair purposes. This interface is valuable because it enables the technician to access and manipulate the system without the presence of the system's GUI, which can mask symptoms and complicate the diagnostic troubleshooting procedure.

TEST TIP

Know how to access the Command Prompt interface in Windows 2000/XP.

Windows 2000 and Windows XP systems provide a **Command Prompt** emulator. When this feature is engaged in Windows 2000/XP, no separate DOS version is being accessed. They simply provide a DOS-like interface that enables users to perform some command-line functions. To access the MS-DOS emulator in Windows 2000 or Windows XP, you must select the *Run* option from the Start menu and then type the command **CMD** (or **COMMAND**) into the dialog box.

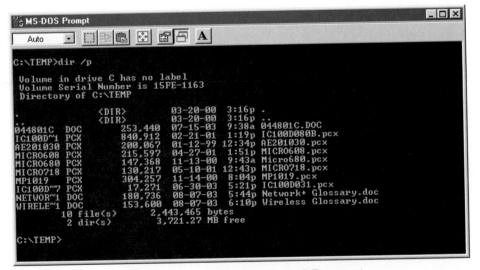

The command line is the space immediately following the command line's drive letter prompt on the screen. All command-line functions and actions are typed in the space immediately to the right of the prompt. These commands are executed by pressing the ENTER key on the keyboard. The command prompt for using the C: hard-disk drive as the active directory is displayed in Figure 9-22.

Figure 9-22: The Command Prompt

From the command prompt, all command-line functions can be entered and executed. Application programs can also be started from this prompt. These files can be discerned by their filename extensions. Files with **.COM**, **.EXE**, or **.BAT** extensions can be started directly from the prompt. The .COM and .EXE file extensions are reserved by Microsoft operating systems and can only be generated by programs that can correctly configure them. BAT files are simply ASCII text files that have been generated using command-line functions. Because .BAT files contain operating system commands mixed with .COM and .EXE files, Microsoft operating systems can execute them from the command line.

Programs with other types of extensions must be **associated** with one of these three file types to be executed. The user can operate application software packages such as graphical user interfaces, word processors, business packages, data communications packages, and user programming languages.

.COM

.EXE

.BAT

associated

┌─ **TEST TIP** ─────────────
Know which file types can be executed directly from the command-line prompt.

As an example, the core component of a word processor could be a file called WORDPRO.EXE. Document files produced by word processors are normally given filename extensions of .DOC (for document) or .TXT (for text file). In order to view one of these documents, you would first need to run the executable file and then use its features to load, format, and display the document.

The user can also enter and execute operating system commands from the command line to perform different functions. These commands can be grouped into *drive-level commands*, *directory-level commands*, and *file-level commands*. The format for using command-line statements in a Microsoft command-line environment is:

COMMAND (space) SOURCE location (space) DESTINATION location

COMMAND (space) location

COMMAND

The first example illustrates how command line operations that involve a source and a final destination, such as moving a file from one place to another, are entered. The second example illustrates how single-location operations, such as formatting a disk in a particular disk drive, are specified. The final example applies to commands that occur in a **default location**, such as obtaining a list of the files on the current disk drive.

default location

You can also place one or more software **switches** at the end of the basic command to modify its actions when executed. A switch is added to the command by adding a space, a *fore-slash* (/), and a single letter after it:

switches

COMMAND (space) option /switch

┌─ **NOTE** ─────────────────────────
Common MS-DOS command switches include /P for page, /W for wide format, and /S for system. Different switches are used to modify different command functions. You can obtain definitions for switches that can be added to a given command by typing "/?" after the command.
└──────────────────────────────────

Drives and Disks

In Microsoft operating systems, each disk drive in the system is identified by a single-letter name (such as A:). This name must be specified when giving the system commands, so that they are carried out using the proper drive. The format for specifying which drive will perform a command-line function uses the drive's identifier letter in the command, followed by a colon (e.g., A: or C:).

Figure 9-23 illustrates how the various disk drives are seen by a typical stand-alone system. Microsoft operating systems reserve the letters A: and B: for the first and second floppy drives. Multiple hard-disk drive units can be installed in the system unit, along with the floppy drives. The Microsoft operating system recognizes a single hard-disk unit in the system as **drive C:**. Disk management utilities can be used to partition a single physical hard-disk drive into two or more **volumes** that the system recognizes as logical drives C:, D:, and so on.

drive C:

volumes

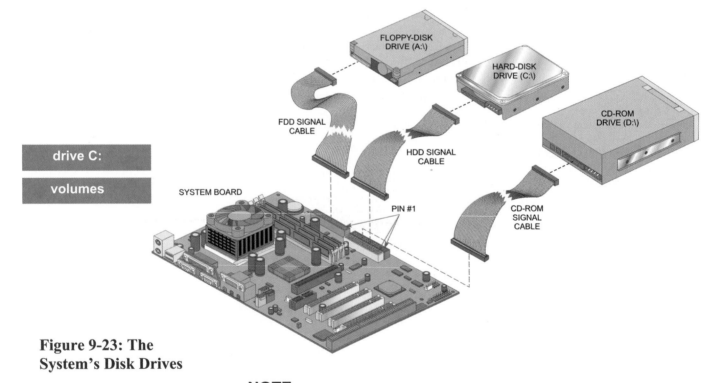

Figure 9-23: The System's Disk Drives

┌─ **NOTE** ─────────────────────────────────────

The figure shows a CD-ROM drive as drive D: because this is becoming the most common PC configuration. In the case of networked systems, logical drive letters may be extended to define up to Z drives. These drives are actually the hard drives located in remote computers. The operating system in the local machine treats them as additional logical drives (i.e., F:, G:, etc.).

└──

Conversely, a second hard-disk drive can be added to the system and set up as logical drive D:. It may also be partitioned into smaller logical drives that the system recognizes as drives E:, F:, and so on.

Some command-line operations are simplified by allowing the system to choose the location for the command to be carried out through the use of **default settings** (special predetermined settings that are automatically used by the system when no specific directions are given to change the settings). These settings are remembered in the operating system and used by the system when the operator does not specify a particular location for events to happen. The default drive in most systems is the A: drive. In systems with two or more drives, it is imperative that the user specify exactly where the specified action is to occur.

default settings

Drive-Level Command-Line Operations

The following command-line function pertains to **drive-level operations**. Although there were several drive level commands available in the MS-DOS environment, there is only one such command of interest in the Windows 2000/XP environment. The command must be typed at the command prompt.

drive-level operations

The only drive level command used with Windows operating systems is the **FORMAT** command. This command is used to prepare a new disk, or a removable storage device, for use with an operating system. Actual data locations are marked off on the disk for the tracks and sectors, and bad sectors are marked. In addition, the directory is established on the disk. New disks must be formatted before they can be used. Typical variations of the FORMAT command include:

FORMAT

> C:\>FORMAT X creates the tracks, sectors, and file system structure on the specified disk (in this case the X: drive).
>
> C:\>FORMAT X:/FS:*file-system* causes system files for the specified file system (FAT, FAT32 or NTFS) to be copied onto the disk after it has been formatted. Floppy disks can only be formatted with FAT.
>
> C:\>FORMAT A:/f:*size* specifies the size of the floppy disk to format.
>
> C:\>FORMAT D:/Q causes the system to perform a quick format operation on the D: disk or device. This amounts to removing the FAT and root directory from the disk.

> **NOTE**
>
> Use the *format /?* entry at the command prompt to review all of the options available with the Format command in Windows 2000 and Windows XP.

Directories

As mentioned earlier, in hard drive−based systems, it is common to organize related programs and data into areas called directories. This makes them easier to find and work with, because modern hard drives are capable of holding large amounts of information. As described earlier, most directories can hold up to 512 directory or filename entries.

> **TEST TIP**
>
> Be aware that Microsoft directories can hold up to 512 directory or filename entries.

The following list of commands is used for **directory-based operations** in Microsoft systems. The format for using them is identical to that for the disk-related commands discussed earlier.

- **DIR**: The Directory command gives a listing of the files on the disk that is in the drive indicated by the drive specifier.

> C:\>DIR or DIR C: If DIR is used without any drive specifier, the content of the drive indicated by the prompt will be displayed. The command may also be used with modifiers to alter the way in which the directory is displayed.
>
> C:\>DIR/W displays the entire directory at one time across the width of the display.
>
> C:\>DIR/P displays the content of the directory one page at a time. You must press a key to advance to the next display page.

- **MKDIR** (**MD**): Will create a new directory in an indicated spot in the directory tree structure.

> C:\>MD C:\DOS\XXX will create a new subdirectory named XXX in the path that includes the ROOT directory (C:\) and the DOS directory.

- **CHDIR** (**CD**): Will change the location of the active directory to a position specified by the command.

> C:\>CD C:\DOS will change the working directory from the C: root directory to the C:\>DOS directory.

- **RMDIR** (**RD**): Remove Directory will erase the directory specified in the command. You cannot remove a directory until it is empty or if it is currently active.

> C:\>RD C:\DOS\forms would remove the DOS subdirectory "forms," provided it were empty.

CREATING AND MANAGING FILES

Disk operating systems handle information in the form of files. Therefore, the computer technician must be aware of the methods that different operating systems use to create and manipulate files. The following sections of the chapter will begin the discussion of files in a disk-based system.

Files and Filenames

Disk-based systems store and handle related pieces of information in groups called files. The system recognizes and keeps track of the different files in the system by their **filenames**. Therefore, each file in the system is required to have a filename that is different from that of any other file in its directory.

If two files having the same name were present within the same directory of the system, the computer would become confused and fail to operate properly. This is because it could not tell which version of the file it should work on. Each time a new file of information is created, it is necessary to give it a unique filename by which the operating system can identify and store it.

Files are created through programming packages, or by applications. When they are created, they must be assigned a filename. In the command-line environment, there were a few rules that you must remember when creating new filenames. As described earlier in this chapter, the filename consists of two parts: a *name* and an *extension*. The filename is a combination of alphanumeric characters and is between one and eight characters in length. The extension is an optional addition to the name that begins with a period, and it is followed by one to three characters.

Extensions are not required on filenames, but they often prove useful in describing the content of a file or in identifying different versions of the same file. If a filename that already exists is used to store another file, the computer will write the information in the new file over that of the old file, because it will assume that they are both the same file. Therefore, only the new file will still exist. The information in the old file will be lost.

Many software packages automatically generate filename extensions for files they create. The software does this so that other parts of the program, which may work with the same file, will be able to identify where the file came from, or what form it is in.

In any event, you should remember the following seven items when assigning and using filenames:

1. All files must have a filename.

2. All filenames must be different than any other filename in the system, or on the disk presently in use.

3. DOS filenames are up to eight characters long with an optional three-character extension (separated from the basic filename by a period).

4. When using a filename in a command, you must also use its extension, if one exists.

5. Some special characters are not allowed in filenames. These are: [,], :, ;, +, =, \, /, <, >, ?, and ,.

6. When telling DOS where to carry out a command, you must tell it on which disk drive the operation is to be performed. The drive must be specified by its letter name followed by a colon (A:, B:, C:, etc.).

7. The complete and proper way to specify a file calls for the drive specifier, the filename, and the filename extension, in that order (i.e., B:filename.ext).

TEST TIP

Know which characters can legally be used in an MS-DOS filename.

The following commands are used to carry out file-level operations. The format for using them is identical to that for the disk and directory-related commands discussed earlier. However, the command must include the filename and its extension at the end of the directory path. Depending on the operation, the complete path may be required, or a default to the currently active drive will be assumed.

COPY

- **COPY**: The file copy command copies a specified file from one place (disk or directory) to another:

  C:\>COPY C:filename.ext E:filename.ext

  > C:\>COPY C:\directory\filename.ext C:\directory\ is used if the file is to have the same name in its new location; the second filename specifier can be omitted.

XCOPY

- **XCOPY**: This command copies all the files in a directory, along with any subdirectories and their files. This command is particularly useful in copying files and directories between disks with different formats (e.g., from a 1.2 MB disk to a 1.44 MB disk):

  C:\>XCOPY C:\Temp A: /s

  > This command would copy all of the files and directories from the \Temp directory on drive C: (except hidden and system files) to the disk in drive A:. The /s switch instructs the XCOPY command to copy directories and subdirectories.

DEL

ERASE

- **DEL** or **ERASE**: This command allows the user to remove unwanted files from the disk when typed in at the command prompt:

  C:\>DEL filename.ext

  C:\>ERASE B:filename.ext

  > A great deal of care should be taken when using this command. If a file is erased accidentally, it may not be retrievable.

REN

- **REN**: Enables the user to change the name or extension of a filename:

  C:\>REN A:filename.ext newname.ext

  C:\>COPY A:filename.ext B:newname.ext

  > Using this command does not change the contents of the file, only its name. The original filename (but not the file) is deleted. If you wish to retain the original file and filename, a copy command, using different filenames, can be used.

- **FC**: This file-compare command compares two files to see if they are the same. This operation is normally performed after a file copy has been performed to ensure that the file was duplicated and located correctly:

    C:\>FC C:\directory\filenameA.ext C:\directory\:filenameB.ext

> If the filename was changed during the copy operation, the command would have to be typed as:
>
>   C:\>FC C:\directory\filename.ext C:\directory\newname.ext

- **ATTRIB**: Changes file attributes such as **Read-only** (+R or –R), **Archive** (+A or –A), **System** (+S or –S), and **Hidden** (+H or –H). The + and – signs are to add or subtract the attribute from the file.

    C:\>ATTRIB +R C:\DocumentsandSettings\My Documents\memos.doc

> This command sets the file MEMOS.DOC as a read-only file. Read-only attributes protect the file from accidentally being overwritten. Similarly, one of the main reasons for giving a file a *hidden* attribute is to prevent it from accidentally being erased. The *system* attribute is reserved for use by the operating system and marks the file as a system file.

A common error message encountered when working with command-line operations is the "bad command or file name" error message. This type of error message generally occurs when the path specified to the location of a file is incorrect, or when the filename is missing or misspelled.

Command-Line Shortcuts

Microsoft operating systems provide some **command-line shortcuts** through the keyboard's function keys. Some of the most notable are the F1 and F3 function keys. The F1 key will bring the previous command back from the command-line buffer, one character at a time. Likewise, the F3 key will bring back the entire previous command through a single keystroke.

When using filenames in command-line operations, the filename appears at the end of the directory path in the source and destination locations.

The * notation is called a **wildcard** and allows operations to be performed with only partial source or destination information. Using the notation as *.* tells the software to perform the designated command on any file found on the disk using any filename and extension.

A question mark (?) can be used as a wildcard to represent a single character in a filename or extension. Multiple question marks can be used to represent multiple characters in a filename or extension.

filter commands

More

Find

Sort

pipe symbol (|)

Data from a command can be modified to fit a prescribed output format through the use of **filter commands**. The main filter commands are **More**, **Find**, and **Sort**. The filter command is preceded by a **pipe symbol** (\|) on the command line when output from another command is to be modified. For example, to view the contents of a batch file that is longer than the screen display can present at one time, type **Type C:\xxx.bat\|more**. If the information to be modified is derived from another file, the less than (<) symbol is used.

Command-Line Utilities

Because technicians must frequently work form the command line, many of the tools you use must also be available from the command prompt. Many of the repair operations used to get the system back up and running (so that it can use the graphical interface) involve disk drive−related problems. The following list describes most of the major tools associated with maintaining and repairing the system's hard-disk drives. They are covered in greater detail, along with the remaining disk drive−related tools, in Chapter 12, *Operating System Troubleshooting*.

- CHKDSK—This hard disk−checking utility inspects the data on a specified disk for errors and corruption. It is used to find and possibly repair cluster chains that make up files that have become disconnected from each other.

- DEFRAG—This disk drive utility organizes disjointed information on hard-disk drives into more efficient patterns to speed up the access and read times associated with finding and reading data from the drive.

- DISKPART—This Windows XP disk-partitioning utility is used to establish logical structures on a hard-disk drive.

Other available *operating system tools* enable administrators and technicians to manage files and memory usage in the PC system. Three such tools are

- EDIT—This command opens the operating system's default text editor package. This editor can be used to alter and repair text-based files.

- MEM—This command-line utility is used to display the amount of used and free memory in a system.

System Configuration Utility

- MSCONFIG—(Also known as the **System Configuration Utility**)This command line utility is used to isolate conflicting items in the startup process. It is typically used after the system has been started using one of the Safe Mode startup options.

- HELP—Typing Help at the command prompt will bring up a list of the commands available for command prompt use, along with a short description of what the command does. You can obtain a more technical description of how the command is used by typing the command at the prompt along with a /? Switch.

Other command-line utilities are available for network troubleshooting purposes. The various Windows operating system versions contain a suite of TCP/IP troubleshooting utilities that are executed from the command prompt. The most widely used TCP/IP commands are

- IPCONFIG—This command-line utility enables you to determine the current TCP/IP configuration (MAC address, IP address, and subnet mask) of the local computer. It also may be used to request a new TCP/IP address from a DHCP server. IPCONFIG is available in both Windows 2000 and Windows XP.

- PING—This TCP/IP networking utility is used to verify network connections between computers.

- Tracert—The Tracert utility is another very important network troubleshooting tool that is used from the command prompt. It provides route information for packets of information being sent across a network.

Be aware that these are only two of several TCP/IP utilities covered in detail in Chapter 12, *Operating System Troubleshooting*.

GEEK SQUAD CASE FILE #87995

The customer from the previous case file in this chapter believes that there may be some corrupt files on the hard drive preventing it from booting up. They have called Special Agent Trent K. back to see if there is some troubleshooting tool that they can use to check out the disk drive and possibly repair any corruption problems present. They think that there is, but they are not sure as to what it is or how to use it. What advice should Trent give them?

KEY POINTS REVIEW

This chapter has discussed basic attributes associated with operating systems. In particular, examples of basic operating system functions, structure, operation, and file management were discussed. Review the following key points before moving into the Review and Exam Questions sections to make sure you are comfortable with each point. Afterward, answer the Review Questions that follow to verify your knowledge of the information.

- There are literally thousands of different operating systems in use with microcomputers. The complexity of each operating system typically depends on the complexity of the application the microcomputer is designed to fill.

- In multiuser and multitasking operations, the appearance of simultaneous operation is accomplished by switching between different tasks in a predetermined order. The multiuser system switches between different users at multiple locations, whereas multitasking systems switch between different applications at a single location.

- The POST is actually a series of tests that are performed each time the system is turned on. The different tests check the operation of the microprocessor, the keyboard, the video display, the floppy- and hard-disk drive units, as well as both the RAM and ROM memory units.

- After the initial set of POST checks, the BIOS routine initializes the system's intelligent devices. During this part of the program, start-up values stored in the ROM chip are moved into the system's programmable devices to make them functional.

- After the initialization and POST are completed, the BIOS checks the area of memory between C0000 and DFFFF for BIOS extension programs.

- If an error or setup mismatch is encountered, the BIOS will issue an error code, either in message form on the display screen, or in beep-coded form through the system's speaker.

- The bootup process starts when the BIOS begins looking through the system for a master boot record (MBR). This record can reside on drive A: or C: or at any other location.

- While the system is operating, the BIOS continues to perform several important functions. It contains routines on which the operating system calls to carry out basic services. These services include providing BIOS interrupt calls (software interrupt routines) for such operations as printer, video, and disk drive accesses.

- The disk's file allocation tables occupy the second section of a FAT disk. This area contains information about how the disk is organized. Basically, the system logs the use of the space on the disk in these tables.

- The next section following the FAT tables is the disk's root directory. This is a special directory that is present on every FAT disk. It is the main directory of every logical disk, and serves as the starting point for organizing information on the disk.

- The command line is the space immediately following the drive letter prompt on the screen. All commands are typed in this space. They are executed by pressing the EN-TER key on the keyboard.

- Disk-based systems store and handle related pieces of information in groups called files. The system recognizes and keeps track of the different files in the system by their filenames. Therefore, each file in the system is required to have a filename that is different from that of any other file in its directory.

- Remember the following seven items when assigning and using filenames: All files must have a filename. All filenames must be different from any other filename in the system, or on the disk presently in use. MS-DOS filenames are up to eight characters long with an optional three-character extension (separated from the basic filename by a period). When using a filename in a command, you must also use its extension, if one exists. Some special characters are not allowed in filenames. These are: [,], :, ;, +, =, \, /, <, >, ?, and ,. When telling MS-DOS where to carry out a command, you must tell it on which disk drive the operation is to be performed. The drive must be specified by its letter name followed by a colon (A:, B:, C:, etc.). The complete and proper way to specify a file calls for the drive specifier, the filename, and the filename extension, in that order (i.e., B:filename.ext).

- The term virtual memory is used to describe memory that isn't what it appears to be. Virtual memory is actually disk drive space that is manipulated to seem like RAM.

- Windows 2000/XP offer their own proprietary NTFS file system that is designed to provide better data security and to operate more efficiently with larger hard drives than do FAT systems.

- The NTFS file system provides security for each file in the system, as well as complete file access auditing information to the system administrator. NTFS files and folders can have permissions assigned to them whether they are shared or not.

- The NTFS system includes security features that allow permission levels to be assigned to files and folders on the disk. These permissions set parameters for activities that users can conduct with the designated file or folder.

- The Windows 2000/XP HAL is a library of hardware drivers that operate between the actual hardware and the rest of the system. These software routines act to make every architecture look the same to the operating system.

- The content of the registry is physically stored in five files referred to as hives. Hives represent the major divisions of all the registry's keys, subkeys, subtrees, and values.

- The Windows 2000/XP registry hive files are stored in the *\Winnt\System32\Config* directory along with a backup copy and log file for each hive.

- The content of the registry can be edited directly using *Regedt32.exe*. This file is located in the *\Winnt\System32* folder. However, most changes to the registry should be accomplished through the wizards in the Windows Control Panel.

- The Windows 2000/XP log-on allows the operating system to configure itself for specific users. Normal log-on involves entering a username and password.

REVIEW QUESTIONS

The following questions test your knowledge of the material presented in this chapter.

1. Which file contains user-related configuration information for Windows 2000/XP systems?

2. What type of operating system breaks the tasks associated with a process into various threads for execution?

3. Ideally, where should all changes to registry items be made from to prevent introducing settings that the operating system cannot deal with?

4. What does the "*" character stand for when used in a Microsoft filename?

5. What is the function of the BOOT.INI file in a Windows XP system?

6. Name three advantages of the Windows NT file system over FAT16 and FAT32 file management structures.

7. Which wildcard characters tell the operating system to perform the designated command on any file found on the disk using any filename and extension?

8. From the system start-up point of view, how do a cold and a warm boot differ?

9. What are the names of the files involved in the Windows 2000/XP boot process, and in what order are they executed?

10. What is the primary function of the NTLDR file?

11. What command-line command is used to view hidden system files?

12. What does the System attribute indicate about the file?

13. A _____ is the standard method of organizing files into directories and subdirectories on magnetic disks.

14. How many files or entries can be included in the root directory?

15. What system components are involved in virtual memory operations?

EXAM QUESTIONS

1. Which command prepares a disk to function as a self-booting disk?
   a. Boot /s
   b. FDISK /s
   c. Format /s
   d. MEM /s

2. In terms of managing processes, what type of operating system is MS-DOS?
   a. A single-process, batch-mode operating system
   b. A multiple-process, interactive-mode operating system
   c. A multiple-process, batch-mode operating system
   d. A single-process, interactive-mode operating system

3. The portion of the Windows 2000/XP structure that communicates directly with the system hardware is _____.
   a. the Win32 Executive
   b. the User Mode
   c. the HAL
   d. the Hardware Subsystem

4. What is an appropriate command that will access the command prompt environment in Windows 2000 and Windows XP?
   a. CMD
   b. Execute
   c. GO
   d. RUN

5. What is the virtual memory file used by Windows XP Professional specifically called?
   a. Winswp.386
   b. Pagefile.sys
   c. Swap File
   d. Winswp.XP

6. Which file is primarily responsible for guiding the Windows 2000/XP bootup process?
   a. NTLDR
   b. NTDETECT.COM
   c. NTOSKRNL.EXE
   d. BOOT.INI

7. Which file is the primary operating system loader looking for during the bootup process?
   a. An OS loader
   b. A primary bootstrap loader
   c. A master boot record
   d. The root directory

8. In a Windows NT/2000 system, the NTBOOTDD.SYS file is used to _____.
   a. boot the system
   b. enable SCSI disk drives
   c. detect bootup errors
   d. enable double-density booting

9. What is the smallest piece of manageable information in a Microsoft disk operating system?
   a. The cluster
   b. The sector
   c. The word
   d. The track

10. The value of having virtual memory is that _____.
    a. it creates more total memory for applications.
    b. it moves applications into the upper memory area.
    c. it shadows applications so that they can be recovered if the operating system crashes.
    d. it creates additional extended memory for applications to operate in.

CHAPTER 10

WINDOWS OPERATING SYSTEMS

OBJECTIVES

Upon completion of this chapter and its related lab procedures, you should be able to perform these tasks:

1. Identify the procedures for installing Windows 2000 and Windows XP and bringing them to a basic operational level on a new system.

2. Upgrade systems from Windows 9x or Windows NT 4.0 to Windows 2000 or Windows XP.

3. Identify procedures for changing options, configuring, and using the Windows 2000/XP printing subsystem.

4. Navigate through the Windows 2000/XP system, including Internet Explorer.

5. Differentiate between the capabilities of Windows XP Professional, Home Edition and Media Center Edition.

6. Identify the procedures for loading/adding device drivers and the necessary software for certain devices in a Windows 2000/XP system.

7. Identify the components of the Windows 2000/XP registry structure.

8. Install and access printers in Windows 2000 and XP.

9. Install and access software applications in Windows 2000 and XP.

10. Install and configure hardware devices and drivers in Windows 2000 and XP.

11. Install and configure local area networking functions in Windows 2000 and XP.

12. Install and configure wide area networking and Internet functions in Windows 2000 and XP.

13. Describe security systems associated with Windows 2000 and Windows XP systems.

14. Identify procedures for establishing Internet connectivity.

15. In a given scenario, configure the operating system to connect to and use Internet resources.

WINDOWS OPERATING SYSTEMS

FROM THE GEEK SQUAD

Geek Squad Agent 475 is working the counter in store 101 when a customer asks him about desktop computer systems for his home. The customer wants to use the computer to download and play music. He would also like to use the system for Internet browsing, e-mail and general office work. Finally, the customer wants this computer to exchange information with his existing home computer.

The customer is confused about the difference between all the Windows XP operating system versions available. What should Agent 475 recommend to the customer? He must know and be able to explain the differences between the different operating systems available. He must also be able to guide the customer to the proper operating system version to carry out the operations the customer has outlined.

Operating systems represent half of the personal computer system. By some accounts, they represent the most complex portion of modern PC systems.

INTRODUCTION

While Microsoft developed and improved its consumer-oriented Windows 3.x and Windows 9x products for the desktop, it also developed a more robust and complicated operating system for corporate client/server networking installations. This new operating system was introduced as **Windows New Technology**, or **Windows NT**. The new operating system was built around a completely new kernel that focused on enhanced reliability, scalability, and security elements required for corporate applications, while retaining the ease-of-use strengths associated with the Windows operating system.

Windows New Technology

Windows NT

In like manner, the Windows NT line of operating systems made no attempt to be compatible with a wide array of hardware and software components. Instead, the Windows NT line of operating systems offered fairly specific sets of software and hardware requirements that must be met for proper operation.

The Windows NT product was originally developed in two parts—the **NT Workstation** and the **NT Server** operating systems. The server software has retained the Server nomenclature through several iterations—NT 4.0 Server, Server 2000, and Server 2003. However, with the advent of Windows 2000 and then Windows XP, Microsoft changed the name of the workstation software to **Windows 2000 Professional** and **Windows XP Professional**. It also introduced market-specific variations of the Windows XP operating system—Windows XP Home Edition and Windows XP Media Center Edition. In this chapter we will examine the most current Windows NT workstation operating system versions—Windows 2000 Professional and all the varieties of Windows XP.

NT Workstation

NT Server

Windows 2000 Professional

Windows XP Professional

THE WINDOWS NT PRODUCT LINE

While the original Windows NT product was based on a related server and workstation versions, subsequent Windows NT operating system versions have actually existed as three distinct products:

- A Workstation operating system

- A Server operating system

- An Extended Server operating system to manage large enterprise networks

Microsoft designed the Windows NT operating system for corporate business networking environments. Unlike its consumer-oriented Windows 3.x and 9x packages that included peer-to-peer networking functions, the Windows NT line of operating systems has been designed specifically to perform in **client/server network** environments preferred by businesses.

A client/server network is one in which stand-alone computers, called **clients**, are connected to, and administered by, a master computer called a **server**. Collectively, the members of the group make up a network structure called a **domain**. Figure 10-1 depicts a typical domain-based network arrangement. The members of the domain share a common directory database and are organized in levels. Each domain is identified by a unique name and is administered as a single unit having common rules and procedures.

client/server network

clients

server

domain

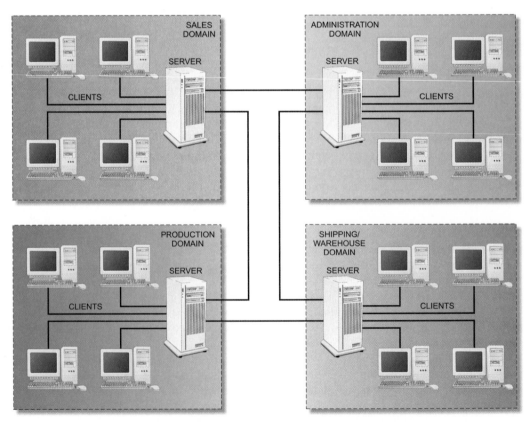

**Figure 10-1:
A Client/Server or
Domain-Based
Network**

Recall from Chapter 5 that in peer-to-peer workgroup settings, all of the nodes may act as servers for some processes and clients for others. In a domain-based network, the network is controlled from a centralized server (**domain controller**). In Windows NT networks, this concept is embodied by the location where the *Administration and Security databases* are kept. In the workgroup, each machine maintains its own security and administration databases. In a domain environment, the server is responsible for keeping the centralized user account and security databases.

Enterprise networks are designed to facilitate business-to-business or business-to-customer operations. Because monetary transactions and customers' personal information travel across the network in these environments, enterprise networks feature additional highly protective security functions. These networks consist of multiple domains (called trusted domains) that are linked together but are managed independently.

Most enterprise networks are actually **intranets**.

An intranet is a network built on the TCP/IP protocol that belongs to a single organization. It is, in essence, a private Internet. Like the Internet, intranets are designed to share information and services, but they are accessible only to the organization's members, with authorization. Figure 10-2 depicts an intranet structure where a local Web server provides Internet applications, such as e-mail, FTP, and Web browsing, for the network without using the public telephone system.

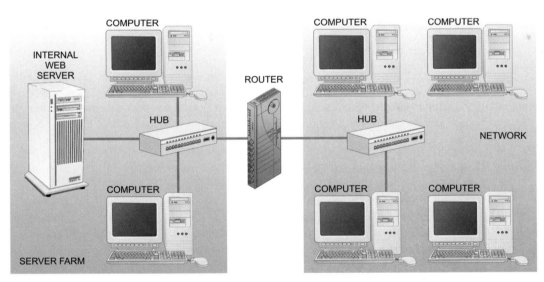

Figure 10-2: An Intranet

A relatively new term, **extranet**, is being used to describe intranets that grant limited access to authorized outside users such as corporate business partners, as illustrated in Figure 10-3. This makes the extranet a partially private, partially public network arrangement. In this example, a customer Web server is placed between the company's intranet and the Internet. Part of this server's job is to authenticate users from the outside by asking them for a valid password before they can access the contents of the server. A hardware or software **firewall** is typically employed to block unauthorized outside users from accessing the intranet site.

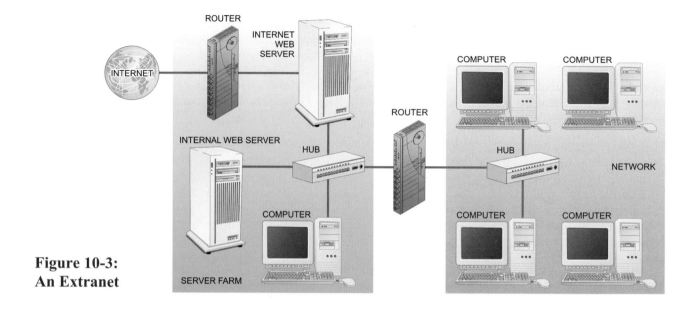

Figure 10-3:
An Extranet

Windows 2000

Windows 2000 is the successor of the Windows NT 4.0 operating system. As a matter of fact, it was originally titled Windows NT 5. This operating system brought together the stability and security of the Windows NT 4.0 product and the Plug-and-Play capabilities of Microsoft's Windows 9x consumer-oriented operating system.

Windows 2000 also brought built-in support for many new technologies including DVD drives, USB devices, accelerated graphics ports, multifunction adapter cards, and a full line of PC Cards. Finally, Windows 2000 provides a new distributed directory service for managing resources across an enterprise, FAT 32 support, and the Internet Explorer 5 Web browser.

Windows 2000
Advanced Server

Windows 2000
Datacenter Server

As with previous NT versions, Windows 2000 comes in two basic variations: the corporate workstation version, titled Windows 2000 Professional, and the network server version, called Windows 2000 Server. The server product is also available in two extended enterprise versions—**Windows 2000 Advanced Server** and **Windows 2000 Datacenter Server**.

Windows 2000 Professional

The workstation side of Windows 2000 is named **Windows 2000 Professional**. This operating system is designed to be the reliable, powerful desktop for the corporate computing world. It has been designed to be easier to set up and configure than its predecessors. Windows 2000 Professional employs several wizards, such as the New Hardware Wizard and the Network Connection Wizard, to make installation and configuration processes easier for users.

Windows 2000 Professional extended and improved the Windows 95/98 user interface and brought Plug-and-Play to the NT workstation line. The hardware supported by Windows 2000 Professional was upgraded significantly from previous workstation versions. While it offered many improvements over previous Windows NT versions, Windows 2000 Professional proved to be too complex for most general consumer usage. For this reason, Microsoft continued to upgrade its Windows 9x product for the general consumer market with its release of Windows Me.

Windows 2000
Professional

Windows 2000 Server

On the server side, Windows 2000 offers a more scalable and flexible server platform than its Windows NT predecessors. **Windows 2000 Server** actually comes in three versions that correspond to the size and complexity of the network environment in which they are used. These versions include the standard Server edition, the Advanced Server edition, and the Windows 2000 Datacenter Server edition.

Windows 2000 Server

The Standard Server edition offers a more scalable and flexible file server platform. It also functions as an application server that handles large data sets. It can be used to implement a standards-based, secured Internet/intranet server.

NOTE

Recall that an intranet is simply a private, Web-based network, typically established by an organization for the purpose of running an exclusive Web site not open to the public (i.e., company Web sites for internal company use only). Intranets can be based on local or wide area networks, or constructed as combinations of the two.

The standard Windows 2000 Server package can manage up to 4 GB of RAM and is capable of distributing work between two microprocessors at a time. This type of operation is referred to as **symmetrical multiprocessing (SMP)**. If Windows 2000 Server has been installed as an upgrade to an existing Windows NT 4.0 Server, it can support up to four different microprocessors simultaneously.

symmetrical
multiprocessing
(SMP)

The Advanced Server edition can support up to eight symmetrical processors and up to 8 GB of memory. These features enable it to function well in medium-sized networks running between 100 and 500 concurrent users.

In other respects, the Advanced Server product is the same as the standard Server version. However, some enterprise versions of applications will run only on the Enterprise version of the operating system.

The Windows 2000 Datacenter Server edition can handle up to 64 GB of RAM and 32 processors. This will enable it to support up to 1000 simultaneous users with heavy processing demands.

Both the Advanced and Datacenter Server editions employ a pair of high-availability features that allow them to effectively handle the traffic levels found on medium and large Web sites. These features are **Network Load Balancing (NLB)** and **Microsoft Cluster Server (MSCS)**. The load-balancing feature enables the operating system to distribute IP requests to the most available Web server in a cluster of up to 32 Web servers.

| **Network Load Balancing (NLB)** |
| **Microsoft Cluster Server (MSCS)** |

Windows XP

Windows XP is the current version of Microsoft's desktop operating system. Windows XP represents another level of meshing the stable kernel of the Windows NT operating system line with the consumer-oriented ease of use associated with its Windows 9x line of products. The Windows XP operating system is available in four versions:

| **XP Home Edition** |

- *Windows XP Home Edition*—The Windows **XP Home Edition** is designed to replace the Windows 95/98/Me operating systems. It is primarily intended for consumer and entertainment markets and provides many enhancements, such as more powerful and streamlined Internet access than any of its predecessors. The networking element has been downgraded in the Home Edition. It has been restricted to peer-to-peer networking and cannot be joined to a client/server domain network.

| **XP Professional** |

- *Windows XP Professional*—Windows **XP Professional** is designed and positioned to compete with Windows NT Workstation and Windows 2000 Professional operating systems. It contains features that make it more suitable as a client in an enterprise network. These features include such items as simpler remote access and domain membership, enhanced security and reliability features, multiple processor support, and multiple language availability. The A+ certification focuses primarily on this Windows XP version.

| **Windows XP 64-bit edition** |

- *Windows XP 64-bit Edition*—The **Windows XP 64-bit edition** is a high-end version of the operating system designed to run on Intel Itanium processors. These processors are employed in high-data-volume environments. This Windows XP version supports up to 16 GB of physical memory and 16 TB of virtual memory. Unlike its NT predecessors, Windows XP does not feature matching workstation and server operating system versions.

| **Windows XP Media Center Edition (XP MCE)** |

- *Windows XP Media Center Extension*—**Windows XP Media Center Edition (XP MCE)** is a special version of Windows XP Professional that includes a special multimedia-centered application, called the *Media Center*, which provides a TV remote control interface for viewing and recording television, a DVD player, and an audio/video record/playback system. Like the Home Edition, MCE's networking capabilities have been limited to the peer-to-peer environment.

Windows XP Media Center Edition

The **Windows XP Media Center Edition (MCE)** is a special extension to the Windows XP Professional operating system that is designed to turn the *Media Center PC* into a device that users can use to watch and record TV programming, store videos, and create electronic picture albums as well as download, manipulate, and listen to music.

Windows XP Media Center Edition (MCE)

MCE is actually a Microsoft exclusive, preinstalled application that provides a large-font user interface to accommodate television viewing from across a room. The 72 pt. font used in the MCE menus is referred to as the "10-foot" font. Microsoft has developed its own infrared remote control, receiver, and IR blaster, along with new wireless keyboard to work with the MCE interface. In addition to watching televison, users can remotely access an interface for video recording and playback, DVD playback, photo viewing, and music playback.

The MCE portion of the operating system converts the system's hard drive and video products into a PVR (a Personal Video Recorder), as described in Chapter 5, *Mass Storage Systems*.

In most other respects, Media Center Edition is a Windows XP Professional system. However, the networking options for MCE are limited to workgroup connections. Computers running Media Center Edition cannot be connected to a domain-based network.

Microsoft has limited distribution of XP Media Center Edition to *OEM System Builders* and *Microsoft Developer Network* (*MSDN*) subscribers, but not to retail distributers. This has been done primarily to insure that MCE is associated with high-quality products and produces high levels of consumer happiness with Microsoft's efforts in the consumer entertainment market.

Microsoft also supports the addition of up to five dedicate hardware devices, referred to as **Media Center Extenders**, to the MCE system through Ethernet networking links. Extenders include items such as game consoles and handheld devices.

Media Center Extenders

Windows 2003 Server

Although Microsoft decided to call their next workstation operating system Windows XP, the next version of the Server product line is called **Windows Server 2003**. As with the Windows 2000 series of server operating systems, the 2003 series will include Standard, Enterprise (advanced), and Datacenter editions. The capabilities and qualities of these editions are similar to those stated for their Windows 2000 predecessors.

Windows Server 2003

In addition to those editions already mentioned, Microsoft is producing a **Windows Server 2003—Web edition** that is designed for Web services and hosting support. It only contains features required specifically to support development and deployment of Web services and applications.

Windows Server 2003 —Web edition

> **— NOTE —**
>
> Remember that information about specific server operating systems is not part of the A+ certification objective map. These systems are mentioned here for your information and knowledge base.

NAVIGATING WINDOWS 2000/XP

When Windows 2000 or Windows XP is started, it produces the basic **desktop** screen depicted in Figure 10-4. The desktop is the primary graphical user interface for all Windows versions. As with previous Windows products, the desktop uses **icons** to quickly locate and run applications. In Windows 9x, however, the **Start button** provides the starting point for most functions.

**Figure 10-4:
The Windows 2000
Desktop**

Windows is a **task-switching** environment. Under this type of environment, several applications can run at the same time. In some cases, a particular application might be running on the desktop while others are running out of view. When you have multiple applications open in Windows, the window currently being accessed is called the active window and appears in the *foreground* (on top of the other windows). The activity of the other open windows is suspended, as denoted by their gray color, and their applications run in the *background*.

Select key combinations can be used to navigate through the Windows environment using the keyboard. The most common keys include the ALT, ESC, TAB, and ENTER keys. These keys are used to move between the different Windows structures and make selections (that is, the TAB key is used to move forward through different options, whereas the SHIFT+TAB combination is used to move backward through available options).

Special key combinations enable the user to move between tasks easily. By pressing the ALT and TAB keys together, you can quickly select one of the open applications. Similarly, the ALT+ESC key combination enables the user to cycle through open application windows. Pressing the CTRL+ESC keys will pop up the Start menu.

┌─ **TEST TIP** ─────
Memorize the desktop's
shortcut key combinations.
└────────────────────

Windows 2000/XP Desktops

The desktop interface provides an easy method for starting tasks and making resource connections. Small graphic symbols called **icons** are used to represent programs and utility that can be accessed by double clicking on the icon. *Double-clicking* the icon starts the application, or brings up its window. The standard icons generated when Windows is installed are located along the left border of the screen. Notice that the standard desktop icons for Windows 2000 include *My Computer*, *My Network Places*, and the *Recycle Bin*. However, If the operating system is installed on a stand-alone unit that does not have a network card installed, the My Network Places icon will not be presented on the desktop.

A separate screen area called the **Taskbar** runs across the bottom of the screen, and the **Start menu** pops up from the **Start button** on the Taskbar. The desktop icons are referred to as *shortcuts*, because the primary method of accessing applications is through the Start menu. Figure 10-5 depicts the Windows 2000 desktop with the Start menu expanded.

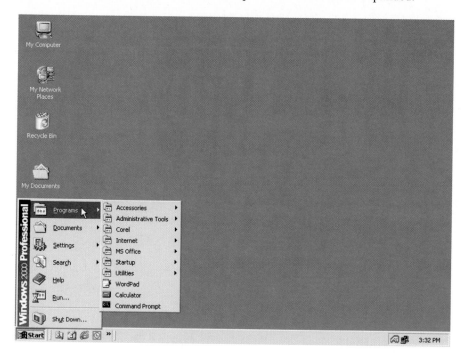

Figure 10-5: Windows 2000 Desktop Start Menu

In addition to the normal Windows left-click and double-click functions, Windows 2000 and all versions of Windows XP employ the right mouse button for some activities. This is referred to as **right-clicking**, or as **alternate clicking** for right-handed users, and is used to pop up a menu of functions on the screen. The right-click menus in Windows are context sensitive, so the information they contain applies to the item that is being clicked on.

Right-clicking techniques are employed to access context-sensitive options on the screen. Right-clicking on a **folder** or file produces a pop-up menu, similar to the left-hand menu in Figure 10-6. These menus enable the user to open, cut, or copy a folder (an icon that represents a directory), create a **shortcut**, delete or rename a folder, or examine **properties** of the folder. In the case of clicking on one of the system's hardware devices, the menu will permit you to perform such functions as sharing the device or checking its properties. These menus may have additional items inserted in their lists by applications that they serve.

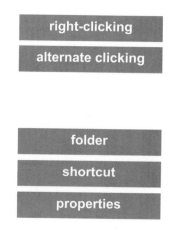

**Figure 10-6:
Right-Click Menus**

Right-clicking in an open area of the desktop produces a pop-up menu, similar to the one displayed in the right-hand side of Figure 10-6. This menu enables the user to arrange icons on the desktop, create new folders and shortcuts, and see the properties of the system's video display.

Essentials 3.1

Locating, Accessing, and Retrieving Information in Windows 2000 and XP

The major Windows 2000/XP user interfaces are

- My Computer
- Start menu/Taskbar
- Windows Explorer

- Internet Explorer
- My Network Places
- Windows 2000/XP dialog boxes (windows)

These interfaces provide user access to all of the major areas of the system. In the following discussions we will treat them as the same except where we specifically point out differences between operating system versions. Most of the time, these occurrences will involve the Windows XP version.

My Computer

My Computer

The **My Computer** icon is the major user interface for Windows 2000 and XP. It enables the user to see the local system's contents and manage its files.

Double clicking the *My Computer* icon will produce the Windows 2000 *My Computer* window, shown in Figure 10-7. This window displays all the system's disk drives as icons and represents the Control Panel as a folder. Double clicking one of the drive icons produces a display of its contents on screen.

Right clicking the *My Computer* icon produces a menu listing that provides options for opening the *My Computer* window, exploring the system drives and files through Windows Explorer, working with network drives, creating shortcuts, renaming the selected folders and files, and accessing the properties of the system's installed devices.

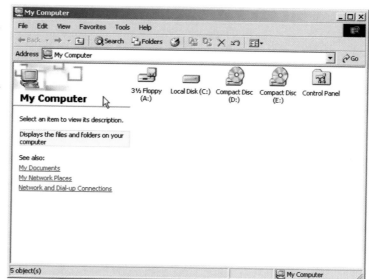

Figure 10-7: My Computer Window

Because Windows 2000 and Windows XP are designed to permit multiple users on a single machine, they both include a **My Documents** folder that acts a central repository for user's files. In reality, each user who has a profile on a given computer has their own, dedicated *My Documents* folder for their files. The *My Documents* folder in Windows 2000 and Windows XP includes a *My Pictures* subfolder that acts as the default location to hold graphic files. Windows XP also adds *My Music* and *My Videos* folders to the *My Documents* folder family. Windows XP Media Center Edition has gone even farther and provided *My TV*, *My Photos*, *My Video*, and *My Radio* folders to provide each user with personal storage areas for these types of files.

| My Documents |

TEST TIP
Know how to navigate to various parts of Windows through the *My Computer* icon.

The Recycle Bin

The **Recycle Bin** is a storage area for deleted files that enables you to retrieve files if they are deleted by mistake. When you delete a folder or file from the Windows system, it removes the first three letters of its name from the drive's FAT so that it is invisible to the system. However, the system records its presence in the Recycle Bin. The system is free to reuse the space on the drive, because it does not know that anything is there. As long as it hasn't been overwritten with new data, or it hasn't been removed from the Recycle Bin, it can be restored from the information in the Recycle Bin. If it has been thrown out of the bin but has not been overwritten, it can be recovered using a third-party software utility for recovering deleted files.

| Recycle Bin |

TEST TIP
Know what happens to files moved into the Recycle Bin.

The *Recycle Bin* icon should always be present on the desktop. It can only be removed through the registry. If its icon is missing, there are two alternatives for restoring it: establish a shortcut to the Recycle Bin using a new icon, or just reinstall Windows. This action will always place the Recycle Bin on the desktop.

TEST TIP
Know how to replace the Recycle Bin's icon in a Windows 9x system.

In the case of removable media, such as floppy disks and removable hard drives, the Recycle Bin does not retain the files deleted from these media. When a file or folder is removed from one of these devices, the information is deleted directly from the system.

My Network Places

My Network Places

network share

The **My Network Places** icon opens an applet, depicted in Figure 10-8, that enables the user to create shortcut icons to network shares on the desktop. A **network share** is an existing shared resource (i.e., printer, drive, modem, or folder) located on a remote system. The new icon acts as an alias to link the system to the share point on the remote unit.

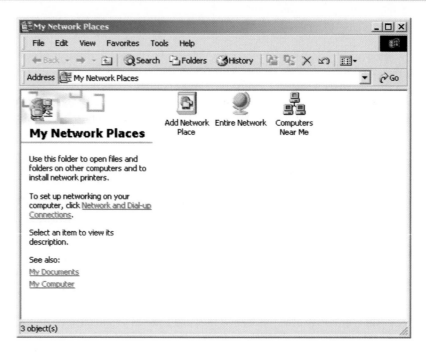

**Figure 10-8:
My Network Places**

The *Network and Dial-up Connections* option enables you to see all of the network connections that exist for the local computer. The *My Network Places* folder includes a convenient *Computers Near Me* view that identifies local area network devices. The *Add Network Place* options enable you to more easily establish connections to other servers on the network. The user can establish shortcuts to virtually every server on the network.

In the Windows XP operating system, the *My Network Places* icon opens to a display of the local network as shown in Figure 10-9. As the figure illustrates, the Network Tasks pane offers options to *Add a network place* and *View network connections*. In larger network environments, you may also have a *Search Active Directory* option.

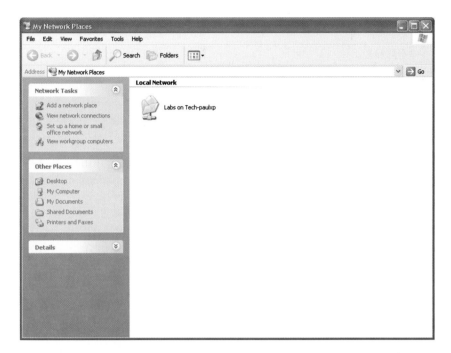

Figure 10-9: The Windows XP Local Network Window

The *Add a network place* option can be used to create shortcuts to network locations and Web sites. It can also be used to sign up for personal Web storage space. As its name indicates, the *Search Active Directory* option enables the user to search the Active Directory structure for network shares, computers, and users.

┌─ **TEST TIP** ──────────────────────
Be aware that information deleted from a removable media is not moved into the Recycle Bin. Therefore, no recovery is possible for this information.
└────────────────────────────────────

GEEK SQUAD CASE FILE #32993

A customer has called the Counter Intelligence help desk to complain that she has mistakenly removed a project that she has been working on for several months from her hard drive. She wants to know if your company can extract erased data from disk drives. With good questioning techniques, you determine that she is using a Pentium 4 machine with lots of RAM and a huge hard-disk drive. In addition, she has a R/W CD-ROM drive and she is running Windows 2000 Professional. She does not have a tape drive for backup and because the system is very new, she has never performed a backup on it. What, if anything, can you do to help this customer?

Drop-Down Menus

Most Windows 2000 and XP dialog boxes include **menu bars** that provide pop-up menus when you click on their titles. You can also press the ALT key and their underlined character (e.g., the ALT/F combination will pop up the File menu). Typical menu bar options on most windows include *File*, *Edit*, *View*, and *Help*. Options that apply to the current window are displayed as dark text. Options that are not applicable to the window are grayed out.

menu bars

┌─ **TEST TIP** ──────
Know what is indicated when menu options are grayed.
└────────────────────

File Menus

File menu

The Windows drop-down **File menu** performs basic file management—related functions for files and folders. These functions include Open, Close, and Save operations that users constantly perform on files. In addition, the menu provides options that enable the user to rename the file or folder, create a shortcut for it, or establish properties for it.

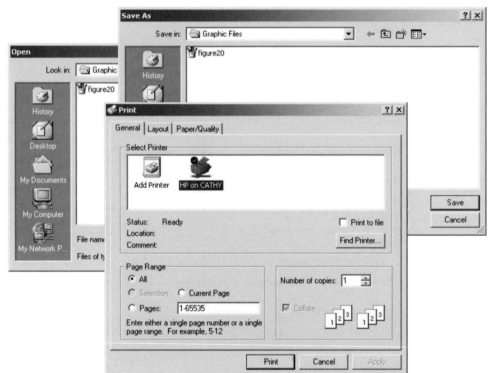

Windows 2000 and XP offer extended common dialog boxes for *File/Open*, *File/Print*, and *File/Save* options. These dialog boxes provide easy organization and navigation of the system's hard drives, as well as navigation columns that grant quick access to frequently used folders, such as the *My Documents* and *My Pictures* folders. Figure 10-10 depicts the *File/Open*, *File/Save As*, and *File/Print* common dialog boxes. The navigation column also provides easy access to the *My Network Places* folder.

The File menu also includes an entry at the top of the menu titled *New*. Clicking on this option produces the *New* options submenu shown in Figure 10-11. This menu is used to create new folders, shortcuts, and files.

**Figure 10-10:
Windows 2000/XP
Common Dialog
Boxes**

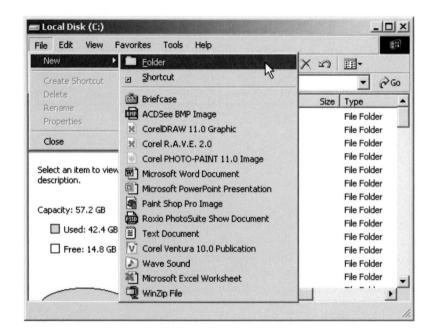

**Figure 10-11:
The New Option**

The *File* option on the My Computer and Windows Explorer menu bars can be used to perform many disk maintenance procedures. When a disk drive icon is selected, clicking on the *File* option will produce a menu that includes provisions for *Opening*, *Exploring*, *Formatting* the drive, *Sharing* the drive with the network community, *Searching* the contents of the drive, or displaying its *Properties*.

The File menu's *Properties* option displays general information about the drive, such as file system type, capacity, free space, and used space. This option also has tabs that provide you with access to the system's drive maintenance tools and utilities through the *Tools* tab.

View Menu

The **View** menu option, shown in Figure 10-12, is one of the most used features of the menu bar. It can be used to alter the manner in which the contents of the window are displayed. The drives and folders in Figure 10-12 are displayed as *Small Icons*. However, they can be changed to *Large Icons*, displayed as a *List*, or displayed with *Name*, *Type*, *Size*, and *Free Space Details*. Windows 2000 and XP dialog boxes also include an image preview function that enables users to locate graphic files efficiently. This is made possible through the use of *Thumbnail* views. The dialog boxes can be resized to accommodate as many thumbnail images as desired.

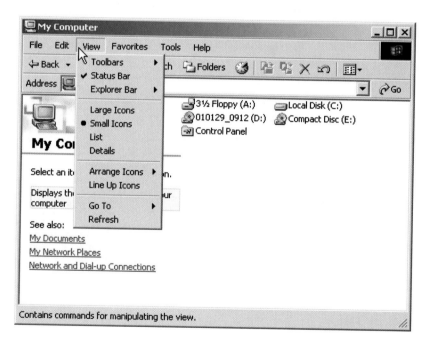

**Figure 10-12:
The Windows 2000
View Menu**

Other options in the menu can be used to organize the icons within the window. A checkmark located next to the menu option indicates that the item is currently in use. A large dot next to the item indicates that it is the currently selected option.

```
┌─ TEST TIP ─────────────────────┐
│ Be aware of what the checkmark and the dot │
│ in a pop-up menu indicate about the option. │
└────────────────────────────────┘
```

Tools Menu

This information can also be displayed in several different formats using the *View* option. Selecting the *Folder Options* entry in the *Tools* menu produces the *Folder Options* window displayed in Figure 10-13. This window consists of four tabs (screens): *General*, *View*, *File Types*, and *Offline Files*.

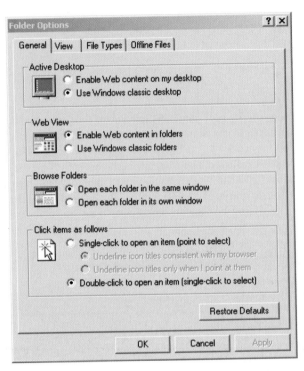

Figure 10-13: The Folder Options Window

The *General* tab supplies information about how the desktop will display windows as the user browses through multiple windows. The *View* tab is used to define how the folders and files in the selected window will be displayed on screen. This screen also determines which types of files will be displayed. To see hidden and system files, select the *View* tab and click on the *Show Hidden Files and Folders* radio button. Files with selected extensions will be hidden. The *File Types* tab lists the types of files that the system can recognize. New file types can be registered in this window.

The Taskbar

task-switching

Across the bottom of the display is an area called the **Taskbar**. This area employs icons to display all the applications currently running in the system. Each time a program is started, or a window is opened, a corresponding button appears on the Taskbar. To switch between applications, just click on the desired program button to make it the active window. The button will disappear from the Taskbar if the program is closed. Right-clicking on the Taskbar at the bottom of the screen produces a menu that can be used to control its appearance and open windows on screen.

A small window at the extreme right side of the Taskbar shows programs and events that occur in the background (mouse drivers, antivirus programs, volume control, etc.). This area is referred to as the **notification area** or more commonly as the **Systray**. On most systems at least the clock will be displayed here. The icons in this area provide quick links to programs and services, such as the volume control icon, that are running in the background.

notification area

Systray

In Windows 2000 and XP, the Taskbar is located at the bottom of the display by default. However, it can be moved around the display by clicking and dragging it to the left, right, or top of the screen. When moved to the top of the screen, the Start menu will drop down from above instead of pop up from the bottom. It can also be hidden just off screen by clicking on its edge and then dragging it toward the edge of the display.

If the Taskbar is hidden, pressing the CTRL+ESC key combination will retrieve it. This will pop up the Start menu along with the Taskbar. Enter the *Start/Settings/Taskbar and Start Menu* option to change the Taskbar settings so that it will not be hidden. You can also locate an absent Taskbar by moving the mouse around the edges of the screen until the shape of the cursor changes. Likewise, pressing the TAB key will cycle control between the Start menu, the Quick launch icons, the Taskbar, and the desktop icons. The TAB key can be helpful in navigating the system if the mouse fails.

TEST TIP

Know how to move around the desktop, Start menu, and Taskbar using the keyboard.

Start Menu

Windows 2000 and Windows XP operations typically begin from the **Start menu** that pops up when the Start button is clicked. The Start menu provides the user with access to the system regardless of what else is occurring in the system. In doing so, it provides access to the system's installed applications, a search engine for finding data in the system, and the operating system's Help file structure.

Start menu

Figure 10-14: The Windows 2000 Start Button Menu

The Windows 2000 Start menu contains entries for *Programs, Documents, Settings, Find, Help, Run,* and *Shut Down* options. Placing the cursor over designated menu items will cause any submenus associated with that option to pop up onscreen, as illustrated in Figure 10-14. An arrow to the right of the option indicates a submenu is available. To open the selected item, just left-click on it, and its window will appear on the desktop.

The Programs submenu, depicted in Figure 10-15, has several options that include *Accessories, Startup,* and *Windows Explorer*.

Figure 10-15: The Programs Submenu

The *Programs/Accessories* entry is of particular interest to technicians, because it provides access to some of the most frequently used Windows operating system tool groups and utilities. These groups include the Communications utilities, Accessibility tools, the Entertainment controls, and the System Tools. The System Tools group contains many utilities that are used to maintain and optimize the system, as illustrated in Figure 10-16. All of the tools in this area are covered in detail in Chapter 12, *Operating System Troubleshootin*g.

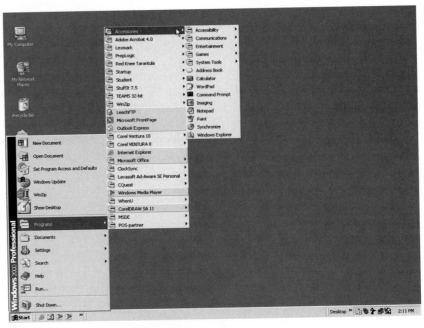

Figure 10-16: The Programs/Accessories/ System Tools Menu

Windows 2000 and Windows XP feature intelligent, personalized Programs menus. These operating systems monitor the user's program usage, and after the first six accesses arrange the menu options according to those most frequently used. The menu options displayed change based on their usage. Less frequently used programs are not displayed in the list but can be accessed by clicking on the double arrow at the bottom of the list. The hidden portion of the list will appear after a short delay. When this occurs, the six most frequently used applications are highlighted. This reduces screen clutter and makes it easier for users to access their most used items.

The Start menu's *Documents* entry displays a list of documents previously opened and provides direct access to the user's **My Document** folder.

The *Settings* option displays values for the system's configurable components. It combines previous Windows functions, such as copies of the **Control Panel**, Network and Dialup Connection and Printers (Print Manager) folders, as well as access to the Taskbar. The contents of the Windows 2000 and Windows XP Control Panels can be cascaded as a submenu of the Start button for quick access. The My Documents menu can also be cascaded off the Start menu for fast access to documents.

The Windows 2000 and XP *Search* utility includes powerful search capabilities for searching the local hard drive and the Web to locate folders, files, mail messages, and shared computers. The HTML-like **Search** *function* in Windows 2000 and XP replaces the Start menu's *Find* option from previous Windows desktops. The Search feature provides three distinct search options:

1. For Files and Folders   2. On the Internet   3. For People

My Document

Control Panel

Search

The *For Files and Folders* option opens a powerful search function with advanced search options, such as case-sensitive searches. These options are available through the *Advanced* button. Selecting the *On the Internet* option brings up a search bar that establishes a link to a predetermined Internet search engine such as Yahoo or Google. The *Search for People* option opens a *Lightweight Directory Access Protocol (LDAP)* dialog window.

Indexing Service

Enabling the *Microsoft Index Server* function produces particularly fast searches. The **Indexing Service** runs in the background to provide content indexing on the local hard drive. Windows 2000 and XP Professional versions include a local version of the indexing service that operates with the local hard drive. In a network environment that uses Windows 2000 Servers, the server can perform the content indexing service. The *Index Service Management* tools are located in the *Start/Programs/Administrative Tools* path.

Searching with the context index feature enabled allows the user to write Boolean logic expressions (such as AND, OR, and NOT) for finding specific content quickly.

The *Help* file system provides extensive information about many Windows functions and operations. It also supplies an exhaustive list of guided troubleshooting routines for typical system components and peripherals.

The *Run* option is used to start programs or open folders from a command-line dialog box. To start an executable file, simply type its filename in the dialog box and click on the *OK* button. The *Browse* button can be used to locate the desired file by looking through the system's file structure.

Start button

The **Start button** is also used to correctly shut down Windows. The *Shut Down* option shuts down the system, restarts the computer, or logs the user off. It must be used to avoid damaging files and to ensure that your work is properly saved. When it is clicked, the *Shut Down Windows* dialog box shown in Figure 10-17 appears. After you select an option from the dialog box, the operating system will tell you to wait, and then it will give you a screen message telling you that it is okay to turn off the system.

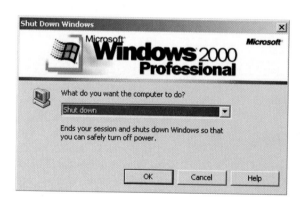

Figure 10-17: The Shut Down Windows Dialog Box

Windows 2000 and XP enable individuals in multiuser systems to log on to, and operate in personalized Windows environments specifically configured to their work needs. The *Log Off User* option is used to return the system to its natural setup. The *Log Off* entry may not appear in some installations, such as stand-alone machines that are not connected to a network environment.

Start menu items can easily be renamed in Windows 2000. You can accomplish this by right-clicking on the menu item and choosing the *Rename* option from the context-sensitive pop-up menu. Then, the user types the new name in the text entry box. This is all accomplished without opening the Start menu.

Additional items can be added to the Start menu so that they can be used directly from the menu. By doing so, the normal method of clicking on *Start*, pointing to the *Program* option, and moving through submenus can be avoided. To move a frequently used item to the top of the Start menu, simply drag its icon to the *Start* button on the Taskbar. It is also possible to move all of your frequently used programs to the Programs submenu. Frequently used items can be moved to the Taskbar, the QuickLaunch toolbar, or user-created toolbars for easy access.

Windows 2000 Control Panel

Control Panel

Properties dialog box

The Windows **Control Panel**, shown in Figure 10-18, is the primary user interface for configuring and managing the Windows system. It contains a collection of Windows-specific applications and utilities (referred to as *applets*) that control different components of the operating system. The Control Panel can be accessed through the *Start\Settings* path.

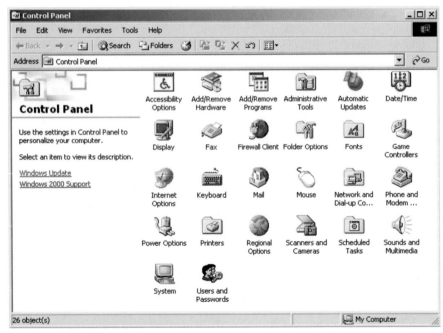

Figure 10-18: Windows 2000 Control Panel Icons

The *Control Panel* icon provides access to the configuration information for each of the system's installed devices specific to its type. Double clicking on any of the device icons will produce a **Properties dialog box** for that device. Each dialog box is different in that it contains information specific to the selected device. The boxes will also have a number of different folder tabs along their tops. These tabs are labeled with the type of information the folder holds and can be used to review and change settings and drivers for the device. Clicking on a tab will display additional information and options for the designated topic.

The Control Panel also provides support for infrared device control, an Internet configuration tool, a Power Management utility, support for scanners/digital cameras, and additional modem and communication control functions in the form of a *Phone and Modem* utility. The final addition to the Control Panel is the *Users and Passwords* icon that provides tools to establish and manage profiles for multiple users on the system.

However, the most important uses of the Control Panel tools are

- Adding or removing new hardware or software components to the system
- Modifying system device settings
- Modifying desktop items

These functions are performed through two configuration wizards—*Add/Remove Hardware* and *Add/Remove Programs*. Windows 2000 and XP bring the most widely used administrative tools together in the *Administrative Tools* applet. The other control panel widely used by technicians is the *System* applet.

Installation Wizards

The **Add/Remove Hardware** icon brings the Add/Remove Hardware wizard into action. It will initially ask you whether you want to *Add/Troubleshoot a device* or *Uninstall/Unplug a device*. Next, the wizard will run a new PnP enumeration on the system to see if it can detect any new hardware. If the system does not detect any new hardware, it will ask you to *Choose a Hardware Device to Troubleshoot*.

Add/Remove Hardware

The Devices list also offers a "*Add a new device*" option. If you select this option, you are given the choice of having Windows conduct another search for the new hardware through a PnP-style detection process, or of selecting the hardware from a list of Windows-supported hardware products.

If the device must be installed manually because Windows could not detect it, Windows will produce a *Choose a Hardware Device* component list similar to the one shown in Figure 10-19. The Add New Hardware wizard will guide the manual installation process from this point and prompt the user for any necessary configuration information. If the device is not present in the list, click on the **Have Disk button** to load drivers supplied by the device's manufacturer.

Have Disk button

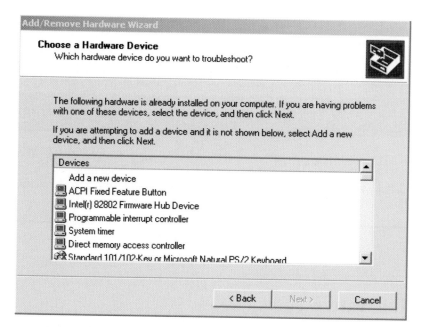

TEST TIP

Know what action is required to install hardware devices not directly supported by Windows.

Figure 10-19: The Hardware Wizard's Device Selection Page

The **Add/Remove Programs** icon leads to the *Change or Remove Programs* screen illustrated in Figure 10-20. This page can be used to install new programs by simply clicking on the *Add New Programs* button and specifying where to look for the program files. Conversely, programs listed in the programs window can be removed from the system by highlighting their title and clicking on the *Change or Remove Programs* button.

Add/Remove Programs

Figure 10-20: The
Change or Remove
Programs Wizard
Window

Add/Remove Windows Component

The **Add/Remove Windows Component** button is used to add or remove selected Windows components, such as communications packages or additional system tools.

GEEK SQUAD CASE FILE #32993

A friend gave you a copy of several quaint old MS-DOS-based games on CD. When you put the CD into the drive, there is no Auto-run action. You want to install the game on your PC, but you're not sure how to go about it. Where should you look first to install the game under Windows 2000?

Administrative Tools

Administrative Tools

Computer Management Console

Microsoft Management Consoles (MMCs)

The Windows 2000 and Windows XP operating system versions have taken a different approach to system administration and preventive maintenance by concentrating many of the system's administration tools in a single location, under the Control Panel's **Administrative Tools** icon. The tools are combined in the Windows 2000/XP **Computer Management Console**, shown in Figure 10-21. You can access the Management Console by right clicking the *My Computer* icon and selecting the *Manage* option from the pop-up menu. As the figure illustrates, the console includes three primary **Microsoft Management Consoles** (MMCs):

- System Tools
- Storage
- Services and Applications

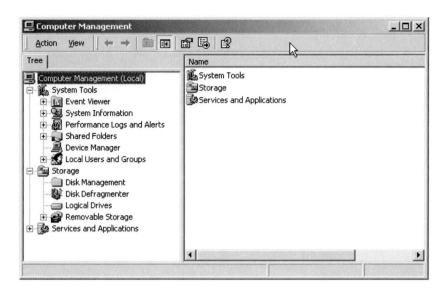

Figure 10-21: The
Windows 2000 Computer
Management Console

The contents of the different consoles vary depending on which snap-in tools administrators decide to add to them.

The **System Tools** console, shown in Figure 10-22, provides a collection of tools that can be used to view and manage system objects. They can also be used to track and configure all of the system's hardware and software and to configure network options and view system events.

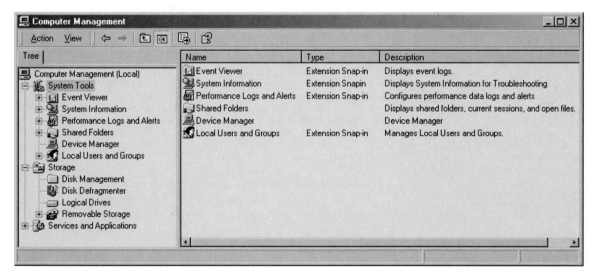

Figure 10-22:
The System
Tools Options

Likewise, the *Storage* console provides a standard set of tools for maintaining the system's disk drives. These tools include the **Disk Management** tool, the **Disk Defragmenter** utility, and a **Logical Drives** utility.

The *Disk Management* tool enables the user to create and manage disk partitions and volumes. The organization of the Storage console is illustrated in Figure 10-23. The *Disk Defragmenter* is used to optimize file operations on disks by rearranging their data into the most effective storage pattern for reading and writing. Finally, the *Logical Drives* tool shows a listing of all the logical drives in the system, including remote drives that have been mapped to the local system.

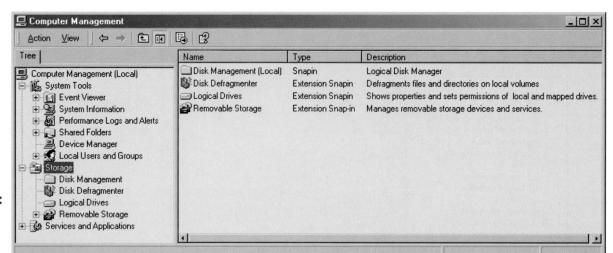

Figure 10-23:
The Storage
Console
Options

The *Services and Applications* entry includes an advanced set of system management tools. These tools include the **Windows Management Instrumentation (WMI)** tools, a listing of all the system's available services, and access to the Windows 2000 Indexing functions, as shown in Figure 10-24. The WMI tools are used to establish administrative controls with another computer, provide logging services, view user security settings, and enable the Windows 2000/XP advanced scripting services.

┌─**TEST TIP**──────────────┐
│ Be aware of where the Disk Management │
│ tools are located in Windows 2000. │
└──────────────────────────────┘

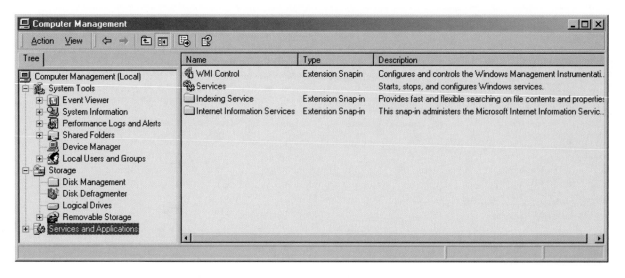

Figure 10-24:
The Services and
Applications Options

Some of the Windows 2000/XP management consoles are not loaded when the operating system is installed. However, they are available for installation from the Windows 2000/XP CDs. These consoles are referred to as snap-ins. In addition to the Control Panel path, all of the installed MMCs can be accessed under the *Start/Programs/Administrative_Tools* path. Extended discussions of these tools are presented throughout the remainder of the text as they apply to managing and troubleshooting the operating system.

Windows 2000/XP Device Manager

Both the Windows 2000 and Windows XP operating systems employ the **Device Manager** utility illustrated in Figure 10-25. This utility provides a graphical representation of the devices configured in the system. It also plays a major role in modifying hardware configurations and troubleshooting hardware problems encountered in Windows 2000 and Windows XP systems.

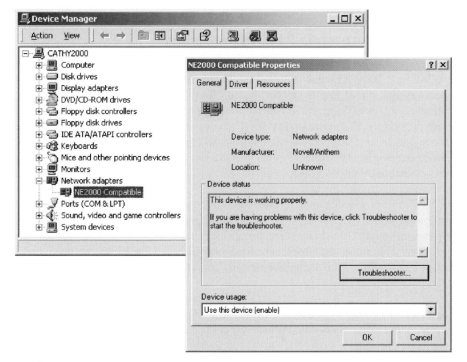

**Figure 10-25:
The Windows 2000
Device Manager**

You can access the Windows 2000 or Windows XP *Device Manager* utilities by clicking on their buttons located under the *Hardware* tab of the Control Panel's System *Properties* page. However, in Windows 2000 and Windows XP, the Device Manager is usually accessed through the *Computer Management Console*.

The Device Manager can be used to identify installed ports, update device drivers, and change I/O settings for hardware installed in the system. Even though entries in the registry can be altered through the RegEdt32 and RegEdit utilities, the safest method of changing hardware settings is to change their values through the Device Manager. Steps for using the Device Manager are covered in some detail in Chapter 12, *Operating System Troubleshooting*.

It can also be used to manually isolate hardware and configuration conflicts. The problem device can be examined to see where the conflict is occurring. The Device Manager will display an exclamation point (!) inside a yellow circle whenever a device is experiencing a direct hardware conflict with another device. Similarly, when a red "X" appears at the device's icon, the device has been disabled due to a User Selection Conflict.

> **TEST TIP**
>
> Know that the safe method of changing registry entries is to let the system do it through the Device Manager.

If a conflict is suspected, click on the offending device in the listing, make sure that the selected device is the current device, and then click on the *User Selection Conflict* tab to examine its *Conflicting devices* list. Make sure that the device has not been installed twice.

WINDOWS OPERATING SYSTEMS   579

Typical Device Manager's *Properties* pages provide tabs that can be used to access general information, device settings, device drivers information, and device resources requirements and usage. Each device may have some or all of these tabs available depending on what type of device it is and what its requirements are. The information under the tabs can be used to change the properties associated with the selected device. This often becomes necessary when resource conflicts occur in a system that has legacy devices installed. The Device Manager can be used to identify possible causes of these IRQ, DMA, I/O, and memory settings conflicts.

Managing Symmetric Multiprocessing

The Windows 2000/XP task scheduling capabilities enable it to control multiple microprocessors on a single system board. In the case of hardware with multiple microprocessors, the Windows NT Microkernel provides synchronization between the different processors. The **symmetrical multiprocessing (SMP)** function enables threads of any process to be applied to any available processor in the system. The SMP function also enables microprocessors within a system to share memory space with and assign threads to the next available microprocessor.

symmetrical multiprocessing (SMP)

asymmetrical multiprocessing (AMP)

Using SMP, the processing load is distributed evenly among all the installed processors, regardless of what type of task is being performed. However, in an **asymmetrical multiprocessing (AMP)** scheme, each processor is capable of processing only a particular type of task. Therefore, the processing load is distributed based on the tasks that each processor can perform. This technique permits conditions to occur where one processor is very busy while others are idle.

Windows 2000 Professional and XP Professional both offer SMP support for dual (2x) processor operations. Similarly, Windows 2000 Server can support up to four (4x) simultaneous processors, while the Advanced and Datacenter versions of the Server package support 8x and 16x SMP, respectively (or 32 processors using a special OEM version of Windows 2000 Datacenter). With versions of the Server running more than four processors, the hardware manufacturer must supply a special, proprietary version of the Windows 2000 HAL.DLL file for their machines.

If you upgrade a system to use additional processors, or you upgrade the existing processors on a multiprocessor board, you will need to update the HAL file. This operation is performed through the *Device Manager* utility as follows.

1. Access the *Device Manager* and expand the Computer node. The currently installed HAL will be displayed, as illustrated in Figure 10-26.

2. To update the installed HAL, right click on the existing HAL and select the *Update Driver* option from the menu.

Figure 10-26: Updating the HAL in a Multiple-Processor System

The System Icon

One of the main Control Panel icons is the **System icon**. Clicking this icon produces the *System Properties* window displayed in Figure 10-27. This window features tabs for *General* information, *Network Identification*, *Hardware*, *User Profiles*, and *Advanced*.

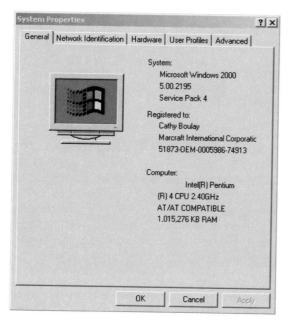

Figure 10-27: The System Properties Window

- The *General* tab supplies information about the system's operating system version, microprocessor type, and RAM capacity, as well as its ownership and registration.

- The *Network Identification* tab provides information about the system's full computer name and network relationship. It also provides access to the *Network Identification* wizard, which is used to join the computer to a workgroup or domain network structure.

- The *Hardware* tab provides three important utilities used to manage the system's hardware components—the *Hardware Wizard*, the *Device Manager*, and *Hardware Profiles*. The hardware wizard is the same tool described earlier in this chapter in connection with the Add/Remove Hardware wizard in the Control Panel. The *Device Manager* is a major hardware device configuration and troubleshooting tool discussed in detail later in this chapter. The *Hardware Profiles* button provides a window that can be used to establish different hardware configuration profiles to be implemented at start-up. Normally, only multiple user systems require additional profiles.

- The *User Profiles* tab identifies the profiles that have been configured for all the different users defined in the system. These profiles contain tailored desktop settings and other information specific to each user.

- The *Advanced* tab provides access to the system's *Performance Options*, *Environmental Variables*, and *Startup/Recovery* configurations. The *Performance Options* button is used to configure how applications use memory, which ultimately affects the speed of the system. *Environmental Variables* direct the system to certain types of information they need to operate. The *Startup and Recovery* options direct the computer's operation on start-up and define a course of action for when errors cause the computer to stop processing.

┌─ **TEST TIP** ─────────

Memorize the types of information provided by the *General* tab of the System Properties page.

└────────────────────────

The Display Icon

The final major Control Panel function is to enable users to customize the Windows desktop. This customization is performed through the *Display* icon and includes such things as setting screen colors, changing the Windows *wallpaper*, and selecting *screen savers*. Wallpaper is the pattern that shows behind the various application windows. **Screen savers** are screen displays that remain in motion while the system is setting idle. This utility prevents a single display from remaining on the screen for a prolonged time. This keeps the image from being "burned into" the screen. When this happens, the image becomes a permanent ghost on the screen, and the monitor is ruined.

Screen savers

Technical Support 2.1

IT Technician 3.1

Windows Explorer

Windows Explorer

File Management functions in Windows are performed through the **Windows Explorer** interface. The Windows 2000/XP Windows Explorer graphically displays the entire computer system in a hierarchical tree structure on the left side of the screen. This enables the user to manipulate all of the system's drives and software. The inclusion of the *My Network Places* icon links Windows Explorer directly to the *My Network Places* dialog window and extends the Windows Explorer structure to include network and domain structures. Likewise, the *Internet Explorer* icon supplies the system with a tightly linked Web connection.

This manager is located under the *Start/Programs/Accessories* path in Windows 2000 and XP. By clicking on the *Windows Explorer* entry, the system's directory structure will appear, as shown in Figure 10-28. You can access the Windows Explorer by right-clicking on the *Start* button, or by clicking on the *My Computer* icon and selecting the *Explore* option.

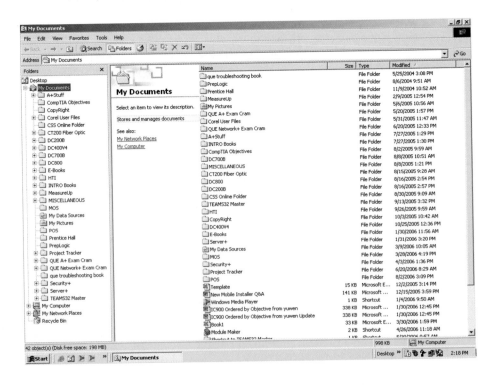

Figure 10-28: The Windows Explorer Screen

Windows Explorer enables the user to copy, move, and erase files on any of the system's drives. Its screen is divided into two parts. The left side displays the system's directory tree, showing all of the directories and subdirectories of its available drives.

In the Windows environment, directories and subdirectories are referred to, and depicted as, folders (and **subfolders**). Any drive or directory can be selected by clicking on its icon or folder. You can expand the content of a folder by clicking on the (+) sign beside it. Conversely, you can contract the same folder by clicking on the minus (−) sign in the same box.

Windows Explorer is not limited to simply showing the directories, subdirectories, and files on local drives. It will also display drives and folders from throughout the network environment. The contents of the local drives are displayed at the top of the directory tree. If the system is connected to a network, the additional resources available through the network are displayed below those of the local system as a continuation of its tree structure.

The right side of the *Windows Explorer* screen displays the files of the selected directory. Applications can be started from this window by double clicking their executable file. Double clicking on a file produced by an associated application will cause Windows to open the application and load the selected file.

The Windows 2000/XP Explorer **toolbar**, depicted in Figure 10-29, comes with a collection of about 20 add-on buttons that can be used to customize its available options. You can modify the toolbar by right clicking on the toolbar, and then selecting the *Customize* option from the pop-up menu. Additional buttons include *Move To*, *Copy To*, *Search*, *Map Drive*, *Favorites*, and *Full Screen*. The *Full Screen* option is new and can be used to toggle between maximized and normal window sizes.

The *Status bar* at the bottom of the screen provides information about the number and size of the files in the selected directory. The View menu on the Windows Explorer menu bar can be used to set the display for large or small icons, as well as simple or detailed lists. The Explorer's View functions are the same as those described for the My Computer menu bar.

**Figure 10-29:
Windows 2000
Explorer Toolbar**

Windows Explorer is also used to perform functions, such as formatting and copying disks. Right-clicking on a folder icon will produce a menu that includes a *Send To* option, as shown in Figure 10-30. Moving the mouse to this entry will produce a submenu that can be used to send a selected folder or file to a floppy drive or to the desktop. Several files or folders can be selected for copying using the SHIFT key.

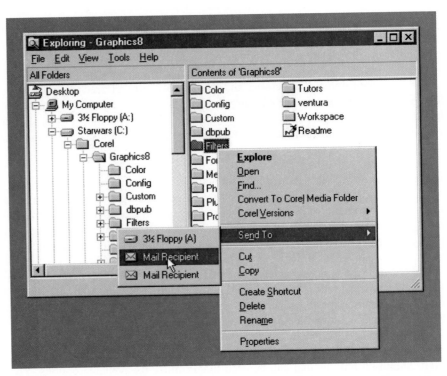

Figure 10-30: The Send To Option

The contents of the right-click menu change in Windows Explorer, depending on the item that is selected. Because the right-click function is context sensitive, the menu produced for a folder will be different than the one displayed for a document file. Each menu will have options that apply to the selected item. Right-clicking on a document file will produce options that enable the user to *Copy*, *Cut*, *Rename*, *Open*, or *Print* the document from the Windows Explorer. This menu also provides options to *Create a Shortcut* for the document or to *Change its Attributes*.

┌─ **TEST TIP** ─────────────┐
Be familiar with efficient methods of changing file attributes from the Windows Explorer.
└────────────────────────────┘

By default, Windows Explorer does not show SYS, INI, or DAT files. To change file attributes from the Explorer, right click on the desired file, select the *Properties* option from the pop-up list, move to the *General* page, and click on the desired attribute boxes. To see hidden and system files in Windows Explorer, click on the *Tools* menu option, select the *Folder Options* entry, click on the *View* tab, and check the *Show All Files* box. If you experience difficulty with this operation from the Windows environment, you can always access the file from the command prompt and change its attributes with the ATTRIB command.

┌─ **TEST TIP** ─────────┐
Know which file types are normally not shown in Windows Explorer.
└────────────────────────┘

If Windows cannot identify the application associated with the selected file, the operator will need to start the application and then manually open the file. However, the user can also register the file's extension type under the *Tools/Folder Options/File Types* path from the Menu bar. This will produce the registered file types dialog box shown in Figure 10-31.

┌─ **TEST TIP** ──────────────┐
Know how to navigate to various parts of the Windows operating system using Windows Explorer.
└─────────────────────────────┘

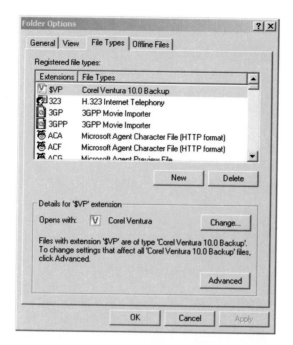

**Figure 10-31:
The Registered
File Types Window**

To create a new folder in Windows Explorer, select a parent directory by highlighting it in the left window. Then click the *File* menu button, move the cursor to the *New* entry, slide across to the *Folder* option, and click on it. A new unnamed folder icon will appear in the right Explorer window.

The same process is used to create new files. A file icon can be produced for any of the file types registered. Right-clicking on the new icon will produce the menu with options for renaming the icon, creating a shortcut for it, and establishing its properties (including its attributes).

┌─ **TEST TIP** ───────────────────────────
│ Be aware of the different locations in Windows where new
│ folders can be created and remember the primary method of
│ creating a new folder.
└──

A small arrow in the lower-left corner of an icon identifies it as a **shortcut**. When a shortcut is created, Windows does not place a copy of the file or application in every location that references it. Instead, it creates an icon in each location and defines it with a link to the actual location of the program in the system. This reduces the amount of disk space required to reference the file from multiple locations.

shortcut

Windows XP Interface Variations

Technical Support 2.1

IT Technician 3.1

Even though the Windows XP desktop and Start menu can be configured to look like the old Windows 2000 Start menu (referred to as the *Classic* theme), they have really been redesigned to offer a more compartmentalized arrangement as illustrated in Figure 10-32.

To be more appealing to consumers, the "My..." collection has been expanded to include *Documents* (and *Recent Documents*), *Pictures*, *Music*, *Favorites*, *Computer*, and *Network Places*. These represent the personalized settings for the logged-in user. They also make up one of the biggest sections of the revised Start menu.

Figure 10-32:
The Windows XP
Start Menu

Most of the other Start menu items are similar to those that users are familiar with from previous versions of Windows. This includes quick-access applications along the left side of the menu, the *Control Panel/Printers and Faxes* options, and the *Help and Support/Search and Run* options at the bottom right side of the menu. The *Log off* and *Shut Down* buttons have been set off to themselves at the bottom of the menu. The one item that looks significantly different is the *All Programs* entry. This button is the new version of the *Programs* option from the Windows 2000 menu.

Simply resting the cursor over the green arrow icon will pop up the *All Programs* menu, as illustrated in Figure 10-33. As the figure shows, the Windows XP All Programs menu contains the usual entries from previous Programs menus. Technicians should be most familiar with the contents of the *Accessories* and *Administrative Tool*s options. These two locations provide the most direct access to most of the diagnostic and maintenance tools provided by the Windows XP operating system.

Remote Assistance

One additional technician-related entry to note in the *All Programs* menu is the **Remote Assistance** icon. This utility can be used to let remote computer users, such as remote technicians or administrators, take over the local computer and operate it from their desktop. This feature must be activated locally and usually involves turning control over to a trusted individual for assistance purposes.

Figure 10-33:
The Windows XP
Programs Menu

Figure 10-34 shows the *Accessories* menu listings. The most interesting entries in the *Accessories* menu include *Communications*, *Entertainment*, and *System Tools*.

- The *Communications* entry provides tools and wizards that assist in setting up local area and dial-up networking functions. The **Remote Desktop Connection Wizard** in this menu enables you to access desktops on remote computers and use them as if you were setting in front of those machines.

Remote Desktop Connection Wizard

- The *Entertainment* option primarily involves audio and video functions associated with the PC.

- The **System Tools** submenu is a very important area for technicians. This entry can be used to access the disk and system management tools used to perform preventive maintenance on the system and to optimize its performance.

System Tools

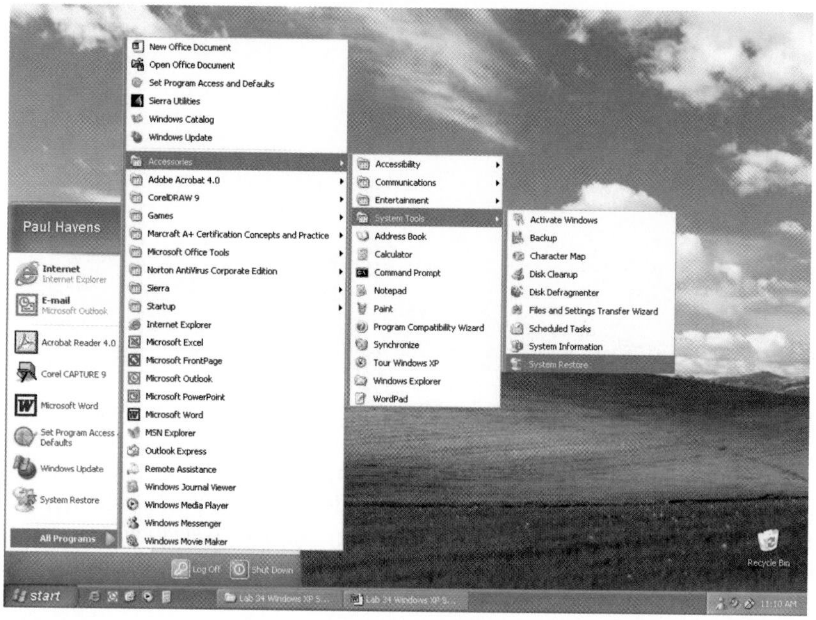

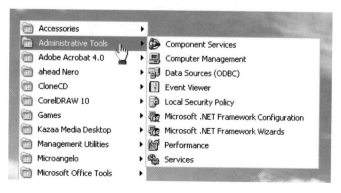

Figure 10-34: Key XP Programs Menu Extensions

One other entry that you may need to be aware of in the *Accessories* menu is the *Accessibility* option. This entry provides system customization features that can be implemented to accommodate users who have physical barriers to using the computer system.

Administrative Tools

Computer Management applet

The **Administrative Tools** menu, whose contents are displayed in Figure 10-35, is another key location for technicians. This applet provides access to the system's major administration and management tools. Important entries in this submenu include the **Computer Management applet** that has tools for managing the system's disk systems as well as both local and remote computers, the *Local Security Policy* option that is used to configure local security policies, and the *Event Viewer* and *Performance* tools that are used to monitor system events and performance so that problems can be spotted and corrected before major failures occur. These tools and their usage are described in greater detail in Chapter 12, *Operating System Troubleshooting*.

Figure 10-35: Windows XP Administrative Tools

Windows XP Control Panel

The Windows XP Control Panel, depicted in Figure 10-36, also offers some additional features and functionality not found in previous versions. In Windows XP, the *Control Panel* option is included directly on the Start menu instead of in a submenu. Under the native Windows XP version of the Control Panel, the applets are organized into nine related categories.

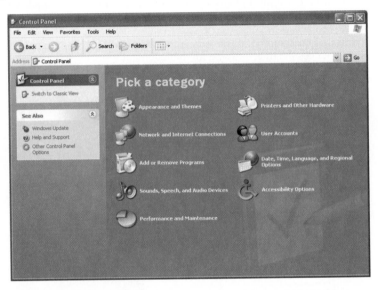

**Figure 10-36:
Windows XP
Control Panel**

When you access some of these options, two corresponding dialog windows pop up in the left window—*See Also* and *Troubleshooters*. The *See Also* window lists other related topics that might be important to the activity you are attempting to perform. The *Troubleshooters* window provides direct access to related Windows Help Troubleshooters to solve context-specific problems. The *Add or Remove Programs* and *User Accounts* options do not have either of these two options when they are accessed. Similarly, the *Date, Time...* and *Accessibility Options* only provide a *See Also* window.

If you select the *Switch to Classic View* option in the upper left dialog box, you should see all of the normal Windows 2000−type Control Panel options for adding and removing hardware and software components, as well as a collection of individual control panels for different devices and Windows services. The Windows XP Control Panel also features a Windows 2000 Administrative Tools applet that performs the same function as the entry from the Start/Programs menu of the same name.

In addition, the Classic View Control Panel includes advanced applets for *Wireless Networking* and *Speech* functions not found in other versions. There are also *Taskbar* and *Start Menu* options that can be used to customize these structures and control what items are displayed through them, such as the ability to lock the Taskbar so that it cannot be moved or changed.

For the technician, one of the most important options in the Windows XP Control Panel is the *Performance and Maintenance* group depicted in Figure 10-37. This group contains the *Administrative Tools* and *System* icons. The Administrative Tools are discussed in detail in Chapter 12, *Operating System Troubleshooting*. However, the *System* icon is the link to information about the computer system and to the Device Manager that is used to change the properties of the system's hardware devices.

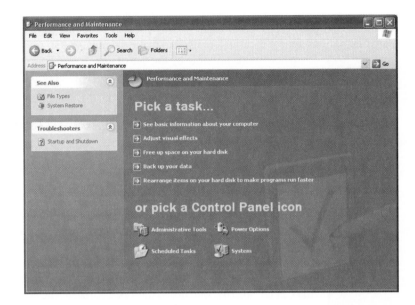

Figure 10-37: Windows XP Control Panel/ Performance and Maintenance Group

Windows XP Media Center Interfaces

The major features of the **Windows XP Media Center Edition** are appropriately connected to using the computer to handle multimedia functions such as viewing and recording television and other video sources; recording and listening to music; and storing, manipulating, and viewing pictures and graphics. Microsoft has accomplished this by adding a new *Media Center* option to the Start menu as illustrated in Figure 10-38.

Windows XP Media Center Edition

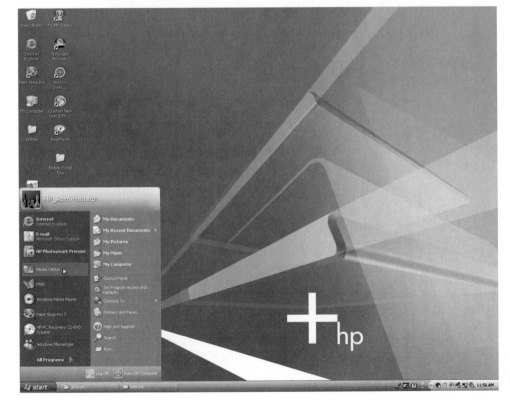

Figure 10-38: Media Center Start Menu

The Media Center *Start* page, depicted in Figure 10-39 provides a listing of content areas sorted by type. The options appear in large font used to make the menu easier to read from a

distance (made possible by the use of an infrared TV remote control). As you move the cursor across the menu options, most will pop up icons that represent recently used content for that content area. These pop-up icons enable users to move directly to desired content more quickly (i.e., they do not have to click on the main menu item to access the desired content area).

On earlier versions of Media Center Extension, Microsoft used the standard *Minimize*, *Maximize*, and *Close* buttons in the upper-right side of the Start Page. However, in the 2005 version of MCE, they changed to a single *Shut Down* button located just to the left of the on-screen clock. When you move the cursor over this button, it turns red and pops up a Shut Down message. Click on the button to open the *Close Media Center* options box depicted in Figure 10-40. From this options box, you can close Media Center, log off, shut down the system, restart the computer, or enter standby mode in order from left to right.

Figure 10-39: Media Center Start Page Options

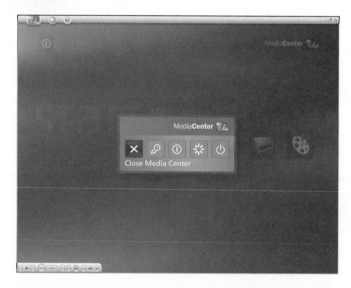

Figure 10-40: Media Center Close Media Center Options

When you right click on an object in MCE, a context-sensitive menu pops up on the display. This pop up also occurs when you press the *Details/More Info* button on the remote control. The menu provides access to the object's details, as well as activity options for what actions can be performed on the object.

My TV

My TV

When you select the **My TV** option from the Start menu, the My TV main screen, depicted in Figure 10-41 appears. This screen provides a menu of TV options that includes *Live TV*, *Recorded TV*, *Guide*, *Search*, and *Movies*. It also displays listings of recently recorded shows and upcoming scheduled recordings. These lists provide direct access to these categories of content. The idea is that these two areas represent the content that users are most likely to be looking for.

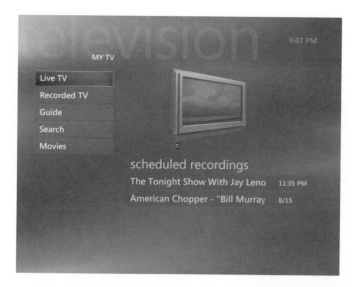

Figure 10-41: My TV

The *Live TV* option brings up the current programming on the selected television channel. It also features a small control overlay that is used to pause a *live* show, navigate through it, or view the remaining time in a show.

The *Recorded TV* option brings up the *Recorded TV* page depicted in Figure 10-42. This screen provides a small menu that includes *Sort by Date* and *Sort by Title* options. The *Sort by Date* option lists your recorded TV programs alphabetically and combines each episode of a recorded TV series into a single title.

The *Scheduled* option produces the Scheduled screen depicted in Figure 10-43. Like the *Recorded TV* page, the *Scheduled* page presents a Sort by…/Series/History menu. It also displays information about the shows you have scheduled to record in the future. The *History* option provides access to the complete list of recorded TV shows on the machine.

**Figure 10-42:
Recorded TV**

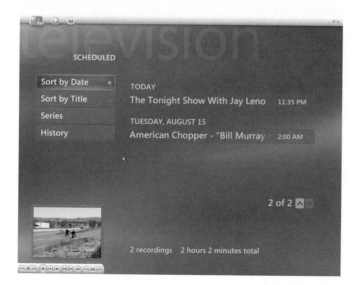

**Figure 10-43:
Scheduled TV**

program guide

program guide

My TV also features a *conflict resolution* interface. If the user attempts to schedule two programs to be recorded at the same time, this interface reminds you that "Only one show can be recorded at one time" and asks you to select the program you prefer to record. However, MCE will attempt to find another instance of the same episode at a different time in the **program guide**. If so, it will automatically reschedule the recording for that time. This problem can be overcome in MCE systems by using TV capture cards that feature multiple TV tuner capabilities. Windows XP MCE is capable of handling up to three logical TV tuners simultaneously.

The My TV **program guide**, depicted in Figure 10-44, allows users to search through the channels they receive for TV programming that they want to watch or record. It also features a user interface for editing TV channel information. This feature permits users to navigate through their TV channel listings while they are viewing the channels and remove any channels that they do not receive through their service. You can also access viewing filter settings that enable users to limit the types of programming that can be viewed through the system. Unlike competing TV services, the Media Center Edition program guide does not charge a monthly fee for usage.

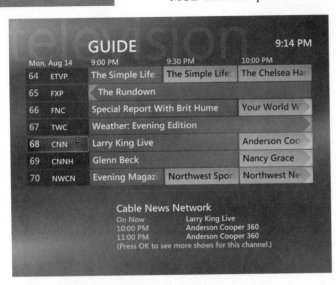

Figure 10-44: My TV Program Guide

My Music

When you select the **My Music** option from the MCE Start menu, the *My Music* main page, depicted in Figure 10-45, is displayed. It includes a selection menu and a graphical album list. The menu enables users to change the view to display all their music by artist, playlist, song, or genre. The menu also lets the user search for music. As with the other Start menu options, the *My Music Start* option presents the user's recent music. If you access the *My Music* page, the entire album list will be displayed along with the albums' cover art.

Figure 10-45: My Music

Under MCE, users can add music to a playlist while it is being played. To add more music to a list, you simply navigate to where the new music to be added is located and click on the *Add to Queue* button. This will attach the new music to the end of the playlist. The same operation can be performed from the remote control. Simply press the *More Info* button on the remote, and then select the *Add to Queue* option. Users can also use the menu to edit the playlist queue to move songs up or down the queue or remove them from the list.

You can save the updated playlist as a *Media Player–compatible playlist* using the *Save as Playlist* button. This button brings up the *Queue* screen illustrated in Figure 10-46. This enables users to access the playlist from both the Media Center and the **Windows Media Player (WMP)** utility. Availability in the WMP enables users to copy that music to portable devices for mobile listening purposes.

The playlist can also be burned to a CD or DVD using the *Create CD/DVD* option. This will bring up the *Create CD/DVD* page illustrated in Figure 10-47. At this point, you must specify whether you are burning an audio CD or a data CD if you've placed a blank CD in the drive, or a data DVD, video DVD, or DVD slide show if you've loaded a blank recordable DVD disc in the drive.

Figure 10-46: My Music Queue Screen

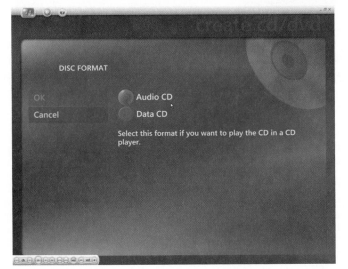

Figure 10-47: The Create CD/DVD Page

You can also use MCE to load music and save it to the hard drive. To accomplish this, place an audio CD in the drive with MCE open. The title appears at the top of the My Music main screen where you can choose to copy the music to the drive.

My Pictures

The MCE **My Pictures** option, depicted in Figure 10-48, allows users to view and edit graphics through the MCE interface. Users can choose to play all pictures, or particular folders of pictures, in a slide-show fashion. They can also view and *Import* graphics from CompactFlash cards, digital camera interfaces, or other portable storage formats.

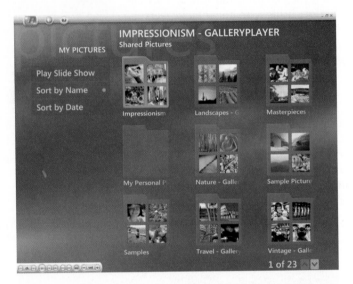

Figure 10-48: My Pictures

Right clicking on an image brings up a menu of actions you can perform on the image. If you select the *Picture Details* option from the menu, the image will be displayed in the *Picture Details* page with a menu of editing options. These options include the following:

- *Rotate*—This option will rotate the picture.

- *Print*—Printing from this option will send the photo directly to the default printer without any prompting or configuration choices. To achieve greater printer control you must resort to Windows XP's more traditional print management tools.

- *Touch Up*—The photo *Touch Up* screen includes photographic enhancement features such as automatic *red eye reduction* and contrast enhancement. It also provides an intelligent photo-cropping feature that allows users to improved poorly framed photographs. The *Crop* feature enables users to zoom in and zoom out, as well as to move the crop area left, right, up, and down. They can also use this feature to change the photograph's landscape/portrait orientation.

- *Delete*—Delete the picture from the system.

- *Next*—Navigate to the next picture.

- *Previous*—Navigate to the previous picture.

The *Create CD/DVD* option in My Pictures can be used to store pictures, folders, and slide shows on optical discs. The slide-show storage option is only available if the *DVD* option is chosen.

Other Features

The **My Videos** option is used to play digitized video stored on the system. Windows XP Media Center Edition includes version 2.1 of the Windows Movie Maker application. Likewise, the *Play DVD* option simply plays DVDs. Windows XP MCE includes FM and **Internet radio** playback support with the ability to time-share FM radio. For example, you can pause, rewind, and fast forward through FM radio transmissions. However, MCE does not allow you to save FM recordings. A third-party Internet radio service is required to access Internet radio through the *Radio* option.

My Videos

Internet radio

Essentials 3.1

Technical Support 3.1

WINDOWS 2000/XP FILES

Filenames in Windows 2000 and XP can be up to 215 characters long (NT 4.0 names could be a maximum of 256 characters long) including spaces. Windows 2000 and XP employ a proprietary method for reducing long filenames to MS-DOS−compatible 8.3 filenames. Instead of simply truncating the filename, inserting a tilde, and then assigning a number to the end of the filename, the Windows 2000 and XP systems perform a mathematical operation on the long name to generate a truly unique MS-DOS−compatible filename. Windows 2000/XP filenames cannot contain the following characters:

/\:*?"|.

Basically, the Windows 2000 and Windows XP algorithms employed to produce MS-DOS−compatible filenames remove any characters that are illegal under MS-DOS, remove any extra periods from the filename, truncate the filename to six characters, insert a tilde, and add an ID number to the end of the name.

However, when five or more names are generated that would result in duplicate short names, Windows NT changes its truncation method. Beginning with the sixth filename, the first two characters of the name are retained, the next four characters are generated through the mathematical algorithm, and, finally, a tilde with an ID number is attached to the end of the name. This method is used to create MS-DOS−compliant short filenames for MS-DOS, Windows 3.x, and Windows 9x−compliant FAT systems, as well as the proprietary NTFS file systems.

Windows 2000 and XP create properties sheets for each file and folder in the system. These sheets contain information about the file (or folder) such as its size, location, and creation date. When you view the file's properties, you can also see its attributes, file type, the program that is designed to open it, and when the file was last opened or modified.

┌─ **TEST TIP** ─┐
Know which characters can legally be used in a Windows 2000 filename.

GEEK SQUAD CASE FILE #32993

A customer has an important business file on his Windows 2000 machine that has boot problems. He can gain access to the drive using a Start disk. However, when he views the disk from the command line, he cannot find the *FutureBusinessPlansandMarketing.doc* file. He has asked the local Geek Squad agents to help him locate the file because he must give a presentation based on it in 1 hour. When you view the drive, there are literally several hundreds of files on the drive. What can his local Geek Squad precinct do for him?

File Encryption and Compression

encrypted files

compressed files

encrypted file system (EFS)

The NTFS file system employed in Windows 2000 and Windows XP Professional provides two new file types that technicians must deal with. These are **encrypted files** and **compressed files**. The Windows 2000 NTFS system provides an **encrypted file system (EFS)** utility that is the basis of storing encrypted files on NTFS volumes. Once a file or folder has been encrypted, only the user who encrypted it can access it. The original user can work with the file or folder just as they would a regular file. However, other users cannot open or share the file (although they can delete it).

> **NOTE**
>
> Windows XP Home does not provide the ability to encrypt files, as does Windows XP Professional.

For other users to be able to access the file or folder, it must first be **decrypted**. The encryption protection disappears when the file or folder is moved to a non-NTFS partition. Only files on NTFS volumes can be encrypted. Conversely, system files and compressed files cannot be encrypted.

decrypted

cipher

Files and folders can be encrypted from the command line using the **cipher** command. Information about the cipher command and its many switches can be obtained by typing **cipher /?** at the command prompt.

> **TEST TIP**
>
> Know how to encrypt a file from the Windows 2000 command line.

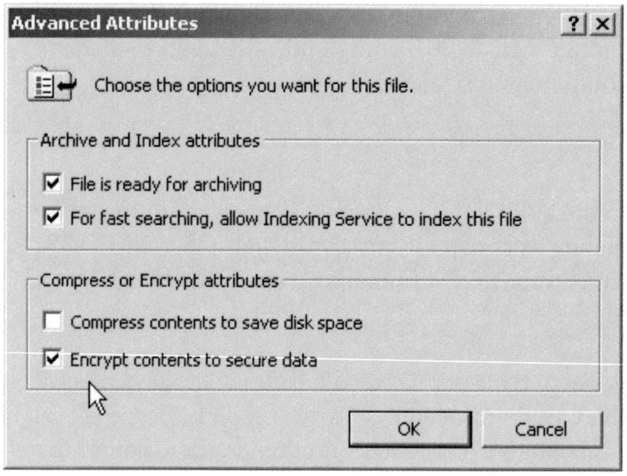

Files can also be encrypted through Windows Explorer. Encryption is treated as a file attribute in Windows 2000 and Windows XP. Therefore, to encrypt a file, you simply need to access its properties page by right clicking on it and selecting its *Properties* option from the pop-up menu. Move to the *Advanced* screen under the *General* tab and click on the *Encrypt contents to secure data* check box, as illustrated in Figure 10-49. Decrypting a file is a simple matter of clearing the check box.

Figure 10-49: Encrypting a File

NTFS compression

Windows Explorer can also be used to compress files and folders on NTFS volumes. Like encryption, Windows 2000 and Windows XP treat **NTFS compression** as a file attribute. To compress a particular file or folder, right click on it in the Windows Explorer, and then select the *Properties* option, followed by the *Advanced* button to access its advanced properties screen, as illustrated in Figure 10-50. Click in the *Compress contents to save disk space* check box to compress the file or folder. Likewise, an entire drive can be compressed through the *My Computer* icon. From the File menu, select the *Properties* option, and click in the *Compress drive to save disk space* check box.

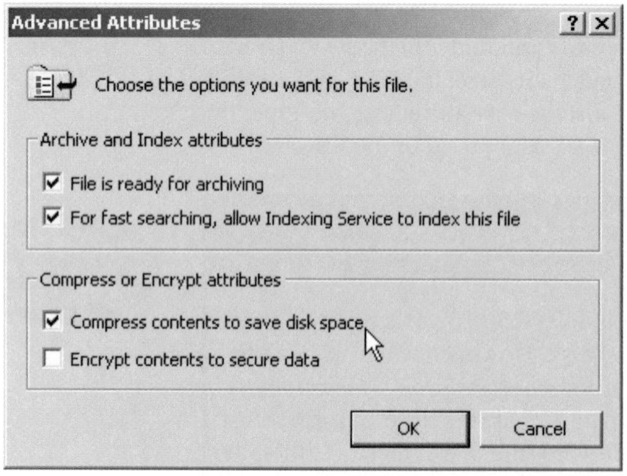

Figure 10-50: Compressing a File

As with the encryption function, Windows 2000 and XP files and folders can only be compressed on NTFS volumes. If you move a file into a compressed folder, the file will be compressed automatically. These files cannot be encrypted while they are compressed. Compressed files can be marked so that they are displayed in a second color for easy identification. This is accomplished through the *Folder Options* setting in the Control Panel. From this page, select the *View* tab and click in the *Display compressed files and folder with alternate color* check box. The only other indication that you will have concerning a compressed or encrypted file or folder is an attribute listing when the view setting is configured to display in Web style.

┌─ **TEST TIP** ─────────────
Know how to identify a compressed file
in Windows 2000.

Managing Windows 2000/XP NTFS

Essentials 3.1

As mentioned earlier, Windows 2000 and Windows XP are based on NTFS Version 5.0. This version of NTFS enables the user to establish disk space quotas for users and locate files by owner. The new NTFS system provides the administrator with tools to manage user access and usage rights to individual files and directories. As mentioned earlier, file-level control was not possible in earlier NT versions. A special administrative list called the **Access Control List (ACL)** is used to view which files a user can have access to. This feature was new to the NT environment but had been available in the Novell NetWare products for some time.

The Windows 2000/XP **Disk Management** utility contains a **Dynamic Volume Management** feature that permits the capacity of an existing volume to be extended without rebooting or reformatting. The Disk Management utility also features a new user interface that enables administrators to configure drives and volumes located in remote computers. Disk Management is a graphical tool that handles two distinctive types of disks—**basic disks** and **dynamic disks**. This tool enables the administrator to handle **dynamic volumes**, created on dynamic disks.

A basic disk is a physical disk that contains partitions, drives, or volumes created with Windows NT 4.0 or earlier operating systems.

Dynamic disks are physical disks created through the Windows 2000 Disk Management utility. These disks can hold only dynamic volumes (not partitions, volumes, or logical drives). However, with dynamic disks, the four-volume limit inherent with other Microsoft operating system versions has been removed. There are five different types of dynamic volumes:

- Simple
- Spanned
- Mirrored
- Striped
- RAID 5

Only systems running Windows 2000 or Windows XP Professional can access dynamic volumes. Therefore, basic volumes should be established on drives that Windows 9x or Windows NT 4.0 systems need to access. If a dynamic volume is present on a drive, the file management systems associated with the other operating systems will not be able to see or access the dynamic drives or volumes.

Access Control List
(ACL)

Disk Management

Dynamic Volume
Management

basic disks

dynamic disks

dynamic volumes

┌─ **NOTE** ─────────────
Windows XP Home Edition
does not support spanned
volumes.

To install Windows 2000 or Windows XP on a dynamic volume, it must be either a simple or a mirrored volume, and it must be a volume that has been upgraded from a basic volume. Installing Windows 2000 on the volume requires that it have a partition table, which dynamic volumes do not have unless they have been upgraded from a basic volume. Basic volumes are upgraded by upgrading a basic disk to a dynamic disk. Under Windows 2000, basic volumes are converted to dynamic volumes using the Disk Management tool (follow

┌─ **TEST TIP** ─────────────
│ Know what the requirements are for creating
│ a dynamic volume in Windows 2000.
└────────────────────────────

the path *Start/Run*, enter *DISKMGMT.MSC* into the text box, and then click on the *OK* button). Windows 2000 and XP will not support dynamic volumes on portable computers. Likewise, mirrored and RAID-5 volumes are only supported on Windows 2000 Servers.

Disk Management snap-in

Administrators group

┌─ **TEST TIP** ─────────────
│ Know what is required to
│ install Windows 2000/XP
│ in a dynamic volume.
└────────────────────────────

Dynamic volumes are managed through the Windows 2000/XP **Disk Management snap-in** tool, depicted in Figure 10-51, located under the Computer Management console. To access the Disk Manager, follow the *Start/Settings/Control Panel/Administrative Tools* path. Double click the *Computer Management* icon and click on the *Disk Management* entry. Because working with dynamic volumes is a major administrative task, you must be logged in as an administrator or as a member of Windows 2000's **Administrators group** in order to carry out the procedure. Also, system and boot volumes cannot be formatted as dynamic volumes.

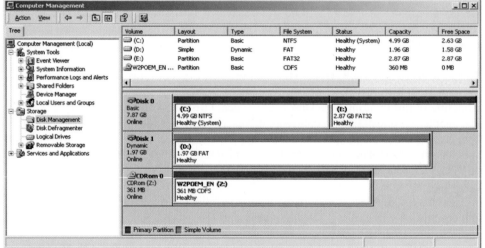

Figure 10-51:
Windows 2000 Disk
Management Snap-In

Formatting Volumes in Windows 2000/XP

Formatting a partition or volume prepares the logical structure to accept data by creating the file system in it. If a partition or volume has not been formatted, it does not contain a file system and cannot be accessed through the operating system or any applications. In the Windows 2000/XP environment, many actions can be performed to initiate formatting. These include the following:

- Use the Volume Creation wizard in the Disk Management utility when the volume is created

- In the Disk Management utility, right click on a volume that has already been created, and select the *Format* option from the action menu

- In Windows Explorer, right-click on the desired drive letter, and select the *Format* option from the action menu

- At a command prompt, type the command *Format* along with the appropriate switches

If you format an existing partition or volume, any data residing in the structure will be lost. The Windows XP Professional operating system protects its system files by preventing the system and boot partitions from being formatted.

Typical options that will be presented during the formatting process include:

- *Volume label*—An 11-character name for the volume that will be displayed in Disk Management, Windows Explorer, and other utilities to identify it. You should make the label descriptive of the type of information that is stored on the volume.

- *File system*—This option permits you to choose FAT (for FAT16), FAT32, or NTFS for the file system type that will be installed in the partition or volume.

- *Allocation unit size*—This setting enables you to manipulate the default cluster size for any of the file systems. This setting should be left at the default value unless you are highly skilled at manipulating disk parameters.

- *Perform a quick format*—This option is used when you want to remove the files and folders on the volume without checking for bad sectors. This should only be selected if you have previously performed a full format and verified that the disk does not have damaged areas.

- *Enable file and folder compression*—The compression option is only available for partitions or volumes that are formatted with NTFS. It specifies that all files placed on the disk will be compressed by default. The compression option is always available on NTFS volumes and can be enabled at any time.

Essentials 3.2

INSTALLING WINDOWS 2000/XP

The installation process for Windows NT versions, including Windows 2000/XP, can be a little more difficult than that of the Windows 9x versions. In particular, the lack of extensive hardware and software compatibilities requires some advanced planning before installing or upgrading to Windows NT/2000/XP.

The first issue to deal with is hardware compatibility. Windows 2000 makes no claim to maintaining compatibility with a wide variety of hardware devices. Check to ensure that the hardware being used is supported by the intended version of Windows 2000 or Windows XP. If the current hardware does not appear in the Microsoft **Hardware Compatibility List** (**HCL**) of the new version, you are on your own for technical support.

Hardware Compatibility List (HCL)

The second factor to sort out is which file management system should be used. Windows 2000/XP can be configured to use either a typical FAT-based file system, or its own proprietary NTFS file system. Review the NTFS Advantages section from earlier in this chapter to determine which file system is better suited to the particular situation.

Installation Methods

Windows 2000/XP operating systems can be installed using two different methods. These are

- Attended installations from the Windows distribution CD of a USB flash drive

- Unattended installations across a network connection using a copy of the installation files obtained from a network server

In both cases, the installer must have access to the operating system's installation files. This primarily means the equivalent of the \I386 folder on the distribution CD. If the local unit has a bootable CD-ROM drive, you can simply insert the CD in the drive and boot directly to it. When the system starts, the CD will load, and the installation can take place locally straight from the CD. If the system does not support a bootable CD, then you will need to start the system using a boot floppy, load the CD-ROM drivers, and run the setup utility from the CD. This will require running the *Winnt.exe* or *Winnt32.exe* files from the \I386 folder on the Windows CD.

The requirements for installing an operating system from a USB flash drive are similar to those associated with installing from a CD-ROM. The major difference is that a BIOS capable of booting from a USB device is required. Otherwise the process is the same. Typically, the operating system must be loaded into the flash drive using a third party program that condenses the Windows Setup files into a smaller operating system that will fit on the flash drive. In some cases it is also possible to add additional utilities to the drive such as anti-virus and other anti-malware products.

distribution server

destination

computer

In a network environment, it is possible to perform installs from a network server across the network connection. This is particularly efficient when you need to perform multiple installations of the operating system around the network (such as when a new operating system version is rolled out across a business or office environment). In these settings, the operating system files are placed on a **distribution server** and executed from the **destination** (receiving) **computer**.

To do this, you simply boot the destination computer to a start disk (floppy, USB, CD, or HDD) that has the *MS-DOS Client for Microsoft Networks* utility on it, connect to the shared folder on the server that holds the setup files, and execute the *Winnt.exe* or *Winnt32.exe* file, as illustrated in Figure 10-52. Of course, the disk drive of the destination drive must be partitioned and formatted before engaging the installation routine.

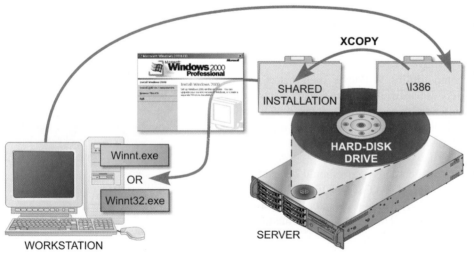

Figure 10-52: Network-Based Windows Installation

Unattended Installations and Disk Images

In a large corporate network, it could literally take weeks to perform a network operating system upgrade for all the systems on the network. For these environments, network operating system manufacturers have provided options for automating the installation process using the network and one or more *distribution servers*. Two automation methods are offered for Windows NT4.0, 2000, and XP networks:

- Unattended automated installations using answer files

- Disk cloning using disk images

Using Answer Files

In an unattended installation using **answer files**, administrators run scripted answer files that have been created to provide automatic answers to all the questions normally asked by the setup/install routine. An administrator can run multiple installations across the network at one time.

If there are circumstances that require different answers for different computers on the network, a **uniqueness database file (UDF)** must also be created to supply the unique settings required for those computers.

The Windows 2000/XP **Setup Manager wizards** can be used to create answer files for unattended Windows installations and for Sysprep disk image cloning. In addition, this wizard can be used to create answer files for use with Windows **Remote Installation Services (RIS)** server. This service is available to conduct RIS image-based installations across the network. It can only be used to deploy Windows 2000 Professional and Windows XP Professional operating systems. This system involves establishing an RIS server in the network and then booting up systems as RIS clients that can download the image from the server. These images can be **CD-based** images or **Remote Installation Preparation (RIPrep)** images created with the Windows RIPrep wizard.

This book deals primarily with attended, local installations of the Windows 2000 and XP operating systems. Automated installations are normally the responsibility of the network administrator. However, even newer technicians may be asked to create images for different types of computers and roll them out on an as-needed basis.

answer files

uniqueness database file (UDF)

Setup Manager wizards

Remote Installation Services (RIS)

CD-based

Remote Installation Preparation (RIPrep)

> **— NOTE —**
>
> Be aware that RIS can only be used to deploy Windows XP Professional and Windows 2000 Professional.
>
> It cannot be used to deploy Windows 2000 Server or any down-level operating systems, including *Windows XP Home Edition* and *Windows XP Media Center Edition*.

Disk Cloning

The second high-volume automated installation method employs clone copies of a given installation and simply re-creates that exact installation on multiple computers across the network. **Disk cloning** requires that a disk image be created of a **reference computer**. This computer must be an exact copy of the hardware and software that you want to clone. The **Sysprep** tool is used to prepare the reference computer for cloning. Third-party cloning software is required to actually create and distribute the **disk image** file that is used to clone the installation process on the remote computers.

Disk cloning

reference computer

Sysprep

disk image

Remote Installation Services Images

You must establish a RIS server in the network and then boot up systems as RIS clients that can download the image from the server.

The general procedure for creating RIPrep images is as follows:

1. Install and configure the RIS service on a Windows server using the *Windows Components* option under the Control Panel's *Add/Remove Programs* icon.

2. Execute the command *Risetup.exe* from the *Run* option of the Start menu on the RIS server. The RIS wizard will install the RIS software, create an initial CD-based image of the system, create RIS answer files in the form of setup information (.sif) files, and configure the Client Installation menu required for remote installation operations.

3. Authorize the RIS server. This is performed through the Server's Administrative Tools and requires that the DHCP administrative utility be configured to *Authorize* the server.

4. Create a reference computer as a template for the clone image. Configure this system with "most common denominator" user and system settings. Also, install and configure any application programs that will be part of the disk image.

5. Copy the Administrator profile into the Default User profile to ensure that everyone will be able to use the settings applied in the previous step.

6. From the command prompt, run *RIPrep* to prepare the system for duplication and create a disk clone image. This will create an exact snapshot of the reference system that can be stored on the RIS server and copied to as many different computers as desired.

7. On the RIS client end, you must boot the system to an RIS boot disk containing the PXE protocol and network adapter card. The RIS boot disk is created using the Remote Boot Floppy Generator (*Rbfg.exe*) utility under the *\Remoteinstall\Admin* folder of the RIS server. The network adapter card will automatically request an IP address from the network's DHCP server and attempt to locate the RIS server in the network.

8. When the client machine locates the RIS server and connects to it, it will automatically download the image—provided the administrator has signified that the computer should receive that image.

Creating Disk Images

The *Sysprep* tool is used to prepare the reference computer for cloning. Third-party cloning software is required to actually create and distribute the *disk image* file that is used to clone the installation process on the remote computers.

The basic steps for creating a disk image include

1. Install the Windows 2000 or Windows XP operating system on the reference computer and log on as Administrator.

2. Install and configure any application packages that are to be part of the disk image.

3. Configure a default set of User settings and Windows components that can be applied to everyone who will use the computers being cloned (i.e., Start menu, Desktop, etc.).

4. Under the Control Panel's *System* icon, copy the Administrator profile to the Default User profile to ensure that everyone who logs on to one of the clone computers will receive the proper settings.

5. Copy the *Sysprep.exe*, *Setupcl.exe*, and *Sysprpe.inf* files into the Sysprep directory of the reference computer (or on a floppy disk).

6. From the command prompt, run the *Sysprep* utility to prepare the system for cloning.

7. Run a disk cloning utility (such as Norton Ghost from Symantec or Casper XP from Future Systems Solutions) to create an exact snapshot of the system. This snapshot can be stored on a distribution server and then be copied to as many different computers as desired. Because the snapshot contains an exact picture of the reference system, including its registry and configuration files, the copies must be installed on systems that either have the same or similar hardware configurations. It is particularly important that the hardware abstraction layers (HALs) and disk controller types match. Differences in Plug-and-Play devices will automatically be detected and corrected during the first start up.

8. When the clone system is started for the first time, the system will request information about several user and computer-specific settings such as licensing, user and company names, computer name and administrator password, product key, regional options, and time zone settings.

The general steps for using a third-party disk cloning program to make disk images is as follows:

1. Install the disk cloning software on a computer system.

2. As part of the installation process, the disk imaging software provides for making a boot floppy that can be used to run the software on the reference and target computers.

3. Prepare a reference computer with the exact installation that you want to clone.

4. Boot the reference computer using the disk imaging boot disk.

5. Follow the instructions presented by the imaging software to create the bit-by-bit clone image of the system. This is typically a menu selection to create an image for the system. You must inform the cloning software where to store the image after it is completed (i.e.. a CD-ROM or remote network drive).

6. Allow the image to be copied to the destination (CD or network drive). This may take a few minutes.

7. Boot the target computer using the boot disk and create a new partition on the drive.

8. Tell the disk-cloning client where to get the image and tell it where to write the image on the target. This is normally a menu function as well.

9. Configure the target computer after the cloning process has concluded.

Hard-Disk Drive Preparation

When a disk is manufactured, its surface is electronically blank. Several levels of preparation must take place to prepare the disk for use by the system. Installing the operating system on a new hard drive has evolved into the four basic steps that follow:

1. Partition the drive for use with the operating system.

2. Format the drive with the basic operating system files.

3. Run the appropriate setup utility to install the complete operating system.

4. Load all the drivers necessary to enable the operating system to work with the system's installed hardware devices.

Therefore, before you can install Windows 2000 or XP on a drive, it must contain as least one partition to hold the system and boot files.

Several disk partition options are available when performing Setup from the Windows XP distribution CD. Partitioning can also be performed with a partitioning utility prior to the installation of Windows 2000 or XP Professional. Some partitioning utilities, such as the FDISK utility, are limited in the size and number of partitions that they can create. Third-party disk partitioning utilities tend to be much more flexible.

When you are partitioning the disk during the Setup process, you will be given the following options:

> **┌─ NOTE ─────**
>
> During the Setup procedure, you should only create the partition that will hold the operating system. In Windows 2000 or XP, it is more efficient to create any additional partitions using the Disk Management utility after the installation has been completed.

- *Create a new partition* if the hard disk does not have any partitions, or if it has existing partitions but also has free (unpartitioned) space.

- *Delete partitions* if the hard disk has existing partitions that you do not want to preserve. Then you can create a new partition in which to install the operating system. However, when you delete a partition, all the existing information in it is lost.

- *Bypass the partitioning process* if the hard disk has existing partitions that you want to install Windows XP into. Any other existing partitions will remain intact.

Patches and Service Packs

In the Windows environment, there are actually three parts of the operating system that you must address when installing a new version or upgrade. These are

- The operating system release version
- Operating system patches and service packs
- Third-party device drivers

operating system release

The **operating system release** is the version of the installation media produced and distributed as a complete unit. However, due to the nature of product development and the pressures on software producers to bring new products to the market, new releases never seem to be complete or perfect. Therefore, manufacturers continue to develop and upgrade their operating systems after they have been released.

Rather than provide customers with a new version of the operating system when new features are added or major problems are corrected, software manufacturers provide **OEM patches** for their products. Microsoft typically releases patches in the form of updates, or in collections that include additional functionality or new device drivers, that they refer to as **service packs**. Patches and service packs are not typically required to run an operating system release. The fact that an operating system exists as a release means that it is a complete operating system.

OEM patches

service packs

When you install a fresh copy of an operating system that has been on the market for some time, or when you upgrade an existing operating system to a new version, there is a definite order for installing the new components:

1. Install the Operating System release.

2. Install the OEM patches or the latest service pack.

3. Install the best device driver choices.

When the new version or the upgrade is installed, it should automatically install its own drivers for the devices it detects. In most cases, these drivers are the best choice for the installed devices, because they have been tested to work with the operating system and should provide the least amount of problems. OEM drivers may not be written as well and tested as thoroughly as those supplied with the operating system.

If the device is not listed in the operating system's HCL, the device manufacturer's driver offers the only choice for operating the device. The other condition that calls for using the equipment manufacturer's driver occurs when the device does not operate correctly with the Windows-supplied drivers. New drivers delivered in service packs may offer a better choice than using the original operating system drivers. However, if they do not produce the operation desired, then the OEM drivers must be reinstalled.

Installing Windows 2000 Professional

Essentials 3.2

The minimum hardware requirements for installing Windows 2000 Professional on a PC-compatible system are

- Microprocessor—133 MHz Pentium (P5 equivalent or better)
- RAM—64 MB (4 GB maximum)
- HDD space—650 MB or more free on a 2 GB drive
- VGA monitor

For installation from a CD-ROM, a 12x drive is required. If the CD-ROM drive is not bootable, a high-density 3.5-inch floppy drive is also required.

┌─ **TEST TIP** ─┐
Memorize the minimum system requirements for installing Windows 2000 Professional.
└────────────────┘

Before installing Windows 2000 Professional from the CD, it is recommended that the Windows 2000 version of the **checkupgradeonly** be run. This file is located on the installation CD under *\i386\winnt32* and checks the system for possible hardware compatibility problems. The program generates a text file report named **upgrade.txt** that can be found under the *\Windows* folder. It contains Windows 2000 compatibility information about the system along with a list of potential complications.

If your system has hardware devices that are not on the Windows 2000 Hardware Compatibility List, you should contact the manufacturer of the device to determine whether they have new, updated Windows 2000 drivers for their device. Many peripheral makers have become very proactive in supplying updated drivers for their devices. Often, they post their latest drivers and product compatibility information on their Internet Web sites, where customers can download them. This is a good place to begin looking for needed drivers. The second alternative is to try the device with Windows NT or Windows 9x drivers to see if it will work. The final option is to get a device that is listed on the Windows 2000 HCL.

A Windows 2000 Professional—compatible NIC is required to install Windows Professional across a network.

A list of Microsoft-verified network cards can be obtained from the **HCL.TXT** file on the Windows 2000 Professional distribution CD. The system must also have access to the network share that contains the Setup files.

If several machines in an organization are being upgraded to the same status, the Windows 2000 Scripting capabilities can be put to good use. This feature can be used to create installation routines that require no user interaction. Microsoft has also increased support for third-party disk copying and imaging utilities that perform multiple installs within a networked system.

To conduct a New Windows 2000 Professional installation, you will need the Windows 2000 Professional distribution CD. If the installation is being performed on a system that cannot boot to the CD-ROM drive, you will also need the Windows 2000 Professional Setup disks.

Hands-on Activity

1. To initiate the installation from a floppy disk, turn the system off, place the Windows 2000 Professional Startup Disk #1 in the floppy drive, and turn the system on. When the Setup program starts, it brings the Windows 2000 Setup Wizard, shown in Figure 10-53, to the screen. The Setup Wizard collects information, including names, passwords, and regional settings, and writes the information to files on the hard drive. Afterward, the wizard checks the system's hardware and properly configures the installation.

2. The first step in the Setup process is to choose whether the installation is a *Clean Install* or an *Upgrade*. If a new installation is being performed, the Setup program will install the Windows 2000/XP files in the *\WINNT* folder.

3. Follow the instructions the Wizard places on the screen, entering any information required. The choice made concerning the type of setup being performed and user-provided input determines the exact path the installation process will take.

4. Verify the operation of the operating system and its components.

Hands-on Activity

1. For a CD-ROM install, boot the system to the existing operating system and then insert the Windows 2000 Professional distribution CD into the CD-ROM drive.

2. If the system detects the CD in the drive, simply click on the *Install Windows 2000 (XP)* option.

3. At the prompt, enter the location on the Windows 2000/XP start file (*Winnt.exe* or *Winnt32.exe*) on the distribution CD (i.e., *d:\i386\Winnt32.exe*). In the case of Windows 3.x, the *Winnt.exe* option should be used.

4. Choose whether the installation is a *New Install* or an *Upgrade*.

5. Follow the instructions the wizard places on the screen, entering any information required.

6. Paste in verification step from last hands on.

> ┌─ **TEST TIP** ─┐
> Know which files are used to start a Windows 2000 install from 16-bit and 32-bit operating systems.

To install Windows 2000 or Windows XP Professional across a network, it will be necessary to establish a shared connection between the local unit and the system containing the Windows 2000/XP Professional Setup files.

Hands-On Activity

1. Boot the local unit to the existing operating system, and establish a connection with the remote unit.

2. At the command prompt, enter the path to the remote *Winnt32.exe* file (use the *Winnt.exe* file if an older 16-bit operating system is being used on the local unit).

3. Choose whether the installation is a *Clean Install* or an *Upgrade*.

4. Follow the instructions the Setup Wizard places on the screen, entering any information required.

5. Paste in verification step.

The Windows 2000 Setup Wizard collects information about the system and the user during the installation process. The most important information that must be provided includes the type of file management system that will be used (FAT or NTFS), Computer Name and Administrator Password, Network Settings, and Workgroup or Domain operations.

GEEK SQUAD CASE FILE #29896

You have been tasked with changing one of your office computers that had been running Windows 98SE to Windows XP Professional. The company has purchased a new, high-capacity hard drive for the machine. As you move through the preinstallation preparation, you notice that the machine contains a modem and a LAN card that you cannot find on the Microsoft HCL for Windows XP Professional. What should you do to get the system running and back in service?

Essentials 3.2

Upgrading to Windows 2000

Systems can be upgraded to Windows 2000 Professional from older Windows 3.x and 9x operating systems, as well as from Windows NT 3.5 and 4.0 workstations. This includes older NTFS, FAT16, and FAT32 installations. When you install Windows 2000, it can recognize all three of these file system types.

If the computer is running a different Microsoft operating system, that OS version must be upgraded to one of these versions before it can be upgraded to Windows 2000. Otherwise, a clean install must be performed from a full version of the operating system. Table 10-3 lists the acceptable Windows 2000 upgrade routes.

CURRENT OPERATING SYSTEM	UPGRADE PATH
Windows 95 and Windows 98	Windows 2000 Professional only
Windows NT 3.51 and 4.0 Workstation	Windows 2000 Professional only
Windows NT 3.51 and 4.0 Server	Any Windows 2000 product
Windows NT 3.1 and 3.5	Must be upgraded to NT 3.51 or 4.0 first, and then to Windows 2000
Windows 3.x	Must be upgraded to Windows 95 or 98 first, then to Windows 2000 Professional

Table 10-3: Windows 2000 Upgrade Routes

The easiest upgrade path to Windows 2000 is from the Windows NT 4.0 operating system. Upgrading from Windows 9x is potentially more difficult.

The process of upgrading to Windows 2000 can be performed in incremental steps. This enables network administrators to bring network machines up to Windows 2000 status over time. During the system upgrade process, the Windows NT 4.0 units can interact with the Windows 2000 units because they see them as NT 4.0 systems. Upgrading Windows 2000 from a Windows NT 4.0 or Windows 9x base is quicker than performing a new installation. When a system is upgraded to Windows 2000 Professional, the Setup utility replaces any existing Windows files with Windows 2000 Professional versions. However, existing settings and applications will be preserved in the new environment.

Windows 2000 does not attempt to remain compatible with older hardware and software. Therefore, some applications may not be compatible with Windows 2000 and may run poorly, or may fail completely after an upgrade.

GEEK SQUAD CASE FILE #28833

A corporate customer has an office network made up of a Windows 4.0 Server with three Windows NT 3.5 workstations, two Windows 98 workstations, one Windows NT 4.0 workstation, and one Windows 3.51 workstation. He wants to test out Windows 2000 Professional on one of his computers to see how it works and to begin getting his users accustomed to Windows 2000. He wants to do this with as little hassle as possible. What would you suggest he do to accomplish these goals?

Upgrading to Windows 2000 is suggested for those using an existing Windows operating system that is compatible with Windows 2000 and who wish to maintain their existing data and preference settings.

Hands-on Activity

1. To upgrade a system to Windows 2000 from a previous operating system using a CD-ROM install, boot the system to the existing operating system, and then insert the Windows 2000 Professional distribution CD in the CD-ROM drive.

2. If the system detects the CD in the drive, simply click on the Install Windows 2000 option. If not, start Setup through the *Run* command. In Windows 9x and NT 4.0, click on *Start* and then *Run*. In Windows 3.x and NT 3.51, click on *File* and then *Run*.

3. At the prompt, enter the location on the Windows 2000 start file (*Winnt.exe* or *Winnt32.exe*) on the distribution CD (i.e., *d:\i386\Winnt32.exe*). In the case of Windows 3.x, the *Winnt.exe* option should be used.

4. Choose whether the installation is a *Clean Install* or an *Upgrade*.

5. Follow the instructions the wizard places on the screen, entering any information required.

6. Verify the operation of the expanded OS.

To upgrade Windows 2000 Professional from a previous operating system across a network, it will be necessary to establish a shared connection between the local unit and the system containing the Windows 2000 Professional Setup files.

Hands-on Activity

1. Boot the local unit to the existing operating system and establish a connection with the remote unit.

2. At the command prompt, enter the path to the remote *Winnt32.exe* file (use the *Winnt.exe* file if an older 16-bit operating system is being used on the local unit). The Winnt command is used with 16-bit operating systems such as DOS or Windows 3.x. The Winnt32 version is used with 32-bit operating systems including Windows 95, 98, NT 3.5, and NT 4.0

3. Choose the *Upgrade your computer to Windows 2000* option.

4. Follow the instructions the Setup Wizard places on the screen, entering any information required.

5. Verify the operation of the expanded OS.

During the installation process, the Windows 2000 Setup Wizard collects information about users and the system. Most of this information is collected automatically. However, some information must be provided by the user or technician. The most important information required during the setup process is the file management system to be used, the computer name and administrator password, network settings, and Workgroup/Domain selection.

GEEK SQUAD CASE FILE #55822

You are working the counter at store 663 when you place a Windows 2000 Professional distribution CD into the drive of a Windows 98 machine, and nothing happens. You want to upgrade the system to Windows 2000, but there is no autodetection or self-starting feature for the CD-ROM. What do you need to do to install the Windows 2000 OS?

Installing Windows XP Professional

Essentials 3.2

The installation process for Windows XP is considerably different from previous Windows installation processes in that Windows XP requires you to activate your copy of the operating system within 30 days after installing it. This process is electronic and is meant to ensure that the copy of XP being used is legitimate and that it is being used on only one computer. If you attempt to install it on a second computer and activate it, an error message will be generated notifying you that the registration is already active.

For technicians this does not become a problem until an extensive system upgrade is performed or a hard drive must be replaced. When these events occur, it will be necessary to deal with Microsoft's licensing department to reactivate the license. The licensing agreement that comes with Windows XP enables a single copy to be legally installed on one desktop and one portable computer.

Windows XP Professional Hardware Requirements

The minimum hardware requirements for installing Windows XP Professional on a PC-compatible system are as follows:

- *Microprocessor*—Pentium II 233 MHz or higher or compatible processor required/Pentium II 300 MHz or compatible processor recommended. Dual-processor configurations are also supported with Windows XP.

- *RAM*—64 MB required/128 MB recommended. The more memory installed, the better. Maximum supported RAM is 4 GB.

- *HDD Space*—2 GB with 650 MB of free space required/2 GB of free hard disk space recommended. A 1.5 GB partition size is required, with 2 GB recommended. Additional disk space is required for installing over a network. The maximum hard disk space supported for a partition is 2 TB.

- *Display device*—A VGA-compatible or higher display adapter with a monitor capable of 800 × 600 resolution required/SVGA-compatible display adapter recommended.

- *Input devices*—Keyboard and mouse (or other pointing device) required.

- *CD-ROM*—12x or faster CD-ROM drive recommended (this item is required to perform Setup from CD-ROM). If the CD-ROM drive is not bootable, a high-density 3.5-inch floppy drive is also required.

Other installation hardware requirements associated with network installations include a high-density 3.5" drive for performing Setup across the network using a network client or boot disk along with an appropriate network adapter card.

As with Windows 2000 systems, all hardware devices included in a Windows XP Professional system must be listed on Microsoft's **Windows XP HCL**. These devices have been tested and are supported by Microsoft. Copies of the Windows XP HCL can be obtained at two locations:

- The Windows XP Professional distribution CD contains a file is named *Hcl.txt* in the *\Support* folder.

- On the Microsoft Web site at *http://www.microsoft.com/hcl*. The HCL version on the Microsoft Web site typically represents the most up-to-date listing.

Before installing Windows XP Professional from the CD, you should run the Windows XP version of the *checkupgradeonly* utility. This file is located on the installation CD under *\i386\winnt32* and checks the system for possible hardware compatibility conflicts. It generates a text file report named *upgrade.txt* that contains Windows XP compatibility information, along with potential complications for the system. This report can be accessed in the *\Windows* folder.

If the system has a hardware device that is not on the Windows XP HCL, then Microsoft has not tested or approved it and, therefore, will not support it. You should contact the device manufacturer to determine whether they have new or updated Windows XP drivers for their device. Most peripheral makers are aware of the importance of supplying updated drivers for their devices. So, they typically post the latest drivers and product compatibility information on their corporate Internet sites.

Windows XP MCE Hardware Requirements

Media Center Edition has more stringent hardware requirements than other versions of Windows XP.

- *Microprocessor*—Pentium 4, 1.6 GHz or higher

- *Display Device*—DirectX 9 hardware-accelerated **graphical processing unit (GPU)**. The term *GPU* is used to describe a dedicated graphics rendering device that is optimized to manipulate and display screen images.

- *RAM*—256 MB required (at least 512 MB preferred)

- *HDD*—40 GB (high-speed ATA or better)

- *Input Devices*—Remote Control and Wireless Keyboard preferred. Media Center remote controls are generally standardized in terms of button labels, functionality, and layout.

Windows XP HCL

graphical processing unit (GPU)

- *TV Tuner Card*—required to receive and process television and other A/V signals. MCE 2005 supports up to four tuners—two *analog tuners* and two *HDTV tuners*. Recording is limited to only two programs at a time. Media Center tuners must have standardized driver interface, hardware MPEG-2 encoders, and closed caption support. The 2005 version of MCE is capable of encoding incoming TV signals at a maximum rate of 9 Mbps.

- *Video Output Device*—High-end video card (with S-video, component video, or DVI TV video output). The 2005 version of MCE directly supports DTV displays and can display 720p and 1080i video on large-screen displays.

- *Sound Card/Speakers*—Sound Card with Stereo Speakers or headset minimum, a 5.1 or 7.1 channel surround system is preferred.

> **NOTE**
>
> Additional functionality, such as Media Center Extender support, use of multiple tuners, or HDTV playback/recording capabilities present higher system requirements.

Upgrading to Windows XP

Essentials 3.2

As time passes, many corporate workstations that are already running different versions of Windows will be upgraded to Windows XP Professional. These workstations can be migrated to the new operating system by either upgrading them or by performing a clean install of Windows XP Professional. Upgrading is preferable in many situations, because it provides for the preservation of existing users and groups, user settings, data, and installed applications.

Systems can be upgraded to Windows XP Professional from Windows 98 and Windows Me as well as Windows NT 4.0 (with service Pack 6) workstations and Windows 2000. This includes older FAT16, FAT32, and NTFS systems. As was the case with Windows 2000, the Windows XP operating system can recognize all three file-system types when it is installed.

Check system compatibility

If a computer is currently running Windows 98, Windows Me, Windows NT Workstation 4.0 (with Service Pack 5 installed), or Windows 2000 Professional, it can be upgraded directly to Windows XP. However, systems running Windows 95 or Windows NT Workstation 3.51 operating systems cannot upgrade directly to XP. Instead, they must have intermediate upgrades to bring them up to a Windows version that does support direct upgrading to Windows XP.

> **NOTE**
>
> Although older Windows operating systems can be upgraded using interim upgrades, the computer hardware that they are running on probably does not satisfy the minimum hardware requirements for Windows XP Professional.

As with new Windows operating system installations, it is a good idea to generate a system compatibility report prior to running the upgrade process. This will permit potential problems to be detected and analyzed and allow solutions to be implemented. The report can be generated through the WINNT32 *checkupgradeonly* command, or by selecting the **Check system compatibility** option on the Setup menu. Either action will launch Setup for the purpose of generating the compatibility report only—the computer will not be modified in any way.

Compatibility Report

Some portions of upgrading from Windows 98 to Windows XP Professional can be difficult. While most operating system and user configuration settings upgrade easily, other items such as applications and device drivers may create problems. Most of these issues will show up when the **Compatibility Report** is generated. If any hardware or software incompatibilities are detected, the proper updates should be obtained and applied before proceeding with the upgrade. Any incompatible software detected should be uninstalled from the system until new compatible replacements can be loaded. Because Windows XP is relatively new, you should take the time to check the system BIOS version to verify that it is the latest revision available.

> **NOTE**
>
> As with Windows 2000 upgrades, remember to verify that BIOS-based virus protection is disabled before performing the Windows XP upgrade. This BIOS feature causes the Setup process to fail because it will interpret Setup's attempts to modify the boot sector as a virus activity.

You should always back up any important files and data before performing an upgrade to avoid losing them. You should also scan for viruses and remove them from the system before conducting an upgrade. Finally, make sure to uncompress any drive compressed with anything other than NTFS compression before performing the upgrade. The only compression type supported by Windows XP Professional is NTFS compression. Third-party compression formats are not supported.

Performing Local Upgrades

To initiate a local upgrade from a bootable CD-ROM drive, simply insert the Windows XP Professional distribution CD into the drive and select the *Install Windows XP* option from the Setup menu, as illustrated in Figure 10-54. If the menu is not displayed automatically, run the Setup utility from Windows XP CD. If you are upgrading from a distribution server, run the WINNT32 utility command.

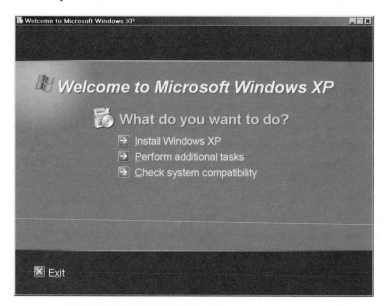

Figure 10-54: Windows XP Setup Menu

Figure 10-55: Windows XP Setup Wizard

The opening Windows Setup page, depicted in Figure 10-55, asks for verification of whether an upgrade of the existing operating system is being conducted or a new version of Windows XP is being installed. If the *New Installation* option is specified, the existing operating system settings will be overwritten along with any existing applications. These applications must be reinstalled to retain their use.

There are two types of upgrades—Express and Custom. An Express upgrade will automatically upgrade the existing Windows installation and maintain all current settings. A Custom upgrade enables you to change the following:

- Installation partition
- Installation folder
- Language options
- File system type (NTFS conversions allowed)

Upgrading to Windows XP requires a minimum of administrative intervention and can be fully automated using answer files as previously discussed in this chapter. The information required to perform a standard upgrade is very similar to that involved with the standard Setup process.

Windows XP has special tools called the **user state migration tools (USMT)** that administrators can use to transfer user configuration settings and files from systems running Windows 9x and NT systems to a clean Windows XP installation. This enables user information to be preserved without going through the upgrade process. In a USMT operation, user state information is backed up from the old operating system to a network server and then restored to the new Windows XP system. The following list describes the default settings transferred from the older system to the new Windows XP system by the USMT utility:

user state migration tools (USMT)

- The contents of all the My Documents, My Pictures, Desktop, and Favorites folders

- Most user interface settings, including display properties, fonts, mapped network drives, network printers, browser settings, folder options, Taskbar options, and files and settings associated with the Microsoft Office applications

- Files with industry standard extensions such as .doc, .ppt, .txt, and .xls

Dual Booting with NT Operating Systems

Windows NT can be set up to dual boot with MS-DOS or Windows 9x operating systems. This provides the option for the system to boot up into a Windows NT environment, or into an MS-DOS/Windows 9x environment. In such cases, a start-up menu appears on the display that asks which operating system should be used. Establishing either of these dual-boot conditions with Windows NT requires that the MS-DOS or Windows 9x operating systems be installed first.

While it is possible for Windows 2000 or Windows XP to share a partition with Windows 9x or Windows NT 4.0, this produces some potentially undesirable situations. Normally, you should install Windows 2000 or XP and the other operating system in separate partitions.

The major drawback of dual booting with Windows NT is that neither operating system is capable of using applications installed in the other operating system's partition. Therefore, software to be used by both operating systems must be installed in the system twice—once for each operating system's partition. Even when you permit Windows 2000 or Windows XP to share the same partition with a Windows 9x or Windows NT operating system, you will need to reinstall the system's applications so that their installation programs can modify the Windows 2000/XP registry.

> **NOTE**
>
> When dealing with dual booting situations, always remember that the Windows 2000 and Windows XP registry structures are not compatible with registries used in Windows 9x/Me products.

TEST TIP

Be aware of which operating system versions are aware of other partition types in a dual-boot situation.

Care must also be taken when formatting a logical drive in a Windows NT dual-boot system. The native file management formats of Windows NT and the other operating systems are not compatible. If the disk is formatted with NTFS, the MS-DOS or Windows 9x operating systems will not be able to read the files in the NTFS partition. These operating systems are not "*NTFS Aware.*" However, Windows 2000 and XP can operate with the FAT file systems. As a matter of fact, they can both be installed on FAT16, FAT32, or NTFS partitions. Windows 2000 and Windows XP also support the CDFS file system used with CD-ROM drives in PCs. Therefore, it is recommended that logical drives in a dual-boot system be formatted with the FAT system.

One reason to configure a dual-boot arrangement occurs when some of your key applications are not Windows XP compatible. In these situations, you can simply boot the computer into an older operating system to use those applications and then run all the other applications under Windows XP. However, there are a few items to consider when dual booting. You should be aware that the system's *active partition* must be formatted with a file system that all the operating systems in the system can use. For example, Windows NT 4.0 does not support the FAT32 file system and cannot boot from a FAT32 partition. Likewise, Windows 98 does not support NTFS and cannot boot from an NTFS partition.

NOTE

If you want to set up a dual-boot configuration with your current operating system, you will need to select the new installation option to preserve the existing operating system.

If drive C: is formatted as NTFS, you will be unable to dual boot with any other operating system without employing a third-party boot manager utility. Therefore, Windows XP Professional should be the last operating system installed. The Windows XP boot manager is backward compatible with previous Microsoft operating systems; however, their boot managers are not compatible with Windows XP. For example, if you were to install Windows NT 4.0 as a second operating system in a dual-boot scenario after Windows XP Professional had been installed, the Windows NT 4.0 boot manager would overwrite the Windows XP boot manager, making it unbootable.

You should make sure that each operating system is installed into a different folder. If possible, they should even be placed in different volumes (drive letters). For example, if you install Windows XP in a folder where another operating system exists, the XP files will overwrite the previous operating system so that it will not boot. However, if you install Windows XP in a different folder on the same volume as an existing operating system, then all the operating systems will function.

While it is possible to dual boot FAT and NTFS volumes, from a security point of view it is recommended that FAT partitions be converted to NTFS partitions. The Windows Setup utility provides you with the option to convert the partition to the new version of NTFS, even though it was previously formatted as FAT or FAT32. This conversion process protects existing files—unlike formatting the partition. The conversion process can also be accomplished form the command line using the CONVERT command.

GEEK SQUAD CASE FILE #75831

You have a physical disk in your computer that has two partitions—both of which are formatted with FAT 16. In one partition you are running Windows 95, and in the other you are running Windows NT 4.0. Because Windows 95 is becoming very old and you do not want to keep it up, you upgrade the Windows 95 partition to Windows 2000 and use the NTFS5 file system. When you start up the system using the Windows 2000 partition, there is no problem. However, when you boot into the Windows NT 4.0 partition, the new partition is not available. What should you do to correct this problem?

WINDOWS 2000/XP DEVICE DRIVERS

Windows 2000 and Windows XP versions offer support for a fairly wide range of disk drive types, VGA video cards, network interface cards, tape drives, and printers. To determine what components the operating system supports, it is necessary to consult the **hardware compatibility list (HCL)** for the version of Windows 2000/XP being used.*

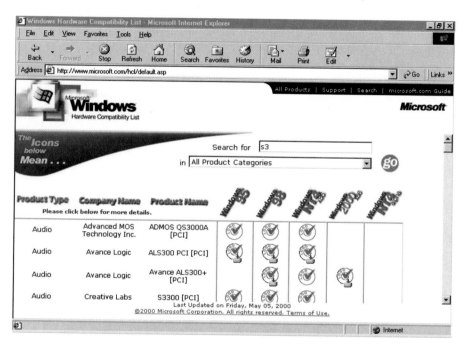

> **hardware compatibility list (HCL)**

> **NOTE**
>
> *This information can be obtained from the Microsoft Web site (*www.microsoft.com/st/hcl*), shown in Figure 10-56.

Figure 10-56: Windows 2000/XP Drivers Page

If drivers for the device being installed are not listed at this location, there is a good chance the device will not operate well, if at all, in the Windows 2000/XP environment. If this is the case, the only recourse is to contact the device's manufacturer for their *Windows 2000* or *Windows XP drivers*. It is a good idea to check the manufacturer's Web site for updated drivers that can simply be downloaded.

> **TEST TIP**
>
> Know where to begin looking for Windows device drivers that are not supplied directly from Microsoft.

GEEK SQUAD CASE FILE #79844

You have been deployed to a music production facility that uses high-end MIDI devices (high-end professional sound cards and devices) to generate and manipulate musical instruments and sounds. They want you to upgrade their production computers, but you worry that these specialized sound cards will not be compatible with the Windows 2000 Professional operating system. The cards and devices work under Windows 98 and they tend to be somewhat expensive compared to other computer devices. How can you determine whether this is a good thing to do?

Adding new devices to Windows 2000 or Windows XP is typically performed automatically through the system's Plug-and-Play process. However, devices can be manually added to a Windows 2000 system through the *Add /Remove Hardware* icon located in the Control Panel. In Windows XP, the icon is simply labeled *Add Hardware*. Double clicking this icon will produce the Add/Remove Hardware (Add Hardware) Installation Wizard that will guide the installation process or aid in troubleshooting problems with the new hardware component. In cases where the device came with an Installation CD, Microsoft recommends that you use the CD instead of the Add Hardware Wizard.

NOTE

Be aware that in an administrated client/server network, you need to have proper administrative permissions to add drivers to a system. If you are working in someone else's network, you normally need to contact the network administrator for a user account with permission levels and rights that will permit you to carry out the driver install/update.

After installing or upgrading a device driver you should verify that it works properly with the hardware it supports. The most straightforward method of verifying the functionality of the driver is to use the device to make sure that it does everything it is supposed to. You can also verify the installation of the driver through the Device Manager utility.

SATA Drivers

Drivers for SATA interfaces and devices are not native to Windows 2000 or Windows XP. If you are installing a SATA drive in an existing system that already has a boot drive, the drivers can be installed at any time. However, if the SATA drive is being installed as the boot drive, the SATA drivers will be loaded into the operating system during the Windows installation process.

In either case, you will need to check the CMOS configuration setup to make sure the SATA communication channel and controller have been enabled. There should be no problem mixing SATA and PATA drives in a system that has the physical interfaces to do so. The operating system will prompt you for the SATA drivers during the installation process. At this point, you need to insert the disk/disc that has the driver on it in an accessible drive and press the F6 function key.

To confirm the presence of the new SATA drivers, access the *Device Manager* utility and look for SCSI and RAID controller device entries. Click on the + sign next to the SCSI device icon to reveal the presence of the Serial ATA Controller. With the drivers installed, you can move into the *Computer Management* console and select the *Disk Management* utility to partition the drive for use.

Finding Drivers

Device manufacturers often continue to develop improved device drivers for their products after they have been released into the market. In addition, there is relatively little cooperation between hardware manufacturers and operating system companies. Therefore, you may need to locate new drivers for existing equipment that is not included in an early release of an operating system such as Windows 2000 or Windows XP.

To find new or updated drivers for a specific device, you should contact the product vendor's web site and search for your specific network operating system. Typically, you will need to know the specific make and model of your device. In most cases, the appropriate device drivers can be downloaded directly from the vendor's Web site or obtained through mail. However, some vendors will only supply their drivers by shipping them to the user on CD.

There are also several third-party Web sites on the Internet where device drivers can be obtained for various pieces of hardware. These sites tend to be especially useful for finding device drivers for older pieces of hardware, where original copies of drivers have been lost.

Driver Signing

Windows 2000 and Windows XP support a relatively wide array of newer hardware devices. These devices include DVD, USB, and IEEE-1394 devices. Microsoft works with hardware vendors to certify their drivers. These drivers are digitally signed so that they can be loaded automatically by the system.

Because poorly written device drivers had traditionally been a third-party problem for Microsoft, they created a *Windows Hardware Quality Labs* (*WHQL*) approval system for hardware manufacturers. Manufacturers who want to insure their customers that their products will work with Windows 2000 and XP operating systems can submit their equipment and drivers to Microsoft for certification. Microsoft grants tested drivers a digital signature that is embedded in the driver to show that it has been approved. When Windows 2000 or Windows XP load the driver, they check it for the signature.

Driver signing is controlled through the Windows 2000/XP Control Panel's System icon. In the *System* applet, select the *Hardware* tab and click the **Driver Signing** button. The *Driver Signing Options* page will appear. On this page, you can establish how the system should react when it detects an unsigned driver. The options are as follows:

- *Warn*—This setting will cause Windows to notify the user when an unsigned driver has been detected. It will also produce an option to load or not load the driver.

- *Block*—As its title implies, this option will not permit any unsigned drivers to be loaded into the system.

- *Disable*—This option disables the digital signature check and automatically loads any driver without providing a warning to the user.

If you check the *Apply setting as system default* check box, the signature verification setting will be applied to anyone who logs onto the system. Otherwise, only the currently logged-on user will be affected.

Because Windows 2000 and Windows XP are designed with centralized network security in mind, there are some administrative control issues that may be encountered when loading device drivers into one of these systems. If the system detects a valid digital signature, or the Designed for Windows Logo, when it checks the driver, it will normally accept the driver without any problems. However, if there is no digital signature or logo, then administrative privileges are required to load the driver into the system.

You must also be a member of the Administrators group to install drivers using the Add Hardware Wizard or when a network policy setting has been established to restrict who can install devices.

Driver Signing

PRINTING IN WINDOWS 2000/XP

Windows 2000 and Windows XP employ a print spooler processing architecture that provides smooth printing in a background mode and quick return-to-application time. The key to this operation is in how the print spooler sends data to the printer. Data are moved to the printer only when it is ready to receive more. Therefore, the system never waits for the printer to digest data that has been sent to it.

print spooler

The Windows 2000 **print spooler**, depicted in Figure 10-57, is actually a series of 32-bit virtual device drivers and DLLs. In the figure, the spooler consists of the logical blocks between the client computer and the print device. These blocks process threads in the background and pass them to the printer when it is ready. In essence, the application prints to the Windows printer driver, the driver controls the operation of the spooler, and the driver prints to the printer from the spooler.

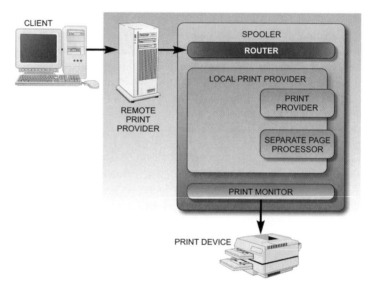

Figure 10-57: The Windows 2000 Print Spooler

Figure 10-58: Windows XP Print Spooler Properties

In a network printing operation, the print spooler must run on both the local server and the remote client systems. The user can start and stop the local print spooler process in Windows 2000 and XP through the Control Panel's *Administrative Tools/Services* icon. Clicking on this icon produces the Services listing that contains the *Print Spooler* entry. Simply select the *Print Spooler* entry from the list to access the Print Spooler Properties, as illustrated in Figure 10-58. After the user stops the spooler service, it will be necessary to restart it before printing can occur again, unless the printer driver has been configured to bypass the spooler. Also, the local user is not capable of controlling the print operation to a server. The server print function is managed independently.

To print an open file in Windows 2000 or Windows XP, simply move to the application's File menu as usual and click on the *Print* option. If the file is not open, it is still possible to print files in Windows 2000 and Windows XP. Under the *My Computer* icon, access the desired file, right click on it, and select the *Print* option from the pop-up menu as shown in Figure 10-59. Files can be printed from the *Windows Explorer* screen by employing the same right-click menu method. The document can also be dragged and dropped onto a printer icon in the *Printers* folder, in the My Network Places listing, or on the desktop. Obviously, this option can be performed with both local and remote networked printers.

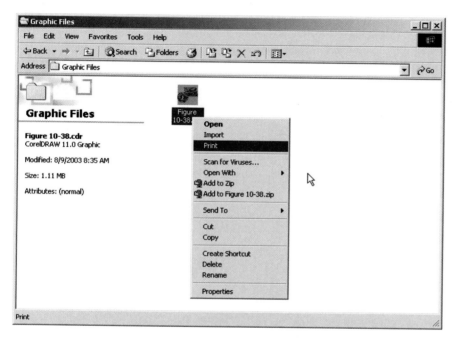

**Figure 10-59:
Printing from My
Computer Pop-up
Menu**

In Windows 2000, the settings for any printer can be changed through the *My Computer* icon on the desktop or through the *Printers* option under the Start menu's *Settings* entry. The process is the same for both routes: simply double click on the *Printer* folder, right click on the desired printer, and select its *Properties* entry from the menu. In Windows XP, you can access these settings through the *Printers and Faxes* option in the Start menu. The rest of the process is the same as that used in Windows 2000.

To view documents waiting to be printed from the print spooler, double click on the desired printer's icon in the *Printer* folder. This will display the existing print queue, as illustrated in Figure 10-60. Closing the print window does not interrupt the print queue in Windows 2000 or XP. The fact that the print spooler runs in its own virtual environment means that printer hang-ups will not lock up the system. The print jobs in the queue will be completed unless they are deleted from the list.

Document Name	Status	Owner	Pages	Size	Subm
COVER178.cdr	Printing	Cathy	1	8.25 MB/10.8 MB	2:17:
FORMS226.cdr		Cathy	1	135 KB	2:18:
ic100f.vp	Spooling	Cathy	1	13.9 MB	2:19:

3 document(s) in queue

**Figure 10-60:
Windows 2000
Print Queue**

GEEK SQUAD CASE FILE #77383

You have sent a document to your local printer for printing when you notice that you have not included some key information in the document. Nothing has come out of the printer, so you check the Windows 9x printer queue in an attempt to delete the document before it prints. However, nothing is there. What can you do to get the document back?

The print spooler window's menu options permit printing to be paused and resumed. They can also be used to delete print jobs from the queue. Right-clicking a printer icon will produce a pop-up menu that can also be used to control printing operations that are performed by that printer. Both options offer a *Properties* option that can be used to access the printer's configuration and connection information.

Internet printing protocol (IPP)

The Windows 2000 and Windows XP Printers dialog boxes enable users to sort between different printers based on their attributes. Windows 2000 Professional possesses the capability of printing across the Internet using the new standards-based **Internet printing protocol (IPP)**. Using this protocol, Windows 2000 Professional and Windows XP can print to a URL, view the print queue status using an Internet browser, and install print drivers across the Internet.

Establishing Printers in Windows 2000/XP

Add Printer Wizard

Windows 2000 and Windows XP will automatically adopt any printers that have been established prior to their installation in the system. If no printers have been installed, the Setup routine will run the **Add Printer Wizard**, shown in Figure 10-61, to enable a printer to be installed. Each printer in the system possesses its own print window and icon to work from. The wizard can be accessed at any time through the Start menu.

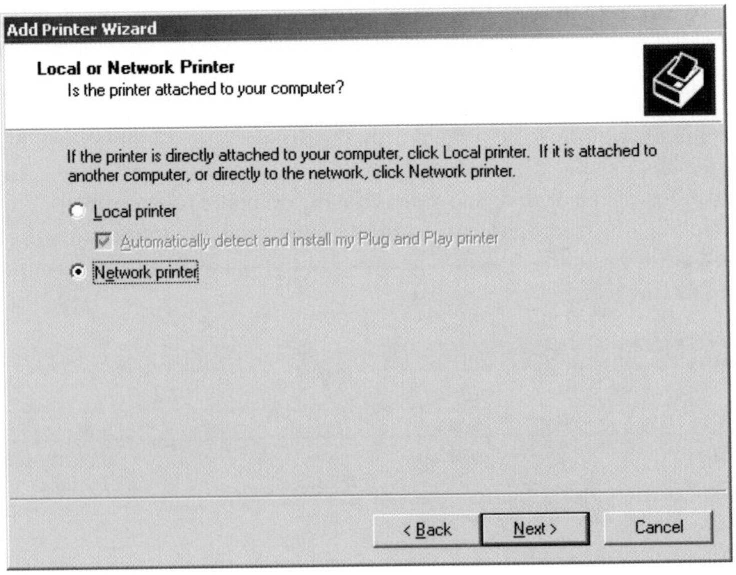

Figure 10-61: The Windows 2000/XP Add Printer Wizard

To use the Start menu in Windows 2000 for this purpose, move to the *Settings* entry and click on *Printers*. To install a printer, open the *Printers* folder and double click the **Add Printer icon**. In Windows XP, click on the *Start* button and then click on the *Printers and Faxes* icon. To access the Printer wizard in Windows XP, select the *Add a Printer* option from the *Printer Tasks* window. From this point, the Printer Wizard guides the installation process. Because Windows 2000 and Windows XP have built-in networking support, the printer can be a local unit (connected to the computer) or a remote unit located somewhere on the network.

To install local printers, choose the *Local Printer* (*Local printer attached to this computer in XP*) option, and click on the *Next* button. In the Windows XP dialog window, you should also have the *Automatically detect and install my Plug and Play printer* option checked. Normally, the LPT1 options should be selected from the list of **Printer Port** options. Next, the Add Printer Wizard will produce a list of manufacturers and models to choose from. This list will be similar to the one shown in Figure 10-62. Simply select the correct manufacturer and then the desired model from the list and inform the wizard about the location of the \I386 directory to fetch the driver from. If the \I386 directory has been copied to the hard drive, it will be faster to access the driver there. If not, the Windows 2000 or Windows XP distribution CD will be required.

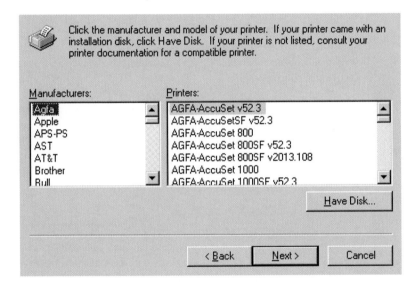

Figure 10-62: A List of Printer Manufacturers and Models

If the printer is not recognized as a model supported by the Windows 2000 or Windows XP driver lists, OEM drivers can be installed from a disk containing the OEMSETUP.INF file. Select the *Have Disk* option from the *Add Printer Wizard* screen. In Windows XP, you can also select the *Windows Update* option to search for updated drivers. After loading the driver, the wizard will request a name for the printer to identify it to the network system. Enter a unique name or use the default name supplied by Windows and continue.

Finally, the Add Printer Wizard will ask whether the printer is to be shared with other units on the network. If so, the printer must have a unique name to identify it to others on the network and must be set as *Shared*. The shared printer must also be set up for the different types of operating systems that may want to use it. The wizard will display a list of operating system types on the network. Any or all of the operating system types may be selected. The installation process is completed when the *Finish* button is clicked.

In Windows 2000, the Add Printer Wizard can also be accessed through the *My Computer* icon, the Control Panel, or by double clicking on the *Printers* folder or icon. However, in Windows XP, the My Computer path does not exist.

TEST TIP
Know how to install device drivers in Windows 2000 if the particular device is not listed in the standard Windows driver listings.

Printer Properties

Printer properties are all of the defining features about a selected printer and include information that ranges from which port it uses to what security features have been implemented with it.

To examine or change the properties of a printer in Windows 2000, select the *Printers* option from the Start/Settings menu. In Windows XP the path is *Start/Printers and Faxes*. Inside the printer window, click on the desired printer to select it. From the *File* menu option, select the *Properties* entry to display the printer's properties sheet, as depicted in Figure 10-63. Right-clicking on the printer icon and then selecting the *Properties* option from the menu will also access the printer Properties.

The *General* tab provides general information about the printer. This includes such information as its description, physical location, and installed driver name. The *Ports* tab lists the system's physical ports and the *Scheduling* tab displays the printer's availability, priority level, and spooling options. In Windows XP, the *Scheduling* tab has been replaced with a tab named *Advanced*. The *Sharing* tab shows the printer's share status and share name.

The *Security* tab provides access to three major components. These are the *Permissions* button, the *Auditing* button, and the *Ownership* button. The *Permissions* button enables the system administrator to establish the level of access for different users in the system. The *Auditing* button provides user and event tracking capabilities for the administrator. Finally, the *Ownership* button displays the name of the printer's owner.

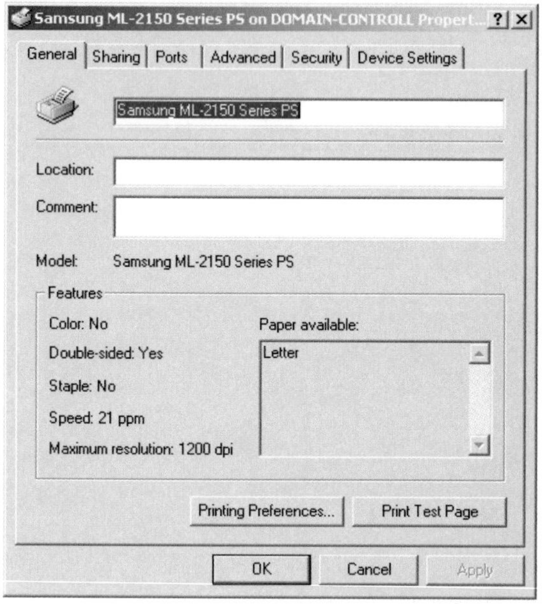

Figure 10-63: Printer Properties Sheet

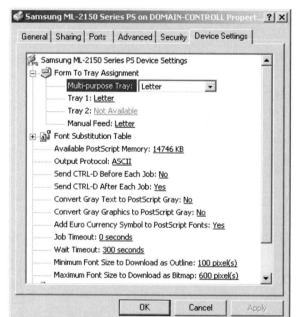

Figure 10-64: Windows 2000 Printer Properties/ Device Settings Tab

---

NOTE

Access to files and folders on NTFS volumes can be audited, allowing the tracking and discovery of potential security violations. However, this feature is not available on Windows XP Home Edition.

The *Device Settings* tab provides a wide array of information about the printer, including such items as paper tray sizes and font substitution tables. This feature is used to import downloadable font sets, install font cartridges, and increase the printer's virtual memory settings. The *Device Settings* tab, shown in Figure 10-64, is one of the most important tabs in the *Printer Properties* page.

WINDOWS 2000/XP APPLICATIONS

The Windows 2000 and Windows XP environments employ an **Add/Remove Programs wizard** (actually *Add or Remove Programs* in Windows XP) to assist users in installing new applications. The Windows 2000/XP Add/Remove Programs icon is located in the Control Panel.

Double clicking on the *Add/Remove Programs* icon produces the *Add/Remove Programs* dialog window, as illustrated in Figure 10-65. Any application that employs a Setup.exe or Install.exe installation routine can be installed through this window. Clicking on the *Install* button will cause the system to request the location of the installation program.

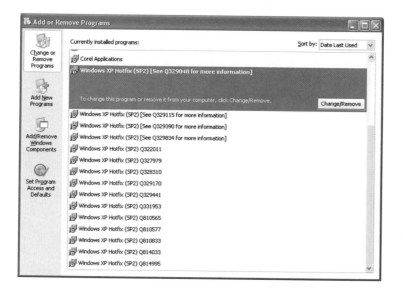

Figure 10-65: Windows XP Add or Remove Programs Window

In addition to third-party applications, the Windows Components wizard can be used to install or remove **optional components** of the Windows 2000/XP operating system. Clicking on the *Windows 2000* or *Windows XP Setup* tab under the *Properties* box produces a list of components, like the one shown in Figure 10-66. The individual components can be selected for inclusion in or removal from Windows 2000 or Windows XP systems.

In Windows 2000 networks, application software can be installed remotely across the network. This enables the network administrator to control user application software across the network and keep it uniform throughout an enterprise. Likewise, the network administrator can assign applications to users so that they appear on their Start menus. When the application is selected for the first time, it will be installed on the local machine. The administrator can also place optional applications on the *Add/Remove Programs* dialog box in the Control Panel. The user can install these applications from this location at any time.

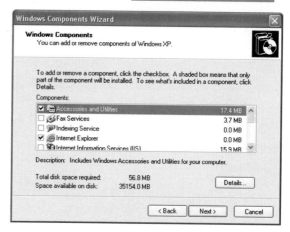

Figure 10-66: Windows XP Optional Components

NOTE

Be aware that in an administrated client/server network, you need to have proper administrative permissions to add software to a system. If you are working in someone else's network, you normally need to contact the network administrator for a user account with permission levels and rights that will permit you to carry out the application install/update.

Windows 2000/XP Application Installer

Application Installer

Windows 2000 and Windows XP both feature a versatile MSI applications installer called the Windows Application Installer. This program is designed to better handle DLL files in the Windows 2000/XP environments. In previous versions of Windows, applications would copy similar versions of shared DLL files, and other support files, into the \Windows folder. When a new application overwrites a particular DLL file that another application requires for proper operation, a problem is likely to occur with the original software package.

The Windows 2000 **Application Installer** enables applications to check the system before introducing new DLLs to the system. Software designers who want their products to carry the Windows 2000/XP logo must write code that does not place proprietary support files in the \Windows directory, including DLL files. Instead, the DLL files are located in the application's folder.

Windows Installer—compatible applications can repair themselves if they become corrupted. When the application is started, the operating system checks the properties of its key files. If a key file is missing, or appears to be damaged, it will invoke the Installer and prompt the user to insert the application distribution CD. When the CD has been inserted, the Installer automatically reinstalls the file in question.

Launching Applications in Windows 2000/XP

In Windows 2000 and Windows XP, there are several acceptable methods of launching an application. These include

- *Select the application from the extended Start menu*, click on the folder containing the application, and double click its filename.

- *Select the Run entry from the Start menu*, and then enter the full path and filename for the desired executable file.

- *Double click the application's filename* in the Windows Explorer or in My Computer.

- *Click on the File menu option* from the My Computer menu bar, or through the Windows Explorer, and select the *Open* option. (You can also alternate-click on the application and choose *Open*).

- *Create a shortcut icon* on the desktop for the application, so that simply double clicking on its icon will start it.

Figure 10-67: The Windows 2000 Open With Dialog Box

Open With

In the Windows 2000/XP operating systems, an application can also be set up to run by association. Using this method, the application will be started whenever an associated file is double clicked. This is accomplished by defining the file's type in the **Open With** dialog box. The first time you attempt to open a nonassociated application, the *Open With* dialog box, shown in Figure 10-67, will appear. Holding down the left SHIFT key and right-clicking the file's icon will access the *Open With* option.

WINDOWS 2000/XP NETWORK STRUCTURE

The central feature of the Windows 2000 network architecture is the **Active Directory (AD)** structure. Active Directory is a distributed database of user and resource information that describes the makeup of the network (i.e., users and application settings). It is also a method of implementing a distributed **authentication process**. **Authentication** is the process of identifying individuals as being who they claim to be. This process is normally based on usernames and passwords.

Windows 2000 remains a domain-dependent operating system. It uses domains as boundaries for administration, security, and replication purposes. Each domain must be represented by at least one **domain controller**. The domain controller is a server set up to hold the directory database for the network. This database contains information about **User Accounts**, **Group Accounts**, and **Computer Accounts**. It tracks the names of all of the objects and requests for resources within the domain. You may also find this database referred to as the **Security Accounts Manager (SAM)**. This feature helps to centralize system and user configurations, as well as data backups on the server in the Windows 2000 network.

The Active Directory structure employs two common Internet standards—the **lightweight directory access protocol (LDAP)** and **domain name service (DNS)**. The LDAP protocol is used to define how directory information is accessed and exchanged. DNS is the Internet standard for resolving domain names to actual IP addresses. It is also the standard for exchanging directory information with clients and other directories.

Active Directory (AD)

authentication process

Authentication

domain controller

User Accounts

Group Accounts

Computer Accounts

Security Accounts Manager (SAM)

lightweight directory access protocol (LDAP)

domain name service (DNS)

The Active Directory arranges domains in a hierarchy and establishes trust relationships among all of the domains in a tree-like structure, as illustrated in Figure 10-68.

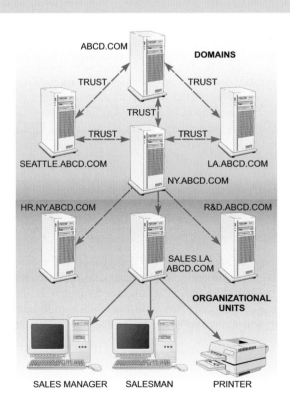

Figure 10-68: Basic Active Directory Structure

tree

A **tree** is a collection of objects that share the same DNS name. Active Directory (AD) can subdivide domains into organizational units (sales, administration, etc.) that contain other units, or leaf objects, such as printers, users, and so on.

forest

Conversely, Windows 2000 can create an organizational structure containing more than one tree. This structure is referred to as a **forest**. Figure 10-69 expands the AD structure to demonstrate these relationships.

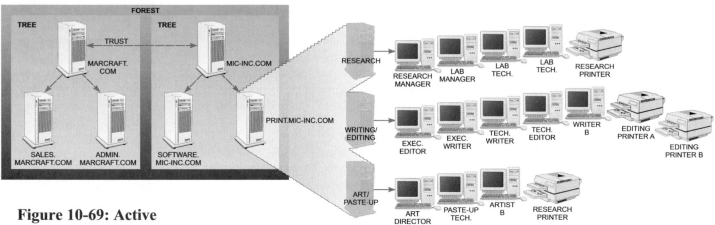

Figure 10-69: Active Directory Relationships

The Windows 2000 operating system automatically joins all of the domains within a tree through two-way trusts.

Trusts

Trusts are relationships that enable users to move between domains and perform prescribed types of operations.

If a trust relationship is established between the sales and marketing domains in the example and a similar trust exists between the sales and administration domains, then a trust relationship also exists between the marketing and administration domains. Trusts enable administrators to provide users and groups with different rights to objects.

Rights
Administrative rights

Rights are permission settings that control a user's (or groups of users') authority to access objects and perform operations (such as reading or writing a file). **Administrative rights** provide authority to users down to the organizational unit (OU) level.

Administrative rights do not cross boundaries established at the domain level but can be inherited by other OUs having subordinate positions within the same tree. On the other hand, **user rights** must be established for individual users or for members of groups. Using groups allows common rights to be assigned to multiple users with a single administrative action (as opposed to setting up and maintaining rights for each individual in, say, a 150-person accounting staff).

user rights

Configuring Windows 2000/XP Networking

During the Windows 2000 or Windows XP setup processes, the system must be configured to function as a workgroup node, or as part of a domain. A workgroup is a collection of networked computers assigned the same workgroup name. Any user can become a member of a workgroup by specifying the particular workgroup's name during the setup process. Conversely, a domain is a collection of networked computers established and controlled by a network administrator. As mentioned earlier in this chapter, domains are established for security and administration purposes.

The Setup routine requires that a computer account be established before a computer can be included in the domain. This account is not the same as the user accounts that the system uses to identify individual users.

If the system has been upgraded from an existing Windows NT version, Windows 2000 or XP will adopt the current computer account information. If the installation is new, the Setup utility will request that a new computer account be established. The network administrator normally assigns this account prior to running Setup. Joining the domain during setup requires a username and password.

In Windows 2000 or Windows XP systems using the TCP/IP protocol, computer names can range up to 63 characters in length and should be made up of the letters A through Z, numbers 0 through 9, and hyphens.

┌ TEST TIP ┐
Know the specifications for setting up computer names in a given operating system.

Administering Windows 2000/XP Networks

Essentials 6.1

IT Technician 6.1

Windows 2000 and XP Professional are both designed for use in an administrated LAN environment. As such, they must provide network administrators with the tools necessary to control users and data within the network. To empower the network administrator, Windows 2000 and XP furnish five powerful administrative tools:

- System Policies
- User Profiles
- Groups and Group Policies
- Network Share Permissions
- NTFS Rights

Each of these tools is designed to enable administrators to limit, or grant, users' access to files, folders, services, and administrator-level services.

Windows 2000/XP Policies

As with other Windows versions, the overall operation of the Windows 2000 and Windows XP environments is governed by **System Policies**. Basically, policies give administrators control over users. Using System Policies, the network administrator can give or limit users' access to local resources, such as drives and network connections. Administrators can establish policies that force certain users to log in during specified times and lock them out of the system at all other times. System Policies also enable the administrator to send updates and configure desktops for network clients. Fundamentally, any item found in the Control Panel can be regulated through System Policies.

User Profiles

Each Windows 2000/XP user is assigned a profile directory under their username the first time they log in to a given Windows 2000/XP system. This **profile** contains system information and settings that become particular to the user and are stored under the Documents and Settings directory. Inside the directory, the system creates the **Ntuser.dat** file, along with various other data files. As discussed previously, this file contains the User portion of the Windows registry. This file contains the user-specific settings that have been established for this user. When the user logs onto the system, the User and System hive portions of the registry are used to construct the user-specific environment in the system.

The first time a user logs onto a system, the default **User Profile** directory is copied into the directory established under the user's name. When the user makes changes to the desktop, Start menu, My Documents, and so on, the data are stored in the appropriate files under the username. Windows 2000 and Windows XP provide methods of storing user profiles on the server in a networked environment. This prevents the user's profile directories from being re-created at each machine the user logs in to. Instead, these operating systems provide roaming profiles that are downloaded from the server to the client when the user logs in. Changes made during sessions are uploaded to the server when the user logs out.

As with previous versions of Windows NT, Windows 2000 and Windows XP employ profiles to provide customized operating environments for users. These profiles are stored in different locations, hold more information, and are more customizable than previous Windows NT versions, but they perform the same functions. However, you should be aware that Windows 2000/XP policies work very differently under the Active Directory structure than they do in the Windows NT Domain structure.

The primary tool for working with the Active Directory is the **Active Directory Users and Computers**, depicted in Figure 10-70. The organizational units of a domain contain users, groups, and resources. The Active Directory Manager tool is used to add users, groups, and **organizational units (OUs)** to the directory.

Although the Active Directory structure is designed primarily to help manage a network, it can also be a valuable desktop tool. The Active Directory Service running on a Windows 2000 Server enables Windows 2000 and XP Professional installations to locate printers, disk drives, and other network devices across the network.

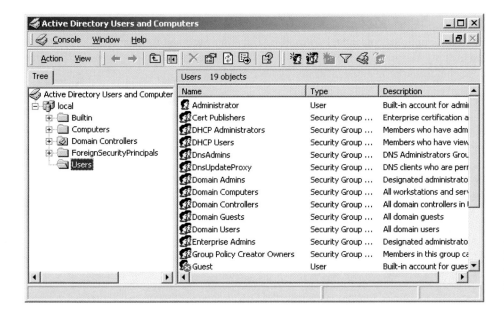

Figure 10-70: Active Directory Users and Computers

Group Policies

Windows 2000 and Windows XP environments function on **Group Policy Objects** (**GPOs**). Group Policies are the Windows 2000/XP tools for implementing changes for computers and users throughout an enterprise. The Windows 2000 and XP Group Policies can be applied to individual users, domains, organizational units, and sites. In addition, the Windows 2000/XP policies are highly secure.

In Windows 2000 and Windows XP systems, policies are established through the Group Policy Editor (GPE) shown in Figure 10-71. Administrators use this editor to establish which applications different users have access to, as well as to control applications on the user's desktop.

> **Group Policy Objects (GPOs)**

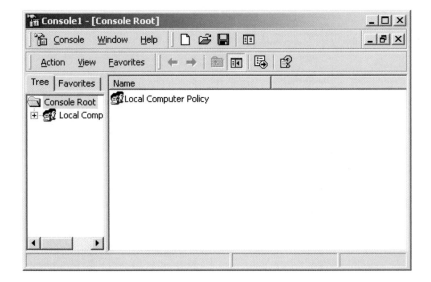

Figure 10-71: The Windows 2000 Group Policy Editor

With Group Policies, administrators can institute a large number of detailed settings for users throughout an enterprise, without establishing each setting manually. GPOs can be used to apply a large number of changes to machines and users through the Active Directory. These changes appear in the GPE under three headings:

- *Software Installation Settings*
- *Windows Settings*
- *Administrative Templates*

Each heading appears in two places—the first version is listed under Computer Configuration and the second copy is found under User Configuration. Values will usually differ between the versions of the headings, because the user and computer settings will be different.

- The *Software Installation Settings* heading can be used to install, update, repair, and remove applications.

- The *Windows Settings* portion of the GPO contains start-up and shutdown scripts as well as security settings. The Security Setting portion of this heading covers such topics as Account policies, Password policies, and User Right Assignments, to name a few.

- The *Administrative Templates* portion of the GPO stores changes to the registry settings that pertain to the HKEY_LOCAL_MACHINE. Figure 10-72 shows the hierarchy of items in the Computer Configuration Administrative Templates window of the Group Policy Editor.

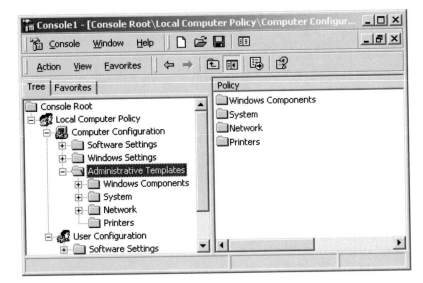

Figure 10-72: Computer Administrative Templates

Network Shares

In a network environment, only network shares (shared directories and resources) can be accessed across the network. The sharing function is implemented at the computer that hosts the folder or resource (resources are devices capable of holding or manipulating data). In Windows operating systems, you can establish sharing for a folder by right clicking on it and selecting the *Sharing* option from the menu. This will produce the *Sharing* tab of the file or folder's Properties page, as illustrated in Figure 10-73.

Similarly, for resources such as disk drives and printers, you can institute sharing by right clicking on the device's icon and select the *Sharing* option from the menu. This will produce the *Sharing* tab from the device's Properties. In both cases, the presence of a hand symbol under the folder or device's icon indicates that it has been shared. To configure a shared folder's Properties, click on the *Share this folder* radio button and fill in the *Share name:* dialog box. Then click on the *Permissions* button to open the folder's *Permissions* dialog box to produce the *Share Permissions* dialog window shown in Figure 10-74.

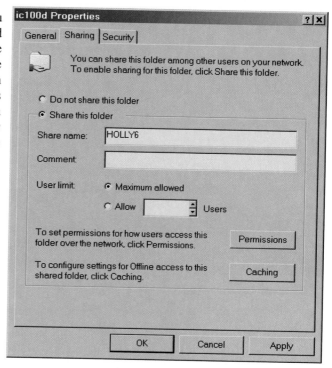

**Figure 10-73:
File and Folder
Sharing Tab**

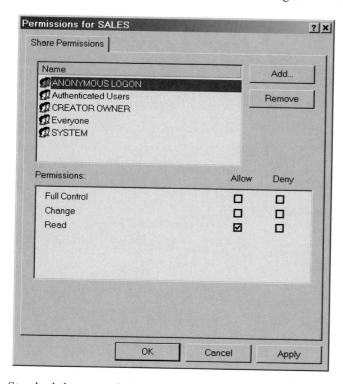

**Figure 10-74: Share
Permissions Dialog**

Standard share permission options in Windows 2000 and XP are as follows:

- *Read*—This setting enables the user to view file and folder names, run applications, read files, view file and folder attributes, and navigate through the directory tree at levels beneath this folder.

- *Change*—This setting provides complete Read permissions, as well as the ability to create and delete files and folders, to edit files, and to change file and folder attributes.

- *Full Control*—This option enables the user to perform all of the functions available through the Change permission and provides the ability to modify permissions and to take ownership of the folder.

It is possible for users to receive these permissions from different sources (i.e., as members of different groups that have been assigned different permissions to the folder or resource). When this occurs, the different settings combine, and the user receives the highest *Allow* option setting. However, *Deny* option settings override any Allow setting. For example, if a user has Full Control permissions for a certain folder from one group and only Read permissions from another group, then the result will be Full Control. However, if a *Deny* permission is assigned for Full Control from another group, then the user will receive only Read permissions for the folder.

To access the shared remote resource, the local operating system must first connect to it. After the connection has been established, the local operating system creates a new logical drive on the system to accommodate the new folder in the system.

Share permissions can only be assigned to the folder level. Windows 2000 and Windows XP NTFS permissions are much more robust than share permissions. NTFS permissions can be set at the file level in NTFS systems. However, share permissions are the only network access control option available for non-NTFS partitions.

NTFS Permissions

NTFS permissions

The NTFS system includes security features that enable permission levels to be assigned to files and folders on the disk. These permissions set parameters for operations that users can perform on the designated file or folder. *Standard* **NTFS permissions** include

- *Read (R)*—This permission enables the user to display the file or folder along with its attributes and permissions.

- *Write (W)*—This permission enables the user to add files or folders, change file and folder attributes, add data to an existing file, and change display attributes.

- *Execute (X)*—The Execute permission enables users to make changes to subfolders, display attributes and permissions, as well as to run executable file types.

- *Delete (D)*—The Delete permission makes it possible for users to remove files and folders.

- *Change (P)*—This permission enables users to change permission assignments of files and folders.

- *Take Ownership (O)*—Ownership permission enables the user to take ownership of the file or folder.

Some of these permission settings apply only to file-level objects, whereas others apply to both files and folders. Some combinations of the permissions are woven together in Standard NTFS file and folder permissions. These include

- *No Access (none)*—File and folder levels

- *Read (RX)*—File and folder levels

- *Change (RWXD)*—File and folder levels

- *Add (WX)*—Folder level only

- *Add & Read (RWX)*—Folder level/*Add & Read (RX)*—File level

- *List (RX)*—Folder level only

- *Full Control (RWXDPO)*—File and folder levels

While the NTFS system provides permission-level security for files and folders, other operating systems under Windows NT do not. For example, when a file is moved from an NTFS partition to a FAT partition, the NTFS-specific attributes are discarded. However, NTFS permissions apply over a network connection.

Permissions can be assigned directly by the administrator, or they can be inherited through group settings. If a user has only Read permissions to a particular file but is assigned to a group that has wider permissions, then that individual would gain those additional rights through the group. In a server environment, the default permission setting for files is *No Access*.

— NOTE —

NTFS is the preferred file system for Windows XP Home. However, several features are not available in the Home edition. For the typical home users, this is not an issue; however, many corporate environments will require the more advanced NTFS features available only in Windows XP Professional. Windows XP Home does not offer any type of File or Folder level security. Sharing permissions are available in the same fashion as Windows XP Professional.

Mapping a Drive

A drive map is a very important tool in a network environment. It allows a single computer to act as though it possesses all the hard drives that reside in the network. The **network file service** (**NFS**) portion of the operating system coordinates the systems so that drives located on other physical machines show up as logical drives on the local machine. This shows up in the Windows Explorer and My Computer screens, as illustrated in Figure 10-75. It also makes the additional drives available through the command-line prompt.

network file service (NFS)

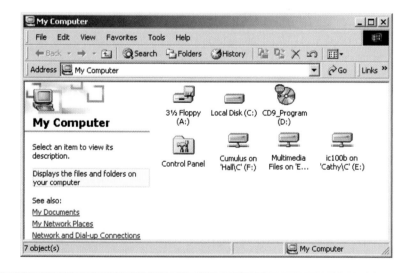

Figure 10-75: A Mapped Drive Display

The primary reason to map a drive in a network environment is because some applications cannot recognize volume names. They can see only drive letters. In Windows, the number of recognizable drive letters is 26 (A–Z).

Some network operating systems can recognize an extended number of drive letters (i.e., A–Z and AA–ZZ). However, by using unique volume names to identify drives, the system is capable of recognizing a large number of network drives.

For a local system to access a remote resource, the resource must be shared, and the local user must have a valid network user ID and password. The user's assigned rights and permissions are tied to his or her password throughout the network, either through individual settings or through group settings.

Installing Network Components in Windows 2000/XP Control Panels

After the network adapter card has been configured and installed, the next step in setting up the computer on the network is to load its drivers, protocols, and services. In most Windows 2000/XP installations, simply rebooting the computer and permitting Windows to detect the network adapter will accomplish the majority of these items.

Network and Dial-up Connections

In Windows 2000, the networking control panel is located under the **Network and Dial-up Connections** icon. It provides access to the *Network and Dial-up Connections* window shown in Figure 10-76. This window provides several key functions associated with local and wide area networking. It is used to install new network adapter cards and change their settings, change network component settings, and install TCP/IP.

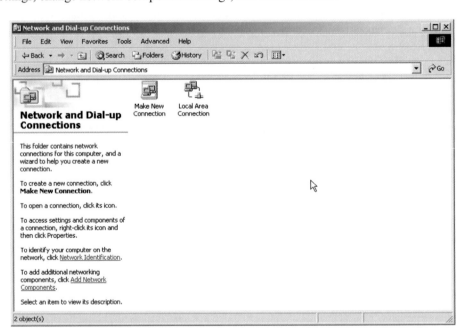

**Figure 10-76:
The Network and
Dial-up Connections
Window**

In Windows XP, the Networking icon has been changed to the **Network Connections** icon. It does not offer the dial-up networking function included in the Windows 2000 applet, but it is used to configure and manage LAN and high-speed Internet access connection (i.e., DSL and cable modem connections). Clicking on the icon produces the *LAN or High-Speed Internet* window shown in Figure 10-77.

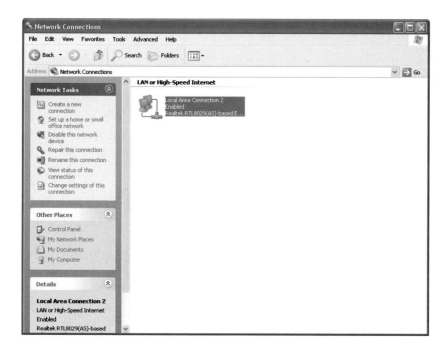

Figure 10-77: Windows XP LAN or High-Speed Internet Window

The *Network Tasks* pane of the *Network Connections* window provides options for creating, viewing, repairing, renaming, and reconfiguring the displayed connection as well as for disabling a network device.

Right clicking on the connection will produce a pop-up menu that contains the *Properties* option for the connection. Selecting this option in either operating system version will produce the connection's Properties window. The organization of the Windows 2000 *Network and Dial-Up Connections* and Windows XP *LAN or High Speed Internet Properties* windows consolidates the Services, Protocols, and Adapters functions under a single tab, as illustrated in Figure 10-78.

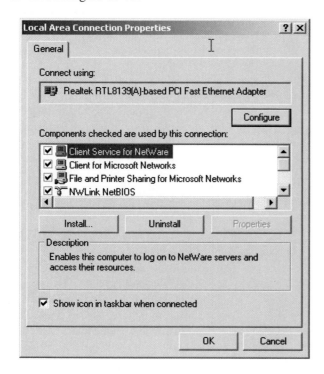

Figure 10-78: Windows 2000/XP Local Area Connection Properties

The functions associated with the Windows 2000 *Local Area Connection Properties* include the following:

Clients

Services

Protocols

- **Clients**—Enables the system to use files and printers shared on other computers

- **Services**—Used to add, remove, or configure network services such as DNS, WINS, and DHCP functions

- **Protocols**—Used to add, remove, or configure network protocols for specific types of network environments

To configure any of these functions for a given component, access the *Local Area Connection Properties* dialog box, highlight the desired component, and click on the *Install* button. Each entry contains a list of primary and alternative drivers, protocols, and services that can be viewed by clicking on the title in the window. These alternatives are included, because there are many non-Microsoft networks in use, and Windows attempts to support the most common ones. If a particular network component type is not supported in the standard listings, each "Select Network..." page features a **Have Disk** button that permits the system to upload Windows-compatible drivers and protocols.

Have Disk

Other functions affecting the networking and dial-up connections in Windows 2000 and Windows XP include the following:

Network Identification

Bindings

- **Network Identification**—Specifies the computer name and the workgroup or domain name to which the computer belongs. Under TCP/IP, computer names can be up to 63 characters but should be limited to 15 characters or less. They can use the numbers 0−9, letters A−Z (and a−z), as well as hyphens. Using other characters may prevent other nodes from finding your computer or the network. This option is located under the System icon in the Control Panel.

- **Bindings**— Establishes a potential pathway between a given network service, a network protocol, and a given network adapter. The order of the bindings can affect the efficiency of the system's networking operations. To establish bindings, access the *Network and Dial-Up Connections* (*Network Connections* in XP) page and click on the *Advanced* entry on its drop-down menu bar. Then select the *Advanced Settings* option from the menu.

┌─ **TEST TIP** ──────────

Memorize which network items can be set through the Windows 2000 *Network and Dial-Up Connections* applet's *Local Area Connections* Properties.

The Windows XP *Local Area Connections* Properties window offers two tabs not available in the Windows 2000 version. These are the *Advanced* tab and the *Authentication* tab. The *Advanced* tab is used to enable the Windows XP **Internet Connection Firewall**. This feature is embedded in Windows XP so that it can act as an Internet firewall for itself or for a local area network attached to it. This feature is described in more detail at the end of this chapter.

Internet Connection Firewall

authentication protocols

The *Authentication* tab is used to configure **authentication protocols** for conducting local area and wide area communications across a network. Recall that authentication is the process of identifying an individual as who they claim to be. This page, shown in Figure 10-79, is used to select standard protocols associated with particular network types, including Ethernet and 802.1x Wireless protocols.

**Figure 10-79:
Windows XP
Authentication Tab**

Configuring Clients in Windows 2000/XP

Any network computer that uses the resources of another computer in the network is acting as its client. To use these resources, the local computer must have client software installed that will enable it to work with the other computer. In some networks, this may mean working with computers that have other types of operating systems running on them. In Windows 9x/Me systems, you are offered Microsoft and Novell clients that will enable the computer to use resources that belong to these types of systems.

To add a new client to the computer, highlight the *Client* option in the *Select Network Component Type* dialog box, select the desired client from the list, and click on the *Add* button. The new Client will appear in the *Installed Network Components* window of the Network page.

Configuring Protocols in Windows 2000/XP

Because the bootup detection process loads the adapter driver, two types of clients to choose from, and a set of sharing parameters, most installation procedures require only that the appropriate protocols be loaded for the network type. In Windows-based client/server LANs, TCP/IP has become the leading choice of networking protocols. Therefore, the TCP/IP protocol must be activated and configured properly for the computer to function on the LAN.

However, you may need to add the NetBEUI, Appletalk, and IPX/SPX (also known as NWLink) protocols if the LAN contains computers with older Windows operating systems, Apple/MAC computers, or computers running Novell operating systems. You should also be aware that Microsoft offers separate TCP/IP protocols for local area and wide area networking. The additional TCP/IP protocol is used for dial-up Internet support.

The procedure for adding protocols is the same as that described for adding clients.

Configuring TCP/IP in Windows 2000/XP LANs

When the TCP/IP protocol is installed, it can require several pieces of configuration information to fully implement. In a simple local area network, such as a peer-to-peer network, only an IP address and a Subnet mask setting are required. However, in multisegmented client/server LANs, you may also be required to provide a Default Gateway (router) address, as well as an IP address for a DNS or WINS server.

TCP/IP is automatically installed in Windows 2000 and XP and configured to automatically obtain an IP address. There are three possible sources for IP addresses—Dynamic Host Configuration Protocol (DHCP), Automatic IP Addressing (AIPA), and manually assigned TCP/IP properties.

Manual TCP/IP Configuration

To manually configure TCP/IP values, from the Local Area Connections Properties page, highlight *Internet Protocol (TCP/IP)* from the listing and click on the *Properties* button. This will produce the *General* tab of the TCP/IP Properties page as illustrated in Figure 10-80.

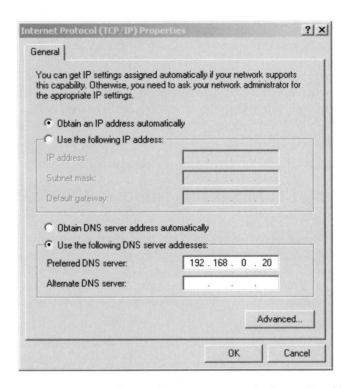

Figure 10-80: The TCP/IP Properties Page

Through this page, you can configure the computer to obtain an IP address using an automatic service, such as DHCP, or you can manually configure a static address for the computer. To manually configure TCP/IP, the *Use the following address* option must be enabled, and you must know the IP address and subnet mask settings you want to use. Remember that every computer on a network must have a unique IP address that identifies who it is. It must also have a subnet mask entry to limit the mobility of the transmission to those nodes within the subnet (without subnets, every TCP/IP communication could range across every connected network link in the world—the traffic would be unbelievable).

If the *Obtain an IP address automatically* option is selected, the computer will attempt to locate a DHCP server when it boots onto the network. The DHCP server has the ability to provide it with all of the TCP/IP configuration information it needs. If no DHCP server is found, Windows computers will default to a random IP address in the range of 169.254.XX.XX and a subnet mask of 255.255.0.0. The APIPA feature is very useful in smaller single-segment networks, because it effectively autoconfigures such a network.

The Preferred and Alternate DNS server boxes can be configured to provide a secondary source for DNS information in the event that the primary DNS server is unavailable.

Click on the *Advanced* button to access the *Advanced TCP/IP Settings* dialog window, as shown in Figure 10-81, where you can configure additional TCP/IP settings.

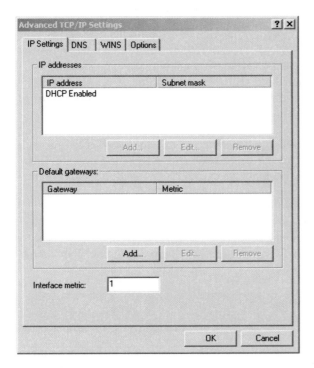

**Figure 10-81:
Advanced TCP/IP
Settings**

Under the *IP Settings* tab, depicted in Figure 10-80, you can configure the following settings:

- *IP Addresses*—This dialog window is used to enter, remove, and edit IP addresses. It can contain multiple IP addresses that may be required for special situations. You can add as many IP addresses to the list as you want.

- *Default Gateways*—This dialog window is used to specify the IP address of the router (or other gateway device) that separates your network segment from other segments. The computer uses this address to communicate with IP addresses outside the local segment.

There are three additional tabs that can be used to configure TCP/IP functions for given implementations:

- *DNS tab*—This tab enables you to specify the IP addresses of Domain Name System servers that are responsible for reconciling DNS computer names to actual IP addresses. In a LAN, this is typically the domain server for your network. In a wide area network environment, such as the Internet, this is typically the IP address of the ISP.

Various DNS suffixes can be attached to enable the DNS system to attempt to resolve incomplete domain names. This listing will attach specified domain suffixes (i.e., *mic-inc.net*, *mic-inc.com*, etc.) to names it receives. These suffixes will be attached to the received name and tried in the order they are entered in the list.

- *WINS tab*—This tab is used to specify the IP addresses of a Windows Name System server that is used to resolve the NetBIOS/NetBEUI names associated with older Windows operating systems to IP addresses.

- *Options tab*—This tab is used to configure TCP, UDP, and IP address filtering. These settings are used to control the type of TCP/IP traffic that can reach the computer.

┌─**TEST TIP**─────────┐
Know where TCP/IP properties are established in Windows 2000 and XP.
└──────────────────┘

Networking with Novell NetWare

Novell NetWare

Network Basic Input/Output System (NetBIOS)

In a **Novell NetWare** system, the root directory of the workstation should contain the files NETBIOS and IPX.COM. The NETBIOS file is an emulation of IBM's **Network Basic Input/Output System (NetBIOS)**, and it represents the basic interface between the operating system and the LAN hardware. This function is implemented through ROM ICs, located on the network card. The Internetworking Packet Exchange (IPX) file passes commands across the network to the file server.

The NETBIOS and IPX protocols must be bound together in order to navigate the Novell network from a computer using a Windows operating system. This is accomplished by enabling the NETBIOS bindings in the IPX protocol Properties in the *Network Properties* window.

The *Open Datalink Interface* (*ODI*) file is the Novell network shell that communicates between the adapter and the system's applications. Older versions of NetWare used a shell program called NETx. These files should be referenced in the *AUTOEXEC.BAT* or *NET.BAT* files.

TEST TIP

Be aware of the elements that are required to navigate through a Novell network from a computer running a Microsoft operating system.

GEEK SQUAD CASE FILE #78921

You have been deployed to ACME to work on their accounting network. You are working on a Windows 2000 Professional client computer that has IPX loaded. You are working in a Novell LAN, however, and you find that you cannot browse the network. What should you check to gain access to the LAN?

Installing NetWare Clients and Protocols

For Windows computers to be able to communicate with Novell servers in a network, they must have the client service for NetWare installed and configured. As indicated earlier in this chapter, clients are installed through the *Select Network Component Type* dialog window. This window is located under the connection's Properties.

Similarly, in Windows 2000 and Windows XP systems, you must install the *Client Service for NetWare (CSNW)* option to provide the Windows client with the ability to communicate with NetWare servers. CSNW requires that the IPX/SPX protocol be installed on the client. It can be installed manually beforehand, or it will be installed automatically when the CSNW client is installed.

There are actually two pieces to the IPX/SPX implementation in Windows—the *NWLink NetBIOS* and *NWLink IPX/SPX/NetBIOS Compatible Transport Protocol* options. Both are required for interaction with Novell systems. To configure the IPX/SPX protocol, select the *NWLink IPX/SPX/NetBIOS Compatible Transport Protocol* option from the list in the dialog window, and click on the *Properties* button.

In certain instances, you may need to enter an internal network number and a frame type setting on the *General* tab of the IPX/SPX Properties page. The network number is used when certain NetWare-specific applications are installed. This number is generally obtained from the NetWare administrator. The *Frame Type* setting is used in Ethernet networks to identify the type of Ethernet packets being used. The *Auto frame-type detection* option permits the IPX function to determine what type of frame is actually being used on the network.

Installing Other Network Protocols

There are two other protocols of interest that you can install in a Windows system—Appletalk and NetBEUI. As mentioned earlier, Appletalk is required for Windows computers to communicate with Apple MACs running Apple operating systems in the network, while NetBEUI is required when the network contains computers running older Windows operating systems. Both of these protocols are available through the *Select Network Component Type* dialog window. As with the other protocols, they are installed by simply clicking on the *Install* button, selecting the *Protocol* option, clicking the *Add* button, selecting the desired protocol from the list, and clicking the *OK* button.

NETWORK PRINTING WITH WINDOWS 2000/XP

Essentials 4.2

Windows 2000 and Windows XP provide installation wizards to guide the network printer installation. If the physical printer is connected to a remote computer, referred to as a print server, the remote unit must supply the printer drivers and settings to control the printer. Likewise, the print server must be set up to share the printer with the other users on the network.

To install the network printer, access the *My Network Places* icon on the desktop, navigate the network to locate and open the remote computer's network name, right click on the remote unit's printer name, select the *Connect* option from the pop-up menu, and follow the directions provided by the Windows *Add Printer Wizard*. When the wizard produces a dialog box asking whether to install the selected printer, click on the *OK* button. This should produce the *Add Printer Wizard* driver selection dialog box, shown in Figure 10-82. After the remote printer has been installed, the local computer can access it through the *My Network Places* icon.

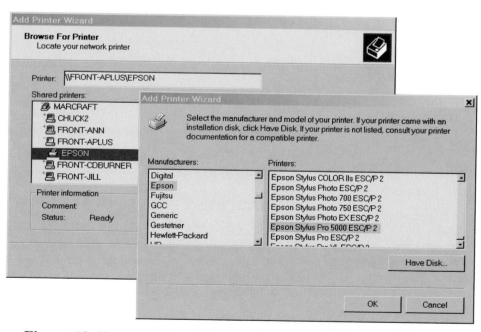

Figure 10-82: Installing a Network Printer in Windows 2000/XP

Windows 2000 includes a printing feature called **Autopublish** (or point and print). This feature enables the user to install a printer driver on a client PC from any application. The Active Directory also enables the user to browse the network for a specific printer type or location.

Windows 2000 and Windows XP both feature Internet printing capabilities. This function enables the user to print to a remotely located printer using the Internet as the network. Microsoft designed this feature to compete with document faxing. Instead of faxing a document to a remote fax machine, just print it out on a printer at that location. Any standard printer can be used for this operation, as long as a Windows 2000 Server is hosting it.

The File/Print window, shown in Figure 10-83, includes a *Find Printer* button that you can use to search for printers locally, connected to the LAN, or connected across the Internet. After a printer has been located, Windows 2000 or XP will automatically install the driver for that printer on the client PC.

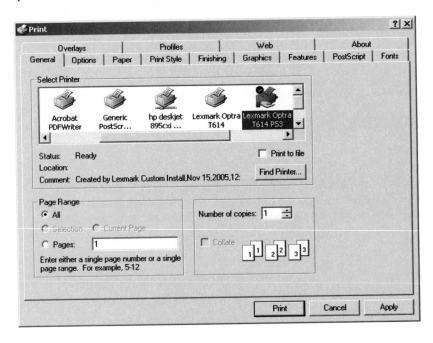

Figure 10-83: The Windows 2000 File/ Print Window

Both Windows 2000 and Windows XP include a library of more than 2500 printer drivers. If the local unit is not set up for the type of printer selected, it is possible to add these files and initiate the print job without leaving the *Print* dialog box.

Sharing Printers in Windows 2000/XP

Shared printers, also referred to as **networked printers**, receive data from computers throughout the network and direct thr data to a local printer. As in other networks, these printers must be configured as shared printers in the Windows 2000/XP environment to allow remote computers to access them.

To share a printer under Windows 2000, select the *Printers* option from the *Start/Settings* path. In Windows XP, select the *Faxes and Printers* option from the Start menu. Alternate-click the printer to be shared and select the *Sharing* option. This action produces the *Sharing* tab shown in Figure 10-84. From this page, click the *Shared As* option, enter a share name for the printer, and click on the *OK* button to complete the sharing process. Unlike the Windows 9x systems, you must have administrative rights to make these changes in Windows 2000.

To connect to a printer on the network in Windows 2000, select the *Printers* option from the *Start/Settings* path and double click the *Add Printer* icon. In Windows XP you must select the *Printers and Faxes* option form the Start menu and click on the *Add a printer* option. The *Welcome to the Add Printer Wizard* page will be displayed. Click on the *Next* button to move forward in the connection process. In the *Local or Network Printer* page, select the *Network Printer* (or *A Network Printer or Printer attached to another computer*) option, and click on the *Next* button to access the *Specify a Printer* dialog window, shown in Figure 10-85.

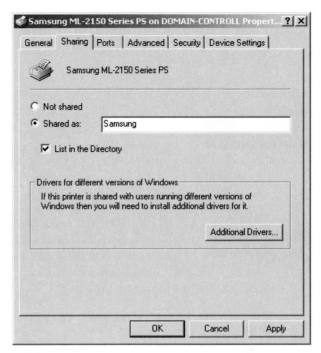

Figure 10-84: Sharing a Printer in Windows 2000

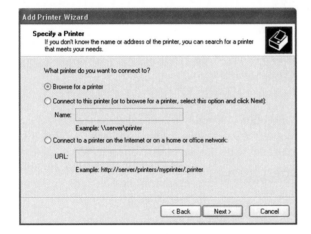

Figure 10-85: The Windows XP Specify a Printer Dialog Window

In Windows 2000, you can enter the network printer name in this window. You should also use the UNC format to specify the path to the printer being connected to (that is, *computer_name\share_name*). If the printer's name is not known, click on the *Type the Printer Name* option or click on the *Next* button to *Browse for a Printer* option.

In Windows XP, you have additional options to enter the UNC path and printer name or connect to a printer on the Internet (or a SOHO network). There is also a radio button that will enable you to find a printer using the Active Directory.

```
┌─ TEST TIP ─────────────────┐
│ Know how to correctly write a UNC │
│ path to a shared directory located on a │
│ remote computer. │
└────────────────────────────┘
```

To link up with a printer over the Internet (or the company intranet), select the *Connect to Printer on the Internet or Your Intranet* option, and enter the URL address of the printer. The URL must be expressed in standard HTTP addressing format (i.e., *http://servername/printer/*). The connection wizard guides the connection from this point.

WIDE AREA NETWORKING WITH WINDOWS 2000/XP

Remote Access Services (RAS)

Older versions of Windows NT referred to all aspects of the dial-up networking function as **Remote Access Services (RAS)**. With Windows NT 4.0, however, Microsoft changed the nomenclature to *Dial-Up Networking* on its client-side elements. The server-side elements are still referred to as RAS. This same convention continues in the Windows 2000 and Windows XP products.

Dial-Up Networking

Windows 2000 and Windows XP provide all the software tools required to establish an Internet connection. These include a TCP/IP network protocol and the Windows NT Workstation **Dial-Up Networking** component. The Dial-Up Networking component is used to establish a link with the ISP over the public telephone system. This link also can be established over an ISDN line. All Windows 2000 and Windows XP versions feature the built-in Microsoft Internet Explorer Web browser and a personal Web server.

The Windows 2000/XP Internet Infrastructure

The Windows 2000 operating systems feature a *New Network Connections* folder, located in the *My Computer* window.

To create a dial-up connection in Windows 2000, click on the *Make New Connection* icon in the *My Computer/Network Connections* folder. Similarly, to create a new connection in Windows XP, you must navigate the *Start/My Network Places/View network connections* path and click on the *Create a new connection* option in the Network Tasks pane as illustrated in Figure 10-86.

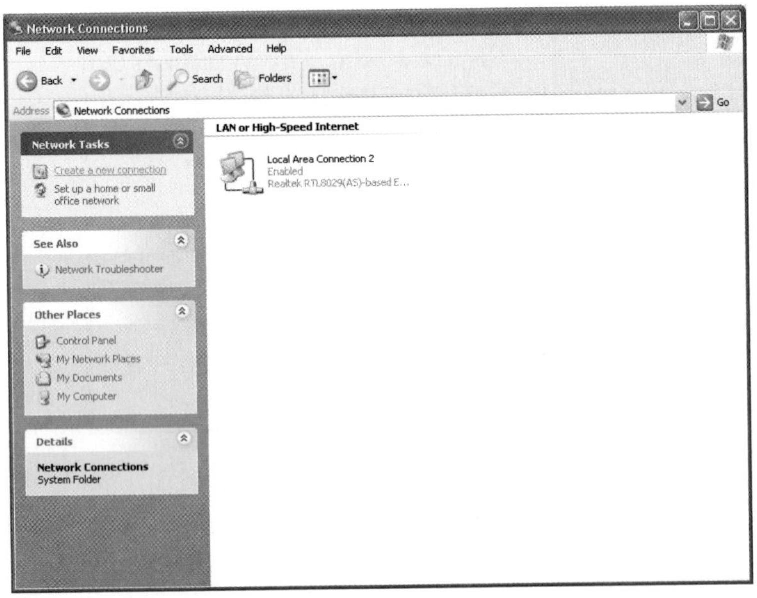

These actions will open the Windows 2000/XP *Network Connection Wizard* (*New Connection Wizard* in XP) that guides the connection process. The wizard requires information about the type of connection, modem type, and the phone number to be dialed. The connection types offered by the wizard include private networks, virtual private networks, and other computers. The *Network Connection Wizard* enables users to employ the same device to access multiple networks that may be configured differently. This is accomplished by enabling users to create connection types based on who they are connecting to rather than on how they are making the connection.

Figure 10-86: Creating a New Network Connection

Establishing the Windows 2000/XP Dial-Up Configuration

Under Windows 2000 and Windows XP, the operating system should detect (or offer to detect) the modem through its Plug-and-Play facilities. It may also enable you to select the modem drivers manually from a list in the Control Panel's *Phone and Modem Options* applet. After the modem has been detected, or selected, it appears in the *Windows 2000* or *Windows XP Modems* tab. The settings for the modem can be examined or reconfigured by selecting it from the list and clicking on its *Properties* tab. In most cases, the device's default configuration settings should be used.

Establishing Dialing Rules

For Windows 2000 or XP to connect to a network or dial-up connection, it must know what rules to follow to establish the communication link. These rules are known as the **dialing rules**. In Windows 2000 and XP, the dialing rules are configured through the *Phone and Modem Options* icon in the Control Panel. If the connection is new, a *Location Information* dialog window displays, enabling you to supply the area code and telephone system information.

dialing rules

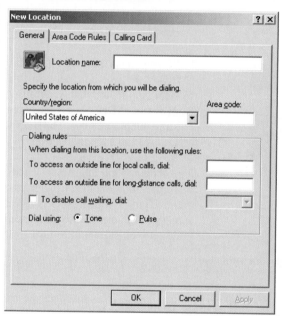

To create a new location, click on the *New* button on the *Dialing Rules* tab and move through the *General*, *Area Code Rules*, and *Calling Card* tabs, shown in Figure 10-87, to add information as required. The default rules for dialing local, long-distance, and international calls are established under the *General* tab. These rules are based on the country or region identified on this page. Ways to reach an outside line (such as dialing 8 or 9 to get an outside line in a hotel or office building) are established here. Similarly, the *Area Code Rules* information modifies the default information located under the *General* tab. As its name implies, the information under the *Calling Cards* tab pertains to numbers dialed using a specific calling card or long-distance company.

Figure 10-87: The Windows 2000 Phone and Modem Options/New Location Dialog Window

Establishing Dial-Up Internet Connections

The Windows 2000 **Internet Connection Wizard**, shown in Figure 10-88, provides an efficient way to establish Internet connectivity. In Windows XP, the Internet connection is established through the New Connection Wizard. You can use the Internet or New Connection Wizard to set up the Web browser, the Internet e-mail account, and the newsgroup reader. To create the Internet connection for an existing account with an ISP, you need to know the following:

Internet Connection Wizard

- The ISP's name
- The username and password
- The ISP's dial-in access number

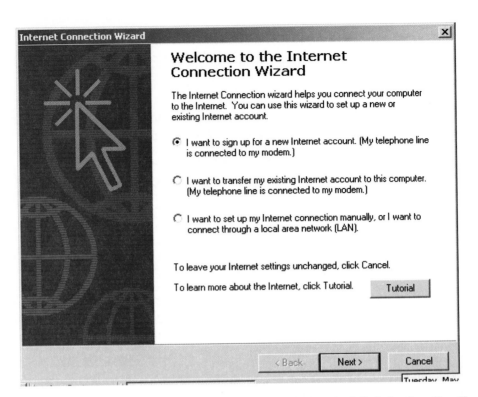

Figure 10-88: The Windows 2000 Internet Connection Wizard

cable modem

asymmetrical digital subscriber line (ADSL)

If the system is equipped with a **cable modem** or an **asymmetrical digital subscriber line** (**ADSL**), the ISP will need to furnish any additional connection instructions. The cable modem is a device that transmits and receives data through cable television connections. Conversely, ADSL is a special, high-speed modem technology that transmits data over existing telephone lines. The Internet Connection Wizard collects this information and then creates the Internet connection.

To connect to the Internet in Windows 2000, select *the Internet Connection Wizard* option from the *Start/Programs/Accessories/Communications* path. Likewise, to connect to the Internet in Windows XP, you must select the *New Connection* option from the Accessories/Communications menu. If the connection is new, the *Location Information* dialog boxes, shown in Figure 10-89, along with the dialing rules defined in the preceding section of this chapter will appear. You also need to click on the *I want to sign up for a new Internet account* option, click on the *Next* button, and follow the wizard's instructions.

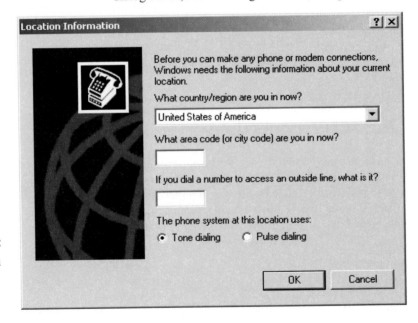

Figure 10-89: The Location Information Dialog Box

In a Windows XP system, the New Connection Wizard produces the *Network Connection Type* screen shown in Figure 10-90. In this screen you can choose to Connect to the Internet, Connect to a network at my workplace, or Set up an advanced connection.

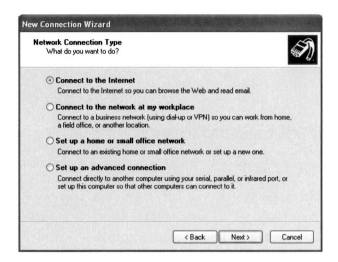

Figure 10-90: Windows XP Network Connection Type Page

Establishing Internet Connection Sharing

Sharing an Internet connection enables several computers to be connected to the Internet through a single dial-up connection. These connections can be made individually, or simultaneously, with each user maintaining the ability to use the same services it did when it was connected directly to the Internet.

Internet connection sharing (ICS)

To establish **Internet connection sharing (ICS)**, you must log on to the computer using an account that has Administrator rights. In a Windows 2000 system, click on *Start/Settings* and select the *Network and Dial-Up Connections* option. Right click the connection to be shared, and then select the *Properties* option from the pop-up menu. The Internet connection's *Sharing* screen displays, as shown in Figure 10-91.

Under the *Internet Connection-Sharing* tab, select the *Enable Internet Connection Sharing for this connection* check box. If the connecting computer is supposed to dial in to the Internet automatically, click on the *Enable on-demand dialing* check box. Clicking on the *OK* button causes protocols, services, interfaces, and routes to be configured automatically.

In Windows XP, access the Network Connections, select the connection you want to share, and then select the *Change settings of this connection* option from the Network Tasks pane. On the *Advanced* tab, enable the *Allow other network users to connect through this computer's Internet connection* setting. On this tab, you can also enable settings that will automatically dial out when another computer on the network tries to access the Internet and permit other network users to control the shared Internet connection.

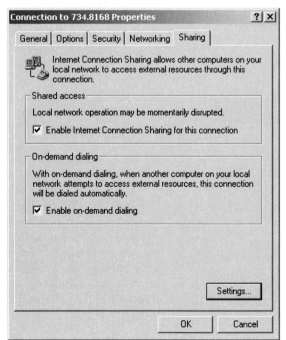

Figure 10-91: The Internet Connection Sharing Screen

WINDOWS SECURITY

One of the main features of the Windows 2000 and Windows XP operating system versions has been their array of security options. As an operating system designed to work in business networks, **data security** is one of the most important functions of the Windows NT line of products.

data security

The Windows 2000 and XP operating systems provide security in four forms:

User Logon

Passwords

- User security in the form of **User Logon** and **Passwords** is required to access the system
- User security between users of the same computer to control access to local data
- Identification of attempted security breaches through audit trails
- Memory usage protection between applications running on the same hardware

User Account

In Windows 2000 Professional and Windows XP Professional systems, a user must have a **User Account** on a particular computer to gain access to its operation. In a workgroup setting, this account must be set up on each computer. However, in a domain environment, the account can be established on the domain server.

Administrator Account

When Windows 2000 or XP is first installed, a master **Administrator Account** is established.

The administrator has rights and permissions to all of the system's hardware and software resources. The administrator, in turn, grants rights and permissions to other users as necessary.

groups

The administrator can deal with users on an individual basis or may gather users into **groups** that can be administered uniformly. In doing so, the administrator can assign permissions or restrictions on an individual or an entire group. The value of using groups lies in the time saved by being able to apply common rights to several users instead of applying them one by one.

profile

Each user and group in the Windows environment has a **profile** that describes the resources and desktop configurations created for them. Settings in the profile can be used to limit the actions users can perform, such as installing, removing, configuring, adjusting, or copying resources. When users log into the system, it checks their profile and adjusts the system according to their information. In Windows 2000, this file has been moved to *\Documents and Settings\login_name\NTuser.dat*.

The Windows 2000 Server operating system can be used to establish profiles for the entire network from a central location. Its administration package can also be used to establish roaming profiles that enable users to log in to any workstation on the network and work under their own profile settings. The administrator can also cause the content of each user's local *My Documents* folder to reside on the server instead of the local desktop. This option provides safe, centralized storage for user files by enlisting the server's security and backup functions to safeguard the data.

Windows Portable Design

The Windows 2000 and XP operating systems provide many features for portable computers. In addition to furnishing the power management and Plug-and-Play features discussed earlier, Windows 2000 and Windows XP both provide increased data security functions and greater administrator control over mobile PCs.

Portable computer users in the business world typically spend some time connected to a company network and other times traveling away from the network connection. The Windows 2000 **Synchronization Manager** enables the user to select network files and folders and to travel without an active connection to a server.

Synchronization
Manager

When the client wishes to take files, the files are moved from the server to the portable and the Synchronization Manager synchronizes the time and date version information concerning the files. While the portable client is off-line, the user can continue to use the files under their network names. When the user returns to the network environment, the client resynchronizes the files with the server versions and the newer copy overwrites the older version. The synchronization process is described in Figure 10-92.

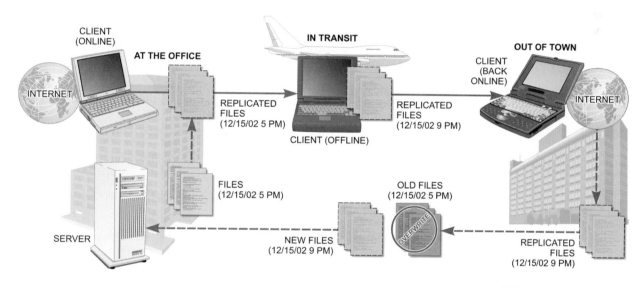

Figure 10-92: Windows 2000 Synchronization Manager

Windows 2000/XP portability features are not limited to mobile computers. Many organizations have mobile employees that work at different computers within a given location. To accommodate this type of mobility, Windows 2000 and Windows XP provide for **roaming profiles** that can be employed to store each user's desktop, Start menu setup, and *My Document* folder on the server and redirect them to the local client where the user logs in. Windows 2000 and XP can also automatically install applications the user requires on the local client when they log on.

roaming profiles

KEY POINTS REVIEW

This chapter has investigated the structure and operation of the Windows 2000 and Windows XP operating systems. Review the following key points before moving into the Review and Exam Questions sections to make sure you are comfortable with each point. Afterward, answer the Review Questions that follow to verify your knowledge of the information.

- Enterprise networks are designed to facilitate business-to-business or business-to-customer operations. Because monetary transactions and personal information travel across the network in these environments, enterprise networks feature facilities for additional, highly protective security functions.

- An intranet is a network built on the TCP/IP protocol that belongs to a single organization—in essence, a private Internet. Like the Internet, intranets are designed to share information and are only accessible to the organization's members, with authorization.

- The Windows 2000 Server product is also available in two extended enterprise versions—Windows 2000 Advanced Server and Windows 2000 Datacenter Server.

- The standard Server package supports four-way symmetrical microprocessor operations (i.e., it can distribute work between four different microprocessors at a time) and can manage up to 4 GB of RAM.

- The Advanced Server edition can support up to eight symmetrical processors and up to 8 GB of memory. These features enable it to function well in medium-sized networks running between 100 and 500 concurrent users.

- The Windows 2000 Datacenter Server edition can handle up to 64 GB of RAM and 32 processors. This enables it to support up to 1000 simultaneous users with heavy processing demands.

- The Windows 2000 desktop includes My Computer, Network Neighborhood, Inbox, and the Recycle Bin icons.

- Windows XP Media Center Edition is not sold through retail software outlets—it is sold to OEM system manufacturers who build Media Center PCs.

- Instead of simply truncating the filename, inserting a tilde, and then attaching a number to the end of the filename, Windows 2000/XP performs a mathematical operation on the long name to generate a truly unique MS-DOS−compatible filename.

- Windows 2000 and Windows XP feature an intelligent, personalized Programs menu. It monitors the user's program usage, and after the first six accesses, arranges the menu options according to those most frequently used.

- A network share is an existing shared resource (i.e., printer, drive, modem, or folder) located on a remote system.

- Windows 2000 and Windows XP offer extended common dialog boxes for the *File/Open*, *File/Print*, and *File/Save* options. These dialog boxes provide easy organization and navigation of the system's hard drives, as well as navigation columns that grant quick access to frequently used folders.

- The Windows 2000/XP registry is not compatible with the Windows 9x registries.

- The overall operation of Windows 2000 and Windows XP systems is governed by System Policies that give administrators control over users. Using System Policies, the network administrator can give or limit users' access to local resources, such as drives and network connections.

- The central feature of the Windows 2000 architecture is the Active Directory structure. Active Directory is a distributed database of user and resource information that describes the makeup of the network (i.e., users and application settings).

- In Windows 2000 and XP, policies are established through the Group Policy Editor. Administrators use this editor to establish which applications different users have access to, as well as to control applications on the user's desktop.

- With Group Policies, administrators can institute a large number of detailed settings for users throughout an enterprise, without establishing each setting manually.

- A member server is most often referred to as a stand-alone server. As such, the member server maintains a local domain database that only it uses. These servers are most commonly used as application and file servers.

- The minimum hardware requirements for installing Windows 2000 Professional on a PC-compatible system are as follows:

  - Microprocessor—133 MHz Pentium (P5 equivalent or better)
  - RAM—64 MB (4 GB maximum)
  - HDD space—650 MB or more free on a 2 GB drive
  - VGA monitor

- For installation from a CD-ROM, a 12x drive is required. If the CD-ROM drive is not bootable, a high-density 3.5-inch floppy drive is also required. If Windows Professional is to be installed across a network, a Windows 2000 Professional−compatible NIC is required.

- Systems can be upgraded to Windows 2000 Professional from Windows 3.x and 9x, as well as Windows NT 3.5 and 4.0 workstations. This includes older NTFS, FAT16, and FAT32 installations. When you install Windows 2000, it can recognize all three of these file system types.

- Windows 2000 does not attempt to remain compatible with older hardware and software. Therefore, some applications may not be compatible with Windows 2000 and may run poorly, or fail completely after an upgrade.

- Windows 2000 and Windows XP support a wide array of newer hardware devices. These devices include DVD, USB, and IEEE-1394 devices. Microsoft works with hardware vendors to certify their drivers. These drivers are digitally signed so that they can be loaded automatically by the system.

- Windows 2000 and Windows XP employ a print spooler processing architecture that provides smooth printing in a background mode and quick return-to-application time.

- Printer properties are all of the defining features about a selected printer and include information that ranges from which port it should use, to what security features have been implemented with it.

- Active Directory arranges domains in a hierarchy and establishes trust relationships among all of the domains in a tree-like structure.

- In an Active Directory, a tree is a collection of objects that share the same DNS name. Active Directory can subdivide domains into organizational units that contain other units, or leaf objects, such as printers, users, and so on.

- Windows 2000 can create an organizational structure containing more than one tree. This structure is referred to as a forest.

- Trusts are relationships that enable users to move between domains and perform prescribed types of operations.

- Rights are the permission settings that control a user's (or group of users') authority to access objects and perform operations (such as reading or writing a file). Administrative rights provide authority to users down to the Organizational Unit level.

- In the Windows 2000 and Windows XP systems, the *Network Neighborhood* folder has been replaced with a more powerful *My Network Places* folder. The new folder includes new *Recently Visited Places* and *Computers Near Me* views.

- The primary reason for mapping a drive in a network environment is that some applications cannot recognize volume names. They can only see drive letters. In Windows 2000/XP, the number of recognizable drive letters is 26 (A – Z).

- Windows 2000 includes a printing feature called Autopublish (or point and print). This feature enables the user to install a printer driver on a client PC from any application. The Active Directory also enables the user to browse the network for a specific printer type, or location.

- Windows 2000 and XP make it possible to share resources such as printers, folders, and Internet connections across a network. Sharing the connection permits several computers to access the Internet through a single dial-up connection. These connections can be made individually, or simultaneously, with each user maintaining the ability to use the same services it did when it was connected directly to the Internet.

- One of the main features of the Windows 2000/XP operating systems is their security capabilities. As operating systems designed to work in business networks, data security is one of the most important functions of Windows 2000 and Windows XP.

- The administrator has rights and permissions to all of the system's hardware and software resources. The administrator, in turn, grants rights and permissions to other users as necessary.

REVIEW QUESTIONS

The following questions test your knowledge of the material presented in this chapter.

1. A user wants to use his new hard drive to store sensitive company data. His computer is running Windows XP Professional. He plans on encrypting all data in his folder so only a few select users may access the data. From the properties window of the folder, what tab do you suggest that the user utilize to protect his data?

2. How can you identify a compressed file in Windows 2000 or Windows XP?

3. Describe four types of security found in the Windows 2000 environment.

4. A new Windows XP Professional workstation is built for the company accountant. The accountant is very concerned about security of his data, and wishes to have his data protected via the Windows XP Firewall. How do you enable the Windows XP Firewall?

5. Describe the steps required to change a file's attributes in the Windows 2000 Windows Explorer environment.

6. How much memory is required to install Windows 2000 Professional?

7. You are installing a new network for a company. They recently acquired workstations with the Windows XP Professional operating system and have a hub and DSL modem. Due to costs, the company does not wish to pay for a new server or a router but would still like to have the Internet available to all workstations and would, therefore, be willing to pay for extra cabling and Network Interface card costs. What is the best solution for this scenario?

8. Which set of Windows tools is employed to check out network-related problems?

9. Where should changes to registry hardware devices be made from?

10. To ensure that existing hardware will work after a Windows 2000 upgrade, what reference should be examined before beginning the upgrade process?

11. Dynamic IP addressing is performed by _____.

12. Name two factors that must be taken into account when considering upgrading a system to a Windows 2000 or Windows XP operating system.

13. _____ is the Windows 2000 tool for implementing changes for computers and users throughout an enterprise.

14. What command is used to encrypt files and folders from the Windows 2000 command line?

15. Which Windows 2000 utility can be used to create a backup copy of the registry? Where is the utility located, and where will the backup copy be stored?

EXAM QUESTIONS

1. In Windows 2000 and Windows XP, the _____ networking components provide the rules that the computer will use to govern the exchange of information across the network.
   a. client
   b. adapter
   c. protocol
   d. service

2. What is required to create a dynamic volume in Windows 2000?
   a. Converting a FAT32 volume using the Disk Management tool
   b. Converting a primary volume using the Disk Management tool
   c. Converting a basic volume using the Disk Management tool
   d. Converting an extended volume using the Disk Management tool

3. What is the safest method of changing registry entries in Windows 2000?
   a. Use REGEDIT.
   b. Use a file editor.
   c. Use Device Manager.
   d. Use REGEDT32.

4. For Windows XP, the Local Connections properties window offers two tabs not available in the Windows 2000 version. What are the two tabs called?
   a. General and Advanced
   b. Authentication and Encryption
   c. Advanced and Encryption
   d. Advanced and Authentication

5. _____ are relationships that enable users to move between domains and perform certain types of operations.
   a. Trusts
   b. Permissions
   c. Rights
   d. Privileges

6. How do you install a hardware device in a Windows system if the operating system does not have the device on its hardware compatibility list and does not have any existing drivers that are compatible with the device?
   a. Install the device, and allow the PnP process to configure the card.
   b. Install the device, and click on the Have Disk button when prompted.
   c. Install the device, and manually configure it through the Device Manager.
   d. Install the device, and access the Add/Remove Hardware applet to install it automatically.

7. How many drives can be mapped in a Windows 2000 system?
   a. 10
   b. 26
   c. 4
   d. 16

8. What is the maximum length of a Windows 2000 filename?
   a. 8 characters
   b. 215 characters
   c. 255 characters
   d. 256 characters

9. Where will the Windows 2000 or Windows XP Setup utility install the Windows operating system files in a typical installation?
   a. The \Winnt directory
   b. The \I386 folder
   c. The \Windows\system folder
   d. The \Windows directory

10. The members of a _____ share a common directory database and are organized in levels.
    a. workgroup
    b. tree
    c. group
    d. domain

CHAPTER

11

BASIC SYSTEM TROUBLESHOOTING

Upon completion of this chapter and its related lab procedures, you should be able to perform these tasks:

1. Describe the characteristics of a good workspace.

2. Outline steps for using a digital multimeter (DMM) to perform voltage, resistance, and current checks on a system, as well as identify common DMM tests associated with personal computers.

3. List preliminary steps for diagnosing computer problems.

4. Perform visual inspections of a system.

5. Describe the three general categories of problems into which symptoms can be grouped, and differentiate between them.

6. Differentiate between software- and hardware-based troubleshooting techniques.

7. Use disk-based diagnostic tools to isolate system problems.

8. Describe the function of a POST card.

9. Describe quick checks that can be used to determine the nature of system hardware problems.

10. Describe FRU-level troubleshooting.

11. Describe the steps for isolating power supply problems.

12. Outline checks to isolate problems that produce a dead system.

13. Discuss methods of dealing with symptoms that are not defined well enough to point to a particular component.

CHAPTER 11

BASIC SYSTEM TROUBLESHOOTING

FROM THE GEEK SQUAD

Lauren B. from store 645 has just been moved from a sales associate position to a new position with the Geek Squad as Agent 99. She is very familiar with the specifications and sales points of the computer products sold in the store. However, she is now in a position where she will need to work on PCs and repair them. The organization provides training in two ways—through a basic vendor neutral PC repair course and then into vendor-specific training on various PC models sold in the store.

Agent 99 knows that she will need to develop a new knowledge base and a new skill set focused on how to maintain, troubleshoot, and repair PC equipment. This training must cover several distinct areas of the PC—its hardware, peripheral devices, operating systems, application software, and preventive maintenance. Fortunately, Agent 99 already has a good bit of PC component knowledge, and now she needs to add knowledge of how to work with diagnostic tools and how to apply that knowledge to PC systems and components when they do not work correctly.

INTRODUCTION

Lots of people know a lot about computer systems. They may be up to date with the latest information concerning different processor specification, RAM types, chipsets, video adapters and displays, operating system capabilities, and software applications. Because of the wide acceptance of PCs in society, the PC industry produces lots of information about these topics. However, this is generally consumer-oriented advertising information designed to get people to buy something. However, fixing broken or malfunctioning PCs is still a profession, not something done by consumers.

Troubleshooting and repairing PC systems and peripherals requires a more complete *knowledge base* and a different *skill set* than those items marketed to the public. You have already endured multiple chapters dedicated to acquiring component knowledge and operational information. In these final three chapters we will build on that component knowledge to develop testing techniques and deductive reasoning skills associated with repairing electronic equipment in general and PC systems in particular. This chapter addresses basic troubleshooting practices associated with hardware-related problems. The following chapter deals with troubleshooting and repairing operating system problems. The final chapter covers preventive maintenance and security procedures used to protect PC systems and their components.

Essentials 1.3

Technical Support 1.2

IT Technician 1.2

BASIC PC TROUBLESHOOTING

To be an effective PC troubleshooter, you must combine good equipment knowledge with proper tools, good diagnostic techniques, and deductive reasoning skills. These skills are based on careful observation and an organized approach to solving problems. They can be applied to the repair of any type of defective equipment. The general process for diagnosing and troubleshooting equipment can be summarized as follows:

1. First, you must *gather information* to identify the nature of the problem. This can involve questioning the user and identifying any changes that have been made to the system. After the problem has been identified, you should *assess* the problem systematically and divide complex problems into smaller components to be analyzed individually. Next, you should *analyze* the potential causes of the individual problems and make an initial assessment of whether they are hardware or software related. During this analysis, you should verify even obvious potential causes—the classic is the unplugged power cord call.

2. *Inspect* components related to the possible cause, including their connections and configuration settings. *Test* the system after each component is checked or modified to see what symptoms it will produce as the system is changed. *Evaluate* the results of all changes, and establish priorities for additional steps. Do not assume anything—*verify* the impact of each step.

3. *Research* manufacturer Web sites and documentation for information related to the problem. Also consider whether you need to *consult* with others to gain insight into the possible cause of the problem you are working on. You may need to involve others in the process as a normal matter of practice. Some problems may require consultation with management or other professionals, such as the network administrator.

4. Finally, *document* your activities, actions, and outcomes. Good notes become a technician's personal knowledge base and can be used over and over. They also provide documentation when questions arise concerning how a problem was handled.

To this end, the following sections of the chapter address all of these topics. The place to start this discussion is with the common tools of the job and the workspace area.

Depot Technician 1.2

Diagnostic and Repair Tools

Anyone who wants to work on any type of equipment must have the proper tools for the task. The following sections discuss the tools and equipment associated with the testing and repair of digital systems. A well-prepared technician's tool kit should contain a wide range of both *flat-blade* and *Phillips-head* **screwdriver** sizes. At a minimum, it should have a small jeweler's and a medium-sized flat-blade screwdriver, along with a medium-size Phillips screwdriver. In addition, you may want to include a set of miniature nut drivers and a set of *Torx drivers*.

screwdriver

You also should have a couple of pairs of **needle-nose pliers**. These pliers are available in a number of sizes. You need at least one pair with a sturdy, blunt nose and one pair with a longer, more tapered nose. You also might wish to get a pair that has a cutting edge built into its jaws. You may perform this same function with a different type of pliers called *diagonals*, or crosscuts. Many technicians carry a pair of surgical forceps in addition to their other pliers.

needle-nose pliers

Other hand tools that you may want to include in your tool kit include:

- A *telescopic magnet* for retrieving screws and nuts that get dropped into the system unit or printer. This tool can save lots of disassembly/reassembly time when metal objects get loose in the system.

- A small *flash light* for examining the insides of enclosed system units and peripherals.

- *Wire crimpers* for fastening connectors to telephone and network cables. There are many times when you may need to make a test cable, or replace a damaged connector in the end of an existing network or telephone cable.

- A *multimeter* for making common electrical tests on computers, peripherals and cabling.

- A *network cable tester* for testing continuity and correct connections.

Figure 11-1 depicts *hand tools* commonly associated with microcomputer repair.

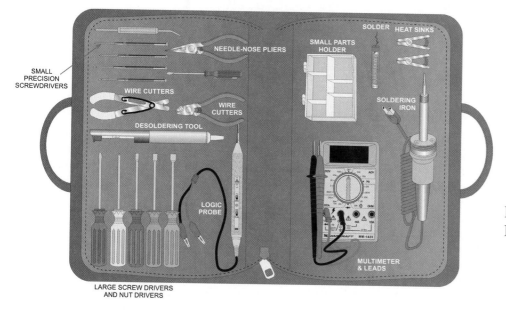

**Figure 11-1:
Hand Tools**

NOTE

You should always make sure to use the correct tools for the job. This lessens the chances of breaking components or ruining screws because tools slipped or did not fit.

In addition to these hardware tools, the technician should have a collection of software tools at his disposal. Typical software tools used by computer technicians include

- Emergency boot/start disks to get broken systems started

- Hardware diagnostic utility packages

- Embedded operating system software tools and utilities

- Antivirus/malware utilities

multimeter

voltage (V)

current

resistance

VOMs (volt-ohm-milliammeters)

DMMs (digital multimeters)

Using a Multimeter

In addition to a good selection of hand tools, there are a number of test instruments that can help you to isolate problems. One of the most basic pieces of electronic troubleshooting equipment is the **multimeter**. These test instruments are available in both analog and digital readout form and can be used to directly measure values of **voltage (V)**, **current** in milliamperes (mA) or amperes (A), and **resistance** in ohms (W). Therefore, these devices are referred to as **VOMs (volt-ohm-milliammeters)** for analog types, or **DMMs (digital multimeters)** for digital types. Figure 11-2 depicts a digital multimeter.

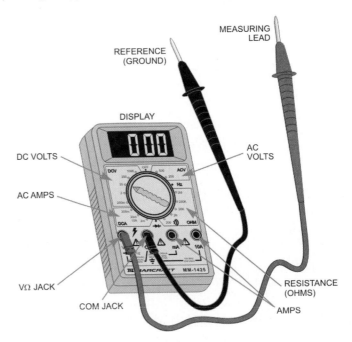

**Figure 11-2:
Digital Multimeter**

With a little practice, you can use this device to check diodes, transistors, capacitors, motor windings, relays, and coils. This particular DMM contains facilities built into the meter to test transistors and diodes. These facilities are in addition to its standard functions of current, voltage, and resistance measurement.

The first step in using the multimeter to perform tests is to select the proper function. For the most part, you should never need to use the current functions of the multimeter when working with computer systems. However, the voltage and resistance functions can be very valuable tools.

In computer and peripheral troubleshooting, fully 99% of the tests made are DC voltage readings. These measurements most often involve checking the DC side of the power supply unit. You can make these readings between ground and one of the expansion slot pins or at any of the different power supply connectors. It is also common to check the voltage level across a system-board capacitor to verify that the system is receiving power. The voltage across most of the capacitors on the system board is 5 Vdc. The DC voltages that can normally be expected in a PC-compatible system are +12 V, +5 V, −5 V, and −12 V. The actual values for these readings may vary by 5% in either direction.

The **DC voltage function** is used to take measurements in live DC circuits. It should be connected in parallel with the device being checked. This could mean connecting the reference lead (black lead) to a ground point and the measuring lead (red lead) to a test point to take a measurement, as illustrated in Figure 11-3.

DC voltage function

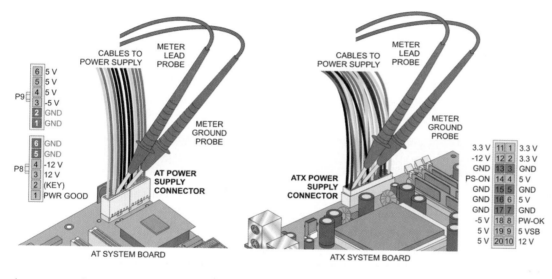

Figure 11-3: DC Voltage Check

As an approximate value is detected, you can decrease the range setting to achieve a more accurate reading. Most meters allow for overvoltage protection. However, it is still a good safety practice to decrease the range of the meter after you have achieved an initial value.

The second most popular test is the resistance or **continuity test**.

continuity test

Failure to turn off the power when making resistance checks can cause serious damage to the meter and can pose a potential risk to the user. Resistance checks also require that you electrically isolate the component being tested from the system. For most circuit components, this means de-soldering at least one end from the board.

The resistance check is very useful in isolating some types of problems in the system. One of the main uses of the resistance function is to test fuses. You must disconnect at least one end of the fuse from the system. You should set the meter on the 1-kilohm resistance setting. If the fuse is good, the meter should read near 0 ohms. If it is bad, the meter reads infinite. The resistance function is also useful in checking cables and connectors. By removing the cable from the system and connecting a meter lead to each end, you can check the cable's continuity conductor by conductor to verify its integrity. You can also use the resistance function to test the system's speaker. To check the speaker, just disconnect the speaker from the system and connect a meter lead to each end. If the speaker is good, the meter should read near 8 ohms. If the speaker is defective, the resistance reading should be 0 for an electrical short or infinite for an open circuit.

Only a couple of situations involve using the **AC voltage function** for checking microcomputer systems. The primary use of this function is to check the commercial power being applied to the power supply unit. As with any measurement, it is important to select the correct measurement range. However, the lethal voltage levels associated with the power supply call for additional caution when making such measurements. The second application for the AC voltage function is to measure ripple voltage from the **DC** output side of the power supply unit. This particular operation is rarely performed in field service situations.

AC voltage function

DC

TEST TIP

Know what readings to expect from a multimeter when testing fuses, speakers, and typical power-supply voltages in a PC.

GEEK SQUAD CASE FILE #23873

The local ACME network administrator has called your precinct about a problem she is having with her computer at home. She is not getting sound from her speaker and has checked all her software. She has asked you to explain to her how to check her speaker hardware. What should you tell her?

Essentials 1.3

Using Software Diagnostic Packages

Many companies produce disk-based diagnostic routines that check the system by running predetermined tests on different areas of its hardware. The diagnostic package evaluates the response from each test and attempts to produce a status report for all of the system's major components. Like the computer's self-tests, these packages produce visual and beep-coded error messages. Figure 11-4 depicts the Main menu of a typical self-booting software diagnostic package.

```
PC-CHECK V5.03 (c) Eurosoft (UK) Ltd 1988,2002

                    MAIN MENU

            System Information Menu
            Advanced Diagnostic Tests
            Immediate Burn-in Testing
            Deferred Burn-in Testing
            SCSI Utilities
            Show Results Summary
            Print Results Report
            About PC-CHECK
            Exit (Save)

        Use ↑↓ to Move Bar, <ENTER> to Select, <ESC> to Exit
```

**Figure 11-4:
The Main Menu**

This menu is the gateway to information about the system's makeup and configuration, as well as the entryway to the program's Advanced Diagnostic Test functions. You can find utilities for performing low-level formats on older hard drive types and for managing SCSI interface devices through this menu. Additionally, options to print or show test results are available here, as is the exit point from the program.

The most common software-troubleshooting packages test the system's memory, microprocessor, keyboard, display monitor, and the disk drive's speed. If at least the system's CPU, disk drive, and clock circuits are working, you may be able to use one of these special software-troubleshooting packages to help localize system failures. They can prove especially helpful when trying to track down non-heat-related intermittent problems.

If a diagnostic program indicates that multiple items should be replaced, replace the units one at a time until the unit starts up. Then, replace any units removed prior to the one that caused the system to start. This process ensures that there were not multiple bad parts. If you have replaced all the parts, and the unit still does not function properly, the diagnostic software is suspect.

For enterprises that repair computers, or build computers from parts, diagnostic programs that perform continuous burn-in tests are valuable tools. After the system has been built or repaired, these programs are used to run continuous tests on the system for an extended **burn-in period**, without any intervention from a technician or operator.

burn-in period

The tests performed in a burn-in situation are similar to standard software utility tests. However, they are normally used for reliability testing instead of general troubleshooting. Different parts of the system can be selected for the burn-in tests. Because the burn-in tests are designed for use in an unattended manner, you must be careful to select only tests that apply to hardware that actually exists in the system. The diagnostic keeps track of how many times each test has been run and how often it failed during the designated burn-in period, as depicted in Figure 11-5.

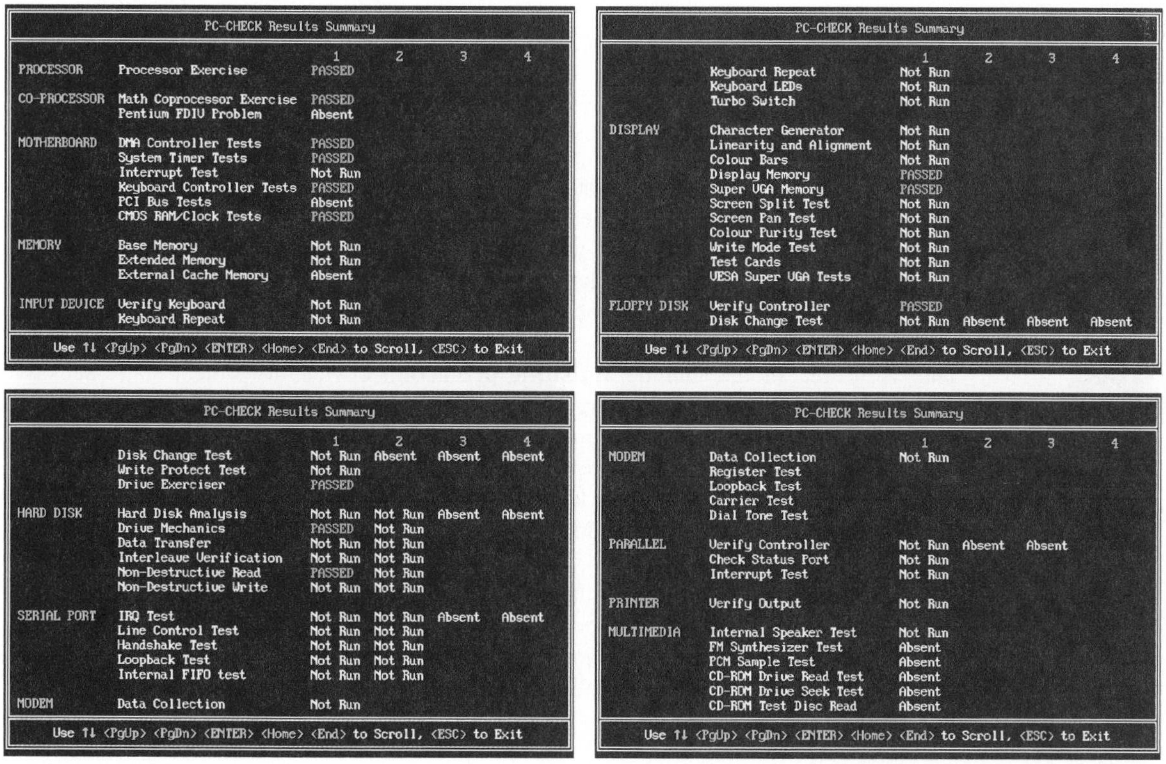

PC-CHECK Results Summary

		1	2	3	4
PROCESSOR	Processor Exercise	PASSED			
CO-PROCESSOR	Math Coprocessor Exercise	PASSED			
	Pentium FDIV Problem	Absent			
MOTHERBOARD	DMA Controller Tests	PASSED			
	System Timer Tests	PASSED			
	Interrupt Test	Not Run			
	Keyboard Controller Tests	PASSED			
	PCI Bus Tests	Absent			
	CMOS RAM/Clock Tests	PASSED			
MEMORY	Base Memory	Not Run			
	Extended Memory	Not Run			
	External Cache Memory	Absent			
INPUT DEVICE	Verify Keyboard	Not Run			
	Keyboard Repeat	Not Run			

Use ↑↓ <PgUp> <PgDn> <ENTER> <Home> <End> to Scroll, <ESC> to Exit

PC-CHECK Results Summary

		1	2	3	4
	Keyboard Repeat	Not Run			
	Keyboard LEDs	Not Run			
	Turbo Switch	Not Run			
DISPLAY	Character Generator	Not Run			
	Linearity and Alignment	Not Run			
	Colour Bars	Not Run			
	Display Memory	PASSED			
	Super VGA Memory	PASSED			
	Screen Split Test	Not Run			
	Screen Pan Test	Not Run			
	Colour Purity Test	Not Run			
	Write Mode Test	Not Run			
	Test Cards	Not Run			
	VESA Super VGA Tests	Not Run			
FLOPPY DISK	Verify Controller	PASSED			
	Disk Change Test	Not Run	Absent	Absent	Absent

Use ↑↓ <PgUp> <PgDn> <ENTER> <Home> <End> to Scroll, <ESC> to Exit

PC-CHECK Results Summary

		1	2	3	4
	Disk Change Test	Not Run	Absent	Absent	Absent
	Write Protect Test	Not Run			
	Drive Exerciser	PASSED			
HARD DISK	Hard Disk Analysis	Not Run	Not Run	Absent	Absent
	Drive Mechanics	PASSED	Not Run		
	Data Transfer	Not Run	Not Run		
	Interleave Verification	Not Run	Not Run		
	Non-Destructive Read	PASSED	Not Run		
	Non-Destructive Write	Not Run	Not Run		
SERIAL PORT	IRQ Test	Not Run	Not Run	Absent	Absent
	Line Control Test	Not Run	Not Run		
	Handshake Test	Not Run	Not Run		
	Loopback Test	Not Run	Not Run		
	Internal FIFO test	Not Run	Not Run		
MODEM	Data Collection	Not Run			

Use ↑↓ <PgUp> <PgDn> <ENTER> <Home> <End> to Scroll, <ESC> to Exit

PC-CHECK Results Summary

		1	2	3	4
MODEM	Data Collection	Not Run			
	Register Test				
	Loopback Test				
	Carrier Test				
	Dial Tone Test				
PARALLEL	Verify Controller	Not Run	Absent	Absent	
	Check Status Port	Not Run			
	Interrupt Test	Not Run			
PRINTER	Verify Output	Not Run			
MULTIMEDIA	Internal Speaker Test	Not Run			
	FM Synthesizer Test	Absent			
	PCM Sample Test	Absent			
	CD-ROM Drive Read Test	Absent			
	CD-ROM Drive Seek Test	Absent			
	CD-ROM Test Disc Read	Absent			

Use ↑↓ <PgUp> <PgDn> <ENTER> <Home> <End> to Scroll, <ESC> to Exit

Figure 11-5: The Burn-in Test Report

Using POST Cards

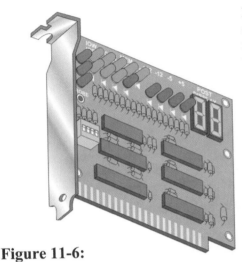

Most BIOS program chips do not have an extensive set of on-board diagnostics built into them. Therefore, several companies produce **POST cards** and diagnostic software to aid in hardware troubleshooting. A POST card is a diagnostic device that plugs into the system's expansion slot and tests the operation of the system as it boots up. These cards can be as simple as interrupt and DMA channel monitors, or as complex as full-fledged ROM BIOS diagnostic packages that carry out extensive tests on the system.

POST cards are normally used when the system appears to be dead, or when the system cannot read from a floppy or hard drive. The firmware tests on the card replace the normal BIOS functions and send the system into a set of tests. The value of the card lies in the fact that the tests can be carried out without the system resorting to software diagnostics located on the hard disk or in a floppy drive.

The POST routines located in most BIOS chips will report two types of errors: fatal and nonfatal. If the POST encounters a fatal error, it stops the system. The error code posted on the indicator corresponds to the defective operation. If the POST card encounters a nonfatal error, however, it notes the error and continues through the initialization routine to activate as many additional system resources as possible. When these types of errors are encountered, the POST card must be observed carefully, because the error code on its indicator must be coordinated with the timing of the error message or beep code produced by the BIOS routines.

Simple POST cards come with a set of light-emitting diodes (LEDs) on them that produce coded error signals when a problem is encountered. Other cards produce beep codes and seven-segment LED readouts of the error code. Figure 11-6 depicts a typical POST card.

**Figure 11-6:
A Typical
POST Card**

Depot Technician 1.2

IT Technician 1.2

flat workspace

antistatic protection

Antistatic mats

Good lighting

Workspace

The first order of business when working on any type of electronic equipment is to prepare a proper work area. You need a clear, **flat workspace** on which to rest the PC and its components. Make sure that your workspace is large enough to accommodate the work piece. Confirm that you have an adequate number of power receptacles to handle all of the equipment you may need. Try to locate your workspace in a low-traffic area.

The work area should include **antistatic protection** devices to protect static sensitive devices from electro static discharges (ESD). These discharges can build up on moving surfaces (including people) and damage the integrated circuit devices in the PC. The most common anti-static device is a grounding strap placed around the wrist or ankle while working on equipment. **Antistatic mats** for the floor and table are advised as well. These devices all work to channel static discharges away from sensitive devices.

Good lighting is a prerequisite for the work area, because the technician must be able to see small details, such as part numbers, cracked circuit foils, and solder splashes. An adjustable lamp with a shade is preferable. Fluorescent lighting is particularly desirable. In addition, a magnifying glass helps to read small part numbers.

Because computers have the potential to produce these kinds of injuries, it is good practice to have a well-stocked **first-aid kit** in the work area. In addition, a **Class-C fire extinguisher** should be on hand. Class-C extinguishers are the type specified for use around electrical equipment. You can probably imagine the consequences of applying a water-based fire extinguisher to a fire with live electrical equipment around. The class, or classes, that the fire extinguisher is rated for are typically marked on its side.

You may think that there's not much chance for a fire to occur with computer equipment, but this is not so. Just let a capacitor from a system board blow up and have a small piece land in a pile of packing materials in the work area. It becomes a fire.

TEST TIP
Remember the type of fire extinguisher that must be used with electrical systems, such as a PC.

Gathering Information

One of the most important aspects of troubleshooting anything is the gathering of information about the problem at hand and the symptoms it is showing. One of the best sources for this type of information is the computer user. The next most important source of information is actually observing the system to see what it is doing. The PC technician should be able to effectively acquire information from the customer (user) and the system concerning the nature of a problem and then be able to practice basic troubleshooting methods to isolate and repair the problem.

Assessing the Situation

The most important task when checking a malfunctioning device is to be observant. Begin by talking to the PC user or the person who reported the problem. You can obtain many clues from this person. Gather information from the user regarding the environment in which the system is being used.

Also note any symptoms or error codes produced by the system, and the situations that existed when the failure occurred. Ask the user to demonstrate the procedures that led to the malfunction in a step-by-step manner. This communication can help you narrow down a problem to a particular section of the computer. It does no good to check the video display when the user is having trouble using the disk drive.

Part of the technician's job is to determine whether the user could be the source of the problem—either trying to do things with the system that it cannot do or not understanding how some part of it is supposed to work. Carefully listening to the user is a good way to eliminate the user as a possible cause of the problem. Attempt to gain a full understanding of the process they are trying to perform.

TEST TIP
Be well aware that the user is one of the most common sources of PC problems. In most situations, your first troubleshooting step should be to talk to the user.

If you suspect that the user is part of the problem, remove him or her from the situation and operate the equipment yourself. This will enable you to personally observe the system's symptoms as they occur. Attempt to limit the problem to the hardware involved, the software package being used, and then to the operator.

Assessing the Environment

Take note of the environment in which the equipment is being used and how heavy its usage is. If the system is located in a particularly dirty area, or an area given to other environmental extremes, it may need to be cleaned and serviced more frequently than if it were in a clean office environment. The same is true for systems subjected to heavy or continuous use. In an industrial environment, check with the management to see whether any office or industry maintenance standards for servicing apply.

Finally, use simple observation of the wear and tear on the equipment to gauge the need for additional or spot maintenance steps. Look for signs of extended use (such as frayed cords, missing slot covers, keyboards with letters worn off, etc.) to spot potential problems resulting from age or usage.

GEEK SQUAD CASE FILE #22294

You have been deployed to a business to repair a printing problem. When you arrive, you are told that the user is having trouble printing spreadsheets from his Microsoft Excel program. You are not an Excel or spreadsheet guru, so how do you go about servicing this problem?

Essentials 1.3

Depot Technician 1.2

IT Technician 1.2

Perform an Initial Inspection

"Check the easy things first." As a general rule, the majority of all equipment problems can be reduced to the simplest things you can think of. The problem is, most people don't think of them. Successful troubleshooting is the result of careful observation, deductive reasoning, and an organized approach to solving problems. These techniques are common to repairing any type of defective equipment. Although we are demonstrating these techniques as they apply to repairing computer systems, it is quite possible to adapt them to other systems as well.

Next, observe the symptoms of a malfunction to associate the malfunction with a section of the system responsible for that operation. If there is no prior knowledge of the type of malfunction, you should proceed by performing a careful visual inspection of the system. Check the outside of the system first. Look for loose or disconnected cables. Consult all of the external front-panel lights. If no lights are displayed, check the power outlet, the plugs, and power cords, as well as any power switches that may affect the operation of the system. You may also want to check the commercial power-distribution system's fuses or circuit breakers to insure that they are functional.

Don't forget to *listen* to the system. Listen for the sounds of the power supply and processor fans, the hard drive spindle motor turning, and the sounds coming from the system speaker.

If part of the system is active, try to *localize the problem* by systematically removing peripheral devices from the system. Try to revive the system, or its defective portion, by restarting it several times. You should try to restart the system after each correctional step is performed.

Consult any additional user's or operations manuals liberally. Indeed, many of the computer's peripheral systems, such as hard drives and printers, have some level of **self-diagnostics** built into them. Generally, these diagnostics programs produce coded error messages. The key to recognizing and using these error messages is usually found in the device's **user's manual**. In addition, the user's manual may contain probable cause and suggested remedy information or specialized tests to isolate specific problems.

self-diagnostics

user's manual

Document the Process

Take the time to *document the problem,* including all of the tests you perform and their outcomes. Your memory is never as good as you think it is, especially in stressful situations such as with a "down" computer. This recorded information can prevent you from making repetitive steps that waste time and may cause confusion. This information will also be very helpful when you move on to more detailed tests or measurements.

Observe the Bootup Procedure

Unless the system is on fire, the first real diagnostic step is normally to turn the system on and carefully observe the steps of the bootup process. This procedure can reveal a great deal about the nature of any problems in a system. Faulty areas can be included or excluded as possible causes of errors during the bootup process.

The observable actions of a working system's cold-boot procedure are listed as follows, in their order of occurrence:

1. When power is applied, the power supply and system fans activate.

2. The system's power light and CD-ROM/DVD power lights come on.

3. The hard-disk drive activity light flashes, and it can be heard spinning up to speed.

4. The BIOS message displays on the monitor (this may occur later on some monitors that take longer to come alive), followed by processor type and memory count information.

5. The video display and keyboard lights flash as the rest of the system components are being reset.

6. The system produces a single beep, indicating that it has completed its Power-On Self-Tests and initialization process. After this point, the operation of the machine has shifted to looking for and loading an operating system.

7. The floppy-disk drive access light comes on briefly (if enabled in the CMOS boot sequence) before switching to the hard drive activity light.

8. HDD and CD-ROM/DVD interface configuration information is displayed on the screen.

9. At this point in the process, the BIOS is looking for additional instructions (boot information)—first from the floppy drive and then from the hard drive (assuming that the CMOS setup is configured for this sequence).

10. When the system finds the boot files, the drive light will come on, indicating that the system is loading the operating system and configuration files.

11. On Windows machines, the "Starting Windows" message appears on the screen.

12. Windows loads its GUI desktop components and takes over control of the system.

TEST TIP

Be familiar with the order of the series of observable events that occur during the normal PC boot/start process.

The exact order of events in the start-up process of a given computer may differ slightly from the list provided here. The order is affected by CMOS setup configurations and the speed of the display when it starts up. The point is, if a section of the computer is defective, you should only observe some (or possibly none) of these events. By knowing which sections of the computer are involved in each step, you can suspect a particular section of causing the problem when the system does not advance past that step.

Note Symptoms and Error Codes

Most PCs have reasonably good built-in POSTs that are run each time the computer is powered up. These tests can prove very beneficial in detecting hardware-oriented problems within the system. Whenever a self-test failure or setup mismatch occurs, the BIOS may indicate the error through a blank screen, or a visual **error message** on the video display (if possible), or an audio response (**beep code**) produced by the system's speaker. It will also produce a POST code that can be read by POST diagnostic cards. If the POST detects problems during the testing phase, it will attempt to continue with the start-up process. However, if the problems are severe, it may be forced to halt the system.

error message

beep code

Some PCs issue numerically coded error messages on the display when errors occur. Conversely, other PCs display a written description of the error. Figure 11-7 defines the error messages and beep codes produced by a BIOS version from *American Megatrends* (*AMI*). The error messages and codes vary among different BIOS manufacturers and from version to version.

If you receive a beep code of one beep, two beeps, or three beeps, reseat the DRAM modules in their slots. If the error continues after restarting the system, replace the memory with known good chips. If the beep code consists of four beeps, five beeps, seven beeps, or ten beeps, troubleshoot the system board. Unless your repair area can support IC level rework, you may have to simply replace the system board.

BEEP CODE MESSAGES

1 beep – DRAM refresh failure

2 beeps – Parity Circuit Failure

3 beeps – Base 64K RAM failure

4 beeps – System Timer Failure

5 beeps – Processor Failure

6 beeps – Keyboard Controller/Gate A20 Failure

7 beeps – Virtual Mode Exception Error

8 beeps – Display Memory Read/Write Failure

9 beeps – ROM BIOS Checksum Failure

10 beeps – CMOS Shutdown Register Read/Write Error

1 long, 2 short beeps – Video controller failure

1 long, 3 short beeps – Conventional and extended test failure

1 long, 8 short beeps – Display test failure

VISUAL DISPLAY ERROR MESSAGES

SYSTEM HALTED ERRORS

CMOS INOPERATIONAL – Failure of CMOS shutdown register test

8042 GATE A20 ERROR – Error getting into protected mode

INVALID SWITCH MEMORY FAILURE – Real/Protected mode change over error.

DMA ERROR – DMA controller failed page register test

DMA #1 ERROR – DMA device # 1 failure

DMA #2 ERROR – DMA device # 2 failure

NON-FATAL ERRORS - WITH SETUP OPTION

CMOS BATTERY LOW – Failure of CMOS battery or CMOS checksum test

CMOS SYSTEM OPTION NOT SET – Failure of CMOS battery or CMOS checksum test

CMOS CHECKSUM FAILURE – CMS battery low or CMOS checksum test failure

CMOS DISPLAY MISMATCH – Failure of display type verification

CMOS MEMORY SIZE MISMATCH – System Configuration and Setup failure

CMOS TIMER AND DATE NOT SET – System Configuration and Setup failure in timer circuitry

NON-FATAL ERRORS - WITHOUT SETUP OPTION

CH-X TIMER ERROR – Channel X (2, 1, or 0) Timer Failure

KEYBOARD ERROR – Keyboard test failure

KB/INTERFACE ERROR – Keyboard test failure

DISPLAY SWITCH SETTING NOT PROPER – Failure to verify display type

KEYBOARD IS LOCKED – Unlock it

FDD CONTROLLER ERROR – Failure to verify floppy disk setup by System Configuration file

HDD CONTROLLER FAILURE – Failure to verify hard disk setup by System Configuration file

C:DRIVE ERROR – Hard disk setup failure

D:DRIVE ERROR – Hard disk setup failure

Figure 11-7: Error Messages and Beep Codes

For six beeps, check parts of the system relating to the keyboard (e.g., swap the keyboard for a known good one and check to see if the system board has a keyboard fuse). Eight beeps indicate a video adapter memory error. Replace the video card (or the memory devices on the video adapter if possible). If the system produces nine beeps, indicating that there is a faulty BIOS device, you must replace or flash the BIOS with an updated version.

- **Hard disk install failure**—Cannot find or initialize the hard drive controller or the drive. Make sure the controller is installed correctly. If no hard drives are installed, be sure the Hard Drive selection in Setup is set to NONE.

- **Hard disk(s) diagnosis fail**—The system may run specific disk diagnostic routines. This message appears if one or more hard disks return an error when the diagnostics run.

- **Primary master hard disk fail**—POST detects an error in the primary master IDE hard drive.

- **Primary slave hard disk fail**—POST detects an error in the secondary master IDE hard drive.

- **Resuming from disk, Press TAB to show POST screen**—Phoenix Technologies offers a save-to-disk feature for notebook computers. This message may appear when the operator re-starts the system after a save-to-disk shut down.

- **Secondary master hard disk fail**—POST detects an error in the primary slave IDE hard drive.

- **Secondary slave hard disk fail**—POST detects an error in the secondary slave IDE hard drive.

Determining Hardware/Software/Configuration Problems

One of the earliest steps in troubleshooting a computer problem (or any other programmable system problem) is to determine whether the problem is due to a hardware failure or to faulty software. In most PCs, you can use a significant event that occurs during the bootup process as a key to separating *hardware problems* from *software problems*—the **single beep** that most PCs produce between the end of the POST and the beginning of the bootup process.

`single beep`

Errors that occur, or are displayed, before this beep indicate that a hardware problem of some type exists. Up to this point in the operation of the system, only the BIOS and the basic system hardware have been active. The operating system does not come into play until after the beep occurs. You can group errors that occur before the beep into two distinct categories:

- Hardware failures

- Configuration errors

Hardware failures associated with the system's basic components are typically the easiest items to troubleshoot. They tend to produce distinct symptoms (such as no video or no lights or no disk drive activities). Depending on how much of the system is working, the POST will normally detect these types of problems and generate a beep-coded message or an error code.

Configuration or setup problems tend to occur whenever a new hardware option is added to the system, or when the system is used for the very first time. These problems result from mismatches between the system's programmed configuration, held in CMOS memory, and the actual equipment installed in the system. The POST typically detects configuration errors and produces error-code messages on the screen to identify them.

Typically, if the bootup process reaches the point where the system's CMOS configuration information is displayed on-screen, you can safely assume that no hardware configuration conflicts exist between the system's basic components.

> **┌─ NOTE ───┐**
>
> If the system produces an error message (such as *The System Has Detected Unstable RAM at Location x*) or a beep code before the beep, for example, the system has found a problem with the RAM hardware. In this case, a bad memory device is indicated.
>
> **└───┘**

In most systems, the BIOS and operating system use Plug-and-Play (PnP) techniques to detect new hardware that has been installed in the system. These components work together with the device to allocate system resources for the device. In some situations, the PnP logic will not be able to resolve all the system's resource needs and a configuration error will occur. In these cases, the user must manually resolve the configuration problem.

In addition, there are several port and device enabling functions controlled through the BIOS' CMOS setup utility. If these settings are not enabled, the device will not be able to interact with the system when its hardware is installed. You may need to access and configure settings in the system's CMOS Setup utility the first time you start a newly constructed system, when you add a new device that is enabled through the CMOS utility, or when it becomes necessary to replace the system board's CMOS backup battery.

If you encounter configuration errors, refer to the installation instructions found in the new component's user manual. Table 11-1 lists typical configuration error codes and messages produced when various types of configuration mismatches occur.

CONFIGURATION ERROR MESSAGE	MEANING
CMOS System Option Not Set	Failure of CMOS battery or CMOS Checksum test
CMOS Display Mismatch	Failure of display type verification
CMOS Memory Size Mismatch	System configuration and setup failure
Press F1 to Continue	Invalid configuration information
CMOS Time and Date Not Set	Failure of CMOS battery

Table 11-1: Common Configuration Error Messages

┌─ TEST TIP ─┐
Know the situations that cause a Press F1 to Continue error message to display.
└───────────┘

It is important to observe the system's symptoms to determine in which part of the system's operation the fault occurs. The configuration error messages described in the table occur and are reported before the single beep tone is produced at the end of the POST routines. If you cannot confirm a configuration error, the problem most likely is a defective component. The most widely used repair method used with PC systems involves substituting known-good components for suspected bad components.

GEEK SQUAD CASE FILE #78734

A friend is having trouble starting up her computer and she has asked you for help. When you turn the system on, the video display comes on, and you can hear the disk drive spinning. Several different screens display and then you hear a single beep from the computer. From your knowledge of system bootups, what can you tell your friend about her system?

After the *beep tone* is produced, the system shifts over to the process of booting up and begins looking for and loading the operating system. Errors that occur between the beep and the presentation of the operating system's user interface (command prompt or Desktop GUI) generally can be divided into three distinct types for troubleshooting purposes. These error types also correspond to three possible sources, which are summarized in the following list that includes the typical error messages types associated with each source.

- *Hard Drive Failure* or *Configuration Problems*—physical or configuration problem with the boot drive

  - General Failure Error Reading Drive x

- *Boot Failure*—corrupted or missing boot files

  - Bad or Missing MBR

  - Non-System Disk or Disk Error

  - Bad File Allocation/Master File Table

- *OS Startup Failure*—corrupted or missing operating system files

  - Bad or Missing NTOSKRNL File

Procedures for diagnosing and troubleshooting problems associated with typical PC hardware components are presented throughout the *Symptoms and Troubleshooting* sections later in this chapter. Conversely, bootup and OS startup problems are typically associated with the hard-disk drive and the operating system. Steps for isolating and correcting operating system problems are presented in Chapter 12, *Operating System Troubleshooting*. In these cases, checking the drive hardware is generally the last step of the troubleshooting process. Unless some specific symptom indicates otherwise, you should check for missing or corrupted boot and operating system files first.

Field-Replaceable Unit Troubleshooting

Field-replaceable units (FRUs) are the portions of the system that you can conveniently replace in the field. Typical PC FRUs are depicted in Figure 11-8. FRU troubleshooting involves isolating a problem within one section of the system. A section consists of one device such as a keyboard, video display, video adapter card, I/O adapter card, system board, disk drive, printer, and so on. These are typically components that can simply be exchanged for a replacement on-site and require no electronic repair work.

> **Field-replaceable units (FRUs)**

> **TEST TIP**
> Know which devices in a typical PC system are FRU devices.

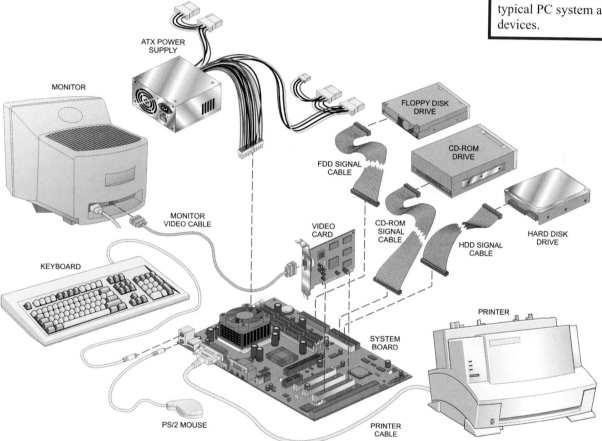

Figure 11-8: The Typical FRUs of a Microcomputer System

Exchanging FRUs is the level of troubleshooting most often performed on PCs. Due to the relative low cost of computer components, it is normally not practical to troubleshoot failed components to the IC level. The cost of using a technician to diagnose the problem further, and repair it, can quickly exceed the cost of the new replacement unit.

> **Exchanging FRU components**—After a hardware error has been indicated, start troubleshooting the problem by exchanging components (cards, drives, etc.) with **known-good ones**. Turn off the power and exchange suspected or indicated devices from the system one at a time. Make sure to restore the power and retry the system after each exchange.

> **known-good ones**

If a diagnostic tool indicates that multiple components have failed, use the one-at-a-time exchange method, starting with the first component indicated, to isolate the original source of the problem. Test and evaluate the system between each component exchange and work backward through the exchanged components after the system has started to function again.

Always check cabling connections after plugging them in. Look for missed connections, bent pins, and so on. Also, check the routing of cables. Try to establish connections that do not place unnecessary strain on the cable. You should attempt to route cables away from major IC devices as much as possible. Some ICs, such as microprocessors, can become so hot that they may eventually damage cables. Avoid routing cables near cooling fans as well, because they produce high levels of EMI that can be introduced into the signal cables as electrical noise.

> **Work backward**—After you have isolated the problem and the computer boots up and runs correctly, work backwards through the troubleshooting steps and reinstall any original adapters and other components removed during the troubleshooting process. Working backwards, one component at a time, through components that have been removed from the system enables you to make certain that only one failure occurred in the machine. If the system fails after installing a new card, check the card's default configuration settings against those of the devices already installed in the system.

COMMON SYMPTOMS AND TROUBLESHOOTING PROCEDURES

One of the primary responsibilities of every PC technician is to diagnose and troubleshoot computer problems. The technician should be able to identify common symptoms associated with computer components and to use those symptoms to effectively troubleshoot and repair the problem. Numerous sources of problems and symptoms are discussed below, beginning with those that relate to the power supply.

Essentials 1.3

Depot Technician 1.2

Technical Support 1.2

IT Technician 1.2

Isolating Power-Supply Problems

Typical symptoms associated with power-supply failures include

- No indicator lights visible, with no disk drive action and no display on the screen. Nothing works, and the system is dead.

- The ON/OFF indicator lights are visible, but there is no disk drive action and no display on the monitor screen. The system fan may or may not run.

- The system produces a continuous beep tone.

The power-supply unit is one of the few components in the system that is connected to virtually every other component in the system. Therefore, it has the ability to affect all of the other components if it fails. Figure 11-9 illustrates the interconnections of the power-supply unit with the other components in the system.

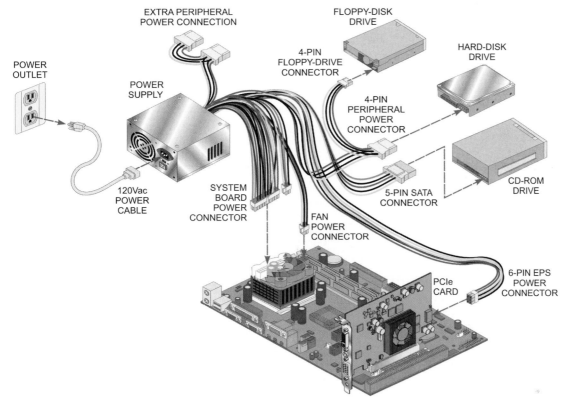

**Figure 11-9:
Power-Supply
Interconnections**

Checking a Dead System

Special consideration must be taken when a system is inoperable. In a totally inoperable system, there are no symptoms to give clues as to where to begin the isolation process. In addition, it is impossible to use troubleshooting software or other system aids to help isolate the problem.

The following discussion is a standard method of troubleshooting dead microprocessor-based equipment. The first step in troubleshooting any dead system is to visually inspect the system. Check for unseated cards, loose cables, or foreign objects within the system unit.

When the system exhibits no signs of life—including the absence of lights—*the best place to start looking for the problem is at the power supply*. The operation of this unit affects virtually every part of the system. Also, the absence of any lights working usually indicates that no power is being supplied to the system by the power supply.

1. Begin by checking the *external connections* of the power supply. This is the first step in checking any electrical equipment that shows no signs of life.

TEST TIP

Remember the first step of checking out electrical equipment that appears dead.

2. Confirm that the power supply cord is plugged into a functioning outlet.

3. Check the position of the ON/OFF switch.

4. Examine the power cord for good connection at the rear of the unit.

5. Check the setting of the 110/220 switch setting on the outside of the power supply. The normal setting for equipment used in the United States is 110.

6. Check the power at the commercial receptacle using a voltmeter, or by plugging a lamp (or other 110-volt device) into the outlet.

If power is reaching the power supply and nothing is happening, the most likely cause of a totally dead system is the power supply itself. However, be aware that in an ATX system, if the cable that connects the system board to the power switch has become loose, the power supply will appear dead. Use a voltmeter to check for the proper voltages at one of the system's option's power connectors. (All system voltages should be present at these connectors.) If any voltage is missing, check the power supply by substitution.

WARNING

Turn It Off First! Before changing any board or connection, always turn the system off first. In ATX/BTX/NLX-style systems, you should disconnect the power cable from the power supply. This is necessary, because even with the power switch off, there are still some levels of voltages applied to the system board in these units.

Other Power-Supply Problems

If the front panel lights are on and the power-supply fan is running but no other system action is occurring, you should consider the power supply as one of the most likely sources of such a problem. The presence of the lights and the fan operation indicate that power is reaching the system and that at least some portion of the power supply is functional. This type of symptom results from the following two likely possibilities:

1. A portion of the power supply has failed or is being overloaded. One or more of the basic voltages supplied by the power supply is missing, while the others are still present.

2. A key component on the system board has failed, preventing it from processing, even though the system has power. A defective capacitor across the power input of the system board can completely prevent it from operating.

Adding and Removing Power Supplies

Figure 11-10 illustrates the steps involved in removing the power supply from a PC. To exchange the power supply, all of its connections to the system must be removed.

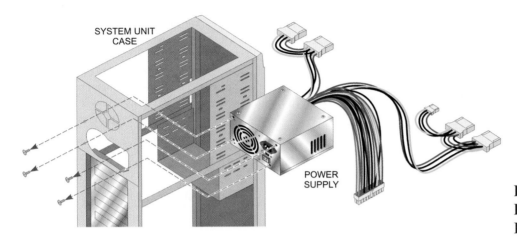

SYSTEM UNIT
CASE

POWER
SUPPLY

**Figure 11-10:
Removing a
Power Supply**

Hands-On Activity

Typical steps for removing a power supply:

1. Disconnect the exterior power connections from the system unit.
   a. Unplug the power cable from the commercial receptacle.
   b. Disconnect the monitor's power cable from the power supply.

2. Disconnect the interior power connections.
   a. Disconnect the power-supply connections from the system board.
   b. Disconnect the power-supply connector from the floppy-disk drive (if installed).
   c. Disconnect the power-supply connector from the hard-disk drive.
   d. Disconnect the power-supply connector from the CD-ROM/DVD drive.
   e. Disconnect the power-supply connector from the front panel switches.

3. Remove the power-supply unit from the system.
   a. Remove the four retaining screws that secure the power-supply unit to the rear of the system unit.
   b. Store the screws properly.
   c. Remove the power supply from the system unit by lifting it out.

These steps would be reversed for the installation of a power supply.

Power-Supply Upgrade Considerations

One consideration that may not be apparent when system components are being upgraded is the power supply each time a new drive or device is added to the system, more current is required from the power supply. The power-supply unit in a computer comes with a given power rating (in watts). The voltage level for a given location in the world is fixed (i.e., 120 or 220 Vac), and the power required can be calculated by multiplying the voltage level by the maximum current rating (in amperes) of all the devices in the system.

In the field, it is difficult to accumulate the current values for all the devices in the system. For example, upgrading the processor can easily increase the power consumption in the system by more than 20 W. A typical Pentium processor may require 65 W of power to operate. Advanced Pentium processors have increased their power consumption to over 80 W.

Likewise, replacing RAM with faster or bigger RAM devices tends to increase power consumption as well. Simply, increasing the installed memory from 128 MB to 256 MB by adding an additional DIMM will almost double the power consumption of the system's memory (i.e., from 6 W to 12 W).

Adding adapter cards to the system also significantly increases the amount of power the power supply must deliver to the system board. A typical adapter card may require 12 to 15 W with good connections to the slot. A high-end video adapter used for games may consume up to 100 W.

However, disk drive devices tend to consume more power than most other system devices, simply because they use motors to spin the disk or disc and to position the read/write mechanism. A typical hard-disk drive can require up to 20 or 30 W each.

As you can see from these paragraphs, it is relatively easy to consume hundreds of watts of power for a normal system. The typical power supply used with basic Pentium desktop systems is 300 W. One-third of this value must be reserved simply for startup of the computer. During this time, the system will require more power than it does when it is running. For systems using the high-end video card mentioned earlier, the power supply might need to be capable of delivering 500 W of power.

As mentioned in Chapter 8, adding peripheral devices to portable systems does not typically present the same load on their power supplies as it does on a desktop system – most portable peripherals come with their own power sources. However, you should still be aware that adding peripherals that do not have their own separate power source to the portable would draw current from the system. This can be exceptionally problematic if the system is running on its battery. That's why the first step in troubleshooting general portable computer problems involves removing any unnecessary peripherals from the system and checking the ac adapter/battery system.

In any event, there are two ways to determine that the system will need a power-supply upgrade. The first is to approximate how much each device will require and double that value to provide for operating safety and the startup surge. The second method involves purchasing all of the upgrade items and turning on the system to discover that it will not start.

TROUBLESHOOTING THE SYSTEM BOARD

Troubleshooting problems related to the system board can be difficult because of the system board's relative complexity. So many system functions at least partially rely on the system board that certain symptoms can be masked by other symptoms. If you suspect a system board problem, you should

- Observe the steps that lead to the failure and determine under what conditions the system failed. Were any unusual operations in progress?

- Note any error messages or beep codes produced.

- Refer to the documentation for the system board and peripheral units to check for symptoms and technical notes related to the symptoms observed.

- Examine the CMOS setup entries for configuration problems. Also check the advanced CMOS setup parameters to make certain that all the appropriate system board–enabling settings have been made.

Remember that the microprocessor, RAM modules, ROM BIOS, and CMOS battery are typically replaceable units on the system board. If enough of the system is running to perform tests on these units, you can replace them. If symptoms suggest that one or more of these devices may be defective, you can exchange them with a known-good unit of the same type.

System Board Symptoms

So much of the system's operation is based on the system board and its components that a problem with it can produce a wide variety of different symptom types. Typical symptoms associated with system board hardware failures include

- The On/Off indicator lights are visible and the display is visible on the monitor screen, but there is no disk drive action and no bootup.

- The On/Off indicator lights are visible, the hard drive spins up, but the system appears dead, and there is no bootup.

- The system locks up during normal operation.

- The system produces a beep code with one, two, three, five, seven, or nine beeps.

- The system produces a beep code of one long and three short beeps.

- The system will not hold date and time.

- An "8042 Gate A20 Error" message displays—Error getting into Protected mode.

- An "Invalid Switch Memory Failure" message displays.

- A "DMA Error" message displays—DMA Controller failed page register test.

- A "CMOS Battery Low" message displays, indicating failure of CMOS battery or CMOS checksum test.

- A "CMOS System Option Not Set" message displays, indicating failure of CMOS battery or CMOS checksum test.

- A "CMOS Checksum Failure" message displays, indicating CMOS battery low or CMOS checksum test failure.

- A 201 error code displays, indicating a RAM failure.

- A parity check error message displays, indicating a RAM error.

Typical symptoms associated with system board's CMOS setup failures include

- A "CMOS Inoperational" message displays, indicating failure of CMOS shutdown register.

- A "Display Switch Setting Not Proper" message displays—Failure to verify display type.

- A "CMOS Display Mismatch" message displays—Failure of display type verification.

- A "CMOS Memory Size Mismatch" message displays—System

- Configuration and Setup failure.

- A "CMOS Time & Date Not Set" message displays—System Configuration and Setup failure.

- An IBM-compatible error code displays, indicating that a configuration problem has occurred.

Typical symptoms associated with failures of the system board's I/O include the following:

- Error initializing hard drive controller. The system has detected a failure related to the IDE hard disk built into the system board. The problem is most likely in the system board's IDE controller circuitry but could be connected to the disk drive unit as well.

- Speaker doesn't work during operation. The rest of the system works, but no sounds are produced through the speaker.

- Keyboard Interface Error. While the message says the problem is with the keyboard controller on the system board, it is more often related to an unplugged or failed keyboard.

- Keyboard does not function after being replaced with a known-good unit.

Most of the hardware problems that occur with PCs involve the system board. Because the system board is the center of virtually all the computer's operations, it is only natural that you must check it at some point in most troubleshooting efforts. The system board is normally the last step at the end of various troubleshooting schemes used for different system components. It occupies this position for two reasons. First, the system board supports most of the other system components, either directly or indirectly. Second, it is the system component that requires the most effort to replace and test.

Configuration Checks

You should recall from the discussions of advanced CMOS setup options in Chapter 3, *Advanced System Boards,* that there are many system board configuration options available in modern BIOS. However, manipulating these settings requires the user to have a good deal of knowledge about the particular function being configured. When users attempt to tweak these settings they often create configurations that the system cannot work with (i.e., data transfer timing errors and speed miss matches). When this happens, the system can crash and refuse to run. In cases where there are serious configuration circumstances, don't forget that you have the option to select default configuration options through the CMOS Setup utility.

A configuration problem occurs when the system is being set up for the first time or when a new option is installed that the PnP process cannot identify. Incorrectly set BIOS-enabling parameters cause the corresponding hardware to fail. Therefore, check for the presence of port and device enabling functions in the *BIOS Features* and *Chipset Features* screens, illustrated in Figure 11-11, as part of every hardware configuration troubleshooting procedure. Advanced CMOS configuration and enabling settings in these screens usually include the disk drives, keyboard, and video options, as well as on-board ports and buses.

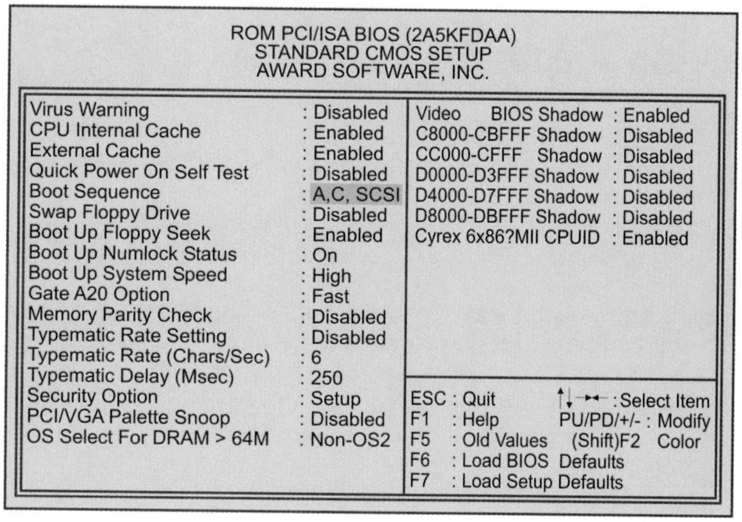

```
                 ROM PCI/ISA BIOS (2A5KFDAA)
                    STANDARD CMOS SETUP
                    AWARD SOFTWARE, INC.

 Virus Warning                : Disabled   Video   BIOS Shadow : Enabled
 CPU Internal Cache           : Enabled    C8000-CBFFF Shadow  : Disabled
 External Cache               : Enabled    CC000-CFFF  Shadow  : Disabled
 Quick Power On Self Test     : Disabled   D0000-D3FFF Shadow  : Disabled
 Boot Sequence                : A,C, SCSI  D4000-D7FFF Shadow  : Disabled
 Swap Floppy Drive            : Disabled   D8000-DBFFF Shadow  : Disabled
 Boot Up Floppy Seek          : Enabled    Cyrex 6x86?MII CPUID : Enabled
 Boot Up Numlock Status       : On
 Boot Up System Speed         : High
 Gate A20 Option              : Fast
 Memory Parity Check          : Disabled
 Typematic Rate Setting       : Disabled
 Typematic Rate (Chars/Sec)   : 6
 Typematic Delay (Msec)       : 250
 Security Option              : Setup      ESC : Quit      ↑↓←→ : Select Item
 PCI/VGA Palette Snoop        : Disabled   F1  : Help      PU/PD/+/- : Modify
 OS Select For DRAM > 64M     : Non-OS2    F5  : Old Values  (Shift)F2  Color
                                           F6  : Load BIOS  Defaults
                                           F7  : Load Setup Defaults
```

Figure 11-11: BIOS Enabling Settings

Another condition that causes a configuration problem involves the system board's CMOS backup battery. If the battery fails, or has been changed, the contents of the CMOS setup will be lost. After replacing the battery, it is always necessary to run the CMOS Setup utility to reconfigure the system. The values stored in CMOS must accurately reflect the configuration of the system; otherwise, an error occurs. Accessing these values to change them normally requires pressing a predetermined key combination during the bootup process.

Hardware Checks

If the system's CMOS configuration setup appears to be correct and a system board hardware problem is suspected, you may need to exchange the system board for a working unit. Because most of the system must be dismantled to exchange it, however, a few items are worth checking before doing so.

Check the system board for signs of physical problems, such as loose cables and devices. If nothing is apparently wrong, check the power-supply voltage levels on the system board. Check for +5 Vdc and +12 Vdc on the system board, as illustrated in Figure 11-12. If these voltages are missing, turn off the system, disconnect power to all disk drives, and swap the power-supply unit with a known-good one.

Figure 11-12: The System Board Voltage Check Location

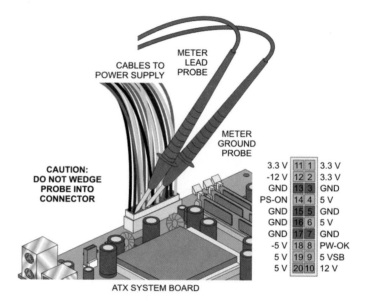

Essentials 1.3

Depot Technician 1.2

IT Technician 1.2

soft-memory errors

hard-memory errors

RAM

The system board's memory is a very serviceable part of the system. RAM failures basically fall into two major categories and create two different types of failures:

- **Soft-memory errors**—Errors caused by infrequent and random glitches in the operation of applications and the system. You can clear these events just by restarting the system.

- **Hard-memory errors**—These errors are caused by permanent physical failures that generate NMI errors in the system and require that the memory units be checked by substitution.

Observe the bootup RAM count to see that it is correct for the amount of physical RAM actually installed in the system. If not, swap RAM devices around to see if the count changes. Use logical rotation of the RAM devices to locate the defective part. The burn-in tests in most diagnostic packages can prove helpful in locating borderline RAM modules.

┌─ **TEST TIP** ────────
Know what type of failures hard- and soft-memory errors are and how they affect the system.
└──────────────────────

You can swap the RAM modules out one at a time to isolate defective modules. These modules are also swapped out when a system upgrade is being performed. Take care when swapping RAM into a system for troubleshooting purposes to make sure that the new RAM is the correct type of RAM for the system and that it meets the system's bus speed rating. Also, make sure that the replacement RAM is consistent with the installed RAM. Mixing RAM types and speeds can cause the system to lock up and produce hard memory errors.

When examining DRAM memory you will encounter some DRAM package configurations designated as SS and some as DS. This refers to **single-sided** modules and **double-sided** modules. Single sided modules place all the DRAM chips on one side of the module, while double sided modules place half of the total memory on each side of the module.

There are many theories about how this impacts memory performance – such as the two sides being two separate banks of memory and taking time to switch between them, or that separating the chips on each side of the module lets them run cooler and perform more efficiently.

In reality, the performance of a DRAM module is controlled by the types of IC devices it employs and how the module designer lays out the physical connections on the printed circuit board. However, you should not mix these two types of memory even if they have the same capacity. You should consult the system board's User's/Installation Guide to determine what types of memory it will support.

Microprocessor

Essentials 1.3

Depot Technician 1.2

IT Technician 1.2

In the case of the microprocessor, the system may issue a slow, single beep, with no display or other I/O operation as a symptom. This indicates that an internal error has disabled a portion of the processor's internal circuitry (usually the internal cache). Internal problems also may allow the microprocessor to begin processing, but then cause it to fail as it attempts operations. Such a problem results in the system continuously counting RAM during the bootup process. It also may lock up while counting RAM. In either case, the only way to remedy the problem is to replace the microprocessor.

If the system consistently locks up after being on for a few minutes, this is a good indication that the microprocessor's fan is not running or that some other heat buildup problem is occurring. You also should check the microprocessor if its fan has not been running, but the power is on. This situation may indicate that the microprocessor has been without adequate ventilation and has overheated. When this happens, you must replace the fan unit and the microprocessor. Check to make certain that the new fan works correctly; otherwise, a second microprocessor will be damaged.

The fact that most microprocessors are mounted in sockets or slots brings up another point. These items should be pulled and reseated in their sockets or slots if they appear to be a possible cause of problems. Sockets and slots are convenient for repair and upgrade purposes, but they can also attract corrosion between the pins of the device, and those of the socket. Over time, the corrosion may become so bad that the electrical connection becomes too poor for the device to operate properly.

> ┌─ **TEST TIP** ─
> Know the effects on the system of heat buildup and microprocessor fan failures.

ROM

As with the microprocessor, a bad or damaged ROM BIOS will typically stop the system completely. When you encounter a dead system board, examine the BIOS chip(s) for physical damage. When these devices overheat, they usually crack or blow a large piece out of the top of the IC package. Another symptom of a damaged BIOS is indicated by the bootup sequence automatically moving into the CMOS configuration, but never returning to the bootup sequence. In any case, you must replace the defective BIOS with a version that matches the chipset used by the system.

In situations where new devices (microprocessors, RAM devices, hard drives, etc.) have been added to the system, there is always a chance that the original BIOS will not be able to support them. In these situations, the system may or may not function depending on which device has been installed and how its presence affects the system. To compensate for these possible problems, always check the Web sites of the device and the system board manufacturers to obtain the latest BIOS upgrade and support information.

Problems with key system board components produce symptoms similar to those described for a bad power supply. Both the microprocessor and the ROM BIOS can be sources of such problems. You should check both by substitution when dead system symptoms are encountered but the power supply is good.

Essentials 1.3

Cooling Systems

Microprocessors-based equipment is designed to provide certain performance levels under specified environmental conditions. One of the key design elements for microprocessor performance is operating temperature. With Pentium-class microprocessors, PC systems are designed to maintain the operating temperature for the device in the range of 30 to 40°C.

To accomplish this, Pentium-class computers employ a microprocessor temperature control system that operates as part of the system chipset. A temperature-sensing **thermocouple** device is embedded in the system board under the microprocessor socket (or in the microprocessor cartridge). The thermocouple senses the current temperature of the microprocessor and produces an analog voltage signal that is proportional to the temperature. A special **health controller** IC monitors this signal and supplies the microprocessor with a digital representation of the temperature measurement.

thermocouple

health controller

The microprocessor compares this reading to an ideal setting established in the CMOS configuration and sends a digital code to the health controller, which in turn generates an analog speed control signal that is applied to the microprocessor fan. This signal slows the fan down if the measured temperature is too low and speeds it up if it's too hot.

The ideal operating temperature setting varies between microprocessor types and manufacturers. In addition, the location of the CMOS configuration setting varies between BIOS versions. Some CMOS setup utilities provide a separate *Health* screen, while others integrate it into their *Power Management* screen. Many systems include an additional fan control circuit for use with an optional chassis (case) fan. In these cases, the system board features additional berg connectors for the chassis temperature sensor and fan control cable.

If temperature-related problems like those described in the previous section occur, you should access the CMOS *Hardware Health* configuration screen, like the one depicted in Figure 11-13, and check the fan speed and processor temperature readings. If they are outside the designated range, you may enter a different value for the temperature set point. If no fan speed measurement is shown, check to see if the fan is actually turning. If not, you should turn the system off as soon as possible, check the operation of the fan, and replace it before the microprocessor is damaged.

Other alternatives when dealing with thermal problems in a PC include installing an additional chassis fan to help move cooler air through the system unit, changing the microprocessor fan for one that runs faster over a given range of temperatures, and flashing the BIOS to provide different fan control parameters.

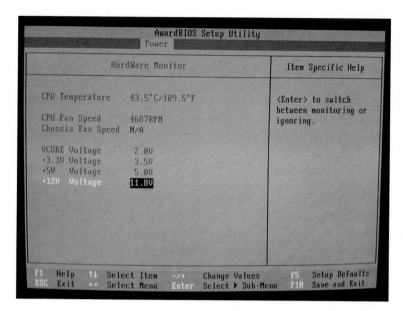

Figure 11-13: The CMOS Setup Health Screen

Also, check for missing slot covers that can disrupt air flow in the case, and route internal signal cables so that they do not block the flow of air through the case.

CMOS Batteries

The second condition that causes a configuration problem involves the system board's CMOS backup battery. If a system refuses to maintain time and date information, the CMOS backup battery, or its recharging circuitry, is normally faulty. After the backup battery has been replaced, check the contacts of the battery holder for corrosion.

If the battery fails or if it has been changed, the content of the CMOS configuration will be lost. After replacing the battery, it is always necessary to run the CMOS Setup utility to reconfigure the system.

┌─ **TEST TIP** ─┐
Be aware that a defective battery can cause the system to continually lose track of time.
└────────────┘

GEEK SQUAD CASE FILE #66346

You are working Counter Intelligence when you receive a call from a customer who complains that his Windows system constantly loses the time and date information. What advice can you give this customer about his system?

Exchanging the System Board

If symptoms indicate that the system board is the source of problems, do the following:

- Use the CMOS Setup utility to check the system's configuration for accuracy (and possibly used default CMOS configuration options to start the system)

- Check the BIOS version to verify that it supports the system's installed hardware components

- Examine the system board's FRU components for possible problem causes

If none of the above steps corrects the problem, then you must exchange the system board with a known-good one. If possible, *back up the contents of the system's hard drive* to some other media before removing the system board. Also, *record the CMOS configuration settings*, along with the settings of any jumpers and switches, before exchanging the system board.

Exchange the system board with a known-good one. Reconnect all of the power-supply, disk drive, and front-panel connections to the system board. Reinstall the video card and any other adapter cards, and try to reboot the system. Reconfigure the system board to operate with the installed peripherals. When the system boots up, reinstall any options removed from the system, and replace the system unit's outer cover.

Essentials 1.3

IT Technician 1.2

Troubleshooting Keyboard Problems

Most of the circuitry associated with the computer's keyboard is contained in the keyboard itself. However, some keyboard interface circuitry is located on the system board. Therefore, the steps required to isolate keyboard problems are usually confined to the keyboard, its connecting cable, and the system board.

This arrangement makes isolating keyboard problems relatively easy. Just check the keyboard and the system board. Figure 11-14 depicts the components associated with the keyboard.

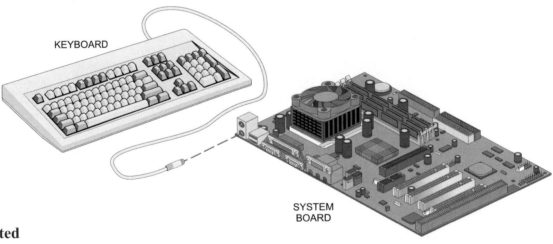

KEYBOARD

SYSTEM BOARD

Figure 11-14: Keyboard-Related Components

Keyboard Symptoms

Typical symptoms associated with keyboard failures include the following:

- No characters appear on-screen when entered from the keyboard.

- Some keys work, whereas others do not work.

- A "Keyboard Is Locked—Unlock It" error displays.

- A "Keyboard Error—Keyboard Test Failure" error displays.

- A "KB/Interface Error—Keyboard Test Failure" error displays.

- An error code of six short beeps is produced during bootup.

- Wrong characters displayed.

- An IBM-compatible 301 error code displays.

┌─ TEST TIP ─┐
Memorize the IBM-compatible error codes.

Keyboard Configuration Checks

Although keyboard configuration settings do not generally cause keyboard failures, you should be aware that several keyboard configuration settings are stored in CMOS that can affect the operation of the keyboard. In most systems, the CMOS setup information includes keyboard enabling, NumLock key condition at startup, typematic rate, and typematic delay. The typematic information applies to the keyboard's capability to repeat characters when the key is held down. The typematic rate determines how quickly characters are repeated, and the delay time defines the amount of time the key can be held before typematic action occurs. A typical typematic rate setting is six characters per second; the delay is normally set at 250 milliseconds.

Basic Keyboard Checks

One quick test to determine basic keyboard problems is to watch the keyboard's NumLock and ScrollLock lights during the bootup process. These lights should flash when the system attempts to initialize the keyboard. The system's POST routines may also return keyboard-related error messages and codes.

The key switches of the keyboard can wear out over time. This may result in keys that don't make good contact (no character is produced when the key is pushed) or ones that remain in contact (stick) even when pressure is removed. A stuck key will produce an error message when the system detects it. However, the system has no way of detecting an open key. If you detect a stuck key, or keys, you can desolder and replace the individual key switches with a good key from a manufacturer or a similar keyboard. However, the amount of time spent repairing a keyboard quickly drives the cost of the repair beyond the cost of a new unit.

┌─ TEST TIP ─┐
Know the most common conditions that will produce a keyboard error message.

If the keyboard produces odd characters on the display in a Windows operating system environment, check the Windows keyboard settings in the Control Panel's Device Manager. If the keyboard is not installed, or is incorrect, install the correct keyboard type. Also, make certain that you have the correct language setting specified under the Control Panel's keyboard icon.

Keyboard Hardware Checks

If you suspect a keyboard hardware problem, you must first isolate the keyboard as the definite source of the problem (a fairly easy task). Because the keyboard is external to the system unit, detachable, and inexpensive, begin by exchanging the keyboard with a known-good keyboard.

If the new keyboard works correctly, return the system to full service, and service the defective keyboard appropriately. Remove the back cover from the keyboard and check for the presence of a fuse in the +5 Vdc supply and check it for continuity. Disconnecting or plugging in a keyboard with this type of fuse while power is on can cause it to fail. If the fuse is present, simply replace it with a fuse of the same type and rating.

TEST TIP

Be aware that standard PS/2 6-pin mini-DIN keyboards cannot be hot swapped, and that doing so can cause damage to the keyboard and system board.

If replacing the keyboard does not correct the problem, and no configuration or software reason is apparent, the next step is to troubleshoot the keyboard receiver section of the system board. On most modern system boards, this ultimately involves replacing the system board with another one. Refer to the system board removal and installation instructions in Chapter 2, *Advanced System Boards* to carry out this task.

Essentials 1.3

IT Technician 1.2

Troubleshooting Mouse Problems

Most of the problems with mice are related to a few items:

- Its port connection

- The mouse driver

- The trackball in a trackball mouse or a trackball unit

- The operation of the mouse buttons

In newer systems, the mouse is typically connected to a USB port or to the dedicated PS/2 mouse port on the back of the unit. Unfortunately, the PC industry forgot an old design problem that they eradicated long ago—they used the same type of connector for two different devices. The original IBM PCs used the same connector for monochrome and color video monitors with sometimes disastrous consequences. In ATX, BTX, and NLX systems, the keyboard and mouse have been given the same 6-pin mini-DIN connector, and unfortunately, they do not work interchangeably. Even though plugging the mouse into the keyboard connector should not cause any physical damage, it will cause problems with the operation of the system. These connections tend to be color coded, so check to make sure the mouse is connected to the *green* connector.

The second reason for mouse failures is using the wrong driver for the mouse or its port. For USB and PS/2 mice, installation and configuration has become a fairly routine process. Connect the mouse to the USB or PS/2 mouse port, and let the system autodetect it and install the basic Windows mouse drivers.

However, specialty mice—including some wireless and infrared mice—along with other pointing devices require special drivers that must be supplied by the manufacturer and loaded from the disk or disc that accompanies the device.

Mouse Hardware Checks

For most systems, the hardware check for the mouse involves isolating it from its connection port. Simply replace the mouse to test its electronics. If the replacement mouse works, the original mouse is probably defective. If its electronics are not working properly, few options are available for actually servicing the mouse. It may need a cleaning or a new trackball. However, the low cost of a typical mouse generally makes it a throwaway item if simple cleaning does not fix it.

If the new mouse does not work either, chances are very high that the mouse's electronics are working properly. In this case, the mouse driver or the port hardware must be the cause of the problem. If the driver is correct for the mouse, the port hardware and CMOS configuration must be checked.

The system board typically contains all of the port hardware electronics and support, so it must be replaced to restore the port/mouse operation at that port. However, if the system board mouse port is defective, another option is to install a mouse that uses a different type of port (e.g., use a USB mouse to replace a PS/2 mouse).

When a trackball mouse is moved across the table, the trackball picks up dirt or lint, which can hinder the movement of the trackball, typically evident by the cursor periodically freezing and jumping onscreen. On most mice, you can remove the trackball from the mouse by a latching mechanism on its bottom. Twisting the latch counterclockwise enables you to remove the trackball. Then you can clean dirt out of the mouse.

The other mechanical part of the mouse is its buttons. These can wear out under normal use. When they do, the mouse should simply be replaced. However, before doing so, be sure to check the *properties* of the mouse in the operating system to make sure that the button functions have not been altered. It would be a shame to throw away a perfectly good mouse because it had been set up for left-hand use in the operating system. Refer to the *Mouse Configuration Checks* section that follows for instructions on checking the mouse configuration settings in a Windows-based system.

> ┌─ **TEST TIP** ─────────┐
> Be aware of the condition that causes the cursor to jump and freeze on the display.
> └──────────────────────────┘

Mouse Configuration Checks

When a mouse does not work in a Windows system, restart the system and move into *Safe Mode*. This is accomplished by pressing the F5 function key while the "Starting Windows" message is displayed. Doing so will start the operating system with the most basic mouse driver available. If the mouse does not operate in this mode, you must check the mouse hardware and the port it is connected to.

If the mouse works in Safe Mode, then the problem exists with the driver you are trying to use with it. The installed driver may be corrupt, or it could be having a conflict with some other driver. To check the driver, consult the *Device Manager* entry under the Control Panel's *System* icon. If the Device Manager shows a conflict with the mouse, remove the driver, and allow the system's PnP process to reinstall it.

If the correct driver for the installed mouse is not available, you will need to install one from the manufacturer. This typically involves placing the manufacturer's driver disk or disc in the appropriate drive and loading the driver using the *Update Driver* (requires disk from OEM) option on the Device Manager *Mouse Properties* page. If the OEM driver fails to operate the mouse in Windows, you should contact the mouse manufacturer for an updated Windows driver.

GEEK SQUAD CASE FILE #86723

When you upgrade your mouse to one of those new two-button wheel mice, you cannot get it to work. You return it to the distributor and exchange it for another one. It also does not work. When you try one from your coworker's machine, it works fine. What should you conclude about the wheel mouse?

Essentials 1.3

IT Technician 1.2

Troubleshooting Video

Figure 11-15 depicts the components associated with the video display. It may be most practical to think of the video information as starting out on the system board. In reality, the keyboard, one of the disk drives, or some other I/O device may be the actual originating point for the information. In any case, information intended for the video display monitor moves from the system board to the video adapter (usually through a video card installed in one of the system board's expansion slots). On the adapter, the screen information is converted into the configured screen image format and stored in the video screen memory. Finally, the information is applied to the monitor through the video signal cable.

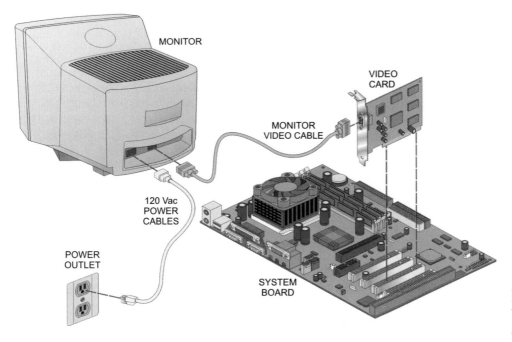

MONITOR

VIDEO CARD

MONITOR VIDEO CABLE

120 Vac POWER CABLES

POWER OUTLET

SYSTEM BOARD

**Figure 11-15:
Video-Related
Components**

Basically, there are two levels of troubleshooting that apply to video problems—configuration and hardware problems. As the figure indicates, in the case of hardware problems, the components involved include the video adapter card, the monitor, and, to a lesser degree, the system board. Common symptoms associated with display problems include the following:

- No display

- Wrong characters displayed on-screen

- Diagonal lines on-screen (no horizontal control)

- Display scrolls (no vertical control)

- An error code of one long and six short beeps is produced by the system

- A "Display Switch Setting Not Proper—Failure to verify display type" error displays

- A "CMOS Display Mismatch—Failure to verify display type" error displays

- An error code of one long and two short beeps is produced by the system (indicates a display adapter problem)

- LCD display blank (backlight failure)

WARNING

The following sections cover the digital portion of the video system. Troubleshooting an actual CRT monitor is discussed immediately following the video adapter troubleshooting sections. Only experienced technicians should participate in troubleshooting internal monitor problems because of the very high voltages present there.

Video Hardware Checks

The video monitor should come on fairly quickly after power has been applied to it. With newer monitors, the monitor is normally only asleep and is awakened through the video adapter card when power is applied to the system. When the system is shut down, the monitor's circuitry senses that no signal is present from the video adapter card and slips into a monitoring mode as long as its power switch is left in the On position.

If the monitor does not wake up early in the system's start-up process and present a display, you should assume that there is some type of hardware problem—the bootup action and operating system have not been introduced to the system before the single beep tone is produced. However, video problems that occur after the single beep are more likely to be related to operating system configuration settings.

If you suspect a video display hardware problem, the first task is to check the display's On/Off switch to see that it is in the On position. Also, check the monitor's power cord to see that it is plugged either into the power supply's monitor outlet, or into an active 120 V (AC) commercial outlet. Also check the monitor's intensity and contrast controls to make certain they are not turned down.

The next step is to determine which of the video-related components is involved. On some monitors, you can do this by just removing the video signal cable from the adapter card. If a raster appears on-screen with the signal cable removed, the problem is probably a system problem, and the monitor is good. If the monitor is an EPA-certified Energy Star–compliant monitor, this test may not work. Monitors that possess this power-saving feature revert to a low-power mode when they do not receive a signal change for a given period of time.

Check the components associated with the video display monitor. Start by disconnecting the monitor's signal cable from the video controller card at the rear of the system unit, and its power cord from the power supply connector or the 120 V (AC) outlet. Then, exchange the monitor for a known-good one of the same type (i.e., VGA for VGA).

If there is still a video problem, exchange the video controller card with a known-good one of the same type. Remove the system unit's outer cover. Disconnect the monitor's signal cable from the video controller card. Swap the video controller card with a known-good one of the same type. Reconnect the monitor's signal cable to the new video adapter, and reboot the system.

Other symptoms that point to the video adapter card include a shaky video display and a high-pitched squeal from the monitor or system unit. If the system still does not perform properly after swapping the video adapter card, the source of the problem may be in the system board.

Windows Video Checks

If you can read the contents of the display through the start-up process, but then cannot see it after the system boots up, you have an operating system–related video problem. Because Windows operating systems are graphically based programs, navigation can be nearly impossible if video problems are severe enough to prevent you from seeing the display.

If the Windows video problem prevents you from being able to work with the display, restart the system, press the F8 function key when the "Starting Windows" message appears, and select the *Safe Mode* option. This should load Windows with the standard 640 × 480 × 16–color VGA driver (the most fundamental driver available for VGA monitors) and should furnish a starting point for installing the correct driver for the monitor being used.

After you have gained access to a display that you can use, the next step in isolating Windows video problems involves checking the installed video drivers. You can access the Windows video information through the Control Panel's *System* icon. Inside the *System Properties* page, access the Device Manager through the *Hardware* tab, and select the *Display Adapters* entry from the list. Click on the node to the left of the monitor icon, and double click on the desired driver under the *Display Adapters* entry.

The adapter's *Properties* page should pop up on-screen. The Device status box normally presents a message that "The device is working properly" if the system hasn't detected a problem. However, if a conflict or error has been detected, the system will note it in this box. You can click on the *Troubleshooters* button to gain access to the Windows troubleshooting guidelines for the display.

Clicking on the *Driver* tab reveals the driver file in use with the display adapter. If the video driver listed is not correct, reload the correct driver. Selecting the *Resources* tab displays the video adapter's register address ranges and the video memory address range, as described in Figure 11-16. You can manipulate these settings manually by clicking on the *Set Configuration Manually* button. You also can obtain information about the monitor through the System icon.

You can also gain access to the Windows video information by double-clicking the Control Panel's *Display* icon. At the top of the *Display* page, there are a series of file folder tabs. Of particular interest is the *Settings* tab. Under this tab, the *Change Display Type* button provides access to both the adapter type and monitor type settings.

In the Adapter type window, information about the adapter's manufacturer, version number, and current driver files is given. Clicking on the *Change* button beside this window brings a listing of available drivers to select from. You also can use the *Have Disk* button with an OEM disk to install video drivers not included in the list. You also can alter the manner in which the list displays by choosing the *Show Compatible Devices* or the *Show All Devices* options.

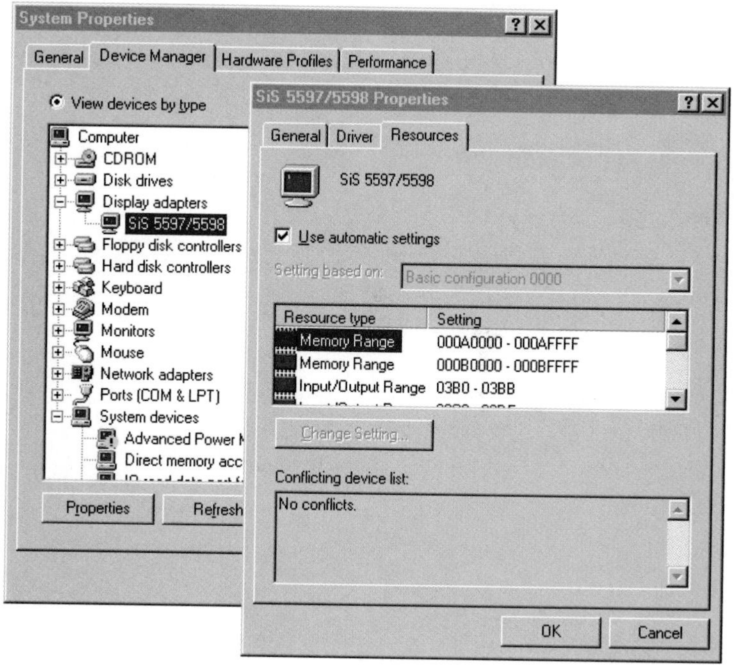

In the *Monitor type* window, there is an option list for both manufacturers and models. You can use this function with the *Have Disk* button to load OEM settings for the monitor.

Figure 11-16: Video Adapter's Resources

Microsoft Download Service (MSDL)

If the video problem disappears when lower settings are selected but reappears when a higher resolution setting is used, refer to the *Color Palette* box under the Control Panel's Display option/Settings tab, and try the minimum color settings. If the problem goes away, contact the **Microsoft Download Service (MSDL)** or the adapter card maker for a compatible video driver. If the video problem persists, reinstall Windows. If the video is distorted or rolling, try an alternative video driver from the list.

One of your customers has called you to his facility to repair a desktop computer that doesn't show anything on the display. When you start it up, you hear the system fans come on and the hard drive spin up. You also hear the system beeps when they are supposed to occur. The monitor power light is on. What piece of equipment should you retrieve from your repair kit for these symptoms?

Working with Monitors

All the circuitry discussed so far is part of the computer or its video adapter unit. The circuitry inside the CRT monitor is responsible for accepting, amplifying, and routing the video and synchronizing information to its electron guns and deflection coils.

Figure 11-17 shows the components located inside a typical CRT color monitor. Of particular interest is the high-voltage anode that connects the tube to the high-voltage sections of the signal-processing board. This is a very dangerous connection that is not to be touched.

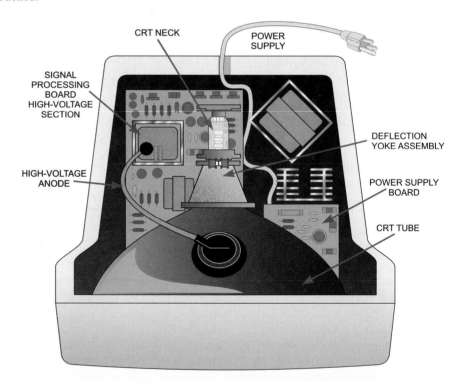

Figure 11-17: The Circuitry Inside a Typical CRT

WARNING

Lethal voltage levels—You must exercise great caution when opening or working inside the monitor. The voltage levels present during operation are lethal. Electrical potentials as high as 25,000 V are present inside the unit when it is operating.

Operation of a monitor with the cover removed poses a shock hazard from the power supply. Therefore, anyone unfamiliar with the safety precautions associated with high-voltage equipment should not attempt servicing.

The high voltage levels do not necessarily disappear because the power to the monitor is turned off. Like television sets, monitors have circuitry capable of storing high-voltage potentials long after power has been removed. Always discharge the anode of the picture tube to the receiver chassis before handling the CRT tube. Due to the high voltage levels, you should never wear antistatic grounding straps when working inside the monitor.

An additional hazard associated with handling CRTs is that the tube is fragile. Take extra care to prevent the neck of the tube from striking any surface. Never lift the tube by the neck—especially when removing or replacing a CRT tube in the chassis. If the picture tube's envelope is cracked or ruptured, the inrush of air will cause a high-velocity **implosion**, and the glass will fly in all directions. Therefore, you should always wear protective goggles when handling picture tubes.

Color monitors produce a relatively high level of **X-rays**. The CRT tube is designed to limit X-rays at its specified operating voltage. If a replacement CRT tube is being installed, make certain to replace it with one of the same type, and with suffix numbers that are the same. You can obtain this information from the chassis schematic diagram inside the monitor's housing.

| implosion |
| X-rays |

Diagnosing Display Problems

Examine the power cord to see that it is plugged in, and check to see that the monitor's power switch is in the On position. Verify the external settings to see that the brightness and contrast settings are not turned off. If the problem produces a blank display, disconnect the monitor's signal cable from its video adapter card. If a raster appears, a video card problem is indicated. The final step in isolating the video display as the source of the problem is to exchange it for a known-good one. If the replacement works, the problem must be located in the monitor.

Some display problems can actually be caused by incorrectly set front panel display settings. The monitor's front panel controls (either analog or digital) establish parameters for brightness, contrast, screen size and position, and focus. Typical problems associated with these controls include

- Fuzzy characters
- Poor or missing colors
- Incomplete displays.

Actually, there can be several causes of fuzzy characters on the display. The first step in troubleshooting this problem is to reset the display resolution to standard VGA values. If the fuzzy characters remain, check the intensity and contrast controls to see if they are out of adjustment. With a CRT display, you may need to remove built-up electromagnetic fields from the screen through a process called **degaussing**. This can be done using a commercial degaussing coil. However, newer monitors have built-in degaussing circuits that can be engaged through their front panel controls. These monitors normally perform a degauss operation each time they are turned on. However, sometimes the user might need to perform this operation.

| degaussing |

The front panel controls can also be used to adjust the red/green/blue color mixture for the display. If the monitor is showing poor colors, or only one color, examine the color settings using the front panel controls. If these settings are responsive to change, the problem exists in either the video adapter or the signal cable (broken or bad pin or conductor), or the monitor's color circuitry is deteriorating.

LCD displays can be calibrated to display correct colors as determined by a color calibration program or by using a set of transparent strips of color film. The transparent strips are standard colors that the screen can be calibrated to. The individual strips are placed on the screen, and the colors are adjusted to match.

Incomplete displays are often the result of improperly set horizontal and vertical placement and size settings. These setting are also adjusted through the display's front panel controls.

Troubleshooting HDDs

Typical symptoms associated with hard-disk drive failures include the following:

- The computer does not boot up when turned on.

- The computer boots up to a distribution CD in the CD-ROM drive (or the Windows 2000 Emergency Start disk in the FDD drive) but not to the hard drive, indicating that the system files on the HDD are missing or have become corrupt.

- No motor sounds are produced by the HDD while the computer is running. (In desktop units, the HDD should always run when power is applied to the system—this also applies to portables because of their advanced power-saving features.)

- An IBM-compatible *17xx* error code is produced on the monitor screen.

- An *HDD Controller Failure* message displays, indicating a failure to verify hard disk setup by system configuration file error.

- A C: or D: *Fixed Disk Drive Error* message displays, indicating a hard-disk CMOS setup failure.

- An *Invalid Media Type* message displays, indicating the controller cannot find a recognizable track/sector pattern on the drive.

- A *No Boot Record Found*, a *Non-System Disk or Disk Error*, or an *Invalid System Disk* message displays, indicating that the system boot files are not located in the root directory of the drive.

- The video display is active, but the HDD's activity light remains on, and no bootup occurs, indicating that the HDD's CMOS configuration information is incorrect.

- An *Out of Disk Space* message displays, indicating that the amount of space on the disk is insufficient to carry out the desired operation.

- A *Missing Operating System*, a *Hard Drive Boot Failure*, or an *Invalid Drive or Drive Specification* message displays, indicating that the disk's master boot record is missing or has become corrupt.

- A *Current Drive No Longer Valid* message displays, indicating that the HDD's CMOS configuration information is incorrect or has become corrupt.

Figure 11-18 depicts the relationship between the hard-disk drive and the rest of the system. It also illustrates the control and signal paths through the system.

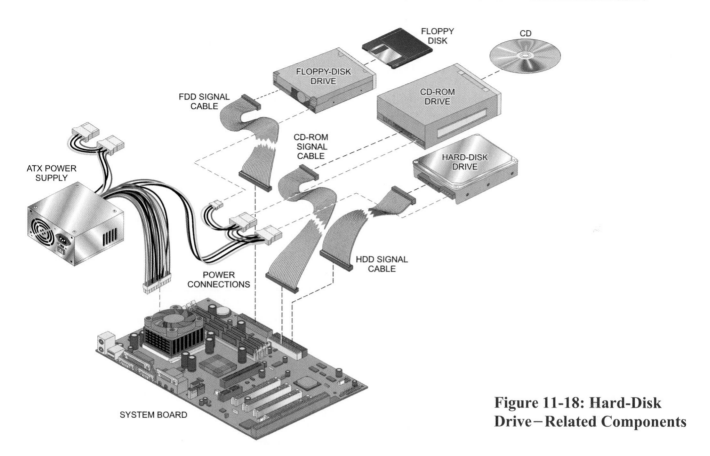

Figure 11-18: Hard-Disk Drive–Related Components

The PC's hard drive subsystems typically consist of a *controller*, one or more signal cables, a *power cable*, and *drive units*. The controller may be an integral part of the system board's chipset (as it is in PATA/SATA systems), or it may be mounted on an adapter card (as is the case with most SCSI and RAID systems). If the controller is integrated into the system board, the system board becomes a logical extension of the components that make up the HDD subsystem. Modern PCs rely on the PnP process and their operating systems to configure the drive and handle its operation.

The troubleshooting procedure typically moves from basic observation to setup and configuration, to formatting, and, finally, into the hardware component isolation process.

Basic HDD Checks

Does the drive spin up? Start the system, and listen for sounds of the hard drive spinning up (a low whine and clicking noise). If you do not hear any drive noises, verify that its power connector and interface cable are securely attached to the drive. Also check the *HDD's activity light* during the start-up sequence. If the light does not come on at any time during the process, the system may not think the drive is installed. Proceed to the *HDD Configuration Checks* and *HDD Hardware Checks* sections that follow.

If you think the hard drive is spinning, or you see the access light come on, the next step is to get the system to boot up to some alternative, such as a simple boot disk, an Emergency Start disk, or a setup/Distribution CD. This will enable you to examine the system to determine how extensive the problem is.

After you get the system started and can look around inside, the next objective is to determine whether the hard-disk drive problem is a simple *boot problem* or something more serious. The quickest way to determine this is to attempt to access the primary partition of the drive. This can be accomplished by executing a Directory (DIR) command from the command prompt to access the C: drive.

Disk Boot Failure

If the system can see the contents of the drive, the boot files have simply been lost or corrupted, but the architecture of the disk is intact. If any of these files are missing, you will typically receive some type of **Disk Boot Failure** message on-screen. The *No (or Missing) ROM BASIC Interpreter* message presented in the symptoms list may also be produced by this condition.

Emergency Repair Disk

You may be able to correct a missing boot or system file problem by reinstalling the specified files from the operating system's **Emergency Repair Disk** or its distribution CD. These operations are performed from the command prompt, so you will need to be familiar with command-line functions and the different files involved in the operating system's boot process. These are covered in detail in Chapter 10, *Windows Operating Systems*, and Chapter 12, *Operating System Troubleshooting*.

NOTE

If the drive can be accessed but it will not boot, you should back up any important information on the drive to a different media before attempting any type of repair. This can involve copying the data to another hard drive that you temporarily install for this purpose, or to a USB thumb drive, a tape drive, or other backup device. You should do this while you still have access to the data—it may not survive some steps you employ to return the drive to service.

Invalid Drive

Invalid Drive Specification

If the system cannot see the drive after booting to an alternative source, an **Invalid Drive** message or an **Invalid Drive Specification** message should be returned in response to any attempt to access the drive. Under these conditions, the drive or its disks have a serious problem, and you will need to examine the HDD subsystem's configuration and hardware components as directed in the following sections.

HDD Configuration Checks

Does the system recognize the drive? While booting up the system, *observe the BIOS's HDD type information* displayed on the monitor. Note the type of HDD(s) the BIOS believes are installed in the system. The values stored in this CMOS configuration must accurately reflect the actual HDD(s) format installed in the system; otherwise, an error occurs. If the drive has a hardware problem, the system may not be able to recognize or configure it.

Possible error messages associated with HDD configuration problems include the **Drive Mismatch Error** message and the **Invalid Media Type** message. If the system produces an error message like these, open the CMOS Setup utility and verify that the drive is enabled there. If not, select the **Autodetect option**, enable it, and attempt to boot the system.

On PATA drives, verify the *Master/Slave* jumper settings, illustrated in Figure 11-19, to make sure that they are set correctly for the drive's logical position in the system. Determine whether the system might be using the **Cable Select** option also depicted in Figure 11-19. This setting requires a special **CSEL** signal cable designed to determine the master/slave arrangements for multiple PATA drives. Likewise, check the ID configuration settings and terminator installations for SCSI drives. Exchange the HDD power connector with another one from the power supply, to make certain that it is not a source of problems.

| Drive Mismatch Error |
| Invalid Media Type |
| Autodetect option |
| Cable Select |
| CSEL |

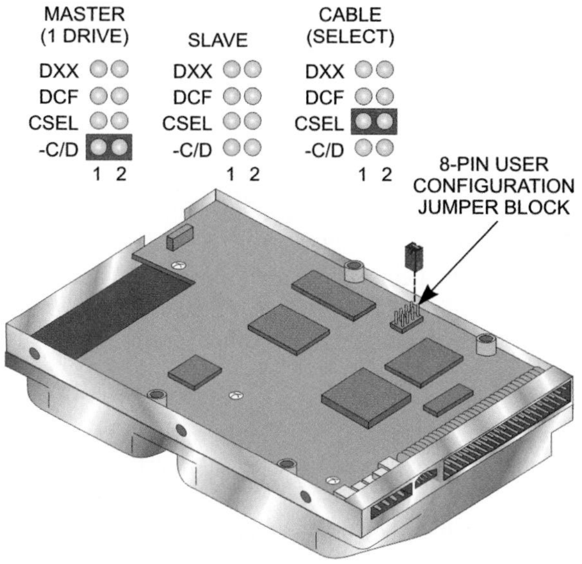

Figure 11-19: PATA Master/Slave Settings

With SATA drives there is no Master/Slave setting to deal with. However, you may need to access the CMOS setup utility to *disable PATA drives* and *enable SATA drives*. You can also experience problems loading drivers for these drive types. If the operating system does not recognize the SATA drive, use the Windows *Device Manager* utility to confirm the latest driver for host adapter has been installed. If the drive is connected to the system board, the drivers should be those provided by the manufacturer. If the drive is connected to the system through a PCI card, then the drivers should be those distributed by the manufacturer of the PCI card. The drive must also be partitioned and formatted through the operating system. This is done through Windows 2000 or Windows XP during the OS installation process.

TEST TIP

Know that there can only be one master drive selection on each PATA channel.

If the drive is a SCSI drive, check to see that its ID has been set correctly and that the SCSI chain has been terminated correctly. Either of these errors will result in the system not being able to see the drive. Also, check the CMOS Setup utility to make sure that SCSI support has been enabled, along with large SCSI drive support.

GEEK SQUAD CASE FILE #62621

You are updating a working computer for the local store manager. The upgrade consists of adding a new microprocessor to the system, along with additional RAM and a second PATA hard drive. When you restart the system, the system will not boot to the original hard drive. As a matter of fact, neither drive will work. What should you check first?

HDD Hardware Checks

If you cannot access the hard-disk drive, and its configuration settings are correct, you must troubleshoot the hardware components associated with the hard-disk drive. These components include the drive, its signal cable, and the HDC (on the system board).

Check the HDD signal cable for proper connection at both ends. Exchange the signal cable for a known-good one. With PATA drives, make certain that the correct type of signal cable is being used. Do not get the newer 80-cable/40-pin version confused with the older and much slower 40-cable/40-pin version.

SATA cables have also been known to be a source of disk drive problems. Because the SATA specification does not use a shielded cable, their cables are susceptible to induced noise from other system components. Therefore, you should not place SATA devices or cables near each other, or near to PATA cables. Also, do not tie wrap SATA cables together or put sharp bends in them, as doing so modifies their insulation and decreases their noise resistance.

Check the drive to make sure that it is properly **terminated**. Each drive type (both IDE and SCSI) requires a termination block somewhere in the interface.

If you have more than one device attached to a single interface cable, make sure that they are of the same type (i.e., all are PATA devices or all are ATA100 devices). Mixing device types will create a situation where the system cannot provide the different types of control information each device needs. The drives are incompatible, and you may not be able to access either device.

The next logical step may seem to be to replace the hard drive unit. However, it is quite possible that the hard drive may not have any real damage. It may just have lost track of where it was, and now it cannot find its starting point. In this case, the most attractive option is to reformat the hard disk. This action gives the hard drive a new starting point to work from. Unfortunately, it also destroys anything that you had stored on the disk.

If the reformatting procedure is not successful, or the system still won't boot from the hard drive, you must replace the hard-disk drive unit with a working one. Disconnect the signal, control, and power cords from the HDD unit, and exchange it with a known-good one of the same type. Reconnect the signal, control, and power cords to the replacement HDD unit.

Troubleshooting CD-ROM and DVD Drives

The troubleshooting steps for CD-ROM and DVD drives are nearly identical to those of an HDD system. The connections and data paths are similar. Basically, three levels of troubleshooting apply to CD-ROM problems. These are the *configuration level*, the *operating system level*, and the hardware level. Figure 11-20 shows the parts and drivers associated with CD-ROMs.

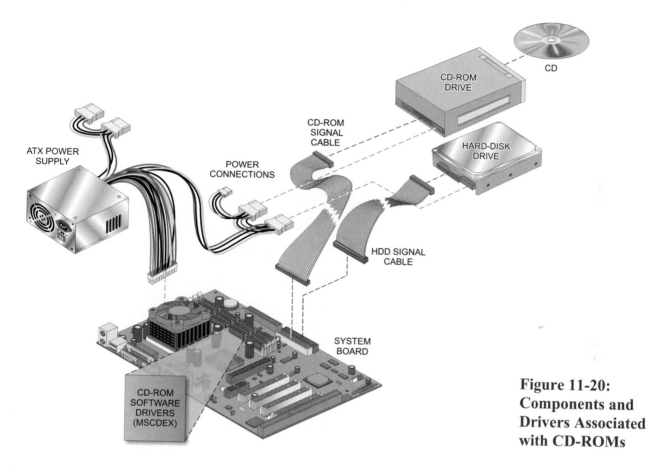

Figure 11-20: Components and Drivers Associated with CD-ROMs

Basic Checks

In most systems, the CD-ROM and DVD drives share a controller or host adapter with the hard-disk drive. If the system is using PATA drives, you should verify their *Master/Slave* jumper settings to make sure that they are set correctly. Normally, the CD-ROM or DVD drive should be set up as the Master on the Secondary PATA channel. In this manner, each drive has its own communications channel and does not need to share. If three or four PATA devices are installed in the system, you must determine which devices can share the channels most effectively.

Windows Checks

In the Windows operating systems, you can access the contents of the CD-ROM or DVD through the *Compact Disc* icon in the desktop's *My Computer* applet. The CD-ROM drive's information is contained in the *Device Manager* utility located under the *Hardware* tab of the Control Panel's *System* icon. The Properties of the installed CD-ROM drive can be viewed by expanding the node beside the *DVD/CD-ROM Drives* icon and double clicking on the driver listed there. Figure 11-21 shows a typical set of CD-ROM specifications.

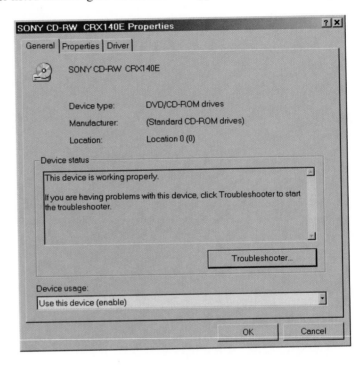

**Figure 11-21:
CD-ROM Properties**

CD-ROM/DVD Hardware Checks

If the configuration and software checks do not remedy the CD-ROM or DVD problem, you must troubleshoot the drive's related hardware. Basically, the hardware consists of the drive unit, the signal cable, the power cord, the media, and the controller or host adapter. The controller may be mounted on a host adapter card or on the system board in a Pentium system. For external drives, you must also check the plug-in power adapter.

In most systems, the CD-ROM and DVD drives share a controller or host adapter with the hard-disk drive. Therefore, if the hard drive is working and the CD-ROM drive is not, the likelihood that the problem is in the CD-ROM or DVD drive unit is very high.

Before entering the system unit, check for simple user problems:

- Is there a CD or DVD in the drive?

- Is the label side of the disk facing upward?

- Is the disk a CD-ROM or some other type of CD?

If the drive is inoperable and there is a CD or DVD locked inside, you should insert a straightened paper clip into the tray-release access hole that's usually located beside the ejection button. This will release the spring-loaded tray and pop out the disc.

If no simple reasons for the problem are apparent, exchange the CD-ROM drive with a known-good one of the same type. For external units, simply disconnect the drive from the power and signal cables, and then substitute the new drive for it. With internal units, you must remove the system unit's outer cover and disconnect the signal and power cables from the drive. Remove the screws that secure the drive unit in the drive bay. Install the replacement unit, start the system, and attempt to access it.

┌─ **TEST TIP** ─┐
Know how to retrieve a CD from a disabled CD-ROM drive.

If the new drive does not work, check the drive's signal cable for proper connection at both ends. Exchange the signal cable for a known-good one.

If the controller is built into the system board and becomes defective, it is still possible to install an IDE or SATA host adapter card in an expansion slot and use it without replacing the system board. This action can also be taken to upgrade PATA systems to SATA systems so they can use additional IDE devices. The on-board IDE controller may need to be disabled before the system will address the new host adapter version.

┌─ **TEST TIP** ─┐
Remember that card-mounted IDE host adapters can be used to repair system boards with defective on-board IDE controllers and to upgrade older PATA systems.

Writable Drive Problems

An additional set of problems come into play when a write or rewrite function is added to the CD-ROM or DVD drive. These problems are concentrated in three basic areas:

- The quality of the drive's controller circuitry

- The makeup and version of the drive's read/write (R/W) application interface software

- Compatibility with the operating system's multimedia support systems

The quality of the drive is actually based on the controller IC that oversees the operation of the drive. In less-expensive drives, the BIOS extension on the drive may not support all of the R/W functions to coordinate with the application package or the operating system's drivers. While all newer CD-ROM and DVD drives are ATAPI compatible, they may not have an effective method of controlling **buffer underrun** errors. These errors occur when the system transfers data to the drive faster than the drive can buffer and write it to the disc. The ATAPI compatibility of the chipset ensures that the CD-ROM and DVD read functions work fine, but the nonstandard writing part of the drive may not produce satisfactory results.

`buffer underrun`

There are a few techniques that can be used to minimize *buffer underruns*. These include placing the CD-ROM or DVD writer on an IDE channel of its own. This keeps the drive from competing with other drives for the channel's available bandwidth. Also, conducting the write operation on the same drive as the read operation and using reduced write speed options in the R/W application software can minimize data flow problems.

In addition, the R/W application software for the drive may not be compatible with the operating system version in use or with the controller chip on the drive. Likewise, the operating system's multimedia enhancement drivers (**DirectX** in Windows operating systems) may not be compatible with the controller or the R/W application. It is best to consult the operating system's hardware and software compatibility lists before buying and installing a CDRW or DVDRW drive in a system. This typically means using a more expensive drive, but for now, you do seem to get what you pay for when it comes to rewritable drives.

If the drive has already been purchased and installed, check the drive's documentation for suggestions and check the drive manufacturer's Web site for newer R/W applications and driver versions. You may also be able to locate a flash program for the drive's BIOS to upgrade it so that it provides better support for the write function.

In the end, there are some CD-ROM and DVD R/W applications that are incompatible with different drive BIOS versions or DirectX versions. Check all of the parties involved to find a collection of components that are all compatible with each other.

Troubleshooting FDDs

Typical symptoms associated with floppy-disk drive (FDD) failures during bootup include the following:

- FDD errors are encountered during bootup.

- The front-panel indicator lights are visible, and the display is present on the monitor screen, but there is no disk drive action and no bootup.

- An IBM-compatible 6xx (i.e., 601) error code displays.

- An FDD Controller Error message displays, indicating a failure to verify the FDD setup by the System Configuration file.

- The FDD activity light stays on constantly, indicating that the FDD signal cable is reversed.

Additional FDD error messages commonly encountered during normal system operation include the following:

- Disk Drive Read Error messages.

- Disk Drive Write Error messages.

- Disk Drive Seek Error messages.

- No Boot Record Found message, indicating that the system files in the disk's boot sector are missing or have become corrupt.

- The system stops working while reading a disk, indicating that the contents of the disk have become contaminated.

- The drive displays the same directory listing for every disk inserted in the drive, indicating that the FDD's disk-change detector or signal line is not functional.

┌─ **TEST TIP** ─┐
Memorize the IBM error codes for different types of hardware devices.
└─────────────┘

A number of things can cause improper floppy-disk drive operation or failure. These items include the use of unformatted disks, incorrectly inserted disks, damaged disks, erased disks, loose cables, drive failure, adapter failure, system board failure, or a bad or loose power connector. Basically three levels of troubleshooting apply to FDD problems: the configuration, the software, and the hardware. No Windows-level troubleshooting applies to floppy-disk drives. Figure 11-22 depicts the components associated with the operation of the floppy-disk drive.

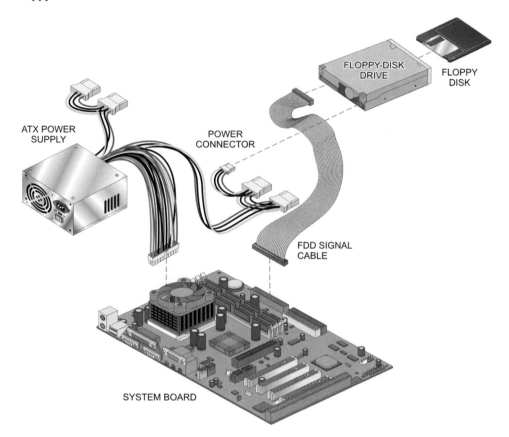

Figure 11-22: FDD-Related Components

Basic FDD Checks

If there is a problem reading or writing to a particular floppy disk, try the disk in a different computer to determine whether it works in that machine. If not, there is most likely a problem with the format of the disk or the files on the disk. In the case of writing to the disk, you could be dealing with a write-protected disk, but the system will normally inform you of this when you attempt to write to it. However, if the other computer can read and write to the disk, you must troubleshoot the floppy drive hardware.

Hardware troubleshooting for floppy-disk drives primarily involves exchanging the FDD unit for another one that is working. If necessary, exchange the signal cable with a known-good one. If neither of these actions repairs the problem, the only other option with most PC-compatible systems is to exchange the system board with a known-good one.

If there is a problem booting the system to the hard drive, you can insert the bootable disk in the A: floppy drive and turn on the system. If the system does not boot up to the floppy, examine the advanced CMOS Setup to check the system's boot order. It may be set so that the FDD is never examined during the bootup sequence.

If the system still will not boot up with the CMOS setting established to check the FDD first in the boot seek order, check the disk drive cables for proper connection at both ends. In many systems, the pin-1 designation is difficult to see. Reversing the signal cable causes the FDD activity light to stay on continuously. The reversed signal cable will also erase the master boot record from the disk, making it nonbootable. Because this is a real possibility, you should always use an expendable backup copy of the boot disk for troubleshooting FDD problems.

Troubleshooting Port Problems

The PC-compatible computer features a wide array of peripheral connection ports. Figure 11-23 illustrates the components involved in the operation of the legacy serial, parallel, and game ports. Failures in these ports tend to end with poor or no operation of the peripheral. Generally, there are only four possible causes for a problem with a device connected to an I/O port:

- The port is defective.

- The software is not configured properly for the port.

- The connecting signal cable is bad.

- The attached device is not functional.

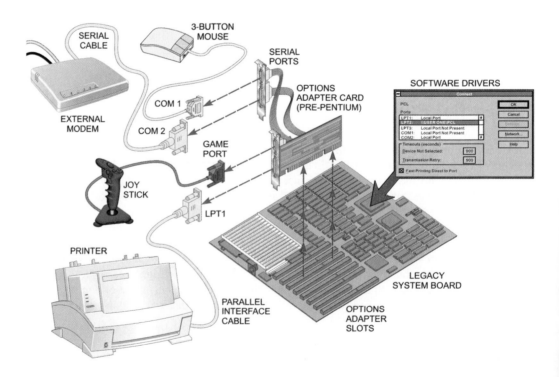

Figure 11-23: Components Associated with I/O Ports

Basic Port Checks

Check the CMOS Setup utility to determine whether the port in question has been enabled, and, if so, whether it has been configured correctly. The system's USB and infrared ports must be enabled in the Peripherals page of the CMOS Setup utility.

A modern parallel port must be enabled and configured with the proper protocol to interface with advanced peripherals. For typical printer operations, the setting can normally be set to SPP mode. However, devices that use the port in a bidirectional manner need to be set to EPP or ECP mode for proper operation. In both cases, the protocol must be set properly for both the port and the device to carry out communications.

If serial or parallel port problems are occurring, the CMOS configuration window is the first place to look. Read the port assignments in the bootup window. If the system has not detected the presence of the port hardware at this stage, none of the more advanced PnP levels will find it either. If values for any of the physical ports installed in the system do not appear in this window, check for improper port configuration.

Because the system has not loaded an operating system at the time the configuration window appears, the operating system cannot be a source of port problems at this time. If all configuration settings for the ports appear correct, assume that a hardware problem exists.

USB Port Checks

Because nearly any type of peripheral device can be added to the PC through the USB port, the range of symptoms associated with USB device can include all the symptoms listed for peripheral devices in this chapter. Therefore, problems associated with USB ports can be addressed in three general areas:

- The USB hardware device

- The USB controller

- The USB drivers

The first step in troubleshooting USB problems is to check the CMOS setup screens to make sure that the USB function is enabled there. If the USB function is enabled in BIOS, check in the Windows Control Panel/System/Device Manager to make certain that the USB controller appears there. In Windows 2000, the USB controller should be listed under the *Universal Serial Bus Controllers* entry or in the *Human Interface Devices* entry (using the default *Devices by Type* setting).

If the controller does not appear in *Device Manager*, or a yellow warning icon appears next to the controller, the system's BIOS may be outdated. Contact the BIOS manufacturer for an updated copy of the BIOS.

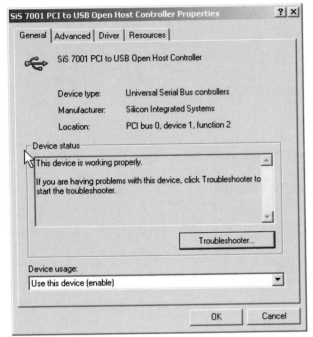

If the controller is present in the *Device Manager*, right-click the *USB controller* entry and click the *Properties* tab. If there are any problems, a message appears in the *Device Status* window, depicted in Figure 11-24, describing any problems and suggesting what action to take.

If the BIOS and controller settings appear to be correct, the next items to check are the USB port drivers. These ports have a separate entry in the Device Manager that you can access by clicking the *Universal Serial Bus Controllers* option, right-clicking the *USB Root Hub* entry, and then clicking the *Properties* tab.

If a USB device does not install itself automatically, you may have conflicting drivers loaded for that device, and you may need to remove them.

Authority Needed—To use the Windows 2000/XP Professional *Device Manager* utility to troubleshoot USB problems in an administered network environment, you must be logged on as an administrator or as a member of the Administrators group.

Figure 11-24: The USB Controller Properties Page

Hands-On Activity

Removing Potentially Conflicting USB Drivers

1. Disconnect any USB devices connected to the system, and start the system in Safe mode.

2. Under Windows 2000, you are asked about which operating system to use. Use the up- and down-arrow keys to highlight Windows 2000 Professional or Windows 2000 Server, and then press *ENTER*.

    If alert messages appear, read each alert and then click the *OK* button to close it.

3. Open the *Device Manager*, click the USB device, and then click the *Remove* option.

    Your particular USB device may be listed under the *Universal Serial Bus Controller*, *Other Devices*, *Unknown Devices*, or a particular device category (such as the Modem entry if the device is a USB modem).

4. Click the Start menu, select the *Shut Down* option followed by the *Restart* entry, and then click the *OK* button.

5. Connect the USB device directly to the USB port on your computer. If the system does not autodetect the device, you must install the drivers manually. You may need to obtain drivers from the device manufacturer to perform this installation.

Legacy Port Problem Symptoms

Typical symptoms associated with legacy serial, parallel, or game port failures include

- A 199, 432, or 90x IBM-compatible error code displays on the monitor (Printer port).

- The on-line light is on, but no characters are printed by the printer.

- An 110x IBM-compatible error code displays on the monitor (Serial port).

- Device not found error message displays, or you have an unreliable connection.

- Input device does not work on the game port.

As you can see from the symptoms list, I/O ports do not tend to generate many error messages on-screen.

Basic Parallel Ports Check

Run a **software diagnostic** package to narrow the possible problem causes. This is not normally a problem, because port failures do not generally affect the main components of the system. Software diagnostic packages normally require you to place a **loopback test plug** in the parallel port connector to run tests on the port. The *loopback plugs* simulate a printer device by redirecting output signals from the port into port input pins. Figure 11-25 describes the signal-rerouting scheme used in a parallel port loopback plug.

software diagnostic

loopback test plug

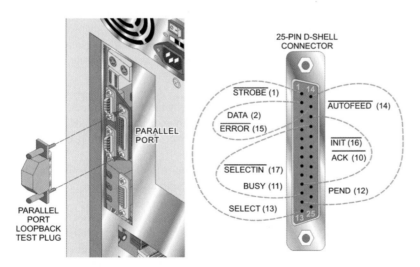

Figure 11-25: Parallel Port Loopback Connections

You can use a live printer with the port for testing purposes. However, this action elevates the possibility that the printer might inject a problem into the troubleshooting process. If there is a *printer switch box* between the computer and the printer, remove the print-sharing equipment, connect the computer directly to the printer, and try to print directly to the device.

─ **TEST TIP** ─

Be aware that print-sharing equipment (such as switch boxes) can be responsible for parallel port/printer problems and should be removed as part of port testing.

Basic Serial Ports

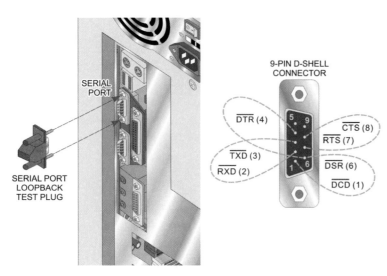

As with parallel ports, diagnostic packages typically ask you to place a loopback test plug in the serial port connector to run tests on the port. Use the diagnostic program to determine whether any IRQ or addressing conflicts exist between the serial port and other installed options. The serial loopback plug is physically connected differently from a parallel loopback plug so that it can simulate the operation of a serial device. Figure 11-26 describes the signal-rerouting scheme used in a serial port loopback plug.

You can use a live serial device with the port for testing purposes, but, as with the printer, this elevates the possibility that nonport problems can be injected into the troubleshooting process.

Figure 11-26:
Serial Port Loopback
Connections

Windows Parallel Ports

Check to determine whether the *Print* option from the application's File menu is unavailable (gray). If so, navigate the Start/Settings/Printers window in Windows 2000 (or the Start/Printers and Faxes window in Windows XP) and right-click on the printer you are trying to use. Select the *Properties* entry in the menu, and click on the *Ports* tab. Verify that the port settings are correct for parallel port being used. You can also check the definition of the printer under the Control Panel's *Printers* folder by right-clicking on the desired printer and selecting the *Properties* option from the menu. The system's printer port configuration information is also available through the *Device Manager* utility.

Click on the *Advanced* tab in the Printer's Properties window to make certain that the correct printer driver is selected for the printer being used. If no printer (or the wrong printer type) is selected, use the *Add Printer* wizard to install and set up the desired printer.

Continue troubleshooting the port by checking the printer's driver to insure that it is the correct driver and version number. Click on the *About* tab to view the driver's name and to verify the driver's version number.

Troubleshooters

Print Troubleshooter

The Windows operating systems come with embedded tools called **Troubleshooters**, one of which is designed to help solve printing problems. To use the Printing Troubleshooter, access the Windows *Help* system through the Start menu, as illustrated in Figure 11-27, and navigate to the **Print Troubleshooter** (or Printing Troubleshooter in Windows XP). The Troubleshooter asks a series of questions about the printing setup. After you have answered all of its questions, the Troubleshooter returns a list of recommendations for fixing the problem.

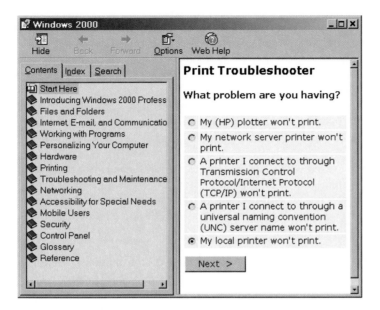

Figure 11-27: Print Troubleshooter

If the conclusions of the *Troubleshooter* do not clear up the problem, try printing a document to a file. This enables you to separate the printing software from the port hardware.

From the Windows 2000 *Printers* folder (or the Windows XP *Printers and Faxes* folder), double-click on the printer in question to open the *Print Manager* screen. Check the Print Manager for errors that have occurred and that might be holding up the printing of subsequent print jobs. If an error is hanging up the print function, highlight the offending job, and remove it from the print spool by clicking the *Cancel* entry of the *Document* menu. You can clear the print spooler of all pending print jobs by clicking on the *Cancel All Documents* option in the Printer menu.

Troubleshooting Tape Drives

Because the fundamentals of recording on tape are so similar to those used with magnetic disks, the troubleshooting process is also similar. The basic components associated with the tape drive include the tape drive, the signal cable, the power connection, the controller, and the tape drive's operating software. The tape itself can be a source of several problems. Common points to check with the tape include the following:

- Is the tape formatted correctly for use with the drive in question?

- s the tape inserted securely in the drive?

- Is the tape write-protected?

- Is the tape broken or off the reel in the cartridge?

As cartridge tapes are pulled back and forth, their mylar base can become stretched over time. This action can cause the tape's format to fail before the tape actually wears out. To remedy this, you should retention the tape periodically using the software's retention utility. Cartridge tapes are typically good for about 150 hours of operation. If the number of tape errors begins to increase dramatically before this time, try reformatting the tape to restore its integrity. After the 150-hour point, just replace the tape.

If the tape is physically okay and properly formatted, the next item to check is the tape software. Check the software setup and configuration settings to make sure they are correct for any hardware settings. Refer to the tape drive's documentation for a list of system requirements, and check the system to make sure they are being met.

If any configuration jumpers or switches are present on the controller, verify that they are set correctly for the installation. Also, run a diagnostic program to check for resource conflicts that may be preventing the drive from operating (such as IRQ and base memory addressing).

The software provided with most tape drives includes some error-messaging capabilities. Observe the system, and note any tape-related error messages it produces. Consult the drive's documentation for error-message definitions and corrective suggestions. Check for error logs that the software may keep. You can view these logs to determine what errors have been occurring in the system.

Because many tape drives are used in networked and multiuser environments, another problem occurs when you are not properly logged in or enabled to work with files being backed up or restored. In these situations, the operating system may not allow the tape drive to access secured files, or any files, because the correct clearances have not been met. Consult the network administrator for proper password and security clearances.

If you have read/write problems with the drive, begin by cleaning its R/W heads. Consult the user's guide for cleaning instructions, or use the process described in Chapter 13, *Preventive Maintenance*, for manual cleaning of floppy and tape drive R/W heads. The R/W heads should be cleaned after about 20 backups or restores.

Also, try to use a different tape to see whether it works. Make certain that it is properly formatted for operation. It should also be a clean tape, if possible, to avoid exposing any critical information to potential corruption. If cleaning does not restore the drive to proper operation, continue by checking the drive's power and signal cables for good connection and proper orientation.

GEEK SQUAD CASE FILE #44863

You have installed a new sound card in a customer's desktop computer. When they attempt to perform a weekly backup to tape, the sound card fails. When they reboot the system, the sound card begins working again. What type of troubleshooting steps should you employ to solve this mystery?

Troubleshooting Modems

A section on troubleshooting modems has to be subdivided into two segments:

- External modems

- Internal modems

An internal modem is checked out in the same basic sequence as any other I/O card. First, check the modem's hardware and software configuration, check the system for conflicts, and check for correct drivers. Improper software setup is the most common cause of modems not working when they are first installed. Inspect any cabling connections to see that they are made correctly and functioning properly, and test the modem's hardware by substitution. If an external modem is being checked, it must be treated as an external peripheral, with the serial port being treated as a separate I/O port. Figure 11-28 shows the components associated with internal and external modems.

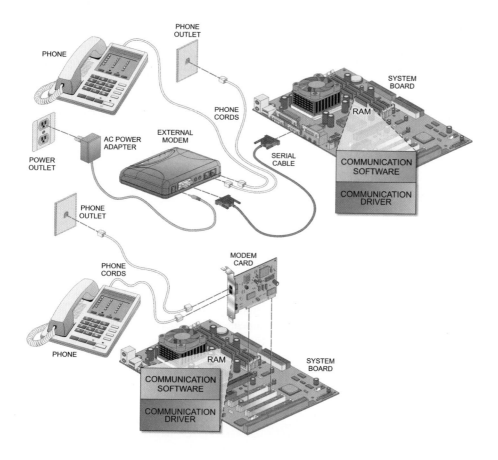

Figure 11-28: Internal and External Modem Components

Modem Problem Symptoms

Typical symptoms associated with modem failures include

- No response from the modem.
- Modem does not dial out.
- Modem does not connect after number has been dialed.
- Modem does not transmit after making connection with remote unit.
- Cannot get modem installed properly for operation.
- Garbled messages are transmitted.
- Cannot terminate a communication session.
- Cannot transfer files.

COM Port Conflicts

As stated earlier, every COM port on a PC requires an IRQ line in order to signal the processor for attention. In most PC systems, two COM ports share the same IRQ line. The IRQ4 line works for COM1 and COM3, and the IRQ3 line works for COM2 and COM4. This is common in PC-compatibles. The technician must make sure that two devices are not set up to use the same IRQ channel. If more than one device is connected to the same IRQ line, a conflict occurs, because it is not likely that the interrupt handler software can service both devices.

Therefore, the first step to take when installing a modem is to check the system to see how its interrupts and COM ports are allocated. You can alleviate this particular interrupt conflict by using a bus mouse rather than a serial mouse, thus freeing up a COM port.

To install a non-PnP device on a specific COM port (i.e., COM2), you must first disable that port in the system's CMOS settings in order to avoid a device conflict. If not, the system may try to allocate that resource to some other device, because it has no way of knowing that the non-PNP device requires it.

Windows Modem Checks

In Windows, you can find the modem configuration information in the Control Panel under the *Modems* icon. There are two tabs that appear on the Modem Properties page—*General* and *Diagnostics*. The *Properties* button on the *General* tab provides port and maximum-speed settings. The *Diagnostics* tab's dialog box, shown in Figure 11-29, provides access to the modem's driver and additional information. The PnP feature reads the modem card and returns its information to the screen, as demonstrated in Figure 11-29.

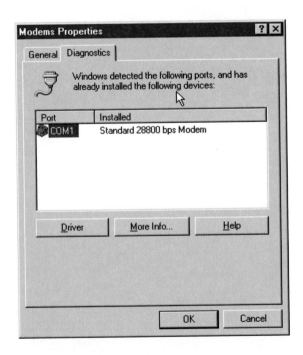

Figure 11-29: The Diagnostics Tab of the Modem Properties Dialog Box

Clicking on the *Properties* button in the Modem Properties page will produce the Standard Modem Properties page. This page contains two or more tabs that apply to the port associated with the selected modem. The *Connection* tab provides character-framing information and Call Preferences information, as illustrated in Figure 11-30. Recall that character-framing information includes items such as the number of data bits to be included in a character frame as well as the number and type of Start and Parity bits to be used. Clicking on the *Advanced* button will provide error and flow-control settings, as well as modulation type.

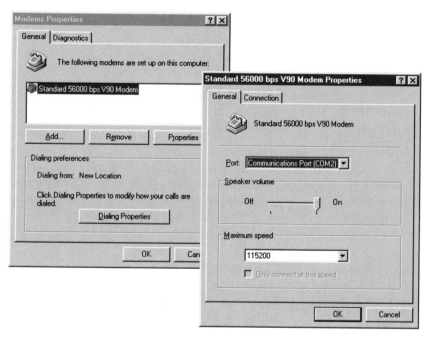

Figure 11-30: The Connection Tab of the Standard Modem Properties Dialog Box

The Windows program contains an application called HyperTerminal that can be used to control the operation of the system's modem with TelNet services. HyperTerminal is capable of operating with several different modem configurations. This flexibility enables it to conduct transfers with a wide variety of other computer systems on the Internet, such as UNIX and LINUX, without worrying about operating system differences.

Using HyperTerminal with TelNet to access other locations is much quicker than browsing Web sites with a graphical browser. The HyperTerminal New Connection window, shown in Figure 11-31, provides the options for configuring the communications settings. This program can be accessed through the *Start/Programs/Accessories/Communications* path in Windows 98.

Windows also provides fundamental troubleshooting information for wide area networking through its system of Help screens. Just select *Help* from the Control Panel's toolbar, and click on the topic that you are troubleshooting.

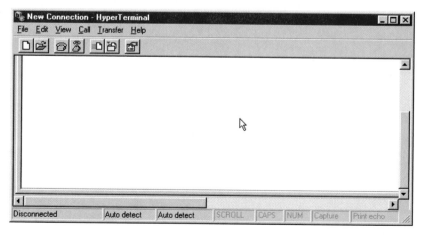

Figure 11-31: HyperTerminal

Communication Software

All modems require software to control the communication session. This software is typically included with the purchase of the modem and must be configured to operate in the system the modem will be used in. To communicate with other computers, some information about how the communication will proceed must be agreed on. In particular, it is necessary to match the protocol of the remote unit, as well as its parity, character framing, and baud rate settings. In the case of online services, the information comes with the introductory package the user receives when joining the service.

At the fundamental instruction level, most modem software employs a set of commands known as the **Hayes-compatible command set**. This set of commands is named for the Hayes Microcomputer Products company that first defined them.

In the Hayes command structure, the operation of the modem shifts back and forth between a Command mode and a Communications mode. In the Command mode, the modem exchanges commands and status information with the host system's microprocessor. In Communications mode, the modem facilitates sending and receiving data between the local system and a remote system. A short guard period between Communications mode and Command mode allows the system to switch smoothly without interrupting a data transmission.

The AT Command Set

The Hayes command set is based on a group of instructions that begin with a pair of attention characters followed by command words. Because the attention characters are an integral part of every Hayes command, the command set is often referred to as the **AT command set**.

AT commands are entered at the command line using an ATXn format. The Xn nomenclature identifies the type of command being given (X) and the particular function to be used (n). Except for ATA, ATDn, and ATZn commands, the AT sequence can be followed by any number of commands. The ATA command forces the modem to immediately pick up the phone line (even if it does not ring). The Dn commands are dialing instructions, and the Zn commands reset the modem by loading new default initialization information into it. Table 11-2 provides a summary of the Hayes-compatible AT command set.

Table 11-2: AT Command Set Summary

COMMAND		FUNCTION
A/		Re-execute command.
A		Go off-hook and attempt to answer a call.
B0		Select V.22 connection at 1200 bps.
B1	*	Select Bell 212A connection at 1200 bps.
C1	*	Return OK message.
Dn		Dial modifier (see Dial Modifier).
E0		Turn off command echo.
E1		Turn on command echo.
F0		Select auto-detect mode (equivalent to N1).
F1	*	Select V.21 of Bell 103.
F2		Reserved.
F3		Select V.23 line modulation.
F4		Select V.22 or Bell 212A 1200 bps line speed.
F5		Select V.22bis 7200 line modulation.
F6		Select V.32bis or V.32 4800 line modulation.
F7		Select V.32bis 7200 line modulation.
F8		Select V.32bis or V.32 9600 modulation.
F9		Select V.32bis 12000 line modulation.
F10		Select V.32bis 14400 line modulation.
H0		Initiate a hang-up sequence.
H1		If on-hook, go off-hook and enter command mode.
I0		Report product code.
I1		Report computed checksum.
I2		Report OK.
I3		Report firmware revision, model, and interface type.
I4		Report response.
I5		Report the country code parameter.
I6		Report modem data pump model and code revision.
L0		Set low speaker volume.
L1		Set low speaker volume.
L2	*	Set medium speaker volume.
L3		Set high speaker volume.
M0		Turn off speaker.
M1	*	Turn speaker on during handshaking, and turn speaker off while receiving carrier.
M2		Turn speaker on during handshaking and while receiving carrier.
M3		Turn speaker off during dialing and receiving carrier, and turn speaker on during answering.
N0		Turn off Automode detection.
N1	*	Turn on Automode detection.
O0		Go online.
O1		Go online and initiate a retrain sequence.
P		Force pulse dialing.
Q0	*	Allow result codes to PC.
Q1		Inhibit result codes to PC.
Sn		Select S-Register as default.
Sn?		Return the value of S-Register n.
=v		Set default S-Register to value v.
?		Return the value of default S-Register.
T		Force DTMF dialing.
V0		Report short form (terse) result codes.
V1	*	Report long form (verbose) result codes.
W0	*	Report PC speed in EC mode.
W1		Report line speed, EC protocol, and PC speed.
W2		Report modem speed in EC mode.
X0		Report basic progress result codes, OK, CONNECT, RING, NO CARRIER (also for busy, if enabled, and dial tone not detected), NO ANSWER, and ERROR.
X1		Report basic call progress result codes and connection speeds such as OK, CONNECT, RING, NO CARRIER (also for busy, if enabled, and dial tone not detected), NO ANSWER, CONNECT XXXX, and ERROR.
X2		Report basic call progress result codes and connection speeds such as OK, CONNECT, RING, NO CARRIER (also for busy, if enabled, and dial tone not detected), NO ANSWER, CONNECT XXXX, and ERROR.
X3		Report basic call progress result codes and connection rate such as OK, CONNECT, RING, NO CARRIER, NO ANSWER, CONNECT XXXX, BUSY, and ERROR.

* Default

Table 11-3: AT Command Result Codes

After a command has been entered at the command line, the modem attempts to execute the command and then returns a result code to the screen. Table 11-3 describes the command result codes.

RESULT	CODE	DESCRIPTION
0	OK	The OK code is returned by the modem to acknowledge execution of a command line.
1	CONNECT	The modem sends this result code when line speed is 300 bps.
2	RING	The modem sends this result code when incoming ringing is detected on the line.
3	NO CARRIER	The carrier is not detected within the time limit, or the carrier is lost.
4	ERROR	The modem could not process the command line (entry error).
5	CONNECT 1200	The modem detected a carrier at 1200 bps.
6	NO DIAL TONE	The modem could not detect a dial tone when dialing.
7	BUSY	The modem detected a busy signal.
8	NO ANSWER	The modem never detected silence (@ command only).
9	CONNECT 0600	The modem sends this result code when line speed is 7200 bps.
10	CONNECT 2400	The modem detected a carrier at 2400 bps.
11	CONNECT 4800	Connection is established at 4800 bps.
12	CONNECT 9600	Connection is established at 9600 bps.
13	CONNECT 7200	The modem sends this result code when the line speed is 7200 bps.
14	CONNECT 12000	Connection is established at 12000 bps.
15	CONNECT 14400	Connection is established at 14400 bps.
17	CONNECT 38400	Connection is established at 38400 bps.
18	CONNECT 57600	Connection is established at 57600 bps.
22	CONNECT 75TX/1200RX	The modem sends this result code when establishing a V.23 Originate.
23	CONNECT 1200TX/75RX	The modem sends this result code when establishing a V.23 answer.
24	DELAYED	The modem returns this result code when a call fails to connect and is considered delayed.
32	BLACKLISTED	The modem returns this result code when a call fails to connect and is considered blacklisted.
40	CARRIER 300	The carrier is detected at 300 bps.
44	CARRIER 1200/75	The modem sends this result code when V.23 backward channel carrier is detected.
45	CARRIER 75/1200	The modem sends this result code when V.23 forward channel carrier is detected.
46	CARRIER 1200	The carrier is detected at 1200 bps.
47	CARRIER 2400	The carrier is detected at 2400 bps.
48	CARRIER 4800	The modem sends this result code when either the high or low channel carrier in V.22bis modem has been detected.
49	CARRIER 7200	The carrier is detected at 7200 bps.
50	CARRIER 9600	The carrier is detected at 9600 bps.
51	CARRIER 12000	The carrier is detected at 12000 bps.
52	CARRIER 14400	The carrier is detected at 14400 bps.
66	COMPRESSION: CLASS 5	MNP Class 5 is active CLASS 5.
67	COMPRESSION: V.42bis	COMPRESSION: V.42bis is active V.42bis.
69	COMPRESSION: NONE	No data compression signals NONE.
70	PROTOCOL: NONE	No error correction is enabled.
77	PROTOCOL: LAPM	V.42 LAP-M error correction is enabled.
80	PROTOCOL: ALT	MNP Class 4 error correction is enabled.

Using the AT Command Set

Run All Tests

ATZ

OK code

Many of the software diagnostic packages available include a utility for testing modems. If such a program is available, run the equivalent of its **Run All Tests** entry to test the modem. If all of the configuration settings are correct, attempt to run the modem's command line–based communications package to test the modem's operation. At the command line, type **ATZ** to reset the modem, and enter the Command mode using the Hayes-compatible command set. You should receive a 0, or OK response, if the command was processed.

If no result code is returned to the screen, check the modem's configuration and setup again for conflicts. Also, check the speed setting of the communication software to make sure it is compatible with that of the modem. On the other hand, a returned **OK code** indicates that the modem and the computer are communicating properly.

Other AT-compatible commands can be used to check the modem at the DOS level. The **ATL2** command sets the modem's output volume to medium, to make sure that it is not set too low to be heard. If the modem dials but cannot connect to a remote station, check the modem's speed and DTR settings. Change the DTR setting by entering **AT&Dn**. When

> n = 0, the modem ignores the DTR line
>
> n = 1, the modem goes to async command state when DTR goes off
>
> n = 2, DTR off; switches modem to off-hook and back to Command mode
>
> n = 3, DTR switching off initializes modem

If the modem connects but cannot communicate, check the character-framing parameter of the receiving modem, and set the local modem to match. Also, match the terminal emulation of the local unit to that of the remote unit. ANSI terminal emulation is the most common. Finally, match the file transfer protocol to the other modem.

> During the data transfer, both modems monitor the signal level of the carrier to prevent the transfer of false data due to signal deterioration. If the carrier signal strength drops below some predetermined **threshold level** or is lost for a given length of time, one or both modems will initiate automatic disconnect procedures.

threshold level

Use the **ATDT*70** command to disable call waiting if the transmission is frequently garbled. The +++ command should interrupt any activity the modem is engaged in and bring it to the Command mode.

ATDT*70

Depot Technician 1.2

Modem Hardware Checks

Most serial ports and modems can perform self-tests on their circuitry. Modems have the capability to perform three different kinds of self-diagnostic tests:

- The local digital loopback test

- The local analog loopback test

- The remote digital loopback test

In a **local digital loopback test**, data are looped through the registers of the port's UART. When testing the RS-232 port, a device called a **loopback plug** (or **wrap-plug**) channels the output data directly back into the received data input, and only the port is tested. Many modems can extend this test by looping the data through the local modem and back to the computer (the **local analog loopback test**). Some modems even possess the ability to loopback data to a remote computer through its modem (**remote digital loopback test**). In this manner, the entire transmit and receive path can be validated, including the communication line (i.e., the telephone line). One of the most overlooked causes of transmission problems is the telephone line itself. A noisy line can easily cause garbled data to be output from the modem. Figure 11-32 illustrates port, analog, and digital loopback tests.

local digital loopback test

loopback plug

wrap-plug

local analog loopback test

remote digital loopback test

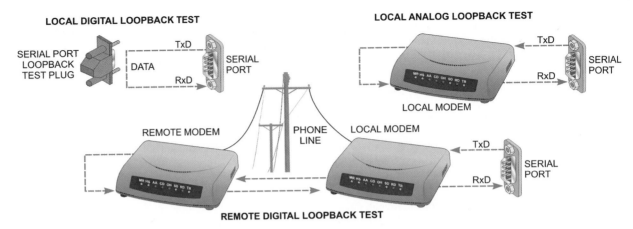

LOCAL DIGITAL LOOPBACK TEST

SERIAL PORT LOOPBACK TEST PLUG

TxD

DATA

RxD

SERIAL PORT

LOCAL ANALOG LOOPBACK TEST

TxD

RxD

SERIAL PORT

LOCAL MODEM

REMOTE MODEM

PHONE LINE

LOCAL MODEM

TxD

RxD

SERIAL PORT

REMOTE DIGITAL LOOPBACK TEST

**Figure 11-32:
Loopback Tests**

If transmission errors occur frequently, you should use the various loopback tests to locate the source of the problem. Begin by running the remote digital loopback test. If the test runs successfully, the problem is likely to be located in the remote computer.

**Local Digital
Loopback Test with
Self Tests**

If the test fails, run the **Local Digital Loopback Test with Self Tests**. If the test results are positive, the problem may be located in the local computer. On the other hand, you should run the local analog loopback test if the local digital test fails.

If the local analog test fails, the problem is located in the local modem. If the local analog test is successful, and problems are occurring, you should run the local analog test on the remote computer. The outcome of this test should pinpoint the problem to the remote computer or the remote modem.

**communications
software**

If the modem is an internal unit, you can test its hardware by exchanging it with a known-good unit. If the telephone line operates correctly with a normal handset, only the modem, its configuration, or the **communications software** can be causes of problems. If the modem's software and configuration settings appear correct, and problems are occurring, the modem hardware is experiencing a problem, and it will be necessary to exchange the modem card for a known-good one.

> With an external modem, you can use the front-panel lights as diagnostic tools to monitor its operation. You can monitor the progress of a call, and its handling, along with any errors that may occur.

Figure 11-33 depicts the front panel lights of a typical external modem.

**Figure 11-33:
Modem Front Panel
Indicators**

FRONT PANEL LIGHTS:
MR - MODEM READY
HS - HIGH SPEED
AA - AUTO ANSWERING
CD - DATA CARRIER DETECT
OH - OFF-HOOK
SD - SEND DATA
RD - RECEIVE DATA
TR - TERMINAL READY

The **Modem Ready (MR)**, **Terminal Ready (TR)**, and **Auto Answer (AA)** lights are preparatory lights that indicate that the modem is plugged in, powered on, ready to run, and prepared to answer an incoming call. The MR light becomes active when power is applied to the modem and the modem is ready to operate. The TR light becomes active when the host computer's communication software and the modem contact each other. The AA light just indicates that the Auto Answer function has been turned on.

The **Off-Hook (OH)**, **Ring Indicator (RI)**, and **Carrier Detect (CD)** lights indicate the modem's online condition. The OH light indicates that the modem has connected to the phone line. This action can occur when the modem is receiving a call or when it is commanded to place a call. The RI light becomes active when the modem detects an incoming **ring signal**. The CD light activates when the modem detects a carrier signal from a remote modem. As long as this light is on, the modem can send and receive data from the remote unit. If the CD light will not activate with a known-good modem, a problem with the data communication equipment exists.

The final three lights indicate the status of a call in progress. The **Send Data (SD)** light flickers when the modem transmits data to the remote unit, while the **Received Data** light flickers when the modem receives data from the remote unit. The **High Speed (HS)** light becomes active when the modem is conducting transfers at its highest possible rate. If an external modem will not operate at its highest rated potential, check the specification for the UART on the adapter card to make certain that it is capable of operating at that speed.

Modem Ready (MR)
Terminal Ready (TR)
Auto Answer (AA)

Off-Hook (OH)
Ring Indicator (RI)
Carrier Detect (CD)
ring signal

Send Data (SD)
Received Data
High Speed (HS)

Essentials 1.3

IT Technician 1.2

Troubleshooting Sound Cards

Some very basic components are involved in the audio output of most computer systems: a *sound card*, some *speakers*, the *audio-related software*, and the *host computer system*. Several software diagnostic packages enable you to test sound card operation. Most sound cards perform two separate functions. The first is to *play* sound files; the second is to *record* them. You might need to troubleshoot problems for either function.

Sound Card Configuration Checks

If sound problems are occurring in the multimedia system, two of the first things to check are the hardware and audio software configuration settings. Refer to the sound card manufacturer's documentation for proper hardware settings.

In the past, sound cards have been notorious for interrupt conflict problems with other devices. Because these conflicts typically exist between peripheral devices, they may not appear during bootup. If the sound card operates correctly except when a printing operation is in progress, for example, an IRQ conflict probably exists between the sound card and the printer port. Similar symptoms would be produced for tape backup operations if the tape drive and the sound card were configured to use the same IRQ channel. Use a software diagnostic program to check the system for interrupt conflicts.

Checking the system for resource conflicts in Windows is relatively easy. Access the *System* icon in the Control Panel and select the *Hardware* tab. From this point, click the *Device Manager* button, and select the *Sound, video, and game controller* option. If the system detects any conflicts, it places an exclamation point within a circle on the selected option.

From the Device Manager, verify that the correct audio driver is installed, and that its settings match those called for by the sound card manufacturer. If the driver is missing, or wrong, add the correct driver to the system through the Control Panels' *Add/Remove Hardware* wizard (simply *Add Hardware* in Windows XP). The main page of the sound card's *Properties* window displays all the resources the driver is using for the card. The *Conflicting devices* list window provides information about any conflicting resource that the system has detected in conjunction with the sound card.

If the Windows PnP function is operating properly, you should be able to remove the driver from the system, reboot the computer, and allow the operating system to re-detect the sound card and assign new resources to it. If the driver is not installed, or is incorrect, add the correct driver from the available drivers list. If the correct driver is not available, reinstall it from the card's OEM disk, or obtain it from the card's manufacturer.

Sound Card Hardware Checks

Figure 11-34 depicts the system's sound card–related components. Provided that the sound card's configuration is properly set, and the software configuration matches it, the sound card and speakers will need to be checked if problems exist. Most of these checks are very simple. They include insuring that the speakers are plugged into the **Speaker** port. It is not uncommon for the speakers to be mistakenly plugged into the card's **MIC** (microphone) port.

Likewise, if the sound card will not record sound, make certain that the microphone is installed in the proper jack (not the speaker jack) and that it is turned on. Check the amount of disk space on the drive, to ensure that there is enough to hold the file being produced.

In the case of stereo speaker systems, it is possible to place the speakers on the wrong sides. This will produce a problem when you try to adjust the balance between them. Increasing the volume on the right speaker will instead increase the output of the left speaker. The obvious cure for this problem is to physically switch the positions of the speakers.

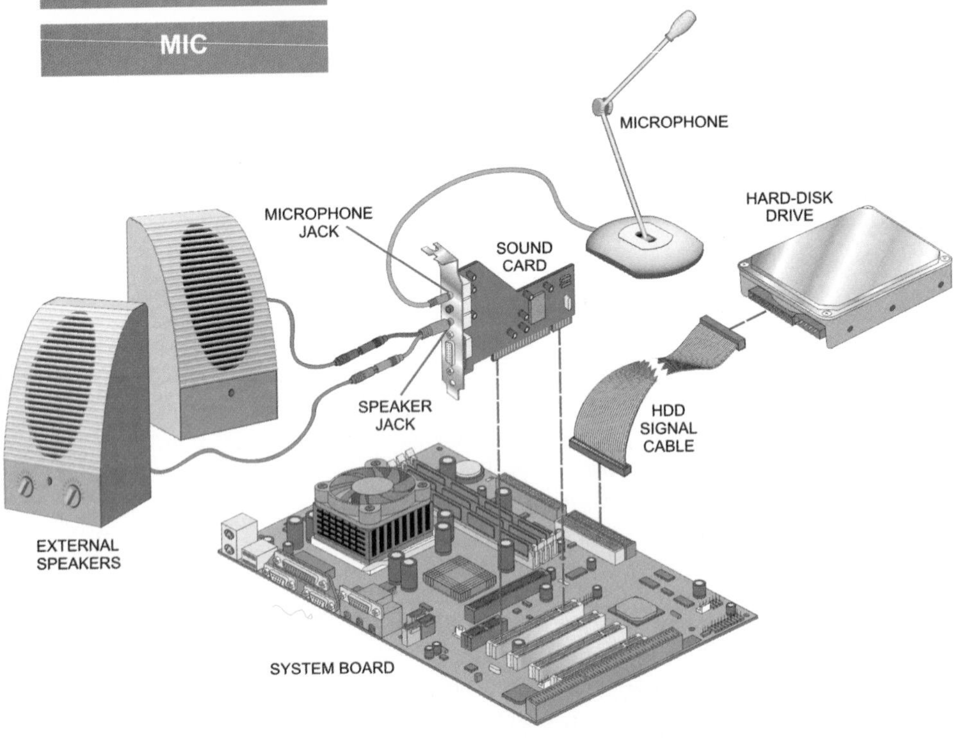

Figure 11-34: Sound Card–Related Components

If the system will not produce sound, troubleshoot the audio output portion of the system. Do the speakers require an external power supply? If so, is it connected, and are the speakers turned on? If the speakers use batteries for their power source, check them to see that they are installed and good. Check the speakers' volume setting to make certain they are not turned down.

┌─ **TEST TIP** ─────
Know how to correct a balance problem that occurs with add on stereo speakers.

NETWORK TROUBLESHOOTING

Essentials 5.3

Begin troubleshooting a general network problem by determining what has changed since it was running last. If the installation is new, it will need to be inspected as a setup problem. Check to determine whether any new hardware or software has been added to the system. Has any of the cabling been changed? Have any new protocols been added? Has a network adapter been replaced or moved? If any of these events has occurred, begin by checking them specifically.

Network Troubleshooting Basics

`network drop cabling`

If the problem does not appear in, or is not related to, the stand-alone operation of the unit, it will be necessary to check the portions of the system that are specific to the network. These elements include the network adapter card, the network-specific portions of the operating system, and the **network drop cabling**. Figure 11-35 depicts the network-specific portions of a computer system.

Be aware that in a network environment, no unit really functions alone. Unlike working on a stand-alone unit, the steps performed on a network computer may affect the operation of other units on the network.

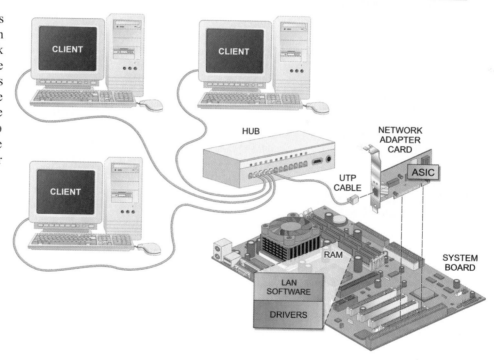

Figure 11-35: Network-Related Components

Diagnostic efforts and tests run across the network can use a lot of the network's bandwidth. This reduced bandwidth causes the operation of all the units on the network to slow down. This is due simply to the added usage of the network.

Because performing work on the network can affect so many users, it is good practice to involve the network administrator in any such work being performed. This person can run interference for any work that must be performed that could disable the network or cause users to lose data.

┌─ **TEST TIP** ─────
Be aware of the effects that running applications across the network can have on its performance.

LAN Configuration Checks

As with any peripheral device, the LAN card's configuration must be correct for the software that is driving the peripheral and for the adapter card it is communicating through. An improperly configured network adapter card can prevent the system from gaining access to the network. Most network adapter cards are PnP compliant, so they are configured automatically.

Security Access Problems

One of the major concerns in most network environments is data security. Because all of the data around the network are potentially available to anyone else attached to the Net, all LAN administration software employs different levels of security. Passwords are typically used at all software levels to lock people out of hardware systems, as well as out of programs and data files.

Log-on passwords and **scripts** are designed to keep unauthorized personnel from accessing the system or its contents. Additional passwording may be used to provide access to some parts of the system and not others (i.e., lower-level accounting personnel may be allowed access to accounts receivable and payable sections of the business management software package but may not be allowed into the payroll section). A series of passwords may be used to deny access to this area.

In other LAN management packages, the **network administrator** is normally responsible for establishing user **access and privileges** to programs and data through the operating system's security subsystem. These settings can be established to completely provide access to everything, deny access to certain information, or allow limited **access rights** to specific resources. An example of limited rights would be the ability to read data from a file but not manipulate it (write, delete, print, or move it) in any way.

The reason for discussing security at this point is because established security settings can prevent the technician from using any, or all, of the system's resources. In addition, having limited access to programs can give them the appearance of being defective. Because of this, the service technician must work with the network administrator when checking a networked machine. The administrator can provide the access, and the security relief, needed to repair the system. The administrator can also keep you away from data that may not be any of your business.

Refer to Chapter 12, *Operating System Troubleshooting*, which covers the Operating System Technologies module for in-depth network software troubleshooting information.

> Log-on passwords
>
> scripts
>
> network administrator
>
> access and privileges
>
> access rights

LAN Hardware Checks

Check the activity light on the back plate of the LAN card (if available) to see if the network recognizes the adapter. If the lights are active, the connection is alive. If not, check the adapter in another node. Check the cabling to make sure that it is the correct type, and that the connector is properly attached. A LAN cable tester is an excellent device to have in this situation.

Check the system for switches, routers, and bridges that may not be functioning properly. Check the protocol's frame settings to make sure that they are compatible from device to device, or that they are represented on the file server. The operation of these devices will have to be verified as separate units.

The first step in troubleshooting local network connectivity is to try to obtain a connection with the network. Check the activity/status lights on the back plate of the LAN card (if available) to determine whether the network recognizes the adapter. If the lights are active, the connection is alive. If not, check the network's local connectivity devices, such as switches, routers, and bridges that may not be functioning properly.

Check the power, status and activity lights on these devices to determine their interaction with the node you are troubleshooting. These network connectivity devices often provide several indicator lights that can be used to troubleshoot hardware connectivity problems. Typical status and activity lights include:

- PWR—showing that the device is receiving power and that its power supply is functioning.

- ACT—The activity light that blinks when the device is transmitting or receiving data to/from the LAN card

- 10M/100M—Speed indicator lights that are illuminated when the device is properly connected to a LAN card—the light corresponding to the operating speed of the link will be illuminated.

If the status lights for the node in question are not present at the connectivity device, check the adapter and cable in another node. Check the cabling to make sure that it is the correct type, and that the connector is properly attached. A LAN cable tester is an excellent device to have in this situation.

If the physical link between the local network card and the connectivity device is good, you will need to check the logical operation of the network. In Windows systems, this involves using the TCP/IP tools that come with the operating system. Refer to the "Windows 2000/XP Networking Problems" section of Chapter 12.

No Network Node Is an Island—In a network, no node is an island, and every unit has an impact on the operation of the network when it is online. Changes made in one part of a network can cause problems and data loss in other parts of the network. You should be aware that changing hardware and software configuration settings on an adapter might have adverse effects when the system is returned to the network. In addition, changing hard drives in a network node can have a negative impact on the network when the unit is brought back online.

GEEK SQUAD CASE FILE #49762

You have been called to a customer site to repair a networking problem. The user cannot see any other computers on her network. You check the drivers for the NIC, and you check the protocols that are installed in the operating system, and they appear to be okay. You also check the NIC and see that the light on its back panel is not glowing. What items should you check next?

associating

authenticating

wireless signal
strength indicator

Troubleshooting Wireless Networks

Communicating across a wireless network link involves two distinct functions—**associating** and **authenticating**. Associating is the process of *establishing a connection* between the local wireless network adapter and the remote AP (or wireless adapter in a peer to peer setting). This means creating a wireless link between the adapter and the AP as indicated in the Installing Wireless LANs sections of Chapter 6.

In a wireless network, or a wireless link in a mixed network, the link status indicator you should refer to for troubleshooting on the client end is the **wireless signal strength indicator**, depicted in Figure 11-36. If the signal strength level is too low the client will not be able to communicate with the network. Also note the number of packets that are sent and received. If packets are sent but not received, the logical configuration of the WLAN adapter or the wireless AP/router is incorrect.

While the signal strength indicator may show a connection exists, if there are no communications occurring between the local unit and remote units, the network link is probably not configured properly. The status indicator only shows that the local adapter sees an AP or another wireless adapter—not that communications are going on.

When dealing with portable PCs, you should check that your wireless network adapter is switched on. Some laptops come with buttons that can be used to disable the wireless network function when not in use. This is a power saving feature used to extend the battery cycle life.

**Figure 11-36:
Wireless Signal
Strength Indicator**

Use the Device Manager to insure that the wireless adapter is enabled. In Device Manger, right click the wireless network adapter and click on *Properties*. On the *Advanced* tab select the *Channel Property* option and insure that the number corresponds to the channel setting of the Access Point. Disable and then re-enable the wireless connection.

The other key factor in wireless network communications is *Association*. In Windows XP, you should navigate to the wireless connection's *Properties* dialog window and select the *Association* tab. Check the Service Set Identifier (SSID) setting. This setting should match the configuration of the wireless AP/router. In a Peer-to-Peer environment (or one without an access point), this value should be the same on all the computers in the wireless network.

Check the local IP settings. If your AP is also acting as a router, it may be configured to automatically provide IP addressing through its DHCP function. If the IP addressing is incorrect, you must troubleshoot the DHCP problem at the network router or server to reestablish connectivity. In Peer-to-Peer environments (those without an access point) all the wireless clients should be using static IP addresses on the order of:

- PC-A IP address—192.168.0.2

- PC-B an IP address—192.168.0.3

- Router/Gateway address—192.168.0.1 (usually reserved for the gateway)

- Each PC should have the same Subnet mask (i.e., 255.255.255.0)

Make sure that the security settings are set to the same encryption type (WEP/WPA), level (64 bit, 128 bit and so on) as the AP/router (or the other computers in a peer to peer setting), and that they are using identical encryption keys. If possible, you may want to disable encryption long enough to get the connection up and running—however this will leave the network more vulnerable to outside access while it is disabled. Both WEP and WPA can make establishing a connection more difficult—fight one battle at a time.

Other wireless network items to check include making sure that the network adapter is in the right mode—ad-hoc mode for peer-to-peer operations, or **Infrastructure mode** for use in wireless networks with APs or AP/routers. Make sure the access point is enabled. If it is using the access list (ACL) function make sure the list contains the correct MAC address for the local wireless adapter.

It is also a good idea to remove any unused network connections from Preferred Networks list on the Wireless Network's tab. This will speed up connection time by eliminating the need to move through unavailable network connections (they are checked in the order they are listed.)

Testing Cable

Essentials 5.3

As we mentioned earlier in this chapter, the most frequent hardware-related cause of network problems involves bad cabling and connectors. There are several specialized, handheld devices designed for testing the various types of data communication cabling. These devices range from inexpensive continuity testers to moderately priced Data Cabling testers to somewhat expensive **time domain reflectometry (TDR)** devices.

time domain reflectometry (TDR)

The inexpensive continuity testers can be used to check for broken cables. This function can also be performed by the simple DMM described in Chapter 2. Data cabling testers are designed to perform a number of different types of tests on twisted pair and coaxial cables. These wiring testers normally consist of two units—a master test unit and a separate load unit, as illustrated in Figure 11-37.

The master unit is attached to one end of the cable, and the load unit is attached at the other. The master unit sends patterns of test signal through the cable and reads them back from the load unit. Many of these testers feature both RJ-45 and BNC connectors for testing different types of cabling. When testing twisted pair cabling, these devices can normally detect such problems as broken wires, crossed-over wiring, shorted connections, and improperly paired connections.

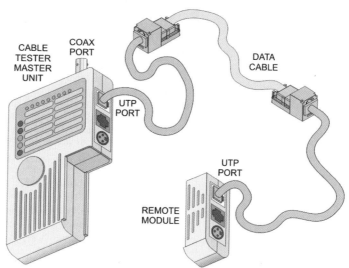

Figure 11-37: Cable Tester

optical time domain reflectometers (OTDRs)

TDRs are sophisticated testers that can be used to pinpoint the distance to a break in a cable. These devices send signals along the cable and wait for them to be reflected. The time between sending the signal and receiving it back is converted into a distance measurement. The TDR function is normally packaged along with the other cable testing functions just described. TDRs used to test fiber optic cables are known as **optical time domain reflectometers (OTDRs)**.

KEY POINTS REVIEW

This chapter has discussed basic troubleshooting and diagnostic methods associated with the system hardware. Review the following key points before moving into the Review and Exam Questions sections to make sure you are comfortable with each point. Afterward, answer the Review Questions that follow to verify your knowledge of the information.

- It is normal practice to first set the meter to its highest voltage range to make certain that the voltage level being measured does not damage the meter.

- Unlike the voltage check, resistance checks are always made with power removed from the system.

- Whenever a self-test failure or setup mismatch is encountered, the BIOS may indicate the error through a blank screen or through a visual error message on the video display or through an audio response (beep codes) produced by the system's speaker.

- The most important thing to do when checking a malfunctioning device is to be observant. Begin by talking to the person who reported the problem. Many clues can be obtained from this person. Careful listening is also a good way to eliminate the user as a possible cause of the problems occurring. Part of the technician's job is to determine whether the user could be the source of the problem—either trying to do things with the system that it cannot do, or not understanding how some part of it is supposed to work.

- Carefully observing the steps of a bootup procedure can reveal a great deal about the nature of problems in a system. Faulty areas can be included or excluded from possible causes of errors during the bootup process.

- The majority of all problems that occur in computer systems are in the area of configuration settings.

- In most newer systems, the BIOS and operating system use Plug-and-Play techniques to detect new hardware that has been installed in the system. These components work together with the device to allocate system resources for the device. In some occasions, the PnP logic will not be able to resolve all of the system's resource needs and a configuration error will occur. In these cases, the user will be required to manually resolve the configuration problem.

- Field replaceable units (FRUs) are the portions of the system that can be conveniently replaced in the field.

- Once you have isolated the problem, and the computer boots up and runs correctly, work backwards through the troubleshooting routines, reinstalling any original boards and other components removed during the troubleshooting process.

- Special consideration must be taken when a system is inoperable. In a totally inoperable system, there are no symptoms to give clues where to begin the isolation process. In addition, it is impossible to use troubleshooting software or other system aids to help isolate the problem.

- In Pentium-based systems, check the Advanced CMOS configuration and enabling settings in the BIOS and Chipset Features screens. These settings usually include the disk drives, keyboard, and video options, as well as on-board serial and parallel ports.

- Hard drive systems have a controller, a signal cable. a power cable, and a drive unit. The troubleshooting procedure typically moves from setup and configuration, to formatting, and, finally, into the hardware component isolation process.

- Typically, if the bootup process reaches the point where the system's CMOS configuration information is displayed on the screen, it can be assumed that no hardware configuration conflicts exist in the system's basic components. After this point in the bootup process, the system begins loading drivers for optional devices and additional memory. If the error occurs after the CMOS screen is displayed and before the bootup tone, it will be necessary to clean boot the system and single-step through the remainder of the bootup sequence.

- A number of things can cause improper floppy-disk drive operation or disk drive failure. These items include the use of unformatted diskettes, incorrectly inserted diskettes, damaged disks, erased disks, loose cables, drive failure, adapter failure, system board failure, or a bad or loose power connector.

- The troubleshooting steps for a CD-ROM drive are almost identical to those of an HDD system. The connections and data paths are similar. There are basically three levels of troubleshooting that apply to CD-ROM problems—the configuration level, the operating system level, and the hardware level.

- It is necessary to check the Advanced CMOS Setup to determine whether the port in question has been enabled, and, if so, whether it has been enabled correctly.

- The basic components associated with the tape drive include the tape drive, the signal cable, the power connection, the controller, and the tape drive's operating software.

- Every COM port on a PC requires an IRQ line in order to signal the processor for attention. In most PC systems, two COM ports share the same IRQ line. The IRQ4 line works for COM1 and COM3, and the IRQ3 line works for COM2 and COM4. This is common in PC-compatibles. The technician must make sure that two devices are not set up to use the same IRQ channel.

- During the data transfer, both modems monitor the signal level of the carrier to prevent the transfer of false data due to signal deterioration. If the carrier signal strength drops below some predetermined threshold level or is lost for a given length of time, one or both modems will initiate automatic disconnect procedures.

- With an external modem, the front panel lights can be used as diagnostic tools to monitor its operation. The progress of a call, and its handling, can be monitored along with any errors that may occur.

- The components involved in the audio output of most computer systems are very simple. There is a sound card, some speakers, the audio-related software, and the host computer system. Several software diagnostic packages are available with the capability of testing sound card operation.

- Be aware that in a network environment, no unit really functions alone. Unlike working on a stand-alone unit, the steps performed on a network computer may affect the operation of other units on the network.

- One of the major concerns in most network environments is data security. Because all of the data around the network are potentially available to anyone else attached to the Net, all LAN administration software employs different levels of security. Passwords are typically used at all software levels to lock people out of hardware systems, as well as out of programs and data files.

- In a network, no node is an island, and every unit has an impact on the operation of the network when it is online. Changes made in one part of a network can cause problems and data loss in other parts of the network. You should be aware that changing hardware and software configuration settings for the adapter can have adverse effects when the system is returned to the network. In addition, changing hard drives in a network node can have a negative impact on the network when the unit is brought back online.

- All modems require software to control the communication session. This software is typically included with the purchase of the modem and must be configured to operate in the system the modem will be used in. At the fundamental instruction level, most modem software employs a set of commands known as the Hayes-Compatible Command Set.

REVIEW QUESTIONS

The following questions test your knowledge of the material presented in this chapter.

1. If the system issues a single beep and the C:\> prompt appears on the screen, what condition is indicated?

2. List the FDD-related hardware components that should be checked when floppy-disk problems are suspected.

3. List three situations that would normally require that the CMOS Setup routines be run.

4. What type of problem is indicated by a "Press F1 to continue" message during bootup?

5. What is the recommended method of using a digital multimeter to check voltage in a computer system?

6. If you are replacing components one at a time and the system suddenly begins working properly, what can be assumed?

7. List three items commonly tested using the resistance function of a multimeter.

8. What resistance reading would normally be expected from a fuse if it is functional?

9. If you are measuring across a capacitor on the system board with a DMM, what voltage reading would you normally expect to see?

10. Which noncomputer possibility should be eliminated early in the troubleshooting process?

11. What range should the voltage function of a DMM be set to for an initial measurement?

12. Log-on passwords and scripts are designed to _____.

13. In a LAN environment, access and privileges to programs and data can be established by the _____.

14. What is the first step in checking a networked computer?

15. To what type of communications products do Hayes-compatible commands pertain?

EXAM QUESTIONS

1. If an error occurs before the single beep tone in the bootup sequence, what type of failure is probable?
    a. The problem is probably associated with the operating system.
    b. The BIOS code has become corrupted.
    c. A setup or configuration problem.
    d. The problem is hardware related.

2. If an error occurs after the single beep in the bootup process, what type of problem is likely?
    a. The problem is probably associated with the operating system.
    b. The BIOS code has become corrupted.
    c. A setup or configuration problem.
    d. The problem is hardware related

3. If the system refuses to boot up after a new component is installed, what type of problem is normally assumed?
    a. The problem is probably associated with the operating system.
    b. The BIOS code has become corrupted.
    c. A setup or configuration problem has occurred.
    d. A hardware-related problem has occurred.

4. What component has the ability to affect the operation of all the other sections of the computer system?
    a. The power supply
    b. The ROM BIOS
    c. The microprocessor
    d. The system board

5. What multimeter reading would be appropriate for checking a system's speaker?
    a. Infinity
    b. Near 0 ohms
    c. 4 ohms
    d. 8 ohms

6. What type of problem is indicated by a continuous beep tone from the system?
    a. A power supply failure
    b. An undefined problem
    c. A configuration problem
    d. A bootup problem

7. If a system appears to be completely dead, what item should logically be checked first?
   a. The system board
   b. The microprocessor
   c. The hard-disk drive
   d. The power supply

8. The error message "Bad File Allocation Table" indicates _____ problem.
   a. an operating system
   b. a Run Time
   c. a configuration
   d. a bootup

9. If a "CMOS" Display Type Mismatch" message appears on the screen, what type of error is indicated?
   a. An operating system problem
   b. A Run Time error
   c. A setup or configuration problem
   d. A bootup failure

10. Which of the following is not normally considered an FRU that would be changed in the field?
    a. A system board
    b. A floppy-disk drive
    c. A power supply
    d. A video controller IC

CHAPTER 12

OPERATING SYSTEM TROUBLESHOOTING

OBJECTIVES

Upon completion of this chapter and its related lab procedures, you should be able to perform these tasks:

1. Apply basic diagnostic procedures and troubleshooting techniques to operating system-related problems.

2. Describe common Windows disk management utilities.

3. Describe common Windows system management tools.

4. Identify Windows file management tools.

5. Explain common error messages associated with Windows.

6. Identify and solve Windows 2000/XP setup problems.

7. Locate and solve Windows 2000/XP start-up problems.

8. Locate and solve Windows 2000/XP operational problems.

9. Describe Windows 2000/XP system tools, disk management tools, and TCP/IP tools.

10. Use the Policy Editor to change Windows 2000/XP policy settings.

11. Describe various Windows 2000/XP Safe Mode start-up scenarios.

12. Use the Windows XP Automated System Recovery and System Restore functions.

13. Use log files to determine the location of Windows 2000/XP operating system problems.

14. Employ Microsoft On-line Help utilities in Windows 2000/XP.

OPERATING SYSTEM TROUBLESHOOTING

FROM THE GEEK SQUAD

Lauren B., Agent 99 from store 645, has completed her PC hardware troubleshooting and repair training. However, she realizes that this is only half the battle in getting ready to repair PCs efficiently. She still needs to extend her product knowledge of operating systems and application programs to include knowledge about what to do when these items do not perform properly.

Agent 99's most important task as someone who services PCs is to become familiar with the operating system products that control the operation of the entire system—both system hardware and software applications packages. In her store, these products are basically Microsoft Windows operating systems—Windows 2000 Professional and Windows XP—Professional, Home Edition, and Media Center Edition. However, she also knows that if she continues to advance in the Geek Squad, she will eventually have to deal with other non-Windows operating systems. Fortunately, she has been told that what she learns from being involved with Windows at a diagnostic and troubleshooting basis will help her to understand other operating system types later.

INTRODUCTION

The Windows operating systems provide a wealth of troubleshooting tools that can be used to isolate and correct operating system problems. In the first half of this chapter, we will investigate the most widely used Windows system utilities.

Troubleshooting operating system problems involve the same steps as any other logical troubleshooting procedure. The steps are just adapted to fit the structure of the operating system. Analyze the symptoms displayed, isolate the error conditions, correct the problem, and test the repair. The second half of the chapter is dedicated to using the tools presented in the first half of the chapter to solve common Windows operating system problems.

OPERATING SYSTEM UTILITIES

Essentials 3.0

Technical Support 2.0

IT Technician 3.0

Successful troubleshooting of operating systems requires tools. The Windows operating system includes a wide variety of different tools designed to help users and administrators optimize and repair problems related to the operating system, its peripherals, and applications. The major Windows diagnostic and management tools can be divided into three general categories:

- Disk management tools
- System management tools
- File management tools

Windows Disk Management Tools

The operation of hard drives can slow down with general use. Files stored on the drive can be erased and moved, causing parts of them to be scattered around the drive. This causes the drive to reposition the R/W heads more often during read and write operations, thereby requiring more time to complete the process.

There are three important Windows utilities that can be used to optimize and maintain the operation of the hard-disk drive. These are the CHKDSK, defrag, and backup utilities. All of these utilities have been available since early MS-DOS versions.

In Windows 2000 and Windows XP, these disk drive tools are located in the Computer Management console under the Control Panel's *Administrative Tools* icon. The Storage node in the Computer Management console offers direct access to the *Disk Management* and *Defragmentation* utilities. The Backup and Defrag utilities are available through the *Start/Programs/Accessories/System Tools* menu path. The executable file for the Defrag program is under *C:\Windows*. The actual Windows 2000/XP NT Backup utility is located in the *C:\WINNT\SYSTEM32* folder.

Another way to access the HDD tools in Windows 2000/XP is to open *My Computer* and right-click on the icon for the hard-disk drive you want to use. Next, select the *Properties* option from the context-sensitive pop-up menu. Then, simply click on the *Tools* tab to gain access to the most useful Windows HDD utilities.

┌─ **TEST TIP** ─────────────┐
Remember where the main HDD utility programs are located in the Windows 2000/XP environments.
└───────────────────────────┘

┌─ **NOTE** ──┐
Microsoft does not supply a built-in antivirus utility with its operating systems, so a third-party add-on must be used.
└──┘

You should use these HDD utilities periodically to tune up the performance of the system. To do so, perform these steps:

1. Periodically remove unnecessary TMP and BAK files from the system.

2. Check for and remove lost file chains and clusters using the CHKDSK utility.

3. Use the Defrag utility to realign files on the drive that may have become fragmented after being moved back and forth between the drive and the system.

CHKDSK

CHKDSK (Check Disk)

The **CHKDSK (Check Disk)** command is a command-line utility that has remained in use with Windows 3.x, 9x, NT, 2000, and XP and is used to recover lost allocation units from the hard drive. Lost allocation units occur when an application terminates unexpectedly and causes the file management system to lose track of where some parts of the file are stored. The total file becomes segmented into undefined pieces that can still be read by the utility but cannot be associated with a particular filename in the FAT or MFT.

Files can also become cross-linked when the file management system loses track of some portion of the file. In these cases, part of a second file might be written into a sector that actually belonged to another file, and they become linked to each other at that spot. Figure 12-1 depicts a typical CHKDSK display. CHKDSK locates lost clusters and, when used with an /F switch, converts them into files that can be viewed with a text editor.

Over a period of time, lost units can pile up and occupy large amounts of disk space. To remove these lost units from the drive, an /F modifier is added to the command so that the lost units will be converted into files that can be investigated, and removed if necessary. In some cases, the converted file is a usable data file that can be rebuilt for use with an application.

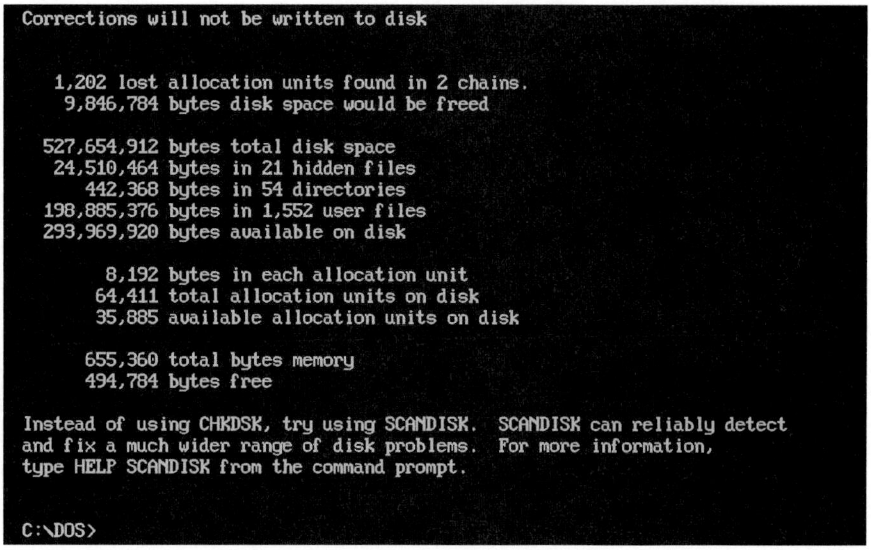

```
Corrections will not be written to disk


    1,202 lost allocation units found in 2 chains.
    9,846,784 bytes disk space would be freed

527,654,912 bytes total disk space
 24,510,464 bytes in 21 hidden files
    442,368 bytes in 54 directories
198,885,376 bytes in 1,552 user files
293,969,920 bytes available on disk

      8,192 bytes in each allocation unit
     64,411 total allocation units on disk
     35,885 available allocation units on disk

    655,360 total bytes memory
    494,784 bytes free

Instead of using CHKDSK, try using SCANDISK.  SCANDISK can reliably detect
and fix a much wider range of disk problems.  For more information,
type HELP SCANDISK from the command prompt.

C:\DOS>
```

Figure 12-1: A CheckDisk Display

The CHKDSK command can be run from the command prompt at any time. However, in Windows 2000 and Windows XP, the CHKDSK command is only available when working from the command line in the Recovery Console. The Windows 2000/XP version provides only the /P switch for performing an exhaustive check of the drive, and /R for finding bad sectors and recovering readable information from them if possible. The Windows 2000/XP version also requires that the file *Autochk.exe* be present in the root directory of the drive to operate.

HDD Defragmentation

In the normal use of the hard-disk drive, files become fragmented on the drive, as illustrated in Figure 12-2. This file fragmentation creates conditions that cause the drive to operate more slowly. Fragmentation occurs when files are stored in noncontiguous locations on the drive. This happens when files are stored, retrieved, modified, and rewritten due to differences in the sizes of the before and after files.

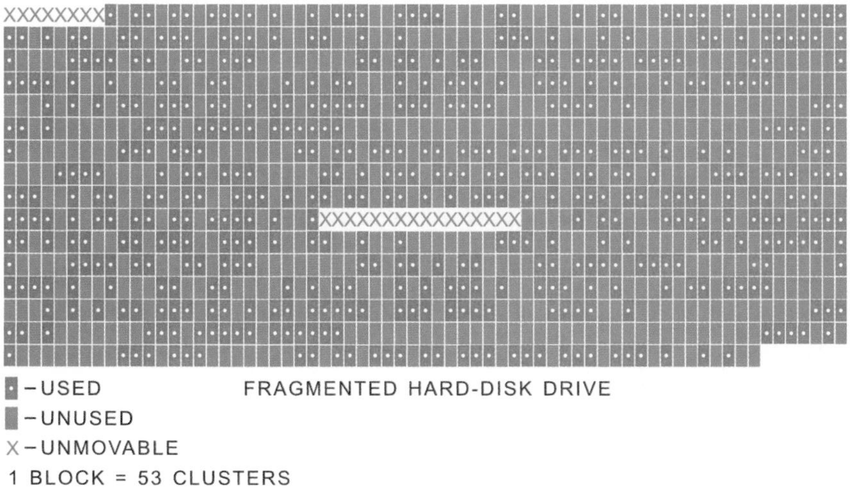

XXXXXXXX

XXXXXXXXXXXXXXXX

■ – USED
■ – UNUSED
X – UNMOVABLE
1 BLOCK = 53 CLUSTERS

FRAGMENTED HARD-DISK DRIVE

Figure 12-2: Data Sectors

defragmentation

Because the fragmented files do not permit efficient reading by the drive, it takes longer to complete multisector read operations. The **defragmentation** process optimizes the operation of the disk drive by reorganizing its data into logically contiguous blocks. With data arranged in this manner, the system does not need to reposition the drive's read/write heads as many times to read a given piece of data.

Some portions of files may become lost on the drive when a program is unexpectedly interrupted (such as when software crashes, for example, or during a power failure). These lost allocation units (chains) will also cause the drive to operate slowly. Therefore, it is customary to use the command-line CHKDSK command to find these chains and remove them before performing a defrag operation.

It may also be necessary to remove some data from the drive to defragment it. If the system is producing "Out of Disk Space" error messages, the defragmentation utility will not have enough room on the drive to realign clusters. When this happens, some of the contents of the drive will need to be transferred to a backup media (or discarded) to free up some disk space for the realignment process to occur.

Disk Defragmenter utility

The Defrag utility has been available since the later versions of MS-DOS (with the exception of Windows NT). In Windows 2000 the **Defragmenter utility** is located under the *Start/Programs/Accessories/System_Tools* path. In Windows XP the correct path is *Start/All Programs/ Accessories/System_Tools*. In Windows 2000 and Windows XP, the Defragmenter can also be accessed through the *Control Panel/Administrative Tools/Computer Management* path. To use the Defrag tool from this point:

1. Click the Disk Defragmenter option

2. Click the desired drive to highlight it

3. Click the Defragment button to begin the operation

DEFRAG

The **DEFRAG** main screen should appear, similar to that shown in Figure 12-3.

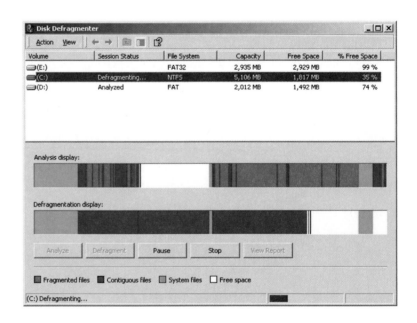

Figure 12-3: The DEFRAG Main Screen

The Defragmenter contains a disk analysis tool that reports the current status of the volume's key parameters. Figure 12-4 shows a sample analysis report.

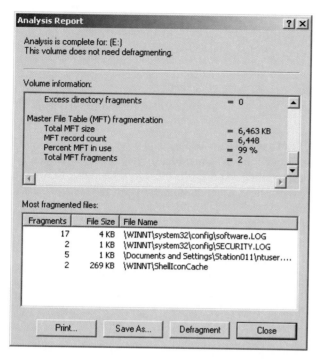

Figure 12-4: The Defrag Analysis Report

Viewing the defragmentation operation is possible through the *My Computer* window. Just right-click the drive icon, and select the *Properties* option. From this point, click the *Tools* option and select *Defrag*. However, viewing the operation of the defragmentation process makes the operation longer. It is better to run this utility in a minimized condition.

Backups

Backup utilities enable the user to quickly create extended copies of files, groups of files, or an entire disk drive. This operation is normally performed to create backup copies of important information, for use if the system's hard drive crashes, or when its content becomes corrupt.

The **Backup and Restore** utilities can be used to back up and retrieve one or more files to another disk.

Backup and Restore

Because a backup of related files is typically much larger than a single floppy disk, serious backup programs allow information to be backed up to a series of disks; they also provide file compression techniques to reduce the size of the files stored on the disk. Of course, it is impossible to read or use the compressed backup files in this format. To be usable, the files must be decompressed (expanded) and restored to their original format.

Backup Types

Most backup utilities provide a number of different options for conducting backups. Typically, backups fall into four categories:

- Full or total
- Incremental
- Selective
- Differential (or modified only)

total backup

In a full or **total backup** process, depicted in Figure 12-5, the entire contents of the designated disk are backed up. This includes directory and subdirectory listings and their contents. This backup method requires the most time each day to backup, but requires the least time to restore the system after a failure. Only the most recent backup copy is required to restore the system.

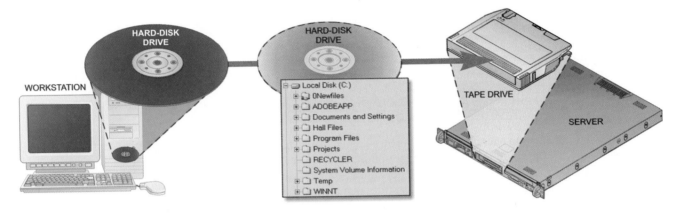

**Figure 12-5:
Full Backup**

Partial backups are often used instead of full backups to conserve space on the backup media and consume less time for the administrator. Three partial backup techniques are used to store data but yet conserve space on the storage media: incremental backups, selective backups, and differential backups.

incremental backup

- *Incremental Backup*—In an **incremental backup** operation, shown in Figure 12-6, the system backs up those files that have been created or changed since the last backup. Restoring the system from an incremental backup requires the use of the last full backup and each incremental backup taken since then. However, this method requires the least amount of time to backup the system but the most amount of time to restore it.

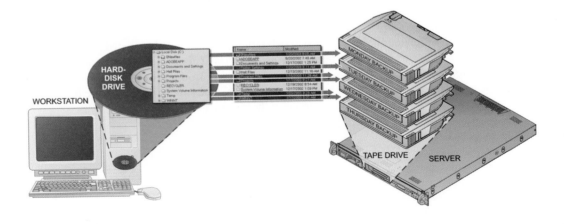

**Figure 12-6:
Incremental
Backup**

- *Selective or Copy Backup*—To conduct a **selective backup**, the operator moves through the tree structure of the disk marking, or tagging, directories and files to be backed up. After all the desired directories/files have been marked, they are backed up in a single operation. This form of backup is very labor intensive and may inadvertently miss important data. A selective backup is illustrated in Figure 12-7.

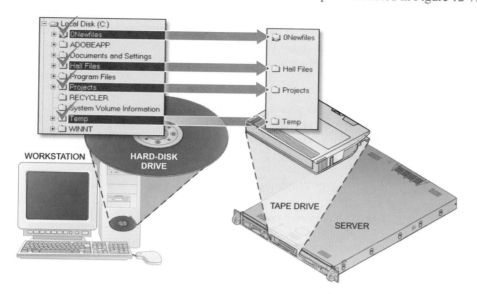

Figure 12-7:
Selective Backup

- *Differential or Modified Only Backup*—Specifying a **differential backup** causes the backup utility to examine each file to determine whether it has changed since the last full backup was performed. If not, it is bypassed. If the file has been altered, however, it will be backed up. This option is a valuable time-saving feature in a periodic backup strategy. To restore the system, you need a copy of the last full backup and the last differential backup. A Differential or Modified Only Backup operation is depicted in Figure 12-8.

— TEST TIP —

Know which backup type requires the least amount of time to perform and the least amount of effort to restore the system.

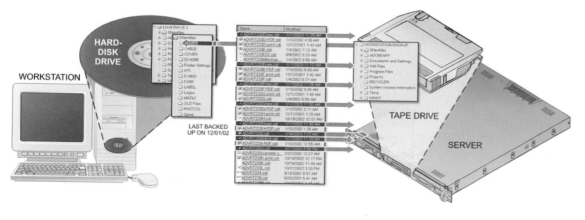

Figure 12-8:
Differential Backup

Windows Data Backup

Backup utility

You must be a member of the *Administrator* or *Backup Operators* groups or have appropriate permissions to the information they are attempting to back up to use the Windows 2000 or XP **Backup utility**. Members of these groups can back up and restore all data on a Windows computer, regardless of their permissions level. These groups are automatically assigned the *Back up files and directories* and *Restore files and directories* user rights.

Any user can back up any files they have at least the Read permission for. Likewise, they can restore anything they have at least the Write permission for. Users generally have these permissions to their own files, so they can perform backups and restores of their data as necessary.

The operation of the Microsoft Windows 2000/XP Backup utility is as follows.

To perform a backup of all data on a computer:

1. Log on as a user with appropriate permissions to back up the system.

2. Use the CHKDSK/F command to clean up lost file clusters. Instruct the program to convert any lost chains into files that can be checked later.

3. From the Start menu, select *Programs* (*All Programs in Windows XP*), then *Accessories*, followed by *System Tools*, and then *Backup*.

Backup Wizard

4. From the *Welcome* window, launch the **Backup Wizard** in Windows 2000. In Windows XP, click on the *Advanced mode* link to switch into *Advanced mode*. You could perform the Backup using Wizard mode, but Advanced mode will provide more backup options to choose from.

5. From the *Welcome* tab, launch *Backup Wizard or Backup Wizard (Advanced)*.

6. At the *Welcome* window, click on the *Next* button.

7. At the *What to Back Up* window, shown in Figure 12-9, select the *Back up everything on my computer* option, and click on the *Next* button.

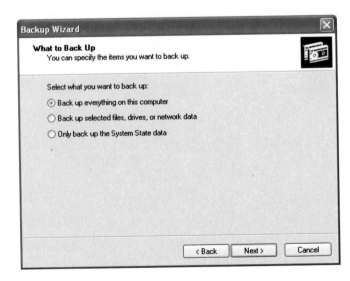

Figure 12-9: Choosing What to Backup

8. At the *Where to Store the Backup* (*Backup Type, Destination, and Name* in Windows XP) window, configure the type, location, and name for the backup, and then click on the *Next* button.

9. At the *Completing the Backup Wizard* window, click on the *Advanced* button to modify the Advanced settings, if necessary, and then click on the *Finish* button to start the backup process.

> ┌─ **NOTE** ──────────────────────────────
> You can also access the Windows Backup utility through the command prompt. Simply type *Ntbackup* in the *Start/Run* dialog window. The *Ntbackup.exe* utility can also be used to write scripts to automate the backup and restore process. For additional information about this option, type *Ntbackup /?* at the command prompt.

Advanced Backup Settings

Essentials 3.4

Choosing the *Advanced* backup option will lead you through the following configuration pages:

- *Type of Backup* page, displayed in Figure 12-10, includes normal, differential, incremental, copy, or daily backup options.

- *How to Back Up* includes options for verifying the backup and enabling compression (if it's supported by your backup device). Verifying the backup means to compare the data on the tape with the data that were backed up, to make certain that all information was copied properly during the backup.

- *Media Options* (*Backup Options* in Windows XP) enables you to specify whether to replace the existing data on the backup media or append the new data to the end of the media.

- *Backup label* enables you to assign a name to the backup. You should normally label backups with the date and time that the backup was performed, and the contents of the backup.

- *When to Back Up* enables you to launch the backup operation immediately or specify a later time and date for the backup.

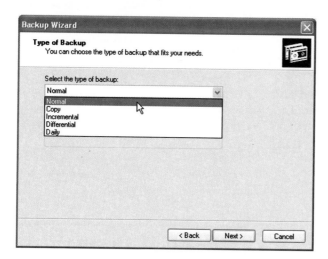

Figure 12-10: Type of Backup Window

You can schedule backups to occur repetitively at a designated time through the *Schedule Jobs* tab, as shown in Figure 12-11. Double clicking on any date in the calendar will launch the Backup Wizard, with the option to specify the time that the backup operation will start. You will also be prompted to set up a repetitive schedule during the process.

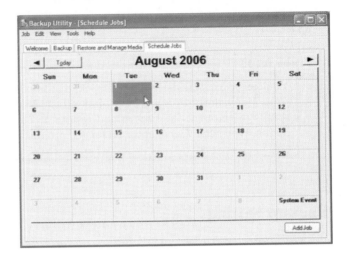

Figure 12-11: The Scheduled Jobs Tab

Restoring Data

To restore data from a backup, start the Backup/Restore utility from the System Tools submenu:

1. From the *Welcome* window, select the *Restore Wizard* option (switch to *Advanced* mode in Windows XP and from the *Welcome* tab, launch the *Restore Wizard* (Advanced).

2. At the *Welcome* window, click on the *Next* button.

3. In the *What to Restore* window, select the appropriate backup file, and the files and folders to be restored as illustrated in Figure 12-12. Click on the *Next* button to continue.

4. In the *Completion* window, click on the *Advanced* button to specify additional options if necessary.

5. Click on the *Finish* button to start the restore process.

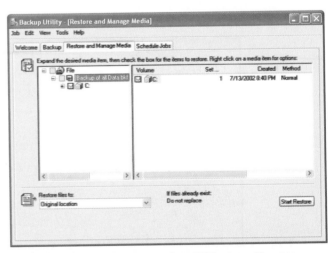

Figure 12-12: Choosing What to Restore

Advanced Restore Settings

If you choose to configure Advanced restore settings, you will be presented with the following series of configuration pages:

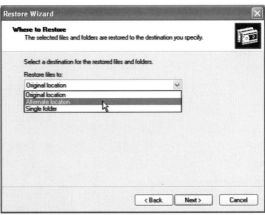

- *Where to Restore*—This option enables you to restore to the *original location*, an *alternate location*, or a *single folder*, as illustrated in Figure 12-13. If you choose to *Restore to an alternate location*, the wizard will ask you to supply a path to restore the files. The folder structure of the backup will be maintained. Selecting the *Restore to a single folder* option will also require a path to use for the restore. However, this option will not preserve the existing folder structure.

- *How to Restore*, this option enables you to determine how the restore will handle files that already exist on the disk. The options include not replacing files on the disk (this is the default option), replacing the files on the disk only if they are older than the backup copy, and always replacing the files on the disk, as illustrated in Figure 12-14.

Figure 12-13: Selecting Where to Restore

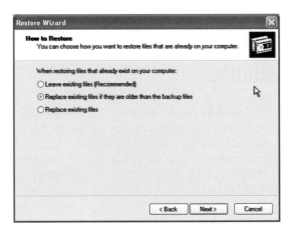

Figure 12-14: Determining How to Restore

System State data

System State Data Backups

In addition to backing up data files and applications, it is often convenient to back up the key system configuration and information as well. This type of data is called **System State Data** and is stored so that the system can be rebuilt quickly in case of a failure. Windows 2000 and Windows XP Backup utilities provide an option specifically to perform System State data backup, as illustrated in Figure 12-15. The System State data can be backed up by itself or as part of the regularly scheduled system backup operation.

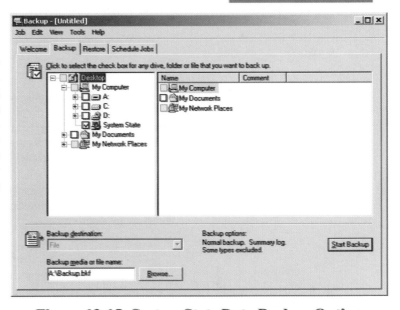

Figure 12-15: System State Data Backup Option

The System State data to be backed up includes

- The contents of the registry

- The System startup files

- Files under Windows File Protection in Windows XP

- The COM+ Class registration database (a database of information about Component Services applications)

When the System State data check box is checked, its individual components are listed in the details pane of the display. The components are dependent on one another and can only be backed up and restored as a set (i.e., there is no way to back the components up individually).

When the System State data are restored to a machine, any existing system state information will be overwritten and destroyed. This can be a problem if an older version of the System State data is copied back into the system (any newer configuration information would be lost).

Backup Scheduling

In business environments, backup operations are a very important part of most company preventive maintenance programs. In these environments, the backup process is scripted into a schedule and a method for performing the backup function. To develop an acceptable backup schedule, you must consider a variety of issues, including when and what type of backup is required to ensure acceptable recovery in case of system failure. At a minimum, you must ask yourself the following questions when considering what type of backup method to use:

- How critical is your data?

- Can the business tolerate losing financial records for the past 24 hours?

- What systems must be reinstated first?

- How far back should you retain system settings?

- How far back might you be asked to go to recover a file?

Time is also a critical element in deciding your Backup Schedule. A full system backup would give you the best assurance of a quick system recovery, but it takes a fair amount of server downtime to perform. Can you afford to have productivity stop just to perform backups? This may not be an issue when backing up a small server system that is measured in megabytes, but when your overall system's data amount is large, measured in multiple gigabytes or terabytes, your server downtime for full backups could adversely affect overall company productivity.

When determining your backup mythology, you must consider when to do your backups and the form of media rotation you will use. The following provides you with a brief discussion on these issues.

- *Daily Backup*—Daily full-system backup provides the best assurance of at least being able to quickly recover all but the last 24 hours of your data. This is only feasible for small systems or portions of a system. For larger systems, a daily regiment of incremental or differential backups would at least assure recovery of your system, again excluding up to the last 24 hours. If your organization determines that specific data are too critical to potentially lose 24 hours worth of information, you may need to backup that specific data on a more rigorous schedule.

- *Weekly Backup*—Normally you can schedule weekly full-system backups during weekends, as long as your company requirements for uptime allow. The overall time required for your weekly backups will depend upon the size of your system and the frequency you apply. Very large companies may require maximum uptime, even during weekend time frames. In these incidences, more aggressive data distribution, backup methods, and more controlled backup scheduling needs to be applied.

- *Unscheduled Backups*—Unscheduled backups occur whenever there is a need that is either unanticipated or does not fit into your regular schedule of backups. A good example is when your server is exhibiting symptoms of potential failure or you are upgrading portions of the system. At these times, or any time you are concerned that the normal backup schedule may not cover a potential loss of data, you should perform an unscheduled backup.

Backup Media Rotation

backup media rotation

Once you ensure that your Backup Plan has the necessary attributes to ensure initial system recovery, you must determine the need of your company to retrieve historical copies of their data. The **backup media rotation** method you employ will determine the historical time frame that you will be able to retrieve data. There are numerous media rotation methods that can be employed, each having its own time frame of recovery. The *Grandfather-Father-Son* method, shown in Figure 12-16, is the most common method employed today.

The Grandfather-Father-Son method uses three different groupings of backup tapes: The *Grandfather* for monthly backups, the *Father* for weekly backups, and the *Son* for daily backups.

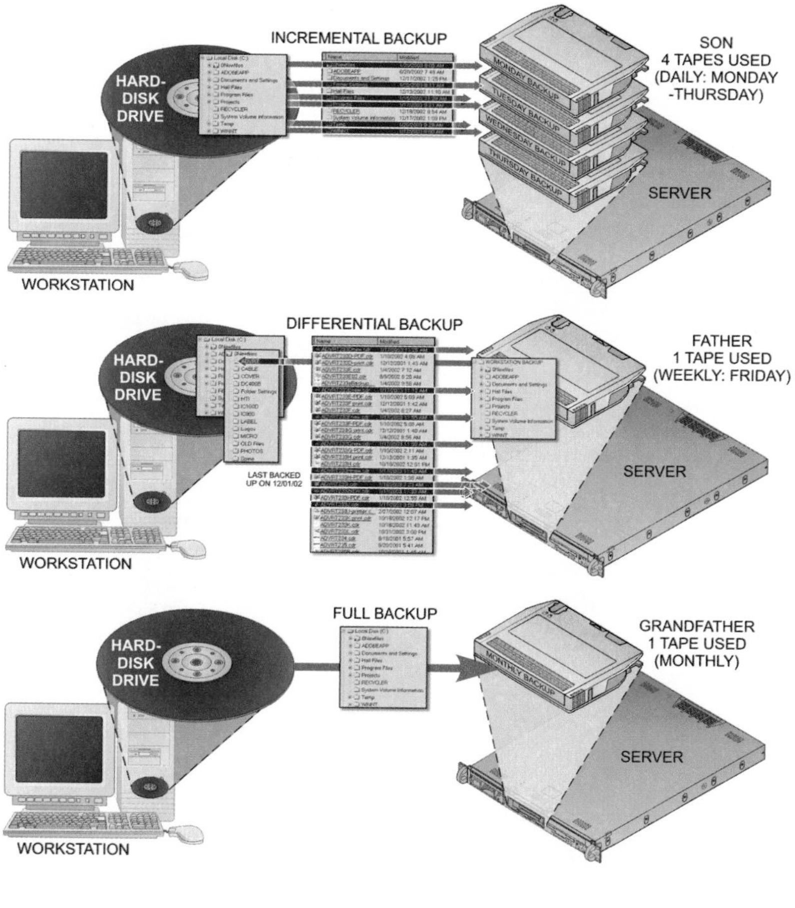

Figure 12-16: The Grandfather-Father-Son Method

The Son uses four tapes, one for every weekday normally covering Monday through Thursday, typically applying the incremental backup method. The Father's weekly backup, normally performed on Friday, uses one tape applying the differential method of backup. After this, you reuse the corresponding Son tapes for the following daily backups. At month's end, you will use one tape to run the Grandfather backup. This backup would be a full backup of the system. Depending upon your company's needs, you may store these tapes to support an ongoing historical backup library, or reuse the tape for future backups.

┌─ NOTE ──┐
It is a good idea to periodically perform restore operations from backups to diverse locations. This will enable you to validate the backups. It would be really bad to wait until the system fails to find out that the backups you've been making on a regular basis don't work. Also, the worst time to learn how to restore data is when you are in the middle of a crisis.
└──┘

Removable Storage Utility

Removable Storage utility

Windows 2000 and XP provide a **Removable Storage utility**, shown in Figure 12-17, that provides a variety of services to system administrators. It enables them to set up, share, and manage the removable media devices attached to the computer. Both the Windows 2000 and third-party Backup applications use the Removable Storage utility to keep track of the identity of all backup media they use. The utility facilitates the actual mounting of the media when requested by the application, while the application keeps track of the actual data written or retrieved from the media.

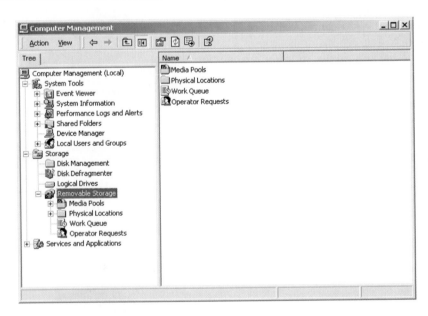

**Figure 12-17:
Microsoft Removable
Storage Utility**

Windows 2000/XP System Management Tools

Essentials 3.3

Technical Support 2.1

IT Technician 3.1

The Windows operating systems also include a number of tools and utilities designed to manage and troubleshoot the Windows environment. These tools typically include utilities for managing system configuration settings, device drivers, and system resources. In Windows 2000 and XP, a number of administrative, diagnostic, and troubleshooting tools are clustered under the Control Panel's **Microsoft Management Console**.

**Microsoft
Management Console**

The System Tools console consolidates a number of utilities that can be used to configure and track all of the system's hardware and software components, in addition to configuring network options and viewing system events. The major tools gathered in this console by default include

- Event viewer

- System information

- Performance logs and alerts

- Device manager

- Local users and groups

Event Viewer

In Windows 2000 and Windows XP, significant events (such as system events, application events, and security events) are routinely monitored and stored. These events can be viewed through the **Event Viewer** utility depicted in Figure 12-18. As described earlier, this tool is located under the *Control Panel/Administrative Tools/Computer Management* path.

IT Technician 3.1

Event Viewer

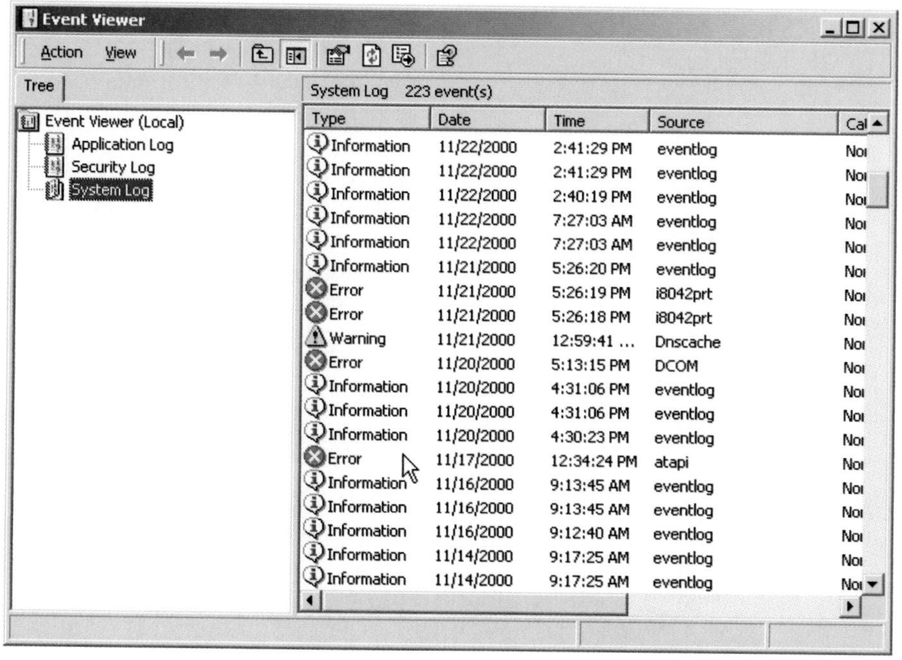

**Figure 12-18:
Windows 2000
Event Viewer**

System events include items such as successful and failed Windows component start-ups, as well as successful loading of device drivers. Likewise, application events include information about how the system's applications are performing. Not all Windows applications generate events that the Event Viewer will log. Finally, security events are produced by user actions such as log-ons and log-offs, file and folder accesses, and creation of new Active Directory accounts.

Three default event logs track and record the events just mentioned. The system log records events generated by the operating system and its components. The application log tracks events generated by high-end applications. Likewise, the security log contains information generated by audit policies that have been enacted in the operating system. If no audit policies are configured, the security log will remain empty.

In addition to the default logs, some special systems such as domain controllers and DNS systems will have specialized logs to track events specifically related to the function of the system.

The Event Viewer produces three categories of system and application events:

- *Information events*—Events that indicate an application, service, or driver has loaded successfully. These events require no intervention.

- *Warning events*—Events that have no immediate impact but that could have future significance. These events should be investigated.

- *Error events*—Events that indicate an application, service, or driver has failed to load successfully. These events require immediate intervention.

System Information

Notice in the figure that the Information events are denoted by a small "i" in a cloud, whereas exclamation marks (!) and Xs are used to identify Warning and Error events, respectively.

Windows 2000/XP System Information

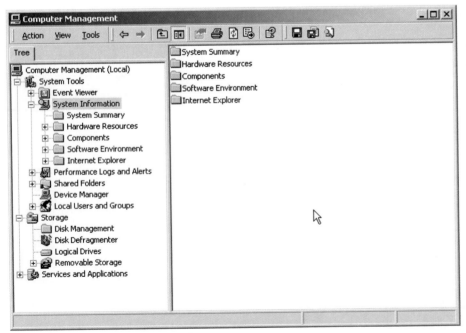

The Windows 2000 **System Information** utility, depicted in Figure 12-19, provides five subfolders of information about the system. These folders include a System Summary, a list of Hardware Resources being used, a list of I/O Components in the system, a description of the system's current Software Environment, and a description of the Windows Internet Explorer.

Figure 12-19: The Windows 2000/XP System Information Utility

The System Information tool can be used to enable remote service providers to inspect the system's information across a LAN environment. To save system information to a file, right-click the *System Information* entry and select the *Save As* option from the resulting menu. Saving this information enables you to document events and conditions when errors occur. You can use the results of different system information files to compare situations and perhaps determine what changes may have occurred to cause the problem.

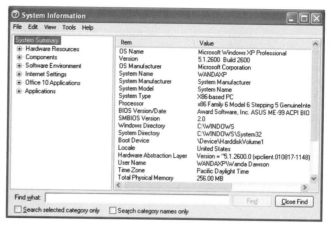

In Windows XP systems, the System Information tool can be accessed through the Start/Run menu by typing *msinfo32.exe* in the *Run* dialog box. You can also access the Windows XP System Information tool by navigating the *Start/All Programs/ Accessories/ System Tools* path and selecting the *System Information* option. Both methods will produce the Windows XP System Information console depicted in Figure 12-20.

Figure 12-20: Windows XP System Information

The contents of the System Information utility can be saved or exported to a file so it can be saved for troubleshooting or optimization purposes. Both of these functions can be performed through the utility's File menu. Using the *Save* option stores the data in a .NFO format that can read again by the System Information utility. The export function saves the information to a text file that can be read with any standard text editor (i.e., Notepad).

One of the biggest reasons to save the System Information is for troubleshooting use when system errors occur. By saving System Information when the system is functioning properly, you can compare it to information obtained when a failure occurs. The other reason to save System information is to establish performance baselines that can be used to measure the effectiveness of changes that are made to the system. If an upgrade is performed and the System Information report shows diminished performance characteristics, then you can reverse the upgrade effort.

The Windows XP System Information Tools menu, depicted in Figure 12-21, provides additional access to many of the system's troubleshooting and administrative tools.

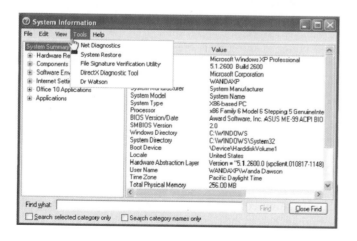

Figure 12-21: Windows XP System Information/ Tools Menu

Task Manager

In Windows 2000 and Windows XP, the **Task Manager** is a utility that can be used to determine which applications in the system are running or stopped, as well as which resources are being used. You can also determine general microprocessor and memory usage levels using this tool.

When a Windows application hangs up, the system may **lock up** and stop working. When this occurs, you can access the Task Manager window depicted in Figure 12-22 and remove it from the list of tasks. The Windows 2000 and Windows XP Task Managers can be accessed by pressing CTRL+ALT+DEL or by pressing CTRL+SHIFT+ESC.

TEST TIP

Be able to access the Task Manager in Windows 2000 and Windows XP and be aware that it can be used to remove nonfunctioning applications from the system.

Figure 12-22: Task Manager

You can also access the Task Manager by right-clicking the system tray and selecting *Task Manager* from the pop-up contextual menu. The CTRL+SHIFT+ESC key sequence moves directly into Task Manager, while the CTRL+ALT+DEL selection opens the Windows Security menu screen, which offers Task Manager as an option.

To use the Task Manager, select the application from the list on the *Applications* tab and press the *End Task* button. If prompted, press the *End Task* button again to confirm the selection. The *Performance* tab provides a graphical summary of the system's CPU and memory usage. The *Process* tab provides information that can be helpful in tracking down problems associated with slow system operation.

Device Manager

Hardware and configuration conflicts also can be isolated manually using the Windows 2000/XP **Device Manager** from the Control Panel's *System* icon. This utility is basically an easy-to-use interface for the Windows 2000/XP registries. You can use the Device Manager, depicted in Figure 12-23, to identify installed ports, update device drivers, and change I/O settings. From this window, the problem device can be examined to see where the conflict is occurring.

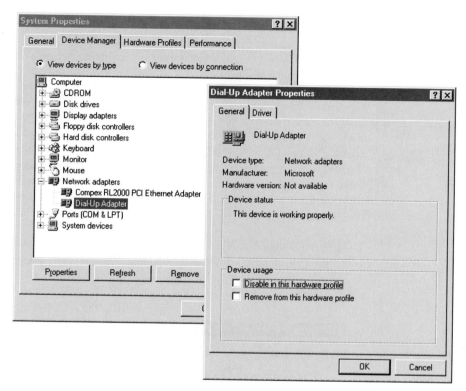

Figure 12-23: The Device Manager's Display

Two radio buttons on the *Device Manager* page can be used to alter the way it displays the devices installed in the system. Clicking the left button (the page's default setting) displays the system's devices alphabetically by device type. The rightmost radio button shows the devices by their connection to the system. As with the registry and Policy Editors, the presence of plus (+) and minus (−) signs in the nodes of the devices indicates expandable and collapsible information branches at those nodes.

The Device Manager will display an exclamation point (!) inside a yellow circle whenever a device is experiencing a direct hardware conflict with another device. The nature of the problem is described in the device's Properties dialog box. Similarly, when a red X appears at the device's icon, the device has been disabled due to a user-selection conflict.

```
┌─ TEST TIP ─────────────┐
│ Memorize symbols used by the │
│ Windows Device Manager.      │
└──────────────────────────────┘
```

This situation can occur when a user wishes to disable a selected device without removing it. For example, a user who travels and uses a notebook computer may want to temporarily disable device drivers for options that aren't used in travel. This can be accomplished through the Device Manager's *Disable in this hardware profile* option. This will keep the driver from loading up until it is reactivated. Clicking the *Properties* button at the bottom of the *Device Manager* screen produces the selected device's Properties sheet. The three tabs at the top of the page provide access to the device's General information, Driver specifications, and System resource assignments.

```
┌─ TEST TIP ─────────────────────┐
│ Be aware of how to temporarily disable device │
│ drivers that are not needed in certain situations, │
│ yet retain them in the system for future use.    │
└──────────────────────────────────┘
```

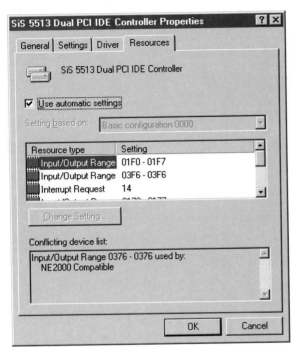

Figure 12-24: The Device Manager Resources Page

Figure 12-25: The Device Manager Computer Properties Page

When a device conflict is suspected, just click the offending device in the listing, make sure that the selected device is the current device, and then click the *Resources* tab to examine the conflicting device's list, as depicted in Figure 12-24.

To change the resources allocated to a device, click the resource to be changed, remove the checkmark from the *Use Automatic Settings* box, click the *Change Setting* button, and scroll through the resource options. Take care when changing resource settings. The *Resource Settings* window displays all the available resources in the system, even those that are already spoken for by another device. You must know which resources are acceptable for a given type of device and which ones are already in use.

To determine what resources the system already has in use, click the *Computer* icon at the top of the Device Manager display. The *Computer Properties* page, depicted in Figure 12-25, provides ways to view and reserve system resources.

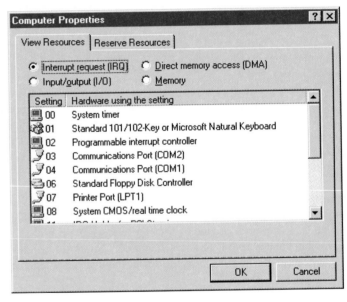

Through this page, you can click radio buttons to display the system's usage of four key resources: IRQ channels, DMA channels, I/O addresses, and memory addresses. The *Reserve Resources* page is used to set aside key resources to avoid conflicts with the PnP configuration operations. If a resource is reserved and Windows detects it as already in use, a warning dialog box displays on-screen and asks for a confirmation.

Normal causes for conflict include devices sharing IRQ settings, I/O address settings, DMA channels, or base memory settings. The most common conflicts are those dealing with the IRQ channels. Nonessential peripherals, such as sound and network adapters, are most likely to produce this type of conflict.

When a device conflict is reported through the *Resource* tab's *Conflicting Device* list, record the current settings for each device, refer to the documentation for each device to determine what other settings might be used, and change the settings for the most flexible device. If either device continues to exhibit problems, reset the configurations to their original positions, and change the settings for the other device.

Make sure that the device has not been installed twice. When this occurs, it is normally impossible to determine which driver is correct. Therefore, it will be necessary to remove both drivers and allow the PnP process to redetect the device. If multiple drivers are present for a given device, remove the drivers that are not specific to the particular device installed in the system.

Using MSCONFIG.EXE

If a startup problem disappears when the system is started using any of the Safe modes, use the command line **System Configuration Utility (MSCONFIG.EXE)** to isolate the conflicting items. The Windows XP System Configuration utility, depicted in Figure 12-26, provides several tabs that can be used to selectively omit startup sequences and actions that may be preventing the system from starting up normally.

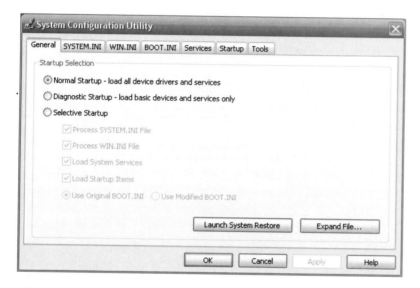

Figure 12-26: The System Configuration Utility

Select the **Diagnostic Startup** option to start the system using only the basic device drivers and services. This option is equivalent with the standard Safe Mode startup. If the system starts using this option, advance to the **Selective Startup** option and restart the system. The *Selective Startup* option interactively loads device drivers and software options according to the check boxes enabled on the *General* tab.

Start the troubleshooting process with only one box checked. If the system starts up with that box checked, add another box to the list and restart. When the system fails to start, move into the tab that corresponds to the last option you enabled and step through the check boxes for that file, one at a time until the system fails again. You can use the *Edit* button to manually edit the lines of the file. This step-by-step process is used to systematically enable or disable items until all the problem items are identified.

The *Expand File* button is used to extract individual Windows files directly from the cabinet files on the distribution/installation media, under the I386 folder. The *Launch System Restore* button can be used to restore the system if changes made to the configuration increase the level of the problem. You should use this button to create a Restore Point before you begin troubleshooting.

┌─ **TEST TIP** ─────
Know what types of problems the MSCONFIG.EXE utility is used for.
└────────────────────

Windows XP Driver Rollback Feature

The Windows XP operating system includes a new option that can be used to revert to an older device driver when a driver upgrade causes problems with a device. This feature is called **Driver Rollback** and can be implemented through the Windows XP Device Manager. To roll back the driver, simply right-click on the device in the Device Manager listing and select the *Properties* option. Click on the *Driver* tab followed by the *Roll Back Driver* button, depicted in Figure 12-27.

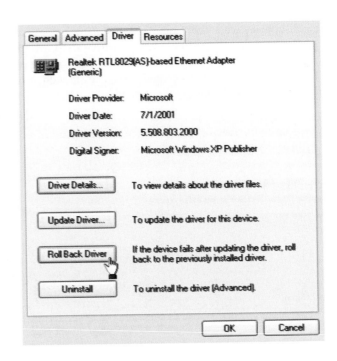

**Figure 12-27:
Device Manager/
Roll Back Driver
Option**

File Management Tools

The primary file management tool in all Windows versions is the *Windows Explorer* described in Chapter 10. Its File and Edit menus enable you to create, delete, rename, and reposition files and folders in the Windows system. It also provides access to the attributes associated with each file and folder in the system. This is a feature primarily intended for technicians. During many repair processes, technicians need to access system files that are typically hidden from view. To show the hidden files in Windows 2000 and XP Explorer, select the drop-down Tools menu, click on the *Folder Options*, click on the *View* tab, and select the *Show hidden files and folders* option.

The command line also provides very powerful file management capabilities. You can always access a file from the command prompt and change its attributes with the ATTRIB command. Another command-line tool that PC technicians should be aware of is the Extract command. This utility is used to pull needed files from the Windows distribution media, so that they can be used to replace corrupted or missing files that are preventing the system from working.

System Editors

The Windows 2000 and XP operating systems contain several important editors:

- Two *text editors—Edit* and *System Editor* (*SysEdit*)
- Two *registry Editors—RegEdit* and *RegEdt32*
- The *Group Policy Editor* (*GPE*)

The two command line–based text editor programs, **EDIT.COM** and the *System Editor* (**SYSEDIT.EXE**) program, depicted in Figure 12-28, enable users to easily modify text files such as the BOOT.INI and other initialization files as needed.

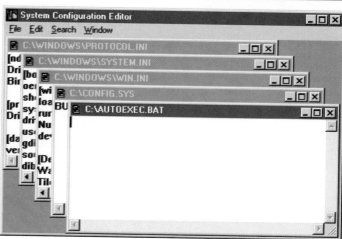

You can start the Edit version of the text editor by typing the EDIT command and the filename at the command prompt. To start the SysEdit function, select the *Run* option from the Start menu. Type *SYSEDIT* in the *Run* dialog box, and click the *OK* button. The SysEdit commands are similar to those of other Windows-based text editing programs, such as Notepad or Write.

The Windows registry is a very complex structure that can accumulate invalid entries and become corrupt. These are typically caused by incorrect removal of applications, missing or corrupt device drivers, or non-existent startup programs. Still other registry problems are caused by viruses and spyware programs that track system activity. Over time this corruption can cause the system to simply crash and not run, provide unpredictable operation, or cause it to issue an error message indicating that a particular type of problem has occurred. Common registry corruption errors include:

Figure 12-28: The Windows System Editor Screen

- Different Stop errors
- .dll errors
- Runtime errors
- Missing file or program errors

When these symptoms or error messages appear you will need to repair the registry to get back to normal operations. This can be accomplished by performing a restore point operation, restoring the registry from a backup, editing the registry, or by reinstalling Windows.

TEST TIP

Be aware of which Windows utilities can be used to make changes to the registry in Windows 2000 and Windows XP.

Windows 2000 and Windows XP include two registry editors—**RegEdit** and **RegEdt32**. RegEdit is an older registry editor that was used with previous Windows versions but retains some features not available in the newer RegEdt version. Both utilities enable you to add, edit, and remove registry entries and to perform other basic functions. However, specific functions can be performed only in one editor or the other. RegEdt32 presents each subtree as an individual entity in a separate window. The subtrees are presented as being part of the same entity in a single window, as illustrated in Figure 12-29.

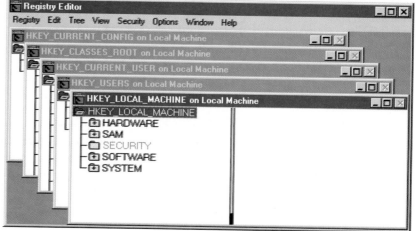

Figure 12-29: RegEdt32 Registry Editor

The registry has a permissions system that is similar to NTFS permissions, which enables you to control access to the keys and assigned values. RegEdt32 enables you to view and set permissions through the *Security* menu. RegEdit does not allow you to access the permissions system.

The Find capabilities of RegEdt32 are accessed from the View menu and are very limited. You can search only for keys, not assigned values or their corresponding data. This is the equivalent of being able to search for folders in the file system but not for files. Also, you can initiate a search in only one subtree at a time. The Find capabilities of RegEdit are accessed through the Edit menu and are very strong. You have the option to search for keys and assigned values, and you can search all subtrees at once. RegEdit also enables you to save frequently accessed registry locations as favorites to enable quicker access.

> ## WARNING
>
> Editing the registry with RegEdit or RegEdt32 should be done only when you have no other alternative. These editors bypass all the safeguards provided by the standard utilities and allow you to enter values that are invalid or that conflict with other settings. Incorrect editing of the registry can cause Windows 2000 to stop functioning correctly, prompting a significant amount of troubleshooting or a reinstall of the operating system.

Dr. Watson

The main tool for isolating and correcting *application errors* is the *Dr. Watson* utility provided in all Windows versions. It is used to trace problems that appear under certain conditions, such as starting or using a certain application. When Dr. Watson is started, it runs in the background with only an icon appearing on the taskbar to signify that it is present. For problems that cannot be directly attributed to the Windows operating system, an application program might be the source of the problem, and the Dr. Watson utility should be set up to run in the background as the system operates.

DRWATSON.LOG

As the system operates, the Dr. Watson utility monitors the code moving through the system and logs its key events in the **DRWTSN32.LOG** file. When a system error occurs, the Dr. Watson log contains a listing of the events that were going on up to the time of the failure. This log provides programmers with a detailed listing of the events that led up to the failure. The information is automatically stored in the log file that can be provided to software developers, or to Microsoft, so that they can debug their software and produce patches for it. In many cases, the program will describe the nature of the error and possibly suggest a fix.

┌ TEST TIP ──
Know which Windows utility can be used to monitor the operation of application packages and log errors so that they can be reported to software developers for repairing their programs.

drwtsn32

The Dr. Watson utility is not located in any of the Windows 2000/XP menus. To use it, you must execute the program from the Start menu's *Run* option by typing the name **drwtsn32** in the dialog box and clicking *OK* to start the log file.

┌ TEST TIP ──
Be aware of where the Dr. Watson utility is located and what it is used for.

System File Checker

The **System File Checker utility (SFC.EXE)** is a Windows 2000/XP command-line utility that checks the system's protected files for changed, deleted, or possibly corrupt files. If it finds such files, it attempts to extract the original correct versions of the files from Windows files in the *\system32\dllcache* folder. **SFC** can be used to verify that the protected system files are the appropriate versions and to verify and replace files in the *dllcache* folder. The latter insures that files used to replace invalid operating system files are actually valid.

The System File Checker can be run manually, or can be configured to run automatically when the system starts up. You can also use the **Scheduled Tasks** utility to configure SFC to run at specified intervals. You must have administrative privileges to run System File Checker. Table 12-1 lists the switches that can be used to modify the SFC operation. The actual run process is very quick on modern PCs and only flashes on the screen for an instance.

> System File Checker utility (SFC.EXE)
>
> SFC
>
> Scheduled Tasks

SWITCH	ACTION PERFORMED
/scannow	This switch immediately scans all protected system files when it is activated. This operation is only carried out one time and requires access to the Windows 2000 or XP installation source files.
/scanonce	Scans all protected system files, once at the next boot. Requires access to the Windows XP installation source files.
/scanboot	Scans all protected system files, every time the system is booted. Requires access to the Windows XP installation source files.
/revert	This switch returns scan to the default setting.
/purgecach	This switch purges the dllcache folder and immediately scans all protected file system files.
/cachesize=x	Sets the maximum size of the dllcache folder.

Table 12-1: SFC Switches

Windows Troubleshooting Help Files

Windows 2000 and Windows XP come with built-in troubleshooting **Help file systems**. The **Windows Troubleshooters** are a special type of context-specific help that is available in Windows 2000 and XP. These interactive files enable you to pinpoint problems and identify solutions to problems by asking a series of questions and then providing you with detailed troubleshooting information based on your responses to those questions. This feature includes troubleshooting assistance for a number of different Windows problems.

> Help file systems
>
> Windows Troubleshooters

In both systems, the *Troubleshooter* utilities can be accessed from the Start menu, from the Help menu entry on the toolbar, or through the Device Manager. Selecting the *Help* entry from the Start or toolbar menus produces the Windows 2000 *Help Topics* window, shown in Figure 12-30.

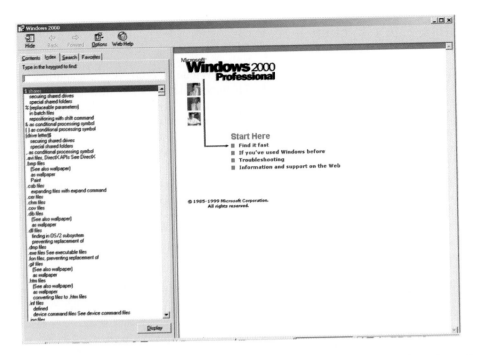

Figure 12-30: The Windows 2000 Help Topics Window

The Windows 2000 local Help screens are manipulated by making selections from the various tabs (i.e., Contents, Index, Search, and Favorites). Double-clicking the *Troubleshooting and Maintenance* entry on the *Contents* tab menu will expose the *Windows 2000 Troubleshooters* option. Selecting this option will produce the list of *Troubleshooter* routines depicted in the right-hand pane of Figure 12-31.

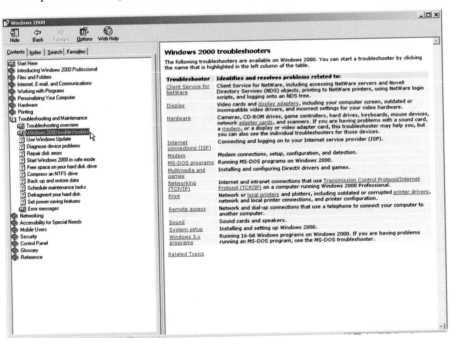

Figure 12-31: Windows 2000 Troubleshooter Options

This window contains a list of several entries with information about common Windows problems and situations. Clicking on one of the listed topics will produce an interactive troubleshooting process in the right-hand pane of the window that is associated with that particular problem (for instance, modem problems). The interactive text contains a step-by-step procedure for isolating the problem listed. Simply follow the questions and suggestion schemes provided.

The *Index* tab provides an index of topics that can be searched using keywords (i.e., Hardware/Conflict Troubleshooting) as illustrated in Figure 12-32. Several troubleshooting procedures can be accessed through this tab. Simply type the word "troubleshooting" in the keyword dialog box, and select the appropriated topic from the list.

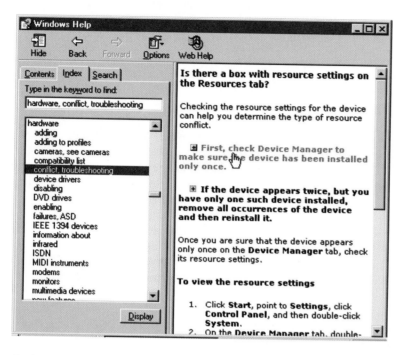

Figure 12-32: Using the Help/Index Tab

The *Search* tab can be used to conduct a search of all the Windows help and support materials for key topics such as troubleshooting. Enter the word, and click on the *List Topics* button to conduct the search.

In Windows XP, clicking the *Help and Support* option from the Start menu produces the *Help and Support* window depicted in Figure 12-33. This window looks considerably different than the Windows 2000 version. It also brings several new tools to the Help function.

One of the most significant improvements to the Help system in Windows XP is the search option that checks its local help files and produces a suggestion list of material as well as provides access to its full local text file. In addition, the search function will search the *Microsoft Knowledge Base* for extended information about the topic you enter.

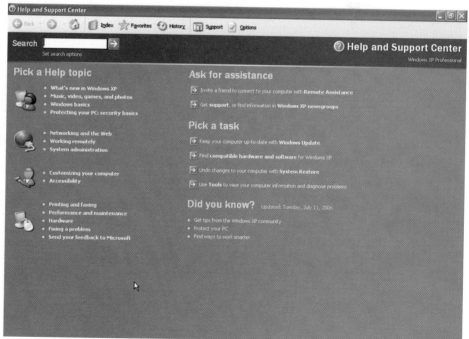

Figure 12-33: Windows XP Help and Support Center

Other Information and Troubleshooting Resources

You can turn to many resources outside of the operating system for information and troubleshooting assistance, such as Windows Resource Kits, the Internet, and Microsoft TechNet. The following sections discuss these additional resources.

Windows Resource Kits

Resource Kits

The Windows 95, 98, NT 4.0, 2000, and XP **Resource Kits** provide thousands of pages of in-depth technical information on these Windows operating systems, as well as hundreds of additional utilities that you can use to enhance deployment, maintenance, and troubleshooting of your Windows network. The Resource Kits are excellent printed references for Windows and also come with searchable electronic versions.

There are two different versions of the Resource Kit for each NT operating system—one for Windows NT Workstation and one for Windows NT Server (as well as one for Windows 2000 or Windows XP Professional, and one for Windows 2000 Server). The Resource Kits are published by Microsoft Press and are available from major book retailers.

Internet Help

online Help

You can activate the Windows 2000 or Windows XP **online Help** functions by selecting a topic from the menu and then clicking the menu bar's *Web Help* button. Afterward, you must click on the *Support On-line* option at the lower right of the Help window. This action brings up the Internet Sign-In dialog box, if the system is not already logged on to the Internet. After signing in, the Microsoft technical support page appears, as depicted in Figure 12-34.

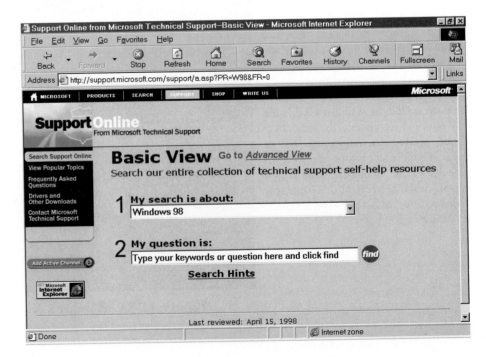

**Figure 12-34:
Microsoft Online
Help Window**

Microsoft's online **Product Support Services** can provide a wealth of information about Microsoft products, including their operating systems. The URL for Product Support Services is *www.Microsoft.com/support*. Features of Microsoft Product Support include the following:

Product Support Services

- The **Microsoft Knowledge Base** is a searchable database of information and self-help tools. The Knowledge Base is used by Microsoft Technical Support to support their customers and is made available to you free of charge.

Microsoft Knowledge Base

- The **Download Center** enables you to search all available downloads for any Microsoft product, including service packs, patches, and updates.

Download Center

- *Facts by Product* enables you to browse for information by product, and it includes a list of most frequently asked questions about each product.

- A listing of support phone numbers is given that can be used to access live assistance. A charge applies for phone support.

- *Online Support Requests* permits you to submit questions to Microsoft support personnel. A charge applies for online support.

Microsoft TechNet

Microsoft's **TechNet** Web site is designed to support IT professionals. The URL for this site is www.Microsoft.com/technet. This is an excellent site for getting the latest information about Windows 2000 or XP (and all other Microsoft products and technologies).

TechNet

TechNet features include the following:

- Search capabilities for the Technical Information database and the Knowledge Base.

- A What's New section that highlights new issues every month.

- Access to the Product Support Services Web site.

- Information categorized by product to help you troubleshoot, maintain, and deploy software.

- Chats, user groups, and Feedback Central for communicating with your peers and with Microsoft.

Microsoft also provides a TechNet subscription service. For an annual fee, the Technical Information database, Knowledge Base, service packs, patches, fixes, software utilities, product enhancements, Resource Kits, beta versions of future Microsoft products, training information, and many other useful items will be shipped to you each month in CD-ROM format. A TechNet subscription can be purchased at the TechNet Web site.

TROUBLESHOOTING WINDOWS

The general procedures for troubleshooting operating system problems are similar to those presented in the previous chapter for hardware failures. Begin by talking to the operator to determine what has been done to the system, or what they are trying to do that might cause the failure.

Perform tests and make changes to the operating system one at a time, taking time to evaluate the effects of the change before making additional changes. Also take time to document the steps you take along with the outcome of each step.

Finally, refer to any available information and troubleshooting resources to assist in the troubleshooting and repair process. These resources include users manuals, online tutorials and vendor documentation.

As you have seen in previous chapters, operating systems are tremendous collections of complex programming code brought together to control every operation of the computer hardware and link it to the software applications that users want to employ. As with anything so complex, operating systems fail from time to time—some more than others—and although potentially millions of things can go wrong with complex software systems, you should be happy to know that you can group operating system problems into three basic areas:

- Setup problems (those that occur during installation or upgrading)

- Start-up problems (those that occur when the system is booting up)

- Operational problems (those that occur during the normal course of operations)

By isolating a particular software problem to one of these areas, the troubleshooting process becomes less complex.

Setup problems typically involve failure to complete an OS install or upgrade operation. In some cases, this can leave the system stranded between an older OS version and a newer OS version, making the system unusable.

Start-up problems usually produce conditions that prevent the system hardware and software from coming up and running correctly. These problems fall into two major groups:

- Hardware configuration problems

- OS bootup problems

Operational problems are problems that occur after the system has booted up and started running. These problems fall into three main categories:

- When performing normal application and file operations

- When printing

- When performing network functions

TROUBLESHOOTING SETUP PROBLEMS

Setup problems are those errors that occur during the process of installing the operating system on the hard-disk drive. With early MS-DOS versions, installation was a simple matter of making a \DOS directory on the hard drive and copying the contents of the DOS disks into it. For operating system versions from MS-DOS 5.0 forward, however, the installation procedure became an automated process requiring an Install or Setup program to be run.

One of the most common OS setup problems involves situations in which the system's hard drive does not have enough free space to carry out the installation process. When this occurs, you must remove files from the disk until you have cleared enough room to perform the installation. Unless you can remove enough obsolete files from the drive to make room for the new operating system, it is recommended that the files be backed up to some other media before erasing them from the drive.

Setup problems also occur when the system's hardware will not support the operating system that is being installed. These errors can include the following:

- Microprocessor requirements
- Insufficient memory problems
- Memory speed mismatches
- Incompatible device drivers

The memory speed mismatch or mixed RAM-type problem produces a **Windows Protection Error** message during the installation process. This error indicates that the operating system is having timing problems that originate from the RAM memory used in the system. Correcting this problem involves swapping the system's RAM for devices that meet the system's timing requirements.

Windows Protection Error

It is not uncommon for mouse or video drivers to fail during the installation of an operating system. If the video driver fails, you must normally turn off the system and attempt to reinstall the operating system from scratch. Conversely, if the mouse driver fails during the install, it is possible to continue the process using the keyboard. This problem is normally self-correcting after the system reboots.

A similar problem occurs when the operating system is looking for a PS/2 mouse and the system is using a serial mouse. It will not detect the serial mouse, and you will need to complete the installation process using the keyboard. Afterward, you can check the CMOS *Port Settings* for the serial port the mouse is connected to, and install the correct driver for the serial mouse if necessary.

The best way to avoid hardware-compatibility problems is to consult Microsoft's Web site to verify that the hardware you are using is compatible with the operating system version you are installing.

Most error messages produced during an operating system installation stop the system. However, some errors offer to continue the process. It is our experience that continuing the installation rarely works out. Instead, just shut down the system, attempt to clear the problem, and then reinstall the operating system.

Windows 2000 Setup Problems

Blue Screen of Death (BSOD)

When an attempt to install Windows 2000 or Windows XP fails, a *Stop screen* error will normally result. Stop errors occur when the Windows operating system detects a condition from which it cannot recover. The system stops responding, and a screen of information with a blue or black background displays, as illustrated in Figure 12-35. Stop errors are also known as Blue Screen errors, or the "**Blue Screen of Death (BSOD)**." Troubleshooting these types of errors is discussed in more detail later in the chapter.

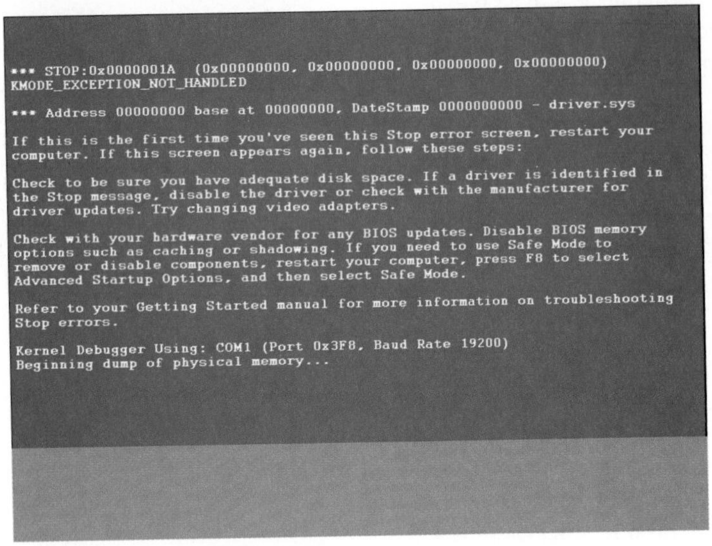

Some other problems can typically occur during the Windows 2000 installation process. These problems include items such as the following:

- Noncompliant hardware failures
- Insufficient resources
- File system type choices
- The installation process starts over after rebooting
- WINNT32.EXE will not run from the command-line errors

Figure 12-35: Stop Error or Blue Screen Error

blue screen error

Hardware Compatibility List

TEST TIP

Be aware that you should check hardware manufacturer's web sites for updated device drivers before installing Windows 2000.

Ways to correct these particular installation-related problems include the following:

- *Verify Hardware Compatibility*—The hardware-compatibility requirements of Windows 2000 and Windows XP are more stringent than those of the Windows 9x platform. When either of these operating systems encounters hardware that is not compatible during the setup phase, they fail. In some cases, the system incorrectly detects the hardware, whereas in other cases, the system produces a **blue screen error**.

  Make certain to check the **Hardware Compatibility List** to ensure that your hardware is compatible with Windows 2000. If the hardware is not listed, contact the hardware vendor to determine whether they support Windows 2000/XP before starting the installation.

- *Verify Minimum System Resource Requirements*—Also, make certain that your hardware meets the minimum hardware requirements, including the memory, free disk space, and video requirements. When the Windows 2000 or Windows XP Setup routine detects insufficient resources (that is, processor, memory, or disk space), it either informs you that an error has occurred and halts or it just hangs up and refuses to continue the install.

- *Establish the File System Type*—During the installation process, you must decide which file system you are going to use. If you are going to dual-boot to Windows 9X, and have a drive that is larger than 2 GB, you must choose FAT32. Choosing NTFS for a dual-boot system renders the NTFS partition unavailable when you boot to Windows 9X. FAT16 does not support drives larger than 2 GB. You can upgrade from FAT16 to FAT32 or from FAT32 to NTFS; however, you can never revert to the older file system after you have converted it. You should also be aware that Windows NT 4.0 does not support FAT32 partitions. Therefore, Windows NT 4.0 or earlier cannot be used on a Windows 9x drive. Consider using the lowest common file system during installation and upgrade later.

- *Installation Process Reboots*—If you discover after the initial installation of Windows 2000, and the subsequent rebooting of the system to finish the installation, that the installation program seems to start over again, check the CD-ROM drive for the installation disc. Leaving the bootable CD-ROM in the CD player normally causes this condition, because the BIOS settings instruct the computer to check for a bootable CD-ROM before looking on the hard drive for an operating system. To correct this problem, remove the Windows 2000 CD from the player, or change the CMOS Setup configuration's boot sequence so that it does not check the CD player during bootup.

- *WINNT32 Will Not Run from the Command Prompt*—The **WINNT32.EXE** program is designed to run under a 32-bit operating system and will not run from the command line. It is used to initiate upgrades from Windows 9x or Windows NT to Windows 2000 or Windows XP. If you attempt to upgrade to Windows 2000 or Windows XP from a 16-bit operating system, such as MS-DOS or Windows 95a, you must run the **WINNT.EXE** program from the command line to initiate the installation.

WINNT32.EXE

WINNT.EXE

In most cases, a failure during the Windows 2000 setup process produces an unusable system. When this occurs, you usually must reformat the disk and reinstall the system files from the Windows 2000 Setup (boot) disks.

Windows XP Setup Problems

As with the other operating system version, there are many things that can cause Windows XP installations to fail. If a setup attempt fails during the installation process, you will be left with a system that has no workable operating system in place. If this occurs, determine whether there are any hardware/software application conflict problems that could keep the system from starting. If not, you should start up the system from some type of bootable media and attempt to determine what might be happening that would keep Windows XP from installing. Finally, if nothing appears as a likely cause of the problem, attempt to reinstall the Windows XP operating system from scratch.

If the Windows Setup wizard does not detect sufficient hard disk space on the drive, a *Stop error* will be created. If this occurs, try to remove files and programs to free up the needed disk space. You can also create an additional partition to hold Windows XP, or delete the existing partition and create a larger partition.

You should also verify that the system's hard drive and CD-ROM drives are on the **Windows XP HCL**. If the drives are not acceptable to the system, it will be difficult to conduct the install. You should receive errors during the text-based portion of the Windows XP Setup routine. If the drives are not on the HCL, you can attempt to load **OEM drivers** for the devices from an OEM CD-ROM or floppy by pressing the F6 key when prompted and accessing the drivers on the disk.

Windows XP HCL

OEM drivers

BIOS-based antivirus utilities can prevent operating systems from being installed or upgraded. When the Setup utility attempts to make the hard disk Windows XP bootable, a **BIOS-based virus scanner** will interpret this action as an attempt by a virus to infect the system. In these cases, the system will produce an error message indicating that a virus is attempting to infect the boot sector. To prevent this from happening, disable the virus protection through the CMOS Setup utility and then enable it again after the operating system has been installed.

BIOS-based virus scanner

Generally, most other failures during the installation process involve hardware detection problems or component installation errors. If the Windows XP installation process fails during the hardware detection phase of the process, check the system for devices that are not listed on the Windows XP HCL. Because of Windows 2000 and Windows XP's relative intolerance for unapproved devices, you should verify that all the system's hardware components are listed on the HCL. If any component is not on the list, remove it, restart the installation process, and see whether the process advances past the error.

Upgrade Problems

You will encounter many of the same problems performing an operating system upgrade that you do when performing a clean install. To review, these problems are normally related to the following:

- Insufficient hard drive or partition sizes

- Memory speed mismatches

- Insufficient memory problems

- Incompatible device drivers

version incompatibilities

Incompatible Version error

While performing upgrade operations, you can also encounter problems created by **version incompatibilities**. New versions of operating systems are typically produced in two styles—full versions and upgrade versions. In some cases, you cannot use a full version of the operating system to upgrade an existing operating system. Doing so will produce an **Incompatible Version error** message telling you that you cannot use this version to upgrade. You must either obtain an upgrade version of the operating system or partition the drive and perform a new installation (losing your existing data).

┌─ **TEST TIP** ─────────────┐
Know how to display the current version of
Windows information for a system.
└──────────────────────────┘

In order to determine the current version and service pack level of a Windows operating system running on a computer, right-click on the *My Computer* icon, select the *Properties* option from the pop-up menu, and view the *General* tab of the System Properties window. Another way to get the version of Windows is to open Windows Explorer, click on the *Help* menu, and select *About Windows*.

Technical Support 2.3

IT Technician 3.3

TROUBLESHOOTING START-UP PROBLEMS

Fortunately, only a few problems can occur during the start-up process of a disk-based computer. These problems include the following:

- Hardware problems

- Configuration problems

- Bootup (or Operating System start-up) problems

- Operating system desktop GUI won't load.

All four of the previously listed problem types can result in start-up failures. Some prevent any activity from appearing in the system, others produce symptoms that can be tracked to a cause, and yet others produce error messages that can be tracked to a source. When dealing with starting up a disk operating system, the following four things can prove very useful to help you isolate the cause of start-up problems:

- Error messages and beep codes

- Clean boot disks (Emergency Start Disks)

- Operating system start-up tools

- System log files

If the system will not boot up correctly, there are two possible actions you can take:

- Boot the system into an alternative boot mode

- Boot the system to a different device, such as a floppy-disk drive or a CD-ROM drive

If the system fails to start-up properly, the Windows operating systems offer a variety of alternative start-up tools to work with. These tools can be used to start the system in minimized configurations or to look around the system after an *alternative boot mode* has been successful. They typically boot the system to some minimized configuration level that bypasses selected unnecessary configuration and GUI-related settings to establish a point at which to begin troubleshooting the problem.

If the system boots up from one of the minimized conditions, the problem exists in the bypassed files. You must replace these files to get the system up and running normally. Different Windows tools can be used to manually copy files back to the disk, or you may wind up reinstalling the operating system to restore the corrupt or missing files.

If none of the alternative boot methods get the system to a level where you can work with it, you must try to boot the system to an alternative device. To boot to an alternative drive, you must insure that the system is configured to search for that drive in the CMOS Setup utility and have a bootable disk in that drive when you turn it on. This normally involves using some type of *clean boot disk* or the *Setup disk* to start the system. A **boot disk** (or disc) is one that has an operating system that can be used to start the system.

boot disk

As we discussed in Chapter 11, if the system boots to another device and you can see the drive, you may be able to save the data on the disk by repairing its boot files. If you cannot access the drive structure after booting to an alternative device, you have two possible alternatives—you can try to repartition and reformat the drive, or you can physically replace the drive. If the drive has a physical hardware failure, you will not be able to restructure the drive. In either case, you will not be able to save the data from the drive—you can only hope there is a current backup on a different media.

Windows 2000 Start-Up and Emergency Repair Disks

In the Windows 2000 arena, there are two different types of troubleshooting-related disks that the technician should have on hand. These are

- The setup disks
- The Emergency Repair disk

MAKEBT32.EXE

Windows 2000 creates a four-disk set of the Setup disks do not bring the system to a command prompt. Instead, they initiate the Windows Setup process. Under Windows 2000, you must place the distribution CD in the drive and launch the MakeBootDisk utility to create the four disk images for its Windows 2000 Setup disks. You can also create Setup disk from the command prompt using the **MAKEBT32.EXE** file for Windows 2000. These disks can also be made from the *Start/Run/Browse/CD-ROM* path. From the CD, select the BOOTDISK option followed by the MAKEBT32.EXE command.

┌─ **TEST TIP** ─────────┐
│ Be aware of the different ways that │
│ Setup disks are created in Windows │
│ NT 4.0 and Windows 2000. │
└────────────────────┘

Emergency Repair Disk (ERD)

Windows 2000 provides for an **Emergency Repair Disk (ERD)** to be produced. The ERD is different than the Setup disks in that it is intended for use with an operational system when it crashes. It is not a bootable disk and must be used with the Setup disks or the distribution CD. While the Setup disks are uniform for a given version of Windows 2000, the ERD is specific to the machine it is created from. It contains a copy of the registry in Windows 2000. When dealing with the Windows 2000 ERD, it is necessary to manually copy the registry files to the disk.

Creating the Windows 2000 ERD

The Windows 2000 Setup routine prompts you to create an ERD during the installation process. The ERD can also be created using the Windows 2000 Backup utility located under the *Programs/Accessories/System_Tools* path. Choosing this option will activate the Windows 2000 ERD Creation Wizard, depicted in Figure 12-36. The Windows 2000 ERD disk contains configuration information that is specific to the computer that will be required during the emergency repair process.

┌─ **TEST TIP** ─────────┐
│ Know where ERDs are cre- │
│ ated in Windows NT 4.0 and │
│ in Windows 2000. │
└────────────────────┘

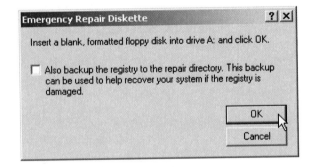

Figure 12-36: The ERD Creation Screen

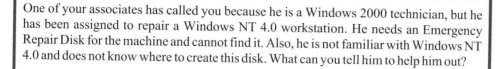

GEEK SQUAD CASE FILE #30201

One of your associates has called you because he is a Windows 2000 technician, but he has been assigned to repair a Windows NT 4.0 workstation. He needs an Emergency Repair Disk for the machine and cannot find it. Also, he is not familiar with Windows NT 4.0 and does not know where to create this disk. What can you tell him to help him out?

Windows XP Boot Disk

Although not Microsoft's recommended way of starting a failing Windows XP system, it is possible to make a Windows XP boot disk that can be used to bypass corrupted boot files at the root of the system volume and start the PC.

To create a Windows XP boot disk:

1. Start Windows XP, and move into the My Computer windows.

2. Place a blank floppy disk in the disk drive.

3. Right-click on the floppy drive icon in My Computer, and select the *Format* option from the menu.

4. Verify the floppy parameters in the Format 3 1/2 Floppy (A:) page, and click the *Start* button.

5. When the format operation is complete, copy the system's *Ntldr*, *Ntdetect.com*, and *Boot.ini* files to the floppy disk.

6. If *Bootsect.dos* or *Ntbootdd.sys* exists in the system, copy it (or both) to the floppy disk as well.

Ntldr and *Ntdetect.com* are generic files and can be used with any Windows XP installation. However, *Boot.ini* and *Ntbootdd.sys* are specific to the system that created them. Therefore, Windows XP boot disks may not work on different systems. *Bootsect.dos* cannot be used on any system other than the one that created it.

Troubleshooting Windows 2000/XP Start-Up Problems

If Windows 2000 or Windows XP fails to boot, the first troubleshooting step is to determine whether the computer is failing before or after the operating system takes control. If the start-up process makes it to the beep that indicates the end of the POST, but you do not see the operating system's Advanced Options Menu, the problem is probably one of the following:

- System partition
- Master Boot Record
- Partition boot sector

These types of problems are usually the result of hard-disk media failure, or a virus, and must be repaired before the operating system can function. Typical symptoms associated with these failures include the following:

Essentials 3.3

IT Technician 3.3

- Blue screen or Stop message appears.
- Bootup stops after the POST.
- The Boot Selection menu is never reached.
- An error message is produced.

Windows displays a number of error messages related to these problems, including the following:

- Missing Operating System
- Disk Read Error
- Invalid Partition Table
- Hard Disk Error (or Absent/Failed)
- Insert System Disk
- Error Loading Operating System
- At lest one service or driver failed during startup

"Error Loading Operating System" message

BOOT.INI

The **"Error Loading Operating System" message** indicates that the system partition was located but could not start the operating system. The system partition on that drive could be missing or misidentified.

The **BOOT.INI** file enables Windows 2000/XP to boot to separate operating systems. If this file is missing or corrupt, you will not be able to boot to the *Previous version* of Windows. The computer will boot only to Windows 2000/XP. To correct this condition, copy the BOOT.INI file from a backup or from another machine running the same setup and using the same installation directories.

NTDETECT.COM

NTLDR files

NTLDR is missing

NTDETECT failed

Recovery Console

Missing Operating System

Invalid Partition Table errors

FIXMBR

The **NTDETECT.COM** or **NTLDR files** could also be missing or have become corrupt. If you receive the message "**NTLDR is missing**" or "**NTDETECT failed**," the partition boot sector is OK, but the NTLDR or NTDETECT.COM file is missing or corrupt. To correct these errors, you must reinstall Windows 2000 or Windows XP or boot to the **Recovery Console** and copy replacements for the missing or corrupt files from a backup or from the distribution CD.

The **Missing Operating System** and **Invalid Partition Table errors** indicate a problem with the Master Boot Record. Use the **FIXMBR** command in the Recovery Console to replace the Master Boot Record. Although this works well on a stand-alone drive, it does not work with disks that contain partitions or logical drives that are part of striped or volume sets. You also should not perform this procedure on drives that use third-party translation, partitioning, or dual-boot programs.

┌─ **TEST TIP** ─────────
Know which files must be present to boot Windows 2000/XP and how to correct problems associated with the Windows NT boot sequence.
└──────────────────────

Figure 12-37 illustrates the Windows 2000/XP start-up process. In addition to listing the order of events that occur in each distinct start-up stage, it also describes various types of problems typically encountered during each stage.

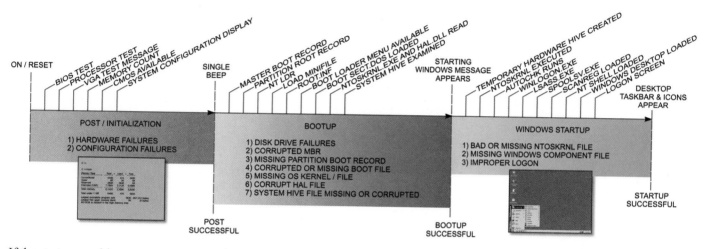

If the start-up problem occurs at some point after the screen clears and the operating system selection menu appears, or after selecting Windows 2000 or Windows XP from the OS boot menu, the issue is probably with the operating system. Most likely, some necessary files are missing or have been corrupted.

Figure 12-37: The Windows 2000/XP Start-Up Sequence

With some errors that occur during this time, the system will place a "…**Service or Driver Failed During Startup**" message on the screen. This indicates that some information about a device or service that the system was looking for during the startup process was missing from the registry or was corrupt. There are several tools you can use to investigate this problem—the *Event Viewer* utility, the **Boot Logging** option available through the Advanced Options menu, and the **LISTSVC** command in the Recovery Console.

Service or Driver Failed During Startup

Boot Logging

LISTSVC

Start the system in Safe mode and access the Event Viewer through the *Start/Control Panel/Administrative Tools* path. In the Event Viewer, open the *System log* and locate the offending service. Double click on the service to view a description of the error and obtain a link to the *Microsoft Help and Support Center* where an extended explanation is presented, along with possible corrective actions to be taken.

GEEK SQUAD CASE FILE #99285

A remote customer calls and complains that she is receiving a *Missing \System32\system file* error message, and the system stops operating. She thinks she should replace her hard drive and wants you to order it for her. What should you tell her?

Windows 2000/XP Start-Up Tools

Windows 2000 and Windows XP provide a wealth of tools for recovering from a start-up problem, including the following:

- Windows 2000/XP Safe-mode options

- Windows 2000/XP Recovery console

- Windows 2000 Emergency Repair Disk

- Windows XP System Restore Function

- Windows XP Automated System Recovery

- Windows XP Driver Roll-back option

The following sections describe these tools and their use in detail.

Altering BOOT.INI

OS Choices Boot Options

The BOOT.INI file in Windows 2000/XP systems is a special, hidden read-only boot text file that is used to generate the **OS Choices Boot Options** menu during the 2000/XP start-up process. The system reads the settings in the BOOT.INI file during the bootup process and places the menu on the screen to permit the user to select an operating system to boot to.

The menu can support the starting of different Windows 2000/XP versions as well as provide for starting one non-Windows 2000/XP operating system. There is also an option on the menu that enables users to enter an *Advanced Boot Options* menu by pressing the F8 function key. If no selection is made within a specified time frame, the bootup process continues in default mode.

The BOOT.INI file contains two sections of text that can be read and modified. The default values of the BOOT.INI file are generated automatically by the system when the Windows 2000/XP operating system is installed. You can access this file using a text editor. Before doing this, you must change its attributes so that it becomes visible and so you can open it. This can be done through My Computer or Windows Explorer or by using the Attrib command.

Essentials 3.3

Technical Support 2.3

IT Technician 3.3

Advanced Options Menu

Windows 2000/XP Start-Up Modes

The Windows 2000 and Windows XP operating systems incorporate a number of start-up options that can be engaged to get the system up and running in a given state to provide a starting point for troubleshooting operations. The **Advanced Options Menu**, depicted in Figure 12-38, contains several options that can be of assistance when troubleshooting Windows start-up failures. To access this menu, hold down the F8 function key when the *Starting Windows...* message is displaying on-screen.

```
Windows 2000 Advanced Options Menu
Please select an option:

    Safe Mode
    Safe Mode with Networking
    Safe Mode with Command Prompt

    Enable Boot Logging
    Enable VGA Mode
    Last Known Good Configuration
    Directory Services Restore Mode (Windows 2000 domain controllers only)
    Debugging Mode

    Boot Normally
    Return to OS Choices Menu


    Use ↑ and ↓ to move the highlight to your choice.
    Press Enter to choose.
```

**Figure 12-38:
The Advanced
Options Menu**

Safe Modes

The Advance Boot Options menu basically provides several variations of Safe Mode options that can be used to start the system using a minimized subset of the complete system. Windows 2000/XP has three Safe Mode start-up options:

- Boot Normally
- Safe Mode
- Safe Mode with Networking
- Safe Mode with Command Prompt

Each option is customized for specific situations and disables selected portions of the system to prevent them from interfering with the start-up process.

If Windows determines that a problem that prevents the system from starting has occurred, or if it senses that the registry is corrupt, it automatically attempts to restart the system in **Safe Mode**. This mode bypasses several start-up files to provide access to the system's configuration settings.

> **What's active in Safe Mode?** In Safe Mode, the minimal device drivers (keyboard, mouse, and standard-mode VGA drivers) are active to start the system. However, the CD-ROM drive will not be active in Safe mode.

Unless modified, the *Safe Mode* screen appears as depicted in Figure 12-39. Active functions appear on-screen along with the "Safe-mode" notice in each corner. However, there is no taskbar in Safe Mode.

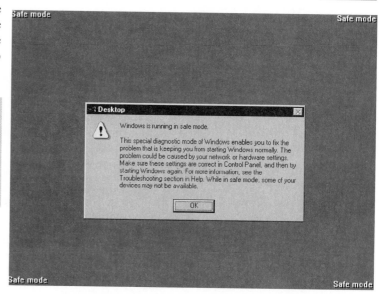

Figure 12-39: The Safe Mode Start-Up Screen

The standard Safe Mode *Start-Up* option is used when the system:

- Will not start after the Starting Windows… message appears on-screen

- Stalls repeatedly or for long periods of time

- Cannot print to a local printer after a complete troubleshooting sequence

- Has video display problems

- Slows down noticeably or does not work correctly

The only device drivers loaded in Safe Mode are the mouse driver, the standard keyboard driver, and the standard VGA driver. This should enable enough of the Windows structure to operate so that the offending portions can be isolated and repaired using step-by-step checking procedures.

Safe Mode with Network Support

The **Safe Mode with Network Support** option loads the normal Safe mode files and includes the basic network driver files. This mode is used in networked environments when the system

- Stops responding when a remote network is accessed

- Cannot print to a remote printer

- Stalls during start-up and cannot be started using a normal Safe Mode start-up

Safe Mode with Command Prompt

CMD.EXE

If the Safe mode option will not start the system, reboot the computer, and select the **Safe Mode with Command Prompt** option from the menu. Selecting the *Command Prompt* mode causes the system to boot up to the command line, using the start-up files and the registry. The system will start in Safe Mode with minimal drivers (while not executing any of the start-up files) and will produce the command-line prompt. It does load the command interpreter **CMD.EXE**. You can also use this mode to

- Employ command-line switches, such as WIN d/x

- Employ command-line instructions and text editors

Other Windows Start-Up Options

In addition to the different Safe Mode options, the menu also provides a number of other start-up options carried over from previous Windows NT versions:

Enable Boot Logging

- **Enable Boot Logging**—Creates a log file called NTBTLOG.TXT in the root folder. This log is similar to the BOOTLOG.TXT file described earlier in that it contains a listing of all the drivers and services that the system attempts to load during start-up and can be useful when trying to determine what service or driver is causing the system to fail.

Enable VGA Mode

- **Enable VGA Mode**—When selected, this option boots the system normally but uses only the standard VGA driver. If you have configured the display incorrectly and are unable to see the Desktop, booting into VGA Mode will enable you to reconfigure those settings.

- **Last Known Good Configuration**—This option will start Windows 2000 or XP using the settings that existed the last time a successful user log-on occurred. All system setting changes made since the last successful start-up are lost. This is a particularly useful option if you have added or reconfigured a device driver that is causing the system to fail.

- **Debugging Mode**—This will start Windows 2000 or XP in a kernel debug mode that will enable special debugger utilities to access the kernel for troubleshooting and analysis.

Last Known Good
Configuration

Debugging Mode

These start-up modes play an important role in getting a Windows 2000 or Windows XP operating system up and running when it fails to start. You must press the SPACEBAR while they are displayed on the screen to select one of the optional start-up modes. If no selection is made, the system will continue with a normal start-up sequence as previously outlined, using the existing hardware configuration information.

GEEK SQUAD CASE FILE #69356

While you are working on a customer's Windows 2000 system, you notice that the display resolution is running well below what you expect from his video card. When you attempt to change the video driver to get better display performance out of it, you see only horizontal streaks across the screen after you reboot the machine. Which Windows 2000 start-up mode provides the best choice for quickly accessing the display setup so you can correct it?

Windows 2000/XP Recovery Console

Essentials 3.3

IT Technician 3.3

Recovery Console

The **Recovery Console** available in Windows 2000 and Windows XP is a command-line interface that provides you with access to the hard disks and many command-line utilities when the operating system will not boot (i.e., after the *Last Known Good Configuration* and *Safe Mode* options have been tried). The Recovery Console can access all volumes on the drive, regardless of their file system type. However, if you have not added the *Recovery Console* option prior to a failure, you will not be able to employ it and will need to use the Windows 2000 Setup disks or the Windows 2000/XP distribution CD instead. You can use the Recovery Console to perform tasks such as the following:

- Copy files from a floppy disk, CD, or another hard disk to the hard disk used for booting, enabling you to replace or remove files that may be affecting the boot process. Because of the security features in Windows 2000 and Windows XP, you are granted only limited access to certain files on the hard drive. You cannot copy files from the hard drive to a floppy or other storage device under these conditions.

- Control the start-up state of services, enabling you to disable a service that could potentially be causing the operating system to crash.

- Add, remove, and format volumes on the hard disk.

- Repair the MBR or boot sector of a hard disk or volume.

- Restore the registry.

The Recovery Console can be permanently installed on a system so that it is accessible from the Advanced Options menu. It can be started at any time by booting from the Windows 2000 Setup disks or the Windows 2000/XP distribution CDs, choosing to repair an installation, and selecting Recovery Console from the repair options.

To install the Recovery Console on a computer, follow these steps:

1. Put the Windows 2000 or Windows XP distribution CD in the CD-ROM drive, or connect to an installation share on the network.

winnt32 /cmdcons

2. Run the **winnt32 /cmdcons** command. Windows 2000/XP Setup will start up, as illustrated in Figure 12-40, and install the Recovery Console.

3. The Recovery Console will automatically be added to the Advanced Options menu.

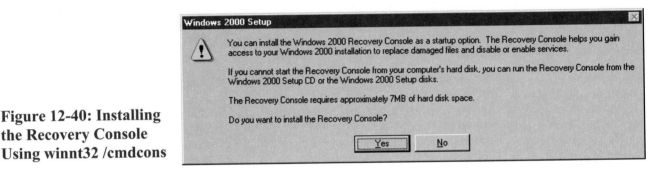

Figure 12-40: Installing the Recovery Console Using winnt32 /cmdcons

You can run the Recovery Console from the distribution CD for both Windows 2000 and Windows XP. To do so, start the system with the distribution CD in the drive, and choose the option to repair (Press the R key) the installation. Enter the administrator's password to access the Recovery Console. The password protection for the Recovery Console permits only two incorrect attempts by default. On the third incorrect attempt, the system will stop accepting further entries for a predetermined amount of time (referred to as **lockout time**).

lockout time

Calling for Help—When you start the Recovery Console, you are prompted to choose the folder that contains the Windows 2000 or Windows XP installation that you are trying to repair, and then to log on as Administrator. The commands that can be used with the Recovery Console include most of the MS-DOS-based commands covered in Chapter 8, *Operating System Fundamentals*. After you have logged on to the system, you can type HELP at the command line to obtain a list of available commands.

One of the primary uses of the Recovery Console is to restore the registry. Every time you back up the system state data with the Windows 2000 or Windows XP Backup utilities, a copy of the registry is placed in the *\Repair\RegBack* folder. If you copy the entire contents of this folder or only particular files to *\System32\Config* (which is the folder where the working copy of the registry is stored), you can restore the registry to the same condition as the last time you performed a **System State Data backup**. It is recommended that you create a copy of the files in *\System32\Config* prior to restoring the other files from backup so that you can restore the registry to the original condition if necessary.

System State data backup

Table 12-2 displays the list of Recovery Console commands along with a brief description of each.

Table 12-2: Recovery Console Commands

COMMAND	DESCRIPTION
ATTRIB	Changes attributes on one file or directory (wildcards not supported)
BATCH	Executes commands specified in a text file
BOOTCFG	Scans hard disks to locate Windows installations and modifies or re-creates Boot.ini accordingly
CD or CHDIR	Displays the name of the current directory, or switches to a new directory
CHKDSK	Checks a disk and displays a status report
CLS	Clears the screen
COPY	Copies a single file to another location (wildcards not supported)
DEL or DELETE	Deletes one file (wildcards not supported)
DIR	Displays a list of files and subdirectories in a directory
DISABLE	Disables a Windows system service or driver
DISKPART	Manages partitions on a hard disk, including adding and deleting partitions
ENABLE	Enables a Windows system service or driver
EXIT	Quits the Recovery Console and restarts the computer
EXPAND	Expands a compressed file
FIXBOOT	Writes a new boot sector to the system volume
FIXMBR	Repairs the Master Boot Record of the system volume
FORMAT	Formats a disk for use with Windows XP
HELP	Displays a list of available commands
LISTSVC	Lists all available services and drivers on the computer
LOGON	Lists the detected installations of Windows XP, and prompts for Administrator logon
MAP	Displays drive letter to physical device mappings
MAP ARC	Displays the ARC path instead of the Windows XP device path for physical device mappings
MD or MKDIR	Creates a directory
MORE	Displays a text file to the screen
RD or RMDIR	Removes a directory
REN or RENAME	Renames a single file (wildcards not supported)
SET	Used to set Recovery Console environment variables
SYSTEM_ROOT	Sets the current directory to system_root
TYPE	Displays a test file to the screen (same as the MORE command)

One of the major Windows 2000/XP *Recovery Console* commands is the *Bootcfg* command. This command can be used to change the configuration of the *BOOT.INI* file or to recover from bootup problems. The *Bootcfg* file is only available for use in the Recovery Console.

There are many switches available for use with the Recovery Console items to change the bootup process. Some of the switches that are particularly interesting for troubleshooting purposes are the

- */BASEVIDEO* switch that forces the computer to start up using the Standard VGA driver

- */DEBUG* switch that starts the system in Debug mode as described in the Alternative Windows 2000/XP Startup Modes section earlier in this chapter

- *MAXMEM:n* switch that can be used to specify the maximum amount of RAM that the system will start up with

- */SOS* switch that displays the different drive names as they are loaded to provide a step-by-step start-up option where individual start-up entries can be skipped

Windows XP System Restore

System Restore

roll back

restore points

The Windows XP **System Restore** utility enables administrators to **roll back** the Windows XP Professional operating system to a previous operational state and configuration—without affecting any user's personal data. This feature extends the Last Known Good Configuration mode by allowing the system to be rolled back to predetermined **restore points**.

Restore points are records of information that are created at specific intervals and when certain events occur. Some restore points are created automatically on a 24-hour/daily basis. Others are created when significant events occur, such as when you upgrade the system hardware or software, perform a recovery operation, or when a new driver is loaded. However, restore points can also be created manually as a method of preserving the current state of the operating system prior to performing management activities. Such activities include

- When you are updating a driver and it appears to cause a problem with the system that rolling back the driver does not resolve

- When you are installing a new software program and it creates problems with the system that uninstalling the software does not resolve

- Anytime you need to get back to a point where you know the system was functioning correctly

You should create a Restore point any time that you are making changes to the system that might make it unstable or that might disable it.

Using System Restore

To activate the Windows XP **System Restore wizard**, navigate the *Start/All Programs/Accessories/System Tools* path, and then select the *System Restore* option from the menu. The *Welcome* screen will be displayed as shown in Figure 12-41.

System Restore
wizard

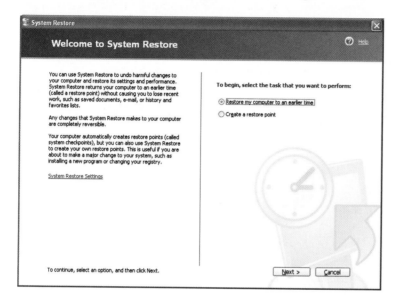

**Figure 12-41:
System Restore
Welcome Screen**

To manually create Restore points, simply select the *Create a restore point* option from the *Welcome to System Restore* screen. (The *Create a restore point* option can also be accessed through the Start menu's **Help and Support Center** option.) Click the *Next* button and enter the name for the restore point in the *Point Description* dialog box, as illustrated in Figure 12-42. The System Restore utility will automatically add this name, along with the time and date, to the restore point list. Click on *Create* to finish the process.

> **NOTE**
>
> You must be a member of the Administrators group to use the System Restore feature.

Help and Support
Center

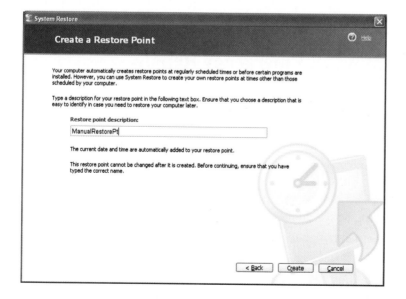

**Figure 12-42:
Creating a Restore
Point**

Selecting the *Restore my computer to an earlier time* option from the Welcome screen will enable you to select a restore point from a calendar and a listing, as illustrated in Figure 12-43. Unless you simply need a restore point from earlier in the day, select the date on the calendar that you wish to roll the system back to, and if there are multiple restore points for that day, choose the restore point you want to use.

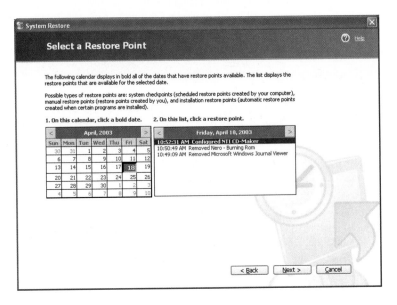

Figure 12-43: The Select a Restore Point Screen

After you have confirmed the restore point, the system will conduct the rollback, and the system will automatically restart. There is an *Undo* option (undo my last restoration) available that can be used if the restore operation did not solve the problem or the problem became worse.

To access the System Restore wizard through the Start menu's *Help and Support* option, select the *Performance and Maintenance* option from its menu, click the *Using System Restore to Undo Changes* entry, and click the *Run the System Restore Wizard* option.

IT Technician 3.3

Performing an Emergency Repair

The Windows 2000 ERD provides another troubleshooting tool that can be used when Safe Mode and the Recovery Console do not enable you to repair the system. If you have already created an ERD, you can start the system with the Windows 2000 Setup CD or the Setup floppy disks, and then use the ERD to restore core system files. The **emergency repair process** enables you to perform the following operations:

emergency repair process

- Repair the boot sector
- Replace the system files
- Repair the start-up files

Limited to the Operating System—The emergency repair process is designed to repair the operating system only, and cannot be of assistance in repairing application or data problems.

To perform an emergency repair, follow these steps:

Hands-On Activity

1. Boot the system from the Window 2000 CD. If the system will not boot from the CD, you must boot with the Setup Boot Disk, which is the first of four Setup floppy disks that are required. You create the Setup floppy disks with *MAKEBOOT.EXE*, which is in the *\BOOTDISK* folder in the Windows 2000 CD root directory.

2. When the text-mode portion of the setup begins, follow the initial prompts. You will reach the *Welcome to Setup* screen, as shown in Figure 12-44.

3. When prompted, choose the *Emergency Repair Process* by pressing *R*.

4. When prompted, press *F* for *Fast Repair*.

5. Follow the instructions, and insert the Emergency Repair Disk into the floppy-disk drive when prompted.

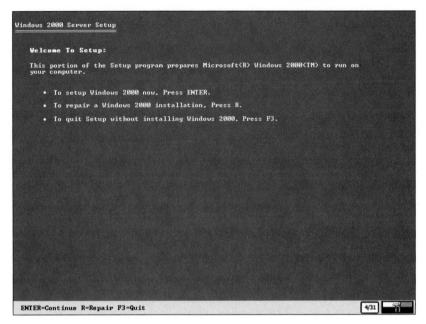

Figure 12-44: The Welcome to Setup Screen

Essentials 3.3

Windows XP Automated System Recovery

In the Windows XP Professional operating system, the Emergency Repair Disk has been replaced with an emergency start-up tool called the **Automated System Recovery (ASR)**. The ASR tool can be used to back up and restore the system state information, along with all the files stored on the system volume. As with the Windows 2000 ERD, the ASR feature is considered to be the last resort used when you have been unable to recover the system using other methods, including Safe Mode, Last Known Good configuration mode, and the Recovery Console.

> **Automated System Recovery (ASR)**

┌─ **NOTE** ───┐
ASR is only available in Windows XP Professional—ASR is not available in Windows XP Home Edition. You can use the ASR Wizard if you install the Ntbackup program from the *\Valueadd* folder on the Windows XP Home Edition CD-ROM.
└──┘

┌─ **TEST TIP** ─────────────┐
Be aware that the ASR function replaces the Emergency Repair process that was used in Windows 2000.
└────────────────────────────┘

ASR backups

ASR restore

The ASR utility is a function of the (NTBackup.exe) backup utility. As with other backup options, ASR is a two-part system—back up and restore operations. **ASR backups** should be performed periodically to keep them up to date. On the other hand, an **ASR restore** operation is normally only performed in the case of a system failure. The contents of an ASR backup operation include

- The system state data

- The system services

- The system components for all disks

In addition, an ASR floppy disk is created during the backup operation that contains additional information required for the ASR restore process. This disk contains two files:

- *Asr.sif*—contains hard disk, partition, and volume configuration information along with general system information.

- *Asrpnp.sif*—contains PnP device configuration data.

NOTE

Be aware that the ASR function can be used only to back up and restore *system* information. Therefore, you must make sure that you perform regular applications and back up data as well.

Conducting ASR Backups

ASR back up operations are performed through the Windows XP backup utility as follows:

1. Access the Windows XP backup utility and press the *Next* button on the *Backup and Restore Wizard Welcome* window.

2. From the *Welcome* window, switch to *Advanced mode*.

3. Click on the *Automated System Recovery* Wizard button, as shown in Figure 12-45, and click the *Next* button.

4. Select a backup media type, specify the backup name, and click the *Finish* button to complete the ASR backup operation.

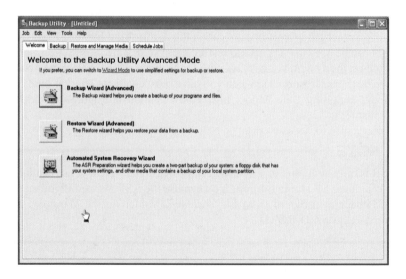

Figure 12-45: Launching the ASR Wizard

You should not place the ASR backup on the system or boot volume when specifying a location for the backup. The system volume is reformatted during an ASR restore, and depending on the condition of the system, the boot volume may be reformatted as well. You should also be aware that performing a restore operation from network shares is not an option with ASR. You must use local devices such as another hard disk, a CD-ROM, or a tape drive to hold the ASR backup.

> **NOTE**
>
> If the ASR backups are being used as a method of system restore, make sure that they are performed on a regular schedule.

ASR Restore Operations

The ASR restore process is launched from Windows XP Professional Setup as a part of the operating system install process (i.e., the operating system is reinstalled, and then the ASR backup information is used to complete the restoration of the system).

There are three items required to conduct the ASR restore operation. These items are

- The Windows XP distribution CD
- The ASR floppy disk
- The ASR backup

You should make sure that you have access to these items prior to launching an ASR restore operation.

To perform an ASR restore, boot the system using the Windows XP Professional CD, and press the F2 function key when the *Welcome to Setup* screen is displayed. The ASR process should automatically start at this point. Then, when prompted, insert the ASR floppy disk and simply follow the on-screen prompts.

In the event that the ASR floppy disk is lost or damaged, the *Asr.sif* and *Asrpnp.sif* files can be recovered from the ASR backup. The *Asf.inf* and *Asrpnp.inf* files must reside at the root of the ASR floppy disk in order for them to be found during the ASR restore process.

Network Start-Up Problems

For network clients, such as Windows 2000 and Windows XP systems, there is one additional start-up phase that could produce errors. This is the network log-on phase (which is automatic in client/server network environments). During this period, the desktop should appear on the screen. However, there are still several communication services being loaded into the system behind the scene. Failure to load one of these services (or the device that supports them) will result in a *Device or service has failed to start* error message being displayed on the screen.

In most of these cases, you should still have a desktop display to work from. However, the system is working in a stand-alone fashion. In Windows 2000 or Windows XP systems, access the Event Viewer utility, and expand the System node to view the event log of system events, such as loading the networking services. Even if no desktop is available, you can restart the system in Safe mode and access the Event Viewer to use these logs to isolate the cause of the error.

Authentication Problems

log-on problem

One last problem that can occur during start-up (even though it is not actually a start-up problem) is a **log-on problem**. Basically, users cannot log on to systems unless they have the proper authorization to do so. These problems tend to be very common in secure environments such as those that use Windows 2000 or Windows XP.

The most common log-on problem is a forgotten or invalid username and password. Invalid usernames and passwords typically result from poor typing or from having the Caps Lock function turned on. Users also can be prevented from logging on due to imposed station or time restrictions. Check with the network administrator to see whether the user's rights to the system have been restricted.

Administrator account

Guest account

When Windows 2000 or Windows XP is first installed, the only usable account is the **Administrator account**; the **Guest account** is disabled by default. If a user cannot log on, check their password. The password is case sensitive, so verify that the Caps Lock key is not an issue.

If you have forgotten the Administrator password and you have not created any other accounts with Administrator privileges, you must reinstall Windows 2000 or XP. Some third-party utilities may be able to help you recover the Administrator password, but you will usually find it easier to just reinstall the operating system at this point.

Essentials 3.3

Technical Support 2.3

IT Technician 3.3

Common OS Operational Problems

The technician should be able to recognize common problems and determine how to resolve them. Once the operating system has been started up and is functional, there are particular types of problems that come into play. You must be able to identify and correct **operational problems** associated with the operating system. To this end, the following sections deal specifically with OS operational symptoms and problems, including the following:

- Optional devices
- Application
- Printing
- Networking

Optional Devices Will Not Operate

The system's basic devices are configured as part of the system's PnP start-up process in both Windows 2000 and Windows XP systems. However, this doesn't mean that all the system's devices are in working order or that they will remain in working order while the system is on. Optional devices such as modems, sound cards, and advanced I/O devices might configure properly as part of the PnP process and then fail to operate after the system starts.

operational problems

As an example, many video cards are capable of displaying very high-resolution screens at high refresh rates. However, some monitors do not have the same capabilities. When you configure the video card with settings that the monitor cannot display, symptoms can range from a simple blank screen to several ghost images being displayed on-screen. After the initial installation, the video drivers are always changed while Windows is operating. In a Windows 2000 or Windows XP system, you should select the *VGA Mode* option to gain access to the video configuration by loading a standard VGA driver.

Similarly, adding input devices, such as a new mouse or joystick, can create problems where the new device does not work under the Windows environment. In the Windows operating system, there are several tools to help identify and isolate hardware-related problems. These tools include the Device Manager (located under the Control Panel's *System* icon), the Hardware Troubleshooter procedures (located under the *Help* entry of the Start menu), and the various hardware-related icons in the Control Panel.

GEEK SQUAD CASE FILE #26359

You believe your video display can produce a much higher resolution display than it is currently providing, so you change the video driver in your Windows 2000 Professional system. When you apply the new setting, you cannot see anything on the display. What should you do to regain control of your display?

As mentioned earlier, Windows XP offers *Device Driver Roll Back, System Restore,* and *Disable the Device* options that can be used to replace an updated driver (other than a printer driver) that may be causing problems. This option reinstalls the driver that was being used previous to the current driver and restores any driver settings that were updated when the driver was installed.

The *System Restore* feature can be used to restore the system and its applications to a previous operating configuration that was known to be working correctly at that point. You would resort to this method of changing the device driver in Windows XP after the Device Driver Roll Back option did not repair the system.

The *Disable the Device* option should be used when you believe that a specific device is causing a system problem. This option simply disables the device and its drivers so that you can verify that it is the cause of whatever problem the system is experiencing.

Troubleshooting Stop Errors

Stop errors occur most frequently when new hardware or their device drivers have been installed, or when the system is running low on disk space. Also, stop errors can occur on a system that has been running without a problem for months, but for whatever reason experiences a hardware error of some sort that causes the system to crash. You need to be aware that they can happen for a variety of other reasons and can be very difficult to troubleshoot.

In Windows XP, stop errors may produce a condition where the system reboots seemingly for no reason. This is caused by a combination of a blue screen error and an **Auto Restart** setting in Windows XP. The setting is designed to automatically reboot Windows when it detects a critical error in the system. Because the setting automatically kicks in when the system stops you do not get to see the blue screen error message.

Essentials 3.3

Technical Support 2.3

IT Technician 3.3

Auto Restart

If the system is displaying this symptom, you must either check the error logs in the Event Viewer, or disable the Automatic Restart feature to get to the error message so that you can begin to correct the problem causing the error. To disable the setting, right-click on the *My Computer* icon and select *Properties*. In the Startup and Recovery section of the *Advanced* tab, click *Settings* and then remove the check from the *Automatic restart* option in the System Failure section. You can also access the setting through the *Advanced* tab of the Control Panel's *System* icon. This will allow the blue screen error message to be displayed on the screen when it occurs.

There is no set procedure for resolving Stop errors, but you can do many things to potentially eliminate the error, or to gain additional information about what caused the error.

Use the following steps to troubleshoot stop errors:

1. Restart the system to see whether the error will repeat itself. In many cases, an odd series of circumstances within the system can cause the error, and simply restarting it will correct the condition. However, if the Stop Error appears again, you will need to take additional action.

2. If you have recently installed new hardware in the system, verify that it has been installed correctly, and that you are using the most current version of its device drivers.

3. Check the HCL to verify that any newly installed hardware and device drivers are compatible with Windows 2000 or Windows XP.

4. Remove any newly installed hardware to see whether that relieves the Stop error. If Windows 2000 starts, immediately use the Event Viewer to view any additional error messages that were generated before the Stop error occurred. These messages will provide further information as to why the hardware caused the system to crash.

5. Try to start the operating system in Safe Mode. If you can start the system in Safe Mode, then you can remove any newly installed software that could be causing the Stop error. You can also remove or update device drivers that could be causing the Stop error.

6 Attempt to start the system using the Last Known Good configuration. This resets the system configuration to whatever the hardware configuration was the last time you were able to successfully boot the system, and it gives you the opportunity to try to install or configure a new hardware device again.

7. Verify that the latest operating system **Service Pack** has been installed.

8. Use TechNet or visit the Microsoft Support Center Web site and search for the particular Stop error number to see whether you can get any additional information. The Stop error number is noted in the upper-left corner of the Stop screen.

9. Disable memory caching or shadowing options in the system CMOS Setup.

10. If possible, run diagnostic software on the system to check for memory errors.

11. Use a virus utility to check for viruses, and eliminate any viruses if found.

12. Verify that the system's BIOS is the latest revision. If not, contact the manufacturer of your system to determine how to update the BIOS.

Service Pack

One of these steps should enable you to resolve the error or pinpoint it to a particular component that you can eliminate from the system to clear up the symptom.

Windows 2000/XP Application Problems

Windows application problems tend to fall into two categories—the *application will not install* or the *application will not start*. There is a trio of Windows utilities that are very useful for troubleshooting application problems:

- Event Viewer

- Task Manager

- System Monitor

Applications Will Not Install

Technical Support 2.3

IT Technician 3.3

Autorun feature

In Windows 2000 and Windows XP systems, most applications will run when their distribution CD is placed in the drive. The **Autorun feature** presents a user interface on the display that will guide the user through the installation process. If the Autorun feature in Windows 2000 or Windows XP systems can be disabled in the drive's *Properties* page, the automatic interface will not start, and the installation will not be performed.

You should check the distribution CD for the presence of the Autorun.inf file. If it is present and no Autorun action occurs, you should examine the CD-ROM drive's Properties page to ensure that the Autorun function is enabled.

Some applications do not include the Autorun function as part of their installation scheme and are typically installed through the Control Panel's *Add/Remove Programs* applet. If the application is not on the *Windows 2000 Application Compatibility Toolkit (ACT)*; the software equivalent of the HCL listing), the application might not install on the system or operate properly. This tool can be downloaded from the Microsoft Upgrade Web page.

Application Will Not Start

Technical Support 2.3

IT Technician 3.3

Application Properties

As with other GUI-based environments, Windows applications hide behind icons. The properties of each icon must correctly identify the filename and path of the application's executable file; otherwise, Windows will not be able to start it. Likewise, when a folder or file, accessed by the icon or by the shortcut from the Windows Start menu, is moved, renamed, or removed, Windows will once again not be able to find it when asked to start the application. Check the application's properties to verify that the filename, path, and syntax are correct. **Application Properties** can be accessed by right-clicking on their desktop icon, as well as by right-clicking their entry in the Start menu, My Computer page, or Windows Explorer screen.

TEST TIP

Be aware of the different methods of accessing an application's properties.

Most applications require registry entries in order to run. If these entries are missing or corrupt, the application will not start. Corrupted or conflicting DLL files prevent applications from starting. To recover from these types of errors, you must reinstall the application. If an application will not start in Windows, you have several possibilities to consider. These include:

TEST TIP

Know what items to look for when applications will not start.

- The application is missing or its path is incorrect.

- Part or all of the application is corrupted.

- The application's executable file is incorrectly identified.

- The application's attributes are locked.

- There are incorrect application properties (filename, path, and syntax).

- There are missing or corrupt registry entries.

- There are conflicting DLL files.

Starting Applications from the Command Prompt

In Microsoft operating systems, applications with .BAT, .EXE, or .COM file extensions should start when their names are properly entered at the command prompt. If such an application (including any of the command line−based troubleshooting tools) will not start in a command-line environment, you have a few basic possibilities to consider: it has been improperly identified, it is not located where it is supposed to be, or the application program is corrupted.

Check the spelling of the filename, and reenter it at the command prompt. Also, verify that the path to the program has been presented correctly and thoroughly. If the path and filename are correct, the application may be corrupted. Reinstall it, and try to start it again.

Other possible reasons for application programs not starting in a command-line environment include low conventional memory or disk space and file attributes that will not let the program start. In client/server networks, permission settings may not permit a user to access a particular file or folder.

GEEK SQUAD CASE FILE #36452

You have just installed a new Windows 2000 Professional operating system upgrade on a coworker's machine. In the process of testing it, you discover that her word processor application will not start from the desktop icon. How should you go about troubleshooting this problem?

Locating Hidden Files

By default, Windows 2000 hides known filename extensions. If you cannot see filename extensions, open the Windows Explorer, click Tools, click *Folder Options*, click the *View* tab, and then locate and deselect the *Hide File Extensions for Known Files* option.

Likewise, Windows 2000 and Windows XP, by default, do not display hidden or system files in Explorer. To see hidden or system files in Windows 20000, open the Windows Explorer, click *Tools*, click *Folder Options*, click the *View* tab, and then locate and select the *Show Hidden Files and Folders* option.

┌─ **TEST TIP** ─────────────────────────────┐

Be aware that Windows 2000 does not show hidden and system files by default. Also, know how to display these file types from the Windows environment.

└──┘

Applying Task Manager to Application Problems

Technical Support 2.3

IT Technician 3.3

In Windows 2000 and XP, the Task Manager can be used to monitor the condition and operation of application programs and key Windows operating system services and components. In these operating systems, the Task Manager is available at any time and can be accessed by pressing the CTRL+ALT+DEL key combination.

When the Task Manager appears, the *Applications* tab will show by default. The tab displays the applications that are currently running in the system along with a description of their status (i.e., Running or Not Running). When an application is present in this window and shows a Not Running status, it has stalled, and you should remove it. You can use this tab to remove these applications from the active system by highlighting the task and clicking the *End Task* button.

You should consult the Task Manager's *Processes* tab if the system is running slow to determine whether an application is using more of the system's resources than it should. If the memory usage number for a given application consistently grows, the application may have a programming problem known as a memory leak. Over time, memory leaks can absorb all of the system's free memory and crash the system.

┌───┐
│ **GEEK SQUAD CASE FILE #74594** │
├───┤
│ You are using a commercial customer tracking database application on a Windows 2000 │
│ Professional system when the system hangs up and will not do anything. What is the best │
│ method with which to safely gain control of the system and remove the offending │
│ application? │
└───┘

Applying Event Viewer to Application Problems

Although Blue Screen Stop Errors are primarily associated with Setup and configuration problems involving new hardware or software products, they can happen at any time. When they occur during the normal operation of a Windows 2000/XP system, you should restart the system and see if it reoccurs. When the system restarts, use the Event Viewer utility to look for the source of the problem.

The Windows 2000 and Windows XP application logs can be used to examine the operation of the higher-end applications and some operating system services. The contents of this log can be examined through the Event Viewer utility to determine what conditions the system logged leading up to a failure, such as an application failing to start or stalling. The Event Viewer will show whether the application or service ran correctly or not. It may also indicate that there are conditions present that you should take note of before they become failures.

Another indicator of application-related problems is the appearance of an **Event Log full** error message. The event logs have a specified maximum file size that they can become before they are considered full. By default, the event logs are set to overwrite any log data more than seven days old if they become full. Therefore, if events are occurring so quickly that the logs fill up before the default time, this indicates that an excessive number of system errors (events) are occurring. You should examine the full event log to determine what activity is accounting for so many loggable events.

In the case of failure events, the system will normally generate a user alert through a pop-up dialog box on the screen. The information in the box will indicate the nature of the problem and refer you to the Event Viewer for details. The Event Viewer is available through the *Start/Programs/Administrative Tools/Event Viewer* path.

Event Log full

Monitoring Application Performance with System Monitor

Most applications do not create significant performance problems as long as the system has sufficient processing power, hard disk space, and memory. If an application is running abnormally slow, and there are no virus problems, you probably have a system configuration problem, but you may also need to analyze application performance with the **System Monitor**. You may find that the system has a **bottleneck** that is the result of any particular application that is running on the system, or a group of applications.

System Monitor

bottleneck

performance counters

The *Process object* in System Monitor, depicted in Figure 4-46, is used to monitor selected **performance counters** on a per-application basis. Performance counters can be established for quantities such as % Processor Time, IO Data Bytes/sec, Page Faults/sec, Page File Bytes, and Thread Count. These counters can help to identify the resource usage of each application.

The System Monitor utility has no repair or problem-solving capabilities. However, carefully analyzing process counters will give you a better idea of how resources are being used. If the system doesn't have enough memory, processor, or hard disk resources, you will have to address these issues to correct the problem (i.e., either upgrade the device causing the bottleneck or move applications to another location).

Figure 4-46: Monitoring Application Performance with System Monitor

Other Operational Problems

Because Windows 2000 and XP are typically used in client/server networks, some typical administrative problems are associated with files, folders, and printers and can pop up during their normal operations. These problems include such symptoms as

- Users cannot gain access to folders.

- Users send a print job to the printer but cannot locate the documents.

- Users have Read permissions to a folder, but they can still make changes to files inside the folder.

- Users complain that they can see files in a folder but cannot access any of the files.

- Users complain that they cannot set any NTFS permissions.

- You cannot recover an item that was deleted by another user.

- You cannot recover any items deleted.

A user's inability to gain access to folders can come from many places. In the Windows 2000/XP environment, they might not have permissions that will enable them to access different files and folders. This is an administrative decision and can only be overcome by an administrator establishing **permission levels** that will permit access.

permission levels

If the print job is not still in the local spooler or the **print server**, but **Print Pooling** is enabled, check all the printers in the pool. You cannot dictate which printer receives the print job. If the print job is visible in the spooler but does not print, this can be caused by the printer availability hours being set for times other than when you submitted the print job.

print server

Print Pooling

If users have Read permission for a folder but can still make changes to files inside the folder, their file permissions must be set to Full Control, Write, or Modify. These permissions are set directly to the file and override the folder permissions of Read. You can correct this by changing the permissions on the individual files or at the folder level and allowing the permissions to propagate to files within the folder.

TEST TIP

Know what items to look for when applications will not start.

TEST TIP

Be aware that files deleted from remote and removable storage devices do not appear in the Recycle Bin.

When users complain that they can see files in a folder but cannot access any of the files, they have most likely been assigned the List permission at the folder level. The List permission enables users to view the contents of the folder only and denies them all other permissions, including Read and Execute.

If you cannot set any **NTFS permissions**, the first item to check is that the file or folder is on an NTFS partition. FAT16 and FAT32 have no security options that can be assigned. If the partition is NTFS, the user must have *Full Control permission* to set any security permissions to a file or folder.

If the system cannot see files in a folder but cannot access any of the files, they might have been assigned the List permission at the folder level. The List permission enables users to view the contents of the folder only, denying them all other permissions, including Read and Execute.

In Windows, you cannot recover an item that was deleted by another user, because the Recycle Bin is maintained on a user-by-user basis. If one user deletes something, only that user can recover it. You must log on as the user who deleted the items. Files and folders deleted from a floppy disk or network drive are permanently deleted and cannot be recovered. When the Recycle Bin fills to capacity, any newly deleted file or folder added causes older deleted items to be automatically deleted for the Recycle Bin.

REMOTE DESKTOP AND REMOTE ASSISTANCE

Windows XP Professional offers two utilities that provide remote access to other computers. The first is the **Remote Desktop** utility that enables users to connect to *their own Windows XP computer* from a remote location. The second is **Remote Assistance** that enables technicians and mentors to remotely control *another user's computer*.

Using Remote Desktop, the user can gain access to his or her remote Windows XP Professional desktop, applications, data, and network resources from another computer on the network. In addition, users who have been granted permission can remotely connect to the system.

For technicians and help desk personnel, the Remote Assistance feature is the more interesting utility. Instead of sometimes awkwardly trying to give less technical users directions over a phone (or worse yet in person), the Remote Assistance feature provides the user with the ability to electronically permit you to take control of their system from your remote location. Both systems must be configured for Remote Assistance before a connection can be made. After the Remote Assistance connection has been established, the communications provide interactive cooperation between the user and the *helper*.

Using Remote Desktop

Remote Desktop enables users who work from various locations, such as PC Repair book authors, to access their main Windows XP Professional system running at the home office. This provides access to all the resources needed to write this book—source materials and research materials. Packing all this material in a suitcase and dragging it around the world can produce tennis elbow and numerous back pain problems. As I'm sure you are probably aware at this point in this book, books can be quite heavy.

When the remote user is accessing the remote computer, its desktop is locked down, and local access by other users is not possible, except by an administrator. Users with administrative privileges can log on locally during the remote session. However, the remote session will be terminated.

Configuring the Remote Desktop Function

You must configure the Remote Desktop function in two parts—first, configure the *remote target computer* to accept Remote Desktop connections; second, configure the local computer with *Remote Desktop Connections* or *Terminal Services* client software.

To configure the remote target computer to allow Remote Desktop connections

1. Right-click the *My Computer icon*, and select the *Properties* option from the pop-up menu.

2. In the Remote Desktop window of the *Remote* tab, select *Allow users to connect remotely to this computer*, as shown in Figure 12-47.

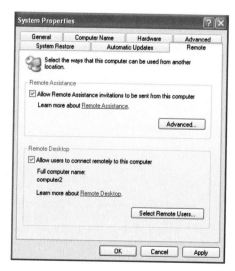

Figure 12-47: Enabling Remote Desktop

3. Click on the *Select Remote users* button and add the appropriate user accounts (local administrators automatically on the list can access remote sessions without being invited). Verify that the accounts entered have passwords, as these are required for remote Desktop activities.

4. Click on the *OK* button to return to the System Properties *Remote* tab. Click on the *OK* button again to exit the *Properties* window.

Conducting Remote Desktop Sessions

To establish a Remote Desktop session from a Windows XP Professional computer

1. Navigate the *Start/All Programs/ Accessories/Communications* path on the local computer to launch the *Remote Desktop Connections* client.

2. When the *Remote Desktop Connection* dialog box appears, as depicted in Figure 12-48, simply enter the name of the remote computer to access and click on the *Connect* button.

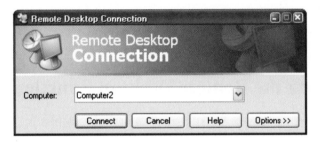

Figure 12-48: Establishing a Remote Desktop Session

Figure 12-49: Remote Desktop Connection Properties

Clicking on the *Options>* button will display several tabs of configurable options, shown in Figure 12-49. These options include the following:

- *General options*—On this tab, you can specify the username, password, and domain names that will be used for authentication. The tab also provides for saving and opening connection settings.

- *Display options*—This tab includes options for configuring the parameters for the remote connection display. One of the key settings is how much of the local screen will be taken up by the remote desktop display. You want to be able to see the details of the remote screen but still have some access to the local desktop.

- *Local Resources options*—This tab enables sound and keyboard configurations in addition to which local devices to connect to when logged on to the remote computer.

- *Programs options*—This tab provides the ability to automatically launch a program when a remote connection is established.

- *Experience options*—This performance tab enables you to optimize the connection speed and to control the display of the desktop background, themes, menu, and windows animation, and other items that can affect performance.

NOTE

To use Remote Desktop connections, TCP port 3389 must be enabled if ICS, ICF, or another type of firewall is in use. The Windows Firewall link on the bottom of the System Properties/Remote page will automatically configure the Windows ICF for Remote Desktop operation.

---

3. Enter a username and password, and click on the *OK* button to log on to the remote computer.

4. If another user is also logged on to the remote system, a *Logon Message* dialog box will be displayed. In order to continue, you must click on the *Yes* button. However, the other user will be logged off, and any unsaved data they have will be lost.

5. The Remote Desktop session like the one depicted in Figure 12-50 is established. In this case, the remote window is a fraction of the total display. It is possible to make the remote desktop cover the entire display. This setting is configured under the *Options>* button described earlier.

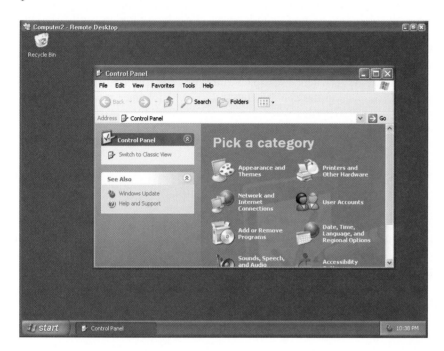

Figure 12-50: A Remote Desktop Session

NOTE

Once a connection has been established, the local desktop is locked for security reasons, preventing anyone from viewing the tasks that are being performed remotely.

---

6. Perform all the tasks you normally would if you were seated in front of the other computer.

7. When finished, end the remote session.

There are two acceptable methods of ending a remote session—*log off* the remote computer normally (which will close all programs, log the user off, and then close the Remote Desktop connection) or *disconnect* by closing the *Remote Desktop* window or selecting *Disconnect* from the Start menu (this will leave the user logged on at the remote computer, and all programs will continue processing—the user will be reconnected to the same session the next time they connect).

NOTE

One technique that does not work the same in a remote desktop as it does in the local setting is the CTRL-ALT-DEL key combination. To access the *Windows Security* dialog box or the task manager utility on the remote unit, you must select the *Windows Security* option from the remote Start menu. Pressing CTRL-ALT-DEL still brings up the local *Security/Task Manager* window.

Using Remote Assistance

If you've never tried to give troubleshooting information to someone over the phone, you probably can't imagine how many ways the conversation can head off in a wrong direction. Most technicians would rather be right there looking at what's going on. This is much less tiresome than trying to remember what you've already asked the other person to do and trying to understand and guide the feedback they are giving you.

Remote Assistance enables you to get online with the user and do just that—see what happens on the other end without having to run everything through another less technical person. Once you're connected to their desktop, you can view and take shared control of their desktop, chat with them, and send and receive files.

helper

Conducting a Remote Assistance session requires that both the user and the **helper** actively participate in establishing the connection. A Remote Assistance session is established in three phases:

1. The user requiring support sends a Remote Assistance invitation to the helper.

2. The helper responds to the invitation.

3. The user accepts the helper user's assistance.

Establishing Remote Assistance Sessions

To send a Remote Assistance invitation, the user must perform the following steps:

1. Access the *Help and Support* screen from the Start menu.

2. Under the *Ask for assistance option*, select *Invite a friend to connect to your computer with* **Remote Assistance**, followed by the *Invite someone to help you* option.

3. Select the utility you want to create the invitation with, as shown in Figure 12-51.

    invitations

    As Figure 12-51 illustrates, **invitations** can be sent directly to the helper using a Windows Messenger account, or as an e-mail attachment using Outlook. You can also create the invitation as a file and save it to a folder that the helper has access to, or send it as an e-mail attachment. The e-mail attachment or saved file will be given a *.msrcindicent* extension.

4. When prompted, enter the requested information, including your name, a message, when the invitation should expire, and a password that the helper can use to establish the connection in a more secure fashion.

5. Click on the *Send Invitation* option.

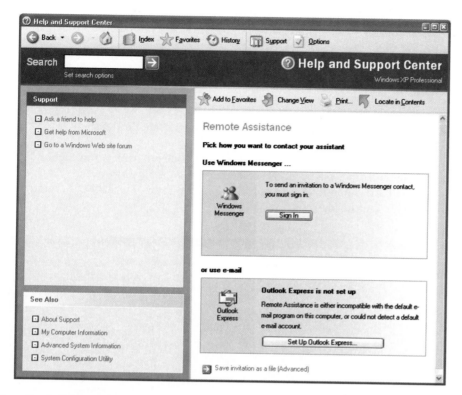

Figure 12-51: Creating an Invitation

When the helper receives the invitation, they must respond in like kind to continue the process. If the invitation was sent through Windows Messenger, the helper must accept the invitation using the Messenger pop-up window. Conversely, if the invitation is sent via e-mail, or as a file, the attached invitation must be accessed and opened to notify the user that the request has been accepted. When the user receives the confirmation they must click on the *Yes* button in the *Remote Assistance* dialog box to establish the connection.

The Remote Assistance Consoles

After the Remote Assistance connection has been established, the user will receive the **User's Console** displayed in Figure 12-52. The console provides a *Chat History* and *Message Entry* window for online chatting. The *Connection Status* window displays the connected helper information, along with the capabilities of the connection—*View Only* or *In Control*.

There are several other functions available to the user through the buttons on the right side of the screen. These options include the following:

- *Stop Control (ESC)*—This button enables the user to regain control of his or her system after the helper has taken control.

- *Send a File*—You can use this option to send a file to the helper's computer.

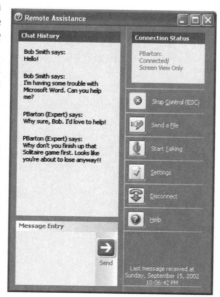

User's Console

Figure 12-52: Remote Assistance User's Console

- *Start Talking*—This feature is used to enable voice communications between computers with voice capabilities.

- *Settings*—The Settings button enables the user to adjust sound quality.

- *Disconnect*—This button is used to terminate the Remote Assistance connection.

- *Help*—This provides access to Remote Assistance help features.

Helper's Console

On the helper end of the connection, the **Helper's Console** depicted in Figure 12-53 is displayed. This end of the connection has a corresponding *Chat History* and *Message Entry* window for online chatting. The other user's desktop is displayed in the *Status* window at the right-hand side of the display.

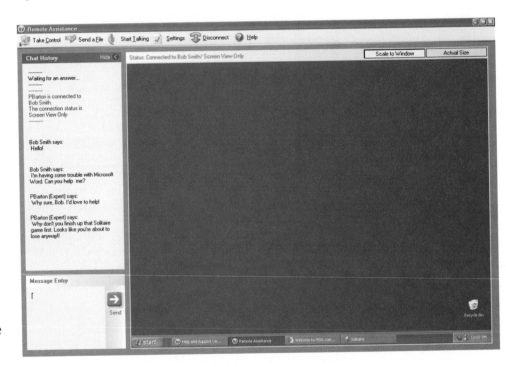

Figure 12-53:
Remote Assistance
Helper's Console

For the most part, the Helper Console has a corresponding set of button options for those provided in the User Console. However, the notable exception is the *Take Control/Release Control* button. This button sends a request to the user to take *shared control* of the desktop. The user must accept the request to grant the helper access to the system. The user can cancel the connection at any time by clicking on the *Disconnect* button or by pressing the *ESC* key.

When the helper establishes shared control of the user's system, he or she can fully manipulate the remote system as if he or she was physically setting at it. This includes manipulating drivers, launching applications, and viewing event logs. However, the helper cannot move files from the user's computer to the helper's computer. The user's data is secure during the Remote Assistance connection.

OPTIMIZING WINDOWS 2000/XP PERFORMANCE

Windows operating systems have evolved to the point where they adapt well to most system settings and changes. Most of these adaptations are automatic in nature. However, there are still some areas of the Windows system that can be optimized by users and administrators. These areas involve the following activities:

- Optimizing Virtual Memory Management
- Performing Disk Defragmentation
- Maintaining Files and Buffers
- Establishing and Optimizing various memory caches
- Effective Temporary file management
- Managing System Services
- Optimizing the Startup process
- Managing Applications

Even using the setup steps just listed, the system's performance will deteriorate over time. Most of this deterioration is due to unnecessary file clutter and segmentation on the system's hard-disk drive. The following steps can be used to periodically tune up the performance of the system.

- Periodically remove unwanted or unused TMP and .BAK files from the system, and maintain the operating system's various caches. Temporary (TMP) files and backup (BAK) files are special versions of files that the operating system creates when it is performing functions where it needs to store an original copy of the file along with an updated copy. Over time, these types of files can accumulate and take up space on the hard drive.

The Windows 2000/XP **Windows Cleanup** utility can be used to identify optional applications and certain types of temporary files that are not required for operation of the system. The temporary files that you can normally afford to remove from the system to gain needed disk space include Windows, Internet, and multimedia temp files.

Windows Cleanup

- Check for and remove lost file chains and clusters using the CHKDSK and CHKDSK /f commands. Cross-linked files can accumulate and cause the system to slow. Use the Chkdsk utility to find and remove, or repair, cross-linked files that may be using up disk space.

- Use the DEFRAG utility to realign files on the drive that may have become fragmented after being moved back and forth between the drive and the system. The Defragmenter utility is available through the *Administrative Tools/Computer Management* console and is used to reposition related files/sectors on a disk drive so that they are located in the most advantageous pattern for being found and read by the system. Performing a defrag operation can improve the disk drive's access and delivery times dramatically.

- Conduct post-installation updates and product activation. Windows features an **Updates** service that provides improvements to the installed Windows system. These updates include system security updates, device driver updates, and **Service Packs**.

Updates

Service Packs

The Windows Update service is offered through the Internet and enables the system to periodically check the Microsoft updates site for enhancements. When the system connects with the site, the service compares the current status of the local Windows installation to the latest information on the site. It then provides a list of available updates for the computer. The user can select which updates are applicable to his or her use. The user can also access the Windows Update service at any time through the Start menu or through the Internet Explorer *Tools* menu.

The Windows Update service is also used to obtain *Service Packs*. These additions are important, because they address major issues that have been detected in the operating system version since it was launched (or since the last Service Pack was issued). For larger network environments, administrators typically work through the Microsoft subscription service to automatically receive Service Packs when they are released.

Essentials 3.2

Technical Support 2.2

IT Technician 3.2

SERVICES.MSC

Unused *system services* should be stopped or disabled to optimize system responsiveness and performance. In Windows XP, you can launch the Services control applet either through *Control Panel/Administrative Tools/Services* path, or by running the **SERVICES.MSC** command line utility. This utility will produce a listing of all the user controllable services running in the system. From this list you can *Stop* or switch services to *Manual* startup configuration—you should not *Disable* any service unless you are absolutely sure that you will not need it and that no other vital service needs it.

You can double click on any of the services to open its Properties page, as illustrated in Figure 12-54. The Properties page contains a *General* tab, a *Log On* tab, a *Recovery* tab and a *Dependencies* tab. On the *General* tab you can Start, Stop, Pause or Resume a service as part of the optimization or troubleshooting process. On the *Recovery* tab you can specify what action to take if the service fails. You can check the *Dependencies* tab to see what other services this service relies on for proper operation to make sure that you don't turn off services that it needs.

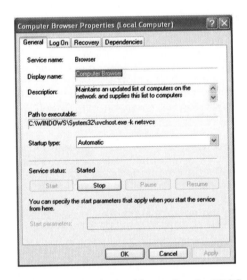

Figure 12-54:
Service Properties

The Windows startup process can be optimized by tuning the BIOS, modifying the timeout setting in the BOOT.INI file and limiting the number of applications and programs that launch automatically when Windows starts up. Applications designated to run at start up are located in the *Startup* folders for both user profiles (*UserProfile\Start Menu\Programs\Startup*) and for the All Users profile (*All Users\Start Menu\Programs\Startup*) under *C:\Documents and Settings*. You should delete any program shortcuts that are no longer needed.

You can also use the MSCONFIG.EXE command line utility to fine-tune the applications that run at startup. Load MSCONFIG from the command prompt and move to the *Startup* tab. Remove the checks from any applications that you do not want to run at startup. This action should be performed with some forethought—generally you do not want to disable anything in the *\Windows* folder. Using the MSCONFIG utility allows you to disable applications, try the system and then restore them if you need to—as apposed to deleting them from the *Startup* folder.

Monitoring System Performance

There are two Windows utilities that can be useful in monitoring the system's performance. These utilities are the Task Manager and the System Monitor. The three areas of the system that are most commonly monitored include memory, processor, and disk usage.

Of these entities, the amount of memory in the system has the most impact on its overall performance. Insufficient memory negatively impacts the operation of applications and services and can affect the performance of other hardware resources in the system. Next to memory usage, *processor activity* is the next most important component to monitor. If the processor becomes overloaded, requests for processor time begin to back up, and the overall system performance is degraded. Finally, the performance of the hard disk system can also greatly impact the overall performance of the system.

Monitoring Performance with Task Manager

The Task Manager *Performance* tab, displayed in Figure 12-55, provides a quick summary of CPU and memory usage. Its History charts enable you to view recent trends in both statistics. The Totals, Physical Memory, Commit Charge, and Kernel Memory sections display summary processor and memory information.

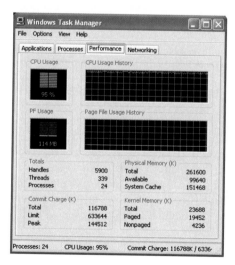

**Figure 12-55:
Task Manager
Performance Tab**

While the *Performance* tab can provide a quick view of the system's overall processor and memory usage, the *Processes* tab of Task Manager or the System Monitor utility can be used to obtain a better view of the system changes over time.

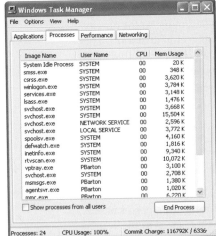

**Figure 12-56:
Task Manager
Processes Tab**

The Task Manager's *Processes* tab, depicted in Figure 12-56, displays the processor activity and memory usage of individual system processes and application programs. If you notice that a process or application appears to be taking up a disproportionate amount of processor time, you should identify the process or application's role and determine how to handle it—remove it or treat it as normal.

> ## NOTE
>
> It is not uncommon for the System Idle Process to show a high percentage of CPU usage. This indicates that the processor is lightly loaded and does not represent a problem—to the contrary, a very low processor idle time reading indicates that the processor may be overloaded. If the report continually shows a low reading, corrective action should be taken.

Essentials 3.2

Technical Support 2.2

Monitoring Performance with System Monitor

The **System Monitor** utility is designed to collect performance information. It provides more detailed information than the Task Manager display can generate. In addition, it enables you to monitor other systems remotely, to log information for future analysis, and to configure alerts to notify you of potential error conditions.

The System Monitor classifies information in three categories—as objects, instances, and counters:

- *Objects*—Objects are major hardware or software components of the system or the operating system. Typical objects include microprocessors, memory allocations, and OS services.

- *Instances*—Each occurrence of an object is considered an instance. For example, dual-processor systems would show two instances of processors.

- *Counters*—A counter is a particular aspect of an object that can be measured.

System Monitor

counters

Using the System Monitor to track and analyze system performance involves creating and monitoring **counters** for different system objects. In Windows 2000 and XP, there are literally hundreds of counters to choose from. You can select counters to use through the *Performance* option under the Control Panel's *Administrative Tools* icon. Figure 12-57 illustrates adding counters to the System Monitor display. Which objects you choose to monitor depends on whether you are trying to collect general baseline information, troubleshoot a performance problem, diagnose an issue with an application, and so forth.

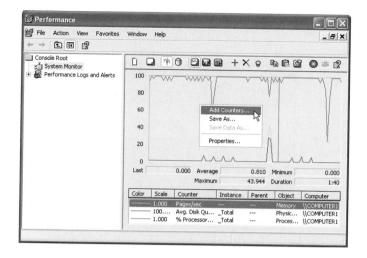

Figure 12-57: The System Monitor

Using Performance Logs and Alerts

You can configure the **Performance Logs and Alerts** utility to log System Monitor counter information in a file and to generate alerts based on **event** levels that you configure. The *Performance* logs can be viewed and analyzed through the System Monitor. This utility contains three components:

- *Counter logs*—These logs compile activity information for selected System Monitor counters taken at regular intervals.

- *Trace logs*—These logs monitor and record activity for selected System Monitor counters when a configured event occurs.

- *Alerts*—These logs monitor and record activity and notify administrators when a particular counter exceeds a configured threshold.

To enable performance logging:

1. Access *Performance* from the Control Panel's *Administrative Tools* icon.

2. Expand the *Performance Logs and Alerts* node, right-click on the *Counter Logs* option and select the *New Log Settings* option.

3. In the *New Log Setting* dialog window, enter a name for the log, and click the *OK* button.

4. On the *General* tab, depicted in Figure 12-58, add the counters that you wish to log, and modify the sampling interval if necessary.

5. You can modify the name and location of the log file as well as the type of file on the *Log Files* tab, if necessary.

Performance Logs and Alerts

event

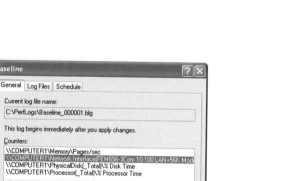

Figure 12-58: Configuring General Log Properties

6. Configure the start and stop times for logging on the *Schedule* tab, as illustrated in Figure 12-59.

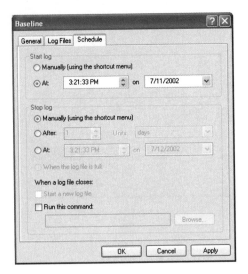

Figure 12-59: Configuring Log Scheduling Properties

7. Click on the *OK* button to save the log configuration and exit.

To view a performance log:

1. Open the *Performance* utility, and select *System Monitor*.

2. Right-click the data display, and select the *Properties* option from the menu.

3. On the *Source* tab, select the *Log files* option, and enter the name of the log file to be viewed, as illustrated in Figure 12-60, and click on the *OK* button to continue.

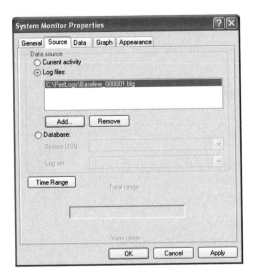

Figure 12-60: Configuring the Data Source

4. Right-click the data display, and select the *Add Counters* option.

5. Add the counters to be viewed, and click on the *OK* button. The available counters will be limited to those that are present in the log.

Correcting Memory Performance Issues

One good indicator of low system memory is a high number of virtual memory accesses. This indicates that there is not enough memory, and the system is having to transfer data back and forth between RAM and the disk drive. This condition also negatively impacts the performance of the drive system. Insufficient system RAM also puts an unnecessary load on the microprocessor and can severely degrade its performance.

The most straightforward way to handle memory problems is to add more memory. However, if the system's RAM capacity is maxed out, or adding RAM is not cost effective, there are still several steps you can take to improve memory-related performance:

- Remove unused or unnecessary operating system components.
- Remove unused or unnecessary network services.
- Minimize the number of applications that are opened simultaneously.
- Minimize the number of programs in the Start-up group.
- Increase the initial size of the paging file to equal its maximum size setting.
- Increase the paging file size if usage approaches 100%.
- Ensure that there is sufficient hard-disk space to support the growth of the paging file.
- Move the paging file to a volume other than the system and boot volumes.
- Offload resources to another system to reduce memory usage

Correcting Processor Performance Issues

There are several key counters that you can monitor to detect processor **bottlenecks**. These counters include measurements of the percent of processor time counter, the Interrupts/sec counter, and queue length.

bottlenecks

If these counters indicate that there is a processor usage problem, there are several steps you can take to correct the problem:

- Verify that the system has enough memory.
- If the rate of system interrupts is high, determine which device is causing the issue.
- Upgrade to a faster processor or add another processor.
- Offload processes that are overloading the system to another computer.

To some degree, working with these counters requires that you be aware of what types of applications the system is running. For example, if single-threaded applications are using large amounts of processing time, upgrading to a faster processor will increase performance more than adding another processor, due to the fact that a single-threaded application can only make use of one processor at a time. On the other hand, if multithreaded applications are using large amounts of processing time, installing an additional processor will increase performance more than a faster processor. Multithreaded applications can take advantage of multiple processors simultaneously.

Correcting Disk System Performance Issues

You can detect disk bottlenecks by monitoring and evaluating physical and logical disk counters. Physical disk counters provide information about activity for the entire disk. Logical disk counters monitor performance of the individual volumes on the disks. If these counters indicate that there is a disk issue, there are several steps you can take to correct them:

- If the page file usage is high, add more RAM.

- Analyze and defragment the drive.

- Add an additional drive to the system, and create a spanned volume to increase contiguous disk space.

- Add disk compression to increase space if processor performance is not an issue.

- Install faster drives.

- Configure stripe sets to increase performance.

- If one drive is used significantly more than others, distribute the workload evenly across all the disks in the system.

- Install additional HDD controllers if you have multiple disks attached to a single controller.

Technical Support 2.3

IT Technician 3.3

Troubleshooting Windows Printing Problems

In a Windows-based system, the Windows environment controls the printing function through its drivers. Check the printer driver using the Control Panel's Print icon to make certain that the correct driver is installed. Determine whether the *Print* option from the application's File menu is unavailable (gray). If so, check the printer's Port settings through the *Ports* tab of the Windows Control Panel/Printers (or Printers and Faxes under Windows XP) Properties. Make certain that the correct printer driver is selected for the printer being used. If no printer type or the wrong printer type is selected, simply set the desired printer as the default.

If a printer is not producing anything in a Windows 2000/XP environment, even though print jobs have been sent to it, check the Print Spooler to see whether any particular type of error has occurred. To view documents waiting to be printed, double-click the desired printer's icon. Return to the *Printer* folder, right-click the printer's icon, click *Properties*, and then select *Details*. From this point, select *Spool Settings*, and select the *Print Directly to the Printer* option. If the print job goes through, there is a spooler problem. If not, the hardware and printer driver are suspect.

To check spooler problems, examine the system for adequate hard-disk space and memory. If the **Enhanced Metafile (EMF) Spooling** option is selected, disable it, clear the spooler, and try to print. To check the printer driver, right-click the printer's icon, select the *Properties* option, and click the *Details* option. Reload or upgrade the driver if necessary.

Enhanced Metafile (EMF) Spooling

If a Windows printer operation *stalls*, or *crashes*, during the printing process, some critical condition must have been reached to stop the printing process. The system was running but stopped. Restart the system in Safe Mode, and try to print again. If the system still will not print, check the print driver, the video driver, and the amount of space on the hard-disk drive. Delete backed up spool and temp files (SPL and TMP) in the System/Spool/Printers directory.

Check to determine whether there is a printer switch box between the computer and the printer. If so, remove the print sharing equipment and connect the computer directly to the printer.

GEEK SQUAD CASE FILE #35353

When you arrive at the customer's machine, he tells you that he has been sending files to the local printer but nothing comes out. When you check the local print queue, you see the files sitting there and determine that they are not moving. What steps should you take to get the printer back into operation?

Technical Support 4.3

Troubleshooting Local Area Networks

Figure 12-61 depicts the system components associated with LAN troubleshooting. Generally, the order of isolating LAN problems is as follows:

1. Check the local networking software

2. Check the cabling and connectors

3. Check the NIC adapter

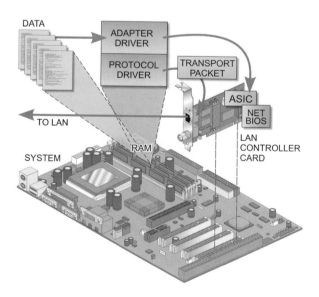

Figure 12-61:
LAN Components

The order of checking is based on convenience and speed of isolating problems. The configuration checks performed on the operating system do not require that any hardware be disassembled. Likewise, cables and connectors are easier and faster to check than internal hardware.

Most network adapter cards come from the manufacturer with a disk, or CD-ROM, of drivers and diagnostic utilities for that particular card. You can run these diagnostic utilities to verify that the LAN hardware is functioning properly. However, it may be easier to run the Windows **PING utility** from the command prompt and attempt to connect to the network. In a LAN environment, you will need to know the IP address or the name of a computer in the network that you can direct the PING to. Both PING and TRACERT can be used to identify the IP address of a known network address. These utilities are discussed in detail later in this chapter.

> **TEST TIP**
> Know which network utility can be used to identify the address of a known remote location.

> **TEST TIP**
> Be aware that cabling faults represent the number one reason for LAN failures.

Cabling is one of the biggest problems encountered in a network installation. Is it connected? Are all the connections good? Is the cable type correct? Has there been any termination, and if so, has it been done correctly? The most efficient way to test network cable is to use a line tester to check its functionality.

> **TEST TIP**
> Know what type of device is commonly used to make checks on LAN cables.

With UTP cabling, simply unplug the cable from the adapter card and plug it into the tester. If coaxial cable is used, you must unplug both ends of the cable from the network, install a terminating resistor at one end of the cable, and plug the other end into the tester. The tester performs the tests required to analyze the cable and connection.

Windows 2000/XP Networking Problems

Some typical networking problems can occur during normal Windows 2000 or Windows XP operations, including the following:

- The user cannot see any other computers on the local network.

- The user cannot see other computers on different networks.

- The clients cannot see the DHCP server but have an IP address.

- The clients cannot obtain an IP address from a DHCP server that is on the other side of a router.

> **TEST TIP**
> Know what the presence of a light on the NIC card indicates.

As mentioned earlier, a major cause of connectivity problems is the physical layer. Check to see that the computer is physically connected to the network and that the status light is glowing (normally green). The presence of the light indicates that the NIC sees network traffic.

If a client cannot see any other computers on the network, improper IP addressing may be occurring. This is one of the most common problems associated with TCP/IP. Users must have a valid IP address and subnet to communicate with other computers. If the IP address is incorrect, invalid, or conflicting with another computer in the network, you will be able to see your local computer but will not be able to see others on the network.

One reason for an incorrect IP address problem would be that the local system in a **TCP/IP network** is looking for a **DHCP Server** that is present. In some LANs, a special server called a DHCP Server is used to dynamically assign IP addresses to its clients in the network. In large networks, each segment of the network would require its own DHCP Server to assign IP addresses for that segment. If the DHCP Server were missing, or not functioning, none of the clients in that segment would be able to see the network.

Likewise, if a DHCP client computer were installed in a network segment that did not use DHCP, it would need to be reconfigured manually with a static IP address. The DHCP settings are administered through the *TCP/IP Properties* window. This window is located under the *Start/Settings/Networking and Dial-Up Connections* option. From this point, open the desired Local Area or Dial-Up Connection, and click the *Properties* button. DHCP operations are covered in more detail later in this chapter.

Begin the troubleshooting process for this type of problem by checking the TCP/IP Properties under the *Network* icon. Next, check the current TCP/IP settings using the command-line **IPCONFIG/ALL** utility. They will display the current IP settings and offer a starting point for troubleshooting. Afterwards, use the PING utility to send test packets to other local computers that you find. The results of this action indicate whether or not the network is working.

TEST TIP

Know the primary TCP/IP tools used to troubleshoot network problems.

GEEK SQUAD CASE FILE #83855

You have installed a new Windows 2000 Professional client in your network and manually assigned it a valid IP address. However, when you try to browse the network, nothing shows up. What network utilities should you use to get the new system into operation?

If users can see other local computers in a TCP/IP network but cannot see remote systems on other networks, the problem may be routing. Check to make certain that the address for the default gateway listed in the TCP/IP properties is valid. Use the NET VIEW command to see whether the remote computer is available. If the user is relying on the My Network Places feature to see other computers, a delay in updating the Browse list may cause remote systems to not be listed. The **NET VIEW** command directly communicates with the remote systems and displays available shares.

If the clients have an IP address of 169.254.xxx.xxx, it is because they cannot communicate with the DHCP server. Windows 2000 automatically assigns the computer an IP address in the 169.254 range if it cannot be assigned one from a DHCP server. Check the previously discussed procedures to determine what the problem may be.

Many routers do not pass the broadcast traffic generated by DHCP clients. If clients cannot obtain an IP address from a DHCP server that is on the other side of a router, the network administrator must enable the forwarding of DHCP packets or place a DHCP server on each side of a router.

You are a Geek Squad Secret Agent who has been deployed to work in the ACME corporation office that has just converted all of its Windows NT Workstation client computers in your network over to Windows 2000 Professional. The network uses a DHCP server to provide IP addresses for the clients. In the process of upgrading the system, you have also moved one of the workstations to a new location in the network. However, when you bring the network back up, all the clients come up perfectly except the unit that was relocated—it cannot connect to the network. What should you look for as you try to get the unit back in operation?

Troubleshooting Network Printing Problems

The complexity of conducting printer operations over a network is much greater because of the addition of the network drivers and protocols. Many of the problems encountered when printing over the network involve components of the operating system. Therefore, its networking and printing functions must both be checked.

print server

When printing cannot be carried out across the network, verify that the local computer and the network printer are set up for remote printing. In the Windows operating systems, this involves sharing the printer with the network users. The local computer that the printer is connected to, referred to as the **print server**, should appear in the *My Network Places* window of the remote computer. If the local computer cannot see files and printers at the print server station, the *file and print sharing* function may not be enabled there.

> **TEST TIP**
>
> Be aware that not having File and Print sharing enabled will cause computers to not "see" the other computers across the network.

printer sharing

In Windows, **printer sharing** can be accomplished at the print server in a number of ways. First, double-click the printer's icon in the *Printer* (or *Printers and Faxes*) dialog box, navigate the *Printer/Properties/Sharing* path, and then choose the desired configuration. The second method uses a right-click on the printer's icon, followed by selecting the *Share* entry in the pop-up context menu, and choosing the desired configuration. The final method is similar except that you right-click the printer's icon and click *Properties*, *Sharing* tab, and then choose the configuration.

Run the printer's self-test to verify that its hardware is working correctly. If it will not print a test page, there is obviously a problem with the printer hardware. Next, troubleshoot the printer hardware. When the operation of the hardware is working, attempt to print across the network again.

Next, determine whether the print server can print directly to the printer. Open a document on the print server and attempt to print it. If the file will not print directly to the local printer, there is a problem in the local hardware. Troubleshoot the problem as a local, stand-alone printer problem.

If the local print server operation is working, verify the operation of the network by attempting to perform other network functions, such as transferring a file from the remote unit to the print server. In Windows 9x, open the Control Panel's *Printer* folder and select the *Properties* entry in the drop-down File menu. Check the information under the *Details* and *Sharing* tabs.

If other network functions are operational, verify the printer operation of the local computer. If possible, connect a printer directly to the local unit and set its print driver up to print to the local printer port. If the file prints to the local printer, a network/printer driver problem still exists. Reload the printer driver, and check the network print path, as depicted in Figure 12-62. The correct format for the UNC network path name is *computer_name**shared device_name*.

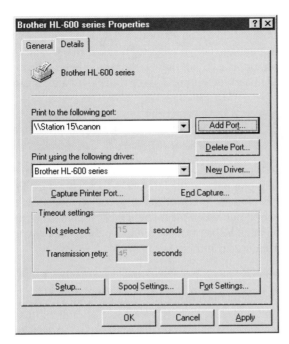

Figure 12-62:
Checking the
Printer Path

If the printer operation stalls, or crashes, during the printing process, a different type of problem is indicated. In this case, the remote printer was functioning, the print server was operational, and the network was transferring data. Some critical condition must have been reached to stop the printing process. Check the print spooler in the print server to see whether an error has occurred. Also, check the hard-disk space and memory usage in the print server.

┌─ **TEST TIP** ─────────────────────────┐
│ Know how to create a UNC path from a local computer │
│ to a remote printer or a directory located on a remote │
│ computer. │
└──────────────────────────────────────┘

Troubleshooting WAN Problems

The quickest items to check in a WAN application are the dial-up network software settings. Check the spelling of the **Fully Qualified Domain Names** to make sure they are spelled exactly as they should be. If the spelling is wrong, no communications will take place. The major difference in checking WAN problems occurs in checking the Internet-specific software, such as the browser.

Fully Qualified
Domain Names

Most of the WAN troubleshooting steps from the local computer level involve the modem. The modem hardware should be examined as described in Chapter 11. If the hardware is functional, the operating system's driver and resource configuration settings must be checked.

Each user should have received a packet of information from their ISP when the service was purchased. These documents normally contain all the ISP-specific configuration information needed to set up the user's site. This information should be consulted when installing and configuring any Internet-related software.

The ISP establishes an Internet access account for each user. These accounts are based on the user's account name and password that are asked for each time the user logs on to the account. Forgetting or misspelling either item will result in the ISP rejecting access to the Internet. Most accounts are paid for on a monthly schedule. If the account isn't paid up, the ISP may cancel the account and deny access to the user. In either of these situations, if the user attempts to log on to the account, they will repeatedly be asked to enter their account name and password until a predetermined number of failed attempts has been reached.

GEEK SQUAD CASE FILE #88223

A customer has called your precinct because he cannot get on the Internet and he doesn't know enough about his computer or the Internet to fix his problem. When you ask him to describe what is happening, he tells you that he gets to the log in screen that asks for his username and password, but each time he puts them in, the same screen reappears. He wants to know if you think he has a virus. What two things can you tell him to check? Is one of those items running an antivirus program?

The most common communication error is the *Disconnected* message. This message occurs for a number of reasons, including a noisy phone line or random transmission errors. You can normally overcome this type of error by just retrying the connection. Other typical error messages include the following:

- *No Dial Tone*—This error indicates a bad or improper phone-line connection, such as the phone line plugged into the modem's line jack rather than the phone jack.

- *Port In Use*—This error indicates a busy signal or an improper configuration parameter.

- *Can't Find Modem*—This error indicates that the PnP process did not detect the modem, or that it has not been correctly configured to communicate with the system.

If the *system cannot find the modem*, you should reboot the system and allow Windows to redetect it. If rebooting does not detect the modem, run any diagnostics available for the modem. In particular, use the Utility disk, or CD-ROM, that comes with the modem to perform tests on the modem hardware. Check the modem documentation for any manufacturer-specified hardware configuration settings for the modem and compare them to the settings in the Control Panel's Hardware Device Manager. Check the modem manufacturer's Web site for updated drivers that will work with the operating system you have.

If the *modem is present*, move into Device Manager and check the modem for resource conflicts. If there is a conflict with the modem, an exclamation point (!) should appear beside the modem listing. If a conflict is indicated, double-click on the modem driver under the Modems node to move into the *General* tab of the Modem's *Properties* page. Check the message in the *Device status* window to see what type of conflict is indicated. The conflict must be resolved between the modem and whatever device is sharing its resources. Click on the *Troubleshooter* button to access and run the *Windows Modem Troubleshooter*.

If no conflict is indicated, move into the *Diagnostics* tab. Click the *Query Modem* button to cause Windows to communicate with the modem hardware. If no problems are detected by this test, Windows displays a listing of the AT communications commands that it used to test the hardware, as illustrated in Figure 12-63. If an error is detected during the Windows testing, an error message displays on-screen. These messages are similar to those previously listed.

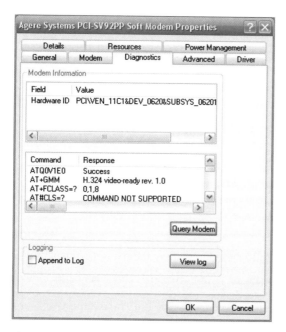

Figure 12-63: Modem Properties Query Modem Response

If the modem tests are OK, check the *user name* and *password* settings. This can be accomplished through the *Start/Settings/Network and Dial-Up Connections* path in Windows 2000. In Windows XP, the path is *Start/Connect To/Show all connections*.

In the *Network and Dial-Up Connections* (or *Show all connections*) window, right-click the desired connection icon, and select *the Properties* option from the list. Check the phone number and modem type on the *General* tab. Next move into the *Networking* tab and confirm the "*Type of Dial-Up Server I am calling*" setting. For Windows Internet dial-up service, this is typically a "PPP, Windows 95/98NT4/2000, Internet" connection. Also, disable the NetBEUI and IPX/SPX components on the page, and make certain that the TCP/IP component is enabled.

Most ISPs use DHCP to assign IP, DNS, and Gateway addresses to clients for dial-up accounts. Therefore, in a dial-up situation, the *Server Assigns IP Address* option and the *Server Assigns Name Server Address* option are normally enabled. Check the ISP-supplied package to make sure that these settings do not need to be set manually. If they are, set up the page to match the ISP-specified settings. In the case of intranets with "in-house" clients, the network administrator determines how the values are assigned—statically or via DHCP.

Network Troubleshooting Tools

When TCP/IP is installed in a Windows system, a number of TCP/IP troubleshooting tools are automatically installed with it. All TCP/IP utilities are controlled by commands entered and run from the command prompt. These TCP/IP tools include the following:

- **Address Resolution Protocol (ARP) command**—This utility enables you to modify IP-to-Ethernet address-translation tables.

- **FTP**—This utility enables you to transfer files to and from FTP servers.

- **PING**—This utility enables you to verify connections to remote hosts.

- **NETSTAT**—This utility enables you to display the current TCP/IP network connections and protocol statistics. A similar command, called NBTSTAT, performs the same function using NetBIOS over the TCP/IP connection.

- **Trace Route (TRACERT)**—This utility enables you to displays the route, and a hop count, taken to a given destination. The route taken to a particular address can be set manually using the ROUTE command.

┌─ **TEST TIP** ───┐
Know where TCP/IP utilities are run from.
└────────────────────────────────┘

Address Resolution Protocol (ARP) command

FTP

PING

NETSTAT

Trace Route (TRACERT)

IPCONFIG

┌─ **TEST TIP** ───┐
Know which TCP/IP utility can be used to display the path of a transmission across a network.
└──┘

- **IPCONFIG**—This command-line utility enables you to determine the current TCP/IP configuration (MAC address, IP address, and subnet mask) of the local computer. It also may be used to request a new TCP/IP address from a DHCP server. IPCONFIG is available in both Windows 2000 and Windows XP.

  The IPCONFIG utility can be started with two important option switches—*/renew* and */release*. These switches are used to release and update IP settings received from a DHCP server. The */all* switch to view the TCP/IP settings for all the adapter cards that the local station is connected to.

┌─ **TEST TIP** ───┐
Know which TCP/IP utilities can be used to release and renew IP address information from a DHCP server.
└──┘

┌─ **TEST TIP** ─────────────┐
Know which TCP/IP utilities show the host IP address.
└────────────────────────────┘

- **NSLOOKUP.EXE**—This is a Windows 2000/XP TCP/IP utility that can be entered at the command prompt to query Internet (DNS) name servers interactively. It has two modes—*interactive* and *noninteractive*. In interactive mode, the user can query name servers for information about various hosts and domains. Noninteractive mode is used to print just the name and requested information for a host or domain. *NSLOOKUP* is available only when the TCP/IP protocol has been installed.

NSLOOKUP.EXE

┌─ **TEST TIP** ─────────────────┐
Know where TCP/IP utilities are run from.
└────────────────────────────────┘

GEEK SQUAD CASE FILE #54353

You have been deployed to set up a network of old Windows 95 and 98 computers that have been donated to a school by a local company. Which utilities must you use to view the TCP/IP settings for all the adapter cards in the network?

Although all of these utilities are useful in isolating different TCP/IP problems, the most widely used commands are PING and TRACERT.

The **PING** utility sends **Internet Control Message Packets (ICMP)** to a remote location and then waits for echoed response packets to be returned. The command waits for up to 1 second for each packet sent and then displays the number of transmitted and received packets. You can use the command to test both the name and IP address of the remote unit. A number of switches can be used to set parameters for the PING operation. Figure 12-64 depicts the information displayed by a typical PING operation.

PING

Internet Control Message Packets (ICMP)

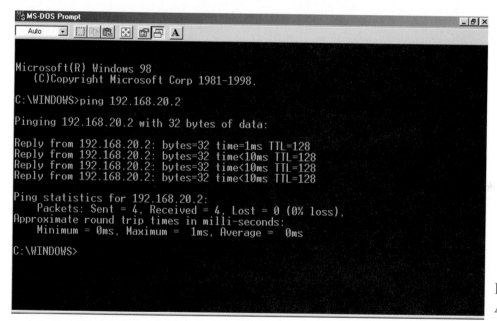

**Figure 12-64:
A PING Operation**

Most Internet servers do not respond to ICMP requests created by pinging. However, you can use the PING utility to access *www.somewebsitename.com*. By doing so, you can get a reply that will verify that TCP/IP, DNS, and gateway are working. The **TRACERT** utility traces the route taken by ICMP packets sent across the net, as described in Figure 12-65. Routers along the path return information to the inquiring system, and the utility displays the host name, IP address, and round-trip time for each hop in the path.

TRACERT

Figure 12-65:
TRACERT
Operation

Because the TRACERT report shows how much time is spent at each router along the path, it can be used to help determine where network slowdowns are occurring.

Verifying TCP/IP Configurations

There are two TCP/IP utilities that are particularly important in confirming and troubleshooting a new TCP/IP configuration. These are the IPCONFIG and PING utilities. To verify the configuration of a new TCP/IP installation, begin by running the IPCONFIG utility from the command prompt to verify that the connection has been properly initialized.

Then use the PING utility to test the TCP/IP operations. This is accomplished by pinging different IP addresses in order:

1. PING address 127.0.0.1 to perform a loopback test that will verify that TCP/IP has successfully been loaded in the local computer.

2. PING the local adapter's IP address to insure that it has been initialized.

3. PING the default gateway (router) address to verify that TCP/IP is working on both devices.

4. PING the address of another computer on the same network segment to make sure that the default gateway is functional.

┌─ **TEST TIP** ─────────┐
│ Know which Windows tools to │
│ use to check out network-related │
│ problems. │
└──────────────────────┘

If only one of the PINGed devices does not return a reply, then it has a problem. If neither device replies, then the local computer may have a problem. Have someone else check your TCP/IP configuration settings to make sure no values have been transposed as they were being entered.

Troubleshooting Software Firewall Issues

Some connection problems can be the result of misconfigured Proxy or firewall settings. While corporate and business environment rely on hardware firewalls and have skilled administrators to manage them, personal and residential networks typically rely on software firewalls, such as Zone Alarm or the Windows XP ICF. For typical PC users, these utilities can often be difficult to configure correctly.

If you are having Internet connectivity problems getting WAN access, or some services, such as incoming or outgoing mail do not function, you should try temporarily disable your security software and setting their Internet Explorer security level to its default. This should minimize interference with the connection. If you are able to connect to the Internet, or use the desired service under this condition, you must reconfigure the firewall settings. This will involve identifying services (or ports) that are being blocked and configuring them to allow communications to take place, or the identified service to function. Proxies and software firewalls are described in detail in Chapter 13.

KEY POINTS REVIEW

This chapter has discussed troubleshooting and diagnostic methods associated with the Windows operating systems. Review the following key points before moving into the Review and Exam Questions sections to make sure you are comfortable with each point. Afterward, answer the Review Questions that follow to verify your knowledge of the information.

- During the bootup process, an interesting troubleshooting point occurs at the single beep in the bootup process of most computers. If the system produces an error message, such as "The system has detected unstable RAM at location XXXX", or a beep-coded error signal before the beep, the problem is hardware related.

- If the error message or beep code is produced after the single beep occurs, the problem is likely to be associated with starting up the operating system. At this point, the problem becomes an operating system start-up problem.

- If nothing is being produced by the printer, even though print jobs have been sent to it, check the Print Spooler to see if any particular type of error has occurred.

- To view documents waiting to be printed, double-click on the desired printer's icon. Return to the *Printer* folder, right-click on the printer's icon, click *Properties*, and then select *Details*. From this point, select *Spool Settings* and select the *Print Directly to the Printer* option. If the print job goes through, there is a spooler problem. If not, the hardware and printer driver are suspect.

- The complexity of conducting printer operations over a network becomes much greater due to the addition of the network drivers and protocols. Many of the problems encountered when printing over the network involve components of the operating system. Therefore, its networking and printing functions must both be checked.

- Windows comes with a built-in Troubleshooting Help file system. This feature includes troubleshooting assistance for a number of different Windows problems.

- Hardware and configuration conflicts can also be isolated manually using the Windows Device Manager from the Control Panel's *System* icon. This utility is basically an easy-to-use interface for the Windows registry.

REVIEW QUESTIONS

The following questions test your knowledge of the material presented in this chapter.

1. How is a stalled application cleared in the Windows 2000/XP environment?

2. How is a UNC path specified to create a path from a local computer to a remote printer, or to a directory located on a remote computer?

3. Which utility is used to view real-time system performance in Windows 2000/XP?

4. Which Windows XP utility can be used to monitor the operation of application packages and log any errors?

5. Why are defragmentation programs run on computers?

6. What is the purpose of running a CHKDSK operation before performing a backup or defrag operation on the hard drive?

7. Which Windows utility can be used to examine and change text files such as the BOOT.INI file?

8. If an application will not start in Windows when its icon is clicked, what action should be taken?

9. How can the Print Spooler be isolated as a cause of printing problems in a Windows environment?

10. Where are the disk-drive management tools located in Windows 2000?

11. Which devices are loaded in Safe Mode start-up?

12. If a printer is not producing anything in a Windows 2000 environment, even though print jobs have been sent to it, what should you check first?

13. What is a common reason for not seeing a remote printer in the Windows Network Neighborhood?

14. In Windows 2000, which utility can be used to access hard drives and command-line utilities when the system does not boot?

15. Which TCP/IP utility can be used to display the current TCP/IP network connections and protocol statistics?

1. Which of the following is not a function of the Emergency Repair Process in Windows 2000? (Select all that apply.)
   a. Repairing the disk drive's boot sector
   b. Repairing the system's Start-up files
   c. Repairing corrupted data files
   d. Repairing failed applications

2. A Windows XP Professional workstation has had problems during normal operations lately. What sort of application will enable you to review any sort of conflicts and problems that have occurred over time?
   a. ASR
   b. Device Manager
   c. Event Viewer
   d. Services and Applications

3. Where are the Backup and Restore functions accessed in a Windows 2000 system?
   a. Start/Programs/Accessories/System Tools and then select Backup
   b. Start/Settings/Control Panel/System and then click on the Backup tab
   c. Start/Settings/Control Panel and then double-click the Backup tool
   d. Start/Programs/Accessories and then select Backup

4. Which backup methodology requires the least amount of time to perform and the most amount of time to restore the system?
   a. Full
   b. Differential
   c. Incremental
   d. Daily

5. If an "X" is displayed by an entry in the Windows Device Manager, what is indicated?
   a. The device has been disabled by a user selection conflict.
   b. The device is experiencing a direct hardware conflict with another device.
   c. The device's real-mode driver is not being loaded.
   d. The device's virtual-mode driver is not being loaded.

6. How can you remove a stalled application in a Windows 2000 system? (Select all that apply.)
   a. Right-click the system tray, select Task Manager from the contextual menu, click on the Applications tab, highlight the application, and click on End Task.
   b. Press CTRL+ALT+ESC, click on Task Manager, click on the Applications tab, highlight the application, and click on End Task.
   c. Press CTRL+SHIFT+ESC, click on the Applications tab, highlight the application, and click on End Task.
   d. Press CTRL+ALT+DEL, click on Task Manager, click on the Applications tab, highlight the application, and click on End Task.

7. If one computer cannot see another computer on the network, what might the most logical problem be?
   a. The Device Manager does not recognize the adapter.
   b. The IP address is incorrect, invalid, or conflicting with another computer.
   c. The Network Control Panel has not been enabled.
   d. The Networking Services have not been installed.

8. If Plug-and-Play is not working in a Windows 9x system, where can a device driver be installed from?
   a. The Start Menu
   b. The Device Manager
   c. The Add/Remove Programs wizard
   d. The Add New Hardware wizard

9. If a modem listed in the Device Manager indicates a resource conflict, what action should be taken to clear up the situation?
   a. Run MSD.EXE.
   b. Run MEM.EXE.
   c. Click the Resources tab and check for conflicts.
   d. Change the IRQ setting for the device.

10. What is the proper path to activate the Windows XP System Restore wizard?
    a. Start/All Programs/Accessories/System Tools
    b. Start/Programs/Accessories/System Tools
    c. Start/All Programs/Administrative Tools/Backup
    d. Start/All Programs/Backup/System Restore

CHAPTER
13

SECURITY AND PREVENTIVE MAINTENANCE

Upon completion of this chapter and its related lab procedures, you should be able to perform these tasks:

1. Demonstrate proper cleaning procedures for various system components.

2. Describe electrostatic discharge hazards and methods of preventing ESD.

3. List the steps for proper IC handling.

4. Define the term ground.

5. Describe the two types of uninterruptible power supplies (UPSs) and state their qualities.

6. State typical precautions that should be observed when working on computer equipment.

7. Perform generic preventive maintenance routines as required.

8. Detail routine preventive maintenance procedures as they apply to hard and floppy disks.

9. Perform basic disk-management functions, including using CHKDSK and Defrag utilities.

10. Use backup software to create backups of important data.

11. Use software utilities to identify and remove viruses from computer systems.

12. List precautionary steps that should be taken when handling floppy disks.

13. List steps to clean a dot-matrix, ink-jet, or laser printer.

14. Establish and maintain preventive maintenance schedules for users.

15. Differentiate between various UPS specifications and state how they apply to a given situation.

16. State potential hazards present when working with laser printers, monitors, and other equipment.

17. Identify hardware- and software-based authentication methods used with PCs.

18. Describe malware and grayware products used to access PCs, and identify common prevention tools and techniques used against them.

19. Recognize social engineering efforts and respond to them.

CHAPTER 13

SECURITY AND PREVENTIVE MAINTENANCE

FROM THE GEEK SQUAD

Bill is Agent 31, a brand new Geek Squad Special Agent. He is working the desk at store number 455 in Scottsdale, Arizona, customizing PCs to fill specific customer orders. The number one activity Agent 31 performs is installing antivirus, antispyware, and antispam utilities on the systems.

These utilities change often, and Agent 31 must stay abreast of not only the products but the types of problems driving the changes. Because these products tend to be after-sales add-ons, Bill needs to be able to tell customers what products they need, why they need them, and how to use them. He has found that this information works well with the preventive maintenance discussion he has with the customers when they pick up their new computers.

INTRODUCTION

Modern printed circuit board and chipset technologies coupled with fairly mature PnP technology has made the PC fairly stable over a predictable life cycle. In addition, Microsoft's efforts to control the relationship between their operating systems and application software manufacturers have led to relatively problem-free software. However, increased connectivity through networks and the Internet have made PCs vulnerable to an array of different types of *malware* and *grayware*. One of the greatest threats to computer operations has become the proliferation of malware intended to interfere with the operation of systems or to steal information that may be stored on them.

The second half of the chapter covers safety issues and preventive maintenance procedures associated with personal computers. The safety portion of the chapter includes information about the potential hazards to personnel and equipment when working with lasers, high-voltage equipment, ESD, and items that require special disposal procedures that comply with environmental guidelines. The preventive maintenance sections include information about preventive maintenance products, procedures, environmental hazards, and precautions when working on microcomputer systems.

PC SECURITY

Computer **security** is implemented on multiple levels that include physical denial of use, limited access to system resources, and active protection against individuals and software intent on corrupting or stealing data. When dealing with server systems, it is common to strictly limit physical access to the server hardware by placing it in protected rooms that have automatic locks on the door and computer chassis. These systems also include audible alarms and escalating security notices if anyone attempts to get past these safeguards. However, this is not practical with PC systems that may be used by different users and, in many cases, are portable.

There are three levels of security commonly associated with desktop and portable PCs:

- Hardware-oriented possession and access limitation

- Local and network policies and permissions governing access to information on a PC

- Protection from external sources seeking to steal, damage, or disrupt data on the PC

In the following sections of this chapter, we will concentrate on two of those security levels—common hardware security devices and protection from **malware** and **grayware**. Information about local and network policies and permissions was covered in Chapter 10, *Windows Operating Systems*.

security

malware

grayware

polarizing films

Hardware Security

While it is not practical to limit physical access to PCs in most situations, there are several hardware methods commonly used to limit possession of the computer and to limit what unauthorized people can do with the computer. These methods can be as simple as installing **polarizing films** over displays to prevent people other than the user from being able to view information displayed on the screen, or as extreme as chaining computer equipment to furniture or other suitable structures to keep it from being removed.

Polarizing screens are placed in front of displays and permit the user setting directly in front of the display to view the information on the screen. The polarizing feature prevents others from viewing the screen from an angle.

Some portable systems also have lockable docking stations that secure the notebook and docking station to a structure such as a desk. Other organizations encase the system units inside furniture to keep them from being removed. Access doors provide access to the drive openings and the on/off switch. This leaves only the keyboard, video display and pointing devices vulnerable to removal.

When it's not feasible to physically lock up the hardware as described above, there are hardware devices that can be used to make the system unusable by people other than authorized users. These devices include such items as *smart cards* and *biometric devices*.

Smart Cards

Smart cards are authentication tools that contain information about their owners, such as their *passwords*, **personal identification numbers (PINs)**, network keys, digital certificates, and so forth. Physically, smart cards exist as smart, credit card–like devices, ID badges, and plug-in devices that communicate with a smart card reader.

The smart card reader may communicate with the reader through magnetic stripes or wirelessly. Generally, the reader is installed in the PC, or it attaches to or plugs in to one of the PC's serial, USB, or PCMCIA ports. Figure 13-1 depicts a typical smart card device used with PCs.

Essentials 6.1

Depot Technician 4.2

Technical Support 5.2

IT Technician 6.0

Smart cards

personal
identification
numbers (PINs)

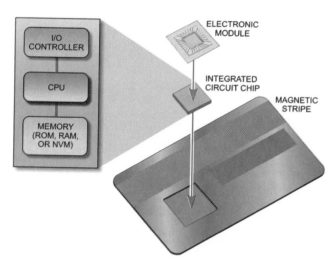

**Figure 13-1:
Smart Cards**

Internally, all smart card designs contain a microprocessor and memory devices that are embedded in the card structure. The memory section of the smart card holds user-specific identification information, as well as all the programming it needs to communicate with the host system—the **card operating system (COS)**. The programmability of the smart card enables it to work with changing password strategies and to pass *tokens* and certificates back and forth with network hosts to provide secure network interactions.

card operating
system (COS)

Some organizations that use smart cards issue their employees smart cards that they can use to get into their buildings, log on to their PCs, and access appropriate applications. The card system combines the users' secret PINs (i.e., something the users alone know) with tokens generated by the network's Certificate Authority *authentication system* to generate a unique **pass code**. The pass code validates the user and his or her access to different resources.

pass code

The IC devices in smart cards are embedded in a manner that makes them resistant to tampering. Tampering with a smart card generally disables it. In addition, some care must be taken with smart cards as even bending one may render it unusable.

Windows 2000 and XP support *Personal Computer/Smart Card (PC/SC)* compliant smart card readers through the PnP process. Therefore, no external device drivers need to be loaded for these smart card readers. However, the Windows Smart Card Services must be enabled in the Computer Management console. Windows also provides smart card secured log in support when authenticating to Active Directory domains.

In Windows 2000, right-click on the connection (dial-up, VPN, or incoming) that you want to use the smart card in the *Network and Dial-Up Connections* window and choose *Properties*. In Windows XP, click on the desired connection in *Network Connections*, and select the *Change Settings of this connection* option under Network Tasks. In both Windows 2000 and XP, click the *Typical (recommended settings)* option on the *Security* tab, depicted in Figure 13-2. Next, click the *Use smart card* option in the *Validate my identity as follows* dialog box.

**Figure 13-2:
Selecting Smart
Card Validation**

Checking the *Advanced (custom settings)* check box and clicking the *Settings* button will bring up the *Advanced Security Settings* window depicted in Figure 13-3. On this page you can configure custom security settings for *data encryption* and *logon security*. Under the *Logon security* entry, click the *Use Extensible Authentication Protocol (EAP)* option, then click *Smartcard or other certificate (encryption enabled)*, click *Properties*, and then choose the appropriate setting for the certificate you want to use—*Use my smartcard* or *Use a certificate on this computer*.

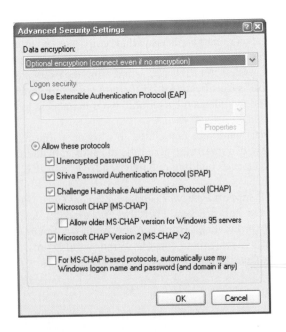

**Figure 13-3:
Advanced Security
Settings Window**

Biometric Authentication Devices

Depot Technician 4.2

Technical Support 5.2

Biometric authentication

Biometric authentication involves using uniquely personal physiological characteristics to verify people are who they say they are. Each person possesses unique physical characteristics that differentiate him or her from everyone else. Even identical twins have separate and distinctive DNA, voice patterns, fingerprints, eye features, and other characteristics. The qualities most often involved in biometric authentication include voice patterns, fingerprints, palm prints, signatures, facial features, and retinal and iris scans, as shown in Figure 13-4.

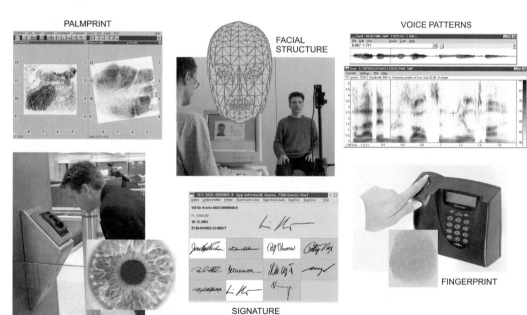

Figure 13-4: Typical Biometric Authentication Methods

In each case, a *biometric scanning device* is required to convert the physiological quantity into a digital representation. The results are stored in a database where they can be used in an authentication process. The underlying application will use the truly unique qualities of the data as a basis to compare future access requests to. If the data from a future authentication request match the key points of the stored version, then access will be granted.

Not all biometric scanning devices are equally accurate at authenticating users. The characteristics of the human eye—iris and retinal scans—tend to make it the most reliable source of authentication. Although fingerprint readings tend to be more accurate than voice scans, fingerprints can be stored on a clear surface and used later. On the other hand, illnesses and user stress levels can affect voiceprints.

Biometric scanners are becoming significantly more sophisticated, including facial scanning devices, searchable databases, and supporting application programs. However, the biometric authentication device most widely used with PCs is the **fingerprint scanner**. Some manufacturers offer miniature touch pad versions that set on the desk and connect to the system through a cable and USB connector. Other fingerprint scanners are built into key fobs that simply plug directly into the USB port. Some manufacturers even build these devices into the top of the mouse. Figure 13-5 shows different fingerprint scanner devices designed for use with PCs.

NOTEBOOK

KEYBOARD

DESKTOP TOUCH PAD

USB

MOUSE

**Figure 13-5:
Fingerprint Scanners**

Most fingerprint scanners come with password management software that enables users to manage access to Internet accounts, encrypted documents, and other options secured with a password. For USB-based scanners, the scanners' application software is generally installed in the host machine first. Next, the scanner is physically attached to one of the system's USB ports. When the system is started up, the PnP process should detect the new hardware component and bring up its installation configuration wizard to guide you through the setup process.

The setup process typically involves entering passwords and usernames for different accounts. Because the users will not be asked to input their passwords, passwords can be long and quite complex. This makes it much harder for the password to be *cracked*.

The password manager's enrollment wizard will prompt you to identify which finger, or fingers, you intend to use. Afterward, it will ask you to place that finger firmly and securely on the scanner pad and press selected keys to submit the scan into the system. The fingerprint scanner application uses the image to build the authentication database. The reason for scanning multiple fingerprints is to provide log-in options for occurrences such as injured/bandaged fingers. The other finger scans serve as a backup for these occasions. The user may also be asked to repeat the scanning process multiple times on each finger to insure that a good print is taken and stored. Likewise, you can use multiple fingerprint reads to identify multiple users for a single computer.

─ **NOTE** ─────────────

Some fingerprint scanners actually store the scanned images and the account access information on the device. This allows the identification file to travel with the user if the user works with different computers at different locations.

After the fingerprint scanner software has been installed and configured, the password manager will prompt you to scan in your finger rather than type a password on future log-in attempts. Software supplied with some fingerprint scanner models can log users into local Windows systems as well as into a domain environment with a quick, simple finger scan. This feature undermines keystroke-logging spyware that attempts to monitor and steal passwords and usernames.

The fingerprint scanner support software typically includes encryption functions that incorporate the fingerprint as the key. The supporting applications often include utilities for storing other information routinely used in authenticated transactions.

Microsoft provides a proprietary fingerprint scanner for stand-alone and home computers. However, this scanner does not work with domain log-ins. Therefore, they are not practical for use in domain-based business environments. In addition, they will not work with non-IE Web browsers such as *Firefox*.

Essentials 6.1

Information Disposal/Destruction Policies

People and businesses generate and collect piles of information each day in the normal course of living and working. Without proper forethought and planning, these piles can become a source of information for unauthorized and malicious people and businesses. Access to certain types of information can enable these people to commit crimes such as identity theft, intellectual property theft, and monetary theft. For this reason, it is a good idea to have an information disposal and destruction policy.

This policy should address the handling of information in the following areas:

- Wastepaper handling policy
- Electronic file storage policy
- Network information policy

Wastepaper includes documents, notes, memos, files, and folders that are no longer useful in day-to-day activities. All of these items should be shredded and removed or shredded and burned, as they may contain information that others could use to do damage.

However, not all old files and folders should be destroyed. Some types of information are required to be stored for different periods of time after they are no longer current. Files such as tax records, bank records, personnel files, and audit files may need to be protected rather than destroyed.

Essentials 6.2

Depot Technician 4.1

Software Security

Files and folders of electronic information can collect on hard drives, backup tapes, floppy disks, and CD-ROMs. As with waste paper products, old floppies, backup tapes, and CD-ROMs should be erased and destroyed when they are no longer useful. Methods used to destroy storage media such as outdated floppy disks and tape backups include incineration, shredding, using acid, or preferably by demagnetizing.

You can demagnetize floppy disks and backup tapes using strong magnets to electronically erase them. Simply erasing the files from the disk or tape does not actually remove the recorded data from them. There are several commercially available software tools that can restore erased data from a magnetic disk. There are other stronger tools that can be used to raise old data from magnetic disks even after they have been overwritten.

Wastepaper and obsolete magnetic storage materials cannot simply be disposed of without being destroyed first. Unscrupulous individuals called **dumpster divers** go through trash receptacles trying to find items such as credit card information, account information, shipping receipts, phone numbers, and even scribbled passwords that they can use to undermine people's lives and businesses.

Another major security threat that is often overlooked occurs when systems are updated with new hard-disk drives. It is a simple matter to migrate any desired data over to the new drive and put the old drive away in case it can be used for something else later. However, that information still resides on the old drive, and left alone, it can remain for many years. Because the drive is no longer in a machine where physical and electronic access to its data is controlled, it becomes a security risk.

Data migration operations can become a security problem when the data is not removed from the old machine and it is assigned to a new user. For example, if a manager receives a new notebook and transfers his data from the old machine to the new machine without removing the data when he is finished, and that machine is reissued to an employee, the employee can gain access to the data. Its not difficult to see how this could be a problem since the employee has access to potentially sensitive information.

As mentioned in Chapter 10, when information from an NTFS partition is moved to a FAT partition, the NTFS attributes and security features are lost. Even moving files between different NTFS partitions on different drives can change the security level of data. Migrating NTFS data to a partition that has lower permission levels than the original partition will cause the data to inherit the lesser permissions of the target folder.

It is a good security move to convert any FAT or FA32 partitions to NTFS so that the stronger NTFS and share permissions can be used to provide stronger control over access to data on the drive. This will also allow you to use the NTFS encrypting file system to protect files on the drive.

Disposal and Destruction Policies

Without a disposal and destruction policy, the same thing can happen when old computers are decommissioned and replaced. The drives still hold their information for a long time, and no one is generally paying attention to where they are and who might be accessing them. At a minimum, the data on these drives need to be erased. There are also commercially available software tools for cleaning information from drives. However, these tools generally do not conduct the **low-level format** procedure on the hard drive required to completely erase it. Many hard drive manufacturers provide downloadable low-level format tools that can be used to remove any remnant of data from their drives.

> If a hard drive is to be stored or reused in a different capacity, it should be low-level formatted before it is removed from the original system. This will provide some measure of security for the data it originally held.

If a hard-disk drive is not going to be reused, it should be destroyed to the point where it is physically unusable. This can involve *opening the outer cover of the drive* and physically *scarring* its disk surfaces. Scratching the surface with a sharp implement, hammering the disks, or pouring acid on the disk surfaces will render the drive and the information in it useless. You can also use a powerful magnet to magnetically erase data from the disks. However, this method must be applied thoroughly to the disks, as some **data remnants** may remain on the disk surfaces that professional data collectors can still detect.

data remnants

Backup tapes and discs pose the same security risks as hard drives do. Old backup tapes contain information that in the wrong hands can be used in a mischievous or malicious manner. The network administrators, or their designated subordinates are typically responsible for controlling access to backup tapes. Current tapes should be kept in a physically secure place (in a locked cabinet or in a locked room) away from general access. However, this copy should be handy to the administrators in case they need access to them to restore the system.

In many companies multiple backup copies are created. At least one copy is kept off site so that it will survive any catastrophic failures such as fires or floods. In some cases, copies are performed over the Internet to remote third-party facilities to add additional physical security to the data.

When the tapes become obsolete they should be physically and logically destroyed in the same manner as hard disk drives.

Network Security

IT Technician 6.2

The sheriff on any network is the **network administrator**. As described in Chapter 10, these individuals create *user and group accounts* for network members that include specific access rights and permissions to the network and its resources. Network users are *allowed* or *denied* access to read, modify, and examine files and folders based on the access control policy that is established for them either as individuals or by their position in different network groups.

network administrator

In most organizations, the network administrators establish policy statements that control "who" has access to the network and its resources and what they can do with them. The tools for implementing such policy statements in a Windows environment were covered in Chapter 10, *Windows Operating Systems*.

Administrative Security Settings

Essentials 6.1

Depot Technician 4.1

Technical Support 5.1

IT Technician 6.1

Administrative activities associated with implementing network security policies include

- Establishing user and group accounts
- Implementing authentication options

- Enabling system auditing and event logging
- Establishing firewall settings
- Establishing and implementing malicious software protection policies

Establishing User and Group Accounts

These accounts are configured to Allow or Deny access to system and network resources. In a Windows environment, the administrator can use local and group policies, share permissions, and NTFS permissions to restrict access to resources to just those individuals or groups who need them. Even if a user is granted access to certain resources, the administrator can limit the scope of activities the user can conduct with different files and folders.

Local users and groups exist in the local Windows 2000 or XP accounts database. They are used to gain initial access to the computer, control access to its local resources, and control access to network resources. These accounts are created and managed through the **Local Users and Groups** utility under Computer Management, as depicted in Figure 13-6.

Local Users and Groups

Figure 13-6: Managing Local User and Group Accounts

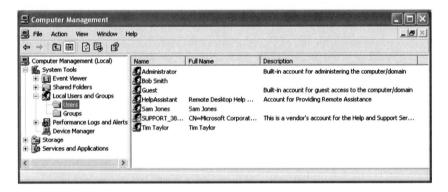

There are several default user accounts in Windows 2000 and XP. These accounts include the following:

- *Administrator*—the main administrative management account that has full access to the system and all of its management tools.

- *Guest* account—a catchall account used to provide access to users that do not have a user account on the computer. This account should be disabled after user accounts have been established.

- *HelpAssistant*—a special Windows XP account used with its Remote Assistance utility to authenticate users connecting through it. This account is enabled whenever a remote assistance invitation is created and automatically disabled when all invitations have expired.

- *SUPPORT_XXXXX*—a special Microsoft account used to provide remote support through their *Help and Support Service* utility.

The Windows default user accounts can be renamed but not deleted. The initial Windows Administrator accounts password is set up during the Windows installation process.

Administrators use **group accounts** to collectively deal with user accounts that have common needs. Groups save administrators time by allowing them to issue user rights and resource access permissions to everyone in the group at once. You cannot use a group account to log on to a computer. You can only gain access to a system by logging on with a legitimate user account.

group accounts

The default *group accounts* in Windows 2000 and XP Professional include the following:

- *Administrators*—Members of this group have full access to the computer and its tools and can perform all management functions. This group automatically includes the Administrator user account as a member.

- *Guests*—This default group has minimized access to the system, and all members share the same user profile. The Guest user account is automatically a member of this group.

- *Power Users*—Power Users is a special group that has permissions to perform many management tasks on the system but does not have the full administrative privileges of the Administrator account. Power Users can create and manage users and groups they create. Also, they do not have access to files and folders on NTFS volumes unless they are granted permissions to them through other sources. There are no members in this group when it is created.

- *Backup Operators*—As the name implies, members of this group can back up and restore all files on the computer. Through the backup utility, members of this group have access to the system's entire file system. There are no members in this group when it is created.

- *Network Configuration Operators*—Members of this group can manage different aspects of the system's network configuration. In particular, they can modify TCP/IP properties; enable, disable, and rename connections; and perform IPCONFIG operations. This group is empty when it is created.

- *Users*—This is a catchall group with limited default permissions. Except for the Guest account, all user accounts created on the system, including the administrator account, are made members of this group by default.

- *Remote Desktop Users*—Members of this Windows XP group have user rights to log on to the system remotely in order to perform Remote Desktop activities. The group has no members by default.

> **NOTE**
>
> Whenever possible, the default group accounts in Windows should be used to assign permissions. Creating additional groups generates additional system management requirements.

Windows 2000 and XP systems also support **domain user and group accounts** when used in a domain environment. **Domain accounts** are created on Windows domain controllers through their *Active Directory Users and Computers* utility and are stored in the Active Directory database. When a Windows 2000 or Windows XP computer is placed in a domain environment, some group memberships are automatically changed to reflect this:

domain user and
group accounts

Domain accounts

- The *Domain Admins* group is added to the local Administrators group so that domain administrators will have administrative control over all the computers in their domain.

- A *Domain Users* group is added to the local Users group.

- A *Domain Guests* group is added to the local Guests group.

These groups are all a function of the Windows domain controllers and exist only in Windows domain environments. The automatic addition of these groups in domain environments makes it easier for domain administrators to configure access to the local computer's resources. The groups are not permanent additions and can be removed at the administrator's discretion.

Implementing Authentication Options

Windows 2000 and Windows XP offer much improved security structure over previous Windows versions. The new security features apply to both LAN and wide area communications. The main security improvement is the adoption of the **Kerberos** authentication protocol. **Authentication** is a process that determines that users on the network are who they say they are.

The Kerberos protocol enables users to authenticate without sending a password over the network. Instead, the user acquires a unique key from the network's central security authority at log-in. The domain controller referred to as the **Key Distribution Center (KDC)** provides the security authority.

When a client makes a request to access a network resource or program, it authenticates itself with the KDC as described in Figure 13-7. The KDC responds by returning a session ticket to the client that is used to establish a connection to the requested resource. The ticket can be used only to authenticate the client's access to services and resources for a limited amount of time. During that time, the client presents the ticket to the application server that verifies the user and provides access to the requested program.

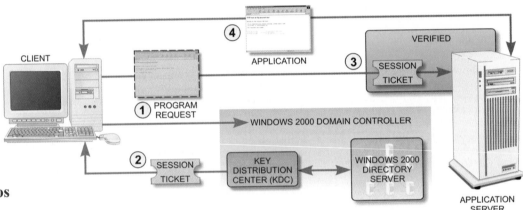

Figure 13-7: Kerberos Protocol Operations

The key is cached on the local machine so that the user can reuse the key at a later time to access the resource. Keys are typically good for about 8 hours, so there is no need for repeated interaction between the user and the KDC. This reduces the number of interactions that must be made across the network and, thereby, reduces the traffic load on the network in general. In addition, no passwords are circulated during the process, so there is no chance of compromising them.

Digital certificates are another major security feature in the Windows 2000 and Windows XP operating systems. Digital certificates are password-protected, encrypted data files that include data that identify the transmitting system and can be used to authenticate external users to the network through **virtual private networks (VPNs)**.

VPNs use message encryption and other security techniques to ensure that only authorized users can access the message as it passes through public transmission media. In particular, VPNs provide secure Internet communications by establishing encrypted data tunnels across the WAN that cannot be penetrated by others.

When the certificates are combined with security standards, such as the **IP security protocol (IPSec)**, secure, encrypted TCP/IP data can be passed across public networks, such as the Internet. IPSec is a secure, encrypted version of the IP protocol. IPSec client software connects remote users to a VPN server by creating an encrypted tunnel across the Internet to the remote user as illustrated in Figure 13-8.

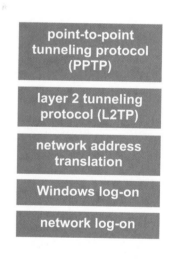

IP security protocol (IPSec)

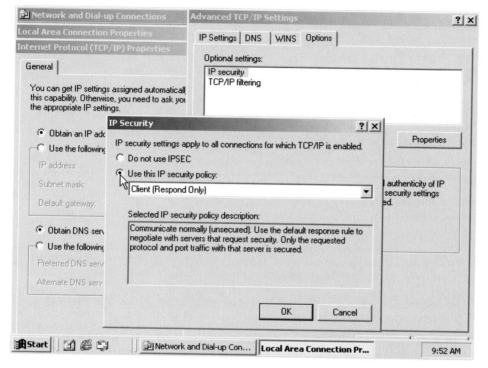

Figure 13-8: IP Security Protocol Operations

In addition to IPSec, Windows 2000 and Windows XP continue to offer **point-to-point tunneling protocol (PPTP)** and **layer 2 tunneling protocol (L2TP)** as alternative security technologies for VPNs. L2TP can be used in conjunction with IPSec to pass the IPSec packets through routers that perform **network address translation**.

The main user authentication tool is the username and password log-in. In Windows 2000 and XP Professional there are two types of user-related log-ons to contend with—the interactive **Windows log-on** to the local machine and the **network log-on**. The first log-on validates the user for local computer resources, while the latter confirms the user's credentials for accessing remote resources. Figure 13-9 shows the *Windows Interactive* and *Network log-on* dialog boxes.

point-to-point tunneling protocol (PPTP)

layer 2 tunneling protocol (L2TP)

network address translation

Windows log-on

network log-on

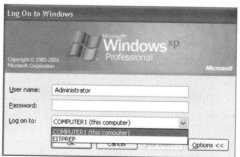

Figure 13-9: Windows Log-On Dialog Boxes

The administrator also sets the network **password policy** for how often users must change their passwords as well as setting length and complexity requirements. The options in the *Password Policy* folder, shown in Figure 13-10, enable administrators to make user accounts and passwords more secure. Password policies apply to all users who log on to the system and cannot be configured for individual users.

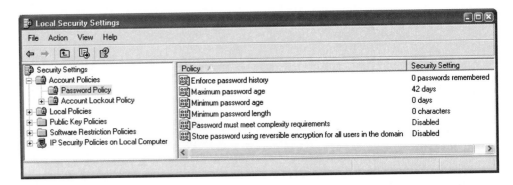

Figure 13-10: Password Policies

As the figure indicates, the *Password Policy* folder is accessed through the Local Security Settings utility. From this folder, administrators can configure the following settings:

- *Enforce password history*—This option is used to specify the number of passwords that will be tracked for each user. When users attempt to change their password, they will not be permitted to reuse any of the passwords being tracked.

- *Maximum password age/Minimum password age*—These two settings enable administrators to set passwords so that they expire after the specified number of days, and also to prevent users from changing their passwords for some specific number of days. When the password expires, the user is prompted to change it, insuring that even if a password becomes public, it will be changed within a short period of time to close the security breach.

- *Minimum password length*—This option is used to specify the minimum number of characters that a password may contain. This allows the administrator to force users to employ passwords that are longer and harder to guess. A password of at least eight characters is recommended for secure systems.

- *Passwords must meet complexity requirements*—Administrators can use this option to force users to use more secure, complex passwords that include some combination of lowercase letters, numbers, symbols and capitalized characters. The administrator sets the level of complexity by establishing password filters at the domain controller level.

- *Store password using reversible encryption for all users in the domain*—This is a special Active Directory domain option that permits passwords to be recovered in emergency cases.

Enabling System Auditing and Event Logging

In a Windows network, auditing is established at the server level while event logging can be set up at the local level. The auditing functionality of Windows 2000 and Windows XP enables the user and operating system activities on a computer to be monitored and tracked. This information can then be used to detect intruders and other undesirable activity.

The auditing system consists of two major components—an **audit policy**, which defines the types of events that will be monitored and added to the system's security logs, and **audit entries**, which consist of the individual entries added to the security log when an audited event occurs. The system administrator implements audit policy. Audit entries are maintained in the **security log**, which can be viewed through the *Event Viewer*. Figure 13-11 shows a typical security log displayed in the Event Viewer utility. For auditing to be an effective security tool, the security log should be reviewed and archived regularly.

audit policy

audit entries

security log

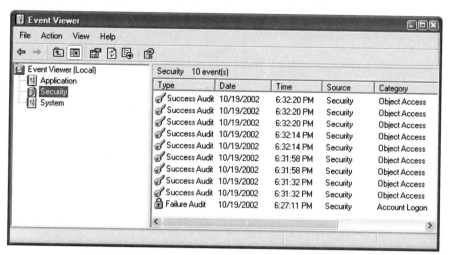

Figure 13-11: Viewing Security Audit Logs

Auditing is configured through the *Local Security Policy* option located under the *Administrative Tools menu*, as shown in Figure 13-12.

In the right-hand pane, open the policy to be configured (or right-click it and select *Properties*). This will produce the *Local Security Setting* window, depicted in Figure 13-13. Place checkmarks beside the option, or options, that should be tracked and audited—Success, Failure, or both—and click on the *OK* button to save the setting and close the policy setting window.

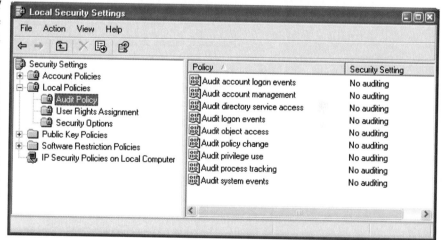

Figure 13-12: Configuring Auditing

Figure 13-13: Establishing a Local

In domain-based environments, auditing can be automated through *Active Directory Group Policy* to save administrators the time that would be involved in setting up audit policies on all the computers in their network.

NOTE
You must be logged in as an administrator to configure audit

Auditing must be configured both as a general system policy setting and on each *object* (file, folder, and printer) that requires auditing. With this in mind, when you are configuring an audit policy, you must consider what effect the policy will have on the system and its performance. If you were to set up auditing on every file, folder, and printer in a system, the auditing process would place so much extra work on the system that the system could literally slow to a halt.

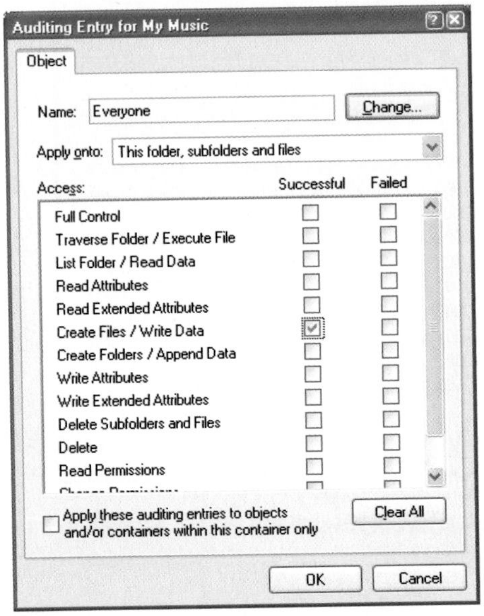

Figure 13-14: Configuring an Auditing Entry

To configure auditing on a file or folder on an NTFS disk, open Windows Explorer, right-click on the file or folder to be audited, and select the *Properties* option. Move to the *Security* tab and click on the *Advanced* button. From the *Auditing* tab, click on the *Add* button to bring up the *Select User or Group* window. Add the users or groups whose access should be audited (if you want to audit all accesses, select the Everyone group) and click the *OK* button. This will bring up the *Auditing Entry* window depicted in Figure 13-14. Select the items to configure the type of accesses that you wish to audit for the object and then click on the *OK* button to exit.

NOTE
To audit files and folders, they must exist on an NTFS disk.

The process for configuring auditing on a printer is similar. The printer's properties are accessed through the *Printer* folder, and the options for event to audit include *successful* and *failed* attempts to

- Print
- Manage printers
- Manage documents
- Read permissions
- Change permissions
- Take ownership

Establishing Firewall Settings

Essentials 6.1

Technical Support 5.2

IT Technician 6.2

Firewalls are configured to pass only those services actually needed and used by the network's users. In a business network environment, the administrator controls firewall installations and configurations. This is done at the router/gateway and server levels of the network. In Windows XP, the local user can configure the built-in *Internet Connection Firewall (ICF)*.

Internet Connection Firewall (ICF)

Windows XP Professional provides a new **Internet Connection Firewall (ICF)** feature that is designed to provide protection from outside attacks by preventing unwanted connections from Internet devices. Computers connected directly to the Internet are vulnerable to attacks from the outside. Recall that a firewall is a device (or program) that is placed between an internal network, such as a corporate intranet, and an outside network (i.e., the Internet). The firewall is used to inspect all traffic going to and coming from the outside network and can be programmed to control traffic flow between the networks based on desirable properties.

The Windows XP ICF service is designed to protect individual computers that are directly connected to the Internet through dial-up, LAN, or high-speed Internet connections. Proper installation and configuration of the ICF service can provide a strong protective barrier between Windows XP Professional and the outside network. When combined with the Windows ICS service, the XP firewall can be configured to provide Internet access to multiple computers through a single connection. ICF should be enabled on the shared external connection to secure communication for all internal clients.

Firewalls work by examining the front end (header) of network packets as they are received. Depending on how the firewall is configured, it may look at the header information and permit it to pass through the firewall or block it from going through. By default, the Windows XP ICF service will block all connection requests initiating from outside its network. It will only permit incoming traffic to come through that it recognizes as a response to a request from inside the network. The ICF knows which responses are acceptable, because it maintains a table of outgoing connection information for itself and any computers on the local network that are sharing the ICF connection.

However, the ICF function can be configured with filters to enable specific traffic to enter the network. For example, if there are services such as Web or FTP services running on the internal network that must be made available to external customers, then you can configure a filter to open the firewall to let just that service pass through.

Normally, these filters are configured around services recognized by the TCP and UDP networking protocols. These protocols use port numbers to identify specific processes such as HTTP or FTP. These ports are 16-bit numbers that refer incoming messages to an application that will process them. Many of the port numbers are standardized and are referred to as **well-known ports**. Similarly, their associated applications are called *well-known services*.

well-known ports

Internet Assigned Numbers Authority (IANA)

Table 13-1 lists several well-known port numbers and their provided services. The **Internet Assigned Numbers Authority (IANA)** has assigned standard port numbers ranging from 0 to 1023 to specific services. Port numbers from 1024 through 65535 are called ephemeral ports and are not assigned by the organization. Instead, they are frequently employed in user-developed programs.

Table 13-1: Well-Known Ports

When the firewall examines the incoming packet, it can read the source and destination IP addresses of the packet and any TCP/UDP port numbers. It will use the IP address and port information in the packet headers to determine if an incoming packet should be routed into the internal network. If you have configured the firewall with the IP address of an internal computer that provides FTP services and opened ports 20 and 21, the firewall will recognize the IP address and port numbers in the incoming header as valid and route the packet to that computer. However, all other incoming requests will still be blocked.

SERVICE	WELL-KNOWN PORT NUMBER
FTP	21, 20
Telnet	23
SMTP Mail	25
HTTP (WWW)	80
POP3 (Mail)	110
News	144
HTTP	443
PPTP	1723
IRC	6667

To enable the ICF function in Windows XP, open the *Network Connections* applet, right-click the connection (dial-up, LAN, or high-speed Internet) that you want to protect, and select the *Properties* option from the menu. Then, in the *Internet Connection Firewall* section of the *Advanced* tab, check the *Protect my computer and network by limiting or preventing access to this computer from the Internet* check box and click on the *OK* button.

Internet connection sharing (ICS)

In a network that is using **Internet connection sharing (ICS)**, only the outgoing Internet connection should use the ICF feature. The other computers in the internal network should not have their ICF enabled.

Essentials 6.2

Technical Support 5.2

IT Technician 6.2

Using the Encrypting File System

Windows 2000 and Windows XP both provide effective local hard drive security through their **encrypting file system (EFS)** feature. The EFS feature enables the user to encrypt files stored on the drive using keys only the designated user (or an **authorized recovery agent**) can decode. This prevents theft of data by those who do not have the password or a decoding tool.

> **NOTE**
>
> EFS prevents files from being accessed by unauthorized users, including those trying to by-pass the operating system and gain access using third-party utilities. However, EFS is not available on Windows XP Home Edition.

encrypting file system (EFS)

authorized recovery agent

encryption key

public key

private key

Windows 2000 and XP Professional users can implement the EFS option to encrypt their files and folders on NTFS drives. They can open these files and folders just as they would any ordinary files or folders. However, if someone gains unauthorized access to the computer, they will not be able to open the encrypted files or folders. EFS is simple to use, because it is actually an attribute that can be established for files or folders.

The EFS feature further enhances the security of files on portable computers by enabling users to designate files and folders so that they can only be accessed using the proper **encryption key**. Public key encryption techniques employ two keys to ensure the security of the encrypted data—a **public key** and a **private key**. The public key (known to everyone) is used to encrypt the data, and the private or secret key (known only to the specified recipient) is used to decrypt it. The public and private keys are related in such a way that the private key cannot be decoded simply by possessing the public key.

IT Technician 5.2

Establishing Internet Browser Security Options

There are a variety of user-selectable options that can be established for Web browsers. Some of these options are personal preferences, such as colors, fonts, and toolbars. However, there are a variety of security-related activities that involve the browser and searching the Internet. These include configuring scripting, proxies, and security levels through the user's browser. In Microsoft IE these functions are located on the *Security* tab under the *Tools/Internet Options* path, depicted in Figure 13-15.

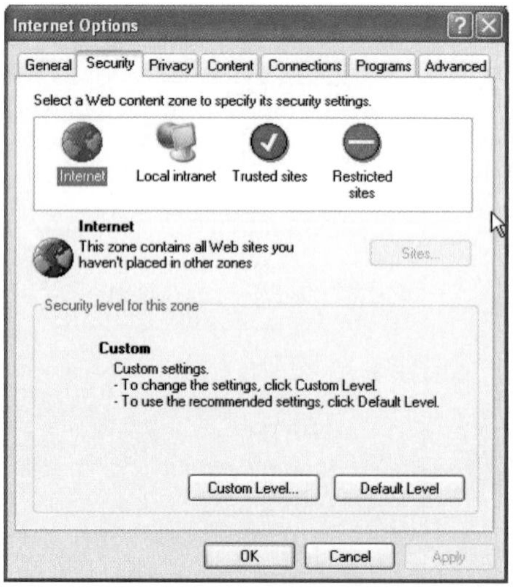

Figure 13-15: IE Security Tab

Highlighting the *Intranet*, *Trusted Sites*, or *Restricted* sites icons will enable the *Sites* button. This button can be used to add or remove sites to each of these different zone classifications. The security settings attached to these different zone types can be modified by clicking the *Custom Level* button. The Internet icon enables security settings to be established for all Web sites that have not been classified as one of the other zone types.

In each zone type, clicking the *Custom Level* button will produce a list of individual controls that can be enabled, disabled, or configured to present a user prompt when the browser encounters related objects. These objects represent Web page components that may be encountered by accessing or viewing a given Web site (such as animated scripts, file downloads, user identification log-ins).

The *Reset Custom Settings* dialog box features a drop-down window for establishing general levels of security settings for all of the items in the selected zone type's list.

Configuring Script Support

Scripts are executable applications that provide interactive content on Web sites. They are also capable of retrieving information in response to user selections. However, the user may not have to do anything to run a script program—they are simply embedded in the Web site that they access. There are a couple of reasons why you would consider controlling scripts encountered on Web sites. Scripts are one of the main sources of virus infections. Hackers configure scripts to contain viruses that clients may download unwittingly. Scripts also facilitate automatic pop-up windows that appear without warning on the client's browser. These windows normally contain unrequested advertisements that tend to annoy users.

The ability to load and run scripts in a browser can be controlled through the browser's *Tools/Internet Options/Security* tab. The list of individual Web page components that you can control includes different script types, such as ActiveX and Javascript. As with the other Security objects, you can configure the browser to enable, disable, or present a user prompt whenever it encounters one of these scripted items.

> Scripts

Configuring Proxy Settings

A **proxy server** is a barrier that prevents outsiders from entering a local area network. All addressing information sent to the Internet will use the IP address of the proxy server. Because the IP address of the workstation that's connecting to the Internet isn't used, an outside intruder has no way of accessing the workstation.

> proxy server

Client access is configured from the Web browser of the workstation. To configure a workstation using the Microsoft Internet Explorer browser for a proxy server, follow these steps:

1. Start Microsoft Internet Explorer. From the toolbar menu, choose *Tools,* then *Internet Options*.

2. Select the *Connection* tab, and click on the *LAN Setting* button. This will produce the *Local Area Network (LAN) Settings* dialog box similar to that shown in Figure 13-16.

3. Check the *Use a proxy server for your LAN* option and enter the name of the proxy server in the *Address* field. An IP address may be entered in the *Address* field instead of the server name.

4. Enter the port number of the server in the *Port* field. The port number is usually a well-known port number.

5. Click on the *Apply* button, followed by the *OK* button.

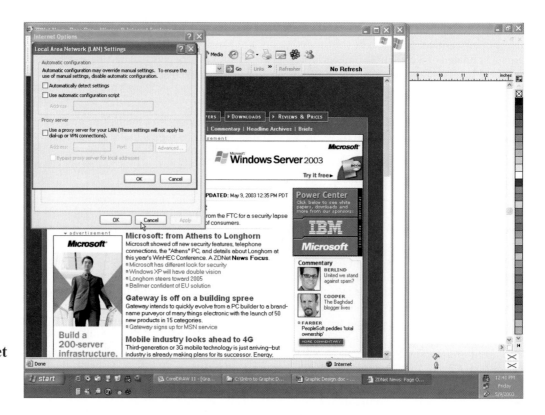

Figure 13-16: Internet Explorer Proxy Configuration

When fully configured, the proxy server will supply the client with the addresses and port numbers for Internet services (i.e., HTTP, FTP, etc.) that are available to it.

Most commercial Web browsers provide for proxy configuration in a manner that's similar to the steps described above. For example, follow these steps to configure the workstation proxy settings for Netscape Navigator:

1. From the Netscape Navigator toolbar menu, choose *Options*, and then select the *Network Preferences* entry from the menu. Click on the *Proxies* tab in the *Preferences* dialog box.

2. Click on the *Manual Proxy Configuration* radio button, then click on the *View* button.

3. Enter the name or IP address of the proxy server for each service, along with the port number of the service.

4. Click on the *Apply* button, followed by the *OK* button.

Navigator also permits you to use an automatic proxy configuration for workstations by entering the address where the proxy configuration file is located. Enter the address in the *Automatic Proxy Configuration* field of the *Preferences* dialog box.

Locking the Computer

Users should never leave their computer unattended after they have logged on. Doing so opens the door for others to access and manipulate their computer, data, and network. All users should be trained to either log off or **lock** their computers when they are away from them, even if only for a few minutes. Locking the computer protects it from intruders and preserves the current system state. When the computer is unlocked, the applications and data that were active in the system are still open, making it much easier for the user to pick up where he or she left off. Users should also be instructed to make sure they log off at the end of the day. This closes all applications and ensures that data files are saved.

In Windows 2000 and XP, the computer can be locked from the keyboard by pressing *CTRL+ALT+DEL* to open the *Windows Security* dialog box as shown in Figure 13-17. Simply click on the *Lock Computer* button. The *Unlock Computer* dialog box will appear, and the user will need to enter his or her username and password in the *Unlock Computer* dialog box and click the *OK* button to unlock the computer. If the user who locked the computer is unavailable to unlock it, an administrator will have to do so. In this event, the current user will be logged off, all applications will be closed, and any unsaved data will be lost.

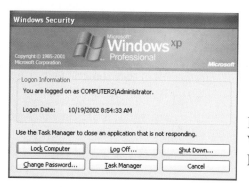

Figure 13-17: The Windows Security Dialog Box

Users can also click on the *Change Password* button on the *Windows Security* dialog box to change their password at any time. Doing so will bring up the *Change Password* dialog box, as shown in Figure 13-18, with the user's *Username* and *Log on to* information already present. The user simply needs to enter the old and new passwords as indicated, and click the *OK* button. If all the information was entered correctly, a message will appear indicating that the password was successfully changed. If not, a different message will be displayed indicating that there is a problem and that the information needs to be entered again.

Figure 13-18: Change Password Dialog Box

Administrators can use this dialog box to change users' passwords but in Windows-based networks, they can use their much more powerful *Local Users and Groups* utility or *Active Directory Users and Computers* utility to change user passwords without knowing the old ones. In either utility, the administrator can change a user's password by right-clicking on their account and selecting the *Set Password* entry in the action menu.

Establishing and Implementing Malicious Software Protection

It is common to install a number of different defensive products to protect PCs and their data from unauthorized access and malicious interference. The products most widely used for these purposes include

- Antivirus programs
- Antispyware programs
- Spam blockers
- Pop-up blockers

All of these program types are covered in detail in the next sections of this chapter.

MALICIOUS PROGRAM SECURITY

Malware

grayware

As is true of most things in life, with anything good comes its antagonist. In the case of networked and internetworked computing systems that allow users to freely interact and to access nearly limitless amounts of information, comes *malware* and *grayware*. **Malware** is the term used to describe programs designed to be malicious in nature. The term **grayware** describes programs that have behavior that is undisclosed or that is undesirable. The following are common malware and grayware programs:

- Viruses
- Trojan horses
- Worms
- Spyware
- Adware
- Hacking tools

The first three entries in the list belong to the malicious malware category and are generally associated with computer viruses. The last three entries fall into a category of mischievous and obnoxious grayware programs.

Viruses

Computer viruses

Computer viruses are destructive programs designed to replicate and spread on their own. Viruses are created to sneak into personal computers. Sometimes these programs take control of a machine to leave a humorous message, and sometimes they destroy data. After they infiltrate one machine, they can spread into other computers through infected disks that friends and coworkers pass around or through local and wide area network connections.

There are basically three types of viruses, based on how they infect a computer system:

- **Boot-sector virus**—This type of virus copies itself onto the boot sector of floppy and hard disks. The virus replaces the disk's original boot-sector code with its own code. This allows it to be loaded into memory before anything else is loaded. Once in memory, the virus can spread to other disks.

Boot-sector virus

- **File infector**—File infectors are viruses that add their virus code to executable files. After the file with the virus is executed, it spreads to other executable files. A similar type of virus, called a **macro virus**, hides in the macro programs of word-processing document files. These files can be designed to load when the document is opened or when a certain key combination is entered. In addition, these types of viruses can be designed to stay resident in memory after the host program has been exited (similar to a terminate and stay resident virus), or they might just stop working when the infected file is terminated.

File infector

macro virus

- **Trojan horses**—This type of virus appears to be a legitimate program that might be found on any system. Trojan horse viruses are more likely to do damage by destroying files, and they can cause physical damage to disks. In newer definitions *trojan horses* are not referred to as viruses because they do not replicate or attach themselves to other files. Instead, they are made to appear to be applications so that users will be tricked into using them. Although they appear to work properly, they have a malicious code hidden inside that gathers information by monitoring network behavior.

Trojan horses

  Some Trojan horses establish an additional user or administrator account while others remain dormant in the background until a *back door* becomes available for an attack. **Back-door** Trojan horses make use of specific service port numbers to invade systems. Therefore, a firewall or router must be used to limit access to these ports to reduce the threat of these types of attacks. As an example, a Trojan horse might be designed to mimic the operation of the system's telnet service. If a user opens the telnet service, they would be unaware that the malicious code was recording each activity that occurred.

Back-door

A number of different viruses have been created from these three virus types. They have several different names, but they all inflict basically the same damage. After the virus file has become active in the computer, it basically resides in memory when the system is running. From this point, it might perform a number of different types of operations that can be as complex and damaging as the author designs them to be.

As an example, a strain of boot-sector virus, known as **CMOS virus**, infects the hard drive's Master Boot Record and becomes memory resident. When activated, the virus writes over the system's configuration information in the CMOS area. Part of what gets overwritten is the HDD and FDD information. Therefore, the system cannot boot up properly. The initial infection comes from booting from an infected floppy disk. The virus overwrites the CMOS once in every 60 bootups.

CMOS virus

A similar boot-sector virus, referred to as the **FAT virus**, becomes memory resident in the area of system memory where the IO.SYS and MSDOS.SYS files are located. This allows it to spread to any non-write-protected disks inserted into the computer. In addition, the virus moves the system pointers for the disk's executable files to an unused cluster and rewrites the pointers in the FAT to point to the sector where the virus is located. The result is improper disk copies, inability to back up files, large numbers of lost clusters, and all executable files being cross-linked with each other.

FAT virus

In another example, a file-infector virus strain, called the **FAT table virus**, infects EXE files but does not become memory resident. When the infected file is executed, the virus rewrites another EXE file.

FAT table virus

Likewise, **terminate and stay resident (TSR) viruses** create copies of themselves in system memory. Then, they intercept system events such as a disk access and use this operation to infect files and sectors on the disk. In this manner TSR viruses are active both when an infected program runs and after it terminates. Because the resident copies of these viruses remain viable in memory, even if all the infected files are deleted from the disk, it is very difficult to fully remove these viruses from the system. Removing TSR viruses by restoring all the files from distribution disks or backup copies does not work well, because the resident copy of virus remains active in RAM and infects the newly created files.

Computer worms are malicious programs that destroy the host by replicating until the disk space, memory, and other system resources have been consumed. They do not infect other programs like viruses. Worms are typically introduced into the system when users view an e-mail attachment that contains the worm.

Terminate and Stay
Resident (TSR)
viruses

Computer worms

Essentials 6.3

Virus Symptoms

Because viruses tend to operate in the background, it is sometimes difficult to realize that the computer has been infected. Typical virus symptoms include the following:

- Hard disk controller failures.

- Disks continue to be full even when files have been deleted.

- System cannot read write-protected disks.

- The hard disk stops booting, and files are corrupted.

- The system will boot to floppy disk but will not access the HDD.

- An Invalid Drive Specification message is displayed when attempting to access the C: drive.

- CMOS settings continually revert to default even though the system board battery is good.

- Files change size for no apparent reason.

- System operation slows down noticeably.

- Blank screen when booting (flashing cursor).

- Windows crashes.

- The hard drive is set to DOS compatibility, and 32-bit file access suddenly stops working.

- Network data transfers and print jobs slow dramatically.

Common practices that increase the odds of a machine being infected by a virus include use of shareware software, software of unknown origin, or bulletin board software. One of the most effective ways to reduce these avenues of infection is to buy shrink-wrapped products from a reputable source.

Antivirus Software

Another means of virus protection involves installing a **virus-scanning (antivirus) program** that checks disks and files before using them in the computer. Several other companies offer third-party virus-protection software that can be configured to operate in various ways. If the computer is a stand-alone unit, it might be nonproductive to have the antivirus software run each time the system is booted up. It would be much more practical to have the program check floppy disks or writable CD-ROM disks, only because this is the only possible nonnetwork entryway into the computer.

A networked or online computer has more opportunity to contract a virus than a stand-alone unit, because viruses can enter the unit over the network or through the modem. In these cases, setting the software to run at each bootup is more desirable. Most modern antivirus software includes utilities to check e-mail and files downloaded to the computer through dial-up connections.

Most of these suppliers provide their products in multiple formats. They usually sell boxed commercial versions as well as Internet download versions. In addition, they typically provide automatic update services that periodically notify you of new threats and provide new virus definition databases. (These programs work by comparing the characteristics of received files to profiles associated with known virus types.) A subscription service is normally provided to continue the update service after the initial usage period has expired.

As indicated earlier, when an antivirus application is installed on the system, it can be configured to provide different levels of virus protection. You will need to configure when and under what circumstances you want the virus software to run.

> **GEEK SQUAD CASE FILE #89321**
>
> A customer calls you to his site complaining that the wide-carriage, dot-matrix printer in his accounting department is running very slowly and that they cannot get all their invoices printed for today's shipping purposes. When you check their print queue, you see that the print jobs for the invoices are stacked up in the queue but that they are being processed. The accounting manager tells you that they typically don't have any problems getting their invoices printed and that nothing out of the ordinary has been done to the computer to make it slow down. What items should you check to determine the cause of the slowdown?

Boot-sector virus protection provided through the system CMOS is *not exactly a virus protection* tool. What this feature does is provide a warning whenever the boot sector is accessed for writing. The warning screen allows you to disable the access or to continue. This feature can be extremely annoying if you use programs that need to write to the boot sector as part of their normal operation. Boot-sector virus protection is completely useless for SCSI drives, as they use their own BIOS on the controller.

virus-scanning (antivirus) program

Boot-sector virus protection

Grayware

As mentioned earlier in this chapter, **grayware** is a general classification for applications that have behavior that is *undisclosed* or that may be *annoying* or *undesirable*. Grayware programs can perform a variety of undesired and threatening actions such as irritating users with pop-up advertising, logging user key strokes, and exposing computer vulnerabilities to attack. The different categories of grayware include the following:

- *Spyware*—programs that hide and record Internet surfing habits, typically without the user's consent.

- *Adware*—programs that display unintentional advertising on the system's screen.

- *Dialers*—programs that invade and change Internet configuration settings. The infected system dials preconfigured numbers through a modem. These numbers are typically billed or international numbers that leave the host with large telephone bills.

- *Jokes*—programs that invade the system and alter the operation of the system in a nondestructive way.

- *Password crackers*—programs designed to steal usernames, passwords, and account information.

- *Spam*—undesirable junk e-mail and unsolicited advertisements.

Even though grayware programs do not harm the performance of infected computers, they do adversely affect their operation. In addition, they can introduce significant security, confidentiality, and legal risks to an organization.

Spyware

Spyware programs are generally introduced to the system through Internet downloads that appear to be useful programs (similar to Trojan horses). They can also be acquired through music sharing downloads. Unlike viruses and Trojan horses, spyware programs typically don't self-replicate. Once spyware is installed on the system, it monitors the system's operation and collects information such as usernames, passwords, credit card numbers, and other confidential information. The program then transmits the information to its author while the host system is online.

While most spyware is used to gather marketing information, it can also be used in malicious activities, such as identity theft and credit card fraud. Some spyare has been delivered to user computers in the form of rogue *antispyware programs* that actually contain spyware. Some spyware products are designed so that they can disable antivirus and firewall software. Others can alter browser security settings to open the system to other types of attacks.

One particularly troubling method of distributing spyware is when programmers create fake notices that tell users they have been infected and that they need to download their antispyware product. The downloaded product is actually a spyware product.

Some spyware programs include other programs designed to protect them. In these cases, the protective program watches for efforts, either by software or by the user, to uninstall or terminate it. When this occurs, the protective program simply reinstalls the spyware or regenerates the registry key that starts it. One way to circumvent this type of spyware is to start the system in Safe Mode and run the antispyware program.

Spyware-infected computers can accumulate a number of spyware components after the initial infection. This leads to degraded system performance due to elevated microprocessor, disk, and network activity created by the spyware. Users may also encounter problems connecting to the Internet due to spyware activity. Some spyware versions even disable competitor's spyware programs when they find them in a system. If a system becomes infected with several pieces of spyware, there may be no alternative but to back up its important data and perform a full clean install of the operating system and applications.

Because of its popularity, Microsoft Windows presents the biggest target for both mischievous and malicious malware and grayware writers. Therefore, Windows receives an unrivaled percentage of all the attacks associated with viruses and spyware. This fact has led some Windows customers to adopt other operating system platforms such as Linux or Mac OSX, which are much less of a malware target.

Spyware Prevention

Several companies have created **antispyware** products. These include companies that specialize in antispyware products, companies that already specialize in antivirus products, and, most recently, Microsoft. Microsoft has licensed an antivirus product it relabeled as *Windows Defender* that will ship free with its future operating system versions. (It is currently available as a free download for Windows XP, Windows 2000, and Windows 2003.)

antispyware

There are basically two types of antispyware products available—those that *find and remove* spyware after it has been installed, and those that *block* spyware when it is trying to install. Both of these methods stand a better chance of keeping computers free from spyware when they are combined with user information about how to *avoid* spyware.

The *detect and remove* method is by far the simpler type of antispyware product to write. Therefore, there are several commercially available products that use this method. Like antivirus software packages, this type of antispyware product relies on databases of existing definitions to recognize spyware threats. These databases must be updated frequently to recognize new spyware versions that have been identified.

The real-time prevention type of antispyware product does not rely on historical data to identify spyware. Instead, this type monitors certain configuration parameters and notifies the user when suspicious installation activity occurs. The user then has the option to *allow* or *block* the installation effort. Some antispyware products incorporate both methods of dealing with spyware.

In addition to installing antispyware applications, users can fight spyware in a number of other ways:

- Install a Web browser other than Internet Explorer (e.g., Mozilla Firefox)

- Work with an ISP that uses their firewalls and proxies to block sites that are known to distribute spyware

- Only download software from reputable sites to prevent spyware downloads that come attached to other programs

Adware

Adware

Adware programs introduce unwanted, unsolicited advertising displays to Web browser screens. They can also be designed to gather user selection information from the browser. This information is used to tailor future advertising to the user. Adware is typically introduced to the system through downloads such as free software. Users actually agree to install these programs by accepting the *End User Licensing Agreement* (*EULA*) included in most software packages. Other adware programs are packaged with spyware so that they can do double duty to collect user preference information and tailor ads to take advantage of the acquired knowledge.

One of the problems with adware is that those who create adware products believe they are doing nothing wrong by clogging up people's computers with unasked for pop-up advertising. They also don't think there is anything wrong with placing things on other people's property without the owner's knowledge.

Spam

spam

SMTP relay

denial of service (DoS) attacks

spam filters

spam blockers

The term **spam** is used to describe the distribution of unsolicited, undesirable e-mail and advertisements. Spam is easy to create and cheap to distribute, so spammers use **SMTP relay** servers to flood the Internet with multiple copies of the same spam message. Getting rid of spam is time-consuming for the receivers. Because spam is legal in many places, it is difficult to regulate or eliminate.

Malicious spammers can use SMTP relay techniques to flood e-mail servers and create **denial of service (DoS) attacks**. The attack directs so many e-mail messages at the server that it cannot handle the level of traffic. This effectively prevents clients who use that server from sending or receiving real e-mail.

On a local level, users can establish **spam filters** and **spam blockers** through their ISPs or e-mail service providers. These filters examine key features of e-mail received to determine whether each piece is likely to be real e-mail or spam. Suspected e-mails are rerouted to a holding area and do not show up in the user's e-mail program.

Social Engineering

Essentials 6.1 and 6.4

Technical Support 5.4

IT Technician 6.4

Social engineering

There are some malicious computer activities for which the only prevention method is to educate customers about them. **Social engineering** is one of these activities. *Social engineers* exploit people's human nature to fool them into providing information about themselves, their business, or their computer/network. They accomplish this by using trickery, deceit, lies, gifts, or acts of kindness to first establish a level of trust. They then use this trust relationship to gain information.

Typical social engineering ploys include using free sales pitches or personal notes of affection to get users to click on something that downloads malicious code to their system. Other social engineering efforts can go to great lengths to get users to surrender their log-in information. For instance, the programmer may design a log-in screen that exactly mimics a log-in screen that you expect to see from a trusted site or company. In the background, the log-in screen passes your information back to the programmer.

Social engineering activities aren't limited to just the computer and network. They can also be used on a personal basis. For example, humans as a group typically desire to be helpful and friendly, particularly when the other person is in a position of importance to them (employers, coworkers, potential clients, relatives, or friends). The social engineer uses this fact to establish apparent relationships with people in order to gain their confidence and trust. Once trust is established, the target feels freer to divulge personal and potentially secret information to the social engineer.

To combat such activities in the workplace, employees must be educated to the fact that these attacks occur and must be given examples of strategies used to get information from them. Organizations should have social engineering awareness training programs to bring these activities to their employees' attention. They should also have an **incidence reporting policy** that tells employees how to report suspicious efforts to obtain information from them.

incidence reporting policy

PREVENTIVE MAINTENANCE

Essentials 7.0

Depot Technician 5.0

IT Technician 7.0

It has long been known that one of the best ways to fix problems with complex systems is to prevent them before they happen. This is the concept behind preventive maintenance procedures. Breakdowns never occur at convenient times. By planning for a few minutes of nonproductive activities, hours of repair and recovery work can be avoided.

The environment around a computer system, and the manner in which the computer is used, determines greatly how many problems it will have. Occasionally dedicating a few moments of care to the computer can extend its **mean time between failures (MTBF)** period considerably. This activity, involving maintenance not normally associated with a breakdown, is called **preventive maintenance (PM)**.

mean time between failures (MTBF)

preventive maintenance (PM)

The following sections of this chapter describe PM measures for the various areas of the system. As with any electronic device, computers are susceptible to failures caused by dust buildup, rough handling, and extremes in temperature.

┌─ **TEST TIP** ─────────────────┐
Know what environmental conditions, or activities, are most likely to lead to equipment failures.
└────────────────────────────────┘

Cleaning

Essentials 7.1

Cleaning is a major part of keeping a computer system healthy. Therefore, the technician's tool kit should also contain a collection of cleaning supplies. Along with hand tools, it will need a lint-free, soft cloth (*chamois*) for cleaning the plastic outer surfaces of the system.

TEST TIP

Know the common methods of cleaning various computer components.

Outer surface cleaning can be accomplished with a simple soap and water solution, followed by a clear water rinse. Care should be taken to make sure that none of the liquid splashes, or drips, into the inner parts of the system. A damp cloth is easily the best general-purpose cleaning tool for use with computer equipment.

antistatic spray

antistatic solution

The cleaning should be followed by the application of an **antistatic spray** or **antistatic solution** to prevent the buildup of static charge on the components of the system. A solution composed of 10 parts water and one part common household fabric softener makes an effective and economical antistatic solution. To remove dust from the inside of cabinets, a small paintbrush is handy.

TEST TIP

Know what types of materials/techniques can be used to clean different areas of the computer sys-

oxidation

Another common problem is the buildup of **oxidation**, or corrosion, at electrical contact points. These build-ups occur on electrical connectors and contacts and can reduce the flow of electricity through the connection. Some simple steps can be used to keep corrosion from becoming a problem. The easiest step in preventing corrosion is observing the correct handling procedures for printed circuit boards and cables, as shown in Figure 13-19. Never touch the electrical contact points with your skin, because the moisture on your body can start corrosive action.

electrical contact cleaner

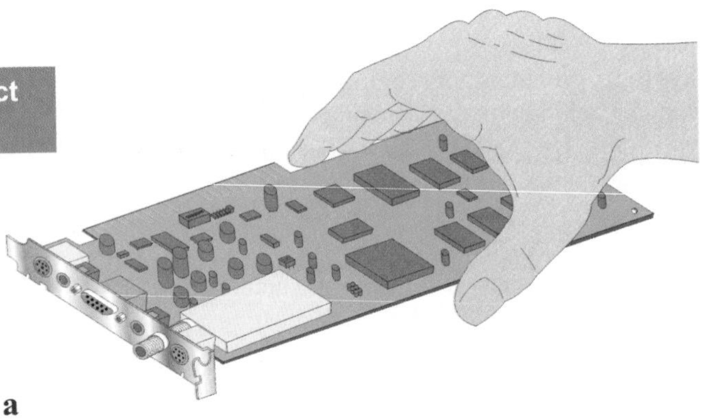

Figure 13-19: How to Handle a PC Board

Even with proper handling, some corrosion may occur over time. This oxidation can be removed in a number of ways. The oxide buildup can be sanded off with emery cloth, rubbed off with a common pencil eraser or special solvent-wipe, or dissolved with an **electrical contact cleaner** spray. Socketed devices should be reseated (removed and reinstalled to establish a new electrical connection) as part of an anticorrosion cleaning. However, they should be handled according to the MOS Handling guidelines in this chapter to make certain that no static discharge damage occurs.

If you use the emery cloth, or rubber eraser, to clean your contacts, always rub toward the outer edge of the board, or connector, to prevent damage to the contacts. Rubbing the edge may lift the foil from the PC board. Printed-circuit board connectors are typically very thin. Therefore, rub hard enough to remove only the oxide layer. Also, take time to clean up any dust or rubber contamination generated by the cleaning effort.

Cleaning other internal components, such as disk drive Read/Write heads, can be performed using lint-free foam swabs and isopropyl alcohol or methanol. It is most important that the cleaning solution be one that dries without leaving a residue.

Dust

Over time, dust builds up on everything it can gain access to. Many computer components generate static electrical charges that attract dust particles. In the case of electronic equipment, dust forms an insulating blanket that traps heat next to active devices and can cause them to overheat. Excessive heat can cause premature aging and failure. The best dust protection is a dust-tight enclosure. However, computer components tend to have less than dust-tight seals. Power supply and microprocessor fans pull air from outside through the system unit.

Another access point for dust is uncovered expansion slot openings. Missing expansion slot covers adversely affect the system in two ways. First, the missing cover permits dust to accumulate in the system, forming the insulating blanket described above, which causes component overheating. Second, the heat problem is complicated further by the fact that the missing slot cover interrupts the designed airflow patterns inside the case, causing components to overheat due to missing or inadequate airflow.

Smoke is a more dangerous cousin of dust. Like dust particles, smoke collects on all exposed surfaces. The residue of smoke particles is sticky and clings to the surface. In addition to contributing to the heat buildup problem, smoke residue is particularly destructive to moving parts such as floppy disks, fan motors, and so forth.

Dust buildup inside system components can be taken care of with a soft brush. A **static-free vacuum** can also be used to remove dust from inside cases and keyboards. Be sure to use a static-free vacuum, because normal vacuums are by their nature static generators. The static-free vacuum has special grounding to remove the static buildup it generates. Dust covers are also helpful in holding down dust problems. These covers are simply placed over the equipment when not in use and removed when the device is needed.

TEST TIP

Be aware of the effect that missing expansion slot covers have on the operation of the system unit.

Smoke

static-free vacuum

TEST TIP

Know that computer vacuums have special grounding to dissipate static buildup that can damage computer devices.

Heat Buildup Problems

Identifying and controlling heat buildup problems can require some effort and planning. Microcomputers are designed to run at normal room temperatures. If the ambient temperature rises above about 85°F, heat buildup can become a problem. High humidity can also lead to heat-related problems.

To combat heat problems, make sure that the area around the system is uncluttered so that free airflow around the system can be maintained. Make sure the power supply's fan is operational. If it is not, replace the power supply unit. Likewise, be sure that the microprocessor fan is plugged in and operational. It is very easy for a high-speed microprocessor to fry if its fan fails. A good rule of thumb is to install a fan on any microprocessor running above 33 MHz.

If heat buildup still exists, check to make sure that the outer cover is secured firmly to the machine and that all of the expansion slot covers are in place. These items can disrupt the designed airflow characteristics of the case. Finally, add an additional case fan to draw more air through the system unit.

Depot Technician 5.1

Technical Support 7.1

Handling Techniques

Rough handling is either a matter of neglect or a lack of knowledge about how equipment should be handled. Therefore, overcoming rough handling problems requires that technicians be aware of proper handling techniques for sensitive devices, such as hard-disk drives and monitors, and that they adjust their component handling practices to compensate.

Protecting Display Systems

The PM associated with video display monitors basically consists of **periodic cleaning**, **dusting**, and good, **common-sense practices** around the monitor. The monitor's screen and cabinet should be dusted frequently and cleaned periodically. Dust and smoke particles can build up very quickly around the monitor's screen, due to the presence of static charges on its face. When cleaning the screen, some caution should be used to avoid scratching its surface and, in the case of antiglare screens, to preserve its glare-reduction features.

Aerosol sprays, solvents, and commercial cleaners should be avoided, because they can damage the screen and cabinet. The simple cleaning solution, described earlier, is also fine for cleaning the monitor. Make sure that the monitor's power cord is disconnected from any power source before washing. The monitor's screen should be dried with a soft cloth after rinsing.

The monitor should not be left on for extended periods with the same image displayed on the screen. Over a period of time, the image will become permanently "burnt" into the screen. If it is necessary to display the same information on the screen for a long period of time, turn the intensity level of the monitor down or install a **screen saver** program to alter the screen image periodically.

Inside the monitor's housing are very dangerous voltage levels (in excess of 25,000 volts, more than enough to kill or badly injure someone). Therefore, you should remove the monitor's outer cabinet only if you are fully qualified to work on CRT-based units. Even if the monitor has been turned off and unplugged for a year, it may still hold enough electrical potential to be deadly. Figure 13-20 shows the areas of the monitor that should be avoided if you must work inside its housing.

periodic cleaning

dusting

common-sense practices

screen saver

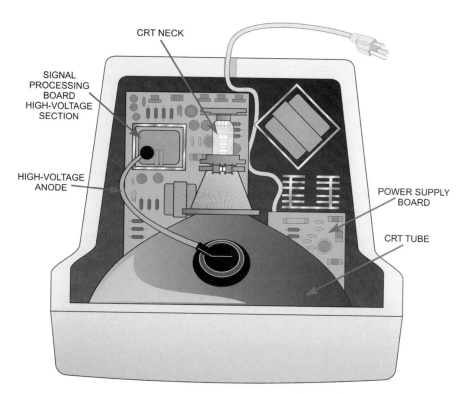

CRT NECK

SIGNAL
PROCESSING
BOARD
HIGH-VOLTAGE
SECTION

HIGH-VOLTAGE
ANODE

POWER SUPPLY
BOARD

CRT TUBE

**Figure 13-20: Caution
Areas Inside the Monitor**

Video display monitors often include a tilt/swivel base that allows the users to position it at whatever angle is most comfortable. This offers additional relief from eyestrain by preventing the users from viewing the display at an angle. Viewing the screen at an angle causes the eyes to focus separately, which places strain on the eye muscles.

Protecting Hard-Disk Drives

Hard-disk drives don't require much preventive maintenance, because the Read/Write (R/W) heads and disks are enclosed in sealed, dust-tight compartments. However, there are some things that can be done to optimize the performance, and life span, of hard-disk systems. Rough handling is responsible for more hard-disk drive damage than any other factor.

The drive should never be moved while you can still hear its disks spinning. The disk is most vulnerable during start-up and shut-down, when the heads are not fully flying. Even a small jolt during these times can cause a great deal of damage to both the platters and the R/W heads. If the drive must be moved, a waiting period of one full minute should be allotted after turning the system off.

If the drive is to be transported, or shipped, make sure to pack it properly. The forces exerted on the drive during shipment may be great enough to cause the R/W heads to slap against the disk surfaces, causing damage to both. Pack the drive unit in an oversized box, with antistatic foam all around the drive. You may also pack the drive in a **box-within-a-box** configuration, once again using foam as a cushion. This concept is illustrated in Figure 13-21.

box-within-a-box

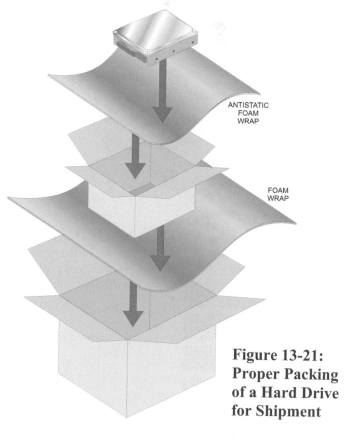

ANTISTATIC
FOAM
WRAP

FOAM
WRAP

**Figure 13-21:
Proper Packing
of a Hard Drive
for Shipment**

At no time should the hard drive's housing, which protects the platters, be removed in open air. The drive's disks and R/W heads are sealed in the airtight housing under a vacuum. The contaminants floating in normal air will virtually ruin the drive. If the drive malfunctions, the electronic circuitry and connections may be tested, but when it comes to repairs within the disk chamber, factory service or a professional service facility with a proper **clean room** is a must!

To recover quickly from hardware failures, operator mistakes, and acts of nature, some form of **software backup** is essential with a hard-disk system. The most common backup for larger systems is high-speed, streaming-tape cartridges, which can automatically back up the contents of the entire disk drive on magnetic tape. In the event of data loss on the disk, a full reinstall from the tape is possible in a matter of a few minutes.

High-volume disk-based devices, such as **optical drives** and **removable hard drives**, have become attractive methods for backing up the contents of large hard drives. CD-R and CD-RW drives provide an attractive option for storing limited amounts (680 MB) of critical data. Their high capacities allow large amounts of information to be written on a single disc. The major drawback of using a CD-R disc is that after the disc has been written to, it cannot be erased or reused. Various backup methods are depicted in Figure 13-22. In any case, failure to maintain backups will eventually result in a great deal of grief when the system goes down due to a hardware or software failure.

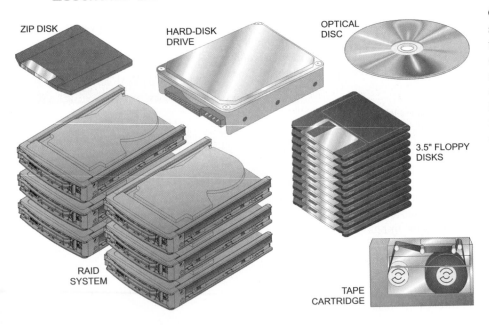

ZIP DISK
HARD-DISK DRIVE
OPTICAL DISC
3.5" FLOPPY DISKS
RAID SYSTEM
TAPE CARTRIDGE

Copies of the system backup should be stored in a convenient but secure place. In the case of secure system backups, such as client/server networks, the backup copies should be stored where the network administrators can have access to them, but not the general public (i.e., a locked file cabinet). Left unsecured, these copies could be used by someone without authority to gain access to the system, or to its data. Even Emergency Repair Disks associated with Windows NT and Windows 2000 should be stored in a secure location. These disks can also be used by people other than administrators to gain access to information in client/server networks. Many companies maintain a copy of their backup away from the main site. This is done for protection in case of disasters such as fire.

Figure 13-22: Data Backup Systems

There are a number of hard-disk drive software utilities designed to optimize and maintain the operation of the hard-disk drive. They should be used as part of a regular preventive maintenance program. The primary HDD utilities are the **CHKDSK**, **Defrag**, **Backup**, and **Antivirus** utilities.

> **TEST TIP**
>
> Be aware of the precautions that should be employed with storing system backups.

Protecting Removable Media Drives

Unlike hard-disk drives, tape drives, floppy drives, and CD-ROM/DVD drives are at least partially open to the atmosphere, and their media may be handled on a regular basis. This opens these drive units up to a number of maintenance concerns not found in hard-disk drives. Also, the removable cartridges, disks, or discs can be adversely affected by extremes in temperature, exposure to magnetic and electromagnetic fields, bending, and airborne particles that can lead to information loss.

Protecting Removable Media

Because magnetic tapes and floppy disks store information in the form of magnetized spots on their surfaces, it is only natural that external magnetic fields will have an adverse effect on their stored data. Never bring tape cartridges or floppies near magnetic field–producing devices, such as CRT monitors, television sets, or power supplies. They should also never be placed on or near appliances such as refrigerators, freezers, vacuum cleaners, and other equipment containing motors. All of these items produce electromagnetic fields that can alter the information stored on their media.

Proper positioning of the drive, and proper connection of peripheral interface cables, helps to minimize noise and **radio frequency interference (RFI)**. RFI can cause the drive to operate improperly. Magnetic fields generated by power supplies and monitors can interfere with the magnetic recording on disks and tapes. The drive and signal cables should be positioned away from these magnetic-field sources as well. Magnets should never be brought near any type of computer-related drive unit.

radio frequency interference (RFI)

Additional measures to protect tape cassettes, disks, and discs include storing them in a cool, dry, clean environment, out of direct sunlight. Excessive temperature will cause the disk and its jacket or the tape and cartridge to warp. Also, you should never physically touch the surface of the magnetic tape, floppy disk, or CD\DVD disc. In all cases, the natural oils from your skin can cause physical damage to the floppy's coating and partially block the laser in a CD-ROM or DVD drive causing it to be unreadable. Take care when inserting the disk into the drive so as not to damage the disk, its jacket, or the drive's internal mechanisms.

Maintaining Removable Media Drives

So far, each preventive action has involved the storage media. However, periodic manual cleaning of the R/W heads of tapes and floppies, or the laser reading mechanism in CD-ROMs and DVDs can prevent failures and bigger maintenance problems. Cleaning the R/W heads in tape and floppy drives removes residue and oxide buildups from the face of the head to ensure accurate transfer of data from the head to the disk. Likewise, cleaning CD-ROM and DVD drives removes contaminants and buildup from the laser lens in the drive.

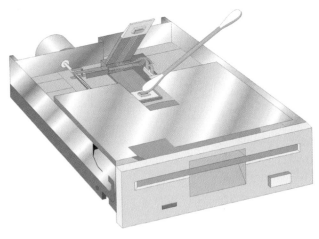

Figure 13-23: Cleaning the R/W Heads

alcohol

cellular foam swabs

lint-free cloths

dusting

soft brush

lint-free swab

There are cleaning kits available for both floppy drives and CD/DVD drives, as well as for different types of tape drives. In the case of floppies and tape drives, cleaning should be done by manually cleaning the heads, as depicted in Figure 13-23. Automatic cleaning kits often include abrasive disks that scrub the faces of the R/W heads to remove buildup. These kits can eventually wear away the R/W head and damage it. On the other hand, CD-ROM/DVD drive cleaning kits offer cleaning discs that brush the laser lens to remove dust and other contaminants. It is also common practice to keep discs free from smudges and dust by wiping them gently with a soft cloth.

Manual cleaning operations involve removing the cover of the drive, gaining access to the R/W heads, and cleaning them manually with a swab that has been dipped in **alcohol**. Together, these steps provide an excellent preventive maintenance program that should ensure effective, long-term operation of the drive.

The cleaning solution for manual cleanings can be isopropyl alcohol, methanol, or some other solvent that does not leave a residue when it dries. Common cotton swabs are not recommended for use in manual cleaning, because they tend to shed fibers. These fibers can contaminate the drive and, in certain circumstances, damage the R/W mechanisms. Instead, **cellular foam swabs** or **lint-free cloths** are recommended for manual head cleaning. The interval of time between cleanings is dependent on several factors, such as the relative cleanliness of your computer area and how often you use your disk drive.

Protecting Input Devices

Input peripherals generally require very little in the way of preventive maintenance. An occasional **dusting** and cleaning should be all that's really required. There are, however, a few commonsense items to keep in mind when using input devices that should prevent damage to the device and ensure its longevity.

The keyboard's electronic circuitry is open to the atmosphere and should be vacuumed, as described in Figure 13-24, when you are cleaning around your computer area. Dust buildup on the keyboard circuitry can cause its ICs to fail due to overheating. To remove dirt and dust particles from inside the keyboard, disassemble the keyboard, and carefully brush particles away from the board with a **soft brush**. A **lint-free swab** can be used to clean between the keys. Take care not to snag any exposed parts with the brush or swab. To minimize dust collection in the keyboard, cover your keyboard when not in use.

Never set keyboards or pointing devices on top of the monitor or near the edge of the desk where they may fall off. To prevent excessive wear on special keys, avoid applications and game programs that use keys in a repetitive manner. For these applications, use an appropriate pointing device, such as a mouse or joystick, for input.

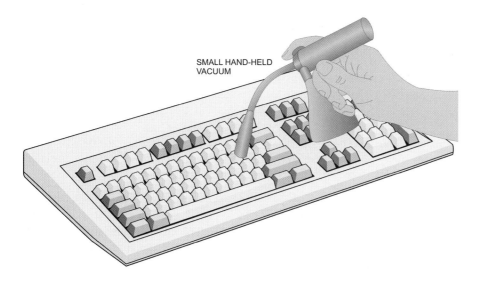

SMALL HAND-HELD VACUUM

Figure 13-24: Cleaning the Keyboard

When using a mouse, keep its workspace clear, dry, and free from dust. With a trackball mouse, the trackball should be removed and cleaned periodically. Use a lint-free swab to clean the X and Y trackball rollers inside the mouse, as described in Figure 13-25.

As with detachable keyboards, keep the connecting cables of all pointing devices out of harm's way.

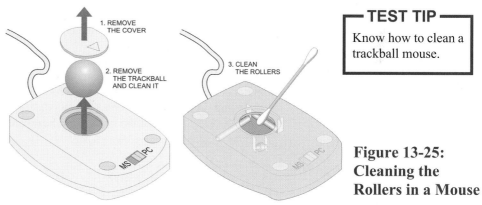

1. REMOVE THE COVER

2. REMOVE THE TRACKBALL AND CLEAN IT

3. CLEAN THE ROLLERS

┌─ **TEST TIP** ─┐
Know how to clean a trackball mouse.
└──────────────┘

Figure 13-25: Cleaning the Rollers in a Mouse

Essentials 6.4

IT Technician 4.4

Software PM

Make sure to keep the system software updated with the latest service packs and patches. Microsoft offers an automated online update service that scans your system, downloads updates and security patches, and then installs them without your intervention. This same service can be run manually at any time. Simply access the Microsoft.com Web site and select the Microsoft Updates option. Many software application providers offer similar Web-based update services for their products.

Likewise, you should either set up protective utilities to automatically run periodically, or set a schedule to manually run these utilities yourself. These utilities include antivirus programs and backup operations. In addition, antivirus programs require periodic updating to stay current with new viruses and worms releases. Most commercial antivirus solutions provide automatic Web-based update functions to keep their products up to date. Finally, take time to educate the user about preventing malicious software attacks, as the well-informed user is the most effective antivirus solution available.

In a Windows XP environment you should periodically establish Restore Points while the system is running correctly. You should also make it a practice to set a new Restore Point just before you make a change to the system, and just after you have verified that the update is performing correctly.

PRINTER PM AND SAFETY ISSUES

Because printers tend to be much more mechanical than other types of peripherals, they require more effort to maintain. Printers generate pollutants, such as paper dust and ink droplets, in everyday operation. These pollutants can build up on mechanical parts and cause them to wear. As the parts wear, the performance of the printer diminishes. Therefore, printers require periodic cleaning and adjustments to maintain good performance.

The best preventive maintenance practice for printers involves performing scheduled maintenance according to the manufacturer's guidelines. These activities include cleaning and lubricating the system, installing update kits to renew print mechanisms and supplies (such as ink or toner cartridges). While you may be able to save you or your customer some money by using third party supplies. However, you should never have a problem using manufacturer-recommended kits and supplies.

The conditions and environment around the printer or scanner will also affect its usefulness and life cycle. The environmental requirements for printers are identical to those of a computer or any other electronic device. Provide ample free air space around the printer, run its power and signal cables in such a manner that they are not a trip or catch hazard, and keep them out of direct sunlight and away from heat sources.

Dot-Matrix Printers

If the printhead is too far away from the platen, the print should appear washed out. The tension on the printhead positioning belt should be checked periodically. If the belt is loose, the printer's dot positioning will become erratic. The belt should be reset for proper tension.

Use a damp, soft cloth to clean the surface of the platen. Rotate the platen through several revolutions. Do not use detergents or solvents on the rollers.

WARNING

Cleaning the printer and its mechanisms periodically adds to its productivity by removing contaminants that cause wear. Vacuum the inside of the unit, after applying antistatic solution to the vacuum's hose tip. Wipe the outside with a damp cloth, also using antistatic solution. Brush any contaminant buildup from the printer's mechanical components, using a soft-bristled brush. *Never lubricate the platen assembly of the printer.*

Use a nonfibrous swab, dipped in alcohol, to clean the face of the dot-matrix printhead. This should loosen paper fiber and ink that may cause the print wires to stick. Apply a small amount of oil to the face of the printhead.

Clean the paper-handling motor's gear train. Use a swab to remove buildup from the teeth of the gear train. If the gear train has been lubricated before, apply a light oil to the gears, using a swab. Turn the platen to make sure the oil gets distributed throughout the gear train. Apply a light coating of oil to the rails that the head-positioning carriage rides on. Move the carriage assembly across the rails several times to spread the lubricant evenly.

The steps to cleaning a dot-matrix printer are described as follows:

Hands-On Activity

Cleaning a Dot-Matrix Printer

1. Adjust the printhead spacing.

2. Check the tension on the printhead positioning belt.

3. Clean the printer and its mechanisms.

4. Clean the printer's roller surfaces.

5. Clean the surface of the platen.

6. Clean the surface of the dot-matrix printhead.

7. Clean the paper-handling motor's gear train.

8. Apply light oil to the gears using a swab.

9. Turn the platen to distribute the oil.

10. Apply a light coating of oil to the rails.

11. Move the carriage assembly to distribute the oil.

Ink-Jet Printers

The printheads in some ink-jet printers require cleaning and adjustment similar to those described for dot-matrix printers. Clean the paper-handling motor's gear train. Use a swab to remove buildup from the teeth of the gear train. If the gear train has been lubricated before, apply a light oil to the gears using a swab. Turn the platen to make sure the oil gets distributed throughout the gear train. Apply a light coating of oil to the rails that the printhead-positioning carriage rides on. Move the carriage assembly across the rails several times to spread the lubricant evenly.

The steps to cleaning an ink-jet printer are provided as follows:

Hands-On Activity

Cleaning an Ink-Jet Printer

1. Adjust the printhead spacing.

2. Check the tension on the printhead positioning belt.

3. Clean the printer and its mechanisms.

4. Clean the printer's roller surfaces.

5. Clean the surface of the platen.

6. Clean the surface of the ink-jet printhead.

7. Clean the paper-handling motor's gear train.

8. Apply light oil to the gears using a swab.

9. Turn the platen to distribute the oil.

10. Apply a light coating of oil to the rails.

11. Move the carriage assembly to distribute the oil.

Laser Printers

Use a vacuum cleaner to remove dust buildup and excess toner from the interior of the laser printer. Care should be taken to remove all excess toner from the unit. Vacuum the printer's ozone filter. Because water can mix with the toner particles in the printer, using wet sponges or towels to clean up toner inside the laser printer can create a bigger mess than the original one you were cleaning up. Remove the toner cartridge before vacuuming.

Clean the laser printer's rollers using a damp cloth or **denatured alcohol**. Also, clean the paper-handling motor's gear train. Use a swab to remove buildup from the teeth of the gear train. If the gear train has been lubricated before, apply a light coating of oil to the gears using a swab. Make sure the oil gets distributed throughout the gear train.

Clean the writing mechanism thoroughly. Use **compressed air** to blow out dust and paper particles that may collect on the lenses and shutters. If possible, wipe the laser lens with lint-free wipes to remove stains and fingerprints.

If accessible, use a swab dipped in alcohol to clean the corona wires. Rub the swab across the entire length of the wires. Take extra care not to break the strands that wrap around the corona. If these wires are broken, the printer will be rendered useless until new **monofilament wires** can be reinstalled.

denatured alcohol

compressed air

monofilament wires

TEST TIP
Remember acceptable methods for cleaning laser printers.

Steps to cleaning a laser printer are described in the following hands-on activity:

Hands-On Activity

Cleaning a Laser Printer

1. Remove dust buildup and excess toner from the interior.

2. Clean the laser printer's rollers.

3. Clean the paper-handling motor's gear train.

4. Apply light oil to the gears, using a swab.

5. Distribute the oil throughout the gear train.

6. Clean the corona wires.

As with other printer types, you should maintain laser printers in accordance with the manufacturer's guidelines. This includes installing the manufacturer's maintenance kit designed for that printer. Don't forget to reset the *page counter* on those copiers and laser printers that have them.

In some laser printer models, the toner cartridges are designed so that they can be refilled. At this time, the **third-party refill cartridges** are not typically as good as those from the manufacturer. However, they tend to be much cheaper than original equipment cartridges. If the output from the printer does not have to be very high quality, then refilled toner cartridges might be an interesting possibility to consider. To date, there are no regulations governing the disposal of laser printer cartridges.

third-party refill
cartridges

Preventive Maintenance Scheduling

There is no perfect preventive maintenance schedule; however, the following is a reasonable schedule that can be used to effectively maintain most computer equipment. The schedule is written from the point of view of a personal computer. From an outside maintenance perspective, some of the steps will need to be shared with the daily users. For the most part, users carry out the daily and weekly PM activities.

Daily Activities

Back up important data from the unit. This can be done to floppy disks, backup tape, another network drive, or some other backup media. Check computer ventilation to make sure that papers and other desk clutter are not cutting off airflow to the unit. Check for other sources of heat buildup around the computer and its peripherals. These sources include

- Direct sunlight from an outside window
- Locations of portable heaters in the winter
- Papers/books piled up around the equipment

Weekly Activities

Clean the outside of the computer, and its peripheral equipment. Wipe the outsides of the equipment with a damp cloth. The cloth can be slightly soapy. Wipe dry with an antistatic cloth. Clean the display screen using a damp cloth with the antistatic solution described earlier in this chapter. An antistatic spray can also be used for static buildup prevention.

CHKDSK/f

Run **CHKDSK/f** on all hard drives to locate and remove any lost clusters from the drives. The CHKDSK command must be run from the command prompt in all versions. Run a current virus-check program to check for hard drive infection. Back up any revised data files on the hard drive. Inspect the peripherals (mice, keyboard, and so on), and clean them if needed.

Monthly Activities

Clean the inside of the system. Use a long-nozzle vacuum cleaner attachment to remove dust from the inside of the unit. Wipe the nozzle with antistatic solution before vacuuming. A soft brush can also be used to remove dust from the system unit.

Clean the inside of the printer using the same equipment and techniques as those used with the system unit. Check system connections for corrosion, pitting, or discoloration. Wipe the surface of any peripheral card's edge connectors with a lubricating oil to protect it from atmospheric contamination.

Vacuum the keyboard out. Clean the X and Y rollers in the trackball mouse using a lint-free swab and a noncoating cleaning solution, as illustrated in Figure 13-24.

.TMP

Defragment the system's hard drive using the Defrag utility. Remove unnecessary temporary (**.TMP**) files from the hard drive. Check software and hardware manufacturers for product updates that can remove problems and improve system operation. Back up the entire hard-disk drive.

Six Months' Activities

Every six months, perform an extensive PM check. Apply an antistatic wash to the entire computer/peripheral work area. Wipe down books, the desktop, and other work area surfaces with antistatic solution. Disconnect power and signal cables from the system's devices, and reseat them. Clean the inside of the printer. Run the printer's self-tests.

Use a software diagnostic package to check each section of the system. Run all system tests available, looking for any hint of pending problems.

Annual Activities

Reformat the hard drive by backing up its contents and performing a high-level format. Reinstall all the application software from original media, and reinstall all user files from the backup system. Check all floppy disks in the work area with a current antivirus program.

Clean the R/W heads in the floppy drive, using a lint-free swab. (Cotton swabs have fibers that can hang up in the ceramic insert of the head and damage it.) Perform the steps outlined in the monthly and semiannual sections.

This is a good model PM schedule, but it is not the definitive schedule. Before establishing a firm schedule, there are several other points to take into consideration. These points include any manufacturer's guidelines for maintaining the equipment. Read the user's guides of the various system components and work their suggested maintenance steps into the model.

Over time, adjust the steps and frequency of the plan to effectively cope with any environmental or usage variations. After all, the objective isn't to complete the schedule on time, it's to keep the equipment running and profitable.

SYSTEM PROTECTION

power variations

Computer technicians should be aware of potential environmental hazards and know how to prevent them from becoming a problem. A good place to start checking for environmental hazards is with the incoming power source. The following sections of the chapter deal with power line issues and solutions.

Power Line Protection

Avoid power variations—Digital systems tend to be sensitive to power variations and losses. Even a very short loss of electrical power can shut a digital computer down, resulting in a loss of any current information that has not been saved to a mass storage device.

Transients

spikes

surges

Sags

voltage sags

brownouts

Typical power supply variations fall into two categories:

- **Transients**—an overvoltage condition; sags are an undervoltage condition. Overvoltage conditions can be classified as **spikes** (measured in nanoseconds) or as **surges** (measured in milliseconds).

- **Sags**—can include **voltage sags** and **brownouts**. A voltage sag typically lasts only a few milliseconds, while a brownout can last for a protracted period of time.

The effects of these power supply variations are often hard to identify as power issues. Brownouts and power failures are easy to spot because of their duration. However, faster-acting disturbances can cause symptoms that are not easily traced to the power source. Spikes can be quite damaging to electronic equipment, damaging devices such as hard drives and modems. Other occurrences will simply cause data loss. Sags may cause the system to suddenly reboot, because it thinks the power has been turned off. These disturbances are relatively easy to detect, because they typically cause any lights in the room to flicker.

In general, if several components go bad in a short period of time, or if components go bad more often than usual at a given location, these are good indicators of power-related issues. Likewise, machines that crash randomly and often could be experiencing power issues. If "dirty" power problems are suspected, a voltage-monitoring device should be placed in the power circuit and left for an extended period of time. These devices observe the incoming power over time and will produce a problem indicator if significant variations occur.

Surge Suppressers

power line filters

surge suppressors

Inexpensive **power line filters**, called **surge suppressers**, are good for cleaning up dirty commercial power. These units passively filter the incoming power signal to smooth out variations. There are two factors to consider when choosing a surge suppresser:

- Clamping speed
- Clamping voltage

These units will protect the system from damage, up to a specified point. However, large variations, such as surges created when power is restored after an outage, can still cause considerable data loss and damage. In the case of start-up surges, making sure that the system is turned off, or even disconnected from the power source, until after the power is restored is one option. In the case of a complete shutdown, or a significant sag, the best protection from losing programs and data is to use an **uninterruptible power supply** (**UPS**).

uninterruptible power supply (UPS)

Uninterruptible Power Supplies

UPS

Uninterruptible power supplies are battery-based systems that monitor the incoming power and kick in when unacceptable variations occur in the power source. The term **UPS** is frequently used to describe two different types of power backup systems.

The first is a **standby power system**, and the second is a truly **uninterruptible power system**. A typical UPS system is depicted in Figure 13-26.

standby power
system

uninterruptible power
system

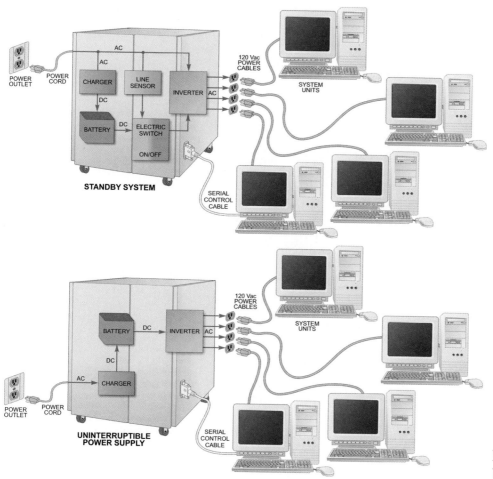

**Figure 13-26:
UPS System**

The standby system monitors the power input line and waits for a significant variation to occur. The batteries in this unit are held out of the power loop and draw only enough current from the AC source to stay recharged. When an interruption occurs, the UPS senses it and switches the output of the batteries into an inverter circuit that converts the DC output of the batteries into an AC current and voltage that resemble the commercial power supply. This power signal is typically applied to the computer within 10 milliseconds.

The uninterruptible systems do not keep the batteries off-line. Instead, the batteries and converters are always actively attached to the output of UPS. When an interruption in the supply occurs, no switching of the output is required. The battery/inverter section simply continues under its own power. Figure 13-27 shows how a UPS connects into a system.

Standby systems don't generally provide a high level of protection from sags and spikes. However, they do include additional circuitry to minimize such variations. Conversely, an uninterruptible system is an extremely good power-conditioning system. Because it always sits between the commercial power and the computer, it can supply a constant power supply to the system.

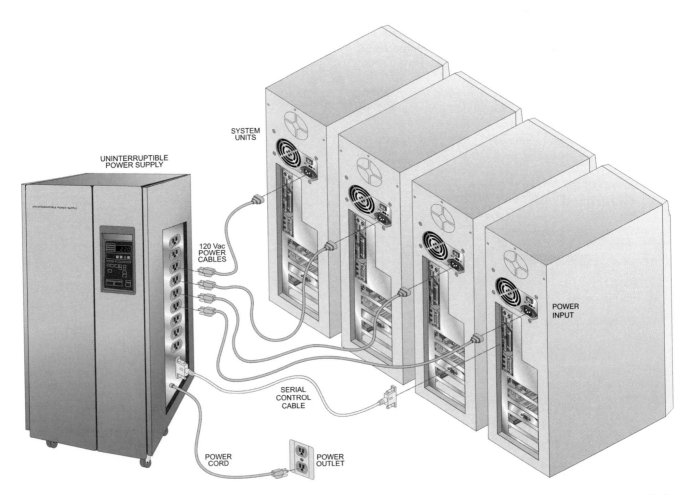

SYSTEM
UNITS

UNINTERRUPTIBLE
POWER SUPPLY

120 Vac
POWER
CABLES

POWER
INPUT

SERIAL
CONTROL
CABLE

POWER
CORD

POWER
OUTLET

**Figure 13-27:
Connecting the
UPS in the System**

volt-ampere (VA)

wattage rating

out-of-phase

When dealing with either type of UPS system, the most important rating to be aware of is its **volt-ampere (VA)** rating. The VA rating indicates the ability of the UPS system to deliver both voltage (V) and current (A) to the computer, simultaneously. This rating is different than the device's **wattage rating**, and the two should not be used interchangeably.

The wattage power rating is a factor of multiplying the voltage and current use, at any particular time, to arrive at a power consumption value. The VA rating is used in AC systems, because peak voltage and current elements do not occur at the same instant. This condition is referred to as being **out-of-phase** and makes it slightly more difficult to calculate power requirements. In general, always make sure that the UPS system has a higher wattage capability than the computer requires, and likewise that the VA rating of the UPS is higher than that required by the computer.

┌─ **NOTE** ─────────────────────────────────────
│ High power—consumption peripheral devices, such as laser printers,
│ should not be connected directly to the UPS. These devices can overload
│ the UPS and cause data loss.
└──

ampere-hour rating

The other significant specification for UPS systems is the length of time they can supply power. Because the UPS is a battery-powered device, it uses an **ampere-hour rating**. This is the same time notation system used for automobile batteries and other battery-powered systems. The rating is obtained by multiplying a given current drain from the battery by a given amount of time (i.e., a battery capable of sustaining 1.5 amps of output current for 1 hour would be rated at 1.5 amp-hours).

The primary mission of the UPS is to keep the system running when a power failure occurs (usually, long enough to conduct an orderly shutdown of the system). Because it's battery based, it cannot keep the system running indefinitely. For this reason, you should not connect nonessential, power-hungry peripheral devices such as a laser printer to the UPS supply. If the power goes out, it is highly unlikely that you will really have to print something before shutting the system down. If the UPS is being used to keep a critical system in operation during the power outage, the high current drain of the laser printer would severely reduce the length of time that the UPS could keep the system running.

If the UPS were simply connected in line with the computer's power source, when a power line disruption occurred, the UPS would simply kick in and keep the computer running until the batteries were drained or the power was restored. However, UPS systems have the ability to communicate with a host computer so that an orderly shutdown of the system can be performed. The host computer can be a stand-alone desktop/tower unit that the UPS is guarding, or in a network environment, it can be a server that has network management capabilities for all of the computers on the network. The host computer is typically connected to the UPS typically through a serial interface cable.

When a disruption occurs, the UPS notifies the power management system in the host computer's operating system of the failure. The power management utility for most operating systems can be configured to begin a prescribed shutdown schedule. This option is designed to give the system enough time to safely store any key information and prepare to be shut down. In the case of a server-managed network situation, the server can shut down different programs, computers, and support equipment at different times to conserve the battery life of the UPS, yet stay online as long as possible.

The server can also be configured to notify system users that a shutdown will be occurring so that they can complete their tasks and shut down properly. At the same time, the host computer can issue a page or e-mail alert to an administrator or service person to notify them that a problem has occurred and needs to be investigated.

The host computer sees the UPS device as another peripheral device. When the UPS is first installed, the system's PnP process should detect the UPS as it would any other peripheral attached to one of its serial ports. Afterward, the system will simply see the UPS as another one of its installed devices.

Checking UPS Operation

A UPS system is a major component of any server system that must have a high level of availability. The UPS provides continued operation when power problems arise and provides safety for data in process. However, a UPS is still an electronic device and is subject to failure. If the safety component of a system fails, then the entire system becomes vulnerable.

Therefore, the UPS should be tested at regular intervals to insure that it is functioning properly. The simplest UPS test is to unplug the UPS from the wall while the computer is running to make it supply power to the system through its batteries alone. You should measure the performance of the system against its configured shutdown schedule.

If the UPS does not supply the expected amount of backup time when it's tested, it may be overloaded, or its batteries may be wearing out. The first option is to unplug less important equipment, such as laser printers, from the UPS. Afterward, attempt to recharge the batteries and retest the system. If this does not restore backup time to acceptable levels, consider replacing the batteries in the UPS.

Other common problems that can occur with UPS systems include the UPS not turning on, the UPS not turning off, host computer running only on the UPS batteries, and the UPS not controlling the shutdown of the host computer. If the UPS system will not come on, there are several items that should be checked. These items include

- The on/off switch

- The commercial AC power supply

- The UPS input circuit breaker

- The UPS battery connector

All of these items can cause the UPS to fail. Verify the function of the UPS on/off switch. If it functions properly, check the AC supply to the UPS by substituting a lamp or other handheld AC device in its outlet to verify that power is reaching the outlet. If power is available at the outlet, check the AC power cord at the outlet and the UPS. Next, check the input circuit breaker UPS, if present, to determine whether it is set or tripped. Finally, check the battery connector to make certain that it is fully engaged.

If the UPS operates on battery power even though AC power is available, the input circuit breaker may be tripped or the unit's input voltage sensitivity may be set to high. You should reduce the load on the UPS by unplugging any unnecessary items. After the auxiliary devices have been removed, reset the breaker. Some inexpensive power generators can distort the input voltage to the UPS. To combat this, you may need to move the UPS to a different outlet on a different power circuit, or adjust the UPS unit's voltage sensitivity setting.

Likewise, if the UPS will not turn off, an internal UPS fault has occurred, and the unit should not be used. Instead, the UPS unit should be replaced and serviced immediately.

UPS systems do not always use standard serial cables for communication. If the cable is incorrect, loose, or missing, the computer's power management functions will not be able to communicate with the UPS to control it.

Protection During Storage

The best storage option for most computer equipment is the original manufacturer's box. These boxes are designed specifically to store and transport the device safely. They include form-fitting protective foam to protect the device from shock hazards. The device is normally wrapped in a protective antistatic bag or wrapper to defeat the effects of ESD.

Printed circuit boards are normally shipped on a thin piece of antistatic foam. The board is typically placed solder-side down on the foam. Both the foam and the board are placed in an antistatic bag and then into a storage box.

Hard-disk drives are usually placed directly into a static bag and then placed in a thick foam box. The foam box is then inserted into a storage carton. FDDs typically receive less padding than do HDD units.

Monitors, printers, scanners, and other peripheral equipment should be stored in their original boxes, using their original packing foam and protective storage bag. The contours in the packing foam of these devices are not generally compatible from model to model or device to device. If the original boxes and packing materials are not available, make sure to use sturdy cartons and cushion the equipment well on all sides before shipping.

All electronic devices should be stored in dry cool areas away from heat sources and direct sunlight. Low-traffic areas are also preferable for storage, because there is less chance of incidental damage from people and equipment passing by.

> **TEST TIP**
> Know that the best device for transporting computer equipment is the original manufacturer's packaging, including the antistatic foam and bags used to pack it.

HAZARDS AND SAFETY PROCEDURES

Essentials 7.1

Depot Technician 5.1

IT Technician 7.1

CRT display

In most IBM-compatibles, there are only two potentially dangerous areas. One of these is inside the **CRT display**, and the other is inside the power supply unit. Both of these areas contain electrical voltage levels that are lethal. However, both of these areas reside in self-contained units, and you will normally not be required to open either unit.

You should never enter the interior of a CRT cabinet unless you have been trained specifically to work with this type of equipment. The tube itself is dangerous if accidentally cracked. In addition, ***extremely high voltage levels*** (in excess of 25,000 volts) may be present inside the CRT housing, even up to a year after electrical power has been removed from the unit.

Never open the power supply unit either. Some portions of the circuitry inside the power supply carry extremely high voltage levels and have very high current capabilities.

Generally, there are no open shock hazards present inside the system unit. However, you should not reach inside the computer while power is applied to the unit. Jewelry and other metallic objects pose an electrical threat, even with the relatively low voltage present in the system unit.

> **TEST TIP**
> Be aware of the voltage levels that are present inside a CRT cabinet.

Never have liquids around energized electrical equipment. It's a good idea to keep food and drinks away from all computer equipment at all times. When cleaning around the computer with liquids, make certain to unplug all power connections to the system, and its peripherals, beforehand. When cleaning external computer cabinets with liquid cleaners, take care to prevent any of the solution from dripping or spilling into the equipment.

Do not defeat the safety feature of three-prong power plugs by using two-prong adapters. The equipment ground of a power cable should never be defeated or removed. This plug connects the computer chassis to earth ground through the power system. This provides a reference point for all of the system's devices to operate from, as well as supplys protection for personnel from electrical shock. In defeating the ground plug, a very important level of protection is removed from the equipment.

trip

catch hazards

Periodically examine the power cords of the computer and peripherals for cracked or damaged insulation. Replace worn or damaged power cords promptly. Never allow anything to rest on a power cord. Run power cords and connecting cables safely out of the way, so that they don't become **trip** or **catch hazards**. Remove all power cords associated with the computer and its peripherals from the power outlet during thunder storms or if there is lightning.

Don't apply liquid or aerosol cleaners directly to computer equipment. Spray cleaners on a cloth, and then apply the cloth to the equipment. Freon-propelled sprays should not be used on computer equipment, because they can produce destructive electrostatic charges.

Check equipment vents to see that they are clear and have ample free-air space to allow heat to escape from the cabinet. Never block these vents, and never insert or drop objects into them.

Essentials 7.2

Depot Technician 5.1

IT Technician 7.1

Avoiding Laser and Burn Hazards

Laser printers contain many hazardous areas. The laser light can be very damaging to the human eye. In addition, there are multiple high-voltage areas in the typical laser printer and a high-temperature area to contend with as well.

The technician is normally protected from these areas by interlock switches built into the unit. However, it is often necessary to bypass these interlocks to isolate problems. When doing so, proper precautions must be observed, such as avoiding the laser light, being aware of the high temperatures in the fuser area, and taking proper precautions with the high-voltage areas of the unit. The laser light is a hazard to eyesight, the fuser area is a burn hazard, and the power supplies are shock hazards.

┌─ **TEST TIP** ─────────────────┐
Know the areas of the computer system that are dangerous for personnel and how to prevent injury from these areas.
└───────────────────────────────┘

Another potential burn hazard is the printhead mechanism of dot-matrix, thermal-wax, and dye-sublimation printers. During normal operations, these elements become hot enough to be a burn hazard if touched.

Because computers do have the potential to produce these kinds of injuries, it is good practice to have a well-stocked **first-aid kit** in the work area. In addition, a **Class-C fire extinguisher** should be on hand. Class-C extinguishers are the type specified for use around electrical equipment. You can probably imagine the consequences of applying a water-based fire extinguisher to a fire with live electrical equipment around. The class, or classes, that the fire extinguisher is rated for are typically marked on its side.

You may think that there's not much chance for a fire to occur with computer equipment, but this is not so. Just let a capacitor from a system board blow up and have a small piece land in a pile of packing materials in the work area. It becomes a fire.

first-aid kit

Class-C fire extinguisher

TEST TIP
Remember the type of fire extinguisher that must be used with electrical systems, such as a PC.

ELECTROSTATIC DISCHARGE

What is ESD—Electrostatic discharges (ESD) are the most severe form of **electromagnetic interference (EMI)**. The human body can build up static charges that range up to *25,000 volts*. These buildups can discharge very rapidly into an electrically grounded body or device. Placing a 25,000-volt surge through any electronic device is potentially damaging to it.

Electrostatic discharges (ESD)

electromagnetic interference (EMI)

Static can easily discharge through digital computer equipment. The electronic devices that are used to construct digital equipment are particularly susceptible to damage from ESD. ESD is the most damaging form of electrical interference associated with digital equipment.

TEST TIP
Remember what the acronym ESD stands for.

The most common causes of ESD are

- Moving people
- Improper grounding
- Unshielded cables
- Poor connections
- Moving machines
- Low humidity (hot and dry conditions)

TEST TIP
Memorize the conditions that make ESD more likely to occur.

Elementary school teachers demonstrate the principles of static to their students by rubbing different materials together. When people move, the clothes they are wearing rub together and can produce large amounts of electrostatic charge on their bodies. Walking across carpeting can create charges in excess of 1000 volts. Motors in electrical devices, such as vacuum cleaners and refrigerators, generate high levels of ESD.

TEST TIP
Be aware that compressed air can be used to blow dust out of components and that it does not create ESD.

ESD is most likely to occur during periods of **low humidity**. If the relative humidity is below 50%, static charges can accumulate easily. ESD generally does not occur when the humidity is above 50%. Anytime the charge reaches around 10,000 volts, it is likely to discharge to grounded metal parts.

low humidity

ESD won't hurt humans, but it will destroy certain electronic devices. The high-voltage pulse can burn out the inputs of many IC devices. This damage may not appear instantly. It can build up over time, and cause the device to fail. Electronic logic devices, constructed from **metal oxide semiconductor (MOS)** materials, are particularly susceptible to ESD. The following section describes the special handling techniques that should be observed when working with equipment containing MOS devices.

metal oxide semiconductor (MOS)

You may be a little confused by the fact that we warn you about the lethal 25,000 volts present inside the monitor and then say that the 10,000 to 25,000 volts of ESD is not harmful to humans. The reason for this is the difference in current-delivering capabilities created by the voltage. For example, the circuitry in the monitor and the power supply is capable of delivering amps of current, while the current-producing capability of the electrostatic charge is less than a thousandth of that. Therefore, the 120 Vac, 1 amp current produced by the power supply unit is lethal, while the 25,000 Vdc, microamp current produced by ESD is not.

TEST TIP

Remember that the current capabilities of electrical devices establish the potential danger levels associated with working around them.

GEEK SQUAD CASE FILE #22232

Your precinct has been hired to consult on the design of ACME's new repair facility outside of Phoenix, Arizona. In particular, ACME management wants to know how to equip the work areas of their new facility. You have not been to the site, but you know that it is in a hot desert environment. Also, the building will be air-conditioned. How should you advise them about precautions that should be taken with the work area?

MOS Handling Techniques

In general, MOS devices are sensitive to voltage spikes and static electricity discharges. This can cause many problems when you have to replace MOS devices, especially **complementary-symmetry metal oxide semiconductor (CMOS)** devices. The level of static electricity present on your body is high enough to destroy the inputs of a CMOS device if you touch its pins with your fingers.

complementary-symmetry metal oxide semiconductor (CMOS)

In order to minimize the chances of damaging MOS devices during handling, special procedures have been developed to protect them from static shock. ICs are generally shipped and stored in special **conductive-plastic tubes** or trays. You may want to store MOS devices in these tubes, or you may simply ensure their safety by inserting the IC's leads into aluminum foil or **antistatic** (conductive) **foam**—not styrofoam. PC boards containing static-sensitive devices are normally shipped in special **antistatic bags**. These bags are good for storing ICs and other computer components that may be damaged by ESD. They are also the best method of transporting PC boards with static-sensitive components.

conductive-plastic tubes

antistatic foam

antistatic bags

Professional service technicians employ a number of precautionary steps when they are working on systems that may contain MOS devices. These technicians normally use **grounding straps**, like the one depicted in Figure 13-28. These antistatic devices may be placed around the wrists or ankles to ground the technician to the system being worked on. These straps release any static present on the technician's body and pass it harmlessly to ground potential.

Antistatic straps should never be worn while working on higher-voltage components, such as monitors and power supply units. Some technicians wrap a copper wire around their wrist or ankle and connect it to the ground side of an outlet. This is not a safe practice, because the resistive feature of a true wrist strap is missing. As an alternative, most technicians' work areas include **antistatic mats** made out of rubber or other antistatic materials that they stand on while working on the equipment. This is particularly helpful in carpeted work areas, because carpeting can be a major source of ESD buildup. Some antistatic mats have ground connections that should be connected to the safety ground of an AC power outlet.

To avoid damaging static-sensitive devices, the following procedures will help to minimize the chances of discharging destructive static:

- Before touching any components inside the system, touch an exposed part of the chassis or the power supply housing with your finger, as illustrated in Figure 13-29. Grounding yourself in this manner will ensure that any static charge present on your body is removed. This technique should be used before handling a circuit board or component. Of course, you should be aware that *this technique will only work safely if the power cord is attached to a grounded power outlet*. The ground plug on a standard power cable is the best tool for overcoming ESD problems.

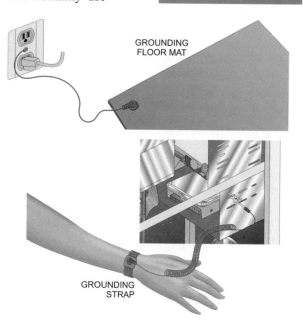

grounding straps

GROUNDING FLOOR MAT

GROUNDING STRAP

Figure 13-28: Typical Antistatic Devices

antistatic mats

┌─ **TEST TIP** ─┐
Know when not to wear an antistatic wrist strap.
└─────────────┘

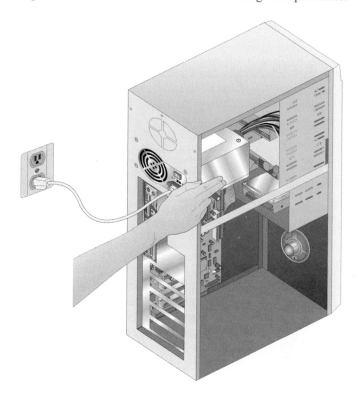

Figure 13-29: Discharging Through the Power Supply Unit

- Do not remove ICs from their protective tubes (or foam packages) until you are ready to use them. If you remove a circuit board or component containing static-sensitive devices from the system, place it on a conductive surface, such as a sheet of aluminum foil.

- In the event that you have to replace a hard-soldered IC, you may want to install an IC socket along with the chip. Be aware that normal operating vibrations and **temperature cycling** can degrade the electrical connections between ICs and sockets over time. This gradual deterioration of electrical contact between chips and sockets is referred to as **chip creep**. It is a good practice to reseat any socket-mounted devices when handling a printed circuit board. Before removing the IC from its protective container, touch the container to the power supply of the unit in which it is to be inserted.

- Use antistatic sprays or solutions on floors, carpets, desks, and computer equipment. An antistatic spray or solution applied with a soft cloth is an effective deterrent to static.

- Install **static-free carpeting** in the work area. You can also install an antistatic floor mat. Install a conductive tabletop to carry away static from the work area. Use antistatic table mats.

- Use a room humidifier to keep the humidity level above 50% in the work area.

Understanding Grounds

The term **ground** is often a source of confusion for the novice, because it actually encompasses a collection of terms. Generically, ground is simply any point from which electrical measurements are referenced. However, the original definition of ground actually referred to the ground. This ground is called **earth ground**.

The movement of the electrical current along a conductor requires a path for the current to return to its source. In early telegraph systems and even modern power transmission systems, the earth provides a return path and, hypothetically, produces an electrical reference point of absolute zero. This type of ground is shown in Figure 13-30.

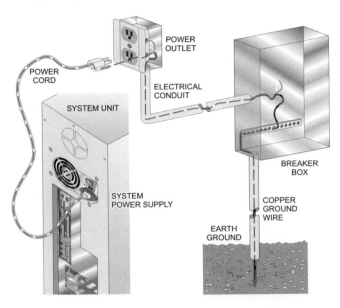

Figure 13-30: Power Transmission System

Many electronic circuits use an actual conductor as a return path. This type of ground is referred to as a **signal ground**. Electronic devices may also contain a third form of ground called **chassis ground**, or **protective ground**. In any event, ground remains the reference point from which most electrical signals are measured. In the case of troubleshooting computer components, measurements referenced to ground may be made from the system unit's chassis.

signal ground

chassis ground

protective ground

The other measurement reference is the signal ground point on the printed circuit board, where the test is being performed. This point isn't too difficult to find in a circuit board full of ICs, because most DIP-style chips use the highest-numbered pin for the positive supply voltage and the last pin on the pin-1 side of the chip as the ground pin. This type of ground is illustrated in Figure 13-31. Some caution should be used with this assumption, because not all ICs use this pin for ground. However, if you examine a number of ICs and connectors on the board, you should be able to trace the ground foil and use it as a reference.

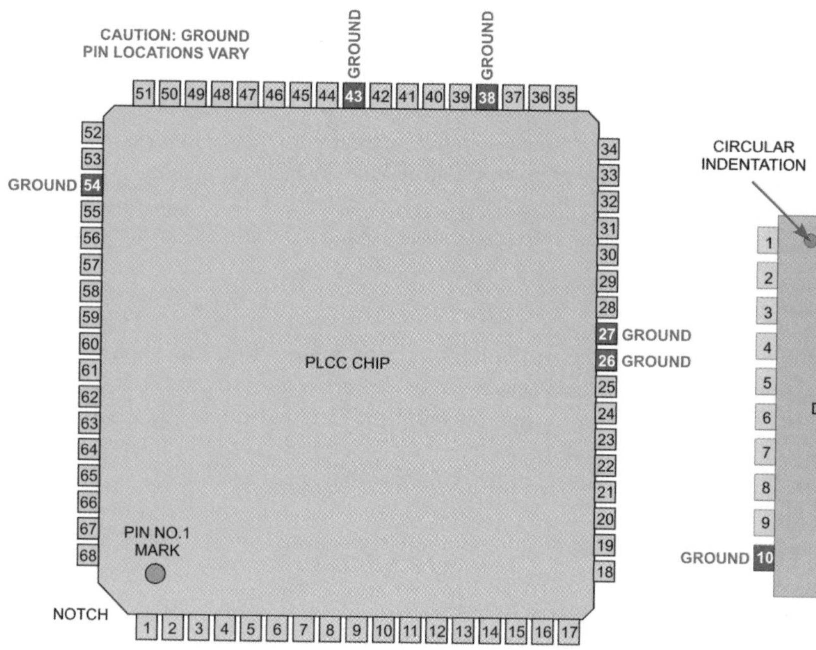

Figure 13-31: Grounds on IC Chips

Grounding is an important aspect of limiting EMI in computer systems. Left unchecked, EMI can distort images on the video display, interfere with commercial communication equipment (such as radios and televisions), and corrupt data on floppy disks. In addition, EMI can cause signal deterioration and loss from improper cable routing. If a signal cable is bundled with a power cable, radiation from the power cable may be induced into the signal cable, affecting the signals that pass through it. Good grounding routes the induced EMI signals away from logic circuitry and toward ground potential, preventing them from disrupting normal operations. Unlike ESD, which is destructive, the effects of EMI can be corrected without damage.

Because the computer system is connected to an actual earth ground, it should always be turned off and disconnected from the wall outlet during electrical storms. This includes the computer and all of its peripherals. The electrical pathway through the computer equipment can be very inviting to lightning on its way to earth ground. The extremely high electrical potential of a lightning strike is more than any computer can withstand.

TEST TIP
Remember that ESD is destructive, and EMI is not.

TEST TIP
Know the best protection for a computer system during an electrical storm.

HARDWARE DISPOSAL PROCEDURES

As with any mechanical device, a computer eventually becomes obsolete in the application that it was originally intended for. Newer machines, with improved features, arise to replace earlier models. And, slowly, but surely, components fail and get replaced. Then comes the question: What do we do with the old stuff? Can it simply be placed in the garbage bin so that it is hauled to the landfill and buried?

In today's world of environmental consciousness, you might not think so. Computers and peripherals contain some environmentally unfriendly materials.

Even though all of these materials can be classified as hazardous materials, so far there are no widespread regulations when it comes to placing them in the landfill. Conversely, **local regulations** concerning acceptable disposal methods for computer-related components should always be checked before disposing of any electronic equipment.

> Most computer components contain some level of **hazardous substances**. Printed circuit boards consist of plastics, precious metals, fiberglass, arsenic, silicon, gallium, and lead. CRTs contain glass, metal, plastics, lead, barium, and rare earth metals. Batteries from portable systems can contain lead, cadmium, lithium, alkaline manganese, and mercury.

Laser printer toner cartridges can be refilled and recycled. However, this should only be done in draft mode operations where very good resolution is not required. Ink cartridges from ink-jet printers can also be refilled and reused. Like laser cartridges, they can be very messy to refill and often do not function as well as new cartridges do. In many cases, the manufacturer of the product will have a policy of accepting spent cartridges.

For both batteries and cartridges, the desired method of disposal is **recycling**. It should not be too difficult to find a **drop site** that will handle recycling these products. On the other hand, even **nonhazardous, subtitle D dumpsites** can handle the hardware components if need be. Subtitle D dumpsites are nonhazardous, solid waste dumpsites that have been designed to meet EPA standards set for this classification. Subtitle C dumpsites are those designed to hold hazardous materials safely.

Fortunately, there seem to be several charitable organizations around the country that take in old computer systems and refurbish them for various applications. Contact your local **Chamber of Commerce** for information about such organizations. The Internet also has several computer disposal organizations that will take old units and redistribute them. In addition, there are a few companies that will dispose of your old computer components in an "environmentally friendly" manner—for a fee.

In addition to the computer parts that provide hazardous materials, many of the **cleaning substances** used on computer equipment can be classified as hazardous materials. When it comes to the chemical solvents used to clean computers, as well as the containers they come in, it will normally be necessary to clear these items with the local waste management agencies before disposing of them. Many dumpsites will not handle **free liquids**. Free liquids are those substances that can pass through a standard paint filter. If the liquid will pass through the filter, it is a free liquid and cannot be disposed of in the landfill. Therefore, solvents and other liquid cleaning materials must be properly categorized and disposed of at an appropriate type of disposal center.

local regulations

hazardous substances

TEST TIP
Remember that toner cartridges from a laser printer should be recycled.

recycling

drop site

nonhazardous, subtitle D dump sites

TEST TIP
Remember that the proper disposal method for batteries is to recycle them.

Chamber of Commerce

cleaning substances

free liquids

All hazardous materials are required to have **Material Safety Data Sheets (MSDS)** that accompany them when they change hands. They are also required to be on hand in areas where hazardous materials are stored and commonly used. The MSDS contains information about

Material Safety Data Sheets (MSDS)

Essentials 7.1

- What the material is

- Its hazardous ingredients

- Its physical properties

- Fire and explosion data

- Reactivity data

- Spill or leak procedures

- Health hazard information

- Any special protection information

- Any special precaution information

The supplier of the hazardous material must provide this information sheet. If you supply this material to a third party, you must also supply the MSDS for the material. The real reason for the sheets is to inform workers and management about hazards associated with the products and how to handle them safely. It also provides instructions about what to do if an accident occurs involving the material. For this reason, employees should know where the MSDS are stored in their work area.

KEY POINTS REVIEW

The focus of this chapter has been to present important points for inclusion in the preventive maintenance programs associated with personal computer systems. Review the following key points before moving into the Review and Exam Questions sections to make sure you are comfortable with each point. Afterward, answer the Review Questions that follow to verify your knowledge of the information.

- Cleaning is a major part of keeping a computer system healthy. Therefore, the technician's tool kit should also contain a collection of cleaning supplies. Along with hand tools, it will need a lint-free, soft cloth (chamois) for cleaning the plastic outer surfaces of the system.

- The environment around a computer system and the manner in which the computer is used determine greatly how many problems it will have. Occasionally dedicating a few moments of care to the computer can extend its mean time between failures (MTBF) period considerably. This activity, involving maintenance not normally associated with a breakdown, is called preventive maintenance (PM).

- Unlike hard-disk drives, floppy drives are at least partially open to the atmosphere, and they may be handled on a regular basis. This opens the floppy-disk drive to a number of maintenance concerns not found in hard-disk drives. Also, the removable disks are subject to extremes in temperature, exposure to magnetic and electromagnetic fields, bending, and airborne particles that can lead to information loss.

- Input peripherals generally require very little in the way of preventive maintenance. An occasional dusting and cleaning should be all that's really required.

- Because printers tend to be much more mechanical than other types of computer peripherals, they require more effort to maintain. Printers generate pollutants, such as paper dust and ink droplets, in everyday operation. These pollutants can build up on mechanical parts and cause them to wear. As the parts wear, the performance of the printer diminishes. Therefore, printers require periodic cleaning and adjustments to maintain good performance.

- Digital systems tend to be sensitive to power variations and losses. Even a very short loss of electrical power can shut a digital computer down, resulting in a loss of any current information that has not been saved to a mass storage device.

- Uninterruptible power supplies are battery-based systems that monitor the incoming power and kick in when unacceptable variations occur in the power source. The term UPS is frequently used to describe two different types of power backup systems.

- In most IBM-compatibles, there are only two potentially dangerous areas. One of these is inside the CRT display, and the other is inside the power supply unit. Both of these areas contain electrical voltage levels that are lethal. However, both of these areas reside in self-contained units, and you will normally not be required to open either unit.

- Laser printers contain many hazardous areas. The laser light can be very damaging to the human eye. In addition, there are multiple high-voltage areas in the typical laser printer and a high-temperature area to contend with as well.

- Most computer components contain some level of hazardous substances. Printed circuit boards consist of plastics, precious metals, fiberglass, arsenic, silicon, gallium, and lead. CRTs contain glass, metal, plastics, lead, barium, and rare earth metals. Batteries from portable systems can contain lead, cadmium, lithium, alkaline manganese, and mercury.

- Electrostatic discharges (ESD) are the most severe form of electromagnetic interference (EMI). The human body can build up static charges that range up to 25,000 volts. These buildups can discharge very rapidly into an electrically grounded body or device. Placing a 25,000-volt surge through any electronic device is potentially damaging to it.

- In general, MOS devices are sensitive to voltage spikes and static electricity discharges. This can cause many problems when you have to replace MOS devices, especially complementary-symmetry metal oxide semiconductor (CMOS) devices. The level of static electricity present on your body is high enough to destroy the inputs of a CMOS device if you touch its pins with your fingers.

- The term *ground* is often a source of confusion for the novice, because it actually encompasses a collection of terms. Generically, ground is simply any point from which electrical measurements are referenced. However, the original definition of ground actually referred to the ground. This ground is called earth ground.

- One of the main features of the Windows 2000/XP operating systems is their security capabilities. As operating systems designed to work in business networks, data security is one of the most important functions of Windows 2000 and Windows XP.

- Authentication is a process that determines that users on the network are who they say they are.

- Digital certificates are password-protected, encrypted data files that include data that identify the transmitting system and can be used to authenticate external users to the network through virtual private networks.

The following questions test your knowledge of the material presented in this chapter.

1. List the two most dangerous areas of a typical microcomputer system, and describe why they are so dangerous.

2. Name three devices used to minimize ESD in the repair area.

3. The best general-purpose cleaning tool for computer equipment is _____.

4. List at least three environmental conditions that can adversely affect microcomputer equipment.

5. A short undervoltage condition, lasting milliseconds, is called _____.

6. Are there any restrictions on disposing of a spent toner cartridge?

7. Which type of IC device is most likely to be damaged by ESD?

8. Can an effective ESD strap be constructed by simply wrapping a grounded bare wire around your wrist?

9. What is the most effective method of dealing with EMI problems?

10. The best method of protecting computer equipment from a thunderstorm is to _____.

11. The best method for transporting electronic devices is _____.

12. List computer-related PM items that should be performed annually.

13. Name two characteristics that should be checked carefully before purchasing a UPS for a given computer system.

14. Describe the normal duration of a voltage spike.

15. Once a virus has infected a computer, where does it normally reside?

EXAM QUESTIONS

1. Do viruses normally attack the system's CMOS settings?
   a. Yes, this is how a virus attacks most computers.
   b. No, viruses do not normally attack CMOS settings.
   c. Yes, this is how viruses attack all computers.
   d. No, viruses never attack CMOS settings.

2. How are most computer viruses spread from computer to computer?
   a. By downloading programs from networks
   b. By sharing infected files between individuals
   c. By not formatting disks before use
   d. By transferring files over modems

3. What is the most common cause of ESD in microcomputer systems?
   a. Moving people
   b. High humidity
   c. Rubber mats
   d. Grounded power supply cables

4. Where would it be inappropriate to use an ESD wrist strap?
   a. While working on hard-disk drives
   b. While working on system boards
   c. While working on CRT video monitors
   d. While working on printers

5. What is one of the best methods for protecting computer systems from ESD?
   a. A water and fabric softener solution
   b. A water and ammonia solution
   c. A water and bleach solution
   d. A hydrogen tetrachloride solution

6. A short overvoltage occurrence (nanoseconds) is called _____.
   a. a spike
   b. a surge
   c. a brownout
   d. a sag

7. ESD is most likely to occur during periods of _____.
   a. low humidity
   b. high humidity
   c. medium humidity
   d. rain

8. The best protection against power-failure data loss is _____.
   a. a tape backup
   b. a surge suppresser
   c. a UPS
   d. a line filter

9. Define a voltage sag.
   a. An overvoltage condition that lasts for a few milliseconds
   b. An undervoltage condition that lasts for an extended period
   c. An overvoltage condition that lasts for an extended period
   d. An undervoltage condition that lasts for a few milliseconds

10. The most effective grounding system for a microcomputer is _____.
    a. an ESD wrist or ankle strap
    b. the safety ground plug at a commercial AC receptacle
    c. the ground plane of the system board
    d. the chassis ground provided by brass standoffs

A+ OBJECTIVE MAP

The **A+ Essentials Exam** is the fundamental exam that can be coupled with any of three other exams to complete the A+ certification. The A+ Essentials exam focuses on fundamental knowledge associated with Personal Computer hardware, printers and Windows operating systems.

The options for the second certification exam include the 220-602 **IT Technician** exam, the 220-603 **Tech Support Technician** exam and the 220-604 **Depot Technician** exam. The 220-602 exam is targeted for technicians who work in a mobile or corporate technical environment with high levels of personal client interaction. The 220-603 exam is intended for individuals who work in remote work environment where client interaction, client training, operating system and connectivity issues are important. Finally, the 220-604 exam is designed for technicians who work in environments where hardware repair is emphasized and customer interaction is minimal.

The CompTIA organization has established the following objectives for the A+ Certification exams.

A+ ESSENTIALS EXAMINATION

The Essentials examination measures necessary competencies for an entry-level IT professional with the equivalent knowledge of at least 500 hours of hands-on experience in the lab or field. Hands-on experience or equivalent knowledge includes installing, building, upgrading, repairing, configuring, troubleshooting, optimizing, diagnosing, and performing preventive maintenance of basic personal computer hardware and operating systems.

Domain 1.0   Personal Computer Components

The topics covered by this domain are included in approximately 21% of the questions in the A+ Essential exam.

1.1 Identify the fundamental principles of using personal computers

- Identify the names, purposes and characteristics of storage devices
    - FDD - Chapters 2 & 5, Lab Procedures 1 & 2
    - HDD - Chapters 2 & 5, Lab Procedures 1 & 2
    - CD / DVD / RW (e.g., drive speeds, media types) - Chapters 2 & 5, Lab Procedures 1 & 2

- Removable storage (e.g., tape drive, solid state such as thumb drive, flash and SD cards, USB, external CD-RW and hard drive) - Chapters 4 & 5

- Identify the names, purposes and characteristics of motherboards

  - Form Factor (e.g., ATX/BTX, micro ATX/NLX) - Chapter 3, Lab Procedure 1

  - Components

    - Integrated I/Os (e.g., sound, video, USB, serial, IEEE 1394/firewire, parallel, NIC, modem) - Chapters 2 & 3, Lab Procedure 1

    - Memory slots (e.g., RIMM, DIMM) - Chapters 2 & 3

    - Processor sockets - Chapters 2 & 3

    - External cache memory - Chapter 3

    - Bus architecture - Chapters 2 & 3

    - Bus slots (e.g., PCI, AGP, PCIe, AMR, CNR) - Chapters 2 & 3

    - EIDE/PATA - Chapters 2 & 5, Lab Procedure 2

    - SATA - Chapters 2 & 5

    - SCSI Technology - Chapters 2 & 5

  - Chipsets - Chapters 2 & 3

  - BIOS CMOS/Firmware - Chapters 2 & 3, Lab Procedures 1, 3, & 4

  - Riser card / daughter board - Chapters 2 & 4

- Identify the names, purposes and characteristics of power supplies, for example: AC adapter, ATX, proprietary, voltage - Chapter 2, Lab Procedure 1

- Identify the names purposes and characteristics of processor/CPUs - Chapter 3, Lab Procedure 1

  - CPU chips (e.g., AMD, Intel) - Chapters 2 & 3

  - CPU technologies - Chapter 3

    - Hyperthreading - Chapter 3

    - Dual core - Chapter 3

    - Throttling - Chapters 3 & 8

    - Micro code (MMX) - Chapter 3

    - Overclocking - Chapter 3

    - Cache - Chapters 2 & 3

    - VRM - Chapter 3

    - Speed (real vs. actual) - Chapter 3

    - 32 vs. 64 bit - Chapter 3

- Identify the names, purposes and characteristics of memory

    - Types of memory (e.g., DRAM, SRAM, SDRAM, DDR/DDR2, RAMBUS) - Chapter 3

    - Operational characteristics

        ○ Memory chips (8, 16, 32) - Chapter 3

        ○ Parity versus non-parity - Chapter 3

        ○ ECC vs. non-ECC - Chapter 3

        ○ Single-sided vs. double-sided - Chapter 11

- Identify the names, purposes and characteristics of display devices, for example: projectors, CRT and LCD - Chapters 2, 4, & 8, Lab Procedure 1

    - Connector types (e.g., VGA, DVI / HDMi, S-Video, Component/RGB) - Chapter 4

    - Settings (e.g., V-hold, refresh rate, resolution) - Chapters 2, 4, & 11

- Identify the names, purposes and characteristics of input devices for example: mouse, keyboard, bar code reader, multimedia (e.g., web and digital cameras, MIDI, microphones), biometric devices, touch screen. - Chapter 4, Lab Procedures 1 & 2

- Identify the names, purposes and characteristics of adapter cards

    - Video including PCI / PCIe and AGP - Chapter 2, Lab Procedure 1

    - Multimedia - Chapter 2

    - I/O (SCSI, serial, USB, Parallel) - Chapter 2, Lab Procedure 1

    - Communications including network and modem - Chapter 2, Lab Procedure 1

- Identify the names, purposes and characteristics of ports and cables for example: USB 1.1 and 2.0, parallel, serial, IEEE 1394/firewire, RJ45 and RJ11, PS2/Mini-DIN, Centronics (e.g., mini, 36) multimedia (e.g., 1/8 connector, MIDI Coaxial, SPDIF) - Chapter 4, Lab Procedure 1

- Identify the names, purposes and characteristics of cooling systems for example heat sinks, CPU and case fans, liquid cooling systems, thermal compound - Chapters 2 & 3

1.2 Install, configure, optimize and upgrade personal computer components

- Add, remove and configure internal and external storage devices

    - Drive preparation of internal storage devices including format / file systems and imaging technology - Chapter 5, Lab Procedures 2 & 5

- Install display devices - Chapter 4, Lab Procedure 2

- Add, remove and configure basic input and multimedia devices - Chapter 4, Lab Procedure 2

1.3 Identify tools, diagnostic procedures and troubleshooting techniques for personal computer components

- Recognize the basic aspects of troubleshooting theory for example: - Chapter 11, Lab Procedure 7

  - Perform backups before making changes - Chapter 11

  - Assess a problem systematically and divide large problems into smaller components to be analyzed individually - Chapter 11, Lab Procedure 7

  - Verify even the obvious, determine whether the problem is something simple and make no assumptions - Chapter 11

  - Research ideas and establish priorities - Chapter 11

  - Document findings, actions and outcomes - Chapter 11

- Identify and apply basic diagnostic procedures and troubleshooting techniques for example: - Lab Procedures 5 & 7

  - Identify the problem including questioning user and identifying user changes to computers - Chapter 11

  - Analyze the problem including potential causes and make an initial determination of software and / or hardware problems - Chapter 11, Lab Procedures 5 & 7

  - Test related components including inspection, connections, hardware/software configurations, device manager and consult vendor documentations - Chapter 11

  - Evaluate results and take additional steps if needed such as consultation, use of alternate resources, manuals - Chapter 11

  - Document activities and outcomes - Chapters 1 & 11, Lab Procedures 5 & 7

- Recognize and isolate issues with display, power, basic input devices, storage, memory, thermal, POST errors (e.g., BIOS, hardware) - Chapter 11

- Apply basic troubleshooting techniques to check for problems (e.g., thermal issues, error codes, power, connections including cables and/or pins, compatibility, functionality, software/drivers) with components for example: - Lab Procedure 7

  - Motherboards - Chapter 11

  - Power supply - Chapter 11

  - Processor/CPUs - Chapter 11

  - Memory - Chapter 11

  - Display devices - Chapter 11

  - Input devices - Chapter 11

  - Adapter cards - Chapter 11

- Recognize the names, purposes, characteristics and appropriate application of tools for example: BIOS, self-test, hard drive self-test and software diagnostics test - Chapter 11, Lab Procedures 3 & 4

- Identify and apply basic aspects of preventive maintenance theory for example:

    - Visual/audio inspection - Chapter 11

    - Driver firmware updates - Chapter 4

    - Scheduling preventive maintenance - Chapter 13

    - Use of appropriate repair tools and cleaning materials - Chapter 13

    - Ensuring proper environment - Chapters 11 & 13

- Identify and apply common preventive maintenance techniques for devices such as input devices and batteries - Chapter 13

Domain 2.0   Laptops and Portable Devices

The topics covered by this domain are included in approximately 11% of the questions in the A+ Essential exam.

- Identify names, purposes and characteristics of laptop-specific:

    - Form factors such as memory and hard drives - Chapter 8

    - Peripherals (e.g., docking station, port replicator and media/accessory bay) - Chapter 8

    - Expansion slots (e.g., PCMCIA I, II and III, card and express bus) - Chapter 8

    - Ports (e.g., mini PCI slot) - Chapter 8

    - Communication connections (e.g., Bluetooth, infrared, cellular WAN, Ethernet) - Chapter 6

    - Power and electrical input devices (e.g., auto-switching and fixed-input power supplies, batteries) - Chapter 8

    - LCD technologies (e.g., active and passive matrix, resolution such as XGA, SXGA+, UXGA, WUXGA, contrast ratio, native resolution) - Chapters 4 & 8

    - Input devices (e.g., stylus/digitizer, function (Fn) keys and pointing devices such as touch pad, point stick/track point) - Chapter 8

- Identify and distinguish between mobile and desktop motherboards and processors including throttling, power management and WiFi - Chapter 8

2.2 Install, configure, optimize and upgrade laptops and portable devices

- Configure power management
    - Identify the features of BIOS-ACPI - Chapter 8
    - Identify the difference between suspend, hibernate and standby - Chapter 8
- Demonstrate safe removal of laptop-specific hardware such as peripherals, hot-swappable devices and non-hot-swappable devices - Chapter 8

2.3 Identify tools, basic diagnostic procedures and troubleshooting techniques for laptops and portable devices

- Use procedures and techniques to diagnose power conditions, video, keyboard, pointer and wireless card issues, for example:
    - Verify AC power (e.g., LEDs, swap AC adapter) - Chapter 8
    - Verify DC power - Chapter 8
    - Remove unneeded peripherals - Chapter 8
    - Plug in external monitor - Chapter 8
    - Toggle Fn keys - Chapter 8
    - Check LCD cutoff switch - Chapter 8
    - Verify backlight functionality and pixilation - Chapter 8
    - Stylus issues (e.g., digitizer problems) - Chapter 8
    - Unique laptop keypad issues - Chapter 11
    - Antenna wires - Chapter 8

2.4 Perform preventive maintenance on laptops and portable devices

- Identify and apply common preventive maintenance techniques for laptops and portable devices, for example: cooling devices, hardware and video cleaning materials, operating environments including temperature and air quality, storage, transportation and shipping. - Chapter 13

Domain 3.0 Operating Systems

(Unless otherwise noted, operating systems referred to within include Microsoft Windows 2000, XP Professional, XP Home and Media Center.)

The topics covered by this domain are included in approximately 21% of the questions in the A+ Essential exam.

3.1 Identify the fundamentals of using operating systems

- Identify differences between operating systems (e.g., Mac, Windows, Linux) and describe operating system revision levels including GUI, system requirements, application and hardware compatibility - Chapter 2

- Identify names, purposes and characteristics of the primary operating system components including registry, virtual memory and file system - Chapter 9

- Describe features of operating system interfaces, for example:

  - Windows Explorer - Chapter 10, Lab Procedures 10 & 12

  - My Computer - Chapter 10

  - Control Panel - Chapter 10, Lab Procedure 19

  - Command Prompt - Chapter 9

  - My Network Places - Chapter 10

  - Task bar/systray - Chapter 10, Lab Procedures 10 & 12

  - Start Menu - Chapter 10, Lab Procedures 10 & 12

- Identify the names, locations, purposes and characteristics of operating system files for example:

  - BOOT.INI - Chapter 9, Lab Procedures 43 & 44

  - NTLDR - Chapter 9

  - NTDETECT.COM - Chapter 9

  - NTBOOTDD.SYS - Chapter 9

  - Registry data files - Chapter 9, Lab Procedure 23

- Identify concepts and procedures for creating, viewing, managing disks, directories and files in operating systems for example: - Lab Procedures 10 & 12

  - Disks (e.g., active, primary, extended and logical partitions) - Chapter 9

  - File systems (e.g., FAT 32, NTFS) - Chapters 9 & 10

  - Directory structures (e.g., create folders, navigate directory structures) - Chapters 9 & 10

  - Files (e.g., creation, extensions, attributes, permissions) - Chapters 9 & 10

- Identify procedures for installing operating systems including:

    - Verification of hardware compatibility and minimum requirements - Chapter 10, Lab Procedure 9

    - Installation methods (e.g., boot media such as CD, floppy or USB, network installation, drive imaging) - Chapter 10, Lab Procedure 9

    - Operating system installation options (e.g., attended/unattended, file system type, network configuration) - Chapter 10, Lab Procedure 9

    - Disk preparation order (e.g., start installation, partition and format drive) - Chapter 10

    - Device driver configuration (e.g., install and upload device drivers) - Chapter 10

    - Verification of installation - Chapter 10

- Identify procedures for upgrading operating systems including:

    - Upgrade considerations (e.g., hardware, application and/or network compatibility) - Chapter 10

    - Implementation (e.g., backup data, install additional Windows components) - Chapter 10

- Install/add a device including loading, adding device drivers and required software including:

    - Determine whether permissions are adequate for performing the task - Chapter 10

    - Device driver installation (e.g., automated and/or manual search and installation of device drivers) - Chapter 10, Lab Procedure 11

    - Using unsigned drivers (e.g., driver signing) - Chapter 10

    - Verify installation of the driver (e.g., device manager and functionality) - Chapter 10

- Identify procedures and utilities used to optimize operating systems for example, virtual memory, hard drives, temporary files, service, startup and applications - Chapter 12

- Identify basic boot sequences, methods and utilities for recovering operating systems - Lab Procedure 15

    - Boot methods (e.g., safe mode, recovery console, boot to restore point) - Chapter 12, Lab Procedure 15

    - Automated System Recovery (ASR) (e.g., Emergency Repair Disk (ERD)) - Chapter 12

- Identify and apply diagnostic procedures and troubleshooting techniques for example:

    - Identify the problem by questioning the user and identifying user changes to the computer - Chapters 11 & 12

    - Analyze problem including potential causes and initial determination of software and/or hardware problem - Chapters 11 & 12, Lab Procedures 43 & 44

    - Test related components including connections, hardware/software configurations, device manager and consulting vendor documentation - Chapter 12, Lab Procedures 43 & 44

    - Evaluate results and take additional steps if needed such as consultation, alternate resources and manuals - Chapters 11 & 12, Lab Procedures 43 & 44

    - Document activities and outcomes - Chapters 1, 11, & 12, Lab Procedures 43 & 44

- Recognize and resolve common operational issues such as bluescreen, system lock-up, input/output device, application install, start or load and Windows-specific printing problems (e.g., print spool stalled, incorrect / incompatible driver for print) - Chapter 12

- Explain common error messages and codes for example:

    - Boot (e.g., invalid boot disk, inaccessible boot drive, missing NTLDR) - Chapter 12

    - Startup (e.g., device/service failed to start, device/program in registry not found) - Chapter 12

    - Event Viewer - Chapters 12 & 13

    - Registry - Chapter 12

    - Windows reporting - Chapter 12

- Identify the names, locations, purposes and characteristics of operating system utilities for example:

    - Disk management tools (e.g., DEFRAG, NTBACKUP, CHKDSK, Format) - Chapters 10, 12, & 13

    - System management tools (e.g., device and task manager, MSCONFIG.EXE) - Chapters 9 & 12, Lab Procedure 22

    - File management tools (e.g., Windows Explorer, ATTRIB.EXE) - Chapters 9, 10, & 12

3.4 Perform preventive maintenance on operating systems

- Describe common utilities for performing preventive maintenance on operating systems for example, software and Windows updates (e.g., service packs), scheduled backups/restore, restore points - Chapters 12 & 13

Domain 4.0 Printers and Scanners

The topics covered by this domain are included in approximately 9% of the questions in the A+ Essential exam.

4.1 Identify the fundamental principles of using printers and scanners

- Identify differences between types of printer and scanner technologies (e.g., laser, inkjet, thermal, solid ink, impact) - Chapter 7

- Identify names, purposes and characteristics of printer and scanner components (e.g., memory, driver, firmware) and consumables (e.g., toner, ink cartridge, paper) - Chapter 7

- Identify the names, purposes and characteristics of interfaces used by printers and scanners including port and cable types for example:

    - Parallel - Chapters 4 & 7, Lab Procedure 13

    - Network (e.g., NIC, print servers) - Chapters 6 & 7

    - USB - Chapters 4 & 7

    - Serial - Chapters 4 & 7

    - IEEE 1394/firewire - Chapters 4 & 7

    - Wireless (e.g., Bluetooth, 802.11, infrared) - Chapters 6 & 7

    - SCSI - Chapters 5 & 7

4.2 Identify basic concepts of installing, configuring, optimizing and upgrading printers and scanners

- Install and configure printers/scanners - Lab Procedure 21, Lab Procedure 13

    - Power and connect the device using local or network port - Chapter 7, Lab Procedure 13

    - Install and update device driver and calibrate the device - Chapters 4 & 7, Lab Procedure 13

    - Configure options and default settings - Chapters 7, Lab Procedure 13

    - Print a test page - Chapters 7, Lab Procedure 13

- Optimize printer performance for example, printer settings such as tray switching, print spool settings, device calibration, media types and paper orientation - Chapter 7

4.3 Identify tools, basic diagnostic procedures and troubleshooting techniques for printers and scanners

- Gather information about printer/scanner problems

- Identify symptom - Chapter 7

- Review device error codes, computer error messages and history (e.g., event log, user reports) - Chapter 7

- Print or scan test page - Chapter 7

- Use appropriate generic or vendor-specific diagnostic tools including web-based utilities - Chapter 7

- Review and analyze collected data

  - Establish probable causes - Chapter 7

  - Review service documentation - Chapter 7

  - Review knowledge base and define and isolate the problem (e.g., software vs. hardware, driver, connectivity, printer) - Chapter 7

- Identify solutions to identified printer/scanner problems

  - Define specific cause and apply fix - Chapter 7

  - Replace consumables as needed - Chapter 7

  - Verify functionality and get user acceptance of problem fix - Chapter 7

Domain 5.0 Networks

The topics covered by this domain are included in approximately 12% of the questions in the A+ Essential exam.

5.1 Identify the fundamental principles of networks

- Describe basic networking concepts - Lab Procedure 35

  - Addressing - Chapter 6

  - Bandwidth - Chapter 6

  - Status indicators - Chapter 6

  - Protocols (e.g., TCP/IP including IP, classful subnet, IPX/SPX including NWLINK, NETBEUI/NETBIOS) - Chapter 6, Lab Procedures 26, 27, 28, & 30

  - Full-duplex, half-duplex - Chapter 6

  - Cabling (e.g., twisted pair, coaxial cable, fiber optic, RS-232, USB, IEEE 1394/Firewire) - Chapter 6

  - Networking models including peer-to-peer and client/server - Chapter 6

- Identify names, purposes and characteristics of the common network cables

  - Plenum/PVC - Chapter 6

- UTP (e.g., CAT3, CAT5 / 5e, CAT6) - Chapter 6

- STP - Chapter 6

- Fiber (e.g., single-mode and multi-mode) - Chapter 6

- Identify names, purposes and characteristics of network connectors (e.g., RJ45 and RJ11, ST/SC/LC, MT-RJ) - Chapter 6

- Identify names, purposes and characteristics (e.g., definition, speed and connections) of technologies for establishing connectivity for example:

  - LAN/WAN - Chapter 6

  - ISDN - Chapter 6

  - Broadband (e.g., DSL, cable, satellite) - Chapter 6

  - Dial-up - Chapter 6

  - Wireless (all 802.11) - Chapter 6, Lab Procedure 33

  - Infrared - Chapters 4, 6, & 7

  - Bluetooth - Chapter 6

  - Cellular - Chapter 6

  - VoIP - Chapter 6

5.2 Install, configure, optimize and upgrade networks

- Install and configure network cards (physical address) - Chapter 6

- Install, identify and obtain wired and wireless connection - Chapter 6

5.3 Identify tools, diagnostic procedures and troubleshooting techniques for networks

- Explain status indicators, for example speed, connection and activity lights and wireless signal strength - Chapter 11

Domain 6.0   Security

The topics covered by this domain are included in approximately 11% of the questions in the A+ Essential exam.

6.1 Identify the fundamental principles of security

- Identify names, purposes and characteristics of hardware and software security for example:

  - Hardware deconstruction/recycling - Chapter 13

  - Smart cards/biometrics (e.g., key fobs, cards, chips and scans) - Chapter 13

  - Authentication technologies (e.g., user name, password, biometrics, smart cards) - Chapters 10 & 13

  - Malicious software protection (e.g., viruses, Trojans, worms, spam, spyware, adware, grayware) - Chapter 13

  - Software firewalls - Chapter 13

  - File system security (e.g., FAT32 and NTFS) - Chapter 10

- Identify names, purposes and characteristics of wireless security for example:

  - Wireless encryption (e.g., WEP.x and WPA.x) and client configuration - Chapter 8

  - Access points (e.g., disable DHCP/use static IP, change SSID from default, disable SSID broadcast, MAC filtering, change default username and password, update firmware, firewall) - Chapter 8

- Identify names, purposes and characteristics of data and physical security

  - Data access (basic local security policy) - Chapters 10 & 13

  - Encryption technologies - Chapters 10 & 13

  - Backups - Chapters 12 & 13

  - Data migration - Chapter 13

  - Data/remnant removal - Chapter 13

  - Password management - Chapter 13

  - Locking workstation (e.g., hardware, operating system) - Chapter 13

- Describe importance and process of incidence reporting - Chapters 1 & 13

- Recognize and respond appropriately to social engineering situations - Chapter 13

6.2 Install, configure, upgrade and optimize security

- Install, configure, upgrade and optimize hardware, software and data security for example:

  - BIOS - Chapter 3

  - Smart cards - Chapter 13

  - Authentication technologies - Chapter 13

  - Malicious software protection - Chapter 13, Lab Procedures 24 & 42

  - Data access (basic local security policy) - Chapter 13

  - Backup procedures and access to backups - Chapters 12 & 13

- Data migration - Chapter 13

- Data/remnant removal - Chapter 13

- Diagnose and troubleshoot hardware, software and data security issues for example:

    - BIOS - Chapter 3

    - Smart cards, biometrics - Chapter 13

    - Authentication technologies - Chapters 10, 12, & 13

    - Malicious software - Chapter 13

    - File system (e.g., FAT32, NTFS) - Chapter 10

    - Data access (e.g., basic local security policy) - Chapter 13

    - Backup - Chapters 12 & 13

    - Data migration - Chapter 13

- Implement software security preventive maintenance techniques such as installing service packs and patches and training users about malicious software prevention technologies - Chapter 13

Domain 7.0   Safety and Environmental Issues

The topics covered by this domain are included in approximately 10% of the questions in the A+ Essential exam.

- Identify potential safety hazards and take preventive action - Chapter 13

- Use Material Safety Data Sheets (MSDS) or equivalent documentation and appropriate equipment documentation - Chapter 13

- Use appropriate repair tools - Chapter 13

- Describe methods to handle environmental and human (e.g., electrical, chemical, physical) accidents including incident reporting - Chapter 13

7.2 Identify potential hazards and implement proper safety procedures including ESD precautions and procedures, safe work environment and equipment handling - Chapter 13

7.3 Identify proper disposal procedures for batteries, display devices and chemical solvents and cans - Chapter 13

Domain 8.0 Communication and Professionalism

The topics covered by this domain are included in approximately 5% of the questions in the A+ Essential exam.

8.1 Use good communication skills including listening and tact/discretion, when communicating with customers and colleagues

- Use clear, concise and direct statements - Chapter 1

- Allow the customer to complete statements – avoid interrupting - Chapter 1

- Clarify customer statements – ask pertinent questions - Chapter 1

- Avoid using jargon, abbreviations and acronyms - Chapter 1

- Listen to customers - Chapter 1

8.2 Use job-related professional behavior including notation of privacy, confidentiality and respect for the customer and customers' property

- Behavior

    - Maintain a positive attitude and tone of voice - Chapter 1

    - Avoid arguing with customers and/or becoming defensive - Chapter 1

    - Do not minimize customers' problems - Chapter 1

    - Avoid being judgmental and/or insulting or calling the customer names - Chapter 1

    - Avoid distractions and/or interruptions when talking with customers - Chapter 1

- Property

    - Telephone, laptop, desktop computer, printer, monitor, etc. - Chapter 1

A+ 220-602 EXAMINATION

The A+ 220-602 examination is targeted for individuals who work or intend to work in a mobile or corporate technical environment with a high level of face-to-face client interaction.

Domain 1.0   Personal Computer Components

The topics covered by this domain are included in approximately 18% of the questions in the A+ 220-602 exam.

1.1 Install, configure, optimize and upgrade personal computer components

- Add, remove and configure personal computer components including selection and installation of appropriate components for example:
    - Storage devices - Chapter 5, Lab Procedures 2 & 5
    - Motherboards - Chapter 3, Lab Procedure 2
    - Power supplies - Chapter 11, Lab Procedure 2
    - Processors/CPUs - Chapter 3
    - Memory - Chapter 3
    - Display devices - Chapter 4, Lab Procedure 2
    - Input devices (e.g., basic, specialty and multimedia) - Chapter 4, Lab Procedure 2
    - Adapter cards - Chapter 4, Lab Procedure 2
    - Cooling systems - Chapter 3

1.2 Identify tools, diagnostic procedures and troubleshooting techniques for personal computer components

- Identify and apply basic diagnostic procedures and troubleshooting techniques
    - Isolate and identify the problem using visual and audible inspection of components and minimum configuration - Chapter 11
    - Recognize and isolate issues with peripherals, multimedia, specialty input devices, internal and external storage and CPUs - Chapter 11
- Identify the steps used to troubleshoot components (e.g., check proper seating, installation, appropriate components, settings and current driver) for example:
    - Power supply - Chapter 11

- Processor/CPUs and motherboards - Chapter 11

- Memory - Chapter 11

- Adapter cards - Chapter 11

- Display and input devices - Chapter 11

- Recognize names, purposes, characteristics and appropriate application of tools for example:

  - Multimeter - Chapter 11, Lab Procedure 6

  - Anti-static pad and wrist strap - Chapter 13

  - Specialty hardware/tools - Chapter 11

  - Loop back plugs - Chapter 11

  - Cleaning products (e.g., vacuum, cleaning pads) - Chapter 13

1.3 Perform preventive maintenance of personal computer components

- Identify and apply common preventive maintenance techniques for personal computer components for example:

  - Display devices (e.g., cleaning, ventilation) - Chapter 13

  - Power devices (e.g., appropriate source such as power strip, surge protector, ventilation and cooling) - Chapter 13

  - Input devices (e.g., covers) - Chapter 13

  - Storage devices (e.g., software tools such as Disk Defragmenter and cleaning of optics and tape heads) - Chapter 13

  - Thermally sensitive devices such as motherboards, CPU, adapter cards memory (e.g., cleaning, air flow) - Chapter 13

Domain 2.0   Laptops and Portable Devices

The topics covered by this domain are included in approximately 9% of the questions in the A+ 220-602 exam.

2.1 Identify fundamental principles of using laptops and portable devices

- Identify appropriate applications for laptop-specific communication connections such as Bluetooth, infrared, cellular WAN and Ethernet - Chapter 8

- Identify appropriate laptop-specific power and electrical input devices and determine how amperage and voltage can affect performance - Chapter 11

- Identify the major components of the LCD including inverter, screen and video card - Chapter 8

- Removal of laptop-specific hardware such as peripherals, hot-swappable and non-hot-swappable devices - Chapter 8

- Describe how video sharing affects memory upgrades - Chapter 8

2.3 Use tools, diagnostic procedures and troubleshooting techniques for laptops and portable devices

- Use procedures and techniques to diagnose power conditions, video, keyboard, pointer and wireless card issues for example:

  - Verify AC power (e.g., LEDs, swap AC adapter) - Chapter 8

  - Verify DC power - Chapter 8

  - Remove unneeded peripherals - Chapter 8

  - Plug in external monitor - Chapter 8

  - Toggle Fn keys - Chapter 8

  - Check LCD cutoff switch - Chapter 8

  - Verify backlight functionality and pixilation - Chapter 8

  - Stylus issues (e.g., digitizer problems) - Chapter 8

  - Unique laptop keypad issues - Chapter 11

  - Antenna wires - Chapter 8

Domain 3.0   Operating Systems

(Unless otherwise noted, operating systems referred with within include Microsoft Windows 2000, XP Professional, XP Home and Media Center.)

The topics covered by this domain are included in approximately 20% of the questions in the A+ 220-602 exam.

3.1 Identify the fundamental principles of operating systems

- Use command-line functions and utilities to manage operating systems, including proper syntax and switches for example:

  - CMD - Chapter 9

  - HELP - Chapter 9

  - DIR - Chapter 9

- ATTRIB - Chapter 9

- EDIT - Chapter 9

- COPY - Chapter 9

- XCOPY - Chapter 9

- FORMAT - Chapter 9

- IPCONFIG - Chapter 9, Lab Procedure 28

- PING - Chapter 9, Lab Procedure 28

- MD/CD/RD - Chapter 9

- Identify concepts and procedures for creating, viewing and managing disks, directories and files on operating systems

    - Disks (e.g., active, primary, extended and logical partitions and file systems including FAT32 and NTFS) - Chapter 9

    - Directory structures (e.g., create folders, navigate directory structures) - Chapter 9

    - Files (e.g., creation, attributes, permissions) - Chapter 9

- Locate and use operating system utilities and available switches for example:

    - Disk management tools (e.g., DEFRAG, NTBACKUP, CHKDSK, Format) - Chapter 12

    - System management tools

        ° Device and Task Manager - Chapter 12, Lab Procedures 17, 20 & 37

        ° MSCONFIG.EXE - Chapters 9 & 12

        ° REGEDIT.EXE - Chapter 12

        ° REGEDT32.EXE - Chapter 12, Lab Procedure 23

        ° CMD - Chapter 9

        ° Event Viewer - Chapter 12, Lab Procedure 40

        ° System Restore - Chapter 12, Lab Procedure 25

        ° Remote Desktop - Chapter 12, Lab Procedure 39

    - File management tools (e.g., Windows EXPLORER, ATTRIB.EXE) - Chapters 9 & 10

3.2 Install, configure, optimize and upgrade operating systems – references to upgrading from Windows 95 and NT may be made

- Identify procedures and utilities used to optimize operating systems for example:

    - Virtual memory - Chapter 12

    - Hard drives (e.g., disk defragmentation) - Chapter 12

    - Temporary files - Chapter 12

- Services - Chapter 12

- Startup - Chapter 12

- Application - Chapter 12

3.3 Identify tools, diagnostic procedures and troubleshooting techniques for operating systems

- Demonstrate the ability to recover operating systems (e.g., boot methods, recovery console, ASR, ERD) - Chapter 12

- Recognize and resolve common operational problems for example:

  - Windows specific printing problems (e.g., print spool stalled, incorrect/incompatible driver form print) - Chapter 7

  - Auto-restart errors - Chapter 12

  - Bluescreen error - Chapter 12

  - System lock-up - Chapter 12

  - Device drivers failure (input/output devices) - Chapter 12

  - Application install, start or load failure - Chapter 12

- Recognize and resolve common error messages and codes for example:

  - Boot (e.g., invalid boot disk, inaccessible boot drive, missing NTLDR) - Chapter 13

  - Startup (e.g., device/service failed to start, device/program in registry not found) - Chapter 3

  - Event Viewer - Chapter 12

  - Registry - Chapter 12

  - Windows reporting - Chapter 12

- Use diagnostic utilities and tools to resolve operational problems for example:

  - Bootable media - Chapter 12

  - Startup modes (e.g., safe mode, safe mode with command prompt or networking, step-by-step/single step mode) - Chapter 12

  - Documentation resources (e.g., user/installation manuals, Internet/Web based, training materials) - Chapters 11 & 12

  - Task and Device Manager - Chapter 12, Lab Procedures 17, 20 & 37

  - Event Viewer - Chapter 12, Lab Procedure 40

  - MSCONFIG command - Chapters 9 & 12

  - Recover CD / recovery partition - Chapter 12

  - Remote Desktop Connection and Assistance - Chapter 12, Lab Procedure 39

  - System File Checker (SFC) - Chapter 12

3.4 Perform preventive maintenance for operating systems

- Demonstrate the ability to perform preventive maintenance on operating systems including software and Windows updates (e.g., service packs), scheduled backups/restore, restore points - Chapter 13, Lab Procedure 41

Domain 4.0   Printers and Scanners

The topics covered by this domain are included in approximately 14% of the questions in the A+ 220-602 exam.

4.1 Identify the fundamental principles of using printers and scanners

- Describe processes used by printers and scanners including laser, ink dispersion, thermal, solid ink and impact printers and scanners - Chapter 7

4.2 Install, configure, optimize and upgrade printers and scanners

- Install and configure printers/scanners

    - Power and connect the device using local or network port - Chapters 7 & 10, Lab Procedure 13

    - Install and update device driver and calibrate the device - Chapter 7, Lab Procedure 13

    - Configure options and default settings - Chapter 7

    - Install and configure print drivers (e.g., PCL^{TM}, Postscript^{TM}, GDI) - Chapter 7

    - Validate compatibility with operating system and applications, Lab Procedure 4

    - Educate user about basic functionality, Lab Procedure 4

- Install and configure printer upgrades including memory and firmware, Lab Procedure 4

- Optimize scanner performance including resolution, file format and default settings, Lab Procedure 4

4.3 Identify tools and diagnostic procedures to troubleshooting printers and scanners

- Gather information about printer/scanner problems - Chapter 11

- Review and analyze collected data - Chapter 11

- Isolate and resolve identified printer/scanner problem including defining the cause, applying the fix and verifying functionality - Chapter 7

- Identify appropriate tools used for troubleshooting and repairing printer/scanner problems - Chapter 11

  - Multimeter - Chapter 11, Lab Procedures 5 & 6

  - Screwdrivers - Chapter 11, Lab Procedures 2 & 5

  - Cleaning solutions - Chapter 13

  - Extension magnet - Chapter 11

  - Test patterns - Chapter 7

4.4 Perform preventive maintenance of printers and scanners

- Perform scheduled maintenance according to vendor guidelines (e.g., install maintenance kits, reset page counts) - Chapter 13

- Ensure a suitable environment - Chapter 13

- Use recommended supplies - Chapter 7

Domain 5.0   Networks

The topics covered by this domain are included in approximately 11% of the questions in the A+ 220-602 exam.

5.1 Identify the fundamental principles or networks

- Identify names, purposes and characteristics of basic network protocols and terminologies for example:

  - ISP - Chapter 6

  - TCP/IP (e.g., gateway, subnet mask, DNS, WINS, static and automatic address assignment) - Chapter 6, Lab Procedure 28

  - IPX/SPX (NWLink) - Chapter 6

  - NETBEUI/NETBIOS - Chapter 6

  - SMTP - Chapter 6

  - IMAP - Chapter 6

  - HTML - Chapter 6

  - HTTP - Chapter 6

  - HTTPS - Chapter 6

- SSL - Chapter 6

- Telnet - Chapter 6

- FTP - Chapter 6

- DNS - Chapter 6

- Identify names, purposes and characteristics of technologies for establishing connectivity for example:

  - Dial-up networking - Chapter 6

  - Broadband (e.g., DSL, cable, satellite) - Chapter 6

  - ISDN networking - Chapter 6

  - Wireless (all 802.11) - Chapter 6, Lab Procedure 33

  - LAN/WAN - Chapter 6

  - Infrared - Chapter 6

  - Bluetooth - Chapter 6

  - Cellular - Chapter 6

  - VoIP - Chapter 6

5.2 Install, configure, optimize and upgrade networks

- Install and configure browsers

  - Enable/disable script support - Chapter 13, Lab Procedure 32

  - Configure proxy and security settings - Chapter 13, Lab Procedure 32

- Establish network connectivity

  - Install and configure network cards - Chapter 6

  - Obtain a connection - Chapter 6

  - Configure client options (e.g., Microsoft, Novell) and network options (e.g., domain, workgroup, tree) - Chapter 6, Lab Procedure 31

  - Configure network options - Chapter 6, Lab Procedure 34

- Demonstrate the ability to share network resources

  - Models - Chapter 6

  - Configure permissions - Chapters 10 & 13

  - Capacities/limitations for sharing for each operating system - Chapter 10

5.3 Use tools and diagnostic procedures to troubleshoot network problems

- Identify names, purposes and characteristics of tools for example:

  - Command line tools (e.g., IPCONFIG.EXE, PING.EXE, TRACERT.EXE, NSLOOKUP.EXE) - Chapters 9 & 12, Lab Procedures 29 & 45

  - Cable testing device - Chapter 11

- Diagnose and troubleshoot basic network issue for example:

  - Driver/network interface - Chapters 10 & 12

  - Protocol configuration - Chapters 10 & 12, Lab Procedure 45

- TCP / IP (e.g., gateway, subnet mask, DNS, WINS, static and automatic address assignment) - Chapters 10 & 12, Lab Procedure 29

- IPX / SPX (NWLink) - Chapter 10

  - Permissions - Chapters 10 & 13

  - Firewall configuration - Chapters 10 & 13

  - Electrical interference - Chapter 13

5.4 Perform preventive maintenance of networks including securing and protecting network cabling

Domain 6.0   Security

The topics covered by this domain are included in approximately 8% of the questions in the A+ 220-602 exam.

6.1 Identify the fundamentals and principles of security

- Identify the purposes and characteristics of access control for example:

  - Access to operating system (e.g., accounts such as user, admin and guest. Groups, permission actions, types and levels), components, restricted spaces - Chapters 10 & 13, Lab Procedure 16

- Identify the purposes and characteristics of auditing and event logging - Chapter 13

6.2 Install, configure, upgrade and optimize security

- Install and configure software, wireless and data security for example:

  - Authentication technologies - Chapter 13

  - Software firewalls - Chapters 10 & 13

  - Auditing and event logging (enable/disable only) - Chapter 13

- Wireless client configuration - Chapter 6, Lab Procedure 33

- Unused wireless connections - Chapter 11

- Data access (e.g., permissions, basic local security policy) - Chapters 10 & 13

- File systems (converting from FAT32 to NTFS only) - Chapters 9, 10, & 13

6.3 Identify tool, diagnostic procedures and troubleshooting techniques for security

- Diagnose and troubleshoot software and data security issues for example:

  - Software firewall issues - Chapter 12

  - Wireless client configuration issues - Chapter 11

  - Data access issues (e.g., permissions, security policies) - Chapters 11 & 13

  - Encryption and encryption technology issues - Chapter 13

6.4 Perform preventive maintenance for security

- Recognize social engineering and address social engineering situations - Chapter 13

Domain 7.0   Safety and Environmental Issues

The topics covered by this domain are included in approximately 5% of the questions in the A+ 220-602 exam.

7.1 Identify potential hazards and proper safety procedures including power supply, display devices and environment (e.g., trip, liquid, situational, atmospheric hazards and high-voltage and moving equipment) - Chapter 13

Domain 8.0   Communication and Professionalism

The topics covered by this domain are included in approximately 18% of the questions in the A+ 220-602 exam.

8.1 Use good communication skills including listening and tact/discretion, when communicating with customers and colleagues

- Use clear, concise and direct statements - Chapter 1

- Allow the customer to complete statements – avoid interrupting - Chapter 1

- Clarify customer statements – ask pertinent questions - Chapter 1

- Avoid using jargon, abbreviations and acronyms - Chapter 1

- Listen to customers - Chapter 1

> 8.2 Use job-related professional behavior including notation of privacy, confidentiality and respect for the customer and customers' property

- Behavior

    - Maintain a positive attitude and tone of voice - Chapter 1

    - Avoid arguing with customers and/or becoming defensive - Chapter 1

    - Do not minimize customers' problems - Chapter 1

    - Avoid being judgmental and/or insulting or calling the customer names - Chapter 1

    - Avoid distractions and/or interruptions when talking with customers - Chapter 1

- Property

    - Telephone, laptop, desktop computer, printer, monitor, etc. - Chapter 1

A+ 220-603 EXAMINATION

The A+ 220-603 examination is targeted for individuals who work or intend to work in a remote-based work environment where client interaction, client training, operating system and connectivity issues are emphasized.

Domain 1.0   Personal Computer Components

The topics covered by this domain are included in approximately 15% of the questions in the A+ 220-603 exam.

> 1.1 Install, configure, optimize, and upgrade personal computer components

- Add, remove, and configure display devices, input devices and adapter cards including basic input and multimedia devices. - Chapter 4, Lab Procedure 3

1.2 Identify tools, diagnostic procedures, and troubleshooting techniques for personal computer components

- Identify and apply basic diagnostic procedures and troubleshooting techniques, for example:
    - Identify and analyze the problem/potential problem - Chapter 11
    - Test related components and evaluate results - Chapter 11
    - Identify additional steps to be taken if/when necessary - Chapter 11
    - Document activities and outcomes - Chapter 11
- Recognize and isolate issues with display, peripheral, multimedia, specialty input device and storage - Chapter 11, Lab Procedure 7
- Apply steps in troubleshooting techniques to identify problems (e.g., physical environment, functionality and software/driver settings) with components including display, input devices and adapter cards - Chapter 11, Lab Procedure 7

1.3 Perform preventive maintenance on personal computer components

- Identify and apply common preventive maintenance techniques for storage devices, for example:
    - Software tools (e.g., Disk Defragmenter, Check Disk) - Chapters 10, 12, & 13
    - Cleaning (e.g., optics, tape heads) - Chapter 13

Domain 2.0 Operating Systems

(Unless otherwise noted, operating systems referred to within include Microsoft Windows 2000, XP Professional, XP Home and Media Center.)

The topics covered by this domain are included in approximately 29% of the questions in the A+ 220-603 exam.

2.1 Identify the fundamental principles of using operating systems

- Use command-line functions and utilities to manage Windows 2000, XP Professional and XP Home, including proper syntax and switches, for example:
    - CMD - Chapter 9
    - HELP - Chapter 9
    - DIR - Chapter 9
    - ATTRIB - Chapter 9

- EDIT - Chapter 9

- COPY - Chapter 9

- XCOPY - Chapter 9

- FORMAT - Chapter 9

- IPCONFIG - Chapter 9

- PING - Chapter 9

- MD/CD/RD - Chapter 9

- Identify concepts and procedures for creating, viewing, managing disks, directories and files in Windows 2000, XP Professional and XP Home, for example: - Lab Procedure 22

  - Disks (e.g., active, primary, extended and logical partitions) - Chapter 9

  - File systems (e.g., FAT 32, NTFS) - Chapters 9 & 10

  - Directory structures (e.g., create folders, navigate directory structures) - Chapters 9 & 10

  - Files (e.g., creation, extensions, attributes, permissions) - Chapters 9 & 10

- Locate and use Windows 2000, XP Professional and XP Home utilities and available switches

  - Disk Management Tools (e.g., DEFRAG, NTBACKUP, CHKDSK, Format) - Chapters 10, 12, & 13, Lab Procedure 22

  - System Management Tools

    ◦ Device and Task Manager - Chapter 12, Lab Procedures 20 & 37

    ◦ MSCONFIG.EXE - Chapters 9 & 12

    ◦ REGEDIT.EXE - Chapter 12

    ◦ REGEDIT32.EXE - Chapter 12

    ◦ CMD - Chapter 9

    ◦ Event Viewer - Chapter 12, Lab Procedure 40

    ◦ System Restore - Chapter 12, Lab Procedure 25

    ◦ Remote Desktop - Chapter 12, Lab Procedure 39

  - File Management Tool (e.g., Windows Explorer, ATTRIB.EXE) - Chapters 9 & 10

2.2 Install, configure, optimize and upgrade operating systems

- Identify procedures and utilities used to optimize the performance of Windows 2000, XP Professional and XP Home, for example: - Lab Procedure 40

  - Virtual memory - Chapter 12

  - Hard drives (e.g., disk defragmentation) - Chapter 12

- Temporary files - Chapter 12

- Services - Chapter 12

- Startup - Chapter 12

- Applications - Chapter 12

2.3 Identify tools, diagnostic procedures and troubleshooting techniques for operating systems.

- Recognize and resolve common operational problems, for example:

  - Windows-specific printing problems (e.g., print spooler stalled, incorrect/incompatible driver form print)

  - Auto-restart errors - Chapter 12

  - Bluescreen error - Chapter 12

  - System lock-up - Chapter 12

  - Device drivers failure (input/output devices) - Chapter 12

  - Application install, start or load failure - Chapter 12

- Recognize and resolve common error messages and codes, for example:

  - Boot (e.g., invalid boot disk, inaccessible boot device, missing NTLDR) - Chapter 13

  - Startup (e.g., device/service has failed to start, device/program references in registry not found) - Chapter 13

  - Event viewer - Chapter 12, Lab Procedure 40

  - Registry - Chapter 12

  - Windows - Chapter 12

- Use diagnostic utilities and tools to resolve operational problems, for example:

  - Bootable media - Chapter 12

  - Startup Modes (e.g., safe mode, safe mode with command prompt or networking, step-by-step/single step mode) - Chapter 12

  - Documentation resources (e.g., user/installation manuals, Internet/Web-based, training materials) - Chapters 11 & 12

  - Task and Device Manager - Chapter 12, Lab Procedures 20 & 37

  - Event Viewer - Chapter 12, Lab Procedure 40

  - MSCONFIG command - Chapters 9 & 12

  - Recovery CD / Recovery partition - Chapter 12

  - Remote Desktop Connection and Assistance - Chapter 12, Lab Procedure 39

  - System File Checker (SFC) - Chapter 12

- Perform preventive maintenance on Windows 2000, XP Professional and XP Home including software and Windows updates (e.g., service packs) - Chapter 13, Lab Procedure 41

Domain 3.0   Printers and Scanners

The topics covered by this domain are included in approximately 10% of the questions in the A+ 220-603 exam.

3.1 Identify the fundamental principles of using printers and scanners

- Describe processes used by printers and scanners including laser, ink dispersion, impact, solid ink and thermal printers - Chapter 7

3.2 Install, configure, optimize and upgrade printers and scanners

- Install and configure printers and scanners
  - Power and connect the device using network or local port - Chapters 7 & 10, Lab Procedure 13
  - Install/update the device driver and calibrate the device - Chapter 7, Lab Procedure 13
  - Configure options and default settings - Chapter 7
  - Install and configure print drivers (e.g., PCL™, Postscript™ and GDI) - Chapter 7
  - Validate compatibility with OS and applications - Chapter 6
  - Educate user about basic functionality - Chapter 6
- Optimize scanner performance for example: resolution, file format and default settings - Chapter 6

3.3 Identify tools, diagnostic procedures and troubleshooting techniques for printers and scanners

- Gather information required to troubleshoot printer/scanner problems - Chapter 11
- Troubleshoot a print failure (e.g., lack of paper, clear queue, restart print spooler, recycle power on printer, inspect for jams, check for visual indicators) - Chapter 7

Domain 4.0   Networks

The topics covered by this domain are included in approximately 11% of the questions in the A+ 220-603 exam.

4.1 Identify the fundamental principles of networks

- Identify names, purposes, and characteristics of the basic network protocols and terminologies, for example:

    - ISP - Chapter 6

    - TCP/IP (e.g., Gateway, Subnet mask, DNS, WINS, Static and automatic address assignment) - Chapter 6, Lab Procedure 28

    - IPX/SPX (NWLink) - Chapter 6

    - NETBEUI/NETBIOS - Chapter 6

    - SMTP - Chapter 6

    - IMAP - Chapter 6

    - HTML - Chapter 6

    - HTTP - Chapter 6

    - HTTPS - Chapter 6

    - SSL - Chapter 6

    - Telnet - Chapter 6

    - FTP - Chapter 6

    - DNS - Chapter 6

- Identify names, purposes, and characteristics of technologies for establishing connectivity, for example:

- Dial-up networking - Chapter 6

- Broadband (e.g., DSL, cable, satellite) - Chapter 6

- ISDN Networking - Chapter 6

- Wireless - Chapter 6, Lab Procedure 33

- LAN/WAN - Chapter 6

4.2 Install, configure, optimize and upgrade networks

- Establish network connectivity and share network resources - Chapters 6 & 10, Lab Procedures 27 & 30

4.3 Identify tools, diagnostic procedures and troubleshooting techniques for networks

- Identify the names, purposes, and characteristics of command line tools, for example:
    - IPCONFIG.EXE - Chapters 9 & 12, Lab Procedure 45
    - PING.EXE - Chapters 9 & 12, Lab Procedure 45
    - TRACERT.EXE - Chapters 9 & 12, Lab Procedure 45
    - NSLOOKUP.EXE - Chapter 12

- Diagnose and troubleshoot basic network issues, for example:
    - Driver/network interface - Chapters 10 & 12
    - Protocol configuration - Chapters 10 & 12
        - TCP/IP (e.g., Gatway, Subnet mask, DNS, WINS, static and automatic address assignment) - Chapters 10 & 12
        - IPX/SPX (NWLink) - Chapter 10
    - Permissions - Chapters 10 & 13
    - Firewall configuration - Chapters 10 & 13
    - Electrical interference - Chapter 13

Domain 5.0   Security

The topics covered by this domain are included in approximately 15% of the questions in the A+ 220-603 exam.

5.1 Identify the fundamental principles of security

- Identify the names, purposes, and characteristics of access control and permissions
    - Accounts including user, admin and guest - Chapters 10 & 13
    - Groups - Chapters 10 & 13
    - Permission levels, types (e.g., file systems and shared) and actions (e.g., read, write, change and execute) - Chapters 10 & 13

5.2 Install, configure, optimizing and upgrade security

- Install and configure hardware, software, wireless and data security, for example:
    - Smart card readers - Chapter 13

- Key fobs - Chapter 13

- Biometric devices - Chapter 13

- Authentication technologies - Chapter 13

- Software firewalls - Chapters 10 & 13

- Auditing and event logging (enable/disable only) - Chapter 13

- Wireless client configuration - Chapter 6

- Unused wireless connections - Chapter 11

- Data access (e.g., permissions, security policies) - Chapter 13

- Encryption and encryption technologies - Chapter 13

5.3 Identify tools, diagnostic procedures and troubleshooting techniques for security issues

- Diagnose and troubleshoot software and data security issues, for example:

  - Software firewall issues - Chapter 12

  - Wireless client configuration issues - Chapter 11

  - Data access issues (e.g., permissions, security policies) - Chapter 13

  - Encryption and encryption technology issues - Chapter 13

5.4 Perform preventive maintenance for security

- Recognize social engineering and address social engineering situations - Chapter 13

Domain 6.0   Communication and Professionalism

The topics covered by this domain are included in approximately 20% of the questions in the A+ 220-603 exam.

6.1 Use good communication skills, including listening and tact/discretion, when communicating with customers and colleagues

- Use clear, concise and direct statements - Chapter 1

- Allow the customer to complete statements – avoid interrupting - Chapter 1

- Clarify customer statements – ask pertinent questions - Chapter 1

- Avoid using jargon, abbreviations and acronyms - Chapter 1

- Listen to customers - Chapter 1

> 6.2 Use job-related professional behavior including notation of privacy, confidentiality and respect for the customer and customers' property

- Behavior
  - Maintain a positive attitude and tone of voice - Chapter 1
  - Avoid arguing with customers and/or becoming defensive - Chapter 1
  - Do not minimize customers' problems - Chapter 1
  - Avoid being judgmental and/or insulting or calling the customer names - Chapter 1
  - Avoid distractions and/or interruptions when talking with customers - Chapter 1
- Property
  - Telephone, laptop, desktop computer, printer, monitor, etc. - Chapter 1

A+ 220-604 EXAMINATION

The A+ 220-604 examination is targeted for individuals who work or intend to work in settings with limited customer interaction where hardware related activities are emphasized.

Domain 1.0 Personal Computer Components

The topics covered by this domain are included in approximately 45% of the questions in the A+ 220-604 exam.

> 1.1 Install, configure, optimize and upgrade personal computer components

- Add, remove and configure internal storage devices, motherboards, power supplies, processor/CPU's, memory and adapter cards, including:
  - Drive preparation - Chapter 5, Lab Procedure 2
  - Jumper configuration
  - Storage device power and cabling - Chapters 2 & 5, Lab Procedure 2
  - Selection and installation of appropriate motherboard
  - BIOS set-up and configuration - Chapter 3, Lab Procedures 2, 3, & 4
  - Selection and installation of appropriate CPU - Chapter 3

- Selection and installation of appropriate memory - Chapter 3, Lab Procedure 2

- Installation of adapter cards including hardware and software/drivers - Chapter 3, Lab Procedure 2

- Configuration and optimization of adapter cards including adjusting hardware settings and obtaining network card connection

- Add, remove and configure systems

1.2 Identify tools, diagnostic procedures and troubleshooting techniques for personal computer components

- Identify and apply diagnostic procedures and troubleshooting techniques, for example:

  - Identify and isolate the problem using visual and audible inspection of components and minimum configuration - Chapter 9

- Identify the steps used to troubleshoot components (e.g., check proper seating, installation, appropriate component, settings, current driver), for example:

  - Power supply - Chapter 11, Lab Procedure 7

  - Processor/CPU's and motherboards - Chapter 11, Lab Procedure 7

  - Memory - Chapter 11, Lab Procedure 7

  - Adapter cards - Chapter 11, Lab Procedure 7

- Recognize names, purposes, characteristics and appropriate application of tools, for example:

  - Multimeter - Chapter 11

  - Anti-static pad and wrist strap - Chapter 13

  - Specialty hardware/tools - Chapter 11

  - Loop back plugs - Chapter 11

  - Cleaning products (e.g., vacuum, cleaning pads) - Chapter 13

1.3 Perform preventive maintenance of personal computer components

- Identify and apply common preventive maintenance techniques, for example:

  - Thermally sensitive devices (e.g., motherboards, CPU's, adapter cards, memory) - Chapter 13

  - Cleaning - Chapter 13

  - Air flow (e.g., slot covers, cable routing) - Chapter 13

  - Adapter cards (e.g., driver/firmware updates) - Chapter 13

Domain 2.0 Laptop and Portable Devices

The topics covered by this domain are included in approximately 20% of the questions in the A+ 220-604 exam.

2.1 Identify the fundamental principles of using laptops and portable devices

- Identify appropriate applications for laptop-specific communication connections, for example:
  - Bluetooth - Chapter 8
  - Infrared devices - Chapter 8
  - Cellular WAN - Chapter 8
  - Ethernet - Chapters 6 & 8
- Identify appropriate laptop-specific power and electrical input devices, for example:
  - Output performance requirements for amperage and voltage - Chapter 8
  - Identify the major components of the LCD (e.g., inverter, screen, video card) - Chapter 8

2.2 Install, configure, optimize and upgrade laptops and portable devices

- Demonstrate the safe removal of laptop-specific hardware including peripherals, hot-swappable and non hot-swappable devices - Chapter 8
- Identify the affect of video sharing on memory upgrades - Chapter 8

2.3 Identify tools, diagnostic procedures and troubleshooting techniques for laptops and portable devices.

- Use procedures and techniques to diagnose power conditions, video issues, keyboard and pointer issues and wireless card issues, for example:
  - Verify AC power (e.g., LED's, swap AC adapter) - Chapter 8
  - Verify DC power - Chapter 8
  - Remove unneeded peripherals - Chapter 8
  - Plug in external monitor - Chapter 8
  - Toggle Fn keys - Chapter 8
  - Check LCD cutoff switch - Chapter 8
  - Verify backlight functionality and pixilation - Chapter 8
  - Stylus issues (e.g., digitizer problems) - Chapter 8

- Unique laptop keypad issues - Chapter 11
- Antenna wires - Chapter 8

Domain 3.0   Printers and Scanners

The topics covered by this domain are included in approximately 20% of the questions in the A+ 220-604 exam.

3.1 Identify the fundamental principles of using printers and scanners

- Describe the processes used by printers and scanners including laser, inkjet, thermal, solid ink, and impact printers - Chapter 7

3.2 Install, configure, optimize and upgrade printers and scanners

- Identify the steps used in the installation and configuration processes for printers and scanners, for example:
  - Power and connect the device using network or local port - Chapter 7, Lab Procedure 13
  - Install and update the device driver - Chapter 7, Lab Procedure 13
  - Calibrate the device - Chapter 7
  - Configure options and default settings
  - Print test page - Chapter 7
- Install and configure printer/scanner upgrades including memory and firmware

3.3 Identify tools, diagnostic methods and troubleshooting procedures for printers and scanners

- Gather data about printer/scanner problem - Chapter 11
- Review and analyze data collected about printer/scanner problems - Chapter 11
- Implement solutions to solve identified printer/scanner problems - Chapter 7
- Identify appropriate tools used for troubleshooting and repairing printer/scanner problems
  - Multimeter - Chapter 11
  - Screw drivers - Chapter 11
  - Cleaning solutions - Chapter 13

- Extension magnet - Chapter 11

- Test patterns - Chapter 7

3.4 Perform preventive maintenance of printer and scanner problems

- Perform scheduled maintenance according to vendor guidelines (e.g., install maintenance kits, reset page counts) - Chapter 13

- Ensure a suitable environment - Chapter 13

- Use recommended supplies - Chapter 13

Domain 4.0   Security

The topics covered by this domain are included in approximately 5% of the questions in the A+ 220-604 exam.

4.1 Identify the names, purposes and characteristics of physical security devices and processes

- Control access to PC's, servers, laptops and restricted spaces

  - Hardware - Chapter 13

  - Operating systems - Chapter 13

4.2 Install hardware security

- Smart card readers - Chapter 13

- Key fobs - Chapter 13

- Biometric devices - Chapter 13

Domain 5.0   Safety and Environmental Issues

The topics covered by this domain are included in approximately 10% of the questions in the A+ 220-604 exam.

5.1 Identify potential hazards & proper safety procedures including power supply, display devices and environment (e.g., trip, liquid, situational, atmospheric hazards, high-voltage and moving equipment) - Chapter 13

GLOSSARY

An Extended Glossary can be found in the electronic Reference Shelf located on the CD that accompanies this book.

A

accelerated graphics port (AGP) A newer 32-bit video interface specification based on the PCI bus design. Rather than using the PCI bus for video data, the AGP system provides a dedicated point-to-point path between the video graphics controller and system memory. The AGP bus was designed specifically to handle the high data-transfer demands associated with 3D graphic operations.

ACK (ACKnowledge) A data communications code used by the receiver to tell the transmitter it is ready to accept data. During a data transfer this signal is continually used to indicate successful receipt of the last data character or block and to request more.

Active Directory Active Directory (AD) is the central feature of the Windows 2000 architecture. It is a distributed database of user and resource information that describes the makeup of the network (i.e., users and application settings). It is also a method of implementing a distributed authentication process. The Active Directory replaces the domain structure used in Windows NT 4.0. This feature helps to centralize system and user configurations, as well as data backups on the server in the Windows 2000 network.

active partition The disk partition that possesses the system files required to boot the system. This is the logical drive that the system reads at bootup.

adapter A device that permits one system to work with and connect to another. Many I/O device adapters interface with the microcomputer by plugging into the expansion slots on the system board. These specialized circuit boards are often called adapter cards.

Add New Hardware Wizard Windows 9x/2000 applet designed to guide the installation process for non-PnP hardware. When installing Plug-and-Play devices, the Add New Hardware wizard should not be used. Instead, the Windows PnP function should be allowed to detect the new hardware. The new hardware must be installed in the computer before running the wizard.

Add/Remove Programs Wizard Windows 9x/2000 applet designed to guide the installation or removal of application programs. This utility can also be used to install or remove optional Windows components, such as Accessibility options, or to create a Windows Start disk.

Add/Remove Windows components Windows 9x/2000 utilities that can be used to change optional hardware (Add New Hardware) and software (Add/Remove Programs) components installed in the system. These utilities are located in the Windows Control Panel.

address The unique location number of a particular memory storage area, such as a byte of primary memory, a sector of disk memory, or a peripheral device itself.

address bus A unidirectional pathway that carries address data generated by the microprocessor to the various memory and I/O elements of the computer. The size of this bus determines the amount of memory a particular computer can use and, therefore, is a direct indication of the computer's power.

A: drive The commonly understood term designating the first floppy-disk drive in Microsoft's DOS microcomputer operating system.

ASCII (American Standard Code for Information Interchange) The 7-bit binary data code used in all personal computers, many minicomputers, and also in communications services. Of the 128 possible character combinations, the first 32 are used for printing and transmission control. Because of the 8-bit byte used in digital computers, the extra bit can be used either for parity checking, or for the extended ASCII set of characters, which includes foreign language characters and line-draw graphic symbols.

ASIC (application specific integrated circuit) A very large-scale integration device designed to replace a large block of standardized PC circuitry. Once the parameters of the device have achieved a pseudo standard usage status, IC manufacturers tend to combine all of the circuitry for that function into a large IC custom designed to carry out that function. Examples include integrated VGA controllers, integrated MI/O controllers, and integrated peripheral controllers.

asynchronous transmission A method of serial data transmission in which the receiving system is not synchronized by a common clock signal with the transmitting system.

AT attachment (ATA) Also known also as IDE. A system-level interface specification that integrates the disk drive controller on the drive itself. The original ATA specification supports one or two hard drives through a 16-bit interface using Programmed IO (PIO) modes. The ATA-2 specification, also known as EIDE or Fast ATA, supports faster PIO and DMA transfer modes, as well as logical block addressing (LBA) strategies.

AT bus Also referred to as the ISA (Industry Standard Architecture) bus. The 16-bit data bus introduced in the AT class personal computer that became the industry standard for 16-bit systems.

ATTRIB The DOS command used to change attributes assigned to files (i.e., system, read-only, and hidden status).

attributes Properties of DOS files. Special file attributes include system, read-only, and hidden status. These conditions can be altered using the external DOS command ATTRIB.

ATX form factor A newer system board form factor that improves on the previous baby AT form factor standard by reorienting the system board by 90 degrees. This makes for a more efficient design, placing the IDE connectors nearer to the system unit's drive bays and positioning the microprocessor in line with the output of the power supply's cooling fan.

AUTOEXEC.BAT An optional DOS program that the system's command interpreter uses to carry out customized startup commands at bootup.

B

backup An operation normally performed to create backup copies of important information in case the drive crashes, or the disk becomes corrupt. Backup utilities allow the user to quickly create extended copies of files, groups of files, or an entire disk drive.

Backup Domain Controller (BDC) Backup Domain Controllers are servers within the network that are used to hold read-only backup copies of the directory database. A network may contain one or more BCDs. These servers are used to authenticate user logons.

Backup Wizard An automated software routine in Windows 2000 designed to lead users through a step-by-step process of configuring and scheduling a backup job.

BAT file (batch file) A filename extension used to identify a batch file in Microsoft DOS versions. A batch file, created by a word processor, contains a list of DOS commands that are executed as if each were typed and entered one at a time.

baud rate The number of electrical state changes per second on a data communication line. At lower speeds, the baud rate and the bits-per-second rate are identical. At higher speeds, the baud rate is some fraction of the bits-per-second rate.

binary This means base two. In digital computers, all data is processed only after being converted to binary numbers consisting of the two digits 0 and 1.

BIOS (basic input output system) See *ROM BIOS*.

bit (binary digit) One digit of a binary number (0 or 1). Groups of bits are manipulated together by a computer into various storage units called nibbles, bytes, words, or characters.

bit map A term used in computer graphics to describe a memory area containing a video image. One bit in the map represents one pixel on a monochrome screen, while in color or grayscale monitors, several bits in the map may represent one pixel.

Blue Screen A kernel-mode stop that indicates a failure of a core operating system function. Also known as the Blue Screen of Death because the system stops processing and produces a blue screen, rather than risking catastrophic memory and file corruption.

boot To start the computer. It refers to the word bootstrap, since just as straps help in pulling boots on, the bootable disk helps the computer to get its first instructions.

bootable disk A disk that starts the operating system. Normally refers to a floppy disk containing the computer operating system.

Boot Menu The Startup options screen menu displayed during the Windows 2000 bootup process. This menu is produced when the F8 function key is depressed while the "Starting Windows" message is on the screen. This menu is generated by the Boot.ini Boot Loader Menu file. Options in this menu include the variety of operating systems installed on the computer. If no selection is made from this menu after a given time, the default value is selected.

boot partition The disk partition that possesses the system files required to load the operating system into memory. Also referred to as the *active partition*.

boot sector The first sector on a disk (or partition). On bootable disks or partitions, this sector holds the code (called the boot record) that causes the system to move the operating system files into memory and begin executing them.

boot.ini Boot.ini is a special, hidden boot-loader menu file used by the NTLDR during the bootup process to generate the Boot Loader Menu that is displayed on the screen. If no selection is made from this menu after a given time, the default value is selected.

bootsect.dos A Windows NT file used to load operating systems other than Windows NT. If an entry from the Boot Loader Menu indicates an operating system other than Windows NT is to be loaded, the NTLDR program loads the BOOTSECT.DOS file from the root directory of the system partition and passes control to it. From this point, the BOOTSECT file is responsible for loading the desired operating system.

bootstrap loader A term used to refer to two different software routines involved in starting a system and loading the operating system. The primary bootstrap loader is a firmware routine that locates the boot record required to load the operating system into memory. The OS loader takes over from the primary bootstrap loader and moves the operating system into memory (known as booting the OS).

bps (bits per second) A term used to measure the speed of data being transferred in a communications system.

bus A parallel collection of conductors that carry data or control signals from one unit to another.

bus master Any class of intelligent devices having the ability to take control of the system buses of a computer.

byte The most common word size used by digital computers. It is an 8-bit pattern consisting of both a high- and a low-order nibble. Computers of any size are frequently described in terms of how many bytes of data can be manipulated in one operation or cycle.

C

cache An area of high-speed memory reserved for improving system performance. Blocks of often-used data are copied into the cache area to permit faster access times. A disk cache memory is an area of RAM used to hold data from a disk drive that the system may logically want to access, thereby speeding up access.

cache controller A highly automated memory controller assigned the specific task of managing a sophisticated cache memory system.

carriage The part in a printer or typewriter that handles the feeding of the paper forms.

cartridge A removable data storage module, containing disks, magnetic tape, or memory chips, and inserted into the slots of disk drives, printers, or computers.

C: drive This is the commonly understood term designating the system or first hard-disk drive in the DOS and OS/2 microcomputer operating systems.

Centronics interface The 36-pin standard for interfacing parallel printers, and other devices, to a computer. The plug, socket, and signals are defined.

certificate A security service used to authenticate the origin of a public key to a user possessing a matching private key.

character printer Any printer that prints one character at a time, such as a dot-matrix printer or a daisy wheel.

chip The common name for an integrated circuit (IC). Preceded by the development of the transistor, ICs can contain from several dozen to several million electronic components (resistors, diodes, transistors, etc.) on a square of silicon approximately 1/16th to 1/2 inch wide and around 1/30th of an inch in thickness. The IC can be packaged in many different styles depending on the specific use for which it is intended.

chipset A group of specifically engineered ICs designed to perform a function interactively.

chkdsk DOS disk maintenance utility used to recover lost allocation units from a hard drive. These lost units occur when an application terminates unexpectedly. Over a period of time, lost units can pile up and occupy large amounts of disk space.

clients Workstations that operate in conjunction with a master server computer that controls the operation of the network.

client/server network A network in which workstations or clients operate in conjunction with a master server computer to control the network.

clock An internal timing device. Several varieties of clocks are used in computer systems. Among them are the CPU clock, the real-time clock, a timesharing clock, and a communications clock.

cluster Clusters are organizational units used with disk drives to represent one or more sectors of data. These structures constitute the smallest unit of storage space on the disk.

CMOS (complementary metal oxide semiconductor) A MOS technology used to fabricate IC devices. It is traditionally slower than other IC technologies, but it possesses higher circuit-packing density than other technologies. CMOS ICs are very sensitive to voltage spikes and static discharges and must be protected from static shock.

CMOS setup A software setup program used to provide the system with information about what options are installed. The configuration information is stored in special CMOS registers that are read each time the system boots up. Battery backup prevents the information from being lost when power to the system is removed.

cold boot Booting a computer by turning the power on.

color monitor Also known as an RGB monitor, this display type allows the user to run text and/or color-based applications such as graphics drawing and CAD programs. There are two basic RGB-type monitors: digital (TTL) and analog. Analog RGB monitors allow the use of many more colors than digital RGB monitors.

color printer Any printer capable of printing in color, using thermal-transfer, dot-matrix, electro-photographic, electrostatic, ink-jet, or laser printing techniques.

COM1 The label used in Microsoft DOS versions assigned to serial port #1.

COMMAND.COM COMMAND.COM is the DOS command interpreter that is loaded at the end of the bootup process. It accepts commands issued through the keyboard, or other input devices, and carries them out according to the command's definition. These definitions can be altered by adding switches to the command.

command prompt A screen symbol that indicates to the user that the system is ready for a command. It usually consists of the current drive letter, followed by a colon and a blinking cursor.

compatible A reference to any piece of computer equipment that works like, or looks like a more widely known standard or model. A PC-compatible, or clone, is a PC that, although physically differing somewhat from the IBM-PC, runs software developed for the IBM-PC and accepts its hardware options.

Computer Management Console A Windows 2000 Management Console, that enables the user to track and configure all of the system's hardware and software. It can also be used to configure network options and view system events.

computer name A name created for a computer by a network administrator. This name identifies the computer to other members of the network. It is generally recommended that computer names be 15 characters or less. However, if the computer has the TCP/IP networking protocol installed, its name can range up to 63 characters long but should only contain the numbers 0-9, the letters A-Z and a-z, and hyphens. It is possible to use other characters, but doing so may prevent other users from finding your computer on the network.

CONFIG.SYS A Microsoft operating system configuration file that, upon startup, is used to customize the system's hardware environment. The required peripheral device drivers (with SYS file extensions) are initialized.

configuration A customized computer system or communications network composed of a particular number and type of interrelated components. The configuration varies from system to system, requiring that some means be established to inform the system software about what options are currently installed.

Configuration Manager A component of the Windows Plug-and-Play system that coordinates the configuration process for all devices in the system.

continuous forms Paper sheets that are joined together along perforated edges and used in printers that move them through the printing area with motorized sprockets. Sprockets may fit into holes on both sides of the paper.

control bus A pathway between the microprocessor and the various memory, programmable, and I/O elements of the system. Control bus signals are not necessarily related to each other and can be unidirectional or bi-directional.

control character A special type of character that causes some event to occur on a printer, display, or communications path such as a line feed, a carriage return, or an escape.

Control Panel The Windows component used to customize the operation and appearance of Windows functions. In Windows 9x and Windows NT/2000 the Control Panel can be accessed through the Start button/Settings route, or under the My Computer icon on the desktop.

control protocols Protocols that configure the communication interface to the networking protocols employed by the system. Each network transport supported under Windows 2000 has a corresponding control protocol.

CPU (Central Processing Unit) The part of the computer that does the thinking. It consists of the control unit and the Arithmetic Logic Unit. In personal computers, the CPU is contained on a single chip, whereas on a minicomputer it occupies one or several printed circuit boards. On mainframes, a CPU is contained on many printed circuit boards. Its power comes from the fact that it can execute many millions of instructions in a fraction of a second.

CRC (cyclic redundancy check) The error-checking technique that ensures communications channel integrity by utilizing division to determine a remainder. If the transmitter and receiver do not agree on what the remainder should be, an error is detected.

CRT (cathode ray tube) The vacuum tube that is used as the display screen for both TVs and computer terminals. Sometimes the term is used to mean the terminal itself.

CTS (clear to send) An RS-232 handshaking signal sent from the receiver to the transmitter indicating readiness to accept data.

cursor The movable display screen symbol that indicates to the user where the action is taking place. The text cursor is usually a blinking underline or rectangle, whereas the graphics cursor can change into any predetermined shape at different parts of the screen.

cursor keys Special keyboard keys that can be used to move the cursor around the display screen. Enhanced keyboards have two clusters of cursor keys so that the numeric keypad portion of the keyboard can be used separately.

cylinder The combination of all tracks, normally on multiple-platter disk drives, that reside at the same track number location on each surface.

D

data Information assembled in small units of raw facts and figures.

data bus A bi-directional pathway linking the microprocessor to memory and I/O devices, the size of which usually corresponds to the word size of the computer.

data compression Most compression algorithms use complex mathematical formulas to remove redundant bits, such as successive 0s or 1s, from the data stream. When the modified word is played back through the decompression circuitry the formula reinserts the missing bits to return the data stream to its original state.

Data Encryption Standard (DES) A U.S. standard method of encrypting data into a secret code. Down-level clients employ the DES standard to encrypt user passwords.

DCE (Data Communications Equipment) A communications device, usually a modem, that establishes, maintains, and terminates a data transfer session. It also serves as a data converter when interfacing different transmission media.

default The normal action taken, or setting used, by hardware or software when the user does not otherwise specify.

defragmentation Disk maintenance operation performed to optimize the use of disk space by moving scattered file fragments into continuous chains to speed up data retrieval from the drive.

demodulator A device that removes the data from the carrier frequency and converts it to its originally unmodulated form.

DEVICE= CONFIG.SYS commands used to load specified device drivers into memory at bootup (e.g., the statement DEVICE=C:\MOUSE\MOUSE.SYS loads a mouse driver from the MOUSE directory). Used as "DEVICEHIGH=", the command will load the specified device driver into the Upper Memory Blocks, thereby freeing up conventional memory space.

device driver Special memory-resident program that tells the operating system how to communicate with a particular type of I/O device, such as a printer or a mouse.

Device Manager A Windows 95/98/2000 Control Panel utility that provides a graphical representation of devices in the system. It can be used to view resource allocations and set hardware configurations properties for these devices. This utility can also be used to identify and resolve resource conflicts between system devices. The Device Manager is located under the Control Panel's System icon.

diagnostics Software programs specifically designed to test the operational capability of the computer memory, disk drives, and other peripherals. The routines are available on disks or on ROM chips. Errors may be indicated by beep codes or visual reports. They can normally point to a board-level problem, but not down to a particular component, unless the routine has been written for a particular board being used in the system under test. A complete system failure would require a ROM-based diagnostic program as opposed to a disk-based routine.

dial-up networking Methods of accessing the public telephone system to carry on data networking operations. These methods include modem, ISDN, and DSL accesses.

DIMMs Dual in-line memory modules. DIMMs are 168-pin plug-in memory modules similar to SIMMs.

direct I/O An I/O addressing method that uses no address allocations but requires extra control lines.

directory A hierarchical collection of disk files organized under one heading and simulating the concept of a drawer in a file cabinet. In the structure of a disk drive system, the directory is the organizational table that holds information about all files stored under its location. This information includes the file's name, size, time, date of when it was last changed, and its beginning location on the disk.

disk arrays A collection of multiple disk drives operating under the direction of a single controller for the purpose of providing fault tolerance and performance. Data files are written on the disks in ways that improve the performance and reliability of the disk drive subsystem, as well as to provide detection and corrective actions for damaged files. Redundant Array of Inexpensive Disks (RAID) 5 in Windows 2000 is an example.

disk drive The peripheral storage device that reads and writes data to spinning magnetic or optical disks. The drive can either hold removable disks or contain permanent platters.

diskette A term usually applied to a removable, floppy-disk memory storage device.

DMA (direct memory access) The ability of certain intelligent, high-speed I/O devices to perform data transfers themselves, with the help of a special IC device called a DMA controller.

docking station Special platforms designed to work with portable computers to provide additional I/O capacity. The docking station is designed so that the portable computer inserted into it can have access to the docking station's expansion slots, additional storage devices, and other peripheral devices, such as full-size keyboards and monitors. No standards exist for docking stations, so they must be purchased for specific types of portable computers.

domain Collectively, a domain is a group of members that share a common directory database and are organized in levels. Every domain is identified by a unique name and is administered as a single unit having common rules and procedures.

domain name A unique name that identifies a host computer site on the Internet.

domain name service (DNS) A networking service that resolves computer names to IP addresses in a TCP/IP network environment. This service is one of the standard networking services available in the Windows operating systems.

domain name system (DNS) A database organizational structure whereby higher-level Internet servers keep track of assigned domain names and their corresponding IP addresses for systems on levels under them. The IP addresses of all the computers attached to the Internet are tracked with this listing system. DNS evolved as a method of organizing the members of the Internet into a hierarchical management structure that consists of various levels of computer groups called domains. Each computer on the Internet is assigned a domain name, which corresponds to an additional domain level.

DOS (disk operating system) Can be a generic term, but in most cases it refers to the Microsoft family of computer operating systems (PC-DOS for IBM equipment or MS-DOS for compatibles).

dot-matrix printer A type of printer that forms its images out of one or more columns of dot hammers. Higher resolutions require a greater number of dot hammers to be used.

dot pitch A measurement of the resolution of a dot-matrix. The width of an individual dot in millimeters describes a display's resolution, with the smaller number representing the higher resolution. The number of dots per linear inch describes a printer's resolution, with the higher number representing the higher resolution.

DRAM (dynamic random access memory) A type of RAM that will lose its data, regardless of power considerations, unless it is refreshed at least once every 2 milliseconds.

drive (1) An electromechanical device that moves disks, discs, or tapes at high speeds so that data can be recorded on the media, or read back from it. (2) In the organizational structure of a DOS system, a drive can be thought of as the equivalent of a file drawer that holds folders and documents. (3) In electronic terms, it is a signal output of a device used to activate the input of another device.

DSR (data set ready) An RS-232 handshaking signal sent from the modem to its own computer indicating its ability to accept data.

DTR (data terminal ready) An RS-232 handshaking signal that is sent to a modem by its own computer to indicate a readiness to accept data.

dual booting A condition that can be established on a hard-disk drive that holds two or more operating systems. A pre-boot option is created that enables the system to be booted from one of the designated operating systems (e.g., Windows 98 or Windows 2000 Professional).

dynamic host configuration protocol (DHCP) Software protocol that dynamically assigns IP addresses to a server's clients. This software is available in both Windows 9x and Windows NT/2000 and must be *located* on both the server and the client computers (installed on servers and activated on clients). This enables ISPs to provide dynamic IP address assignments for their customers.

Dynamic Link Library (DLL) files Windows library files that contain small pieces of executable code that can be shared between Windows programs. These files are used to minimize redundant programming common to certain types of Windows applications.

E

edge connector The often double-sided row of etched lines on the edge of an adapter card that plugs into one of the computer's expansion slots.

EEPROM (electrically erasable programmable read only memory) A type of nonvolatile semiconductor memory device that allows erasure and reprogramming from within a computer using special circuitry. These devices allow specific memory cells to be manipulated, rather than requiring a complete reprogramming procedure as in the case of EPROM's.

EIA (Electronics Industries Association) An organization, founded in 1924, made up of electronic parts and systems manufacturers. It sets electrical and electronic interface standards such as the RS-232C.

EISA (Extended Industry Standard Architecture) A PC bus standard that extends the AT bus architecture to 32 bits and allows older PC and AT boards to plug into its slot. It was announced in 1988 as an alternative to the IBM Micro Channel.

electron gun The device by which the fine beam of electrons is created that sweeps across the phosphor screen in a CRT.

electrostatic discharge (ESD) As it applies to computer systems, a rapid discharge of static electricity from a human to the computer, due to a difference of electrical potential between the two. Such discharges usually involve thousands of volts of energy and can damage the IC circuits used to construct computer and communications equipment.

Emergency Repair Disk A disk created to repair the Windows NT/2000 system when its boot disk fails. The Emergency Repair Disk (ERD) provides another option if Safe Mode and the Recovery Console do not provide a successful solution to a system crash. If you have already created an ERD, you can start the system with the Windows NT/2000 Setup CD or the Setup floppy disks, and then use the ERD to restore core system files.

EMI (electromagnetic interference) A system-disrupting electronic radiation created by some other electronic device. The FCC sets allowable limits for EMI in Part 5 of its Rules and Regulations. Part A systems are designed for office and plant environments, and Part B systems are designed for home use.

EMM (Expanded Memory Manager) Any software driver that permits and manages the use of expanded memory in 80386 and higher machines.

EMS (Expanded Memory Specification) A method of using memory above one megabyte on computers using DOS. Co-developed by Lotus, Intel, and Microsoft, each upgrade has allowed for more memory to be used. EMS is dictated by the specific application using it. In 286 machines, EMS is installed on an adapter card and managed by an EMS driver. See *EMM*.

enhanced cylinder head sector (ECHS) format B I O S translation mode used to configure large hard drives (over 504 MB) for operation. This mode is an extended CHS mode and is identical to Large and LBA modes. However, reconfiguring drives to other configuration settings risks the prospects of losing data.

enhanced IDE (EIDE) An improved version of the Integrated Drive Electronics interface standard. The new standard supports data-transfer rates up to four times that of the original IDE standard. It also makes provisions for supporting storage devices of up to 8.4 GB in size, as opposed to the old standard's limit of 528 MB. The new standard is sometimes referred to as Fast ATA or Fast IDE.

enterprise networks Enterprise networks are designed to facilitate business-to-business, or business-to-customer operations. Because monetary transactions and customers' personal information travels across the network in these environments, enterprise networks feature facilities for additional highly protective security functions.

EPROM (erasable programmable read only memory) A type of nonvolatile semiconductor memory device that can be programmed more than once. Selected cells are charged using a comparatively high voltage. EPROMs can be erased by exposure to a source of strong ultraviolet light, at which point they must be completely reprogrammed.

ergonomics The study of people-to-machine relationships. A device is considered to be ergonomic when it blends smoothly with a person's body actions.

error checking The act of testing the data transfer in a computer system or network for accuracy.

ESC key (Escape key) This keyboard key is used to cancel an application operation or to exit some routine.

Ethernet A popular network topology that uses Carrier Sense Multiple Access with Collision Detection (CSMA/CD) for collision detection and avoidance. Ethernet can be physically implemented as either a bus, or a star network organization.

expanded memory (EMS) A memory management strategy for handling memory beyond the 1 MB of conventional memory. Using this strategy, the additional memory is accessed in 16K pages through a window established in the upper memory area.

expansion slot The receptacle mounted on the system board into which adapter cards are plugged to achieve system expansion. The receptacle interfaces with the I/O channel and system bus, and so the number of slots available determines the expansion potential of the system.

extended memory The memory above one megabyte in Intel 286 and higher computers, and used for RAM disks, disk caching routines, and for locating the operating system files in later versions of Microsoft DOS.

extended memory (XMS) A memory management strategy for handling memory beyond the 1 MB of conventional memory. Using this strategy, Windows and Windows-based programs directly access memory above the 1 MB marker. Extended memory requires that the HIMEM.SYS memory manager be loaded in the DOS CONFIG.SYS.

extended partition A secondary partition that can be created after the drive's primary partition has been established. It is the only other partition allowed on a disk once the primary partition has been made using FDISK. However, an extended partition can be subdivided into up to 23 logical drives.

Extended System Configuration Data (ESCD) The portion of CMOS memory that holds PnP configuration information.

F

FAT (file allocation table) The part of the DOS file system that keeps track of where specific data is stored on the disk.

FDISK command The disk utility program that performs the partitioning of the hard disk into several independent disks.

file Any program, record, table, or document that is stored under its own filename.

file allocation table (FAT) A special table located on a formatted DOS disk that tracks where each file is located on the disk.

File menu A drop-down menu attached to Windows graphical interfaces whose options enable users to Open, Move, Copy, and Delete selected folders, files, or applications.

file system File management system. The organizational structure that operating systems employ to organize and track files. Windows 2000 employs the NTFS5 file system to perform these functions. A file system is a hierarchical directory system that employs directories to organize files into a tree-like structure.

filenames Names assigned to files in a disk-based system. Disk-based systems store and handle related pieces of information in groups called files. The system recognizes and keeps track of the different files in the system through their names. Therefore, each file in the system is required to have a filename that is different from that of any other file in the directory.

Firewire Also known as IEEE-1394, Firewire is a very fast I/O bus standard designed to support the high bandwidth requirements of real time audio/visual equipment. The IEEE-1394 standard employs streaming data transfer techniques to support data-transfer rates up to 400 Mbps. A single Firewire connection can be used to connect up 63 external devices.

firmware A term used to describe the situation in which programs (software) are stored in ROM ICs (hardware) on a permanent basis.

floppy disk Also called a diskette, a removable secondary storage medium for computers, composed of flexible magnetic material and contained in a square envelope or cartridge. A floppy disk can be recorded and erased hundreds of times.

flow control A method of controlling the flow of data between computers. The receiving system signals the sending PC when it can and cannot receive data. Flow control can be implemented through hardware or software protocols. Using the software method, the receiving PC sends special code characters to the sending system to stop or start data flow. Xon/Xoff is an example of a software flow control protocol.

Folder Options Options that enable the user to change the appearance of their desktops and folder content, and to specify how their folders will open. Users can select whether they want a single window to open, as opposed to cascading windows, and they can designate whether folders will open with a single-click or double-click. Folder Options can also be used to turn on the Active Desktop, change the application used to open certain types of files, or make files available when they're not on-line with the network. Changes made in Folder Options apply to the appearance of the contents of Windows Explorer (including My Computer, My Network Places, My Documents, and Control Panel) windows.

folders Icons that represent directories. In Windows 9x/NT/2000, directories and subdirectories are referred to and depicted as folders.

font One set of alphanumeric characters possessing matching design characteristics such as typeface, orientation, spacing, pitch, point size, style, and stroke weight.

forests A group of one or more Active Directory domain trees that trust each other. Unlike directory trees, forests do not share a contiguous namespace. This permits multiple namespaces to be supported within a single forest. In the forest, all domains share a common schema, configuration, and global catalog.

form feed The moving of the next paper form into the proper printing position, accomplished either by pressing the form feed (FF) button on the printer or by sending the printer the ASCII form feed character.

FORMAT command An MS-DOS utility that prepares a disk for use by the system. Track and sector information is placed on the disk while bad areas are marked so that no data will be recorded on them.

formatting The act of preparing a hard or floppy disk for use with an operating system. This operation places operating system−specific data tracking tables on the media and tests its storage locations (sectors or blocks) to make certain they are reliable for holding data.

FQDN (fully qualified domain name) A name that consists of the host name and the domain name, including the top-level domain name (e.g., www.mic-inc.com where www is the host name, mic-inc is the second-level domain name, and com is the top-level domain name).

fragmentation A condition that exists on hard-disk drives after files have been deleted or moved, and areas of free disk space are scattered around the disk. These areas of disk space cause slower performance because the drive's read/write heads have to be moved more often to find the pieces of a single file.

frame (1) A memory widow that applications and the operating system exchange data through, such as the EMS frame in Upper Memory that Expanded Memory managers use to move data between conventional memory and additional memory beyond the 1 MB mark. (2) The construction of a complete package of data with all overhead (headers) for transferring it to another location (e.g., an Ethernet frame). (3) One screen of computer graphics data, or the amount of memory required to store it.

FRU (field-replaceable unit) The components of the system that can be conveniently replaced in the field.

FTP (file transfer protocol) An application layer protocol that copies files from one FTP host site to another.

full-duplex A method of data transmission that allows data flow in both directions simultaneously.

function keys A special set of keyboard keys used to give the computer special commands. They are frequently used in combination with other keys, and can have different uses depending on the software application being run.

G

GDI.EXE A Windows core component that is responsible for managing the operating system's/environment's graphical user interface.

General Protection Fault (GPF) A Windows memory usage error that typically occurs when a program attempts to access memory currently in use by another program.

GHz (gigahertz) One billion hertz or cycles per second.

graphics The creation and management of pictures using a computer.

ground (1) Any point from which electrical measurements are referenced. (2) *Earth* ground is considered to be an electrical reference point of absolute zero, and is used as the electrical return path for modern power transmission systems. This ground, often incorporated by electronic devices to guard against fatal shock, is called *chassis* or *protective* ground. (3) An actual conductor in an electronic circuit being used as a return path, also called a *signal* ground.

group The administrative gathering of users that can be administered uniformly. In establishing groups, the administrator can assign permissions or restrictions to the entire body. The value of using groups lies in the time saved by being able to apply common rights to several users instead of applying them one by one.

group policies Administrators use these tools to institute large numbers of detailed settings for users throughout an enterprise, without establishing each setting manually.

Group Policy Editor Utility employed to establish policies in Windows 2000. Administrators use this editor to establish which applications different users have access to, as well as to control applications on the user's desktop.

GUI (graphical user interface) A form of operating environment that uses a graphical display to represent procedures and programs that can be executed by the computer.

H

HAL.DLL HAL.DLL is the Hardware Abstraction Layer driver that holds the information specific to the CPU that the system is being used with.

half-duplex communication Communications that occur in both directions, but can occur in only one direction at a time. Most older networking strategies were based on half-duplex operations.

handshaking A system of signal exchanges conducted between the computer system and a peripheral device during the data transfer process. The purpose of these signals is to produce as orderly a flow of data as possible.

hard disk A metal disk that is used for external storage purposes. It is coated with a ferromagnetic coating and is available in both fixed and removable formats.

hardware Any aspect of the computer operation that can be physically touched. This includes IC chips, circuit boards, cables, connectors, and peripherals.

Hardware Abstraction Layer (HAL) The Windows NT HAL is a library of hardware drivers that operate between the actual hardware and the rest of the system. These software routines act to make every architecture look the same to the operating system. The HAL occupies the logical space directly between the system's hardware and the rest of the operating system's Executive Services. In Windows NT 4.0, the HAL enables the operating system to work with different types of microprocessors.

hardware compatibility list (HCL) The list of Microsoft-certified compatible hardware devices associated with Windows 2000 Professional and Windows 2000 Server products.

HIMEM.SYS The DOS memory manager that enables Expanded and Extended Memory strategies for memory operations above the 1 MB conventional memory range.

hives The five files that hold the content of the Windows NT Registry. Hives represent the major divisions of all the Registry's keys, subkeys, subtrees, and values. The hives of the Windows NT Registry are the SAM hive, the Security hive, the Software hive, the System hive, and the Default hive. These files are stored in the \Winnt\System32\Config directory along with a backup copy and log file for each hive.

host Any device that communicates over the network using TCP/IP and has an assigned (dedicated) IP address.

I

IC (integrated circuit) The technical name for a chip. See *chip*.

icons Graphical symbols that are used to represent commands. These symbols are used to start and manipulate a program without the user having to know where that program is, or how it is configured.

IDE (integrated drive electronics) A method of disk drive manufacturing that locates all the required controller circuitry on the drive itself, rather than on a separate adapter card. Also known as the AT Attachment interface.

impact printer Any printer that produces a character image by hammering onto a combination of embossed character, ribbon, and paper.

Infrared Data Association (IrDA) A data transmission standard for using infrared light. IrDA ports provide wireless data transfers between devices. These ports support data transfer rates roughly equivalent to those of traditional parallel ports. The only down side to using IrDA ports for data communications is that the two devices must be within one or two meters of each other and have a clear line of sight between them.

INI files Windows text files that hold configuration settings that are used to initialize the system for Windows operation. Originally these files formed the basis of the Windows 3.x operating environments. They were mostly replaced in Windows 9x and NT/2000 by the Registry structure. However, some parts of the INI files still exist in these products.

initialization The process of supplying startup information to an intelligent device or peripheral (e.g., the system board's DMA controller, or a modem), or to a software application, or applet.

ink-jet printer A high-resolution printer that produces its image by spraying a specially treated ink onto the paper.

input device Any input-generating peripheral device such as keyboard, mouse, light pen, scanner, or digitizer.

instruction word A class of binary coded data word that tells the computer what operation to perform and where to find any data needed to perform the operation.

intelligent controller Usually an IC, or series of ICs, with built-in microprocessor capabilities dedicated to the controlling of some peripheral unit or process. Single-chip controllers are sometimes referred to as *smart chips*.

interface The joining of dissimilar devices so that they function in a compatible and complementary manner.

interlaced The method of rewriting the monitor screen repeatedly by alternately scanning every other line and then scanning the previously unscanned lines.

Internet This most famous wide area network is actually a network of networks working together. The main communication path is a series of networks established by the U.S. government that has expanded around the world and offers access to computers in every part of the globe.

Internet printing protocol (IPP) A protocol included with Windows 2000 that enables users to sort between different printers based on their attributes. This standards-based Internet protocol provides Windows users with the capability of printing across the Internet. With IPP, the user can print to a URL, view the print queue status using an Internet browser, and install print drivers across the Internet.

Internet Protocol (IP) address A 32-bit network address consisting of four dotted-decimal numbers separated by periods that uniquely identifies a device on the network. Each IP address consists of two parts—the network address and the host address. The network address identifies the entire network, while the host address identifies an intelligent member within the network (a router, a server, or a workstation).

interrupt A signal sent to the microprocessor from the interrupt controller, or generated by a software instruction, which is capable of interrupting the microprocessor during program execution. An interrupt is usually generated when an input or output operation is required.

interrupt controller A special programmable IC responsible for coordinating and prioritizing interrupt requests from I/O devices, and sending the microprocessor the starting addresses of the interrupt service routines so that the microprocessor can service the interrupting device and then continue executing the active program.

intranet An intranet is a network built on the TCP/IP protocol that belongs to a single organization. It is in essence a private Internet. Like the Internet, intranets are designed to share information and are accessible only to the organization's members, with authorization.

I/O (input/output) A type of data transfer occurring between a microprocessor and a peripheral device. Whenever any data transfer occurs, output from one device becomes an input to another.

I/O port The external window or connector on a computer, used to create an interface with a peripheral device. The I/O port may appear as either parallel data connections or serial data connections.

IO.SYS A special hidden, read-only bootup file that the bootstrap loader finds and moves into RAM to manage the bootup process. After the bootup has been completed, this file manages the basic input/output routines of the system. This includes communication between the system and I/O devices such as hard disks, printers, floppy-disk drives, and so on.

IP (Internet Protocol) The Network layer protocol where logical addresses are assigned. IP is one of the protocols that make up the TCP/IP stack.

IPCONFIG A TCP/IP networking utility that can be used to determine the IP address of a local machine.

IPX/SPX (internetwork packet exchange/sequenced packet exchange protocol) A proprietary transport protocol developed by Novell for the NetWare operating system. The IPX portion of the protocol is a connectionless, Network layer protocol, which is responsible for routing. The SPX portion of the protocol is a connection-oriented, Transport layer protocol that manages error checking. These protocols are primarily found on local area networks that include NetWare servers.

IRQ (interrupt request) Hardware interrupt request lines in a PC-compatible system. System hardware devices use these lines to request service from the microprocessor as required. The microprocessor responds to the IRQ by stopping what it is doing, storing its environment, jumping to a service routine, servicing the device, and then returning to its original task.

ISA (Industry Standard Architecture) A term that refers to the bus structures used in the IBM PC series of personal computers. The PC and XT use an 8-bit bus, and the AT uses a 16-bit bus.

ISDN (integrated services digital network) A digital communications standard that can carry digital data over special telephone lines at speeds much higher than those possible with regular analog phone lines.

ISPs (Internet service providers) Companies that provide the technical gateway to the Internet. An ISP connects all of the users and individual networks together.

J

joystick A computer input device that offers quick, multidirectional movement of the cursor for CAD systems and video games.

jumper Typically, a 2- or 4-pin BERG connector, located on the system board or an adapter card, which permits the attachment of a wired hardware switch or the placement of a shorting bar to implement a particular hardware function or setting.

K

kernel The Windows 3.x and 95 core files that are responsible for managing Windows resources and running applications.

kernel mode The Kernel Mode is the operating mode in which the program has unlimited access to all memory, including those of system hardware, the user mode applications, and other processes (such as I/O operations). The Kernel Mode consists of three major blocks, the Win32k Executive Service module, the Hardware Abstraction Layer, and the Microkernel.

keyboard The most familiar computer input device, incorporating a standard typewriter layout with the addition of other specialized control and function keys.

L

LAN (local area network) A collection of local computers and devices that can share information. A LAN is normally thought of as encompassing a campus setting, a room, or a collection of buildings.

laser printer Any printer that utilizes the electro-photographic method of image transfer. Light dots are transferred to a photosensitive rotating drum, which picks up electrostatically charged toner before transferring it to the paper.

LCD (liquid crystal display) The type of output display created by placing liquid crystal material between two sheets of glass. A set of electrodes is attached to each sheet of glass. The horizontal (row) electrodes are attached to one glass plate, and the vertical (column) electrodes are fitted to the other plate. These electrodes are transparent and let light pass through. A pixel is created in the liquid crystal material at each spot where a row and a column electrode intersect. When the pixel is energized, the liquid crystal material bends and prevents light from passing through the display.

LED (light emitting diode) A particular type of diode that emits light when conducting. It is used in computers and disk drives as active circuit indicator.

legacy devices Adapter cards and devices that do not include plug-and-play capabilities. These are typically older ISA expansion cards that are still being used for some reason.

letter quality Refers to a print quality as good or better than that provided by an electric typewriter.

logical block addressing (LBA) A hard-disk drive organizational strategy that permits the operating system to access larger drive sizes than older BIOS/DOS FAT-management schemes could support.

logon The process of identifying oneself to the network. Normally accomplished by entering a valid user name and password that the system recognizes.

loopback A modem test procedure that allows a transmitted signal to be returned to its source for comparison with the original data.

lost allocation units Also referred to as lost clusters. File segments that do not currently belong to any file in the file allocation table. The DOS command CHKDSK/F can be used to locate and free these segments for future use.

LPT1 The label used in Microsoft DOS versions to refer to parallel port #1, usually reserved for printer operation.

M

magnetic disk The most popular form of secondary data storage for computers. Shaped like a platter and coated with an electromagnetic material, magnetic disks provide direct access to large amounts of stored data, and can be erased and rerecorded many times.

magnetic tape Traditionally, one of the most popular forms of secondary data storage backup for computers. However, Windows 2000 offers a number of other backup capabilities that may render tape an undesirable backup media in the future. Since access to data on tape is sequential in nature, magnetic tape is primarily used to restore a system that has suffered a catastrophic loss of data from its hard disk drive.

mapped drives A technique employed to enable a local system to assign a logical drive letter to the remote disk drive or folder. This is referred to as *mapping the drive letter* to the resource. This will enable applications running on the local computer to use the resource across the network.

master boot record (MBR) Also referred to as the Master Partition Boot Sector. This file is located at the first sector of the disk. It contains a Master Partition Table that describes how the hard disk is organized. This table includes information about the disk's size, as well as the number and locations of all partitions on the disk. The MBR also contains the Master Boot Code that loads the operating system from the disk's active partition.

master file table (MFT) The core component of the NTFS system, this table replaces the FAT in an MS-DOS compatible system and contains information about each file stored on the disk.

MEM.EXE The DOS command that can be used to examine the total and used memory of the system.

memory Computer components that store information for future use. In a PC, memory can be divided into two categories: primary and secondary (i.e., semiconductor RAM and ROM and other devices). Primary memory can be divided into ROM, RAM, and cache groups. Likewise, secondary memory contains many types of storage devices—floppy drives, hard-disk drives, CD-ROM drives, DVD drives, tape drives, and so on)

memory management Methodology used in handling a computer's memory resources, including bank switching, memory protection, and virtual memory.

memory map A layout of the memory and/or I/O device addressing scheme used by a particular computer system.

memory-mapped I/O An I/O addressing method where I/O devices are granted a portion of the available address allocations, thus requiring no additional control lines to implement.

menu A screen display of available program options or commands that can be selected through keyboard or mouse action.

MHz (megahertz) One million hertz, or cycles per second.

microcomputer A personal computer, or a computer using a microprocessor as its CPU.

Microsoft Management Console (MMC) A collection of manageability features that accompany Windows 2000. These features exist as "Snap-in" applets that can be added to the operating system through the MMC.

mirroring A RAID fault tolerance method in which an exact copy of all data is written to two separate disks at the same time.

MMX (Multimedia Extensions) technology An advanced Pentium microprocessor that includes specialized circuitry designed to manage multimedia operations. Its additional multimedia instructions speed up high-volume input/output needed for graphics, motion video, animation, and sound.

modem (modulator-demodulator) Also called a DCE device, a modem is used to interface a computer or terminal to the telephone system for the purpose of conducting data communications between computers often located at great distances from each other.

monitor (1) A name for a CRT computer display. (2) Any hardware device, or software program, such as the Windows 95 System Resource Monitor, that checks, reports about, or automatically oversees a running program or system.

MOS (metal oxide semiconductor) A category of logic and memory chip design that derives its name from the use of metal, oxide, and semiconductor layers. Among the various families of MOS devices are PMOS (P-Type semiconductor material), NMOS (N-Type semiconductor material), and CMOS (Complementary/Symmetry MOS material). The first letter of each family denotes the type of construction used to fabricate the chip's circuits. MOS families do not require a highly regulated +5 V dc power supply like TTL devices.

mouse A popular computer I/O device used to point or draw on the video monitor by rolling it along a desktop as the cursor moves on the screen in a corresponding manner.

MSD (Microsoft Diagnostics) Microsoft diagnostic program that can be used from the command prompt to examine different aspects of a system's hardware and software configuration. The MSD utility has been included with MS-DOS 6.x, Windows 3.x, and Windows 9x.

MSDOS.SYS One of the hidden, read-only system files required to boot the system. It is loaded by the IO.SYS file during the bootup process. It handles program and file management functions for MS-DOS systems. In Windows 95, its function is changed to that of providing pathways to other Windows files and supporting selected startup options.

multimedia A term applied to a range of applications that bring together text, graphics, video, audio, and animation to provide interactivity between the computer and its human operator.

multitasking The ability of a computer system to run two or more programs simultaneously.

N

NAK (Negative Acknowledge) A data communications code used by a receiver to tell the transmitter that its last message was not properly received.

NetBEUI (NetBIOS Extended User Interface) The Microsoft networking protocol used with Windows-based systems.

NetBIOS An emulation of IBM's *NETwork Basic Input/Output System*. NetBIOS represents the basic interface between the operating system and the LAN hardware. This function is implemented through ROM ICs located on the network card.

NetWare The Novell client/server network operating system.

Network Connection Wizard Automated setup routine in Windows 2000 that can be invoked to guide the user through the process of creating a network connection.

Network Neighborhood The Windows 95 utility used to browse and connect multiple networks, and to access shared resources on a server without having to map a network drive.

nibble A 4-bit binary pattern, which can easily be converted into a single hexadecimal digit.

NLQ (near-letter quality) A quality of printing nearly as good as that of an electric typewriter. The very best dot-matrix printers can produce NLQ.

NMI (nonmaskable interrupt) A type of interrupt that cannot be ignored by the microprocessor during program execution. Three things can cause a nonmaskable interrupt to occur: (1) A numeric coprocessor installation error. (2) A RAM parity check error. (3) An I/O channel check error.

nonimpact printer Any printer that does not form its characters by using a hammer device to impact the paper, ribbon, or embossed character.

nonvolatile memory Memory that is not lost after the power is turned off, such as ROM.

NT File System (NTFS) The proprietary Windows NT file system. The NTFS structure is designed to provide better data security and to operate more efficiently with larger hard drives than FAT systems do. Its structure employs 64-bit entries to keep track of storage on the disk (as opposed to the 16- and 32-bit entries used in FAT and FAT32 systems).

NTDETECT NTDETECT.COM is the Windows NT hardware detection file. This file is responsible for collecting information about the system's installed hardware devices and passing it to the NTLDR program. This information is later used to upgrade the Windows NT Registry files.

NTLDR NT Loader is the Windows NT bootstrap loader for Intel-based computers running Windows NT. It is the Windows NT equivalent of the DOS IO.SYS file and is responsible for loading the NT operating system into memory. Afterwards, NTLDR passes control of the system over to the Windows NT operating system.

NTOSKRNL NTOSKRNL.EXE is the Windows NT kernel file that contains the Windows NT core and loads its device drivers.

NTSC (National Television Standards Committee) This organization created the television standards in the United States, and is administered by the FCC.

ntuser.dat The Windows NT/2000 file that contains the User portion of the Windows NT Registry. This file contains the user-specific settings that have been established for this user. When a user logs onto the system, the User file and System hive portions of the Registry are used to construct the user-specific environment in the system.

null modem cable A cable meeting the RS-232C specification, used to cross-connect two computers through their serial ports by transposing the transmit and receive lines. The computers must be physically located very close to one another, eliminating the need for a modem.

O

odd parity The form of parity checking in which the parity bit is used to make the total number of 1's contained in the character an odd number.

Off-Hook (OH) A condition existing on a telephone line that is capable of initiating an outgoing call, but unable to receive an incoming call.

off line Any computer system or peripheral device that is not ready to operate, not connected, not turned on, or not properly configured.

On-Hook A condition that exists on any telephone line that is capable of receiving an incoming call.

online Any computer system or peripheral device that is not only powered up, but also ready to operate.

operating system A special software program, first loaded into a computer at powerup, and responsible for running it. The operating system also serves as the interface between the machine and other software applications.

optical mouse A mouse that emits an infrared light stream to detect motion as it is moved around a special x-y matrix pad.

output device Any peripheral device, such as a monitor, modem, or printer, that accepts computer output.

P

paging file Also known as the swap file. The hidden file located on the hard disk that makes up half of the Windows 2000 virtual memory system. This file holds the programs and data that the operating system's virtual memory manager moves out of RAM memory and stores on the disk as virtual memory.

parallel interface The multi-line channel through which the simultaneous transfer of one or more bytes occurs.

parallel mode The mode of data transfer in which an entire word is transferred at once, from one location to another, by a set of parallel conductors.

parallel port The external connector on a computer that is used to create an interface between the computer and a parallel peripheral such as a printer.

parity bit Used for error checking during the sending and receiving of data within a system and from one system to another. The parity bit's value depends on how many 1 bits are contained in the byte it accompanies.

parity checking A method to check for data transmission errors by using a ninth bit to ensure that each character sent has an even (even parity) or odd (odd parity) number of logic 1's before transfer. The parity bit is checked for each byte sent.

parity error This error occurs when a data transfer cannot be verified for integrity. At least one data bit or the parity bit has been corrupted during the transfer process.

partition A logical section of a hard disk. Partitioning allows a single physical disk to be divided into multiple logical drives that can each hold a different operating system. Most disks contain a single partition that holds a single operating system.

partition boot sector The boot sector of that partition located in the first sector of the active partition. Here the MBR finds the code to begin loading the secondary bootstrap loader from the root directory of the boot drive.

partition table The table present at the start of every hard disk that describes the layout of the disk, including the number and location of all partitions on the disk.

partitioning Partitioning establishes the logical structure of the hard disk in a format that conforms to the operating system being used on the computer. It is a function of the operating system being used. In the case of Microsoft operating systems, the FDISK utility is used to establish and manipulate partitions.

password Unique code pattern associated with a user's logon account that is used to access the resources of a network.

path The location of the file on the disk in reference to the drive's root directory. The file's full path is specified by a logical drive letter and a listing of all directories between the root directory and the file.

PC bus Refers to the bus architectures used in the first IBM PCs, the original 8-bit bus, and the 16-bit bus extension used with the AT.

PCI (peripheral component interconnect) bus A low-cost, high-performance 32-/64-bit local bus developed jointly by IBM, Intel, DEC, NCR, and Compaq.

PCMCIA (Personal Computer Memory Card International Association) card A credit-card-sized adapter card designed for use with portable computers. These cards slide into a PCMCIA slot and are used to implement modems, networks, and CD-ROM drives.

peer-to-peer network A network that does not have a centralized point of management and in which each computer is equal to all the others. In this scenario, all of the members can function as both clients and servers.

peripherals Also called I/O devices, these units include secondary memory devices such as hard-disk drives, floppy-disk drives, magnetic tape drives, modems, monitors, mice, joysticks, light pens, scanners, and even speakers.

permissions Settings that enable security levels to be assigned to files and folders on the disk. These settings provide parameters for activities that users can conduct with the designated file or folder.

personal digital assistant (PDA) Handheld computing devices that typically include telephone, fax, and networking functions. A typical PDA can function as a cell phone, a fax, and a personal organizer. Most are pen-based devices that use a wand for input rather than a keyboard or mouse. PDAs are a member of the palmtop class of computers.

PIFs (Program Information Files) Windows 3.x information files used to identify resources required for DOS-based applications.

pin feed A method of moving continuous forms through the print area of a printer by using mounting pins on each side of a motorized platen to engage the holes on the right and left sides of the paper.

PING Network troubleshooting utility command that is used to verify connections to remote hosts. The PING command sends Internet Control Message Packets to a remote location and then waits for echoed response packets to be returned. The command will wait for up to one second for each packet sent and then display the number of transmitted and received packets. The command can be used to test both the name and IP address of the remote unit. A number of switches can be used to set parameters for the ping operation.

pixel Also called a PEL, or picture element, it is the smallest unit (one dot for monochrome) into which a display image can be divided.

Plug and Play (PnP) A specification that requires the BIOS, operating system, and adapter cards to be designed so that the system automatically configures new hardware devices to eliminate system resource conflicts.

pointing device Any input device used for the specific purpose of moving the screen cursor or drawing an image.

point-to-point protocol (PPP) A connection protocol that controls the transmission of data over the wide-area network. PPP is the default protocol for the Microsoft Dial-Up adapter. In a dial-up situation, Internet software communicates with the service provider by embedding the TCP/IP information in a PPP shell for transmission through the modem in analog format. The communications equipment, at the ISP site, converts the signal back to the digital TCP/IP format. PPP has become the standard for remote access.

point-to-point tunneling protocol (PPTP) The de facto industry standard tunneling protocol first supported in Windows NT 4.0. PPTP is an extension of the point-to-point protocol (PPP) and takes advantage of the authentication, compression, and encryption mechanisms of PPP. PPTP is installed with the Routing and Remote Access service. By default, PPTP is configured for five PPTP ports that can be enabled for inbound remote access and demand-dial routing connections through the Windows 2000 Routing and Remote Access wizard. PPTP and Microsoft Point-to-Point Encryption (MPPE) provide the primary security technology to implement Virtual Private Network services of encapsulation and encryption of private data.

polarizer An optical device that will either block or allow the passage of light through it depending on the polarity of an electrical charge applied to it.

POLEDIT The system policy editor that is used to establish or modify system policies that govern user rights and privileges. The Policy Editor is another tool that can be used to access the information in the Registry. However, unlike the RegEdit utility, Poledit can only access subsets of keys. The Registry editor can access the entire Registry.

policies Network administrative settings that govern the rights and privileges of different users in multi-user operations.

polling A system of initiating data transfer between a computer system and a peripheral in which the status of all the peripherals is examined periodically under software program control by having the microprocessor check the READY line. When it is activated by one of the peripherals, the processor will begin the data transfer using the corresponding I/O port.

POST (Power-On Self-Tests) A group of ROM BIOS-based diagnostic tests that are performed on the system each time it is powered up. These tests check the PC's standard hardware devices including the microprocessor, memory, interrupts, DMA, and video.

power supply The component in the system that converts the AC voltage from the wall outlet to the DC voltage required by the computer circuitry.

preventive maintenance Any regularly scheduled checking and testing of hardware and software with the goal of avoiding future failure or breakdown.

Primary Domain Controller (PDC) Primary Domain Controllers contain the Directory Databases for the network. These databases contain information about User Accounts, Group Accounts, and Computer Accounts. PDCs also are also referred to as Security Accounts Managers.

primary partitions Bootable partitions created from unallocated disk space. Under Windows 2000, up to four primary partitions can be created on a basic disk. The disk can also contain three primary partitions and an extended partition. The primary partition becomes the system's boot volume by being marked as "Active". The free space in the extended partition can be subdivided into up to 23 logical drives.

printer A peripheral device for the printing of computer text or graphics output.

printer font A prescribed character set properly formatted for use by the printer.

profiles Information about each user and group defined in the system that describes the resources and desktop configurations created for them. Settings in the profiles can be used to limit the actions users can perform, such as installing, removing, configuring, adjusting, or copying resources. When users log in, the system checks their profile and adjusts according to their information. This information is stored in the
\WINNT*login_name*\NTUSER.DAT file.

program Any group of instructions designed to command a computer system to perform a specific task. Also called *software*.

programmed I/O A system of initiating data transfer between a computer system and a peripheral in which the microprocessor alerts the specific device by using an address call. The I/O device can signal its readiness to accept the data transfer by using its Busy line. If Busy is active, the microprocessor can perform other tasks until the Busy line is deactivated, at which time the transfer can begin.

prompt A software-supplied message to the user, requiring some specific action or providing some important information. It can also be a very simple symbol, indicating that the program has successfully loaded and is waiting for a command from the user.

protected mode An operational state that allows an 80286 or higher computer to address all of its memory, including memory beyond the 1 MB MS-DOS limit.

protocol A set of rules that govern the transmitting and receiving of data communications.

Q

queue A special and temporary storage (RAM or registers) area for data in printing or internal program execution operations.

quotas Windows 2000 security settings that enable administrators to limit the amount of hard drive space users can have access to.

QWERTY keyboard A keyboard layout that was originally designed to prevent typists from jamming old-style mechanical typewriters, it is still the standard English language keyboard. The name spells out the first six leftmost letters in the first alphabetic row of keys.

R

RAID (redundant array of inexpensive disks) A set of specifications for configuring multiple hard drives to store data to increase storage capacity and improve performance. Some variations configure the drives in a manner to improve performance, whereas others concentrate on data security.

RAM (random access memory) A type of semiconductor memory device that holds data on a temporary or volatile basis. Any address location in the RAM memory section can be accessed as fast as any other location.

RAM disk An area of memory that has been set aside and assigned a drive letter to simulate the organization of a hard disk drive in RAM memory. Also referred to as a virtual disk.

raster graphics A graphics representation method that uses a dot-matrix to compose the image.

raster scan The display of a video image, line by line, by an electron beam deflection system.

read only (1) A file parameter setting that prevents a file from being altered. (2) Refers to data that is permanently stored on the media or to such a medium itself.

read/write head Usually abbreviated "R/W head," the device by which a disk or tape drive senses and records digital data on the magnetic medium.

real mode A mode of operation in 80286 and higher machines in which the computer functions under the same command and addressing restrictions as an 8086 or 8088.

reboot To restart the computer or to reload the operating system.

refresh A required method of re-energizing a memory cell or display pixel in order for its data to continually be held.

RegEdit The editing utility used to directly edit the contents of the Registry (Regedit.exe and Regedit32.exe). This file is located in the \Winnt\System32 folder.

registry A multipart, hierarchical database established to hold system and user configuration information in Windows 9x, NT, and 2000.

registry keys The registries in Windows 9x, NT, and 2000 are organized into headkeys, subkeys, and values.

RESET A control bus signal, activated by either a soft or a hard switch, which sets the system microprocessor and all programmable system devices to their startup, or initialization, values. This allows the computer to begin operation following the application of the RESET input signal.

resolution A measurement of the sharpness of an image or character, either of a printer or a display monitor. For a monitor, resolution consists of the number of dots per scan line times the number of scans per picture. For a printer, resolution consists of the number of dots present per linear inch of print space.

ROM (read only memory) A type of semiconductor memory device that holds data on a permanent or nonvolatile basis.

ROM BIOS A collection of special programs (native intelligence) permanently stored in one or two ROM ICs installed on the system board. These programs are available to the system as soon as it is powered up, providing for initialization of smart chips, POST tests, and data transfer control.

root directory The main directory of every logical disk. It follows the FAT tables and serves as the starting point for organizing information on the disk. The location of every directory, subdirectory, and file on the disk is recorded in this directory.

RS-232C The most widely used serial interface standard, it calls for a 25-pin D-type connector. Specific pins are designated for data transmission and receiving, as well as a number of handshaking and control lines. Logic voltage levels are also established for the data and the control signals on the pins of the connector.

RS-422 An enhancement to the original RS-232C interface standard and adopted by the EIA, it uses twisted-pair transmission lines and differential line voltage signals, resulting in higher immunity for the transmitted data.

RS-423 Another enhancement to the original RS-232C interface standard and adopted by the EIA, it uses coaxial cable to provide extended transmission distances and higher data-transfer rates.

S

Safe Mode A special Windows 95/98/2000 startup mode that starts the system by loading minimum configuration drivers. This mode is used to allow the correction of system errors when the system does not boot up normally. Safe Mode is entered by pressing F5 or F8 when the "Starting Windows 9x" message is displayed during bootup.

scan rate The total number of times per second that a video raster is horizontally scanned by the CRT's electron beam.

SCSI (small computer system interface) bus A system-level interface standard used to connect different types of peripheral equipment to the system. The standard actually exists as a group of specifications (SCSI, SCSI-2, and SCSI-3) featuring several cabling connector schemes. Even within these three specifications there can exist major variations—Wide SCSI, Fast SCSI, and Fast/Wide SCSI. Apple was the first personal computer maker to select the SCSI interface as the bus standard for peripheral equipment that can provide high-speed data transfer control for up to seven devices, while occupying only one expansion slot. The standard is gaining more widespread support in the PC market, particularly in the area of portable PCs. See *system-level interface*.

sector One of many individual data-holding areas into which each track of a disk is divided during the format process.

serial interface A channel through which serial digital data transfer occurs. Although multiple lines may be used, only one of these will actually carry the data. The most popular serial interface standard is the EIA RS-232C.

serial mode The mode of data transfer in which the word bits are transferred one bit at a time along a single conductor.

serial mouse A type of mouse that plugs into a serial port rather than an adapter card.

serial port The external connector on a computer that is used to create an interface between the computer and a serial device such as a modem. A typical serial port uses a DB-25 or a DB-9 connector.

servers Powerful network computers (or devices) that contain the network operating system and manage network resources for other computers (clients). Some servers take on special management functions for the network. Some of these functions include print servers, web servers, file servers, database servers, and so on.

setup disks Disks created to restart a failed Windows NT/2000 system. These disks are created by the Windows 2000 Backup utility and contain information about the system's current Windows configuration settings.

shadow RAM An area of RAM used for copying the system's BIOS routines from ROM. Making BIOS calls from the RAM area improves the operating speed of the system. Video ROM routines are often stored in shadow RAM also.

shared resource A system resource (device or directory) that has been identified as being available for use by multiple individuals throughout the network environment.

shares Resources, such as printers and folders, which have been made available for use by other network users.

SIMM (Single In-line Memory Module) A circuit board module containing eight (without parity) or nine (with parity) memory chips, and designed to plug into special sockets.

simplex communications Communications that occur in only one direction. An public address system is an example of simplex communications.

SLIP (Serial Line Internet Protocol) Older units running UNIX employ this Internet connection protocol for dial-up services. The protocol wraps the TCP/IP packet in a shell for transmission through the modem in analog format. The communications equipment, at the service provider's site, converts the signal back to the digital TCP/IP format.

SMARTDRV.EXE (SmartDrive) A DOS driver program that establishes a disk cache in an area of extended memory as a storage space for information read from the hard-disk drive. When a program requests more data, the SMARTDRV program redirects the request to check in the cache memory area to see if the requested data is there.

software Any aspect of the computer operation that cannot be physically touched. This includes bits, bytes, words, and programs.

speaker The computer system's audio output device. Measuring 2-1/4 inches in diameter and rated at 8 ohms, 1/2 watts, the speaker is usually used as a system prompt and as an error indicator. It is also capable of producing arcade sounds, speech, and music.

SRAM (static random access memory) A type of RAM that can store its data indefinitely as long as power to it is not interrupted.

start bit In asynchronous serial data transmission, this bit denotes the beginning of a character and is always a logic low pulse, or space.

static electricity This is often a serious problem in environments of low humidity. It is a stationary charge of electricity usually caused by friction, and potentially very damaging to sensitive electronic components.

stop bit The bit, sent after each character in an asynchronous data communications transmission, that signals the end of a character.

stop errors Errors that occur when Windows 2000 detects a condition that it cannot recover from. The system stops responding, and a screen of information with a blue or black background is displayed. Stop errors are also known as blue screen errors, or the blue screen of death (BSOD).

subnet mask The decimal number 255 is used to hide, or mask, the network portion of the IP address while still showing the host portions of the address. The default subnet mask for Class A IP addresses is 255.0.0.0. Class B is 255.255.0.0, and Class C is 255.255.255.0.

swap file A special file established on the hard drive to provide virtual memory capabilities for the operating system. Windows 3.x can work with temporary or permanent swap files. Windows 95 uses a dynamically assigned, variable-length swap file.

synchronous transmission A method of serial data transmission in which both the transmitter and the receiver are synchronized by a common clock signal.

SYSEDIT.EXE A special Windows text editor utility that can be used to alter ASCII text files such as CONFIG.SYS, AUTOEXEC.BAT, WIN.INI, and SYSTEM.INI.

system board The large printed circuit board (mother board) into which peripheral adapter boards (daughter boards) may plug into, depending on the number of devices working with the system. The system board is populated with 100 or more IC chips, depending on how much on-board memory is installed. Besides RAM chips, the system board contains the microprocessor, BIOS ROM, several programmable controllers, system clock circuitry, switches, and various jumpers. Also, most system boards come with an empty socket into which the user may plug a compatible co-processor chip to give the computer some high-level number crunching capabilities.

system files Files that possess the system attribute. These are normally hidden files used to boot the operating system.

system-level interface An interface that allows the system to directly access the I/O device through an expansion slot without an intermediate interface circuit. The system is isolated from the peripheral device and only sees its logical configuration.

system partition Normally the same as the boot partition. More precisely, the disk partition that contains the hardware-specific files (Ntldr, Osloader, Boot.ini, and Ntdetect) required to load and start Windows 2000.

system software A class of software dedicated to the control and operation of a computer system and its various peripherals.

system unit The main computer cabinet housing containing the primary components of the system. This includes the main logic board (system or mother board), disk drive(s), switching power supply, and the interconnecting wires and cables.

T

tape drive The unit that reads, writes, and holds the tape being used for backup purposes.

task switching The changing of one program or application to another either manually by the user, or under the direction of a multitasking operating system environment.

TCP/IP (transfer control protocol/Internet protocol) A collection of protocols developed by the U.S. Department of Defense in the early days of the network that became the Internet. It is the standard transport protocol used by many operating systems and the Internet.

telephony In the computer world, this term refers to hardware and software devices that perform functions typically performed by telephone equipment. Microsoft offers the TAPI interface for both clients and servers. See *Telephony API*.

Telephony API (TAPI) Telephony Application Programming Interface. This software interface provides a universal set of drivers that enable modems and COM ports to control and arbitrate telephony operations for data, faxes, and voice. Through this interface, applications can cooperatively share the dial-up connection functions of the system.

toner A form of powdered ink that accepts an electrical charge in laser printers and photocopying machines. It adheres to a rotating drum containing an image that has been given an opposite charge. The image is transferred to the paper during the printing process.

TRACERT A network troubleshooting utility that displays the route and a hop count taken to a given destination. The route taken to a particular address can be set manually using the ROUTE command. The TRACERT utility traces the route taken by ICMP packets sent across the network. Routers along the path return information to the inquiring system, and the utility displays the host name, IP address, and round trip time for each hop in the path.

track A single disk or tape data storage channel, upon which the R/W head places the digital data in a series of flux reversals. On disks, the track is a concentric data circle, whereas on tapes it is a parallel data line.

track ball (1) A pointing device that allows the user to control the position of the cursor on the video display screen by rotating a sphere (track ball). (2) The sphere inside certain types of mice that the mouse rides on. As the mouse moves across a surface, the trackball rolls, creating X-Y movement data.

tractor feed A paper-feeding mechanism for printers that use continuous forms. The left and right edges of the forms contain holes through which the tractor pins pull the paper through the print area.

transmit Although this term usually means to send data between a transmitter and receiver over a specific communications line, it can also describe the transfer of data within the internal buses of a computer or between the computer and its peripheral devices.

transport control protocol (TCP) TCP is a Transport layer protocol used to establish reliable connections between clients and servers.

trees In Active Directory, a collection of objects that share the same DNS name. All of the domains in a tree share a common security context and global catalog.

Troubleshooters A special type of Help utilities available in Windows 9x and 2000. These utilities enable the user to pinpoint problems and identify solutions to those problems by asking a series of questions and then providing detailed troubleshooting information based on the user's responses.

U

UART (universal asynchronous receiver transmitter) A serial interface IC used to provide for the parallel-to-serial and serial-to-parallel conversions required for asynchronous serial data transmission. It also handles the parallel interface to the computer's bus, as well as the control functions associated with the transmission.

Ultra DMA A burst mode DMA data transfer protocol, used with Ultra ATA IDE devices to support data transfer rates of 33.3 MBps. While the official name of the protocol is Ultra DMA/33, it is also referred to as UDMA, UDMA/33, and DMA mode 33.

Ultra SCSI A series of advanced SCSI specifications that include: (1) Ultra SCSI, which employs an 8-bit bus and supports data rates of 20 MBps; (2) SCSI-3 (also referred to as Wide Ultra SCSI) that widens the bus to 16-bits and supports data rates of 40 MBps; (3) Ultra2 SCSI that uses an 8-bit bus and supports data rates of 40 MBps; and (4) Wide Ultra2 SCSI that supports data rates of 80 MBps across a 16-bit bus.

uninterruptible power supply (UPS) A special power supply unit that includes a battery to maintain power to key equipment in the event of a power failure. A typical UPS is designed to keep a computer operational after a power failure long enough for the user to save their current work and properly shut down the system. Many UPSs include software that provides automatic backup and shutdown procedures when the UPS senses a power problem.

Universal Naming Convention (UNC) A standardized method of specifying a path to a network computer or a device (i.e., \\computername\sharename).

universal serial bus (USB) A specification for a high-speed, serial communication bus that can be used to link various peripheral devices to the system. The standard permits up to 127 USB-compliant devices to be connected to the system in a daisy-chained, or tiered-star configuration.

upgrading The process of replacing an older piece of hardware or software with a newer version of that hardware or software. Upgrading also serves as an interim solution for bugs discovered in software.

upper memory area (UMA) The area in the DOS memory map between 640 kB and 1 MB. This memory area was referred to as the Reserved Memory Area in older PC and PC-XT systems. It typically contains the EMS Page Frame, as well as any ROM extensions and video display circuitry.

upper memory blocks (UMBs) Special 16 kB blocks of memory established in the upper memory area between the 640 kB and 1 MB marks.

URL (universal resource locator) A unique address on the World Wide Web used to access a Web site.

USART (universal synchronous asynchronous receiver transmitter) A serial interface IC used to provide for the parallel-to-serial and serial-to-parallel conversions required for both asynchronous and synchronous serial data transmission. It also handles the parallel interface to the computer's bus, as well as the control functions associated with the transmission.

user name The public portion of the user login name that identifies permissions and rights to network resources.

user profiles User profiles are records that permit each user that logs on to a computer to have a unique set of properties associated with them, such as particular desktop or Start menu configurations. In Windows 2000, user profiles are stored in C:\Documents and Settings by default. User profiles are local, meaning that they reside only on that computer. Therefore, users may have different profiles created and stored for them on each computer they log on to.

utility program A term used to describe a program designed to help the user in the operation of the computer.

V

VESA (Video Electronics Standards Association) bus A 64-bit local bus standard developed to provide a local bus connection to a video adapter. Its operation has been defined for use by other adapter types, such as drive controllers, network interfaces, and other hardware.

VGA (video graphics array) Another video standard, developed by IBM, providing medium and high text and graphics resolution. It was originally designed for IBM's high-end PS/2 line, but other vendors have created matching boards for PC and AT machines also, making it the preferred standard at this time. Requiring an analog monitor, it originally provided 16 colors at 640x480 resolution. Third-party vendors have boosted that capability to 256 colors, while adding an even greater 800x600 resolution, calling it Super VGA.

video adapter Sometimes referred to as a display adapter, graphics adapter, or graphics card, it is a plug-in peripheral unit for computers, fitting in one of the system board option slots, and providing the interface between the computer and the display. The adapter usually must match the type of display (digital or analog) it is used with.

View menu A Windows 2000 dialog box drop-down menu that enables the user to toggle screen displays between Large and Small Icons, Details, and Thumbnail views. The dialog boxes can be resized to accommodate as many Thumbnail images as desired.

virtual disk A method of using RAM as if it were a disk.

virtual memory A memory technique that allows several programs to run simultaneously, even though the system does not have enough actual memory installed to do this. The extra memory is simulated using disk space.

virtual memory manager (VMM) The section of the Windows 9x, NT, and 2000 structure that assigns unique memory spaces to every active 32-bit and 16-bit DOS/Windows 3.x application. The VMM works with the environmental subsystems of the User mode to establish special environments for 16-bit applications to run in.

virtual private network (VPN) Virtual Private Networks use message encryption and other security techniques to ensure that only authorized users can access the message as it passes through public transmission media. In particular, VPNs provide secure Internet communications by establishing encrypted data tunnels across the WAN that cannot be penetrated by others.

virus A destructive program designed to replicate itself on any machine that it comes into contact with. Viruses are spread from machine to machine by attaching themselves to (infecting) other files.

VLSI (very large-scale integration) IC devices containing a very large number of electronic components (from 100,000 to approximately 1,000,000).

volatile memory Memory (RAM) that loses its content as soon as power is discontinued.

volumes Portions of disks signified by single drive designators. In the Microsoft environment, a volume corresponds to a partition.

VOM (volt ohm milliammeter) A basic piece of electronic troubleshooting equipment that provides for circuit measurements of voltage, current, and resistance in logarithmic analog readout form.

W

warm boot Booting a computer that has already been powered up. This can be accomplished by pressing the Reset switch on the front of most computers, or by selecting one of the Restart options from the Windows Exit options dialog box.

Web site A location on the World Wide Web. Web sites typically contain a home page that is displayed first when the site is accessed. They usually contain other pages and programs that can be accessed through the home page.

wild cards Characters, such as * or ?, used to represent letters or words. Such characters are typically used to perform operations with multiple files.

Windows A graphical user interface from Microsoft. It uses a graphical display to represent procedures and programs that can be executed by the computer. Multiple programs can run at the same time.

Windows Explorer The Windows 95, Windows 98, and Windows NT/2000 utility that graphically displays the system as drives, folders, and files in a hierarchical tree structure. This enables the user to manipulate all of the system's software using a mouse.

WINNT32 WINNT32.EXE or WINNT.EXE are the programs that can be run to initiate the installation of Windows 2000. The WINNT32.EXE program is designed to run under a 32-bit operating system and will not run from the command line. The WINNT.EXE program is designed to run under a 16-bit operating system and will not run from within a 32-bit operating system such as Windows NT.

WINS A Microsoft-specific naming service that resolves IP addresses to NetBIOS names within a LAN environment. The LAN must include a Windows NT name server running the WINS server software that maintains the IP address/domain name database for the LAN. Each client in the LAN must contain the WINS client software and be WINS enabled.

wizards Special Windows routines designed to lead users through installation or setup operations using a menu style of selecting options. The wizards carry out these tasks in the proper sequence, requesting information from the user at key points in the process.

word The amount of data that can be held in a computer's registers during a process. It is considered to be the computer's basic storage unit.

workgroups A network control scenario in which all of the nodes may act as servers for some processes and clients for others. In a workgroup environment, each machine maintains its own security and administration databases.

X

x-axis (1) In a two-dimensional matrix, the horizontal row/rows, such as on an oscilloscope screen. (2) The dimension of width in a graphics representation.

Xmodem A very early, and simple, asynchronous data communications protocol developed for personal computers that is capable of detecting some transfer errors, but not all.

Xon-Xoff An asynchronous data communications protocol that provides for synchronization between the receiver and transmitter, requiring the receiver to indicate its ability to accept data by sending either an Xon (transmit on-buffer ready) or Xoff (transmit off-buffer full) signal to the transmitter.

x-y matrix Any two-dimensional form or image, where x represents width and y represents height.

Y

y-axis (1) In a two-dimensional matrix, the vertical column/columns, such as on an oscilloscope screen. (2) The dimension of height in a graphics representation.

Ymodem An improvement of the Xmodem protocol that increases the data block size from 128 bytes to 1024 bytes. An offshoot known as Ymodem Batch includes filenames in the transmission so that multiple files can be sent in a single transmission. Another variation, labeled Ymodem G, modified the normal Ymodem flow control method to speed up transmissions.

Z

Zmodem This dial-up protocol can be used to transmit both text and binary files (such as .EXE files) across telephone lines (but not the Internet). It employs advanced error checking/correcting schemes and provides Autofile Restart crash recovery techniques.

INDEX

.BAT, 541
.COM, 540, 541
.EXE, 541
.FOT, 399
.SYS, 540
.TMP, 868
.TTF, 399
/documents/, 382
"Error Loading Operating System" message, 774
10/100Base-F, 339
1000Base-LX, 339
1000Base-SX, 339
100Base-FX, 339
100VG (Voice Grade) AnyLAN, 339
10Base-FL, 339
10Base-FP, 339
6-pin mini-DIN, 200
802.11, 341
802.11a, 341
802.11g, 341
802.11x, 341
80286 CPUs, 42
80386DX CPUs, 42
80386SX CPUs, 42
80586 CPUs. See Pentium CPUs, 42
8088 CPUs, 42
9-in-1, 31

A

AC power, 414
AC voltage function, 664
A-cables, 288
Accelerated graphics port (AGP), 50, 107
Access and privilege, 726
Access Control List (ACL), 597
Access point, 329, 348
Access rights, 726
Access Time, 307
Active, 301
Active Directory (AD) , 627
Active Directory Users and Computers, 630
Active heat sinks, 142
Active matrix display, 477
Active partition, 529
Active Termination, 299

Actively listen, 8
Adaptable, 12
Adapter cards, 32, 51
Adaptive frequency hopping spread spectrum (AFHSS), 331
Add Printer icon, 623
Add Printer Wizard, 622
Add/Remove Hardware, 575
Add/Remove Programs, 575
Add/Remove Programs wizard, 625
Add/Remove Windows Component, 576
Address Resolution Protocol (ARP) command, 818
Addresses, 189
Administrative Password, 346
Administrative rights, 628
Administrative Tools, 576, 587
Administrator account, 650, 788
Administrators group, 598
ADSL terminal unit (ATU), 366
Advanced BIOS Features, 158, 162
Advanced Boot Options Menu, 520
Advanced Chipset Features Setup, 158
Advanced configuration and power interface (ACPI), 494
Advanced Micro Devices (AMD), 132
Advanced Options Menu, 776
Advanced Power Management (APM), 493
Advanced technology (AT) bus, 50
Advanced technology extended (ATX), 39
Advanced technology PC (PC-AT), 24
Advanced Television Systems Committee (ASTC), 237
Adware, 854
Alcohol, 862
Allocation units, 532
Alternate clicking, 563
AMD dual-core Opteron processors, 137
AMD64, 133
America Online (AOL), 353
American Micro Devices (AMD), 43
Ampere-hour rating, 872
Analog telephone adapter (ATA), 380
Anonymous authentication, 384
Answer files, 601
Answer the phone, 15
Antispyware, 853
Antistatic bags, 878
Antistatic foam, 878
Antistatic mats, 666, 879
Antistatic protection, 666

Antistatic solution, 856
Antistatic spray, 856
Antivirus, 860
Apple Macintosh, 78
Apple OS X, 78
Appletalk, 334
Applets, 388
Application Installer, 626
Application key, 479
Application programming interface (API), 122, 523
Application Properties, 791
Application-specific integrated circuits (ASICs), 47
Archive, 547
ARPA, 342
Ask permission, 14
Aspect ratio, 237
ASR backups, 786
ASR restore, 786
Assembler, 82
Assembly language, 82
Associated, 541
Associating, 728
Asymmetric DSL (ADSL), 368, 369
Asymmetrical digital subscriber line (ADSL), 648
Asymmetrical multiprocessing (AMP), 580
Asynchronous SRAM, 151
AT attachment (ATA), 281, 282
AT attachment packet interface (ATAPI), 283
AT command set, 718
AT&Dn, 721
ATA PIO modes, 283
ATA-2, 283
ATAPI (AT attachment packet interface), 111
ATDT*70, 721
Athlon, 132
Athlon 64, 133, 134
Athlon 64 FX, 134
Athlon 64 X2 Dual-Core, 134
ATL2, 721
Attachment unit interface (AUI), 325
Attended installations, 600
Attenuation, 320
ATTRIB, 547
Attribute list, 536
Attributes, 533
ATX form factor, 39, 90
ATX specification, 90
ATZ, 720
Audio connection methods, 208
Audio modem riser (AMR), 50, 108
Audit entries, 841
Audit policy, 841
Authenticating, 351, 728
Authentication, 627, 838
Authentication process, 627
Authentication protocols, 638
Authorized recovery agent, 844

Auto Answer (AA), 723
Auto Configuration, 159, 163
Auto Configure with BIOS Defaults, 159
Auto Configure with Power-On Defaults, 159
Auto Detect, 161
Auto mode, 164
Auto Restart, 789
Autodetect, 108, 263
Autodetect option, 701
Autodetection, 293
Automated System Recovery (ASR), 785
Autopublish, 644
Autorun feature, 791

B

B channels, 365
Baby AT form factor, 90
Back plane, 27
Back side bus (BSB), 98
Backbone, 352
Back-door, 849
Background, 562
Backlight, 477
Backlighting, 477
Backslashes (), 539
Backup, 860
Backup and Restore, 741
Backup copies, 61
Backup media rotation, 749
Backup utility, 744
Backup Wizard, 744
Balanced technology extended (BTX), 39
Bandwidth, 158, 320
Banias, 469
Bank-0, 174
Bank-1, 174
Bar code scanners, 227
BASIC, 82
Basic disks, 597
Basic input/output system (BIOS), 45, 70
Basic rate interface (BRI), 365
Batch mode, 514
B-cable, 288
Be precise, 15
Beam detector sensor, 418
Bearer, 365
Beep code, 670
BERG connectors, 48
Bindings, 638
Biometric authentication, 831
BIOS ACPI error, 494
BIOS extension, 516
BIOS parameter block, 535
BIOS-based virus scanner, 769

Bit-mapped fonts, 399
Bit-mapped images, 81
Black, 442
Black page, 450
Blue Book, 59
Blue screen error, 768
Blue Screen of Death (BSOD), 768
Bluetooth, 227, 331
Body language, 8
Bold, 399
Boot disk, 771
Boot files, 76
Boot Logging, 775
Boot ROM, 342
Boot sector, 518
BOOT.INI, 520, 774
Bootable disk, 518
Booting up, 72
BOOTSECT.DOS, 520
Boot-sector virus, 849
Boot-sector virus protection, 851
Bootstrap, 515
Bootstrap loader, 515
Bootstrapping, 515
Bootup, 517
Bottleneck, 794, 809
Box-within-a-box, 859
Brightness, 442
Broadband, 370
Broadband ISDN (BISDN), 365
Broadband phones, 380
Broadband wireless Internet, 375
Brownouts, 870
Browsers, 386
BTX, 93
BTX form factor, 39
BTX thermal module, 143
Buffer overflow attack, 128
Buffer underrun, 705
Built-in self-test, 434
Bulk data transfers, 204
Bulletin board service (BBS), 351
Burn-in period, 665
Burst-mode SRAM, 151
Bus, 316
Bus enumerating, 204
Bus speed, 98
Bus topology, 316

C

C8000, 516
C8800, 516
Cable, 360
Cable modems, 370, 648

Cable Select, 701
Cable TV (CATV), 370
Cabling, 441
Cache memory, 40, 45
Caching, 154
Call processor, 381
Call waiting, 363
Caller ID, 363
Carbon copies, 397
Card operating system (COS), 829
Carriage motor/timing belt , 401
Carriage position sensor, 403
Carrier Detect (CD), 723
Carrier sense multiple-access with collision detection
    (CSMA/CD), 335
Cartridge processors, 41
Case-closed switch, 499
CAT, 321
CAT 5, 322
CAT 5e, 322
CAT6, 322
Catch hazards, 876
Category (CAT) ratings, 321
Cathode-ray tube (CRT), 66, 231
CD input, 303
CD-based, 601
CDFS (Compact Disk File System), 537
CDMA (code division multiple access), 329
CD-R/W, 59
CD-recordable (CD-R), 274
CD-ROM drives, 273
CD-ROM/DVD drive, 56
CD-ROMs, 59
CD-RW disc, 274
Celeron, 122
Celeron M, 470
Celeron Mendocino, 122
Cells, 329
Cellular, 375
Cellular foam swabs, 862
Centrino, 350, 469
Centronics connector, 212
Centronics parallel port, 423
Centronics standard, 212
Certificate authority (CA), 351, 385
Chamber of Commerce, 882
Character cells, 398
Character generators, 403
Character pitch, 435
Character printer, 63, 69, 395
Characters per inch (cpi), 401
Chassis ground, 881
CHDIR (CD), 544
Check system compatibility, 613
Checksum, 516
Checkupgradeonly, 606
Chemically reactive paper, 397

Chip, 43
Chip creep, 880
Chipsets, 47, 97
CHKDSK, 307, 860
CHKDSK (Check Disk), 738
CHKDSK/f, 868
Chrominance, 209
Cinematic video, 238
Cipher, 596
Class A addresses, 355
Class B addresses, 356
Class C addresses, 356
Class-C fire extinguisher , 667, 877
Clean room, 860
Cleaning pad, 417
Cleaning substances, 882
Client/server network, 332, 556
Clients, 348, 556, 638
Clock multiplier, 98
Clone processors, 43
Cluster links, 532
Clusters, 532
CMD (or COMMAND) , 540
CMD.EXE, 778
CMOS RAM, 48, 75
CMOS Setup utility, 75
CMOS virus, 849
CMYK color, 408, 442
Coaxial cable, 324
Code section, 535
Coder/decoder (codec), 109
Cold boot, 72
Collation, 442
Collators, 447
Color component, 229
Color CRT monitor, 66
Color laser printers, 417
Color management, 430-431
Color scanners, 225
Color space conversion, 230
Color Super-Twist Nematic (CSTN), 477
Column address strobe (CAS), 156
Command line, 518
Command Prompt, 540
Command-line interpreter, 514
Command-line shortcuts, 547
Common courtesy, 8
Common-sense practices, 858
Communicate clearly, 9
Communications and networking riser (CNR), 50, 109
Communications software, 722
Compact disc (CD), 58
Compact disk file system, 537
Compact Disk File System (CDFS), 537
Compact Flash (CF), 278
Compact form factor (CFX), 93
Compatibility, 71

Compatibility Report, 613
Compilers, 81
Complementary-symmetry metal oxide semiconductor (CMOS), 878
Complete, 6
Component Video, 208
Composite TV, 229
Composite video, 67, 208
Compressed air, 866
Compressed files, 596
Compression rollers, 416
Computer, 441, 600
Computer Accounts, 627
Computer Management applet, 587
Computer Management Console, 576
Computer system, 441
Computer viruses, 848
Computer worms, 850
Computer-aided instruction (CAI), 83
Computer-based instruction (CBI), 83
Computer-to-computer VoIP, 381
Conditions, 415
Conductive-plastic tubes, 878
Configuration settings, 47
Configure the computer, 448
Configure the printer, 448
Configure the software, 448
Connection concentrators, 338
Continuity test, 663
Continuous forms, 401
Continuous-stream, 409
Contrast, 442
Contrast ratio, 477
Control board, 441
Control buttons, 30
Control panel, 429, 572, 574
Control Panel wizards, 528
Control transfers, 204
Controllers, 191
Convergence, 331
Coppermine, 123
Coppermine 128, 123
COPY, 546
Core Duo, 471
Core routers, 319
Core Solo, 472
Core speed, 98
Core voltage, 100
Corona wire, 416
Correspondence quality (CQ), 400
Counters, 806
CPU cooling block, 144
CPU cooling fan, 116
Cross talk, 287, 321
Cross-linked, 532
CRT display, 875
CSEL, 701

Current, 662
Customer education, 4
Customer satisfaction, 5
Customer satisfaction skills, 4
Customer service, 4
Cyan, 442
Cyclic redundancy check (CRC), 204
Cyl/Hds/Sec (CHS), 161
Cylinder, 254

D

D channel, 365
DAC (digital-to-analog converter), 233
Data disk, 518
Data Integrity, 164
Data migration, 834
Data packet, 203
Data remnants, 835
Data runs, 536
Data security, 650
Data Terminal Ready , 425
Data Transfer Rate, 307
Database management systems, 80
Databases, 80
DC, 664
DC operating voltages, 414
DC voltage function, 663
DDR2, 148
DDR-SDRAM, 148
DDS standards, 271
DEBUG, 82
Debugging Mode, 779
Decrypted, 596
De-escalate, 14
Default hive, 527
Default location, 541
Default settings, 159, 543
Default values, 160
Defrag, 860
DEFRAG, 307, 740
Defragmentation, 740
Defragmenter utility, 740
Degaussing, 697
DEL, 546
Demand priority, 339
Denatured alcohol, 866
Denial of service (DoS) attacks, 854
Desktop, 562
Desktop cases, 26
Desktop organizers, 81
Destination, 600
Detection phase, 104
Developer roller, 415
Developer unit, 417

Developing roller, 416
Device driver, 194, 222, 284
Device Manager, 579, 754
DHCP Server, 346, 813
Diagnostic Startup, 757
Diagonals, 661
Dialing rules, 647
Dial-up connections, 359
Dial-up networking (DUP), 361, 646
Die, 125
Differential, 289
Differential backup, 743
Digital audiotape (DAT), 271
Digital cameras, 242
Digital certificates, 838
Digital data storage (DDS), 271
Digital linear tape (DLT), 271
Digital loop carrier (DLC), 370
Digital modem, 359
Digital rights management (DRM), 280
Digital subscriber line (DSL), 359, 366
Digital versatile disc, 60
Digital video disc, 60
Digital Video Interface (DVI), 209
Digital video recorders (DVRs), 263
Digital visual interface (DVI), 67, 234
DIR, 544
Direct connect architecture, 134
Direct memory access (DMA), 196
Direct Rambus DRAM (DRDRAM), 150
Direct sequence spread spectrum (DSSS), 329
Direct thermal printers, 407
Direction, 259
Directories, 539
Directory tree, 534
Directory-based operations, 544
DirectX, 706
Disk Boot Failure, 700
Disk cloning, 601
Disk Defragmenter, 577
Disk drives, 33, 539
Disk image, 601, 602
Disk Management, 302, 577, 597
Disk Management snap-in , 598
Disk operating system (DOS), 70, 76
Disk quotas, 537
Distribution server, 600
Distributions, 78
DMA, 193
DMA channel allocations, 197
DMA controller, 196
DMA request (DRQ), 196
DMMs (digital multimeters), 662
DNS client, 358
DNS database, 358
DNS name server, 358
DNS server, 358

Docking port, 496
Docking station, 496
DOCSIS (data over cable service interface specification), 371
Domain, 556
Domain accounts, 837
Domain controller, 557, 627
Domain name, 357
Domain name service (DNS), 378, 627
Domain name system (DNS), 357
Domain user and group accounts, 837
Domains, 357
Dot pitch, 236
Dothan, 469
Dot-matrix, 396
Dot-matrix characters, 398
Dot-pitches, 401
Dotted decimal notation, 355
Double data rate (DDR), 158
Double transition (DT) clocking, 288
Double-layer Super-Twist Nematic (DSTN), 477
Double-sided , 685
Double-Sided, High-Density (DS-HD), 62
Downlinked, 373
Download Center, 765
Downloadable type fonts, 403
Downloaded, 45
Downstream rate, 368
Doze, 166
Draft mode, 400
Draft quality, 396
DRAM tests, 516
Drive array, 265
Drive C:, 542
Drive Mismatch Error, 701
Drive-level operations, 543
Driver Rollback, 758
Driver Signing, 619
Drop site, 882
Drum, 413
Drum assembly, 416
Drum unit, 417
Drwtsn32, 760
DRWTSN32.LOG, 760
D-shell connector, 67
DSL modem, 366
Dual boot, 531
Dual in-line memory module (DIMM), 46, 174
Dual scan, 477
Dual-channel, double data rate 2 (DDR2), 158
Dual-core Pentium chipsets, 131
Dual-core processors, 125
Dumpster divers, 834
Duplexers, 447
Duron, 134
Dusting, 858, 862
DVD, 60

DVD drives, 275
DVD Recordable (DVD+R), 276
DVD Recordable (DVD-R), 276
DVD Rewritable (DVD+RW), 276
DVD Rewritable (DVD-RW), 276
DVD-RAM, 60, 276
DVD-ROM, 60
Dye sublimation printer, 419
Dynamic disks, 597
Dynamic host configuration protocol (DHCP), 379
Dynamic IP addressing, 378
Dynamic RAM (DRAM), 146
Dynamic Volume Management, 597
Dynamic volumes, 597

E

Earth ground, 880
Earthlink, 353
EDDR-SDRAM, 148
Edge connector, 52
Edge router, 319
EDIT.COM, 759
Efficient, 6
EIA/TIA-568, 321
Electrical contact cleaner, 856
Electromagnetic field interference (EFI), 34, 213
Electromagnetic interference (EMI), 877
Electron gun, 231
Electronic Industry Association (EIA), 215
Electronic mail (e-mail), 384
Electrophotographic cartridge, 416
Electrostatic discharge (ESD), 175, 293, 877
EM64T, 128
Emergency Repair Disk (ERD), 700, 772
Emergency repair process, 784
Enable Boot Logging, 778
Enable VGA Mode, 778
Encrypted file system (EFS), 537, 596
Encrypted files, 596
Encrypting, 351
Encrypting file system (EFS), 844
Encryption key, 844
End-of-paper sensor, 403
Enhanced cylinder, heads, sectors (ECHS), 302
Enhanced DRAM (EDRAM), 147
Enhanced IDE (EIDE), 111, 283
Enhanced Metafile (EMF) Spooling, 810
Enhanced parallel port (EPP), 213
Enhanced-Definition TV (EDTV), 238
Enterprise networks, 557
Entry-level power supply (EPS), 36
EPS, 37
ERASE, 546
Ergonomics, 462

Error checking and correcting (ECC), 153, 164
Error detection, 152
Error message, 670
Error-detection and correction algorithm, 266
Error-detection and correction functions, 266
eSATA, 113
ESD (electrostatic discharge), 878
ESDRAM, 148
Ethernet, 335
Even parity, 152
Event, 807
Event Log full, 794
Event Viewer, 751
Exam Map, xi
Exam Tip, xi
Execute-in-place mode, 484
Expansion bus specifications, 109
Expansion slot, 31, 49
Expansion slot connectors, 33
Explicitly parallel instruction computing (EPIC), 124
Extended capabilities port (ECP), 166, 213
Extended data out (EDO), 150
Extended graphics array, 235
Extended parallel port (EPP), 166
Extended partition, 301, 529
Extended system configuration data (ESCD), 74
Extended technology (XT), 24
Extensible authentication protocol (EAP), 351
Extension, 540
External modem, 363
External SATA, 113
Extranet, 557

F

Faint print, 451
Fan heat sink (FHS), 121
Fast ATA (fast AT attachment), 111
Fast Ethernet, 338
Fast SCSI-2, 287
FAT partitions, 531
FAT table virus, 849
FAT virus, 849
FATs (file allocation tables), 531
FC, 547
Federal Communications Commission (FCC), 34
Feedback, 4
Fiber distributed data interface (FDDI), 340
Fidelity, 240
Field, 232
Field-replaceable units (FRUs), 675
File allocation tables (FATs), 303, 519, 531
File infector, 849
File management files, 76
File menu, 568

File server, 332
File transfer protocol (FTP), 383, 384
File://, 383
Filename, 540, 545
Files, 539
Filter commands, 548
Find, 548
Fingerprint scanner, 832
Fire buttons, 216
Firewall, 356, 361, 557
Firewire, 205
Firewire bus, 197
Firmware, 25, 45
First in/first out (FIFO) buffering, 165
First-aid kit, 667, 877
FIXMBR, 774
Flash, 178
Flash drives, 278
Flash memory, 276
Flash ROM, 45
Flat memory model, 524
Flat workspace, 666
Flatbed scanner, 225
Flexible, 12
Flicker, 233
Flip chip, 140
Flip chip LGA775, 140
Flip chip pin grid array (FC-PGA), 123, 140
Floppy connector, 37
Floppy disk drives troubleshooting, 708
Floppy-disk controller (FDC), 268
Floppy-disk drive controller (FDC), 110
Flow control, 426
Flow control/expansion device, 145
Fn, 478
Folder, 563
Font, 399
Forced Perfect Termination (FPT), 299
Foreground, 562
Forest, 628
Form factor, 38, 96
Form feed (FF), 403
FORMAT, 543
Formatting, 255
Frame, 336
Free liquids, 882
Frequency hopping spread spectrum (FHSS), 329
Friction-feed, 401
Friction-feed paper handling, 407
Front side bus (FSB), 98
FTP, 818
Fuel cell, 492
Full Duplex, 321
Full-duplex communication, 340
Full-duplex mode, 362
Full-speed USB, 204
Fully formed, 396

Fully formed characters, 397
Fully qualified domain names (FQDN), 358, 815
Fuser unit, 417
Fusing area, 447
Fusing roller, 416
Fusing unit, 416

G

G.lite ADSL, 369
Game control port, 216
Game-port, 69
Gate A20, 162
Gateway, 360
Gear lash, 441
Gear train, 407
General support, 4
Gimbal, 221
Good communications, 6
Good lighting, 666
Good rapport, 13
Gopher://, 383
Grandfather-Father-Son, 749
Graphical processing unit (GPU), 612
Graphical user interface (GUI), 77, 514, 540
Graphics device interface (GDI), 428
Graphics programs, 81
Grayscale, 442
Grayscale scanners, 225
Grayware, 828, 848, 852
Green Book, 59
Green mode, 493
Ground, 880
Grounding straps, 879
Group accounts, 627, 837
Group Policy Objects (GPOs), 631
Groups, 650
Guest account, 788

H

HAL.DLL, 521
Half Duplex, 321
Half-duplex mode, 362
Halftone color, 442
Hand tools, 661
Handle, 104
Handshake packet, 203
Handshakes, 194
Hard-disk drive (HDD), 56-57
Hard-memory errors, 684
Hardware Abstraction Layer (HAL), 523
Hardware compatibility list (HCL), 599, 617, 768
Hardware handshaking, 426

Hardware hive, 521
Hardware ports, 31
Hardware profile, 521
Have Disk, 638
Have Disk button, 575
Hayes command set, 718
Hayes-compatible command set, 718
Hazardous substances, 882
HCL.TXT, 606
HDD format values, 263
HDD upgrading, 307
Head crash, 257
Head gap lever, 438
Header fields, 376
Head-locking lever, 438
Head-to-disk interference (HDI), 257
Health, 142
Health controller, 686
Heat sink, 41
Heat sink devices, 29
Heat spreader, 150
Heat-sensitive, 397
Help and Support Center, 783
Help file systems, 761
Help.com, 382
Helper, 800
Helper's Console, 802
Hexadecimal (hex), 192
Hibernate mode, 493
Hidden, 547
High Data Rate DSL (HDSL), 370
High Data Rate DSL (HDSL2), 370
High Speed (HS), 396, 723
High-data-rate DSL (HDSL), 368
High-definition multimedia interface (HDMI), 67, 234
High-definition television (HDTV), 207, 234, 238
High-level format, 300
High-voltage DC supply, 414
High-Voltage Differential (HVD), 290
Hit, 154
Hives, 527
Home position, 439
Home position sensor, 403, 445
Horizontal (HSYNC), 233
Horizontal retrace, 232
Host bridge, 102
Host computer, 434, 441
Host name, 358
Hot insertion, 484
Hot swappable, 276
Hot swapping, 65
Hotspot, 348, 375
Hot-swap, 204
HTTP, 382
Hub, 317-318
HyperTerminal, 717
Hypertext links, 386

Hypertext markup language (HTML), 386
Hypertext transfer protocol (HTTP), 382
Hypertext transfer protocol secure (HTTPS), 383
Hyperthreading, 126, 131
Hyperthreading technology (HTT), 124
Hypertransport (HT), 133
Hypertransport controller, 135

I

I/O, 41
I/O devices, 49
I/O port addresses, 190
I/O unit, 188
IC cooler fans, 29
ICC profiles, 431
Icons, 77, 562, 563
IEEE (Institute of Electrical and Electronic Engineers), 205
IEEE-1284, 424
IEEE-1384 Firewire, 54
IEEE-1394, 197, 205
IEEE-1394 Firewire adapters, 54
IEEE-802.15.1, 331
IEEE-802.3 Ethernet protocol, 335
IEEE-803, 339
Impact, 396
Implosion, 697
Incidence reporting policy, 855
Incompatible Version error, 770
Incremental backup, 742
Indexing Service, 573
Indicator lights, 30
Indoor receive unit (IRU), 374
Indoor transmit unit (ITU), 374
Industry Standard Architecture (ISA), 24, 50
Infrared (IR), 68, 221
Infrared Data Association (IrDA), 206
Infrared data association (IrDA) ports, 166, 197
Infrared Monitor, 246
Infrastructure mode, 729
Initial program load (IPL), 517
Initialization, 71
Ink cartridge, 444
Ink-jet printers, 397, 409
Input devices, 25, 218
Input systems, 63, 217
Input/output (I/O), 25
Installable file system (IFS), 528
Installing, 245
Instruction Set, 133
Insulation displacement connector (IDC), 323
Integrated circuit (IC), 46
Integrated drive electronics (IDE), 110, 281
Integrated Peripherals, 159, 165
Integrated service digital network (ISDN), 359

Integrated Services Digital Network DSL (ISDL), 370
Integrated video controller, 53
Integrity, 13
Intel, 42
Intel dual-core processors, 126
Intel Pentium microprocessors, 131
Interactive mode, 514
Interface, 441
Interface adapter cards, 49
Interface cable, 441, 447
Interface circuitry, 188
Interface/controller, 402
Interlaced displays, 237
Interlaced scanning, 232
Interleaving, 156
Interlock switch, 418
Internal fuses, 449
Internal modem, 363
Internal Modem cards, 54
International Color Consortium (ICC), 430
International Electrical and Electronic Association (IEEE), 335
Internet, 352
Internet Assigned Numbers Authority (IANA), 843
Internet Connection Firewall (ICF), 638, 842
Internet connection sharing (ICS), 360, 649
Internet Connection Wizard, 647
Internet Control Message Packets (ICMP), 819
Internet Engineering Task Force (IETF), 379
Internet gateways, 319
Internet printing protocol (IPP), 622
Internet radio, 595
internetwork packet exchange/sequenced packet exchange (IPX/SPX), 334, 342
Interpreters, 81
Interrupt request (IRQ), 194
Interrupt service routine, 194
Interrupt transfers, 204
Interrupt-driven I/O, 193
Interrupted-stream (drop-on-demand), 409
Intranets, 356, 557
Invalid Drive , 700
Invalid Drive Specification, 700
Invalid Media Type, 701
Invalid Partition Table errors, 774
Inverter, 499
Invitations, 800
IO channel check (IOCHCK), 195
IP addresses, 355
IP addressing, 378
IP header, 376
IP phones, 380
IP security protocol (IPSec), 839
IP telephony, 380
IPCONFIG/ALL, 813
IrDA, 328
IrDA LAN protocol, 207

IrLPT, 422
Isochronous transfers, 204
Italic, 399
Itanium, 124

J

Java, 388
Joysticks, 69
Jumper blocks, 48

K

Katmai, 122
Keep an inventory, 16
Kerberos, 838
Kernel, 520
Kernel file, 521
Kernel mode, 522
Key Distribution Center (KDC), 838
Keyboard, 63
Keyboard controller, 219
Keyboard encoder, 219
Kiosks, 223
Knowledge bases, 434
Known-good ones, 675

L

L1 cache, 155
L2 Burst SRAM, 121
L2 cache, 155
L3 cache, 125, 155
LAN switches, 319
Land grid array (LGA) 775, 127
Lands, 273
Landscape printing, 442
Lane, 105
Laptops, 462
Laser printer, 412
Laser printer sensors, 417
Laser/scanning module, 449
Last Known Good Configuration, 528, 779
Layer 2 tunneling protocol (L2TP), 839
LCD panel, 499
Legacy cards, 53
Legacy devices, 198
Legacy ports, 211
Letter boxing, 237
Letter quality (LQ), 396, 400
Lightweight directory access protocol (LDAP), 627
Limitations of Ethernet, 336
Line feed (LF), 403

Line In, 241
Link, 106, 352
Lint-free cloths, 862
Lint-free swab, 862
Linux, 78
Liquid crystal display (LCD), 66, 231, 476
LISTSVC, 775
Lithium-ion (Li-ion), 492
Lithium-ion polymer, 492
Local analog loopback test, 721
Local area network (LAN), 54, 64 315
Local buses, 101
Local computer , 421
Local digital loopback test, 721
Local Digital Loopback Test with Self Tests, 722
Local regulations, 882
Lock, 847
Lock up, 754
Lockout time, 780
Logical block addressing (LBA), 161, 302
Logical cluster numbers (LCNs), 537
Logical drives, 56, 300, 301, 529, 577
Logical topology, 317
Log-on passwords, 726
Log-on problem, 788
Loopback plug, 721
Loopback test plug, 711
Low Definition TV (LDTV) , 238
Low Frequency Effect (LFE), 241
Low humidity, 877
Low noise block (LNB), 374
Low speed, 396
Low-level format, 300, 303, 834
Low-profile, 95
Low-profile desktops, 27
Low-profile extended (LPX), 95
Low-profile form factor (LFX), 93
Low-speed USB, 204
Low-Voltage Differential (LVD), 290
LPX, 40
Luggables, 461
Luminance, 208, 229

M

Macintosh (Mac), 24
Macro virus, 849
Magenta, 442
Mailto:, 383
Maintenance mode, 446
MAKEBT32.EXE, 772
Malware, 828, 848
Manchester core, 135
Mapping, 530
Marketing, 4

Maskable interrupts (IRQs), 194
Mass storage, 45
Master, 282, 294
Master boot record (MBR), 72, 301, 517
Master boot sector, 301
Master device, 331
Master file table (MFT), 303, 535
Material Safety Data Sheets (MSDS), 883
MDI (media dependent interface), 345
Mean time between failures (MTBF), 855
Mechanical vibration, 409
Media access control (MAC) address, 318
Media Center Extenders, 561
Media centers, 207
Media rotation, 749
Media servers, 92
Medium attachment unit (MAU), 325
Memory card reader/writer, 31
Memory Stick, 279
Memory Stick Duo, 279
Memory Stick Micro (M2), 279
Memory Stick Pro, 279
Memory Stick Pro Duo, 279
Memory systems, 63, 217
Menu bars, 567
Mesh, 316
Mesh design, 317
Metal oxide semiconductor (MOS), 878
Metropolitan area networks (MANs), 352
Mezzanine bus, 102
MIC, 724
Micro BTX, 93
Micro FCBGA, 469
Micro FCPGA, 469
MicroATX, 95
Microcontroller, 403
MicroDIMM, 473
Microdrive cards, 279
Microkernel, 523
Microprocessor, 40, 99
Microprocessor characteristics, 138
Microprocessor upgrade paths, 176
MicroSD, 280
Microsoft Cluster Server (MSCS), 560
Microsoft Disk Operating System, 25
Microsoft Download Service (MSDL), 695
Microsoft Knowledge Base, 765
Microsoft Management Consoles (MMCs), 576, 751
Mid towers, 28
MIDI, 166
MIDI cable connections, 210
MIDI Machine Control (MMC), 209
MIDX (media independent interface crossover), 345
Mini Centronic, 212
Mini PCI, 487
Mini towers, 28
MiniATX, 95

Minifile, 520
MiniSD, 280
Mirrored drive array, 265
Miss, 154
Missing Beam, 449
Missing Operating System, 774
Missing print, 451
MKDIR (MD), 544
Mnemonics, 82
Mobile daughter card (MDC), 108
Mobile module (MMO), 467
Mobile Pentium processors, 466
Mobile Voltage Positioning (MVP IV), 469
Modem, 361
Modem Ready (MR), 723
Monofilament wires, 866
More, 548
Motherboard, 33
Mouse, 63, 67, 220
Multi Media Card (MMC), 280
Multimeter, 662
Multimode, 290
Multimode fiber-optic cable, 327
Multimode LVD, 299
Multipath, 330, 348
Multiple-process systems, 514
Multiprocessor, 514
Multitasking, 514
Multiuser, 514
Musical instrument digital interface (MIDI), 209
My Computer, 564
My Document, 572
My Documents, 565
My Network Places, 566
My Pictures, 594
My TV, 590
My Videos, 595

N

Name resolution, 378
NanoBTX, 92
Narrow SCSI, 286
National Center for Supercomputing Applications, 386
National Science Foundation (NSF), 352
National Television Standards Committee (NTSC), 232
Native resolution, 478
Near-letter quality (NLQ), 396, 400
Needle-nose pliers, 661
Negative electrical charge, 413
NET VIEW, 813
NetBIOS enhanced user interface (NetBEUI), 333
NETSTAT, 818
Network access point (NAP), 354
Network adapter card, 341

Network address translation, 839
Network administrator, 726, 835
Network and Dial-up Connections, 636
Network architectures, 334
Network Basic Input/Output System (NetBIOS), 642
Network bridge, 319
Network drop cabling, 725
Network file service (NFS), 635
Network Identification, 638
Network interface adapter, 318
Network interface card (NIC), 64, 341
Network Load Balancing (NLB), 560
Network log-on, 839
Network operating systems (NOS), 77
Network packets, 376
Network printers, 421
Network protocol, 333
Network share, 566
Network switch, 319
Networked printers, 644
Network-ready printers, 421
New low-profile extended (NLX), 95
News:, 383
Nickel cadmium (Ni-Cad), 492
Nickel metal-hydride (NiMH), 492
NLX, 40
NLX form factor, 39
Nodes, 316
No-execute (NE), 133
Noise immunity, 201, 320
Nonhazardous, subtitle D dumpsites, 882
Nonimpact, 396
Noninterlaced scanning, 232
Nonmaskable interrupt (NMI), 153, 194-195
Nonresident attributes, 536
Nonvolatile, 45
Normal, 399
North bridge, 97
Not moving paper, 447
Not printing, 447
Not printing correctly, 447
Notebook computer, 32, 462
Notification area, 571
Novell NetWare, 78, 642
NT Loader, 520
NT Server, 555
NT Workstation , 555
NTDETECT failed, 774
NTDETECT.COM, 520, 774
NTFS (NT File System), 537
NTFS compression, 596
NTFS partitions, 531
NTFS permissions, 538, 634, 796
NTFS5, 537
NTLDR, 520, 535
NTLDR files, 774
NTLDR is missing, 774

NTOSKRNL.EXE, 521
Ntuser.dat, 630
Null modem, 216
NWLink, 639

O

Odd parity, 152
OEM drivers, 769
OEM patches, 605
Off-Hook (OH), 723
OK code, 720
On/off line, 403
Onboard RAM, 403
Onboard ROM, 403
Online Help, 764
Open systems interconnection (OSI), 334
Open With, 626
Operating system boot record, 518
Operating system loader, 518
Operating system release, 604
Operating systems, 76
Operational problems, 788
Operator control panel, 404
Opteron, 137
Optical drives, 860
Optical mouse, 221
Optical time domain reflectometers (OTDRs), 730
Optional components, 625
Orange Book, 59
Organizational units (OUs), 630
OS Choices Boot Options, 776
Out-of-phase, 872
Output devices, 25, 453
Output systems, 63, 217
Overclocking, 100
OverDrive, 139
Oxidation, 856

P

P54Cs, 116
P55Cs, 118
Packet ID (PID), 204
Page description languages (PDLs), 428
Page orientation, 442
PAGEFILE.SYS, 525
Page-mode RAM, 156
Pages, 156
Paging, 156
Palmtop computers, 462
Palmtop PCs, 462
Paper feed motor, 407
Paper feed selector lever, 441

Paper handling mechanism, 401
Paper jams, 447
Paper size, 442
Paper transport mechanics, 417
Paper trays, 452
Paper weight, 419
Paper-Out error, 452
Parallax errors, 224
Parallel advanced technology attachment (PATA), 110
Parallel ATA (PATA), 41
Parallel mode, 189
Parallel printer, 423
Parallel printer ports, 212
Parallel printers, 69
Parallel processing, 514
Parity check (PCK) error, 195
Parity checking, 152, 162
Partition, 300
Partition boot record, 301
Partition boot sector, 519, 535
Partition loader, 518
Partition table, 301, 518, 530
Partitioning, 300, 529
Pass code, 829
Passive heat sinks, 142
Passive matrix, 477
Passive Termination, 299
Password Maintenance Services, 159
Password policy, 840
Passwords, 167, 650
PATA, 281
Path, 539
Patronizing, 10
PC Card, 483
PC clones, 25
PC Health Status, 159
PC look-alikes, 25
P-cable, 288
PC-based PVR, 263
PC-compatibles, 25
PCI bus, 99
PCI express (PCIe), 37, 50, 105
PCI extended (PCI-X), 50
PCI IRQ Map-to, 164
PCIe switch, 107
PCI-to-ISA bridge, 102
PCI-to-PCIe bridge, 107
PCMCIA Type I, 484
PCMCIA Type II, 484
PCMCIA Type III, 484
Peer-to-peer network, 332
PELs, 232
Pen drives, 278
Pentium, 43, 114, 115
Pentium 4, 124
Pentium 4 Extreme Editions , 124
Pentium CPUs, 42, 99

Pentium D, 126
Pentium Extreme Edition (EE), 126
Pentium II, 121
Pentium II CPUs, 42
Pentium III, 122
Pentium M, 468
Pentium MMX (Multimedia Extension), 118
Pentium Pro, 119
Pentium Pro CPUs, 42
Pentium Xeon, 123
Performance counters, 794
Performance Logs and Alerts, 807
Periodic cleaning, 858
Peripheral component interconnect (PCI), 50 101
Peripheral device, 188
Peripheral power connector, 37
Peripherals, 63
Permission levels, 795
Persistence, 232
Personal area networks (PANs), 331
Personal computer (PC), 24
Personal Computer Memory Card International
    Association's (PCMCIA) , 483
Personal digital assistants (PDAs), 462
Personal identification number (PIN), 829
Personal productivity programs, 81
Personal service, 4
Personal video recorders (PVRs), 263
Phone support, 15
Phone tag, 15
Physical topologies, 317
Pickup, 453
Pickup area, 447
Pickup roller, 452
PicoBTX, 92
Piconet, 331
Picture element, 476
Pin #1 indicator stripe, 285
Pin grid array (PGA), 43
Pin-1 notch, 44, 172
Pin-feed, 401
PING, 818, 819
PING utility, 812
Pipe symbol (|), 548
Pipeline SRAM, 151
Pipelining, 116
Pitch, 398
Pits, 273
Pixel, 81, 232, 235, 476
Placing a call, 15
Plain old telephone system (POTS), 360
Plasma flat panel displays, 66
Plastic pin grid array (PPGA), 122, 140
Platen assembly, 407
Plenum, 328
Plenum rated cables, 328
Plug and Play (PnP), 48, 72, 74, 516

PnP manager, 523
PnP registry, 104
PnP/PCI Configuration, 159
Point, 399
Point of sale (POS), 223
Pointing devices, 67, 220
Pointing stick, 482
Point-to-point protocol (PPP), 207, 378
Point-to-point protocol over Ethernet (PPoE), 373
Point-to-point tunneling protocol (PPTP), 839
Polarizer, 476
Polarizing films, 828
Politeness, 6
Polling, 193
Polygonal mirror, 413
POP3, 384
Port connector, 188
Port replicators, 497
Portable PCs, 32
Portrait printing, 442
POST, 71
POST cards, 666
Postscript, 428
POTS (plain old telephone system), 368
POTS splitter, 366
Power cord, 449
Power line filters, 870
Power Management, 166
Power Management Setup, 159
Power manager, 523
Power outlet, 449
Power supply, 35
Power variations, 869
Power-on self-tests, 71
Precharge, 156
Preshared keys, 351
Preventive maintenance (PM), 855
Primary bootstrap loader, 518
Primary corona, 450
Primary corona wire, 415
Primary memory, 45
Primary partition, 301, 529
Primary rate interface (PRI), 365
Print Pooling, 795
Print quality, 442
Print server, 795, 814
Print server port, 421
Print sharing, 421
Print spooler, 424, 620
Print Troubleshooter, 712
Printer, 434, 441
Printer control language (PCL), 429
Printer drivers, 427
Printer FRU modules, 431
Printer initialization programs, 403
Printer Not Ready, 424
Printer Port, 623

Printer sharing, 814
Printer's configuration, 441
Printhead, 406
Printhead carriage, 400
Printhead carriage assembly, 406
Printhead positioning motor, 406
Private FTP sites, 384
Private key, 844
Private network, 356
Processing system, 25
Processor core, 120
Product, 5
Product Support Services, 765
Professional, 6
Profile, 630, 650
Program guide, 592
Programmed I/O (PIO), 193, 283), 293
Programmed input/output (PIO), 165
Progressive displays, 237
Promptness, 6
Properties, 563
Properties dialog box, 574
Protective ground, 881
Protocol, 316
Protocol stack, 377
Protocols, 638
Proxy server, 361, 845
PS/2 connector, 200
Pseudo-standards, 24
Public FTP sites, 384
Public key, 844

Q

Q-cable, 288
Quad Word, 115
Quad-pumped bus, 124
Quarter inch cartridge (QIC), 270
Query, 358
Qword, 115

R

Radio frequency interference (RFI), 861
RAID, 265
RAID 0, 265
RAID 1, 266
RAID 10, 267
RAID 2, 266
RAID 3, 267
RAID 4, 267
RAID 5, 267
RAID 53, 267
RAID 6, 267

RAID Advisory Board, 265
Rambus, 150
Rambus DRAM (RDRAM), 150
Rambus Inline Memory Modules, 150
Random access memory (RAM), 40, 45
Raster line, 232
Rate Adaptive DSL (RADSL), 369
RCA mini jacks, 240
Read only memory (ROM), 40, 45
Read operation, 261
Read/write (R/W), 57
Read/Write (R/W) head, 256
Read-only, 547
Real time clock (RTC), 48
Received Data, 723
Recovery Console, 774, 779
Recycle Bin, 565
Recycling, 882
Red Book, 59
Redundant addressing, 189
Redundant arrays of inexpensive disks, 265
Reference computer, 601
Reference Shelf, x
Refreshed, 152
Refreshing, 152
RegEdit, 528, 759
RegEdt32, 759
Regedt32.exe, 528
Registered jack, 363
Registration, 414, 419
Registration area, 447
Registry, 520, 526
Relative intensities, 477
Remote Access Services (RAS), 646
Remote Assistance, 586, 796
Remote computers, 421
Remote Desktop, 796
Remote Desktop Connection Wizard, 587
Remote digital loopback test, 721
Remote Installation Preparation (RIPrep), 601
Remote Installation Services (RIS), 601
Removable hard drives, 860
Removable storage, 276
Removable Storage utility, 750
REN, 546
Research, 5
Reset, 72
Resident attributes, 536
Resistance, 662
Resolution, 53
Resource conflicts, 104, 516
Resource Kits, 764
Restore points, 782
Restricting blade, 415
Retention mechanism, 121
RG rating, 325
RGB monitor, 66

Ribbon cartridge, 437
Ribbon mask, 439
Right-clicking, 563
Rights, 628
Ring, 316
Ring Indicator (RI), 723
Ring signal, 723
Ring topologies, 317
RMDIR (RD), 544
Roaming profiles, 651
Roll back, 782
ROM BIOS, 70
Roman Gothic, 406
Root directory, 303, 531
Root hub, 203
Router IP Address, 346
Routers, 317
Row address strobe (RAS), 156
RS-232 communication (COM) ports, 213
RS-232C, 215
Run, 82
Run All Tests, 720

S

Safe Mode, 777
Safe Mode with Command Prompt, 778
Safe Mode with Network Support, 778
Sags, 870
SAM hive, 527
SATA connectors, 37
Satellite receiver, 374
Satellite services, 360
Saturation, 442
SC connector, 327
SCANDISK, 307
Scanners, 225
Scheduled Tasks, 761
Screen memory, 233
Screen saver, 582, 858
Screwdriver, 660
Scripting languages, 388
Scripts, 726, 845
SCSI adapters, 54
SCSI host adapter, 286
SCSI ID numbers, 298
SCSI-0, 298
SCSI-1, 286
SCSI-7, 298
SCSI-In, 298
SCSI-Out, 298
Scuzzy, 286
SDRAM types, 148
SDR-SDRAM, 147
Search, 572

Search engines, 387
SECC-2, 139
Secondary bootstrap loader, 518
Sectors, 58, 254
Secure Digital (SD), 280
Secure socket layer (SSL), 385
Security, 828
Security Accounts Manager (SAM), 627
Security descriptor, 536
Security hive, 527
Security log, 841
Security options, 167
Security.txt, 382
Selective backup, 743
Selective Startup, 757
Self-diagnostics, 669
Send Data (SD), 723
Sense of urgency, 11
Serial AT attachment (SATA), 110
Serial ATA (SATA), 37, 41, 281, 284
Serial Line Internet Protocol (SLIP), 378
Serial mode, 189
Serial printers, 69
Server, 556
Service, 5
Service or Driver Failed During Startup, 775
Service Pack, 605, 790, 803
Service set identifier (SSID), 349
Services, 638
SERVICES.MSC , 804
Setup Manager wizards, 601
SFC, 761
SGRAM, 148
Shadow mask, 232
Share permissions, 538
Shared video memory, 474
Shielded twisted pair (STP), 321
Shortcut, 563, 585
Signal cable, 67, 434, 441
Signal ground, 881
Simple mail transfer protocol (SMTP), 383, 384
Simplex, 320
Simplex mode, 362
Single beep, 672
Single connector attachment (SCA), 288
Single edge contact (SEC) cartridge, 121
Single edged processor package (SEPP), 122
Single-drive, 294
Single-ended (SE), 289
Single-mode fiber-optic cable, 327
Single-process systems, 514
Single-sheet forms, 401
Single-sided, 685
Single-speed (1X) drives, 59
Site survey, 348
Slave, 282, 294
Slave devices, 331

Sleep mode, 493
Slim line form factor, 95
Slot 1, 121, 139
Slot 2, 123, 139
Slot A, 132, 139
Small computer system interface (SCSI), 64, 281, 286
Small outline DIMM (SODIMMs), 472
Small scale integration (SSI), 47
Smart cards, 829
Smoke, 857
SMTP relay , 854
Smudged print, 451
Social engineering, 854
Socket 1, 139
Socket 3, 139
Socket 370, 122, 140
Socket 478, 140
Socket 5, 139
Socket 6, 139
Socket 8, 139
Socket services, 484
Socket specifications, 141
Socket-4, 139
Socket-7, 139
Sockets, 43, 172
Soft brush, 862
Soft skills, 5
Soft switch, 36, 381
Soft-memory errors, 684
Software, 70
Software backup, 860
Software diagnostic, 711
Software handle (name), 516
Software handshaking, 426
Software hive, 527
Solid ink-jet printers, 410
Sony/Philips Digital Interface Format (S/PDIF), 241
Sort, 548
Sound cards, 54, 239
South bridge, 97
Spam, 854
Spam blockers, 854
Spam filters, 854
Speaker, 724
Specks, 450
Spikes, 870
Spiral track, 274
Splitter-based DSL, 366
Splitter-less DSL, 366
Spread spectrum, 329
Spreadsheets, 80
Spyware, 852
SSE, 133
Stages, 116
Staggered pin grid array (SPGA), 116
Stains, 450
Standard CMOS Features, 158, 160

Standard information, 536
Standard parallel port (SPP), 166, 212
Standard transmission control protocol/Internet protocol (TCP/IP), 342
Standard-Definition TV (SDTV), 238
Standby, 166
Standby mode , 493
Standby power system, 871
Star, 316
Star topology, 317
Start button, 562, 563, 573
Start menu, 563, 571
Start-of-frame (SOF), 203
Static charges, 414
Static RAM (SRAM), 146
Static-column RAM, 156
Static-free carpeting, 880
Static-free vacuum, 857
Stations, 316
Step, 259
Straight tip (ST) connector, 327
Stylus, 501
Subdirectories, 539
Subfolders, 583
Subnets, 356
Subnotebook PCs, 462
Subtrees, 526
Super digital linear tape (SuperDLT), 272
Super VGA (SVGA), 235
Super XGA (SXGA), 235
Superscalar, 116
Supervisory passwords, 167
Supplier, 5
Surge suppressers, 870
Surges, 870
Suspend, 166
Suspend mode, 493
S-video, 67, 209, 229
Swap Floppy Drive, 162
Swapping files, 525
Switches, 317-318, 541
Symmetric DSL (SDSL), 368-369
Symmetric HDSL (SHDSL), 370
Symmetrical multiprocessing (SMP), 559, 580
Synchronization, 208
Synchronization Manager, 651
Synchronous DRAM (SDRAM), 147
Synchronous SRAM, 151
SYSEDIT.EXE, 759
Sysprep, 601
System, 547
System board, 33, 38
System Configuration Utility, 548
System Configuration Utility (MSCONFIG.EXE), 757
System disk, 518
System File Checker utility (SFC.EXE), 761
System hive, 521, 527

System icon, 581
System Information , 752
System interrupt levels, 195
System memory map, 190
System Monitor, 794, 806
System Policies, 630
System Restore, 782
System Restore wizard, 783
System software, 70
System State Data, 747
System State Data backup, 780
System Tools, 577, 587
System unit, 25
Systray, 571

T

T1 and T3 lines, 359
Tablet PCs, 375
Tag parts, 16
Tag RAM, 121
Tape Carrier Package (TCP), 466
Tape cartridges, 60
Tape drive units, 60
Tape drives, 269
Task Manager, 754
Taskbar, 563, 570
Tasks, 514
Task-switching, 562
TCP header, 376
TCP/IP network, 813
TechNet, 765
Technical support, 4
Telnet, 385
Telnet://, 383
Temperature cycling, 880
Temporary key integrity protocol (TKIP), 351
Terminal adapters (TAs), 365
Terminal Ready (TR), 723
Terminate and stay resident (TSR) viruses, 850
Terminated, 299, 702
Test image , 430
Thermal compound, 179
Thermal fuse, 418
Thermal module, 92
Thermal sensor, 418
Thermal shock, 409
Thermal wax transfer printer, 407-408
Thermocouple, 686
Thermotropic, 476
Thicknet, 325, 338
Thin film transistor (TFT), 477
Thinnet, 326, 338
Third-party refill cartridges, 867
Threads, 514

Threshold level, 721
Throughput, 158
Thumb drives, 278
Time division multiple access (TDMA), 329
Time division multiplexing (TDM), 329
Time domain reflectometry (TDR), 729
Timing belt, 406
Timing sensors, 439
Token packet, 203
Toledo core, 135
Toner cartridge, 417
Toner material, 413
Toner powder, 415
Toner supply, 416
Toolbar, 583
Topology, 316
Torx drivers, 660
Toslink, 241
Total backup, 742
Touch pads, 69, 480
Touch panels, 69
Touch screen monitor, 480
Touch-sensitive screens, 223
Tower cases, 28
Trace Route (TRACERT), 818-819
Trackball, 221, 480
Trackball mouse, 68
TrackPoint, 482
Tracks, 58, 254
Track-seek, 259
Track-Seek Time, 307
Tractor assembly, 407
Tractor feeds, 402
Transfer corona wire, 415
Transfer roller, 415
Transients, 870
Translation modes, 161
Transmission control protocol/Internet protocol (TCP/IP), 334, 375
Transport protocol, 342
Tree, 526, 628
Trip, 876
Trojan horses, 849
Troubleshooters, 712
TrueType fonts, 399
Trusts, 628
Tualatin, 123
Type-110 termination blocks, 323
Type-66 termination blocks, 323
Typematic Action, 163
Typematic Delay, 163
Typematic Rate, 163

U

Ultra 320 SCSI, 288
Ultra DMA (UDMA), 283

Ultra extended VGA (UXGA), 234-235
Ultra SCSI, 287
Ultra XGA (UXGA), 234-235
ULTRA160 SCSI, 288
Ultra2 SCSI, 288
ULTRA640 SCSI, 288
Unattended installations, 600
Uniform resource locator (URL), 382
Uninterruptible power supply (UPS), 870
Uninterruptible power system, 871
Uniqueness database file (UDF), 601
Universal asynchronous receiver transmitter (UART), 109, 214
Universal Plug and Play, 347
Universal serial bus (USB), 54, 64, 197, 200
UNIX, 378
Unshielded twisted pair (UTP), 64, 321, 338
Updates, 84, 803
Upgrade.txt, 606
Upgrades, 84
U-pipe, 116
Uplinked, 373
UPS, 870
Upstream rate, 368
USARTs (universal synchronous/asynchronous receiver/transmitters), 214
USB 2.0, 204
USB adapters, 54
USB controller, 197
USB flash drive, 277
USB keys, 278
User Accounts, 627, 650
User interface, 540
User Logon, 650
User mode, 522
User Profile, 630
User rights, 628
User state migration tools (USMT), 615
User's Console, 801
User's manual, 669
Utility, 400
Utility files, 76
UTP cable category ratings, 322

V

Values, 526
Variable print modes, 403
VCM-SDRAM, 148
Vector images, 81
Vector-based fonts, 399
Version incompatibilities, 770
Vertical (VSYNC), 233
Vertical hold, 233
Vertical refresh rate, 232
Vertical retrace, 232

Very High Bit Rate DSL (VDSL), 369
Very large-scale integration (VLSI), 47
Video adapter card, 34, 53
Video BIOS, 517
Video BIOS ROM, 234
Video cable, 499
Video capture cards, 228
Video editing cards, 230
Video graphics array (VGA), 53, 64, 230
Video monitor, 63
Video standards, 236
View, 569
Viiv, 471
Virtual cluster numbers (VCNs), 536
Virtual memory, 525
Virtual memory manager (VMM), 524
Virtual private networks (VPNs), 838
Virtual servers, 346
Virtualization technology (VT), 128
Virus warning utility, 162
Virus-scanning (antivirus) program, 851
Visual Basic, 82
Voice over IP (VoIP), 380
Voice-over-DSL, 370
Volatile memory, 45
Voltage (V), 662
Voltage Reduction Technology, 466
Voltage regulator module (VRM), 117, 139
Voltage sags, 870
Volt-ampere (VA), 872
Volumes, 56, 302, 542
VOMs (volt-ohm-milliammeters), 662
V-pipe, 116

W

Wallpaper, 582
Warm boot, 72, 516
Wattage rating, 872
Wax-jet printers, 410
Web, 386
Web servers, 382
Weight, 419
Well-known port number, 385
Well-known ports, 843
Wheel mouse, 68
White lines, 451
White page, 450
Wide area network (WAN), 351
Wide Fast SCSI-2, 287
Wide SCSI-2, 287

Wide Ultra SCSI, 287
Wide Ultra2 SCSI, 288
Wide UXGA (WUXGA), 235
WiFi (wireless fidelity), 375
WiFi Protected Access (WPA), 351
Wildcard, 547
WIN keys, 479
Windows 2000 Advanced Server, 558
Windows 2000 Datacenter Server, 558
Windows 2000 Professional, 555, 559
Windows 2000 Server, 559
Windows CE, 463
Windows Cleanup, 803
Windows desktop, 522
Windows Explorer, 582
Windows Internet Naming Service (WINS), 378
Windows log-on, 839
Windows Management Instrumentation (WMI), 578
Windows Media Player (WMP), 593
Windows New Technology, 555
Windows NT, 519, 555
Windows NT File System (NTFS), 519
Windows Protection Error, 767
Windows Server 2003, 561
Windows Server 2003 - Web edition, 561
Windows socket, 388
Windows Troubleshooters, 761
Windows XP 64-bit edition, 560
Windows XP HCL, 612, 769
Windows XP Media Center Edition, 264, 589
Windows XP Media Center Edition (MCE), 561
Windows XP Media Center Edition (XP MCE), 560
Windows XP Professional, 555
WINNT.EXE, 769
Winnt32 /cmdcons, 780
WINNT32.EXE, 769
Wired equivalent privacy (WEP), 330, 351
Wireless LAN (WLAN) adapters, 330
Wireless local area networking (WLAN or LAWN), 329
Wireless mice, 68, 221
Wireless network adapters, 54
Wireless networking adapter, 54
Wireless print server, 422
Wireless signal strength indicator, 728
Word processors, 79
Workstation, 332
World Wide Web (WWW), 382
WPA-PSK, 351
Wrap-plug, 721
Write command, 260
Write once, read many (WORM) drive, 274
Write Protected, 62

X

XCOPY, 546
XD-bit, 128
xDSL, 368
XGA, 235
XP Home Edition, 560
XP Professional, 560
X-rays, 697

Y

Yellow, 442
Yellow Book, 59
YUV, 229

Z

Zero insertion force (ZIF), 44

Maintaining & Repairing PCs
Classroom Support

PC Troubleshooting Trainer

THIS TRAINER INCLUDES:
- Faultable System Board
- Pentium Processor
- DIMM, 128 MB
- Case, ATX Full Tower w/Power Supply
- FDD, 3.5"
- HDD, 10 GB
- Video Card, 4 MB
- Keyboard, 101-key
- PS2 Mouse, 3-Button
- Fax Modem, 56k
- Network Card, 10/100 Mbps
- Speakers
- VGA Monitor
- Hardware/Software Fault Set

The ETG/Marcraft troubleshooting system board is custom designed with hundreds of built-in faults that can be controlled by the instructor. This makes a great platform for teaching diagnostic and repair techniques. It's fast, easy, and realistic.

Complete and Affordable Classroom Management

TEAMS 32 will relieve you from many of the mundane and time-consuming tasks involved in managing a classroom. It can even eliminate a lot of the paperwork…maybe all of it! And you get back the time to do what you actually want to do: teach. *TEAMS 32* is flexible enough to fit any classroom size or style, whether traditional or a more complex rotational system. Classroom records are kept and updated automatically, including individual student test performance,

attendance, class rosters, and other student information. For more details and a sample CD, simply call *(800) 441-6006*.

Universal Fault Sets
For Hands-On Troubleshooting

HARDWARE/SOFTWARE FAULT SET:
- FDD Cable
- HDD Cable
- Modem Cable
- Network Cable
- DIMM
- Y-Power Cable
- 3-Button Clear Mouse
- Software Faults, 3 disk set
- Molded Storage Case

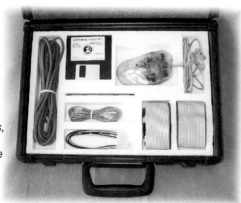

OPTIONAL EXTENDED HARDWARE FAULT SET:
- Keyboard
- Power Supply
- Video Card
- Floppy Drive, 3.5"

To order call Toll Free 1-800-441-6006 or go to: www.etg-corp.com

MARCRAFT
an ETG Brand

ETG/Marcraft 100 N. Morain - 302, Kennewick, WA 99336

Other Great ETG/Marcraft Training Courses

Network+ Certification
Network+ is a CompTIA vendor-neutral certification that measures the technical knowledge of networking professionals with 18-24 months of experience in the IT industry. The test is administered by NCS/VUE and PrometricTM. Discount exam vouchers can be purchased from ETG/Marcraft. Earning the Network+ certification indicates that the candidate possesses the knowledge needed to configure and install the TCP/IP client. This exam covers a wide range of vendor and product neutral networking technologies that can also serve as a prerequisite for vendor-specific IT certifications. Network+ has been accepted by the leading networking vendors and included in many of their training curricula. The skills and knowledge measured by the certification examination are derived from industry-wide job task analyses and validated through an industry wide survey. The objectives for the certification examination are divided in two distinct groups, Knowledge of Networking Technology and Knowledge of Networking Practices.

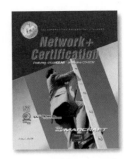

i-Net+ Certification
The i-Net+ certification program is designed specifically for any individual interested in demonstrating baseline technical knowledge that would allow him or her to pursue a variety of Internet-related careers. i-Net+ is a vendor-neutral, entry-level Internet certification program that tests baseline technical knowledge of Internet, Intranet, and Extranet technologies, independent of specific Internet-related career roles. Learning objectives and domains examined include: Internet basics, Internet clients, development, networking, security, and business concepts. Certification not only helps individuals enter the Internet industry, but also helps managers determine a prospective employee's knowledge and skill level.

The Complete Data Cabling Installers Certification provides the IT industry with an introductory, vendor-neutral certification for skilled personnel that install Category 5 copper data cabling. The ETG/Marcraft Complete Data Cabling Installers Certification Training Guide provides students with the knowledge and skills required to pass the Data Cabling Installers Certification exam and become a certified cable installer. The DCIC is recognized nationwide and is the hiring criterion used by major communication companies. Therefore, becoming a certified data cable installer will enhance your job opportunities and career advancement potential.

Server+ Certification
The Server+ certification deals with advanced hardware issues such as RAID, SCSI, multiple CPUs, SANs, and more. This certification is vendor-neutral with a broad range of support, including core support by 3Com, Adaptec, Compaq, Hewlett-Packard, IBM, Intel, EDS Innovations Canada, Innovative Productivity, and ETG/Marcraft. This book focuses on complex activities and solving complex problems to ensure servers are functional and applications are available. It provides an in-depth understanding of installing, configuring, and maintaining servers, including knowledge of server-level hardware implementations, data storage subsystems, data recovery, and I/O subsystems.

Fiber Cabling Installers Certification prepares technicians for the growing demand for qualified cable installers who understand and can implement fiber-optic technologies. These technologies cover terminology, techniques, tools, and other products in the fiber-optic industry. This text/lab book covers the basics of fiber-optic design, installations, pulling and prepping cables, terminations, testing, and safety considerations. Labs will cover ST-compatible and SC connector types, both multi- and single-mode cables and connectors. Learn about insertion loss, optical time domain reflectometry, and reflectance. This text covers mechanical and fusion splices and troubleshooting cable systems. This text/lab covers the theory and hands-on skills needed to prepare you for fiber-optic entry-level certification.

Wireless Networking Certification technology is one of the hottest technologies available today, used in electronic devices, such as cell phones and Personal Digital Assistants (PDA), to enable access to e-mail and the Internet. Wireless technology is also utilized in wireless Local Area Networks (LANs). With ETG/Marcraft's Wireless Networking Certification, you learn the entire process of designing, building, configuring, and managing a wireless network. This text combines in one place everything needed to successfully design, install, and troubleshoot a simple wireless solution. Keep on the cutting edge of wireless with ETG/Marcraft.

Home Technology Integrator+ (HTI+) is an exciting new certification by CompTIA in partnership with Internet Home Alliance (IHA). The HTI+ Certification fills the niche for home technicians as technology in the home environment continues to grow. There is an increasing demand for skilled technicians to install, integrate, and troubleshoot various home sub-systems. This enables consumers to take advantage of and fully enjoy the "Connected Home" sub-systems, such as; home security and surveillance, audio/video, computer networks, control processors, electrical wiring (low andhigh voltage), heating and air conditioning, cable/satellite, access entry control, broadband, telecommunications, systems infrastructure and integration, lighting management, user interface, water control, and commercial wiring. The course is broken into two major certification exam areas, Residential Systems and Systems Infrastructure.

The Complete Introductory Computer Course is an entry-level course. It prepares students for the more challenging A+ Certification course. It also provides a careerport™ into the fast-growing IT industry. The MC-2300 is a 45-hour, easy-to-understand exploration of basic computer hardware, software, and troubleshooting. This course helps build students' confidence and basic computer literacy. The fully-illustrated 198-page Theory Text/Lab Guide provides an easy-to understand exploration of the basics of computers: basic computer architecture and operation, step-by-step computer hardware assembly, computer hardware and functions, common software packages, consumer maintenance practices, and troubleshooting a "sick" computer. The reusable MC-2300 Intro Computer Trainer comes with all the necessary hardware, software, and tools to perform over 30 hands-on Lab Explorations.

The Complete Introductory Networking Course is a superbly illustrated theory text and lab guide all in one. It not only provides a great way for students to explore over 45 hours of easy-to-understand basic networking topics, but also develops job skills for starting them on the path towards a new high-tech career!
This manual guides you through such activities as: installation and configuration of local area network hardware, peer-to-peer networking functions, sharing computer resources, mapping to remote resources, and consumer-level network troubleshooting. The Complete Introductory Networking Course provides an excellent starting point for IT Certification including Microsoft's MCSE, Novell's CNA, and Cisco's CCNA.

The Complete Introductory Internet Course takes advantage of the growing demand for qualified Internet technicians. This 45-hour course explores easy-to-understand basic Internet topics and helps develop Internet skills.
This manual guides you through such activities as: configuring e-mail accounts, designing a basic HTML page, setup of a basic firewall for security, and establishing Internet connection slaving. The Complete Introductory Internet Course provides an excellent starting point for IT Certification including CompTIA's i-NET+ and Prosoft's Certified Internet Webmaster (CIW).

MARCRAFT Electronics Kits

RC Jet Cobra Race Car Kit

RC Jet-Cobra Race Car SE-1030

Leave the competition in the dust.....build this 1/18 scale, 2 wheel drive Baja racer from ETG/Marcraft. Select one of two forward speeds, punch the turbo power and go for it. The Jet-Cobra features a 5-function pistol grip controller that incorporates a turbo-boost circuit. Independent front and rear suspension provide excellent handling on sharp, high-speed corners. You'll find state-of-the-art IC technology coupled with fundamental transistor circuitry to demonstrate important electronics components such as: RF signal transmission and reception, digital information encoding and decoding, and motor control theory. A 72-page manual provides a thorough understanding of the electronics principles. As low as $36.95.

PC Technician's Tool Kit IC-345

This professional technician's kit contains 29 of the most popular PC service tools to cover most PC service applications. Zipper case is constructed out of durable vinyl with room for an optional DMM and optional CD-ROM service disks. Includes: case (with zipper) has external slash pocket for extra storage (13 1/2" L x 9 3/4" H x 2 3/8" W), slotted 3/16" screwdriver, IC Inserter, slotted 1/8" screwdriver, 3-prong parts Retriever, Phillips # 1 screwdriver, self-locking tweezers, Phillips # 0 screwdriver, tweezers, precision 4 pc (2 slotted / 2 Phillips) screwdriver set, inspection mirror, driver handle, penlight, # 2 Phillips / slotted 1/4" screwdriver bits, 6" adjustable wrench, # T-10 Torx / T-15 Torx screwdriver bits, 4 1/2" mini-diagonal, 1/4" nut driver, 5" mini-long nose, 3/16" nut driver, anti-static wrist strap, 5" hemostat, part storage tube, IC Extractor. (Note: Meter not included) As low as $36.95

To order call Toll Free 1-800-441-6006 or go to: www.etg-corp.com

MARCRAFT
an ETG Brand
ETG/Marcraft 100 N. Morain - 302, Kennewick, WA 99336

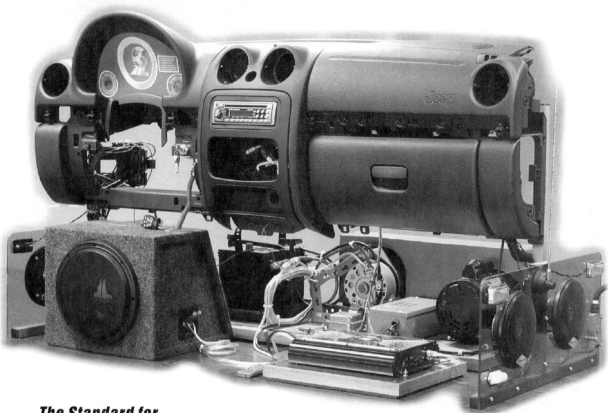